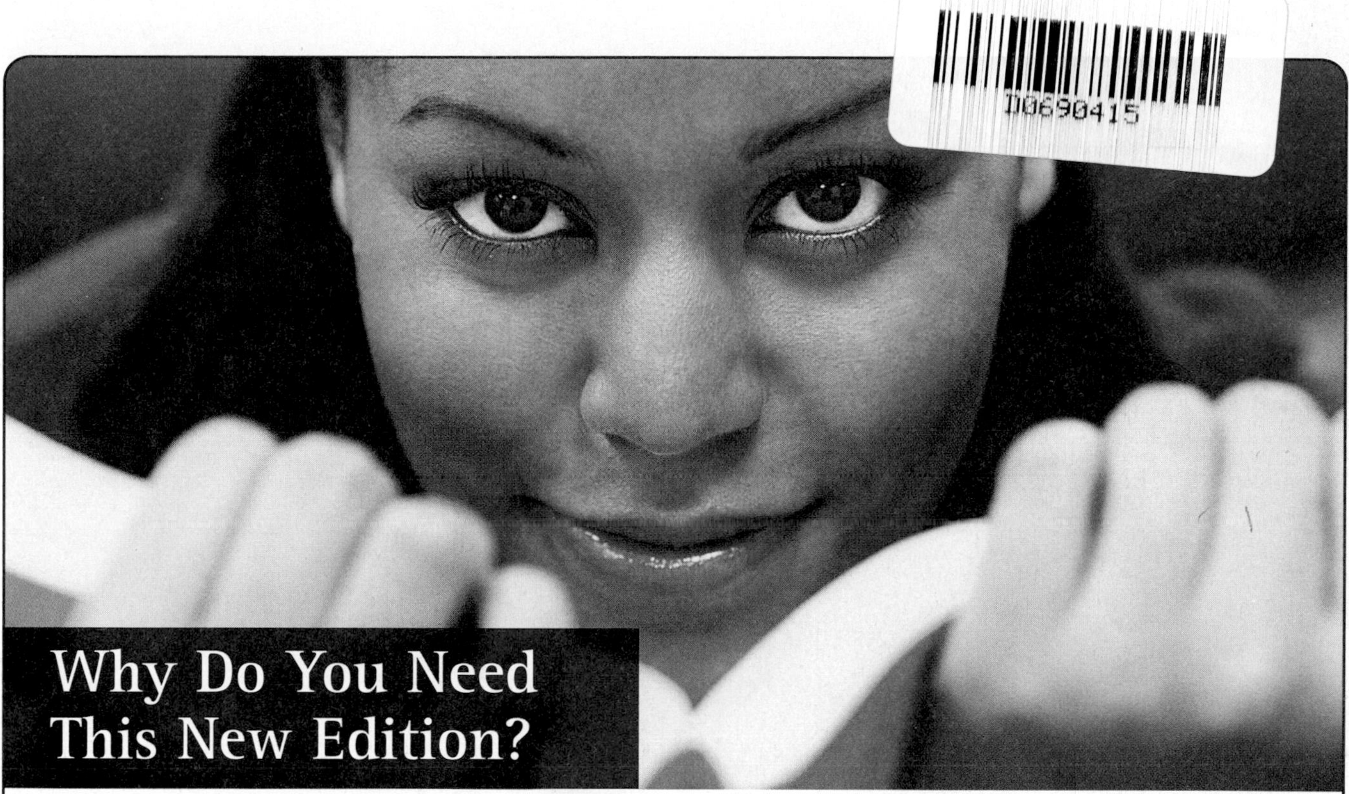


# Why Do You Need This New Edition?

1. This edition of *The World of Children* now contains new chapter-opening stories based on a real family or a child who is in a situation where more knowledge of child development can be helpful. These real-life stories are referenced throughout the chapter through the use of notes and questions, and recapped at the end. You can log onto MyDevelopmentLab (www.mydevelopmentlab.com) to watch video interviews with these individuals and learn what steps they have taken to overcome their real-life problems!

2. Additional videos, simulations, and assessments can be found at MyDevelopmentLab. Icons in the margins indicate that additional features are available online. An exciting new feature of this edition is the collection of exclusive podcasts, recorded by us, your authors, which further explore specific topics referenced in the text. These podcasts are a great way for students to explore topics they are really interested in, while allowing us to keep a manageable amount of content in the textbook.

3. Also new to this new edition, we have highlighted four central research themes: nature/nurture interaction, neuroscience, diversity and multiculturalism, and positive development/resilience. These themes have been integrated into the narrative to help illustrate the link to personal and professional applications of the research. The themes are then revisited and summarized briefly at the end of each chapter in the Revisiting Themes section for easy review.

4. We also updated many topics and areas of coverage throughout the text to keep the research in this edition current. We added updated information on artificial insemination, risks for prenatal testing, and teen sexual activity and pregnancy. We also added sections on sleep patterns and co-sleeping in infants and toddlers, plasticity in brain development, and the ADHD medication controversy. We hope these and the many other changes we have made to this edition (for a complete list of changes, see pages xxii-xxv of the Preface) will teach students to think critically about the content and about other people's perspectives, backgrounds, and beliefs. With this new edition, professors and students alike can expect real people, real experiences, real learning.

PEARSON

# THE WORLD OF CHILDREN

second edition

**GREG COOK**
**University of Wisconsin, Whitewater**

**JOAN LITTLEFIELD COOK**
**University of Wisconsin, Whitewater**

Allyn & Bacon
Boston Columbus Indianapolis New York San Francisco Upper Saddle River
Amsterdam Cape Town Dubai London Madrid Milan Munich Paris Montréal Toronto
Delhi Mexico City São Paulo Sydney Hong Kong Seoul Singapore Taipei Tokyo

**Editorial Director:** *Leah Jewell*
**Editor in Chief:** *Jessica Mosher*
**Executive Acquisitions Editor:** *Stephen Frail*
**Editorial Assistant:** *Kerri Hart-Morris*
**Development Editor:** *Deb Hanlon*
**Director of Development:** *Sharon Geary*
**Associate Editor:** *Kara Kikel*
**Director of Marketing:** *Brandy Dawson*
**Marketing Manager:** *Nicole Kunzmann*
**Marketing Assistant:** *Amanda Olweck*
**Senior Managing Editor:** *Maureen Richardson*
**Project Manager:** *Marianne Peters-Riordan*
**Copy Editor:** *Kerry Beeaker*
**Proofreader**: *David Heath*
**Senior Operations Supervisor:** *Sherry Lewis*
**Senior Art Director:** *Nancy Wells*
**Text Designer:** *Carole Anson*
**Cover Designer:** *Anne DeMarinis*
**Manager, Visual Research:** *Beth Brenzel*
**Photo Researcher:** *Kathy Ringrose*
**Manager, Rights and Permissions:** *Zina Arabia*
**Image Permission Coordinator:** *Jan Marc Quisumbing*
**Manager, Cover Visual Research & Permissions:** *Karen Sanatar*
**Cover Art:** *Isolated Butterfly credit: Neo Edmund/ Shutterstock; Girl Painting Floral Pattern credit: March Rimmer/Corbis*
**Media Director:** *Karen Scott*
**Senior Media Editor:** *Paul DeLuca*
**Full-Service Project Management:** *Martha Wetherill*
**Composition:** *Macmillan Publishing Solutions*
**Printer/Binder:** *Webcrafters, Inc.*
**Cover Printer:** *Lehigh-Phoenix Color*

This book was set in 10.5/13, AGaramond.

Credits and acknowledgments borrowed from other sources and reproduced, with permission, in this textbook appear on pages 559–561.



**Library of Congress Cataloging-in-Publication Data**
Cook, Greg (Greg L.)
The world of children/Greg Cook, Joan Littlefield Cook. -- 2nd ed.
p. cm.
Prev. ed. entered under: Cook, Joan Littlefield.
Includes bibliographical references and index.
ISBN 13: 978-0-205-68592-9 (alk. paper)
ISBN 10: 0-205-68592-7 (alk. paper)
1. Child development. 2. Children. I. Cook, Joan Littlefield. II. Title
HQ767.9.C666 2010
305.23—dc 22

2009033183

10 9 8 7 6 5 4 3 2 1

**Allyn & Bacon**
is an imprint of

Student Version:
ISBN-13: 978-0-205-68592-9
ISBN-10: 0-205-68592-7

Exam Version:
ISBN-13: 978-0-205-76283-5
ISBN-10: 0-205-76283-2

To our children: Will, Rachel, Lily, and Andy.
They enrich our lives and remind us that the most important thing in life is the development of children.

# Brief Contents

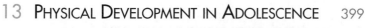

# Contents

# CHAPTER 11 Cognitive Development in Middle Childhood 321

# Preface

Our students often ask us at the beginning of the term why they should study child development and how it will be useful in their lives. As child development instructors for more than 20 years, we have tried our best to follow the example of great teachers who have come before us. We believe that *how* you teach is as important as *what* you teach. We teach to our students' interests and needs, and we resist the temptation to cover everything we *could* cover, and instead treat what we do cover in a scientific and intellectually honest way. How do we decide what to cover and what can be left out? We start by asking how much impact the material is likely to have on the lives of our students, whether they become parents, teachers, nurses, social workers, or child development researchers themselves. We then make sure that we cover both the current science and applications of the material to ensure that students have an accurate view of where the field is today.

As researchers and university professors we have witnessed exciting changes in the field of child development. From new research on brain development to behavior genetics to new theories of the intricacies of social interactions, developments in this area of psychology continue to provide great insights, challenges, and debates. We are continually inspired by the impact the field of child development has on real lives. Every day, health-care professionals, educators, social workers, day care workers, parents, and, yes, psychologists rely upon developmental science research to perform their professional and personal duties, as they nurture, educate, and otherwise care for the children in their lives. It is this connection between the science and **real people facing real issues** that that we try to convey to our students and to the reader of this textbook.

Our mission in writing this textbook was to ensure we answered the "why" and "how" clearly throughout. We also believe strongly in learning outcomes and in applying principles of educational psychology, learning, and cognitive science to help our students get more out of the course. After all, if we want them to leave the course with a strong appreciation of how developmental science can be a force for positive change in people's lives, we must ensure that they are truly learning, not merely memorizing, the concepts presented in this course. Most of our text focuses on contemporary science and on what is happening in the field today—but in order to understand the present, we must reflect on the past. Included in the text are both the classic studies within their historical context and an overview of how these studies have influenced, and continue to influence, how psychologists think about the field of child development. This review helps explain how particular scientific approaches emerged or were adapted or rejected over time. We want to remind students that just as adults are influenced by childhood experiences, the science of child development has been shaped by its past.

## Goals of the Text

*The World of Children* adopts three important goals for the text and the user:

- Focus on real people facing real issues;
- Teach students to think critically about the research;
- Help students make connections between science and practice.

Every feature in our text is thoughtfully designed as part of an integrated system to support active learning, and we hope you will agree that our textbook satisfies these goals.

### GOAL 1 Focus on Real People Facing Real Issues

We want students to see an important purpose in studying child development. We are convinced that the science of child development can be very useful in helping real families and real children, and we want students to think about the research in the context of the real issues real families face. To that end, every chapter begins with a case about a real family or a child who is in a situation where more knowledge of child development can be helpful. Supporting the chapter opening cases are video interviews with these same families on MyDevelopmentLab (www.mydevelopmentlab.com). These real cases encourage students to take what they are learning in each chapter and apply it to creating advice for the profiled individuals.

### GOAL 2 Teach Students to Think Critically about the Research

We want students to learn new facts and information, but more important, we want students to understand how these new facts and information are generated in our field. Throughout the textbook, we take opportunities to show students how research methods work in our field, and we remind them of the important limitations in the methods. The chapter opening cases and the *Think About . . .* questions that appear throughout the chapter are designed to jumpstart the critical thinking process by putting students in the shoes of others and asking them to think about how the research might apply to those individuals' situations. Throughout the chapter we use *Thinking Critically* questions in the margins to provoke deeper, more personal reflection on the content of the chapter.

### GOAL 3 Help Students Make Connections between Science and Practice

The field of child development has much to offer students and society in terms of practical advice for parents and professionals as well as guidance on social policy issues, and this advice is based on a solid foundation of research.

## Exploring Different Perspectives

### Professional Perspective

In each **Professional Perspective** box, a real professional discusses how he or she uses child development information. Using an interview format, each of these features introduces students to a different career; by the end of the book, students have explored 15 different career paths (among them social work, genetic counseling, clinical and counseling psychology, school psychology, and marketing) that involve work with children, adolescents, and development.

| CHAPTER | PROFESSIONAL PERSPECTIVE BOX |
|---|---|
| 1 | Career Focus: Meet a Child Social Worker |
| 2 | Career Focus: Meet a Genetic Counselor |
| 3 | Career Focus: Meet a Certified Nurse-Midwife |
| 4 | Career Focus: Meet a Physical Therapist |
| 5 | Career Focus: Meet a Speech-Language Pathologist |
| 6 | Career Focus: Meet a Toy Company Executive |
| 7 | Career Focus: Meet a Family Nutrition Counselor |
| 8 | Career Focus: Meet a Constructivist Teacher |
| 9 | Career Focus: Meet the Director of a Child Care Center |
| 10 | Career Focus: Meet a Pediatrician |
| 11 | Career Focus: Meet a Child and Family Therapist |
| 12 | Career Focus: Meet a Marketing Executive |
| 13 | Career Focus: Meet an Eating Disorders Counselor |
| 14 | Career Focus: Meet a School Psychologist |
| 15 | Career Focus: Meet a Juvenile Probation Officer |

## Personal Perspective

Also presented as an interview, **Personal Perspective** boxes allow students to connect with the personal feelings of an actual parent, child, or adolescent who is experiencing an issue discussed in the chapter. This feature allows students to see how real people of all backgrounds relate to child development issues.

| CHAPTER | PERSONAL PERSPECTIVE BOX |
|---|---|
| 1 | Meet First-Time Parents |
| 2 | Meet a Mother Who Used Artificial Insemination |
| 3 | Meet a Family Who Adopted a Child with Fetal Alcohol Syndrome |
| 4 | Meet the Parents of a Very Premature Baby |
| 5 | Where Did It Go? |
| 6 | Meet the Parent of a Difficult Child |
| 7 | Living with Cerebral Palsy |
| 8 | Meet a Bilingual Family |
| 9 | Carrots or Sticks? Family Discipline at Different Ages |
| 10 | Child Sexual Abuse: One Survivor's Story |
| 11 | Meet a Literacy Volunteer |
| 12 | We Are Best Friends |
| 13 | Meet a Young Adolescent |
| 14 | I Graduated—Now What? |
| 15 | Developing an Ethnic Identity |

## Social Policy Perspective

We designed **Social Policy Perspective** boxes to give students an understanding of how work in the field of child development can inform government officials, community service agencies, and others who have wide-ranging effects on the lives of children. This feature focuses on many of the controversial issues in society, examining the perspectives of both sides of each debate. It highlights the ways in which programs, laws, regulations, and other factors can affect children and asks students to think about the impact of social policies.

| CHAPTER | SOCIAL POLICY PERSPECTIVE BOX |
|---|---|
| 1 | Every Day in America |
| 2 | Protecting the Genetic Privacy of Citizens |
| 3 | The Case of Malissa Ann Crawley |
| 4 | Can Mozart Stimulate Neural Connections in Infants? |
| 5 | Assessing Infant Intelligence: A Good Idea? |
| 6 | Parental Leave Policies in the United States and Other Nations |
| 7 | Protecting Children from Neglect |
| 8 | Project Head Start: What Lies Ahead? |
| 9 | Should Parents Have to Be Licensed? |
| 10 | Educating Children with Exceptional Needs |
| 11 | Children's Eyewitness Testimony: The Truth, the Whole Truth, and Nothing but the Truth? |
| 12 | Bilingual Education in the Schools |
| 13 | The Sex Education Debate |
| 14 | Ethnicity and IQ |
| 15 | How Should We Deal with Aggressive Students? |

Taken together, these different *perspective* features help students see how child development information is useful in a wide variety of professional, personal, and social situations. They also help students understand the real-life challenges faced by professionals, parents, volunteers, and policy makers whose work relates to the field of child development.

## Changes Made to the Second Edition

In addition to the new features mentioned previously, we are pleased to list the following chapter-by-chapter changes made to this edition:

### Chapter 1:

- Added a new opening story and video interview: Sheryl
- Introduced the recurring themes (repeated throughout the text) of *nature and nurture*, the *role of neuroscience*, *diversity and multiculturalism*, and *positive development and resilience*
- Added a "Revisiting Themes" section at the end of the chapter—this section will occur at the end of every chapter to review connections for that chapter to the recurring themes
- Included a new example of path analysis that shows variables that predict loneliness in children

### Chapter 2:

- Added a new opening story and video interview: Juan and Tracey
- Updated information on number of clinical trials testing gene therapy
- Updated Social Policy box with passage of GINA law
- Updated discussion on artificial insemination (outcome of children, who does/doesn't reveal info on AI to their children)
- Revised Figure 2.10 on Down syndrome risk with age with new data
- Added information on Tay–Sachs disease
- Added information on sickle cell disease
- Added information on ethnic differences in lifespan for those with Down syndrome
- Updated information on risks for prenatal testing (amniocentesis vs. chorionic villus sampling [CVS])
- Added information on new approaches to prenatal testing (blood test being developed)
- Updated data in Table 2.4 on heritabilities

### Chapter 3:

- Added a new opening story and video interview: Elizabeth and Stephanie
- Added information on miscarriages and stillbirths, including rates of incidence
- Updated information on the statistics and use of alcohol, cocaine, cigarette smoking, and other teratogens during pregnancy
- Added research on amount of alcohol that can be harmful (small amounts cause brain damage) and how cocaine relates to reduced brain volume later in childhood
- Added example of how an alcohol counseling program can save lives and reduce birth defects
- Added newer examples of research showing how fathers' age (teens), alcohol use, and exposure to pollutants are related to birth defects
- Added section on cultural differences in birthing practices
- Reorganized the last two sections of the chapter to improve flow of chapter

### Chapter 4:

- Added a new opening story and video interview: Jess and Darran
- Added sections on sleep patterns, co-sleeping, and sudden infant death syndrome (SIDS), with cross-cultural examples
- Improved organization and clarity of several sections (e.g., reflexes, sensory capabilities)

### Chapter 5:

- Added a new opening story and video interview: Chi Hae and Cara
- Added neuroscience work on face processing by typically developing children and those with autism spectrum disorder
- Added information on neuroscience modification of habituation procedure
- Updated and expanded the criticisms of Piaget's theory (sensorimotor stage)
- Added figure on *violation of expectation* studies (to study object permanence)
- Added neuroscience work on infant language processing, infant discrimination of speech sounds
- Updated information on assessing infant intelligence

### Chapter 6:

- Added a new opening story and video interview: Lisa
- Updated longitudinal research on attachment
- Added mention of neuroscience studies on emotion processing in infancy
- Added mention of behavior genetics research on attachment and temperament
- Added mention of sympathy and empathy in toddler emotions
- Added mention of toddler conflict with parents

### Chapter 7:

- Added a new opening story and video news clip: The Rodriguez children
- Combined some sections to improve chapter organization
- Updated statistics on malnutrition, childhood deaths, and child maltreatment
- Reorganized section on the effects of child abuse and neglect to improve organization and readability

### Chapter 8:

- Added a new opening story and video interview: Sujatha and RK
- Streamlined coverage of information processing
- Updated sections on:
  -Early childhood education (added Montessori; added Reggio Emilia; updated Head Start)
  -Kindergarten readiness
  -Theory of mind
- Added neuroscience research:
  -Attention genes
  -Mirror neurons (in theory of mind section)

-Myelination and vocabulary increase

-Neural work on bilingualism

-Added new key term (mirror neurons)

Chapter 9:

- Added a new opening story and video interview: Julie and Tom
- Combined some sections to improve chapter organization
- Created a new table on theories of gender segregation
- Added brief information on theories of self development, including heritability estimates for self-concepts and self-esteem
- Updated research on punishment/discipline and other topics throughout

Chapter 10:

- Added a new opening story and video interview: Brad
- Updated statistics on the increasing percentages of children who are overweight
- Added a section on plasticity in brain development
- Added new neuroscience research on the damaging effects of child sex abuse on the brain
- Added discussion of the controversy about whether too many children are being medicated with stimulants to control ADHD behaviors

Chapter 11:

- Added a new opening story and video interview: Linda and Gianluca
- Combined language subsections (metalinguistic awareness, changes in how language is used)
- Updated sections on:

  -STS forgetting due to interference rather than decay

  -Autobiographical memory

  -Fuzzy trace theory

  -Development of writing skills
- Added neuroscience research:

  -Executive function

  -Autobiographical memory

  -Neural processes in reading

Chapter 12:

- Added a new opening story and video interview: Laurel and Pam
- In the peer popularity sections, added discussion of how researchers use the term "peer popularity" differently than how many children and adolescents use the term "popular" in school
- Added discussion of how peer popularity and unpopularity relate to racial discrimination in some schools
- Added neuroscience work on TV and video game violence
- Added paragraph on TV viewing in infancy and early childhood

### Chapter 13:

- Added a new opening story and video interview: Josh
- Condensed section on puberty
- Added new Table 13.1 (on physical changes during puberty)
- Updated and condensed section on sexual activity (cut old Table 13.2)
- Condensed section on teen pregnancy
- Updated section on brain development
- Updated data throughout (sexual activity, teen pregnancy, drug use, causes of death)
- Updated info on use of antidepressants in children and teens.

### Chapter 14:

- Added a new opening story and video interview: Leo
- Shortened section on adolescent egocentrism
- Revised section on evaluating Piaget's theory
- Updated section on intellectual disabilities
- Added neuroscience research on gifted/talented individuals
- Condensed section on assessing intelligence
- Added brief section on new approaches to assessing intelligence
- Updated section on decision making, added new research on analytic and intuitive decision-making processes

### Chapter 15:

- Added a new opening story and video interview: Camila
- Updated stats throughout:
  -Sexual orientation
  -Ethnic population growth
  -Leisure time activities
  -Academic achievement differences (international, ethnic)
  -Poverty (overall, urban vs. rural)
- Updated section on sexual orientation:
  -Added newer view of identity development
  -Added concept of *fluid sexual identities*
  -Added newer neuroscience info
  -Shortened "exotic becomes erotic" theory description
- Added neuroscience work on teen–parent conflict
- Updated research on gay/lesbian family structure
- Shortened section on transition to dating, restructured it as part of another subheading
- Revised Figures 15.3 (activities in adolescence), 15.4 (ethnic group differences in achievement), 15.5 (percent in poverty)
- Revised Table 15.2 (growth in U.S. ethnic diversity)

## Our Own Personal Perspective

In addition to our training and research in child development, we call on our practical experience from raising our own four children. As this book is going to press, our oldest son, Andy, is 19 and a sophomore in college. He's studying engineering, and he loves to work with motors and mechanical devices. Our second son, Will, is 14. He looks up to his older brother, loves sports, and excels in most school topics. He's a freshman in high school, enjoying his new freedoms and responsibilities. Our twin daughters, Rachel and Lily, are 13. They are fraternal twins and couldn't be more different from each other. Rachel is quiet and shy at first, and she is very coordinated and graceful in athletic activities. Lily is more rambunctious and outgoing, and she is the first one to volunteer for a new challenge or experience. Our girls are best friends in many ways, but they are also learning to be their own separate selves. We have thoroughly enjoyed watching our children's first steps, first words, first days of school, first dates, and all the many joys of living with children and (now four!) teenagers. Like most families, we have also struggled as we try to balance home life with work, and we have dealt with premature infants, speech and physical therapy, minor school problems, sibling rivalry, and many of the other challenges that can appear in family life.

Through our children we have learned the practical side of child development. We know that even the grandest theories fail to capture the challenges, complexities, practicalities, joys, and fulfillment of real life with children. We have used these experiences to inform our writing—they helped us focus on the practical applications of what we teach and what we write. We encourage students to bring their personal perspective to the study of child development; and we do the same thing, including our personal perspective at times throughout the book. We hope that our own experiences will offer students another perspective to consider.

# How to Use This Book

WHEN READING TEXTBOOK CHAPTERS, STUDENTS OFTEN ASK:
"WHY SHOULD I KNOW THIS MATERIAL?"
OR
"HOW IS IT USEFUL IN REAL LIFE?" LET US SHOW YOU.

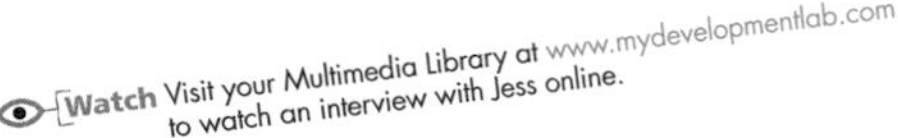
Watch Visit your Multimedia Library at www.mydevelopmentlab.com to watch an interview with Jess online.

4 INFANTS AND TODDLERS

Physical Development in Infants and Toddlers

Infants at Risk: Prematurity and Infant Mortality
- What Is Prematurity?
- Infant Mortality
- Prenatal Care: Having a Healthy Baby

Growth of the Body and Brain
- Physical Growth, Sleep Patterns, and Sudden Infant Death Syndrome
- Feeding and Nutrition
- Structure of the Brain and Nervous System
- Forming the Brain and Nervous System

Sensory Capabilities
- Basic Components of Vision
- How Well Do Infants Hear?
- Smell and Taste

Motor Development
- Reflexes: The Infant's First Coordinated Movements
- Voluntary Movements: The Motor Milestones
- Cultural Differences in Early Experience
- Toilet Training

Jess is six months into her first pregnancy, and she is very excited about becoming a new mother. Now that she's pregnant, Jess has modified her diet to include more foods that are organic and healthy. Jess also walks and goes to the gym two or three times per week for exercise; she wants to improve her strength and stamina to help her through labor and delivery. So far, everything is looking great during her prenatal care visits—the baby is growing well and looks healthy. Jess's mother went into premature labor when she had Jess, so Jess is a bit concerned about her baby being born prematurely.

Jess's husband Darran reads a bedtime story to her abdomen every night. "We've read studies that show that newborns recognize sounds they hear in the womb, so this is Darran's way of bonding with the baby as early as he can," Jess said. "Plus, we're hoping to establish a calming bedtime routine early—there's no way of knowing if it will work or not, but wouldn't it be great if it did!" They are decorating the baby's area with plenty of bright colors, but they also don't want it to be overwhelming for their newborn. After the baby is born, Jess and Darran plan to enroll the family in baby exercise classes for fun and extra stimulation for the baby. Jess plans to breastfeed the baby for at least six months and maybe up to two years depending on the baby's needs.

Like most new and prospective parents, Jess and Darran are eager to support their baby's development. What would you suggest? Can babies really recognize sounds they hear in the womb? Would baby exercise classes be helpful? How long should babies continue to breastfeed? After studying this chapter, you should be able to give sound advice about these and many other questions. Using at least a dozen research findings or concepts, you should be able to help Jess and Darran sort out fact from the fiction and get their baby off to a great start.

108

As you read this chapter, look for the "Think About Jess and Darran . . ." questions that ask you to consider what you're learning from their perspective.

Every chapter in the book begins with a story of life from another person's perspective—a real, often challenging situation that shows you how child development relates to you or to the people around you. In addition, students can watch videos with these individuals and learn more about their situations and what steps they took to overcome their challenges. These videos can be found on www.mydevelopmentlab.com.

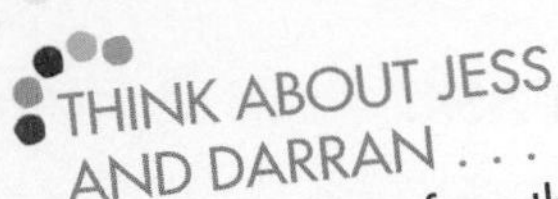

**THINK ABOUT JESS AND DARRAN . . .**

Describe three or four things that Jess can do during her pregnancy to reduce her risk of having a premature baby.

Each of these stories is linked to **Think About . . .** margin questions placed at critical points throughout the chapter. **Think About . . .** questions ask you how you might advise the people described in the opening story, based on what you have learned thus far. By the time you finish studying the chapter, you should have a good idea about how to answer all of the questions.

We include several other perspectives as well, to help you think about the content from personal, professional, and social policy points of view. To support the personal perspective, we offer **Thinking Critically** notes in the margins where you can stop and think about how the chapter material relates to your own life.

**THINKING CRITICALLY**

In your opinion, does brain growth allow children's thought processes to improve, or does exercising thought processes stimulate the brain to grow? What kinds of evidence would you need to have to address this question?

**THINKING BACK TO JESS AND DARRAN . . .**

Like most expectant parents, Jess and Darran would like to do what they can to stimulate their baby's development. With all the excitement generated by popular press reports about research on brain development, parents are eager to learn how experience helps to shape the communication pathways in the brain. During pregnancy, neurons will grow in the baby's brain, and synapses will begin to form to connect the neurons. The brain grows an overabundance of neurons, and half of the baby's neurons will die off in programmed cell death. Which neurons survive and which will die is determined partly by experience and the relative activity of the neurons, but this neuron loss is normal. Infants' brains use the variety of sights, sounds, and other sensations stimulated by the environment to govern brain growth and development, and Jess and Darran should understand that stimulation is important throughout childhood, not just during the first year or two.

At the end of the chapter, **Thinking Back to . . .** summarizes some of the possibilities for how you could have answered the margin questions—but try answering the questions yourself before checking our summary!

Listen: Why are the infant mortality rates in the U.S. so high? (Author Podcast)
www.mydevelopmentlab.com


Watch a video about Breastfeeding.
www.mydevelopmentlab.com

Throughout each chapter, you will be reminded by marginal icons to go online for additional study and practice within **MyDevelopmentLab**. Videos, podcasts, animations, simulations, and other tools help you better understand the concepts presented in the chapter, while practice quizzes and a personalized study plan help you prepare for your exams.

**Listen**: How many neurons are created in the human brain, and how fast? Are any new neurons created after birth? (Author Podcast)
www.mydevelopmentlab.com

**Watch** a video on The Newbornís Reflexes.
www.mydevelopmentlab.com

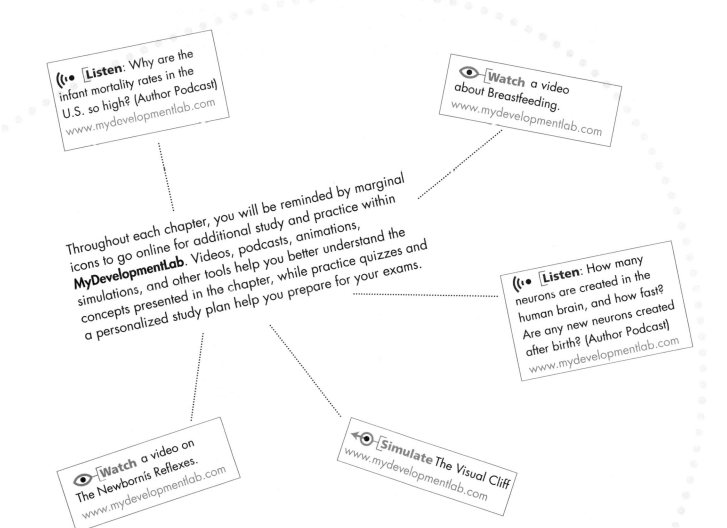

**Simulate** The Visual Cliff
www.mydevelopmentlab.com

## Perspective PROFESSIONAL — CAREER FOCUS: MEET A PHYSICAL THERAPIST

Deanna Walsh
Madison, WI
Physical therapist at Meriter Hospital

**What ages of children and what types of conditions do you work with? Are families involved in the children's therapy?**
The youngest children I treat are premature infants, and the oldest may be up to 16 or 17 years old. I see children who are having a variety of movement problems. I see babies and children with torticollis (a tight muscle in their neck that restricts their movement), cerebral palsy, autism with associated movement difficulties, delays in their gross motor development (difficulty learning to crawl, walk, jump, etc.), spina bifida, muscular dystrophy, Down syndrome, other genetic syndromes that impact movement, and after surgery or fractures. The children I see may have problems with their balance or coordination, muscle weakness, muscle tightness, difficulty with mobility, or difficulty with specific movements. Some children require special equipment to make movement easier. This might include special braces or inserts in their shoes, crutches, walkers, adapted bicycles, or wheelchairs.

Typically, I see a child for one or two treatments per week, depending on the child's and family's needs. A great deal of my job is teaching families what they can do to help their child, since they are the people who are with the child most of the time. By involving families in their child's treatment, greater improvements are seen. Instead of working on an activity for one hour per week, the child will be incorporating it into his or her day, every day.

**How do you determine whether a child is exhibiting delayed motor development?**
I routinely use many different standardized tests when assessing a child's motor skills. Most tests address certain age groups and look at certain types of skills (e.g., balance, locomotor, coordination, and ball skills). I also observe the quality of a child's movements to determine whether she or he is having difficulty with mobility skills.

**What education and training are needed to become a physical therapist?**
Most physical therapy programs are now master's degree programs, and many are moving toward the doctorate level. Most include extensive clinical experience as part of the training, and this is typically where most students gain some hands-on experience working with children. Physical therapy is an excellent career for people who like to be involved with patients and their families. There are many practice settings in physical therapy—such as school-based therapy, hospital-based therapy, outpatient clinics, home health agencies, academics, research, nursing homes, and rehab centers. The great thing about all areas of physical therapy is that you get to help people meet their individual goals. Working with great kids and their families is an added benefit of working with pediatrics.

QUESTION **What are some initial signs that parents can look for to determine whether their infant or toddler needs to see a physical therapist?**

To help you understand the professional side of this field, each chapter has a **Professional Perspective**, a one-on-one interview with someone whose job is related to child development. These professional interviews will not only allow you to understand how professionals view children, but they will also show you many of the career options that exist. Working with children is extremely rewarding, and we are excited to be able to show you numerous ways in which you can contribute to children's healthy development.

## Perspective PERSONAL — MEET THE PARENTS OF A VERY PREMATURE BABY

Kim Powell and Larry Sikkink
Decorah, IA
*Parents of Senia, born at 28 weeks' gestation weighing 1 pound, 15 ounces*

**When did you learn that your baby would be premature? What were your first thoughts? Do you know what caused the prematurity?**
*Kim:* I experienced a healthy pregnancy up to my sixth month. Then, at a prenatal exam, the doctor found I had high blood pressure as well as protein in my urine. The next day I was admitted to a hospital with a neonatal intensive care unit (NICU). At 28 weeks' gestation, on the way to my first ultrasound, I began feeling light-headed and felt a sudden pain in my upper abdomen. I began throwing up and had a severe headache. The doctor said I had to have an emergency Caesarean section if my baby and I were to live. I had HELLP syndrome (hemolysis, elevated liver enzymes, low blood platelets). There is no known cause or predictor for HELLP syndrome, and some mothers and babies die from the complications. I knew my baby would be born prematurely, but I was too sick to realize what that meant. Immediately after her birth, Senia was whisked away to the NICU, intubated, placed on a warming table, and connected to an IV feeding tube and breathing and heart monitors. My husband was still on the 90-minute drive from our home. Senia's left lung collapsed after birth, requiring three days of lung massage therapy. At 2 weeks she was moved to an incubator, where she stayed for 4 weeks.

*Larry:* Senia had been delivered about 15 minutes before my arrival. The NICU team was attending to her, and I was told I would be allowed to see her in about 30 minutes. I was shocked. How could I be the father of a baby girl already? An NICU doctor assured me that given time, care, and love, our daughter's chances for survival were very good.

**Has your baby needed or used any special services? What is your baby like today?**
*Kim:* At 4 pounds and 1 ounce, after seven weeks in the NICU, Senia came home on an apnea and bradycardia monitor. For 2½ months, Senia had episodes in which her breathing would stop and her heart rate would lower. She also had several bouts of pneumonia in her first year. It took 2 years for Senia to perform like others her age, but she is now all caught up. She is tall for her age and is at the 50th percentile in weight. Cognitively, she tests above age level. Senia started kindergarten at age 5 and loves writing, books, music, and dancing.

**What advice do you have for other parents who may have a premature or low-birth-weight baby?**
*Kim:* Educate yourself and read about other premature babies. Kim Wilson and I wrote *Living Miracles: Stories of Hope from Parents of Premature Babies* (Griffin Trade Paperbacks) so parents could share their situation. Above all else, though having a preemie is very stressful, parents should try to focus on the baby and enjoy every minute of watching the baby develop.

QUESTION **What can parents do to reduce their risk of having a premature baby? Which risk factors can they control in their lives?**

In addition, each chapter contains a **Personal Perspective**, an interview feature that introduces you to real-life parents and children.

## Perspective SOCIAL POLICY — CAN MOZART STIMULATE NEURAL CONNECTIONS IN INFANTS?

In his 1999 budget, then Georgia Governor Zell Miller proposed that the state spend $105,000 to send a CD or cassette of classical music home with every baby born in the state. Miller commented that "[n]o one questions that listening to music at a very young age affects the spatial, temporal reasoning that underlies math and engineering and even chess" and that "[h]aving that infant listen to soothing music helps those trillions of brain connections to develop" (Sack, 1998).

Does research evidence support Miller's claims? Frances Rauscher and her colleagues published a series of intriguing studies suggesting that extensive music training significantly enhanced the spatial-temporal skills of preschool children. These researchers also found that listening to a Mozart sonata improved college students' spatial-reasoning IQ scores by 8 to 9 points (Rauscher, Shaw, & Ky, 1993, 1995; Rauscher, Shaw, Levine, Wright, Dennis, & Newcomb, 1997). The spatial-reasoning scores involved were on tests of reasoning about proportions, ratios, and other concepts in mathematics. Improvements in these skills after exposure to classical music has been labeled the "Mozart effect." Reports about the Mozart effect and about how early experience wires the developing brain led the proactive governor of Georgia to propose jump-starting infants' brain development with classical music.

But will it work? For the college students, the benefit of listening to classical music was temporary, lasting only 10 to 15 minutes (Rauscher et al., 1997), and several other researchers have been unable to replicate the Mozart effect (e.g., Nantais & Schellenberg, 1999; Steele, Bass, & Crook, 1999). Still, the excitement over the initial findings prompted the Florida legislature to pass a law requiring that toddlers in state-run schools hear classical music every day (Goode, 1999).

QUESTION **On the basis of information in this chapter, how would you suggest that state and local governments, other agencies, schools, and parents enhance brain development in infants and toddlers? What information would you use to support new social policies in this area?**

To demonstrate the importance of child development information for current social issues and policies, we include a **Social Policy Perspective**. This feature highlights many specific controversies and debates surrounding children in our society. After reading these, you will see that different perspectives and opinions are everywhere. What's your take on these issues?

AS YOU STUDY THIS SECTION, ASK YOURSELF THESE QUESTIONS:

4.4 What are the main patterns of growth and sleep, and what do researchers know about Sudden Infant Death Syndrome?

4.5 What are the benefits of breastfeeding, and how long should children continue to breastfeed?

4.6 What are the main parts of the brain, and what are their basic functions?

4.7 What major patterns are seen in the formation of the brain and nervous system?

There are many tools in this book to help you check your learning. As you begin each major section of every chapter, you'll find **Learning Objective questions,** designed to help you preview the important concepts you are about to study.

The marginal glossary offers you a quick way to find definitions. Because the glossary terms are set in the margin of the text, you can study the important vocabulary and definitions for each chapter without having to hunt for them.

**synaptogenesis**
One form of neuron maturation in which dendrites and axons branch out to form an enormously large number of connections with neighboring neurons.

**myelination**
A form of neuron maturation in which the fatty insulation (myelin sheath) grows around the axons.

**programmed cell death**
Process by which many neurons die during periods of migration and heavy synaptogenesis.

LET'S REVIEW . . .

1. Children reach about half of their adult height by the time they are:
   a. 1 year old.
   b. 2 years old.
   c. 5 years old.
   d. 8 years old.
2. In the United States, how many mothers follow the recommendation of the American Academy of Pediatrics and breastfeed their infants until the infants are at least 12 months of age?
   a. fewer than one-quarter
   b. about half
   c. a little more than half
   d. about two-thirds
3. According to health experts, when should parents first introduce juices, soft foods, or other supplements to their breastfed infants?
   a. after the first month
   b. after 3 months
   c. after 6 months
   d. after 12 months
4. The first synapses form in the brain at around:
   a. 10 weeks of gestation
   b. 15 weeks of gestation
   c. 23 weeks of gestation
   d. 30 weeks of gestation
5. True or False: The American Academy of Pediatrics recommends co-sleeping, where infants sleep with the parents during the night.
6. True or False: Programmed cell death is nature's way of improving the efficiency of the brain as it develops.

Answers: 1. b, 2. a, 3. c, 4. c, 5. F, 6. T

Then, at the end of each section, you'll find **Let's Review** questions to help you make sure you've mastered the material. The answers to these questions accompany them, printed upside down.

4

## CHAPTER REVIEW . . .

**4.1 What are the different ways that prematurity is defined, and what are the developmental risks for each category of prematurity?**
Premature infants can be defined as preterm (born before 37 weeks' gestation), low birth weight (weighing less than 5½ pounds), very low birth weight (weighing less than 3½ pounds), or small for gestational age (born below the 10th percentile for weight for their gestational age). SGA babies are especially at risk because something has prevented them from growing as well as would be expected, given the amount of time they spent in the uterus. A number of risk factors for preterm and low-birth-weight births have been identified. Several, such as lack of prenatal care, malnutrition, smoking, alcohol and drug use, and young maternal age, are controllable.

**4.2 What are the infant mortality rates in the United States, and why are they so high?**
Infant mortality refers to the number of infants who die before reaching 1 year of age. The rate is relatively high in the United States. Increasing access to and use of good prenatal care would reduce the rates of preterm and low-birth-weight

**4.4 What are the main patterns of growth and sleep, and what do researchers know about Sudden Infant Death Syndrome (SIDS)?**
At birth, newborns average 7½ pounds in weight and 20 inches in length. Weight doubles by 5 months of age, and children reach almost half of their adult height by 2 years of age. Newborns sleep for two-thirds of the day, and most are sleeping through the night by six months. Co-sleeping is common in some cultures. SIDS is the leading cause of death in infants from 1 month to 1 year of age. There are no known causes of SIDS, but several risk factors are involved.

**4.5 What are the benefits of breastfeeding, and how long should children continue to breastfeed?**
Health experts agree that human breast milk provides optimal nutrition and additional health benefits for infants and toddlers. Unless other conditions prevent healthy breastfeeding, infants should receive breast milk alone until 6 months; then juices and soft foods can gradually be introduced. Breastfeeding can continue as a supplement to other foods.

**4.6 What are the main parts of the brain, and what are their**

The **Chapter Review** reminds you of the main questions addressed in the chapter and gives you a quick review of the most important concepts. This summary is not meant to be a replacement for reading the chapter, but it is an effective study tool.

The chapter review also contains a **Revisiting Themes** section, recapping where the four new research themes (nature/nurture interaction, neuroscience, resilience/plasticity, diversity and multiculturalism, and positive development/resilience) can be found in each chapter.

## REVISITING THEMES

The roles of *nature* and *nurture* can be seen as infants learn to adjust their sleep patterns (p. 114) and when they learn new motor skills such as walking and toilet training (pp. 129–131, 132). The interplay of nature and nurture is also evident as our early experiences in life help shape connections in the brain and nervous system (pp. 120–121).

*Neuroscientists* study the growth and development of the brain and nervous system, and pediatricians and other experts use the appearance and disappearance of infant reflexes as an indication of neurological maturity (pp. 130–131).

*Diversity and multiculturalism* are reflected in a many topics in this chapter. Cultural differences were noted in co-sleeping (p. 115), breastfeeding (pp. 117–118), and the role of exercise in motor development (pp. 129–131). Ethnic and racial differences were highlighted for rates of infant mortality (p. 111), prenatal care (pp. 112–113), and SIDS (p. 116), and for the timing of toilet training in toddlers (pp. 132–133).

*Positive development and resilience* are connected to the increasing use of prenatal care by pregnant women in the U.S. (p. 112) and by the resilience of preterm infants who survive and eventually catch up to their peers along many developmental milestones (p. 110).

## KEY TERMS

colostrum (116)
co-sleeping (115)
fine motor development (127)
gross motor development (127)
infant mortality (111)
myelination (120)
neurons (119)
programmed cell death (120)
reflexes (126)
small for gestational age (SGA) (111)
synaptogenesis (120)
Sudden Infant Death Syndrome (SIDS) (116)
very low birth weight (109)
visual acuity (123)

In addition, a list of key terms with page references included at the end of each chapter allows a quick flip to check key concepts and test comprehension.

All of these features work together as a learning system, designed to be educational, enlightening, thought-provoking, and memorable. Take what you learn here with you in life: It could help you in your next job, could improve your relationships at home, and surely will influence how you interact with every child you meet.

# Teaching and Learning Package

Pearson Education is pleased to offer the following supplements to qualified adopters.

## For Instructors

**Instructor's Manual** (**ISBN:** 0-205-77862-3) Created by David Wakefield, California State University, Northridge, this robust teaching resource gives you unparalleled access to a huge selection of classroom-proven assets. Each chapter offers integrated teaching outlines to help instructors seamlessly incorporate all the ancillary materials for this book into their lectures. Instructors will also find an extensive bank of lecture launchers, handouts and activities.

**Test Bank** (**ISBN:** Pearson MyTest 0-205-76640-4; Print TB 0-205-77860-7) Matthew Schlesinger, Southern Illinois University and Colleen Fawcett, Palm Beach Community College have created a comprehensive test bank featuring more than 150 questions per chapter and fully reviewed by experienced professors. The test bank includes multiple choice, true/false, fill-in-the-blank, and essay questions, and questions tied to some of the multimedia assets in MyDevelopmentLab, each coded with difficulty rating (easy/medium/difficult), page references, skill type (conceptual/factual/analytical), and rationales for the correct answer.

The test bank is available in a computerized format called **Pearson MyTest,** a powerful assessment generation program that helps instructors easily create and print quizzes and exams. Questions and tests can be authored online, allowing instructors ultimate flexibility and the ability to efficiently manage assessments anytime, anywhere. Instructors can easily access existing questions, edit, create, and store using simple drag and drop and Word-like controls. Data on each question provides information on difficulty level, page number, and skill type. In addition, each question maps to the text's major section and learning objective. For more information go to www.pearsonmytest.com.

**MyDevelopmentLab** This multimedia resource can be used to supplement a traditional lecture course or to administer a course entirely online. It is an all-inclusive tool, including a Pearson eText, plus multimedia tutorials, audio, video, simulations, animations, and controlled assessments to completely engage students and reinforce learning. Fully customizable and easy to use, MyDevelopmentLab meets the individual teaching and learning needs of every instructor and every student. Visit the site at www.mydevelopmentlab.com.

**My Virtual Child** My Virtual Child is an interactive Web-based simulation that allows you to raise a child from birth to age 18 and monitor the effects of your parenting decisions over time. This engaging Web site lets you apply the key concepts that you are learning in class. Just like in real life, certain unplanned events will be presented to you. You can access My Virtual Child within MyDevelopmentLab, or separately at www.myvirtualchild.com.

**PowerPoint™ Presentation** (**ISBN:** 0-205-76637-4) Katherine Norris, West Chester University of Pennsylvania, has created an exciting interactive tool for use in the classroom. The PowerPoint slides are available for download at the Instructor's Resource

Center (http://pearsonhighered.com/irc/) or on the Instructor's Resource DVD. The **PowerPoint lecture presentation** highlights major topics from the chapter, pairing them with select art images. In addition we offer a **PowerPoint collection of the complete art files** from the text which allows customized lectures with any of the figures from the text. Finally, included is a set of lecture **PowerPoints with art and embedded videos**.

Pearson Transparencies for Human Development (**ISBN:** 0-205-46853-5) Designed to enhance your classroom presentations, these transparencies contain color acetates drawn from the figures in *The World of Children* and other Pearson textbooks.

Digital Media Archive for Child Development (**ISBN:** 0-205-40746-3) This comprehensive source of images includes charts, graphs, tables, and figures to enhance your lecture.

Pearson Teaching Films Lifespan Development Video (**ISBN:** 0-205-65602-1) This new video highlights important high-interest topics in human development across the lifespan, including imagination in early childhood, motivation and school success, and aggression in adolescent romantic relationships. A video user's guide with critical-thinking questions and Web resources is available to support the use of the video in the classroom.

## For Students

Study Guide with Practice Tests (**ISBN:** 0-205-77861-5) Developed by Martha Mendez-Baldwin, Manhattan College, each chapter of this comprehensive and interactive study guide includes: "Before You Read," with a brief chapter summary and chapter learning objectives; "As You Read," a collection of demonstrations, activities, and exercises; "When You Have Finished," containing two short practice quizzes and one comprehensive practice test with Web links for further information, and crossword puzzles using key terms from the text. An appendix includes answers to all practice tests and crossword puzzles.

MyDevelopmentLab (www.mydevelopmentlab.com) This online all-in-one study resource offers a dynamic, electronic version of *The World of Children* textbook (eText) with more than 160 embedded video clips (2 to 4 minutes in length) and more than 60 embedded animations and simulations that dynamically illustrate chapter concepts. With more than 100 text-specific practice test questions per chapter, MyDevelopmentLab helps students master the concepts and prepare for exams. After a student completes a chapter pre-test, MyDevelopmentLab generates a customized Study Plan for that student to help focus study efforts where they are needed the most. MyDevelopmentLab is available in both course management and Web site versions and can be used as an instructor-driven assessment program and/or a student self-study learning program.

Development Journey through Childhood and Adolescence CD-ROM (**ISBN:** 0-205-39568-6) This multimedia learning tool includes eight interactive units that cover development from the prenatal period through adolescence and literally brings development to life. Through the use of unscripted, real video footage, students will see everything from live births to a toddler taking his first steps to a teen mom discussing how her life has changed since becoming a mother. The Flash and 3-D video animations teach students visually about the inner workings of the human body, including the reproductive organs, conception, and pregnancy. Written by Dr. Kelly Welch of Kansas State University, the CD-ROM includes several exercises for students, such as "drag-and-drop" activities, multiple-choice quizzes, flash-cards of glossary terms, journal writing, and instant feedback exercises called "Mad Minutes."

Study Card for Child Development (**ISBN:** 0-205-43508-4) Colorful and packed with useful information, the Study Card makes studying easier, more efficient, and more enjoyable.

# Acknowledgments

Literally hundreds of great people have contributed their time, skill, and passion in creating this textbook. We thank our many partners at Pearson Education—they are the leaders in innovation in higher education, and we are proud to be associated with their company. Our Executive Editor, Stephen Frail, has a unique sense of what really works in psychology textbooks, and we benefited greatly from his perspective. He keeps our projects moving, connects us with the latest technologies in the field, and motivates us with his positive enthusiasm. Our development editor, Deb Hanlon, worked with us every day to improve our writing, organize the many pieces of the project, and keep everyone focused on creating a high-quality textbook. Thanks, Deb! Executive Editor, Susan Hartman, and Sharon Geary, director of development, both do great work at Pearson Education in keeping everything organized and on track. Kerri Hart-Morris recruited participants for our Personal Perspective and Professional Perspective interview boxes, and we thank her for finding such intriguing and informative interviews. Marianne Peters-Riordan was our project manager, Nancy Wells was our senior art director, and Kara Kikel was the associate editor for our excellent package of textbook supplements, and they all provided critical leadership on the project. Dr. Lisa Scott from the University of Massachusetts Amherst provided valuable assistance as a content expert with our neuroscience material, and we thank her for her expertise. The marketing team at Pearson Education is terrific! We thank Jeanette Koskinas, our executive marketing manager, and Nicole Kunzmann, marketing manager in psychology. We also thank Katie Toulmin, Mary Clarke, Nick Kaufman, and their colleagues at NKP media for producing the terrific videos that open every chapter in our book. Martha Wetherill and the people at MPS Content Services provided helpful copyediting. We send a big thanks to all of the wonderful sales representatives at Pearson Education—without their expert help, we wouldn't be able to accomplish our goal of connecting a wide range of students and instructors to the field of child development. Communicating the field is our passion, and we couldn't do it without the support, skills, and wisdom of all of these contributors.

We also acknowledge the love and support we received from our family and friends throughout this project. Their patience and understanding helped us push through the long hours and tight deadlines. They both inspire us and keep us grounded in real life. We are especially grateful to our children, Andy, Will, Rachel, and Lily. They help us understand child development with our hearts as well as with our minds.

## Manuscript Reviewers

Of course, the most important part of the book is the content, and we want to express our deep appreciation for all of the time and effort provided by the faculty and instructors who reviewed our manuscript pages and offered feedback. Many of their suggestions became the strengths of our chapters and our supplements. These individuals include:

Carolyn Adams-Price, Mississippi State University
Kimberley F. Alkins, Queens College
Kathleen Bey, Palm Beach Community College
Jean Burr, Colby College
Victoria Coad, College of Marin
Jacquline Cottle, Texas Tech University
Marcie Coulter-Kern, Manchester College
Steven A. Dennis, Brigham Young University–Idaho
Diana Deutsch, Los Angeles Pierce College
Linda Dove, Western Michigan University
Ruth Doyle, Casper College
Patricia S. Eason, Monroe Community College
Michelle M. Englund, University of Minnesota

Karen Falcone, San Joaquin Delta College
Colleen Fawcett, Palm Beach Community College
William R. Fisk, Clemson University
Sherry Forrest, Craven Community College
Judith M. Geary, University of Michigan–Dearborn
Sabine Ferran Gerhardt, University of Akron
Ellis Gesten, University of South Florida
Sara Goldstein, Montclair State University
Gladys Green, Manatee Community College
Rebecca Griffith, College of the Sequoias
Belinda Hammond, Los Angeles Mission College
Myra Harville, Holmes Community College
Darbi Haynes-Lawrence, Western Kentucky University
Loreen Huffman, Missouri Southern State University
David P. Hurford, Pittsburg State University
Lindsay Jernigan, University of Vermont
Brandis Brooke Judkins, Indiana University of Pennsylvania
Jyotsna Kalavar, Pennsylvania State University
Caroline Ketcham, Elon University
Carol LaLiberte, Westfield State College
Sara Lawrence, California State University
Jennifer Leszczynski, Eastern Connecticut State University
Ronald Mulson, Hudson Valley Community College
Annette Nolte, Tarrant County College
Amy Obegi, Grossmont College
Cathy Pollock, Asheville Buncombe Technical Community College
Sandra Portko, Grand Valley State University
Linda S. Raasch, Normandale Community College
Mary Kay Reed, York College of Pennsylvania
Mark P. Rittman, Cuyahoga Community College
Betsye Robinette, Indiana Wesleyan University
Holly Schiffrin, University of Mary Washington
Matt Schlesinger, Southern Illinois University
Ariane Schratter, Maryville College
Whitney Scott, California State University–Northridge
Donna Smith, University of Kentucky
Eric Snader, Rutgers University
Lila Snow, Los Angeles Pierce College
April Taylor, California State University, Northridge
David Townsend, Pittsburg State University
Teraesa Vinson, Bronx Community College

## Perspective Boxes and Chapter Opening Vignette Interviewees

Our special thanks go to the individuals, professionals, and families who were incredibly generous enough to share their stories, experiences, challenges, and advice in an effort to inform and educate. We believe their insightful contributions will help students further their understanding of the text's concepts as well as help shape their personal and career decisions. These contributors are: Lea Adams, Nola and Akindele Akala, Stacie Anderson, Robin L. Bennett, Deena Bernstein, Abbi Beuby, Brad, Sharon Buenaventura, Douglas Bunnell, Camila, Betsy Carroll, Chi Hae and Cara, Jamie Commissaris, Kim Davenport, Dawn, Vivian Dobrinsky, Harlan Gephardt, Patrick, David, and Lori Glenn, Mariana Hertel, Jess and Darran, Josh, Juan and Tracey, Julie and Tom, Deborah Koshansky, Carolyn and Bob Landers, Leo, Paul, Jacqueline, and Paul David Lewis, Linda, Lisa, Nancy Magowan, Sophia Martin, "Mary Jane," Iris and Manual Matos, Kim Miller, Pam, Kristin and Marc Petraluzzi, Kim Powell, the Rodriguez children, Sandy Roland, Donna Rowland, Cheri and Allan Scott, Hannah and Asher Shapiro, Sheryl and Adam, Larry Sikkink, Jan Craige Singer, Sujatha and RK, Pamela Talbot, Susan Tice, Kathryn Tromblay, Anne Upgrove, Hanna Lee Vestal, Deanna Walsh, Angela Watkins.

## Survey Participants

We are grateful to the following instructors who responded to our survey and reviewed several pre-publication chapters of the first edition. Their input helped finalize the manuscript and we are grateful to them. Thanks to the following participants:

Melanie Arpaio, Sussex County Community College
Jane Baker, Tennessee Tech University
Alfred W. Baptista, Massasoit Community College
Dr. Terri Barrett, Lenoir-Rhyne College
Lynne A. Bond, University of Vermont
Dr. Janine P. Buckner, Seton Hall University
Janice Cataldo, Henry Ford Community College
Mary Anne Chalkley, University of St. Thomas
Sarah Changnon, Southeast Community College
Donna Cohn, Pima Community College

Susan Eilason, Anna Maria College
Miriam Folk, Florida Community College at Jacksonville
Sabine Ferran Gerhardt, University of Akron
Bonnie Good, Delta College
Jill A. Harrison, Delta College
Sharon Hirschy, Collin College
Gary E. Krolikowski, State University of New York at Geneseo
Mary Mallory, Chapman University College
Michael Martinsen, Edgewood College
Cathleen McGreal, Michigan State University
Kelly McKown, Saint Paul College
Maryam Mehran, Chapman University College at Concord
Elizabeth Page, Lurleen B. Wallace Community College
Samantha Ramsay, University of Idaho
Elizabeth Kelley Rhoades, West Texas A&M University
Dr. Betsye Robinette, Indiana Wesleyan University
Carole L. Sanetti, Eastern Connecticut State University
Eulis Sawney, Howard University
Maria K. Schmidt, Indiana University
Pamela Schuetze, Buffalo State College
Stephanie Scroggins, Tarrant County College, Northeast
Chris Seifert, Montana State University
Jamie Simpson, Iowa Lakes Community College
Paulo Sudhaus, University of Arizona
Kim Sutton, Ozarks Technical Community College
April Taylor, California State University at Northridge
Margaret Torrie, Iowa State University
Susan Walker, University of Maryland at College Park
Elizabeth Wall, Wilmington College
Kathryn M. Westcott, Juniata College
Glenna Zeak, Penn State

## Class Testers

The following instructors deserve special thanks for their willingness to class test the chapters with their students. Their enthusiasm for teaching and by extension our text is contagious, and we thank the following individuals for their participation:

Dr. Gregory Boers, West Los Angeles College
Juanita Cordero, De Anza College
Tim Croy, Eastern Illinois University
Bonnie Good, Delta College
Janet Hale, Porterville College
Nancy Hartshorne, Central Michigan University
Barbara J. Myers, Virginia Commonwealth University
Cathy Proctor-Castillo, Long Beach Community College
April Taylor, California State University at Northridge
Bonnie L. Voth, University of Central Oklahoma
Angela Williamson, Tarrant County College, Northwest

# About the Authors

**Greg Cook** is a Professor of Psychology at the University of Wisconsin–Whitewater where he also serves as the campus Director of Academic Assessment and works in the Dean's Office. Greg majored in psychology at the University of Dayton and later received his PhD in psychology at Vanderbilt University. For the past 24 years he has taught courses in child development, research methods, statistics, and related topics at Whitewater as well as at Vanderbilt University and at the Madison and Richland Center campuses in the University of Wisconsin system. At Whitewater Greg received a college award and a departmental award for teaching excellence. Students consistently comment on his ability to present difficult information in a clear and understandable way. Greg's research on cognitive development has been published in scholarly journals such as *Child Development, Developmental Psychology,* and the *Journal of Experimental Child Psychology.* He has also collaborated with colleagues in the College of Education on studies published in the *Journal of Experimental Education*, the *Journal of Research and Development in Education,* and the *Journal of Reading Education.*

**Joan Littlefield Cook** is Professor and Chairperson of the Psychology Department at the University of Wisconsin–Whitewater. As an undergraduate she majored in psychology at Tennessee Technological University. She earned a Master's degree and PhD in psychology and human development at Vanderbilt University. Over the past 23 years she has taught courses related to child and adolescent development, educational psychology, and cognitive psychology at the University of Wisconsin–Whitewater, the University of Wisconsin–Madison, and Middle Tennessee State University. Her classes have ranged from large lecture courses (with 250 or more students) to small seminars. Joan's students have always appreciated her knowledge of the field and her ability to present information in a way that is useful, motivating, and friendly. The Student Association at the University of Wisconsin–Madison voted her as one of their most outstanding professors, and the psychology students at University of Wisconsin–Whitewater also gave her their teaching award. Joan's research is on mathematical problem solving and cognitive development. She and her colleagues have published papers in the *Journal of Educational Psychology, Cognition and Instruction, Memory & Cognition, Intelligence,* the *Gifted Child Quarterly, Reading Psychology*, and the *Journal of Experimental Psychology.* She has co-authored three other books and numerous instructional materials.

Greg and Joan also co-authored *Child Development: Principles and Perspectives,* a fresh and widely acclaimed textbook (published by Allyn & Bacon) that explores child development within a topical framework.

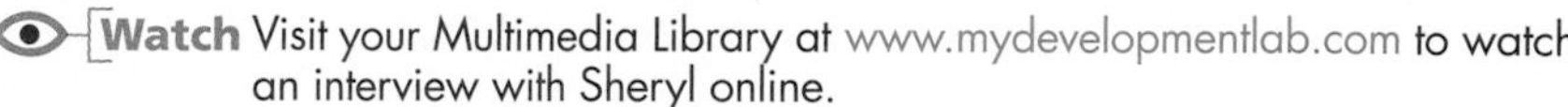

Watch Visit your Multimedia Library at www.mydevelopmentlab.com to watch an interview with Sheryl online.

# 1 BEGINNINGS
# Exploring Child Development

Sheryl and Adam recently welcomed their third child into the family, and their lives have really changed. They used to have more time to spend one-on-one with their children, but now they are finding that it's quite a challenge to keep up with the basic care of a new baby and all of the activities that their other children are in. Max, their oldest, is 9 years old. He's really smart and loves school and video games, and he's an excellent skier for his age. He sometimes has a mind of his own, however, and loves demonstrating his independence. Isabella is 6, and she's very active in gymnastics, dance, acting, and music. Although she's only in first grade, she's ambitious with all of her activities, and she also shows a soft spot in caring for other people. It's really cute to watch her cuddle with her new baby sister. Zoey, the new addition, is already very different from her older brother and sister. Zoey is more relaxed and laid back than the others were as infants. She isn't rolling over yet or showing the kinds of muscle coordination that the other children did at her age, but she is more sociable—she loves to smile and coo anytime people are near. Zoey also looks different than the others. Her hair and eyes are a lighter color, and her skin has a more delicate complexion.

Sheryl wonders what her children will be like when they get older. She doesn't mean to compare them, but she is surprised at how different they are. She and Adam don't think they are treating the children all that differently, but they certainly do have different interests and personalities. How does that happen? Sheryl tries not to worry too much. Like most parents, she wants her children to be happy and to do their best at whatever they try. Raising children is a challenge, but Sheryl and Adam are both excited when they look into the future and wonder how their children will turn out. They wonder what they can do to help their children the most and want to enjoy each one of them as a unique and special individual.

As you read through this introductory chapter, think about the information from the perspective of these parents. What advice could you give to Sheryl and Adam as they think about the best ways to care for their children? What do researchers know about children's development, and why do children from the same family sometimes seem so different? What are the stages of development children go through as they grow and mature? What are the forces that drive development? After studying this chapter, you should be able to use at least a dozen concepts about child development to give Sheryl and Adam specific answers to these questions.

As you read this chapter, look for the "Think About Sheryl and Adam . . ." questions that ask you to consider what you're learning from their perspective.

There are few things more amazing to watch than the growth and development of a child. Babies are tiny and helpless at birth, but in just a few short months they are crawling about, feeding themselves, and exploring everything in sight. Before long, they are starting their first day of kindergarten, and later they are going on first dates, learning to drive a car, and eventually starting their own jobs and young adult lives. Their progress through childhood and adolescence is remarkable.

THINKING CRITICALLY
In what ways are you different as an adult than you were as a young child? In what ways are you still the same?

Have you had the opportunity to closely watch a child grow and mature? If not, you can reflect on your own development. You are obviously larger, stronger, and more coordinated than you were as a young child. You also have much more factual knowledge and more effective and efficient problem-solving skills. Your social relations are very different, especially if you have moved away from your family or have started a family of your own. Yet in other ways you have kept many of the qualities you had at the outset. For example, maybe you were shy as a child and continue to be reserved and reflective today, or perhaps you were very active as a child and are still energetic and athletic.

This chapter introduces you to the field of child development. First we'll define the field of child development, examining the basic issues and questions it addresses. Then we will give you a brief overview of some of the most important theories and research methods used in the field and show you how this information applies to the real lives of children.

▲ Differences in physical development are obvious when you compare the children in this photo. Size, strength, and coordination all increase with development.

## Defining the Field

In the field of **child development**, professionals from psychology, education, sociology, anthropology, social work, biology, medicine, economics, and other related fields work together. Their shared purpose is to describe and understand the important changes that take place as children move from infancy through childhood and adolescence. Children are changing every day—growing, gaining knowledge, and learning new skills. Yet in some ways children remain the same across their development. For example, a child who was happy and outgoing as a toddler may remain happy and outgoing throughout the rest of his childhood.

Understanding child development is important for everyone who wants to work with or help children. Parents naturally have a personal stake in providing the best environment and support they can. Teachers, counselors, social workers, psychologists, nurses, and other professionals who help children also need to understand the fundamental principles of development as well as the various ways that development can be disrupted or affected. Understanding child development can also help you understand your own progression into adulthood: Knowing more about where you came from can help you appreciate your current phase of life and may give you insights about where you are headed next.

**child development**
Field of study in which researchers from many disciplines work to describe and understand the important changes that take place as children grow through childhood.

**physical development**
Component of development related to growth in size, strength, and muscle coordination.

AS YOU STUDY THIS SECTION, ASK YOURSELF THESE QUESTIONS:

1.1 What characteristics and processes do child development researchers study?

1.2 What are several main themes that run across child development research today?

### What Develops?

A child's development is multifaceted. The most visible component is **physical development**. Children grow in size, and their muscles become stronger and more coordinated. At birth, newborn babies cannot even hold their heads up, but over the following months, they will make tremendous gains in muscle strength and coordination. Later they will crawl, take their first steps, and eventually learn to ride bicycles and play sports. Many children go through a "lanky" period—a time when a rapid gain in height outpaces the gains in weight and muscle mass. During adolescence, sexual maturity is attained, and the adolescent's physical appearance becomes more adult-like. The brain and nervous system grow and mature across childhood too, contributing to many of the changes we see in coordination and skill.

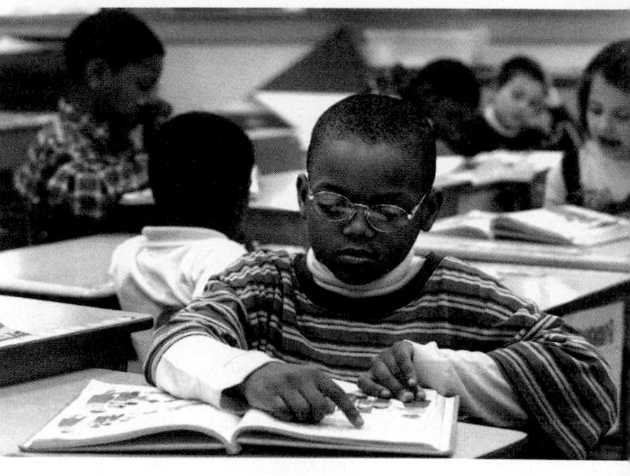

▲ How do cognitive activities change with development? Researchers study how perception, memory, intelligence, problem solving, language, and other thinking skills develop during childhood and adolescence.

**Cognitive development** consists of numerous changes in how children perceive the world, process information, store and retrieve memories, solve problems, and communicate with language. Infants explore the world all around them, and they begin to speak their first words as they learn names for common objects and events. Later, we see cognitive growth most easily in the progress children and adolescents make in their academic work: learning to read and write and gaining mastery of mathematics, social studies, science, art, and other topics. Underlying and supporting this growth are gains in perception, information processing, memory, and problem solving.

Children also make rapid progress in **socioemotional development**. As infants, they depend on their parents and other family members for food, safety, and entertainment. As they grow, they begin to meet and interact with childhood peers, and this helps improve communication and emotional skills. Toddlers play readily with mates of both genders, but by middle childhood true friendships are established and most playmates are same-sex. Later, most adolescents will struggle with the challenges of meeting potential partners and dating, exploring their own sexual identities, and forming intimate relationships.

**THINK ABOUT SHERYL AND ADAM . . .** What examples of physical, cognitive, and socioemotional development did you notice in the descriptions of Sheryl and Adam's children? What other examples might you expect to see for each type of development?

This text explores the many changes and similarities we see as we track child development from birth through childhood and the adolescent period. After these first chapters on beginnings, we will divide the text into the following parts:

- *Infants and Toddlers: The First Years* covers birth through age 2, as infants and toddlers get their starts in life;
- *Early Childhood: The Playful Years* covers ages 3 through 6, as children play, make friends, and explore the world around them;
- *Middle Childhood: The School Years* covers ages 7 through 11, as children focus on school and learning; and
- *Adolescence: The Transition toward Adulthood* covers ages 12 and up, as children move into puberty and teenagers emerge into adulthood.

Each section includes one chapter on physical development, one chapter on cognitive development, and one chapter on socioemotional development. Putting these chapters together will give you a feel for the developmental challenges and advances that take place within each age level.

## Themes in Child Development

Children's lives are complex, and their growth and development is influenced by a vast array of influences. As you read through this text, you will learn many of the details that researchers have learned about child development. For some of the topics, we trace the research back to its origin—as authors, we understand that students often have a better appreciation of what the research looks like today if they understand where the research started. For most topics, however, we concentrate on the most current research. To help you keep all of this information in perspective, we'd like to think about four major

**cognitive development** Component of development related to changes in how children perceive the world, think, remember information, and communicate.

**socioemotional development** Component of development related to changes in how children interact with other people (e.g., family members, peers, and playmates) and manage their emotions.

▲ How do social skills change with age? Friendship patterns, play, and cooperation are just a few of the topics that researchers study in the area of socioemotional development.

themes that we see in child development today. Although these themes have been emerging for many years, they have now risen to a level of prominence that helps us define the modern approach to the study of child development.

**Nature and Nurture.** First, children's growth and development is influenced by both nature and nurture. **Nature** refers to the biological forces that govern development. Just as a seed contains genetic information that controls how a seedling will grow into a beautiful flower, children also have genetic information coded deep inside all of the cells in their bodies. This genetic information controls how the body forms and grows, and it also influences many of our important human traits. By now you know that genes influence the color of your eyes, but did you also know they play a role in determining your height and weight, your level of intelligence, and even your basic personality?

**Nurture** refers to the supports and conditions that surround children and influence their development. For healthy development, children need the love and support of parents, siblings, extended family, teachers, peers, and other people important in the child's life. Children are also influenced by the cultural and socioeconomic environment surrounding them. Poverty, malnutrition, and a lack of adequate medical care can have negative effects on their growth and development. Cultural heritage and diversity can enrich their lives, and the neighborhood where the child lives can determine the types of schools and peer groups the child will have. All of these influences lie outside the child's own biology, and they are all considered part of nurture. Nurture also includes the experiences the children have and the things they learn from their environments.

**THINKING CRITICALLY**

Think back to your own childhood, and identify several examples of nature and nurture and how they influenced your development. In what ways did these two forces interact? How would you explain this interaction to someone who asks whether nature or nurture is the more important force?

Throughout history, philosophers and scientists have debated the relative roles of nature and nurture. John Watson, a renowned American psychologist of the early twentieth century, was a strong proponent of the nurture school. He wrote:

> [G]ive me a dozen healthy infants, well formed, and my own specified world to bring them up and I'll guarantee to take any one at random and train him to become any type of specialist I might select—doctor, lawyer, artist, merchant-chief and, yes, even beggar-man and thief, regardless of his talents, penchants, tendencies, abilities, vocations, and ancestors (1930/1924, p. 104).

Watson argued that experience and learning—nurture—determined what children would become. But other researchers have disagreed, pointing out that characteristics such as intelligence and personality are determined more by genetics (nature) than by nurture. For example, researchers have shown that the IQ scores of identical twins are more similar than the IQ scores of fraternal twins (Bouchard & McGue, 1981). Identical twins have the same genes as each other but fraternal twins have only about half of their genes in common, so these researchers argue that the increase in similarity in intelligence is controlled by the increase in genetic similarity between the twins. A similar conclusion comes from studies of children who were adopted as young infants. By the time adopted children grow up to age 18, their IQs are more similar to the IQs of the biological mothers who gave birth to them than they are to the adoptive parents who raised and nurtured them (Loehlin, Horn, & Willerman, 1994; Scarr, Weinberg, & Waldman, 1993). On the other hand, the IQs of identical twins are more similar when the twins are raised together than when they are adopted and reared apart (Bouchard & McGue, 1981). This demonstrates that IQ is controlled by more than genetics—it is also influenced by nurture.

**nature**
The biological forces (e.g., genetics) that govern development.

**nurture**
The environmental supports and conditions that impact development. Also refers to learning and experience.

The debate about nature and nurture can be traced back to the very beginnings of psychology and philosophy. However, with the technologies being used today scientists are uncovering fascinating new details about the functions of genes and genetic inheritance. Consequently, the nature–nurture issue is again rising to be one of the hottest issues studied in the field. Modern researchers understand that nature and nurture work together, and it is impossible to distinguish their separate effects (Lerner, 2006; Rutter, 2002). Rather than arguing about which one is most important, researchers are shifting their focus to studying exactly how the two groups of factors interact with each other. We will have much more to say about nature, nurture, and their interactions in Chapter 2.
**Listen** on **mydevelopmentlab**

**neuroscience**
Study of the brain and the nervous system.

**Listen**: What is the importance of both biological and environmental influences on development? (Author Podcast)
www.mydevelopmentlab.com

The Role of Neuroscience. **Neuroscience** is a growing field in which psychologists, biologists, and other scientists study the structure and function of the brain and nervous system. Scientists are busy studying which areas of the brain are most responsible for speaking, reading, solving problems, coordinating muscles, and performing many other tasks and skills. We have learned how children's speed and coordination improve as pathways in the brain mature, and we are learning more about how hormones, genes, and other biological features influence children's behaviors, cognitive processes, and even emotions.

Technological advances in recent decades have allowed more direct observation of the brain and nervous system than was ever possible before. *Computerized tomography (CT)* scans give computer-enhanced three-dimensional X-ray images of the brain. With *positron emission tomography (PET),* clinicians inject radioactive markers in a person's bloodstream and then trace them through the brain as the person engages in certain cognitive tasks. For example, with PET scans researchers can tell which areas of the brain are most active when a student is reading versus speaking, or doing math versus trying to recall vocabulary words. One problem with PET scans is that they are not precise—they only indicate which gross areas are involved in processing. *Functional magnetic resonance imaging (fMRI)* can detect changes in the rate of metabolism, or energy consumption, in smaller areas of the brain. With fMRI researchers can precisely identify the specific parts of the brain that become more active as people process different types of information. As this research continues, we will learn more about how biological changes impact child development and also about the reverse—how children's experiences influence their own biological development.

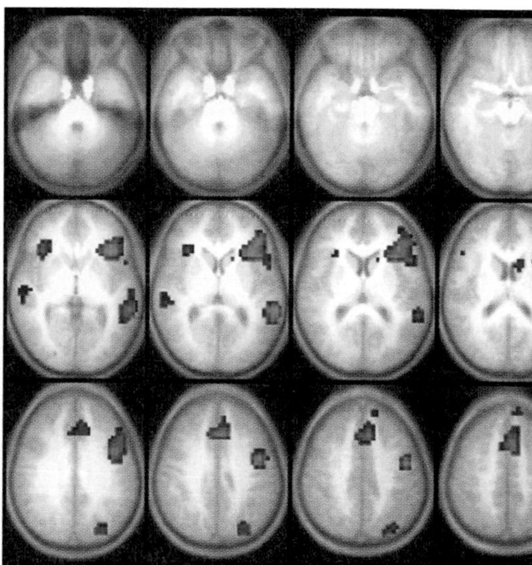

▲ This fMRI scan shows a composite image of brain activity taken as children think about a problem. Notice how the frontal lobe is especially active in this task. Neuroscientists use technologies like this to study how the brain functions and changes as children grow and learn new skills.

Diversity and Multiculturalism. A third theme that we want to emphasize is that researchers are now spending more time studying how diversity enriches children's lives. More than ever before, we are seeing research on children from racial and ethnic minority families, from immigrant families, and from families speaking two or more languages. Researchers are interested in the issues faced by gay and lesbian parents, by divorced and single parents, and by parents who adopt children from the U.S. or from abroad. On an even larger level, psychologists, sociologists, and other researchers are investigating how cultures and cultural values impact society, and then in turn how society influences family life and children. As our nation becomes even more multicultural, the increasing diversity we see in our neighborhoods, schools, and families will no doubt pose many challenges, but it will also add richness to all of our lives.

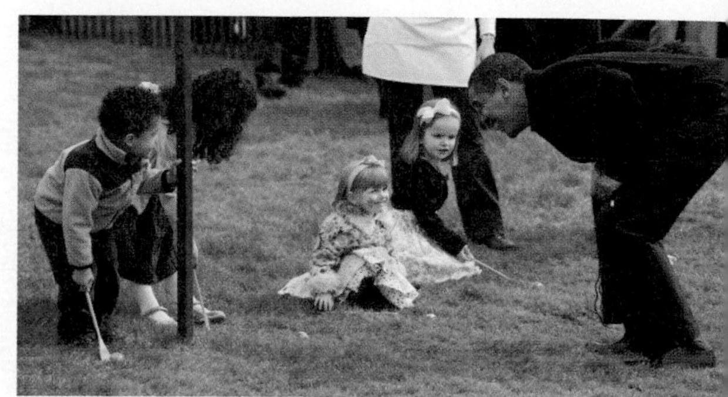

▲ Children growing up today experience even more diversity and multiculturalism than ever before.

Positive development and resilience. Finally, we want to emphasize that most children experience positive growth and development. Most children are happy and healthy; teenagers more often than not report that they enjoy their relationships with their parents, and most go on to be successful in school, careers, and life. Throughout this text, you will read about research on birth defects, mental illnesses, family problems, forms of abuse, and many other topics related to negative pathways of development. Researchers need to investigate these important issues so we can all understand how to better help children and their families. In recent years, however, there has been a move toward increasing research in **positive psychology** and in understanding when and how children develop in positive ways. Even when the odds seem stacked against children, as when they have serious health problems or live in poverty, many children prove to be **resilient**—they rise above adversity and beat the odds. In this text, we will discuss many of the problems that can occur in development, but we will also emphasize the positive paths that most children take.

**positive psychology**
Refers to a new emphasis in psychology on the study of happiness and positive development.

**resilient children**
Children who rise above adversity to become successful or otherwise develop in positive ways.

These four themes represent some of the most vibrant and cutting-edge research in the field of child development. We highlight examples of this research throughout the text. For easy access, we also summarize these topics at the end of each chapter in our Revisiting Themes section (see page 35, after the Chapter Review).

## LET'S REVIEW . . .

1. Which of the following professions contributes to the field of child development?
   - **a.** psychology
   - **b.** sociology
   - **c.** economics
   - **d.** all of the above
2. Learning new strategies for solving problems and remembering information is part of:
   - **a.** cognitive development.
   - **b.** physical development.
   - **c.** social development.
   - **d.** natural development.
3. What was John Watson's position on the nature–nurture debate?
   - **a.** Nature plays the biggest role in child development.
   - **b.** Nurture plays the biggest role in child development.
   - **c.** Nature and nurture play equal roles in child development.
   - **d.** You can never tell which force (nature or nurture) is playing the biggest role.
4. The general conclusion that researchers draw from studies of twins and adopted children is that:
   - **a.** nature governs most of child development.
   - **b.** nurture governs most of child development.
   - **c.** nature and nurture both interact to govern child development.
   - **d.** neither nature nor nurture play strong roles in child development.
5. True or False: Genetics is an example of how nature can influence a child's development.
6. True or False: The fact that IQ scores are more similar between identical twins than between fraternal twins shows the influence of nurture on children's intellectual development.

Answers: 1. d, 2. a, 3. b, 4. c, 5. T, 6. F

# Theories of Child Development

Now that we've outlined common issues studied in child development, let's take a look at the main theories that have been offered to explain how child development occurs. Over the years, researchers have gathered countless observations and facts about all facets of children's development. There are data on everything from average heights and weights to IQ scores to friendship and play patterns to the effects of discipline and divorce. This vast array of facts would be incomprehensible if the data were not organized in some coherent fashion. In this section, we will explain why researchers develop theories to organize the facts. We will also describe some of the most important theories that have influenced the field of child development.

AS YOU STUDY THIS SECTION, ASK YOURSELF THESE QUESTIONS:

**1.3** What is a theory, and why are theories useful?

**1.4** How have the psychoanalytic, behavioral, and social learning theories contributed to the field of child development?

**1.5** How have the cognitive, biological, and contextual and systems theories contributed to the field of child development?

## What Is a Theory, and Why Are Theories Useful?

A **theory** is an explanation of how facts fit together. Theories provide frameworks that show how the facts are organized and related, and these frameworks can serve several useful functions (Thomas, 2000):

- *Theories summarize the facts as currently known.* By understanding contemporary theories you can see what researchers currently know about child development. By tracing important theories through history, you can see what experts once thought and how knowledge and ideas have changed over time.
- *Theories allow prediction of future behavior and events.* Theories tell us how the facts or events tend to be related in most situations; so if we know that one of the events is occurring now, then we can predict that the related events will soon follow. For example, an accurate theory of discipline should tell us how children tend to respond to harsh punishment versus milder forms of punishment. Then, if we know that a particular child is receiving harsh punishment now, we can predict what the child's response might be (soon or in the near future).
- By allowing prediction, *theories provide guidance* to parents, teachers, counselors, therapists, social workers, and others who work with children.
- *Theories also stimulate new research and discoveries.* By definition theories cannot be directly verified, so researchers test theories by drawing specific inferences, or **hypotheses**, from the general theories and then collecting scientific observations to find out if the hypotheses are valid. In the course of testing hypotheses, researchers make observations, collect facts, and may make new discoveries. This process often leads to revisions in the initial theories and sometimes to the development of new theories.
- Finally, *theories act as filters* for identifying relevant information, observations, and relationships. Theories influence how we look at children and their development, and the kinds of questions researchers ask about development. In this way, theories act to filter out questions and observations that don't seem relevant to the theory; what does seem relevant is allowed to pass on to the next level of consideration. A researcher will see the simple act of a child's helping his or her father, for example, very differently depending on whether the researcher views the behavior through the filtering lens of a psychoanalytic, behavioral, or ecological theory.

Table 1.1 on page 10 provides an overview of some of the major theories of child development. Psychoanalytic theories were among the earliest in the field; they had a major influence in shaping our early notions of child development. The development field has largely discarded these theories, however, as the newer theories have proved to be more accurate and useful. The behavioral and social learning theories were prominent in the mid-twentieth century. Although newer approaches have emerged since, professionals who work with children still rely on these theories to design programs to modify children's behavior. Cognitive theories rose to prominence in the late 1900s. Contextual and systems theories, such as dynamic systems, are relatively new and their potential is still being explored.

**theory**
An explanation of how facts fit together, allowing us to understand and predict behavior.

**hypotheses**
Specific inferences drawn from theories; researchers test hypotheses by collecting scientific observations.

**TABLE 1.1**
An Overview of Major Developmental Theories

| PSYCHOANALYTIC THEORIES | BEHAVIORAL AND SOCIAL LEARNING THEORIES | COGNITIVE THEORIES | BIOLOGICAL THEORIES | SYSTEMS THEORIES |
|---|---|---|---|---|
| Focus on personality development and effects of conscious and unconscious mind on behavior and development | Focus on observable conditions in environment and how they relate to observable behaviors | Focus on how children learn to think | Focus on biological and physical explanations of development | Focus on complex interactions among layers of systems and variables |
| **Psychoanalytic (Sigmund Freud)** | **Classical Conditioning (Ivan Pavlov, John Watson)** | **Cognitive Developmental (J ean Piaget)** | **Ethology (Konrad Lorenz)** | **Ecological Systems (Urie Bronfenbrenner)** |
| • Mind contains the id, ego, and superego; all are in constant conflict<br>• Five stages of psychosexual development<br>• Personality is well developed by end of adolescence | • Behavior controlled by stimulus–response connections<br>• Unconditioned stimulus reflexively elicits unconditioned response; unconditioned stimulus paired with neutral stimulus; conditioned stimulus comes to elicit conditioned response<br>• Explains the development of many fears | • Children actively construct their own understanding<br>• Children develop mental schemes to represent their understanding<br>• Children assimilate and accommodate their schemes<br>• Four major stages of cognitive development | • Based on Darwin's theory of evolution and natural selection<br>• Study behaviors that help animals (including humans) compete and survive | • Layers of systems affect the development of the child<br>• Layers include interactions among family, friends, schools, neighborhoods, government agencies, parents' workplace, and the values, laws, and customs of the larger society<br>• These interactions change over time |
| **Psychosocial (Erik Erikson)** | **Operant Conditioning (B. F. Skinner)** | **Sociocultural (Lev Vygotsky)** | **Neuroscience** | **Dynamic Systems** |
| • Focus on development of healthy ego identity<br>• Series of eight psychosocial crises<br>• More positive or more negative crisis resolution dependent on interactions with other people<br>• Personality development is lifelong | • Behavior influenced by the consequences of actions<br>• Reinforcement increases probability of a behavior being repeated; punishment decreases the probability of a behavior being repeated<br>• Children adjust behavior to gain reinforcement and avoid punishment | • Emphasized roles of culture and social interaction in cognitive development<br>• Children adopt the psychological tools created and encouraged by their cultures<br>• Social speech is internalized as private speech; eventually becomes inner speech | • Direct observation of brain and nervous system structures and functions during thought<br>• Uses technological advances to identify specific areas of brain activity related to mental functions and behaviors | • Theories based on models used by mathematicians and physicists to understand complex systems<br>• Complex interactions of multiple factors can appear chaotic, but stable patterns can emerge as the system self-organizes<br>• Patterns change over time |
| | **Social Learning (Albert Bandura)** | **Information Processing** | | |
| | • Children learn by observing and imitating others' behavior; they do not always need reinforcement or punishment<br>• Reinforcement and punishment give information to help children think about which behaviors to imitate | • Detailed analysis of processes used in thinking<br>• Emphasis on roles of basic processing efficiency, prior knowledge, and memory | | |

As you read about these various theories, keep in mind that each one offers a summary of what researchers knew and suspected about child development at a given time. Theories change as science progresses. Also, don't expect any one theory to explain everything about child development. Most theories are targeted at certain aspects of child development—such as how children learn, how they think about things in the world, or how they interact with the people around them. No theory by itself is sufficient to explain every process and change that occurs as children grow and develop. Today, many psychologists and researchers take an eclectic view that combines the main concepts across several theories at once. With these thoughts in mind, let's explore some developmental theories. We'll begin with the earliest and end with the most recent.

## Psychoanalytic, Behavioral, and Social Learning Theories

**Psychoanalytic Theories.** **Psychoanalytic theories** focus on the structure of personality and on how the conscious and unconscious portions of the self influence behavior and development. The two most prominent psychoanalytic theories were developed by Sigmund Freud and Erik Erikson.

**psychoanalytic theories** Theories that focus on the structure of personality and how the conscious and unconscious portions of the self influence behavior and development.

Sigmund Freud (1856–1939) was an Austrian physician, specializing in neurology, who treated patients for a variety of ailments. Some of his patients experienced symptoms (e.g., paralysis) that seemed to be caused by neurological abnormalities, but when Freud carefully examined these patients he found no evidence of physical problems. After puzzling over these cases, Freud concluded that the symptoms sprang from unconscious psychological conflicts. They were similar to what we might today call psychosomatic illnesses. Over several decades, Freud used hypnosis, free association, dream interpretation, and detailed clinical interviews with his patients to explore their unconscious desires and conflicts. In the process he created his famous (and controversial) theory of psychoanalysis and child development.

According to Freud, the mind contains three basic components: the id, the ego, and the superego. Explore on mydevelopmentlab

Explore The Id, Ego, and Superego. www.mydevelopmentlab.com

- The *id* lies completely below the level of conscious awareness and represents the primitive sexual and aggressive instincts that humans inherited through evolution.
- The *ego* is the rational branch of personality; it tries to negotiate realistic ways to satisfy the id's impulses.
- The *superego* represents the moral branch of personality and contains our ethical principles, ideals, and conscience.

Freud proposed that these three components are in a perpetual state of conflict. When arguing with another person, for example, you might experience an impulse (from the id) to shove the person. At the same time you would recall (thanks to the superego) that it is not polite to assault people. You might arrive at a compromise (negotiated by the ego) to let a few angry words fly and then avoid seeing the person for a while. To have a healthy personality, we need the morality of the superego to balance the primitive instincts of the id. We also need an ego that is strong, realistic, and able to conduct swift and delicate negotiations among the id, the superego, and the demands of the world at large.

▲ Sigmund Freud, the originator of psychoanalysis, proposed five stages of personality development.

How do these components develop during childhood? Freud believed that we are born with the id, inherited from our evolutionary ancestors. He then proposed five stages of psychosexual development to explain how the ego and superego emerge to tame the id. Figure 1.1 summarizes these stages. During the oral and anal stages, feedback from parents helps infants and toddlers curb their instincts

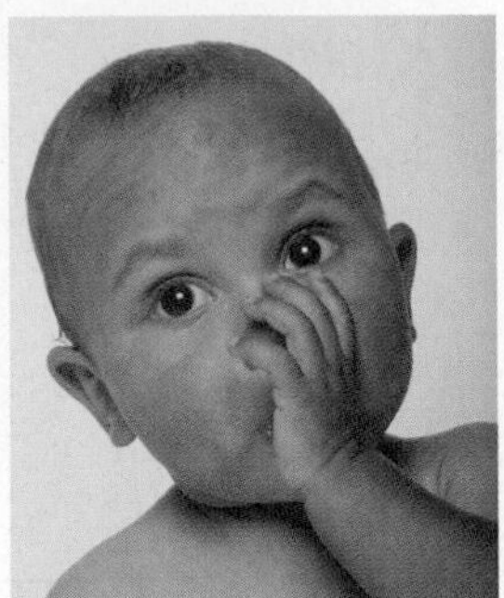

**Oral: Age 0 to 2**
Infant seeks oral gratification by sucking, biting, and babbling.

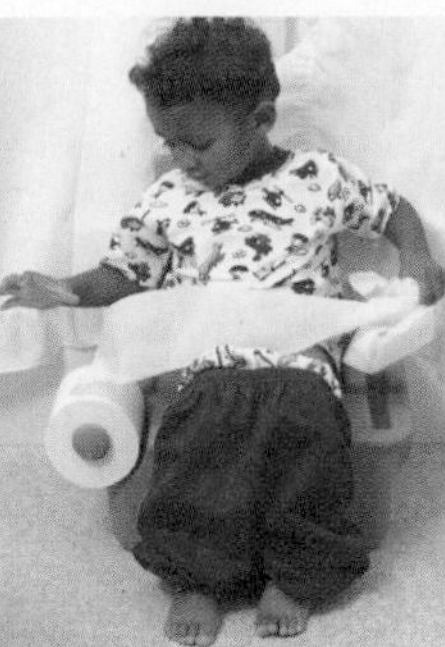

**Anal: Age 2 to 3**
Potty training helps toddlers balance their needs for anal gratification with society's demand to be clean and neat.

**Phallic: Age 3 to 7**
In early childhood an unconscious desire for the opposite-sex parent is controlled by identification with the same-sex parent.

**Latency: Age 7 to 11**
Sexual urges are repressed, and the child prefers same-sex companions.

**Genital: Age 11 to adult**
With puberty sexual urges reappear, and the adolescent learns about mature relationships.

▲ FIGURE 1.1
**Freud's Five Stages of Psychosexual Development**

for oral and anal gratification. Freud believed that children need an appropriate amount of stimulation in these erogenous zones (pleasure-sensitive zones). Receiving too much or too little stimulation can cause a fixation where development is blocked and the child's psychological energy becomes stuck at that developmental level. As young children learn to delay gratification—for example, to use the bathroom appropriately and to wait until morning to eat—the ego gradually begins to emerge to help keep the id in check.

Freud's most controversial proposal involved the phallic stage. He proposed a phenomenon he called the *Oedipus complex*, after the Greek literary character Oedipus who killed his father and married his mother. According to this theory, children in the phallic stage have unconscious sexual desires for their opposite-sex parent. Eventually they realize that they cannot have the parent for themselves, in part because the other parent is too big and powerful to remove. Children then resolve the Oedipus complex by accepting a compromise solution: They identify with their same-sex parents. Boys begin to mimic their fathers and girls their mothers. This way, they avoid confrontation (which the child would surely lose) and "join ranks" with the same-sex parent (who is having sex with their opposite-sex parent—the true object of their desires). Through identification, the child acquires the superego of the same-sex parent. In other words, to be like these parents, children copy their morals, ideals, and values—these become the conscience of the child.

THINK ABOUT SHERYL AND ADAM . . .
From a Freudian perspective, what would you want to know about the dynamics in Sheryl and Adam's family in order to understand their children's development?

Along with children's new sense of morality come feelings of shame and guilt for the incestuous feelings they have had. So the phallic stage is followed by a period of latency, or dormancy. During the latency stage, sexual feelings are repressed, and children prefer to play with same-sex peers and engage in pursuits that are not sexually threatening. Sexual desires will reawaken in the genital stage as children mature into adolescents and begin to explore their sexual identities.

THINKING CRITICALLY
Considering Freud's five psychosexual stages and Erikson's eight psychosocial stages, which theory do you think is more helpful in understanding children's development? Explain the reasons for your choice.

Freud proposed his theory to account for his patients' difficulties—many of which involved anxieties about sexuality or about sexual disturbances from childhood. Critics of Freud have argued that his theory focuses too much on the unconscious mind and sexual impulses, and many experts today do not view his theory as an adequate explanation for normal development in children. Still, Freud was one of the earliest thinkers to propose an elaborate theory of child development. Many of Freud's concepts have become permanent fixtures in our popular culture—the id, the ego, the superego, and the Oedipus complex are just a few examples. There is no question that Freud's theory has had an enormous impact on how we think about child development and psychology.

Erik Erikson (1902–1994) offered a revision of Freud's psychoanalytic theory. Erikson focused more on healthy child development, especially the development of ego identity. Erikson's psychosocial theory involves

> conflicts, inner and outer, which the vital personality weathers, re-emerging from each crisis with an increased sense of inner unity, with an increase of good judgment, and an increase in the capacity to "do well" according to his own standards and to the standards of those who are significant to him (Erikson, 1968, p. 92).

▲ Erik Erikson proposed eight stages of psychosocial development.

Erikson believed that our identity develops as we pass through a series of psychosocial stages. He proposed eight stages, representing eight major crises (Table 1.2, p. 12). As children interact with significant other people in their social environments, they resolve the stage at hand by adopting an identity oriented more toward one end of the crisis than the other. For example, in Stage One, infants struggle with trust versus mistrust. If they have positive interactions with nurturing parents or caretakers, infants learn that the world is dependable and that people are basically trustworthy. If their parents neglect or mistreat them, however, infants learn to mistrust and will tend to mistrust almost everyone they meet. Erikson also believed that resolutions in earlier stages affect later stages. For example, a child who develops a basic sense of trust in Stage One is more likely to develop a healthy sense of autonomy, or independence, in Stage Two, and so forth. Unlike Freud, Erikson believed that personality development continued long after adolescence, and he proposed stages that covered early, middle, and later adulthood periods.

**behaviorism**
A movement to develop a psychology that was objective and scientific, based on principles of classical and operant conditioning.

**classical conditioning**
Learning through association where neutral stimuli are paired with unconditioned stimuli until they come to evoke conditioned responses.

**Behavioral Theories.** A major criticism of psychoanalytic theories is that the concepts of these theories are difficult, if not impossible, to test scientifically. How do we observe, measure, or verify the existence of the id, for example? **Behaviorism** began as an American movement aimed at developing a more objective and scientific psychology. John Watson (1878–1958) was the "father of American behaviorism." Watson argued that psychology needed to focus on observable conditions in the environment and how they are related to overt, or observable, behaviors.

Watson began by adapting Ivan Pavlov's work on **classical conditioning**. Pavlov, a Russian physiologist, conducted experiments on the digestive system in dogs. He showed that when a dog tastes or smells meat powder, which in this case is what he called the *unconditioned stimulus,* the dog automatically salivates, or what he called the *unconditioned response.* Further, when a researcher repeatedly pairs a previously neutral stimulus, like the tone of a tuning fork, with the meat powder, the tone can begin to elicit salivation even when the meat powder is no longer present. The tone has become a *conditioned stimulus* and elicits salivation as a *conditioned response.*

**THINKING CRITICALLY**
Think of one or more times in your life when you learned something as a result of classical conditioning. Identify the unconditioned stimulus, unconditioned response, conditioned stimulus, and conditioned response in your examples.

Watson studied how children learn stimulus–response connections by classical conditioning. In his most famous demonstration, Watson conditioned an 11-month-old named Albert to fear a white rat (Watson & Rayner, 1920). At first, Albert showed no fear and would readily reach out to touch the rat. When Albert reached for the rat, however, Watson clanged a steel bar loudly with a hammer behind Albert's head, frightening him. After several interactions like this, Albert would not touch the rat and began to cry whenever he saw it. Albert's fear was a conditioned response. Later, Albert generalized, or extended, this fear to a rabbit, a fur coat, a dog, and even a Santa Claus mask! Watson warned that children might learn a great many fears through classical conditioning. He argued that parents and others should harness the powers of conditioning to set children on positive developmental paths. If environments could be controlled properly, children had unlimited potential. Remember Watson's guarantee about "a dozen healthy infants," quoted earlier?

▲ John Watson demonstrated that children can learn fears through classical conditioning. Here, Watson and his research assistant demonstrate Little Albert's conditioned fears.

**TABLE 1.2**
**Erikson's Eight Stages of Psychosocial Development**

| STAGE (CRISIS) | AGE | POSITIVE RESOLUTIONS | NEGATIVE RESOLUTIONS |
|---|---|---|---|
| Basic trust versus mistrust | 0 to 1 year | With responsive caregiving, infant learns to trust parents or primary caregivers; acquires basic sense that the world and other people are trustworthy; develops self-confidence. | If caregiving is unresponsive or neglectful, infant can develop a basic sense of mistrust in caregivers, other people, and self. |
| Autonomy versus shame and doubt | 2 to 3 years | Child gains independence from caregivers by walking, talking, toilet training; learns pride in independence ("Me do it!"). | When independence is stifled or punished, child can develop basic sense of shame in self and doubt about his/her abilities. |
| Initiative versus guilt | 4 to 5 years | Child initiates activities to meet larger goals; learns to take initiative to set own goals, design projects, interact with peers. | When initiative is stifled, child can learn guilt that own desires conflict with those of parents. |
| Industry versus inferiority | 6 to 12 years | School years involve frequent comparisons with peers; confidence and sense of industry emerge when comparisons are favorable. | When comparisons are unfavorable, a sense of inferiority can develop; children feel their work and abilities do not measure up. |
| Identity versus role confusion | Adolescence | Sense of central identity emerges through sexual, emotional, educational, ethnic/cultural, and vocational exploration. | Sense of self can be confused or diffuse if a core identity does not solidify. |
| Intimacy versus isolation | Early adulthood | One or more intimate relationships form; may lead to marriage and family. | Without intimate relationships, feeling of isolation can develop; sense of being alone. |
| Generativity versus stagnation | Middle adulthood | Individual makes a positive contribution to the next generation by raising children, teaching, or volunteering. | Without a positive connection to others, can feel sense of stagnation, fear that life is wasted on selfish pursuits. |
| Integrity versus despair | Later adulthood | When other stages are resolved positively, an integrated sense of self has emerged; positive view of life and healthy attitude about death. | When other stages are resolved negatively, a negative sense of self emerges; despair that life was wasted, goals unfulfilled; fear of death. |

**operant conditioning**
A type of learning where a person's actions are reinforced or punished.

**social learning**
A type of learning where children observe and imitate the behaviors of others.

**cognitive developmental theory**
A theory that focuses on how children adjust their own understanding as they explore and learn about the world.

Whereas Watson focused on children's reflexive responses to stimuli, B. F. Skinner (1904–1990) pointed out that children also learn through the consequences of their actions. He called this process **operant conditioning**. As an example, consider a girl who happens to clean her room. Her father, seeing the great deed, gives her a big hug and says, "What a great job—thanks for being so helpful!" After receiving such praise, the child may be more likely to clean her room again in the future. If so, Skinner would say that the child's helpful behavior has been "reinforced" by the hug and praise. In operant conditioning terms, *reinforcement* is any characteristic in the environment that serves to increase the probability that a person will repeat a behavior in the future. *Punishment,* on the other hand, is any characteristic that decreases the probability that a person will repeat a behavior. When a 17-year-old boy comes home late, missing his curfew, his parents may ground him or suspend his driving privileges. If these punishments are effective, the boy will be less likely to come home late in the future. According to Skinner, children "operate" on their environments (hence the term operant conditioning), adjusting their behaviors to attract more reinforcements and to avoid punishments.

▲ B. F. Skinner explored the principles of operant conditioning. He is shown here giving reinforcement for a rat's correct behavior.

**Social Learning Theory.** Adding to the theories of classical and operant conditioning, Albert Bandura (1925– ) demonstrated that children also learn by **social learning**—by observing and imitating the behaviors of other people. For example, when Tamika's father smiles at a visitor, young Tamika smiles too. After watching a television superhero battle with evil villains, Jamie solves his problem at school the next day by picking a fight. After seeing another girl drop a coin into a donation box, Sara asks her mother for a coin that she can donate. Bandura emphasized that children do not always need reinforcements or punishments to shape their behavior; sometimes they act in imitation of the behaviors that they observe around them.

In more recent years, Bandura's social learning theory has evolved into a social cognition theory. The social cognition approach emphasizes how children think about the behaviors and interactions they observe. In this view, reinforcements and punishments provide information that can help the child decide which behaviors to imitate. If children see someone receive reinforcement for a behavior, they are more apt to imitate that behavior in the future. This emphasis on how children think about events is part of a trend away from behavioral theories and toward cognitive theories of development.

**THINK ABOUT SHERYL AND ADAM . . .**
Using the behavioral and social learning theories, what advice could you give Sheryl and Adam to help them work more effectively with their children?

## Cognitive, Biological, and the Contextual and Systems Theories

**Cognitive theories.** Jean Piaget (1896–1980), a Swiss psychologist, created a **cognitive developmental theory** to explain how children actively adjust their own understandings as they learn about the world. Piaget proposed that children represent what they understand about the world in cognitive structures that he called *mental schemes.* For example, the infant in Figure 1.2 on page 14 understands how to grasp the ball—he has a grasping scheme. As the baby acquires new experiences, however, his grasping scheme may be challenged. What would happen, for example, if he tried to grasp a larger ball? Most likely, he would first try to grasp the larger ball with one hand, as he had grasped the smaller ball before. But the one-hand-grasp scheme would not work. To hold the larger ball successfully, the infant would need to use trial-and-error practice to learn to use two hands.

In this scenario Piaget would say that the infant tried to assimilate the larger ball into his grasping scheme.

- *Assimilation* is the process of bringing new objects or information into a scheme that already exists in the mind. If the assimilation is not successful (e.g., if the infant drops the ball), then the scheme needs to be accommodated.
- *Accommodation* is the process of adjusting or adapting a scheme so it better fits the new experience. Through accommodation the infant would learn that grasping sometimes requires two hands. Now the infant has a more powerful and flexible grasping scheme. He understands how to grasp smaller objects with one hand and larger ones with two hands.

▲ Albert Bandura developed a theory of social learning that focuses on how children learn new behaviors by observing and imitating the actions of other people.

As children continue to gain new experiences, they adapt their cognitive structures, or schemes, through a continual cycle of assimilation and accommodation. Piaget also believed

FIGURE 1.2 ▶ **Assimilation and Accommodation** This infant seems pleased to be able to grasp and hold the ball. How would he adjust his grasping scheme to assimilate a larger ball?

▲ Jean Piaget (standing between the two children) created a theory of cognitive development that focused on how children adjust their mental schemes as they learn to understand the world. His theory included four major stages of development.

**sociocultural theory** A theory that focuses on how language and culture influence the growth of thought in children.

**information-processing approach** A theoretical approach focusing on how children perceive, store, and retrieve information, and on how they solve problems and communicate with others.

that children's cognitive structures develop through four major stages or phases of development: *sensorimotor, preoperational, concrete operational,* and *formal operational* thought. We'll look more closely at these stages, and at the rest of Piaget's cognitive developmental theory, in Chapter 5.

Another cognitive theory that we'll discuss in Chapter 5 is Lev Vygotsky's **sociocultural theory**. Vygotsky (1896–1934) was a Russian psychologist and a contemporary of Piaget. Vygotsky's theory emphasized how children adopt the thought structures represented in the language and culture that surrounds them. Cultures create psychological tools to solve problems and handle information, and these tools become reflected in the language of the culture. As children acquire the language, they also adopt the psychological tools embedded in it. Children in the United States, for example, often hear the words *freedom* and *democracy.* As they learn and internalize these words, they may become optimistic that they can shape their own destinies and make contributions to society.

Vygotsky's theory reminds us that language is a powerful tool that we all use when thinking. Children take the social speech spoken by people around them and turn it into their own private speech. At first children speak private speech aloud, as in "Now I cross the laces, then I make a bow." Later this private speech becomes silent inner speech, or what most of us would consider true mental thinking. Our inner thoughts therefore derive from the social speech that we hear in the culture around us. Vygotsky's theory emphasizes the important role that culture and society plays in the cognitive growth of children.

Piaget and Vygotsky had a tremendous impact on our understanding of child development. Piaget, in particular, wrote hundreds of books and articles on children's cognitive development, and his work stimulated countless investigations by other researchers. Since Piaget, researchers have continued investigating cognitive development, often using an **information-processing approach**. This approach focuses on how children perceive information in the world, store and retrieve information from their memory systems, and learn and use strategies to solve complex problems. Information-processing psychologists often emphasize the roles of basic processing efficiency, or a child's speed and accuracy in carrying out cognitive processes, and of changes in the knowledge base, or changes in the knowledge a child already has. Researchers also have studied how children process academic information such as spelling, science, and mathematics. Although this newer research has not always supported Piaget's theory (see criticisms of Piaget's theory in Chapter 5), the field is indebted to Piaget, the founder of cognitive developmental theory.

▲ Lev Vygotsky was a prominent Russian psychologist notable for developing a sociocultural theory of child development.

**Biological Theories.** We mentioned *neuroscience* earlier in this chapter. Although it is not a theory *per se*, neuroscience is an area of study that focuses on the growth and development of the brain and nervous system, and it gives us a biological view of child development.

**Ethology** is a classic biological theory that examines the adaptive significance or survival value of behaviors. Ethology has its roots in Charles Darwin's (1809–1882) theory of evolution and his concept of natural selection ("survival of the fittest"). Ethologists often study animals in their natural environments, carefully observing behavior patterns and instincts that help the animals compete and survive. Konrad Lorenz (1903–1989), a European zoologist, was especially important in formulating the basic tenets of ethology. Lorenz is most known for his work on *imprinting*. He showed that baby goslings become attached to the first guardian figure they observe after hatching from their eggs (Lorenz, 1973/1977). In his famous demonstration, Lorenz himself served as the guardian, and the goslings imprinted on him, following him everywhere. Ethologists believe that the purpose of imprinting is to create a bond of attachment between offspring and parents so the offspring will be more likely to remain close for protection. Extending ethology to humans, researchers have investigated bonding between human infants and their mothers. Some have speculated that the first hours after birth represent a critical period for developing a healthy bond (Klaus & Kennell, 1976). Other researchers believe that attachment bonds develop more gradually in humans, extending across the first year or so of life. We will have much more to say about attachment in Chapter 6.

▲ Konrad Lorenz is one of the "fathers of ethology." In this demonstration of imprinting, these baby geese follow him as if he is their father too!

Beyond bonding and attachment, ethologists have wondered if other behavior patterns have adaptive significance for humans. Aggression, dating rituals, and emotional responses are just a few of the areas they have studied. *Sociobiology*, a subarea within ethology, focuses on the evolutionary development of social interactions among humans and among animals. *Behavior genetics* is another area related to ethology. As we discussed earlier in this chapter, behavior genetics asks to what degree particular behaviors are genetic (inherited) as opposed to learned. Each of these areas of study contributes to our knowledge by helping us understand the biological origins and history of important traits and behaviors.

**Contextual and Systems Theories.** As children develop, their behaviors become very complex. Clearly, development cannot be explained by a single concept such as genes, instinct, reinforcement, or the id. The newest wave of theories attempt to capture the complexity of child development by focusing on the rich network of systems that operate in and around the child. These newer theories recognize that children live and grow within a context of family, society, and culture, and we cannot understand the development of any child without understanding how these contexts operate.

Urie Bronfenbrenner's (1917–2005) **ecological systems theory** is an excellent example of this type of theory. Bronfenbrenner (1989, 1995, 2005) emphasized how

**ethology**
An area of study focusing on the adaptive significance and survival value of behaviors.

**ecological systems theory**
Theory focusing on the complex set of systems and interacting social layers that can affect children's development.

the systems and interrelationships that surround a child affect all aspects of a child's development. Figure 1.3 shows the layers of systems described in Bronfenbrenner's theory:

- The *microsystem,* or inner layer, represents the direct relationships and interactions children have with people in their immediate environment (parents, siblings, friends, teachers, etc.). Parents who are warm and nurturing have a different effect on a child's development than do parents who are cold and distant. Aggressive friends have a different effect than friends who are more peaceful. These relationships go both ways, because a child's own characteristics can influence how others respond to him or her. An easygoing child, for example, may elicit increased warmth and affection from parents. Parents may respond to a child with a difficult temperament by becoming more harsh and punishing.
- The *mesosystem* represents the connections among home, neighborhood, school, day care, and other elements in the larger social environment. Parental involvement in school and increased communication between home and school can have a positive effect on children's school performance. Although children may not take part directly

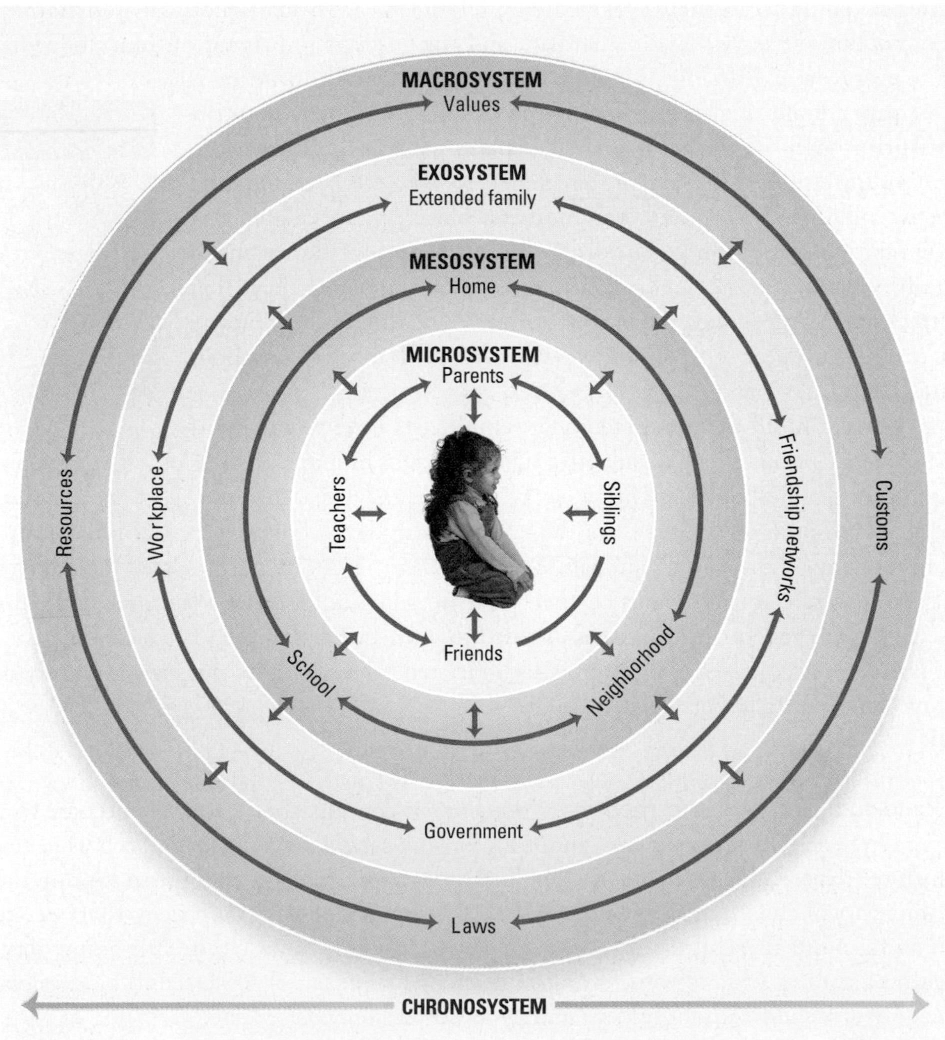


FIGURE 1.3 ▶ **Ecological Systems Theory** Urie Bronfenbrenner proposed layers of systems that influence a child's development.

in such communications, the interactions among these larger elements certainly affect their development.

- The *exosystem* represents even larger social settings and networks. Extended family networks, friendship networks, governmental regulations, social service programs, and even workplace rules regarding family leave and flexible hours are examples of elements in the larger social environment that have bearings on child development.
- At the widest level, the *macrosystem* represents the values, customs, laws, and resources of the culture at large. Cultures that are more individualistic (e.g., that of the United States) tend to stress early independence in children and competition with peers. In collectivist cultures (e.g., those of China and Japan), however, the emphasis is on community and cooperation. In impoverished countries, malnutrition and inadequate health care can compromise children's development. Affluent nations, where resources abound, can offer more support for optimal development (provided that children have access to the resources).
- The *chronosystem* represents how the effects of these systems, and the interrelationships among them, change over time. The birth of a new sibling can significantly alter the relationship between child and parents. When families move, children must deal with new schools, neighborhoods, and peer groups. Economies change, moving through cycles of boom and bust and rising and falling employment rates. Any of these changes can influence child development. Bronfenbrenner's theory serves as an important reminder about the variety of forces that can alter a child's developmental path in both positive and negative ways.

▲ Urie Bronfenbrenner proposed the ecological systems theory of child development.

THINK ABOUT SHERYL AND ADAM . . .
How could Sheryl and Adam use Bronfenbrenner's ecological systems theory to better understand their children's development? What factors within this theory will be the same for all three of their children? What factors might differ?

**Dynamic systems theories** also focus on how layers of systems interact with one another and change over time. These theories are based on models mathematicians and physicists use to understand complex and dynamic systems (Thelen & Smith, 2006). We saved this type of theory for last because it has gained a lot of popularity in recent years and it shows promise for helping researchers integrate many of the ideas they gained from the other theories and other research.

As you know, human behavior is extraordinarily complex and rich in variety. It is virtually impossible to predict exactly how any one child will respond to a given situation, and we can rarely explain any specific behavior by pointing to a single cause. As an example, think about how children respond to the divorce of their parents. We can make general statements about how most children become sad or depressed, or how many children's grades drop in school, but obviously these statements are not true for all children whose parents divorce. (You can read much more about the effects of divorce in Chapter 12.) Some children may seem unaffected by divorce; and some may even become happier or more successful after divorce.

When effects do occur, can we ever identify their precise cause? Usually not. For example, suppose a boy shows an increase in aggressiveness (fighting at school and arguing with friends) following his parents' divorce. The reason could be the loss of his father figure, his mother's depression, a reduction in family income, a move to a rougher neighborhood, a shift to a new school, or a whole host of other variables. In reality, it was likely some combination of multiple variables and conditions that caused the increase in aggression, not any single variable alone.

According to dynamic systems theory, then, the boy's response to divorce emerges from the complex interaction of elements from multiple layers both in and around the child. Inside the child, we would consider his self-esteem, his ability to cope with intense emotions, and his skills in interacting with peers. Outside the child, factors

**dynamic systems theories** Theories that use models from mathematics and physics to understand complex systems of development.

might include a network of extended family, the aggressiveness of his peers, the quality of his school interactions, and the types of interactions he has with his parents. At the broadest level, the prevailing attitudes about divorce in his culture and society may be important. At the most elemental levels, we could look at genetic tendencies toward aggression and at how the child's emotions relate to biochemical changes in his brain and nervous system. At first, combining all of these variables may yield a picture that is too chaotic to interpret. But eventually patterns begin to emerge out of the chaos. For example, soon after the divorce, the child may be confused and his behavior may be erratic. Later, as he digests the various pushes and pulls from all of these levels of variables, he may settle into a stable pattern of behavior—such as meeting common frustrations with acts of aggression. Other children, experiencing different combinations of pushes and pulls, may settle into different patterns, such as withdrawal or depression.

Researchers are interested in how systems become stable, when they change, and what makes them change. As Thelen and Smith (2006) put it,

> [All] components of the developing system are continually linked and mutually interactive in the individual and between the individual and the environment. . . . [M]ental and physical activity are assembled in the moment and always as a function of the system's history. Actions done in this moment, in turn, set the stage for behavior in the next second, minute, week, and year. With this formulation, it makes no sense to ask what part of behavior comes from stages, mental structures, symbol systems, knowledge modules, or genes because these constructs do not exist in timeless, disconnected form. There is no time and no level when the system ceases to be dynamic (p. 307).

In recent years dynamic systems theories have helped us understand how infants learn to walk, reach for objects, and perceive forms, as well as how children learn new word meanings, understand emotions, and move across Piaget's stages of cognitive development (Fischer & Bidell, 1998; Gershkoff-Stowe & Thelen, 2004; Thelen & Smith, 2006). Researchers are just beginning to use dynamic systems thinking to model the complexity of child development. Rather than debating nature versus nurture, we now have the opportunity to consider how all of the elements affecting development work in complex interaction. In the coming years it will be interesting to see how well this type of theory performs.

As you can see, theorists have proposed a wide variety of ideas to explain how children and adolescents develop. We hope that these brief sketches have given you a glimpse of the different theories' usefulness in explaining what is (or was) known about children. Each theory offers some degree of prediction and guidance for people working with children. These theories also guide future research efforts by suggesting new factors and variables that need to be explored. As you consider these theories, don't expect any single approach to be the only one that is "right" or "correct." Many theories address narrow or specific aspects of child development. For example, Piaget's cognitive developmental theory focused on how children think, whereas Bronfenbrenner's ecological systems theory focuses more on how children interact with other people. So it wouldn't make sense to pit these two theories against each other and ask which one is better. Each theory offers at least some valuable insight about children and adolescents, yet no single theory captures all of the complexities of human development. As research continues, we will continue to gain information that favors (or discredits) one or another line of thought, and new theories will continue to emerge. In the next section we will describe the most important research techniques used to study child development.

## LET'S REVIEW . . .

1. Which of the following is *not* one of the useful functions served by theories?
   a. Theories summarize the facts as currently known.
   b. Theories allow prediction of future behavior and events.
   c. Theories contradict the facts gathered by scientific observation.
   d. Theories stimulate new research and discoveries.
2. Who proposed that an important component of personality forms when a child identifies with the same-sex parent?
   a. Sigmund Freud
   b. Erik Erikson
   c. B. F. Skinner
   d. Urie Bronfenbrenner
3. A focus on how observable conditions in the environment relate to observable behaviors in people was the emphasis of:
   a. behaviorism.
   b. cognitive theory.
   c. contextual theory.
   d. psychoanalytic theory.
4. The microsystem, mesosystem, and macrosystem are parts of:
   a. Erikson's psychoanalytic theory.
   b. Bandura's social learning theory.
   c. Bronfenbrenner's ecological systems theory.
   d. Vygotsky's sociocultural theory.
5. True or False: The CT scan, PET scan, and fMRI are tools used in neuroscience to study brain development.
6. True or False: Dynamic systems theories are useful in isolating variables like nature and nurture and determining which one has the most influence on development.

Answers: 1. c, 2. a, 3. a, 4. c, 5. T, 6. F

# Research in Child Development

How do researchers identify patterns in child development? How do we know what types of behaviors are typical of children at different ages? How do we gather information to test theories and to generate solutions to the practical problems faced by children and families? In the field of child development, we rely on the scientific method. With the **scientific method**, researchers collect data by making systematic observations of children and their behaviors, and they use these data to test their research hypotheses. When their hypotheses are confirmed by the data, then the researchers have reason to believe that their theories are correct. If their hypotheses are not confirmed, then they need to modify or replace their theories. In this section, we introduce you to the research methods that are used most commonly in child development research.

**scientific method**
Process where researchers test hypotheses by making systematic observations.

AS YOU STUDY THIS SECTION, ASK YOURSELF THESE QUESTIONS:

- **1.6** What are some examples of descriptive research methods, and how are they useful in studying development?
- **1.7** What is the proper way to interpret a correlation, and what are the advantages and disadvantages of correlational research?
- **1.8** How do researchers use experimental methods to determine cause and effect?
- **1.9** How do cross-sectional, longitudinal, and hybrid research designs differ in how they assess developmental effects?
- **1.10** What steps do researchers take to protect the rights and privacy of children who participate in their studies?

## Descriptive Research Methods

**Descriptive methods** attempt to describe something about a behavior, such as how often and under what conditions it occurs. One way to describe a behavior is simply to observe it. In *naturalistic observation* researchers watch children in their natural environments (such as at home, in school, or on the playground) and record what they do, when, with whom, and other details. For example, if you want to know how often preschoolers look at books and engage in "prereading" activities, you can go to a day care center and watch the children. But what if the children never show the behavior? Or what if the particular setting or the activities going on while you observe aren't conducive to reading (such as nap time or group playtime)? The biggest advantage of naturalistic observation is that a researcher can gather information about real-life behaviors—but a major disadvantage is that the researcher cannot control the situation to ensure that the behavior of interest will occur.

With another descriptive method, *structured observation,* the researcher creates a suitable situation, arranges for children to be placed in it (often in a laboratory or in a specially prepared space within the home or school), and observes their behavior. For example, to observe reading interest and prereading activities, you could set up a room with a variety of toys, including many interesting books. You could watch children and see if they chose to look at the reading materials, for how long, and in what ways. So in structured observation the researcher has more control than in naturalistic observational settings. However, this method does not answer questions about the real-life occurrences and forms of the behavior. In both types of observation, it's very important that the person collecting the information not know what the expected results are. Otherwise, that person's knowledge could influence his or her observations and the outcome of the research—a situation called *observer bias.*

As an alternative to observing children, researchers can also ask children to give *self-reports*, or direct answers to questions about a topic or process. For example, you could ask children how much they like to read, how often they look at books, and the like. You could do this in face-to-face interviews or through written questionnaires. The major drawback of self-reports involves participants' abilities to remember accurately and to verbalize their answers. Some children are stronger in these abilities than others are, and these differences can lead to inaccurate conclusions. In addition, children will sometimes give the answers they think the interviewer wants to hear, rather than answers that are more accurate but that they believe are less desirable in some way. Interviewers must also be very careful to not lead children to give certain kinds of responses. This kind of unintentional prompting can occur through the kinds of questions asked, through the phrasing of questions, or through unconscious nonverbal signals such as body movements or facial expressions.

Finally, researchers can do *case studies*—intensive studies of one child or a small number of children. The goal of a case study is to create a detailed description of the individual(s), usually focusing on some particular behaviors. Case studies often focus on children who are exceptional in some way, such as children with some sort of developmental delay or unusually high level of competence or achievement. These studies may employ a variety of different measures. Examples include detailed and repeated observations (both naturalistic and structured); standardized tests and informal assessments; self-reports; and/or physiological measures such as brain activity, heart rate, or respiration patterns during specific activities. For example, you could study a child who is clearly advanced in reading skill so as to understand why and how the skill is developing, or a child who is delayed in reading in order to identify factors that might be contributing to the delay.

Descriptive research methods are valuable in providing information about a behavior, and they are often a useful starting point for understanding some aspect of development.

**descriptive methods**
Research methods that describe a behavior of interest, such as how often it occurs and under what conditions.

These methods often help researchers develop hypotheses, or specific predictions, about what causes or affects a given behavior. But these methods do not answer questions about relationships among variables; other methods are needed for this.

## Correlational Research Methods

Suppose we wanted to answer this question: Is reading ability in the early grade school years related to the amount of time parents spend reading to children during the preschool years? What kinds of observations would we need to make? One approach we might take would be to ask parents of preschoolers to keep careful notes (reading logs) on the number of minutes they spent each time they read to their children. After six weeks we could collect the logs and calculate the average number of minutes per week that each child was read to by a parent. Later, when the children were in second grade, we could take each child's score on a standardized reading test and match it with his or her average number of minutes of preschool reading. Figure 1.4 presents hypothetical data like those that we might collect if we actually conducted this study. The graph shows that the children who were read to most in preschool tended to have higher reading scores in second grade. The children read to least tended to have lower scores. With the **correlational method**, researchers measure the degree to which two or more variables are related or associated.

A *correlation coefficient* is a number that indicates the direction and strength of an association between two or more variables. In our example, we could compute a correlation coefficient for the association between average minutes of preschool reading and second-grade reading scores. Correlation coefficients (symbolized by the letter *r*) can range from −1.0 to +1.0. *Positive coefficients* ($r = 0.0$ to $+1.0$) indicate that the scores on the two variables tend to run in the same direction. In other words, higher scores on one variable tend to be linked with higher scores on the other variable, and lower with lower. Figure 1.4 shows a positive correlation, and the coefficient is +.81. The *magnitude* of the coefficient indicates the strength of the correlation. Figure 1.4 shows a strong positive relationship (+.81)—a strong tendency for greater preschool reading time to be linked with higher second-grade reading scores.

**correlational method**
Research method that measures the degree to which two or more variables are related or associated.

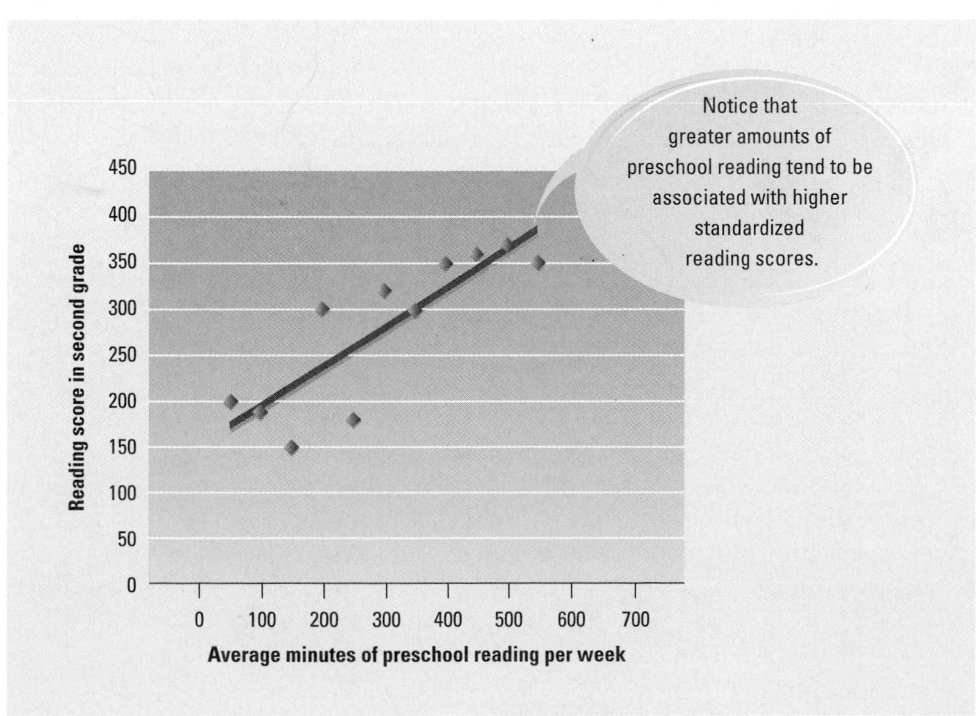


◀ FIGURE 1.4
**Positive Correlation**
A hypothetical correlation (+.81) where higher reading scores in second grade tend to be associated with families who read more to children at preschool age. The blue line shows the best fitting line through the data points.

Now consider an example of a negative correlation. What if we asked mothers of newborn babies to estimate the number of alcoholic beverages they drank per week, on average, during their pregnancies? Would their alcohol consumption be related to the birth weights of their babies? Figure 1.5 shows hypothetical data with a correlation coefficient of –.84. *Negative coefficients* ($r$ = 0.0 to –1.0) indicate that the two variables have an inverse relationship: Higher scores on one variable tend to be linked with lower scores on the other variable and vice versa. You can see that there is a relatively strong pattern in the data—birth weights tend to decrease as alcohol consumption increases.

From these examples you can see the usefulness of correlational studies. If these were actual studies, we could learn that children tend to score higher in reading in second grade when their parents read more to them as preschoolers, and that alcohol consumption is related to lower birth weights in newborn babies. Both of these results would suggest important advice for parents. But at this point we need to emphasize a key limitation of correlational studies: *Correlation does not prove causation!* On the basis of correlational studies alone, we can determine that two variables are linked but we cannot determine what is the cause and what is the effect. For example, compared to nondrinkers, women who drink larger amounts of alcohol also tend to smoke more cigarettes and tend to have poorer nutrition. Was it the alcohol that caused the reduction in birth weight, or was it the cigarette smoking, or poor nutrition, or some other factor that we did not measure? In the reading study, it seems plausible that reading more to preschoolers would enhance their reading ability—but the real causal direction might be the reverse. For example, children might inherit "reading aptitude," with some children destined to become better readers and some poorer readers. Children with greater "reading aptitude" might be more fun to read to; they might be more attentive, ask more interesting questions, and otherwise behave in ways that would encourage their parents to spend more time reading to them. If so, then increased "reading aptitude" (as measured in the second-grade standardized tests) would be the cause, not the effect, of increased parental reading time. Explore on **mydevelopmentlab**

**THINK ABOUT SHERYL AND ADAM . . .** How would correlational research help you understand the factors involved in Zoey's, Isabella's, and Max's development? Given that this research method cannot determine cause and effect, how would this type of research still be useful?

Explore why Correlations Does not Show Causation. www.mydevelopmentlab.com

Researchers recognize the complex ways that variables can interrelate to influence the behavior and development of children. As we mentioned in our discussion of systems theories, more and more research is trying to describe this complexity by measuring

FIGURE 1.5 ▶ **Negative Correlation** A hypothetical correlation (−.84) where lower birth weights tend to be associated with babies born to mothers who consumed more alcoholic beverages during pregnancy. The blue line shows the best fitting line through the data points.

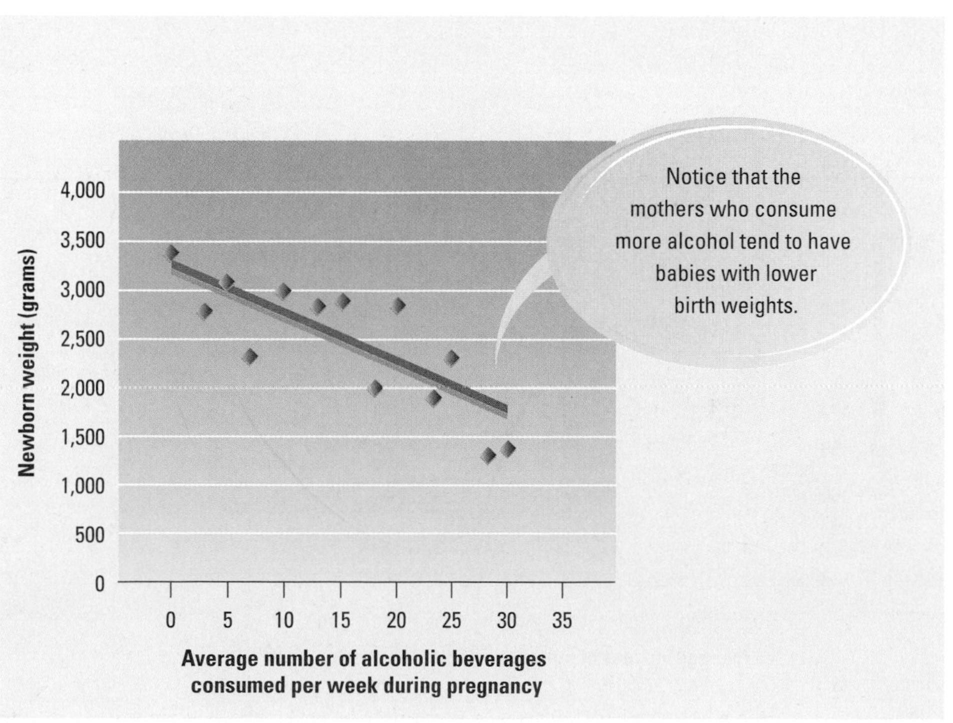

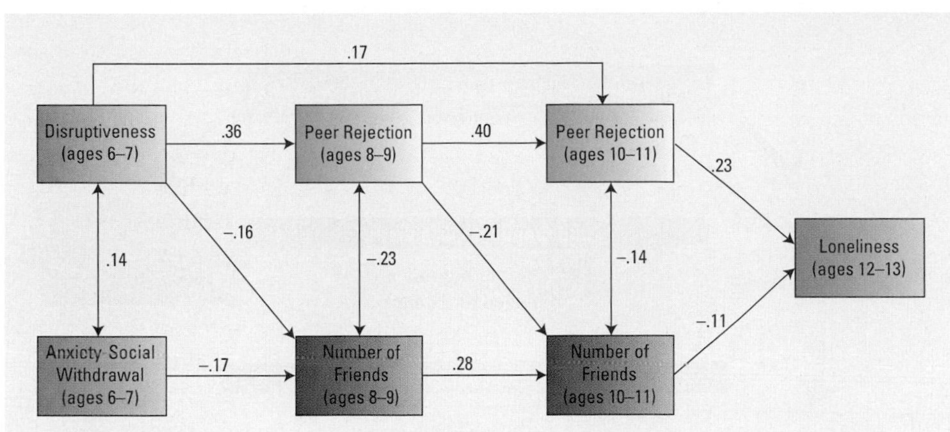


◄ FIGURE 1.6
**An Example of Path Analysis**
This diagram shows correlations among several variables that are related to how lonely children feel when they are 12 or 13 years old.

*Source*: Pedersen, Vitaro, Barker, & Borge (2007). Reprinted with permission.

multiple variables. Sometimes researchers compute *path analyses*—sets of multiple correlations that show how several variables relate to each other. Sara Pedersen and her colleagues (2007), for example, measured several variables that they hypothesized would predict how lonely children feel when they are 12 to 13 years old. When the children were 6 and 7 years old, their mothers and teachers rated how disruptive they were and how anxious and socially withdrawn they were. The researchers also created measures that showed if (and for how long) children were rejected (or disliked) by their peers in school and how many mutual friendships they had, and these measures were taken when the children were 8 or 9 years old and again when they were 10 or 11. Figure 1.6 shows correlations among these variables. For example, disruptiveness at age 6 or 7 correlated positively with peer rejection at age 8 or 9 ($r = .36$), and it correlated negatively with children's numbers of friends at age 8 or 9 ($r = -.16$). The strongest relationship was between peer rejection at age 8 or 9 and peer rejection again at 10 or 11 ($r = .40$). By looking to the far right of the model, you can see that children rated themselves as being more lonely when they had higher ratings of peer rejection and had fewer friends. The model also shows that the path to loneliness can be traced back to how disruptive and anxious/withdrawn the children were at a younger age. Path analyses such as this one can tell us a lot about how multiple variables interrelate.

THINKING CRITICALLY
What other factors can you think of that might have direct or indirect relationships with children's feelings of loneliness? How would a path analysis help you understand the relative contributions of these factors and their interactions?

Even when we measure an array of complicated relationships, we still cannot be sure which are the causes and which are the effects. Do children feel lonely because they are rejected by their peers, or are children rejected because they feel lonely and sad and stay off to themselves? We can hypothesize several different ways to explain the same correlation. So again, correlation in itself is not sufficient for determining cause and effect. But ultimately, of course, researchers would like to determine cause and effect. To accomplish this they use the experimental method.

## Experimental Research Methods

How could we demonstrate that increasing alcohol consumption during pregnancy actually *causes* a reduction in birth weight? Consider the hypothetical experiment diagrammed in Figure 1.7 on page 24. Researchers randomly assign 50 pregnant rats either to an experimental group or to a control group. The 25 rats in the experimental group have water bottles that contain a mixture of water and pure grain alcohol. The 25 rats in the control group have bottles with pure water. Other than this difference, the researchers treat all 50 rats as much alike as possible. They provide identical cages, offer the same food, and follow the same feeding schedules with all the rats. Their aim is to have the two groups differ systematically along only one variable: water with alcohol versus pure water. This variable is the *independent variable*—the variable that the researchers systematically manipulate in the experiment. The idea is to manipulate this variable independently of other factors (e.g., diet)

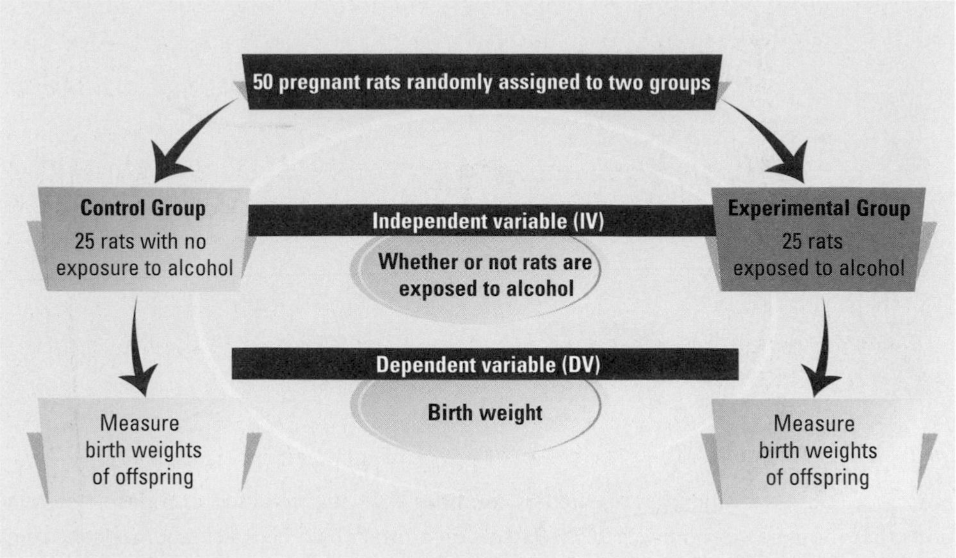

FIGURE 1.7 ▶
**Hypothetical Experiment**
To study the effects of alcohol consumption during pregnancy on the birth weight of newborns, the researcher systematically manipulates the independent variable (IV) to determine its effects on the dependent variable (DV). If the only difference between the control and experimental groups is alcohol exposure versus nonexposure, then any reliable difference in birth weights can be attributed to the alcohol exposure. Experiments are the only method that can determine cause–effect relationships. Why would this experiment never be conducted with human participants?

that might affect pregnancy. In the hypothetical experiment, after the rat pups are born, we can weigh each pup and compare the average birth weights in the experimental and control groups. Birth weight is the *dependent variable.* That is, it represents the outcome that we measure, an outcome that is dependent on the manipulation of the independent variable. **Simulate** on **mydevelopmentlab**

**Simulate** Distinguishing Independent and Dependent Variables. www.mydevelopmentlab.com

With **experiments**, then, researchers systematically manipulate the independent variable to determine if it causes a difference in the dependent variable. If we conduct this experiment properly, the only systematic difference between the two groups will be exposure to alcohol: The experimental group is exposed to alcohol, and the control group is not. If we observe that the pups in the groups differ reliably in birth weight (e.g., if the birth weights in the experimental group are substantially lower than those in the control group), then we can conclude alcohol exposure caused this difference. What else could be the cause? Rats in both groups got the same diet, were on the same feeding schedules, and had the same experience in every way possible other than alcohol exposure.

Of course, researchers cannot perfectly control every factor in the experiment. Individual rats will differ in their metabolisms and appetites, for example. And each mother rat will weigh a different amount even before pregnancy. Because these factors may affect the birth weights, we use *random assignment* to groups to prevent such factors from differing systematically between the groups. With random assignment, each participant (in this case, each rat) has an equal chance of being assigned to any of the groups in an experiment. It is therefore unlikely that all of the heavier mother rats would be assigned to the control group or that all of the rats with lighter appetites would be assigned to the experimental group.

If experimenters can show a systematic relationship between an independent variable and a dependent variable, then they can demonstrate cause and effect. In our example, we might be able to show that alcohol consumption during pregnancy actually causes reduced birth weight in rat offspring. But of course, we experimented on rats, not humans. It would obviously be unethical for us to require that some women consume alcohol during pregnancy just so we could observe the effect on human newborns.

This highlights the main disadvantage of the experimental method: Researchers always must ask whether it is ethical to manipulate the independent variable that is of interest in the experiment. For example, think back to the discussion of a correlation between preschool reading and second-grade reading scores. The correlation was not sufficient to establish cause and effect. Would it be appropriate or ethical to conduct an experiment in this situation? Could we, for example, require that some parents read more

**experiment**
Method where researchers systematically manipulate an independent variable to determine if it causes a difference in a dependent variable.

to their preschool children and that some parents read only a little or not at all? Could we, ethically, randomly assign parents and their children to these two experimental conditions? If any of the experimental conditions might conceivably have a negative effect on a child's development, then ethically it is difficult to justify the experiment.

Sometimes we turn to animal research to study variables that would be unethical to manipulate with humans. Research on the effect of alcohol consumption on pregnancy, for example, has utilized rats and other animal species. (Animal rights activists have argued that those types of experiments are also unethical, and there are now strict guidelines for conducting research using animals.) In other situations, however, animal research would not be appropriate. For example, it wouldn't make sense to study the effects of preschool reading with monkeys or rats. When questions arise asking if it would be unethical or impractical to conduct human experiments, we have to stick to correlational research methods. **Listen** on **mydevelopmentlab**

In summary, correlational methods have the advantage of demonstrating and measuring associations among variables, even for variables that we cannot ethically manipulate. The main disadvantage of correlational research is that correlations alone cannot prove causation. A major advantage of the experimental method is that experiments, if conducted properly, can demonstrate cause-and-effect relationships. A disadvantage is that it is sometimes unethical or impractical to conduct experiments in child development research.

**Listen**: Why do researchers use so many correlational studies? (Author Podcast) www.mydevelopmentlab.com

## Methods for Assessing Development

One of the main objectives in child development research is to determine how children do and do not change as they grow through childhood. Whether they use descriptive methods, correlations, or experiments, researchers need some way to compare observations across different ages of children or across time. To do this, they typically use either the cross-sectional method or the longitudinal method.

With the **cross-sectional method**, researchers compare groups of children of different ages against one another at the same point in time. As an example, consider a cross-sectional study that investigated developmental changes in short-term memory for single-digit numbers (Cowan, Nugent, Elliot, Ponomarev, & Saults, 1999). The participants were groups of first graders, fourth graders, and young adults. Each participant heard recordings of lists of single-digit numbers (e.g., 3, 7, 5, 9). Later the researchers asked them to recall the lists as accurately as possible. At the time the participants heard the lists, the researchers also asked them to play a game on a computer screen; this activity was intended to distract them from verbally repeating, or rehearsing, the series of digits. The goal was to see how well the participants could remember the digits when they couldn't rehearse them. On average, the first graders recalled approximately 3.6 digits correctly, the fourth graders 4.5 digits, and the adults 5.4. Using this cross-sectional study design, these researchers were able to demonstrate that increasing age coincides with increases in short-term memory.

Another approach is to use the **longitudinal method** by comparing performance or observations across ages by taking repeated measurements from the same people across time. Researchers can then compare the measurements or observations to see how they are changing (or remaining the same) as the participants age. Consider, for example, a longitudinal study conducted by Nancy Eisenberg and her colleagues (1999). These researchers used a variety of measures to assess how frequently children engaged in prosocial, or helping, behaviors. They followed a group of 32 children, taking measurements approximately every two years from the time the children were 4 years old until they reached 24 years. The results? Individual differences in prosocial behavior tended to be relatively consistent and stable across development. The children who tended to be the most helpful during preschool (age 4) also tended to show more prosocial behaviors and attitudes during later childhood, in adolescence, and even into early adulthood.

**cross-sectional method**
A type of research design that studies development by comparing groups of children of different ages against one another at the same point in time.

**longitudinal method**
A type of research design that studies development by measuring or observing the same children across time as they grow and mature.

The cross-sectional and longitudinal methods offer different advantages and disadvantages to researchers. The longitudinal method allows a more direct test of development. By following the same children as they age, researchers can observe how behaviors, attitudes, and other dispositions change or remain the same in those children. A disadvantage, however, is that it is difficult to get participants to remain in a study across long periods of time. For example, Eisenberg and her colleagues actually began their study with 37 children. Over the years a few children moved away and could not be contacted; one person participated all the way through adolescence and then refused to complete the study as an adult. You can imagine that participants might drop out of a study for a variety of reasons—from simple boredom and loss of interest to a lack of time due to expanding responsibilities as participants mature to illness or even death.

One factor, called *differential dropout,* poses an especially serious problem with longitudinal studies. If the reason for the dropout is related to the nature of the study itself, then the validity of the results is compromised. If the least prosocial participants were the ones who dropped out of Eisenberg's study, for example, then the results would represent an overestimate of how prosocial most people tend to be. Further, some people might start out being helpful (and agree to participate as children) but then become less helpful (and therefore drop out of the study). If this happened, then the researchers would end up with an overestimate of the stability of prosocial behaviors: The participants who would have demonstrated the most instability would have removed themselves from the study. Clearly, the longer it takes to conduct a longitudinal study, the more likely it is that participants will drop out. Also, the sheer time that it takes to conduct this type of study can make it impractical. Can most researchers really wait 20 years to finish their study? Will they (or the field) even be interested in the same developmental questions 20 years in the future?

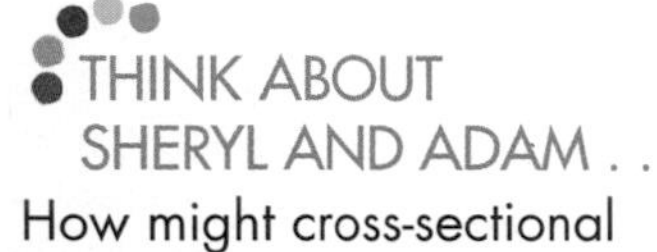
THINK ABOUT SHERYL AND ADAM . . .

How might cross-sectional and longitudinal research help Sheryl and Adam understand their children's development? What concerns should they have with these methods?

The main advantage of the cross-sectional study is that it can be completed in a relatively short period of time. Instead of waiting until participants grow and develop, researchers using the cross-sectional approach take a "cross section" of different ages at one point in time. A disadvantage of this approach, however, is that the participant groups will differ not only in age but also in intelligence, physical strength, and many other qualities that make people unique—and these differences could affect the study results. In the short-term memory study we described, obviously the first graders were not the same children as the fourth graders, and the adults were still another group of people. When we compare the groups on memory performance, how can we be sure that the differences were due to differences in age rather than simply to differences among individuals?

When the age groups differ substantially, as they did in the short-term memory study, there also can be a problem with cohort effects. *Cohort effects* are differences in behavior or other attributes that result from the unique experiences of people who grow up in different periods. Changes in education, technology, medicine, the economy, and the cultural climate are just a few of the factors causing children growing up today to have a different developmental experience than did children several decades ago. For example, we cannot assume that the first graders of today will grow up in the same way as children did during the Great Depression of the 1930s or during the Vietnam War era. Consider the terrorist attacks on the United States on September 11, 2001. Some claim that September 11 was "the day the world changed forever" or the day that freedom and innocence were lost. Would it be fair to compare children raised after the attacks to children raised before? In what ways might their experiences differ?

Some researchers try to balance the advantages and disadvantages of cross-sectional and longitudinal research by using *hybrid designs.* Figure 1.8 shows an example. When the study begins (in the year 2002), groups of 4-, 8-, 12-, and 16-year-olds are all studied at the same time. This part of the study is cross-sectional. Then the researchers track the children's progress by repeating the study with the same children every 4 years. Notice

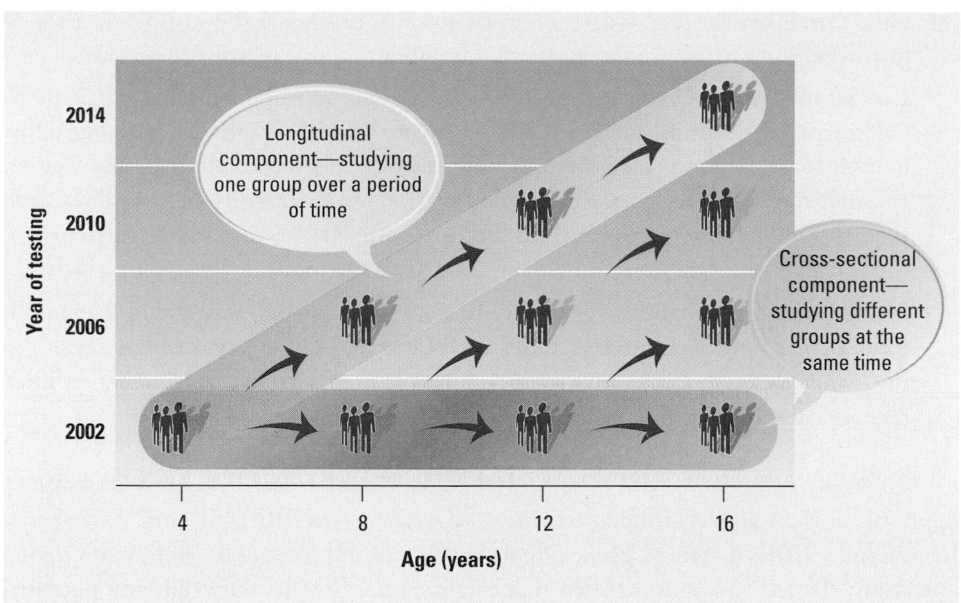


◀ FIGURE 1.8
**Hybrid Research Design**
In a hybrid design, researchers study children of different ages at the same time (the cross-sectional component), then follow and retest the same children as they age (the longitudinal component). These designs are rare in developmental research, in part because they are complicated and time consuming.

that the children who were 4 years old in 2002 are 8 years old in 2006, and so on. This is the longitudinal component. These types of designs are sometimes called *cross-lag* or *sequential designs.*

Whether researchers use the correlational or experimental method, and whether they use cross-sectional, longitudinal, or hybrid designs, they need to carefully protect the rights of everyone who participates in their studies. Let's turn now to the ethical treatment of children in research.

## Ethics in Research with Children

Researchers who work with children must follow the ethical guidelines of the American Psychological Association and the Society for Research in Child Development. The full text of their guidelines can be found at the following Web sites: www.apa.org/ethics and www.srcd.org (click on "About SRCD" then "SRCD Ethical Standards"). Here is a summary of the most important ethical standards. **Simulate** on **mydevelopmentlab**

**Simulate** Ethics in Psychological Research
www.mydevelopmentlab.com

- *Risks versus benefits.* Researchers should conduct studies only when the potential benefits outweigh any known risks. Research designs and procedures must be sound enough that the information to be gained has sufficient value to outweigh any harm, stress, or inconvenience that participants might experience. In some cases participants even receive compensation or other benefits for taking part in the study.
- *Nonharmful procedures.* Researchers should avoid using procedures that could harm a child either physically or psychologically. They must use the least stressful research procedures at all times. If there is any question about possible harm to a child, researchers must consult with appropriate authorities or colleagues.
- *Informed consent.* Researchers must explain the purposes, procedures, and all known risks and benefits of their studies to the potential participants. When working with minors, researchers must obtain informed consent from both the children and their parents or guardians. Children over 6 and their parents must give written consent. Younger children must give verbal consent.
- *Unforeseen consequences.* If a research procedure results in any negative consequence for a child, the researcher must do whatever is necessary to correct the situation. Also, if during the study the researcher collects information that could have a bearing on a

child's well-being, the researcher must discuss this with the child's parents or guardians and with appropriate experts who might be able to assist the child.

- *Confidentiality.* Researchers must keep all information obtained from participants confidential. They must never reveal participants' names or other identifying information to anyone else, and they may not include this information in any written research reports unless the participants have given prior consent. Most research reports give only group averages or scores accumulated across many participants. Reports that give data from individuals must be anonymous.
- *Implications of research.* Researchers must be aware of social, political, and human implications—not only of their research but also of how it is presented to colleagues and to the public. Research on sensitive topics is certainly not forbidden, but researchers must take special care when the results may be alarming to groups or individuals.

THINKING CRITICALLY

Regarding the ethics of conducting research with children, do you think these guidelines provide enough protection to child participants? Why or why not?

To ensure compliance with these ethical guidelines, all researchers must get advance approval for their projects from an *institutional review board* (IRB). At most universities, for example, IRBs of trained professionals review research proposals. Before approving any study, the IRB must be satisfied that the potential benefits outweigh any potential risks and that the researchers will follow proper procedures for obtaining informed consent, protecting confidentiality, and adhering to all other ethical standards. Ethical guidelines also exist for research conducted with animals.

## LET'S REVIEW . . .

1. Attendance in school tends to decline as drug use increases. This is an example of:
   - **a.** a positive effect.
   - **b.** a negative correlation.
   - **c.** lack of a correlation.
   - **d.** a cohort correlation.
2. Which of the following is the most important limitation of correlational research?
   - **a.** It is difficult to obtain positive correlations.
   - **b.** Correlation does not prove causation.
   - **c.** Correlational research cannot describe the complex relations among three or more variables.
   - **d.** Correlation coefficients do not tell you anything about the strength of the relationship between variables.
3. Dr. Jorgenson conducted an experiment to test the effectiveness of a new parent training program. She randomly assigned 40 parents to two groups. One group received the new parent training program, and the other group received the old standard program. After the training programs were finished, Dr. Jorgenson asked each parent to rate their interactions with their children. In this scenario, what is the *independent variable*?
   - **a.** The two parent training programs (new versus standard).
   - **b.** The interaction rating given by each parent after the training.
   - **c.** The number of parents assigned to each training program.
   - **d.** The amount of time each parent spent in the training program.
4. Which of the following research methods is capable of demonstrating a cause-and-effect relationship?
   - **a.** correlational methods
   - **b.** experimental methods
   - **c.** path analysis methods
   - **d.** all of the above
5. True or False: Differential dropout is a problem that plagues the cross-sectional method of assessing development.
6. True or False: Before working with children, all researchers must have their studies approved by an institutional review board so that the rights and privacy of the children will be protected.

Answers: 1. b, 2. b, 3. a, 4. b, 5. F, 6. T

# Applications and Careers Related to Children

One goal of science is to advance knowledge for its own sake, but another important goal is to provide information that can help people with practical challenges in life. We can't think of any practical challenge that is more important than raising and educating children! You may already have a clear idea about the work you would like to do, perhaps as a teacher, counselor, psychologist, social worker, or researcher. If you have not yet chosen a career but do have an interest in working with children, then we hope that this section will give you several interesting ideas. What could be more rewarding than a job in which you have the opportunity to help the next generation attain a healthy and satisfying life?

AS YOU STUDY THIS SECTION, ASK YOURSELF THESE QUESTIONS:

**1.11** How can child development research be used to help parents, government agencies, teachers, psychologists, counselors, and other people who work with children?

**1.12** What career opportunities are available for people who want to work with or for children?

## Practical Applications of Child Development Research

The questions that can be explored in child development research are almost limitless, and the answers that research reveals are, similarly, many and varied. But if research findings were only communicated among researchers, they would not be of much benefit for children, parents, and the many adults whose work involves children. Anyone who works with children can benefit from what researchers have learned in the science of child development. Child development research has important applications to family and parenting, social policy, education, and a wide variety of other fields.

**Family and Parenting.** How can parents be certain what is best for their children in a given situation? How can a parent discipline children while at the same time showing love and caring for them? How can parents help children make friends, learn good social skills, and be popular among their peers? How does divorce affect children? And what about children in blended stepfamilies or with single parents? An infinite number of questions and concerns are involved in family life and parenting. Parenting a child is the most important responsibility that most of us will ever have, and most parents want to improve their knowledge and skills. Almost all of the topics in this text can offer some advice to parents. Researchers continue to collect new data to answer the latest questions (e.g., how to protect children from the dangers of the Internet) and to continue to probe the age-old issues (e.g., whether genes or upbringing influence children more). We will cover many of these issues as we move through this text. Also, in each chapter of this text, a feature called *Personal Perspective* will present interviews with people about their real-life experiences with children. These interviews give examples of how people think about child development or of how people can use topics in child development to improve their understanding of children or their work with children. For this introductory chapter, look at the Personal Perspective called "Meet First-Time Parents."

**Social Policy.** What are our responsibilities as a society for promoting the health and welfare of children? How does living in poverty affect children's development, and how can we all work together to reduce the negative effects? When parents have new babies, should they receive paid time off from work to stay home? What should the role of the federal government

## Perspective PERSONAL — MEET FIRST-TIME PARENTS

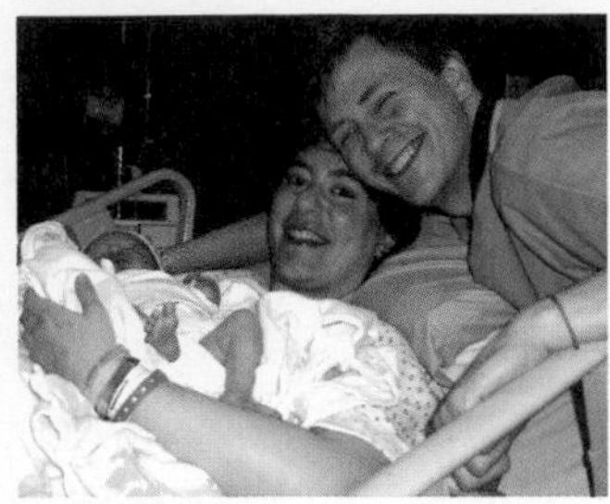

Carolyn and Bob Landers
Dallas, Texas
Just gave birth to their first child, Connor

**What is the biggest question that you have about your child's future and development?**
We wonder what we can do on a daily basis that will enhance our son's development. We want to offer a variety of new experiences without creating a rigid schedule or to-do list for him. It seems like children get overcommitted and spread very thin at an early age—it seems to start shortly after birth. But we also worry we'll miss something that everyone else is doing that gives their child an advantage, and as a result, Connor will be behind in some way. It's all of the short-term things that can have very long-term consequences that concern us.

**What are the main hopes and worries you have for your child?**
Above everything, we wish good health for our son. That is the foundation that makes everything else possible. We also hope to impart to him at an early age a love of learning and an understanding of the importance of a good education that ultimately results in a fulfilling career. We also hope that he'll find his own path (even if it's different from our vision) so he'll know real happiness and be true to himself. We hope to give him a happy childhood full of wonderful memories and the knowledge that he is very loved and cherished. This will hopefully give him a sense of self-worth and confidence, help him make his own decisions, and develop true friendships. A friend sent a beautiful blessing which sums it up nicely: "May love be the first awareness of Connor's life, and the last. And may all that lies between be filled with discovering its many faces."

Our son's personal safety and health are our main worries. Childhood is a more dangerous time now than it was for both of us. We didn't worry (much) about abduction, molestation, weapons at school, etc. I hope we can give him enough information to be aware and to protect himself without taking away the innocence of his childhood or making him afraid of everyone he meets.

**Where will you go for answers to practical questions about raising your child?**
We'll go mainly to family and friends who have children. We'll do a lot of reading, too, but there's nothing like those who have gone before for getting the real scoop about what to expect and how to solve problems. I know we'll rely on our gut instincts a lot, too.

QUESTION **If you were expecting your first child, what questions, hopes, and worries would you have? Where would you turn for information about raising children? What would you say to reassure new parents like Carolyn and Bob?**

be in testing and monitoring children's progress in school? When children are being abused or neglected, when should government agencies step in and remove the children from their environment? These are just a few of the many questions that relate to the relationship between child development and government policies. In the area of **social policy,** officials at the federal, state, and local levels try to use knowledge provided by child development research to improve the lives of children and families. From President Lyndon B. Johnson's "War on Poverty" in the 1960s to George W. Bush's "No Child Left Behind" legislation, government agencies have tried to intervene to improve the lives of children. Private organizations and individuals can also affect social policy. Charities, service organizations, and private individuals contribute by donating money or offering services to children and families in need.

THINKING CRITICALLY

When you vote in elections, do you consider the impact of social policy on children's lives? What political issues now being debated in your local area might have an impact on children?

**social policy**
Attempts to improve the lives of children and families by using child development research to affect laws, regulations, and programs.

Research in child development affects social policy in two ways. First, research findings can stimulate changes in social policy. Research showing that children from disadvantaged families fared poorly in school, for example, stimulated the creation of Project Head Start, an enrichment program designed to give disadvantaged preschoolers the skills they will need in the classroom. Second, after public policies and programs have come into being, child development researchers play an important role in evaluating their effectiveness.

Every chapter in this text includes a *Social Policy Perspective* box that highlights an important social policy issue relevant for that chapter. For this chapter, take a look at the Social Policy Perspective box called "Every Day in America." As you will see, more can be done to protect the lives and healthy development of children.

**Education, Psychology, Counseling, and Other Uses.** Child development research also has many practical uses in educational, therapeutic, and other settings. Classroom teachers and special education instructors need to understand development so they can help all children maximize their learning potential. It is important that teachers know how children learn new information, how they work independently and in groups, and how they relate with friends and peers, and it's important that they know how to work with children who have special needs. Child therapists and counselors need to have a thorough understanding of the typical (and atypical) pathways that child development can take. They must be able to tailor their interventions and therapy techniques to the developmental needs of the individual child. Pediatricians, nurses, physical therapists, and other health-care experts work with children every day, and knowledge of all aspects of child development can help them be more effective with their jobs. Day care providers, athletic instructors, camp counselors, and anyone else who works professionally with children can benefit by studying what researchers have learned about children and their development.

## Careers Related to Children

Another feature you will encounter in each chapter is a box called *Professional Perspective* in which we present interviews with professionals who work with children. For this chapter, see the Professional Perspective box on page 34 called "Career Focus: Meet a Child Social Worker." Many careers allow you to work with children or on behalf of children. In school settings, teachers, special education instructors, guidance counselors, principals, and classroom aides work with children on a daily basis. In therapeutic settings, psychiatrists, clinical psychologists, school psychologists, counselors, and clinical social workers help children who suffer from mental illness or from the abuse or stress they face in life. Social service agencies also employ people to work with

## Perspective SOCIAL POLICY — EVERY DAY IN AMERICA

- 5 children or adolescents commit suicide
- 8 children are killed by firearms
- 78 babies die before their first birthdays
- 155 children are arrested for violent crimes
- 367 babies are born to mothers who had late or no prenatal care
- 928 babies are born low in birth weight
- 1,154 babies are born to teen mothers
- 2,145 babies are born without health insurance
- 2,421 children are confirmed as abused or neglected
- 2,467 teens drop out of high school
- 2,483 babies are born into poverty
- 3,477 children are arrested
- more than 9 million children live without health insurance
- 12.4 million children live in poverty

QUESTION **Think about how these statistics are reflected in the city, neighborhood, or area where you live. Which of these problems is most significant in your area? Why do you think these problems exist? Have welfare reforms or any other changes in social policy been effective in reducing these numbers? What government programs, policies, or laws would you enact to address these problems?**

(From the Children's Defense Fund, 2008.)

children—for example, in domestic violence shelters, at boys and girls clubs, in halfway houses, and in criminal justice or delinquency programs. Child care providers help families manage the balance between work and child care. Many corporations also hire people to work with children or to help inform the corporation about children. Marketing, advertising, and the development of children's products are a few examples of business applications. Government agencies hire people trained in child development to direct, manage, or supervise projects designed to help children and families. To keep the field up to date, scientists and researchers conduct new studies and develop and test new theories of child development. Research scientists provide the database that all of the other professionals can use to decide how best to help children.

## Perspective PROFESSIONAL — CAREER FOCUS: MEET A CHILD SOCIAL WORKER

Pamela Talbot
Flat Rock, MI
Social worker who evaluates foster homes for licensing in the state of Michigan

**What do you do in your work to help children and families?**

I review the financial stability, safety, and suitability of homes for people who want to be foster parents. This involves social history interviews, getting state and local criminal clearances, and medical clearances, then making a recommendation as to whether the person should receive a foster care license. I also provide training to potential foster parents to help prepare them for dealing with children, birth parents, the court system, and our agency. I investigate allegations of abuse, neglect, or rule noncompliance and make recommendations about what to do if an allegation is true.

**What aspects of child development do you use in your work?**

I use information on family structures, discipline, abuse and neglect, separation and attachment, and the effects of drug and alcohol abuse as I train prospective foster parents, with a strong emphasis on discipline. We also address how all of the factors within the family affect the child's stage of development so foster parents can be better prepared to deal with the children's behaviors and needs. Most foster children are not at an average stage of development due to environmental, educational, and/or emotional neglect and physical abuse. Many people expect the children to adjust to their homes with no problems and be just like their own kids were. They don't understand the life the kids were exposed to.

**From what you see, what is the most important problem faced by children and families?**

Drug and alcohol abuse, physical abuse, and neglect. Kids come into care for a lot of different reasons, usually more than one. It's not uncommon for a drug-addicted parent to be physically abusing a child and leaving him home alone. Educational and environmental neglect are also issues; the kids aren't going to school and the house is unsafe (for example, with excessive roaches, no heat or lights, and no furniture). Sexual abuse is also fairly common, but not nearly as common as the other areas.

**What advice do you have for students who are considering a career in your field?**

First you have to clear up any unresolved personal issues. A lot of people are not able to work effectively with all parties involved because of biases, and some even end up in therapy themselves. Also, you can't personalize the things that are going on, and you can't expect to save the world. But it is very rewarding when you are able to make that difference! To know that you have helped to break the cycle and hopefully made the future better for many generations is wonderful. It's just a long road to get there.

**What education and training is needed to work in your area?**

You need at least a bachelor's degree in a related area (social work, psychology, child development, etc). State-mandated training (in Michigan, about 24 hours for caseworkers and 16 hours for licensing workers) and ongoing yearly training is required. There is also training at the agency.

QUESTION **If you were working in a career like Pamela's, what information would you need about child development? What do you think are the most important problems faced by children and families today? How can families best be helped?**

In this chapter we introduced the field of child development. We described the basic issues and theories that have shaped the field, and we explained how researchers use the scientific method to study child development. In the remaining chapters you will learn about many of the important trends and research findings in this exciting field. Along the way you will discover many interesting things that can guide your work with children—and perhaps as a bonus, you will gain insight into your own development.

## LET'S REVIEW . . .

**1.** Research findings about child development have been used:
   **a.** to offer practical advice to parents about raising children.
   **b.** to stimulate new laws, government regulations, and other social policies.
   **c.** to help professionals work with children in therapeutic, educational, and other settings.
   **d.** all of the above.

**2.** An overall theme of this chapter is that the best and most reliable information about child development comes from:
   **a.** casual observation of children.
   **b.** the personal opinions of authorities.
   **c.** the personal stories told by parents.
   **d.** research that uses the scientific method.

**3.** True or False: Child development researchers are often responsible for evaluating how changes in social policy affect children.

**4.** True or False: People interested in working with children, or working to improve the lives of children, can find employment in social service agencies, government agencies, and many corporations.

Answers: 1. d, 2. d, 3. T, 4. T

*Students: Now that you have finished the chapter, look back to the questions we posed about Sheryl and Adam at the beginning of this chapter. You should be able to use a large amount of the chapter material to answer the questions. Use the "Think About" notes in the margin as a guide to help you. After you have considered your own answers, check them against the suggestions in the "Thinking Back" summary below.*

## THINKING BACK TO SHERYL AND ADAM . . .

Now that you have studied this chapter, you should be able to give Sheryl and Adam some general guidance on raising their children, answer the questions they had, and explain how researchers study child development. Compare your thoughts to the following comments.

Raising three children, Sheryl and Adam have a lot of questions about their children's physical, cognitive, and socioemotional development. Researchers have used naturalistic observations, correlational studies, experiments, and other methods to collect scientific data about these areas of child development, and we will cover all of these areas in the other chapters of this textbook. Sheryl and Adam will be able to use this information to understand how Zoey will progress from infancy to toddlerhood in the next year or two, how she will become more proficient in walking and talking, how her attachment to her parents will form and develop, and how she will begin to have significant interactions with other children. The information will also help them understand how Isabella and Max will adjust to school, what they will learn as they participate in school and in their many other activities, and how well they will make new friends and get along with classmates.

Sheryl and Adam can use several of the major developmental theories to guide their parenting. For example, behaviorism can help them learn to reinforce appropriate behaviors for for their children. Social learning theory can give Sheryl and Adam ideas on modeling appropriate behavior for their children to imitate. They can also be mindful of how negative fears and anxieties can be classically conditioned. With an awareness of psychoanalytic theories, Sheryl and Adam can encourage positive ego development in their children by helping Zoey establish trust and helping Isabella and Max express their initiative and industry. Sheryl and Adam can draw on ecological systems theory to understand how their neighborhood, schools, family and friendship networks, and other elements of the larger social systems affect their children's development.

As they notice the similarities and differences among their children, Sheryl and Adam can also think about how nature and nurture interact to influence development. Their children share a similar genetic heritage, so their paths of development will be similar in many ways. Their genes differ, however, and their environmental experiences and free choices will also differ, so the children's developmental paths will not be identical. These are just a few of the insights that Sheryl and Adam and other parents can gain by studying the amazing dynamics of child development.

# 1

## CHAPTER REVIEW . . .

**1.1 What characteristics and processes do child development researchers study?**

Child development is a multidisciplinary field that studies physical, cognitive, and socioemotional development in children and adolescents.

**1.2 What are several main themes that run across child development research today?**

Today, researchers study how nature and nurture interact to influence child development, and more emphasis is being placed on neuroscience (study of the brain and nervous system), diversity, multiculturalism, positive development, and resilience. All of these are key features in understanding how children grow and develop.

**1.3 What is a theory, and why are theories useful?**

A theory is an explanation of how the facts fit together. Theories provide frameworks that summarize the facts as currently known, allow prediction of future behavior and events, provide guidance, stimulate new research and discoveries, and give researchers filters for identifying relevant information and relationships.

**1.4 How have the psychoanalytic, behavioral, and social learning theories contributed to the field of child development?**

The psychoanalytic theories of Sigmund Freud and Erik Erikson focused, respectively, on unconscious processes and the development of ego identity. Freud described five stages of personality development that involved the id, ego, and superego. Erikson described eight stages of identity development. Behavioral theories focused on observable behaviors and environmental conditions. Classical conditioning theories (Ivan Pavlov and John Watson) described how organisms learn reflexive responses, and the theory of operant conditioning (B. F. Skinner) described how reinforcement and punishment affect behavior. Albert Bandura's social learning theory emphasizes imitation and modeling of behavior.

**1.5 How have the cognitive, biological, and contextual and systems theories contributed to the field of child development?**

Jean Piaget's cognitive developmental theory proposed that children actively construct and adapt their own structures of thought and logic through four stages of cognitive growth. Lev Vygotsky described how the internalization of language brings the culture's psychological tools to the developing minds of children. Neuroscientists use modern technology to study the structure and function of the brain and nervous system, and ethologists study the adaptive and survival values of behaviors. Urie Bronfenbrenner's ecological systems theory identifies layers of systems that influence the child, from the child's interaction with immediate family members to the larger context of culture and society. Dynamic systems theories use math and physics models to understand the complex systems that affect child development. Each theory gives you a different perspective on how children develop.

**1.6 What are some examples of descriptive research methods, and how are they useful in studying development?**

Descriptive research methods include observation, self-reports, and case studies. The goal of descriptive methods is to provide information and describe some aspect of development. These methods help researchers gather information and develop hypotheses, but they do not answer questions about relationships among variables.

**1.7 What is the proper way to interpret a correlation, and what are the advantages and disadvantages of correlational research?**
With the correlational method, researchers measure the degree to which two or more variables are related or associated. Correlation is especially useful in situations in which it would be unethical to manipulate an independent variable experimentally. This method also can be used to describe the complex array of interactions among many variables. Its main weakness is that correlation alone does not prove causation.

**1.8 How do researchers determine cause and effect?**
With the experimental method, researchers manipulate an independent variable to test its effect on a dependent variable. The main strength of experimentation is that, if conducted properly, experiments can determine cause-and-effect relationships. The main weakness is that it would be unethical to manipulate many of the variables that are of interest in child development.

**1.9 How do cross-sectional, longitudinal, and hybrid research designs differ in how they assess developmental effects?**
The cross-sectional method compares groups of children of different ages against one another at the same point in time. With the longitudinal method, researchers follow the same children across time and retest or evaluate them as they age. The longitudinal method provides a more direct test of development, but it can be very time-consuming and is compromised when participants drop out of the study. The cross-sectional method is more efficient, and participants are less likely to drop out, but cohort effects can be a problem when the groups differ substantially in age. Hybrid designs try to use the strengths of both types of methods.

**1.10 What steps do researchers take to protect the rights and privacy of children who participate in their studies?**
All researchers must get approval for their studies from an institutional review board. The IRB evaluates proposals to determine if the potential benefits outweigh the risks. Researchers must use nonharmful procedures, obtain informed consent from participants (and from parents or guardians of minor participants), report unforeseen consequences, protect the privacy of information, and consider the implications of their research.

**1.11 How can child development research be used to help parents, government agencies, teachers, psychologists, counselors, and other people who work with children?**
The knowledge provided by child development research can help people deal with family and parenting concerns. It also has important implications for all social policy involving children. It also improves the services offered to children in therapeutic, educational, and medical settings.

**1.12 What career opportunities are available for people who want to work with or for children?**
A wide variety of careers involve work with children. Education, therapy, social service, education, and day care are examples of settings that involve direct work with children and families. Corporations and government agencies hire people to develop products or programs that affect children. Scientists and researchers investigate child development and evaluate the impact that social policies have on children and families.

## REVISITING THEMES

In this chapter, we introduced you to four themes that define the modern study of child development.

*Nature and nurture* have been important issues since the very beginning of child development research. In the past, the debate focused on which was more important (nature *or* nurture), but today researchers are making great progress in understanding how these forces interact (it's really nature *and* nurture) as they influence children's development (p. 4).

*Neuroscience* is a field where researchers study the brain and nervous system, and great strides are being made in understanding how these structures grow and develop (p. 5).

The theme of *diversity and multiculturalism* is becoming increasingly important. Today, more than ever before, families and children can enjoy a rich variety of cultural traditions, ethnicities, languages, and ways of life. Researchers are studying how this variety is expressed in the ways that children develop (p. 5).

Today, researchers also focus more on *positive development* and on the *resilience* shown by many children who grow up in unfortunate circumstances. These stories are both informative and uplifting (pp. 5–6).

We will emphasize these themes throughout this textbook. As we discuss modern research on child development, watch for places where we point out these themes. For your convenience, we include a *Revisiting Themes* section at the end of every chapter, providing a brief outline of the important topics related to each theme.

## KEY TERMS

behaviorism (11)
child development (2)
classical conditioning (11)
cognitive development (3)
cognitive developmental theory (13)
correlational method (21)
cross-sectional method (25)
descriptive methods (20)
dynamic systems theories (17)
ecological systems theory (15)
ethology (15)
experiment (24)
hypotheses (7)
information-processing approach (14)
longitudinal method (25)
nature (4)
neuroscience (5)
nurture (4)
operant conditioning (12)
physical development (2)
positive psychology (6)
psychoanalytic theories (9)
resilient children (6)
scientific method (19)
social learning (12)
social policy (30)
sociocultural theory (14)
socioemotional development (3)
theory (7)

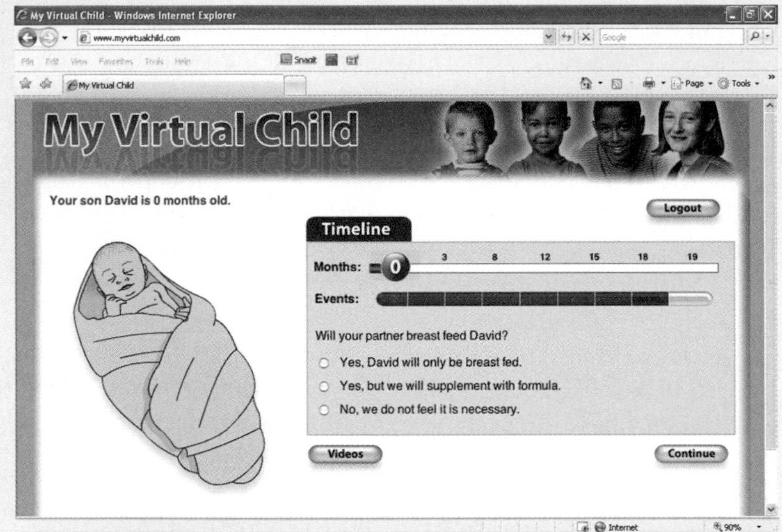


**"What decisions would you make while raising a child? What would the consequences of those decisions be?"**

Find out by accessing My Virtual Child at
**www.mydevelopmentlab.com**
and raising your own virtual child
from birth to age 18.

Watch Visit your Multimedia Library at www.mydevelopmentlab.com to watch an interview with Juan and Tracey online.

# 2 BEGINNINGS

# Heredity and the Environment

Juan and Tracey had a deep desire to have children, but they could not have biological children of their own. They decided to adopt, and they now have two beautiful children! Both Cassandra and John were adopted from Colombia, Juan's home country. Juan and Tracey don't know very much about either of the children's birth parents, other than that Cassandra's mother was only 20 when she gave birth and did not go past the fourth grade in school, and she already had three children. The birth fathers were not involved in either case. The children share a cultural and ethnic background with Juan, but not much is known about their physical or mental health histories or their biological family's skills or challenges.

Sometimes Juan and Tracey wonder who has more of an influence on their children's behaviors and traits—them or the biological parents. Cassie's physical features are noticeably different from Tracey's, but not from Juan's; the physical similarities are reversed for John. But what about their psychological features? Tracey used to think that Cassie's temper was biological—but then realized that she and Juan have an important impact on this trait through the situations in which they put Cassie and how they react to Cassie's behaviors. Will the children's temperaments, personalities, and levels of intelligence resemble Juan and Tracey's? Or will they grow up to be more like their biological parents in these characteristics? What influence will Juan and Tracey have on the development of their children?

As you read through this chapter, think about the information from Juan and Tracey's perspective. What would you tell Juan and Tracey to help them understand how their children will be influenced by the nurturing care that they provide and by the genes inherited from their biological parents? What roles will both nature and nurture play in determining the children's developing temperaments, personalities, and intelligence? After studying this chapter, you should be able to give Juan and Tracey a relatively detailed and concrete explanation of how genetics and the environment will influence their children's physical and psychological traits. You should be able to use at least a dozen specific concepts in your answer.

As you read this chapter, look for the "Think About Juan and Tracey . . ." questions that ask you to consider what you're learning from their perspective.

The questions Juan and Tracey face cut to the very core of child development research. How much do a child's personality, intellectual functioning, and other characteristics depend on genes inherited from the child's biological parents? To what extent are these characteristics learned or modified from experiences with the parents who raise the child or with teachers, peers, and other elements of the environment? In Chapter 1 we introduced the nature–nurture question—a question that philosophers have debated for centuries and that is still one of the most fundamental questions scientists study today. This second chapter explores many aspects of the nature–nurture issue. We begin by focusing on the *nature* side. We review what we know about genes, chromosomes, human reproduction, and cell division. Then we discuss how these elements of nature interact with the nurture side. How does the environment interact with genetics to influence child development? Will the way Juan and Tracey raise their children have an influence on the children's personalities, levels of intelligence, and other traits? How will the nurturing care they provide interact with the children's genes to govern their development? This chapter will help you appreciate human inheritance and illustrate the important interactions between genes and the environment.

THINKING CRITICALLY

In general, do you believe that traits like intelligence and personality are more inherited or more learned? Why do you believe this?

# Genes and Human Reproduction

Each one of us began as a single cell—a fertilized egg cell. By the time we reach adulthood, that cell has multiplied into several trillion cells. The structure and function of every cell in the body is governed by genes, which are molecules that dictate how our cells develop. We inherit some of these genes from our mother and some from our father, but the specific combination of genes that governs our cells is unique to each one of us and distinguishes us from other living things as well as all other human beings. What are genes, and how are they passed down from one generation to the next?

AS YOU STUDY THIS SECTION, ASK YOURSELF THESE QUESTIONS:

**2.1** What are chromosomes, DNA, and genes, and how do they function to determine our genetic codes?

**2.2** What is the difference between mitosis and meiosis?

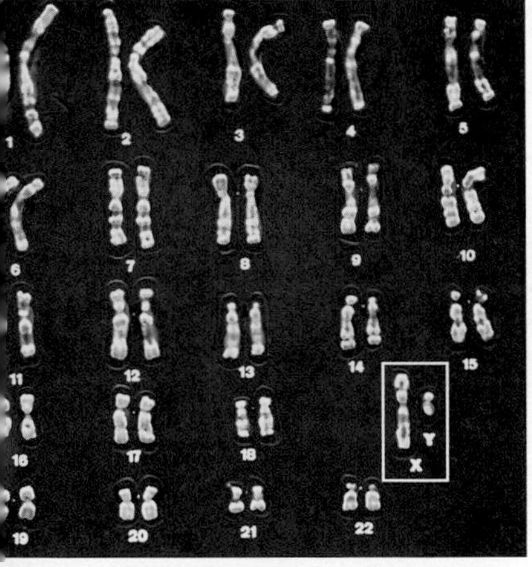


▲ FIGURE 2.1
**Karyotype Showing 46 Paired Chromosomes**
In this karyotype (or picture of chromosomes), there are 22 similar pairs and 1 with different X and Y chromosomes (the boxed pair).

## Genes and the Magical Four-Letter Code

Inside the nucleus of most any cell in the human body are 46 chromosomes. **Chromosomes** are structures made of long strands of deoxyribonucleic acid (DNA). Chromosomes operate in pairs, so we have 23 pairs of chromosomes, as you can see in Figure 2.1. Twenty-two of these pairs are the same across males and females—these are called *autosomes*. The remaining pair is the *sex chromosomes*, and they differ between the sexes. Females have two X chromosomes and males have one X and one Y chromosome. Figure 2.1 shows a male.

**chromosomes**
Strands of deoxyribonucleic acid (DNA) molecules that contain the genetic codes.

**DNA**
Two strands of molecules that twist around each other like a spiral staircase, connected by a series of nucleotide bases (adenine, thymine, guanine, and cytosine).

As the British researchers James Watson and Francis Crick first discovered in 1953, **DNA** consists of two strands of sugar and phosphate molecules that twist around each other like a spiral staircase. In Figure 2.2, you can see the staircase and the "stairs" that connect the two sides. Each step of the staircase is made up of a specific pair of different varieties of a nucleotide base molecule, called adenine (A), thymine (T), guanine (G), and cytosine (C). As you can see in the figure, the DNA strand is simply a series of these connecting stairs or base pairs. You should note that *adenine always pairs with thymine (A-T), and guanine always pairs with cytosine (G-C).* Thus, if you have a sequence of ACCACT on one side of the staircase, the complementary sequence on the other side will be TGGTGA.

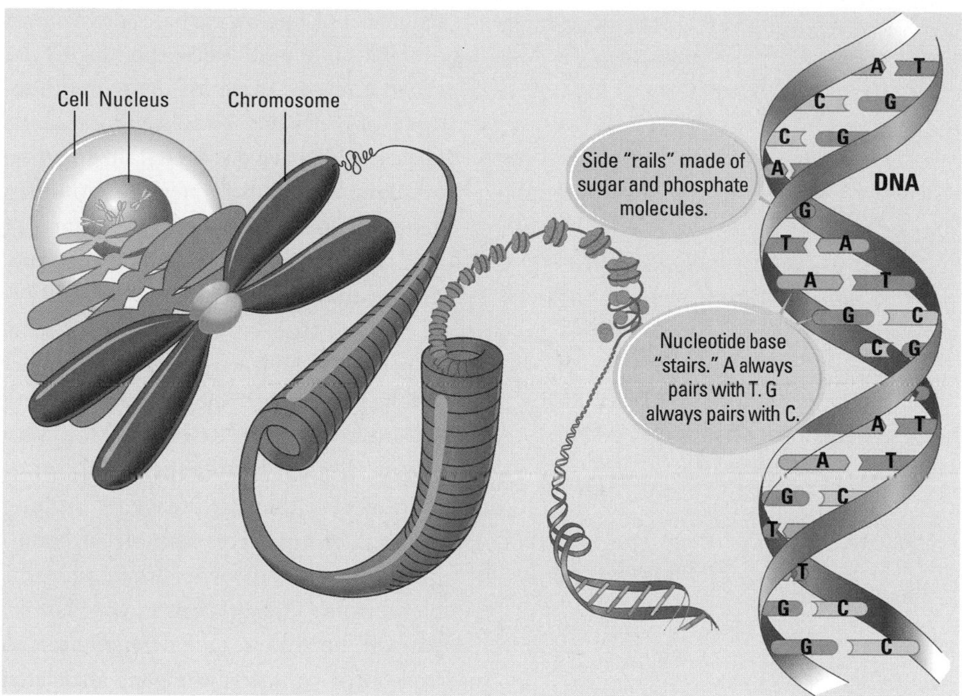


◀ FIGURE 2.2
**Chromosomes, DNA, and Genes**
The nucleus of each cell contains the chromosomes. Chromosomes are made up of highly twisted strands of DNA. The DNA is constructed like a staircase, each side of which is connected by "stairs" made up of pairs of nucleotide bases. Adenine (A) always pairs with thymine (T), and guanine (G) always pairs with cytosine (C). Genes are shorter segments of chromosomal DNA, usually several thousand base pairs in length.

Within the 46 chromosomes in each human cell, there are approximately 3 billion pairs of nucleotide bases (Human Genome Project, 2008a; Venter et al., 2001). It is the specific sequence of these base pairs that makes up our individual genetic code, or *genome*, which is a set of instructions that determines which traits and characteristics are inherited. The entire code is divided up into smaller pieces called genes. A **gene** is a segment of the DNA strand that provides an instruction for a particular trait, tissue, or other structure. There are approximately 20,000 to 30,000 genes (depending on how they are identified and counted) aligned somewhere along the set of 46 chromosomes in each human cell. It is also important to note that less than 2% of the nucleotide base pairs actually provide active instructions. Some of the inactive sequences play a role in cell division, but the function of many of the remaining sequences is not yet known (Human Genome Project, 2008a). Explore on mydevelopmentlab

Explore the Building Blocks of Genetics.
www.mydevelopmentlab.com

Finding specific genes and discovering their functions is a hugely complicated task. For example, Figure 2.3 (p. 40) shows part of the sequence of bases on one side of the DNA strand that makes up just one of the genes related to one form of mental retardation. This form of mental retardation is associated with fragile X syndrome, a genetic disorder we'll discuss later in the chapter. This particular gene contains 39,057 bases. And remember, this is only one side of the DNA strand! To complete the picture, you need to add the complementary strand (the complementary strand is not shown in the figure) where each A connects to a T, each G to a C, and so on. So this gene actually has 39,057 base *pairs*, or a total of over 78,114 base molecules. Can you imagine how complicated it must be to decode this type of sequence for every human gene?

**gene**
A segment of DNA that provides an instruction for a particular structure, function, or trait.

Perhaps you have heard about the **Human Genome Project**, a multinational effort among governments and scientists to map the order of every nucleotide base (AGCT) and locate the position of every gene in the human genome. In April 2003, scientists with the Human Genome Project announced that the sequencing was complete, and further detailed analyses of all human chromosomes was completed in May 2006 (Gregory et al., 2006; Human Genome Project, 2008a). Though these scientists have mapped the positions of approximately 3 billion pairs of nucleotide bases in the human genome, they still don't know what all of the base sequences mean. Scientists still need to determine which

**Human Genome Project**
A multinational effort by governments and scientists to map the 3 billion pairs of nucleotide bases and the genes contained in human chromosomes.

FIGURE 2.3 ▶

**One-Tenth of the Sequence of Nucleotide Bases Needed to Form One of the Genes Related to Fragile X Mental Retardation (FMR1 on Chromosome X)**

The total sequence contains 39,057 bases, and this represents only one side of the DNA strand. Each of these bases would be paired with its complementary mate on the second strand, resulting in 39,043 base pairs (or 78,086 individual base molecules) for the gene. (National Center for Biotechnology Information, 2009)

sequences of nucleotide bases define most of our 20,000 to 30,000 genes. Figure 2.4 shows a few examples of the many thousands of genes that have been located. So far, scientists have discovered the function of about half of the genes in the human genome. Researchers are still working hard to identify and determine the function of many of the remaining genes.

Over the coming decades, the impact of the Human Genome Project will be staggering. Scientists are working toward finding genetic markers for every disease that can be inherited. This information may then help save or prolong millions of lives. For example, if hemophilia (a rare disorder that prevents blood from clotting) runs in your family, you will be able to take a genetic test to find out if you carry the gene associated with this disease. The location of this gene on the X chromosome is marked in Figure 2.4. If you do carry the gene, you will know to work with your physician to learn how to prevent injuries that might otherwise lead to fatal bleeding. In addition, physicians might be able to use gene therapy to alter some of your cells' genetic functions. What if they could give you an injection of healthy genes to counteract the destructive effects of disease genes in your body, or even replace destructive genes entirely? Or what if they could selectively turn off the function of disease genes, preventing you from developing the diseases in the first place? As of 2008 researchers were conducting almost 1,500 clinical trials using gene therapy. Most are in the early stages of testing, but there is keen interest in developing these types of treatments (Journal of Gene Medicine, 2008).

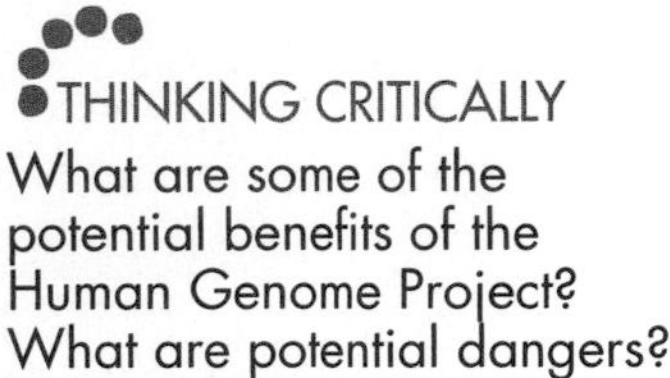

THINKING CRITICALLY

What are some of the potential benefits of the Human Genome Project? What are potential dangers?

Already, parents can select the sex of embryos by using certain reproductive technologies. Clinicians first grow embryos in test tubes using the mother's eggs and the father's sperm. The embryos with the preferred set of sex chromosomes (XX for a female or XY for a male) can then be implanted in the mother's uterus. Embryos carrying disease genes can be selected out in a similar manner. Embryos conceived by more "natural" means can also be tested while they are in the mother's womb. Based on the results, couples can make informed decisions regarding their developing embryo. In the future, couples could have their embryos tested for a variety of genetically based diseases before birth. Coming generations could potentially escape the devastating effects of a large number of genetically determined diseases.

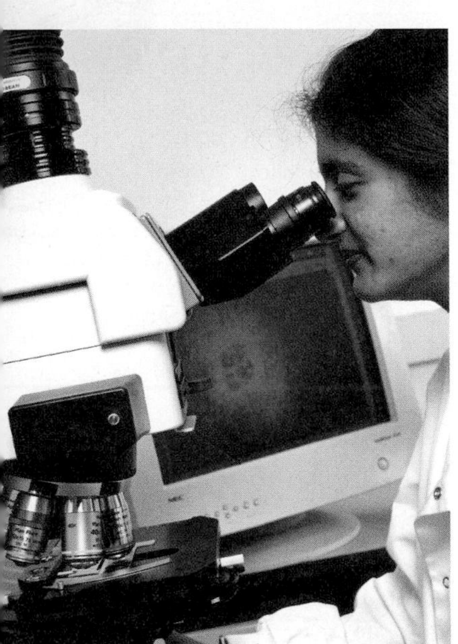

▲ Researchers from around the world are working to decipher the human genetic code, one of the most complex tasks scientists have ever attempted.

But where do we draw the line? As you read the preceding paragraphs, it may have occurred to you that there are profound moral questions in this area that will test our abilities to make sound ethical decisions. Inheriting a disease gene usually just gives us the tendency to develop the disease at some time in our life. It does not guarantee that we will develop the disease, given that the onset of many diseases can depend on additional changes, diet, exposure to risk factors, and other environmental factors. Should parents selectively discard embryos that have tendencies toward certain diseases? Maybe we can agree that future generations should be spared from diseases that lead to early and painful deaths, but what about diseases such as colon cancer or Alzheimer's that tend to emerge

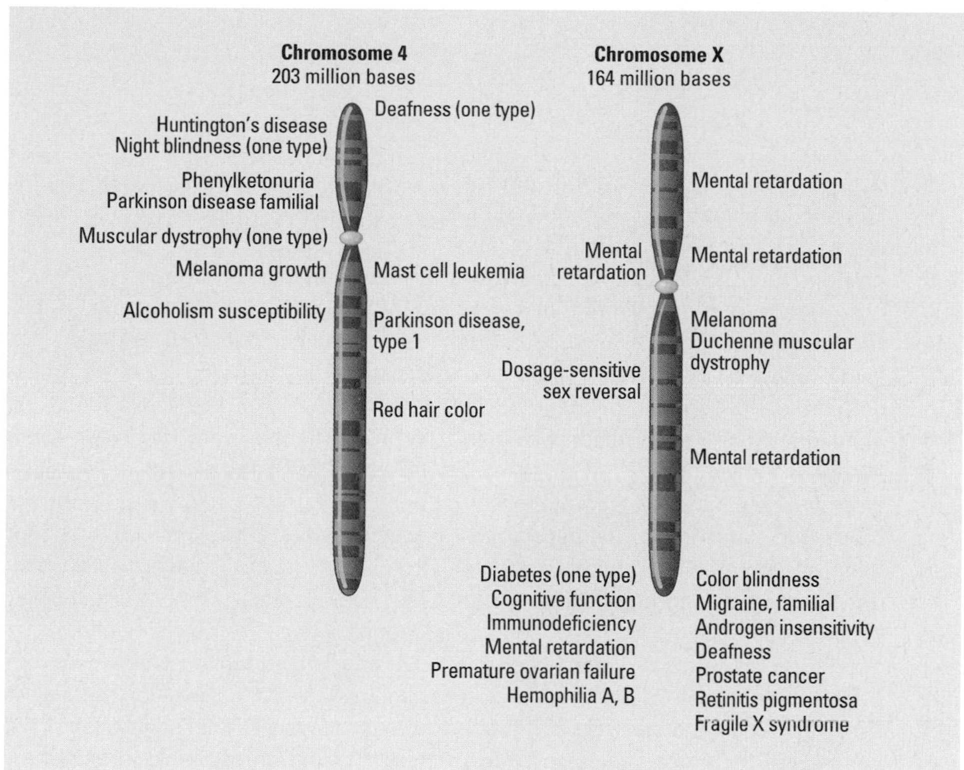


◀ FIGURE 2.4
**Human Chromosomes 4 and X Showing a Few of the Many Thousands of Gene Locations That Have Been Identified**
Later in the chapter, we will discuss Huntington's disease (on chromosome 4) and sex-linked genes (on X). For a more complete catalog, see McKusick (1998) or the online version that is kept up to date through the Genome Data Base at Johns Hopkins University (U.S. Department of Energy, 2008).

late in life? What about embryos carrying other traits that are not desirable? What if an embryo has genes related to low intelligence or a violent personality? Remember, too, that genetic tests are not foolproof. What if an embryo falsely tests positive for a fatal disease? Our growing understanding of genetics raises exciting possibilities but also brings many complicated questions.

Another issue relates to the privacy of individuals after they have had genetic tests. To read more about privacy and ethics in genetic research, read the Social Policy Perspective on page 42, "Protecting the Genetic Privacy of Citizens."

▲ As we learn more about the genes related to inherited diseases and medical conditions, physicians will be able to help patients identify their predispositions and perhaps help them avoid the risks. Designer medications may also be produced to more effectively handle multiple health conditions.

## Human Reproduction and Cell Division

In human reproduction, a new embryo is formed when a sperm cell from the father fertilizes an egg cell from the mother. In **fertilization** the sperm and egg cells join and chromosomes from the father and mother combine to give the embryo a unique combination of genes. Each matching pair of the chromosome contains two different versions of each gene—one from the mother and one from the father. They differ somewhat in the sequence of nucleotide bases (A, T, G, and C). These versions are called the **alleles** of a particular gene and their combination determines the unique traits of each individual.

It isn't always easy for this unique embryo to develop, however. A variety of problems can cause some couples to have difficulty conceiving babies. Low sperm count in the father and damage to the mother's reproductive system are two of the more common problems. In other situations, single individuals or gay or lesbian couples may want to have children. In all these cases, artificial insemination and the other alternative techniques described in Table 2.1 (p. 43) can help people conceive. To learn about one couple's experience with alternative techniques, read the Personal Perspective on page 44, "Using Artificial Insemination."

**fertilization**
The union of the father's sperm cell with the mother's egg, yielding one fertilized cell with a unique combination of genes along 46 chromosomes—23 from the father and 23 from the mother.

**allele**
An alternative version of a gene; alleles operate in pairs across matched chromosomes.

## Perspective SOCIAL POLICY — PROTECTING THE GENETIC PRIVACY OF CITIZENS

Wouldn't it be helpful to know if you were carrying genes linked to a serious disease like diabetes, breast or prostate cancer, or heart disease? If you knew at a young age that you inherited the tendency to develop one or more of these diseases, you could alter your lifestyle to avoid the risk factors that might trigger the onset of the disease. With diet, exercise, and the early use of hypertension medication, for example, you might be able to avoid a heart attack that might otherwise have surprised you at age 48.

But what if your genetic predisposition were revealed to your employer or your health insurance company? Could you be fired from your job or lose the next big promotion because your employer was afraid you couldn't take the pressure of the work? Might future employers be reluctant to hire you for fear you would become sick or disabled? Could your health insurance company drop your coverage because it saw you as too great a risk? Would anyone give you health coverage?

These questions are at the center of a national debate about the privacy of genetic information. Even before the first draft of the human genome was complete, the U.S. government issued an order prohibiting federal agencies from using genetic information in any decisions to hire, promote, or dismiss workers. Legislatures in 23 states quickly followed suit by passing laws against "genetic discrimination" in hiring (Uhlmann, 2000). After much debate and compromise, the federal Genetic Information Nondiscrimination Act of 2008 (GINA) was signed into law on May 21, 2008. This law protects people from genetic discrimination with regard to health insurance and employment, and it forbids insurers and employers to request or demand a genetic test (National Human Genome Research Center, 2009).

How should genetic information be used, and what limits are necessary? From one perspective, many employers and insurance companies already use health-risk assessments when considering applicants. How many times have you been asked about "preexisting conditions" or about your smoking and drinking habits? If cigarette smoking causes health problems, isn't it reasonable to ask smokers to pay more for their health insurance? Who pays more for car insurance, a 20-year-old single male or a 40-year-old married female? So we already classify people into groups based on relative risks.

Lacking reliable ways to predict the future for any individual, we lump together all of those who share certain risk-related characteristics. Is it really fair to lump every 20-year-old male into a high-risk driving category? Some argue that genetic testing will allow us to assess risks in a way that is more fair, reliable, and objective. An editorial in *The New York Times* suggested that "as the potential for rational discrimination grows, the space for old-fashioned bias may shrink. Men and women will increasingly be judged not by the color of their skin but by the content of their chromosomes" (Sullivan, 2000).

Francis Collins, head of the Human Genome Project in the United States, presented another perspective. Collins predicted that the main legacy of the project will be the use of genetics to tailor and improve health care for individuals (Altman, 2000). But he warned that these benefits will not occur unless we pass effective laws to prevent organizations from denying individuals insurance or jobs based on genetic information. Many people already fear the potential negative effects of genetic testing. One telephone poll found that 63% of respondents would not want to take genetic tests if the results would be available to employers and insurers (Uhlmann, 2000). If people avoid genetic tests, they will lose the opportunity for early detection of risks. Millions may suffer or die from diseases that could have been prevented.

QUESTION **Even with the passage of GINA, how effective will the federal and state laws be? Will companies find loopholes? Can we really force employers to overlook health risks when choosing among applicants? How will insurance companies remain profitable if they are forced to accept more risky and costly applicants? How do you think we should balance the need for early risk detection against other potential uses and misuses of genetic information?**

THINKING CRITICALLY
Do you know anyone who has used an alternative method of conception? If so, why do you believe they chose that particular method? How did it work for them?

So far, research on alternative techniques for conception does not indicate any particular developmental problems when children are conceived by these methods (Golombok et al., 2004a; Golombok, MacCallum, & Goodman, 2001; Golombok, MacCallum, Goodman, & Rutter, 2002; Hahn, 2001; Squires & Kaplan, 2007). Children have been studied all the way into adolescence, and they are well adjusted in their emotions, friendships, school performance, and other behaviors as rated by themselves, their parents, and their teachers. One difference that has been noted is that mothers who use these techniques tend to be more warm and involved with their children, compared to other mothers. This may reflect the difficulties they had conceiving children or their strong desire to overcome barriers in having their own children. There is some evidence that parents of children born via embryo donation (in which a donated embryo is implanted in a woman who plans to raise the child) can be somewhat overinvolved in their children's emotional lives and more defensive regarding their child (Golombok et al., 2004b; MacCallum, Golombok, & Brinsden, 2007).

▲ Here human sperm and embryos are being frozen in liquid nitrogen to preserve them to be used later for in vitro fertilization. When parents have fertility problems, this is one of several techniques they can use to conceive a baby.

Most of the parents who have been studied have not told their children about how they were conceived, and many say they regret not telling them. They worry that their children may hear details of their conception from another source, or they worry that it will only get more difficult for them to reveal this information as time goes on. However, attitudes toward openness in telling children how they were conceived may be changing. One recent study found that about half the parents surveyed planned to tell their children about the artificial insemination, often because they believed the child had a right to know. More than 75% had told at least one other person, and fewer than 25% of these parents said they would definitely not disclose information about their child's conception (Golombok et al., 2004a). Single women are more likely than married women to disclose such information to their child, family, and friends, and those who used embryo donation were less likely to tell others about the donation (MacCallum et al., 2007; Murray & Golombok, 2005).

To fully appreciate genetic inheritance, you need to understand a few facts about cell division. After the sperm and egg unite, the fertilized cell begins to divide. After the first division occurs, the organism is referred to as a **zygote**. Cells within the zygote will then

**zygote**
Term used to refer to the human organism after the fertilized egg cell begins to divide.

**TABLE 2.1**
**Alternative Techniques for Conception**

| Technique | Description |
|---|---|
| Artificial insemination | • Sperm are collected from the father and then injected into the mother's reproductive system for fertilization.<br>• If the father cannot produce viable sperm, sperm can be collected from another man or a sperm bank. |
| In vitro fertilization | • Several eggs are removed from the mother's ovary.<br>• Eggs and sperm are placed in a petri dish for fertilization and initial cell divisions.<br>• Several embryos (each with four to eight cells) are placed in the mother's uterus for further development. |
| Cryopreservation | • Sperm can be collected and frozen and are still viable even if thawed several years later.<br>• Embryos from in vitro fertilization can be frozen and thawed later to be placed in the mother's uterus. |
| Assisted in vivo fertilization | • Eggs are collected from the mother's ovary.<br>• Sperm are collected from the father.<br>• Eggs and sperm are injected into the fallopian tube of the mother for fertilization and further development. |
| Surrogate mothers | • In vitro fertilization is used to combine the sperm and eggs from a mother and father.<br>• The embryo is placed into the uterus of another woman (surrogate) who then grows and delivers the baby for the biological parents.<br>• Sometimes the surrogate mother also provides the egg; the father's sperm are injected into the surrogate to conceive the embryo. |

(Moore & Persaud, 1998.)

## Perspective PERSONAL — USING ARTIFICIAL INSEMINATION

Jamie Commissaris
Allegan, MI
Mother of a child conceived through in vitro fertilization.

**Why did you decide to use an assisted reproduction technique?**
I have polycystic ovarian syndrome, so I needed to take hormone injections to assist with ovulation. Intra-uterine insemination (IUI) with the injections increased my chances of conception to 20% each cycle, which was the same as a "normal" woman. The IUI procedures never resulted in a pregnancy, so we moved on to in vitro fertilization.

**Can you give us a brief description of the procedure that enabled you to have your baby?**
We were able to conceive our son through in vitro fertilization (IVF). After several weeks of hormone pills and injections, my ovaries produced multiple follicles that contained mature eggs. The eggs were retrieved from the follicles, fertilized in the laboratory, and two were transferred back to the uterus as two-day-old embryos. The remaining embryos were cryopreserved for the future.

**Was it successful on the first try, what were the side effects like, how did you feel about it overall?**
During our first IVF attempt, we conceived a pregnancy that ended at five weeks. Our second IVF resulted in a triplet pregnancy; our sons were born at 24 weeks gestation and died of extreme prematurity. Our final IVF attempt resulted in a healthy singleton birth. The side effects during the procedures were hot flashes and moodiness from the hormones, bloated abdomen from the overstimulated ovaries, and bruises from the injections. I was also emotional at the prospect of the procedures not being successful. I think IVF was a positive experience, because we conceived a pregnancy every time. However, we did have a higher order pregnancy which had a very devastating end. IVF is a wonderful option for any couple experiencing infertility.

**What kinds of support or reactions have you had from friends, family, and others?**
All of our family and friends know about the IUI and IVF attempts and are very supportive. We are open to talking about it, and we have never received any negative feedback.

**What advice do you have for other people who might be considering IUI or IVF?**
Understand the procedures, including side effects and possible outcomes. Research through reputable Web sites and forums, talk to a fertility counselor and ask your doctor lots of questions. It is important for both the man and the woman to agree on which procedures to do and for how long they want to try to conceive a child. Know your limits, and trust your instincts.

QUESTION **Would you consider artificial insemination or another alternative to conception? Do you think parents should inform their children about their use of these techniques? Why or why not?**

**mitosis**
"Copy division," the type of cell division that occurs when chromosomes are copied into each new cell.

**meiosis**
"Reduction division," the type of cell division that occurs during the formation of gametes (sperm and eggs).

**monozygotic (MZ) twins**
Identical twins. These twins form when one zygote divides to make two zygotes.

continue to divide countless times, and with each division, an exact copy of the genetic material is created in each new cell.

To explore this process, let's first look at how genes are copied into every cell in your body. **Mitosis** ("copy division") occurs when a cell copies its own chromosomes, then divides to form new cells. During cell division the DNA material on each chromosome "unzips." The weak bonds between the nucleotide bases on opposite sides of the staircase break. Figure 2.5 diagrams how the DNA strand first unzips and then replicates itself. It forms two new strands that then link up with the two old strands and wrap up again to make two new chromosomes. When this process is completed, we have a duplicate set of chromosomes. If all goes well, an exact copy of the DNA goes into each new cell. Mitosis doesn't just occur in a developing embryo, it occurs continually throughout the body as it grows, functions, and heals. Except in

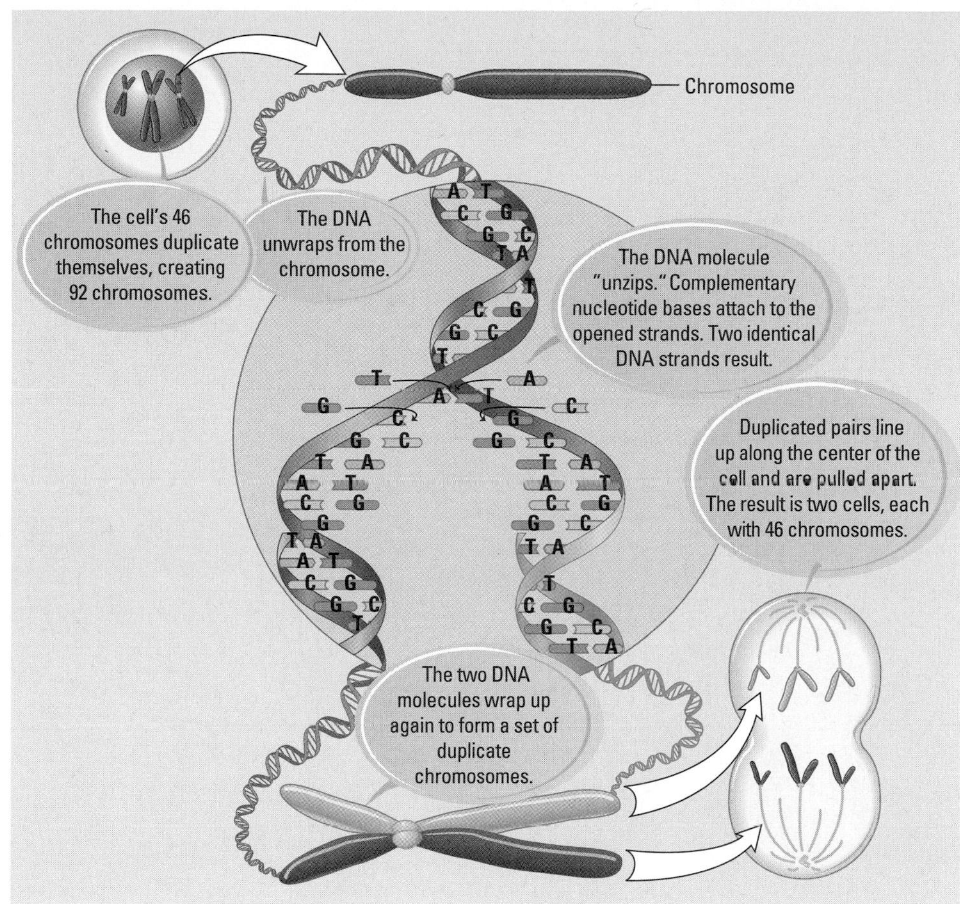
Chromosome
The cell's 46 chromosomes duplicate themselves, creating 92 chromosomes.
The DNA unwraps from the chromosome.
The DNA molecule "unzips." Complementary nucleotide bases attach to the opened strands. Two identical DNA strands result.
Duplicated pairs line up along the center of the cell and are pulled apart. The result is two cells, each with 46 chromosomes.
The two DNA molecules wrap up again to form a set of duplicate chromosomes.

◀ FIGURE 2.5
**Mitosis**
During replication the DNA strand "unzips," and a new complementary strand forms for each original parent strand. This is how each chromosome duplicates itself (with its genetic code) during cell division.

THINK ABOUT JUAN AND TRACEY . . .
Explain to Juan and Tracey how their children inherited a unique combination of chromosomes from their biological parents. What events happened during meiosis to ensure that the genetic material inherited by each child was unique to each?

mutations—changes in the order of nucleotide bases—and sex cells, every cell in our body contains an exact copy of the 46 chromosomes that originated from our single fertilized egg cell.

One exception to mitosis occurs with our sex cells, or *gametes*. Gametes are the cells that make up our sperm and eggs, and they form through a different process called meiosis. The entire process of meiosis is shown in Figure 2.6. **Meiosis** is also called "reduction division" because it reduces the number of chromosomes in each cell by half. That is, it reduces the number of chromosomes to 23 in each gamete so that, when sperm and egg unite in conception, the resulting fertilized egg will have the standard number of 46 chromosomes. Meiosis ensures diversity in the gene pool because during this process, genetic material can be traded among chromosome pairs (a process called crossing over) and then randomly distributed among the gametes. Thus, even when the same parents have several children, the children have plenty of genetic differences from one another because they do not inherit the same combinations of chromosomes or genes.

*Identical twins* are the one exception—these children do have the same genetic codes. Identical twins are two individuals who grow from a single zygote. At some point early in the pregnancy, as cells in the zygote divide, it separates into two separate zygotes that develops into two babies. Scientists refer to identical twins as **monozygotic (MZ) twins**, because they come from one zygote. Because they develop from the same fertilized egg, MZ twins have copies of each

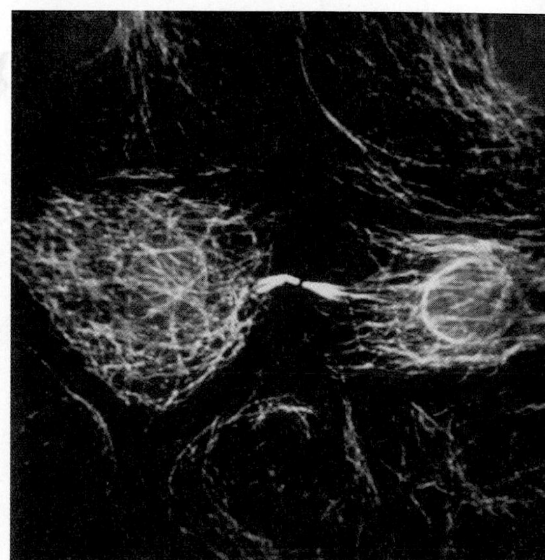

▲ This human cell is finishing the process of mitosis. It has copied itself and all its genetic material to form a second cell.

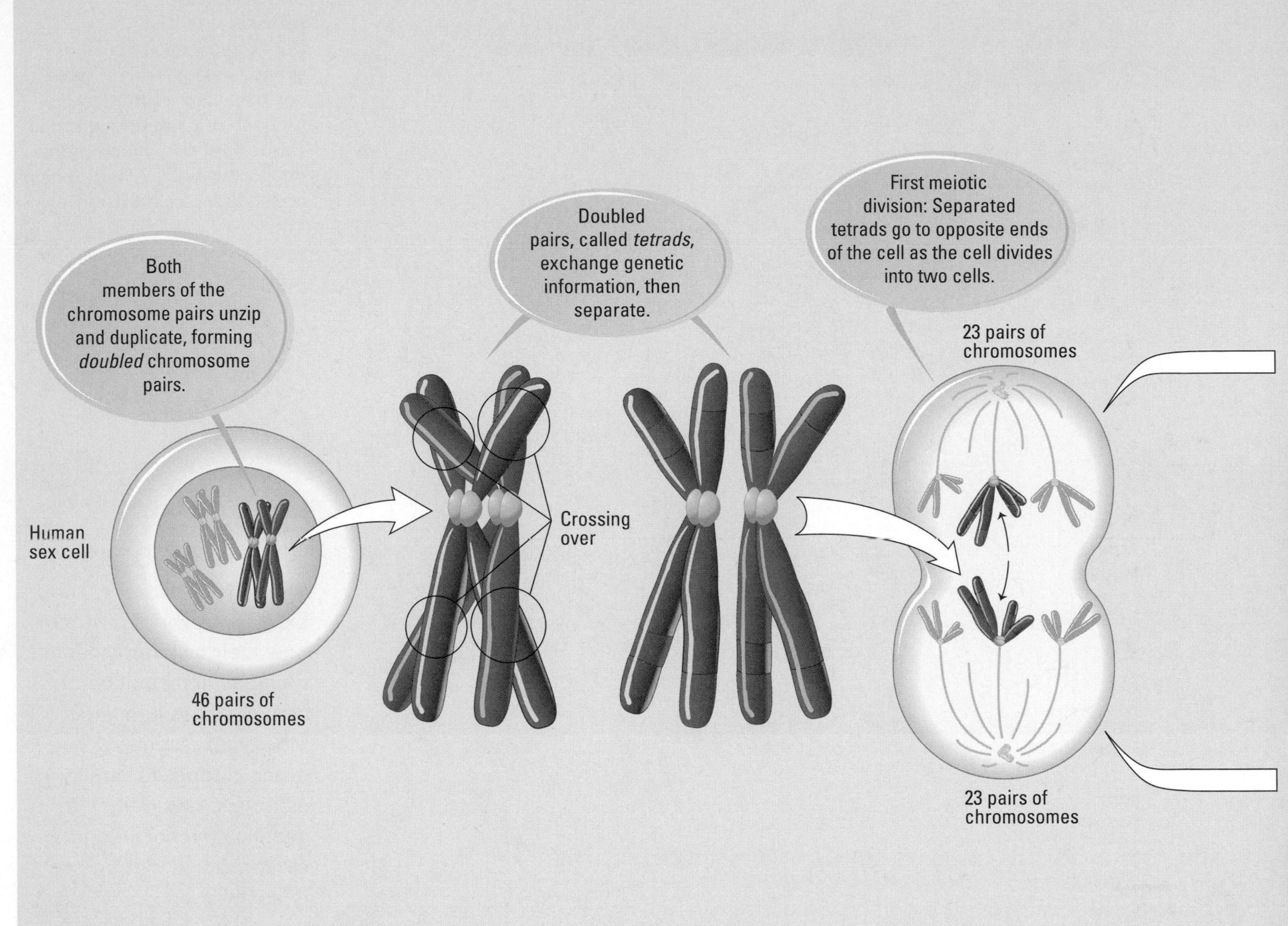

Both members of the chromosome pairs unzip and duplicate, forming *doubled* chromosome pairs.
Doubled pairs, called *tetrads*, exchange genetic information, then separate.
First meiotic division: Separated tetrads go to opposite ends of the cell as the cell divides into two cells.
23 pairs of chromosomes
Human sex cell
Crossing over
46 pairs of chromosomes
23 pairs of chromosomes

▲ FIGURE 2.6
**Meiosis**
The gametes (sperm and egg cells) form via meiosis. Meiosis reduces the number of chromosomes from 46 to 23 in each cell. Crossing over of chromosome segments and random shuffling of chromosomes to cells ensure genetic diversity in the species. After fertilization, cell division occurs with mitosis, where all 46 chromosomes are copied into each new cell.

other's 46 chromosomes and therefore share the same genetic code. MZ twins are always the same sex and tend to be very similar in appearance. MZ twins occur in about 1 in every 260 births (this rate is virtually the same in all segments of the population), and MZ twins do not seem to run in families (Thompson, McInnes, & Willard, 1991).

**dizygotic (DZ) twins**
Fraternal (fraternal) twins. These twins form when two eggs are fertilized by two different sperm cells.

*Fraternal twins*, sometimes called *nonidentical twins*, grow from two separate conceptions. That is, the mother releases two eggs, and two different sperm from the father fertilize them. Because they come from two separate conceptions and therefore form two separate zygotes, we refer to fraternal twins as **dizygotic (DZ) twins**. DZ twins are no

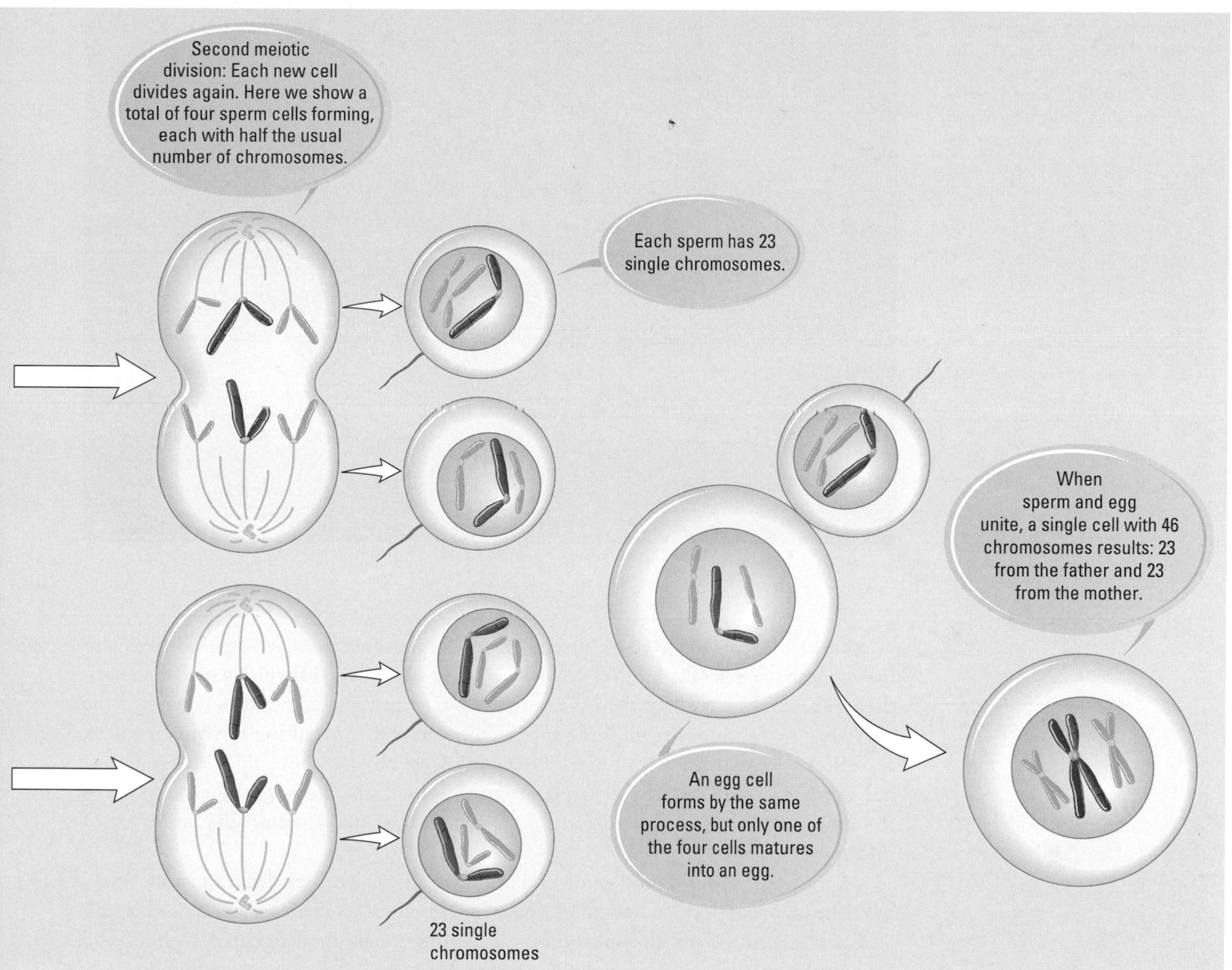


more alike genetically than are any other brothers or sisters from the same parents. They can be different sexes, and their appearances can also be very different. Theoretically, they could even have different fathers. How? If the mother has intercourse with two different men within a short span of time, it is possible that two eggs she released could be fertilized by different fathers. Although this doesn't happen very often, it demonstrates just how different fraternal twins can be.

For reasons that scientists don't yet understand, different ethnic groups have different rates of DZ twinning. DZ twins occur in about 1 in every 500 births for Asians, in 1 in 125 births for Caucasians, and in as many as 1 in 20 births in some African populations (Thompson et al., 1991). Because DZ twinning results from the release of multiple eggs, the mother's genetics and the functioning of her ovaries and reproductive system govern its occurrence. Consequently, higher rates of DZ twinning tend to run on the mother's side of the family. DZ twinning also increases as the mother ages.

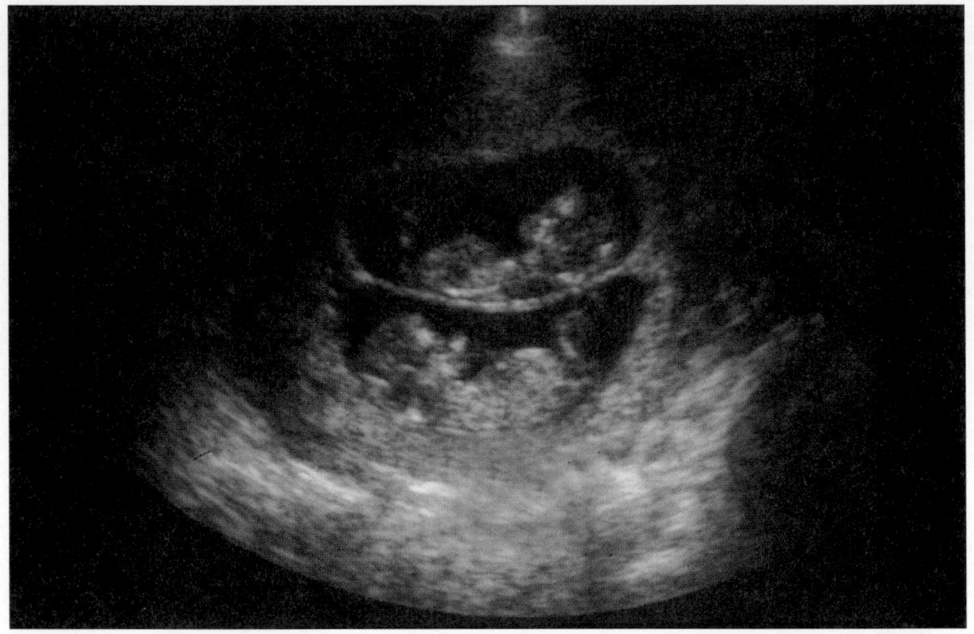

This ultrasound image shows ▶ twins. If they are identical twins, they will have the same genetic code as each other. If they are fraternal, they will share only 50% of their genes, on average.

Earlier in this chapter we discussed fertility problems that some couples can have. Some women take fertility drugs when they are having difficulty conceiving children. The drugs stimulate the ovaries to release extra eggs. Sometimes several of the eggs become fertilized by multiple sperm from the father, resulting in twins, triplets, quadruplets, and other sets of multiple births. Most children born this way are fraternal (fraternal twins, fraternal triplets, etc.). Sometimes, however, one or more of the fraternal zygotes divide to form a set of identical twins within the larger set of multiples.

A final note about reproduction and cell division concerns sex determination. As we have already mentioned, among the 23 pairs of chromosomes in a normal cell is a specialized pair, called the **sex chromosomes**. Sex chromosomes are designated as the X and Y chromosomes. Females have two X chromosomes, and males have one X and one Y. When the sex cells form, females can pass only X chromosomes to their eggs. Males, however, pass the X chromosome to half of their sperm and the Y to the other half. The sex of the offspring therefore depends on which type of sperm fertilizes the egg. If the sperm is carrying an X chromosome, the fertilized egg will be XX and will produce a girl. If the sperm is carrying a Y chromosome, the fertilized egg will be XY and will produce a boy. X and Y chromosomes also have implications for genetic defects, as you will see in the next section.

**sex chromosomes**
The 23rd pair of chromosomes (in humans), specialized to determine the sex of the child and other characteristics. Males are XY and females are XX.

Identical twins *(left)* are ▶ much more alike genetically than are fraternal twins *(right)*. Later in the chapter, you will see that these differences are used to estimate how much influence genetics has on people's traits and characteristics.

## LET'S REVIEW . . .

1. Each cell in the human body typically has 46:
   a. genes. b. gametes.
   c. chromosomes. d. nucleotide base pairs.
2. If one strand of base pairs has the sequence of A, T, C, C, G, what will the complementary sequence be on the other strand?
   a. A, T, C, C, G b. G, C, T, T, A
   c. C, G, A, A, T d. T, A, G, G, C
3. Mitosis is the type of cell division that ensures that:
   a. almost every cell in the human body has 23 chromosomes.
   b. almost every cell in the human body has 46 chromosomes.
   c. crossover occurs to exchange genes across chromosomes.
   d. random shuffling of chromosomes occurs to increase genetic diversity.
4. What is the name of the type of cell division that creates sperm and egg cells?
   a. meiosis b. mitosis
   c. crossing over d. NA replication
5. True or False: Each pair of nucleotide bases forms one gene.
6. True or False: The rate of dizygotic (fraternal) twins varies across ethnic groups and tends to be higher in some family lines.

Answers: 1. c, 2. d, 3. b, 4. a, 5. F, 6. T

# How Traits and Genetic Abnormalities Are Inherited

Imagine how complicated the genetic code that forms each unique individual human being must be. More than 3 billion pairs of nucleotide bases must be ordered properly to form thousands of genes stretched across our 46 chromosomes. All of this code must be copied accurately into each one of our trillions of cells. Errors, or mutations, do occur, and some of these then get passed down to the next generations. In some cases the errors involve only a few base pairs; sometimes, however, whole chromosomes are damaged, lost, or duplicated too many times.

In this section we describe a few examples of diseases and conditions that people can inherit when genetic errors occur. Scientists have identified several thousand such diseases, but here we'll present just a few examples to give you a better understanding of how genes can cause human diseases and abnormalities. As the Human Genome Project progresses, we continue to learn more about the specific codes involved. There is hope that someday genetic therapies or other interventions may provide cures or treatments for these terrible and sometimes deadly conditions.

AS YOU STUDY THIS SECTION, ASK YOURSELF THESE QUESTIONS:

2.3 How do dominant–recessive disease traits work and how do X-linked (or sex-linked) traits work?

2.4 What are the major chromosomal abnormalities, and why are they important for child development?

2.5 What are the most common procedures doctors use to test the health of fetuses?

## Dominant–Recessive Traits

We have already mentioned that chromosomes come in pairs. Many human traits are governed by **dominant–recessive relationships** between alleles—the two different versions of a gene—acting across pairs of chromosomes. That is, if a person inherits a dominant

**dominant–recessive relationship**
Relationship between genes where the dominant allele will govern a particular trait, and the recessive allele will be repressed. To express a recessive trait, the individual needs to inherit two recessive alleles—one on each chromosome.

**TABLE 2.2**
**Common Traits Governed by Dominant–Recessive Gene Relationships**

| DOMINANT TRAITS | RECESSIVE TRAITS |
|---|---|
| Detached earlobes | Attached earlobes |
| Ability to roll tongue | Inability to roll tongue |
| Dimpled cheeks | Nondimpled cheeks |
| Longer eyelashes | Shorter eyelashes |
| Larger eyeballs | Smaller eyeballs |
| Arched feet | Flat feet |

(Starr & Taggart, 1998.)

Explore Dominant and Recessive Traits. www.mydevelopmentlab.com

allele on one chromosome and a recessive allele on the corresponding chromosome, the dominant allele will rule and determine the trait. For example, the allele for arched feet is dominant, and the allele for flat feet is recessive (Starr & Taggart, 1998). If you inherit two dominant alleles, or a mix of one dominant and one recessive allele, your feet will be arched. To inherit flat feet, you would need to inherit two of the recessive alleles, one on the chromosome that came from your father and one on the chromosome from your mother. Because of this dominant–recessive relationship, traits governed by dominant alleles are much more likely to be expressed than are traits from recessive alleles. Other examples of dominant-allele traits are given in Table 2.2. Which of these traits do you have? Explore on mydevelopmentlab

**Dominant Gene Diseases** Huntington's disease is the most common example of a genetic disorder that is governed by a dominant allele. Although Huntington's disease is genetic, the symptoms usually do not appear until age 30 or after. The disease causes progressive damage to the brain and nervous system, leading to deteriorating intelligence, muscle control, balance, and speech. The gene for Huntington's disease has been identified on chromosome 4 (refer back to Figure 2.4). The disease is rare: It occurs in only about 4 to 7 out of every 100,000 births, with the highest rate among populations from western Europe (Gulli, 2005; Thompson et al., 1991). At this time there is no cure for Huntington's disease.

Let's take a close look at Figure 2.7, which shows the likelihood that offspring will inherit Huntington's disease when one or both parents have the disorder. On the left side

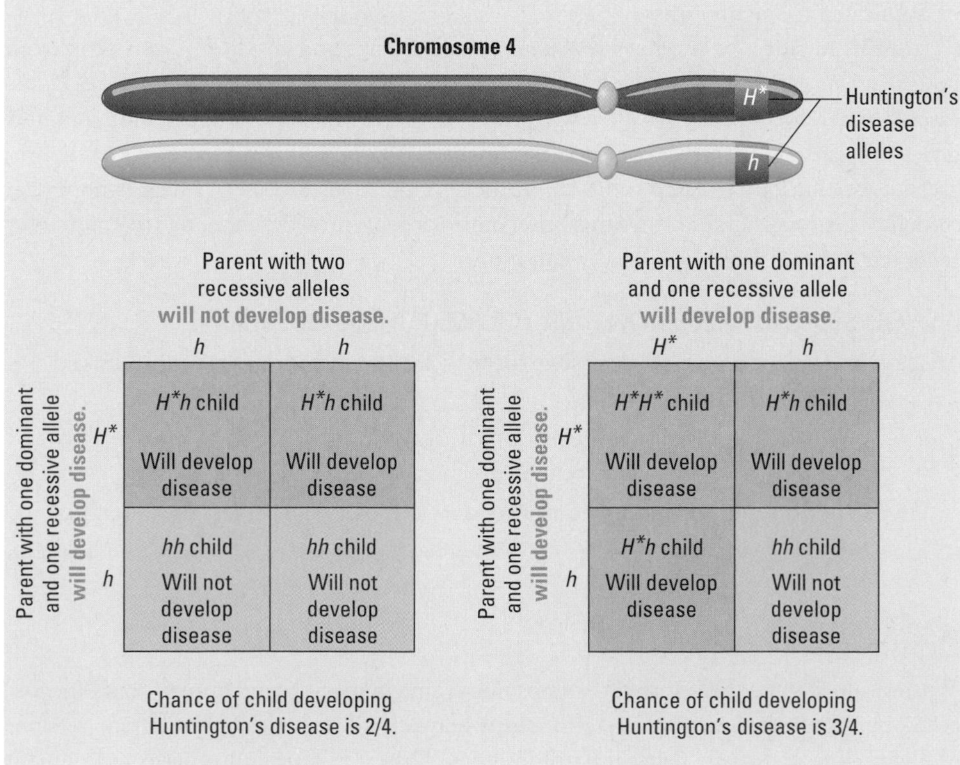


FIGURE 2.7 ▶ **Dominant Disease Alleles** With dominant allele traits, individuals only need one dominant allele to inherit the trait. Here, the dominant allele causes Huntington's disease. Dominant alleles are represented by the uppercase H and recessive alleles by the lowercase h. The asterisk is a reminder of which allele causes the disease (H*). On the left, one parent with the disease (H*h) and one healthy parent (hh) have a 50% chance of having a child who inherits the disease. On the right, both parents have the disease (both are H*h), and they have a 75 percent chance. What would be the odds if one parent carries two dominant disease genes (H*H*)?

of the figure, one parent has the dominant allele for Huntington's (H) and also has one recessive allele (h) that is healthy. Because the disease gene is dominant, this parent will develop the disease. The other parent carries two recessive healthy alleles (hh), so this parent will not develop Huntington's disease. When these two parents have children, we would expect half of their offspring (on average) to inherit the dominant allele and therefore the disease. On average, we would expect the remaining half to inherit two recessive alleles and be healthy. On the right side of the figure, you can see that having both parents with the dominant allele dramatically increases the likelihood that their children will inherit the disease.

**Recessive Gene Diseases** Recessive gene diseases work a bit differently because two recessive alleles need to be inherited before the individual shows the condition. Thus, for a child to inherit a recessive trait, both parents must either have the trait (with two recessive alleles) or at least carry the trait (with one recessive allele). One relatively common recessive disorder is cystic fibrosis, which is controlled by genes on chromosome 7. Cystic fibrosis affects tissues in the body that produce mucus secretions. The lungs, gastrointestinal tract, pancreas, and liver are often affected. People with cystic fibrosis usually experience serious respiratory problems and lung infections, and without lung transplants most do not live past the age of 30. Cystic fibrosis is the most common recessive disease among Caucasians, occurring in approximately 1 in every 2,000 Caucasian children (Thompson et al., 1991). Nearly 1 in every 25 Caucasians carries the recessive allele (Rosick, 2005). The disease is virtually unknown in Asian populations and is very rare among people of African descent. Figure 2.8 shows the inheritance patterns for recessive traits such as cystic fibrosis.

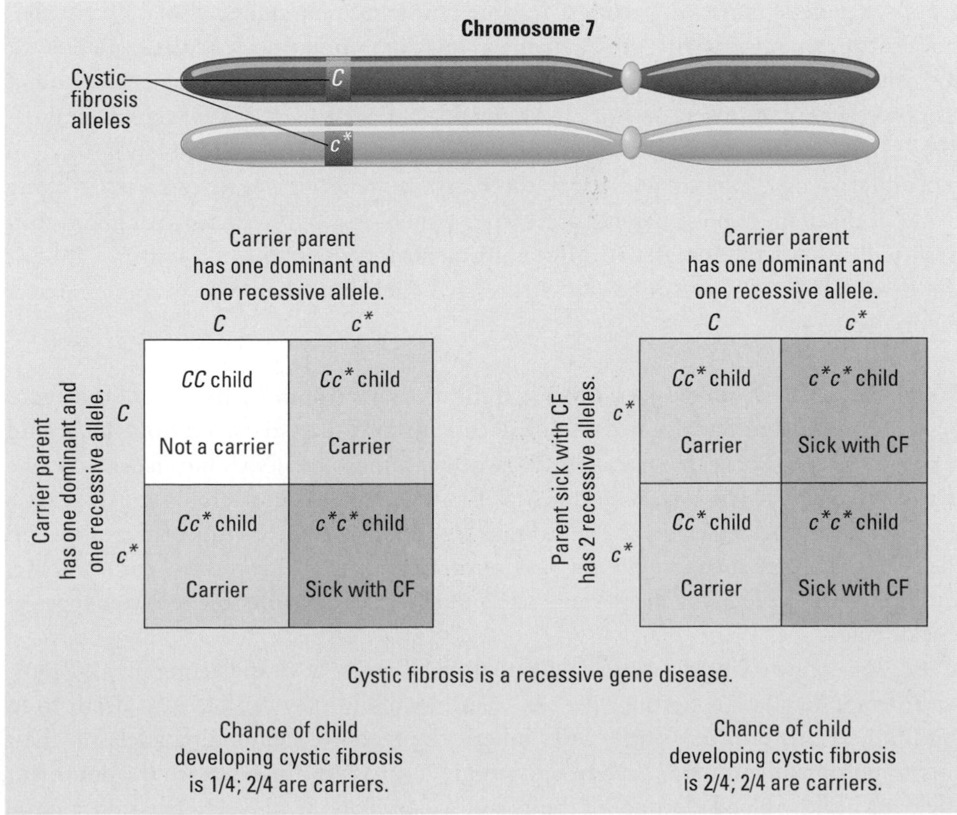


◀ FIGURE 2.8
**Recessive Disease Alleles**
With recessive allele traits, individuals must inherit two recessive alleles (one from each parent) to show the trait. Here, inheriting two recessive alleles (c*c*) causes cystic fibrosis. On the left, both parents are carriers (Cc*), but neither has the disease because they both have the dominant healthy allele. Their children, however, have a 25% chance of inheriting two recessive alleles (c*c*) and developing the disease. On the right, the risk is increased to 50% when one parent has the disease. What would the risk be if both parents had the disease? What if one parent carried the disease (Cc*) but the other parent did not (CC)?

Sickle cell disease (SCD) is the most common genetic disorder worldwide (Embury, Hebbel, Mohandas, & Steinberg, 1994). SCD is actually a group of diseases involving defective hemoglobin, the substance in all red blood cells that carries oxygen from the lungs to the rest of the body. The best-known form of the disease is sickle cell anemia. SCD is most common in people of African and Hispanic descent. About 1 in 400 African American babies and 1 in 1,000 Hispanic babies are affected (Bojanowski, 2005). It also occurs in people with Mediterranean, Middle Eastern, and Native American heritage. In SCD a gene on chromosome 11 causes the production of a defective form of hemoglobin. Unlike normal red blood cells, which are soft and round, red blood cells with the defective form of hemoglobin become stiff and distorted after they deliver oxygen, curving into the shape of a sickle (a tool used to cut wheat). Sickled cells are sticky and can form clots in small blood vessels throughout the body, causing damage to the tissues. Hospitals in many states routinely test newborns for SCD using a simple blood test, and the condition can even be detected through prenatal genetic testing. Several treatments are available to manage SCD but the only potential cure as of now is a bone marrow transplant, a risky procedure that requires a suitable donor. Genetic researchers hope to develop a cure through gene therapy, either correcting the gene itself or finding a way to turn off the action of the defective gene and reactivate a different gene which can produce healthy hemoglobin (Samakoglu et al., 2006; "Sickle Cell Anemia," 2008; Vichinsky, 2002).

Tay–Sachs disease is another recessive allele disorder. Tay–Sachs is controlled by a gene on chromosome 15 that causes damage to the brain and central nervous system. The body lacks an enzyme for metabolizing fats; the gradual accumulation of these fats damages cells. The disease begins in infancy and causes mental retardation, blindness, and loss of muscle control; it is usually fatal by the age of 2 or 3 years (McKusick, 1998; Starr & Taggart, 1998). At present there is no effective cure or treatment. This disease is extremely rare except among certain populations such as Ashkenazi (German) Jews, French Canadians, Louisiana Cajuns, and Pennsylvania Dutch. In each of these groups, a genetic mutation occurred at some point and reproductive isolation (in central European regions for the Ashkenazi Jewish population, in other places for the other groups) lead to a high degree of intermarriage and an increase in the rate of recessive genetic diseases (Desnick & Kaback, 2001; "What Is Tay–Sachs Disease?," 2007). Because Tay–Sachs is fatal in childhood, people with the disease do not live to reproductive age. Parents who carry the recessive gene, however, can pass it along to their children. If both parents are carriers, there is a 25% chance that their children will inherit the disease. If only one is a carrier, their children will not inherit the disease, but they can inherit the recessive allele and therefore become carriers themselves.

THINKING CRITICALLY

As you can imagine, families who carry fatal diseases like Huntington's disease, cystic fibrosis, sickle cell disease, or Tay–Sachs can face serious ethical dilemmas. Would you have your fetus tested for potential fatal diseases during pregnancy if you knew you were a carrier? What information would you use to make such a decision?

### X-Linked Traits

**X-linked (sex-linked) traits** are traits that differ in rate of occurrence between males and females because of dominant and recessive alleles on the X and Y chromosomes. Recall that females have two X chromosomes (XX), but males have one X and one Y (XY). The Y chromosome is very small and does not contain much genetic material (look back at Figure 2.1 and find the Y chromosome). Most of the alleles on the X chromosome therefore do not have a corresponding allele on the Y chromosome, and this causes males to be much more likely than females to suffer the recessive types of disease traits.

**X-linked (sex-linked) traits** Traits that differ in rate of occurrence between males and females, caused by dominant and recessive alleles on the X and Y chromosomes.

A well-known X-linked disease is hemophilia (Type A, or classic hemophilia). People with hemophilia lack a clotting agent in their blood and they can bleed to death from cuts and serious bruises. When males inherit the recessive hemophilia allele on their X chromosome, they do not have an opportunity to mask the disease with the dominant allele for healthy blood clotting on the Y, so they develop the disease. Females are more fortunate. Even if they inherit the recessive hemophilia allele on one X, they almost always have the dominant allele for normal blood clotting on their other X. These females will not get the disease, although they can pass the allele to their children. To have hemophilia, a female would need to inherit the recessive allele on both X chromosomes—a very rare occurrence. Other examples of X-linked recessive traits include Duchenne muscular dystrophy, color blindness, and some forms of retinitis pigmentosa (a major form of blindness). All of these conditions are more common among males than females.

Dominant disease alleles on the X chromosome are another matter. Females have two chances to inherit these disease alleles (having two X chromosomes), but males have only one chance (one X chromosome). Because the allele is dominant, having the allele on either X can cause the disease in females. Females are therefore twice as likely as males to show these diseases. Fortunately, dominant X-linked diseases are very rare. Vitamin D–resistant rickets is one example, occurring twice as often among females as among males (Thompson et al., 1991). With this form of rickets, children have kidney problems that block the production of calcium for bone growth. By 1 year of age, infants begin showing limb deformities and decreased growth (D'Alessandro, 2002). Rett syndrome (causing severe mental retardation) is another example; it occurs only among females, because the few males who do inherit the disease die before birth (Smith, 2001). Females who have the disease allele on one X chromosome usually have the recessive (nondisease) allele on their other X chromosome. The nondisease allele operates enough to allow survivability for female fetuses. With male zygotes, however, the small Y chromosome does not carry the nondisease allele, so only the disease allele operates. The allele causes such severe damage that these male zygotes are miscarried.

Fragile X syndrome is another special case involving the sex chromosomes. It is linked to a defective part of the X chromosome—the chromosome is weakened at the tip and also contains a defective allele that contributes to the syndrome. This syndrome causes facial deformities as well as damage to the brain which results in mental retardation. Fragile X syndrome occurs in about 1 in every 4,000 to 6,000 males, twice as often as the rate for females (Quercia, 2005). It is one of the leading inherited causes of mental retardation among males, second only to Down syndrome (described in the next section).

**Down syndrome**
Trisomy 21, a genetic disorder that occurs when there is an extra 21st chromosome. Low IQ, facial defects, heart problems, and shortened life span are characteristic problems.

## Chromosome Abnormalities

Abnormalities in the structure or number of whole chromosomes are present in 1 of every 160 live births. These abnormalities account for the majority of all miscarriages (Thompson et al., 1991). Normally, each sperm and egg cell has 23 chromosomes. As the gametes form during meiosis, however, errors can occur that cause the sperm or egg cell to be missing a chromosome or contain an extra chromosome. In most cases, this causes a miscarriage early in pregnancy.

One exception of an abnormality that triggers miscarriage is with chromosome 21, one of the smallest chromosomes (look back to Figure 2.1). **Down syndrome** occurs when babies are born with an extra 21st chromosome. Another name for Down syndrome is trisomy 21, as the disorder is due to the presence of three (tri) chromosomes (somy) at location 21. Individuals with Down syndrome typically are short in stature, have short and broad hands, and tend to have heart problems and a shortened life span (see Figure 2.9). People with Down syndrome also have mental retardation, with IQs typically between 25 and 50 (compared to the average IQ of 100 in the rest of the population). Down syndrome is the most common genetic cause of mental retardation,

▲ FIGURE 2.9
**Down Syndrome Features**
Down syndrome is caused by an extra chromosome at the 21st pair. Flattened nose, tightened eyelids, low-set ears, and short neck are typical features. Lower IQ is one of the main problems faced by children with Down syndrome.

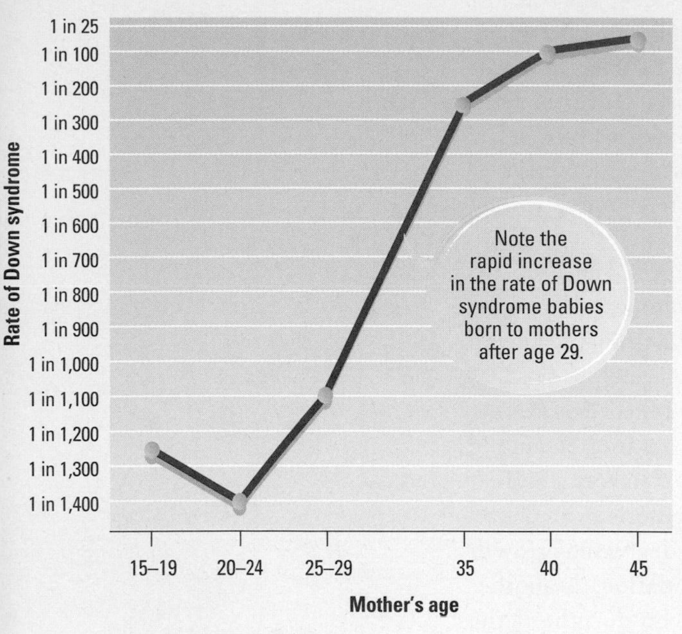


▲ FIGURE 2.10
**Risk of Down Syndrome Due to the Mother's Age**
The rate of Down syndrome births increases dramatically as mothers age. (Based on U.S. births reported in 2004; data from Martin, Hamilton, Sutton, Ventura, Menacker, & Kirmeyer, 2006.)

accounting for 40% of the moderate to severe cases of retardation in the general population (Pennington, Moon, Edgin, Stedron, & Nadel, 2003). In adulthood, the typical person with Down syndrome has the mental ability of an average 7- or 8-year-old child and lives to around 50 years of age. However, lifespan varies greatly depending on the person's ethnicity. The median age at death for Caucasians with Down syndrome is 50 years, while it is 25 years for African Americans, and only 11 years for other ethnicities (Centers for Disease Control and Prevention, 2001). At least some of the difference is likely due to differences in care received (e.g., access to medical or surgical treatment of complications, quality of preventative care) (Centers for Disease Control and Prevention, 2001).

In about 95% of Down syndrome cases, the extra 21st chromosome exists because the 21st chromosome pair did not separate properly when the egg was formed. As Figure 2.10 indicates, the risk of this occurring increases dramatically with the increased age of the mother. We still do not know the reasons for this increase. Perhaps the eggs have deteriorated in older mothers, leading to problems in chromosome formation. Once the mother reaches 35, the risk is high enough that doctors usually recommend genetic testing early in pregnancy to determine if the fetus has the extra chromosome. We'll describe the methods and alternatives for genetic testing later in this chapter. Although most sources emphasize the increased risk for women of "advancing age," you should keep in mind that the birthrate for younger women is so much higher that more than half of all babies with Down syndrome are born to mothers who are actually younger than 35 (Thompson et al., 1991). **Watch** on **mydevelopmentlab**

**Watch** a video on Down Syndrome: Enhancing Development.
www.mydevelopmentlab.com

**Sex Chromosome Abnormalities** With the exception of trisomy 21 (Down syndrome), having an extra chromosome usually leads to pregnancy loss or death of the infant within the first few months of life. Another exception, however, involves the X and Y chromosomes. Babies can survive with extra or missing sex chromosomes—in fact, abnormalities in the number of sex chromosomes are among the most common of all human genetic disorders. They occur in about 1 in every 500 live births (Thompson et al., 1991). Table 2.3 describes several sex chromosome abnormalities. In the next section we describe the most common techniques doctors use to determine if a developing fetus has inherited or developed any of these or other genetic disorders.

## Prenatal Screening and Genetic Testing

It is common for parents to be concerned and anxious during pregnancy, especially if a genetic disorder runs in the family or the baby is at risk in some other way. Fortunately, medical experts today can assist expectant parents who have these concerns. Several procedures can detect genetic diseases and abnormalities, and many other potential problems, before the baby is born. Ultrasonography, amniocentesis, and chorionic villus sampling (CVS) are the procedures most frequently used. An obstetrician may recommend these tests during the mother's prenatal visits. Other procedures are being developed that involve analysis of fetal cells within the mother's blood (Sekizawa et al., 2007). Because these newer approaches do not involve inserting a needle into the uterus, they are expected to have a lower risk to both mother and fetus.

**ultrasonography (ultrasound)**
Images of the fetus inside the mother's womb produced by sound waves. Ultrasound can be used to help physicians monitor fetal growth and detect physical defects.

**amniocentesis**
Procedure used to detect chromosomal and genetic abnormalities in the fetus. A needle is inserted through the mother's abdomen and uterus and into the amniotic sac, and fetal cells are withdrawn from the amniotic fluid.

With **ultrasonography (ultrasound)**, a technician uses an instrument that sends sound waves into the mother's abdomen. By reading the return of the sound waves, the

**TABLE 2.3**
Summary of Sex Chromosome Abnormalities

| DISORDER | SEX CHROMOSOME ARRANGEMENT | FREQUENCY | MAJOR CHARACTERISTICS |
|---|---|---|---|
| Klinefelter syndrome (in males) | XXY, extra X chromosome | 1/650 males | Small testicles, infertility; learning problems, shyness, and social immaturity |
| XYY syndrome (in males) | XYY, extra Y chromosome | 1/1,000 males | Tall stature; learning problems; individuals remain fertile |
| Trisomy X (in females) | XXX, extra X chromosome | 1/1,000 females | Tall stature; individuals remain fertile |
| Turner syndrome (individual develops as female) | X, missing chromosome | 1/2,000 females | Short stature, webbed neck, broad shoulders, spatial perception and motor skill deficits; infertility; various other health problems |
| XX males (reversal) | XX | 1/20,000 males | Sex reversal (normally males are XY). A part of the Y chromosome breaks off during meiosis and attaches to one of the X chromosomes. Because this part of the Y chromosome contains the genes that determine male sexual development, the individual develops male sexual characteristics. All XX males are infertile. |
| XY females (reversal) | XY | 1/20,000 females | Sex reversal (normally females are XX). Part of the Y chromosome breaks off and is lost during meiosis. Now the XY individual does not have the genes required for normal male development, and the default is to develop female sexual characteristics. XY females do not develop secondary sex characteristics and are infertile. |

(Gale Encyclopedia of Genetic Disorders, 2005; Thompson et al., 1991.)

instrument produces an image of the fetus and the surrounding structures. Ultrasound measurements help physicians determine if the fetus is growing properly. They also can reveal many structural defects (e.g., heart defects or neural tube or spinal defects). Ultrasounds can be performed any time during pregnancy. In the ultrasound picture shown in Figure 2.11, you can clearly see the shape of the fetus.

We will never forget the ultrasound session from our third pregnancy (we already had two boys). As the technician moved the instrument over the abdomen, an image of two tiny side-by-side fetuses appeared on the monitor. At first we thought we were seeing an echo of one baby—echoes are common with ultrasounds. But the technician assured us that it was no echo. Instead, we were seeing the first picture of our twin girls, DZ twins. Two boys, and now two girls! Once we knew that both fetuses looked healthy, our thoughts immediately turned to other things . . . like how to feed and diaper two babies at once and how to fit six people into our small car. (We traded it in for a van.)

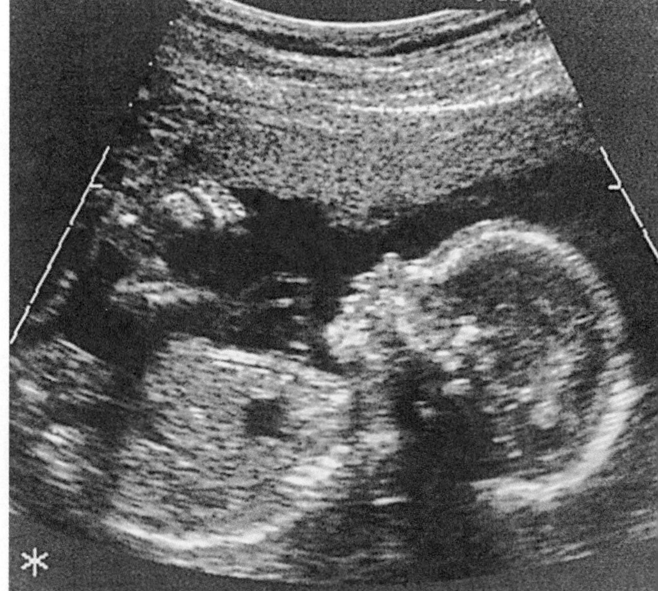

▲ FIGURE 2.11
**Ultrasound Image of a Fetus**
Using ultrasound, physicians can monitor the growth of the fetus and can detect hundreds of potential defects.

If the parents are at high risk for passing a genetic defect to the baby, or if the mother's age is 35 or older, the doctor will usually suggest genetic screening. With **amniocentesis**, a doctor or technician inserts a needle through the mother's abdomen and uterus and into the amniotic sac that surrounds the fetus. The technician also uses ultrasound during this process to show the position of the fetus and to guide the needle to an open pocket of amniotic fluid. The needle draws a small amount of fluid from the amniotic sac. Cells that the fetus has sloughed off into the fluid are then cultured in a laboratory for genetic

THINK ABOUT JUAN AND TRACEY. . .

What would Juan and Tracey be able to learn if they had access to the results of genetic tests that may have been performed with their children? If they knew in advance which diseases or conditions their children may be susceptible to, what might they be able to do to intervene or help?

**chorionic villus sampling (CVS)** Procedure used to detect chromosomal and genetic abnormalities in the fetus. A catheter (tube) is inserted into the uterus, and cells are taken from the chorionic layer of the placenta around the fetus. Chromosomes are removed to conduct genetic tests.

testing. Technicians remove the chromosomes from these cultured cells and arrange them by size to form a picture called a karyotype. The picture of chromosomes in Figure 2.1 on page 38 is a karyotype. By examining the karyotype, experts can detect any of several hundred disorders, especially those caused by missing, extra, or broken chromosomes. If a single-gene disease or other genetic disorder runs in the family, specific tests can check for DNA markers or other indications of the disease.

Amniocentesis can be conducted after the 14th week of pregnancy, and the results are usually available in 1 to 2 weeks. There is about a 1 in 200 chance that the procedure itself will cause a serious problem. Inserting the needle near the fetus can cause early labor contractions and a miscarriage, and bacteria or injury caused by the needle can lead to serious infection. Because of these risks, doctors usually do not perform amniocentesis unless the fetus is already at a higher risk for a serious genetic disorder or other complication.

**Chorionic villus sampling (CVS)** can be performed earlier than amniocentesis, beginning around the 9th week of pregnancy. With CVS the results can be available in just a few days. In this procedure a technician usually inserts a long catheter (tube) through the vagina and into the uterus. Sometimes a needle may be used instead and inserted through the abdomen and uterus (similar to amniocentesis). The technician takes a few cells from the chorionic layer of the placenta that surrounds the fetus. As you will see in the next chapter, this layer of cells originates from the zygote, so the chromosomes and genetic

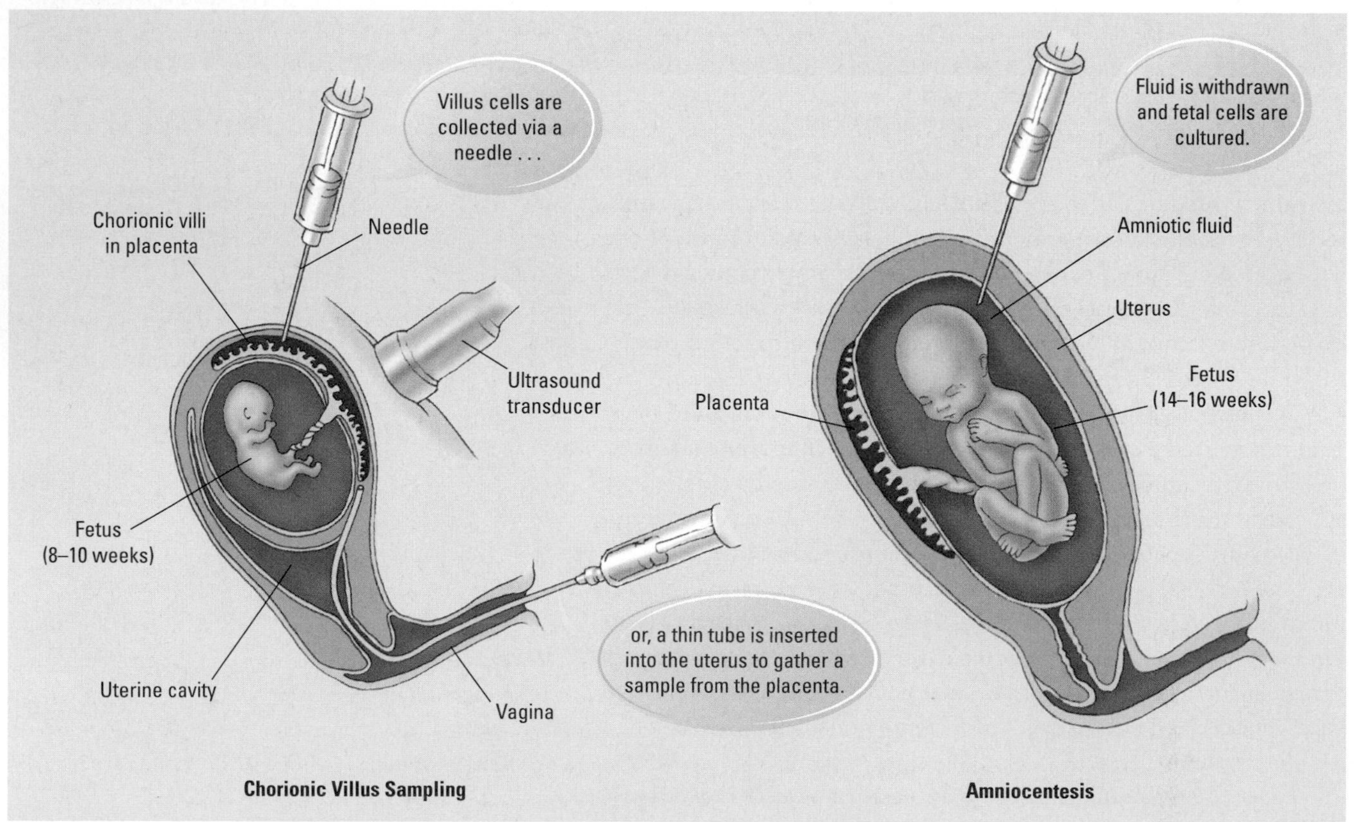


▲ FIGURE 2.12

**Two Ways Fetal Cells Are Collected for Genetic Testing During Pregnancy**

With chorionic villus sampling (CVS) (*left*), either a catheter is inserted through the vagina and into the uterus to take placental villus cells for testing or villus cells are extracted using a needle inserted into the placenta. With amniocentesis (*right*) a needle is inserted through the mother's abdomen and into the amniotic sac. Amniotic fluid is withdrawn, containing cells from the fetus. (Bee & Boyd, 2006.)

## Perspective PROFESSIONAL — CAREER FOCUS: MEET A GENETIC COUNSELOR

Robin L. Bennett, MS, CGC
Seattle, WA
Genetic counselor; president of the National Society of Genetic Counselors (www.nsgc.org); and author of *The Practical Guide to the Genetic Family History* (1999), published by John Wiley & Sons

**What are the main roles and job duties of genetic counselors?**
We help people at risk for or affected with a genetic disorder. We translate complicated genetic facts into practical information to help clients understand a disorder, the available courses of action, how heredity contributes, and the testing options that are available. During a visit, we create a family pedigree, which is a summary of the medical conditions and family relationships over at least three generations. A critical role is discussing the feelings and concerns the clients have about genetic and prenatal testing as well as potential consequences. We also refer clients to community resources and appropriate medical specialties.

**When a serious disease or defect is detected, how do counselors inform and assist clients?**
The diagnosis is discussed face to face, and clients are strongly encouraged to have a support person with them (a partner, relative, or friend). Genetic counselors are trained in grief and crisis counseling. They try to anticipate clients' reactions and refer clients to specialists (such as individual and family therapists) and support groups as needed (see www.geneticalliance.org for information on support groups).

**What are the newest techniques and trends in your field?**
Presymptomatic or susceptibility genetic testing is now available, where people can be tested for the potential of a genetic disorder. Genetic counseling for these individuals is extremely important, because these are healthy individuals at risk of developing the condition, but the tests do not predict when a person will be affected or how their disease will progress. Interpreting these tests is quite complex both medically and emotionally. Pharmacogenomics, where people can be tested for a cluster of susceptibilities so that "designer medications" can be prescribed, is also new. Hopefully this will significantly reduce the incidence of adverse reactions to drugs, but it's very expensive. Gene therapy continues to be in the news, but these therapies are still a ways off in terms of clinical practice.

**What training and education are needed to work in your field?**
A master's degree in genetic counseling is required, which involves course work in medicine, psychology, and human genetics, as well as over a thousand hours in fieldwork. Genetic counselors work in a variety of settings including medical centers, private practice, medical research, public health and policy, pharmaceutical companies, genetic testing laboratories, and in instructional settings. If they work in clinical practice, they must be certified by the American Board of Genetic Counseling.

QUESTION **Do any genetic disorders run in your family? Would you like to be tested to see if you have the predisposition for developing any of the diseases that are linked to genetics? Why or why not?**

codes in these cells will be the same as those in the fetus. By culturing these cells, specialists can construct a karyotype and perform genetic tests as with amniocentesis. The advantage of CVS is that it can be conducted earlier in pregnancy, allowing parents to have results several weeks sooner than with amniocentesis. If parents must decide whether to terminate the pregnancy because of a serious defect found in the fetus, this earlier diagnosis is helpful. In the past, CVS has been associated with a greater risk of inducing miscarriage (about twice as high as with amniocentesis) and with a slight risk of limb deformities, but its safety has improved. Recent research shows that the risks are similar for the two procedures (Caughey, Hopkins, & Norton, 2006; Cederholm, Haglund, & Axelsson, 2005; Furman & Appelman, 2005). Though limb deformities are rare with CVS, experts generally recommend waiting until week 10 of pregnancy to do the procedure. Figure 2.12 shows how technicians collect cells using CVS and amniocentesis. To learn more about a career that involves working with genetic tests, read the Professional Perspective above, "Career Focus: Meet a Genetic Counselor." **Listen** on **mydevelopmentlab**

THINKING CRITICALLY
If you were considering prenatal genetic screening, which test would you select, and why? What information would you need to make an informed decision? Would there be any information that could cause you to decide *against* having the screening?

**Listen**: Are there fetal problems that these prenatal tests cannot identify? (Author Podcast)
www.mydevelopmentlab.com

## LET'S REVIEW . . .

1. Which combination of alleles below is necessary for a person to inherit a disease such as cystic fibrosis? (*Note:* In this example, "C" refers to the healthy allele and "c" refers to the disease allele.)
   **a.** cc **b.** Cc
   **c.** cC **d.** CC
2. Hemophilia, Duchenne muscular dystrophy, and color blindness are examples of:
   **a.** X-linked dominant diseases.
   **b.** X-linked recessive diseases.
   **c.** diseases caused by missing chromosomes.
   **d.** diseases caused by a broken X chromosome.
3. Which of the following is more common among females than males?
   **a.** X-linked recessive traits
   **b.** X-linked dominant traits
   **c.** fragile X syndrome
   **d.** Klinefelter syndrome
4. Which test below could be used earliest in pregnancy to identify missing or extra chromosomes?
   **a.** amniocentesis
   **b.** ultrasonography
   **c.** chorionic villus sampling
   **d.** human genome mapping
5. True or False: Children will inherit Huntington's disease if they inherit a disease allele from one parent and a healthy allele from the other parent.
6. True or False: Down syndrome is caused by a missing chromosome.

Answers: 1. a, 2. b, 3. b, 4. c, 5. T, 6. F

# How Genes and Environments Interact

The first part of this chapter introduced you to some of the basic concepts of genetics and inheritance. Any human trait requires more than genetics, however. An environment of some kind is necessary for development to occur. In this context, environment refers to the interactions children have with the people, events, and situations in their lives. Children are nurtured by parents, educated by teachers, and influenced in countless ways by their siblings, playmates, and role models. Even the temperature, sunlight, and the presence or absence of toxic chemicals can influence development, and these too are considered part of the child's environment. In this section, we discuss how genetics and the environment interact to produce the complex traits, characteristics, and behaviors that we observe in children.

### AS YOU STUDY THIS SECTION, ASK YOURSELF THESE QUESTIONS:

2.6 What are the concepts of range of reaction, canalization, and niche-picking, and how does each concept help explain the interaction of genetics and environment?

2.7 What is probabilistic epigenesis and how does it help explain developmental outcomes?

THINKING CRITICALLY

How do genes and the environment act together to determine our traits?

Developmental psychologists call the interaction of genetics and the environment the **G x E interaction**. Pronounced "G by E interaction," this term refers to the nature–nurture interaction introduced in Chapter 1: The ways in which nature (represented by genetics and heredity) combines with nurture (the influences from a person's environment) to produce a given outcome. As you learned in Chapter 1, philosophers and scientists have long been interested in the relative roles of nature and nurture. For centuries the emphasis has shifted back and forth between nature and nurture, but it is now clear that both are essential for development to take place (de Waal, 1999). There are several ways to think about how genes and the environment interact. Next, we will describe three common ways—range of reaction, canalization, and niche-picking. Then we'll introduce one newer approach, probabilistic epigenesis.

**G x E interaction**
The interacting effects of genetics and the environment on the development of traits and characteristics.

## Range of Reaction, Canalization, and Niche-Picking

**Range of Reaction** One way to understand the interaction between genes and the environment is to recognize that an individual's **genotype** (or actual genetic code) establishes boundaries on the possible **phenotype** (or observable traits) that can occur. For any individual, the various possible phenotypic outcomes are the **range of reaction** for that genotype (Gottesman, 1963). The key idea is that genes set the boundaries for the range of reaction, but influences from the environment determine which possible outcomes actually materialize. Figure 2.13 illustrates the hypothetical range of reaction for cognitive skills for three children. Remember that the range of reaction is a theoretical construct. It is useful for helping us think about the ways in which genes and the environment interact, but we can never know for certain the range of reaction for a specific individual because it is impossible to know or manipulate all of the environmental possibilities during the limited time of one person's development.

THINKING CRITICALLY
What are some implications of the range of reaction for programs that attempt to enrich children's environments? Given that we cannot know which children have larger and which have smaller ranges of reaction, what should policy makers do to optimize the developmental outcomes of as many children as possible?

**Canalization** A second way to think about G x E interactions emphasizes how genetics can help protect children from the effects of the environment. **Canalization** refers to the way genes limit developmental paths and outcomes (Waddington, 1942, 1957). In other words, genes provide a strong buffer against environmental variations, limiting the effects that the environment can have. The result is that development can proceed along only a few species-specific paths and can produce only outcomes that are typical for that species. Figure 2.14 (p. 60) diagrams this concept using the idea of development as a hypothetical landscape. Genetics allows for a small number of pathways, or canals, through the hills and valleys of the developmental landscape. The environment can be thought of as a force (like the wind) that moves the individual around within the developmental landscape. The deeper the canal, the more genes predetermine the developmental pathway. In this model, choice points (where one canal splits into two and offers two different developmental directions) represent critical periods in development.

The view of canalization presented in Figure 2.14 (p. 60) emphasizes the protective role of genetics (especially the landscape on the right side of the figure). It explains how an individual can physically and psychologically survive despite fairly extreme environmental conditions. Can you see how the concept of canalization relates to the theme of *resilience*

**genotype**
The genetic code a person inherits.

**phenotype**
The observable trait a person shows, resulting in part from the genotype they inherit.

**range of reaction**
The range of possible phenotypes that exist for a particular genotype.

**canalization**
Genetic limits on the effects of the environment. In experiential canalization, in contrast, it is the environment that limits the expression of genes.

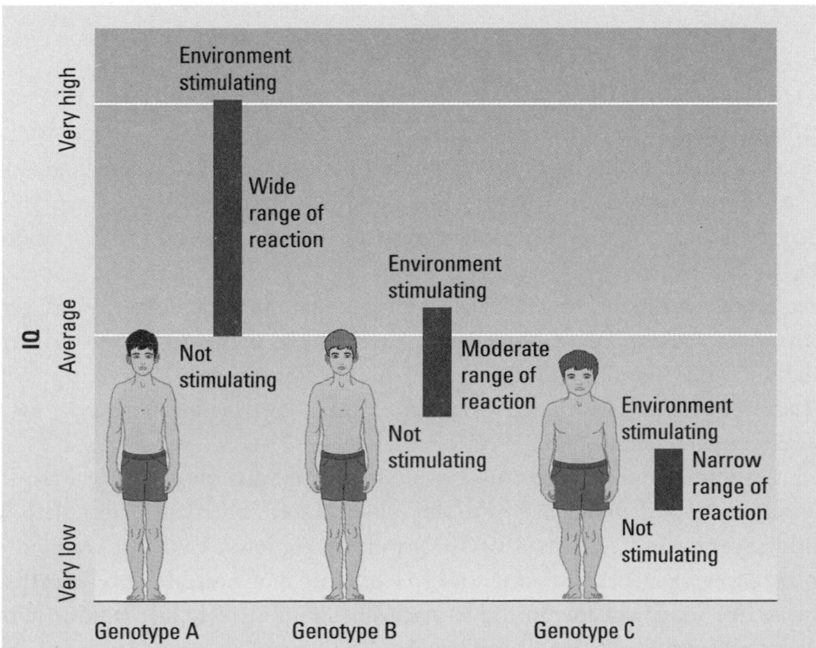


FIGURE 2.13
**Range of Reaction for Cognitive Skills (IQ) of Three Children (Hypothetical)**
Child A shows a large range of reaction (RR). When the environment is not stimulating, his IQ is average. But if the environment was more stimulating, this child's IQ could be much higher. Child C, however, has a very limited RR. The genotype for this child has set narrow limits, and his IQ will be low regardless of environment. A child with Down syndrome might have such a genotype, leading to low IQ. The RR for Child B falls in between these two, with more moderate changes as the environment is altered.

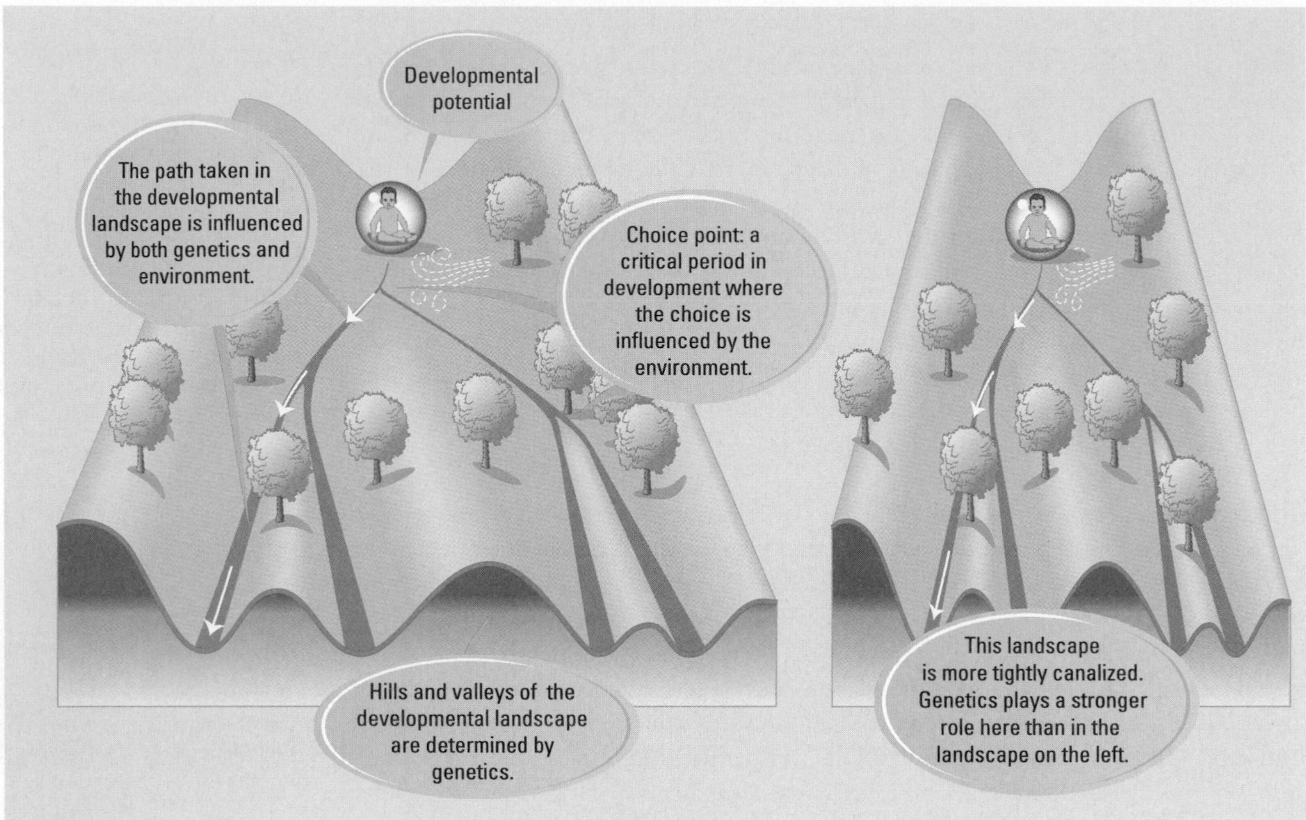


▲ FIGURE 2.14
**Canalization**
The hills and valleys in the diagram represent the developmental "landscape" through which an individual progresses. The individual's development is represented by the path of the ball moving through this landscape. Genetics determines the shape of the landscape, while forces in the environment move the ball through the critical choice points. The width of each valley represents the range of phenotypes possible for that genotype (as with range of reaction). Notice that the landscape on the right is more strongly canalized—genetics plays a stronger limiting role in the individual's development. (Adapted from Waddington, 1974.)

*in development* that we introduced in Chapter 1? Genetic limits may protect the individual from more negative environments. For example, most infants begin walking at about one year of age, and this holds true pretty much regardless of whether the infant receives relatively supportive or unsupportive parenting and regardless of whether the infant receives poor, mediocre, or excellent nutrition. In this way we say that walking is a relatively canalized activity—it occurs at about one year of age across a wide spectrum of environmental conditions. It would take a severe environmental influence to alter this genetic timetable; walking might be delayed, for example, if the infant was severely abused or malnourished. Notice, however, that this theory places a heavy emphasis on *genetic determinism*—environmental conditions must be strong to change an individual's developmental path.

A more recent interpretation places less emphasis on genetic determination. This newer model gives more weight to the role of the environment, particularly prenatal and early experiences (Gottlieb, 1997). This interpretation is called *experiential canalization.* In this view, genetics provides a fairly wide range of possible developmental outcomes (more like the landscape on the left side of Figure 2.14) and it is the environment that plays the limiting role. For example, think about speech perception. Until about one year

**niche-picking**
The tendency to pick activities and environments that fit with our genetic predispositions.

of age, infants respond similarly to the basic sounds used in all languages. After that, they can detect subtle differences in language sounds only in their native languages—the languages they experienced during their first year (Werker & Tees, 1984). In other words, genetics endow all humans with the ability to perceive language sounds, but individuals' linguistic environment eventually limits the sounds they can distinguish.

These two views of canalization lead to quite different implications for a variety of practical problems. For example, all parents wonder from time to time if they are having any important impact on their children's developmental outcomes. The view of canalization that emphasizes the protective effects of genetics would say that unless a parent is providing extreme conditions in some way, the child's outcome is going to proceed along a genetically determined path. Small to moderate variations in parenting style and day-to-day living conditions will have little impact on the child's outcome (Scarr, 1992). The experiential canalization view would offer a different opinion. According to this view, early experiences and opportunities that parents offer would have a significant impact in the child's developmental outcome.

THINK ABOUT JUAN AND TRACEY. . .
How would your response to Juan and Tracey be different depending on whether you emphasize canalization or experiential canalization? What would the implications of each concept be for Juan and Tracey?

**Niche-Picking: I Gotta Be Me . . .** It may surprise you to learn that one way a child's genes interact with the environment is by affecting the kinds of environments that are available (Bouchard, 1997; Scarr, 1992, 1993; Scarr & McCartney, 1983). This is because a child's genes make it more or less likely that the child will be placed in, or will select, a certain kind of environment. First, during infancy, genes primarily operate in a *passive* manner. At this stage, the infant's environment is almost totally controlled by his or her parents. However, the child and parents share many genes, so the home environment is usually consistent with and supportive of the child's genes. Second, as the child gets older, genes play a more *evocative* role. This means that the child's genetic tendencies evoke certain responses from parents and others. For example, if a child likes to be physically active, parents tend to provide more opportunities for physical activities. They may offer more frequent trips to the playground, or encourage the child to join sports teams. These activities are evoked by and tend to support the child's genetic tendencies.

▲ People who inherit high activity levels tend to select activities and environments to suit this disposition. Can you see here how genetics has an influence on the role played by the environment?

Third, as children get older and have more freedom to choose their own activities, genes work in an *active* way. Older children can actively seek out the specific niches, or activities and environments, that suit them best. That is, they engage in **niche-picking**. Given a choice, shy children tend to choose more quiet and passive activities, such as going to movies and reading books. Active children gravitate to physical sports and noisy settings. A child's genetic predisposition toward being shy or active leads the child to pick niches that support his or her tendencies. So, genes influence behavior not only by predisposing children to develop certain traits or characteristics, but also by affecting the kinds of environments that surround them.

THINK ABOUT JUAN AND TRACEY. . .
How will the genetics of Juan and Tracey's children affect the environment that they provide for them? What about when each child begins picking their own activities and environments?

Our twin daughters offer an example of passive, evocative, and active gene influences. When they were infants, we provided an environment that suited our own interests—we read lots of books to them, played music for them, and held and rocked them. Our interests and skills reflected our own genes, and given that we shared a lot of genes with our daughters, the environment we provided was reasonably consistent with their genetic tendencies. But as the girls grow older, they are clearly evoking different kinds of influences from their environments. Rachel is very active and prefers fast-paced physical activities. Lily is much happier playing with computer games or with Barbie dolls, or sitting in someone's lap. We respond to the differences so that Rachel is able to spend more time in physical activities and Lily more time in quieter kinds of play. The girls are now old enough to begin active niche-picking, and their different preferences will almost certainly lead them to select different kinds of environments as they develop hobbies, choose friends, and decide how to spend their spare time.

THINKING CRITICALLY
Identify examples of passive, evocative, and active gene influences on your development. How have your genes affected the niches you have picked?

## Probabilistic Epigenesis: Activating Your Genes

Researchers are continuing to discover increasingly complex ways in which genes and environment interact to influence our traits and characteristics. The concept of probabilistic epigenesis provides a good example. The term *epigenesis* refers to the emergence of a trait, characteristic, or behavior over the course of development (as opposed to its presence from the beginning). *Probabilistic* means that there is some probability that a given characteristic or trait will develop depending on certain conditions in the environment (as opposed to a certainty that it will occur regardless of the environment). According to the concept of **probabilistic epigenesis**, the likelihood of a given behavioral outcome depends on the existence of specific genetic potential that must be activated by specific environmental conditions, or *life experiences* (Gottlieb, 1997, 2003). For example, if an individual inherits a genetic tendency to develop a certain type of cancer, this does not mean that the person will inevitably develop the cancer. The lifestyle the person chooses to lead (for example, diet and exercise patterns, smoking/not smoking, sun exposure, etc.) may impact whether or not the genetic potential for this disorder is activated, and therefore whether the cancer develops.

THINK ABOUT JUAN AND TRACEY. . .

How can the concept of probabilistic epigenesis explain differences in the outcomes of Juan and Tracey's children in their adopted environment, and potential outcomes in other possible environments?

**probabilistic epigenesis**
The likelihood that specific environmental conditions will activate specific genes that lead to particular traits or behavioral outcomes.

The idea of such an interaction is not new, but awareness of the central role of the environment in activating specific genes is. Researchers agree that only about 10–15% of an individual's total genome is actually expressed, or made active. This means that every individual has many more potential developmental pathways than are ever realized, and *it is the individual's environment that controls which parts of the genome are activated.* Figure 2.15 illustrates the complex interactions that take place. For example, we know that certain environmental conditions (e.g., light, stress, nutrition, and length of the day) affect levels of numerous hormones in the body. Hormones in turn enter the nuclei of cells and affect protein production, which essentially "turns on" or "turns off" certain genes. So not only do our genes affect behavior, as we have long realized (see the upper-left arrow in Figure 2.15), but our environment influences which parts of our vast genetic potential are actually activated and expressed (the lower two arrows in Figure 2.15).

Let's examine some important research that has been done to test the theory of probabilistic epigenesis. A key implication of probabilistic epigenesis is that a significant change in the environment will change which genes are expressed. Thus, we can expect that if researchers expose an organism to an environment very different from its natural environment, then characteristics or behaviors not normally seen in that species can develop *even though its actual genetic material has stayed the same.* And indeed, this is a result that some research has produced. For example, certain changes of the developmental environment of bird embryos can result in the birds' developing teeth (Kollar & Fisher, 1980). Because the embryos were already formed, the genetic potential for this abnormal characteristic must already have been present, but the

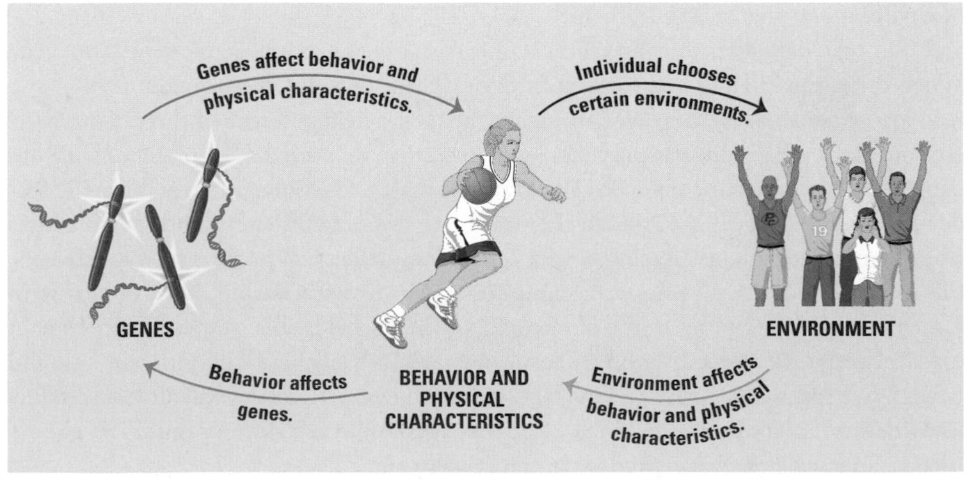


FIGURE 2.15 ▶ **Probabilistic Epigenesis**
Genes can determine physical and behavioral characteristics (such as high activity level) causing the child to select certain environments (e.g., active and stimulating sports). But the environment also stimulates changes in the body (e.g., hormones) that selectively turn genes on and off. (Based on Gottlieb, 1991.)

characteristic does not appear in the normal course of development for birds. The environmental changes activated genes that are normally "turned off." In another experiment, researchers briefly exposed fruit fly eggs to ether vapor, which caused the flies to grow an extra set of wings after they hatched (Ho, 1984). The altered genetic activation can be passed along to future generations as well—the offspring of fruit flies with extra wings also developed the second set of wings (though some researchers argue that the environmental change must be maintained for the genes to continue to be activated in subsequent generations; Rowe, 2003).
((• **Listen** on **mydevelopmentlab**

((• **Listen**: Probabilistic epigenesis: How can the environment activate and deactivate genes? (Author Podcast) www.mydevelopmentlab.com

What does this mean for human development? Clearly humans have a vast genetic potential, and only a small portion of it is expressed. Which portion is expressed depends on the child's environment (both prenatal and after birth). Though researchers continue to make progress, we do not yet have a good understanding of which environmental factors are most important in affecting gene expression. Nor can we pinpoint (yet) precisely how environmental factors shape complex traits like intelligence and personality. But the concept of probabilistic epigenesis makes a strong statement about the relationship between genes and the environment. It emphasizes that this relationship does affect development—that the two factors of nature and nurture are truly interdependent.

### LET'S REVIEW . . .

1. In the range of reaction concept, which of the following sets the upper and lower boundaries for the range of possible developmental outcomes?
   - **a.** genes
   - **b.** environment
   - **c.** G x E interactions
   - **d.** proximal processes
2. A child likes to draw and sketch pictures whenever she can. This is an example of:
   - **a.** canalization.
   - **b.** passive G x E interaction.
   - **c.** evocative G x E interaction.
   - **d.** active G x E interaction.
3. Canalization is different from experiential canalization in that:
   - **a.** canalization emphasizes that limits are set by the environment.
   - **b.** canalization emphasizes that limits are set by genetics.
   - **c.** experiential canalization emphasizes that limits are set by genetics.
   - **d.** experiential canalization places equal emphasis on both genetics and the environment in setting limits.
4. Which of the following best describes the concept of probabilistic epigenesis?
   - **a.** Genes determine behavior.
   - **b.** Genes do not affect behavior.
   - **c.** Genes activated by the environment affect behavior.
   - **d.** The environment activated by genes affects behavior.
5. True or False: The concept of niche-picking is the idea that our genes can influence the kinds of environments that we select for ourselves.
6. True or False: We never know what the range of reaction will be for any particular child.

Answers: 1. a, 2. d, 3. b, 4. c, 5. T, 6. T

# Behavior Genetics: Measuring the Heritability of Traits

How different are you from your siblings and parents? What accounts for the differences and similarities? Behavior genetics is a field that tries to answer these questions.

AS YOU STUDY THIS SECTION, ASK YOURSELF THESE QUESTIONS:

**2.8** What are shared and nonshared environments, and how does each contribute to development?

**2.9** How is a heritability estimate obtained, and what does it mean?

**2.10** What are the heritabilities of cognitive skills and personality, and what do they tell us about the causes and developmental courses of these traits?

## Behavior Genetics, Heritability, and Shared and Nonshared Environments

THINKING CRITICALLY

In what ways are you and your siblings or other close relatives similar and different? Identify environmental factors you have shared with these relatives, then ones you have not shared. How do these shared and nonshared environmental factors contribute to the behavioral similarities and differences you identified?

What is behavior genetics, and how does this field help explain development? In Chapter 1, we introduced you to the field of behavior genetics to show you the relationship between nature and nurture. Behavior geneticists often talk about the heritability of certain behavioral outcomes. **Heritability** is a mathematical estimate of the degree of genetic influence for a given trait. Later in this chapter we will discuss the details of how heritability is estimated. To grasp the general concept, you will want to know that heritability estimates range from 0.00 to 1.00; higher values mean that there is a stronger genetic influence on the trait. For example, the estimated heritability for height is .90, which means that a great deal of the variance in height in a population is due to genetic variation in the population. Contrast this with the estimated heritability of some attitudes, such as religiosity or attitudes toward racial integration. The heritability estimate for religiosity ranges from .04 to .22, depending on how religiosity is assessed; for attitudes on integration it is .06 (Loehlin & Nichols, 1976). These low heritability estimates mean that very little, if any, of the variation in these attitudes is due to genetic variation. Instead, the variation is due mostly to learning experiences and other differences in the environment.

▲ These twins are genetically identical and they will share some features of their environments. Not all of their life experiences will be identical, however, so there will be features of their environments that they do not share.

It's important to resist the temptation to interpret heritability estimates as meaning that a trait is or is not "genetic." Instead, a heritability estimate is a statistic that describes how much of the *variation* in a trait is due to variations in genes within a given population. It is also important to remember that, even if a trait has a very high heritability estimate, this does not mean that one is destined to develop the trait. To understand why, think back to the concept of probabilistic epigenesis—environmental conditions are needed to activate (or deactivate) genetic potential. Though it is theoretically possible for heritability estimates to be as high as 1.0, the complex traits that behavioral geneticists study never show heritabilities this high. In general, heritability estimates over .50 are considered fairly high (Plomin, 1990).

In recent decades, behavior geneticists have become more interested in estimating the influence of the environment on development. As we will point out many times in this book, an actual developmental outcome reflects both a genetic influence and an environmental influence. But there are two types of environments that we must consider when explaining differences in behavioral outcomes. **Shared environment** consists of experiences and aspects of the environment that are common to all individuals living together (Plomin, 1986). These shared experiences tend to produce similarities in behavioral outcomes. Within a family, shared environments include such things as the availability of reading material at home, the cultural or sporting events the family attends, or the overall socioeconomic level of the household.

The shared environment cannot explain behavioral *differences* among family members, however. To explain differences we must examine the aspects of the environment that differ from one person to another. The **nonshared environment** consists of experiences and aspects of the environment that are unique to an individual (Hetherington, Reiss, & Plomin, 1994). Nonshared environments differ from one person to another, and they produce differences in behavioral outcomes. For example, perhaps one child in a family spends lots of time listening to music and playing musical instruments, whereas another spends more time watching and participating in sports activities. Although they are growing up in the same family, these children spend much of their time in different types of environments.

**heritability**
A mathematical estimate of the degree of genetic influence for a given trait or behavior.

**shared environment**
Experiences and aspects of the environment that are common across all individuals who are living together.

**nonshared environment**
Experiences and aspects of the environment that differ across people.

**twin studies**
Comparisons between measurements of identical and fraternal twins, used to estimate the genetic contribution to traits and characteristics.

## How Is Heritability Estimated?

Two methods that researchers have used to estimate heritability are twin studies and adoption studies. **Twin studies** estimate the genetic contribution to a given trait by comparing measurements from identical and fraternal twins. Think about the genetic makeup of these two different kinds of twins and you will see the logic of this method. As you recall from earlier in this chapter, identical twins form when a single zygote splits, resulting in two zygotes. The two individuals that develop from these zygotes are genetically identical—they must be, because they came from the same fertilized egg. Fraternal twins, on the other hand, come from two different eggs fertilized by two different sperm. Therefore, they are no more genetically alike than are any other siblings, having on average 50% of their genetic material in common.

In twin studies, researchers estimate heritability by taking measurements (e.g., IQ or personality measures) of both kinds of twins. They compute correlations between the members of each pair of twins; then they compare the correlations for identical twins to the correlations for fraternal twins. (Recall from Chapter 1 that a correlation is a number representing the degree of association between two scores.) If there is an important genetic influence on the trait measured, then the correlation for the identical twins should be significantly higher than the correlation for the fraternal twins.

**Adoption studies** estimate the genetic contribution to a given trait by studying adopted children, their biological parents and siblings, and their adoptive families. Correlations between the children and their biological relatives are compared with correlations between the children and their adoptive families. If there is an important genetic influence on the trait measured, the correlation with the biological relatives should be significantly higher than the correlation with the adoptive relatives.

These two methods provide a way to estimate heritabilities. They are sometimes combined, as in studies that calculate estimates of heritability from measures of identical twins adopted into different families. But remember that both twin studies and adoption studies, no matter how they are used, provide only estimates of heritability. Remember, too, that several factors can affect these estimates. For example, many adoption agencies engage in *selective placement*, the practice of placing adopted children in homes that are similar in important ways to those of the biological parents. Agencies may well take into consideration factors such as racial and cultural background, overall socioeconomic status, and level of education when they select adoptive homes for children. What effect do you think selective placement would have on heritability estimates? Some adoption studies have reported that selective placement was not an important factor for the traits under consideration. Many, however, provide no information on this question (Plomin, 1990). Another factor to consider is that, in twin studies, there is an assumption of *equal environments*. This means that researchers generally assume the similarity of the environment for identical twins to be the same as for fraternal twins. Do you think this assumption is valid? Or are identical twins likely to share a more similar environment than fraternal twins? If identical twins share a more similar environment, then heritability estimates may well be inflated (Kendler, Neale, Kessler, Heath, & Eaves, 1993; Pam, Kemker, Ross, & Golden, 1996).

THINKING CRITICALLY
What does heritability mean, and what does it *not* mean?

Finally, remember that in many cases children are exposed to, or select, certain environments based on their genetic tendencies, and that different environmental features may activate or deactivate a gene's functioning, as described by the concept of probabilistic epigenesis discussed earlier (Richardson & Norgate, 2006; Partridge, 2005). These interactions lead to a correlation between genetics and environment that current research methods are not able to unravel. It is difficult to say how heritability estimates are affected, because such correlations are not clearly the effect of either heredity or the environment but result from their interaction. Newer statistical techniques such as path analysis, which you learned about in Chapter 1, can help describe these kinds of relations between genetics and heredity and account for the possible effects of selective placement and unequal environments (e.g., Crosnoe & Elder, 2002). We can now obtain more accurate heritability estimates through these techniques than through simple comparison of correlations.

**adoption studies**
Comparisons between measurements of children and their adoptive and biological parents used to estimate the genetic contribution to traits and characteristics.

## Heritability of Complex Characteristics

Using the methods just described, researchers have studied a wide variety of different human characteristics to understand the influences of genetics and the environment. Table 2.4 summarizes the estimated heritability for various traits or behaviors. Almost all show small to moderate heritability.

**TABLE 2.4**
**Heritability Estimates for a Variety of Traits and Characteristics**

| TRAIT OR CHARACTERISTIC | HERITABILITY ESTIMATE | SOURCE |
|---|---|---|
| **COGNITIVE SKILLS** | | |
| General intelligence | .52 | 1 |
| Verbal reasoning | .50 | 1 |
| Perceptual speed | .46 | 2 |
| Vocational interests (in adolescence) | .42 | 1 |
| Spatial reasoning | .40 | 1 |
| Scholastic achievement (in adolescence) | .38 | 1, 2 |
| English usage | .40 | 3 |
| Mathematics | .52 to .56 | 4 |
| Social studies | .34 | 3 |
| Natural sciences | .38 | 3 |
| Processing speed | .22 | 1 |
| Divergent thinking | .22 | 2 |
| **PERSONALITY AND TEMPERAMENT** | | |
| Anxiety | .70 | 5 |
| Sociability | .64 | 5 |
| Activity-impulsivity | .62 | 5 |
| Emotionality | .54 | 5 |
| Extraversion | .51 | 1 |
| Conservatism | .50 | 6 |
| Neuroticism | .46 | 1 |
| Antisocial behavior | .40 to .50 | 7, 13 |
| Masculinity/femininity | .40 | 8 |
| Religiousness | .40 | 7 |
| Sexual orientation | .30 to .70 | 9 |
| Belief in God | .22 | 3 |
| Attitude toward racial integration | .06 | 3 |
| Involvement in religious affairs | .04 | 3 |
| **PROBLEM CONDITIONS** | | |
| Hyperactivity (adolescent males) | .75 | 10 |
| Autism spectrum disorders | .90 | 13 |
| Bipolar disorder | .70 | 13 |
| Schizophrenia | .80 | 13 |
| Obesity (body mass index) | .50 to .90 | 12 |
| Alcoholism (risk of) | .50 to .71 | 9 |

(1. Plomin, Owen, & McGuffin, 1994; 2. Nichols, 1978; 3. Loehlin & Nichols, 1976; 4. Walker, Petrill, Spinath, & Plomin, 2004; 5. McCartney, Harris, & Bernieri, 90; 6. Martin, Eaves, Heath, Jardine, Feingold, & Eysenck, 1986; 7. Koenig, McGue, Krueger, & Bouchard, 2007; 8. Loehlin, Jönsson, Gustavsson, Stallings, Gillespie, Wright, & Martin, 2005; 9. Rose, 1995; 10. Stevenson, 1992; 11. Plomin, 1990; 12. Maes, Neale, & Eaves, 1997. 13. Rutter, 2006.)

**TABLE 2.5**
**Correlations Used to Estimate the Heritability of IQ**

| RELATIONSHIP | AVERAGE CORRELATION IN IQ SCORES |
|---|---|
| Identical twins, raised together | .85 |
| Fraternal twins, raised together | .59 |
| Identical twins, adopted apart | .74 |
| Biological parent with child, living together | .41 |
| Biological parent with child, adopted apart | .24 |
| Adoptive parent with adopted child | .20 |
| Biological siblings, living together | .46 |
| Adoptive siblings | .24 |

(Devlin et al., 1997.)

THINK ABOUT JUAN AND TRACEY. . .

According to these data, would we expect Juan and Tracey's children to have an IQ that is more similar to Juan and Tracey's or more similar to their biological parents'?

**Heritability of Cognitive Skills** Probably the most extensively studied behavioral trait is intelligence. Researchers often measure intelligence using scores on standardized intelligence tests (e.g., IQ scores). Table 2.5 shows the average IQ correlations taken across 216 different studies. These data indicate that heredity has a significant influence on IQ scores. The correlations for identical twins are substantially higher than those for fraternal twins, and the correlations for biological relatives are higher than the correlations for adoptive relatives. Based on data like these, behavior geneticists generally estimate that the heritability of IQ is about .50 (Devlin, Daniels, & Roeder, 1997; Plomin & DeFries, 1998; Rose, 1995). As Table 2.4 shows, there have been similar findings for a variety of specific cognitive skills (such as spatial reasoning, verbal reasoning, and perceptual speed) and achievement scores (such as English usage, mathematics, social studies, and natural sciences).

So it seems that a variety of cognitive skills have a significant hereditary component. Does this component change across age? After all, different genetic systems may become more or less important at different ages, and environmental influences change as children age. Several studies have shown that heritability estimates for some cognitive skills do change—they *increase* with age (Bishop, Cherny, Corley, Plomin, DeFries, & Hewitt, 2003; Plomin & DeFries, 1998; Plomin & Spinath, 2004). As you can see in Figure 2.16 (on p. 68), the relative influence of genetics on cognitive skills appears to become stronger the older a person gets. Why would this be so? Think back to the idea of niche-picking. This concept says that individuals' genes affect their environment by guiding the environments they select. This effect then becomes stronger as people become older and more independent, making more of their own choices of environments. Perhaps the increase in heritability estimates reflects this indirect influence of genetics. Also keep in mind that although the overall influence of genetics seems to increase, we do not know which genes are involved. It is possible that the specific genes exerting their effects are different at different points in the life span, with some genes becoming more influential and others becoming less important.

Further work is needed to identify the contributions and interactions of specific genes at different points in time. It's also important to understand that research on heritability of cognitive skills is often controversial. There are concerns about such issues as bias or inappropriate measures used to assess the skills. We will return to this controversy when we talk about intelligence in Chapter 14.

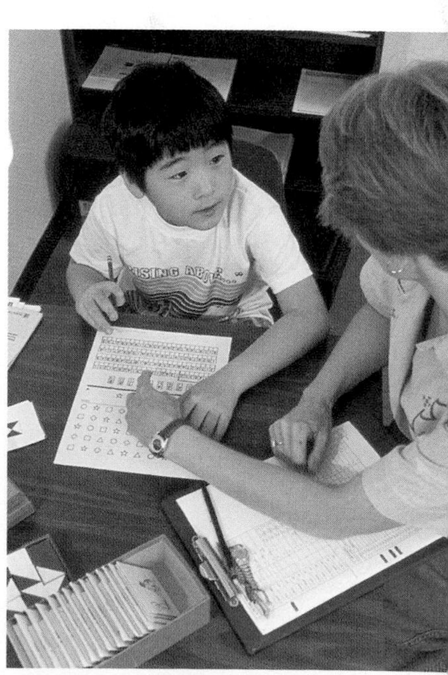

▲ Scores from IQ tests tend to be more similar among identical than among fraternal twins. Generally speaking, scores are more similar when the genetic relationship is more similar.

**Heritability of Personality and Temperament** Behavior geneticists also have studied the heritability of many aspects of personality. As with research on cognitive skills, most studies of personality indicate that genetics is an important influence. Heritability

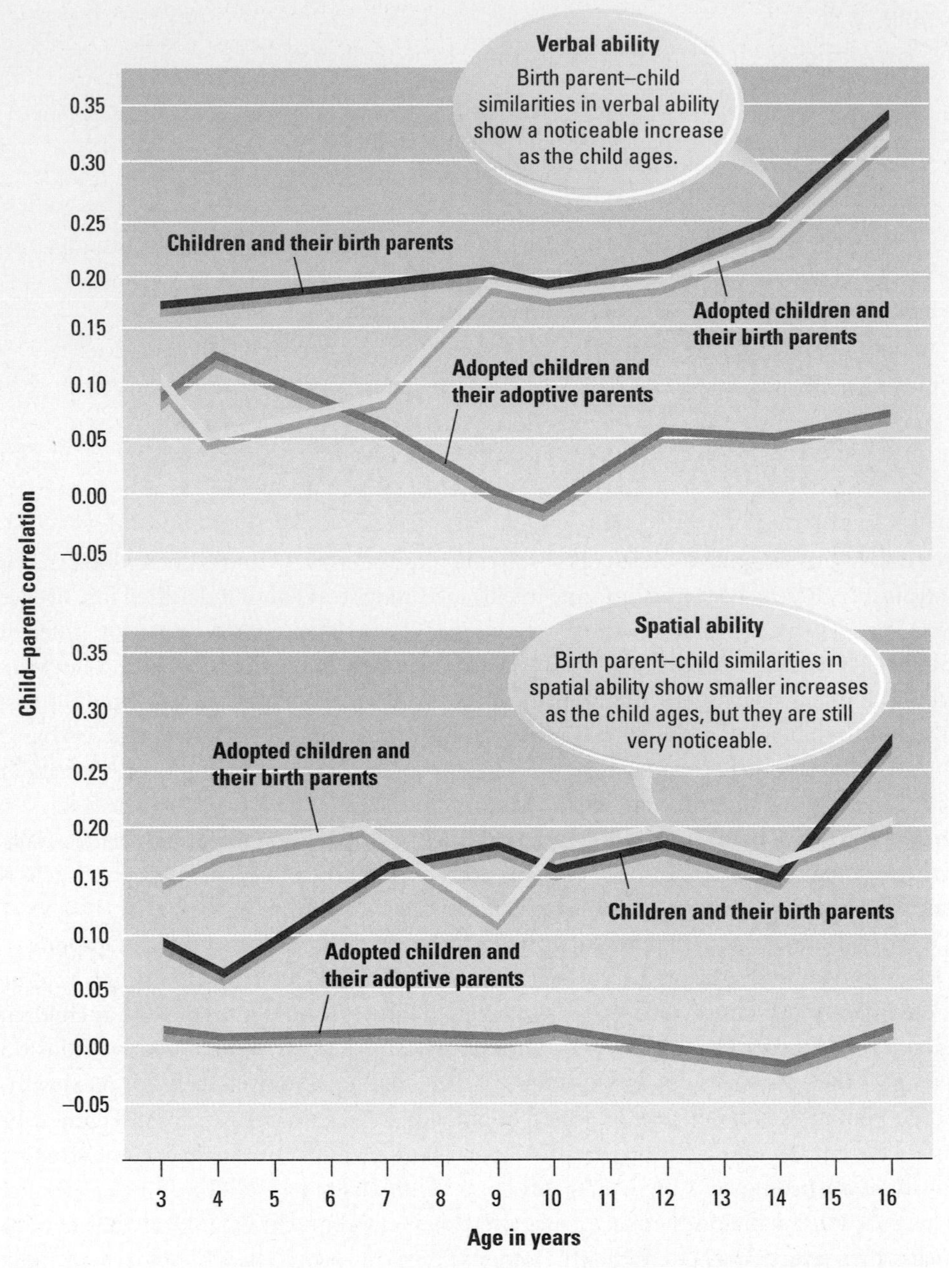


FIGURE 2.16 ▶
**Heritability of Verbal and Spatial Abilities**
Heritability estimates for some cognitive skills increase with age, perhaps because niche-picking increases. The specific genes exerting their effects may also differ at various points in the life span (Plomin & DeFries, 1998).

estimates from twin and adoption studies go as high as .70, as summarized in Table 2.4. Averaging across the major dimensions of personality, it seems that 40–50% of variation in personality is due to genetic factors (Bouchard, 2004; Carey & DiLalla, 1994; Ivkovic et al., 2007; Keller, Coventry, Heath, & Martin, 2005; Plomin, 1990).

Estimated heritabilities for personality measures also change across age, but not as consistently as cognitive measures. For example, for such measures as extraversion, neuroticism, emotionality, activity level, and sociability, heritability estimates appear to decline after late adolescence (Loehlin & Martin, 2001; Pedersen, 1993; Viken, Rose, Kaprio, & Koskenvuo, 1994). But other aspects of social development such as prosocial and antisocial behavior, self-esteem, and religiousness show increasing heritabilities across age (Bouchard, 2004; Kamakura, Ando, & Ono, 2007; Knafo & Plomin, 2006; Koenig, McGue, Krueger, & Bouchard, 2007). In general, it seems that genes contribute more to consistency across age in personality measures; changes in these measures are due more to changes in the environment across age. Research into specific genes or gene markers for aspects of personality is only beginning (Luo, Kranzler, Zuo, Wang, & Gelernter, 2007; Plomin, DeFries, Craig, & McGuffin, 2003).

One dimension of personality that has received much attention from developmental psychologists is *temperament*, or a child's activity level and pattern of response to stimulation. Children clearly differ from an early age in how irritable, sociable, and active they are. Many of these differences have significant effects on a child's interactions, and many persist into adulthood. We will discuss this topic in detail in Chapter 6, but for now consider the evidence for a genetic influence on temperament.

As we saw in Table 2.4, several aspects of temperament show moderate heritability (e.g., anxiety, sociability, activity–impulsivity, and emotionality). Studies with children as young as 3 months of age show persistent genetic influence on traits such as attention, activity, involvement, and shyness (Braungart, Plomin, DeFries, & Fulker, 1992; Cherny et al., 1994; Emde et al., 1992). Temperament differences are important for a child's interpersonal interactions. Perhaps you know from experience how your interactions with a child who is easygoing, smiling, and responsive differ from those with a child who is irritable, fussy, and difficult to soothe.

Some researchers have suggested that the role of genes in temperament has even broader, cultural-level implications. Jerome Kagan has proposed that societies may differ in the typical underlying temperament of their people (an example of the *diversity theme* introduced in Chapter 1). These differences in temperament may then predispose different cultures to adopting certain kinds of philosophical approaches (Kagan, Arcus, & Snidman, 1993; Kagan, Arcus, Snidman, Feng, Hendler, & Greene, 1994). This hypothesis leads to Kagan's suggestion that a basic aspect of cultural difference, each culture's underlying philosophical orientation, may reflect genetic factors. For example, Buddhist philosophies place more emphasis on serenity and harmony than do Western approaches, and those traits are much more common in people in Asian cultures than in Western ones. This may seem far-fetched, but consider the fact that Caucasian and Asian babies consistently show cultural differences in aspects of temperament such as activity level and vocalizing—and many aspects of temperament have a clear genetic influence. Kagan is not suggesting that one philosophical orientation is better than the other. Nor is he arguing that the environment is unimportant for temperament or philosophical orientation. But it is interesting to consider that an aspect of culture that has always been assumed to be environmental in origin may actually reflect some basic genetically influenced tendencies.

THINK ABOUT JUAN AND TRACEY. . .

What can you tell Juan and Tracey about the heritability of personality traits and the role played by the environment?

In Table 2.4 you can see that the heritability estimates for hyperactivity, schizophrenia, obesity, and alcoholism are fairly high. Researchers have reported preliminary evidence for specific genetic markers and linkages for some of these conditions, as well as for some cognitive skills, but much more research is needed before we can draw confident conclusions (Buyske, Bates, Gharani, Matise, Tischfield, & Manowitz, 2006; Cloninger, Adolfsson, & Svrakic, 1996; Dick et al., 2007; Holden, 1995; Luciano et al., 2006; Plomin & McGuffin, 2003; Plomin, DeFries, Craig, & McGuffin, 2003; Rose, 1995).

▲ Could cultural differences in philosophical approaches reflect genetically influenced differences in temperament?

In this chapter we discussed the basics of how genes work. We considered the structure of genes, how they are transmitted from one generation to the next, and how they influence complex traits such as intelligence and personality. The current work in behavior genetics is exciting, and the pace of progress in genetics research virtually ensures that in a few years we will know much more about genetic influences on behavior. We hope you will keep several important points in mind as you think about the information on genes and environment. First, it is becoming increasingly clear that genes and the environment interact in complex ways. The central question for those interested in the development of children has evolved from "Which factor?" to "Which factor has the biggest effect?" to the current "How do the two factors work together to influence complex traits and characteristics?" Second, we must reiterate that just because a trait is influenced by genetics does not mean that the environment is unimportant; nor does it take away an individual's free will. As Gottlieb notes, "genes do not make behavior happen, even though behavior won't happen without them" (1997, p. xiii). Finally, much of the work currently under way investigates genetic contributions to controversial traits and characteristics such as intelligence, sexual orientation, and aggression. Just as important as research on the role of genes is the issue of how societies interpret and use the information that researchers discover. Behavior geneticists hope that society will use new discoveries to develop and implement informed and humane policies—but it is the responsibility of thoughtful policy makers and an informed public to make this happen.

## LET'S REVIEW . . .

**1.** Mr. Cho consistently treats all of his students in the same way, and all of the students respond in the same way to his classroom structure. In this case, Mr. Cho's classroom treatment is part of his students':
- **a.** shared environment.
- **b.** nonshared environment.
- **c.** neither shared nor nonshared environment.
- **d.** nonevocative niche.

**2.** A twin study measured the political attitudes of identical twins and of fraternal twins. Which of the following would be the most reasonable conclusion if the correlation between attitudes for identical twins was not different from the correlation between fraternal twins?
- **a.** Political attitudes are strongly influenced by genetics.
- **b.** Political attitudes are not at all influenced by genetics.
- **c.** Political attitudes are influenced equally by genetics and environment.
- **d.** Political attitudes are more strongly influenced by the environment than by genetics.

**3.** Suppose researchers estimated the heritability of smoking addiction at .95. Based on this heritability estimate, which of the following is true?
- **a.** There is a "smoking" gene.
- **b.** Some people have a genetic predisposition to smoking addiction.
- **c.** If you have the "smoking gene," you will become addicted to nicotine.
- **d.** The environment has no effect on whether smoking addiction develops.

**4.** True or False: The main goal of behavior genetics is to explain why people are similar to one another in their behaviors.

**5.** True or False: In general, most of the cognitive skills that have been assessed show a moderate degree of heritability.

Answers: 1. a, 2. d, 3. b, 4. F, 5. T

### THINKING BACK TO JUAN AND TRACEY . . .

Now that you have studied this chapter, you should be able to give Juan and Tracey a detailed explanation of how nature and nurture will operate together to influence the development of their adopted children. First, you could review the process of meiosis to explain how crossing-over and the random shuffling of chromosomes ensure that each child receives a unique combination of chromosomes and genetic material. The children will not be clones of either of their biological parents, but instead will inherit a portion of the genes from each parent. If the biological parents carry any inherited disease, there is a chance that the child will develop the disease. If Juan and Tracey have access to the results of any genetic tests (e.g., amniocentesis or CVS) that were performed, they could learn if their children are susceptible to certain diseases. With some inherited diseases (e.g., hemophilia) early knowledge and intervention may save the child's life. With others (e.g., Tay–Sachs disease), medical treatments may be of little help, but by knowing the prognosis Juan and Tracey could prepare themselves for parenting a seriously ill child.

Because their children were in good health when they were adopted, Juan and Tracey will likely be especially interested in the effect that the environment they provide will have on the children's development. You can explain the complex kinds of G x E interactions that take place, including the ideas of range of reaction, experiential canalization, and probabilistic epigenesis. Each of these concepts suggests how an enriched environment may help their children realize a greater amount of their genetic potential. In fact, environment can even affect which particular genes are expressed. Yet it is also important to help Juan and Tracey understand that although the environment they provide is critical, even this environment will be affected in important ways by their children's genetics. You can describe how evocative G x E interactions and niche-picking work.

Finally, you can help Juan and Tracey understand the idea of heritability. Remember that heritability estimates indicate genetic influence but do not imply that the environment is unimportant for the development of specific traits or behaviors. By helping Juan and Tracey understand heritability in terms of genetic predispositions that may or may not be activated by the environment, you can help them watch for opportunities to foster skills they see in their children. It will be important to communicate that their children's development depends on their genetics and their environment—neither factor can operate alone.

2

## CHAPTER REVIEW . . .

**2.1 What are chromosomes, DNA, and genes, and how do they function to determine our genetic codes?**
DNA is a string of nucleotide bases (adenine, thymine, guanine, and cytosine) linked in complementary pairs (A–T and G–C). Chromosomes are strands of DNA molecules. Most cells in the human body contain 46 chromosomes (23 pairs). A gene is a segment of DNA, usually several hundred to several thousands of base pairs long. Each gene provides the code for a trait, tissue, or other structure.

**2.2 What is the difference between mitosis and meiosis?**
In mitosis, the 46 chromosomes in the original cell are copied into two cells. With meiosis, however, the number of chromosomes is reduced to 23 in each sex cell (sperm and egg). With crossing-over and the random shuffling of chromosomes to cells, meiosis increases the genetic diversity in offspring.

**2.3 How do dominant–recessive gene traits work and how do X-linked (or sex-linked) traits work?**
Chromosomes operate in pairs, and the genes on each member of the pair work to influence our traits. If you inherit one dominant and one recessive allele, the dominant allele will determine the trait. For a recessive allele to be expressed, you need to carry the recessive allele on both chromosomes. Recessive diseases carried on the X chromosome (e.g., hemophilia, Duchenne muscular dystrophy, color blindness, and some forms of retinitis pigmentosa) are more likely to be expressed in males; because they only have one X chromosome, there is no allele to mask the recessive gene. Dominant X-linked diseases (e.g., vitamin D–resistant rickets, Rett syndrome) occur more in females because they have two X chromosomes.

**2.4 What are the major chromosome abnormalities, and why are they important for child development?**
Chromosome abnormalities involve missing, extra, or damaged chromosomes. Down syndrome occurs when children have an extra chromosome at location 21 (trisomy 21), which causes mental retardation and other problems. In trisomy X (XXX) females are born with an extra X chromosome. Females can also have a missing sex chromosome (only one X), leading to Turner syndrome. Sex reversal sometimes occurs when part of the Y chromosome is lost (leading to XY females) or becomes attached to the X chromosome (leading to XX males).

**2.5 What are the most common procedures doctors use to test the health of fetuses?**
Ultrasonography (ultrasound) sends sound waves through the mother's abdomen to produce images of the fetus. Through ultrasound the doctor can monitor the growth of

the fetus and can detect many structural defects and other problems. In amniocentesis, fluid is removed from the amniotic sac and fetal cells are retrieved for genetic testing. In chorionic villus sampling (CVS), cells are removed from the chorionic layer of the placenta. Amniocentesis and CVS allow clinicians to detect chromosome abnormalities and several hundred genetic diseases. Risk rates for these two procedures are similar.

**2.6 What are the concepts of range of reaction, canalization, and niche-picking, and how does each concept help explain the interaction of genetics and environment?**
Each of these concepts has been proposed to explain how genes and the environment interact. Some concepts, like range of reaction and canalization, emphasize the limits that genes set on possible developmental paths. Niche-picking focuses more on how genes influence traits and behavior differently over age. Experiential canalization emphasizes the role of the environment in limiting outcomes.

**2.7 What is probabilistic epigenesis and how does it help explain developmental outcomes?**
Interactions between genes and environment are complex: Probabilistic epigenesis describes how the environment works to "turn on" or "turn off" certain genes, thus emphasizing the true interdependence of genes and environment. Researchers agree that both genes and the environment are essential and that they interact in very complex ways to produce behavior.

**2.8 What are shared and nonshared environments, and how does each contribute to development?**
A shared environment involves experiences that are shared by all those who live together, whereas a nonshared environment is unique to a particular individual. Behavior geneticists conclude that shared environment contributes to behavioral similarities to only a small degree and that most similarity in behavior is due to shared genetics. The major environmental effect comes from nonshared environment, which contributes to differences between people's behaviors.

**2.9 How is a heritability estimate obtained, and what does it mean?**
Heritability is a numerical estimate of the degree of genetic influence on a particular trait. Twin and adoption studies estimate the heritability of human traits by comparing correlations in various ways. Modern path analyses provide more accurate heritability estimates by statistically accounting for such problems as unequal environments, selective placement, and relations between genes and environments.

**2.10 What are the heritabilities of cognitive skills and personality, and what do they tell us about the causes and developmental courses of these traits?**
Many cognitive skills and personality traits show small to moderate heritabilities. Surprising levels of heritability have been found for some very specific behaviors, probably because of genetic influence on more general underlying traits. Even high heritabilities, however, do not mean that the environment's influence is unimportant.

## REVISITING THEMES

Much of this chapter concerns the *nature and nurture* theme. Several ways in which these two factors interact were described in detail (range of reaction, canalization, niche-picking, and probabilistic epigenesist). The field of behavior genetics and the practice of estimating heritabilities contribute to our understanding of the relative contributions of nature and nurture to specific traits (pp. 59–65).

*Diversity and multiculturalism* can be seen in several places in this chapter. Rates of monozygotic and dizygotic twinning differ for different ethnicities (p. 47), as do the rates of specific genetic disorders such as sickle cell and Tay–Sachs diseases (p. 52). Life span of individuals with Down syndrome also vary by ethnicity, though probably due to the association of ethnicity with access to (or lack of) medical care (pp. 53–54). Jerome Kagan's ideas about the relationship between diversity in underlying temperament and cultural differences in philosophical approaches are interesting to consider (p. 69).

*Resilience in development* was discussed in relation to the concept of canalization. Genetic limits may protect the individual from more negative environments, thus helping individuals show resilience (pp. 59–61).

## KEY TERMS

adoption studies (65)
allele (41)
amniocentesis (54)
canalization (59)
chorionic villus sampling (CVS) (56)
chromosomes (38)
dizygotic (DZ) twins (46)
DNA (38)
dominant–recessive relationship (49)
Down syndrome (53)
fertilization (41)
G x E interaction (58)
gene (39)
genotype (59)
heritability (64)
Human Genome Project (39)
meiosis (44)
mitosis (44)
monozygotic (MZ) twins (44)
niche-picking (60)
nonshared environment (64)
phenotype (59)
probabilistic epigenesis (62)
range of reaction (59)
sex chromosomes (48)
shared environment (64)
twin studies (64)
ultrasonography (ultrasound) (54)
X-linked (sex-linked) traits (52)
zygote (43)

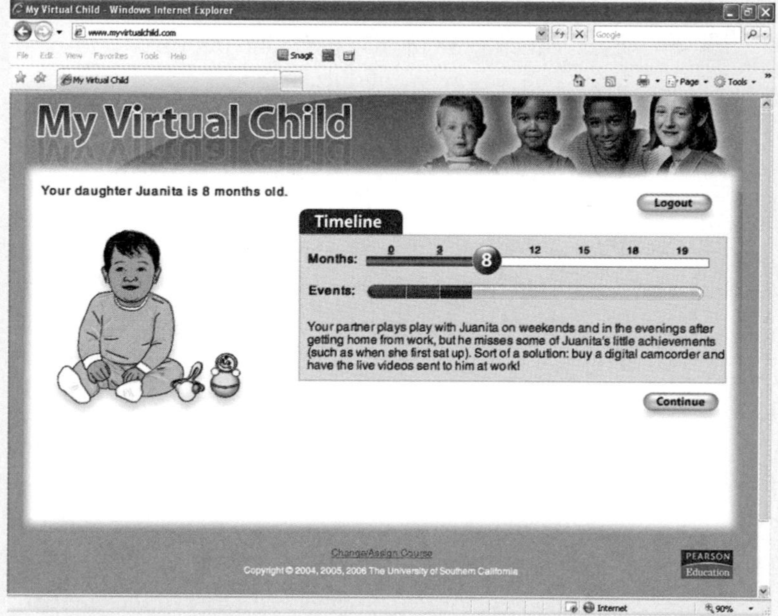

**Watch** Visit your Multimedia Library at www.mydevelopmentlab.com to watch an interview with Elizabeth and Stephanie online.

# 3 BEGINNINGS

# Prenatal Development and Birth

## Prenatal Development

- Conception
- Stages of Prenatal Development

## Teratogens: Health Risks for the Baby

- Alcohol, Cocaine, and Cigarette Smoking During Pregnancy
- The Mother's Health and Age
- Critical Periods
- The Role of Fathers

## The Process of Birth

- Stages of Birth
- Cultural Differences Surrounding Birth
- Modern Birthing Practices in the United States: Choices and Alternatives
- Birthing Complications: Something Isn't Right
- Here's the Newborn!

## Becoming a Family: Psychological Adjustments to Having A Newborn

- The Transition to Parenthood
- Becoming the Big Brother or Sister

Elizabeth cried on the day she found out that her 16-year-old daughter, Stephanie, was pregnant. Elizabeth herself had dropped out of school at 17 years of age and had her first child at 18. She was a bit wild, and she drank alcohol and used illegal drugs. She had two more children by the time she was 22, and life was hard being a single mother with little education or support from family. Now her daughter was following a similar path, but Stephanie is even younger than Elizabeth was when she first became pregnant. What will life be like for Stephanie and her baby? Will Stephanie finish high school?

Elizabeth feels guilty and wonders if she let her daughter down as a parent. Didn't she warn Stephanie about getting pregnant? Didn't she supervise her enough? She also worries about the health of the baby. Is Stephanie too young to have a healthy baby? Is she using drugs and alcohol like Elizabeth did when she was that age? Elizabeth admits that she's made many mistakes in her life, but she does have one piece of advice for other parents: "Educate your children about safe sex."

After reading this chapter, you should be able to identify more than a dozen concepts and research findings that relate to the questions that Elizabeth has about Stephanie and her pregnancy. What do researchers know about teenage pregnancy? What do they know about the effects of alcohol and other drugs on the developing fetus? How can this information be used to help pregnant teens, and how can it also be used to help other mothers who are pregnant?

As you read this chapter, look for the "Think About Elizabeth and Stephanie . . ." questions that ask you to consider what you're learning from their perspectives.

As with many unplanned pregnancies, Elizabeth worries about the health and development of Stephanie's baby. Although Stephanie is young and did not plan to start a family, she wants to do what she can so her baby will be healthy. But many mothers and couples do not have much information about how a baby develops in the womb, or about how their behavior can affect the developing fetus. In this chapter we discuss the basics of conception, prenatal development, and birth. We also detail a variety of factors that can harm the developing fetus. As you read, it may seem that the odds are stacked against a new baby ever being born healthy! It's true that many things can harm a developing fetus, but we hope you will also notice that many important influences are controllable. That is a very positive thing in our view, because it means that any woman and her partner can greatly increase their odds of having a healthy baby—by making positive, healthy lifestyle choices. The truth is that the vast majority of pregnancies do produce healthy, full-term babies.

# Prenatal Development

**Prenatal development** is the development of an organism before (pre) its birth (natal). Prenatal development includes the creation of the organism through fertilization as well as the typical course of development up to birth. In this section we will discuss how conception occurs, then we trace the events that take place as the organism develops.

AS YOU STUDY THIS SECTION, ASK YOURSELF THESE QUESTIONS:

3.1 What happens during conception, and what happens next to begin the developmental process?

3.2 What events mark the beginning and end of each prenatal stage, and what are the main milestones associated with each stage?

## Conception

The intricate dance of nature and nurture begins when one sperm cell unites with one egg cell in the process called **conception**. As you can see in Figure 3.1 (on p. 76), the female reproductive system contains two ovaries. Each ovary will nourish several hundred egg cells (ova) as they mature and become ready for fertilization. During a woman's reproductive years, one egg cell (ovum) will come to maturity approximately every 28 days. When the ovum has matured, the ovary releases it, and this is referred to as **ovulation**. During a typical menstrual cycle, only one ovum matures and is released. But when more than one ovum is released, dizygotic (fraternal) twins, triplets, or other multiples can be conceived. Also recall from Chapter 2 that any of these conceptions can later divide to form monozygotic (identical) twins.

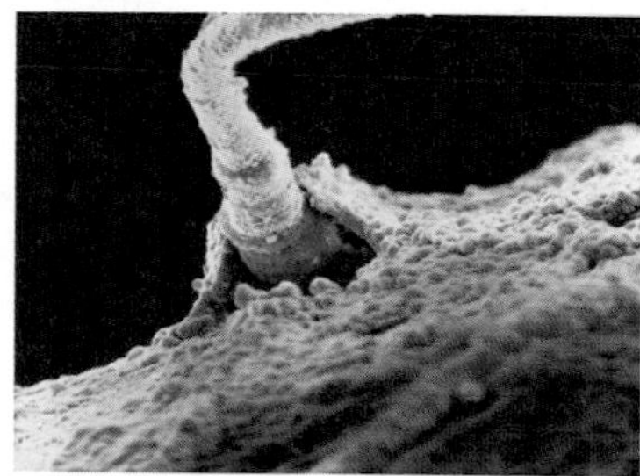

▲ At fertilization, 23 chromosomes from the father's sperm cell join 23 chromosomes from the mother's egg to produce a unique combination.

After ovulation, the ovum moves into the fallopian tube adjacent to the ovary. It is in the upper and wider part of the fallopian tube that conception normally occurs. A man may ejaculate as many as 500 million sperm cells during intercourse, but only a few hundred will survive the journey through the woman's uterus and into the fallopian tube containing the ovum. As soon as the first sperm cell penetrates the ovum's outer membrane, a reaction immediately seals the membrane, making it impermeable to other sperm. This is nature's way of ensuring that only 23 chromosomes from the father, carried by one sperm, join with 23 chromosomes from the mother.

Looking again at Figure 3.1, you can see that cell divisions begin to occur in the zygote even while it is still in the fallopian tube. All of the cell divisions that take place here and throughout the rest of prenatal development occur by mitosis. As we described in Chapter 2, mitosis is a "copy division" that results in a complete copy of the genetic material in all 46 chromosomes in every new cell. The fertilized cell divides and forms 2 identical cells. Then those 2 cells divide forming 4 identical cells, those 4 divide resulting in 8 identical cells, and so on. During this early phase of cell division researchers refer to the organism as a zygote. Notice that mitosis is different from meiosis (the "reduction division" process discussed in Chapter 2).

How do we get from a jumble of cells in the zygote to the formation of a human body by the time the infant is born? **Differentiation** is the important process whereby each

**prenatal development**
Development of the organism that occurs before (pre) its birth (natal).

**conception**
The process of fertilization where a sperm cell combines with an egg cell to create a new organism.

**ovulation**
Release of an egg (ovum) from the female ovary.

**differentiation**
Process that occurs during cell division in which each new cell, as it divides, is committed to becoming a particular structure and serving a particular function.

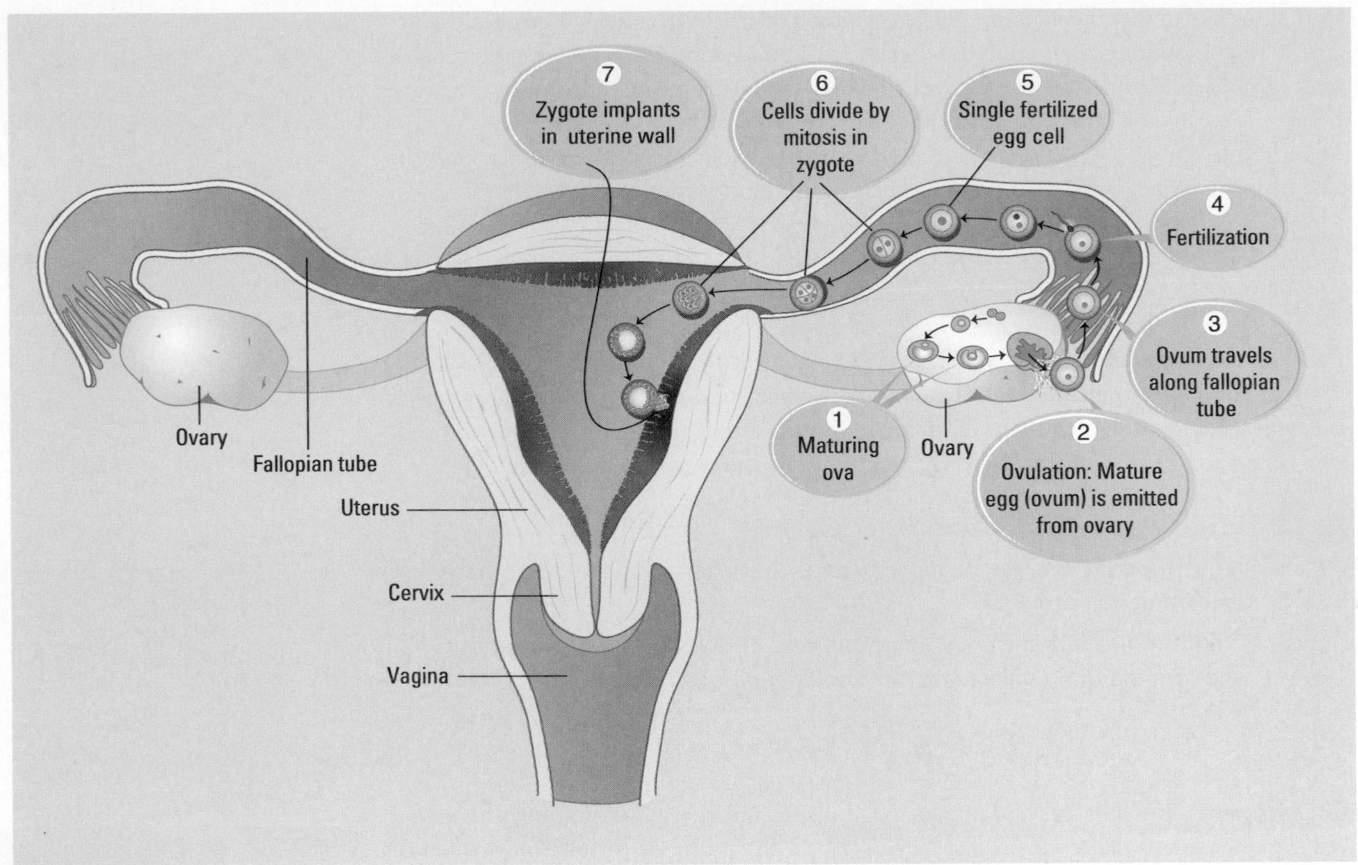


▲ FIGURE 3.1
**Fertilization and Germinal Stage Development in the Female Reproductive System**
When an egg is mature, it is emitted from the ovary and moves through the fallopian tube. If fertilized, the egg will form a zygote that will travel to the uterus and become implanted in the inner lining where it will continue its development.

new cell, as it divides, forms a particular structure—such as a muscle cell, a heart cell, or a brain cell—that serves a particular function. How each dividing cell "knows" which structure and function to acquire is one of the great mysteries of life. Geneticists are trying to discover how certain segments of DNA selectively "turn off" and other segments "turn on" to program the cell for its specialized purpose, and this process is likely controlled by the complex interactions between the genetic codes (provided by nature) and specific conditions that surround the dividing cells (nurture).

## Stages of Prenatal Development

Researchers typically organize the major prenatal events into three stages: the germinal stage, the embryonic stage, and the fetal stage. Table 3.1 provides a summary of the major events and milestones that occur as mitosis and differentiation proceed. The importance of prenatal medical care becomes clear when we consider the remarkable journey the infant makes in 9 months from beginning as a tiny one-celled organism and emerging from its mother's body as a fully formed human being. Let's look at these stages in more detail. **Watch** on **mydevelopmentlab**

**germinal stage**
The first stage of prenatal development, from conception through 2 weeks.

**Watch** a video about the Pregnant Body.
www.mydevelopmentlab.com

**The Germinal Stage: Conception through 2 Weeks.** The **germinal stage** begins at conception and spans the first 2 weeks of pregnancy. Approximately 12 hours after

**TABLE 3.1**
**Major Events and Milestones during Prenatal Development**

| STAGE AND AGE SINCE CONCEPTION | EVENT OR MILESTONE |
|---|---|
| **GERMINAL STAGE (0 THROUGH 14 DAYS)** | |
| 12 hours | First cell division of fertilized egg (zygote is now two cells). |
| 3 to 4 days | Zygote enters the uterus.<br>First cell differentiation leads to trophoblast and blastocyst. |
| 8 to 12 days | Implantation of zygote in uterine lining. |
| **EMBRYONIC STAGE (WEEKS 3 THROUGH 8)** | |
| 14 days | Blastocyst differentiates to form ectoderm, mesoderm, and endoderm.<br>Major genetic and chromosomal abnormalities can cause miscarriage. |
| 3 weeks | Spinal cord and brain begin to form. |
| 3 to 4 weeks | Placenta and umbilical cord form. |
| 4 weeks | Eyes begin to form, heart flutters, and arm buds appear. |
| 5 weeks | Arms develop, and leg buds appear. |
| 8 weeks | Organogenesis complete; all major organs and structures have begun.<br>Embryo weighs 1/30th of an ounce. |
| **FETAL STAGE (WEEKS 9 TO BIRTH)** | |
| 9 to 12 weeks | First arm and leg movements (not detected by mother).<br>First reflexes appear.<br>Sex can be determined with ultrasound. |
| 17 to 20 weeks | Mother feels fetal movements.<br>Heartbeat can be heard with stethoscope.<br>Fetus weighs about 1 pound. |
| 24 weeks | Fat begins to form; rapid weight gain begins. |
| 26 to 28 weeks | Lungs mature enough to support breathing.<br>Fetus weighs approximately 2 pounds. |
| 38 to 40 weeks | Normal gestational age for birth.<br>Newborn weighs 7.5 pounds on average. |

conception, the fertilized egg cell divides for the first time, resulting in two identical cells. The zygote will take 3 to 4 days to travel through the fallopian tube before reaching the uterus, where the first cell differentiation takes place. The outer layer of cells divides rapidly and elongates to form an outer layer called the *trophoblast*. The inner cells, or *blastocyst*, remain more rounded in appearance. Over the next few weeks, cells in the trophoblast will differentiate further to become the placenta, umbilical cord, amniotic sac, and other structures that support the developing baby. The blastocyst will later develop into the fetus itself. The fact that the placenta and other support structures develop from cells in the zygote has important implications for genetic counseling. Recall from Chapter 2 that in chorionic villus sampling (CVS), specialists sample cells from the placental membrane. Because these cells originated from the zygote, they have the same chromosomes and genes as the baby.

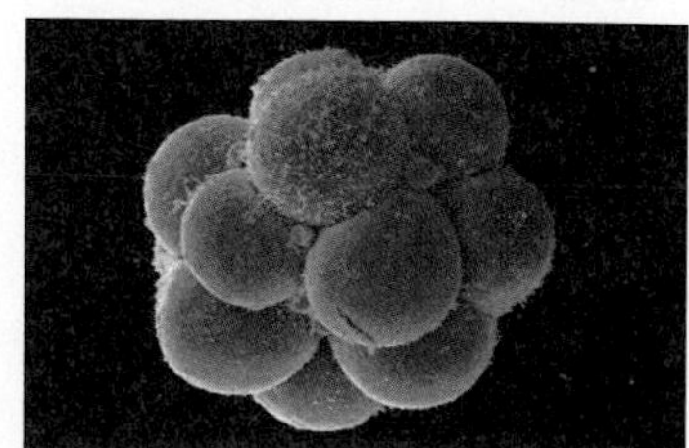

▲ Here is a zygote only 4 days after fertilization. At this point, it contains only about a dozen cells and may still be traveling through the fallopian tube on the way to the mother's uterus.

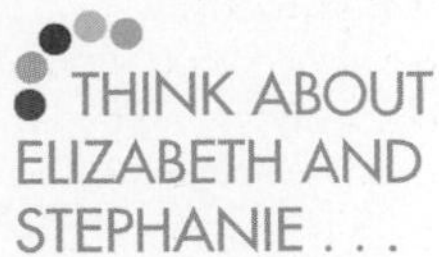

THINK ABOUT ELIZABETH AND STEPHANIE . . .
What would you want to know about Stephanie and her health habits in order to determine if her blood carries the nutrients and oxygen needed for a healthy pregnancy? Will she deliver unhealthy substances to the developing embryo?

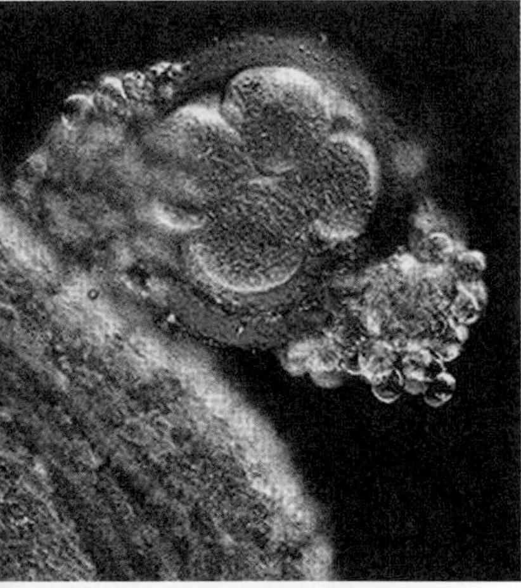

▲ Here is a zygote after it has begun to implant itself into the inner wall of the mother's uterus. Blood supply from the uterus will soon be able to carry more oxygen and nutrients to the growing organism.

**implantation**
Process in which the zygote embeds itself into the inner lining of the mother's uterus.

**embryonic stage**
The second stage of prenatal development, weeks 3 through 8. The embryo forms tissue representing every system and major part of the body.

**miscarriage**
Naturally occurring loss of pregnancy during the first 20 weeks of gestation.

**stillbirth**
Naturally occurring loss of pregnancy after 20 weeks of gestation.

**cephalocaudal pattern**
Pattern of growth where areas in the head and upper body tend to form and grow before the areas in the lower body grow.

Between 8 and 12 days after conception, **implantation** occurs: The zygote embeds itself in the inner lining of the mother's uterus. To generate energy to support the rapid cell divisions that take place in these early days, the zygote can absorb oxygen and nutrients from direct contact with the mother's blood. The zygote irritates the mother's uterine lining, burrowing into the tissue that lines the inner surface of the uterus. Blood from the mother's tissue covers the zygote, and oxygen and nutrients can then "leak" into the zygote. At this point the zygote does not yet have its own circulatory system (a heart or blood vessels). Even when it does, later in development, the mother's blood never mixes directly with the blood in the fetus; the two blood supplies are kept separate within the placenta. Hormonal changes in the mother allow the uterine lining to be most nourishing at about 9 days after conception, so this is the optimal time for implantation. These hormonal changes prevent the uterus from shedding its inner lining through menstruation; they may also make the mother feel tired and drowsy, nauseated with morning sickness and cause her breasts to feel swollen and sore. After 9 days, further hormonal changes cause the uterine lining to be less nourishing. As a result, the risk of pregnancy loss (miscarriage) increases rapidly unless the zygote implants by the ninth day (Wilcox, Baird, & Weinberg, 1999).

After the zygote implants into the uterine lining, the placenta, amniotic sac, umbilical cord, and other support structures begin to grow. Once these structures begin to form, the organism is now referred to as an embryo.

### The Embryonic Stage: Weeks 3 through 8.

The **embryonic stage** begins after the second week of pregnancy. At this point the blastocyst differentiates to form three cell layers in the embryo: the ectoderm, the mesoderm, and the endoderm. The *ectoderm* is the outer layer of the cell mass, and during the embryonic stage it gives rise to the nervous system (including the brain and spinal cord), sensory receptors, and outer skin layers. The *mesoderm*, or middle layer, becomes the circulatory system, skeleton, muscles, excretory system, reproductive system, the outer layer of the digestive tract, and the inner layer of skin. The *endoderm*, or inner layer, will eventually become the respiratory system and the remainder of the digestive system.

This differentiation into ectoderm, mesoderm, and endoderm is critically important, because if major genetic abnormalities exist at this point in development, a miscarriage is likely to occur. A **miscarriage** is any naturally occurring loss of pregnancy that happens during the first 20 weeks of gestation (Centers for Disease Control and Prevention [CDC], 2008). Miscarriages are also referred to as *spontaneous abortions*, and are different from *induced abortions*, which are terminations that are chosen by the parent(s). Remember, the differentiation of the blastocyst occurs early in pregnancy, only 2 weeks or so after conception. A woman who miscarries at this early stage is unlikely even to know that she was pregnant. Because many miscarriages go undetected, it is very difficult for researchers to know how often they happen. A general estimate is that 30–40% of all conceptions end in a miscarriage, with about half of these occurring even before the women were aware of their pregnancies (Michels & Tiu, 2007). More than half of all miscarriages are believed to be caused by genetic problems in the embryo, but others are due to health conditions in the mother, injuries, or for other unknown reasons. A pregnancy that is lost after 20 weeks of gestation is referred to as a **stillbirth**. Stillbirths are more rare, occurring in well less than 1% of pregnancies (Michels & Tiu, 2007).

When the embryo continues to develop normally, it becomes elongated and folds over to form a *neural tube*. During the third week the brain and spinal cord begin to form from the neural tube. At the time when the first brain cells are differentiating from the neural tube, they are extremely vulnerable to toxins in the uterine environment. If the first brain cells are damaged, irreversible alterations can jeopardize normal brain development.

During weeks 3 to 4, the placenta and umbilical cord continue to form. Their function is to provide a more efficient supply of oxygen and nutrients to the growing embryo. The *placenta* is spongy tissue that grows out of the trophoblast layer and into the mother's uterine lining. After just a few weeks, it surrounds most of the embryo and provides a surface where the mother's blood comes into very close proximity to the blood cells from the baby. The *umbilical cord* connects the placenta to the developing embryo. It contains two arteries and one vein that carry materials back and forth between the mother and the developing baby. Oxygen and nutrients are carried to the embryo, and waste materials produced by the embryo (or later the fetus) are carried back to the mother to be excreted.

Now supplied with greater fuel and oxygen, the embryo can undergo even more rapid and complex development. By 4 weeks the eyes begin to form, the torso continues to form, and the heart tissue begins to "flutter" in a primitive heartbeat. Arm buds also appear. By 5 weeks the arms have developed further and leg buds begin to form.

If you look across these early weeks of development, you can see two patterns that describe the formation and growth of the embryo. One of these is the cephalocaudal pattern. *Cephalo* refers to head and *caudal* to tail, so the **cephalocaudal pattern** is the tendency of the areas in the head and upper body to form and grow before the areas in the tail or lower body grow. As you've seen, the brain and eyes form before the arms, and the arms before the legs. The second is the **proximodistal pattern**. *Proximo* refers to nearness (to the body's midline) and *distal* to distance away (from the midline). Heart tissue, for example, is near the midline, and it begins to form before the arms, which are away from the midline. These patterns help us estimate the **critical periods** in development—the times when structures are first forming, and when they are most vulnerable to damage if the initial cell divisions are disrupted by environmental events. While the cell divisions are proceeding according to nature's schedule, they also need the support of the mother's good health (nurture). We will encounter these cephalocaudal and proximodistal patterns again in Chapter 4, because they also describe the pattern that occurs as infants gain control and coordination over their muscles—first in the upper body and along the midline, and later in the lower body and away from the midline.

During the eighth week after conception, organogenesis is complete. **Organogenesis** is the process through which each important body structure differentiates within the embryo. At the conclusion of this process, each structure is represented by its own unique cellular tissue. Brain, heart, lungs, kidneys, fingers, genitals, and even toenails are now identifiable in the embryo. Although most of the important organs are not yet functioning, all of the major structures exist. The embryo is now just over one inch long and weighs only 1/30th of an ounce. The completion of organogenesis signals the end of the embryonic stage, and the organism is then called a *fetus*.

**proximodistal pattern**
Pattern of growth where areas closer to the center of the body tend to form and grow before the areas toward the extremities grow.

**critical periods**
Segments of time when structures are first forming and are most vulnerable to damage.

**organogenesis**
Organ formation: Process where each major organ and system in the body differentiates within the embryo.

**fetal stage**
The third and final stage of prenatal development, lasting from 8 weeks after conception until birth.

▲ Organogenesis is complete by 8 weeks after conception. All of the major structures in the body have already begun to form.

THINKING CRITICALLY
Think of some typical ways for a woman to become aware that she is pregnant. Depending on how she finds out, how far along might she be in these stages of prenatal development?

### The Fetal Stage: Week 9 through Birth (38 to 40 weeks).

The **fetal stage** spans a period of about 30 weeks and represents by far the longest period during prenatal development. During this time, the fetus grows dramatically in size and weight as the tissues and organs differentiate further (gaining detail) and gradually become functional. During weeks 9 through 12, the first arm and leg movements begin, although the mother cannot yet feel them. The first reflexes also appear—usually the startle and sucking reflexes—and the sex organs develop enough that an ultrasound examination can reveal the sex of the fetus. During weeks 17 through 20, the mother begins to feel movements as the fetus rolls around within the amniotic sac and moves its arms and legs. The heartbeat can now be heard with a stethoscope.

At 18 weeks, the fetus weighs less than 1 pound and is not yet mature enough to survive outside the uterus. By week 24, fat begins to form, and now rapid weight gain begins. Weight gain is critically important for survival, as the newborn baby will live off of

THINK ABOUT ELIZABETH AND STEPHANIE . . .
Stephanie will gain weight rapidly while her baby is in the fetal stage. Can you explain why it is important for her baby that Stephanie gains a healthy amount of weight during this stage?

The fetal stage of prenatal ▶ development lasts from 8 weeks until birth. These photos show the fetus at 3 months (*left side*) and at 5 months (*right side*). Notice the growth in size and amount of detail of body structures. You can also see the amniotic sac that surrounds the fetus and the umbilical cord.

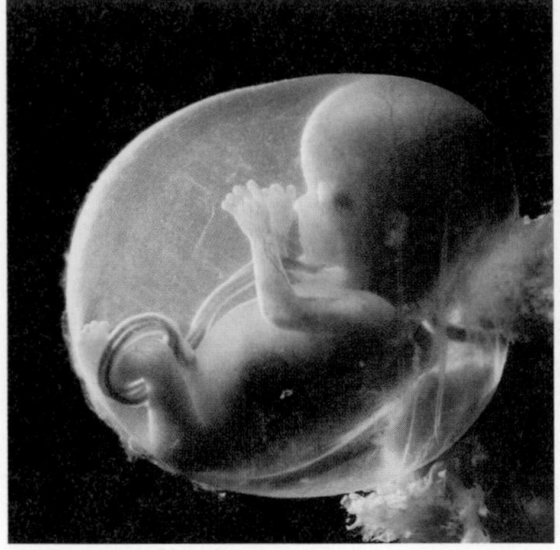

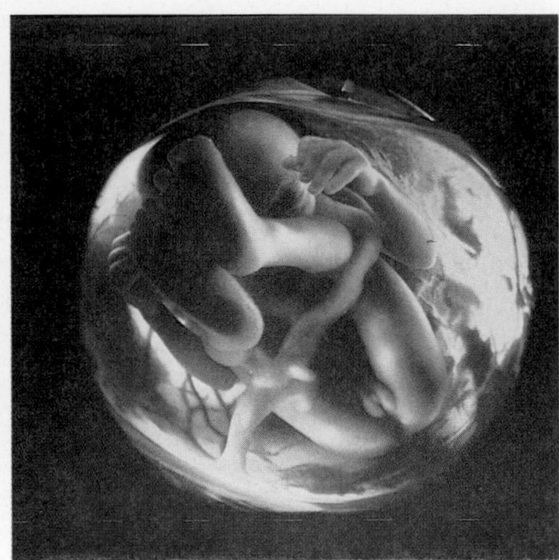

▲ A fetus at 20 weeks. The sucking reflex is evident and the heartbeat can be heard, but the lungs are not yet mature enough to allow breathing. It will be another 18 to 20 weeks before the fetus reaches full term.

accumulated fat during the first few days until the mother's breast-milk supply is well established. By 26 to 28 weeks, the lungs are mature enough to allow successful breathing. At approximately 2 pounds, the fetus may now be viable if born early, but development that occurs during the final weeks is still important, increasing the chances of survival and vastly improving the health of the newborn baby. Some babies who are born this early and this small are resilient and are able to survive if they have intensive medical treatment, but others are more vulnerable and do not survive. During weeks 28 through 40, the fetus typically gains more than 5 pounds. The major organ systems become more functional and strong, and the brain develops very rapidly. At its peak during the fetal stage, the brain produces more than 250,000 new cells per minute (Kolb, 1999), and it will total over 80 billion cells by birth! Neuroscientists are still working to understand this dramatic phase of brain development, and we will have more to say about it in Chapter 4. At the end of a normal gestational period (38 to 40 weeks), the average newborn weighs 7½ pounds and is approximately 21 inches long.

## LET'S REVIEW . . .

1. The process of conception normally occurs in the ______________.
   **a.** ovary **b.** fallopian tube
   **c.** uterus **d.** placenta
2. What is the process whereby each new cell, as it divides and forms, commits to becoming a particular structure and serving a particular function?
   **a.** organogenesis **b.** mitosis
   **c.** implantation **d.** differentiation
3. Major genetic abnormalities normally lead to a miscarriage at the beginning of the ______________.
   **a.** germinal stage **b.** embryonic stage
   **c.** fetal stage **d.** baby's birth
4. All of the major organs and tissues in the body have started to form by the ______________ week after conception.
   **a.** eighth **b.** twelfth
   **c.** twentieth **d.** twenty-fourth
5. True or False: The sex organs of the fetus can be detected by ultrasound beginning around 3 to 4 weeks after conception.
6. True or False: At around 26 to 28 weeks after conception, the lungs are mature enough to support breathing if the baby is born early.

Answers: 1. b, 2. d, 3. b, 4. a, 5. F, 6. T

# Teratogens: Health Risks for the Baby

Each year hundreds of thousands of babies are born with birth defects that threaten their lives or compromise their future development. Some babies are born with malformations of the head, face, heart, or other body tissues. Others are born with seriously low birth weight, and others may not show any defects until later in life when they begin to have problems with memory, attention, physical coordination, or other health problems related to their birth defects. As you learned in Chapter 2, some birth defects are caused by abnormalities in the child's chromosomes or genes. Down syndrome is an example of this type, and it can be traced to a specific cause—inheriting a third chromosome at location 21 (trisomy 21). Most of the time, however, when babies are born with birth defects, the specific cause cannot be determined. Many of the mild to moderate defects such as low birth weight, mental retardation, and attention problems have many potential causes, and they can also occur for reasons that are not yet known or well understood. Still, experts estimate that as many as one-third of all birth defects are related to environmental factors that threaten the fetus while it is still developing in the mother's womb (Moore & Persaud, 1998). Because we have some control over mothers' exposure to these factors, we can greatly reduce the incidence of these birth defects. But to do so, we need to know what the factors are and how people can avoid them. This section will explain some of the most important changes that we can make to protect the health of developing babies.

During most of its prenatal development, the fetus (or earlier, the embryo) is surrounded by structures that support and protect it. The fetus floats within the amniotic sac, where the amniotic fluid buffers it against temperature changes, loud noises, and the mother's sudden movements. The placenta and umbilical cord deliver the oxygen and nutrients the fetus needs. At one time people believed that these structures fully protected the fetus from harmful elements in the environment. Today, however, we know that the fetus is not fully protected. Blood from the mother and baby does not actually mix, but the smaller molecules (such as oxygen and nutrients) move by osmosis into the baby's bloodstream in the placenta. Waste products that build up on the baby's side of the placenta are eliminated in the reverse process—they move into the mother's bloodstream and are processed and eliminated by the mother. These are healthy processes, but there are also some very unhealthy possibilities. For example, when toxins such as alcohol and cocaine get into the mother's bloodstream, they cross the placenta and damage the developing fetus. Pollution in the environment can build up in the mother's tissues, and many of these harmful chemicals can be transmitted to the fetus. Infectious viruses and diseases in the mother also can reach the fetus.

During the 1960s, a new area of research emerged: *teratology*, or the study of teratogens. A **teratogen** is any substance or environmental factor that might affect a pregnancy and cause birth defects. In this section, we discuss several important examples of teratogens and the potential damage that they can cause.

**teratogen**
Any substance or condition that might disrupt prenatal development and cause birth defects.

AS YOU STUDY THIS SECTION, ASK YOURSELF THESE QUESTIONS:

- **3.3** What effects do alcohol, cocaine, and cigarette smoking have on the developing fetus?
- **3.4** What happens when the mother has a contagious disease or illness during pregnancy, and what are the special risks for mothers who are younger or older when they become pregnant?
- **3.5** When are the critical periods during prenatal development, and why are they important?
- **3.6** What about the roles and responsibilities of men and fathers, and are teratogens matters of concern for them too?

The most common teratogens and risk factors are summarized in Table 3.2 (p. 82). In the next several sections, we highlight a few of these risk factors and describe why their associated birth defects occur. **Simulate** on **mydevelopmentlab**

**Simulate** Teratogens and their Effects.
www.mydevelopmentlab.com

**TABLE 3.2**
## Teratogens and Risk Factors

| TERATOGEN OR RISK FACTOR | POTENTIAL EFFECTS |
|---|---|
| **LEGAL AND ILLEGAL DRUGS** | |
| Alcohol | The leading known cause of mental retardation. Fetal alcohol syndrome (FAS) includes growth deficiency, head and facial deformities, and central nervous system dysfunction. Fetal alcohol effects (FAE) include retarded growth, microcephaly (smaller head circumference), hyperactivity, lowered IQ, and other effects occurring alone or in combination. |
| Cocaine | Preterm birth, growth retardation, malformations in brain, intestines, and genital–urinary tract. Hemorrhage, lesions, and swelling in the fetal brain. Irritability, muscle tremors, rigidity, decreased spontaneous movement, visual problems, sleep disturbance in newborns. |
| Cigarette smoking | Low birth weight is the most common problem. Increased risk of spontaneous abortion, stillbirth, neonatal death, hyperactivity, and poor school performance. |
| Marijuana | Low birth weight, muscle tremors, increased startle response, visual problems, lower IQ. Increased risk of leukemia has been reported. |
| Heroin | Low birth weight, jaundice, respiratory distress in newborns. Also withdrawal symptoms that include restlessness, agitation, muscle tremors, and sleep disruption that can continue for 4 to 6 months. Increased fetal and neonatal deaths. |
| **ENVIRONMENTAL POLLUTION** | |
| Mercury | When absorbed by pregnant women, can cause the fetus to develop brain damage, blindness, mental retardation, and cerebral palsy. Found in some industrial settings; accumulates in fish from contaminated waters. |
| Polychlorinated biphenyls (PCBs) | When consumed during pregnancy can cause prematurity, low birth weight, microcephaly, lower scores on infant measures of neurological health, and visual and short-term memory problems. PCBs come from industrial settings and material such as electric insulators and can leach into groundwater. Many water sources and fish in the industrial midwest are contaminated with PCBs. |
| Lead | Lower levels are associated with cognitive impairment in infancy; moderate to higher levels are associated with growth retardation and miscarriage. Lead is found in industrial settings, air pollution, and old paint in many homes. |
| Electromagnetic radiation | No measurable effects have been found for exposure to the small doses associated with computer monitors, microwave ovens, radio waves, or electric blankets or to medical procedures such as ultrasound, magnetic resonance imaging (MRI), and most medical X-rays. Large doses (e.g., as in repeated pelvic X-rays) should be avoided. |
| **MATERNAL DISEASES** | |
| Herpes simplex virus (HSV) | Preterm birth, microcephaly, eye disorders, and mental retardation. |
| Cytomegalovirus (CMV) | Embryonic death, growth retardation, microcephaly, blindness, deafness, mental retardation, and cerebral palsy. |
| Syphilis | Syphilis infection in the infant, deafness, malformations of teeth and bones, facial deformities, excess fluid in the brain, and mental retardation. |
| Human immunodeficiency virus (HIV) | Effects not clear but include infant HIV infection, growth retardation, microcephaly, and head and facial deformities. |
| Rubella (German or three-day measles) | Rubella in the infant, cataracts, heart defects, deafness, glaucoma, and lowered IQ. |
| Chicken pox | Brain damage; mental retardation; muscle atrophy; skin scarring; and malformations of the eyes, limbs, fingers, and toes. |
| **OTHER MATERNAL CONDITIONS** | |
| Stress | Studies are mixed. Some show low birth weight, early labor, and increased labor complications. Animal studies show more serious effects, including pregnancy loss. |
| Age | Teen pregnancy has been associated with low birth weight, early delivery of the baby, and increased rates of neonatal death. Risks of preterm birth, fetal death, and complications during birth increase slightly as women move through their late 30s and into their 40s. |
| **PATERNAL CONSIDERATIONS** | |
| Alcohol | Studies with rats and mice have shown damage to genetic material in sperm and increased activity levels in offspring. |
| Cocaine | May bind to sperm cells and be carried to the egg. May disrupt development in the embryo or jeopardize its survival. |
| Indirect effects | Pregnancies are threatened when fathers or men contribute to the risky behaviors of women. Men must consider the extent to which they encourage or promote women's use of legal or illegal drugs, contribute to environmental pollution, and spread sexually transmitted and other diseases. Healthy pregnancies are the responsibility of men as well as women. |

(*Marijuana*: Dalterio & Fried, 1992; Goldschmidt, Richardson, Willford, & Day, 2008; Robinson, Buckley, Daigle, Wells, Benjamin, & Hammond, 1989. *Heroin*: Kaltenback & Finnegan, 1992; Wilson, 1992. *Environmental pollutants*: Bentur, 1994; Bentur & Koren, 1994; J. Jacobson & S. Jacobson, 1996; J. Jacobson, S. Jacobson, & Humphrey, 1990; Moore & Persaud, 1998. *Maternal diseases*: Moore & Persaud, 1998. *Stress*: Anderson, Rhees, & Fleming, 1985; Barlow, Knight, & Sullivan, 1979; Berkowitz & Kasl, 1983; Burstein, Kinch, & Stern, 1974; Ching & Newton, 1982; DiPietro, Novak, Costigan, Atella, & Reusing, 2006; Falorni, Fornasarig, & Stefanile, 1979; Istvan, 1986; Newton & Hunt, 1984; Standley, Soule, & Copans, 1979.)

As you read further, you will often see the terms premature, preterm birth, and low birth weight, so let's define these now. **Premature** (or **prematurity**) is a general term that refers to babies who are born earlier or smaller than they should be. **Preterm birth** refers more specifically to a baby who is born before 37 weeks of gestation (remember that the normal gestational period is 38 to 40 weeks). **Low birth weight** refers to babies born weighing less than 5½ pounds (2 pounds lighter than average). Babies who are premature—either preterm or low in birth weight—are at greater risk for a variety of serious health problems and even infant death. Many teratogens disrupt fetal growth and are therefore associated with prematurity, preterm births, and low birth weights.

## Alcohol, Cocaine, and Cigarette Smoking During Pregnancy

**Alcohol.** In large national surveys, 60% of women of childbearing age report that they drink alcohol, and 14% report that they consume four or more alcoholic beverages per week (National Center for Health Statistics, 2007). It is difficult to determine how many women continue to drink during pregnancy, but research shows that alcohol use during pregnancy can be catastrophic. Numerous studies with both humans and animals have established that alcohol exposure can cause babies to be born with physical deformities, growth retardation, damage to the central nervous system, and it can even cause miscarriage and fetal death (Cornelius, Goldschmidt, Day, & Larkby, 2002; Institute of Medicine, 1996). In one study, researchers looked at the outcomes of more than 650,000 pregnancies and found that women who consumed alcohol during pregnancy had a miscarriage rate that was 40% higher than the rate for non-drinkers, and when women averaged 5 or more drinks per week, their miscarriage rate was 70% higher than the rate for non-drinkers (Aliyu, Wilson, Zoorob, Chakrabarty, Alio, Kirby, & Salihu, 2008).

Alcohol damages the fetus in several ways. The alcohol in the mother's bloodstream crosses the placenta; once it reaches the fetus it can disrupt cell division and kill fetal cells. Cells in the fetal brain and nervous system are particularly vulnerable to alcohol—and once destroyed, these cells are not replaced. Alcohol in the mother's bloodstream also causes vessels in the placenta to constrict, reducing the flow of blood through the placenta. This reduced blood flow deprives the developing fetus of the oxygen and important nutrients needed for healthy development, and it can also cause the placenta to fail, leading to fetal death.

When children are born to mothers who drank alcohol during pregnancy, they are at greater risk for being impulsive, easily distracted, and hyperactive (Mattson & Riley, 1998; Mick, Biederman, Faraone, Sayer, & Kleinman, 2002). Retarded brain growth and lowered IQ are prominent features of alcohol exposure. In fact, *experts believe that prenatal alcohol exposure is the leading known cause of mental retardation in the United States* (Abel & Sokol, 1987; Institute of Medicine, 1996)! Once a baby is born with mental retardation, there is no cure. Abstinence from drinking during pregnancy, however, would prevent every single case of alcohol-induced mental retardation as well as every case of the even more serious problem—fetal alcohol syndrome.

**Fetal alcohol syndrome (FAS)** was first identified in 1968 (Lemoine, Harousseau, Borteyru, & Menuet, 1968, as cited in Mattson & Riley, 1998). An FAS newborn shows all of the following conditions: (1) overall growth deficiency, (2) head and facial malformations, and (3) dysfunction of the central nervous system (brain and spinal cord) often resulting in some degree of mental retardation (Institute of Medicine, 1996). Babies exposed to alcohol are typically born with low birth weights indicating a disruption in overall growth during pregnancy. Tight eyelids, flattened midface, short nose, and thin upper lip are typical head and face malformations associated with FAS. Lowered IQ, hyperactivity, and poor motor coordination are examples of deficits that indicate

**premature (or prematurity)**
Refers to babies who are born earlier or smaller than average.

**preterm birth**
Births that occur before 37 weeks of gestation.

**low birth weight**
Weight less than 5½ pounds at birth (2 pounds lighter than average).

**fetal alcohol syndrome (FAS)**
A syndrome of birth defects caused by prenatal exposure to alcohol. Includes growth deficiencies, head and facial malformations, and central nervous system dysfunction.

THINKING CRITICALLY

Did you know that the leading known cause of mental retardation is completely preventable? Do you think drinking behaviors would change if more people were aware of this? Why or why not?

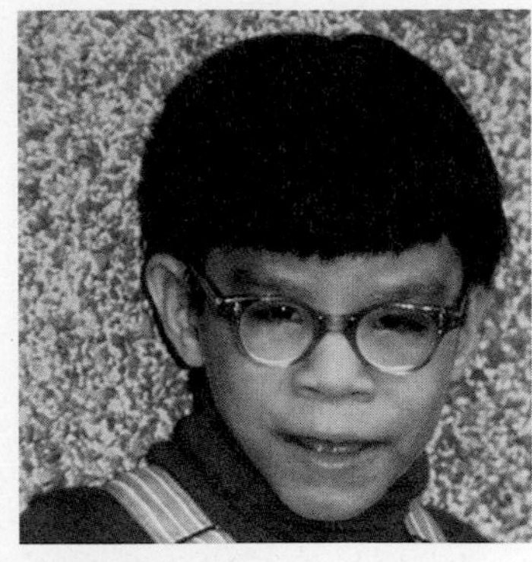

▲ This child has fetal alcohol syndrome (FAS), a combination of birth defects that includes facial deformities (notice the child's tight eyelids and flattened nose), growth deficiency, and nervous system dysfunctions that can include lower IQ and hyperactivity. FAS is completely preventable if women avoid alcohol consumption during pregnancy.

dysfunction of the central nervous system. The combination of these conditions defines the syndrome known as FAS.

In the United States the estimated incidence of FAS is about 1.5 out of every 1,000 live births (Centers for Disease Control [CDC], 2005). FAS is part of *fetal alcohol spectrum disorder* (FASD). In FASD, the effects of alcohol exposure can be severe, as in full-blown FAS we described earlier. More frequently, babies are born without the full syndrome but still show one or more of the individual symptoms, such as lowered IQ and hyperactivity, lowered IQ alone, or problems with specific neuropsychological functions such as attention, cognitive flexibility, planning ability, memory, or language. These conditions are commonly referred to as **fetal alcohol effects (FAE)** (Korkman, Kettune, & Autti-Rämö, 2003; Jacobson & Jacobson, 2002; Sokol, Delaney-Black, & Nordstrom, 2003). The physical defects and the cognitive and behavioral deficits associated with FAE may be subtle and may not even become apparent until later in childhood. As a result, it is hard to estimate their incidence. Still, researchers believe that as many as 6 out of every 1,000 live births show FAS or FAE (Centers for Disease Control [CDC], 2005). Keep in mind that this estimate does not include the number of miscarriages and fetal deaths caused by alcohol damage. To learn about one family's experience with FAS, read the Personal Perspective interview called "Meet a Family Who Adopted a Child with FAS."

THINKING CRITICALLY

Binge drinking and drug use are frequent on college campuses. What dangers are associated with these behaviors?

FAS and the more severe forms of FAE tend to occur when mothers are chronic alcoholics (consuming at least six drinks per day) or engage in regular binge drinking (consumption of four or more drinks per occasion, at least once per week). A woman who drinks less than this, however, may still put her baby at risk, as the effects depend on a variety of factors. These include the genetic health of the fetus and mother, the alcohol metabolism and tolerance of the mother, and the pattern of drinking during pregnancy. You should be aware that one review of the research suggested that even lower levels of drinking during pregnancy were related to increases in childhood hyperactivity, impulsiveness, and delinquency. Drinking as little as one alcoholic beverage per week was related to increases in child aggression, and researchers reported that a single night of binge drinking could cause serious brain damage and learning problems in the child (Huizink & Mulder, 2006). In carefully controlled experiments with mice, neuroscience researchers found that even one-time injections of small amounts of alcohol kill significant numbers of brain cells. When they extrapolate these findings to humans, scientists estimate as many as 20 million fetal brain cells are destroyed each time mothers consume only one or two alcoholic drinks. When it comes to protecting the health and developmental integrity of the baby, there really is no safe level of alcohol consumption. Watch on mydevelopmentlab

Watch a Video on Fetal Alcohol Damage.
www.mydevelopmentlab.com

Fortunately, there is some hope that women can get the message and reduce their drinking during pregnancy. One team of researchers randomly assigned low-income, pregnant women in the Los Angeles area to two groups: one group received a counseling session designed to help them reduce their consumption of alcohol, and the other group was only told that they should stop drinking (O'Connor&Whaley, 2007). Although women in both groups reduced their drinking significantly during their pregnancies, women in the counseling group reduced their drinking by a greater amount. This evidently had a positive effect because the babies born to the women from the counseling group had higher birth weights and birth lengths than babies born to the other mothers. Also, the fetal death rate was lower in the counseling group—out of the 117 women who completed the counseling session, only one pregnancy was lost to miscarriage, but 4 miscarriages or fetal deaths occurred among the 138 women who did not receive counseling. Given these findings, think about the numbers of families and children who could be spared from the devastating effects of alcohol damage if interventions like this were more widely available.

**fetal alcohol effects (FAE)**
Individual or multiple birth defects caused by prenatal exposure to alcohol. Lowered IQ, hyperactivity, growth deficiencies, and physical malformations can exist alone or in combinations but not in a way that indicates FAS.

# Perspective PERSONAL

## MEET A FAMILY WHO ADOPTED A CHILD WITH FETAL ALCOHOL SYNDROME

Cheri and Allan Scott
Anchorage, AK
Adopted a child, Justin, with fetal alcohol syndrome (FAS)

**Cheri and Allan Scott adopted Justin when he was an infant. Justin's biological mother was a chronic alcoholic. She was abused as a child, ran away from home, and lived on the streets. Justin was her third child, and she abused alcohol during all three pregnancies. After Justin she had two more pregnancies that ended in miscarriage due to severe alcohol exposure. Justin was still in the neonatal intensive care unit of the hospital at one month of age, and that is when his biological mother visited him for the last time. She returned to live on the streets. She later died from alcohol and drug abuse when she was only 24 years old.**

**At the time of this interview, Justin had grown up to be 19 years old. Here is some of his story told by his adoptive parents, Cheri and Allan Scott:**

*We were told that Justin had prenatal alcohol exposure and wasn't expected to live to be a year old. He was medically stable and didn't need to take up a hospital bed—he just needed a safe place to be until he died. His birth records described him as a successfully resuscitated spontaneous miscarriage; he was born at 26 weeks of gestation. His blood alcohol level at birth was 0.236.*

*We knew that Justin's brain and body had been affected by prenatal alcohol exposure, but having it finally confirmed that he had FAS meant we couldn't pretend the trouble was going to go away with time and love—these differences would impact him for life. The grief was intense. We cried for the little boy that might have been, for his mom who died and would never see her three surviving children grow up, and for ourselves and our fear that we wouldn't know how to help him learn and grow. We worried that people would judge him based on his diagnosis and not give their best effort to help him achieve all he could do and be. We were also relieved, because now we had an answer to one of the many questions about Justin's development and it gave us some direction as we started to pull together the many players who would support Justin and our family over the years.*

*Justin experiences cerebral palsy, which affects his gross and fine motor skills. He cannot stand or take steps without holding someone's arm, using his crutches, wheelchair, or walker. He can feed himself, but has difficulty using a knife to cut food. He can dress himself, but cannot effectively button, tie, or snap his clothing and shoes. He has vision and hearing problems, brain seizures, and a cleft palate. His preferred communication methods are sign language and his Lightwriter, a handheld electronic voice output device. The hardest thing to deal with is the developmental delay. At 19 years of age, testing shows his cognitive skill level to be between 4 and 7 years. He doesn't have many typically developing friends, and most of the people he spends time with are either family members or paid service providers.*

*The amazing thing is that in spite of all Justin's developmental differences, he is a very loving, happy, and fun kid to be around. He's very empathetic, funny, and musical, and he appreciates any attention.*

*Justin's disabilities have impacted everyone in our family, in both positive and negative ways. We have all learned to work through disagreements without raising our voices, as yelling always startles and frightens Justin. My husband Allan has learned to share his feelings more clearly and to be more animated when showing emotion. He's much more patient now and has learned how good it can feel to offer support to other dads raising children with special needs. Our oldest daughter has been Justin's Independent Care Provider for the last 4 years, helping him learn to get around in the community, work on social, self-help, and independent living skills. She realized before any of the rest of us that Justin needed someone close to him who could use sign language and took it upon herself to sign up for ASL throughout high school.*

**Through their experiences with Justin, the Scotts began working with Stone Soup Group, a nonprofit organization providing support to families of children with special needs and the service providers working with them all over the state of Alaska. The Scotts also created Parent Navigation, a service that pairs families of special needs children with experienced parents who can offer support.**

QUESTION **What do you think it would take to significantly reduce the number of children and families who are affected by prenatal alcohol exposure? What kinds of programs are needed? Will they work?**

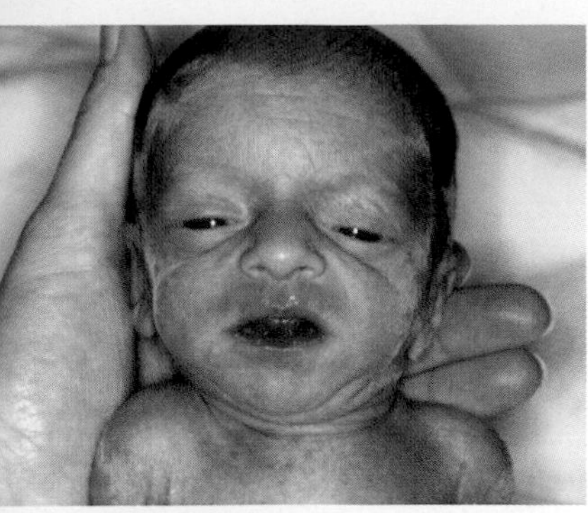

▲ This tiny baby was born too early to a mother who used cocaine during pregnancy. She will be at a very high risk for a variety of health problems. Only time will tell if she can even survive.

**Cocaine.** Approximately 1% of women admit that they used cocaine during pregnancy (National Institute on Drug Abuse, 2001). As you might imagine, however, women tend to underreport use of illegal drugs such as cocaine. When researchers tested newborns in one study, they found that 27% of the babies born to lower-income mothers tested positive for cocaine exposure (Schutzman, Frankenfield-Chernicoff, Clatterbaugh, & Singer, 1991).

Fetal exposure to cocaine retards growth, can cause preterm birth, and can cause malformations in the baby's brain, intestines, and genital–urinary tract (Moore & Persaud, 1998). In one study, mothers who tested positive for cocaine use just before delivering their babies were 2½ times more likely to have a premature baby, and their babies were smaller, had retarded brain growth, and showed more fetal distress at birth than babies born to mothers who did not use cocaine (Doris, Meguid, Thomas, Blatt, & Eckenrode, 2006). Cocaine-exposed newborns can show evidence of hemorrhage, lesions, swelling in the brain, and other brain abnormalities. They have increased irritability, muscle tremors, rigidity, and decreased spontaneous movement. They also have impaired sensory function, decreased visual attention, and trouble regulating their own state of arousal (asleep, awake, or attentive).

Long-term effects of prenatal cocaine exposure have been harder to determine. Some studies indicate negative effects of cocaine exposure on language, visual skill, or overall cognitive development. However, others have found no relationship with problems during early childhood, or that the effect interacts with other factors such as gender or a nonsupportive caregiving environment (Arendt, Short, & Singer, 2004; Delaney-Black, Covington, Nordstrom, Ager, Janisse, Hannigan, et al., 2004; Lewis, Misra, Johnson, & Rosen, 2004; Lewis, Singer, & Short, 2004; Messinger, Bauer, Das, Seifer, Lester, Lagasse, et al., 2004; Morrow, Vogel, & Anthony, 2004; Singer, Arendt, Minnes, Farkas, Salvator, Kirchner, et al., 2002). For example, one recent study showed that boys born to mothers who used cocaine had lower IQs at 9 years of age, but this effect was not found for girls in the sample (Bennett, Bendersky, & Lewis, 2008). Another study showed that children who were 10 to 14 years old had smaller brain volumes when their mothers used cocaine during pregnancy. These differences existed for both boys and girls, and they were especially strong when the mothers also used alcohol, cigarettes, or marijuana during pregnancy (Rivkin et al., 2008).

THINK ABOUT ELIZABETH AND STEPHANIE . . .
What concerns would you have if Stephanie uses alcohol and illegal drugs? What would the potential risks be for the fetus?

**Cigarette Smoking.** Approximately 10% of pregnant women report that they smoked cigarettes during their pregnancies. These rates vary widely by race, age, and education, however. For example, among a large sample of U.S. births registered in 2004, about 18% of Native Americans smoked during pregnancy. The rate was about 11% for whites, 8% for blacks, and only 2% for Asian or Hispanic mothers. Smoking rates were higher for 18- and 19-year-olds who were pregnant (16%) and lower for pregnant women in their 30s (6%). Rates were even higher for pregnant women who never graduated from high school (24%) and very low for those who finished four or more years of college (only 1%) (National Center for Health Statistics, 2007).

Cigarette smoke contains more than 450 different harmful chemicals, including nicotine, carbon monoxide, carbon dioxide, and cyanide (Martin, 1992). These chemicals damage the placenta, reduce the blood supply to the placenta and uterus, and reduce the supply of oxygen and nutrients available to the fetus. They also disrupt normal brain development (Huizink & Mulder, 2006). In addition, nicotine is an addictive stimulant that tends to suppress appetite, so women who smoke tend to eat less and gain less weight during pregnancy. But pregnant women need to gain sufficient weight to properly support the nutritional needs of the baby. During healthy pregnancies, women gain at least 20 to 25 pounds. When they gain less weight, their babies are more likely to be premature and are at greater risk for health complications.

Low birth weight is the most common problem associated with newborns of mothers who smoke. Children born to mothers who smoked during pregnancy are more likely to be hyperactive and to have short attention spans, and they tend to score lower in reading, spelling, and math (Fogelman, 1980; Linnett, Dalsgaard, Obel, Wisborg, Henriksen, Rodriguez, et al., 2003; Naeye & Peters, 1984; Thapar, Fowler, & Rice, 2003). One study showed that women who smoked 10 or more cigarettes per day during pregnancy had children who showed more anxiety, depression, aggression, and delinquent behavior than other children, and these differences were observed consistently from the time the children were 5 to 18 years old (Ashford, van Lier, Timmermans, Cuijpers, & Koot, 2008). Finally, cigarette smoke can damage the placenta. As a result, women who smoke during pregnancy are at increased risk for spontaneous abortions, stillbirths, and neonatal deaths. The good news is that more women are learning about the dangers of smoking. Since 1989, there has been a 48% decrease in the number of women who smoke during pregnancy (National Center for Health Statistics, 2007).

So far, we have discussed the effects of alcohol, cocaine, and cigarettes. The additional effects from marijuana and heroin are summarized in Table 3.2. All of these are drugs of choice, and if pregnant women chose to avoid these substances, many millions of children could be born without related birth defects. As a society, what can we do to reduce drug use during pregnancy? To see how one state tries to protect developing babies, read the Social Policy Perspective on page 88 called "The Case of Malissa Ann Crawley." **Listen** on **mydevelopmentlab**

**Listen**: Alcohol, illegal drugs, and cigarette smoking: Why do so many women still expose their babies to these substances? (Author Podcast) www.mydevelopmentlab.com

## The Mother's Health and Age

**Mother's Health.** If a woman is carrying an infectious disease while pregnant, it can endanger the fetus. The virus or microorganism that causes the disease in the mother will usually cross the placenta to the fetus and can cause harm or infectious disease in the baby. In other cases, the disease can be passed to the baby during the birthing process. Let's look at three sexually transmitted diseases: herpes, syphilis, and HIV/AIDS.

*Herpes.* *Herpes simplex virus (HSV)* is a sexually transmitted disease that, in adults, causes blisters around the mouth and lips ("cold sores") and blisters and sores in the genital areas. HSV is contagious and is passed between partners by oral and genital contact such as kissing, intercourse, and oral sex. The virus spreads most easily when sores are present, but it also can spread before the sores emerge and when there are no noticeable symptoms. About half of the American population is infected with HSV, but two-thirds of those infected are not aware that they have the disease (Herpes.com, 2002). Although HSV is mostly a nuisance disease for adults, it can have serious consequences for developing fetuses and newborn babies. When a woman contracts HSV in early pregnancy, her risk of miscarriage increases threefold (Moore & Persaud, 1998).

Babies born with HSV usually contract the virus during delivery rather than through the exchange of blood elements through the placenta during prenatal development. If they receive antiviral medications, about half of HSV-infected newborns will escape permanent damage. The remaining half are at risk for serious neurological damage, mental retardation, and even death (Herpes.com, 2002). When mothers are not showing symptoms (such as open sores) at the time of birth, the risk of infecting the baby is very small (as low as 4 in 10,000 births). The risks are high, however, if the mother is showing symptoms at birth. In these cases doctors recommend a Caesarean section (C-section) delivery. **Caesarean section** is a surgical procedure in which the baby is removed through an incision made through the mother's abdomen and into the uterus. This reduces the baby's exposure to the virus (Herpes.com, 2002).

**Caesarean section (C-section) births**
Surgical procedure in which the baby is removed through an incision made through the mother's abdomen and into the uterus.

## Perspective SOCIAL POLICY: THE CASE OF MALISSA ANN CRAWLEY

From Anderson, SC: When Malissa Ann Crawley gave birth to her third child, Antwon, his blood tested positive for cocaine. Crawley was arrested for unlawful neglect of a child (Associated Press, 1999). Crawley pleaded guilty to the neglect charge and was sentenced to five years in prison. After serving two months, she was released to appeal her case.

The South Carolina State Supreme Court upheld Crawley's conviction, stating that a pregnant woman can be charged for harming a viable fetus. The United States Supreme Court refused to hear the appeal, so Crawley went back to prison. After serving approximately one year and completing a six-month addiction treatment program, Crawley was released under the conditions that she must find suitable employment and housing and that she must submit to frequent home visits and drug testing.

South Carolina takes a strong stand in prosecuting pregnant women who use illegal drugs, and most other states have passed similar legislation. For example, in Florida, Indiana, Minnesota, Oklahoma, and Utah, mothers can be charged with abuse if their babies are born with FAS or addicted to drugs (Gostin, 2001; Tomkins & Kepfield, 1992). These get-tough policies are gaining wide attention—and raising thorny questions. In light of what we know about the harmful effects of teratogens, it seems that there is a growing trend to hold pregnant women responsible for their unhealthy behaviors. But are these laws appropriate? That is, will they protect the health of developing fetuses?

Many are concerned that the burden falls completely on the mother. In Nebraska the laws focus on the entire family as a unit, and it is possible to prosecute fathers who drink alcohol with their pregnant wives or girlfriends (Roth, 2000; Tomkins & Kepfield, 1992). Does this seem like an appropriate response? And should men be prosecuted for delivering drugs to "minors" (i.e., fetuses) when they provide pregnant women with illegal substances? Finally, there is also concern about the "slippery slope." After we protect fetuses from the harmful effects of illegal drugs and alcohol, where do we stop? Do we prosecute women for smoking cigarettes, eating contaminated fish, working in stressful environments, eating poorly, or exercising too much or too little?

QUESTION **Do you agree that Malissa Ann Crawley should have served time in prison for delivering cocaine to her unborn baby? If so, how far do you think such legal actions should go? In the end, will laws be effective in discouraging people from engaging in behaviors that contribute to unhealthy pregnancies?**

*Cytomegalovirus (CMV)*, another member of the herpes family of viruses, is carried by 50–75% of U.S. adults (Mayo Clinic, 2003). Among adults, CMV spreads the same way as HSV: through kissing and other intimate contact. CMV remains dormant in most adults with healthy immune systems, so infected adults rarely experience any symptoms of the virus. For fetuses, however, the virus is very dangerous (Moore & Persaud, 1998). When a pregnant woman who did not previously carry CMV gets infected with the virus during the third to eighth week (embryonic stage) of pregnancy and the virus also infects the embryo (which happens about one-third of the time), the embryo usually dies. If a woman has an initial CMV infection later in pregnancy and the virus infects the fetus, the baby usually is born alive but is at risk for retarded growth, microcephaly (small head circumference, associated with delayed motor, speech, and mental development), blindness, deafness, mental retardation, and cerebral palsy.

*Syphilis.* *Syphilis* is another sexually transmitted disease, and its effects can be deadly for the fetus. Fetal death occurs in up to 40% of cases in which the mother is infected with syphilis but is not receiving treatment for the disease (Centers for Disease Control [CDC], 2007a). When fetuses do survive, they are likely to be infected with the disease and to suffer other birth defects such as deafness, malformations of teeth and bones, facial deformities, excess fluid in the brain, and mental retardation (Moore & Persaud, 1998). Fortunately, syphilis infection is fairly rare. During 2006, for every 100,000 babies born live, only about 8 had a syphilis infection—but of course this does not include the larger numbers of fetuses who did not survive to birth (Centers for Disease Control [CDC],

2007a). Most of the prenatal damage caused by syphilis can be prevented when women are screened for syphilis and get adequate care early in pregnancy.

*HIV/AIDS.* It is estimated that 140,000 women in the United States are infected with the human immunodeficiency virus (HIV), and this is the virus that causes Acquired Immunodeficiency Syndrome (AIDS) (Centers for Disease Control [CDC], 2007b). Nearly one-quarter of these women are not aware that they are infected, and this puts them at greater risk for passing the virus to their babies. It is tragic for any infant to begin life with this serious, incurable illness. Babies born with HIV usually contract the virus at or near delivery, and the chances of infecting the baby with HIV increase if the mother breastfeeds the baby. For babies who do not contract the virus but whose mothers carry it, the teratogenic effects of HIV are not yet clear, but they may include growth retardation and head and facial deformities. If mothers are not being treated for their HIV, they have a 25% chance of passing the virus to their babies. Fortunately, when both the mothers and babies receive antiretroviral medications, only 2% of babies end up with HIV infections. Since the introduction of these medications, the infection rate for infants has declined 93% (Centers for Disease Control [CDC], 2007b).

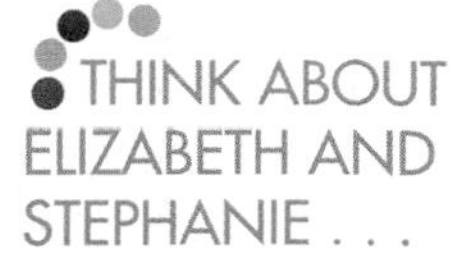

THINK ABOUT ELIZABETH AND STEPHANIE . . .
How can Stephanie reduce the chances of spreading a sexually transmitted disease to her baby?

Mother's Age. In the United States, approximately 750,000 teenage girls become pregnant each year (Guttmacher Institute, 2006). At the other end of the spectrum, many women delay childbirth until their late 30s or 40s to complete their educations and pursue careers. Are infants at greater risk when they are born to younger or older mothers? Is there a biological advantage if a woman gives birth in her 20s or early 30s? For the most part, research has indicated that pregnancies tend to proceed in a healthy manner across all of the reproductive years.

As you can see in Figure 3.2, however, the percentage of babies born low in birth weight is highest for mothers under the age of 15 and over 44. Low birth-weight percentages decline steadily through the teen years and begin to rise again in the 30s. You can also see that non-Hispanic blacks have a greater percentage of low birth-weight babies across the entire range of ages—a racial and ethnic difference that might well be addressed with better prenatal care and education.

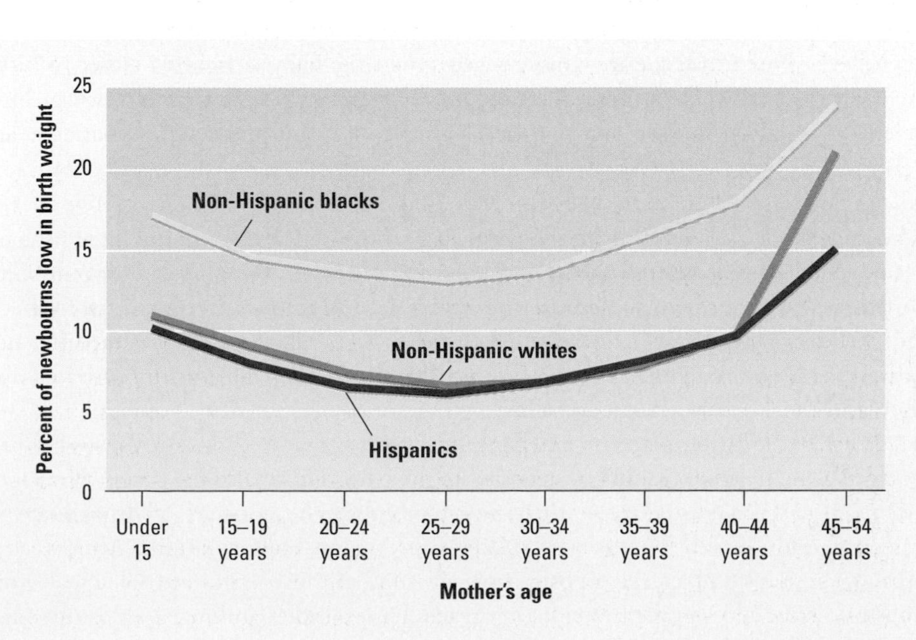


◀ FIGURE 3.2
**Percentage of Newborns Who are Born Low in Birth Weight**
The percentage of babies born low in birth weight (less than 5 ½ pounds) is greatest for mothers under age 15 and 45 and older. Data are based on all births registered in the United States during the year 2005.

*Source*: Martin et al., 2007.

**THINK ABOUT ELIZABETH AND STEPHANIE . . .**
At Stephanie's age, is she at an especially high risk for having a baby who is premature or has other health problems? Why or why not?

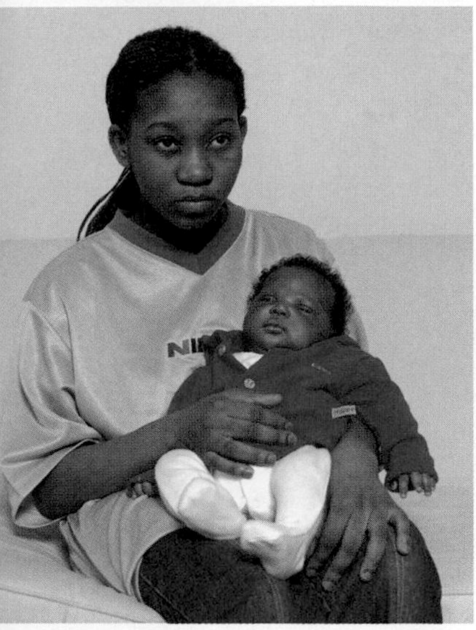

▲ Teenage mothers are at higher risk for giving birth to babies who are premature and low in birth weight. Problems are compounded by factors such as low income, inadequate access to prenatal care, and poor nutrition. Many teens are not psychologically or emotionally prepared for the responsibilities of caring for a new baby.

Many adolescents are not socially and cognitively mature, and this may limit their ability to cope with the stress of pregnancy. Low income, poor education, social isolation, drug and alcohol use, and lack of early prenatal care are factors that tend to be associated with teenage pregnancy—and with negative birth outcomes. There is also some question as to whether young teenagers, who may only recently have started menstruation, are biologically ready to carry a pregnancy to full term. Fortunately, with increases in abstinence and the improved use of contraception, the teenage birth rate has dropped in recent years. It hit a peak in 1991, has declined one-third since then, and is now at its lowest point since the government started recording the statistic in 1976. Since 1991, abortion rates have declined 40%, and the numbers of babies born to teenage mothers has declined more than one-third (Guttmacher Institute, 2006; Martin et al., 2007. We will have much more to say about the risks and developmental effects associated with teenage pregnancy in Chapter 13.

While teens have been having fewer babies in recent years, the birth rates for older women have increased. The birth rates for women over 35 hit a low in the late 1970s, but since then their birth rates have doubled (Martin et al., 2007). Women in the later years of their reproductive lives have many concerns. High blood pressure, diabetes, and other health conditions occur more frequently as women age. Consequently, the risks of prematurity, fetal death, and complications during birth increase slightly as women move through their late 30s and into their 40s (Berkowitz, Skovron, Lapinski, & Berkowitz, 1990; Cnattingius, Forman, Berendes, & Isotalo, 1992; Fretts, Schmittdiel, McLean, Usher, & Goldman, 1995). Among women who give birth in their 40s, mothers who are giving birth for the first time tend to have more problems than those who have already had one or more children. Older mothers have an increased risk of having a baby with Down syndrome (see Chapter 2). Most of the other known chromosomal abnormalities are not associated with increased maternal age, however. Yet even with some increased risks, we should emphasize that the vast majority of pregnancies do proceed normally and result in the birth of a happy and healthy newborn, even when the mother is over 40 years of age.

## Critical Periods

At what point is the developing baby most vulnerable to toxins such as alcohol, cocaine, and cigarette smoke? Are the defects more severe when the exposure occurs early in prenatal development? Or are they more severe when the baby is exposed closer to birth? You will find answers to these questions in Figure 3.3. Notice that the risk of birth defects is small during the first two weeks after conception but rises dramatically and peaks shortly after week 3. By week 8, the risk has declined again, and it will continue to fall until the time the baby is born. Why is the risk so low in the first two weeks? Remember that this period is the germinal stage. This is a time when the zygote has not yet attached itself to the mother's uterine lining and when the placenta and umbilical cord have not yet formed. Because the zygote is not yet getting nutrition from the mother's bloodstream, it is not exposed to most of the harmful compounds that may exist in her blood. If toxins do reach the zygote, however, they may disrupt early cell divisions and cause the pregnancy to be lost.

After week 3, the placenta and umbilical cord provide a conduit through which harmful elements can pass from the mother to the baby. This is also the period when most organs and structures are first forming—remember the concept of organogenesis? Therefore, any disruption at this stage can cause major malformations. After week 8, organogenesis is complete, so exposure now will tend to cause less catastrophic malformations or disturbances in the functions of organs. For example, prolonged exposure to toxins during the fetal stage tends to cause growth retardation and lowered IQ.

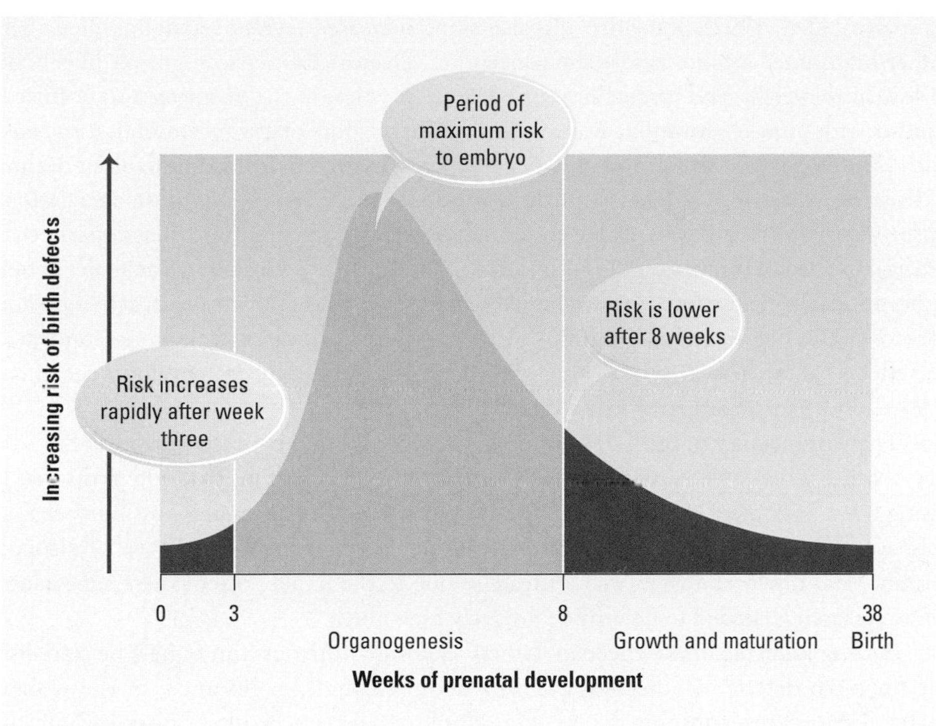


◀ FIGURE 3.3
**Relative Risk of Birth Defects during Prenatal Development**
When exposed to teratogens, the developing organism is at greatest risk while the organs and tissues are forming during the embryonic stage (weeks 3 to 8). Abnormalities during the germinal stage (weeks 1 to 2) are not frequent but are often fatal. Risks are lower during the fetal stage (weeks 8 to birth) after the basic organs and tissues have formed (Moore & Persaud, 1998).

By looking at Figure 3.3, you can see that the early weeks of pregnancy are crucial to the baby's health. The problem, of course, is that many women are not even sure that they are pregnant until they are near (or even past) the eighth week of pregnancy. By then the critical periods for the major organ systems have passed. Ideally, women who think they may be pregnant can make healthy changes in their lifestyles even before they are sure to avoid the harmful effects of teratogens. We hope you can see that, to prevent the harmful effects of teratogens, women with risky habits really need to make changes even before they know that they are pregnant.

THINKING CRITICALLY
What aspects of your current lifestyle would you be willing to change to prevent future birth defects? What changes do you think other people would be willing to make?

## The Role of Fathers

So far, we've discussed problems that can occur when mothers are too young or too old or when they expose their babies to toxic substances and risky conditions during pregnancy. But is all of this burden on women and mothers alone? Certainly not! Recent research shows that babies are more likely to be preterm and low in birth weight when they have fathers who are teenagers (under age 20). These babies also tend to have lower Apgar scores (see later in this chapter), and they are more likely to die during infancy. Surprisingly, these tendencies remain regardless of whether the mothers are 20 years old, 29 years old, or anywhere in between. In this study, the age of the father is predicting poor birth outcomes above and beyond the age of the mother (Chen, Wen, Krewski, Fleming, Yang, & Walker, 2008). Other studies show that miscarriages and a variety of birth defects are more likely to occur when fathers work in settings that expose them to heavy metals such as lead and mercury or when they work in other settings that expose them to pesticides or toxic chemicals (Trasler & Doerksen, 1999).

In most cases, when toxic substances affect sperm cells, the damaged sperm do not survive the long journey to the egg. However, toxins sometimes damage the chromosomes or genes, alter the way the genes operate, or otherwise disrupt the development of the zygote or embryo. Birth defects, miscarriages, and other problems therefore can occur. Studies with rats and mice, for example, show that alcohol damages the genetic material

▲ What can we do to help people realize that drinking alcohol during pregnancy has catastrophic effects? What do you see as men's role in preventing alcohol-related birth defects?

in sperm (Abel, 1992). Rat offspring also show increased levels of activity when their fathers consumed alcohol before the conception. Decreased litter size, greater likelihood of low birth weight, and greater susceptibility to infection in the offspring also occurred. Studies with humans show that alcohol use by fathers before or at conception is associated with children's later learning and memory problems, hyperactivity, and difficulties dealing with stress, though researchers still do not understand exactly how these associations occur (Abel, 1993, 2004). Cocaine accumulates in the testes and can damage sperm cells (Yazigi, Odem, & Polakoski, 1991). In mice, when cocaine is inhaled by the males before conception, the mouse pups show retarded brain growth and problems with attention and memory (He, Lidow, & Lidow, 2006). Although human studies have not yet confirmed the effects, researchers suspect that cocaine can then directly disrupt development in the zygote, probably jeopardizing its survival.

The vast majority of birth defects, however, result from the mother's exposure to toxins, because it is elements in the mother's bloodstream that cross the placenta to the developing baby. Still, these studies on the father's role do raise the intriguing possibility that at least a small portion of the birth defects that we blame on the mother's use of alcohol, cocaine, and other teratogens may instead be due to the father's use of these substances. More research is needed to determine precisely how much.

Putting aside the direct effects of fathers' exposure to toxins, can fathers be responsible for birth defects in other ways? Think about alcohol, for instance. In the United States, 14% of men consume two or more drinks on average per day, but only 3–4% of women drink at this level (Abel, 1992). Also consider that 69% of women who are alcoholics have husbands who are also alcoholics. When men encourage women to drink, don't they share responsibility for the results? Many men do reduce their alcohol consumption, or abstain completely, while their wives or partners are pregnant. But remember that the most serious birth defects occur during organogenesis—that is, during weeks 3 to 8 of the pregnancy, when many women are not even aware that they are pregnant.

THINK ABOUT ELIZABETH AND STEPHANIE . . .
What are several things Elizabeth can do to help Stephanie have a healthy pregnancy?

Men as well as women should realize that many of our exposures to toxins are due to our personal habits, and that these habits develop over the many years before pregnancy occurs. To ensure a healthy pregnancy, a woman of reproductive age can avoid harmful substances even before she knows she is pregnant—or plan her pregnancy so she can take precautions ahead of time. Men, and everyone else who supports women, should strongly consider how their actions, habits, or attitudes might encourage or contribute to women's use of alcohol, drugs, and tobacco. We should all consider how we contribute to other prenatal hazards, from environmental pollution to sexually transmitted diseases. Aren't healthy pregnancies the responsibility of all of us: mothers, fathers, partners, and friends?

## LET'S REVIEW . . .

1. Drugs, environmental pollutants, and viruses are examples of elements in the environment that can cause birth defects when they come into contact with a developing fetus. These elements are more generally referred to as __________.
   **a.** teratogens **b.** oncogens
   **c.** critical periods **d.** differentiation agents
2. The three conditions needed to diagnose a baby as having fetal alcohol syndrome are overall growth deficiency, head and facial malformations, and __________.
   **a.** preterm birth
   **b.** detectable blood alcohol levels
   **c.** central nervous system dysfunction
   **d.** sign of stroke or hemorrhage in the brain
3. Which drug is known to cause babies to be born with hemorrhages, lesions, and swelling in the brain as well as with intestinal and genital–urinary tract disorders?
   **a.** alcohol **b.** cocaine
   **c.** heroin **d.** marijuana

4. What is the most common problem associated with prenatal cigarette exposure?
   a. brain damage in the newborn.
   b. lung damage in the newborn
   c. low birth weight in the newborn
   d. death of the newborn
5. True or False: The leading known cause of mental retardation in the United States is completely preventable—it is prenatal alcohol exposure.
6. True or False: When it comes to teratogens, the most damaging effects tend to occur when babies are exposed during the last few weeks before birth.

Answers: 1. a, 2. c, 3. b, 4. c, 5. T, 6. F

# The Process of Birth

It's been almost 9 months and the time is nearly here. The baby's room is ready, the hospital bag is packed, and everyone is eagerly awaiting the birth of the new baby. The pregnant mother-to-be has been feeling a vague tightening in her uterus off and on for weeks or even months now, but these false labor contractions are only "practice," not as regular as real labor contractions will be. Eventually the contractions become more regular, closer together, and more intense. Within hours the baby will be born.

AS YOU STUDY THIS SECTION, ASK YOURSELF THESE QUESTIONS:

3.7 What are the stages of birth, and what important events take place during each stage?

3.8 How do birthing practices differ across cultures, and what can we learn from these differences?

3.9 What are the most common birthing practices and options practiced in the United States?

3.10 What are some of the potential complications of the birth process, and what can be done to avoid or reduce them?

3.11 What is the newborn baby like?

## Stages of Birth

Exactly what triggers the start of the birth process is still a mystery. Researchers believe that when the fetal brain reaches a certain point of maturity, it sends a signal that prompts hormonal changes in the mother (Nathanielsz, 1992). These changes cause the mother's uterine muscles to contract, and the contractions create an ever-increasing feedback loop of hormones that stimulate more frequent and more intense contractions until the baby is born. As shown in Figure 3.4, (page 94) physicians typically divide the birth process into three stages of labor: dilation, delivery, and afterbirth. **Watch** on **mydevelopmentlab**

**Watch** a video on Labor and Birth.
www.mydevelopmentlab.com

*Stage 1 (dilation)* is the longest stage, lasting on average from 6 to 14 hours. This stage is usually longer for first-time mothers but varies significantly from one woman to another. This stage begins when the uterus starts regular contractions. The contractions are gentle and infrequent at first, but eventually become much more intense, occurring every 2 minutes or so with each contraction lasting up to 2 minutes. The contractions cause **dilation**, the gradual opening of the cervix. The cervix is a tough ring of tissue that has remained tightly closed throughout pregnancy to keep the fetus securely inside the uterus and protect it from infection. During Stage 1 of labor, the cervix must dilate to 10 cm, which is about 100 times its normal diameter, to allow for passage of the baby. Contractions also push the baby downward so the baby's head presses firmly against the cervical opening.

**dilation**
The gradual opening of the cervix caused by labor contractions during the first stage of birth.

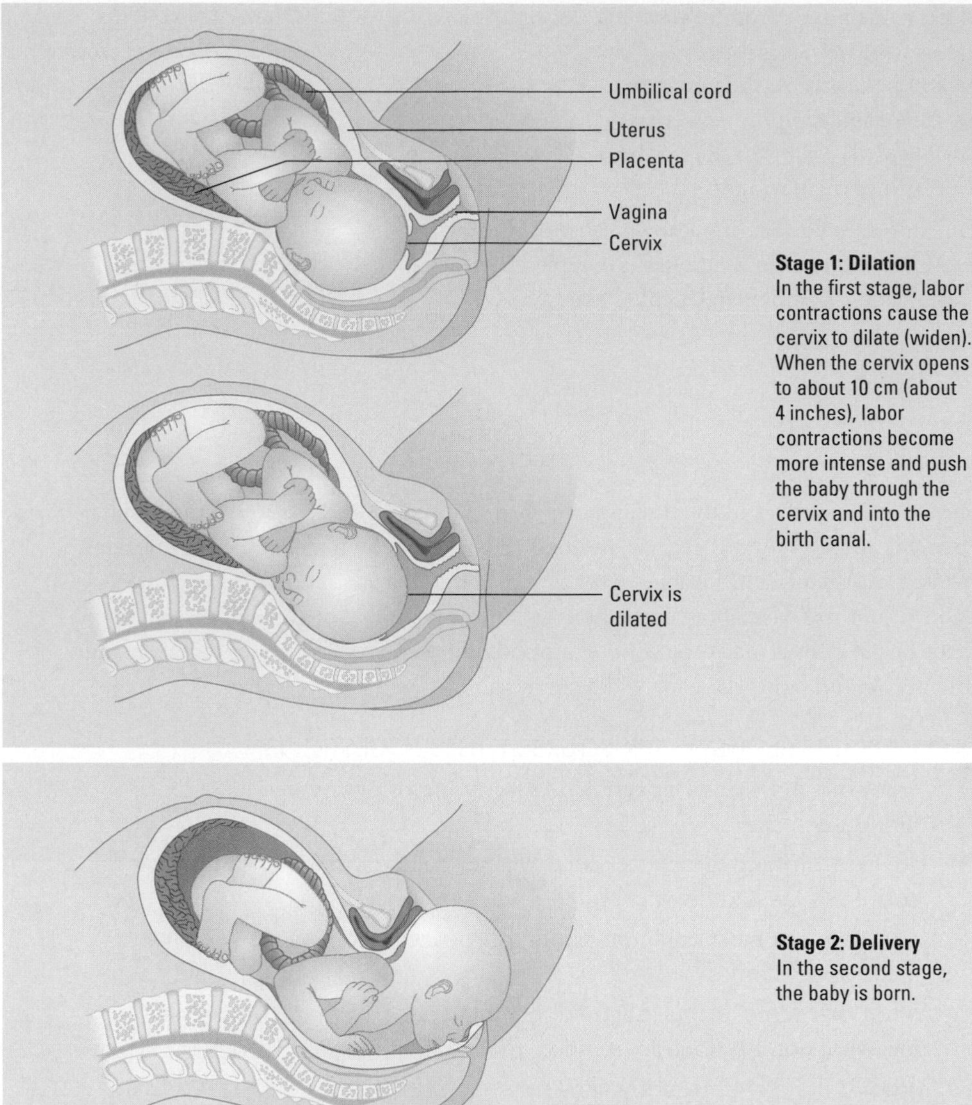
Umbilical cord
Uterus
Placenta
Vagina
Cervix
Cervix is dilated
Stage 1: Dilation
In the first stage, labor contractions cause the cervix to dilate (widen). When the cervix opens to about 10 cm (about 4 inches), labor contractions become more intense and push the baby through the cervix and into the birth canal.
Stage 2: Delivery
In the second stage, the baby is born.

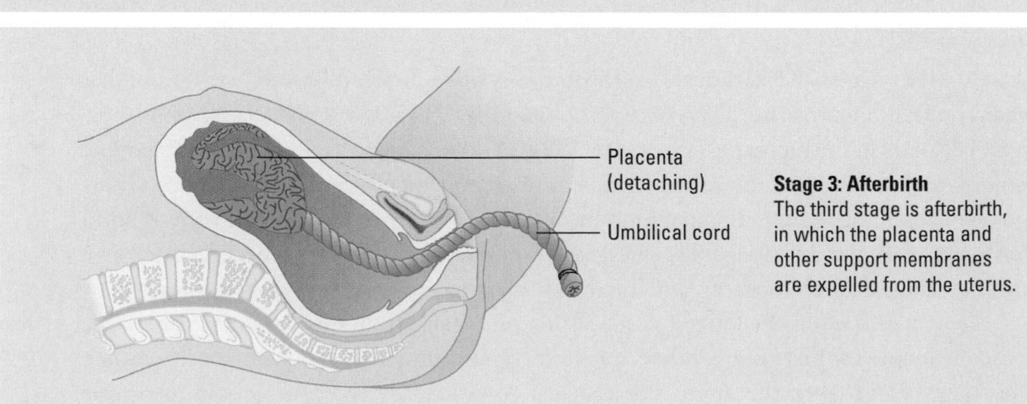
Placenta (detaching)
Umbilical cord
Stage 3: Afterbirth
The third stage is afterbirth, in which the placenta and other support membranes are expelled from the uterus.

▲ FIGURE 3.4
**The Stages of Birth**
In Stage 1, labor contractions cause the cervix to dilate (widen). When the cervix opens to about 10 cm, labor contractions become more intense and push the baby through the cervix and into the birth canal. In Stage 2 the baby is born. Stage 3 is afterbirth, in which the placenta and other support membranes are expelled from the uterus. (Adapted from Moore & Persaud, 1998.)

During *Stage 2 (delivery)*, the baby actually moves through the birth canal and is delivered. This stage is much shorter than the first, lasting an average of 30 minutes to 2 hours. Contractions push the baby through the birth canal for delivery. During this stage the mother feels an overwhelming urge to bear down strongly to help push the baby out. This stage ends with the delivery of the baby.

In *Stage 3 (afterbirth)*, the placenta and other membranes emerge through the birth canal in a process referred to as **afterbirth**. During this stage, which usually lasts less than an hour, the mother continues to experience contractions as her uterus expels the placenta. These contractions are much less intense than those of the first and second stages. Mothers are usually quite preoccupied with their newborn baby, so their attention is not on the contractions.

THINKING CRITICALLY
Think of someone you know who gave birth recently. What did she have to say about her birthing experience? How long was her labor? Was this her first delivery? If not, was her labor shorter this time than it was for her first delivery?

## Cultural Differences Surrounding Birth

The general biology of giving birth is the same for all human beings, but the way that the birthing process is approached varies considerably across cultures. As an example, consider the following two stories.

In rural Mexico, a mother begins to feel contractions so she goes to the home of her local birth attendant. The birth attendant is a woman who has helped hundreds of other women give birth. The attendant has a small amount of medical training, but most of her skill comes from helping other birth attendants and from the traditions that have been handed down for generations in her community. She has some instruments in her home and a room that is prepared for birthing. The attendant uses traditional methods including massage and steam baths that ease the process of birth for the mother. Ceremonial rituals are also followed. For example, if the baby is a girl, it is important that the placenta be buried near the place where tortillas are made at the home—otherwise misfortune may come to the baby and mother. These rituals have had religious or traditional value for many generations in this part of Mexico. The mother did see a medical physician once during her pregnancy. The visit was free of charge, courtesy of the Mexican government, but the mother had to travel all day to get to the clinic, and she felt very uncomfortable being out of her natural surroundings. The thought of a cold, steel medical table brings up images of sterility in her culture ("frio" or "frigid"), so the mother did not return to the clinic (adapted from Camey, Barrios, Guerrero, Nuñez-Urquiza, Hernández, & Glass, 1996).

▲ Upright birthing positions have been used for centuries in many cultures, as seen in this Aztec statue. It was not until the early 1900s that hospital procedures required mothers to lay flat on their backs as a way to ease the process for *physicians*.

In Shanghai, China, a mother goes to a local hospital that is very modern and large. More than 70,000 people visit the hospital every day, and nearly 40 babies per day are born there. Six mothers share one small room during most of their labor contractions, assisted by several nurse midwives. As the birth nears, the mother is transferred to a delivery room where two other mothers are already giving birth. The mothers lay flat on their backs on a plastic bed, and they are assisted by their midwives and physicians. After delivery, the mothers and babies are taken to separate rooms. Mothers recover while their babies have their footprints and photographs taken, and nurses care for the babies. Some mothers have their own mothers stay with them during labor and delivery, but many do not. Fathers and other family members are not allowed in these small birthing rooms—they can stay and help the mother only if they pay a higher price for a private room, but few families can afford that option. For population control, the Chinese government encourages families to limit themselves to only one child, and this may be one reason that the birth process is so centered around hospitals and medical intervention. In some hospitals, as many as half of all babies are born by Caesarean section; if there are any signs of labor problems, physicians are quick to intervene with surgery because they do not want to risk giving the family a baby who has a disability (Franks, 2008). **Listen** on **mydevelopmentlab**

**afterbirth**
The third and last stage of birth, in which the placenta and other membranes are delivered through the birth canal.

**Listen**: How do birthing practices differ around the world? (Author Podcast)
www.mydevelopmentlab.com

These stories present two different pictures of the birthing process. In many cultures, birth is viewed as a natural event that is celebrated with ceremony and traditional rituals. To the other extreme, physicians use modern technology to control the process. The World

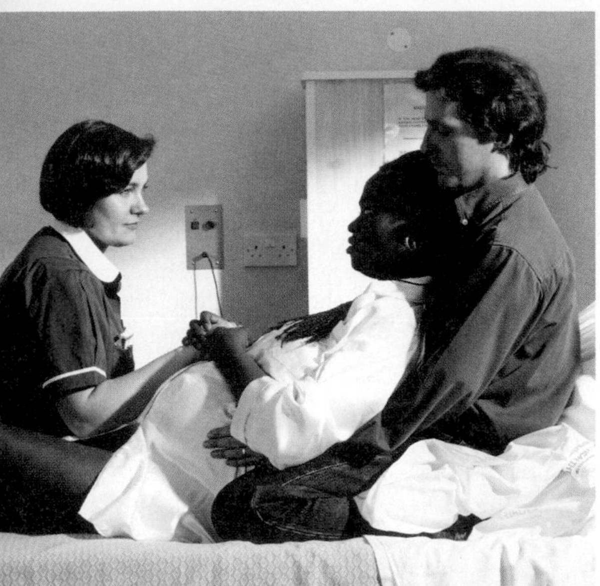

▲ Partners today can be fully involved in the births of their children. This father coached his wife as she delivered their baby.

Health Organization monitors birthing practices and outcomes around the globe and advocates that births should involve the least amount of intervention that still allows for a healthy baby and mother (Zwelling, 2008). In some impoverished nations, too many women and babies die due to infections from unsanitary conditions and unsafe birthing practices. The goal is to use modern technology and safety to save lives while still respecting the natural process of childbirth.

## Modern Birthing Practices in the United States: Choices and Alternatives

In the United States today, 99% of babies are born in hospitals (Martin et al., 2009). The medical profession recognizes the importance of personal support, pain management techniques (both drug- and non-drug-based), and the overall comfort level of the birthing environment. Modern hospitals are equipped with birthing centers where the rooms have rocking chairs and couches, and partners and family members are encouraged to stay with the laboring woman. Lighting is soft, staffers encourage relaxation techniques and moving around during labor, and even whirlpool baths are available in many places. Some women choose to spend much of their labor in a relaxing shower or whirlpool bath, and some even opt to give birth in the bath or underwater. Women can choose from many positions in giving birth, including squatting or kneeling, but most still give birth while lying in a bed. Unless there are complications, labor and birth take place in the same room. *Rooming-in* lets the newborn baby stay in the same room with the mother right from the start so parents can begin getting to know their newest family member as soon as possible. As a society we have come to realize that having a baby is, in most cases, a normal life event rather than a medical condition.

▲ Couples have a wide variety of options to choose from when deciding how to give birth to their babies. This mother has given birth underwater to relieve strain and ease the transition of the baby through the birth canal.

**prepared childbirth**
Classes or training that typically provides education about labor and delivery, selective relaxation and controlled breathing, and the help of a labor coach to help mothers with childbirth.

**Birth Attendants.** About 7% of births today are attended by *certified nurse-midwives* either instead of or in addition to the physician (Martin et al., 2009). A nurse-midwife typically provides prenatal care as well as attending the woman through childbirth. To learn more about the midwifery profession, read the Professional Perspective interview, "Career Focus: Meet a Certified Nurse-Midwife." Women increasingly use another type of birth attendant called a *doula*. Doulas provide non-medical support during labor, such as massage and positioning suggestions, and guide the parents as they adjust to caring for the newborn.

**Prepared Childbirth.** One common approach to labor and delivery is **prepared childbirth**. In prepared childbirth, women and their partners learn about the stages of labor and what to expect during childbirth. They also typically learn specific techniques they can use to cope with the pain of contractions during birth. The *Lamaze method* is one approach. According to Fernand Lamaze (1958), women have been conditioned to believe that labor contractions will be painful. Just the thought of a contraction can cause women to tense up, making the pain of real contractions more intense. To break the conditioning cycle, in Lamaze birthing classes, women learn selective relaxation of muscles and controlled breathing. During labor, the uterine muscles contract strongly—they must, in order to push the baby out. But most women instinctively tense other muscles in the body as the contractions begin. Lamaze training in selective relaxation helps women learn not to tense other muscles during uterine contractions. The tension and therefore the pain are reduced. Controlled breathing during contractions helps reduce pain by serving as a distraction from the contractions. Together, these two Lamaze techniques can greatly reduce the fatigue and pain experienced during childbirth.

# Perspective PROFESSIONAL

## CAREER FOCUS: MEET A CERTIFIED NURSE-MIDWIFE

Abbi Beuby
Kailua, HI
Certified nurse-midwife working in a private OB/GYN practice

**What does a midwife do? Why did you become one?**

Delivering babies makes up about 5% of a typical midwifery practice. I work with pregnant patients from their first visits to their last visits, and I do all the follow-up visits and postpartum checks. I am able to spend more time with them and do far more teaching than the physician has time for. I usually spend a half hour with them on the first visit and then 15 to 20 minutes each subsequent visit. I do the initial ultrasounds and the third-trimester ultrasounds to check fluid and size of the baby. The rest of my day is spent doing annual visits, contraceptive counseling, and some primary care.

I was an RN in labor and delivery for eight years, working with high- and low-risk patients, and I had my master's degree. I mostly thought this was the next step after being a nurse for so long. The most fun part of my job is when I do the first ultrasound that looks like "something" and the parents see their baby for the first time. (On the first ultrasounds the babies are usually too small to see anything.) I used to love doing deliveries, but that's very stressful. Essentially, you have two lives in your hands. It also requires a lot from your family, being on call all the time and up all night sometimes.

**Why do some parents choose midwives? How is the birthing approach different?**

Most women choose a midwife because we take a more natural approach to childbirth. Physicians see what can go wrong all the time, we see what is going right. We are taught that giving birth is a natural thing; women have been doing it forever. These days, doctors realize that women want a more natural birth and have been striving to achieve that, but this is relatively new. We spend more time with women in labor, coaching and helping them through, and in the total care, including office visits and postpartum care. We spend more time talking to them rather than at them. A midwife strives to remember not only their names but the names of their other kids, parents, spouse, what they do for a living, vacation, and so on.

**Are there situations or conditions in which you're not allowed to or would refuse to serve?**

I do not take care of women with pregnancy-induced hypertension (preeclampsia/ toxemia). I do not take care of those who go into preterm labor, before 36 weeks, and those who are severe diabetics. There are some women who come into the pregnancy with problems, and those are chosen case by case.

**What advice would you give to prospective parents who are considering the midwife option?**

Look at their credentials, meet them, and discuss their philosophy. Not all midwives believe the same thing or do things the same. Some are very natural and believe no pain medications should be administered. This works for some, but not everyone can handle that. Some do deliveries at home, others in hospitals, and everything in between, so there are lots of options. I also think it is important for the parents to meet with the midwife's backup physician. If things turn ugly, this is the person who they will need to trust to bring their child into the world.

**What training and education are usually needed to work in your field?**

There are a number of ways to become a midwife. The classic way is to become an RN first then get a master's degree. Certificate-only programs don't give a master's, but both of these routes give the title "certified nurse-midwife." Some programs don't require a nursing degree; those midwives are "certified midwives." Both of these certifications require a national board examination, and the certification must be renewed every eight years. There is the "lay" midwife, which is the "learn-on-the-job" midwife. They are illegal in most states; however, they have a big following. In the midwest, many of the Amish use them. Here in Hawaii they are considered "a-legal"—not illegal, but also not legal.

QUESTION **What do you see as the advantages to using a nurse-midwife during pregnancy and the delivery of a baby? What cautions should you keep in mind? What approach would you prefer to take?**

**THINKING CRITICALLY**
Tighten the muscles in your arm as much as you can. (But don't hurt yourself!) Now hold your muscles tight for a full 2 minutes. Describe the sensations you experienced. Now think about doing this every 3 minutes for 12 hours! How would you cope?

**THINK ABOUT ELIZABETH AND STEPHANIE . . .**
Help Stephanie think about her options during labor and delivery. What preparation does she need? How can Elizabeth help during the birth process?

The final element in prepared childbirth is the presence of a labor coach or companion. This is often the father of the baby, but sometimes mothers or other family members or partners serve as coaches. The coach attends the childbirth preparation classes with the woman, helps her practice the relaxation and breathing techniques, and is on hand and ready to offer assistance throughout labor and delivery. The coach can help the woman remember how and when to use the relaxation and controlled breathing she has learned, and can help talk her through the more difficult contractions (hence the name "coach").

Research shows that women who engage in prepared childbirth tend to experience less pain, need less pain medication, and enjoy childbirth more (Hodnett & Osborn, 1989; Moir, 1986). However, it is not clear whether these positive effects are due to increased knowledge of what to expect during birth, to relaxation techniques and controlled breathing, to the presence of a support person, or to existing differences between women who choose to participate in prepared childbirth and those who do not. Fathers and other partners report benefits as well, expressing more positive feelings about the birth and feeling greater emotional closeness to both the baby and the mother (Bondas-Salonen, 1998; Broome & Koehler, 1986; Cronenwett & Newmark, 1974; Davenport-Slack & Boylan, 1974; Dragonas, 1992; Nettlebladt, Fagerstrom, & Udderberg, 1976; Szeverenyi, Hetey, Kovacsne, & Muennich, 1995).

These approaches to birthing allow families some choice in deciding what their birth experiences will be. Simply having some degree of control over the event may help women and their partners develop a more positive attitude and feel more confident going into labor and delivery. This in turn may enable the mother to relax more; may reduce her tension, anxiety, and perhaps her pain; and may contribute to a more positive birth experience for the entire family.

**Pain Relief during Labor and Delivery.** Even with the use of the prepared childbirth techniques, most women experience significant pain and discomfort as labor contractions continue—sometimes for 12 hours or more—and the baby moves through the birth canal. Various studies have documented that anywhere from 68–95% of all hospital-based deliveries in the United States involve some type of medication for the relief of the mother's pain (Gibbs, Krischer, Peckham, Sharp, & Kirschbaum, 1986; Rosenblith & Sims-Knight, 1985).

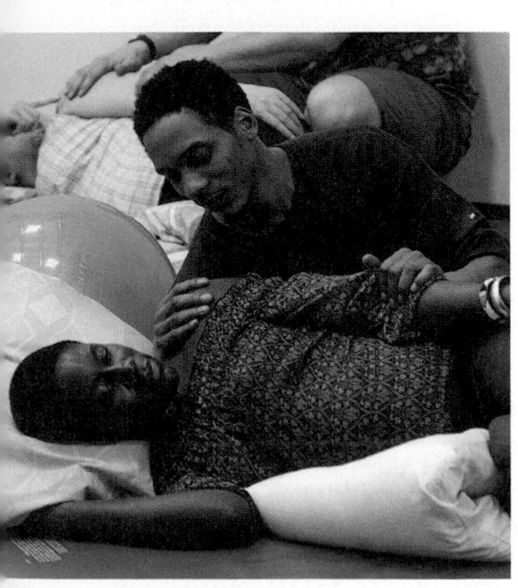

▲ Many expectant mothers attend prepared childbirth classes to learn about techniques they can use to ease the pain and anxiety of childbirth. The birthing partner learns how to be supportive and help the mother relax during labor.

During the middle part of the twentieth century, general anesthetics and major tranquilizers were used for pain relief. However, doctors later realized that many of these drugs crossed the placenta and placed the fetus at significant risk. Today there is a focus on minimizing the use of drugs during labor and delivery. Physicians administer the smallest doses possible and as late in labor as possible, and many women use prepared childbirth techniques to decrease their needs for pain medication. A popular approach is to use *epidural anesthesia*, the injection of a mixture of pain-relieving drugs into spaces along the spine of the mother. Usually physicians give epidurals low in the spine so that the drugs block sensations only from the waist down. Epidural administration seems to be a relatively safe and effective way to deliver pain medication during labor. The most commonly used combinations of medications have not shown significant detrimental effects on the newborn. One complication, however, is that a mother who uses epidural medication loses sensation in the pelvic region and therefore cannot feel the normal urge to push. Women can be instructed when to push, of course, but the use of these medications can still prolong labor. Sometimes practitioners have to use forceps to assist the baby through the birth canal.

## Birthing Complications: Something Isn't Right

The vast majority of pregnancies end happily, producing a healthy infant. Occasionally, however, birthing problems occur. Fortunately, experts in the medical community have learned a tremendous amount in the last half-century about how to deal with these complications.

### Malpresentation.

One complication during birth involves the position of the fetus. The optimal fetal position is head down. This position allows the head to move through the birth canal first and minimizes risk to both mother and baby. About 5% of the time, however, the fetus is positioned differently in the uterus, a situation called **malpresentation** (Martin et al., 2009). In a *breech position* the buttocks or the feet are lowest in the uterus. In a *transverse position* the baby lies sideways inside the uterus. Both of these positions pose serious dangers during delivery.

Physicians or midwives can usually detect malpresentations before delivery by ultrasound procedures or by physical examination. Experienced obstetricians will often try to "turn" an ill-positioned fetus, though this is not always successful. In some cases the fetus turns on its own, sometimes just as labor begins, but it is impossible to predict if and when this change will take place. Malpresentation is a complication of birth, but it need not have serious consequences if it is detected and monitored carefully. To prevent potentially serious harm to the baby and mother, many practitioners choose a planned Caesarean section (C-section) delivery for malpresented babies.

### Fetal Distress.

**Fetal distress** occurs when the fetus experiences a sudden lack of oxygen, change in heart rate, or change in respiration. Any one of these can indicate that the fetus is at risk. Practitioners can identify these conditions by using electrodes or other devices to monitor the fetus during birth. One type of distress that can have very serious consequences is *anoxia*, or deprivation of oxygen. A fetus can withstand brief oxygen deprivation with no ill effects, but more than a few minutes of decreased oxygen can lead to permanent brain damage (Stechler & Halton, 1982). Anoxia can occur for any of several reasons. These include deterioration or premature separation of the placenta, maternal fatigue or hyperventilation during labor, sudden compression of the umbilical cord during labor, or failure of the baby to begin breathing immediately after birth. The possibility of anoxia is one reason practitioners become concerned during longer labors, and it is a major reason for the increased amount of fetal monitoring done during labor. Early identification and prompt treatment of fetal distress are common reasons for C-section deliveries.

## Here's the Newborn!

The long-awaited moment has arrived, and the newest member of the family is here! Physicians and nurses immediately examine the newborn to identify any potential problems. They monitor the baby's breathing and temperature regulation, and often treat the newborn's eyes with silver nitrate; this prevents visual problems due to diseases such as gonorrhea that the baby may have contracted from the mother during birth. Nurses or other staffers also monitor the mother to ensure that she does not experience excessive blood loss or develop infections. They often encourage her to nurse the baby very soon after delivery.

Typical newborn babies' heads may seem huge in comparison to their bodies, and their skulls are usually misshapen from being squeezed during birth. Babies are born wet

**malpresentation**
Improper positioning of the fetus in the mother's uterus.

**fetal distress**
A condition that indicates that the fetus is at risk; usually includes a sudden lack of oxygen (anoxia), a change in fetal heart rate, and/or a change in fetal respiration.

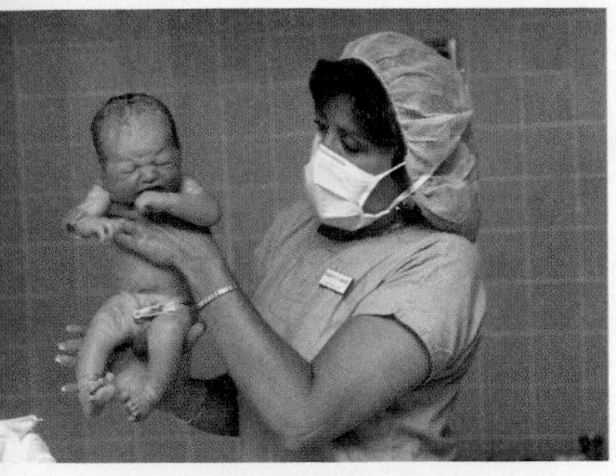

▲ Most newborns are given the Apgar test at 1 and 5 minutes after birth to identify those who need immediate medical attention. This newborn has a healthy pink color.

with amniotic fluid, and some may still have remnants of the white, cheesy coating (called *vernix caseosa*) that protected their skin before birth.

Newborns will turn their heads and eyes toward voices and will gaze into their parents' faces. Although their vision is fuzzy, they can see. They also possess several adaptive reflexes. If you stroke a newborn's cheek, the baby will turn his or her head in the direction of the touch. Touch the newborn's lips, and he or she will suck. Both of these reflexes help a newborn find the nipple and begin feeding. If you put your finger in the newborn's hand, the infant will reflexively grasp your finger and hold on tight. We will give a more complete description of newborns' reflexes and sensory abilities in the next chapter, along with a description of babies' growth and the development of their brains and nervous systems.

The first formal test administered to almost all newborn babies right after birth is the **Apgar test**, by far the most widely used newborn screening assessment (Apgar, 1953). Practitioners conduct this brief assessment 1 minute after delivery and again 5 minutes after delivery. The reason for giving the assessment twice is to make sure that changes in a newborn's condition will be noticed—because subtle changes can be overlooked in the bustle surrounding a delivery. The Apgar test gives the infant a score of 0, 1, or 2 (2 being the best) on each of five dimensions: heart rate, respiration, muscle tone, color, and reflex irritability. The newborn's total score indicates overall condition. The maximum score is 10. A score from 7 to 10 is excellent and means that the baby does not need any immediate assistance or close monitoring. Approximately 89% of all babies born in the United States have 5-minute Apgar scores in this "excellent" range (Martin et al., 2009). A score of 4 to 6 indicates some potential problems: The baby needs close monitoring and possibly some intervention. A score of 0 to 3 indicates a serious risk and calls for immediate action.

**Apgar test**
A brief assessment of the newborn conducted at 1 and 5 minutes after birth; used to identify newborns who are at risk and need medical attention.

## LET'S REVIEW . . .

1. What is the purpose of the contractions during Stage 1 of labor?
   - **a.** to open the cervix
   - **b.** to push the baby through the birth canal
   - **c.** to push the baby into a transverse position
   - **d.** to push the placenta and other membranes through the birth canal
2. In prepared childbirth, the purpose of controlled breathing and selective relaxation is:
   - **a.** to speed up the delivery of the baby.
   - **b.** to slow down the labor contractions.
   - **c.** to improve the effectiveness of pain-relieving drugs.
   - **d.** to reduce the mother's experience of pain during contractions.
3. When partners participate in prepared childbirth, their main role is to:
   - **a.** help the physician deliver the baby.
   - **b.** be available to bond with the baby after birth.
   - **c.** coach the mother through selective relaxation and controlled breathing techniques.
   - **d.** help the mother communicate with the nurses and physicians.
4. What condition exists when a fetus is deprived of oxygen during the birth process?
   - **a.** anoxia
   - **b.** hypoxia
   - **c.** breech birth
   - **d.** malpresentation
5. True or False: The correct order of events during the birth process is dilation of the cervix, delivery of the baby, and afterbirth.
6. True or False: An Apgar score of 5 indicates that the newborn is at serious risk and that immediate attention is needed to save the baby.

Answers: 1. a, 2. d, 3. c, 4. a, 5. T, 6. F

# Becoming a Family: Psychological Adjustments to Having a Newborn

For most families, having a baby is an exciting and happy event. Even so, the addition of a new person to the family requires a great deal of adjustment. Sleeping and eating patterns, family members' amount of free time, and attention to different individuals' needs and desires are all affected. Jealous siblings may even wish that the parents would "take him back"! We finish this chapter with tips and information about families who are making the transition to life with a new baby.

AS YOU STUDY THIS SECTION, ASK YOURSELF THESE QUESTIONS:

**3.12** What are some of the psychological adjustments that parents must make after the birth of a baby?

**3.13** How can parents work with older siblings to help them make the transition to being big brothers and sisters?

## The Transition to Parenthood

A successful transition to this new phase of family life involves a wide range of factors. Parents or partners who are welcoming their firstborn child must adjust their self-perceptions: They are now parents, not simply a couple. They must learn to share their time, energy, and emotion with this very needy newcomer. Success in this transition does not mean that the new parents experience no stress or problems—such a situation is probably impossible. Instead, in a successful transition the couple manages to identify and deal in positive ways with stressors and problems so that all the family members' needs are adequately met. Parents who have a supportive, positive relationship and well-developed coping skills can discuss and solve problems rather than avoid or deny them (Belsky & Isabella, 1985; Frosch, Mangelsdorf, & McHale, 1998; Heinicke & Guthrie, 1996). Families that have made a successful transition show more warmth toward one another, greater sensitivity to one another's needs, and more positive interactions with one another than families that have difficulties with the transition. The amount of time needed for this transition varies depending on the family, but it usually takes about 6 months to a year after the baby's birth.

The transition to parenthood also seems to bring to the forefront any issues that a new parent has with his or her own parents. For example, if a new parent recalls the relationship with his own parents as cold or rejecting, such feelings can cast a shadow on his attitudes toward his new role as a parent (Belsky & Isabella, 1985). The same is true of identity issues. During the period of adjustment new parents incorporate a parental dimension into their self-concepts—sometimes starting this process even before conception if the pregnancy is planned. The more secure each parent is in whom he or she is and in what is important to each person individually and to the family as a whole, the more successful the transition to parenthood seems to be (Diamond, Heinicke, & Mintz, 1996).

The transition is easier if the new parents are realistic in their expectations, both of themselves and of their baby. Having a newborn can certainly be an exciting and joyous experience, but it also involves an incredible amount of hard work and sacrifice. A new parent who believes otherwise is bound to experience frustration and disappointment. In one study conducted in Australia, first-time mothers filled out questionnaires during their pregnancies and again when their infants were four months old. During pregnancy, the women were relatively optimistic about having children and caring for them, and after their babies were born, most of them reported that they were pleasantly surprised by how well things were going and how good they felt about being mothers. Having a positive relationship with their spouse or partner was also important—women who were more optimistic while pregnant tended to have positive relationships with their husbands or

THINK ABOUT ELIZABETH AND STEPHANIE . . .

What can Stephanie do to prepare for the transition to parenthood? What can her family do to help her with this transition?

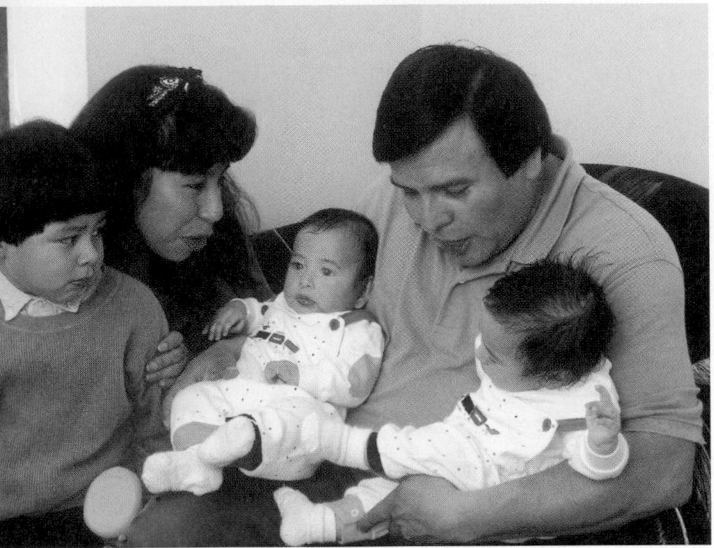

▲ The family system changes dramatically with the introduction of a new family member. Factors to consider in the adjustment include issues between the mother and father, and issues involving siblings who have a new baby (or two!) with whom to share everything. What can a family like this one do to ease their transition?

partners. On the negative side, when mothers' real experiences in caring for their babies did not live up to their positive expectations, they reported more problems with their relationships with their husbands or partners and more symptoms of depression (Harwood, McLean, & Durkin, 2007).

In addition, there are child factors. The transition to parenthood can be made more or less difficult by several aspects of both nature and nurture. For example, infants arrive with temperaments that they largely inherit through genetics, and they have biological needs all their own. Some babies have sweet, compliant, happy temperaments. Some do not. Some babies do not sleep for more than 30 minutes at a time, never nap when the parents would like, do not eat well, spit up their food three times a day, and fuss several hours every night. For the parents of more difficult babies, the transition period can be easier if the parents (either together or alone) can arrange regular breaks from infant care. It's also important for them to remember that most families do find a workable routine eventually (McHale, Kazali, & Rotman, 2004). The transition to family is influenced by the "nature" of what the baby brings to the family and the "nurture" involved in how the parents adapt—we see once again that both nature and nurture are important.

## Becoming the Big Brother or Sister

An older sibling, once the "king of the hill," can have a difficult time coming to grips with the fact that he or she is no longer the center of everyone's concerns after a new baby arrives. Increases in whininess, sleeping difficulties, withdrawal, clinginess, aggressive behaviors, and toileting problems are common in older siblings during the first few months after the birth of a new baby. Most of these changes are short-term, lasting only a few months. Some studies, however, have found correlations between the birth of a sibling and lower levels of verbal development, achievement, and socioemotional adjustment several years later. These findings seem to apply particularly to children in economically disadvantaged families (Baydar & Greek, 1997; Baydar & Hyle, 1997). Such problems are probably due more to changes in the family's overall context and interaction patterns (e.g., poorer parenting strategies, less one-on-one time with the older child, increased financial stress, decreased opportunities for skill development) than to the actual birth of the newborn. Many children adjust quite well to a newborn sibling, showing few negative and even some positive changes. For example, some siblings show greater independence in feeding and toileting habits, improved language abilities, or better peer relations.

Though the transition to being a sibling is not likely to be conflict free, parents can help children adjust. It is important for parents to recognize that becoming a sibling is a major change and can be especially tough for preschool children. It makes sense to prepare the child as much as possible. Parents can try these helpful tips:

- Talk with the child about changes, acknowledge any negative feelings, and try to provide as much one-on-one time as possible.
- Help the child develop coping skills by suggesting positive ways to gain attention.
- Make sure the child has adequate opportunities to play with friends, and encourage more parent–child interaction.
- Point out the many ways in which the older child is needed and can be helpful.
- Finally, parents should model positive coping skills and positive attitudes themselves, thereby helping the child see that the transition can lead to a new phase of family life that is as happy and secure as the phase before.

**THINKING CRITICALLY**

Think of a family you know that had a new baby recently. If this was their first child, how did the couple adjust to becoming parents? If there are older children, how did they adjust to having a new sister or brother? Do you think the adjustment is easier with the second or third child? Why or why not?

**Conclusion.** In this chapter we have gone from the conception through the birth of a baby. We have discussed the normal course of prenatal development, the stages of labor and delivery, and many of the options and choices that a pregnant woman has. We have also covered problems that can occur during the prenatal and birth periods, describing teratogens and other risk factors that can endanger the developing fetus. From these details we hope you clearly see two main points. First, pregnant women and their families can greatly increase their odds of having a healthy baby by making healthy lifestyle choices and avoiding risk factors such as teratogens and teenage pregnancy. Much is under their control! Second, although problems can occur, most of the developmental outcomes are really positive. Most babies are born healthy, robust, and ready to proceed with rapid development of their physical, cognitive, and socioemotional skills. In the next chapters we'll turn to these exciting realms of postnatal development.

## LET'S REVIEW . . .

1. With the arrival of a new baby, parents who make a successful transition to family life most likely:
   - **a.** need only a month or two to make the transition.
   - **b.** experience no real stress or problems in their lives.
   - **c.** show more warmth toward each other than other parents do.
   - **d.** show less sensitivity to each other's individual needs than other parents do.
2. In economically disadvantaged families, there is a correlation between the birth of a sibling and lower levels of cognitive and socioemotional development in the older children. Which factor below do experts believe is *least* involved in driving this correlation?
   - **a.** poor parenting strategies
   - **b.** the actual birth of the sibling
   - **c.** increased financial stress in the family
   - **d.** less parental attention given to the older child
3. True or False: When they first arrive home after birth, all babies have basically the same needs and temperaments as each other.
4. True or False: When a new baby is born, parents can help their older children adjust by giving them one-on-one attention, showing them ways they can help with the new baby, and by modeling a positive attitude and good coping skills.

Answers: 1. c, 2. b, 3. F, 4. T

## THINKING BACK TO ELIZABETH AND STEPHANIE . . .

Now that you have studied this chapter, you should be able to identify more than a dozen risk factors that Stephanie might face with her pregnancy. You should know the possible effects of these risk factors, and you should be able to give her some sound advice on how to reduce her risks.

One factor that you probably noticed is Stephanie's age. In her mid-teens, Stephanie's risk of having a low-birth-weight baby is elevated (compared to that of mothers in their 20s and 30s), but it is not as high as it would have been if she were younger than 15. Like all potential parents, Stephanie should be concerned about her lifestyle and the teratogens to which she may be exposed. Alcohol, cigarette smoke, cocaine, and other illegal drugs can all harm the developing baby. Sexually transmitted and other infectious diseases can cause the baby to be born infected or with birth defects, so Stephanie should take precautions to avoid these diseases.

Elizabeth should make sure that Stephanie receives good prenatal care. She might also go with her to childbirth classes where they can learn about the stages of labor and things they can do to control Stephanie's experience of pain during childbirth. By taking active roles in the birth, they can have a more satisfying experience and enhance their attachment to the new baby. There are things they and their other family members can do to help them make the transition into parenthood.

Like Stephanie, all potential parents should consider the risk factors they might face and take steps to reduce or avoid them. A great many pregnancy problems and birth defects are prevented when parents take the proper precautions.

# 3

## CHAPTER REVIEW . . .

**3.1 What happens during conception, and what happens next to begin the developmental process?**

Conception normally occurs when the ovum and sperm meet in the upper part of the fallopian tube. After fertilization, prenatal development proceeds with mitosis (copy division) and differentiation (in which cells take on specific structures and functions).

**3.2 What events mark the beginning and end of each prenatal stage, and what are the main milestones associated with each stage?**

The three stages are the germinal, embryonic, and fetal stages. During the germinal stage (0 to 2 weeks), the first cell divisions take place, and the embryo implants in the uterine lining. During the embryonic stage (3 to 8 weeks), the ectoderm, mesoderm, and endoderm form and later give rise to the major organs and parts of the body. The placenta, umbilical cord, and other structures form to support the developing baby. The body forms in a cephalocaudal (head-to-tail) and proximodistal (midline-to-outer) pattern. Organogenesis is complete by the end of the embryonic stage, so this stage includes most critical periods in organ and tissue formation. During the fetal stage (9 weeks to birth) the baby grows in size and the body systems gradually become more functional.

**3.3 What effects do alcohol, cocaine, and cigarette smoking have on the developing fetus?**

Several legal and illegal drugs can harm the developing fetus. Alcohol is the leading known cause of mental retardation. It can also cause growth retardation, facial deformities, and FAS. Cocaine can cause growth retardation, cognitive deficits, and defects in the brain, intestines, and genital–urinary tract. Cigarette smoking is associated with low birth weight, hyperactivity, poor school performance, and increased risk of miscarriage, stillbirth, and neonatal death.

**3.4 What happens when the mother has a contagious disease or illness during pregnancy, and what are the special risks for mothers who are younger or older when they become pregnant?**

Several sexually transmitted diseases and other infectious diseases can harm the developing baby. Sometimes the baby is born infected with a disease; in other cases the disease causes birth defects. Infants of teenage mothers are at higher risk for low birth weight and other negative outcomes, especially when the mother is younger than 15. Risks of prematurity, fetal death, and pregnancy complications increase slightly as women enter their late 30s.

**3.5 When are the critical periods during prenatal development, and why are they important?**

Critical periods are times when developing organs and tissues are most vulnerable to defects. They usually occur when the organs and tissues are first forming, differentiating from surrounding cells. Most critical periods occur during the embryonic stage (weeks 3 through 8) and are therefore complete by the time most women know that they are pregnant. Parents should avoid exposure to teratogens during pregnancy.

**3.6 What about the roles and responsibilities of men and fathers, and are teratogens matters of concern for them too?**

Babies born to teenage fathers are at increased risk for low birth weight, prematurity, and infant death. Miscarriages and birth defects are more likely to occur when fathers work in settings with toxic materials. Research with rats indicates that fathers' alcohol consumption may increase activity level in offspring and that cocaine can damage sperm cells and harm the fertilized egg.

**3.7** What are the stages of birth, and what important events take place during each stage?

In Stage 1 the cervix dilates (widens) and the fetus moves downward to the birth canal. In Stage 2 the baby moves through the birth canal and is delivered. In Stage 3 the placenta and all membranes (the afterbirth) are delivered.

**3.8** How do birthing practices differ across cultures, and what can we learn from these differences?

In some cultures, birth is viewed as a natural process and is surrounded by rich traditions and rituals. Especially in impoverished nations, many women give birth with the aid of traditional birth assistants, but they may not have access to medical clinics with physicians and modern technology. In other nations, medical assistance is heavily emphasized. From this variety, we can learn more about respecting the wishes of women and families while still providing a safe birth experience.

**3.9** What are the most common birthing practices and options practiced in the United States?

In the United States, 99% of babies are born in hospitals. Physicians provide assistance, though some mothers use the support of midwives or doulas. The continuous presence of a labor companion, often the baby's father or another partner or relative, has beneficial effects. In prepared childbirth women learn selective relaxation and controlled breathing techniques to help them relax and to reduce the pain of contractions. In the U.S., the majority of mothers use some type of pain medication during delivery. Epidural anesthesia, in which medications are injected into spaces along the spine, is increasingly common and appears to have few negative effects on the baby.

**3.10** What are some of the potential complications of the birth process, and what can be done to avoid or reduce them?

In malpresentation the fetus's position in the womb makes delivery difficult and dangerous. In fetal distress the fetus experiences a serious change in vital signs that put it at risk. Anoxia, a serious birth complication in which the fetus does not receive enough oxygen, can lead to permanent brain damage.

**3.11** What is the newborn baby like?

The newborn baby has a large head and may be covered with a cheesy coating. Newborns can see, but their vision is fuzzy. They have reflexes that help them learn to feed, and they will grasp your finger if you touch their palms. They turn their heads to the sound of voices and gaze into the faces of their parents.

**3.12** What are some of the psychological adjustments that parents must make after the birth of a baby?

Many factors are involved in the transition to parenthood. New parents need to make adjustments in their self-perceptions and identities as parents, issues may arise related to relationships with their own parents, and the needs of the new baby need to be accounted for. The transition is easier when partners show warmth and support for each other. Some newborns are easier to care for than others.

**3.13** How can parents work with older siblings to help them make the transition to being big brothers and sisters?

Parents can help older siblings adjust by providing one-on-one attention, showing them how to help with the new baby, and demonstrating a positive attitude and good family coping skills.

## REVISITING THEMES

Both *nature* and *nurture* have important influences on cell growth in the embryo. Biology and genetics govern the process of cell division and differentiation (p. 75), but teratogens and other aspects of the prenatal environment also have strong effects (pp. 81–92).

*Diversity and multiculturalism* are explored in the different patterns of behavior, such as cigarette smoking (p. 86), that can affect pregnancies, and they are also related to differences in the traditions, rituals, and practices surrounding the birth process (pp. 95–96).

*Positive development and resilience* were emphasized in many areas of this chapter. Alcohol exposure during pregnancy can be catastrophic for developing fetuses, but there is promising research that shows that counseling programs can help women stop or reduce their drinking, and this in turn can save the lives and health of many babies (p. 84). Most people are aware that the risk of Down syndrome increases as mothers get older, but most other chromosome abnormalities do not increase with mother's age and the majority of babies are born healthy even when their mothers are age 40 and older (p. 90). Although many things can go wrong during pregnancy, it is important to keep in mind that the vast majority of babies are born healthy and free from birth defects.

## KEY TERMS

afterbirth (95)
Apgar test (100)
cephalocaudal pattern (78)
Caesarean section (C-section) births (87)
conception (75)
critical periods (79)
differentiation (75)
dilation (93)
embryonic stage (78)
fetal alcohol effects (FAE) (84)
fetal alcohol syndrome (FAS) (83)
fetal distress (99)
fetal stage (79)
germinal stage (76)
implantation (78)
low birth weight (83)
malpresentation (99)
miscarriage (78)
organogenesis (79)
ovulation (75)
premature (or prematurity) (83)
prenatal development (75)
prepared childbirth (96)
preterm birth (83)
proximodistal pattern (79)
stillbirth (78)
teratogen (81)

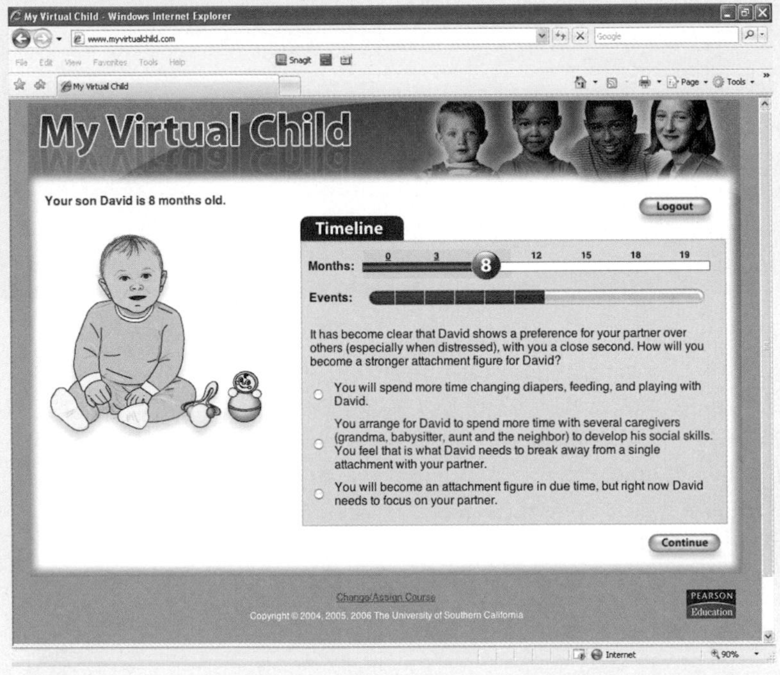


**"What decisions would you make while raising a child? What would the consequences of those decisions be?"**

Find out by accessing My Virtual Child at
**www.mydevelopmentlab.com**
and raising your own virtual child
from birth to age 18.

## Exploring Child Development

Child development is an interdisciplinary field aimed at understanding the important changes that take place as children grow through childhood and into adolescence. At the heart of child development lies the complex interplay between nature (the genes we inherit) and nurture (the environment that supports our growth and development). From Freud to Skinner and from Piaget to Bronfenbrenner, many theorists have shaped the field and advanced our understanding of development. Along the way, researchers have relied on scientific methods to catalog, describe, and explain the developmental processes that shape children's lives. The evidence they gather is very useful for parents and families who are raising children; for government officials and citizens who shape the social policies and laws that affect children and families; and for the many teachers, day care workers, counselors, psychologists, social workers, and others who are involved daily with the important task of helping children learn and grow in healthy ways. The field of child development is varied in its history, in its goals, and in its applications for children's lives, and its study continues to evolve even today.

## Heredity and the Environment

Throughout life, growth and development are shaped by the genes children inherit from their parents and by the environments and situations in which children live. Nature provides the biological blueprints, while nurture provides the physical supports and social interactions that children need to reach their developmental potentials. Unfortunately, some children inherit diseases and conditions that present serious challenges to their positive growth and may even challenge their ability to survive. In an ideal world, children inherit healthy genes and have the support and nurturing care they need to grow, learn, and thrive. Genes and the environment interact in complex ways. To some extent, genes influence the situations and contexts children choose in life, but in other ways the situations and activities children engage in influence the actions of their genes. We cannot separate the forces of nature and nurture into two distinct camps—we must instead understand how they interact so we can enhance the positive growth and development of children in our lives.

## Prenatal Development and Birth

After conception, the cells in the zygote begin dividing and forming the tissues and structures that will become the fetus and later the baby. Along the way, development can be seriously disrupted if the mother consumes alcohol, uses cocaine or other illegal drugs, smokes cigarettes, or has diseases or is otherwise exposed to unhealthy conditions and environments. The most serious risks tend to occur between the third and eighth weeks after conception, during a time when the basic organs and tissues are forming in the embryo. Hopefully all conditions are relatively healthy, and the baby can grow to a healthy size before being born. When birth arrives, the baby will make the transition from the protection of the mother's womb into the welcoming arms of a new family. The baby is ready to enter the phase of ***Infants and Toddlers: The First Years.***

### Periods of Development

**Conception to Birth**
- Prenatal Development
- Birth of the baby

**0–12 months**
- Infancy

**2–3 years**
- The toddler period

**3–7 years**
- Early childhood
- The playful years

**7–12 years**
- Middle childhood
- The school years

**12 years and Up**
- Adolescence
- The transition toward adulthood

**Watch** Visit your Multimedia Library at www.mydevelopmentlab.com to watch an interview with Jess online.

# 4 INFANTS AND TODDLERS

# Physical Development in Infants and Toddlers

### Infants at Risk: Prematurity and Infant Mortality

- What Is Prematurity?
- Infant Mortality
- Prenatal Care: Having a Healthy Baby

### Growth of the Body and Brain

- Physical Growth, Sleep Patterns, and Sudden Infant Death Syndrome
- Feeding and Nutrition
- Structure of the Brain and Nervous System
- Forming the Brain and Nervous System

### Sensory Capabilities

- Basic Components of Vision
- How Well Do Infants Hear?
- Smell and Taste

### Motor Development

- Reflexes: The Infant's First Coordinated Movements
- Voluntary Movements: The Motor Milestones
- Cultural Differences in Early Experience
- Toilet Training

Jess is six months into her first pregnancy, and she is very excited about becoming a new mother. Now that she's pregnant, Jess has modified her diet to include more foods that are organic and healthy. Jess also walks and goes to the gym two or three times per week for exercise; she wants to improve her strength and stamina to help her through labor and delivery. So far, everything is looking great during her prenatal care visits—the baby is growing well and looks healthy. Jess's mother went into premature labor when she had Jess, so Jess is a bit concerned about her baby being born prematurely.

Jess's husband Darran reads a bedtime story to her abdomen every night. "We've read studies that show that newborns recognize sounds they hear in the womb, so this is Darran's way of bonding with the baby as early as he can," Jess said. "Plus, we're hoping to establish a calming bedtime routine early—there's no way of knowing if it will work or not, but wouldn't it be great if it did!" They are decorating the baby's area with plenty of bright colors, but they also don't want it to be overwhelming for their newborn. After the baby is born, Jess and Darran plan to enroll the family in baby exercise classes for fun and extra stimulation for the baby. Jess plans to breastfeed the baby for at least six months and maybe up to two years depending on the baby's needs.

Like most new and prospective parents, Jess and Darran are eager to support their baby's development. What would you suggest? Can babies really recognize sounds they hear in the womb? Would baby exercise classes be helpful? How long should babies continue to breastfeed? After studying this chapter, you should be able to give sound advice about these and many other questions. Using at least a dozen research findings or concepts, you should be able to help Jess and Darran sort out fact from the fiction and get their baby off to a great start.

As you read this chapter, look for the "Think About Jess and Darran . . ." questions that ask you to consider what you're learning from their perspective.

Infancy is an exciting time that contains an impressive run of *firsts:* the first time parents see their baby; the first cuddles, first feeding, and first smiles; and, by the end of the first year, the first steps and the first spoken words. Infants begin life completely helpless and dependent on other people for care. By their second birthday, they are walking, running, climbing, and talking and have developed a sense of autonomy and independence from their parents and caregivers. Most babies end their toddler years with a solid foundation for moving into early childhood. Given the tremendous pace of change during the infant and toddler years, you can understand Jess and Darran's desire to get their baby off to the best start. In this chapter, we focus on physical development during the first 2 years after birth.

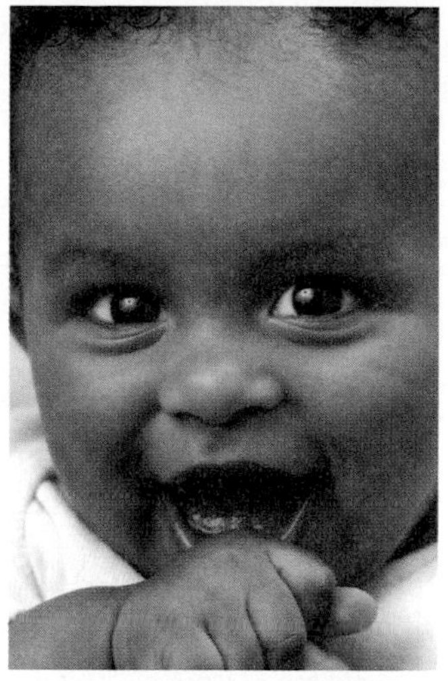

◀ This baby seems healthy, happy, and off to a great start in life. What major developmental milestones can infants be expected to pass through before age 2?

# Infants at Risk: Prematurity and Infant Mortality

Take a look at the premature infant in Figure 4.1. Prematurity is one of the biggest threats faced by infants in our country. In the United States, fewer than 1% of infants are born earlier than 28 weeks of gestation, but these babies account for nearly half of all infant deaths (Mathews & MacDorman, 2006). Although the United States ranks first in the world in health technology, this country ranks seventeenth among industrialized countries in the rate of low-birth-weight births, often associated with preterm birth (Children's Defense Fund, 2001), and the rates of both preterm and low-birth-weight births are increasing. The incidence of preterm birth rose from 9% in 1981 to 12% in 2004. The rate of low-birth-weight births now stands at 8%, the highest level since 1969. The statistics for some groups within the U.S. population are even more grim. For example, African American women have a low-birth-weight rate of 14% while the rate is about 6% for Caucasian and Hispanic women (Martin, Hamilton, Sutton, Ventura, Menacker, & Kirmeyer, 2006).

Clearly, there is reason for concern. But what do we know about the causes and effects of preterm birth and low birth weight? More important, what have we learned about how to prevent these serious problems?

▼ FIGURE 4.1
**Premature Infant**
This baby was born at approximately 27 weeks' gestation and weighs only 2 pounds. Usually, babies born at this age and size experience limbs that jerk and twitch, have erratic breathing, and shrink from human touch. Their tiny bodies can't properly regulate temperature, and their sucking reflex isn't strong enough for breastfeeding or bottle feeding.

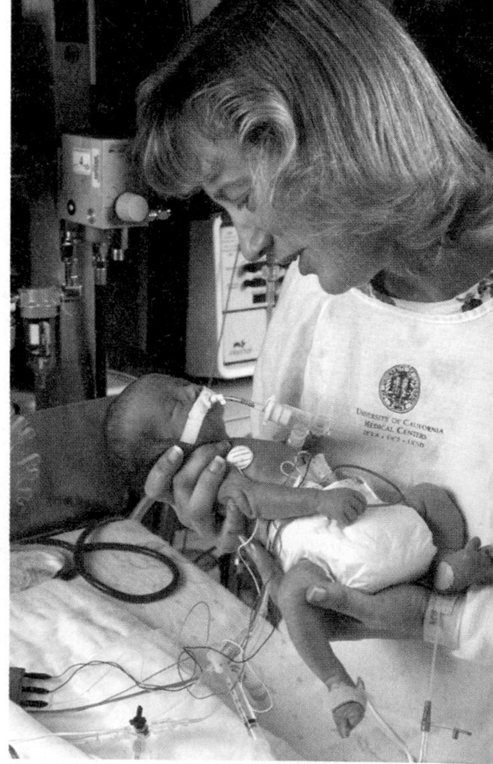

AS YOU STUDY THIS SECTION, ASK YOURSELF THESE QUESTIONS:

**4.1** What are the different ways that prematurity is defined, and what are the developmental risks for each category of prematurity?

**4.2** What are the infant mortality rates in the United States, and why are they so high?

**4.3** How can prenatal care address the issues of prematurity and infant mortality?

## What Is Prematurity?

*Prematurity* is defined in several ways. A full-term pregnancy is about 38 to 40 weeks long, and the average weight for full-term newborns is 7½ pounds. Birth within two weeks of the expected due date (2 weeks early or late) is considered full-term. As we defined in Chapter 3, *preterm birth* is birth before 37 weeks' gestation, or more than 3 weeks before the expected due date. A baby who is born weighing less than 5½ pounds is considered to have a *low birth weight*. Newborns who weigh less than 3½ pounds are classified as being at **very low birth weight** and are at even greater risk for serious problems. Infants

**very low birth weight**
Weight less than 3½ pounds at birth (4 pounds lighter than average); indicates greater potential for health risks.

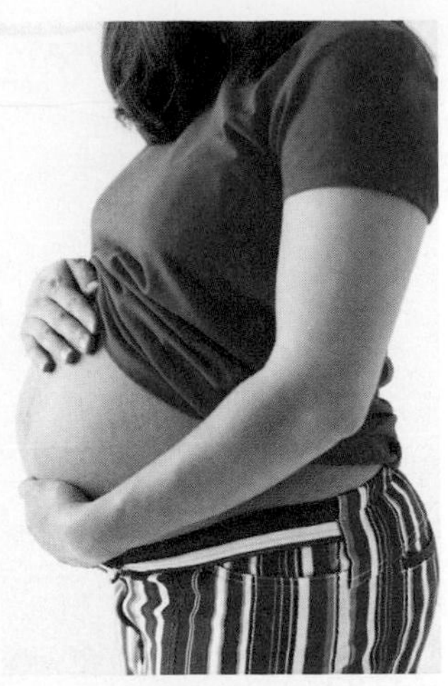

▲ This woman is about 36 weeks along in her pregnancy. If her baby were born now, it would be preterm. Babies need their last few weeks in the womb to gain more size and strength before birth.

THINKING CRITICALLY

Do you know anyone who was or who had a preterm or low-birth-weight baby? What were the suspected causes? What have the long-term effects been?

who are **small for gestational age (SGA)** are those who are below the 10th percentile of birth weight for their gestational age (i.e., among the lightest 10% of infants born at a particular number of weeks since conception).

Why bother to distinguish among all these classifications? The reason is that their outcomes differ. Although preterm birth is certainly not good, many preterm infants are at an appropriate level of development and weight, given their length of gestation. As long as birth weight is not too low and is appropriate for the gestational age—and provided that the infant receives appropriate treatment—many preterm infants are resilient and go on to develop normally. SGA newborns, however, are particularly worrisome. Something has kept them from growing as well as they should have, so they are born smaller than would be expected given their length of gestation. It is difficult to know what has gone wrong in these cases, but poor prenatal nutrition of the fetus is a likely factor. Perhaps the maternal diet was poor, there were problems with the placenta, or problems in the fetus prevented it from being able to utilize nutrients. As you read in Chapter 3, teratogens such as alcohol and cocaine also retard fetal growth, causing infants to be born small for their gestational age. SGA babies fare much worse than other preterm infants. They show greater rates of infection, brain damage, and death during their first year and are more likely to show long-term problems in academic achievement (Copper et al., 1993; Korkman, Liikanen, & Fellman, 1996).

In about half of the cases of preterm birth and low birth weight, the causes are not known. Research has identified numerous risk factors, however. Table 4.1 lists some of these along with the most common effects of prematurity.

If you look closely at the list in Table 4.1, one of the most striking things you should note is that several of the risk factors are controllable. This is good news: It means that it might be possible to reduce the risk of serious birth complications to some extent. To find

**TABLE 4.1**
**Risk Factors and Effects of Premature Births**

| RISK FACTORS WITH PREMATURE BIRTH | EFFECTS OF PREMATURE BIRTHS |
|---|---|
| Lack of prenatal care | Increased risk of infant mortality |
| Vaginal infection | Increased risk of difficulties in:<br>• respiration (e.g., respiratory distress syndrome, apnea, anoxia)<br>• circulation, leading to brain hemorrhage<br>• feeding, due to poor sucking ability<br>• social interactions (difficult to rouse, difficult to calm, ambiguous interpersonal signals)<br>• regulating sleep, awake, alert cycles |
| Short interval between birth and subsequent pregnancy (less than 3 months) | |
| Malnutrition | |
| Cigarette smoking | |
| Drug use (e.g., alcohol, cocaine) | |
| Maternal age (especially younger than age 15) | Increased longer-term risk of:<br>• cerebral palsy<br>• lowered academic achievement, lowered IQ<br>• attentional problems<br>• poor language development<br>• motor and perceptual difficulties<br>• specific learning disabilities |
| Marital status (unmarried) | |
| Maternal illness affecting blood vessels (e.g., diabetes, high blood pressure) | |
| Membership in certain ethnic groups | |
| Genetic background and family history | |
| Personal history of spontaneous abortion or preterm labor | |
| Multiple gestations (i.e., twins, triplets, etc.) | |

## Perspective PERSONAL MEET THE PARENTS OF A VERY PREMATURE BABY

Kim Powell and Larry Sikkink
Decorah, IA
*Parents of Senia, born at 28 weeks' gestation weighing 1 pound, 15 ounces*

**When did you learn that your baby would be premature? What were your first thoughts? Do you know what caused the prematurity?**

*Kim:* I experienced a healthy pregnancy up to my sixth month. Then, at a prenatal exam, the doctor found I had high blood pressure as well as protein in my urine. The next day I was admitted to a hospital with a neonatal intensive care unit (NICU). At 28 weeks' gestation, on the way to my first ultrasound, I began feeling light-headed and felt a sudden pain in my upper abdomen. I began throwing up and had a severe headache. The doctor said I had to have an emergency Caesarean section if my baby and I were to live. I had HELLP syndrome (hemolysis, elevated liver enzymes, low blood platelets). There is no known cause or predictor for HELLP syndrome, and some mothers and babies die from the complications. I knew my baby would be born prematurely, but I was too sick to realize what that meant. Immediately after her birth, Senia was whisked away to the NICU, intubated, placed on a warming table, and connected to an IV feeding tube and breathing and heart monitors. My husband was still on the 90-minute drive from our home. Senia's left lung collapsed after birth, requiring three days of lung massage therapy. At 2 weeks she was moved to an incubator, where she stayed for 4 weeks.

*Larry:* Senia had been delivered about 15 minutes before my arrival. The NICU team was attending to her, and I was told I would be allowed to see her in about 30 minutes. I was shocked. How could I be the father of a baby girl already? An NICU doctor assured me that given time, care, and love, our daughter's chances for survival were very good.

**Has your baby needed or used any special services? What is your baby like today?**

*Kim:* At 4 pounds and 1 ounce, after seven weeks in the NICU, Senia came home on an apnea and bradycardia monitor. For 2½ months, Senia had episodes in which her breathing would stop and her heart rate would lower. She also had several bouts of pneumonia in her first year. It took 2 years for Senia to perform like others her age, but she is now all caught up. She is tall for her age and is at the 50th percentile in weight. Cognitively, she tests above age level. Senia started kindergarten at age 5 and loves writing, books, music, and dancing.

**What advice do you have for other parents who may have a premature or low-birth-weight baby?**

*Kim:* Educate yourself and read about other premature babies. Kim Wilson and I wrote *Living Miracles: Stories of Hope from Parents of Premature Babies* (Griffin Trade Paperbacks) so parents could share their situation. Above all else, though having a preemie is very stressful, parents should try to focus on the baby and enjoy every minute of watching the baby develop.

QUESTION **What can parents do to reduce their risk of having a premature baby? Which risk factors can they control in their lives?**

out what it is like to have a baby who is very premature, read the Personal Perspective box entitled "Meet the Parents of a Very Premature Baby."

### Infant Mortality

The term **infant mortality** refers to deaths that occur before the age of 1 year. In spite of the medical community's best efforts, many infants die each year. As you can see in Figure 4.2, the United States does not rank well when compared to other industrialized countries with respect to infant mortality, even with our sophisticated medical technology. Again, African American infants fare even worse than infants in the rest of the U.S. population. The African American infant mortality rate in 2003 was 13, almost twice the overall rate of 7 deaths per 1,000 live births. The rate for Caucasians and Hispanics was about 5.7 deaths per 1,000 live births (Mathews & MacDorman, 2006). Infant mortality is related to poor or absent prenatal care, teenage pregnancy, poor nutrition, risky health behaviors during pregnancy, and higher rates of prematurity and low-birth-weight births.

THINK ABOUT JESS AND DARRAN . . .

Describe three or four things that Jess can do during her pregnancy to reduce her risk of having a premature baby.

**small for gestational age (SGA)**
Born below the 10th percentile of birth weight for gestational age; indicates serious health risks.

**infant mortality**
Deaths that occur between birth and 1 year of age.

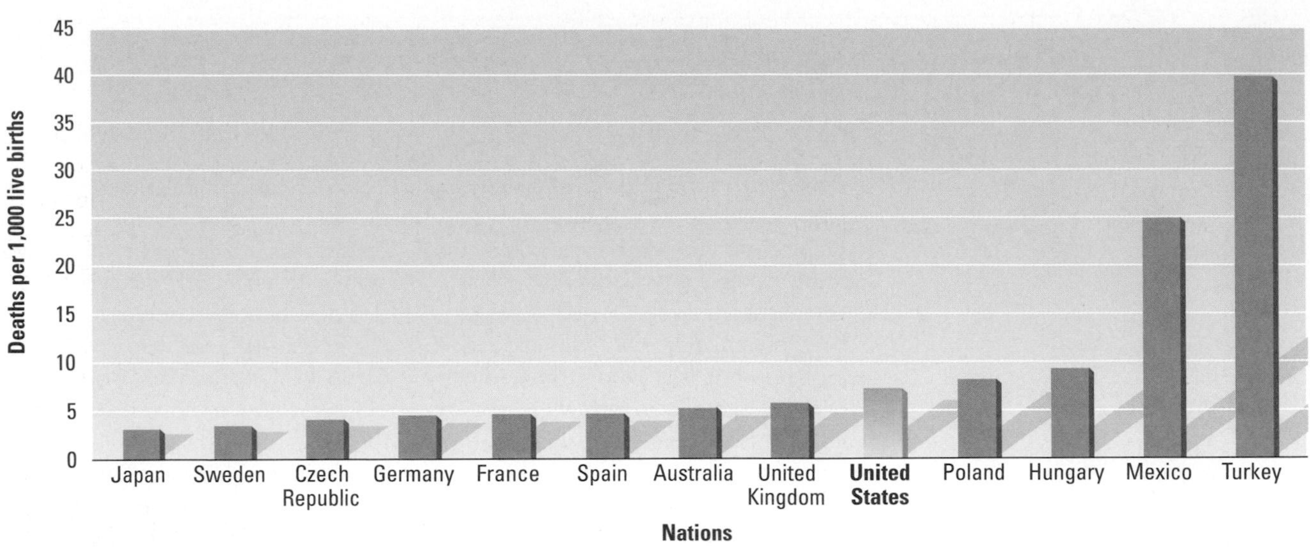


▲ FIGURE 4.2
**Infant Mortality**
This graph shows infant mortality rates for selected nations. All data are for the year 2004 except the data for the United States, for which the latest available data were for 2003. Data for the U.S. from Mathews & MacDorman (2006); all other nations from Organisation for Economic Co-operation and Development (2006).

Experts agree that the steps that would reduce rates of prematurity and low birth weight would also reduce the rates of infant mortality. **Listen** on **mydevelopmentlab**

**Listen**: Why are the infant mortality rates in the U.S. so high? (Author Podcast) www.mydevelopmentlab.com

## Prenatal Care: Having a Healthy Baby

Although it is not possible to prevent all of the problems that newborns face, one thing is for certain: Access to and appropriate use of good-quality prenatal care results in healthier babies. In prenatal visits, practitioners can effectively identify and address many risk factors for problems during pregnancy. Another important component of prenatal care is education. Education can increase the mother's knowledge of how the baby is developing, what she and her partner can do to improve their odds of having a healthy baby, and what

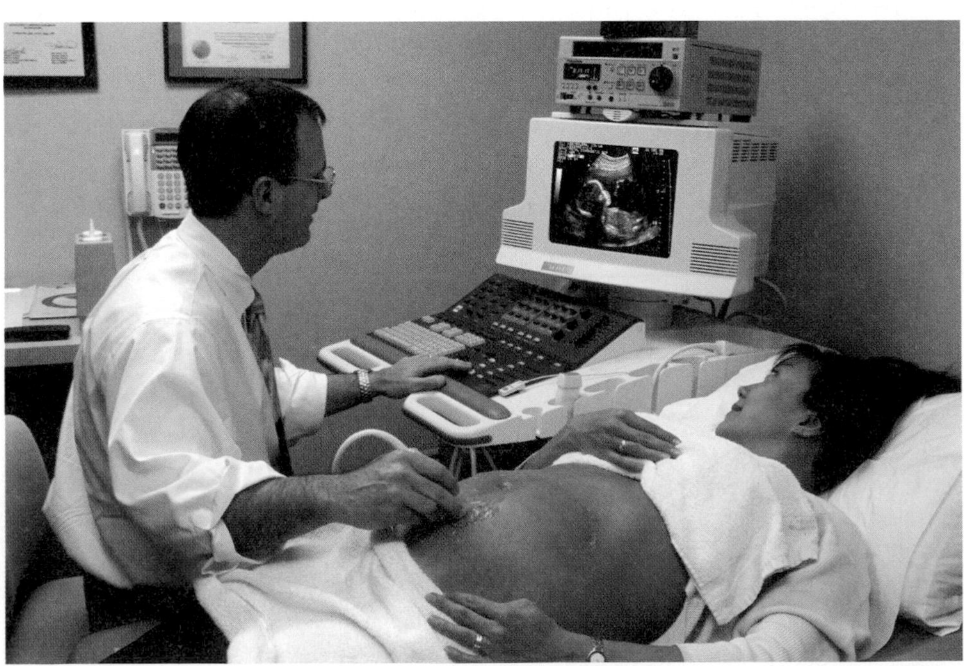

Prenatal care is important for all pregnant mothers and their babies. Physicians can monitor the mother's health and the baby's growth and development, and they can help the mother understand how to avoid risks and maintain a healthy pregnancy.

options she has for labor and delivery. Participation in prepared childbirth classes and the supportive involvement of the woman's partner and family can enhance this education.

We have some good news to report on this point: More women are now getting prenatal care. Overall, in 2005, 84% of pregnant women received prenatal care, and this was up from 76% in 1990. The percentage of Hispanic and African American women who received care increased from about 60% in 1990 to 77% in 2005 (National Center for Health Statistics, 2009). Although there is a way to go before all women have early prenatal care, rates of care are clearly improving.

THINK ABOUT JESS AND DARRAN . . .

How can Jess benefit by receiving good prenatal care? List several specific risks that might be avoided or reduced if she has good care.

LET'S REVIEW . . .

1. Preterm births are defined as all births that occur before ______ weeks of gestation.
   a. 40
   b. 38
   c. 37
   d. 35
2. Very low-birth-weight babies are those who are born weighing less than:
   a. 2 pounds.
   b. 3½ pounds.
   c. 5½ pounds.
   d. 7½ pounds.
3. Generally, the infants who are at the greatest risk are those who are born:
   a. preterm.
   b. low in birth weight.
   c. small for their gestational age.
   d. before 36 weeks of gestation and under 5 pounds.
4. Which of the following is NOT a risk factor related to infant mortality?
   a. poor prenatal care
   b. poor nutrition
   c. premature and low-birth-weight births
   d. births that occur between 38 and 40 weeks of gestation
5. True or False: In the United States, there are no ethnic differences in the rates of prematurity or infant mortality.
6. True or False: With good prenatal care, it is possible to control or avoid some of the risk factors associated with infant mortality and preterm and low-birth-weight births.

Answers: 1. c, 2. b, 3. c, 4. d, 5. F, 6. T

# Growth of the Body and Brain

Whether they are full-term and healthy or premature and small, most infants grow very rapidly during the first year. In this section, we focus on physical growth.

AS YOU STUDY THIS SECTION, ASK YOURSELF THESE QUESTIONS:

- **4.4** What are the main patterns of growth and sleep, and what do researchers know about Sudden Infant Death Syndrome?
- **4.5** What are the benefits of breastfeeding, and how long should children continue to breastfeed?
- **4.6** What are the main parts of the brain, and what are their basic functions?
- **4.7** What major patterns are seen in the formation of the brain and nervous system?

## Physical Growth, Sleep Patterns, and Sudden Infant Death Syndrome

**Physical growth.** At birth, the average newborn weighs 7½ pounds. In Figure 4.3 (on p. 114) you can see that infants double their birth weight by the time they are 5 months old. Changes in length are even more rapid. On average, newborns measure just under

FIGURE 4.3 ▶
**Weight and Length Curves for Boys and Girls, Ages Birth to 36 Months**
(National Center for Health Statistics, 2000.)

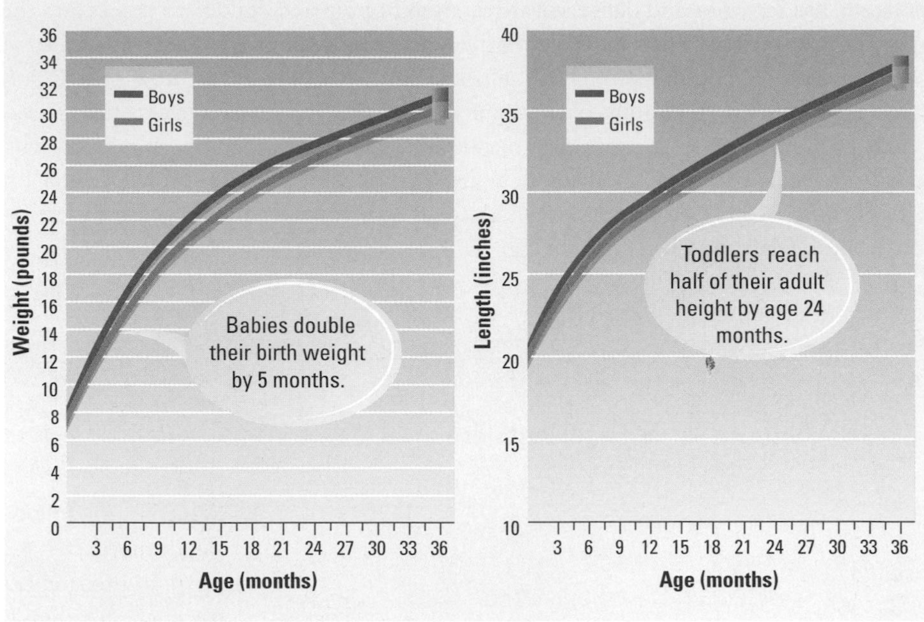


20 inches in length and add another 50 percent in their first year. By 2 years of age, children have already attained about half of their adult height.

**Sleep Patterns.** In Figure 4.4 you can see that the total amount of time spent asleep tends to decrease with age. During the first month, newborns spend nearly two-thirds of their time asleep. They usually sleep for three or four hours at a time, with only brief periods of being awake, and this cycle continues all through the day and night (Burnham, Goodlin-Jones, Gaylor, & Anders, 2002). By six weeks, infants begin to adjust their patterns by staying awake for longer stretches during the day and sleeping more at night—and this is an early indication that cues in the environment (*nurture*) are exerting an influence on the infant's need for sleep (*nature*). During the first few months,

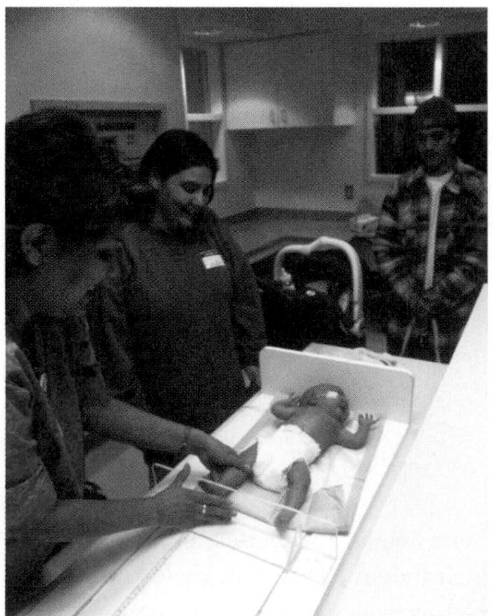

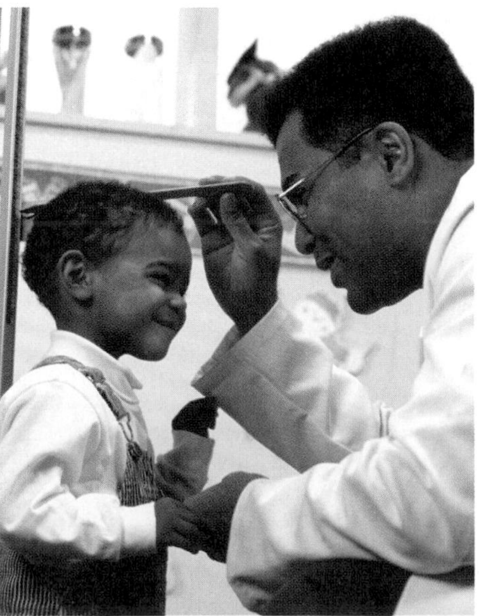

Newborn babies average about 20 inches in length and weigh an average of 7½ pounds. Children reach half of their adult height by the time they are 2 years old.

infants usually get drowsy or fall asleep during or right after feeding, and they often wake up hungry and crying. Parents often struggle with their own nature/nurture issues as they need to wake frequently through the night to feed the baby. Married couples report more strain in their marriages when their infants are waking up and crying more at night, though the strain is reduced when fathers report that they are also providing care and support during nighttime feedings (Meijer & van den Wittenboer, 2007). Although there are great differences among infants, most are sleeping through the night by six months, and 70% are doing so by nine months (National Sleep Foundation, 2009). By two years of age, most toddlers are sleeping through the night and are still taking at least one nap during the day. Toddlers are still sleeping a total of 12 to 14 hours per day, and by this age they have spent more of their life asleep than awake (National Sleep Foundation, 2009).

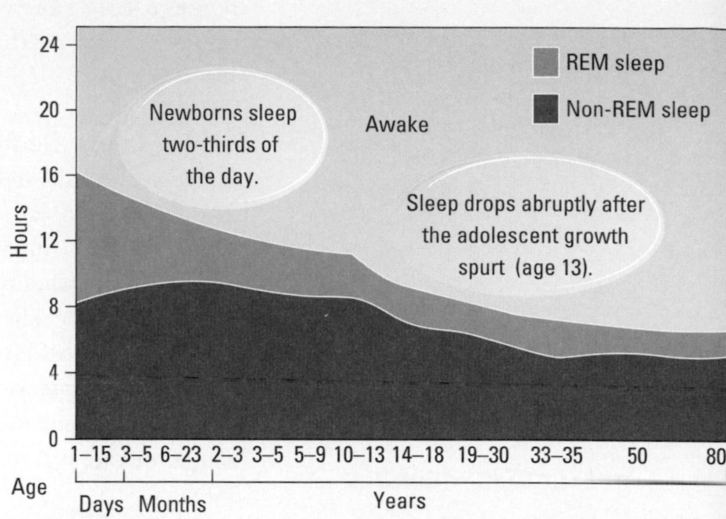


▲ FIGURE 4.4
**Hours of Sleep from Birth through Adulthood**
Total amount of sleep falls as we age. Notice the greater proportion of REM sleep for infants compared to older children and adults. (Adapted from Roffward, Muzio, & Dement, 1966.)

Two types of sleep are shown in Figure 4.4. *REM sleep* (or rapid eye movement sleep) is the phase of sleep where the brain is very active, the eyes are closed but darting around under the eyelids (hence the name "rapid eye movement"), the body sometimes twitches, and breathing is irregular. REM sleep is associated with dreaming and is also important for replenishing mental alertness. As you can see in the figure, infants spend a large portion of time in REM sleep, but this type of sleep diminishes over time. During *non-REM sleep*, the brain and body are less active, and breathing is more regular and rhythmic. This phase of sleep is also called *quiet sleep*, and it's important for restoring energy and stimulating growth. Growth hormones are secreted mostly during quiet periods of sleep. In the figure you can see that the amount of quiet sleep remains high throughout the period of rapid growth, from birth through age 13.

In many countries, it is very common for infants and young children to sleep with one or both parents, a practice called **co-sleeping**. In Sweden, for example, children typically sleep with their parents up to the age when they begin school, and some children continue even longer (Welles-Nystrom, 2005). In Mayan communities of Guatemala, families tend to sleep together, and they believe that making an infant or child sleep alone is terrible and akin to child neglect (Morelli, Rogoff, Oppenheim, & Goldsmith, 1992). Co-sleeping is also common in many Asian countries including China, Japan, Korea, and Thailand (Anuntaseree, Mo-suwan, Vasiknanonte, Kuasirikul, Ma-a-lee, & Choprapawon, 2008; McKenna, Ball, & Gettler, 2007). In many cultures, co-sleeping corresponds to cultural values of family and community.

▲ Co-sleeping is a common practice in many cultures. How does this practice reflect the values of different cultures around the world?

In the United States and many other Western nations, emphasis is placed on helping infants gain independence, and co-sleeping is usually avoided. Although infants might sleep in the same room as their parents, they most often sleep in a separate crib. American families tend to move their children into their own bedrooms, or out of the parents' room, as soon as the infant can sleep through the night. There are variations, however. Compared to other families, co-sleeping tends to occur more often in families with parents who are African American, Hispanic, or Asian American, among Whites in rural Appalachia, and in families where the mothers are breastfeeding younger infants (McKenna, Ball, & Gettler, 2007). Although co-sleeping often reflects a sense of family togetherness, it can also reflect the economic conditions and other factors in the family. Lower-income families, larger families, and families in smaller homes, for example, may engage in co-sleeping out of necessity, and parents may also

**co-sleeping**
Practice where infants and young children sleep with one or both parents.

choose to sleep more with infants who are difficult to sooth or have troubles regulating their own sleep rhythms (Hauk, Signore, Fein, & Raju, 2008; Taylor, Donovan, & Leavitt, 2008).

**Sudden Infant Death Syndrome.** **Sudden Infant Death Syndrome (SIDS)** is defined as the sudden death of an infant under one year of age in which the death cannot be explained after an autopsy, review of medical history, and thorough investigation of the death scene (American Academy of Pediatrics, 2005a). By definition, the cause of death is not known, but research shows that the risk of SIDS increases when infants sleep on their bellies or sides, sleep on a soft surface or with soft objects in their bed, or when they are overheated. SIDS rates increase when mothers are younger (under 20), have late or no prenatal care, or smoke cigarettes during pregnancy. Infants who are preterm or low in birth weight are at greater risk, and the SIDS rates are higher for male infants and infants who are African American or Native American (American Academy of Pediatrics, 2005a).

In 1992, the American Academy of Pediatrics recommended that all infants be positioned on their backs for sleep. The "Back to Sleep" campaign has resulted in a remarkable 50% reduction in the incidence of SIDS deaths in the U.S. and many other nations, but SIDS is still the leading cause of death for infants between one month and one year of age. Approximately one out of every 2,000 infants dies from SIDS, with most SIDS deaths occurring between 1 and 3 months of age (American Academy of Pediatrics, 2005a).

A major controversy in this area is that some studies show that SIDS rates increase when infants co-sleep, but other studies do not. Because co-sleeping occurs more frequently in ethnic minority and lower-income families, it is difficult to determine if the SIDS increase is due to co-sleeping itself or to other factors (such as poor prenatal care) associated with these families. Some experts argue that co-sleeping should actually reduce the rate of SIDS because infants are more likely to be breastfed when they sleep with their mothers, and breastfeeding is linked to lower rates of SIDS. Co-sleeping can facilitate parent–infant attachments, and it might also help parents notice when their infants stop breathing during a near-SIDS incident (McKenna, Ball, & Gettler, 2007). Other experts, however, are concerned that infants might be suffocated or injured accidentally when they sleep with their parents or siblings and this, combined with the possible risk of SIDS, has led the American Academy of Pediatrics to suggest that infants should sleep on their backs and in their own crib placed near to the parents (American Academy of Pediatrics, 2005a).

▲ Breast milk has many benefits for young infants.

**Sudden Infant Death Syndrome (SIDS)**
Sudden death of an infant before 1 year of age that is not explained by autopsy, medical history, or investigation of the scene of death.

**colostrum**
A thick, yellowish substance in breast milk containing important antibodies.

## Feeding and Nutrition

Nearly all health officials agree that human breast milk provides the best form of nutrition for most infants. Breast milk provides all of the nutrients, calories, protein, and fat that young infants need and in a balance that is easy for new babies to digest. During the first few days of breastfeeding, the mother's milk contains a high concentration of **colostrum**, a thick, yellowish substance that contains important antibodies that are passed to the newborn. These antibodies offer infants protection against a variety of infections, viruses, and illnesses. After about three days, mothers produce a higher volume of milk; although it now contains less colostrum, it still provides important antibodies that protect the growing infant.

Babies who are breastfed are at lower risk for a variety of conditions including diarrhea, respiratory infections, ear infections, diabetes, lymphoma, and SIDS (American Academy of Pediatrics, 2005b). Nature has provided an optimal form of nutrition for feeding and nurturing infants. There are also important health benefits for the mother: faster recovery of the uterus, less blood loss after delivery, earlier return to prepregnancy

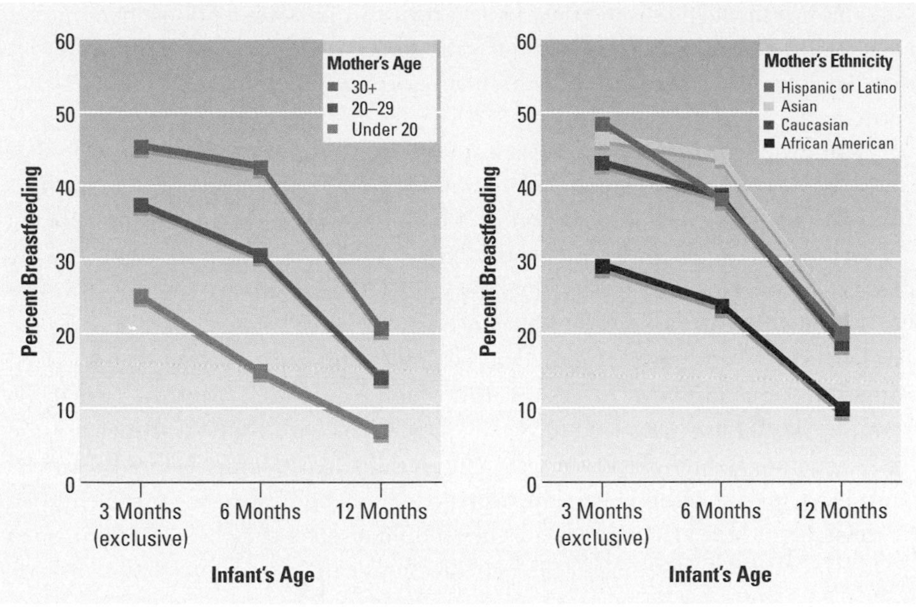


◀ FIGURE 4.5
**Breastfeeding Rates by Age and by Ethnicity**
Percent of U.S. infants being breastfed at 3, 6, and 12 months of age. At 3 months, "exclusive breastfeeding" means that the infant receives breast milk alone (no supplements). At 6 and 12 months, percentages are for infants receiving breast milk as part of their nutrition. (National Center for Chronic Disease Prevention and Health Promotion, 2004.)

weight, reduced risks of ovarian and breast cancers, and a delay in the next ovulation (which can help to increase the spacing to the next pregnancy). The American Academy of Pediatrics noted that by improving the health of both infants and mothers, breastfeeding can reduce health care costs and the number of days parents miss from work to care for themselves or sick infants. Watch on **mydevelopmentlab**

Watch a video about Breastfeeding.
www.mydevelopmentlab.com

The academy also concluded that

- breastfeeding should begin as soon as possible after birth, preferably within the first hour;
- during the first six months after birth, breast milk is usually all that is needed to provide nutrition for optimal growth and development for the infant (water, juice, and other supplements are not necessary these first six months for most infants who are breastfed);
- from 6 to 12 months of age, iron-rich solid foods should be introduced gradually;
- breastfeeding should continue at least until the infant is 12 months of age and as long thereafter as the infant and mother desire.

Infants weaned before 12 months of age should receive iron-enriched infant formula (not cow's milk). Breastfeeding might not be convenient when mothers are working or are away from their newborns for long periods during the day. In many of these situations, mothers can still pump their breast milk and store it so it can be given to infants by bottle.

▲ Breastfeeding rates are low in many of the poorer nations of the world. When mothers use infant formulas, a challenge is to find sanitary water to mix with the formula. Mothers sometimes dilute the formula to try to stretch their supply, but this deprives infants of the calories, nutrients, and other nutritional elements they need.

How many infants are breastfed? Results from a U.S. survey are presented in Figure 4.5. As you can see, fewer than half are being breastfed at 3 months, and well less than one-quarter at 12 months. Younger mothers and mothers who are African American are less likely to breastfeed their infants. Although this is not shown in the figure, the survey also found that mothers are more likely to breastfeed when they are married, have more education, or have higher family incomes. They are also more likely to breastfeed when their choice is supported by their husbands or partners. In one study, mothers' choices to breastfeed were related more strongly to what their partners

**THINKING CRITICALLY**

Think about any families you know that have young babies. Are they feeding breast milk to their babies, or are they using infant formulas? What are the main factors that you think led to their choice?

**THINK ABOUT JESS AND DARRAN . . .**

What would you recommend to Jess about breastfeeding her baby? What would you need to know about her situation to make a good recommendation?

thought they should do than to the mothers' own attitudes or intentions about breastfeeding (Rempel & Rempel, 2004). Although the choice is ultimately the mothers', it is clear that partners play an important role in supporting women's choices to breastfeed or bottle-feed.

Worldwide, there is a push to increase the rates of breastfeeding, especially in poor countries, where many infants are malnourished. In the poorer areas of central Africa, for example, only about 5% of infants under 4 months of age are exclusively breastfed, while in the more affluent countries of Egypt and Saudi Arabia, the rate is just over 60% (World Health Organization, 2003).

Although breast milk is the healthy choice for most infants, there are a few situations in which mothers are advised to use infant formulas instead of breastfeeding. Some infectious diseases can be spread through breast milk. Mothers with HIV, for example, should not breastfeed their babies. Mothers with conditions such as tuberculosis, hepatitis B, and chickenpox should consult their doctors before breastfeeding. Mothers who are receiving medications for high blood pressure, cancer, anxiety, depression, and even migraine headaches should also consult their physicians because harmful products from some of these medications can be passed to the infant through breast milk. In other cases, infants who inherit certain metabolic disorders (e.g., phenylketonuria or galactosemia) might require special formulas designed to help them avoid problems with their disorders.

Except for conditions such as those that we just described, infants should receive only breast milk for the first four to six months. After that, baby cereals, mild-flavored vegetables, and fruits are good choices for first solid foods that can be added to the diet. Avoid foods that are high in sugar, fat, or salt. Foods should be soft or diced small enough to avoid choking. Toward the end of the first year, infants enjoy finger foods such as cheese, plain crackers, cooked vegetables, and sliced fruits. By 2 years of age, most toddlers are having meals at the table, eating most of the same foods as the rest of the family. Although the toddlers might still be breastfeeding, breast milk is no longer their main source of calories and nutrition.

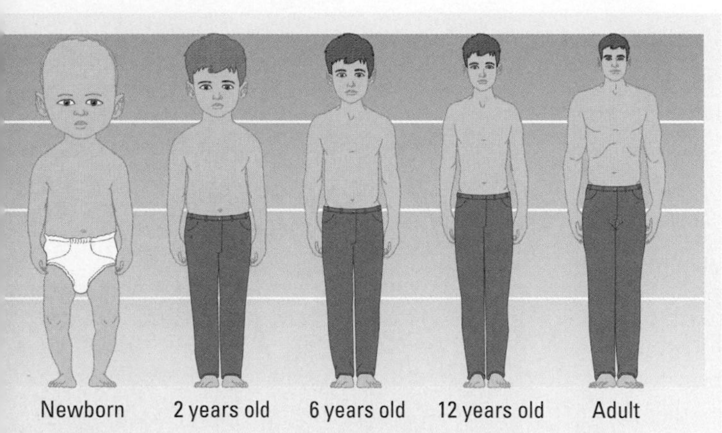
Newborn
2 years old
6 years old
12 years old
Adult
Newborn's head is about one-fourth of the total body length.
Adult's head is about one-eighth of the total body length.

▲ FIGURE 4.6
**Changing Head/Body Proportions**
The newborn's head is relatively large in proportion to the rest of the body. The cephalocaudal pattern of development is apparent here: the head and brain grow early, and the lower body grows more rapidly later. This gives the brain a head start in forming the complicated circuits that will govern movements, thoughts, and emotions.

## Structure of the Brain and Nervous System

The brain and nervous system are the structures that give rise to all of our thoughts, emotions, and behaviors. The most complicated organ in the body, the brain is one of the first structures to form when tissue differentiation begins in the embryo, and at birth, the brain and head are already more than half their adult sizes. In Figure 4.6, you can see that the head represents one fourth of the newborn's total length but only one eighth of the adult's height. The cephalocaudal (head-to-tail) pattern is evident here. At birth, the brain and head region are much further along in growth and development than the trunk and legs are.

The study of how the brain grows and forms the intricate web of connections necessary to code our thoughts, memories, and motor actions is one of the most fascinating areas of science today. How does the brain grow and form internal connections? If the proper experiences are not available for infants, will their brains develop normally? In this section, we outline the major structures in the brain and describe how the brain forms in early development.

The major structures in the human brain are shown in Figure 4.7. The brain and the spinal cord together form the central nervous system. The *spinal cord* is the body's "information superhighway"—it allows vast amounts of information to be exchanged

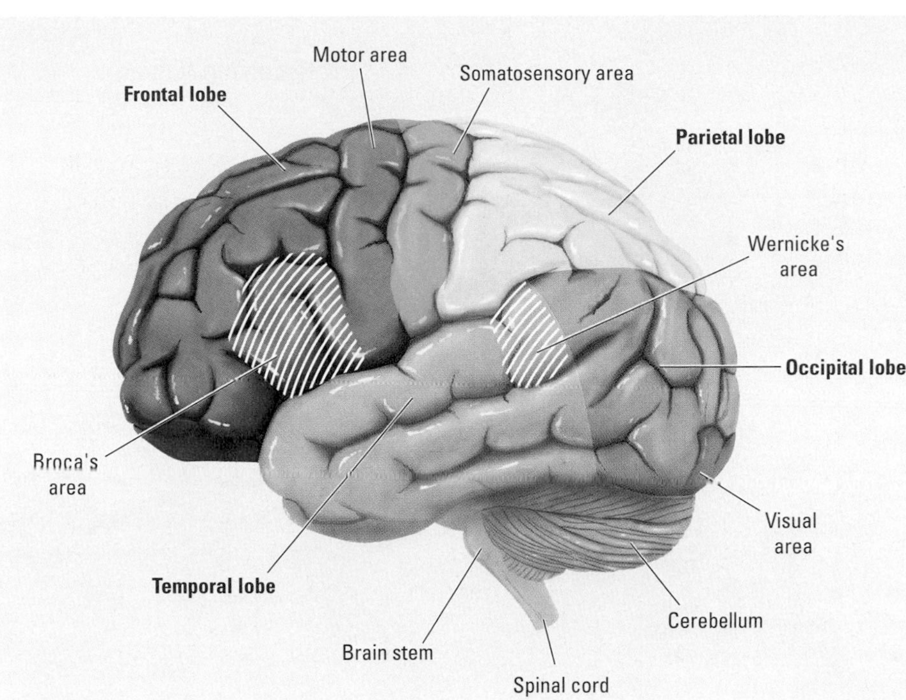


◀ FIGURE 4.7
**The Major Structures in the Brain and Spinal Cord.**
(Adapted from R. Fabes & C. L. Martin, 2003.)

between the body and the brain. At the top of the spinal cord, the *brain stem* controls automatic functions (such as breathing and heart rate) and regulates the general level of alertness throughout the higher levels of the brain. The *cerebellum,* on the back of the brain, controls posture, body orientation, and complex muscle movements. The *cerebral cortex* is the "gray matter" that forms the top portion of the brain; it is divided into four major lobes (frontal, temporal, parietal, and occipital). The many convolutions (folds) in the cortex allow a greater amount of surface area to fit within the confines of the skull.

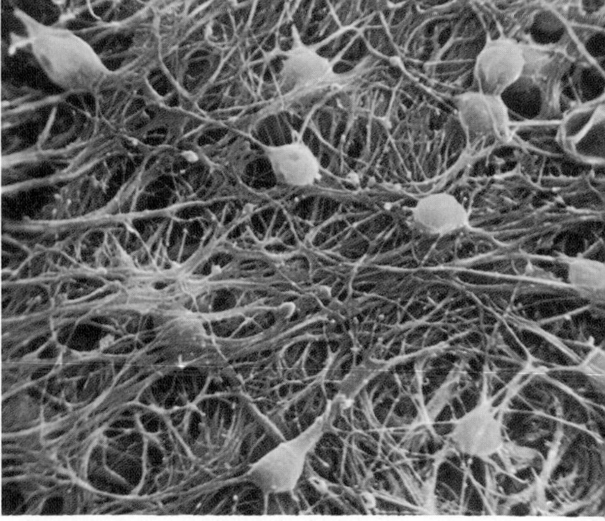

▲ This image from a scanning electron micrograph shows the web of connections that forms among neurons in the human brain. You can see the cell bodies (yellow) and the complex web of axons and dendrites that send messages throughout the web.

Although the various areas within the cortex work together in complex ways, many of them have specialized functions. The large *frontal lobe*, for example, is involved in organizing, planning, higher-level thinking, problem solving, and creativity. The *motor area*, which resembles a band from ear to ear over the middle of the cortex, controls voluntary muscle movements such as raising your eyebrows or wiggling your toes. Just behind the motor area, also shaped like a band, is the *somatosensory area*, which registers sensory input (including touch, pressure, temperature, and pain) from all areas of the body. *Wernicke's area*, a small region on the temporal lobe, processes speech input; and *Broca's area*, at the bottom of the frontal lobe, organizes articulation for speech output. The *visual area* in the back of the occipital lobe receives messages from the eyes for visual processing. Although researchers continue to discover specialized functions of individual parts of the brain, it is also increasingly clear that most of our thoughts, perceptions, emotions, and memories are governed by complex communications occurring throughout the brain.

At the microscopic level, communication throughout the nervous system is controlled by specialized cells called **neurons**. The process involves *neural impulses* (electrical impulses) that travel through the neurons and *neurotransmitters* (chemical messengers) that transmit the impulses from one neuron to another. Neurons have three main parts, as shown in Figure 4.8. *Dendrites* are branchlike structures that receive input from other neurons. The *cell body* contains the nucleus and governs the function of the neuron.

**neurons**
Specialized cells that process information and allow communication in the nervous system.

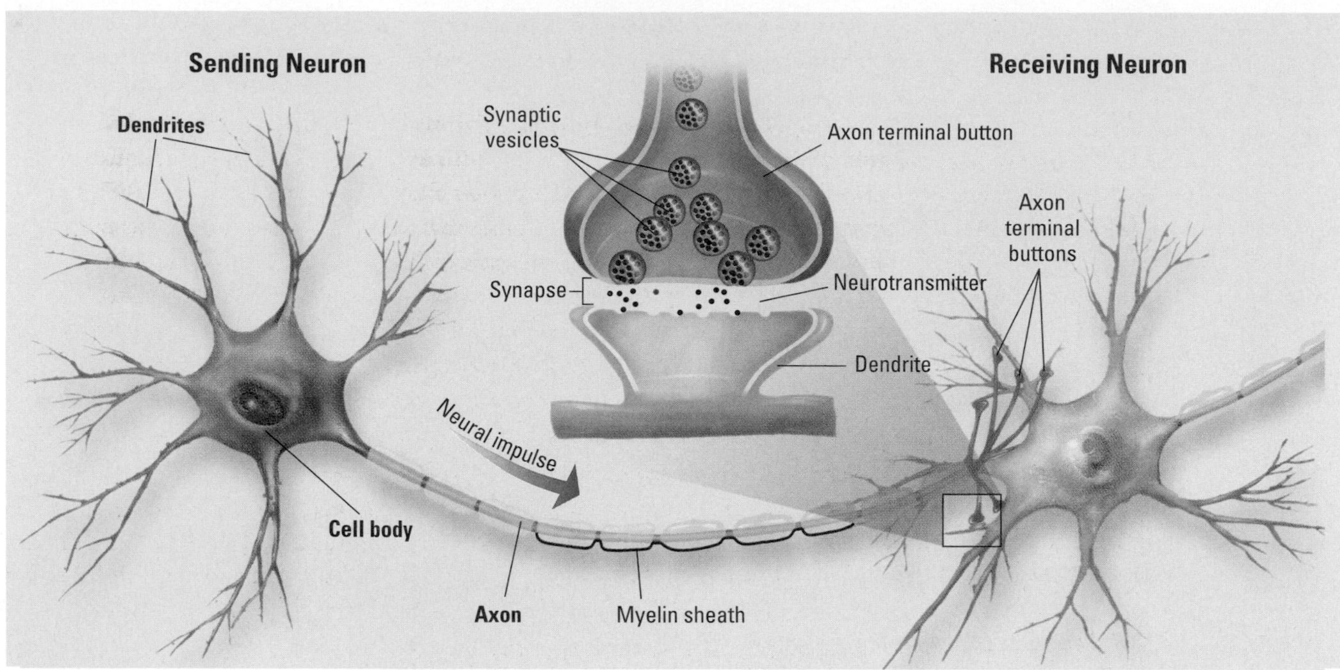


▲ FIGURE 4.8
**Parts of a Neuron**
Each neuron in the brain and nervous system contains a cell body, dendrites, and an axon. Dendrites receive input from neighboring cells. Messages move down the length of the axon to the terminal buttons and across the synapses to neighboring cells.
(Adapted from Fabes & Martin, 2003.)

**synaptogenesis**
One form of neuron maturation in which dendrites and axons branch out to form an enormously large number of connections with neighboring neurons.

**myelination**
A form of neuron maturation in which the fatty insulation (myelin sheath) grows around the axons.

**programmed cell death**
Process by which many neurons die during periods of migration and heavy synaptogenesis.

THINKING CRITICALLY

In your opinion, does brain growth allow children's thought processes to improve, or does exercising thought processes stimulate the brain to grow? What kinds of evidence would you need to have to address this question?

The *axon*, a relatively long fiber, carries electrical impulses that send messages to other cells. Mature axons are covered by a *myelin sheath*, a fatty substance that insulates the axon and speeds the axon's transmission of electrical activity. The end of the axon branches out to form *terminal buttons*. Synapses are the open spaces between terminal buttons of one neuron and dendrites of the next neuron. When the electrical impulse reaches the end of the axon, it causes the release of chemical neurotransmitters from the terminal buttons. The neurotransmitters flow across the synapse to the dendrites, where they can stimulate or inhibit the response of the neighboring cells. This process of electrochemical stimulation allows neurons to communicate throughout the nervous system.

## Forming the Brain and Nervous System

Now that you're familiar with the major (and the microscopic!) parts of the nervous system, let's step back into prenatal development and take a look at how the brain forms and develops. About 4 weeks after conception, the human embryo folds over to form a *neural tube.* The neural tube will later develop into the central nervous system (the brain and spinal cord). By 7 weeks after conception, neurons have begun to form in the neural tube. By 10 weeks, some of the neurons begin migrating to the top of the tube, where they form the first layer of the cerebral cortex. The cortex will eventually have six layers of neurons. The innermost layers form first. As more neurons grow, they migrate past the first layers to create the outer layers. New neurons form at an enormous pace. By 20 weeks of gestation, the cerebral cortex has approximately 80 billion neurons, and this is the approximate number that infants are born with (Kolb, 1999). To reach such a huge number, the brain needs to gain an average of over half a million neurons per minute after neurons begin to form in week 7! Neurons continue to form after this point, but as you will read later, the brain loses about as many as it gains. **Listen** on **mydevelopmentlab**

**Listen**: How many neurons are created in the human brain, and how fast? Are any new neurons created after birth? (Author Podcast) www.mydevelopmentlab.com

The focus of brain development now shifts from the creation of new neurons to the growth of connections among the neurons. By 20 weeks, axons and dendrites have begun growing (Huttenlocher, 1999). By 23 weeks, the first synapses have formed. The formation of new synapses is called **synaptogenesis**. Dendrites and axons grow longer and branch out to form an enormously large number of synapses with neighboring neurons. Thousands of synapses can form rather randomly as the axons of one neuron come into proximity with dendrites from another (Huttenlocher, 1999). Although the first synapses begin to form by the 23rd week of pregnancy, the process of synaptogenesis doesn't accelerate until late in pregnancy, and most synapses form after birth. By 31 weeks into pregnancy (only 7 to 9 weeks before a full-term birth), the cerebral cortex has grown enough that it begins to fold inside the skull, forming the convolutions that characterize this part of the brain. At birth, the newborn's brain has the same outward appearance as an adult's brain, although inside, much growth has yet to occur.

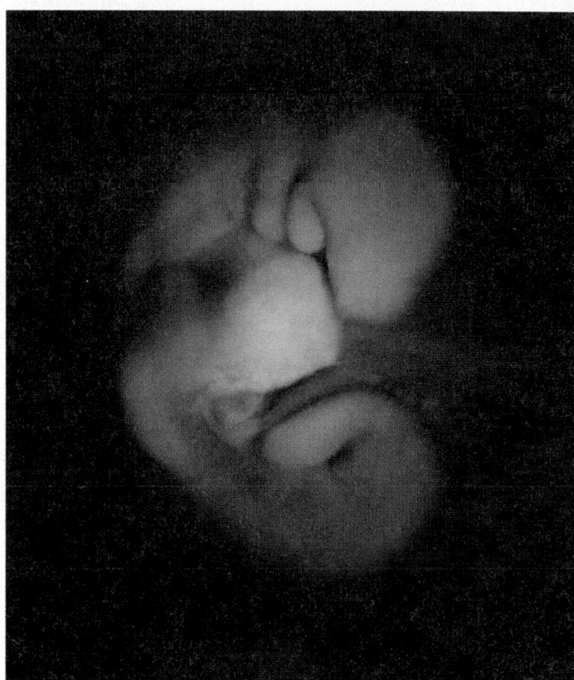

▲ About 4 weeks after conception, the embryo folds over to form the neural tube. In another few weeks, neurons begin to form in the neural tube; later, they migrate to the top of the tube to form the beginnings of the brain.

**Myelination** is the growth of the myelin sheath around the axon. The myelin sheath insulates the axon, which more than triples the speed of transmission of the impulse and communication with other neurons (Bornstein & Arterberry, 1999). Although most axons are myelinated by birth, some areas of the brain are not completely myelinated for several years. For example, the motor and sensory areas in the cortex are still forming myelin until about 4 months after birth. It is not until after the motor areas are myelinated (after 4 months) that infants accomplish coordinated motor actions such as sitting, reaching, and standing. The frontal lobe is probably one of the last areas in the brain to be completely myelinated; some areas in the frontal lobe are still forming myelin all the way into our early 20s (National Research Council and Institute of Medicine, 2000).

Here is an interesting fact: Human beings lose half of their neurons before they are even born! Before birth, neurons multiply at a tremendous rate and migrate to their final destinations, where they form the structures in the brain and the rest of the nervous system. But during migration and during periods of heavy synaptogenesis, about half of our neurons die in a process called **programmed cell death** (Kandel, Schwartz, & Jessell, 2000). Neural activity determines which neurons will survive by diverting the brain's energy supplies toward the neurons that are more useful and active; the neurons that are less important or not very active begin to lose energy and die. Genetics provides an overabundance of neurons, and the brain manages to chisel away the excess until the final form is achieved.

Stimulation from the environment is important in the growth and pruning of synapses, in myelination, and in other aspects of brain development. Nature provides the basic materials (neurons, a brain, and a nervous system), but nurture and experience are needed to sculpt and optimize the system. A little more than a decade ago, a Georgia governor pushed for legislation aimed at enriching the environments of all newborn babies. To see how far his policy went, take a look at the Social Policy Perspective box called "Can Mozart Stimulate Neural Connections in Infants?" on page 122. We will have much more to say in Chapters 7 and 10 about the interplay of nature and nurture in shaping the brain.

THINK ABOUT JESS AND DARRAN . . .

What would you tell Jess and Darran about the development of the brain and nervous system? How could this information be useful as they strive to enhance their baby's development?

## Perspective SOCIAL POLICY — CAN MOZART STIMULATE NEURAL CONNECTIONS IN INFANTS?

In his 1999 budget, then Georgia Governor Zell Miller proposed that the state spend $105,000 to send a CD or cassette of classical music home with every baby born in the state. Miller commented that "[n]o one questions that listening to music at a very young age affects the spatial, temporal reasoning that underlies math and engineering and even chess" and that "[h]aving that infant listen to soothing music helps those trillions of brain connections to develop" (Sack, 1998).

Does research evidence support Miller's claims? Frances Rauscher and her colleagues published a series of intriguing studies suggesting that extensive music training significantly enhanced the spatial-temporal skills of preschool children. These researchers also found that listening to a Mozart sonata improved college students' spatial-reasoning IQ scores by 8 to 9 points (Rauscher, Shaw, & Ky, 1993, 1995; Rauscher, Shaw, Levine, Wright, Dennis, & Newcomb, 1997). The spatial-reasoning scores involved were on tests of reasoning about proportions, ratios, and other concepts in mathematics. Improvements in these skills after exposure to classical music has been labeled the "Mozart effect." Reports about the Mozart effect and about how early experience wires the developing brain led the proactive governor of Georgia to propose jump-starting infants' brain development with classical music.

But will it work? For the college students, the benefit of listening to classical music was temporary, lasting only 10 to 15 minutes (Rauscher et al., 1997), and several other researchers have been unable to replicate the Mozart effect (e.g., Nantais & Schellenberg, 1999; Steele, Bass, & Crook, 1999). Still, the excitement over the initial findings prompted the Florida legislature to pass a law requiring that toddlers in state-run schools hear classical music every day (Goode, 1999).

QUESTION **On the basis of information in this chapter, how would you suggest that state and local governments, other agencies, schools, and parents enhance brain development in infants and toddlers? What information would you use to support new social policies in this area?**

## LET'S REVIEW . . .

1. Children reach about half of their adult height by the time they are:
   a. 1 year old.
   b. 2 years old.
   c. 5 years old.
   d. 8 years old.
2. In the United States, how many mothers follow the recommendation of the American Academy of Pediatrics and breastfeed their infants until the infants are at least 12 months of age?
   a. fewer than one-quarter
   b. about half
   c. a little more than half
   d. about two-thirds
3. According to health experts, when should parents first introduce juices, soft foods, or other supplements to their breastfed infants?
   a. after the first month
   b. after 3 months
   c. after 6 months
   d. after 12 months
4. The first synapses form in the brain at around:
   a. 10 weeks of gestation
   b. 15 weeks of gestation
   c. 23 weeks of gestation
   d. 30 weeks of gestation
5. True or False: The American Academy of Pediatrics recommends co-sleeping, where infants sleep with the parents during the night.
6. True or False: Programmed cell death is nature's way of improving the efficiency of the brain as it develops.

Answers: 1. b, 2. a, 3. c, 4. c, 5. F, 6. T

# Sensory Capabilities

When parents hold their newborns, they often wonder what their babies can see and hear and to what extent they are able to process other senses. In this section, we cover the basic sensory capabilities of newborn babies and track how some of these capabilities change during the infancy period. We will return to this topic again in Chapter 5, where we will describe how researchers study perceptual development and summarize what researchers have learned about how well infants and toddlers coordinate information across different sensory modalities.

AS YOU STUDY THIS SECTION, ASK YOURSELF THESE QUESTIONS:

**4.8** How clearly do infants see, and how well do they see colors and depth?

**4.9** How well can infants hear, and how early can they distinguish different sounds?

**4.10** When do infants begin to recognize smells and react to different flavors?

## Basic Components of Vision

### How Clear Is Their Vision?

One of the fundamental questions in perception concerns **visual acuity**—the ability to see fine detail. You are probably familiar with the standard eye chart used to measure visual acuity. According to this chart, a person with normal, 20/20 vision can read a certain row of letters on the chart from 20 feet away. A person with 20/40 vision would need to be 20 feet away to read what someone with normal vision could read from 40 feet away. But how can researchers test acuity in young infants who do not know the alphabet? To do this, researchers presented infants with the striped patterns shown in Figure 4.9. Each striped pattern was paired with a uniform gray square. If an infant doesn't have sufficient acuity to see the stripes, then the striped pattern blends to gray. As you can see in Figure 4.9, it is harder to see the most closely spaced stripes. (Back up several feet from your textbook, and the stripes will fade even more.) When infants can see the stripes, however, they tend to prefer to look at the stripes over the gray square. At a distance of 10 inches, 6-month-olds can see stripes as thin as 1/64 inch (and they prefer to look at those over the plain gray square), but 1-month-olds need the stripes to be at least 1/8 inch thick before they see them and prefer to look at them.

**visual acuity**
The ability to see fine detail.

Researchers estimate that visual acuity in newborns is somewhere between 20/150 and 20/600. Infants reach 20/20 vision by 6 to 12 months (Cohen, DeLoache, & Strauss, 1979). Even though acuity is poor in the first months, Hainline (1998) reminds us that when "development proceeds normally, infant vision seems perfectly adequate for the things that infants need to do" (p. 42), such as locate a caregiver, see a food source, or lock in on a smiling face.

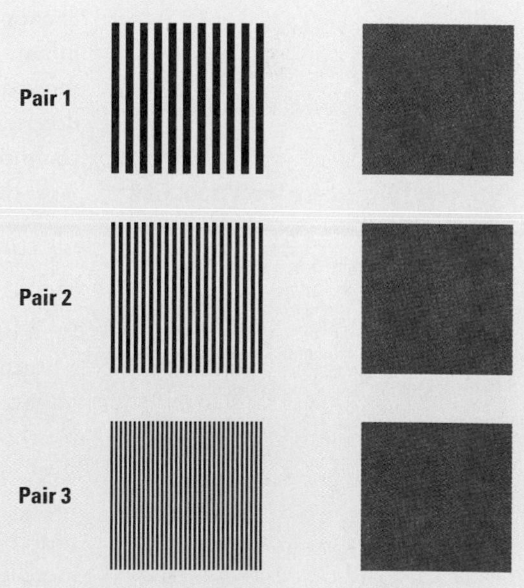


▲ FIGURE 4.9
**Patterns Used to Test Visual Acuity in Infants**
Researchers determine which set of stripes infants differentiate from the plain gray square. (Fantz, 1961.)

### Can They See Different Colors?

It is unclear how well newborn infants are able to distinguish among various colors. Studies have found that newborns prefer to look at green, yellow, or red over gray (Adams, Maurer, & Davis, 1986). However, other evidence indicates that newborns can distinguish red from white but not blue, green, or yellow from white (Adams, Courage, & Mercer, 1994). Most of the evidence collected in the last few decades suggests that the photopigments in the eye that are necessary for normal color vision are present by at least 3 months, and it is safe to say that color vision is relatively mature by 6 months (Kellman & Arterberry, 2006; Suttle, Banks, & Graf, 2002).

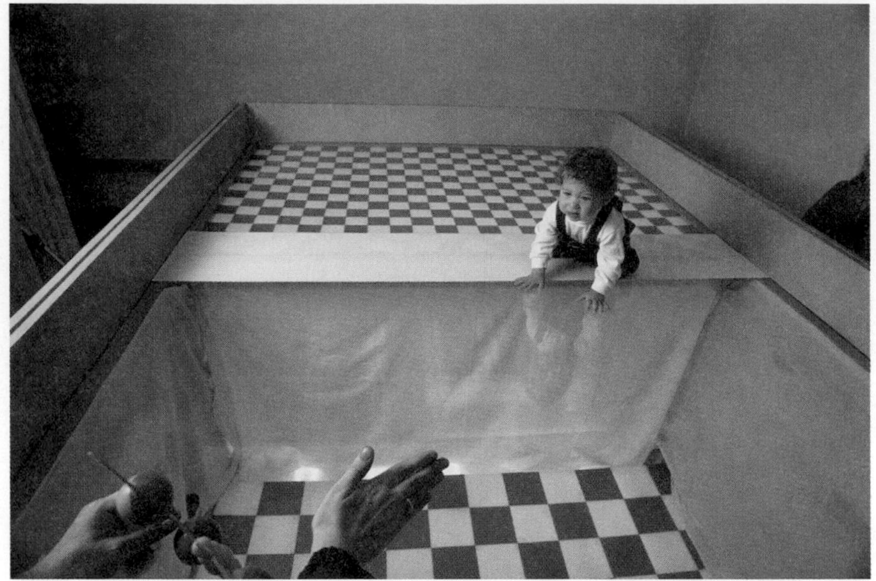

FIGURE 4.10 ▶ **Visual Cliff** A "visual cliff" like this was used in the classic study of depth perception by Gibson and Walk (1960). How can you tell whether the infant can see the deep drop under the glass?

**How Deep Is That Drop? Early Depth Perception.** The classic research on depth perception was Eleanor Gibson and Richard Walk's (1960) *visual cliff* experiment. Similar to the photo in Figure 4.10, a heavy sheet of glass extended across a solid surface and a deep drop-off. Infants from 6 to 14 months of age were tested. The researchers placed each infant in the middle; then the baby's mother called, first from one side and then the other. All of the 6-month-olds crawled out onto the solid side to reach their mothers, but they refused to crawl onto the deep side. Many cried, but still they didn't venture over the visual cliff. Gibson and Walk concluded that depth perception is available by the time infants learn to crawl. A decade later, other researchers demonstrated that infants just under 2 months of age could see the difference between the deep and solid sides (Campos, Langer, & Krowitz, 1970). They placed infants face-down on each side of the visual cliff and measured their heart rates. Infants showed significantly more slowing of their heart rates on the deep side. In infants, heart rate deceleration indicates engrossed attention. Although it was clear that these young infants could perceive depth, it seems that they were more intrigued by than afraid of the "cliff." **Simulate** on **mydevelopmentlab**

**Simulate** The Visual Cliff
www.mydevelopmentlab.com

## How Well Do Infants Hear?

Even before birth, fetuses react to loud noises, and by 6 months of age infants respond to a broad range of sounds including rattles, voices, songs, and many other environmental noises. Researchers have devoted extensive study to infant reactions to the human voice. Newborns prefer the voices of their own mothers to the voices of unfamiliar females (DeCasper & Fifer, 1980). At 4 months, infants prefer to listen to human voices over silence or white noise (Colombo & Bundy, 1981). By 5 months of age, infants can recognize their own names being spoken amid other names but only if their name is spoken more loudly than the other words (Newman, 2005).

A fascinating experiment was conducted by DeCasper and Spence (1986). These researchers asked pregnant women to read aloud a particular children's story (e.g., *The Cat in the Hat*) twice each day during the last six weeks of pregnancy. Two to three days after birth, the experimenters tested the newborns for their recognition of the story. They connected a pacifier to an electronic switch that could activate one of two sound tracks. One sound track was a recording of the newborn's mother reading the familiar story (*The Cat in the Hat*). The other track was a recording of the mother reading a new story (e.g., *The King, the Mice, and the Cheese*). Newborns could choose which story to activate by adjusting their rate of sucking on the pacifier. For some, slower sucking would activate the familiar story; for others, this required faster sucking. In both cases, newborns adjusted their rate of sucking as required to activate the familiar story. Because both sound tracks were recordings of the mother's voice, the infants must have been choosing on the basis of certain qualities (e.g., pace) they heard in the stories. Further, these infants still preferred the familiar story when the stories were recorded by unfamiliar female voices. These results indicate that auditory perception before birth was adequate to process and retain the acoustic qualities of the story and that the newborns' perception and memory were sufficient to differentiate the two sound tracks and recognize which one was familiar. Quite a task for a baby only 2 to 3 days old!

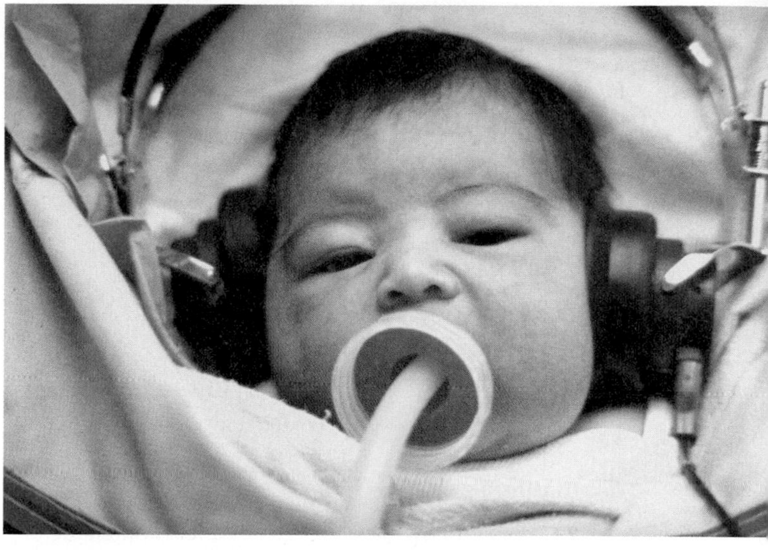

▲ This infant is participating in an experiment on auditory perception. By adjusting how fast he sucks on the pacifier, he can activate one of two tape recordings played into the headphones. If he adjusts his sucking rate, that is evidence that he hears the difference and is working to listen to one sound over the other.

## Smell and Taste

Immediately after birth, their facial expressions show that newborns react to certain odors in a manner similar to adults. Newborns show positive facial expressions in response to the aromas of bananas and butter, positive or indifferent responses to vanilla, some rejection to fishy odors, and complete disgust to rotten eggs (Bornstein & Arterberry, 1999; Steiner, 1979). In other experiments, Richard Porter and his colleagues studied newborns' recognition of their parents' smells. For example, parents in one study wore gauze pads under their arms for several hours; then researchers used the pads in a smelling test with the parents' newborn babies (Cernoch & Porter, 1985). At the age of 2 weeks, breastfed infants turned their heads toward the smell of their mothers more than to the smell of unfamiliar females (mothers of other infants). The newborns did not show recognition of the smell of their fathers, however. Also, bottle-fed newborns did not show a preference for the smell of their mothers. These results demonstrate that infants are capable of discerning small differences in complicated odors, at least when they have close and repeated contact with the odor—as breastfed infants would have with the smell of their mothers.

But the perception of smell might become functional even before this time. Infants as young as 3 to 4 days of age prefer the smell of breast milk to that of formula milk, regardless of whether they are breastfed or bottle-fed (Marlier & Schall, 2005). There is also intriguing evidence that, just as for audition, the fetal system is well enough developed sometime near the end of gestation to sense and store information about odors encountered before birth. For example, newborns prefer the smell of their own amniotic fluid over that of other infants (Schall, Marlier, & Soussignan, 1998).

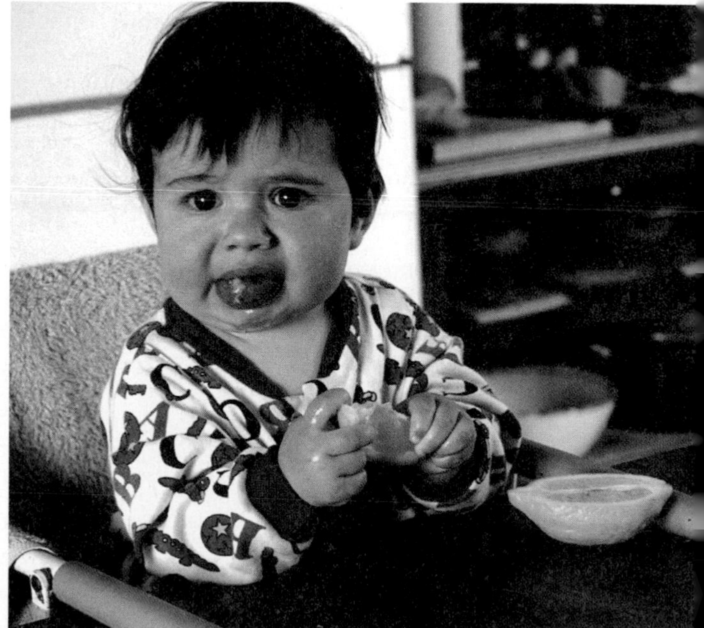

▲ It is obvious that this child does not care for the taste of this lemon. Reactions to basic categories of smell and taste are controlled in the lower brain centers of babies.

Infants show taste preferences immediately after birth, even before their first feedings (Steiner, 1979). When given a sweet solution, newborns smile and make sucking movements. Infants will suck longer to obtain a solution that is sweeter as opposed to one that is less sweet (Crook, 1987). With a sour taste, they purse their lips and wrinkle their noses. A bitter taste causes newborns to spit and make a face that indicates disgust and rejection. These early taste preferences seem to be governed by areas in the lower brain, because they appear even in infants who are born without a cerebral cortex (Steiner, 1979). Reaction to salty flavors develops later, usually by 4 months of age (Beauchamp, Cowart, Mennella, & Marsh, 1994).

## LET'S REVIEW . . .

1. Infants reach adult levels of visual acuity by the time they are:
   a. 1 month old.
   b. 3 to 6 months old.
   c. 6 to 12 months old.
   d. 12 to 18 months old.
2. It is likely that color vision is relatively mature by the time an infant is:
   a. 2 months old.
   b. 6 months old.
   c. 12 months old.
   d. 18 months old.
3. Which of the following is a correct conclusion about the auditory capabilities of infants?
   a. The auditory system becomes functional around 2 weeks of age.
   b. Around 10 months of age, infants are beginning to recognize their own name when it is spoken.
   c. Infants can recognize some sounds that they heard in the womb even before they were born.
   d. Newborns cannot detect the sound of their mother's voice, but infants begin to distinguish one voice from another by 6 months.
4. True or False: Research using the visual cliff indicates that infants as young as 2 months of age can see the depth on the deep side and are intrigued by it, and that by 6 months infants are afraid of the deep side.
5. True or False: Different reactions to sweet, bitter, and sour flavors can be observed in newborns even before they receive their first feedings, so learning is evidently not required to distinguish these flavors.

Answers: 1. c, 2. b, 3. c, 4. T, 5. T

# Motor Development

When infants are born, they can turn their heads in the direction of interesting sounds, and they move their eyes to track the movements of some objects. Even in the first weeks, they are beginning to gain control over muscles in the head and neck area, but it will still be a while before they can coordinate muscles in the rest of their bodies. With some trial and error, newborns may be able to get their hands to their mouths to suck their fingers or thumbs, but they still can't control their arm and hand muscles well enough to reach out and grasp an object. They are months away from being able to stand up, walk, and run.

In this section, we trace the typical patterns of motor development—gains that infants and children make in the ability to control their muscle movements.

**reflexes**
Involuntary movements that are elicited by environmental stimuli.

AS YOU STUDY THIS SECTION, ASK YOURSELF THESE QUESTIONS:

**4.11** What reflexes do infants have, and what is their significance?

**4.12** What patterns are seen as infants and toddlers learn to control their muscles and motor movements, and what are the factors that govern this phase of development?

**4.13** How does motor development compare across cultures, and what can we learn from these comparisons?

**4.14** When are toddlers ready for toilet training, and what is the best approach for parents to use?

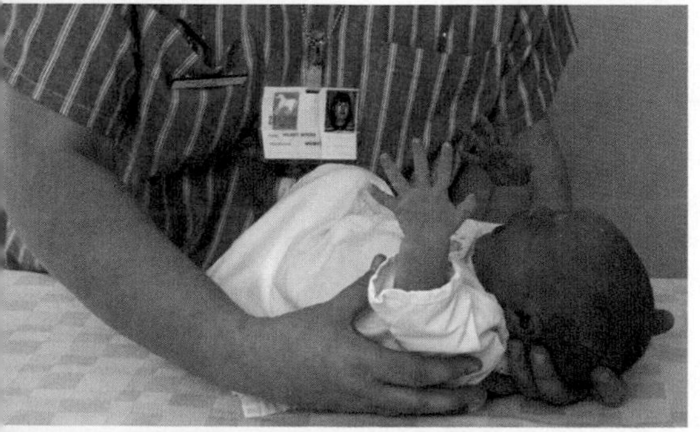

▲ This newborn is demonstrating the Moro reflex. When startled, she extends her arms and legs and spreads her fingers. Why do infants have this reflex?

## Reflexes: The Infant's First Coordinated Movements

Human infants are equipped at birth with several interesting reflexes. **Reflexes** are involuntary movements that are elicited by environmental stimuli such as sound, light, touch, and body position. If you touch a newborn's cheek, the infant's head will turn in the direction of the touch. This is called the *rooting reflex.* If anything touches an infant's lips, the infant automatically begins to suck—the *sucking reflex.* The *Moro reflex* (or startle reflex) occurs when an infant is startled by a loud noise or begins to fall. A sharp bang on the crib will cause infants to extend their arms and legs outward, spread their fingers and toes, then bring their limbs back to their bodies. You will see the same response if you hold an infant in your arms, face upward, and then drop your arms suddenly a few inches. (Be sure to catch the baby!) The *grasping reflex* occurs when an object touches an infant's palm; the baby's fingers will automatically wrap around the object and grip strongly.

As you read earlier in this chapter, the cerebral cortex (the upper part of the brain), which governs voluntary muscle movements, is not well developed at birth. So at first, it is the lower brain centers (spinal cord, brain stem, and midbrain) that control infants' involuntary reflexes. These reflexes tend to disappear by about four months after birth as the higher cortical centers in the brain begin to take over voluntary control of muscle movements. Pediatricians have long used the existence and disappearance of reflexes as early indicators of nervous system function. Remember from Chapter 3 that the Apgar test includes a measure of "reflex irritability" as part of the assessment of early functioning in newborns. The Brazelton Neonatal Behavioral Assessment Scale, designed to assess the health of infants, measures some 20 different reflexes. A lack of reflexive response, or a delay in the emergence or disappearance of certain reflexes, can signal a problem with neurological development. **Watch** on **mydevelopmentlab**

Which reflexes have you observed in infants you have known? What purposes are served by these reflexes?

**Watch** a video on The Newborn's Reflexes. www.mydevelopmentlab.com

## Voluntary Movements: The Motor Milestones

When our children were newborn babies, we loved the way they wiggled and squirmed when we held and played with them. Many of their movements were jerky and somewhat erratic, but it was a joy to watch them stretch and exercise their tiny muscles. Newborns can typically move their eyes and turn their heads to find one's face or track the sound of one's voice. Put your finger in the palm of a newborn's hand, and the strength of the infant's grip (from the grasping reflex) will surprise you. When newborns are awake, their arms and legs seem to be constantly stretching and flexing, their fingers gripping and extending. These early arm and leg movements are spontaneous and involuntary, not directed at reaching at or holding particular objects. It will be several months before the infant can coordinate voluntary and purposeful behaviors like reaching for a toy or dumping out a box of blocks. Over the next months, infants' reflexes, spontaneous movements, and later voluntary movements gradually strengthen the infants' muscles and stimulate neurological development in their brains and nervous systems.

Figure 4.11 (on p. 128) illustrates the major milestones in gross motor development across the first year of life. **Gross motor development** refers to the process of coordinating movements with the large muscles in the body. These muscles control the larger parts of the body such as the head, neck, torso, arms, and legs. Later, we will discuss **fine motor development**, the development of the smaller muscles that control our more intricate movements (e.g., finger movements).

Gross motor development follows the *cephalocaudal* pattern that we discussed earlier in the chapter (Frankenburg et al., 1992). By 1 month of age, the muscles in infants' necks are strong enough to allow the infants to hold their heads upright. Next, the muscles in the trunk become more coordinated. Infants can roll over by 3 months and sit upright without support by 6 months. Around 7 months the legs are strong enough to allow infants to crawl—pushing with their legs and dragging their bodies along the floor. At 7 months, infants also can stand by holding onto a table or other form of support.

For many parents, the most significant of the early motor milestones is the baby's first step. Most infants take their first unaided steps sometime around their first birthday. But it is important to know that these ages are averages, and the rates of development for

**gross motor development**
Process of coordinating movements with the large muscles in the body.

**fine motor development**
Process of coordinating intricate movements with smaller muscles.

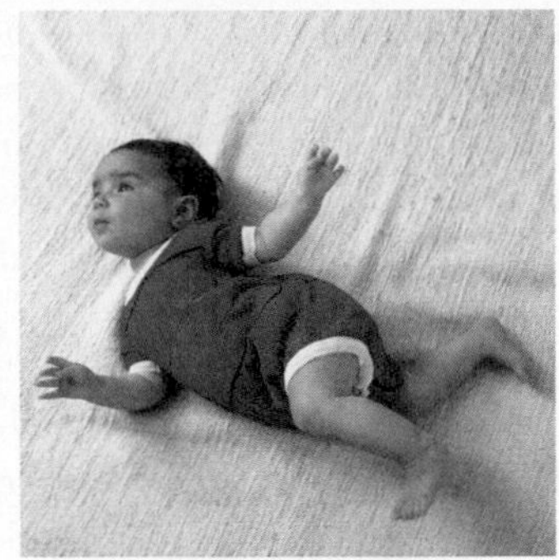

FIGURE 4.11 ▶
**Gross Motor Milestones**
You can see the cephalocaudal (head-to-tail) pattern of development by looking at the average ages at which infants achieve each of these gross motor milestones. Notice that they gain control over the neck and head before the trunk, and the trunk before the legs.

individual babies vary considerably. For example, 25% of infants are walking well at 11 months; another 25% begin walking well at 13 months; and 10% do not walk proficiently until 15 months (Frankenburg et al., 1992). Individual genetics, different rates of neurological development, and opportunities to practice muscle movements all contribute to this variability. Pediatricians will, however, see serious delays in motor development as a potential indication of neurological or muscular deficits. To learn more about how to identify and treat developmental delays in motor development, read the Professional Perspective box on page 130 called "Career Focus: Meet a Physical Therapist."

A *proximodistal*, or nearer-to-farther (from the body's midline), pattern can be seen in the progress infants make in reaching and grasping. At first, they reach with their arms; next come the fine motor skills of grasping with the hands and fingers (Gabbard, 1992). In Figure 4.12, you can see that voluntary control over the upper arm is shown by 4 to 5 months. The infant has voluntary control over the upper arm and can reach out and pull an object in with both arms. At this age, infants wrap all four fingers and the thumb around the object in what is referred to as the *palmar grasp*. By 10 months, infants show the more advanced *pincer grasp*, using the thumb and the opposite forefinger. At 15 months, they can hold a writing implement (although they begin again with the palmar grasp) and make scribbles by using the large muscles in the upper arm. Later, children begin using the more precise *tripod grasp* for holding pencils and other writing implements: They hold the writing tool between the forefinger and thumb, and they steady the bottom of their hand on the writing surface. As you can see, control over the fine motor movements of the hands and fingers comes much later than control over the gross motor movements of the elbows, arms, and shoulders.

The cephalocaudal and proximodistal patterns in motor development mirror the progressive maturation of centers in the brain. Cells and connections in the part of the brain

a.

b.

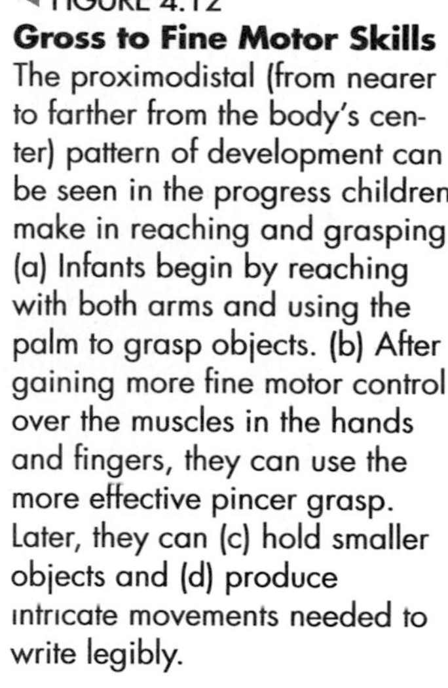

c.

d.

◀ FIGURE 4.12
**Gross to Fine Motor Skills**
The proximodistal (from nearer to farther from the body's center) pattern of development can be seen in the progress children make in reaching and grasping. (a) Infants begin by reaching with both arms and using the palm to grasp objects. (b) After gaining more fine motor control over the muscles in the hands and fingers, they can use the more effective pincer grasp. Later, they can (c) hold smaller objects and (d) produce intricate movements needed to write legibly.

that controls muscle movements in the head and upper body tend to mature first. Neurological development then spreads, allowing control and coordination of muscles to proceed both downward and outward through the body. Of course, there are exceptions to every rule, and we point one out here. When young infants first start reaching for toys and other objects, they actually tend to reach with their feet first and do not try to reach with their hands until they are several weeks older (Galloway & Thelen, 2004). In general, however, motor development does tend to follow the head-to-tail and midline-out patterns of development.

Newborn babies show a *stepping reflex* where they make small stepping motion when they are held up with their feet dangling down and barely touching a table or other surface. This reflex disappears as the motor area of the cortex matures enough to allow coordinated and voluntary movements of the legs. But is brain maturation the only factor driving motor development? Obviously not. For example, the disappearance of the stepping reflex is also related to weight gain during infancy. Infants who gain weight more rapidly tend to lose the stepping reflex earlier.

One group of researchers demonstrated this effect with 1-month-old infants. When they fitted these infants with leg weights that mimicked the amount of weight the infants would gain in the next few weeks, the stepping reflex diminished (Thelen, Fisher, & Ridley-Johnson, 1984). And when the researchers held other infants in water, the infants showed a more vigorous stepping reflex. The fatty leg tissue was more buoyant under

## Perspective PROFESSIONAL — CAREER FOCUS: MEET A PHYSICAL THERAPIST

Deanna Walsh
Madison, WI
Physical therapist at Meriter Hospital

**What ages of children and what types of conditions do you work with? Are families involved in the children's therapy?**
The youngest children I treat are premature infants, and the oldest may be up to 16 or 17 years old. I see children who are having a variety of movement problems. I see babies and children with torticollis (a tight muscle in their neck that restricts their movement), cerebral palsy, autism with associated movement difficulties, delays in their gross motor development (difficulty learning to crawl, walk, jump, etc.), spina bifida, muscular dystrophy, Down syndrome, other genetic syndromes that impact movement, and after surgery or fractures. The children I see may have problems with their balance or coordination, muscle weakness, muscle tightness, difficulty with mobility, or difficulty with specific movements. Some children require special equipment to make movement easier. This might include special braces or inserts in their shoes, crutches, walkers, adapted bicycles, or wheelchairs.

Typically, I see a child for one or two treatments per week, depending on the child's and family's needs. A great deal of my job is teaching families what they can do to help their child, since they are the people who are with the child most of the time. By involving families in their child's treatment, greater improvements are seen. Instead of working on an activity for one hour per week, the child will be incorporating it into his or her day, every day.

**How do you determine whether a child is exhibiting delayed motor development?**
I routinely use many different standardized tests when assessing a child's motor skills. Most tests address certain age groups and look at certain types of skills (e.g., balance, locomotor, coordination, and ball skills). I also observe the quality of a child's movements to determine whether she or he is having difficulty with mobility skills.

**What education and training are needed to become a physical therapist?**
Most physical therapy programs are now master's degree programs, and many are moving toward the doctorate level. Most include extensive clinical experience as part of the training, and this is typically where most students gain some hands-on experience working with children. Physical therapy is an excellent career for people who like to be involved with patients and their families. There are many practice settings in physical therapy—such as school-based therapy, hospital-based therapy, outpatient clinics, home health agencies, academics, research, nursing homes, and rehab centers. The great thing about all areas of physical therapy is that you get to help people meet their individual goals. Working with great kids and their families is an added benefit of working with pediatrics.

QUESTION **What are some initial signs that parents can look for to determine whether their infant or toddler needs to see a physical therapist?**

THINKING CRITICALLY

Have you known an infant who began walking several months earlier or later than the average age of 13 months? What do you think caused this infant's timetable of development to be faster or slower than average?

water, so the reflex revived when the muscles were relieved of the extra weight load. Esther Thelen hypothesized that the normal disappearance of the stepping reflex is affected by the biomechanical load placed on the limbs and not caused entirely by maturation of the higher brain centers.

Philip Zelazo and his colleagues (1972) demonstrated that daily practice could strengthen the stepping reflex. Zelazo (1983) has even suggested that motor development may be subservient to cognitive development. Independent walking, for example, may occur only after toddlers develop certain information-processing and memory skills. According to this view, toddlers need to associate balance with stepping and to remember how to coordinate different body movements to walk successfully. So when it comes to motor development, cognitive practice may be as important as physical exercise and the strengthening of muscles.

Esther Thelen and her colleagues have proposed a dynamic systems theory (see Chapter 1) to describe the myriad interactive processes that are involved in motor development (Gershkoff-Stowe & Thelen, 2004; Thelen, 1989; Thelen & Smith, 2006). In this theory, coordinated movements such as reaching, crawling, walking, and throwing are dynamic actions that emerge from the complex interplay of individual muscles, nerve pathways, physical growth, learning, and motivation:

- *Neurological development* gives infants the ability to exert voluntary control over their muscles.
- *Parental encouragement* and interesting objects in the environment motivate infants to raise their heads, turn their bodies, crawl, and take their first steps.
- *Opportunities to exercise* give babies the muscle strength they need to lift and control their growing limbs.
- *Maturation of cognitive systems* helps babies to remember where interesting objects are located and figure out how to coordinate their movements to get them.

▲ About half of all infants are taking their first steps alone at about 13 months of age. There is a good deal of variability, however, with some infants walking a few months earlier and some a few months later.

The brain, the body, and the environment all work in concert to propel the child toward increased strength and coordination. Without the brain, the muscles won't move. Without muscular exercise, the brain won't develop. Without motivation, the child won't exercise. The important question is not which part of the system develops first, but rather how the various components work together to move the infant and child toward higher levels of development. This is another example of the interplay between nature and nurture in child development.

## Cultural Differences in Early Experience

Because parenting practices differ across cultures, infants in some cultures receive more vigorous physical stimulation than do babies in other cultures. In Mali, for example, mothers often stretch their infants' muscles by suspending them by their arms or legs, and they encourage infants to sit and stand at an early age (Bril & Sabatier, 1986). Researchers have also noted that some African cultures emphasize physical stimulation, and infants who are raised in these cultures are typically ahead of North American infants in the major motor milestones such as sitting up and walking (Ainsworth, 1967; Rabain-Jamin & Wornham, 1993; Super, 1976).

In contrast, in some South American cultures, mothers are more protective of young infants and tend to limit their infants' opportunities to explore and exercise their motor skills. In Brazil, for example, researchers find that mothers carry their infants or hold the babies in their laps for a large part of the day. Many Brazilian mothers reportedly believe that sitting and standing positions can cause damage to the legs and spines of young infants, so they rarely allow their infants to sit or play on the floor by themselves (Santos, Gabbard, & Goncalves, 2001). During the first six months of infancy, these Brazilian babies lag behind their North American age-mates in motor skills such as sitting up and reaching for objects. By 8 months of age, however, they gain more physical exercise and catch up with infants raised in other cultures. Studies have found similar trends in babies in Chile (Andraca, Pino, LaParra, & Castillo, 1998).

▲ Hopi Indians traditionally carried their infants on cradle boards like this one. What was the effect of this practice on their infants' ability to learn to walk?

Infants among the Hopi tribe in Arizona and the Tewa of New Mexico take their first steps at about 14 months of age, or one to two months later than most other infants in North America (Dennis & Dennis, 1939/1991). For their classic study on cultural differences in motor development, Wayne and Marsena Dennis spent two summers living among the Hopi. In some villages, they found that Hopi mothers used the traditional practice of strapping their infants to cradle boards that the mothers then carried on their backs. For the first nine months of life, these infants spent most of their days restrained tightly on these boards, and they remained on the cradle boards even when they were nursing and when sleeping at night. Other Hopi villages were more "Americanized," and mothers in these villages had given up use of the cradle boards. Did the infants in these villages walk at an earlier age than the cradle board babies? Interestingly, the answer was no, not really: Use of the cradle board delayed the onset of walking by only two days on average (Dennis & Dennis, 1939/1991). Whether confined to the board or allowed to play and exercise more freely, all the Hopi infants took their first steps at about 14 months of age. As you can see, studies that investigate different cultures do not agree completely about the roles of nature and nurture regarding the effect of practice and exercise in motor development.

THINK ABOUT JESS AND DARRAN . . .
What advice would you give Jess and Darran about providing exercise for their baby during the first year? Can exercise accelerate motor development significantly?

## Toilet Training

Watching infants and toddlers move through the motor milestones is thrilling. Parents celebrate the first time their infants sit up, crawl, and stand on their own. And who can forget the excitement of those first few wobbly steps the toddler takes? For practical reasons, parents also celebrate a much less glamorous milestone: when their toddlers become toilet trained. As with crawling, walking, and other developmental milestones, toilet training develops from an interaction of physical maturity, cognitive understanding, cues and feedback from the environment, and motivation. Toilet training isn't solely a matter of physical development—it involves both nature and nurture. This is a lesson that can be learned from the dynamic systems theory discussed earlier in the chapter.

Most toddlers gain voluntary control and coordination over the muscles that control their bladder and bowel movements by the time they are 18 to 24 months old. By this time, the toddlers are also walking well enough that they can get through the house and to the potty as the need arises. Once these physical developments have occurred, parents next need to assess their child's emotional and cognitive readiness. Can the child approach toilet training in a way that is positive and fairly relaxed? This is not the time to engage in a major power struggle with a testy 2-year-old, and children are not ready if they show fear of the potty or fear of bodily functions. Cognitive readiness is indicated when the child shows awareness of having soiled diapers, requests to be changed, asks to wear underwear, or shows a positive interest in the bathroom and toilet. It helps if the child is able to follow simple instructions and can stay dry for at least two or three hours during the day.

When the child seems ready for training, it's time to introduce the child to his or her own special potty (usually a child-sized potty chair), demonstrate or teach the basic skill, and be ready with lots of praise and rewards for a job well done. Most experts recommend a child-oriented approach to training, allowing the child to set the pace according to his or her own schedule of readiness (Brazelton, 1962; Stadtler, Gorski, & Brazelton, 1999).

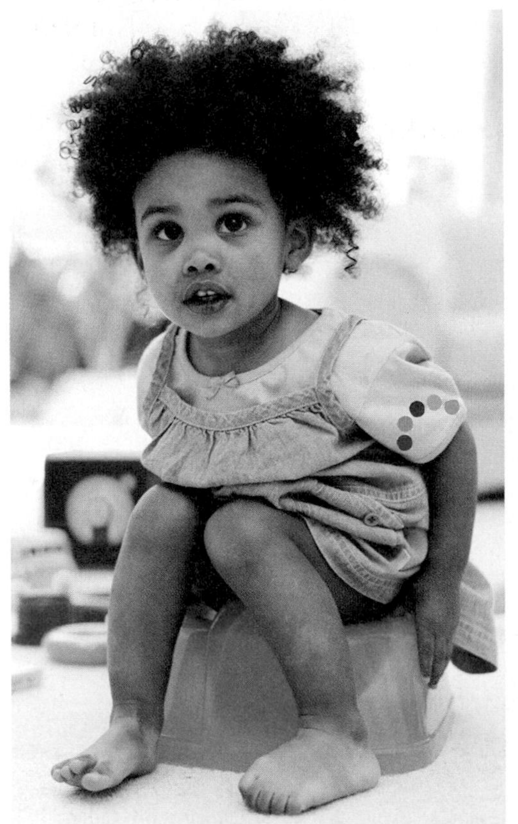

▲ What do experts suggest about the best way to toilet train children?

Researchers studying a group of toddlers in the Milwaukee area found that at least half of girls showed an interest in using the toilet by 24 months of age and stayed dry during the day and night by 34 months (Schum, Kolb, McAuliffe, Simms, Underhill, & Lewis, 2002). Boys achieved these milestones about two months later than girls. It is possible, however, for children to be trained at an even earlier age. In their review of other studies on this topic, the researchers conducting the Milwaukee study noted that the average age of daytime dryness was about 24 months during the 1950s (when parents tended to push children harder and use stricter methods). They also noted that children in some other countries are trained earlier than most U.S. children and that many of the African American toddlers in their Milwaukee sample began training before 15 months of age. Although children can be pushed to train at an earlier age, most experts believe that there are psychological and emotional benefits to using a more child-oriented approach with most toddlers, even though it might delay training success by several months.

THINKING CRITICALLY

Do you think parents should push their toddlers to toilet train earlier, or do you think parents should follow the pace of the child? Why?

## LET'S REVIEW . . .

1. What should you conclude about a 1-month-old infant who does not show the Moro reflex?
   a. This reflex normally does not emerge until 4 months, so the infant is developing normally.
   b. This reflex disappears by 3 weeks of age, so the infant is developing normally.
   c. Most infants do not show the Moro reflex, so there is no reason to be concerned.
   d. The infant may have a neurological problem or immaturity.
2. Which is the correct sequence of motor development for most infants?
   a. roll over, sit up, hold head up, walk
   b. hold head up, sit up, roll over, walk
   c. hold head up, roll over, sit up, walk
   d. hold head up, roll over, walk, sit up
3. Which of the following statements provides the best summary of the dynamic systems theory of motor development?
   a. Motor skills emerge from the combination of physical growth, learning, and motivation.
   b. Motor development is governed primarily by neurological development as maturation in the brain allows more coordinated motor movements.
   c. Motor development is governed primarily by experience as physical exercise stimulates the formation of neural circuits in the brain.
   d. Cognitive development precedes motor development; infants must first understand how to coordinate individual movements before they can execute complex motor skills.
4. True or False: Like most infants, Kelli learned to sit upright on her own before she learned to walk. This is an example of the proximodistal pattern of motor development.
5. True or False: Overall, children are being toilet trained at an earlier age today than they were 50 years ago.

Answers: 1. d, 2. c, 3. a, 4. F, 5. F

THINKING BACK TO JESS AND DARRAN . . .

Like most expectant parents, Jess and Darran would like to do what they can to stimulate their baby's development. With all the excitement generated by popular press reports about research on brain development, parents are eager to learn how experience helps to shape the communication pathways in the brain. During pregnancy, neurons will grow in the baby's brain, and synapses will begin to form to connect the neurons. The brain grows an overabundance of neurons, and half of the baby's neurons will die off in programmed cell death. Which neurons survive and which will die is determined partly by experience and the relative activity of the neurons, but this neuron loss is normal. Infants' brains use the variety of sights, sounds, and other sensations stimulated by the environment to govern brain growth and development, and Jess and Darran should understand that stimulation is important throughout childhood, not just during the first year or two.

What about reading stories to the baby during pregnancy? There is evidence that newborns can recognize something about the sounds they hear while still in the womb, but it's unclear how this might relate to the formation of an attachment to the father. At this point, we can say only that it certainly won't hurt! The same goes for exercise classes for infants. For example, practicing reflexes speeds the emergence of motor skills only slightly, so such classes probably do more for fun and the social interaction between parent and baby than for the motor skills. The infant's nervous system and motor skills will develop well if the typical sources of stimulation are on hand: objects to manipulate, friendly voices and faces, hugs, things to climb on, and encouragement to explore a varied environment.

Unless there are conditions that prevent Jess from breastfeeding, the expert advice is that she should breastfeed her baby for at least the first year. Breast milk is all that her baby will need for the first six months, and then other foods and supplements can be introduced gradually. Experts also recommend that parents such as Jess and Darran follow their children's pace when it comes to toilet training; toddlers learn this task relatively easily once they are physically and cognitively ready for the chore. These are just a few of the concepts and research findings that you might share with Jess and Darran. What other topics in this chapter did you find that would be helpful?

# 4

## CHAPTER REVIEW . . .

**4.1 What are the different ways that prematurity is defined, and what are the developmental risks for each category of prematurity?**

Premature infants can be defined as preterm (born before 37 weeks' gestation), low birth weight (weighing less than 5½ pounds), very low birth weight (weighing less than 3½ pounds), or small for gestational age (born below the 10th percentile for weight for their gestational age). SGA babies are especially at risk because something has prevented them from growing as well as would be expected, given the amount of time they spent in the uterus. A number of risk factors for preterm and low-birth-weight births have been identified. Several, such as lack of prenatal care, malnutrition, smoking, alcohol and drug use, and young maternal age, are controllable.

**4.2 What are the infant mortality rates in the United States, and why are they so high?**

Infant mortality refers to the number of infants who die before reaching 1 year of age. The rate is relatively high in the United States. Increasing access to and use of good prenatal care would reduce the rates of preterm and low-birth-weight births and would help to reduce infant mortality.

**4.3 How can prenatal care address the issues of prematurity and infant mortality?**

With prenatal care, at-risk pregnancies are identified early and parents learn how to reduce their risks by avoiding teratogens and engaging in healthy behaviors.

**4.4 What are the main patterns of growth and sleep, and what do researchers know about Sudden Infant Death Syndrome (SIDS)?**

At birth, newborns average 7½ pounds in weight and 20 inches in length. Weight doubles by 5 months of age, and children reach almost half of their adult height by 2 years of age. Newborns sleep for two-thirds of the day, and most are sleeping through the night by six months. Co-sleeping is common in some cultures. SIDS is the leading cause of death in infants from 1 month to 1 year of age. There are no known causes of SIDS, but several risk factors are involved.

**4.5 What are the benefits of breastfeeding, and how long should children continue to breastfeed?**

Health experts agree that human breast milk provides optimal nutrition and additional health benefits for infants and toddlers. Unless other conditions prevent healthy breastfeeding, infants should receive breast milk alone until 6 months; then juices and soft foods can gradually be introduced. Breastfeeding can continue as a supplement to other foods.

**4.6 What are the main parts of the brain, and what are their basic functions?**

The cerebral cortex is made up of four major lobes (frontal, temporal, parietal, and occipital), and it also contains the motor, somatosensory, and visual areas of the brain. The brain stem controls automatic functions and regulates alertness throughout the higher levels of the brain. The spinal cord relays information between the body and brain. The cerebellum controls posture and complex body movements. Neurons are specialized cells that process information in the brain and nervous system.

**4.7 What major patterns are seen in the formation of the brain and nervous system?**
Development begins with the neural tube, which later forms the brain and spinal cord. Neurons form and migrate to the top of the neural tube to form the cerebral cortex. By 20 weeks of gestation, the cortex has nearly 80 billion neurons. Neurons will continue to proliferate, but many will later be lost through programmed cell death. Synaptogenesis (formation of synapses between neurons) begins after 23 weeks of gestation. Myelination of axons improves the neurons' capability to transmit information.

**4.8 How clearly do infants see, and how well do they see colors and depth?**
Newborn acuity is somewhat limited, with estimates ranging from 20/150 to 20/600. Normal 20/20 vision is achieved by 6 to 12 months of age. It is not clear how well newborns are able to distinguish various colors. Evidence suggests that color vision is adultlike by 3 to 6 months. Experiments with the visual cliff indicate that 2-month-olds can see the difference between the deep and shallow sides, and infants avoid the deep side by the time they can crawl (around 6 months).

**4.9 How well can infants hear, and how early can they distinguish different sounds?**
The auditory system is functional before birth, and young infants can distinguish among a variety of sounds. Newborns prefer the voices of their own mothers, and they can recognize some sounds that they heard while in the womb.

**4.10 When do infants begin to recognize smells and react to different flavors?**
Newborns react positively to the aromas of bananas and butter, but they reject the odors of fish and rotten eggs. Breastfed infants can recognize the smells of their mothers. Newborns prefer sweeter solutions but reject sour and bitter flavors.

**4.11 What reflexes do infants have, and what is their significance?**
Newborns show rooting, sucking, Moro, and grasping reflexes. When reflexes do not appear or disappear according to the usual timetable, neurological problems might be present.

**4.12 What patterns are seen as infants and toddlers learn to control their muscles and motor movements, and what are the factors that govern this phase of development?**
Motor development generally proceeds according to cephalocaudal (head-to-tail) and proximodistal (near-to-far) patterns. Infants hold their heads up before they can sit alone, and they sit before they walk. They coordinate large muscles in the arms before gaining dexterity in the hands and fingers. Neurological development and opportunities to exercise muscle both contribute. According to dynamic systems theory, motor skills emerge from complex interactions among neurological development, physical growth, learning, and motivation.

**4.13 How does motor development compare across cultures, and what can we learn from these comparisons?**
Cultural differences in exercise and stimulation can lead to small differences in attainment of motor milestones.

**4.14 When are toddlers ready for toilet training, and what is the best approach for parents to use?**
Toilet training usually begins around age 2 years, and most toddlers can stay dry during the day by the time they are 3 years old.

## REVISITING THEMES

The roles of *nature* and *nurture* can be seen as infants learn to adjust their sleep patterns (p. 114) and when they learn new motor skills such as walking and toilet training (pp. 129–131, 132). The interplay of nature and nurture is also evident as our early experiences in life help shape connections in the brain and nervous system (pp. 120–121).

*Neuroscientists* study the growth and development of the brain and nervous system, and pediatricians and other experts use the appearance and disappearance of infant reflexes as an indication of neurological maturity (pp. 130–131).

*Diversity and multiculturalism* are reflected in a many topics in this chapter. Cultural differences were noted in co-sleeping (p. 115), breastfeeding (pp. 117–118), and the role of exercise in motor development (pp. 129–131). Ethnic and racial differences were highlighted for rates of infant mortality (p. 111), prenatal care (pp. 112–113), and SIDS (p. 116), and for the timing of toilet training in toddlers (pp. 132–133).

*Positive development and resilience* are connected to the increasing use of prenatal care by pregnant women in the U.S. (p. 112) and by the resilience of preterm infants who survive and eventually catch up to their peers along many developmental milestones (p. 110).

## KEY TERMS

colostrum (116)
co-sleeping (115)
fine motor development (127)
gross motor development (127)
infant mortality (111)
myelination (120)
neurons (119)
programmed cell death (120)
reflexes (126)
small for gestational age (SGA) (111)
synaptogenesis (120)
Sudden Infant Death Syndrome (SIDS) (116)
very low birth weight (109)
visual acuity (123)

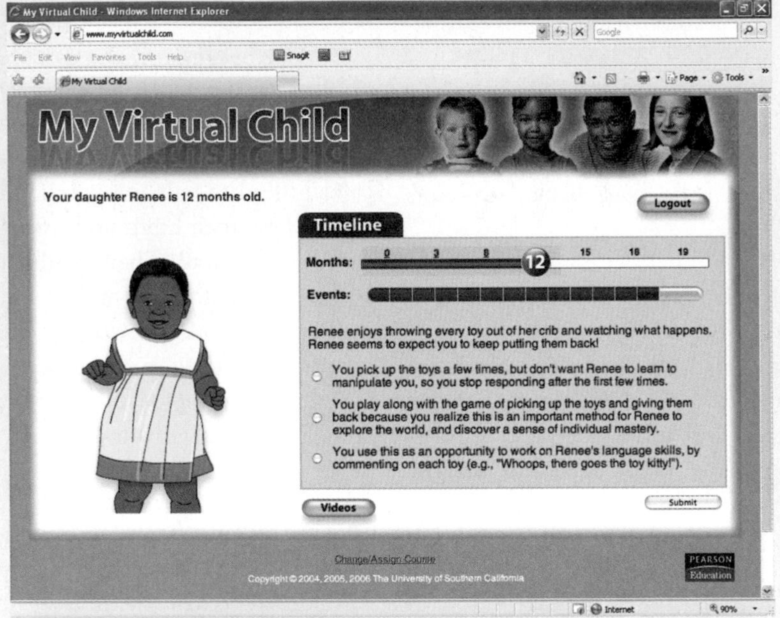


**"What decisions would you make while raising a child? What would the consequences of those decisions be?"**

Find out by accessing My Virtual Child at
**www.mydevelopmentlab.com**
and raising your own virtual child
from birth to age 18.

Watch Visit your Multimedia Library at www.mydevelopmentlab.com to watch an interview with Chi Hae online.

# 5 INFANTS AND TODDLERS

# Cognitive Development in Infants and Toddlers

Chi Hae loves to watch her 11-month-old daughter Cara play. Like most babies, Cara seems eager to touch things, experiment, and experience the world (trying to put most things in her mouth, of course)! Yesterday, Cara was holding a baby rattle. Whereas a few months ago Cara would have shaken the rattle or thrown it, yesterday she looked at it closely and moved it up and down slowly. It was as if Cara was deliberately studying the rattle and experimenting to see what kinds of sounds it would produce. A friend told Chi Hae that babies don't even realize that something continues to exist if they can't see or touch it. Just as her friend predicted, it worked when Chi Hae distracted Cara from playing with a toy by hiding it under a blanket—until recently. Now Cara cries for a few minutes when Chi Hae takes something away from her. Even though Cara hasn't said any "real" words yet, Chi Hae has no trouble understanding what Cara needs, when she's happy, and when she wants another bite of her cereal.

Chi Hae wonders what babies this age understand about their world. Do infants connect the sounds they hear with what they see? Do toys that move and make sounds encourage development, or does all the clamor just confuse a young baby? How do babies come to realize that objects exist whether they can see them or not? And why does it seem so easy for babies to communicate, even before they are able to produce any words? Most important, Chi Hae wonders what she can do to support her daughter's cognitive development.

As you read this chapter, look for the "Think About Chi Hae . . ." questions that ask you to consider what you're learning from Chi Hae's perspective.

Like Chi Hae, you might have wondered what infants really understand about the world. How do babies put together the information from their senses and think about the things they experience? And how do they communicate their needs and thoughts to others? As you will learn in this chapter, even young infants have

surprisingly well-developed capabilities in some areas (such as perceptual skills), and they are able to quickly and easily develop other complex skills (such as understanding the permanence of objects and using language). As you might recall from Chapter 1, *cognitive* refers to mental processes such as perceiving, thinking, remembering, solving problems, and communicating with language. While *sensation* is the physical process of detecting information about a stimulus in the environment through the five senses and transmitting that information to the brain, **perception** is the cognitive process of organizing, coordinating, and interpreting that information. Perception is an important part of cognition; it enables people to use sensory input to think, solve problems, and function in their environments. In this chapter, we will describe the perceptual, cognitive, and language abilities of infants and toddlers, and we will introduce you to some of the major theories that explain these areas of development. You will also see examples of three of the themes we identified in Chapter 1—nature and nurture, the role of neuroscience, and positive development and resilience.

## Perceptual Development

As you read in Chapter 4, the human nervous system is relatively immature at the time of birth. Most of the synapses in the brain have not yet formed, and many of the neurons have not yet acquired the myelin sheath that insulates the axons and speeds transmission of neural impulses. Newborns can move their eyes to locate and track objects in their surroundings, but until they gain better control of the intricate muscles in and around their eyes, infants have trouble focusing on a target and coordinating the images coming from each eye. Early philosophers, most notably John Locke, believed that the newborn's mind was a "blank slate." According to this view, infants need to learn by trial and error to use their senses to form meaningful perceptions. One of the founders of psychology, William James (1890/1950), claimed that the mental experience of the infant was "one great blooming, buzzing confusion" (p. 488).

Do infants really begin life this helpless? Clearly, they do not. As we mentioned in Chapter 4, newborns come equipped with an array of sensory capabilities. The emergence of reliable nonverbal techniques for testing these capabilities in infants has opened the floodgates for research in the past few decades. Since the 1950s, scientists have learned an impressive amount about the perceptual capabilities of infants. It is apparent that, far from experiencing a "blooming, buzzing confusion," even young infants have a tremendous ability to organize and use sensory information in a meaningful way.

AS YOU STUDY THIS SECTION, ASK YOURSELF THESE QUESTIONS:

**5.1** What is the preferential-looking technique, and what has it shown us about infant perception?

**5.2** How is the habituation–dishabituation technique used to test infant perception?

**5.3** Can infants coordinate information across different sensory modalities or avenues of sensation?

**perception**
The cognitive process of organizing, coordinating, and interpreting sensory information.

**preferential-looking technique**
Technique used to test infant visual perception. If infants consistently look longer at some patterns than at others, researchers infer that the infants can see a difference between the patterns.

### Robert Fantz and the Early Work in Testing Visual Preferences

As early as 1951, Robert Fantz was conducting experiments with newly hatched chickens and infant chimpanzees to determine whether perception of different forms (e.g., distinguishing squares from circles) was innate or learned (can you see how this is an example of the nature and nurture theme?) (see Fantz, 1956, 1961). To study human infants, Fantz and his associates used a *looking chamber* (Figure 5.1). The researchers placed infants on the sliding tray at the bottom. A researcher, standing over the chamber, could slide patterns on cards through slots in the top of the chamber. Peering through a hole, the researcher could also observe the infants' eyes and use electronic devices to record the time infants spent fixating on (i.e., looking at) each pattern. "If an infant consistently turns its gaze toward some forms more often than toward others, it must be able to perceive form" (Fantz, 1961, p. 67). This became the logic of the **preferential-looking technique**, a simple but powerful procedure that many researchers have since used to investigate infant perception.

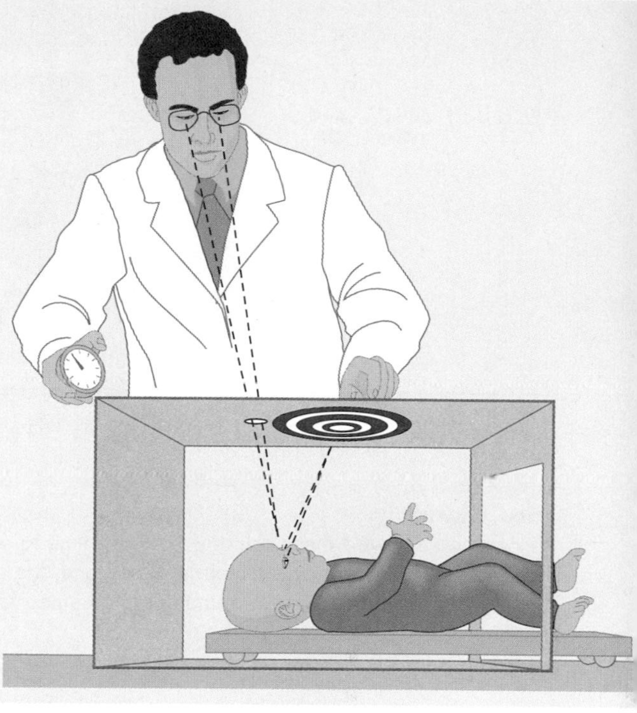

▲ FIGURE 5.1
**Looking Chamber**
Early researchers used the looking chamber to investigate visual preferences in young infants. The infant looked up from the bottom toward stimulus patterns illuminated within the chamber. A researcher monitored the infant's eyes, recording the amount of time the infant's gaze fixated on each stimulus pattern. (Based on Fantz, 1961.)

Figure 5.2 shows the results from one of Fantz's early experiments. Newborns who were only 2 to 5 days old looked more at a drawing of a face than at a bull's-eye or newsprint, but they preferred any of these detailed patterns over plain colored disks (Fantz, 1963). Infants spent approximately equal time looking at the colored disks, especially the yellow and white disks, so the experiment didn't show whether the infants could distinguish between these colors. Using this preferential-looking technique, Fantz collected some of the first scientific data that demonstrated conclusively that human infants are able to perceive form and pattern.

Using Fantz's preferential-looking technique and similar techniques, other researchers have followed with their own studies and found that newborn babies prefer the following types of visual information (see Bjorklund, 1989, for a review):

- Moving stimuli
- Outer contours or edges
- Sharp color contrasts (e.g., where black meets white or where red meets white)
- Patterns with some complexity or detail (but not too complex)
- Symmetrical patterns
- Curved patterns
- Patterns that resemble the human face

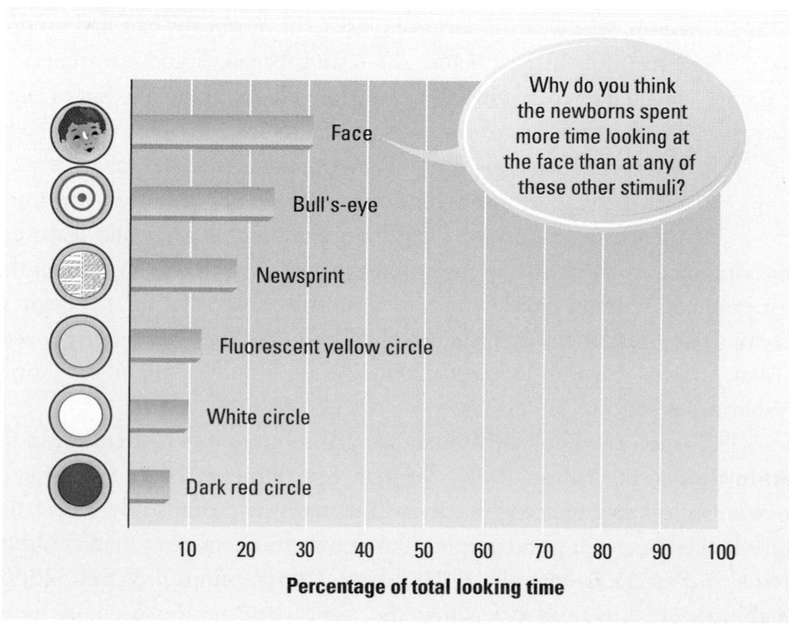


◀ FIGURE 5.2
**Preferential-Looking Results**
This graph shows results from an early preferential-looking study. Stimuli were presented one at a time in random order to newborns who were only 2 to 5 days old. What types of features caught the newborns' eyes? (Based on Fantz, 1963.)

▲ FIGURE 5.3
**Face Stimuli**
Researchers showed these patterns one at a time to newborns who were only a few minutes old. Although they had yet to see their first real face, the newborns preferred to look at the pattern that most resembled the arrangement of the human face. Why do you think this was so? (Goren, Sarty, & Wu, 1975.)

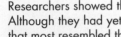

Some of these preferences are evident in Figure 5.2. Parents can use these preferences in shaping their babies' environments. To capture the infant's attention, crib mobiles, baby books, blocks, and other infant toys should feature sharp color contrasts, symmetrical patterns, curves, and even human face patterns. As infants explore these and other patterns, their sensory systems get the input they need to stimulate further growth and development.

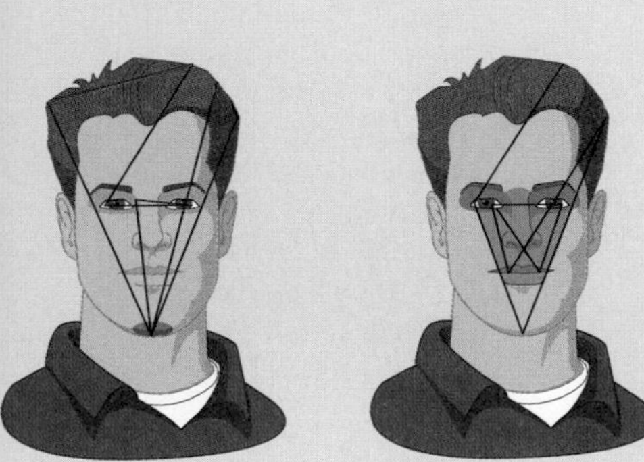
One-month-old's gaze
Fixations are primarily to the chin and outer hairline.
Two-month-old's gaze
Fixations are primarily between the eyes and mouth.

▲ FIGURE 5.4
**Infant Visual Fixation on Facial Patterns**
Tracking their eye movements, you can see that 1-month-old infants spend most of their time looking at the external features of the face—mostly the chin and outer hairline. By 2 months, infants are now looking more at the internal features, especially the eyes. (Based on Maurer & Salapatek, 1976.)

One of the more intriguing findings we've mentioned is that infants tend to prefer patterns that resemble the human face. One group of researchers entered the delivery room when babies were born and showed newborns the patterns in Figure 5.3 (Goren, Sarty, & Wu, 1975). One at a time, in a random series, they placed the patterns about 6 to 10 inches in front of each newborn's nose, then moved the patterns slowly toward the left or right. Although the newborns were only a few minutes old, they reliably turned their heads farther to follow the pattern that most resembled the human face. Because people in the delivery room were wearing surgical masks, the newborns had had no opportunity to see a real human face before the testing began. Some researchers speculate that at birth, babies are already equipped with an innate *schema*, or mental framework, for the structure of the human face. However, other researchers remind us that these newborns might not recognize the patterns as "faces" *per se* (another example of trying to understand the relative roles of nature and nurture in development). Instead, they might be responding to particular features that happen to be contained in faces—left-right symmetry and more details in the top than bottom half, for example. It might not be until 3 to 5 months of age that infants begin recognizing perceptual cues specific to faces (such as the location of the eyes and the space between them) (Bhatt, Bertin, Hayden, & Reed, 2005; Turati, Simion, Milani, & Umtilá, 2002; Turati, Valenza, Leo & Simion, 2005).

The "specialness" of the human face has received much attention in the research literature (Cohen & Cashon, 2006; Kellman & Arterberry, 2006; Quinn et al., 2008). Even newborns are able to recognize individual faces, and one study found that 3-month-old girls looked longer at photographs of their own mothers' faces than at photos of other adult females (Barrera & Maurer, 1981; Turati, Cassia, Simion, & Leo, 2006). Interestingly, 3-month-old boys did not show the same pattern. Research in neuroscience using event-related potentials (ERPs, changes in the brain's electrical activity in response to a stimulus) indicates that our brains process human face information differently than information about objects. For example, stimuli of human faces are processed more quickly than object stimuli, and different brain areas and hemispheres are involved (de Haan & Nelson, 1999). It is interesting to note that children who have autism spectrum disorder (ASD), a disorder characterized by impairments in social interaction and communication, show different ERP patterns for familiar versus unfamiliar toys, but not for familiar versus unfamiliar faces. Normally developing children show different ERPs for familiar versus unfamiliar faces as well as toys (Dawson et al., 2002).

Beyond recognizing their mothers' faces, when do you think infants begin to judge the physical attractiveness of faces? Would you believe that they do this by 2 months of age? In an intriguing study, Judith Langlois and her colleagues asked college students to rate the attractiveness of photos of female adults. Then they slide-projected the photos in pairs on a large screen in front of infants (Langlois et al., 1987). When an "attractive" photo was paired with an "unattractive" photo, 2-month-olds looked longer at the attractive photo. Langlois and her colleagues (1987) concluded that "the tendency to detect and prefer certain faces over others is present very early in life, long before any significant exposure to contemporary standards, definitions, and stereotypes" (p. 367). If beauty is in the eye of the beholder, it's there at a surprisingly early age!

Infant scanning of faces changes significantly from 1 to 2 months of age (Maurer & Salapatek, 1976). As Figure 5.4 shows, 1-month-olds tend to fixate more on the external features of faces (the chin and hairline), whereas 2-month-olds tend to focus on the internal features (especially the eyes and mouth). This change might help to explain why it is in the 2- to 3-month period that infants begin to show recognition of familiar faces (e.g., their mothers) and a preference for attractive faces: It's the internal features that are most helpful in recognizing people. **Watch** on **mydevelopmentlab**

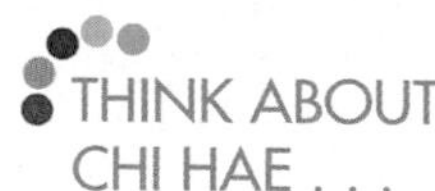

THINK ABOUT CHI HAE . . .

On the basis of the preferential-looking research reviewed so far, what could you tell Chi Hae about her baby's perceptual abilities? What types of patterns or decorations might her baby prefer?

THINKING CRITICALLY

Why do you believe 2-month-olds preferred looking at "attractive" faces? How did they learn or know which faces were more attractive?

**Watch** a video on Infant Perception.
www.mydevelopmentlab.com

## Habituation–Dishabituation Research

Recall from Figure 5.2 that young infants did not show a preference among the plain colored disks. Can infants see the differences among these colors? On the basis of this test alone, it's not possible to know whether infants can visually discriminate between the colors. This is an important limitation of the preferential-looking technique: To show visual discrimination, infants not only must be able to *see* the difference between the stimuli, but also must have some reason to *prefer* one over the other. What if infants can see the difference but find both stimuli to be equally interesting?

To solve this problem, a more stringent test of visual discrimination involves the **habituation–dishabituation technique**, which capitalizes on infants' tendency to look longer at novel (new) stimuli than at familiar (old) stimuli. As an example, consider the experiment conducted by Cohen, Gelber, and Lazar (1971). Imagine that you show a red circle to a 4-month-old infant for several seconds, and you record the amount of time the infant spent looking at the circle. Then you remove the circle, and then you show it again. Repeat this procedure, each time recording how long the infant looks at the circle. Plotting the looking times, you might notice a trend, as shown in Figure 5.5. That is, the infant's interest in the stimulus has likely decreased across trials. The infant has shown **habituation**—the tendency to reduce a response to a stimulus that is presented repeatedly. Habituation indicates that the infant processed the stimulus and recognized it on its repeated appearances.

Now look at what happens during the *dishabituation trials* in Figure 5.5. Here, the same infant sees a series of stimuli with familiar or novel forms and colors. Fixation time for the same familiar red circle remains low, continuing the trend shown in habituation trials. The infant continued to show habituation to the familiar color and form. But a change in color (to a green circle) or a change in form (to a red triangle) produces an

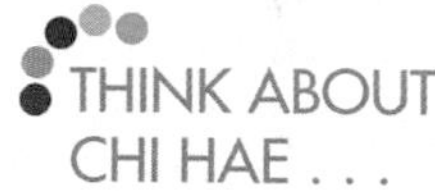

THINK ABOUT CHI HAE . . .

Would you expect Cara to habituate to the decorations, toys, and other stimuli in her environment? Knowing about the habituation–dishabituation tendency, what would you advise Chi Hae to do to enhance the stimulation value of her baby's surroundings?

**habituation–dishabituation technique**
Technique used to test infant perception. Infants are shown a stimulus repeatedly until they respond less (habituate) to it. Then a new stimulus is presented.

**habituation**
The tendency of infants to reduce their response to stimuli that are presented repeatedly.

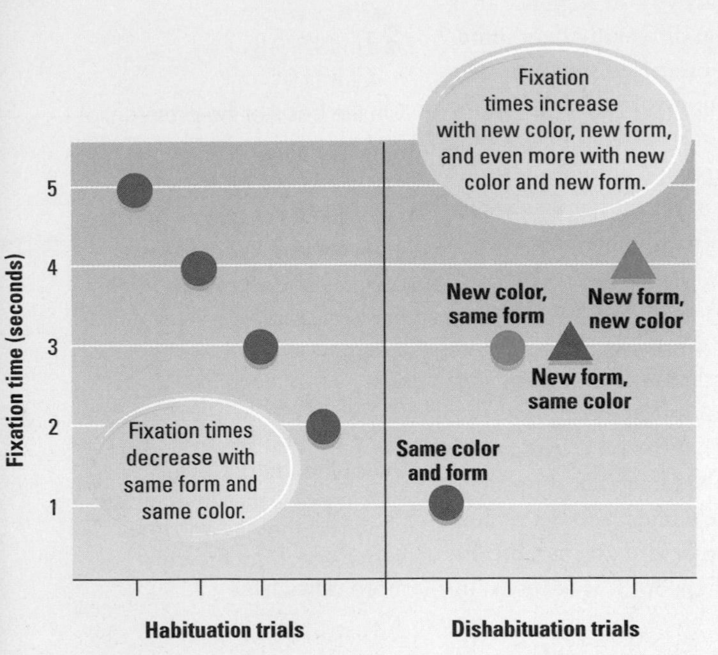


▲ FIGURE 5.5
**Habituation–Dishabituation Example**
This graph shows hypothetical data from a 4-month-old infant using the habituation–dishabituation technique. The infant shows habituation by looking less and less at a red circle that is presented repeatedly, but looking time increases (dishabituation) when novel forms or colors are presented. (Based on Cohen et al., 1971.)

*increase* in fixation time. Changing both color and form (to a green triangle) produces an even greater increase. These increases reflect **dishabituation**—the recovery or increase in response when a new stimulus replaces a familiar stimulus. Dishabituation indicates that the infant can see the difference between the novel and familiar stimuli. In this case, the infant can obviously see the difference between colors (red versus green) and forms (circle versus triangle).

Notice that at the outset of the experiment, there was no reason for the infants to prefer green over red or triangle over circle but that habituating the infants to "red" and "circle" induced such preferences. The habituation–dishabituation technique thus avoids one of the problems with the preferential-looking technique because it can demonstrate visual discrimination even when there is no chance that infants might have an already established preference for one stimulus over another.

An important practical application of these methods of studying infant perception is their use to predict later cognitive skills, even IQ (Fagan, 2000; Kavšek, 2004). Neuroscientists have begun using a modification of the visual habituation procedure, called *habituation of flash evoked potentials*, to assess habituation of electrical activity in the brain as it responds to visual stimulation (González-Frankenberger et al., 2008). The advantage of this newer technique is that infants do not have to actively respond to the stimuli for researchers to determine whether their brains have processed it—in fact, they don't even have to be awake! To read more about issues surrounding the use of habituation techniques to predict cognitive skills, read the Social Policy Perspective box on page 143 called "Assessing Infant Intelligence: A Good Idea?"

## Intermodal Perception: Putting It All Together

Although we have treated the different sensory systems separately so far, in reality, most experiences involve multiple senses. For example, as you walk down the sidewalk, you feel the breeze on your face, see the colors of the sky, hear the voices of people walking around you, and smell the food in restaurants you walk by. In short, you experience the world through combined or integrated sensory inputs, or what researchers refer to as **intermodal perception**. (sometimes also called intersensory perception).

Do human beings need to learn to combine sensory information into unified impressions? According to the *constructivist* view, they do. Jean Piaget (1952b), for example, believed that young infants are not aware that what they see is related to what they hear. He hypothesized that infants need to learn, through experience, to coordinate their sensory systems. (We will discuss Piaget's constructivist theory of cognitive development in the next section.) At the other end of the spectrum, T. G. R. Bower (1974) speculated that infants have to learn to *separate* their sensory impressions. He proposed that in the early months of their lives, infants confuse their sensory impressions—they do not know whether they are seeing or hearing, tasting or smelling. Bower concluded that "the initial primitive unity [of the sensory systems] must go, leaving differentiated sensory systems in place of a unitary perceptual world" (p. 151). In a more moderate view, Eleanor Gibson pointed out that important features in the environment (she called them *invariants*) can be detected by multiple sensory systems (Gibson & Walker, 1984; Rose & Ruff, 1987). For example, you can see that a sidewalk is a solid surface (because its texture continues into the distance), and you can also feel its solidity beneath your feet. Similarly, infants

**dishabituation**
The recovery or increase in infant's response when a familiar stimulus is replaced by one that is novel.

**intermodal perception**
The process of combining or integrating information across sensory modalities.

## Perspective SOCIAL POLICY — ASSESSING INFANT INTELLIGENCE: A GOOD IDEA?

For decades, researchers, educators, and policymakers have tried to find reliable ways to predict intelligence from early childhood, with limited success. Although intelligence test scores change over time, they are reasonably stable starting at about age 5 years of age. But correlations of scores for younger children and infants have typically shown low relationships to later IQ scores.

The habituation–dishabituation procedures that are used to study infant perception have shown promise in predicting cognitive skills later in childhood (Fagan, 2000; Kavšek, 2004; Neisser et al., 1996). Summary studies have found average correlations of about 0.45 between young infants' degrees of dishabituation and the same children's intelligence test scores at 1 to 8 years of age, and .34 with IQ scores in young adulthood (Fagan, Holland, & Weaver, 2007; McCall & Carriger, 1993). This correlation means that infants who show more dishabituation tend to score higher on IQ tests. The memory, discrimination, and recognition skills involved in habituation–dishabituation are related to the kinds of cognitive skills measured in typical intelligence tests. The habituation–dishabituation technique therefore can help researchers to assess cognitive functioning in early infancy and perhaps identify infants who are at risk for developmental delays. Infants who were exposed prenatally to cocaine, for example, show depressed habituation and dishabituation (Mayes, Granger, Frank, Schottenfeld, & Bornstein, 1993). In one study, half of the 3-month-olds who were cocaine-exposed failed to achieve habituation at all (Mayes & Bornstein, 1995). Modifications of the habituation procedure have even found that the rate of habituation *even before birth* is related to being at higher risk of cognitive problems at 6 months of age (Gaultney & Gingras, 2005). Using multiple measures of infant processing speed and memory allows even better prediction of cognitive scores, at least up to three years of age (Domsch, Lohaus, & Thomas, 2009).

Critics point out, however, that researchers do not completely understand what the infant assessments are measuring and how they relate to later cognitive skills. Habituation scores may reflect differences in cognitive speed of processing, but it is also possible that they are measuring differences in temperament or inhibition instead (Neisser et al., 1996). Some studies find that the aspect of the test that correlates with later cognitive skills (i.e., time to habituate versus degree of dishabituation) might be different for different types of infants (Kavšek, 2004). While the infant assessments do predict later scores reasonably well, some studies have found that they do not show good test-retest reliabilities—that is, an individual baby's score changes if more than a few weeks go by before a second test (Andersson, 1996; Slater, 1997; Tasbihsazan, Nettelbeck, & Kirby, 2003). These apparent inconsistencies make it difficult to interpret correlations with later IQ scores. Some critics argue that the best predictor is already known: the home environment. Assessment of early processing abilities might help in understanding specific difficulties, but effective prevention and intervention programs must address multiple factors, including home environments (Meisels & Atkins-Burnett, 2000). Finally, although the researchers who develop these assessments have the best of intentions, the possibility of unfair discrimination against those who are found to be most at risk for later cognitive problems cannot be ignored.

QUESTION **Do you think policymakers should pursue the development of predictive infant assessments? How could this information be useful in developing effective early interventions for children who are at risk? What guidelines would you suggest for the use of these interventions?**

can both smell and taste the sweetness of breast milk or formula and can both see and hear the movement of a rattle. Can infants make connections across these avenues of sensation? Research on intermodal (or intersensory), or cross-modal (or cross-sensory), perception indicates that they can (Bahrick, 2000). **Listen** on **mydevelopmentlab**

One of the classic demonstrations was an experiment conducted by Andrew Meltzoff and Richard Borton (1979). They placed a smooth or a "nubby" pacifier in the mouths of 1-month-old infants, and then removed the pacifier to show both types of pacifiers simultaneously to the infants. The 1-month-olds looked significantly longer at the shape that had been in their mouths—they matched the shape they saw with the one they had felt. In another study, Elizabeth Spelke and her colleagues found that infants can match the dynamic features of moving objects across senses. Infants saw two films side by side

**Listen**: Can researchers really tell what infants are thinking about from what they look at and habituate to? (Author Podcast) www.mydevelopmentlab.com

▲ Does it take a significant amount of trial-and-error learning for infants to connect the voices they hear with the visual images of faces? Evidently not. Using a variety of interesting stimuli, research on intermodal (or intersensory) perception indicates that infants make such connections even when they have had very little experience with the events they are matching.

THINKING CRITICALLY

How do you think infants learn to match information across different sensory modalities? Is this ability available at birth? What real-life examples of intermodal perception have you observed in infants you have known?

(Spelke, 1979). One showed a kangaroo (or donkey) puppet bouncing quickly up and down. In the other film, the puppet bounced more slowly. At the same time the researchers played a slow or fast "thump" or "gong" sound that was synchronized with the bouncing in one of the films. Four-month-old infants looked significantly longer at the film that matched the pace of the sound. Of course, kangaroos do not normally make "thump" or "gong" noises when they jump, and it can be assumed that the infants had no prior experience with kangaroo activities. Still, these young infants matched the pace of the sound with the pace of the bouncing, showing that infants are quite capable of detecting features shared across the different senses.

In related research, 5-month-old infants matched the sound of an engine increasing or decreasing in volume with a video of an automobile coming toward or moving away from them (Walker-Andrews & Lennon, 1985). Five-and-a-half-month-old infants can use information about the hardness or softness of a ball that they touched but could not correctly judge which would fit through a tunnel opening that they saw but did not touch (Schweinle & Wilcox, 2004). In another study, infants 6 to 8 months old matched the number they heard with the number they saw (Starkey, Spelke, & Gelman, 1983). For example, when they heard two drumbeats, they looked longer at a photo of two household objects; when they heard three drumbeats, they preferred to look at three objects.

Again, these findings demonstrate intermodal perception of a variety of complicated events. Intermodal perception is sufficiently evident during infancy that its strength can serve as a reliable indicator of later cognitive functioning. For infants born preterm, scores on intermodal matching at 12 months of age predict cognitive abilities all the way through 6 years of age (Rose & Wallace, 1985). It takes a healthy nervous system to integrate the information flowing to the infant from multiple perceptual modalities.

As you can see, researchers have learned a lot about the perceptual capabilities of human infants. At birth, newborns can locate and track objects, and they can perceive a variety of forms, colors, sounds, tastes, and smells. As their brains and nervous systems continue to develop, their perceptual abilities will become even more refined. With rapidly developing nervous systems and enhanced perceptual capabilities, young children are ready to absorb information and learn amazing amounts about their world. In the next section, we will look at one prominent theory that describes how infants and toddlers conceptualize information and learn to think about all of the wonders they encounter.

## LET'S REVIEW . . .

1. With the preferential-looking technique, when an infant spends more time looking at a checkerboard pattern than at a plain colored square, it can be inferred that:
   a. the infant can see the difference between the checkerboard and the plain square.
   b. the infant is probably color-blind.
   c. the infant's visual acuity is very poor.
   d. the infant has habituated to the checkerboard pattern.
2. On the basis of research described in this section, it seems that infants recognize the configuration of the human face:
   a. by 3 months of age.
   b. by 6 months of age.
   c. by 1 year of age.
   d. immediately after birth.
3. Jamil shows his infant son a teddy bear several times. Each time Jamil shows the teddy bear, his son looks

less at it. The decreased interest shown by Jamil's son shows an example of:
   **a.** habituation.
   **b.** dishabituation.
   **c.** preferential looking.
   **d.** cross-modal perception.

**4.** Which of the following is an example of intermodal perception?
   **a.** Infants prefer to look at faces over most any other stimulus.
   **b.** Infants habituate before they show dishabituation.
   **c.** Infants prefer to look at attractive and happy-looking faces.
   **d.** Infants can match the sound of a happy voice with the film of a happy face.

**5.** True or False: Infants are more likely to show that they can discriminate red from blue when they are tested by using the habituation–dishabituation technique than when they are tested with the preferential-looking technique.

**6.** True or False: Jean Piaget believed that infants need to learn to separate sources of information coming from their different perceptual systems.

Answers: 1. a, 2. d, 3. a, 4. d, 5. T, 6. F

# Explaining Cognitive Development: Piaget's Constructivist View

Vast changes in thinking are evident in every aspect of life as children grow from infants into toddlers, including such things as what they will pay attention to, the kinds of questions they ask, and the explanations they can offer or understand. These changes in thinking, in which children's thought gradually becomes more organized and complex, are collectively called *cognitive development*. The most influential theorist in the study of cognitive development was Jean Piaget (1896–1980). His prolific career in psychology spanned an astonishing seven decades and had an immense impact on the field (Beilin, 1994).

AS YOU STUDY THIS SECTION, ASK YOURSELF THESE QUESTIONS:

5.4 How is Piaget's background in biology reflected in his theory of cognitive development?

5.5 Why is Piaget's theory considered a constructivist view, and how do the main concepts in this theory explain the development of cognitive structures?

5.6 What are the main limitations and advances in cognitive processing at the sensorimotor stage?

## Piaget as a Child Prodigy

Jean Piaget was no ordinary child. From a very early age, he showed tremendous intellectual talent. Born in Neuchâtel, Switzerland, a small university town, Piaget showed an early interest in nature, particularly in observing wildlife in its natural setting. His observations led to the first of his many scientific publications. He was only 10 years old when he published his first article, a one-page report on an albino sparrow he observed in a park. At the Museum of Natural History in Neuchâtel, Piaget began working with a zoologist who specialized in mollusks (clams, oysters, snails, etc.). Piaget "catalogued and studied adaptation" (Bringuier, 1980, p. 8), detailing how mollusks' shells changed in relation to the movement of the water in which they lived. As you will see, the idea of adaptation came to play a central role in Piaget's later theory of human cognitive development.

After earning a Ph.D. degree at age 21, Piaget became interested in psychology. He worked for a time at a psychiatric clinic in Zurich, where he learned about Freudian

▲ Jean Piaget was a pioneer in child development research. His theory revolutionized how children's thinking is viewed.

psychoanalysis and how to conduct a clinical interview. Later, he moved to Paris to work with Theophile Simon in the Binet Laboratory. Simon and Alfred Binet were known for their work on intelligence testing, and Piaget's job in the laboratory was to help develop a standardized French version of some reasoning tasks. These years were important in several ways for Piaget and the development of his theory and methods. First, he realized that children were *active* in their thinking, not passive. He found that even very young children made admirable attempts to understand and answer questions, although their reasoning was far from what an adult would see as logical. Drawing on his biological background, Piaget interpreted these attempts as children's efforts to adapt cognitively to the situations they were in, to understand and succeed in their situations. Second, Piaget began to see that children's thinking showed a striking regularity and consistency, even though the thinking was often incorrect. Piaget noticed that children of the same age tended to give the same wrong answers, whereas children of a different age tended to give different wrong answers. There seemed to be age-related patterns in the children's thinking. These might not seem to be groundbreaking insights today, but at that time, most experts believed that children were passive recipients of information (simply memorizing information without interpreting or modifying it) and did not have coherent or regular ways of thinking. Piaget challenged these well-established views. Finally, Piaget realized that a *clinical method*, in which children are asked to explain the reasons for their answers rather than simply to give an answer, could be an invaluable tool in his efforts to understand children's thinking.

## Constructivism and Interaction with the Environment

Piaget combined his background in biology with his interest in understanding how logic and knowledge develop and spent the rest of his career observing children and articulating his theory of cognitive development. He applied several concepts from biology and used them to explain how knowledge develops.

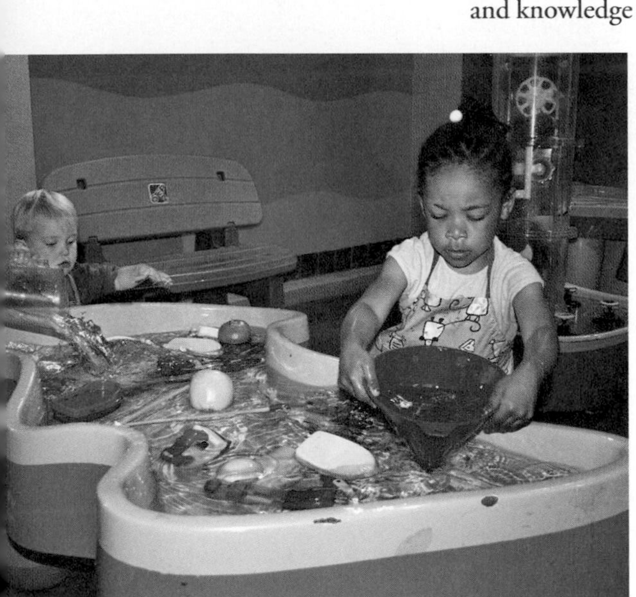

▲ How is this child constructing her own understanding of science concepts?

**constructivist view**
The view that people construct their own knowledge and understanding of the world by using what they already know and understand to interpret new experiences.

Piaget's theory is often described as a **constructivist view**. According to *constructivists*, people interpret their environments and experiences in light of the knowledge and experiences they already have. People do not simply take in an external reality and develop an unchanged, exact mental copy of objects or events. Instead, they build (or "construct") their own individual understandings and knowledge. For Piaget, the essential building block for cognition is the *scheme*. A **scheme** is an organized pattern of action or thought. It is a broad concept and can refer to organized patterns of physical action (such as an infant reaching to grasp an object) or mental action (such as a high school student thinking about how to solve an algebra problem).

As children interact with the environment, individual schemes become modified, combined, and reorganized to form more complex cognitive structures. Think of cognitive structures as the organizing framework of all a child's knowledge and cognitive skills. According to Piaget, structures are essential for understanding new knowledge, but structures are also changed by the new knowledge. As children mature, these structures allow more complex and sophisticated ways of thinking. These, in turn, allow children to interact in qualitatively different ways with their environment. For example, a little girl develops a scheme for noticing similarities between objects (we'll call this a "compare" scheme) and a separate one for noticing differences (a "contrast" scheme). Gradually, she combines the two into a single cognitive structure that allows her to compare and contrast objects at the same time. When she encounters a new object, she uses this coordinated cognitive structure to develop a fuller understanding of the object. The first time she encounters an avocado, for example, she can compare and contrast it to other foods. This process will help her to determine what kind of food it is and will increase her understanding of the overall category (similar in size to an orange but different in shape, similar in color to a lime, different in texture from an apple).

Cognitive structures not only organize existing knowledge, but also serve as filters for all new experiences. That is, people interpret new experiences in light of their already existing cognitive structures. Because no two people ever have exactly the same experiences, no two cognitive structures ever are exactly the same, and no two people ever interpret events in exactly the same way. The way you interpret and understand the information you're learning in this chapter is different, at least slightly, from the way your classmates understand it, because each of you filters and interprets the information through a different cognitive structure.

With respect to the relative roles of nature and nurture in development, Piaget believed that extensive interaction with the environment is absolutely essential for each person's cognitive development. Piaget acknowledged that biological maturation sets the general limits within which cognitive development occurs, but he placed much more emphasis on the role of the environment. Children who have severely limited interactions with their environments simply will not have the opportunities to develop and reorganize their cognitive structures so as to achieve mature ways of thinking. The way people interact with the environment is not random, however. Three common processes guide their interactions: *organization, adaptation*, and *reflective abstraction*. If you have studied biology, you will recognize the influence of Piaget's biology background in the first two of these processes. Both concepts originate in the physical sciences, and Piaget used them in his theory of psychological development.

**Organization** is the tendency of all species to integrate separate elements into increasingly complex higher-order structures. For example, consider the human body. Cells themselves are organized systems of subcellular material; cells also organize into tissues, tissues into organs, organs into organ systems, and organ systems into the body. Piaget believed that the tendency to organize also occurs on the psychological level—that people try to organize their knowledge into coherent systems. In fact, Piaget believed that the tendency to organize is so basic that people cannot keep from trying to organize their knowledge. This explains why you might find yourself thinking about something that didn't make sense to you when you encountered it, even when you don't intend or want to spend time thinking about it. The advantage of this organizational tendency is that it gives people a way to understand and interpret events and objects they encounter; in short, it helps us to function more successfully in our psychological environments. The disadvantage is, of course, that the particular way in which you organize your knowledge might be completely wrong. If enough mistakes and misinterpretations occur, however, you might reexamine your cognitive organization and perhaps make adjustments. Piaget called this later process *adaptation*.

In biology, the term **adaptation** refers to every species' tendency to make modifications in order to survive and succeed in the environment. (Remember how the mollusks' shells adapted to the water currents?) Applied to cognitive development, *adaptation* means changing one's cognitive structure or one's environment (or both to some degree) in order to better understand the environment. Figure 5.6 (p. 148) diagrams the steps involved in adaptation: A child moves from assimilation through cognitive disequilibrium, accommodation, and cognitive equilibrium, then back to a new assimilation.

Let's explore this process using the example of Lily, a 2-year-old who is learning to name animals (see Figure 5.6). Lily has a dog at home, and according to her "dog scheme," "doggies" are animals that have four feet and fur and that bark and fetch balls. One day, riding in the car with her mother, Lily points to a field with several cows and

Can you think of a time when you found yourself wondering about an event, a fact, or a concept that you did not quite understand, even though you did not intend to think about it? As you continued to think about it, did it finally "fall into place" as you were able to integrate it into your cognitive structures?

**scheme**
An organized pattern of physical or mental action.

**organization**
The tendency to integrate separate elements into increasingly complex higher-order structures.

**adaptation**
In cognitive development, the process of changing a cognitive structure or the environment (or both) in order to understand the environment.

exclaims, "Look, Mommy, doggies!" She is excited to see so many "doggies," especially ones that are so large! Lily is trying to understand these new animals by thinking about them as something she already understands: "doggies." This is an example of **assimilation**, the process of bringing new objects or information into a scheme that already exists. ((•• [Listen on **mydevelopmentlab**

((•• [**Listen**: How can confusion be a good thing? (Author Podcast) www.mydevelopmentlab.com

Thinking of these new animals as "doggies," Lily fully expects that they will also bark and fetch balls. Such misunderstandings are common when a person tries to force new objects into an ill-fitting scheme. Lily's mother, however, comments, "No, those are cows. They are bigger than dogs. And see the udders underneath? Cows give us milk." These comments place Lily into cognitive disequilibrium—she is confused. Lily realizes that she has never seen udders under dogs and also has never seen dogs that large. To resolve her cognitive conflict, Lily adjusts her understanding of animals. She adds new information about dogs (they are smaller and don't give us milk), and she learns a new animal (cows are like dogs but larger, and they give us milk). These adjustments are examples of **accommodation**, the process of modifying old schemes or creating new ones to fit better with assimilated information. Now Lily can properly identify dogs and cows, and her new success in naming the animals moves her into cognitive equilibrium. Lily remains in cognitive equilibrium until she visits the zoo and encounters a new animal: an elephant. How will she assimilate this animal?

THINKING CRITICALLY

Think back over your day so far. Can you identify an example of assimilation in your daily activities? Can you think of an example of accommodation?

Piaget claimed that people try to understand new experiences by assimilating these experiences into the schemes or cognitive structures that they already have. If the assimilation does not work completely, there is an imbalance between the new experience and the old scheme. Piaget described this imbalance as a state of *cognitive disequilibrium*. To resolve the disequilibrium, people accommodate, or adjust, their schemes to provide a better fit for the new experience. If this process is successful, they achieve *cognitive equilibrium*. **Equilibration** therefore is the dynamic process of moving between states of cognitive disequilibrium and equilibrium as new experiences are assimilated and schemes are accommodated.

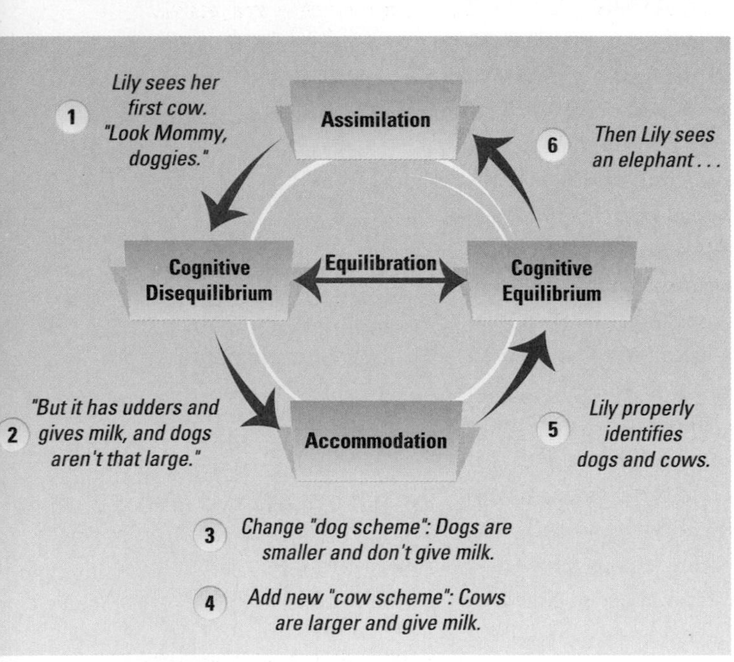


▲ FIGURE 5.6
**Adaptation and Equilibration**
In the cycle of adaptation and equilibration, a new experience is first assimilated into an existing scheme. If it does not fit properly, cognitive disequilibrium results. Accommodating (adjusting) the scheme brings the child to cognitive equilibrium until a new assimilation challenges the scheme again.

Because of the process of organization, human beings are never satisfied with equilibrium. They stretch and extend their cognitive structures by assimilating new and challenging information. According to Piaget, the tendency to seek equilibrium is always present—people are constantly seeking to understand—but equilibration is a dynamic process and is never fully achieved. In other words, although there are certainly periods when a person understands and deals effectively with the environment, no one ever attains perfect, complete, and permanent understanding of everything. Piaget believed that "the normal state of mind is one of disequilibrium—or rather a state of 'moving equilibrium'" (Beilin, 1994, p. 263). There are always new things to learn.

A final process that guides thinking is reflective abstraction. In **reflective abstraction**, a person notices something in the environment (e.g., some specific property of an object or action), then reflects on it (Ginsburg & Opper, 1988; Piaget, 1971). That is, the person tries to relate it to his or her current cognitive structures. As a result of reflection, people modify their current cognitive structures. For example, a boy playing on the beach might notice that the number of rocks he has is the same regardless of whether he arranges them in a line or a circle or piles them on top of one another. Reflective abstraction in this case involves the child's *noticing* that he has the same number of rocks, then *thinking about the implication* of this fact—that number is not affected by how they are arranged.

According to Piaget, people must engage in reflective abstraction to learn from their interactions with the environment. The process enables them to isolate and think about specific properties, compare and contrast them, and think about how they understand them. In this way, reflective abstraction *leads to* the accommodation of cognitive structures. A child can notice something in the environment, but if he does not think about its meaning or its relation to what he already knows, no cognitive reorganization will occur. In our earlier example, Lily would not have accommodated her understanding of "doggies" if she had not (1) *noticed* that the cows were much larger than dogs (and had udders) and (2) reflected or *thought about* what this meant.

THINKING CRITICALLY

Engage in some reflective abstraction: What do you notice and think about Piaget's background in biology and how it relates to the concepts to explain cognitive development?

The processes of organization, adaptation, and reflective abstraction play important roles in children's development. First, children are naturally curious. They are constantly probing and exploring their environments, looking for ways to challenge their existing schemes, and reflecting on whether the things they encounter make sense to them. But without opportunities for exploration and stimulating experiences, there would be nothing new to assimilate. Second, cognitive disequilibrium is a precursor to learning. When children are confused and perplexed, they are ready to make adjustments—they are ready to make accommodations in their schemes. Although it might be tempting to think of confusion as a sign of failure or as something to avoid, in Piaget's system it is a necessary step toward success. Finally, the concept of constructivism is embedded in the cycle. Faced with disequilibrium, children will accommodate their own schemes, engage in reflective abstraction, and improve and reorganize their cognitive structures. In short, children do not passively absorb structures from the adults and other people around them. They actively create their own accommodations and so construct their own understandings.

THINK ABOUT CHI HAE . . .

What kinds of experiences could Chi Hae provide to encourage Cara to engage in adaptation, organization, and reflective abstraction? How can caregivers for infants use constructivist concepts to facilitate cognitive development?

## Piaget's Stage 1: Sensorimotor Thought (Birth to 2 Years)

We have seen that children adapt individual schemes (such as "doggie" and "cow") through equilibration. According to Piaget, our continual organization and adaptation lead to periodic major reorganizations of cognitive structures, which result in four broad stages of cognitive development. After a major reorganization, new and more powerful ways of thinking become possible. Each stage has certain skills and limitations, as summarized in Table 5.1 (page 150). In this chapter, we will focus on Stage 1, sensorimotor thought, which involves developments in infants and toddlers. We will discuss Stages 2, 3, and 4 in detail in later chapters.

According to Piaget, infants can engage only in **sensorimotor thought**. That is, they know the world only in terms of their own sensory input (what they can see, smell, taste, touch, and hear) and their physical or motor actions on it (e.g., sucking, reaching, and grasping). They do not have internal mental representations of the objects and events that exist outside their own body. For example, consider what happens when you give 3-month-old Hyeree a plastic rattle. Hyeree grasps the rattle tightly in her hand, shakes it back and forth, and rubs it against her cheek. Then she brings the rattle to her mouth to explore it in detail by sucking and biting on it. Finally, she flings the rattle to the floor and stares brightly back at you. Now, what does Hyeree "know" about the rattle?

According to Piaget, Hyeree doesn't know anything about the rattle unless she is having direct sensory or motor contact with it. At the time when she is grasping and shaking the rattle, she knows how it feels in her hand and how it moves and sounds when she shakes it. She can feel its smooth surface against her cheek. She knows more about the detailed bumps, curves, and textures when she has it in her mouth. After she flings it to the floor, however, she has no way of maintaining an internalized mental representation of the rattle. She therefore can't "think" about the rattle, and she doesn't know or remember anything about it.

**assimilation**
The process of bringing new objects or information into a scheme that already exists.

**accommodation**
The process of modifying old schemes or creating new ones to better fit assimilated information.

**equilibration**
The dynamic process of moving between states of cognitive disequilibrium and equilibrium.

**reflective abstraction**
The process of noticing and thinking about the implications of information and experiences.

**sensorimotor thought**
Thought that is based only on sensory input and physical (motor) actions.

**TABLE 5.1**
**Piaget's Four Stages of Cognitive Development**

| COGNITIVE STAGE | LIMITATIONS | ACHIEVEMENTS |
|---|---|---|
| Sensorimotor Thought: Birth to 2 years | • No representational thought; infants cannot form internal symbols early in this stage.<br>• Object permanence is lacking early in this stage. | • Representational, symbolic thought gradually emerges as the stage progresses.<br>• Object permanence develops as the stage progresses. |
| Preoperational Thought: 2–7 years | • Intuitive logic leads to egocentrism, animism, artificialism, and an inability to use more objective forms of logic.<br>• Schemes are not reversible, not operational.<br>• Children fail conservation tasks because of centration, focus on static endpoints, and lack of reversibility. | • Flourishing mental representations and symbols are seen in language, art, and play. |
| Concrete Operational Thought: 7–12 years | • Logic is limited to concrete, tangible materials and experiences. | • Logical thought is more objective, allows skills such as class inclusion and transitivity.<br>• Schemes can be reversible, operational.<br>• Children pass conservation problems due to decentration, focus on dynamic transformations, reversibility. |
| Formal Operational Thought: 12 years and up | • Adolescent egocentrism is seen in the imaginary audience and personal fable. | • Hypothetico-deductive reasoning emerges.<br>• Abstract thought emerges. |

Most adults take mental representation for granted. When adults study an object, they form a mental code or image that represents what they know, and they can access this image later when the object is no longer physically available. They are capable of **symbolic (representational) thought**—the ability to form symbols in their minds that represent (or stand for) objects or events in the world. Piaget claimed that young infants cannot form symbols and are therefore stuck in the here-and-now world of their immediate sensory and motor actions. He believed that representational thought gradually emerges as

**symbolic (representational) thought**
The ability to form symbols (or mental representations) that stand for objects or events in the world.

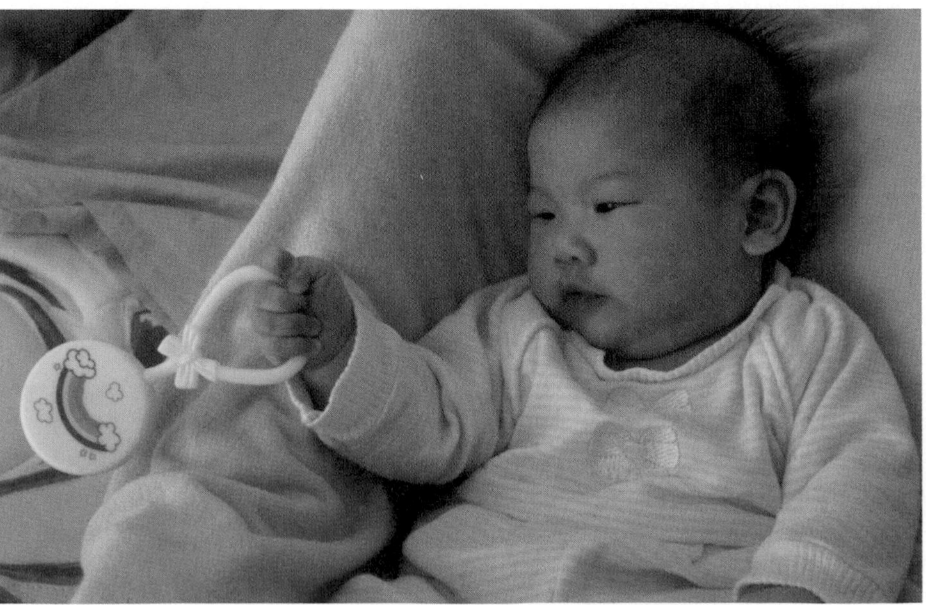

What does this infant understand about her rattle? If she drops the rattle out of sight, will she know that it still exists?

babies develop the ability to form mental symbols. This represents an important achievement, because the emergence of representational thought frees children from the here and now. With representational thought, children can think about past events and anticipate future interactions. Mental representation also allows children to communicate with others, using language. By definition, language of any type requires that arbitrary symbols (words) represent actual things. Without mental representation, it is impossible to learn words and understand what they stand for. **Watch** on **mydevelopmentlab**

**Watch** a video on the Sensorimotor Stage. www.mydevelopmentlab.com

Piaget proposed six substages of sensorimotor thought that describe how representational thought emerges during infancy. These substages are summarized in Table 5.2. If you look carefully across the substages, you will notice a general trend in babies' thinking. Infants begin in the early stages as simply *reflexive*—that is, reacting to environmental stimuli via inborn reflexes. They have no voluntary control over objects or events in their

**TABLE 5.2**
**Piaget's Six Substages of Sensorimotor Thought**

| SENSORIMOTOR SUBSTAGE | AGE | CHARACTERISTIC | EXAMPLES |
|---|---|---|---|
| 1. Basic Reflexes | Birth to 1 month | The first schemes are inborn reflexes. | Rooting, sucking, grasping reflexes. |
| 2. Primary Circular Reactions | 1–4 months | Infants discover actions involving their own bodies by accident, then learn by trial and error to repeat the actions until they become habits (schemes). | At first thumb comes to mouth by accident. Through trial and error, infants learn to reproduce the event until a thumb-sucking scheme becomes established. |
| 3. Secondary Circular Reactions | 4–10 months | Infants discover actions involving objects in the environment by accident, then learn by trial and error to repeat them until they become habits (schemes). | Holding a rattle, an infant might accidentally shake the rattle and enjoy the noise. Through trial and error, the infant learns to reproduce the event until a shaking scheme becomes established. |
| 4. Coordination of Secondary Schemes | 10–12 months | Infants intentionally put two schemes together to solve a problem or reach a goal. Intentionality is a new feature—these new behaviors are no longer discovered by accident. | An infant sees a toy behind a box, pushes the box aside, then reaches for the toy. The infant intentionally combined pushing and reaching schemes to reach the goal (the toy). |
| 5. Tertiary Circular Reactions | 12–18 months | Babies are curious about objects in the world and explore them in a trial-and-error fashion, trying to produce novel reactions. | A baby drops a ball from shoulder height and watches what happens. The baby then explores the dropping scheme by dropping the ball from hip height, then head height, then knee height, observing each new result. |
| 6. Transition to Symbolic Thought | 18–24 months | Toddlers begin to form symbolic representations of events, showing the beginnings of mental thought. Representations still tend to be physical (rather than purely mental), as when toddlers use their own body movements to represent movements of objects in the world. | A 1½-year-old girl would like to open the lid of a box; to think about this, she opens and closes her hand repeatedly. Rather than working directly on the box, she first uses her hand motion as a way to "think" about how to open it. She is thinking about the box using a symbolic representation (her hand). |

environment but can only react to whatever takes place. Gradually, however, infants begin to take more control. These first attempts occur because infants accidentally notice the effects of certain random actions. They begin trying to understand events by using *trial and error*, taking actions and simply observing what happens, then slightly modifying the actions, observing, and so on. Initially, these trial-and-error interactions are observations of effects with no anticipation of what the outcomes might be. Eventually, however, babies show evidence of *intentionality*. That is, they begin to take actions that they expect to have specific outcomes. Intentionality represents an effort to exert control over the environment because it involves taking actions that are intended to produce specific results.

How can parents tell when an infant has achieved representational thought? One line of evidence is the use of language, starting at about 1 year of age—because to use language, the child must have mental representations to which they can attach labels. A second indicator is *deferred imitation*, when a young child observes a behavior and imitates it later, after a period of several hours or days. If the child did not have a mental representation of the behavior, there would be no memory of the event, and imitation would not be possible. Finally, a third line of evidence for representational thought can be seen in babies' grasp of the concept Piaget called *object permanence.*

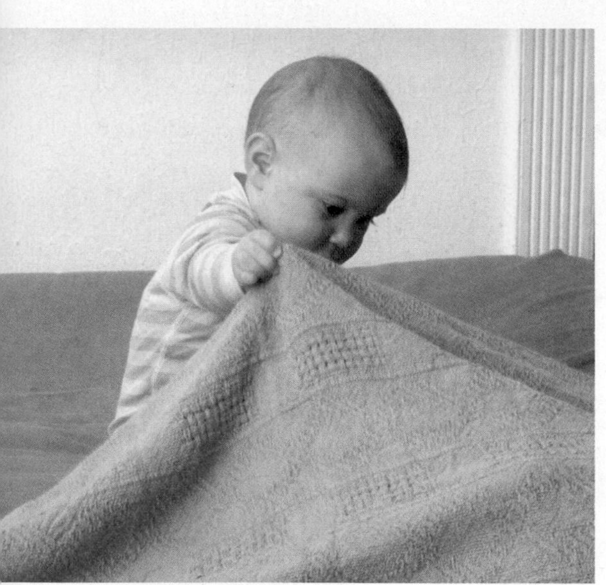

▲ This infant is looking under the blanket for a hidden toy. What does this search behavior tell us about the mental representations formed by infants?

Piaget made the provocative claim that young infants do not understand **object permanence**—the fact that objects, events, or even people continue to exist when they are not in the infant's direct line of sensory or motor action. Recall Hyeree and her rattle. Once Hyeree flung the rattle to the floor, Piaget would say that she had no way to think or know about the rattle. Because she couldn't form a mental representation of it, she couldn't consider its continued existence. She couldn't want it or wonder about it. For Hyeree, "out of sight" was literally "out of mind."

Piaget traced understanding of object permanence through the substages of sensorimotor thought, from nonexistence at birth to its full achievement at about age 2 years (Ginsburg & Opper, 1988; Piaget, 1952a, 1954a). In the earliest substages, infants simply do not look for an object once it is out of their immediate experience. They make no attempt to get the object back, though they might continue looking at the place where they last saw the object. Later, they might actively try to retrieve an object, but only if part of it is still visible (e.g., reaching for a toy that is partially hidden under a blanket). By about 1 year, babies will attempt to retrieve an object that is completely hidden. Interestingly, however, if babies watch the object being hidden in one location, then watch as a researcher moves the object to a different location (this is called a visible displacement problem), they will look in the first location rather than the second even though they witnessed the whole sequence. By about 18 months, babies are able to solve these *visible displacement* problems, but they still cannot find the object when the displacements are invisible. That is, they watch as the object is hidden in one location but when the researcher secretly moves the object to a different location, the babies look only in the first spot. They don't check other possible places nearby. Finally, by 2 years of age, the child is able to solve *invisible displacement* problems. Piaget described this ability as evidence of full mental representation. The Personal Perspective Box entitled "Where Did It Go?" describes three families as their infants solve a visible displacement problem.

THINK ABOUT CHI HAE . . .

Does Cara show evidence of object permanence yet? In a few months, how is she likely to react when Chi Hae hides a toy under a blanket?

**object permanence**
The fact that objects, events, and people continue to exist even when they are out of a child's direct line of sensory input or motor action.

In summary, there are two major developmental trends as an infant moves through the sensorimotor stage. First, the infant progresses from interacting reflexively with the environment through a trial-and-error phase to deliberate and intentional actions on the environment. Second, the child develops the ability to mentally represent objects, events, and people. Infants' early thought processes involve reflexes and immediate sensations and motor actions, but toddlers leave the sensorimotor stage with the ability to internalize

# Perspective PERSONAL WHERE DID IT GO?

Each of these parents was asked to play a game with their child, similar to the game that researchers sometimes use when studying object permanence. The parents showed their child a toy; then, making sure the child watched, they hid the toy under a blanket (Trial 1). They did the same thing a second time, except that they made sure the baby watched as they moved the toy and hid it in a different place (Trial 2). This is the *visible displacement* task that Piaget used. Here's how these children responded and what their parents' thought.

**Hanah Shapiro, mother of Asher, 6 months old**
Hollywood, FL

Trial 1:
Asher grasped for the rattle when I showed it to him. He watched me hide it but cried when he couldn't see it anymore—he didn't even try to look!

Trial 2:
Again, Asher cried when he could not see the rattle.

Parent's thoughts:
I was surprised Asher didn't even try to look for the rattle. He is normally very inquisitive, looking around a room and reaching for things. As Asher has grown, he explores objects more thoroughly—*everything* goes into his mouth! He particularly likes toys that play music and respond to him. Asher recently taught himself how to turn on the aquarium in his crib. He is, however, content to play with whatever is given to him rather than seeking out a favorite toy.

**Paul Lewis, father of Paul David, 11 months old**
Riverside, CA

Trial 1:
Paul David found the toy very quickly—after about 10 seconds.

Trial 2:
He went looking for the toy under the first location. He searched there for about 15 seconds before losing interest. He never looked under the final destination of the toy!

Parent's thoughts:
Paul David is very interactive and inquisitive. On Trial 1, he went after the ball immediately and was eager to find it. We were very surprised that he did not find the ball the second time. He understood the game and found the ball in Trial 1 but had a hard time making a connection to the ball and its new location. Paul David is very hands-on; he likes most of his toys in his mouth. At this age, it's easy to distract him. If we hide "off-limits" items, he will immediately look for them, but he gives up and loses interest if we move them to a new location.

**Nola Akala, mother of Akindele, 25 months old**
Deerfield, IL

Trial 1:
Akindele went directly to retrieve the train underneath the sofa cushion.

Trial 2:
He followed me to both locations and retrieved the toys. He looked for the toy in the new location within seconds. I was not surprised. My son is a determined little fellow!

Parent's thoughts:
Akindele knows where to go to get what he wants. This makes my life easier because I can say "Where is ABCD?" (his dog that sings the alphabet song) or "Where is Thomas the Train?," and he goes to find them with no problems. When he was younger, Akindele played more by exploring with his mouth; he is more physical with his toys now, turning things over and around. Now he likes toys with a "cause and effect," ones that make a sound when you open a door or that speak when you press a button or slide a bar on the toy.

QUESTION **Were you surprised at the 6- and 11-month-olds' reactions? What reaction do you think these three children would have to an invisible displacement problem? Try these games with some babies you know (with a parent's permission). What do their responses indicate about their cognitive development?**

their thought processes into a purely "mental" form. Internal and intentional thought provides the building blocks for the next stage of cognitive development.

Of course, not everyone agrees with Piaget's explanation of infant cognition. In particular, researchers from the information-processing approach (which you read about in Chapter 1 and will learn more about in Chapter 8) have found that Piaget underestimated the cognitive skills of infants and toddlers in many areas (Cohen & Cashon, 2006). Research conducted since the 1970s, using techniques and technologies not available when Piaget was forming his theory, have demonstrated impressive cognitive abilities during infancy. For example, research demonstrates that young infants do code information and store mental representations in the form of memories. Numerous studies have shown that

A. Expected Event

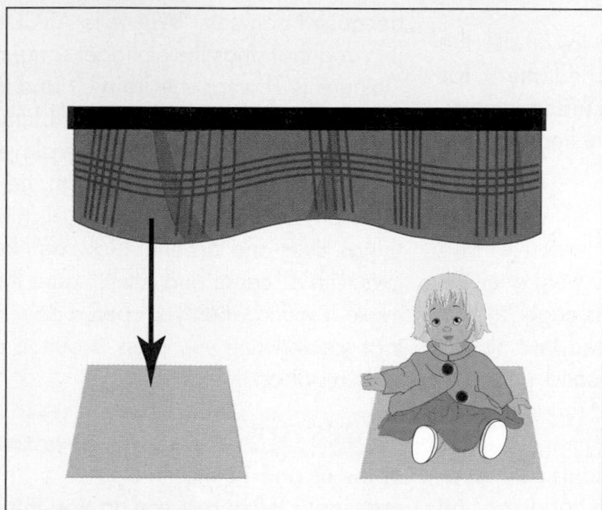

B. Unexpected Event

▲ FIGURE 5.7
**Violation of Expectation Studies:**
*Violation of expectation* studies are used to study the development of object permanence. Infants are shown a toy resting on one of two mats. A curtain hides both mats, then an experimenter's hand retrieves the toy either from the mat where it had been (the expected outcome, shown in Panel A) or the other mat (the unexpected outcome, shown in Panel B). Infants as young as 2½ months look longer at the unexpected outcome.
(*Source*: Wilcox, Nadel, & Rosser [1996], pg. 314.)

infants can remember events for several weeks, or even years, if they're given specific cues. By 6 months, infants can form associations between their memories of two stimuli (i.e., when the two objects were not both present at the same time) and maintain these mental associations for up to two weeks (Cuevas, Rovee-Collier, & Larmonth, 2006; Rovee-Collier & Cuevas, 2009; Rovee-Collier & Gerhardstein, 1997; Wang, 2003). Neuroscience studies that record infants' eye movements have found that 4-month-old infants who have seen an object moving across a computer screen will, when a screen prevents them from seeing the object's movement, anticipate to where the object will move. This indicates that they understand that the object continues to exist *and* continues to move in the expected pattern even when it disappears from view (Johnson, Amso, & Slemmer, 2003).

In addition, many studies have demonstrated that, under the proper conditions, infants as young as 2½ months demonstrate a grasp of object permanence (Baillargeon, 1993, 2008; Spelke, 1991). These studies often use a *violation of expectation* method in which infants are shown two events, as in Figure 5.7. In this example, a toy is shown on one of two mats, then screens hide both mats. An experimenter's hand comes into view and retrieves the toy. In the expected outcome, the toy is retrieved from the mat on which the infant had seen it resting. In the unexpected outcome, the toy is retrieved from the *wrong* mat; i.e., from the one where it had not been before. Infants as young as 2½ months looked longer at the unexpected event, indicating that they realized the toy continued to exist while it was hidden and that it should not be found on one mat when it had been placed on the other. Violation of expectation studies consistently show that young infants look longer at unexpected events. However, the abilities to represent more complex objects, maintain mental representations of objects over longer periods of time, and to mentally coordinate objects and their spatial locations continue to develop (Baillargeon, 2004; Moore & Meltzoff, 2007). We will discuss more aspects of Piaget's theory as well as alternative approaches to understanding cognitive development in Chapters 8, 11, and 14.

## LET'S REVIEW . . .

**1.** Adaptation is an important concept in Piaget's theory of cognitive development, and this concept can be traced back to Piaget's early work in:
- **a.** psychology.
- **b.** biology.
- **c.** philosophy.
- **d.** physics.

**2.** Two-year-old David points to a pickup truck and says, "Look, Mommy, a red car!" Calling the truck a car is an example of what Piaget would call:
- **a.** equilibration.
- **b.** accommodation.
- **c.** abstraction.
- **d.** assimilation.

**3.** When you consider Piaget's cycle of adaptation, what condition comes immediately before accommodation?
- **a.** assimilation.
- **b.** cognitive equilibrium.
- **c.** cognitive disequilibrium.
- **d.** organization.

**4.** According to Piaget, infants in the sensorimotor stage *cannot*:
- **a.** use sensory impressions to understand the world.
- **b.** use motor actions to understand the world.
- **c.** form symbolic representations to understand the world.
- **d.** display reflexes during the first month after birth.

**5.** True or False: Piaget is referred to as a "constructivist" because he believed that children learn primarily by copying the cognitive structures that have been constructed by the adults and other more mature people around them.

**6.** True or False: In Piaget's theory, cognitive equilibrium is achieved when children accommodate their schemes so that the schemes provide a better fit with new experiences.

Answers: 1. b, 2. d, 3. c, 4. c, 5. F, 6. T

# Learning to Communicate

Language has long been a fascinating subject for psychologists. As you have just learned, it is seen as an indicator of mental representation, and it also seems to be one skill that sets humans apart from other species. Other species have many different ways to communicate with one another, that is, to send and receive information or messages. In this section, we will discuss what sets human language apart. Then we will describe theories of language development and how language develops in infants and toddlers.

AS YOU STUDY THIS SECTION, ASK YOURSELF THESE QUESTIONS:

- **5.7** What are the defining characteristics of language?
- **5.8** What is the evidence for and against the theory that language is learned?
- **5.9** What is the evidence for and against the theory that language is genetically programmed in humans?
- **5.10** How do social interactions and general cognitive level affect language development?
- **5.11** How do infants' prelinguistic skills help to prepare them for language, and what are the major developments in vocalizations, semantics, and grammar during infancy?

## What Is Language?

Three key features distinguish human language (Brown, 1973; Gleason, 1997). First, language has *semanticity,* which means that it represents thoughts, objects, and events through specific and abstract symbols. For example, the word *baby* does not look or sound like a real baby. This word is an abstract symbol. Second, language is *productive,* which means that there is no limit to the number or types of utterances that humans can create. As long as people follow the rules that their particular language has for how to put sounds together, their novel communications are completely understandable by others. Third, language has the quality of *displacement,* which means that people can communicate about things that are distant in time or space or even about things that are physically or logically impossible or nonexistent. Displacement allows humans to communicate about a vast range of things instead of being limited to the immediate circumstances.

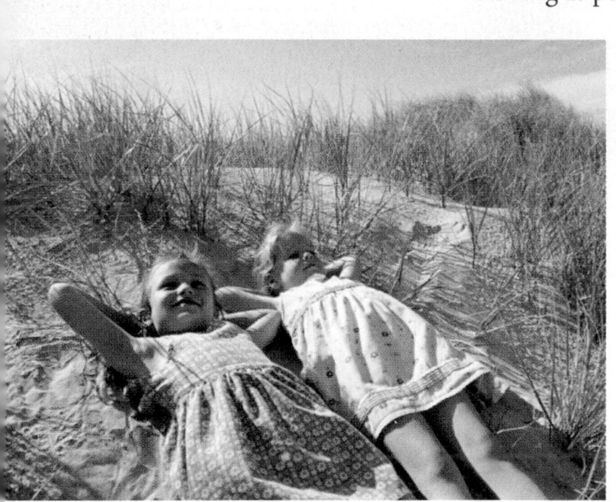

▲ Language uses abstract symbols and allows communication about an infinite number of topics. What fantasies do you think these children could express with their language?

**language**
An arbitrary system of symbols (words) that is rule-governed and allows communication about things that are distant in time or space.

So **language** is an arbitrary system of symbols (words) that is rule-governed and allows communication about things that are distant in time or space. In studying language, it is important to keep in mind the distinction between language *comprehension* and language *production.* Often, young children are able to understand and respond appropriately to spoken language well before they can produce grammatical speech. One point that most researchers agree on is that humans seem to have a very strong instinctive drive to acquire language. Although an impoverished language environment (i.e., one that provides and encourages less language) will affect a child's rate of language acquisition and the quality of the language the child achieves, it is quite difficult to keep humans from developing *any* language (Flavell, 1985; Hulit & Howard, 2006).

How do children grasp the complex rules of language? More intriguing, how are they able to master these rules so quickly? Three basic theories attempt to explain language development. The *learning* theory emphasizes the role of the environment, whereas *nativist* theory emphasizes the role of biology. *Interactionist* perspectives, as you might expect, focus on how various aspects of the environment interact with biological characteristics.

## Learning Theory: Language as a Learned Skill

The **learning theory** of language development is based on behaviorist theories of learning, particularly B. F. Skinner's principles of operant conditioning and Albert Bandura's concept of learning through imitation (Bandura & Walters, 1963; Skinner, 1957). Sometimes referred to as the *environmental view,* this approach views language as a behavior that people learn just like any other skill (Watson, 1924). Learning theorists believe that specific language training governs language development and that biological predispositions do not play an important role.

According to the learning theory, *operant conditioning* principles, particularly the procedure of *shaping* (selectively reinforcing certain behaviors while ignoring or punishing others), explain how children come to produce speech. For example, as a child begins to make sounds, the people around the child tend to reinforce the ones that resemble real words (e.g., "dada") but ignore those that do not (e.g., "gaga"). As a result, the child tends to repeat the reinforced wordlike sounds, and the nonwordlike sounds gradually die out. Caregivers also reinforce simple phrases such as "Me want juice" when they give the child what was requested. The more clearly the child says the phrase, the more likely an adult is to understand and comply with the request. As the child progresses, parents shift from shaping individual words to shaping longer phrases and sentences (Skinner, 1957). Explore on mydevelopmentlab

Explore The Shaping Process. www.mydevelopmentlab.com

*Imitation* and *modeling* are also important. At the same time that parents and others are selectively reinforcing closer approximations to real words and phrases, they also provide models of more advanced language. One way in which they do this is by repeating the word they think the child means to say. For example, if a young child says "Mmmm" while looking at his mother, the mother might respond by saying "Mommy, that's right, I'm your mommy." When the child tries to imitate the *mmmaaa* sound in the word "mommy," the mother reinforces the attempt. Adults also extend words or phrases, elaborating a bit on what the child said. For example, if the child says "Go" as she walks out the door, her father might say, "That's right, we're going bye-bye." Such interactions reinforce the child's language attempts, and they also provide a model of how to produce more mature words and phrases (Moerk, 1992, 2000).

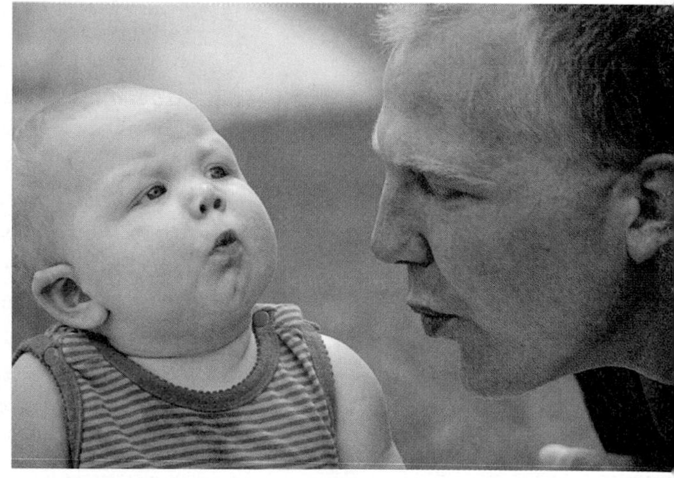

▲ Behaviorists believe that parents use imitation, modeling, and shaping to teach language.

Word meanings can be learned through these conditioning processes. For example, therapists have successfully used shaping techniques to improve the language skills of children with mental retardation or autistic disorder. Simply providing models of language and grammar does not appear to affect these children's language skills, but if the children are actively encouraged to imitate the model, their language often improves (Bohannon & Bonvillian, 1997).

However, there are several criticisms of the learning theory of language development. First, it is not clear how consistent parents are in shaping their children's language. Some studies show that shaping is inconsistent and that parents tend to reinforce or punish the accuracy of the content of children's utterances rather than the grammatical correctness. Also, parents do not appear to explicitly teach their children language rules. In fact, most adults have a great deal of difficulty identifying and describing these complex rules for themselves, much less explicitly teaching them to children. Second, critics argue that much of the language children hear in their everyday lives is incomplete, ill formed, and full of errors—far from being a good model from which to learn. Third, learning principles can't really account for the degree of novelty of children's language utterances, or what linguists call *productivity.* From an early age, children regularly say things that they have never heard before, such as, "I goed to the store." They also express things they have heard in new and innovative ways. Critics argue that it would be impossible for all of children's utterances to

THINKING CRITICALLY

Have you ever used, or seen someone using, language shaping, modeling, or imitation with young children? What did the adult do, and how did the child respond?

**learning theory**
Theory that sees language as a skilled behavior that children learn through operant conditioning, imitation, and modeling.

THINK ABOUT CHI HAE . . .

How could Chi Hae use the learning theory view of language development to improve Cara's language skills?

result from imitation and shaping. Fourth, critics say that children learn language at a very fast pace—too fast to be explained by reinforcement, shaping, and imitation. Finally, critics question the learning theorists' idea that language is "simply another behavior." Research evidence that we will discuss in the next section suggests that humans are biologically predisposed to detect language and process it differently from other types of information (Brown & Hanlon, 1970; Eisenberg, 1976; Morgan, Bonamo, & Travis, 1995; Pinker, 1994).

## Nativist Theory: Born to Talk

The famed linguist Noam Chomsky was one of the first to argue that learning theories could not adequately explain how children are able to master so quickly the complex systems of language. Chomsky proposed a **nativist theory**, the idea that language is an innate human capability. He suggested that humans are born with a **language acquisition device (LAD)**, a brain mechanism that is specialized for detecting and learning the rules of language (Chomsky, 1957, 1981; Lenneberg, 1967). Just as humans are born with specialized organs—a heart and lungs—to carry out the complex tasks of circulation and respiration, they are born with a specialized "language organ" in the brain to carry out the complex task of acquiring language (Siegler, 1998, p. 140). Children must hear some amount of language to activate the LAD, but extensive language input is not necessary. Nor is it essential that the language that is heard be completely grammatically correct. Because the LAD is innate, language acquisition does not require great cognitive skill or cognitive effort. This explains why young children, as well as children with mental retardation and other cognitive delays, all develop at least some language ability quickly and easily. Another strength of the nativist view is that it explains both language acquisition patterns that are similar across different languages and patterns that differ. The LAD is innate but does not preprogram a child to learn a specific language.

Chomsky proposed that the LAD contains an innate knowledge of *universal grammar,* or the aspects of language rule systems that are common across all languages. When a child hears language, the LAD analyzes the language to determine its general type of grammatical construction system. Once the basic grammar of the language is recognized, the child can easily abstract important linguistic information and quickly acquire language. Other nativist theories suggest that the LAD contains more general *operating principles*—assumptions and biases that cause children to treat the language environment in special ways (Slobin, 1982, 1985b). In other words, children are predisposed to pay special attention to certain aspects of the language they hear, such as the ends of words, word order, and differences in intonation. Because of innate operating principles, children notice the subtle patterns their language uses to express things like plurality, possession, or relationships. Children become progressively more sensitive to the features that are most useful in their language (and less sensitive to less useful features). For example, a child learning Russian will gradually focus more closely on word endings to determine relationships between words. In contrast, a child learning English will focus more on the order of words. Regardless of the particular kinds of information contained in the LAD, all nativist theorists agree that a physiologically based LAD exists and that the role of the environment is to trigger its maturation. The environment does not shape or train verbal behavior (Bohannon & Bonvillian, 1997; Saffran, Werker, & Werner, 2006).

**nativist theory**
Theory that sees language as an innate human capability that develops when language input triggers a *language acquisition device* in the brain.

**language acquisition device (LAD)**
A brain mechanism in humans that is specialized for acquiring and processing language.

**Is Language Innate?** If language acquisition is biologically programmed, then it should show developmental patterns similar to those of other biologically based systems, such as physical maturation. On this basis, all humans should develop language, and they should develop it in a fairly consistent way. Language should be easy for humans to develop and hard to prevent, but nonhumans should not develop language. Also, there should be physical structures that specialize in language processing. Finally, language development should show *sensitive periods* (times during which a child is particularly sensitive to some aspect of the environment), as happens with many aspects of physical development. Language development shows several of these characteristics.

THINKING CRITICALLY

Which language features seem most useful in your native language? Have you ever tried to learn a foreign language? If so, were the important features different from or similar to those of your native language?

*Do All Humans Develop Language?* There is strong evidence from cross-cultural comparisons that all physically intact humans develop language easily and quickly and that the order and pace of achieving linguistic milestones are remarkably consistent across different languages (Caselli et al., 1995; Slobin, 1982, 1985a). Only extremely impoverished linguistic environments seem to keep children from developing some kind of language skill. Presumably, these environments simply don't provide enough language experience to trigger the LAD. Even children with significant cognitive delays develop near-average levels of language usage and syntactic knowledge (Bellugi & St. George, 2001; Fowler, 1998; Tager-Flusberg, Boshart, & Baron-Cohen, 1999).

*Can Nonhumans Develop Language?* Whether nonhumans develop language has been an issue of some debate. Through sign language, by manipulating colored plastic tokens, or even by using specially designed computer keyboards, apes can learn to use words to describe things in their environment, ask and answer questions, and make requests. However, apes do not show knowledge of grammar, rarely include new information in their utterances, and show little understanding of language pragmatics such as taking turns in a conversation (Gleason, 1997; Terrace, Petitto, Sanders, & Bever, 1980). Studies with a bonobo chimpanzee named Kanzi show that he became very good at understanding the meaning and grammar of verbal instructions (Goodall, 1986; Savage-Rumbaugh, Shanker, & Taylor, 1998). Although Kanzi's performance was impressive, nativists argue that it is unclear whether he could *produce* grammatically correct phrases, and they point out that it took eight years of intensive training to teach Kanzi his skills. Human children, by contrast, quickly and easily master the rules of grammar, meaning, and the social use of language. What explains the difference? Nativists argue that other species lack the specialized brain mechanism common to all humans: the LAD.

▲ Can primates develop true language?

*Are There Physical Structures That Are Specialized for Language?* Although you might not have thought of them this way, the structures of the human mouth and throat are specially suited for producing the complex sounds of spoken language. Other species are not able to produce these sounds (Lenneberg, 1967). In addition, specific areas within the human brain specialize in processing linguistic information. Figure 5.8 (page 160) shows some of these areas. In most people, the left hemisphere of the brain is chiefly responsible for processing language information. *Wernicke's area,* located in the left temporal lobe for most people, enables human beings to understand spoken words and produce coherent written and spoken language. *Broca's area,* located in the left frontal lobe, directs the patterns of muscle movements necessary for producing speech. Other brain areas that are specialized for language include the *arcuate fasciculus,* a band of fibers that connects Wernicke's area to Broca's area, and the *angular gyrus,* which is involved in processing written language (Gleason, 1997; Maratsos & Matheney, 1994).

So there is evidence of physical structures that are specialized for language processing. However, there does not appear to be a *single area* that is the LAD proposed by Chomsky. Instead, the LAD may be more correctly thought of as several interconnected brain areas

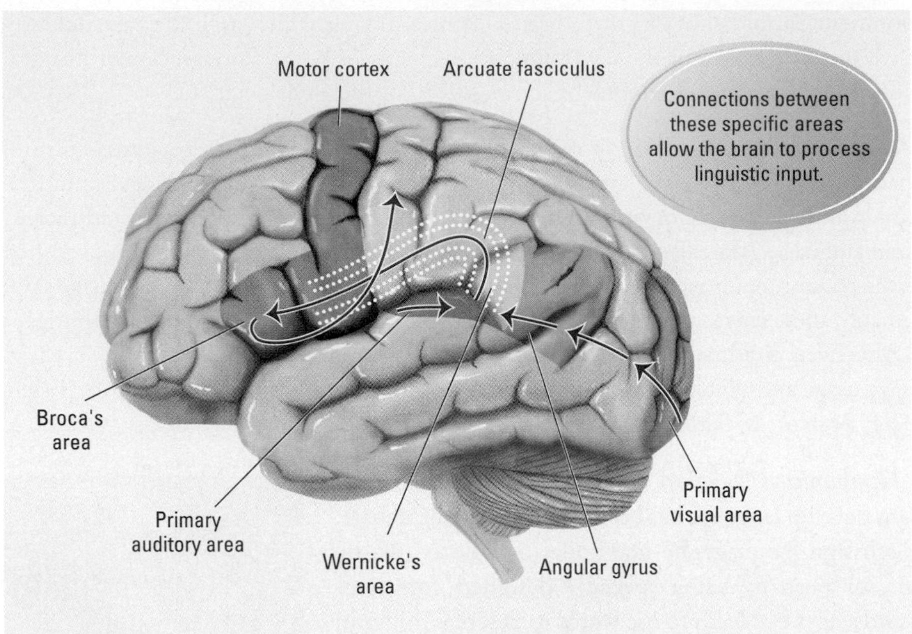


FIGURE 5.8 ▶ **Brain Structures Involved in Language Processing** *Wernicke's area* is important in comprehending spoken words and producing coherent written and spoken language. Nerves connect Wernicke's area to the *primary auditory cortex. Broca's area* directs the patterns of muscle movements necessary to produce speech sounds. The *arcuate fasciculus* connects Wernicke's area to Broca's area. The *angular gyrus* processes written language. (Based on Fabes & Martin, 2003.)

(Cornell, Fromkin, & Mauner, 1993; Krishner, 1995). As of now, there is still no agreement as to what kinds of innately hardwired information might exist within those structures.

Neuroscientists have begun using interesting new methods to study the neurobiological basis for infants' language development (Kuhl & Rivera-Gaxiola, 2008). Direct measures, such as *event-related potentials*, examine the timing and localization of electrical activity within the brain in response to spoken words alone or in combination with visual stimuli. Other measures, such as *near-infrared spectroscopy (NIRS)*, estimate brain activity by projecting near-infrared light through the scalp and into the brain and measuring the reflection of the light (similar to the way sonar is used to detect objects in water through reflection of sound waves and radar is used to detect objects in the sky through reflection of microwaves). When a brain area is activated, blood flow (and so the volume of blood with higher levels of oxygen, or oxygenated blood) is increased to that area because of an increased demand for energy. Infrared light is absorbed differently by oxygenated than by deoxygenated blood; NIRS assesses the change in blood flow to an area by measuring relative levels of oxygenated and deoxygenated blood, thus giving a neurobiological picture of the brain's processing. Using methods like these, researchers have found that 2- to 5-day-old infants show greater processing in the left temporal region of the brain for words spoken normally versus in reverse, indicating that this area of the brain is centrally involved in language processing and is functional very early in life (Peña, et al., 2003). Older infants (6 to 9 months of age) show greater brain activity in the left temporal lobe when they hear speech but not when they see a visual stimulus (Bortfeld, Wruck, & Boas, 2007).

*Are There Sensitive Periods for Language Development?* According to Lenneberg (1967), human beings acquire language almost exclusively during childhood, before the brain's organization becomes specialized and fixed. Areas of the brain are predisposed to respond to linguistic input, but children must experience language to activate these mechanisms. If a child does not receive enough linguistic input, the period of heightened sensitivity goes by. The key brain areas become specialized for other types of processing, and the opportunity for quick and easy language acquisition is lost. If Lenneberg is correct about sensitive periods, then several things should follow:

- Children who have been deprived of language should show poorer language skills, because the brain areas will not be activated.

- Older children and adults should have greater difficulty learning new languages than young children do.
- Older children and adults should recover less fully from damage to language areas of the brain, because the brain is already specialized.

There is evidence to support each of these predictions (Locke, 1993). First, case reports indicate that people who were deprived of linguistic input during childhood do not develop average linguistic skills; they have particular problems with grammar (Curtiss, 1977). Second, learning a new language seems to be more difficult for older children and adults than for younger children. For example, Jacqueline Johnson and Elissa Newport (1989) examined the English language skills of Chinese and Korean immigrants, focusing on the ages at which immigrants arrived in the United States. Figure 5.9 shows that English proficiency clearly relates to the immigrants' age on arrival. Proficiency was not related to the number of years the immigrants had spoken English or to the amount of formal English instruction they had received (Johnson & Newport, 1989). Other research found the same result for deaf children learning American Sign Language: Proficiency in ASL reflected the age at which children first encountered ASL but not how long they had used ASL (Newport, 1990). Finally, recovery of language functions after damage to the left hemisphere of the brain is much faster and more complete for younger children (Stiles & Thal, 1993; Witelson, 1987). In fact, if the left hemisphere is damaged before the age of 1 year, the language functions can shift into the right hemisphere and "crowd out" the perceptual-spatial skills that usually localize there (an example of the theme of resilience in, in this case, brain function). The result is that language survives but perceptual-spatial skills suffer. So it seems that language development is biologically very important (Maratsos & Matheny, 1994; Siegler, 1998).

**Criticisms of Nativist Theory.** One of the major criticisms of nativist theory concerns the kind and amount of linguistic input and feedback that children actually receive. Steven Pinker (1994), a nativist, suggested that language acquisition according to the learning model could occur only if children received explicit corrections of their language errors. Nativists claim that adults do not give this kind of feedback, so language must be innately driven (Morgan et al., 1995; Pinker, 1994). However, some studies show that adults do provide a great deal of corrective feedback (Bohannon & Bonvillian, 1997; Bohannon & Padgett, 1996; Farrar, 1992; Kilani-Schoch, Balčiuniené, Korecky-Kröll, Laaha, & Dressler, 2009; Saxton, 1997). Others argue that the language children hear contains rich enough

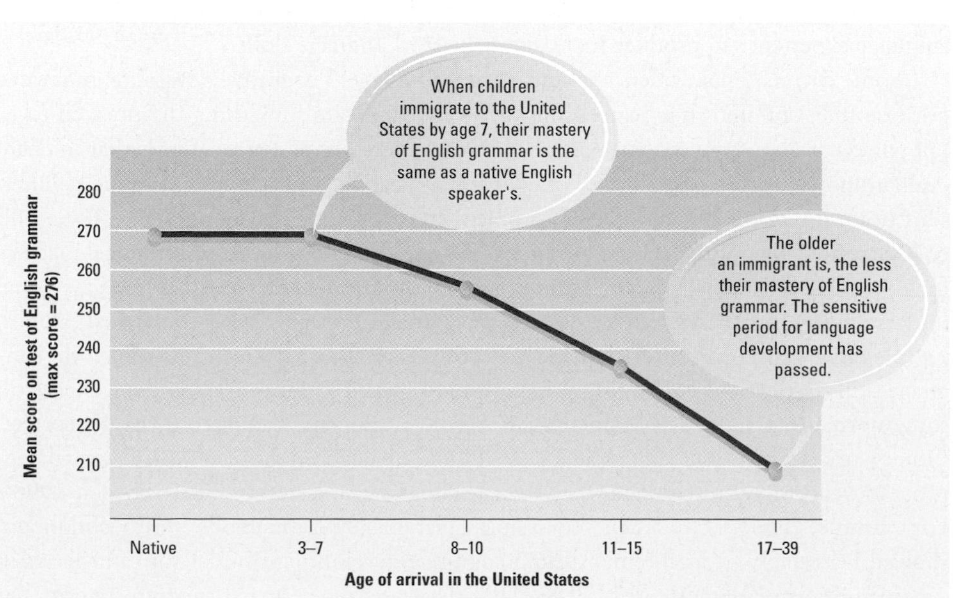


◀ FIGURE 5.9
**Support for a Sensitive Period for Language Development**
Johnson and Newport found that Chinese and Korean immigrants' proficiency in English was related to the age at which the immigrants arrived in the United States but not to the number of years they had spoken English or the amount of formal English instruction the immigrants had received. (Based on Johnson & Newport, 1989.)

information that general learning abilities are sufficient for developing language; therefore a specific *language* acquisition brain module is not needed (Behme & Deacon, 2008). In addition, nativist theory predicts that any kind of exposure to language should activate the LAD and lead to average levels of language, regardless of the level of complexity, abstraction, or grammatical correctness of the linguistic input. But research has found that if language exposure comes only from television, children do not develop typical language skills (Sachs, Bard, & Johnson, 1981). Other critics point out that nativists have not identified a single universal grammar that applies to all known languages—a critical element in any theory that proposes a biologically programmed universal grammar (Tomasello, 1995). Finally, there is ongoing disagreement about whether other species can develop language.

## Interaction Theories: Cognitive and Social Interactionist Approaches

Although both Skinner and Chomsky were right about some aspects of language development, many researchers came to believe that these two opposing theorists were too extreme. Dissatisfaction with both purely learning and purely nativist views led researchers to consider how multiple factors might interact to produce language development. Some interaction approaches emphasize the role of cognitive factors; others emphasize how social interactions contribute to language acquisition.

**Cognitive Approach: Language Depends on Cognition.** Not surprisingly, Jean Piaget stressed the role of the general cognitive abilities of the child in language acquisition. **Piaget's cognitive developmental theory** views language as only one of several different abilities that depend on overall cognitive maturation. Proper cognitive development is a necessary prerequisite for normal language development (Piaget, 1954b). For example, you might remember that one of the major cognitive achievements by the end of Piaget's first stage of cognitive development—the sensorimotor stage—is object permanence, or the understanding that objects and people continue to exist even when the infant cannot directly experience them. If words are symbols that represent objects, then babies in the sensorimotor stage do not need them. Either babies directly experience objects (and so need no symbols) or objects are out of babies' immediate experience and no longer exist (requiring no symbols). Only when children develop cognitively to the point at which they need symbols to represent things do they have a reason to use words and develop language. Cognitive skills then interact with environmental demands and language experience to produce increasingly mature language skills.

Some correlational evidence is consistent with Piaget's cognitive developmental view. For example, children first begin using words that indicate something disappeared (e.g., "all gone") at about the same time they develop object permanence. Words that indicate evaluation of effort (e.g., "uh-oh," or "got it") appear at around the same time children start using intentional, goal-directed, problem-solving strategies (Gopnik, 1984; Gopnik & Meltzoff, 1984). Some research indicates that children do not use grammatical markers for things like past tense or possession in their spontaneous speech until they have some understanding that there is such a thing as the past and that objects can be owned (Slobin, 1982). However, these correlations do not prove that the cognitive skills *caused* the language skills to develop. Interestingly, many children with significant cognitive deficits still show normal language development; this should not occur if Piaget's theory is correct. Other work suggests that some specific aspects of language might result from general cognitive development, but others might not (Bellugi & St. George, 2001; Fowler, 1998). For example, Genie, a child deprived of normal language for much of her early childhood, showed reasonably normal semantic and cognitive development but significant delays in syntax and morphology (Curtiss, 1981). In other cases researchers have found normal or

**Piaget's cognitive developmental theory**
Theory that sees language as one of several abilities that depend on overall cognitive development. Proper cognitive development is a necessary prerequisite for normal language development.

advanced development of syntax and morphology, but delays in semantic and cognitive development (Levy, Tennenbaum, & Ornoy, 2000). Finally, some researchers argue that language development depends on basic cognitive processes, but they focus on the roles of memory, processing speed, and attention rather than more general Piagetian stages or concepts. These researchers have found that basic cognitive processes like these do predict later language skills (Rose, Feldman, & Jankowski, 2009). (We will describe another cognitive approach to language development called the *connectionist view*, which is based on current information-processing theory, in Chapter 11.)

Social Interactionist Theory. **Social interactionist theory** says that language development is the result of a complex interaction between the child's biological predispositions and social interactions. Most social interactionists agree with nativists that humans are biologically prepared to develop language, but they believe that simply hearing language is not enough. Instead, interacting with others is critical: To develop language, children must have conversations with other people. This theory also assumes that children have a strong drive to communicate effectively with others. Because humans are social by nature, children themselves play a significant role by seeking social interactions and trying to communicate with those around them (Akhtar & Tomasello, 2000).

**social interactionist theory** Theory proposing that language development results from the interaction of biological and social factors and that social interaction is required.

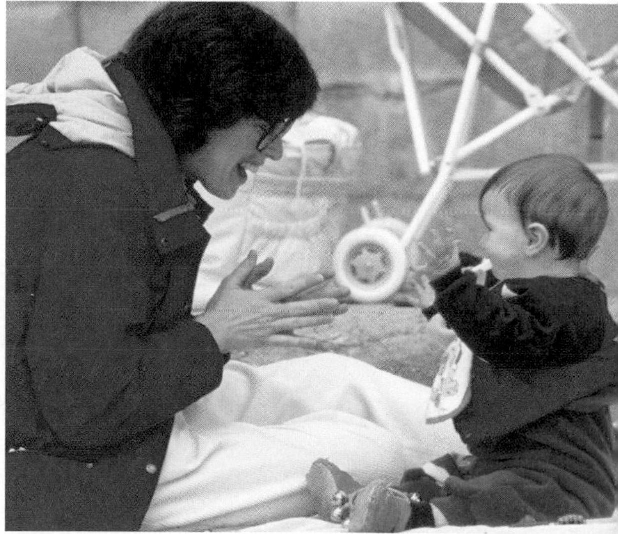

▲ Everyday activities and games serve as social structures that support language development. What language skills is this baby learning?

What role do social interactions play for language development? As we noted earlier, it seems that parents provide much more feedback about language performance than some theorists used to think (Hart & Risley, 1995). Children often initiate language interaction by attempting some kind of sound, word, or phrase. If the utterance is grammatically correct, parents might imitate it—repeat or echo it—exactly. But parents also provide implicit feedback. For example, *recasts* are restatements of what the child said but with corrected grammar. If a child says, "I saw two deers in the yard," her mother might recast this and reply, "You saw two *deer*; that's great!" Parents also use *expansions*, repeating but also correcting and elaborating on the child's utterance. For example, a mother might expand the statement about *deers* by saying, "You saw two deer? Remember when we saw the deer at the forest preserve? Did those deer look like the ones in the yard?" Children respond to feedback by correcting their errors (Bohannon & Bonvillian, 1997; Farrar, 1992; Saxton, 1997, 2000).

Caregivers also present language to children quite carefully and in a structured fashion through social interactions (Bruner, 1983). Examples are joint activities such as songs that have specific gestures, games such as peekaboo, and common daily activities such as baths and meals. These interactions have predictable structures, and all are very common across cultures (Fernald & O'Neill, 1993).

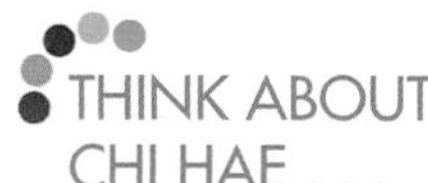

THINK ABOUT CHI HAE . . .

Develop some examples of how Chi Hae might use recasts, expansions, imitation, joint social activities, and child-directed speech to help Cara.

Adults and older children also change their linguistic style when they talk to young children—they use *child-directed speech,* sometimes called *motherese* (Sachs & Devine, 1976; Snow, 1972). As we described in Chapter 4, child-directed speech is slower and higher pitched, has more frequent and more extreme ups and downs in pitch, and includes more questions than does speech directed to adults. Child-directed speech also exaggerates key words and phrases for emphasis and often repeats such words several times. The sentences are short and simple, and they often focus on objects and activities to which the child is actively attending. Child-directed speech occurs in many different cultures and languages (Fernald, 1992; Kuhl et al., 1997). Even deaf mothers use child-directed sign language with their infants, signing more slowly, employing more repetition, and making exaggerated gestures (Masataka, 1996). Infants pay more attention to child-directed speech, and they are more successful in discriminating words both from nonwords and from other words with subtle differences in sound when they hear the words in child-

THINKING CRITICALLY

Have you ever used child-directed speech? What is different about it? What prompted you to use it, and what effect did it have on the child?

directed speech (Cooper & Aslin, 1994; Masataka, 1998; Moore, Spence, & Katz, 1997; Thiessen, Hill, & Saffran, 2005). However, the phenomenon of child-directed speech is not yet fully understood. Although it seems quite useful, it does not have the same features in all cultures. It is not yet known which particular features are most important or whether the central features are different for younger and older children (Bohannon & Bonvillian, 1997; Fee & Shaw, 1998). Watch on **mydevelopmentlab**

**Watch** a video on Child Directed Speech.
www.mydevelopmentlab.com

## Early Communication: How Language Starts

We have explored some of the theories that explain how language develops, but what kinds of changes take place and when do they occur? During the first year of life, important changes relevant to language take place in three areas. First, perceptual skills improve, enabling infants to perceive and discriminate different speech sounds. Second, infants and their caregivers establish a social environment; this encourages babies to turn random sounds into words that communicate specific meanings. Third, having begun life with sounds that are reflexive and unintentional, by 1 year of age, infants begin to use real words.

**Perceptual Skills.** It does not take infants long to start recognizing differences between speech sounds. One classic study used a variation of the habituation procedure you learned about earlier in this chapter (Eimas, Siqueland, Jusczyk, & Vigorito, 1971). The researchers gave infants as young as 1 month of age a pacifier that activated a predetermined sound (e.g., "ba"). Babies gradually habituated to the sound, slowing their rate and intensity of sucking. When the sound was changed (e.g., to "pa"), the babies increased their rate of sucking. As you might recall, this pattern indicates that the babies remembered the first sound and could tell that the second was different. Other studies have shown the same result with a variety of different speech sounds (Aslin, Jusczyk, & Pisoni, 1998; Saffran et al., 2006). By 6 months, infants are able to discriminate among different sequences of sounds—an important skill, because words are made up of sometimes subtly different sound sequences (Goodsitt, Morse, VerHoeve, & Cowan, 1984). Interestingly, it does not matter whether or not the speech sounds come from the infant's "native" language for 6- to 8-month-olds, but older babies have increasing difficulty with sounds from nonnative languages (Trehub, 1976; Werker & Tees, 1984). It seems that experience with language increases the ability to discriminate among speech sounds in one's own language, but the ability to make discriminations that are not required on a regular basis gradually decreases. Neuroscience research that examines changes over time in event-related potentials (a measure of the brain's electrical activity) supports this finding, but adds the interesting result that the differentiation of non-native speech sounds is not completely lost; while the brain shows decreased differentiation of non-native speech sounds, some differentiation at the neural level remains (Rivera-Gaxiola, Silva-Pereyra, & Kuhl, 2005). It is also the case that some subgroups of infants show greater differentiation of non-native sounds than others. Perception of the basic sounds of one's language is a good predictor of later language performance, including important skills such as word comprehension and production (Kuhl, Conboy, Padden, Nelson, & Pruitt, 2005; Tsao, Liu, & Kuhl, 2004). However, it is not yet clear whether and for how long differences in neural-level processing remain or if and how greater differentiation of non-native speech sounds at 11 months is related to speech or language difficulties in later development (Kuhl & Rivera-Gaxiola, 2008).

**Social Interactions.** During the first year, infants are also beginning to understand that they can use sounds to communicate their needs and even to control other people's behavior. Successful communication requires a joint focus of attention; that is, it requires that both people focus their attention on the same object or event at the same time. You can imagine what odd "conversations" would take place if each conversational partner were talking about different objects, events, or topics! Joint focus of attention develops gradually over the first year of life (Carpenter, Nagell, & Tomasello, 1998; Hulit & Howard, 2006). Social interactions during infancy are also essential for developing an understanding of the social rules for language. For example, the games and routines you read about earlier (e.g., peekaboo) help to emphasize when and how the infant is expected to contribute to the conversation or interaction. These interactions help infants learn when it is their turn to talk and what kinds of contributions they should make (Bruner, 1983).

THINK ABOUT CHI HAE . . .

Would you expect Cara to understand anything about taking turns in conversations yet? How can Chi Hae help her to learn this skill?

**From Crying to Words: Speech Production in Infancy.** Table 5.3 summarizes the developmental progression in speech production during the first year. Examine this progression, and you will notice that the sounds become increasingly *differentiated,* which means that specific sounds are produced under specific conditions. The sounds also become increasingly *intentional,* which means that the baby produces them for a specific goal, such as showing a caregiver a toy or getting a caregiver to provide something. Both differentiation and intentionality help to lay the groundwork for the first real words around the age of 1 year.

An infant's first sounds are reflexive, nonintentional sounds such as crying, burping, sneezing, and coughing. Sometimes called *vegetative sounds,* these natural sounds come from many living creatures but are passive and do not convey an intentional meaning (Hulit & Howard, 2006). Also, a baby's first cries are undifferentiated; the cry that is produced because the baby is hungry sounds just like the one that is produced because the baby is wet, tired, angry, or in pain. By 2 months, the baby's cries show much more variation; and by 4 months, the baby is producing distinctive cries to signal such things as discomfort and request. *Cooing,* the production of vowel-like sounds such as "o-o-o-o-u-u-u," is present by 2 months. Cooing communicates an infant's pleasure and comfort; infants often coo during social interactions, such as when their caregivers talk to or smile at them. By 4 months, babies both coo and laugh.

At about 6 months infants show *true babbling,* or repeated consonant–vowel syllables such as "mamama." True babbling occurs most often when infants are exploring their

**TABLE 5.3**
**The Development of Speech Sounds in Infancy**

| AGE | TYPE OF SPEECH SOUND |
|---|---|
| Birth | • Vegetative and undifferentiated sounds: Reflexive, nonintentional sounds such as crying, burps, sneezing, coughing |
| 2 months | • Greater variation in cries |
| | • Cooing to indicate comfort and pleasure |
| 4 months | • Distinctive cries to signal specific states |
| | • Cooing and laughing |
| 5 months | • Transitional babbling: Single syllables with one consonant and one vowel sound ("ma") |
| 6 months | • True babbling: Repeated vowel-consonant pair ("mamama") |
| 8 to 12 months | • Echolalia: Immediate imitation of words |
| 9 to 18 months | • Variegated babbling: Multiple, differing syllables ("bapadaga") |
| | • Jargon babbling: Babbling that includes native language intonation patterns, rhythms, and stresses |
| | • Protowords: Consistent sound patterns used to refer to specific objects and events |
| 1 year | • First true words, usually accompanied by gestures, babbling, and/or protowords |

(Adapted from Hulit & Howard, 1997.)

surroundings and when an infant is alone (Stark, Bernstein, & Demorest, 1993). It includes many different sounds, even sounds that are not part of the infant's native language. Gradually, the babbling comes to resemble more closely the speech sounds of the family's language. This means that all infants have the potential to develop any language. It is the language they experience during the first year or so of life that determines which speech sounds they will continue to produce and which will fade away. True babbling depends heavily on infants' being able to hear themselves clearly. As a result, it is at this point in development that babies with hearing impairments start to show delays, falling behind infants with normal hearing in the amount and variety of speech produced (Oller & Eilers, 1988; Stoel-Gammon & Otomo, 1986).

Between 8 and 12 months, infants start to show *echolalia*, the immediate imitation of others' sounds or words. Echolalia can be very accurate and might lead adults to believe that an infant has learned words, but infants do not understand the sounds they are producing. From 9 to 18 months, infants start to show *variegated babbling*, which includes syllables that differ from one another (e.g., "badagapa"), and *jargon babbling*, which includes the rhythms and stress patterns of the native language. Jargon babbling sounds just like a conversation but without using real words. It indicates that babies are attending to and beginning to master the rhythmic and intonation characteristics of the language they are hearing but haven't put these aspects together with real words yet.

THINK ABOUT CHI HAE . . .

Does Cara's language development during infancy seem to be progressing at an appropriate pace? What skills does she seem to be showing, and what can Chi Hae expect to develop within the next year?

Finally, around 9 to 10 months, infants begin to use *protowords* (also called *vocables*): consistent patterns of sounds that refer to specific people, objects, or events. For example, one of our sons used the protoword "neenee" to refer to his brother Andy, and many children use the protoword "baba" to refer to a baby bottle. Protowords mark an important transition from the random and nonmeaningful vocalizations of babbling to vocalizations that are intentional, consistent, and have specific meaning. Once a child begins using protowords, it is usually not long until the child begins using true words.

**Semantics: Words and Their Meanings.** Around the age of 1 year, children say their first true adult word. The transition from protowords to real words is gradual, and children continue to use gestures, babbling, and protowords along with real words for several months (Goldin-Meadow; 2006; Vihman & Miller, 1988). The average child can produce about 50 words by 18 months of age. Table 5.4 shows the kinds of words typically produced first. As you can see, children's earliest words are usually nouns. They are usually labels for familiar and important objects or people in the environment, such as family members, favorite toys, pets, or favorite foods (Childers & Tomasello, 2002; Nelson, Hampson, & Shaw, 1993; Waxman & Lidz, 2006).

*How Are Early Words Acquired?* Toddlers learn the meanings of new words at an astonishing pace. One way is through their parents' modeling and labeling of objects and events. It is not surprising that the first words children acquire are the ones that are used most often by their parents. In addition, the more parents talk to their children, the faster the children's vocabulary grows. But children also use a process called *fast mapping,* in which they acquire at least a partial understanding of a word after only a single exposure (Carey, 1977; Woodward, Markman, & Fitzsimmons, 1994). Toddlers as young as 18 months show fast mapping if both the child and his or her conversational partner are attending to the object that is being labeled (Baldwin et al., 1996). Despite these impressive abilities, however, children's early words often include errors. Children frequently show *overextensions,* in which they expand a word's meaning to include more objects than it should (Naigles & Gelman, 1995). For example, a young child who is learning the word *parrot* might overextend this label and use it to refer to any feathered creature that flies with wings (what adults would call *birds*) rather than only to a certain type of bird. Children also show *underextensions,* in which they use a word too narrowly. For example, a child might learn

**TABLE 5.4**
**The Nature of Early Words**

| TYPE OF WORD | EXAMPLES | PERCENTAGE OF VOCABULARY WORDS |
|---|---|---|
| Names for *general examples* of a category | Mother, father, grandparent, doggy, kitty, toy | 51 |
| Names for *specific* members of a category | Mommy, Daddy, Grandma, Spot, Fluffy, Teddy | 14 |
| Words for *actions* | Go, up, swing, bounce, run, throw, cry | 13 |
| Words that *describe* objects or events | Big, little, mine, yummy, cold | 9 |
| Words that express *feelings or relationships* | No, sad, please | 8 |
| Words that serve *grammatical functions* | What, where, for, is | 4 |

(Adapted from Nelson, 1973.)

that the family's pet is a parrot and believe that this word applies only to this particular parrot, not to parrots in a zoo, on television, or in other places.

*What Is the Function of Early Words?* As you have read, young children's early words are often labels for familiar objects or people. Their early attempts at communication consist of single words, but these words often convey an entire idea or sentence. Words used in this way are called **holophrases**. For example, a toddler might say the word *hot* when he sees his father opening the oven door. Depending on the context and accompanying nonverbal cues, this single word might stand for several different and more complex ideas. The child could be saying, "Watch out, Dad! The oven is hot!" or "I need to stay away from that hot oven because it can burn me" or even "Is the oven hot?" Holophrases cannot communicate the wide range of meanings that children will be able to express once they start combining words, but holophrases do serve several communication functions, including demands, requests, desires, and questions. To understand holophrases, the listener needs to pay attention to intonational cues (i.e., which parts of a word or phrase are emphasized), gestures, and the specific context (Tomasello, 2006).

Listen carefully to the speech of any 1- to 2-year-olds that you know. Do you hear examples of fast mapping, overextension, underextension, or holophrases?

**Toddler Grammar: Rules for Putting Words Together.** Between 18 and 24 months of age, toddlers start to produce two- and three-word sentences. Many children's earliest sentences are of the form "familiar word + ________," though the particular familiar word differs from child to child (Bloom, Lightbrown, & Hood, 1975; Maratsos, 1983). For example, a child's early sentences might all consist of the phrase "No + ____," to produce "No *milk*," "No *Mommy*," "No *nap*," "No *kitty*," and so forth. The specific functions served by early sentences (e.g., to make demands, ask questions, or claim possession) are very similar across several different languages (Slobin, 1979).

As toddlers expand their language production to sentences, they often use telegraphic speech. Like telegrams, **telegraphic speech** includes words that are essential to get the meaning across but leaves out nonessential words. Instead of saying, "I'm going to watch my brother Will play baseball," a 2-year-old is likely to say, "I watch Will." Interestingly, even such limited utterances follow certain grammatical rules. Young children do not randomly combine words; they choose certain combinations of words and word orders (de Villiers & de Villiers, 1999; Mandel, Kemler Nelson, & Jusczyk, 1996).

**holophrases**
Single words used to express an entire idea or sentence.

**telegraphic speech**
Speech that includes only words that are essential to get the meaning across, leaving out unessential words.

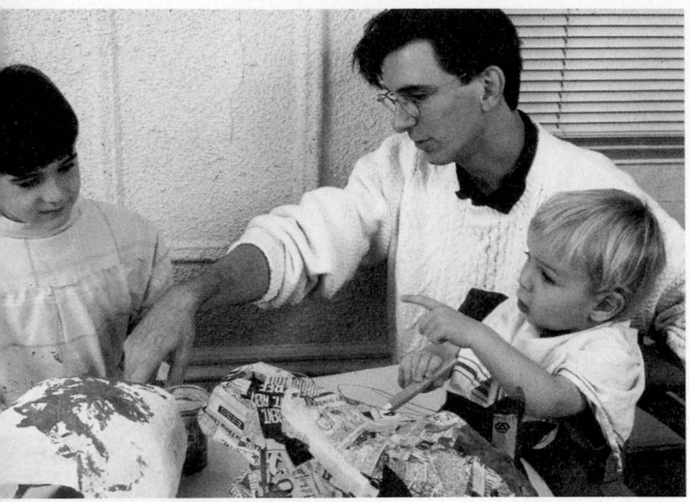

▲ This young child is likely using telegraphic speech to communicate. What words do you think he is saying, and what do you think his full meaning is?

For example, toddlers usually place nouns before verbs, as in "Daddy play" rather than "play Daddy"; and they place possessives before nouns, as in "my kitty" instead of "kitty my." Such combinations indicate a beginning understanding that the ordering of words, not just the words themselves, conveys important information.

The infant and toddler period is one of amazing change in language abilities. It is also a time when many parents might begin to notice the vast individual differences between their child and others in the pace of language development and to worry if their child is not saying words or putting together sentences as quickly as other children of the same age. When should parents worry about their child's pace of language development? What are some common language delays, and what kinds of therapy are available? The field of *speech-language pathology* helps to provide answers to these kinds of questions. To find out more about this field, read the Professional Perspective box called "Career Focus: Meet a Speech-Language Pathologist."

In this chapter, we have discussed some of the surprising capabilities of young infants and toddlers and have described how they integrate their perceptual experiences to support their cognitive and language development. Clearly, infants and toddlers need many more years and support from those around them to become sophisticated thinkers and conversationalists, but they are far from helpless even during infancy.

## LET'S REVIEW . . .

**1.** The LAD refers to:
   **a.** a specific structure in the brain's left hemisphere that governs language development.
   **b.** the process of learning language.
   **c.** the specific structured parent–child interactions that help to teach language rules.
   **d.** several brain areas that together enable humans to detect and learn language rules.

**2.** The term *operating principles* refers to:
   **a.** an innate knowledge of universal grammar.
   **b.** innate predispositions to notice certain elements of language.
   **c.** the strategies that parents use to shape their children's use of grammar.
   **d.** rules that govern how connections between units change in response to external feedback.

**3.** Child-directed speech fosters language development in all of the following ways *except* by:
   **a.** providing feedback about grammar.
   **b.** drawing an infant's attention to the topic of conversation.
   **c.** explaining the operating principles for the native language.
   **d.** emphasizing important features of speech.

**4.** Which of the following provides the best support for the hypothesis that there are sensitive periods in language development?
   **a.** The existence of physical organs that are specialized for language processing.
   **b.** The fact that adults and children are both able to learn second languages.
   **c.** The fact that children are especially sensitive to child-directed speech.
   **d.** The greater degree of language recovery shown by children than by adults after damage to the brain's left hemisphere.

**5.** True or False: Human newborns are able to discriminate between speech sounds of their native language but not between sounds of other languages.

**6.** True or False: The use of protowords marks the first use of adult language.

Answers: 1. d, 2. b, 3. c, 4. d, 5. F, 6. F

## Perspective PROFESSIONAL — CAREER FOCUS: MEET A SPEECH-LANGUAGE PATHOLOGIST

Deena Bernstein, Ph.D.
*Bronx, NY*
*Certified Speech-Language Pathologist, Lehman College/City University of New York; coauthor with Ellenmorris Tiegerman-Farber of* Language and Communication Disorders in Children *(2002), published by Allyn and Bacon*

**What are the early signs of problems in language development?**

Parents are often the first to suspect that a child might be delayed in acquiring language. They might notice that their infant does not do much babbling ("abbababa") or stops producing these playful sounds.

The child might not interact or make eye contact when parents try to talk and play with the child. Some young children will have problems learning to produce the sounds of speech. They will be difficult to understand, even beyond the preschool years. Others might be slow to learn new words, word endings (such as "-ing" or "-ed"), or small functional words (such as "is," "am," "was") or to string words together to make sentences. Some might struggle with how to use language to communicate, not knowing how to ask for objects or actions they want. If parents notice these types of problems, they should seek help. Speech-language pathologists will conduct a speech-language evaluation and work with other professionals to help determine whether a language delay exists, the possible cause(s) for a delay, the skills the child has and/or needs to learn, and intervention strategies that would help the child. It is important that a child receive speech-language therapy as soon as he or she is diagnosed as having a language delay, no matter the cause. The earlier a child receives services, the greater are his or her chances for success.

**What are other common problems that you see in your practice?**

Some parents get concerned when they hear their 3-year-old say things like "I, I, I, I want the red car," but this is very common. Three- to 3-and-a-half-year-olds often repeat not only whole words ("my, my, my, crayon") but also phrases ("Mommy, I want, Mommy I want, Mommy I want a drink,") or even parts of words ("play, play, playschool"). However, if a child repeats the sounds of a word ("p, p, p, pot"), shows signs of struggle behaviors (such as tics, facial tension, or grimaces), or frequently produces a repetition or prolongation ("sssssssit," in more than one out of ten words), then this could indicate a stuttering condition.

Children who have language problems in the first five years of life are at risk for reading and writing problems later. When learning to read and write, children must actively think about all the components of the language system, and this can be difficult for children who have had a difficult time learning the oral language system. Parents should monitor and encourage their child's literacy skills and work with their child's teachers to provide any special help the child might need.

**What causes problems in language development?**

Often, the reason is not known. Some children have conditions that lead to language problems, such as hearing loss, mental retardation, autism, or attention deficit hyperactivity disorder. For some children, there is a genetic component. Researchers now believe that the "wiring" in the child's brain that is used to learn language is not operating at its optimum capacity, but they don't know why some individuals' "wiring" is less efficient than that of others.

**What training is needed to work as a speech-language pathologist?**

One needs a master's degree in speech-language pathology or communication disorders. Different states have different requirements, but some kind of certification and/or licensing is needed.

QUESTION **Do any speech or language problems run in your family? On the basis of what you have learned about language development from this chapter, what techniques do you think might help people with speech and/or language problems?**

### THINKING BACK TO CHI HAE . . .

Now that you have studied this chapter, you should be able to explain how Chi Hae can use concepts about perceptual, cognitive, and language development to understand and support her baby's development. You should be able to list at least a dozen specific concepts and explain how each would relate to Chi Hae and Cara.

Like most parents of infants, Chi Hae is interested in what her baby understands and how she can help to support her baby's learning. She might be interested to know about the perceptual skills that Cara is developing, including the kinds of visual and auditory preferences she might show.

Chi Hae might be especially interested in the fact that newborns really do prefer to look at human faces. This preference and the supportive behavior it elicits from adults might help to keep Chi Hae and Cara looking and "talking" to one another for extended periods, which helps to support Cara's developing cognitive and language skills. It would be useful to tell Chi Hae about infants' abilities to integrate their sensory experiences through intermodal perception. This skill also helps to support Cara's cognitive development: According to Piaget, a critical part of cognitive development is combining and coordinating experiences to construct understanding. Piaget would encourage Chi Hae to provide Cara with as much sensory and motor experience as she can, since infant thought is based on these experiences and they lay the foundation for later stages. As Cara encounters new things in her environment, her natural tendencies to adapt will lead her to construct new understandings of her world. Finally, Chi Hae might be interested to know that even though human infants seem biologically prepared to develop language, the social and language interactions she helps to provide for Cara are essential to support this important human skill.

# 5

## CHAPTER REVIEW . . .

**5.1 What is the preferential-looking technique and what has it shown us about infant perception?**

Infants are shown two or more stimuli, and the amount of time spent looking at each one is recorded. When infants spend more time fixating on some stimuli than on others, it can be inferred that the infants are visually processing and discriminating the stimuli (i.e., they can see the differences among the stimuli). Using this technique, Robert Fantz and other researchers have demonstrated that young infants prefer to look at moving stimuli, outer contours and edges, areas of high contrast, detailed or complex patterns, symmetrical patterns, curves, and human face patterns.

**5.2 How is the habituation–dishabituation technique used to test infant perception?**

Infants are presented with the same stimulus repeatedly until they habituate (show decreased response). When a new stimulus is presented, dishabituation (renewed interest and response) indicates that the infant has processed the difference between the old and new stimuli.

**5.3 Can infants coordinate information across different sensory modalities or avenues of sensation?**

Yes. Research on intermodal perception indicates that young infants can match what they see with what they hear or feel. For example, 1-month-olds look longer at the shape of a pacifier they previously held in their mouths, and older infants can match the sounds of objects with their filmed movements.

**5.4 How is Piaget's background in biology reflected in his theory of cognitive development?**

Piaget was a young scholar in biology, producing his first scientific publication at the age of 10. As a teen, he studied how sea mollusks adapt their shells to changes in water currents, and this image of adaptation formed the core of his theory of cognitive development. Piaget theorized that children create and adapt their own cognitive structures in response to their changing experiences with the world.

**5.5 Why is Piaget's theory considered a constructivist view, and how do the main concepts in this theory explain the development of cognitive structures?**

Piaget's theory is considered a constructivist view because he emphasized that children learn primarily by interpreting their own environment and experiences in light of the knowledge and experiences they already have, thus constructing their own schemes and cognitive structures. Schemes are the cognitive structures that are constructed by the child, and they are modified through adaptation. New experiences are assimilated into existing schemes, and if the experiences do not fit adequately, cognitive disequilibrium results. Children can accommodate or modify their schemes to provide a better fit with the environment, returning themselves to cognitive equilibrium. Organization is the tendency to integrate cognitive structures into larger coherent systems, and reflective abstraction is used to notice patterns and connections among related schemes.

**5.6 What are the main limitations and advances in cognitive processing at the sensorimotor stage?**
In the stage of sensorimotor thought (birth to 2 years), infants begin by understanding the world through inborn reflexes and through their own direct sensory and motor actions. The ability to represent knowledge internally, in symbolic, mental form, develops gradually during this stage.

**5.7 What are the defining characteristics of language?**
Human language has *semanticity* and displacement and is productive. It is made up of arbitrary and abstract symbols and is governed by specific rules for how to communicate.

**5.8 What is the evidence for and against the theory that language is learned?**
Learning theorists argue that language is learned through shaping of behavior, imitation, and modeling. Research indicates that language can be affected by differential reinforcement, but it is not clear how consistently parents shape their children's language or how learning processes could explain the productivity and rate of language acquisition.

**5.9 What is the evidence for and against the theory that language is genetically programmed in humans?**
Nativist theory proposes that humans are endowed with an innate language acquisition device that contains either knowledge of universal grammar or operating principles that guide the processing of language information. Across many languages, children develop language quickly and easily, with marked consistency in the achievement of language milestones. There is disagreement as to whether nonhumans develop language, but the pace of animal language achievements is slower and the effort required is much greater than for humans. There are brain structures that are specialized for language processing, though there does not seem to be a single LAD brain organ. There is some evidence for the existence of sensitive periods in language development.

**5.10 How do social interactions and general cognitive level affect language development?**
Cognitive approaches view language as dependent on other, more general cognitive skills. For Piaget, the broader ability to represent objects leads to the need for language. Social interaction theory emphasizes the importance of social interactions for acquiring language.

**5.11 How do infants' prelinguistic skills help to prepare them for language, and what are the major developments in vocalizations, semantics, and grammar during infancy?**
Infants have at birth or rapidly develop abilities to discriminate speech sounds and sequences of sounds, localize sound direction, and recognize a voice. Their recognition of speech sounds from their native language rapidly improves, but they lose the ability to discriminate sounds of other languages. Social interaction during the first year of life helps infants to learn that sounds can be used to communicate and fosters early pragmatic skills such as turn-taking. Child-directed speech and a developing joint focus of attention between infants and caregivers foster prelinguistic skills. Infants begin life making nonspeech sounds with no consistent meaning, then progress through cooing, babbling, echolalia, and protowords during the first year of life. Toddlers expand their vocabularies and learn grammatical rules for combining words into phrases and sentences.

## REVISITING THEMES

Much of this chapter concerns the *nature and nurture* theme. The complex interactions of nature and nurture were the early motivation for Robert Fantz; this issue led him to develop clever methods to study infant perception that are still in use (pp. 138–139). Research on infant perception of faces (p. 140) and integration of information from different modalities (p. 142) asks about the relative roles of nature and nurture, and the relative influence of nature and nurture is probably the central issue in explaining language development (pp. 156-168). Finally, Piaget's constructivist approach (p. 162) describes how cognitive structures are neither inborn nor taken as a whole from the environment—they are constructed from an interaction of these two factors.

The theme of *neuroscience* is also evident throughout this chapter. Neuroscience methods such as the analysis of event-related potentials (p. 160), flash-evoked potentials (p. 142), eye movements (p. 155), and near-infrared spectography (p. 160) are being used to study infant perception, object permanence, and language development. These methods allow us to "see the brain" as it responds to different types of stimuli.

*Plasticity and resilience in development* was discussed in relation to language development. Even children who experience impoverished early language environments or who sustain damage to the left brain hemisphere early in life still develop some language skills; the brain's plasticity allows children to show at least some recovery from such experiences (pp. 160–161).

## KEY TERMS

accommodation (149)
adaptation (147)
assimilation (149)
constructivist view (146)
dishabituation (142)
equilibration (149)
habituation (141)
habituation–dishabituation technique (141)
holophrases (167)
intermodal perception (142)
language (156)
language acquisition device (LAD) (158)
learning theory (157)
nativist theory (158)
object permanence (152)
organization (147)
perception (138)
Piaget's cognitive developmental theory (162)
preferential-looking technique (138)
reflective abstraction (149)
scheme (147)
sensorimotor thought (149)
social interactionist theory (163)
symbolic (representational) thought (150)
telegraphic speech (167)

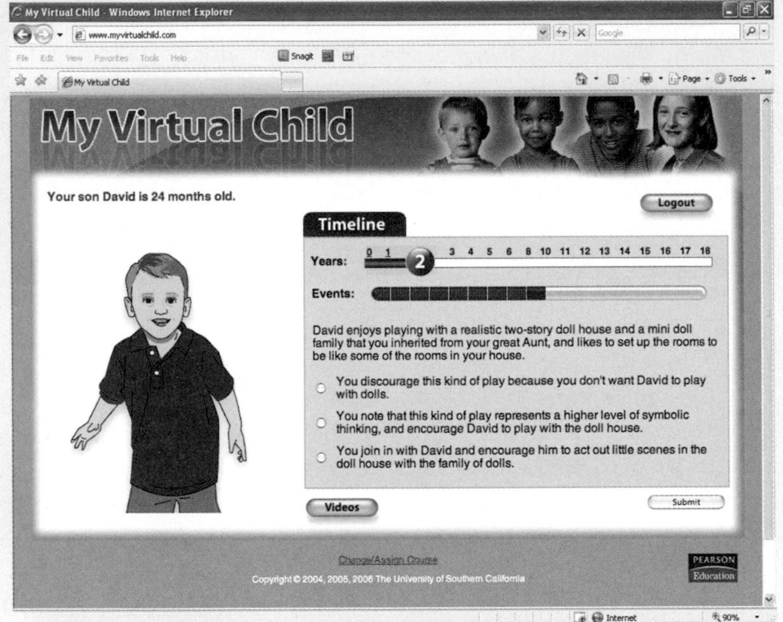


**"What decisions would you make while raising a child? What would the consequences of those decisions be?"**

Find out by accessing My Virtual Child at
**www.mydevelopmentlab.com**
and raising your own virtual child
from birth to age 18.

Watch Visit your Multimedia Library at www.mydevelopmentlab.com to watch an interview with Lisa online.

# 6 INFANTS AND TODDLERS

# Socioemotional Development in Infants and Toddlers

Recently, Lisa dropped off her 10-month-old son, Christopher, at a family day care for the first time. Lisa and her husband Chris both work full time, and Christopher has been staying with Lisa's mother while they work. Lisa wanted to start Christopher in another type of supervised child care because she thought he'd benefit by having a structured learning environment and other children with whom to play, and she was also concerned that Christopher's grandmother was getting older and might not be able to keep up with him after he starts walking and getting into things. Before his first day, Lisa prepared Christopher by taking him twice to visit his new day care home. Christopher was hesitant at first—he is normally wary of new people and new situations—but before long he warmed up and crawled around to explore the toys and check out a few of the other toddlers who were there. His day care provider, Rachel, was warm and helpful, and Christopher seemed to enjoy his visits.

On his first real day at the day care, however, things didn't go quite as smoothly. When Lisa tried to leave, Christopher held tightly to her and cried. After a few minutes, Lisa finally asked Rachel to hold him and give him his bottle, hoping that would comfort Christopher while she left.

Christopher is still having a hard time adjusting to day care. When Lisa drops him off in the mornings, Christopher still whines and looks at her like he's asking "why are you doing this to me?" When Chris picks him up in the afternoons, Christopher often cries and looks at him like he's being "rescued." Lisa and her husband Chris are still torn by the situation. They are very sad when they leave Christopher with Rachel, but they also know that she provides good care and that Christopher will adjust.

After studying this chapter, you should be able to use at least a dozen concepts to help Lisa understand Christopher's reaction to his new setting. You will be able to explain what researchers know about infant–parent attachment and about when and why young children fear strangers and new settings. Does Christopher seem to have a secure attachment to his parents? What clues can you find in the scenario that you just read? How does Christopher's temperament factor into his reaction? What can Lisa and Chris do to help Christopher cope with the emotions he feels?

As you read this chapter, look for the "Think About Lisa . . ." questions that ask you to consider what you're learning from Lisa's perspective.

Most parents remember the first time they left their child in a child care center or with a babysitter. That first time is usually not easy. Some children get very upset; others react more calmly. In this chapter, we explore some of the reasons behind these differences. We begin by looking at how researchers study human attachment and how they classify the various types of attachments that infants form with their parents. We also look at temperament and at the types of temperament that have been identified, and we discuss emotional development in infants and toddlers. We conclude the chapter by exploring the types of social interactions infants and toddlers develop and how they play with friends and peers. As you would imagine, children's attachment styles, temperaments, emotions, and social skills all contribute to their varied responses to situations like Christopher's first morning in day care.

▲ Who could resist this smile? Chubby cheeks, soft skin, and big smiles are just some of the features that induce adults to want to cuddle and take care of babies.

## Attachment

First, we look at the emotional bond that develops between an infant and his or her primary caregivers. Although most of us would call it "love," researchers refer to this bond by its more technical name: *attachment*. **Attachment** is an emotional tie to a specific person or people that endures across time and space (Ainsworth, 1973). Infants don't bond with everyone. They reserve this special emotional attachment for the select few who provide their primary care. From its beginnings in the 1950s, most research in this area has focused primarily on the attachments that infants form with their mothers. Of course, today, many infants receive a substantial amount of care from fathers, older siblings, grandparents, other close relatives, and child care providers, and they can form attachments with anyone who provides consistent and loving care. In our discussion, we will sometimes refer to *caregivers*, though this term sounds too technical for the special emotions and relationships that we will discuss. We'll use the term *mother* when describing research that primarily investigated mother attachments, but we hope that fathers and other caregivers will recognize that their relationships follow a similar path. **Watch** on **mydevelopmentlab**

**Watch** a video on Attachment in Infants.
www.mydevelopmentlab.com

AS YOU STUDY THIS SECTION, ASK YOURSELF THESE QUESTIONS:

- **6.1** What are the historical roots that gave rise to modern research on attachment, and how do these roots affect our thinking about attachment today?
- **6.2** What are the main factors related to healthy and unhealthy attachment relationships between infants and their parents or caregivers?
- **6.3** How do the emotional bonds that are established early in life influence development throughout childhood?

### The History of Attachment Research

Modern-day research on human attachment has been heavily influenced by the ethological theory of John Bowlby, by the classic experiments Harry Harlow conducted with rhesus monkeys, and by the well-known work of Mary Ainsworth, who tested attachments between human infants and their parents.

**attachment**
An emotional tie to a specific other person or people that endures across time and space.

**contact comfort**
The comfortable feeling that infants gain by clinging to a soft attachment figure.

**John Bowlby's Ethological Theory.** In John Bowlby's ethological theory, attachment emerges from a system of traits and behaviors that have evolved over time to increase the infant's chances of survival (Bowlby, 1958, 1988). Unlike some animal species whose young can survive on their own shortly after birth, human infants are entirely dependent on their caregivers for food, protection, and everything else they need. The deep emotional bond of attachment increases the amount of attention and the quality of care that an infant receives. Bowlby (1958) commented, "It is fortunate for their survival that babies are so designed by Nature that they beguile and enslave mothers" (p. 367). Newborns follow adults with their eyes, a behavior that delights new parents. Later, as infants learn to reach, crawl, and then walk, they are able to physically find, follow, and cling to their caregivers. They use smiling, crying, and calling to bring adults closer. Bowlby emphasized the infant's smile as a powerful social releaser of nurturing behavior in adults. Adults typically respond positively to these social cues, and see the infant's round face, bright eyes, and chubby appearance as cute and cuddly. They soon develop a deep emotional bond with the infant. Evolution, then, has provided an interactive system that links nurturing adults to infants who depend on the adults' loving care.

Bowlby believed that attachment is especially evident when an infant seeks nearness to a protective adult in moments of distress or fear. The attachment figure provides a *secure base* of emotional comfort for the infant.

Bowlby (1969) proposed that infants develop attachments in the following four stages:

1. *Orientation without discrimination* (first 2 to 3 months after birth). Infants signal and respond to any available and caring adult. In this initial stage, an attachment to a specific caregiver has not yet formed.
2. *Orientation with discrimination* (2 to 6 months of age). Infants begin to show a decided preference for their primary caregivers, signaling and responding more to the people who take care of them than to other people.
3. *Safe-base attachment* (6 months to 3 years). Infants and toddlers actively seek to be near their favored caregivers. They follow and cling to them, use them as a safe base to explore the environment, and often become visibly distressed when separated from their attachment figures. Fear of strangers also emerges.
4. *Goal-corrected partnerships* (3 years and up). Children begin to understand the feelings and motives of their caregivers. The relationship goes both ways now: Children can adjust their behaviors to the changing needs and desires of their attachment figures, just as attachment figures adapt to children's changing needs. For example, children learn that sometimes their attachment figures are busy or have other demands that conflict with caregiving. There is now a more integrated emotional relationship between child and caregiver.

Since the 1950s, Bowlby's ethological theory has provided the dominant framework for study of the special bonds between infants and adults.

THINKING CRITICALLY
What do you think were the qualities in your parents or other caregivers that made you become attached to them?

THINK ABOUT LISA . . .
Which one of Bowlby's four stages best describes the attachment behaviors that Christopher showed on his first day in day care?

**Harry Harlow's Research with Rhesus Monkeys.** Also during the 1950s, psychologist Harry Harlow conducted one of the most famous series of experiments in child development research. Harlow raised infant rhesus monkeys with the two types of surrogate (substitute) "mothers" shown in Figure 6.1 (Harlow & Zimmermann, 1959). One surrogate was made of bare wire mesh; the other had a soft cloth covering. Would infant monkeys form an attachment to either of these objects? Would the presence of a surrogate provide any emotional support for the infant? The cloth-covered surrogate did. With his experiments Harlow provided a convincing demonstration that the critical ingredient in attachment formation is **contact comfort**—the comfortable feeling that infants gain by clinging to a soft attachment figure.

▲ FIGURE 6.1
**Surrogate Mothers from Harlow's Experiment**
Rhesus monkeys became emotionally attached to the cloth mother that provided contact comfort but not to the wire mother that provided food.

Harlow's finding contradicted the psychoanalytic and behavioral theories that were popular at this time. These theories predicted that infants would form attachments with the caregiver who provided food. In psychoanalytic theory, oral gratification during feeding establishes the initial bond between infant and mother (recall Freud's oral stage, discussed in Chapter 1). In behavioral theory, food serves as a powerful reinforcer for behaviors related to attachment. But feeding was not what determined attachment for

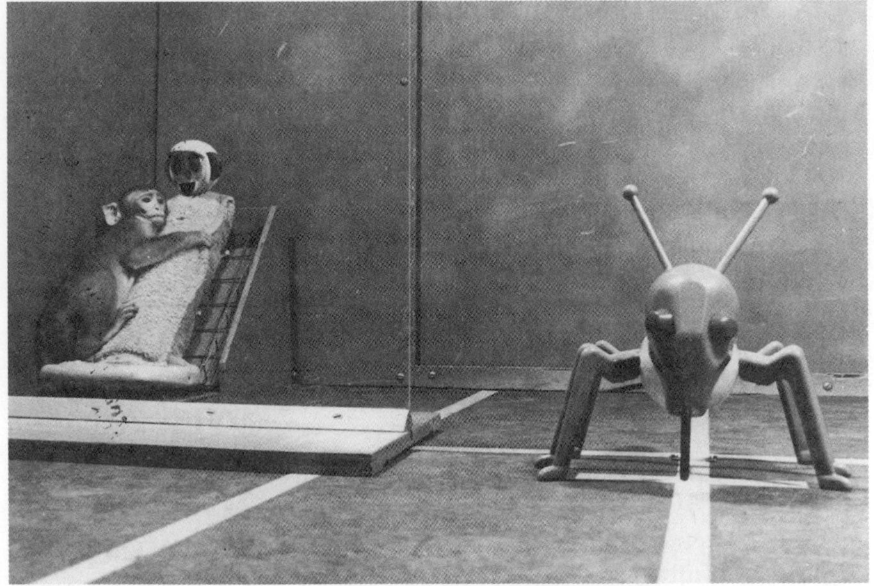

Where do infant monkeys turn when they are frightened? What does this response tell us about the attachment that they have formed with their caregivers?

Harlow's monkeys. Even when the infants received milk from the wire mesh mother, they spent the great majority of their time clinging to the cloth mother. When placed in an open room or an unfamiliar setting, infant monkeys without their cloth mothers showed extreme anxiety. They typically huddled in the corner, rocking and hugging themselves. But when their cloth mothers were in the room, these same infant monkeys showed a very different reaction. They would hug and cling to the mothers, and then, finding security in the mothers' presence, they would explore the room and play freely. When confronted with a fear stimulus (e.g., a clanging robot or a model of a giant insect), the infant monkeys first sought the comfort of their cloth mothers and then turned bravely to face their fears. The mother surrogates that provided contact comfort served as the secure base that these infant monkeys needed. Mere feeding provided no such benefit. Harlow found that it was the cloth mother that provided the infants with the kind of emotional security John Bowlby had described in his ethological theory.

THINK ABOUT LISA . . .
What similarities do you see between the reactions of Harlow's monkeys to strangers and separation and Christopher's behavior on his first day in day care? How were Harlow's experiments similar to situations faced by human children?

Taken together, Bowlby and Harlow's findings provided the lens through which other researchers examine infant–parent attachments. Infants have formed an emotional bond to a specific person when they seek closeness to that person as a secure base. When separated from this person, the infant shows distress. When reunited, the infant clings to the attachment figure and becomes emotionally comfortable again. This is the pattern that Bowlby predicted in his ethological theory, and it is the pattern that Harlow observed with his rhesus monkeys. Can it also be demonstrated with human infants?

Mary Ainsworth and the Strange Situation. To investigate attachment in human infants, psychologist Mary Ainsworth developed the *Strange Situation* test (Ainsworth, 1973; Ainsworth, Blehar, Waters, & Wall, 1978; Ainsworth & Wittig, 1969). Following Bowlby and Harlow, Ainsworth based her procedure on the idea that infants will seek to be near their attachment figure when they are distressed by an unfamiliar setting or an unfamiliar person. Let's look at how this works.

The **Strange Situation** consists of eight episodes strictly scripted to allow researchers to observe attachment behaviors in human infants, as described in Table 6.1. The purpose is to place the infant in a "strange" or unfamiliar setting with the primary caregiver, usually the mother. Does the infant use the mother as a secure base for exploring the new setting? Does the infant become distressed when the mother leaves and

**Strange Situation**
A structured laboratory procedure that is used to observe attachment behavior in human infants.

**TABLE 6.1**
**Mary Ainsworth's Strange Situation Procedure**

| EPISODE | BEHAVIOR OF INFANT SHOWING SECURE ATTACHMENT |
|---|---|
| 1 **INTRODUCTION:** Assistant introduces mother and baby to the room. This episode lasts 30 seconds; the other episodes last approximately 3 minutes each. | Baby is held by mother. |
| 2 **UNFAMILIAR ROOM:** Mother places baby on floor with toys and sits in chair. Mother is told not to direct baby's actions but otherwise to respond normally. | Baby might be wary of room at first but uses mother as a *safe base* of security. Plays with toys while mother is present. Usually maintains visual contact with mother during play. |
| 3 **STRANGER ENTERS:** Unfamiliar female adult knocks on door, then enters. Stranger speaks with mother, then approaches baby to play. | Baby might show *stranger anxiety* and clearly prefers mother over stranger. While mother is present, baby might allow stranger to approach and play. |
| 4 **MOTHER LEAVES:** Mother quietly leaves the room, leaving baby with the stranger. Stranger returns to sit in her chair. | Baby shows *separation anxiety* and renewed *stranger anxiety*. Baby might be somewhat comforted by stranger but clearly wants mother. |
| 5 **REUNION; STRANGER LEAVES:** Mother returns, and stranger leaves. Mother comforts baby if baby wishes and returns baby to play with the toys. | Baby *seeks contact* with mother for joyful reunion. Seeks proximity, clings. Baby might continue playing while mother is present. |
| 6 **MOTHER LEAVES AGAIN:** Mother says "bye-bye" and leaves infant alone in the room. | Baby shows *separation anxiety*, distress. |
| 7 **STRANGER ENTERS AGAIN:** While baby is still alone, the same stranger enters again. Stranger sits in chair, then calls or approaches baby to play. | Baby might show *stranger anxiety* and clearly prefers that mother return. |
| 8 **REUNION; STRANGER LEAVES:** Mother returns and stranger leaves. Mother picks up baby for a reunion that ends the procedure. | Joy on reunion. Baby *seeks proximity and contact* with mother. |

▲ Mary Ainsworth developed the Strange Situation, a method of testing attachment security that has been used by many researchers in the United States and in other countries.

seek her proximity when she returns? Does the infant prefer the mother over an unfamiliar adult?

The procedure begins when the mother brings her infant into a laboratory setting. Infants are normally observed at about 1 year of age. The setting is an average-sized room with a few chairs and interesting toys. A one-way observation mirror on the wall permits observers to videotape the sessions for later analysis. After a 30-second introductory period, the mother places the baby on the floor in the center of the room and sits in one of the chairs. Most infants are wary of the unfamiliar setting and usually situate themselves so they can maintain visual contact with their mothers.

After 3 minutes, an unfamiliar female adult comes in. In a friendly manner, she speaks to the mother and then approaches the infant to play. Most infants show signs of **stranger anxiety**, a wariness or fear of unfamiliar adults. Infants may allow the stranger to approach and play, although most remain wary. Next, the mother calmly leaves the

**stranger anxiety**
Wariness or fear of unfamiliar adults.

Like this baby, most infants go through a period of time when they are afraid of strangers. What does this behavior tell us about the attachment that has formed between the infant and mother?

room. Losing their secure base, most infants show renewed stranger anxiety. They are no longer willing to play with the stranger and instead move to the door (or to the mother's chair), where they whine, cry, or show other visible signs of distress that indicate **separation anxiety**.

THINK ABOUT LISA . . .
How were Christopher's behaviors similar to the ones Ainsworth observed with infants in her Strange Situation test?

**separation anxiety**
Distress infants experience when separated from their primary caregivers.

**secure attachment**
In Ainsworth's classification system, the healthy type of attachment between an infant and a caregiver. It is indicated when the infant seeks contact with the caregiver, clings, and is soothed by the caregiver and when the infant uses the caregiver as a safe base for exploring unfamiliar environments.

**insecure–avoidant attachment**
Unhealthy type of attachment that is indicated when infants do not use their caregivers as a safe base for exploring unfamiliar environments, do not prefer the caregiver over unfamiliar adults, and are not visibly distressed by separation. Infants ignore or avoid their caregivers when reunited after separation.

For the next episode, the mother returns and the stranger leaves. Infants joyfully hug and cling tightly to their mothers. Feeling secure once more, infants resume their play. As the episodes continue, the mother exits again, leaving the infant alone; then the stranger reenters. These episodes allow additional opportunities to observe separation anxiety and stranger anxiety, respectively. The infant is reunited with the mother in the final episode.

Although anxieties are not normally considered positive, you can see from this description that *separation anxiety* and *stranger anxiety* both signify that the infant has formed a special emotional attachment to a specific other person. It is the mother, not the stranger, who provides the security the infant needs to feel comfortable in the new setting. The loss of this security is evident when the mother leaves. Wariness of the stranger and preference for the mother both indicate what Ainsworth termed **secure attachment**. The most reliable indicator of secure attachment, however, is the way in which the infant responds when the mother returns to the room: Securely attached infants seek contact with the mother, cling tightly, and allow the mother to soothe and comfort them. Of the thousands of infants and parents observed by Ainsworth and other U.S. researchers in the Strange Situation procedure, approximately 62% show secure attachment (Thompson, 2006). But what about the other 38%?

Ainsworth identified two patterns of *insecure attachment.* With **insecure–avoidant attachment**, seen in approximately 15% of infants studied in the United States, infants do not seem to use the mother as a secure base. When the stranger enters, these infants do not show a special preference for their mother; they might go directly to the stranger or play with the stranger without first needing to cling to the mother. When the mother leaves, these infants seem undisturbed. They might continue playing rather than going to the door and fussing. When the mother reenters, these infants turn away, ignore her, or avoid her. There is debate about how to interpret this pattern of behavior (Thompson, 1998). Are the infants actively avoiding contact with a parent who has rebuffed them in the past, or are they merely uninterested because they have not developed a special bond?

**TABLE 6.2**
**Different Types of Attachment Identified in the Strange Situation**

| TYPE OF ATTACHMENT | BEHAVIORS |
|---|---|
| Secure | • Baby uses mother as safe base for exploring unfamiliar room.<br>• Baby prefers mother over stranger.<br>• Baby might show distress when separated from mother.<br>• Baby seeks proximity and contact with mother on reunion. |
| Insecure–avoidant | • Baby does not prefer mother over stranger.<br>• Baby avoids contact with mother by turning or looking away. |
| Insecure–resistant | • Baby shows ambivalent approach–resist behavior: seeks proximity with mother but then resists contact.<br>• Baby does not avoid mother.<br>• Some infants show anger; others are passive. |
| Insecure–disorganized/ disoriented | • Babies seem confused or dazed or may show contradictory behaviors.<br>• Babies may be calm, then angry.<br>• Babies may be motionless or show apprehension.<br>• Behaviors are not consistently avoidant or resistant as in other categories. |

**Insecure–resistant attachment** is seen in about 8% of infants (Thompson, 2006). These infants usually seek the proximity of their mother, but they do not seem to gain comfort from the contact. Some show exaggerated stranger and separation anxiety or a strong need to stay close to the parent. But when the mother picks the baby up, some of these infants fight off her efforts to provide comfort, often showing signs of anger or heightened distress. Others seem passive when their mothers try to console them. Some researchers label this category *insecure–ambivalent attachment,* because the infant seeks proximity but then shows ambivalence about contact with the caregiver.

More recently, researchers have added another category called **insecure–disorganized (or disoriented) attachment**, seen in nearly 15% of infants who have been tested (Main & Solomon, 1986, 1990; Thompson, 2006). These infants seem confused or dazed, or they might show contradictory behaviors. They might be calm one moment and angry the next. They might remain motionless or show apprehension as their parent approaches. Their behaviors are not consistently avoidant or resistant, so they do not fall neatly into either of those classifications of insecure attachment. Table 6.2 summarizes the types of attachment that Mary Ainsworth and other researchers have identified.

THINK ABOUT LISA . . .
Do you see any indications of insecure attachment in Christopher's behavior on his first day at day care? Explain.

THINKING CRITICALLY
What kinds of parenting have you observed that might contribute to insecure attachment relationships?

## Factors Related to Attachment

What causes these different types of attachments to develop? Parent, infant, and cultural factors are all involved.

**Parent Factors.** According to Ainsworth, it's the quality of the parenting during the first year of life that determines the type of attachment that is formed—it's due more to nurture than to nature. Through extensive observation of mother–infant behaviors in the home environment, Ainsworth and others found that secure attachment relationships tend to be associated with mothers who respond positively, consistently, and warmly to their infants (Ainsworth, 1973; Ainsworth et al., 1978; Thompson, 2006). They hold their babies frequently, tenderly, and for long enough that the infants seem satisfied when they are put back down. When Ainsworth (1973) observed families in their homes, she found that securely attached infants showed very little distress when their mothers left the

**insecure–resistant attachment**
Unhealthy type of attachment indicated when infants seek the proximity of their caregiver but do not seem to gain comfort from the contact.

**insecure–disorganized (or disoriented) attachment**
Unhealthy type of attachment indicated when infants seem confused or dazed or show contradictory behaviors in the Strange Situation.

room briefly. They seemed conscious of their mothers' whereabouts and confident that the mothers would soon return. This was in contrast to the babies' behavior in the Strange Situation: These same infants showed separation distress when their mothers left them in the unfamiliar laboratory setting. During reunion episodes, securely attached infants gain considerable comfort by being held by their mothers.

A particularly important characteristic of secure attachments is the mother's sensitivity to the calls and signals of her baby. These mothers respond quickly when their infants cry or call out. Their approach is more positive, and they are not worried that their attention will "spoil" the baby. But it is more than just responding quickly and positively. These mothers show **sensitive responsiveness**—they see things from the infant's point of view and adjust their responses to meet the infant's needs. Consider a 1-year-old who opens a book, points to a balloon, and says "dat." The caregiver responds by smiling and saying, "Yes, that's a balloon, and here's another one." The caregiver has noticed the infant's signal and has responded to it by allowing the infant to initiate a game of pointing and naming. Contrast this to the caregiver who takes the book from the baby, turns to the beginning, and proceeds to read the book the "right" way. Which caregiver has shown sensitive responsiveness? Healthy attachments are facilitated when caregivers go along with the games, interactions, and other activities that their infants initiate. They adjust their babies' feeding and sleep schedules according to the signals and rhythms of the baby, and they otherwise show sensitivity toward the infant's perspective. With secure attachments, the relationship is mutual rather than being completely dominated by the caregiver. In a cross-cultural study that compared families in the United States and in Bogotá, Colombia, maternal sensitivity was related to infant security in both countries (Posada et al., 2002; Posada, Carbonell, Alzate, & Plata, 2004). Caregiver sensitivity is also important in child care settings: Infants and young children are more likely to show secure attachments with their child care providers when the providers show sensitive responsiveness (Ahnert, Pinquart, & Lamb, 2006).

▲ How is the attachment relationship affected when parents are frequently hostile or irritable? What if they are abusive?

**sensitive responsiveness**
A quality of infant care in which caregivers respond quickly and warmly to the baby's signals and adjust their responses to allow the infant to direct some of the interactions.

Based on her home observations, Ainsworth (1973) believed that indifferent parenting led to insecure–avoidant attachments and that inconsistent parenting led to insecure–resistant attachments. Other researchers, however, have produced evidence that avoidant attachments arise more from parenting that is intrusive, overstimulating, or even hostile, and that resistant attachments develop when care is unresponsive (Isabella, 1995; Isabella & Belsky, 1991; Isabella, Belsky, & von Eye, 1989; Lyons-Ruth, Connell, Zoll, & Stall, 1987). These researchers describe mothers of insecure–avoidant infants as being tense and irritable, showing little interest in their infants, handling them in a mechanical fashion, failing to adjust feedings to the baby's pace, being less responsive to infants' cries and calls, and otherwise reacting to motherhood in a resentful or negative way (Egeland & Farber, 1984). Whether avoidant or resistant, insecurely attached infants learn that their caregivers will not respond sensitively to their needs. Thus, in times of stress, they might reject their parents' attempts to comfort them by looking away or by showing anger and frustration.

Insecure–disorganized attachments have been associated with parenting that is negative, intrusive, or abusive, and disorganized attachments are also linked to parents who themselves have suffered childhood traumas, have unresolved difficulties with their own parents, or are still mourning the death of their attachment figure (Madigan, Moran, & Pederson, 2006; Main & Hesse, 1990; Main & Solomon, 1990). Infants who have been frightened by their parents might be confused about how to respond when they are in a stressful situation. They might also be fearful of how their parents will respond under stress. Can they use their parent as a safe base of security, or will their parent be dangerous? You can understand how an infant might respond in contradictory ways, such as approaching the parent but also cowering. Or an infant might freeze, immobilized by the dilemma.

**Infant Factors.** Attachment is a two-way relationship, and factors associated with infants themselves also can contribute to their security and insecurity. Infants who become securely attached tend to cry less frequently, greet their mothers more positively, and initiate more bodily contact with their mothers (Ainsworth et al., 1978). Conversely, infants with insecure attachments tend to cry more, often show anger, and show disruptions in bodily contact. Are these differences due to the infant or due to the parenting? Do securely attached infants cry less because their mothers respond more sensitively to them, or do the mothers respond more sensitively because their babies are more pleasant and happy? It is difficult to determine the cause–effect relationships among these correlational associations.

It has been found that insecure–disorganized attachments occur at a higher rate among infants with special needs, such as those with high-risk prematurity, Down syndrome, autism, and physical disabilities (Thompson, 1998; van IJzendoorn, Goldberg, Kroonenberg, & Frankel, 1992). It is very challenging to parent infants with these types of special needs, and parents may have difficulty remaining nurturing over long periods of time. Behavior genetics studies generally show that attachment types are determined more by the ways that infants are nurtured and parented than by the genes that the infants inherited (Pasco Fearon et al., 2006; Roisman & Fraley, 2008). When it comes to attachment, nurture wins out over nature.

▲ How do our cultural values influence the way we parent? How might the expression of attachment differ across cultures?

**Cultural Factors.** Beyond the infant and parent, the values of the larger culture influence parental expectations and behaviors. Table 6.3 shows attachment classifications from the United States and seven other nations. For comparison purposes, note that the data from

**TABLE 6.3**
Cross-National Attachment Data on Infants Observed in the Strange Situation

| COUNTRY OR GROUP | NUMBER OF INFANTS SAMPLED | SECURE ATTACHMENT (PERCENTAGE) | INSECURE–AVOIDANT ATTACHMENT (PERCENTAGE) | INSECURE–RESISTANT ATTACHMENT (PERCENTAGE) |
|---|---|---|---|---|
| Great Britain | 72 | 75 | 22 | 3 |
| Sweden | 51 | 74 | 22 | 4 |
| Netherlands | 115 | 68 | 26 | 6 |
| Germany | 136 | 57 | 35 | 8 |
| Japan | 96 | 68 | 5 | 27 |
| Israel | 166 | 64 | 5 | 31 |
| Chile | 38 | 52 | 24 | 24 |
| U.S.: General population | 1,584 | 67 | 21 | 12 |
| U.S.: Chinese Americans | 36 | 50 | 25 | 25 |
| U.S.: Low-income Hispanics in South Bronx | 50 | 50 | 30 | 20 |

*Source:* Data for U.S. general population taken from a review by van IJzendoorn, Goldberg, Kroonenberg, & Frankel (1992). All other data taken from Thompson (1998), who reviewed studies by Beller & Pohl (1986); Durrett, Otaki, & Richards (1984); Fracasso, Busch-Rossnagel, & Fischer (1993); Goossens & van IJzendoorn (1990); Grossmann, Grossmann, Huber, & Wartner (1981); Lamb, Hwang, Frodi, & Frodi (1982); Li-Repac (1982); Sagi, Lamb, Lewkowicz, Shoham, Dvir, & Estes (1985); Sagi & Lewkowicz (1987); Sagi, van IJzendoorn, Aviezer, Donnell, & Mayseless (1994); Smith & Noble (1987); Takahashi (1986, 1990); Valenzuela (1990); and van IJzendoorn, Goossens, Kroonenberg, & Tavecchio (1985). We excluded data from high-risk groups.

the United States represent three categories: the general population, Chinese-Americans, and low-income Hispanics. In all of these studies the researchers observed infants in the Strange Situation, in most cases between 11 and 22 months of age. The newer category of insecure–disorganized attachment does not appear in the table because most of the studies cited did not include it. You can see that Great Britain and Sweden registered the highest percentages of secure attachments. Chile and Germany showed the lowest national percentages, although the majority of infants observed in both countries were still securely attached. More variability is seen with insecure attachments. In the European countries (Great Britain, Sweden, the Netherlands, and Germany), nearly all of the insecure infants were classified as avoidant, and very few were classified as resistant. The reverse pattern occurred in Japan and Israel. Insecure infants in Chile were evenly divided between the avoidant and resistant categories. **Listen** on **mydevelopmentlab**

**Listen**: Why would attachment categories differ around the world? (Author Podcast) www.mydevelopmentlab.com

What cultural factors might underlie these international differences? Japanese culture encourages close physical contact and intimacy between infants and mothers, and Japanese parents rarely leave their infants alone, especially when strangers are present (Takahashi, 1986). Similarly, Israeli infants are accustomed to close-knit relations and less experience with strangers and separation. When Japanese or Israeli infants encounter the Strange Situation, many show high levels of distress—sometimes to the point at which the researchers need to curtail the separation episodes. In the Strange Situation procedure, infants with high levels of distress level are classified with insecure–resistant attachment. In contrast, German culture stresses early independence in young children (Grossmann, Grossmann, Huber, & Wartner, 1981; Thompson, 1998). German infants learn that their mothers expect independence, so these infants might be less likely to seek proximity to their mothers in stressful situations. Remember that if infants ignore or avoid contact with their parents in the Strange Situation, they are typically classified as insecure–avoidant.

THINKING CRITICALLY
What cultural differences have you observed in how parents interact with their children?

Within the United States, attachment patterns show socioeconomic and ethnic variability. Caucasian mothers tend to value independence and competence in infants and react more negatively to the clingy, dependent behavior that is typical of insecure–resistant infants (Harwood, 1992; Thompson, 1998). Other ethnic groups have somewhat different values. Puerto Rican mothers, for example, value familial love and respect and look most negatively on the independence shown by insecure–avoidant infants (Harwood, 1992). Many African Americans are raised in extended-family arrangements in which caregiving is often shared among the mother, grandmother, aunts, sisters, and other relatives. Might these infants show less fear when their mothers leave?

▲ Some infants spend a considerable amount of time with grandparents or other extended family members. How might these experiences relate to stranger anxiety and separation anxiety and how infants would respond when they are in Ainsworth's Strange Situation test with their mothers?

Parent–infant interactions also change in response to the environment in which the family lives. In urban communities where violence is pervasive, for example, some parents might be more restrictive with their children, allowing the children less independence and freedom to roam. In these situations, young children might be more afraid when their parents leave them and might display this fear in the Strange Situation.

From this discussion, we hope you can see that environmental and cultural differences in parent–infant interactions influence behavior in the Strange Situation. Ainsworth originally developed her procedure with predominantly middle-class white American infants. It might not be appropriate to use the typical behaviors of this group as a normative reference for categorizing infants who are being raised in other circumstances or cultures. Because of cultural differences, the behaviors children show in the strange situation may signify different types of attachments across different countries. Being "clingy," for example, may mean something different in Japan than it does in Germany.

**Attachments with Fathers.** Until now, we have focused mostly on infant–mother attachments. What about fathers? Summing up the data from eleven studies of attachments with both mothers and fathers, researchers concluded that infants were just as likely to form secure attachments with fathers as with mothers (Fox, Kimmerly, & Schafer, 1991). Furthermore, the type of infant attachment tends to be consistent from one parent to the other. That is, infants with secure attachments with their mothers tended also to have secure attachments with their fathers; infants with avoidant attachments with their mothers tended also to have avoidant attachments to their fathers; and so on. It is unclear whether this consistency is due to characteristics in the infant that produce a similar attachment with each parent or whether both parents respond in similar ways to the infant.

▲ Children form attachments with their fathers and other close caregivers when they spend significant time together.

Evidence from a twin study suggests that similarities in father–infant attachment are determined more by the way the twins were fathered than by any genetic predispositions the twins may have shared (Bakermans-Kranenburg, van IJzendoorn, Bokhurst, & Schuengel, 2004). In this case, nurture was more influential than nature. It is clear that the fathering relationship is very important and that infants do reach beyond their relationships with their mothers. When fathers, older siblings, and other important people provide sensitive care for infants, infants begin to rely on them as a secure base for emotional support.

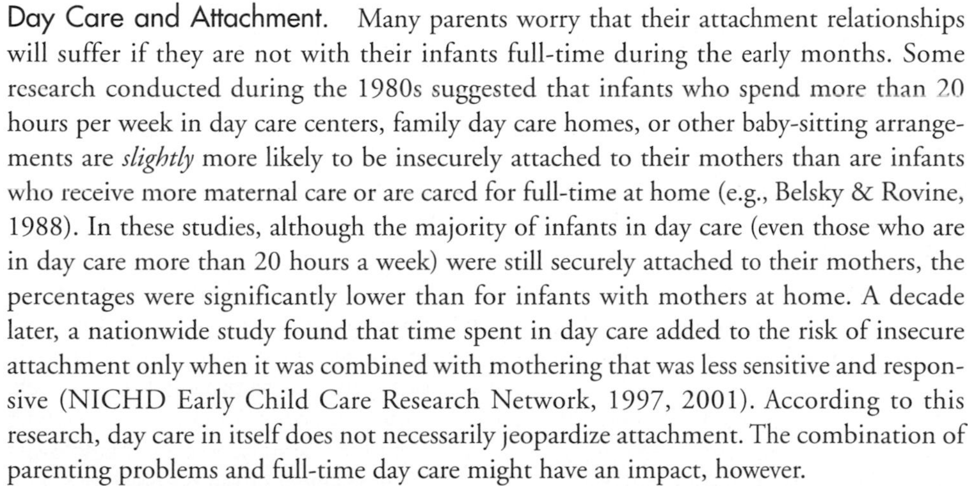

**Day Care and Attachment.** Many parents worry that their attachment relationships will suffer if they are not with their infants full-time during the early months. Some research conducted during the 1980s suggested that infants who spend more than 20 hours per week in day care centers, family day care homes, or other baby-sitting arrangements are *slightly* more likely to be insecurely attached to their mothers than are infants who receive more maternal care or are cared for full-time at home (e.g., Belsky & Rovine, 1988). In these studies, although the majority of infants in day care (even those who are in day care more than 20 hours a week) were still securely attached to their mothers, the percentages were significantly lower than for infants with mothers at home. A decade later, a nationwide study found that time spent in day care added to the risk of insecure attachment only when it was combined with mothering that was less sensitive and responsive (NICHD Early Child Care Research Network, 1997, 2001). According to this research, day care in itself does not necessarily jeopardize attachment. The combination of parenting problems and full-time day care might have an impact, however.

Even if day care itself does not disrupt parent–infant attachment, many parents still wish they could spend more time at home during the months after their babies are born. Many parents must return to work sooner than they would like to avoid losing their jobs and the paychecks they need to pay the bills. In some countries, generous paid parental leave laws let parents spend more time at home with their new babies. To see how the United States compares, see the Social Policy Perspective box called "Parental Leave Policies in the United States and Other Nations."

## Early Attachment and Long-Term Outcomes

So far, we've seen that there is a link between the quality of infant attachment and the quality of care an infant receives during the first year of life. Although interesting, this research would be less important if the effects applied only to the first year. They do not. Alan Sroufe, a psychologist and researcher at the University of Minnesota, and his colleagues continue to report on a longitudinal study of a large group of families who were originally recruited in Minneapolis in the early 1970s (Sroufe, Egeland, Carlson, & Collins, 2005). Researchers observed these families' infants with their mothers in the Strange Situation when the infants were 12 and 18 months of age, and they then collected information on these children as they grew older. The evidence pointed to the positive influence that secure attachments can have on child development. During the preschool

## Perspective SOCIAL POLICY PARENTAL LEAVE POLICIES IN THE UNITED STATES AND OTHER NATIONS

Many families in the United States face a troublesome dilemma when a new baby is born. Does the mother leave her job to stay at home with the baby? If so, how does the family survive her loss of income? What if she also loses her family's health insurance and other benefits? Will she be able to return to her job later, without penalty or loss of advancement? Or does the father leave his job, with all the same issues to consider? As you can imagine, this dilemma is especially acute for single mothers and in two-parent households in which neither parent makes a high wage. How do the parents do what is right for their new child without jeopardizing the family's economic security?

When parents who work outside the home look for day care for their infants, they encounter additional trouble. There are very few licensed care arrangements for infants (and toddlers under 2 years of age) in this country. When a family can find care, it often costs a substantial portion of one parent's wages. Many parents wonder whether it's worth staying at work. But again, can they afford to quit or take substantial time off?

Almost all other industrialized nations have recognized their important role in supporting healthy families. No one benefits when infants are left in substandard care or when families must live in poverty to care for their own children. On average, nations in the European Union provide 36 weeks of *paid leave* to families with new babies (Kamerman, 2000). Most provide similar benefits for adoption. Typically, mothers receive 14 to 16 weeks of maternity leave, paid at a full or substantial rate. An additional 20 or so weeks' leave for the mother (and sometimes for the father or for both parents) is available at a reduced rate of pay. Additional nonpaid time is usually available to one or both parents if they choose. While on leave, parents maintain their job security and full benefits.

Table 6.4 (page 185) summarizes the family leave policies of several industrialized nations. Out of 29 of the world's most developed nations, only the United States, Australia, and New Zealand have no paid leave benefits (Kamerman, 2000). In the United States, the *Family and Medical Leave Act (FMLA)* was signed into law in 1993. The FMLA requires employers that have 50 or more employees to provide up to 12 weeks of *unpaid leave* for the birth or adoption of a child or to care for other family members with serious medical conditions. Leaves are job protected. Employers may require, however, that accumulated sick leave or vacation time be used to cover some or all of the leave. Only about 55% of the U.S. workforce is covered by the FMLA (Kamerman, 2000). And although this statute pales in comparison to the provisions that are made in other nations, passage of the law still met considerable resistance. The impetus for the FMLA began in the 1970s but was not introduced in Congress until 1985. The law passed in Congress twice, in 1990 and 1991, but was vetoed both times by the president (Kamerman, 2000). Many employers were concerned that paid leaves would cripple their companies.

QUESTION **Should the care of young infants be left up to the operation of a free-market economy? Or if paid leave were to be provided, how should it be financed? Should all taxpayers contribute equally, or should employers shoulder most of the burden? What do you think is the best policy?**

years, teachers and observers rated children who had been securely attached as infants as happier and more socially skilled, competent, compliant, and empathetic than were children who were insecurely attached as infants. Preschoolers with secure attachments also were more popular with their peers, had higher self-esteem, and were less dependent and negative.

By age 10 years, children in the securely attached classification were still less dependent and received higher ratings on self-esteem, self-confidence, social skills, and emotional health. They made more friends than did children who had been insecurely attached as infants, and they spent more time with their friends.

Adolescents who had been securely attached were more likely to be leaders in their social groups, they had longer-lasting dating relationships, and in early adulthood they reported greater satisfaction in their romantic relationships. The secure attachment they experienced with their parents had evidently carried through to their relationships with peers in childhood and with romantic partners later in life. Adolescents and adults who had insecure attachments as infants with their parents, however, had more emotional and psychological problems including anxiety disorders and depression. Simulate on mydevelopmentlab

Simulate Adult Attachment.
www.mydevelopmentlab.com

**TABLE 6.4**
**Family Leave Policies in Selected Countries**

| COUNTRY | DURATION OF LEAVE | WAGE PAID |
|---|---|---|
| Sweden | 1 year parental leave | 80% |
| | 3 months' additional leave | Flat rate |
| | 3 more months | Unpaid |
| Norway | 42 weeks' parental leave | 100% |
| | Parental leave until child is 2 years old | Unpaid |
| Portugal | 6 months' maternity leave | 100% |
| | 24 months' additional parental leave | Unpaid |
| Poland | 16–18 weeks' maternity leave | 100% |
| | 24 months' additional leave | Flat rate |
| Spain | 16 weeks' maternity leave | 100% |
| | Parental leave until child is 3 years old | Unpaid |
| Netherlands | 16 weeks' maternity leave | 100% |
| | 6 months' additional leave per parent | Unpaid |
| Luxembourg | 16 weeks' maternity leave | 100% |
| Mexico | 12 weeks' maternity leave | 100% |
| Turkey | 12 weeks' maternity leave | Two-thirds |
| Great Britain | 6 weeks' maternity leave | 90% |
| | 12 weeks' additional maternity leave | Flat rate |
| | 13 weeks' parental leave | Unpaid |
| New Zealand | 52 weeks' parental leave | Unpaid |
| United States | 12 weeks' parental leave | Unpaid |

(Adapted from Kamerman, 2000.)

How do these long-term attachment effects work? Research suggests that secure attachment relationships help children learn to communicate more openly about emotions and learn better language and social skills. These skills help children interact more positively with their peers, leading to higher quality friendships (McElwain, Booth-LaForce, Lansford, Wu, & Dyer, 2008). According to Alan Sroufe, infants internalize the significant relationships that they have early in life and use those early experiences as interpretive filters when they develop later relationships. People come to expect others to interact with them in a way that mirrors their early attachment relationships. Securely attached infants, therefore, grow up to seek and expect others to be supportive and positive, and they behave in ways that elicit these qualities in people around them. Insecurely attached infants, however, might later expect and provoke hostility, ambivalence, or rejection in their relationships.

▲ This preschool child is being a good friend. How is this type of behavior related to the attachments that children form with their caregivers in the first year of life?

Michael Lamb, a researcher at the National Institute of Child Health and Development, provides a different explanation (Lamb, 1987; Lamb, Thompson, Gardner, & Cahrnov, 1985). Lamb points out that parents who show sensitivity early on with their infants tend to be parents who remain warm and sensitive as their children grow older. Warm parenting during these later childhood years might be more important than first-year attachment in helping children to maintain positive behavioral, social, and personality characteristics. When parenting remains warm and supportive, we see secure attachments in infancy and correlations with positive characteristics later in the child's life. When the parenting and family circumstances change, however, these correlations can be disrupted. For example, divorce, illness, and other negative circumstances can disrupt relationships even when children were securely attached as infants. Conversely, insecurely attached infants can benefit from later improvements in the quality of their care. Although the quality of the initial attachment is important in getting the infant off to a good start, Lamb reminds us that the quality and consistency of parental care after infancy also play an important role (Thompson, 2006). **Listen** on **mydevelopmentlab**

**Listen**: How does a secure attachment relationship in infancy relate to the child's continuing social development during childhood and adolescence? (Author Podcast) www.mydevelopmentlab.com

## LET'S REVIEW . . .

1. What is the main point of John Bowlby's ethological theory of attachment?
   - **a.** Infants are attached to the contact comfort they receive from their parents.
   - **b.** Parents have to learn to love and nurture infants.
   - **c.** Attachment behaviors have evolved over time to increase the chances of infant survival.
   - **d.** Evolution has provided a system that causes parents to be attached to infants, but infants must learn to engage in behaviors that draw their caregivers to them.
2. In Ainsworth's Strange Situation, infants who show stranger anxiety and separation anxiety will most likely be classified as having:
   - **a.** a secure attachment.
   - **b.** an insecure–avoidant attachment.
   - **c.** an insecure–disorganized attachment.
   - **d.** no attachment at all.
3. In which of the following cultures are infants expected to show the most independence from parents?
   - **a.** Japanese
   - **b.** Israeli
   - **c.** German
   - **d.** Puerto Rican
4. True or False: According to the research, it appears that nature has more influence than nurture in determining whether infants will form secure or insecure attachments to their parents and caregivers.
5. True or False: Compared to other infants, infants with secure attachments with their parents tend to grow up to be children who are happier, more competent, and popular with their peers.

Answers: 1. c, 2. a, 3. c, 4. F, 5. T

# Temperament and Emotion

When our fraternal twin daughters were about 6 months old, our good friends Steve and Sue volunteered to babysit one evening to give us a much-needed break. After about two hours of quiet dinner and conversation, we returned home to an interesting sight. One of the twins, Lily, was playing on the couch with Steve and Sue. She was bouncing on their laps, giggling, and generally enjoying the attention that was being heaped on her by two loving adults. Our other daughter, Rachel, was gently rocking back and forth in an infant swing, but the swing was facing the wall.

Although our friends had visited several times before, Rachel was still not comfortable interacting with them without us around. She had become upset and cried for quite some time after we left. Our friends are very knowledgeable and experienced with parenting and children. After trying all the standard techniques to comfort Rachel, they came up with a resourceful and effective solution. They settled her in the swing (a familiar and comforting place), turned the swing so that Rachel couldn't see these less-familiar adults, and coached our 7-year-old son (Rachel's familiar and comforting older brother) in playing with her. It worked. By the time we got home, Rachel wasn't crying—though she seemed quite glad to see us when we walked in.

Infants and toddlers differ widely in their emotions and in their reactions to different people, places, and events. In this section, we discuss the research findings in these interesting areas.

AS YOU STUDY THIS SECTION, ASK YOURSELF THESE QUESTIONS:

**6.4** What are the main types of temperaments that have been studied by researchers, and how do these different temperaments develop?

**6.5** What are some of the alternative ways of studying temperament, and what have researchers learned about infants and toddlers who are extremely shy?

**6.6** What are some of the first emotional reactions of newborn infants, and what else do researchers know about infant emotions?

**6.7** When are children first able to feel emotions such as guilt, embarrassment, shame, and pride?

## Types of Temperaments

How can the extremely different reactions shown by our twin girls be explained? As recently as the 1970s, many child development theorists thought that infants entered the world as "blank slates" and that most of their behaviors and reactions were the result of parenting and other experiences (Foreman, 1995). According to this theory, any differences in the way our twins behaved would be caused by their being raised differently. Had we really treated our daughters so differently in their first few months? That's unlikely. Anyone who has spent considerable time with infants or toddlers recognizes that children come into the world with their own behavioral styles and dispositions. Some are more sociable and outgoing and smile frequently. Others are more shy, afraid, or reluctant to engage in new situations. Today, researchers refer to the infant and child's behavioral style, or primary pattern of reacting to the environment, as **temperament**.

The most widely accepted method of classifying temperaments is the system developed by two psychiatrists, Alexander Thomas and Stella Chess (Chess & Thomas, 1995; Thomas & Chess, 1977). In 1956, Thomas and Chess began an extensive longitudinal study with children from New York. Later, they added children of working-class Puerto Rican parents, and they also added children who had been born prematurely or with physical, neurological, or intellectual disabilities. The study has followed most of these children well into adulthood. On the basis of detailed interviews with the parents, Thomas and Chess identified nine temperament dimensions that seemed to capture the diverse behavior patterns exhibited among the infants, as shown in Table 6.5. A child can receive a high, medium, or low score on each dimension. Together, the scores create a profile of the child's primary pattern of reacting to the environment.

Using the nine dimensions, Thomas and Chess (1977) identified three constellations of temperament that are particularly significant:

- The **easy temperament** is displayed when the child is primarily positive, smiles easily, has a positive and flexible approach to new situations, adapts to change, and quickly develops regular patterns of eating and sleeping.
- The **difficult temperament** exists when a child is frequently negative and easily frustrated, withdraws from new situations, is slow to adapt to change, and shows irregular patterns of eating and sleeping.
- The **slow-to-warm-up temperament** is shown when a child has mildly negative responses to new stimuli and situations but with repeated exposure gradually develops a quiet and positive interest. Compared to children with a difficult temperament, these children have less intense emotional reactions and more regular eating and sleeping schedules.

**temperament**
The infant or child's behavioral style or primary pattern of reacting to the environment.

**easy temperament**
Temperament in which a child is primarily positive, smiles easily, is adaptive and flexible, and has regular patterns of eating and sleeping.

**difficult temperament**
Temperament in which a child is frequently negative, is easily frustrated, withdraws from new situations, is slow to adapt to change, and shows irregular patterns of eating and sleeping.

**slow-to-warm-up temperament**
Temperament in which a child shows mildly negative responses to new stimuli and situations but with repeated exposure gradually develops a quiet and positive interest.

THINKING CRITICALLY

Looking at these three types of temperaments and at the dimensions listed in Table 6.5, how would you rate your temperament?

**TABLE 6.5**
**Nine Temperament Dimensions**

| TEMPERAMENT DIMENSION | DEFINITION |
|---|---|
| 1. Activity Level | Degree of motor activity during daily activities such as bathing, eating, playing, and dressing: How *active* is the infant? |
| 2. Rhythmicity | Degree of predictability/unpredictability in sleep, feeding, elimination, and other schedules: How *predictable and regular* are the infant's schedules? |
| 3. Approach or Withdrawal | Degree of positive or negative response to a new stimulus: When the infant is presented with a new person, situation, or toy, how *positive or negative* is the infant's first response? |
| 4. Adaptability | Ease with which infant modifies his or her responses in a desirable way when confronted with new or changing situations: How well does the infant *adapt to change*? |
| 5. Threshold of Responsiveness | Intensity level of stimulation that is needed to cause a response: How strong does the new situation need to be to *cause a change* in the infant's behavior? |
| 6. Intensity of Reaction | Energy level of the response: How *intense* is the infant's response? |
| 7. Quality of Mood | Amount of pleasant or unpleasant response: How *joyful or friendly* is the infant's response? |
| 8. Distractibility | Degree to which environmental stimuli interfere with ongoing behavior: How *distracted* is the infant? |
| 9. Attention Span and Persistence | Degree to which the infant pursues and continues an activity, even in the face of obstacles: How long does the infant *continue activities;* how well does the infant *overcome obstacles* in continuing activities? |

(Thomas & Chess, 1977.)

In Thomas and Chess's original longitudinal sample, 40% of the children were "easy," 10% were "difficult," and 15% were "slow to warm up." The remaining 35% did not fall neatly into any of these three categories, instead showing their own constellations of temperament dimensions. In some cases, a particular dimension—such as an extremely high activity level, high distractibility, or poor attention span—dominated a child's temperament.

**Watch** on **mydevelopmentlab**

**Watch** videos on Temperament.
www.mydevelopmentlab.com

**How Do Different Temperaments Form?** What shapes temperament? Thomas and Chess (1977) proposed an interactionist model that emphasizes the complementary forces of nature and nurture. As we saw in Chapter 2, behavior geneticists have come up with

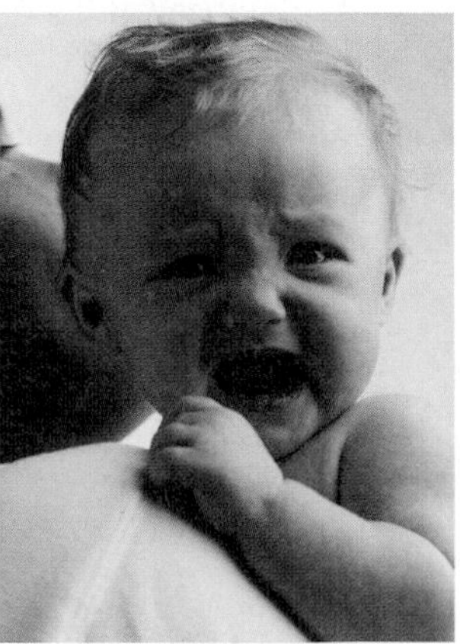

As all parents quickly learn, some infants are more easygoing and peaceful, while others are easily frustrated and difficult. Researchers believe that infants are born with a basic temperament—a style of reacting to new situations and stimuli.

moderately high heritability estimates for temperament and personality. For example, heritability estimates range from about 0.44 to 0.70 for traits such as anxiety, sociability, activity level, emotionality, task orientation, and control (see Table 2.4 in Chapter 2). This means that 44–70% of the variation in these traits across the population is related to genetics—a substantial contribution.

Based on this and other research, most psychologists believe that infants are born with innate tendencies that can be reinforced, channeled, or frustrated by parents, the family, and the larger environment. For example, one family might see a child with a high activity level as "trouble," whereas another family might label such a child "vigorous." With warm and supportive parenting, an active child might learn self-control; harsh and punitive parenting, however, might lead such a child toward aggression (Rubin, Burgess, Dwyer, & Hastings, 2003). This adaptation goes both ways: Parents adapt to the activity level of the child, and the child adapts to the parents' expectations and constraints.

Also recall from Chapter 2 that the philosophical orientation of a whole society could have a relationship to the predominant temperament expressed in that particular gene pool (Kagan, Arcus, & Snidman, 1993; Kagan et al., 1994). The emphasis on serenity and harmony in Asian cultures, for example, might be an expression of a predominant temperament that in turn influences how parents and society treat children. Nature and nurture interact to facilitate some characteristics of temperament and suppress others. "It is a constantly evolving dynamic, as the child and family and society change over time" (Thomas & Chess, 1977, p. 68).

**Goodness of Fit.** As children mature, the key factor in their developmental outcomes will be what Thomas and Chess call the **goodness of fit** between their temperaments and their environments (Chess & Thomas, 1995). Healthy development occurs when a child and his or her environment are compatible. Highly active children, for example, will fare better when their parents are on the outgoing side and value physical activity. Conversely, a poor fit can impair development. Parents who are more reserved might not respond well to highly active children, and slow-to-warm-up children might not adapt well with parents who tend to rush them into new situations. When incompatibilities are severe, behavior disorders can emerge in the child (Chess & Thomas, 1995).

Characteristics of the child and parent don't necessarily need to match to provide a good fit, however. Sometimes, good fits are complementary, as when a highly reactive child benefits from the calming influence of parents who are reflective, flexible, and patient. Children with difficult temperaments can benefit greatly when parenting is supportive and nurturing (Stright, Gallagher, & Kelley, 2008). One study even suggests that children who are born with a gene that is normally associated with risky behavior and aggression can learn to control their negative emotions when they receive sensitive parenting during infancy (Propper et al., 2008). Good fits help children learn positive social skills. Compatibility with peers, teachers, coworkers, and spouses becomes important as the child grows into adolescence and adulthood. Further, one culture might approve of active and assertive children, whereas another might view such children as rude and disrespectful. These relationships among child temperament, parenting, and culture demonstrate the interplay between nature and nurture as children learn to navigate the social world.

To see how one parent provided a good fit for her difficult child, read the Personal Perspective box entitled "Meet the Parent of a Difficult Child."

THINK ABOUT LISA . . .
How can Lisa and Chris find a day care setting that would provide a good fit for Christopher's temperament? What factors should they and other parents consider?

**goodness of fit**
The degree to which the child's temperament and environment are compatible or complementary, leading to better developmental outcomes.

**Consistency over Time.** Measures of temperament are not highly consistent over time. As with most other personality variables, numerous factors can influence temperament (or the behaviors that indicate temperament). With children in their longitudinal study, Thomas and Chess repeatedly collected measures on each of the

## Perspective PERSONAL MEET THE PARENT OF A DIFFICULT CHILD

Mary Jane
Portland, ME
Mother of Maria (15), Rocco (13), John (9), and Maggie (3)

**Describe your child's basic temperament (mood, behavior, outlook on life).**

My concern is John. John has been challenging since he was 6 or 7 years old. He is quite moody, and mostly my concern is with his anger and lack of self-esteem. It seems to me that he has never quite felt that he is talented or good at anything. Most concerning to me was John's recent comment that there was nothing on this earth for him; it was boring and he hated it here.

**Can you describe recent examples of John's behavior that concern you?**

An example is playing family card games. When John loses, he becomes enraged, hitting and kicking everyone else involved. He also has a hard time with sudden changes in schedule. If we announce we are going for ice cream, John will be angry and refuse to go, or if he went, he wouldn't have any ice cream because no one asked whether that was what he wanted to do. John loves to play computer games, but when we ask him to leave the game, he almost always ends up yelling loudly, stomping around, and being sent to his room.

**How have you helped John? Can you give specific examples?**

We did a little counseling to deal with the anger, and it was beneficial. The only way to get John to talk is to wait and go in with a positive attitude. I sit and talk to him (for over an hour sometimes) and validate that I understand that he feels badly. During this time, I make sure we have complete privacy (no other children barging in), and it usually ends nicely with him telling me how glad he is that we talked and could we please do it again. I try to plan something special just with him monthly—a hike or going out to a café for cocoa and cookies, et cetera. I really think time with a parent or grandparent once a week can be great therapy. I try to support him by showing him how much he is loved and cared for.

QUESTION **What other advice would you have for parents who have children with difficult temperaments?**

nine temperament dimensions listed in Table 6.5. When comparing measures taken one year apart, the researchers found reliable correlations for six out of the nine dimensions. But only one dimension (threshold of responsiveness) showed a reliable correlation when measures were taken four years apart (Chess & Thomas, 1995). One reason for this variability is that the ways children express temperament can change over time. As children mature, they develop insight into their own temperaments and can use this self-awareness to adapt to their environments. One child might realize, "I'm shy, but I'm not a pushover." She therefore might assert herself more in social situations. Another might recognize that "I'm excitable, but I know the warning signs" and therefore might show more self-control. In both cases, the children's behavioral output might not reflect their true internal temperament. In some ways, individuals' temperaments change as they adapt to their environments, but in other ways, people learn to control how they express their temperaments. Both processes cause the outward measures of temperament to change across time. As children develop, we see some consistency but also many changes in how their temperaments are expressed (Janson & Mathiesen, 2008).

THINKING CRITICALLY

In what ways has your temperament changed over the years? In what ways is it still the same as it was when you were very young? How have you shaped the way you express your temperament to adapt to your environment?

### Other Approaches to Temperament

Mary Rothbart (1981) developed the *Infant Behavior Questionnaire* which asks parents to report the frequency of specific behaviors shown by their infants, ages 3 to 12 months. An advantage of this method of assessing temperament is that it yields useful information quickly; it does not require extensive interviews. The questionnaire includes 96 items. One example is: "During the past week, when being undressed, how often did your baby smile or laugh?" Parents respond along a six-point scale that ranges from *never* to *always*. The original questionnaire scored six dimensions of temperament: *activity level, smiling and laughter, fear, frustration, soothability,* and *duration of orienting*. The revised version now scores 14 dimensions (Rothbart, 2001). If you compare these dimensions to the ones in Table 6.5 (page 188), you'll see that there is some overlap with the Thomas and Chess system. Among Rothbart's dimensions, *activity level* and *smiling and laughter* show the greatest stability across the first year of life. The other dimensions show only minimal consistency over time. Rothbart developed other questionnaires to measure temperament in children from 18 months to 15 years of age and in adults (Rothbart, 2001; Rothbart, Ahadi, & Hershey, 1994).

▲ This child is very shy. How might shyness be related to thresholds for arousal in the brain? How did shy children react to unfamiliar stimuli when they were infants?

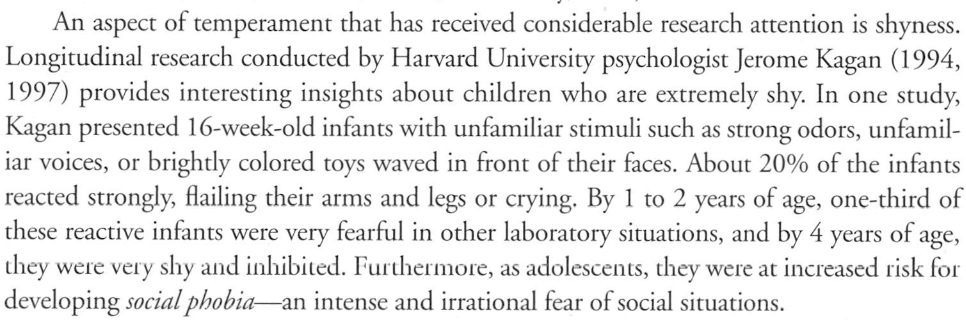

An aspect of temperament that has received considerable research attention is shyness. Longitudinal research conducted by Harvard University psychologist Jerome Kagan (1994, 1997) provides interesting insights about children who are extremely shy. In one study, Kagan presented 16-week-old infants with unfamiliar stimuli such as strong odors, unfamiliar voices, or brightly colored toys waved in front of their faces. About 20% of the infants reacted strongly, flailing their arms and legs or crying. By 1 to 2 years of age, one-third of these reactive infants were very fearful in other laboratory situations, and by 4 years of age, they were very shy and inhibited. Furthermore, as adolescents, they were at increased risk for developing *social phobia*—an intense and irrational fear of social situations.

Kagan suggested that these children had a genetic predisposition to shyness, with the genes affecting the development of particular structures in the brain. He points to the amygdala and the hypothalamus, two structures in the brain that process environmental changes and help to produce our emotional reactions to new stimulation. Children with low thresholds for arousal in these systems tend to react more strongly to unfamiliar stimuli (Kagan & Fox, 2006). It doesn't take much stimulation to arouse fear states in these children. In the face of unfamiliar situations, their heart rates accelerate more than other children's do. Even when they are asleep, these children still show higher heart rates than other children do (Kagan, Reznick, & Snidman, 1988). Shy children learn to back away from social situations and other events that are highly stimulating for them.

What about the other extreme? In Kagan's study, about 40% of infants reacted calmly to unfamiliar odors, voices, and colored toys. They remained relatively still and were not distressed. Presumably, the new stimuli were not strong enough to arouse fear reactions in these infants—the infants had higher arousal thresholds. At 1 to 2 years of age, these children were not afraid of new laboratory situations, and as 4-year-olds, they tended to be sociable and talkative and smiled frequently. Kagan did warn, however, that children with extremely high arousal thresholds might seek intense or dangerous activities. In a small percentage of cases, this inclination might lead to problem behaviors, delinquency, or even violence (Kagan, 1997). Proper socialization and positive role models can help to steer such children away from thrill seeking with risk-prone peers or in dangerous circumstances.

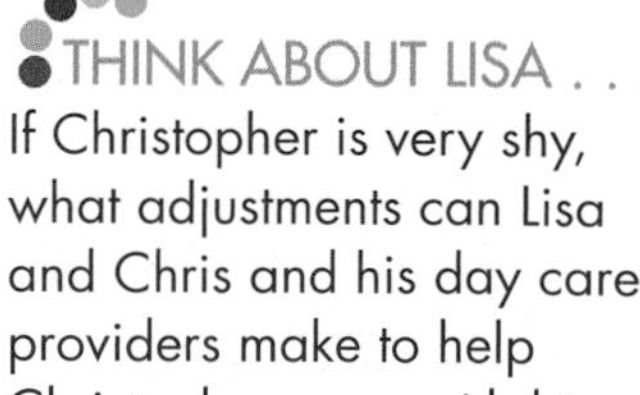

THINK ABOUT LISA . . .

If Christopher is very shy, what adjustments can Lisa and Chris and his day care providers make to help Christopher cope with his new situation?

## Infant Responses to Emotions

Immediately after birth, newborn infants are responsive to certain emotional cues displayed by people around them. Visit any hospital nursery, and you will notice that when one newborn starts crying, they all start crying. This phenomenon is referred to as

**THINKING CRITICALLY**
When was the last time you experienced emotional contagion? Did you start laughing because other people around you were laughing? Did you even know what they were laughing about? Why do you think crying is more contagious for infants but laughter is more contagious for adults?

**emotion contagion**—the tendency of the emotional cues displayed by one individual to generate similar cues or emotional states in other people. For newborns, some types of cries are more contagious than others. Newborns are more likely to cry when they hear other newborns cry than when they hear recordings of their own crying, of older infants' cries, or of artificially produced crying sounds (Martin & Clark, 1982; Sagi & Hoffman, 1976; Simner, 1971).

Newborns also can produce facial expressions that mimic the expressions of adults who are displaying emotions. In the photos in Figure 6.2, the young infant imitates the adult's happy, sad, and surprised expressions remarkably well (Field, Woodson, Greenberg, & Cohen, 1982). Newborns can also imitate adults when the adults open their mouths, move their heads, and stick out their tongues (Meltzoff & Moore, 1983, 1989). In one study, researchers asked mothers to make facial expressions and speak in ways that showed joy, sadness, and anger (Haviland & Lelwica, 1987). The mothers' 10-week-old infants responded differently to each of these emotions. The infants showed more joy and interest when their mothers were joyful. They made "mouthing" movements when their mothers were sad. They showed less interest and less movement when their mothers showed anger. Other researchers have found that 2-month-olds respond differently to happy faces than to faces that show no emotion at all (Nelson & Horowitz, 1983) and that 5-month-olds can tell the differences among anger, sadness, and fear (Schwartz, Izard, & Ansul, 1985). Although young infants can detect these emotion differences in photographs of adult faces, it helps if they also have emotional sounds that correspond to the facial expressions, as when a happy face is also saying, "You're such a beautiful baby!" (Flom & Bahrick, 2007).

**emotion contagion**
The tendency of the emotional cues displayed by one person to generate similar cues or emotional states in other people.

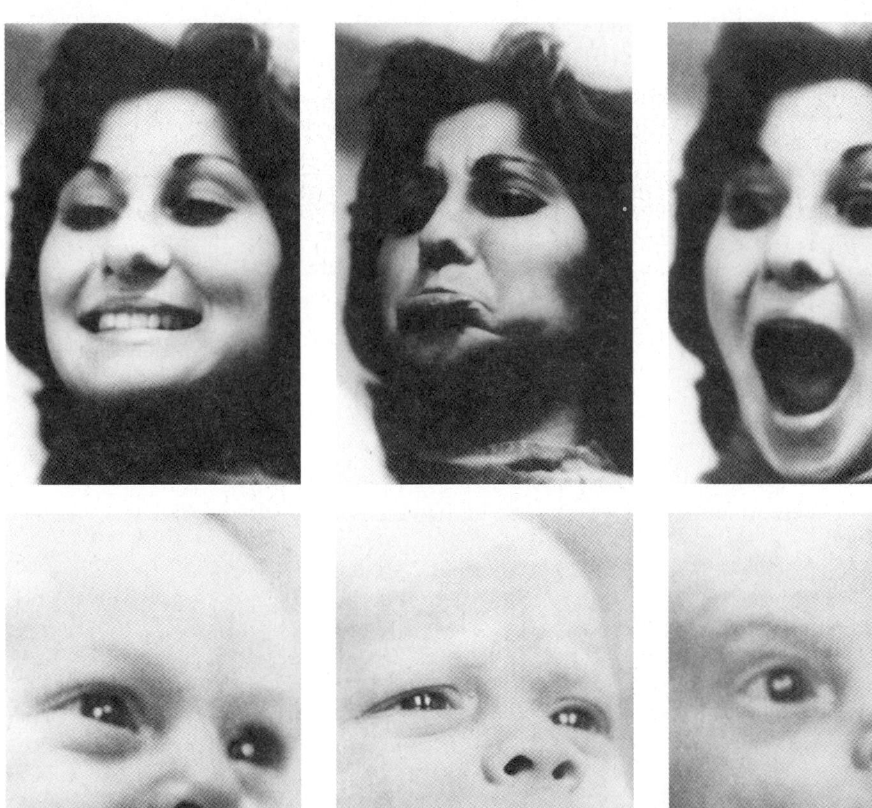

FIGURE 6.2 ▶
**Adult and Baby Facial Expressions**
This newborn baby is imitating the facial expressions made by the adult model. Although they cannot see their own faces, newborns are capable of matching facial movements made by others.

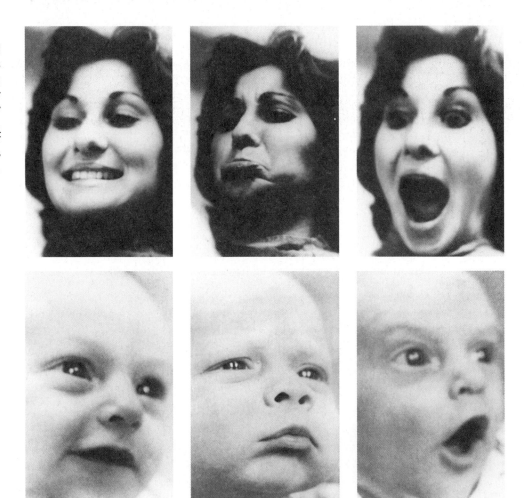

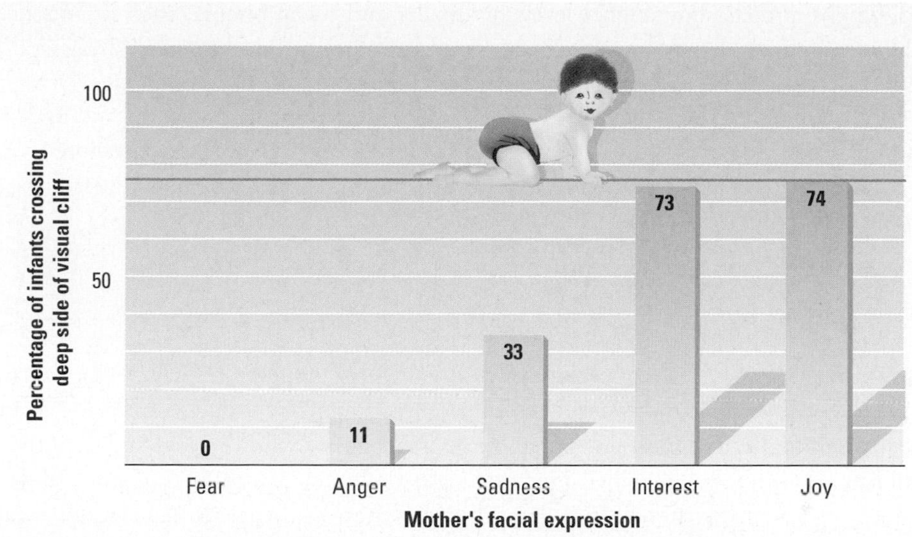


◀ FIGURE 6.3
**Infants' Readings of Facial Expressions**
When 12-month-old infants were deciding whether to cross the deep side of the visual cliff, they relied on their mothers' facial expressions. Infants did not cross when their mothers looked afraid, and infants were reluctant when mothers looked angry or sad. Most of the infants did cross when mothers looked interested or joyful. (Based on Sorce et al., 1985.)

Even if infants can tell different emotional expressions apart, do they understand what the different expressions mean? Evidence suggests that they do: Infants as young as 4 months of age can understand the basic emotions behind facial expressions, including joy, anger, surprise, and sadness (Montague & Walker-Andrews, 2001). When infants view facial expressions, their brains show patterns of activity that are very similar to the patterns shown in adult brains (Hoehl & Striano, 2008; Leppänen, Moulson, Vogel-Farley, & Nelson, 2007). By 12 months of age, the evidence is even clearer. Consider a clever study that used the visual cliff that we described in Chapter 4 (on page 124). The researchers placed 12-month-old infants on the shallow side of the cliff and put an attractive toy at the other end of the deep side (Sorce, Emde, Campos, & Klinnert, 1985). As infants approached the deep side, they looked up at their mothers, who had been instructed to show a joyful, interested, sad, angry, or fearful face. As Figure 6.3 shows, none of the infants crossed the deep side when the mothers showed fear. A few crossed when their mothers looked angry or sad, but many more crossed when the mothers appeared interested or joyful. These infants were doing more than just discriminating among various facial expressions: They were using the expressions to get information to guide their behavior. Trusting their mothers, they crossed the deep side when their mothers showed positive emotions, but they were reluctant or refused to cross when the mothers showed negative emotions. Still, keep in mind how difficult it is to know exactly what infants are understanding about emotional expressions. Are they really responding to the meaning in the expression (e.g., the joy or fear intended by the mother), or are they responding more to other aspects of the communication, such as the loudness of the mothers' voices (Saarni, Campos, Camras, & Witherington, 2006)?

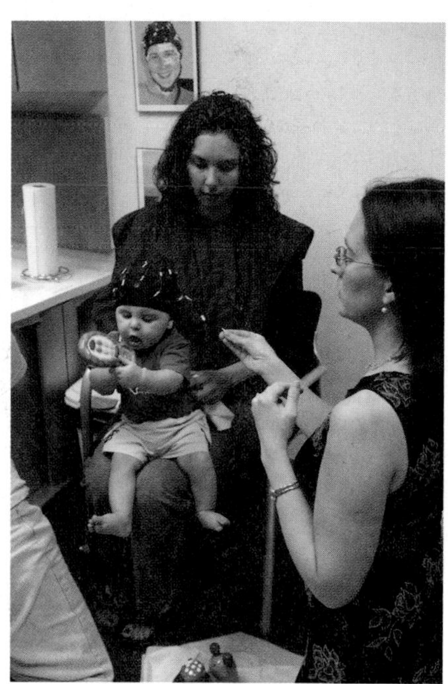

▲ Neuroscience researchers measure patterns of brain activity in infants to determine when the brain circuits are available for processing particular types of information. When it comes to processing emotional expressions in people's faces, the brains of infants respond in ways that are similar to the brains of adults.

Emotions communicate important information about the environment, and infants learn at an early age to use their parents' emotions as a guide in uncertain situations. Researchers refer to this as **social referencing**—the tendency of infants and children to look for emotional cues from parents and other caregivers to get information in uncertain situations (Thompson, 2006). When strangers approach, for example, infants often look to their parents for a cue. If the parent speaks to the stranger in a friendly manner, the infant reacts more positively to the stranger (Boccia & Campos, 1989; Feinman & Lewis, 1983). If the parent looks worried, the infant reacts more negatively. In more extreme

**social referencing**
The tendency of infants and children to look for emotional cues from parents and other caregivers to get information in uncertain situations.

cases, when mothers show higher levels of anxiety and social phobia, their infants use social referencing to learn to avoid strangers and be more fearful of them (Murray et al., 2008). **Watch** on **mydevelopmentlab**

**Watch** a video on Social Referencing.
www.mydevelopmentlab.com

By the time they reach their first birthdays, infants are capable of reading and understanding something about the emotions expressed by other people. Even before they understand a spoken language, infants are already receiving messages through the language of emotion.

▲ "Oops. I made a mess!" Shame is a self-conscious emotion. Children begin to reflect on who they are and who they should be.

## Toddler Self-Conscious Emotions

By 15 months of age, **self-conscious emotions** begin to emerge (Lewis, 1993; Saarni et al., 2006). These are emotions related to people's thoughts about themselves—about how their thoughts and behaviors relate to their images of who they are and who they should be. A toddler who spilled his juice looks down and away, feeling *guilty* about the mess he made. If his siblings or other children are watching, he might feel *embarrassed* by his mistake. If he makes frequent mistakes, he might feel *shame*, believing that he is a "bad boy." If he pours his juice successfully, however, he might feel *pride* in his new accomplishment. By 15 months, he is comparing his own behavior to how he thinks he should behave, and his emotional reaction reflects this self-conscious comparison. At this time, infants also begin to show *sympathy* (concern for other people who are distressed or in trouble), and they begin to show *empathy* by sharing the same happy, sad, and other emotions that other people feel around them (Vaish, Carpenter, & Tomasello, 2009). For self-conscious emotions to emerge, the toddler must first have a sense of his own identity (who he is) and a sense of what others expect of him. As you will see in a later chapter, the self-conscious emotions become more complex as children's sense of self and others continues to develop during the preschool and following years.

**self-conscious emotions**
Emotions that relate to people's self-images or what people think about themselves; include shame, embarrassment, guilt, and pride.

### LET'S REVIEW . . .

1. The most widely accepted system for classifying infant temperaments is the one developed by:
   - **a.** Mary Rothbart.
   - **b.** Jerome Kagan.
   - **c.** John Bowlby.
   - **d.** Alexander Thomas and Stella Chess.
2. Jerome Kagan believes that extreme shyness in children can be traced to:
   - **a.** fear and anxiety shown by parents in social situations.
   - **b.** the punishments children receive from peers and parents.
   - **c.** low thresholds for arousal in the limbic system and hypothalamus.
   - **d.** a dysfunction in the pituitary gland that causes a lack of energy and enthusiasm.
3. Self-conscious emotions (such as guilt and pride) emerge when toddlers:
   - **a.** have a sense of their own identity.
   - **b.** have a sense of what other people expect of them.
   - **c.** have a sense of their own identity AND what other people expect of them.
   - **d.** Research shows that self-conscious emotions do not develop until later childhood.
4. True or False: Compared to children with difficult temperaments, children who are slow to warm up have less intense emotional reactions and more regular eating and sleeping schedules.
5. True or False: Infants cannot imitate the facial expressions that they see in other people until they are approximately 6 months of age.

Answers: 1. d, 2. c, 3. c, 4. T, 5. F

# Social Relations and Play

If you are like most students, your earliest memory of a friend probably dates back to when you were about 5 or 6 years old. The first foundations of friendship began much earlier, however—when you were a small baby. To finish this chapter, we explore the social interactions and forms of play for infants and toddlers.

AS YOU STUDY THIS SECTION, ASK YOURSELF THESE QUESTIONS:

**6.8** What are the first interactions that infants typically have with each other, and how do infants play?

**6.9** What are friendships based on during the toddler period?

**6.10** What should parents and other caregivers do to help toddlers with their interpersonal conflicts, and what are the main themes in the play of toddlers?

## Infant Social Interactions and Sensorimotor Play

By the age of only 2 months, infants show a special interest in other people their own size. When placed near each other, young infants show **mutual gaze**—they look intently at each other as if they are taking in all the information they can about this intriguing new peer (Eckerman, 1979; Fogel, 1979). They often express their excitement by flailing their arms and legs. By 6 months, infants interact with each other by babbling, smiling, and touching (Vandell, Wilson, & Buchanan, 1980). These are often the infants' first social interactions that involve mutual activity with people other than their family members.

Not surprisingly, infants vary greatly in social responsiveness. Some infants initiate interactions with peers frequently; others do so only rarely. Differences in temperament, in parent–infant relationships, and in opportunities to practice social skills all contribute to this variability. When infants have more exposure to other infants their age, they show more frequency and skill in their social interactions than infants with less exposure to peers (Vandell & Wilson, 1982). By the end of the first year, infants play by imitating each other's actions and by sharing and playing together with toys (Mueller & Silverman, 1989; Rubin, Bukowski, & Parker, 2006).

▲ Mutual gaze is one of the early social interactions in infancy. What do you think these infants think of each other?

During the first year of life, play evolves mostly around the practice of sensory activity and the development of new motor actions. Researchers refer to this period of play as **sensorimotor play**, based on the sensorimotor stage in Piaget's theory (refer back to Chapter 5). For the first few months, infants spend most of their awake time lying on their backs and looking around at the world. They seem to be soaking up their new environments by staring at objects and colors and listening intently to the various sounds around them. The first noticeable signs of play involve activities infants discover with their own bodies. After accidentally bringing his fist to his mouth, for example, an infant might work to repeat this action. When he succeeds, the repetitive motion becomes a game that he repeats for several minutes, smiling and squirming with glee at his new discovery. Spitting bubbles and kicking their feet are similar games that infants discover and playfully repeat.

By 3 months of age, infants can reach out and grasp small objects. Now the world of play expands from actions involving infants' own bodies to interactions with objects in the world. Rattles, balls, pieces of cloth, and other small objects can now be grasped, mouthed, banged, and dropped. Infants repeat these playful actions as they develop new motor actions and explore new objects in their environments.

**mutual gaze**
Intent eye contact between two people, as when young infants stare at each other.

**sensorimotor play**
Play that evolves mostly around the practice of sensory activity and the development of new motor actions.

An interesting development occurs between the ages of 6 and 9 months. At 6 months infants usually treat all objects that are about the same size in the same way. Give a 6-month-old a spoon, for example, and the baby will bang the spoon on the table. If you then give the baby a ball, she will bang it, too, and will do the same with a rattle or a small doll (Hughes, 1999). At 6 months, babies incorporate every object into the action pattern they prefer at the moment (e.g., banging). At 9 months, however, infants pay more attention to the specific features of objects and begin treating objects differently (Hughes, 1999; Ruff, 1984). They bring the spoon to their mouth, throw the ball, shake the rattle, and hug the doll. Rather than forcing all objects into a fixed action pattern, 9-month-olds can adjust their play to fit the unique features of each object.

Infants enjoy having a variety of playthings with different shapes, sounds, textures, and actions. They especially delight in toys that respond to their own actions. When babies realize that pushing a particular button produces an exciting sound or a flash of light, a smile of recognition spreads across their faces. They recognize that they are having an influence on their environment and that the environment is now responding to them. It is exciting for parents to watch their infants form these early connections, and the infants derive self-confidence and a general sense of self from the realization that they can influence the environment (Hughes, 1999).

Describe the kinds of sensorimotor play that you have observed in infants. Where do these kinds of play fit within the developmental trends that we presented?

To read more about how toy manufacturers use their knowledge of infant and child development to design interesting and educational toys, see the Professional Perspective box entitled "Career Focus: Meet a Toy Company Executive."

## Toddler Friends

After 1 year of age, emerging language and motor skills allow toddlers to interact in increasingly complex ways. They can seek each other out, follow each other around, and add verbal dialogue to their play. At the age of 2 years, **coordinated imitation** becomes much more frequent. Toddler playmates take turns imitating each other and—a new feature—become aware that they are being imitated (Eckerman, 1993; Rubin, Bukowski, & Parker, 1998). Consider Josh and Jalen, two toddlers playing in a sandbox. Josh pours sand on his legs, and Jalen does the same. Josh throws sand at a toy, and Jalen copies again. Then Jalen throws sand straight up in the air, and Josh does too, both giggling and chuckling all the while. The fun in this toddler game is that each child knows that he is being imitated. Each act becomes an invitation for the other child to copy. This level of coordination rarely appears in children younger than 2 years of age (Eckerman, 1993).

Toddler interactions often evolve around games that children either repeat from prior experiences or create on the spot. Characteristically, these early games include taking turns, playing roles, and engaging in numerous repetitions of the game sequences (Ross, 1982). Common games are stacking and toppling blocks; throwing and catching; putting toys in a pail and pouring; requesting, receiving, and returning items; running and chasing; and climbing and jumping. These early interactions help children to acquire important social skills such as learning to play as equals, maintaining fun and interest for both players, and adapting to the characteristics of different playmates.

Toddlers choose playmates based largely on convenience—on who is available for play and who has interesting toys or materials to play with. By 2 years of age, however, pairs of children begin to select each other as mutually preferred playmates (Vandell & Mueller, 1980). That is, although other familiar peers are available for play, these friends pair off and voluntarily choose to play more with each other than with other children. For most children, this is the first time that a relationship contains all of the qualities of a true friendship: It is voluntary, mutual, and close, and it persists over time.

**coordinated imitation**
Interaction in which toddler playmates take turns imitating each other and are aware that they are being imitated.

## Perspective PROFESSIONAL — CAREER FOCUS: MEET A TOY COMPANY EXECUTIVE

Susan Tice, B.A.
Parsippany, NJ
Public Relations Director and Product Manager for International Playthings, Inc. (http://www.intplay.com).

**What does International Playthings, Inc. (IPI) do, and what is your role at the company?**

IPI is one of the largest suppliers of specialty toys in North America. We make a wide variety of games, infant toys, preschool toys, dolls, educational toys, activity toys, and other playthings. I am the director of public relations and a product manager. I determine what products to submit to various toy testing programs to obtain product recognition and consumer awareness. I also make new product suggestions. I work closely with manufacturers and their factories to bring new product ideas to life.

**How do toy manufacturers decide what kinds of toys to produce?**

Multiple factors are involved, and it depends on the age of the child. We consider the child's developmental skills, the educational benefits, age appropriateness, and how unique or different our toy can be from similar products that are already in the marketplace.

**What do you think infants and toddlers look for in toys?**

Infants respond to toys that can stimulate one or more of their senses. Contrasting colors provide visual stimulation as well as a focal point for developing eyesight. Different materials provide tactile stimulation. Jingles, rattles, crinkle, and music provide auditory stimulation and so on. The product should not overstimulate the senses but should be able to provide multiple experiences. For example, an infant will focus on the toy and then touch it and then mouth it as she learns all she can about it using her senses.

I think toddlers look for toys that "do" more—products with a cause-and-effect reaction that lets them be in control. For instance, if a toy plays music, toddlers want to be the ones who do whatever is necessary to get the music to play. They are more mobile, so they enjoy toys that can go with them, such as a walker, ride-on toy, push toy, and so forth. A great toy at this age is a basic toy that allows the child's play pattern to imitate life that he sees every day, opening his imagination. This can be done with something as basic as a plush animal or a basic plastic car. Here again, the product needs to appeal to the child's initial senses.

**How do you use child development research when designing new toys?**

When we begin the design phase, we want to make sure the toy is appropriate for a child of a certain age. As a result, we need to keep in mind how children develop—what basic skills they possess, what skills they are in the process of developing, and how our toy can encourage these developing skills. It's also extremely important to be aware of a child's environment and exposure to society at that age so that our products can be themed appropriately.

**What education or training does it take to work in your area?**

You need a minimum of a four-year college degree. It's excellent if you have taken marketing classes and have an understanding of childhood development (perhaps taking some child psychology classes could help here). If you are looking to go more into the PR aspect, writing classes are a tremendous asset. As for design of the toy, you will work closely with an art department and/or designers who can turn your ideas into graphics that can be easily understood by factories. For this, studying graphic design is definitely the way to go. Finally, being familiar with how retail works is very important, so your summer job at a retail store can actually become something extremely useful for your career.

QUESTION **As you read through this interview, did you recognize how this toy executive used child development information in her role at the company? If you had a job like hers, what else would you like to know about child development?**

Playmate-by-convenience is still more the norm during the toddler period, however, as most play situations are arranged by parents according to which toddlers happen to be available in social situations such as family gatherings, neighbors, and day care. Toddlers are beginning to identify preferred friends, but they are not yet in a position to actively seek out friends.

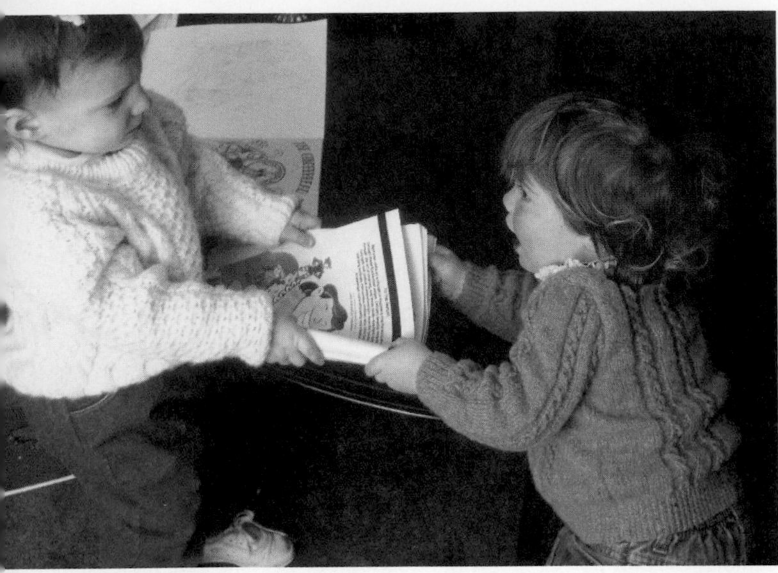

▲ Conflict is common among toddlers. What is the best way to help children of this age handle conflict?

In a longitudinal study, Howes (1988) followed toddlers for up to 3 years as they maintained friends, lost friends, and made new friends. Her observations suggest that children who are more successful at maintaining friendships tend to enter into peer play more easily and to be more cooperative in social pretend play. For example, they are more likely to join in when asked, "You be the baby and I'll be the mommy, okay?" Children who were less successful in maintaining friendships showed less social skill and were more likely to be rebuffed by peers.

## Toddler Conflicts and Symbolic Play

Anyone who has spent much time with toddlers knows that conflict is all too common. In one study, researchers paired up 2-year-old children who had never met before and allowed them to play together in several sessions that lasted 15 minutes each (Hay & Ross, 1982). After carefully analyzing videotapes of the play sessions, the researchers found that playmates averaged just over two instances of conflict for every 15-minute session. Most of the conflicts (84%) were struggles over toys. A few pairs of playmates had no conflicts, but one pair displayed 14 instances of protest, resistance, or retaliation in their 15 minutes of play. Other research suggests that children who are more socially outgoing tend to initiate more conflicts, and children who lose in a conflict are more likely to start another one (Brown & Brownell, 1990; Hay & Ross, 1982; Rubin et al., 2006).

Parents, child care workers, and others who work frequently with young children often need to help toddlers resolve their disputes. Lecturing and moralizing are usually ineffective because toddlers have difficulty understanding abstract reasoning. The question "How do you think she feels?" is largely nonsensical for the average 2-year-old who is motivated more by the concrete benefit of getting his or her hands on a colored marker or a piece of candy. (In Chapter 8, we will describe the egocentric forms of thought that are typical for young children.) Distracting the toddlers with another attractive activity is a more practical way to resolve the dispute. Parents and caregivers can then gradually introduce moral reasoning and conflict resolution skills according to the cognitive and emotional maturity of the individual child. Over time, parents can gradually use toddler conflicts as opportunities to help children learn to negotiate, resolve disputes, and be sensitive to other people. Of course, many conflicts also occur between parents and their toddlers, and the ways that these conflicts are handled are often related to the temperament of the child and to the quality of the attachment relationship between the parent and child (Laible, Panfile, & Makariev, 2008).

As you saw in Chapter 5, a major change during the toddler period is the emergence of symbolic thinking—the ability to form mental representations of objects or events in the world. Symbolic thinking allows **symbolic play**, where children use make-believe and pretend to embellish the objects and actions in their play. Early symbols begin to emerge between 12 and 14 months as toddlers pretend to act out common activities. They might lie on the floor with a small blanket and pretend to go to sleep or use toy dishes to pretend to eat. By 2 to 3 years of age, toddlers pretend that an object is something else: A wooden block is a car, a spoon is an airplane, or the family cat is their baby. Still later, children integrate multiple objects and actions into dramatic play activities. Their bed becomes a castle, their pillow is a magic shield, and they engage in mythical duels with the Evil Knight of Doom (really a chair or their

**symbolic play**
Play in which children use make-believe and pretend to embellish objects and actions.

sister). Their play takes on all of the imagination allowed by their ever-expanding cognitive abilities. It can be terrific fun to watch infants and toddlers as they discover new ways to enjoy play—it's one of the most rewarding ways to observe positive forms of child development.

## LET'S REVIEW . . .

1. Which appears earliest in development?
   **a.** Mutual gaze.
   **b.** Symbolic play.
   **c.** Reaching for toys.
   **d.** Coordinated imitation.
2. An interesting change occurs by 9 months of age in how infants play with toys. What is it?
   **a.** Infants begin to babble at their toys.
   **b.** Infants begin to treat all toys alike.
   **c.** Infants begin to treat different toys differently.
   **d.** Infants temporarily lose interest in toys and prefer to play with other people.
3. At 18 months of age, Lauren is pretending to cook on a toy stove. This type of pretend represents the beginning of:
   **a.** social play.
   **b.** mutual play.
   **c.** symbolic play.
   **d.** coordinated imitation.
4. True or False: During the first three months of sensorimotor play, infants prefer activities that involve their own bodies such as kicking, waving their arms, or spitting bubbles.
5. True or False: Convenient availability is an important factor in determining which toddlers will play together and be friends.

Answers: 1. a, 2. c, 3. c, 4. T, 5. T

## THINKING BACK TO LISA . . .

Now that you've studied this chapter, you should be able to help Lisa understand Christopher's behavior on his first morning at day care. You should begin by explaining how Christopher's reactions reveal his attachment to his mother and father. By clinging to his parents in his new environment and by showing both stranger and separation anxiety, Christopher is demonstrating that he is securely attached to his parents. This is a positive attribute and will have benefits for Christopher as he continues to grow. Lisa and Chris can help by letting Christopher see them interact in a friendly manner with Rachel, signaling to him that she is safe.

You should also discuss with Lisa the research on day care and attachment. Many parents worry that day care will disrupt their child's attachment to them. Some research suggests that full-time day care can reduce attachment, but only if it is combined with parenting that is not sensitive or responsive. The majority of infants in day care still show secure attachments to their mothers, and Christopher's attachment to his parents is even more likely to be secure if they are is sensitive and responsive when caring for Christopher.

Lisa should also consider Christopher's temperament. On the basis of the few details that were provided in the opening story, it does not appear that Christopher has a difficult temperament. He might be slow to warm up; recall that he did eventually begin to crawl around and explore when he first visited the day care home. If Christopher is very shy, the day care provider should introduce new things gradually, doing what she can to reduce his level of arousal. Lisa should also work to find a day care setting that provides a good fit for Christopher's temperament. At day care, Christopher will have opportunities to make friends and learn to play in new ways. What other topics from this chapter did you find that fit Lisa's story?

## CHAPTER REVIEW . . .

**6.1 What are the historical roots that gave rise to modern research on attachment, and how do these roots affect our thinking about attachment today?**
John Bowlby theorized that attachment behaviors evolved to increase survivability in infants. Harry Harlow's research with rhesus monkeys demonstrated that contact comfort was the critical ingredient in attachment formation. Mary Ainsworth and other researchers have used the Strange Situation with human infants to reveal secure attachments and also insecure–avoidant, insecure–resistant, and insecure–disorganized/disoriented attachments. All of this research demonstrates the importance of the infant's sense of security in forming healthy attachments with parents and other important caregivers.

**6.2 What are the main factors related to healthy and unhealthy attachment relationships between infants and their parents or caregivers?**
Ainsworth believed that the key to an infant's attachment style was the quality of parenting and the infant's interaction with his or her caregiver in the first year of life. Infant characteristics are also important. The prevalence of the different types of insecure attachments varies considerably across nations. Researchers believe that these cross-cultural variations are due to differences in the treatment and expectations of infants.

**6.3 How do the emotional bonds that are established early in life influence development throughout childhood?**
Infants who are securely attached tend to become preschoolers who are more well-liked, happy, competent, compliant, and empathetic. Later in childhood, they tend to have higher self-esteem and self-confidence, and they are more sociable and more emotionally healthy. Adolescents who were insecurely attached during infancy tend to have more psychological problems. Early attachment relationships can become internalized models that people use to guide their social relationships throughout life. Continuities in parenting might also contribute to the correlations between early attachment and later development.

**6.4 What are the main types of temperaments that have been studied by researchers, and how do these different temperaments develop?**
The most popular method of classifying temperaments is the system developed by Thomas and Chess, who identified three main temperaments: easy, difficult, and slow to warm up. Thomas and Chess believed that different temperaments result from interactions between genetics, parenting, and culture. They also emphasized the importance of an environment that is a good fit for the temperament of the individual child.

**6.5 What are some of the alternative ways of studying temperament, and what have researchers learned about infants and toddlers who are extremely shy?**
Mary Rothbart's revised Infant Behavior Questionnaire assesses infant temperament along 14 behavioral dimensions rated by parents. The original version scored 6 dimensions. Jerome Kagan observed infants who reacted strongly to unfamiliar stimuli. Later, these infants became children who were afraid in other laboratory situations and were very shy and inhibited. Kagan emphasized genetic and biological components involving brain structures that process changes and new stimulation.

**6.6 What are some of the first emotional reactions of newborn infants, and what else do researchers know about infant emotions?**
Newborn infants show motion contagion and imitation of facial expressions. By 2 months of age, infants can discriminate among various facial expressions and respond differently to them. One-year-olds can use their mothers' facial expressions to gain information about how to respond in ambiguous situations.

**6.7 When are children first able to feel emotions such as guilt, embarrassment, shame, and pride?**
Self-conscious emotions include guilt, embarrassment, shame, and pride. They begin to appear by 15 months of age as toddlers start to understand who they are and what other people expect of them. Sympathy and empathy also emerge at about this time.

**6.8 What are the first interactions that infants typically have with each other, and how do infants play?**
By 2 months of age, infants show mutual gaze—looking intently at other babies their size. By 6 months, they enjoy interacting with other babies by babbling, smiling, and touching. Infants engage in sensorimotor play—using their sensory systems and motor actions to interact with toys and other objects.

**6.9 What are friendships based on during the toddler period?**
By age 2 years, toddlers show coordinated imitation when they imitate each others' actions. They enjoy activities and games that involve taking turns. They make friends mostly by convenience, playing mainly with whoever is readily available. By age 2, they also begin pairing up in mutual friendships.

**6.10 What should parents and other caregivers do to help toddlers with their interpersonal conflicts, and what are the main themes in the play of toddlers?**
Conflicts are common among toddlers, and these are often best handled by distracting the children off into different activities. Toddlers enjoy the beginnings of symbolic play—using make-believe and pretending to embellish objects and activities.

## REVISITING THEMES

The roles of *nature and nurture* are evident in the development of infant-parent attachment and in the development of temperament. John Bowlby highlighted the role of evolution (nature) in the development of attachment behaviors in humans (pp. 174–175), and Mary Ainsworth emphasized the importance of the quality of parenting (nurture) during the first year of life (pp. 176–179). Temperament is believed to have a heavy genetic component, but it is also modifiable depending on parenting and other circumstances in the environment (pp. 188–189).

*Neuroscience* was involved in Kagan's explanation of children who are extremely shy (p. 191), and neuroscience research is also used to investigate how infants and young children process emotional expressions and other social sources of information (p. 193).

*Diversity and multiculturalism* are reflected in the research studies that investigate how attachment categories may differ across countries and among different racial and ethnic groups within the United States (pp. 181–182).

*Positive development* can be seen in the role that sensitive responsiveness plays in forming secure attachments and in the positive influence that secure attachments in infancy can have on development later in life (pp. 183–186). Watching infants and toddlers enjoy their play is an especially rewarding way to observe positive forms of development.

## KEY TERMS

attachment (174)
contact comfort (174)
coordinated imitation (196)
difficult temperament (187)
easy temperament (187)
emotion contagion (192)
goodness of fit (189)
insecure–avoidant attachment (178)
insecure–disorganized (or disoriented) attachment (179)
insecure–resistant attachment (179)
mutual gaze (195)
secure attachment (178)
self-conscious emotions (194)
sensitive responsiveness (180)
sensorimotor play (195)
separation anxiety (178)
slow-to-warm-up temperament (187)
social referencing (193)
Strange Situation (176)
stranger anxiety (177)
symbolic play (198)
temperament (187)

**"What decisions would you make while raising a child? What would the consequences of those decisions be?"**

Find out by accessing My Virtual Child at
**www.mydevelopmentlab.com**
and raising your own virtual child
from birth to age 18.

# PART TWO SUMMARY Infants and Toddlers: The First Years

## Some Developmental Landmarks

### 0–6 months
- Strong sucking reflex
- Imitates facial expressions
- Holds head upright
- Recognizes familiar faces and voices
- Will not look for object after it is hidden
- Coos and babbles
- Rolls over

### 6–12 months
- Sits upright without help
- Begins eating solid foods
- Imitates speech sounds
- Creates own nonsense words
- Crawls
- Afraid of strangers and separation from parents

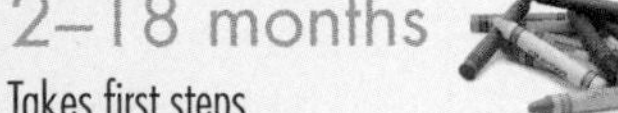

### 12–18 months
- Takes first steps
- Speaks first words
- Can find object, if watches where it was hidden
- Attachment with caregivers has formed
- Can pretend play
- Scribbles on paper

### 18–24 months
- Uses two- and three-word sentences
- Frequent conflicts with other toddlers
- Begins toilet training

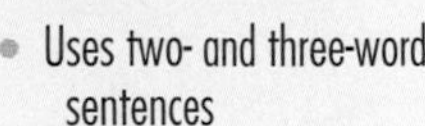

### 24–36 months
- Already reached half of adult height
- Finds object, even if didn't watch where it was hidden
- Imitates other playmates
- Plays turn-taking games
- Makes friends

## Physical Development

With proper prenatal care, babies have the best chance at being born full-term and healthy. Infants are at risk for a variety of developmental problems when they are born preterm, low in birth weight, or small for their gestational age. Experts recommend that infants receive breast milk for at least the first 12 months although that isn't always possible. They grow at an incredible rate, and children have already reached half of their adult height by the time they are 2 years old. Their brains are also developing rapidly as they form connections within the intricate network of neurons, as brain fibers become myelinated, and as they form the complex web of synapses that proliferate in the brain. Right from birth, infants have an impressive ability to see and hear and to distinguish basic odors and flavors. Over the first year, infant reflexes have been replaced by voluntary muscle movements as infants have learned to sit up, crawl, and take their first steps. These forms of physical development pave the way for the cognitive and socioemotional advances we see during these first years.

## Cognitive Development

Even young infants have surprisingly well-developed abilities to remember and integrate sensory information. They can recognize sounds they've heard—even if they heard them before birth! Even as newborns, infants prefer to look at the human face over many other kinds of objects. By 6 months of age they can match information across different senses. Infants build on these experiences and gradually become able to mentally represent things and people in their environment—a significant achievement because it allows toddlers to think about things in the past and future. Their actions on the world become more intentional as well, and by the age of 2 toddlers are doing things on purpose to achieve specific goals. The average infant begins using sounds to communicate during the first year, and speaks the first real words around 1 year. From then on, toddlers' language proceeds at a phenomenal pace. It seems that humans are biologically predisposed to learn language, but the social interactions infants and toddlers have with those around them also help them as they learn words, grammar, and the social rules for using language.

## Socioemotional Development

Over the first year, infants form a special emotional attachment to their parents and primary caregivers. They feel secure and comfortable when they are with their caregivers, and they show fear when they are separated from them or when strangers approach. Infant temperaments vary, and parents will find that some babies are easy to interact with while others are fussy and difficult or slow to warm up to new situations. Infants respond to other people's emotions at an early age. They gaze intently at other infants even before they have the physical coordination to crawl over and play. As children exit the toddler years, they are already playing creatively, forming new friendships, displaying their unique temperaments, and showing continued effects of the attachments they have formed with their parents and other important caregivers. With their physical, cognitive, and socioemotional developments, these toddlers are ready to explore the wider world. They are ready to enter the phase of ***Early Childhood: The Playful Years.***

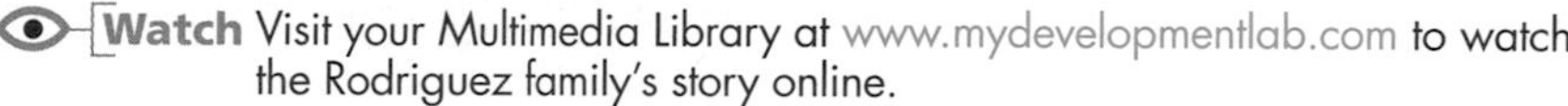
Watch Visit your Multimedia Library at www.mydevelopmentlab.com to watch the Rodriguez family's story online.

7 EARLY CHILDHOOD

# Physical Development in Early Childhood

A few years ago, Kathy and Rod Rodriguez adopted six children: Jesse, Jordan, Joey, Toby, Robbie, and Suzanna. When they were younger, state officials removed the children from their mother who was a chronic alcoholic and abandoned the children for months at a time. They were then placed in a foster home that was perhaps even worse: the children were beaten, tortured, neglected, and severely abused. After five years in this foster home, someone finally called an abuse hotline, and police responded. The children were rescued from a horrifying situation and were then placed with Kathy and Rod Rodriguez. They now have a secure and loving home, but how long will it take for the Rodriguez children to learn to trust other people? Will they ever recover and be able to enjoy normal childhoods?

What should neighbors, teachers, child care workers, and other people do if they suspect that children are being abused or neglected? What should you do if you suspect that children are not being properly cared for or if they are in danger? Are you obligated to report your suspicions to authorities? What effects can abuse and neglect have on children's physical and psychological development? What advice would you give to Kathy and Rod about what they can expect?

After studying this chapter, you should have a better understanding of the typical course of physical development in early childhood, and you should also have a better understanding of abuse and neglect and the terrible toll that it can take. You should be able to relate at least a dozen concepts and research findings to the situation like the one that Kathy and Rod now face with their adopted children.

As you read this chapter, look for the "Think About the Rodriquez children . . ." questions that ask you to consider what you're learning from their perspective.

## Growth of the Body and Brain

- Physical Growth and Nutrition
- Growth and Development of the Brain
- The Role of Experience in Brain Development
- Larger Developmental Patterns in the Brain

## Motor Development and Physical Activity

- Gross-Motor and Fine-Motor Development
- Physical Activity and Exercise
- Cerebral Palsy

## Health and Safety Issues

- Childhood Deaths and Safety Issues
- Child Maltreatment: Abuse and Neglect
- Effects of Abuse and Neglect

Information in this chapter is important for anyone who is in charge of the physical care and well-being of children and for all of us who care about how children grow and develop. As you will see in the next chapters, early childhood is a wonderful period of play, imagination, and intellectual discovery. But to enjoy the magic of these early years, children first need to have their basic needs met. They need proper nutrition and exercise, basic health care, and the love and attention of parents and other caregivers who will keep the children safe and secure. All of these issues are discussed in this chapter along with information about more unfortunate situations like the ones faced by the Rodriguez children and millions of other children who endure less severe forms of abuse and neglect.

# Growth of the Body and Brain

Young children grow at a rapid rate. As parents, we always marveled at how fast our children outgrew their pants and shoes, and even when we were gone on business trips for just a few days we could notice how much they grew while we were away. In this section we describe the rapid changes that occur in height and weight during early childhood, and we discuss the importance of proper nutrition to support this growth. We also cover the growth and development of the child's brain—a type of growth that is less obvious from the outside but clearly important in understanding the many ways that children change, learn, and mature.

AS YOU STUDY THIS SECTION, ASK YOURSELF THESE QUESTIONS:

**7.1** How much do children grow during early childhood, and what are the important issues related to childhood nutrition?

**7.2** In what important ways does the brain grow and change during early childhood?

**7.3** How is brain development influenced by experience and interactions with the environment?

**7.4** What are the larger patterns of development that we see in the brain during this age period?

## Physical Growth and Nutrition

During early childhood, children grow 2 or 3 inches and gain about 5½ pounds per year, on average (National Center for Health Statistics, 2004). Figure 7.1 plots these averages along with the variation in growth we expect for the middle 80% of children. Keep in mind that 10% of children will be smaller than the 10th percentile, while another 10% will be larger than the 90th percentile. The remaining 80% of children will fall somewhere between these two boundaries. By the time children are 6 years old, they have already gained about 70% of their adult height but only about one-third of their adult weight.

▲ You can see how much taller this 6-year-old is than the 3-year-old. Young children grow so quickly!

Children's body proportions also change. The head size becomes smaller relative to the rest of the body, and the chest and legs grow longer. The tummy is now flatter and the body becomes more trim. By the time children enter first grade their body proportions look like those seen in older children (Gallahue & Ozmun, 1995). On the inside, children's bones are getting thicker and children are gaining more muscle mass. Gender differences in growth are minimal. Boys have slightly more muscle mass and thicker bones than girls; otherwise boys and girls are remarkably similar in size and shape at this age.

Adequate nutrition is essential for healthy growth and development. Although young children do not require as much food as adults, their need for a balanced diet is, if anything, greater than that of adults, as their bodies are growing and forming important structures. A healthy diet includes the proper balance of several key nutrients (Gabbard, 1992):

*Proteins* provide our bodies with amino acids, the essential "building blocks" of growth. Proteins are necessary to support new growth in the body, especially in periods of

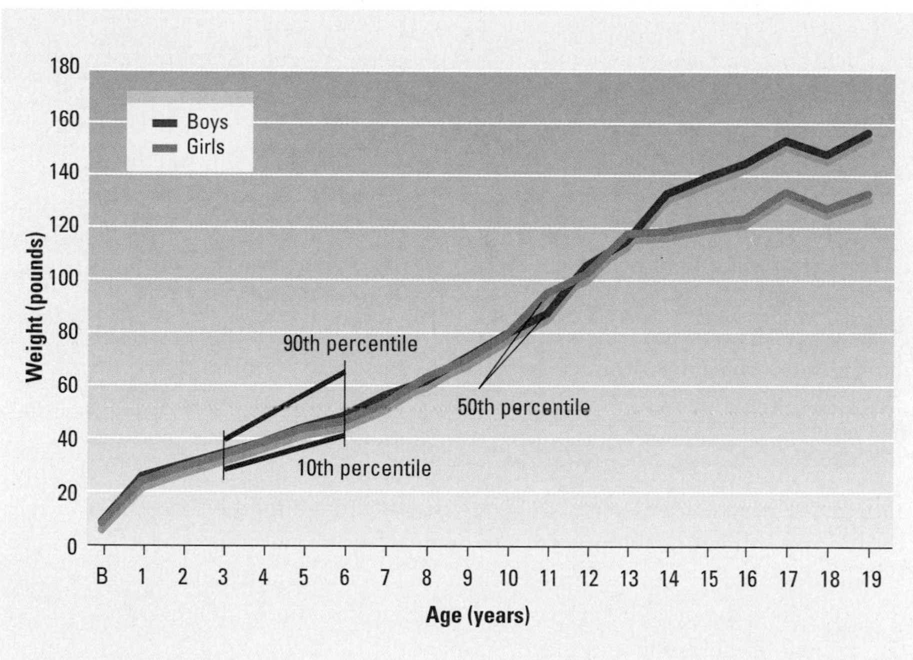


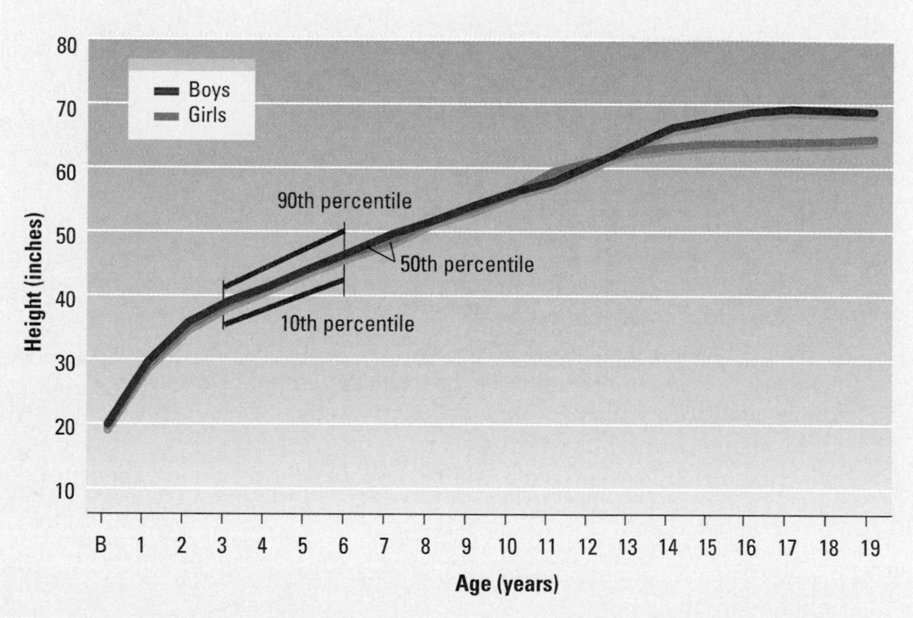


FIGURE 7.1
**Growth in Height (top) and Weight (bottom) from Birth through Adolescence.**
The bracketed areas show the area between the 90th percentiles (largest 10% of children) and the 10th percentiles (smallest 10% of children). The 50th percentiles show where the middle (or average) heights and weights are for each age. (National Center for Health Statistics, 2004.)

rapid growth—in the last trimester of pregnancy, in infancy, and during the adolescent growth spurt. Good sources of protein include meats, fish, cheese, and legumes.

*Carbohydrates* are an important source of fuel for the body, providing energy for muscle activity, the generation of body heat, and the enormous energy demands of the brain and nervous system. Breads, pasta, rice, and fruits are rich in carbohydrates.

*Fats* provide a store of energy, and body fat helps insulate the body from fluctuations in environmental temperature. Vegetable oils are important sources of poly- and monounsaturated fat. Most fats that are solid at room temperature, such as butter, contain saturated fat and should be eaten only in limited quantities, as dietary saturated fat and high blood cholesterol are linked to heart disease and other harmful conditions. However, it is important to know that the body actually produces cholesterol and requires it for many bodily functions, including synthesis of sex hormones (androgens and estrogens).

*Vitamins and minerals* help maintain normal body growth and functions. Calcium, for example, is important for enabling muscles to contract, and for forming bones and teeth and maintaining healthy bones as we age. Dairy products are a rich source of calcium, while vegetables and fruits provide vitamins.

Most young children tend to have a few foods they prefer to eat, and they don't usually like trying new foods. It's often a challenge to get young children to eat a balanced diet. What can parents do to encourage healthy eating in young children? Check out the advice given by a professional nutritionist in the Professional Perspective box called "Career Focus: Meet a Family Nutrition Counselor." Perhaps a career in nutrition is for you?

THINKING CRITICALLY

What were your favorite foods when you were young? Were you a picky eater? What do you or your parents remember?

**Malnutrition** occurs when children do not consume adequate calories, protein, vitamins, and minerals. Although starvation is rare in the United States, many families do not have the money or resources to provide enough food for their children. In the U.S., 11% of all households do not have the quantity or quality of food that they need for healthy nutrition (United States Department of Agriculture, 2008). Twelve million children live in families that are struggling to put enough food on the table, and nearly 4 million children are skipping meals or not getting enough to eat. According to nationwide surveys, 38% of families living in poverty and 30% of families who are headed by single women do not have enough food, and one out of every five black and Hispanic households do not have enough to eat (United States Department of Agriculture, 2008).

**malnutrition**
Nutritional deficiency caused by an inadequate intake of calories, protein, vitamins, and minerals.

**kwashiorkor**
Disease caused by a lack of protein in the diet. Children are severely malnourished, with a swollen belly.

## Perspective PROFESSIONAL — CAREER FOCUS: MEET A FAMILY NUTRITION COUNSELOR

Kathryn Tromblay, RN, BSN
Naperville, IL

**What eating patterns do you deal with most with children ages 3 to 6?**
I work in a pediatrician's office in a suburb of Chicago, and I mostly see children who are constantly snacking. I talk with the parents and discuss using a schedule with three meals plus a morning and afternoon snack. I also stress that they decrease juice and switch to water in the children's sippy cups or drink cups.

**How can parents get children to eat a more balanced and healthy meal?**
Offer fun-looking meals that have all the food groups in them. Parent and family magazines always offer cute ideas for snacks and lunches such as mini pizzas made with whole wheat muffins and decorated with "faces" made of small pieces of vegetables. I always emphasize that parents should continue to offer all the food groups even if their children turn their noses up at the offering. Also, the parents must set good examples by eating healthy!

**How should they handle a picky eater who wants to eat the same thing every day?**
Offer new foods along with small amounts of a food that you know the child will eat. Parents must be consistent and not give in to a child's every request. Include something of what they like but always add the other food group or groups. If new foods are never offered, a child will never eat them! Never make the dinner table a place to argue—be calm, be consistent, and have the child leave the table if he/she becomes upset.

**What education and experience does it take to work in your field?**
I have a bachelor's degree in nursing and a Bachelor of Science degree in psychology. I feel this has been a good mix in working with the children and families. I can be successful only if the parents are willing to change. Eating habits are formed by parents! I tell my families we are not counting calories—we are talking about the food pyramid, how to use it at meals, and also how to change our activity levels in our day-to-day lives.

QUESTION **What other nutrition issues do you think counselors deal with? What do you think the biggest nutrition problems are in the United States?**

What are the short- and long-term effects of malnutrition? Children who lack adequate nutrition tend to show stunted growth. Inadequate calories or lack of a balanced diet can cause lowered intelligence. Malnourished children perform less well in school. As adults, children who were malnourished can continue to suffer physical and intellectual deficits that often limit their ability to earn an adequate income.

In developing countries, the rate of malnutrition is even more alarming. According to the World Health Organization (WHO), 230 million children under the age of 5 are seriously malnourished in the developing countries (de Onis, Monteiro, Akré, & Clugston, 2002; World Health Organization, 2005). These children are significantly underweight and show stunted growth. Approximately 80% live in Asia, 15% in Africa, and 5% in Latin America. As Table 7.1 shows, in various regions of the world, large segments of the population are not able to meet their basic nutritional requirements.

Maybe you have seen photos of children like the one shown in Figure 7.2. This child has **kwashiorkor,** a terrible disease caused by a chronic lack of protein in the diet. Children with kwashiorkor are seriously underweight but have swollen bellies. Their growth is retarded and they often have sores on their bodies and suffer from diarrhea. Untreated, the disease leads to coma and death. This level of malnutrition occurs mostly in developing nations that have suffered severe droughts or political unrest, and people are not able to get the food and nutrition they need. Writing about worldwide problems with nutrition, de Onis and colleagues commented that malnutrition "not only perpetuates the vicious cycle of poverty but also leads to an enormous waste of

▲ Millions of Americans are too poor to provide enough food for their families every day. Many rely on government programs and community food partners for help.

THINK ABOUT THE RODRIGUEZ CHILDREN . . .

What might happen if the Rodriguez children were malnourished? What do children need for proper nutrition?

**TABLE 7.1**
Children under Age 5 in Developing Countries Who Are Significantly Malnourished and Underweight

| REGION | EXAMPLE COUNTRIES | NUMBER OF CHILDREN (UNDER AGE 5) | PERCENTAGE OF CHILDREN (UNDER AGE 5) |
|---|---|---|---|
| South Asia | includes Bangladesh, India, Pakistan | 101 million | 60 |
| East Asia | includes China, Mongolia | 26 million | 21 |
| Southeast Asia | includes Indonesia, Laos, Vietnam, Philippines | 22 million | 38 |
| West Africa | includes Ghana, Namibia, Nigeria | 12 million | 33 |
| East Africa | includes Ethiopia, Rwanda, Uganda | 11 million | 31 |
| South America | includes Bolivia, Brazil, Colombia | 3 million | 8 |
| Central America | includes Mexico, Guatemala, Honduras | 3 million | 18 |
| North Africa | includes Algeria, Egypt | 2 million | 11 |
| Caribbean | includes Dominican Republic, Haiti, Jamaica | 0.6 million | 19 |
| United States (for comparison) | | | Less than 3 |

*Note*: "Underweight" is defined as being two standard deviations below the median weight for that age (equal to the lower 2.27% of a normal curve for children's weights).

(World Health Organization, 2005, and their report written by de Onis, Monteiro, Akré, & Clugston, 2002.)

**THINKING CRITICALLY**
What do you think we need to do to combat the problem of world hunger? What can you and your friends do?

human potential" (2002, p. 10). From our discussion on malnutrition you can see that nature stimulates the growth of the body and brain, but we need proper nutrition (supplied by nurture) to capitalize properly on the growth.

Another growing nutrition-related problem children face is obesity. Obesity problems have risen to epidemic proportions in the United States and elsewhere. We cover this important topic in detail in Chapter 10.

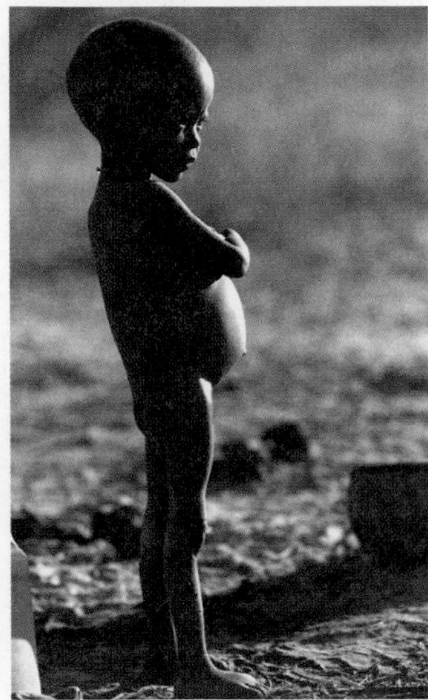

▲ FIGURE 7.2
**Kwashiorkor Disease.** This child has *kwashiorkor*, a terrible disease caused by a chronic lack of protein in the diet.

## Growth and Development of the Brain

The brain grows in spurts (Epstein, 1978; Kolb, 1999; Kolb & Fantie, 1989). The first growth spurt is the greatest—during the infancy period between 3 and 18 months, the weight of the brain increases 30%. Brain weight then increases up to another 10% during each period from the years 2 to 4, 6 to 8, 10 to 12, and 14 to 16. These age periods correspond roughly with the stages of cognitive development Jean Piaget proposed several decades ago. Look back to Chapter 5 for an outline of Piaget's stages and the ages associated with each one.

Remember from Chapter 4 that most neurons are formed midway during pregnancy (by the 20th week of gestation). The rapid brain growth that occurs during postnatal growth spurts is therefore due mostly to an increase in blood vessels to feed the growing brain, the growth of the myelin sheath around axons (in the process of *myelination*), and the proliferation of *glial cells.* **Glial cells** are specialized cells in the nervous system that support neurons in several ways. First, they provide structural support, holding neurons together. The name *glial* refers to this property of "gluing" neurons together. In addition, glial cells provide nourishment, remove waste products, occupy injured sites in the nervous system, and form the myelin sheaths that insulate axons. There are more than 100 billion glial cells in a mature brain, outnumbering neurons (Kolb, 1999).

Although the brain is gaining size and weight, it is actually *shrinking* in another way. In Chapter 4 we explained that *synapses* (connections between neurons) form at a very rapid rate during the later weeks of pregnancy and into the infancy period. Synaptogenesis, governed largely by genetics, leads to a tremendous overabundance of synapses by the time the child reaches the age of 2. But from early childhood into adolescence, heavy **synaptic pruning** means that many more synapses are lost than gained. Synapses that are activated by environmental input and brain activity are maintained, but synapses that are not used are lost or "pruned" (Couperus & Nelson, 2006). Figure 7.3 shows the developmental phases of heavy synaptogenesis followed by synaptic pruning. During childhood, as many as 100,000 synapses can be lost every second! About 40% of the synapses that existed at 2 years of age are lost by adulthood (Kolb, 1999). Explore on mydevelopmentlab

Explore The Synapse
www.mydevelopmentlab.com

**glial cells**
Specialized cells in the nervous system that support neurons in several ways.

**synaptic pruning**
Process in which unused synapses are lost (pruned).

**experience-expectant development**
Development of universal skills (such as hand–eye coordination) in which excess synapses form and are pruned according to experience.

## The Role of Experience in Brain Development

Researchers describe two types of brain development: *experience-expectant* and *experience-dependent* (Black & Greenough, 1986; Greenough & Black, 1999). With **experience-expectant development,** the brain has evolved to "expect" certain basic experiences or activities that all humans share—such as attachment to caregivers, recognition of human faces, hand–eye coordination, and communication by language (Nelson, 2001). The foundations for these types of experiences tend to be hardwired in the brain. Their development follows the pattern we've already described: Excess synapses form early in development ("expecting" the experience) and then are pruned throughout childhood (based on the actual experience). Nature and nurture work together. Genetics governs the rapid multiplication of synapses, and then experience determines which synapses survive.

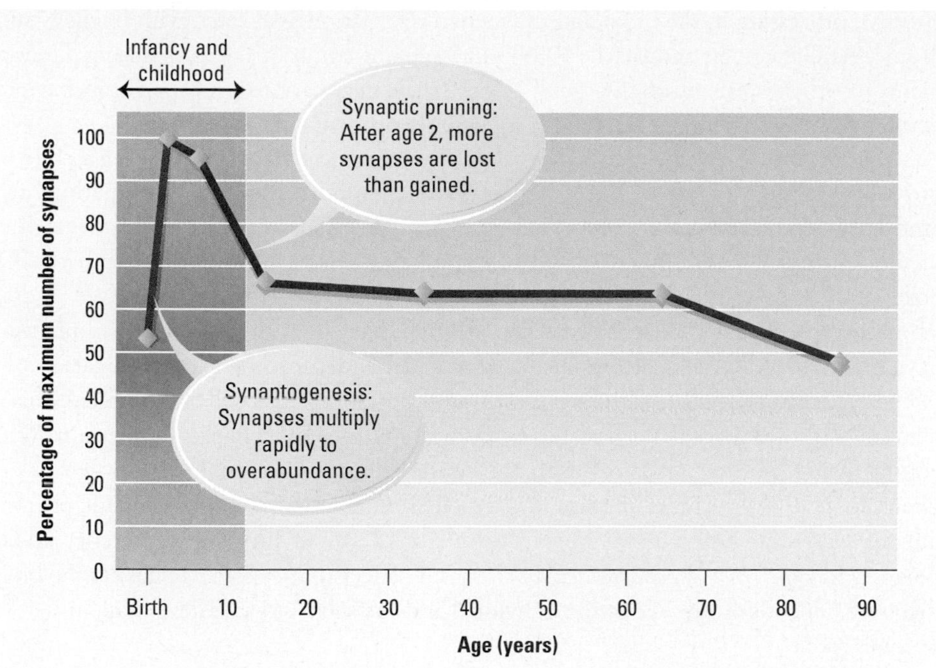


◀ FIGURE 7.3
**Synaptogenesis and Synaptic Pruning.**
New synapses form at an incredible rate during the first two years of life. During childhood, synaptic pruning reduces the total number of synapses. Synaptic density then remains relatively stable until the later years of life. (Adapted from Huttenlocher & Dabholkar, 1997.)

Cycles of synapse overproduction and pruning are staggered across the various skills, yielding a schedule of critical or sensitive periods of development (Couperus & Neslon, 2006; Greenough & Black, 1999). Synapses related to hand–eye coordination, for example, are produced and pruned earlier than synapses for language. With experience-expectant development, every human can develop the same set of basic skills, yet each person can develop his or her own twist on the universal theme.

**Experience-dependent development,** on the other hand, has to do with experiences that are not universal. Examples include the vocabulary of a particular language (e.g., Portuguese), culture-specific behaviors (e.g., a handshake), and specific motor skills (e.g., riding a bicycle). The brain cannot "expect" these particular behaviors, so new synapses must form, stimulated by the experiences themselves, to encode them. As we learn to ride a bicycle, for example, new synapses form to code the motor movements required for this activity. Later some of these synapses may be pruned as we refine our skills. In addition to forming new synapses, researchers are now discovering that some new neurons do form and grow throughout life (especially in the hippocampus region of the brain) as a way to help us code new learning and memories (Schmidt-Hieber, Jonas, & Bischofberger, 2004).

**experience-dependent development**
Development of specific skills (such as riding a skateboard) in which new synapses form to code the experience.

Experience-dependent development occurs throughout the life span, giving us the potential for lifelong learning and the retention of individualized skills, facts, and knowledge. This type of development contributes to the distinctive character coded into every individual's brain and sets each of us apart from all others.

With experience-dependent development, additional synapses tend to form to encode the skills and information learned through experience. In that sense, more synapses code more learning. This is not necessarily true, however, with experience-expectant development. Researchers have learned an interesting lesson by studying brain development in children with fragile X syndrome (Greenough & Black, 1999). As we discussed in Chapter 2, fragile X syndrome is one of the leading inherited causes of mental retardation among males. In this syndrome a defective gene suppresses the normal production of a protein (called FMRP) that is important for synaptic pruning. Without FMRP, the synapses overproduced during experience-expectant development cannot be pruned effectively. Maintaining inefficient synapses adds "noise" to the neural circuits, leading to less

THINKING CRITICALLY
Give an example of something you learned by experience-expectant development. What have you learned recently by experience-dependent development?

effective processing in the brain and the mental retardation associated with fragile X syndrome. As Greenough and Black (1999) put it, "elimination of synapses during development, in other words, is often a good thing that is necessary to proper neurobehavioral development" (p. 35). **Listen** on **mydevelopmentlab**

**Listen**: Would there be an advantage to maintaining more synapses? (Author Podcast) www.mydevelopmentlab.com

Can parents or caregivers enhance synaptogenesis and synaptic pruning in a child by providing stimulating experiences? Consider one experiment in which experimenters randomly assigned laboratory rats to live in "enriched" versus "sterile" environments. Rats in the "enriched" environments lived in cages equipped with numerous ramps, tubes, boxes, and other stimulating toys to explore. Rats in "sterile" environments lived in drab laboratory cages that lacked added stimulation. What effect did the added stimulation have on the development of the rats' brains? It depended on the age of the rats (Kolb, Gibb, & Dallison, 1999). With rats in early adulthood, the enriched environment caused neurons to grow longer dendrites and *increased* the number of synapses per neuron. With young newly weaned rats, however, the enriched environment led to a *decrease* in synapses. That is, for the young rats, the enriched experience facilitated synaptic pruning during *experience-expectant development*, but for the older rats, the experience added synapses in *experience-dependent development*. The effect that experience has on the brain therefore depends on the age of the individual and the stage of brain development that he or she is in.

THINK ABOUT THE RODRIGUEZ CHILDREN . . .
With this information on brain development, what concerns should Kathy and Rod have about the children they adopted? In what ways might the children's brain development be affected by their experiences of abuse and neglect?

From this discussion, you can see that exposure to stimulating environments is important for forming sophisticated neural networks in the young brain. Children deprived of adequate stimulation lose the positive benefits of synaptic pruning during experience-expectant development, and they lose the opportunity to gain new synapses during experience-dependent development. In both ways, they fail to reach their full cognitive potentials. But how far do we need to go to stimulate the developing brain? What does it take to create appropriately "enriched" environments? For children on a healthy developmental path the answer can be found in the everyday environment around them: colorful and varied visual patterns in their toys and books; voices speaking, reading, and singing to them; hugs, cuddles, and tickles; and the stimulation of running, jumping, and climbing. Opportunities to interact in rich and meaningful ways with the environment flood the developing brain with input and stimulate its development. Children deprived of these forms of stimulation, however, will be at greater risk for retarded or immature brain growth.

▲ Safe places to climb, run, and play are part of the "enriched" environment all children need for optimal brain development.

## Larger Developmental Patterns in the Brain

So far, we have described microscopic development in the brain, focusing on individual neurons and synapses. Researchers also track the development of larger areas in the brain, correlating their development with corresponding advances in behavior and thought. The *visual area,* located in the occipital lobe in the back of the brain, develops early. This area reaches its peak in synapse density within 4 months after birth, and synapse density decreases to adult levels by approximately 10 years of age (Huttenlocher, 1990). As the visual area and the whole occipital lobe develop during early childhood, children become better able to process, recognize, and remember visual patterns that are more complex. The abilities to recognize specific faces and the emotional expressions from faces, for example, improve dramatically by the age of 6 to 8 years (Elias & Saucier, 2006; Kolb, Wilson, & Taylor, 1992). At the same time, plasticity in the visual area is decreasing. For example, if a child under the age of 4 has *amblyopia* (one "lazy" eye), it can be corrected by using a patch to block input to the healthy eye, pushing the other eye to process more input. After the age of 4, this intervention is not very effective.

As the *temporal lobes* develop, children make significant progress in learning language. Vocabulary increases sharply after age 3, and young children also absorb the structure and grammar of the language they hear around them. Improved communication between Wernicke's area (in the temporal lobe) and Broca's area (in the frontal lobe) helps children transform the language they hear into a language that they can speak and produce themselves. Language, hand–eye coordination, and the coordination of many other functions in the brain all improve as development continues in the *parietal lobes*. The parietal lobes begin to absorb more energy and become more active after children reach 2 to 3 years of age (Chugani, 1998; Elias & Saucier, 2006; Teeter & Semrud-Clikeman, 1997).

▲ Growth and myelination in the frontal lobes help children learn to pay attention, inhibit temptations, and cooperate in group situations.

Heavy growth in the *frontal lobes* occurs between the ages of 3 and 6 years (Thompson et al., 2000). The frontal lobes are responsible for organizing and planning behavior, so by 3 to 6 years this brain growth helps children to participate more fully in group settings like preschool and kindergarten. As the frontal lobes develop, children become better able to control their emotions, inhibit their first reactions, and coordinate strategies to solve increasingly complex problems.

Areas elsewhere in the brain are also developing during early childhood. The hippocampus, for example, is an area deeper in the brain that is responsible for storing and processing memories. Most people cannot remember anything that happened to them before they were about 3 to 4 years old. **Infantile amnesia** is the term used to describe this type of memory failure, and it is believed to be related to immaturities in the hippocampus and other structures involved in memory (Elias & Saucier, 2006). As the hippocampus matures, our memories become more lasting and easier to retrieve.

These are just a few examples of how development of larger structures in the brain correlate with the improved skills and processes we see during early childhood.

**THINKING CRITICALLY**
What is your earliest memory? Why do you think we don't remember more about our early years?

**infantile amnesia**
Inability to remember things and events occurring before the age of 3 or 4.

## LET'S REVIEW . . .

1. Most of the children who are seriously malnourished live in ___________.
   a. Africa
   b. Asia
   c. Latin America
   d. the urban sections of the United States
2. Which of the following is happening in the brains of typical 3-year-old children?
   a. They lose fatty glial cells as they learn.
   b. Their axons are losing their myelin sheaths.
   c. Neurons are beginning to outnumber glial cells.
   d. They lose more synapses than they gain.
3. Josh gets better grades in spelling and his twin brother gets better grades in reading. These differences in school performance are most likely due to differences in their ___________.
   a. experience-expectant form of development.
   b. experience-dependent form of development.
   c. patterns of myelination in the occipital lobes.
   d. growth of glial cells before age 2.
4. In general, which lobe of the brain shows the earliest maturity?
   a. the frontal lobe
   b. the temporal lobe
   c. the occipital lobe
   d. the parietal lobe
5. True or False: Kwashiorkor is a disease caused by a chronic lack of protein in the diet.
6. True or False: Growth and development in the temporal lobes are primary reasons that children become better able to recognize faces and the emotions expressed by faces.

Answers: 1. b, 2. d, 3. b, 4. c, 5. T, 6. F

# Motor Development and Physical Activity

As toddlers mature into the early childhood period, they are no longer trapped in their uncoordinated and unstable bodies. From birth to age 2 their mobility was very limited, and they stayed mostly in cribs, laps, playpens, and other spaces that were usually confined and safe. By the age of 3, however, most children are much more coordinated in their walking; they can walk up and down stairs, run, and even pedal a tricycle. Their world has opened into wide, new horizons! In this section we explore the major changes that occur in motor development and physical activity from the ages of 3 to 6 years.

AS YOU STUDY THIS SECTION, ASK YOURSELF THESE QUESTIONS:

**7.5** What improvements do young children make in the control and coordination of their gross-motor and fine-motor skills?

**7.6** How physically active are most young children, and how much do children differ in their levels of activity?

**7.7** What is cerebral palsy, and what do we know about this condition?

## Gross-Motor and Fine-Motor Development

With advances in *gross-motor development*, children learn to use the large muscles in their legs, trunk, and upper arms to maintain their balance (Gallahue & Ozmun, 1995). At age 3, children can barely stand on one foot, but most 5-year-olds can hold their balance on one foot for several seconds. At age 3, children use their leg muscles to pedal a tricycle, but they need to gain much more control of all of their large muscles to manage the balance necessary to ride a two-wheel bicycle. As children improve their balance, they also improve their **locomotor skills,** or the skills used to move around, such as walking, running, and climbing. When toddlers walk, they take short, wobbly steps and their legs and arms are rather rigid. By age 4 we see a more mature walk with longer strides, relaxed movements, and a more rhythmic swinging of the arms to improve balance (Gallahue & Ozmun, 1995). By 5 years, children can run more efficiently, jump about 1 foot high, hop 8 to 10 times on one foot, and skip with both feet. In the gross-motor area, children also improve their ability to manipulate large objects with actions such as throwing, catching, and kicking. These skills improve as children gain balance, improve their coordination, and learn to move one arm or leg independently from the other.

**locomotor skills**
Skills used to move around, such as walking, running, and climbing.

By age 3, children have enough leg strength to pedal a tricycle, but it will be another few years before they typically have the balance and coordination to master a two-wheeled bicycle.

It is important to remember that children vary in their rates of progress in motor development. Some children improve their balance, strength, and coordination very quickly while others progress more slowly. The pace of physical development and coordination is controlled in part by genetics. It is also influenced by instruction and encouragement from adults and other children and by the opportunities that children have to practice particular motor skills. Differences in rate of development can be due to differences in nature, in nurture, or both. Even within a particular child, it is common to see uneven development across tasks. For example, one child may jump and skip with ease but be uncoordinated in throwing and catching. Another child may show the reverse pattern. The kinds of play activities children choose can be a major influence. Children who like to skip rope will develop different motor skills than children who prefer to shoot basketballs. Keeping this in mind, parents, teachers, and childcare providers should offer children a variety of large motor activities. Play spaces, toys, and activities should encourage children to run, jump, climb, lift, catch, throw, balance, and otherwise help them strengthen and coordinate the larger muscles of their bodies.

THINKING CRITICALLY

Did you learn some motor skills faster than others? Which forms of motor development were slowest to develop for you? Why?

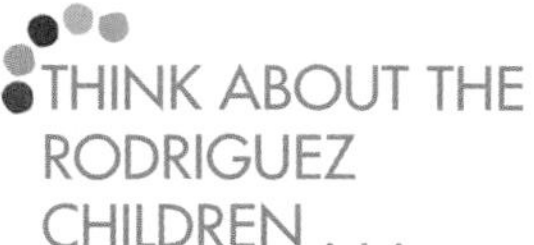

THINK ABOUT THE RODRIGUEZ CHILDREN . . .

What types of abuse and neglect might prevent children from getting proper opportunities to develop their gross-motor skills?

Control over the delicate movements of the hands and fingers is required for *fine-motor* activities such as drawing, writing, typing, sewing, and stringing small beads. Young children are usually clumsy with these small movements. Their fine-motor development lags behind gross-motor development during this early childhood period.

Remember the *proximodistal* (midline-out) pattern of development we discussed in Chapters 3 and 4? You can see this pattern here in the transition children make from gross- to fine-motor development: Children learn to coordinate the larger muscles in their trunks, shoulders, and upper arms before they learn fine control over the smaller muscles further out in the hands and fingers. Coordination is spreading from the middle of their bodies outward into the extremities in a proximodistal pattern. We also see a *cephalocaudal* (head-to-tail) pattern in both gross- and fine-motor development as children learn to control their upper bodies (arms and hands) before their lower bodies (legs and feet). Most children, for example, can roll and catch a ball with their hands before they are very coordinated in kicking a ball with their feet.

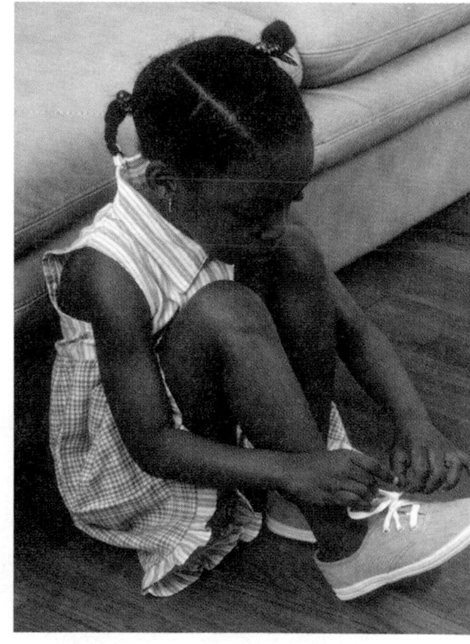

▲ Tying shoes is an example of a skill that requires considerable control over the fine-motor movements in the fingers and hands.

By age 3, children can put their shoes on, work large buttons, wash their hands and face, and pour a drink from a pitcher (Gallahue & Ozmun, 1995). They can use a spoon to feed themselves, though they often spill and get as much food on their faces as in their mouths. By age 4, they can put on pants and shirts without help, brush their teeth, and lace their shoes. By 5 and 6 years of age, most children have gained remarkable control in fine-motor development: they can pour beverages and feed themselves without spilling; they can tie their shoes and work smaller buttons and zippers; and they can use pencils, scissors, and other tools with some precision.

As they enter school, it is important that children learn to use writing implements such as crayons, markers, and pencils. Figure 7.4 (page 214) shows four phases children move through when developing a mature grip with pencils and other writing tools (Keogh & Sugden, 1985). At age 2, they usually use a **palmar grasp** by holding the pencil in the palm and moving the whole arm to draw on the paper. Many children then learn to hold the pencil through the fingers, still using large arm movements for drawing. By age 3, they learn to hold the pencil more delicately between the thumb and forefinger, but they are still using larger movements in the wrist to move the pencil. Finally, by around age 4, children show the **mature tripod grasp**—they place the base of their hands on the writing surface for support, they hold the pencil with the index finger and thumb, and move the wrist along with finer movements in the fingers to more precisely guide the pencil. They have gradually transferred the control of writing and drawing from the larger muscles in the upper arm to the smaller muscles in the hand and fingers. Similar progress can be seen in their coordination with scissors and other school tools.

**palmar grasp**
An immature grasp, holding the pencil in the palm and moving the whole arm to draw.

**mature tripod grasp**
Placing the base of the hand on the writing surface for support, holding the pencil with the index finger and thumb, and moving the wrist along with finer movements in the fingers to guide the pencil more precisely.

As with gross-motor development, opportunity to practice is important. Children need to be encouraged to draw, color, cut, string beads, tie strings, work zippers and buttons, and

FIGURE 7.4 ▶
**Four Stages of Pencil Grip.** (1) Palmar grasp. (2) Pencil through the fingers. (3) Fingers and thumb, moving wrist. (4) Fingers and thumb, moving wrist and fingers. (Keogh & Sugden, 1985.)

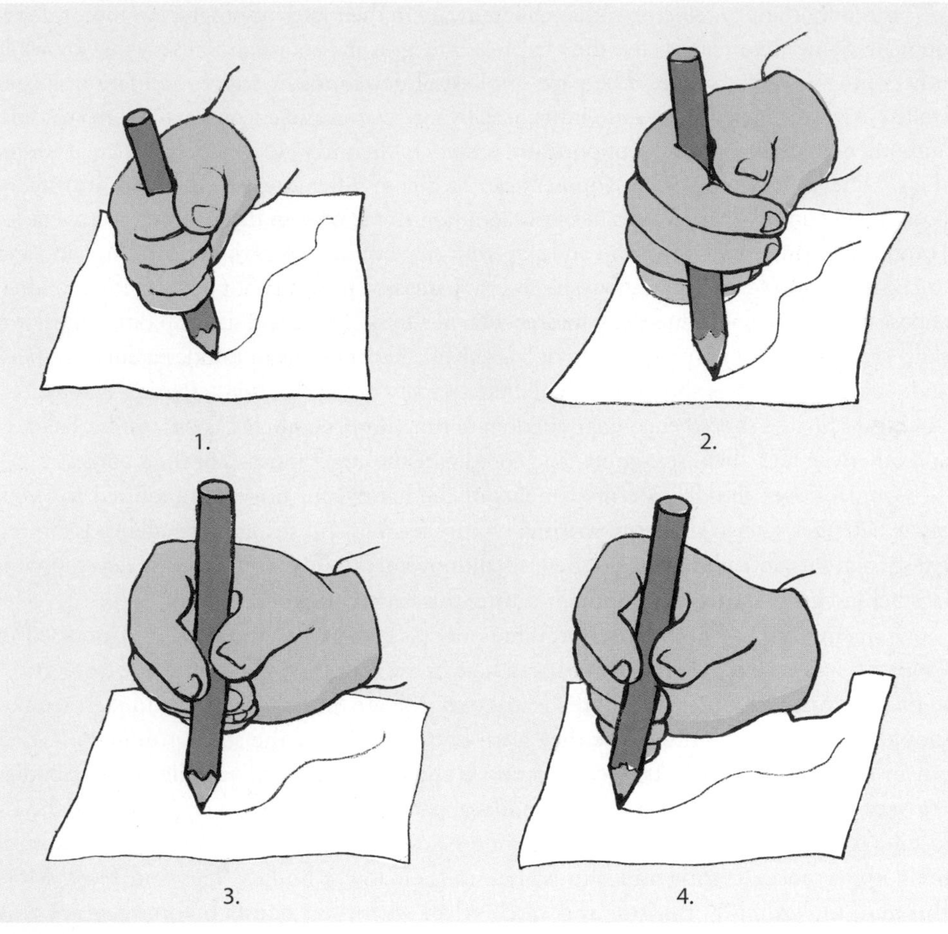

▲ Young children get most of their physical exercise during games and playtime.

practice a variety of other activities that involve fine-motor movements. With practice, they can learn to strengthen and control the smaller muscles that are so important in the many tasks we engage in every day.

Don't forget about the experience-expectant and experience-dependent patterns of brain development (discussed earlier in this chapter). Motor practice is important in helping the brain prune out ineffective synapses. If synapses in the motor areas remain too cluttered, motor movements will be clumsy. Practice also helps children grow new synapses to code the increasingly complex movements and skills that they are learning. Without practice, neither pattern of development can proceed normally.

## Physical Activity and Exercise

Have you ever tried to keep up with young children? One minute they are playing quietly with toys, but the next minute they're running in circles, racing up and down, or climbing over furniture. As we described previously, physical activity is important in helping children strengthen their large muscles and coordinate their balance and fine-motor skills. Physical activity also provides the exercise children need to strengthen their cardiovascular systems (lungs and heart). Like everyone else, young children need to be active to stay healthy, and the active habits they learn while they are young can remain with them as they mature and grow into adulthood.

Health officials recommend that children spend at least 60 minutes each day in physical activities that are structured or organized by parents, teachers, or other people, and they should accumulate at least another 60 minutes of physical activity in their free play sometime during the day (National Association for Sport and Physical Education, 2002). How many young children get this much exercise? In one study, children ages 3 to 5 wore a small watch-like device that recorded their heart rates every minute throughout the day and their parents and child care providers completed logs that described their activities (Benham-Deal, 2005). The researchers looked for evidence of moderate to vigorous physical activity, defined as activity in which the children's heart rates were 130 or more beats per minute (over 65% of a young child's maximum heart rate). What did they find? Overall, about 20% of the children's activities fell into the moderate to vigorous category. Children varied. Some were highly active almost all day, while others did not register any moderate or vigorous activity at all. Children were more active on the weekdays than on the weekend. The children played outside more on weekdays, when their parents and day care workers reported that they played more at parks and on swings, slides, jungle gyms, and in games with other children that involved running and chasing. Overall, children spent 75% of their time indoors where they mostly watched television, played with toys, and worked on arts and crafts. Another important finding was that almost all of the children's moderate to vigorous activities occurred in short bursts, lasting less than 10 minutes at a time. Young children do not pace themselves very well. Anyone working with young children needs to keep in mind that they tend to expend their energy very quickly and then need frequent breaks to rest.

Children get most of their physical activity when they play. Running, climbing, chasing, and throwing are all common elements in young children's play. Parents and others can encourage children's activity by providing jungle gyms and play structures that allow swinging, climbing, and sliding. Push toys and riding toys are popular with young children. Three-year-olds love to pull things around in wagons and ride tricycles, and by the time they are 5 or 6 they are usually riding bicycles, scooters, and skateboards. Sand toys, pails and shovels, balls, and sporting equipment all give children opportunities to strengthen large and small muscles, improve hand–eye coordination, and otherwise enjoy their play and physical activity.

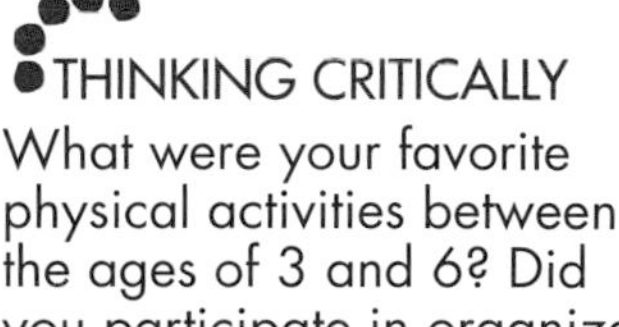

What were your favorite physical activities between the ages of 3 and 6? Did you participate in organized sports or other programs for physical exercise at that age?

As children enter preschool and kindergarten, they have group activities and instruction that teach individual skills and also introduce turn-taking. At this age, most of their instruction in physical activity is incorporated into games, sports, and other fun activities. Music is a good motivator at this age, and one study showed that adding music and rhythmic movement exercises to young children's physical education classes helped them make more progress in their jumping and balance skills (Zachopoulou, Tsapakidou, & Derri, 2004). A similar study showed that 5-year-old boys and girls did not differ in their gross-motor skills or music abilities, but girls did show an advantage over boys in rhythmic movement (Pollatou, Karadimou, & Gerodimos, 2005). Although many young children spend a great deal of time in day care centers and preschools, research suggests that most of this time is spent in activities that are rather quiet or low in energy. One study showed that 3- to 5-year-olds spent 97% of their time at preschool in sedentary or low-energy play, and they spent only 3% of their time in more vigorous types of activities (Brown et al., 2009).

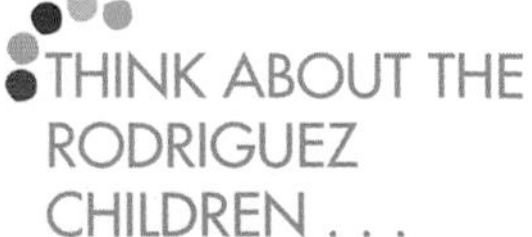

What do children like the Rodriguez children miss when they are not allowed to participate in community sports and exercise programs or other school-related fitness programs? What effect might this have on their physical development?

As they get older, children have gym classes in school and some children participate in dance or exercise programs sponsored by their local parks and recreation organizations. Many choose to join organized sports such as baseball, basketball, and swimming. We will have much more to say about organized sports participation in Chapter 10.

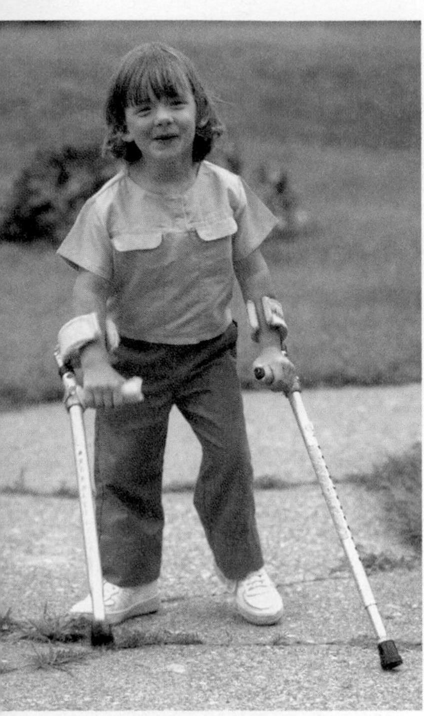

▲ This child has cerebral palsy. The Individuals with Disabilities Education Act (IDEA) requires that all children be given the support they need to be successful in the school setting.

## Cerebral Palsy

So far we have described the typical progress of motor development, but a large number of children have developmental delays or disorders in motor function, and they do not follow the typical pattern of development. **Cerebral palsy** (or CP) is one of the most serious disorders of motor development. It is caused by damage to one or more areas of the brain that control muscle movement and coordination (United Cerebral Palsy, 2005). *Cerebral* refers to the brain, and *palsy* refers to the muscle weakness and loss of muscle control that comes with the disorder. Cerebral palsy is actually a group of disorders, and the symptoms of CP vary depending on the specific areas of the brain that are damaged. Symptoms can include uncontrolled movements of the arms, legs, or other parts of the body. They may also include weak muscles, poor coordination, spastic (or jerky) movements, tight muscles, perceptual problems, and seizures. Children with CP usually have difficulty walking and engaging in many other physical activities (Østensjø, Carlberg, & Vøllestad, 2003, 2004). They may need help with common tasks such as dressing and going to the bathroom. They often have difficulty speaking, eating, and sometimes even breathing and swallowing. Children with CP often show mental retardation or learning disabilities. Read firsthand about a family living with cerebral palsy in our Personal Perspective box called "Living with Cerebral Palsy" on page 217.

Cerebral palsy is a serious disorder, but it is important to remember that it is not a disease. It is not curable, but with training and physical therapy children can learn to improve their muscle control and function. At United Cerebral Palsy (www.ucp.org) you can find a lot of other information about this disorder, including these facts:

- CP was first described by an English surgeon in the 1860s.
- In the U.S., approximately 10,000 new cases of CP are diagnosed in infants and young children each year.
- In about 70% of cases, the brain damage occurs during prenatal development (motor areas of the brain did not form properly); the symptoms may not be noticed for several months after the baby is born.
- In about 20% of cases, the brain is damaged during the process of birth, usually due to a lack of oxygen or severe pressure on the baby's head.
- About 10% of children have CP because of brain damage that occurred in the first months or years after birth, usually due to brain infections or other illnesses that affect the brain, head injuries in car accidents or falls, or damage inflicted from child abuse.

Today, many children with CP attend public schools, and some go on to college. The **Individuals with Disabilities Education Act** (IDEA) is a federal law that requires that services be provided to assist all children with disabilities. When infants and toddlers are diagnosed with disabilities, states are required to work with families to coordinate services to help the children. When the children enter school, services are provided to help them work successfully in the school setting. Before they graduate from high school, plans are developed to help the teens make the transition to life after high school. When it comes to helping children with cerebral palsy, all of this requires a great deal of work and coordination between parents, teachers, aides, pediatricians, physical therapists, social workers, and other helping professionals.

**cerebral palsy (CP)**
A serious disorder caused by damage to one or more areas of the brain that control muscle movement and coordination.

**Individuals with Disabilities Education Act (IDEA)**
Federal law requiring that services be provided to assist all children with disabilities.

## Perspective PERSONAL — LIVING WITH CEREBRAL PALSY

Betsy Carroll
South Berwick, ME
Parent of Jennifer, who has cerebral palsy

**When and how did you first find out that your child had CP?**
Jen was born 12 weeks early, weighing 2 pounds 10 ounces. Because she was born prematurely, we knew she would be delayed but didn't know how much. At 6 months of age they said she had increased tone but it wasn't until she had a 12-month check up with the developmental pediatrician that they said she would need physical therapy. I think it was about six months after that when a social worker handed me a book entitled *Handling the Cerebral Palsied Child at Home* so that I could take it home and read it. It was thick and purple and orange. I hate that book to this day! I cried all the way home.

**What was your reaction?**
Probably shock. The delivery, hospitalization, caring for a sick child, coping with a child who didn't develop like others—it was all very overwhelming. The typical stress accompanying being a first-time parent was magnified by all the questions I had of how to do the best for my child. The thrill and happiness of the birth of a child were coupled with fear and grief. The day she was born, Jennifer was taken by ambulance to another hospital 2 hours away from home, where she stayed for two months. We lived far away from the NICU, it was winter, and I could only visit three times a week. I lived for those visits.

**What treatments and supports has she needed?**
From the time she was 12 months old, she has needed physical therapy and occupational therapy. She has had hip surgery and was in a body cast for six weeks. She has used a walker, a wheelchair, and crutches at various times. She had vision therapy and had "infant stimulation" when she was young. Jennifer has had an Individualized Educational Plan throughout her school years so that modifications and therapies could be provided. I struggled through many meetings at school, determined to get appropriate services for her. I learned about the laws and resources available for people with disabilities.

**What advice do you have for other parents who might have a child with CP?**
Enjoy them as children! You have many hats as a parent of a child with a disability. Don't let your jobs as occupational therapist, physical therapist, and social skills coach take over your job as a parent. The balance is not an easy one. Learn about your child's disability. Learn about special education and then be your child's greatest advocate. Connect with other parents whose children have a similar disability. They are some of the most wonderful, caring, and patient people you'll ever meet, and the support and resources shared by talking with other parents is incomparable. There will be many professionals in your life but as a parent, you know your child the best and don't forget that!

QUESTION **How is the pattern of motor development different for children who have disabilities such as cerebral palsy? What accommodations can be made at home and school to help children with these types of disabilities?**

## LET'S REVIEW . . .

1. The development of gross-motor skills in early childhood is influenced by __________.
   **a.** genetics
   **b.** instruction and encouragement from adults and other people
   **c.** the types of activities in which the child chooses to engage
   **d.** all of the above
2. Which statement is most accurate in describing motor development in young children?
   **a.** Children usually learn to coordinate their fingers and hands before they coordinate the use of their arms.
   **b.** Children usually learn to coordinate their feet and legs before they coordinate their hands and arms.
   **c.** Gross-motor development is usually ahead of fine-motor development.
   **d.** Most children use the tripod grasp before they learn the palmar grasp when using pencils and other writing tools.

3. Which of the following is *not* true about physical activity in early childhood?
   a. Young children tend to get more exercise on weekends than on weekdays.
   b. Young children get most of their exercise while they play.
   c. Young children tend to burn their energy in fast bursts, and they need frequent breaks to rest.
   d. Young children spend more time indoors than outside.
4. Cerebral palsy is __________.
   a. a disease
   b. curable
   c. communicable and can be transferred from person to person
   d. a group of disorders caused by damage to the brain
5. True or False: Health officials recommend that young children spend at least one hour each day in structured activities that encourage physical activity.
6. True or False: In most cases, cerebral palsy is caused by damage that occurs before birth.

Answers: 1. d, 2. c, 3. a, 4. d, 5. T, 6. T

# Health and Safety Issues

Young children are vulnerable and need our protection. They depend on us to keep them safe and to help them stay healthy. We've already discussed what parents and others can do to provide children with proper nutrition and the types of exercise and experiences they need for their growing bodies and brains. This section outlines the most frequent causes of death in early childhood, and we suggest things parents can do to help protect children from illnesses, accidents, and other health and safety problems. Unfortunately, many children are not properly cared for and protected, and we devote a large portion of this section to the issues of child abuse and neglect.

AS YOU STUDY THIS SECTION, ASK YOURSELF THESE QUESTIONS:

**7.8** What are the most common causes of death during early childhood, and how can they be prevented?

**7.9** What is child maltreatment, and what are the different types?

**7.10** What are the effects of child abuse and neglect?

▲ Cancer and other diseases are the most frequent causes of death among young children.

## Childhood Deaths and Safety Issues

Each year, more than 70,000 young people die in the United States (Kung, Hoyert, Xu, & Murphy, 2008). Table 7.2 shows the numbers of deaths that occurred in one year from various causes from infancy into early adulthood. As you can see in the table, the rate of death is highest for infants who are less than one year of age. The vast majority of infant deaths are due to genetic abnormalities, prenatal problems, complications that arise during the birth process, and diseases and illnesses during the first year. Most of these infants were never healthy, and they were not able to survive their first years. After one year of age, the death rates drop significantly, and then rise again during the middle teenage and early adult years. As you can see in the table, automobile accidents are the leading cause of death among 15- to 24-year-olds, claiming nearly one-third of all of the lives that are lost in that age group. Deaths from other types of accidents and from homicides and suicides also rise sharply after age 14. Compared to these numbers, death rates are relatively low during early and middle childhood. Notice that across the 14 years from age 1 to age 14, the total number of deaths was still less than half of the number who died during their first year alone, and it was about one-third of the number who died during the 10-year span from age 15 to 24.

**TABLE 7.2**
Number of Deaths in the United States during 2005

| CAUSE | UNDER 1 YEAR OF AGE | AGES 1–4 | AGES 5–14 | AGES 15–24 |
|---|---|---|---|---|
| Disease, illness, or medical condition | 7,076 | 2,137 | 3,152 | 8,281 |
| Prenatal or birthing problem, including genetic and chromosomal defects | 19,975 | 580 | 422 | 522 |
| Motor vehicle accidents | 146 | 617 | 1,447 | 10,908 |
| Other accidents, including falls, drowning, guns, poisons | 937 | 1,047 | 968 | 4,845 |
| Homicide | 306 | 375 | 341 | 5,466 |
| Suicide | – | – | 272 | 4,212 |
| Total from all causes | 28,440 | 4,756 | 6,602 | 34,234 |
| Rates per year in age range | 28,440 | 1,189 | 660 | 3,423 |

Data are from Kung et al., 2008.

From ages 1 to 4, 45% of all deaths are due to diseases and illnesses. Cancer, heart disease, and pneumonia are the most frequent killers among the major diseases and illnesses. Another 35% of deaths are due to accidents, and the top three killers in this category are motor vehicle accidents, drowning, and fires. Although early childhood is a relatively safe period of life, there are several things parents can do to protect young children:

- Protect children against diseases by making sure they have proper immunizations. Make sure they get a thorough checkup from their pediatrician at least once each year, and have them checked any time they have a high fever or show other symptoms of serious illness.
- When traveling, always make sure children are secured properly in car seats or booster seats appropriate for their ages and sizes. Rear seats are safest. For your safety and theirs, never drink and drive.
- Never leave children unattended around water. It only takes a few inches of water for a young child to drown. As children become more active and play more outdoors, make sure they do not stray into neighbors' pools or nearby ponds or streams.
- Secure all matches and lighters in your home. Always watch children carefully around candles, space heaters, kitchen stoves, and ovens. Keep a working smoke alarm in or near children's bedrooms, and have a family plan for getting everyone out of the house in case of fire.
- Avoid other accidents by keeping all guns, poisons, household cleaners, medications, and other dangerous materials safely locked and secured from children's reach. Cover electric outlets. Keep children safe around stairs, and make sure that the windows and screens on upper levels of the home or apartment are locked securely so children cannot climb or fall out.
- Although homicides and abductions by strangers don't happen often, it's still a good time to talk with young children about "stranger dangers." They need to learn who to trust and what to do when strangers approach them.

▲Automobile accidents are a leading cause of death and injury in young children. Securing children safely in booster seats is an important precaution.

## Child Maltreatment: Abuse and Neglect

Children depend on their parents and other caregivers for the physical, psychological, and emotional support they need for healthy development. Young children in particular are completely dependent on their parents—they can't make it on their own. Unfortunately, there are some parents and caregivers who don't (or can't) live up to their responsibilities, and there are others who exploit the vulnerable and powerless position of children.

Child abuse is a tragedy that is very real and all too frequent in the lives of children. Before they grow up, about 1 in every 5 girls and 1 in every 9 boys in the United States will experience some form of sexual abuse (Finkelhor, 1994; Mash & Wolfe, 2005). In a national survey, 28% of parents reported that they use objects to hit or spank their children, and 13% said they physically shake their toddlers (Straus & Stewart, 1999). Who knows how many children suffer from other emotional and psychological abuses that remain hidden in family privacy?

**Child maltreatment** is a general category that includes all situations in which parents or other persons in charge of a child's well-being harm the child or otherwise neglect the child's needs. There are four standard categories of maltreatment:

- **Physical abuse** includes beating, slapping, hitting, kicking, burning, shaking, and otherwise causing physical harm to a child. Most cases are not intentional but result from discipline or physical punishment that got out of hand (Mash & Wolfe, 2005).
- **Neglect** is failure to provide for a child's basic physical, educational, or psychological needs. Neglect includes child abandonment, inadequate supervision, failing to provide proper nutrition or timely medical attention, failing to enroll a child in school, allowing truancy, failing to provide adequate affection, exposing the child to spousal conflict, and permitting drug or alcohol abuse (Mash & Wolfe, 2005).
- **Sexual abuse** includes fondling a child's genitals or breasts, committing intercourse or other sexual acts with a child, exposing the child to indecent acts, or involving the child in pornography.
- **Psychological abuse** includes verbal put-downs and other behavior that terrorizes, threatens, rejects, or isolates children or damages their self-esteem, thought processing, or ability to manage social interactions. This is also referred to as *emotional abuse*.

When cases of abuse exist, there is typically considerable overlap among these categories. For example, some degree of psychological abuse is present with every case of neglect or physical or sexual abuse.

In the United States, *mandatory reporting laws* require anyone who comes in contact with children in the course of work or volunteer activities to report any suspected case of child maltreatment to child protection authorities or police (Mash & Wolfe, 1999). This requirement applies to teachers, bus drivers, camp counselors, childcare workers, babysitters, physicians, nurses, and anyone else who works with children. They all must report any credible suspicion they have regarding the abuse or neglect of a child. It is then up to child protection authorities to look into each report, investigate the case if it has merit, and take appropriate actions to protect the child.

To get a feel for the dimensions of the abuse problem in this country, consider that in the year 2007 authorities received 3.2 million reports of suspected abuse or neglect (U.S. Department of Health and Human Services, 2009). Out of these, child protection agents investigated nearly 2 million cases and verified that more than 740,000 children had been abused or neglected. This was for one year alone. Keep in mind that these statistics represent only the cases that were actually reported and then verified by child protection agents. How many more cases go unreported in a given year?

**child maltreatment**
A general category including all situations in which parents or other persons in charge of a child's well-being harm the child or otherwise neglect the child's needs.

**physical abuse**
Abuse that causes physical harm to a child.

**neglect**
Failure to provide for a child's basic physical, educational, or psychological needs.

**sexual abuse**
Abuse that includes fondling a child's genitals or breasts, committing intercourse or other sexual acts with a child, exposing the child to indecent acts, or involving the child in pornography.

**psychological abuse**
Abuse that includes verbal put-downs and other behavior that terrorizes, threatens, rejects, or isolates children.

THINKING CRITICALLY
Have you ever witnessed an incident of child maltreatment that you thought should be reported? Did you report it? Would you know whom to contact?

As you can see in Figure 7.5, neglect is by far the most frequently reported type of maltreatment. The rates of child maltreatment increased significantly during the 1980s, but they started to decline slightly after 1993 and they are still declining (U.S. Department of Health and Human Services, 2009; Wekerle & Wolfe, 2003). We suspect that a large portion of the increase was due to wider implementation of the mandatory reporting laws through the 1980s, and that the decrease came as helpful services began to reach more at-risk families. Also remember that psychological abuse co-occurs with every other type of abuse. Psychological abuse does not have its own reporting category in Figure 7.5, and we don't know how many cases go unreported; however, psychological abuse is the most frequent type of child maltreatment (Mash & Wolfe, 2005).

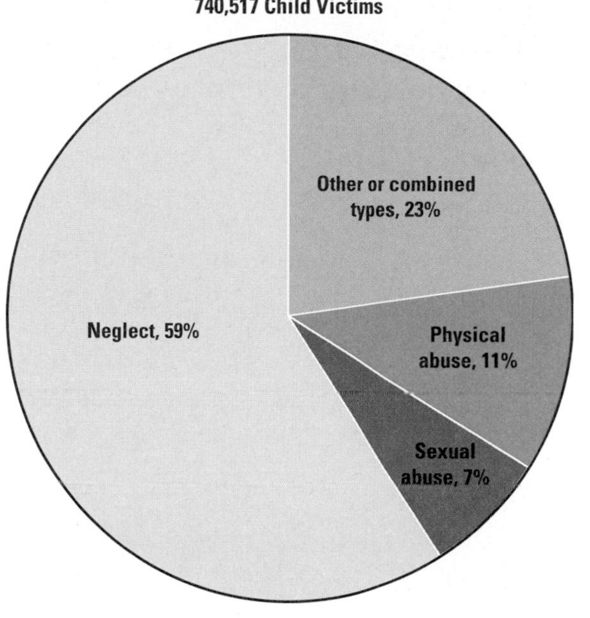


◄ FIGURE 7.5
**Types of Child Maltreatment.**
In the United States, child protection agencies verified that 740,517 children were victims of child maltreatment during 2007. This is approximately 1.2% of all children in the U.S. Most cases were due to neglect or to other or combined types of maltreatment. Data are from the U.S. Department of Human Services (2009).

THINK ABOUT THE RODRIGUEZ CHILDREN . . .

Which categories of maltreatment do you think occurred for the Rodriguez children when they were in their foster home?

Which children are most likely to be abused? You may find it shocking to learn that overall maltreatment rates are highest for infants under the age of 1 (U.S. Department of Health and Human Services, 2009). Rates tend to decline as children grow older. When it comes to physical abuse, boys are most likely to be abused between the ages of 4 and 11, whereas girls most often suffer abuse between 12 and 15. Girls are four times more likely than boys to be sexually abused (U.S. Department of Health and Human Services, 2001; Wekerle & Wolfe, 2003). Nearly half of all of the victims of maltreatment are Caucasian children, but you can see in Figure 7.6 that the rates of abuse and neglect are actually higher in most of the racial and ethnic minority groups.

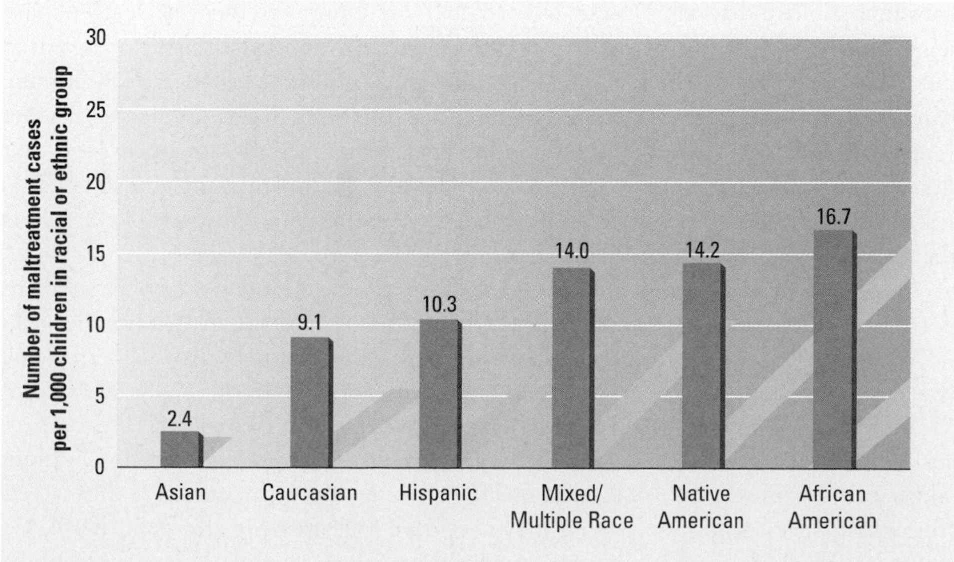


◄ FIGURE 7.6
**U.S. Rates of Child Maltreatment by Race and Ethnicity, 2007**
Rates of child maltreatment vary across racial and ethnic groups. This graph shows patterns of maltreatment reported to authorities during 2007. (U.S. Department of Health and Human Services, 2009.)

**TABLE 7.3**
**Percentages of U.S. Child Maltreatment Cases for Each Type of Perpetrator: 2007**

| PERPETRATOR | PERCENTAGE OF CASES |
|---|---|
| Mother only | 39% |
| Father only | 18% |
| Both parents | 17% |
| Mother and other | 6% |
| Father and other | 1% |
| Other and unknown | 19% |

Note: "Mother," "Father," and "Parent" includes biological, adoptive, and stepparents. Data are from the U.S. Department of Health and Human Services (2009).

Who is most likely to commit abuse? When you think of abuse, you might picture a mean father or stepfather yelling, hitting, or giving harsh punishment to children. It may surprise you to know, however, that mothers commit many more acts of physical abuse and neglect than do fathers (see Table 7.3). This is probably because mothers spend so much more time with children than fathers do. Sexual abuse, however, is one exception: This type of abuse is more likely to be committed by fathers or other people in the child's life (U.S. Department of Health and Human Services, 2001). Isn't it alarming to know that over 80% of all acts of abuse and neglect are committed by parents—the very people who should care most for their children?

During 2007 alone there were 1,700 fatalities due to child abuse or neglect (U.S. Department of Health and Human Services, 2009). Out of these, parents caused 70% of the deaths. As we mentioned before, the youngest children are most vulnerable. A full 42% of the deaths were of infants not yet 1 year old, and 75% were children under age 4.

## Effects of Abuse and Neglect

It is impossible to determine the exact effect that any form of abuse or neglect will have on a given child. Cases of maltreatment vary tremendously, differing in severity, duration, the age of the child, and other circumstances. In some instances well-meaning parents try to "overprotect" their children but use discipline that is too harsh. In other cases violent parents strike their children in anger. Whenever abuse happens, it breaks the trust that should exist between child and caregiver. Although many abused children still claim love and affection for parents who have harmed them, the abuse often shatters their sense of security and well-being.

When abuse occurs early, it threatens the formation of secure bonds of attachment between infants and their parents (recall Chapter 6). Across various studies, between 70% and 100% of abused infants show insecure attachments with their caregivers (Barnett, Ganiban, & Cicchetti, 1999; Cicchetti, Toth, & Bush, 1988; Wekerle & Wolfe, 2003). When children are abused, the experience can cause physical pain, fear, and anxiety; it can lead to feelings of guilt, shame, and embarrassment in children; and it can disrupt children's social interactions as they try to hide their family secrets from their peers. Childhood abuse may also have a permanent effect on the brain's structure. The limbic system, important for regulating emotion and memory, seems to

**TABLE 7.4**
**Outcomes Associated with Physical Abuse and Neglect**

Physical Abuse:

- physical injuries and death;
- increased aggression and hostility;
- reduced sympathy for others, and increased reactivity to anger in others;
- language delays, poor school performance, lower IQ;
- increased risk of committing violent crimes and other criminal offenses;
- increased risk of low self-esteem, depression, self-destructive behaviors, and suicide.

Neglect:

- lack of stimulation, supervision, and support for schoolwork;
- lower cognitive and academic scores;
- language delays and lower IQ;
- poor impulse control and more dependent on teachers or other adults;
- more passive, shy, and socially withdrawn than other children;
- in general, the effects of neglect tend to be even more strong and damaging than those seen with physical abuse.

Sources: Hoffman-Plotkin & Twentyman, 1984; Kim & Cicchetti, 2006; Main & George, 1985; McCord, 1983; Nelson & Crick, 2002; Pollak, Vardi, Putzer Bechner, & Curtin, 2005; Salzinger, Kaplan, Pelcovitz, Samit, & Krieger, 1984; Wekerle & Wolfe, 2003.

be especially affected. Stress is a toxic agent that can disrupt normal brain development (Teicher, 2002).

As we mentioned before, the different types of maltreatment usually overlap. This adds to the difficulty of determining effects. For example, when a child experiences both physical abuse and neglect, any negative effects could result from the physical abuse alone, the neglect alone, the unique combination of both types of maltreatment, or other factors (such as parenting style) that correlate with them. Individual children also have their own individual reactions to the different types of abuse.

▲ Children who are physically abused sometimes develop compulsive compliance—they try to avoid severe punishment by complying with their parents' every demand.

Although we can't specify the exact effects for any particular child, Table 7.4 summarizes what researchers have generally concluded about the outcomes associated with physical abuse and neglect. We will have more to say about sexual abuse in Chapter 10. Remember that psychological abuse co-occurs with all other types of abuse, making it difficult to separate its effects.

Contrary to popular belief, most abused children do not grow up to be abusers themselves. It is estimated that only about 30% of physically abused or neglected children grow up to abuse or neglect their own children. The remaining 70% develop more positive parenting skills (Kaufman & Zigler, 1989).

An interesting behavior pattern seen among some physically abused children is **compulsive compliance**—ready and quick responses aimed at pleasing adults by complying with their demands and wishes (Crittenden & DiLalla, 1988; Wekerle & Wolfe, 2003). Children who experience physical abuse sometimes become especially watchful of their own behavior, trying hard to avoid doing things that will make their abusive parents angry. Researchers report that this pattern is most noticeable in 1- to 3-year-olds. Most nonabused children this age are testing limits, saying no, and developing their own sense of autonomy (you've heard of the "terrible twos"?). Abused children, in contrast, are working to suppress these behaviors. The long-term effects of compulsive compliance are not yet known, but you can imagine the impact on children's sense of well-being, confidence, and self-esteem.

**compulsive compliance**
A behavior pattern seen among some physically abused children, marked by ready and quick responses aimed at pleasing adults by complying with their demands and wishes.

## Perspective SOCIAL POLICY — PROTECTING CHILDREN FROM NEGLECT

Ana Diaz-DeJesus is a child protection caseworker in Bridgeport, Connecticut. She has a daunting caseload of more than 30 families, including nearly 150 children. Today she is visiting Maria R., a young mother of three children who lives in a filthy apartment with no heat and no food. Maria, a high school dropout and drug user, is raising her children alone on welfare. Moving from one cramped apartment to another, she barely stays ahead of eviction. Landlords, neighbors, and even relatives have called authorities to report that she is using drugs, not caring properly for her children, and living with a man who has a record of molesting children. One of the children had to be hospitalized in a coma after falling while unsupervised. At times the family has lived by candlelight because the electricity was turned off. Over many months Ana has often delivered groceries to the apartment and has arranged numerous services for Maria, including drug counseling, domestic violence counseling, and therapy for the children. Maria has never followed through. As she leaves the apartment this time, Ana prays, "God protect this family" (Gross, 1998, p. 1).

Not far from Bridgeport, in New York City, Sabrina Green was found dead several years ago, having suffered untreated burns, gangrene, and blows to the head. Sabrina was only 9 years old. She was living with her half-sister and ten other children in a small apartment. The half-sister and her boyfriend claimed that Sabrina lit a fire and tried to put it out, resulting in the burns. Police, however, arrested the half-sister and boyfriend and charged them with manslaughter (Sexton & Swarns, 1997). A few years later in the Bronx, Ahsianea Carzan died of apparent malnutrition. Blind and disabled, she was not able to fend for herself. When she was found, her tiny body weighed only 17 pounds. Ahsianea was 5 years old (Bernstein & Chivers, 2000).

Abuse and neglect are a leading cause of death of children under the age of 4. The former secretary of Health and Human Services, Donna Shalala, reported that "children are being hurt more often and more seriously" (Pear, 1996, p. 1). Both Sabrina Green's and Ahsianea Carzan's families had numerous encounters with child protection agencies, but in neither case did the agencies put the child in foster care. Should the authorities have been more aggressive in protecting these children? Some people think so, and cases like these have prompted many child protection agencies to become more willing to remove children from their homes. Agencies once tried to keep families intact as long as possible, but they no longer feel they can allow families so many chances.

Other critics, however, believe that child protection agencies remove children too often. In a scathing opinion, one federal judge wrote that agencies are too quick in removing children from homes in which mothers suffer domestic violence, and one group of parents in New York City filed a class-action lawsuit claiming that child protection workers routinely violate the law by removing children from families when they are not in real danger (Glaberson, 2002; Swarns, 1999).

Meanwhile, in Bridgeport, Ana Diaz-DeJesus continues to do her best to provide support and services to families, taking heart in the glimmers of improvement she sometimes sees. The problems families face are complex, and the answers are never easy. Speaking about caseworkers like Ana, the deputy director of the Child Welfare League of America commented that "what they do is not rocket science—it's way harder than rocket science" (Gross, 1998, p. 1).

**QUESTION** **Where do you think child protection authorities should draw the line between supporting families and removing children? What more can be done to ensure children's safety and well-being in cases where children are left in homes where there are substantiated instances of maltreatment?**

It is virtually impossible to distinguish the direct effects of the abuse from the impacts of all of the other factors that surround these children and families. Abusing families tend to isolate themselves from friends and community, keeping the abuse private. They may move frequently, changing the children's schools and networks of friends. Family conflict and family dysfunction are common, so children may witness other acts of violence or abuse in addition to the maltreatment directed at them. Their homes may be overcrowded, and life may be chaotic and unpredictable. Although most abusers do not have officially diagnosed mental disorders, some do. Often, too, the families live in poverty. By interacting with all of these factors, child abuse and neglect can exact a considerable price.
**Listen** on **mydevelopmentlab**

**Listen**: Why is it so difficult to determine the real effects of child abuse and neglect? (Author Podcast)
www.mydevelopmentlab.com

Abused children are usually trapped and powerless to change their environments. As one researcher put it, "She must find a way to preserve a sense of trust in people who are untrustworthy, safety in a situation that is unsafe, control in a situation that is terrifyingly unpredictable, power in a situation of helplessness" (Herman, 1992). Using cognitive and emotional skills that are not yet mature, abused children must struggle to understand their situations and the complex feelings evoked by them. When it comes to pointing fingers for the blame of child maltreatment, we need to focus on parents' lack of understanding of their children's needs, on the undue stressors many parents face, and on the failure of the society to offer families enough support.

One of the difficult decisions child protection authorities often must make is how severe the abuse or neglect needs to be before they remove children from their homes. To learn more about this heart-wrenching issue, read the Social Policy Perspective box (page 224) called "Protecting Children from Neglect."

How can we prevent child maltreatment? Solutions are not easy and must address multiple factors. One program that has been successful in significantly reducing the rate of child maltreatment is the Title I Child–Parent Center program, which began in the Chicago public schools in 1967. This program offers preschool education for low-income children as well as a variety of services to support entire families. For example, training is offered in parenting skills and job-related skills, and the program actively encourages family involvement in children's schooling. The services are continued until the child weathers the transition to school (until second or third grade). Compared to other children, those who have participated in this program do better in school, have higher rates of graduation, and have lower arrest rates. Their parents are more involved in the children's schooling and have higher expectations for their children's academic achievement. Most important for this discussion, the rate of child maltreatment is significantly lower in these families—about 50% lower than in similar families not in the program (Reynolds, 2000; Reynolds & Robertson, 2003; Reynolds, Temple, Robertson, & Mann, 2001).

**THINK ABOUT THE RODRIGUEZ CHILDREN . . .**

Given what the Rodriguez children experienced, what consequences should Kathy and Rod be most concerned about regarding their development? What are the most likely effects of the way they were treated?

## LET'S REVIEW . . .

1. Between 1 and 4 years of age, the most common cause of death is __________.
   - **a.** homicide
   - **b.** some type of accident
   - **c.** a genetic or prenatal problem
   - **d.** an illness, disease, or other type of medical condition
2. What are teachers, nurses, physicians, childcare workers, and other professionals required to do if they suspect that a child has been abused or neglected?
   - **a.** Ignore it; it's a private family matter.
   - **b.** Interview the child to find out what happened.
   - **c.** Contact the parents to find out what happened.
   - **d.** Report it to police or child protection authorities.
3. Who is most likely to physically abuse or neglect a child?
   - **a.** fathers
   - **b.** mothers
   - **c.** childcare workers
   - **d.** other relatives who care for children
4. School achievement and social withdrawal tend to be the worst for children who suffer __________.
   - **a.** neglect
   - **b.** physical abuse
   - **c.** sexual abuse
   - **d.** psychological abuse
5. True or False: Physical abuse increases the chances that children will use violence to solve their own problems.
6. True or False: Children who are neglected tend to become more dependent on their teachers.

Answers: 1. d, 2. d, 3. b, 4. a, 5. T, 6. T

## THINKING BACK TO THE RODRIGUEZ CHILDREN . . .

Now that you have studied this chapter, you should be able to apply at least a dozen concepts and research findings to the situation faced by the Rodriguez children. These children were severely maltreated. Their biological mother was not able to take proper care of them, and the situation with their foster parents was even worse. The different categories of child maltreatment tend to co-occur. You can see that these children suffered from both physical abuse and neglect, and keep in mind that psychological abuse nearly always exists in cases of physical abuse and neglect. Why did it take so long for these children to get help? Ethically, anyone should report their concerns to authorities if they believe children are being seriously mistreated. Legally, people are required to report their concerns if they interact with the children in any capacity of their job or volunteer work. Unfortunately, too many suspicions about maltreatment go unreported, and the foster-care and child protective services are overloaded.

If the children were malnourished, we would have concerns about their growth and physical development. Being neglected, they may miss physical activities in school and not join sports teams or other exercise programs. If they lacked opportunities for exercise, their gross-motor development may be delayed. We should be more concerned, however, with other health and safety issues. Were they getting proper immunizations and health care? Were their illnesses being checked and treated?

Early childhood is an important time for brain development. Synapses are being pruned at a rapid rate as the brain's circuits become shaped by the child's experiences. Axons are myelinating, and glial cells are proliferating in the brain. Without proper care, nutrition, and stimulation, were these processes compromised for the Rodriguez children? What can be done to keep their brain development on the right track?

These are just a few of the concerns Kathy and Rod should have about their adopted children. The concepts you studied in this chapter can help you think about situations in which young children may not be receiving proper care. We can all use these concepts to better understand how children grow and develop and to help all children have an early childhood that is strong, safe, and healthy.

# 7

## CHAPTER REVIEW . . .

**7.1** How much do children grow during early childhood, and what are the important issues related to childhood nutrition?

At this age, children grow about 2 or 3 inches in height and gain just over 5 pounds, on average, per year. To support healthy growth, children need adequate calories and a balance of proteins, carbohydrates, fats, vitamins, and minerals. Malnutrition can result if the diet lacks enough calories or nutrients for proper growth. In developing countries, many millions of children are malnourished.

**7.2** In what important ways does the brain grow and change during early childhood?

Brain weight increases about 10% between the ages of 2 and 4 and again between the ages of 6 and 8. Glial cells are proliferating, and these specialized cells provide structure, hold neurons together, provide nourishment, form myelin, and perform other important functions in the brain. During early childhood, children lose more synapses than they gain in a process called synaptic pruning.

7.3 How is brain development influenced by experience and interactions with the environment?
Basic human capacities develop via experience-expectant development in which the brain overproduces synapses and then prunes them back using experience and feedback from the environment. The unique skills and knowledge that set each of us apart develop more through experience-dependent development in which new synapses are created to code our experiences.

7.4 What are the larger patterns of development that we see in the brain during this age period?
Lobes of the cerebral cortex continue to develop as more axons become myelinated. Various skills and abilities emerge and improve as brain development proceeds. Areas in the occipital lobes tend to mature earlier, and areas in the frontal lobes tend to mature later.

7.5 What improvements do young children make in the control and coordination of their gross-motor and fine-motor skills?
Motor development tends to proceed in a cephalocaudal (head-to-tail) and a proximodistal (inside-out) direction. Children coordinate their arms before their legs, and they learn to control the larger muscles in the arms before the smaller muscles in the hands and fingers. Experience, exercise, and opportunities to practice are all important in facilitating motor development.

7.6 How physically active are most young children, and how much do children differ in their levels of activity?
Young children get most of their physical exercise when they play. Children tend to burn their energy in quick bursts of activity, and they need frequent breaks to rest. Officials recommend that children get at least 60 minutes of physical activity each day in structured activities and another 60 minutes in free play. Children vary. Most meet these recommendations, although they tend to be engaged in vigorous activity only a small percentage of the time.

7.7 What is cerebral palsy, and what do we know about this condition?
Cerebral palsy is a serious disorder of motor development caused by damage to the brain during prenatal development, during birth, or by head trauma or brain illnesses that occur during infancy or childhood.

7.8 What are the most common causes of death during early childhood, and how can they be prevented?
Relatively speaking, death rates are low during early childhood. Among children ages 1 to 4, diseases, illnesses, and accidents are the most common causes of deaths. Auto accidents, drowning, and fires are the top three causes of accidental deaths. Parents and others are responsible for seeing that young children get proper health care and that they are protected as much as possible from accidental injury and death.

7.9 What is child maltreatment, and what are the different types?
Child maltreatment refers to situations where parents or other persons in charge of a child's well-being harm or neglect the child. Physical abuse, neglect, sexual abuse, and psychological abuse are the major categories of child maltreatment. In 2007 there were 3.2 million reports of child maltreatment, and about 740,000 cases were verified.

7.10 What are the effects of child abuse and neglect?
It is impossible to predict or determine the effects for any particular child. For physical abuse, common problems include aggression, hostility, depression, compulsive compliance, language and cognitive delays, and poor school performance. With neglect, delays in language, intelligence, and academic performance are common.

## REVISITING THEMES

*Nature and nurture* are involved as the body is growing and brain is developing. Malnutrition from a lack of food in the environment can stunt growth (pp. 206–207). Nature and nurture interact as the brain experiences experience-expectant and experience-dependent forms of development (pp. 208–209). Nature and nurture are both also involved in determining the different rates of motor development that children show (pp. 212–213).

*Neuroscience* was discussed extensively in this chapter as we covered the growth and development of the brain (pp. 208–211). When children practice motor skills, they refine connections in the brain (p. 214). Child abuse and neglect, however, can disrupt brain development (pp. 222–225).

*Diversity and multiculturalism* are associated with racial, ethnic, and cross-national differences in the rates of malnutrition (pp. 206–208) and also in the rates of child maltreatment (p. 221). These circumstances are unfortunate and need to be addressed to protect more children.

*Positive development and resilience* are highlighted in the suggestions provided for supporting physical growth of the body and the brain (pp. 204–206), in the suggestions for supporting physical activity and motor skills development (pp. 214–215), in the importance of the IDEA legislation in providing positive opportunities for children with disabilities (p. 216), and in the successful program for addressing child maltreatment in the inner city (p. 225).

## KEY TERMS

cerebral palsy (CP) (216)
child maltreatment (220)
compulsive compliance (223)
experience-dependent development (209)
experience-expectant development (208)
glial cells (208)
Individuals with Disabilities Education Act (IDEA) (216)
infantile amnesia (211)
kwashiorkor (206)
locomotor skills (212)
malnutrition (206)
mature tripod grasp (213)
neglect (220)
palmar grasp (213)
physical abuse (220)
psychological abuse (220)
sexual abuse (220)
synaptic pruning (208)

**"What decisions would you make while raising a child? What would the consequences of those decisions be?"**

Find out by accessing My Virtual Child at
**www.mydevelopmentlab.com**
and raising your own virtual child
from birth to age 18.

Watch Visit your Multimedia Library at www.mydevelopmentlab.com to watch an interview with Sujatha and RK online.

8 EARLY CHILDHOOD

# Cognitive Development in Early Childhood

Four-year-old Ashwin will be starting school soon. His parents Sujatha and RK want to pick the best school for their son, so they have been observing and interviewing teachers and school officials at area public, Montessori, Waldorf, and charter schools. Their top priority is a curriculum that promotes thinking, curiosity, and questioning. They are also looking for teachers who are patient and loving and who have a good background in education.

Given Ashwin's behavior and knowledge of letters and numbers, they're sure he is ready for school. They want to make sure that school will challenge Ashwin but not push him too much—they want him to learn out of his own willingness and love for learning. It is also important that the school have art activities and chances for Ashwin to work cooperatively with other children. They believe these activities help develop creativity, offer a chance to express thoughts, and help teach sharing and how to function in a group.

Sujatha and RK both speak their native language of Tamil, and they want their son to continue to learn this language as well as English. They don't expect that their language will be taught at any schools in their area, so they are planning to continue teaching it to Ashwin at home. Sujatha and RK hope the general school environment will support their son being bilingual. At the same time, they don't want learning two languages to interfere with Ashwin's schoolwork and with his mastering English. They'd also like Ashwin to be able to learn other languages at school.

What should Sujatha and RK look for when visiting schools and teachers? What kinds of classroom activities and teaching methods would best foster their son's cognitive development? Will learning two languages interfere with Ashwin's work at school, or will it give him some cognitive advantages?

After studying this chapter, you should be able to identify several important factors that Sujatha and RK should consider. You will know the kinds of educational philosophy and practices that support and stimulate Ashwin's cognitive growth. You will also learn the important aspects of language development that occur in early childhood, including the effects of learning two languages. As you work through this chapter, create a list of at least twelve concepts that might relate to Sujatha and RK's situation. Explain how they could use each concept to identify the best educational environment for their son.

As you read this chapter, look for the "Think About Sujatha and RK . . ." questions that ask you to consider what you're learning from their perspective.

*(Continued)*

The situation Sujatha and RK face is not uncommon. All of us who work with children need to understand cognitive development so that we can advocate for children, recognize their strengths and limitations, and provide stimulating academic and intellectual environments. As you learned in Chapters 4 and 7, children experience tremendous physical changes from birth through early childhood. Less visible but just as important are the enormous changes in children's thinking during these years. In this chapter, we revisit the theory of Jean Piaget to see how he described cognitive development during the early childhood period. We also introduce you to one of his contemporaries—the Soviet psychologist, Lev Vygotsky—who offered a different view of how young children build their knowledge and understanding of the world. Then we cover the more modern perspective offered by the information-processing approach. We end the chapter by exploring language development in early childhood and discussing the issues of early childhood education and kindergarten readiness.

## Piaget's Stage 2: Preoperational Thought

As you saw in Chapter 5, the Swiss psychologist Jean Piaget was very influential in shaping how we think about children's thinking. As toddlers emerge from Piaget's first stage (sensorimotor thought), they are beginning to use their minds to create mental representations that symbolize the objects and events they see in the world. During the early childhood years (roughly ages 3 through 6), children fall into Piaget's second stage: **preoperational thought**. In Stage 2, children can use mental representations to think about objects and events, even when the objects and events are not physically available to see, hear, and touch. According to Piaget, 3-month-old infants, for example, can't think about a toy unless they grab, shake, or mouth the toy. Grabbing, shaking, and mouthing are ways of thinking to a sensorimotor infant. By 3 years of age, however, children can internalize their understanding of the toy and think about it even when it is not physically available. They can remember what the toy looked like yesterday, they can imagine playing with it in a way they have never tried before, and they can even imagine what it tastes like without needing to put it in their mouths. Children's use of mental representations flourishes during this stage of preoperational thought, and Piaget claimed that children also begin to use intuitive logic in their thinking. We describe both of these trends in the next section.

As you will see shortly, children in Stage 2 are still not using full logic in their thinking. In Piaget's theory, **operations** are logical processes that can be reversed. If you pour liquid into a different container, for example, it is logical that you can reverse the process and pour it back into the original container. This logic seems obvious to you as an adult, but Piaget believed that children don't learn this type of logic until they reach middle childhood and Stage 3. During Stage 2, children do not think with *operations,* so Piaget called this level of thought *preoperational.* Explore on mydevelopmentlab

Explore Piaget's Stages of Cognitive Development. www.mydevelopmentlab.com

AS YOU STUDY THIS SECTION, ASK YOURSELF THESE QUESTIONS:

**8.1** What evidence of Stage 2 thinking do we see in children's language, art, and play?

**8.2** What is *intuitive thinking* and what are some examples of this?

**8.3** What do Piaget's conservation problems tell us about children's thinking?

**8.4** How has Piaget's theory influenced how teachers and others think about children's learning?

**preoperational thought**
Thought characterized by the use of mental representations (symbols) and intuitive thought.

**operations**
Logical processes that can be reversed.

### Flourishing Mental Representations

During the preoperational stage children will practice, and even playfully exaggerate, their new mental representation abilities. Let's look at the representations, or symbols, they use in language, art, and play.

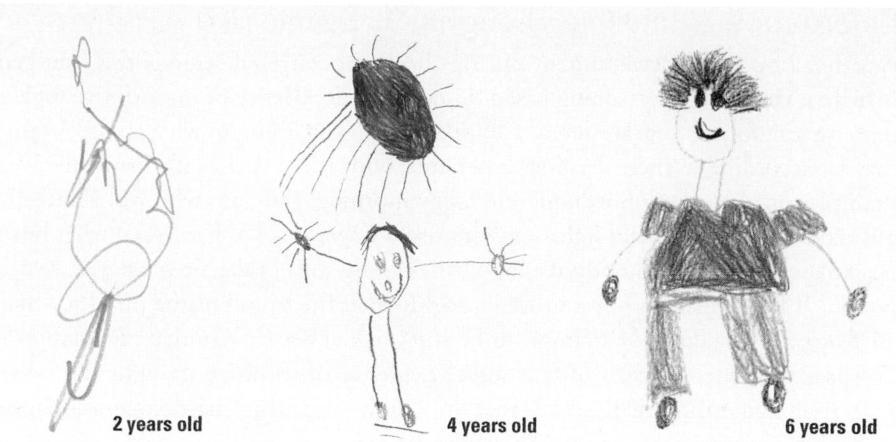


◀ FIGURE 8.1
**Artwork Showing the Development of Mental Representations**
The 2-year-old's drawing of a person is just a scribble. At age 4 the child draws the person as a happy head with arms and legs. By age 6, the body is represented more fully, including the neck and torso. What do these drawings tell us about the developing mental representation of what a person is?

Symbols in Language. Talk to a child who is just turning 2, and the conversation will be pretty simple and limited to objects and events currently present. Talk to a 4-year-old, however, and you'll find yourself engaged in a real conversation! As we discuss later in this chapter, there is an explosive increase in children's language ability after the age of 2 (Anglin, 1993; Ganger & Brent, 2004). What makes this rapid escalation of linguistic skill possible? According to Piaget, language development is based on children's mental representational ability—their ability to let a symbol (e.g., a word) stand for an object in the environment. This ability gives children a way to communicate about the objects in the environment, even when the objects are not actually present. Because children are actively constructing their own language (look back to Chapter 5 for our discussion of constructivism), they often create their own inventive words and phrases. A young child may call a blanket a "winkie," describe a person with short hair as having "little hair," or say that a criminal is "under arrested."

▲ The ability to form mental representations allows these children to use fantasy and symbolism in their play. Using mental symbols, children can escape the reality of the here and now and pretend to be superheroes on exciting adventures in far-off places.

Symbols in Art. Preoperational children's increasing ability to use mental representation is also seen clearly in the art they produce. When one of our daughters was 3 years old, she drew a heavy black horizontal line above a bright red horizontal line. "Look, Mom, I made a picture of you!" she said. "See, there's your head, and your hair on top, and that's your favorite red shirt!" What parent has not admired evidence of mental representation in his or her child? To produce such artwork, the child must have mental representations—not only of the mother's face and hair, for example, but also of her favorite red shirt. Though the initial scribbles of 3-year-olds may not resemble any real object to an adult, they are evidence that the child has developed mental representation. Figure 8.1 exhibits drawings made by children of various ages; you can easily trace the development of more accurate and more complex mental representations in these drawings.

Symbols in Play. Watch children engaged in play and you will soon see clear evidence of symbol use. In *symbolic play,* children use one object to stand for another, such as when they pretend that a blanket is a magic carpet or a banana is a telephone. Children of 18 months seldom show such symbolic play; for example, they'll pretend to talk on a telephone only when they have in hand a quite realistic-looking toy telephone. By the age of 2, children will use objects far less similar to the real item, such as using a banana for a telephone. Finally, by 5 years of age children are capable of using practically anything as a pretend "telephone." Their ability to mentally represent objects has progressed to the point that the symbol no longer has to bear any resemblance to the real thing (Corrigan, 1987; O'Reilly, 1995). Preoperational children use a lot of make-believe and fantasy in their play; we have a lot more to say about children's play in Chapter 9.

How would language, art, and play activities be important in Ashwin's preschool and kindergarten classrooms? Explain.

▲ FIGURE 8.2
**The Three-Mountains Task**
What would the doll see? Can children describe the perspective that would be seen from a different location? (Boyd & Bee, 2006).

## Emergence of Intuitive Thought: "It *Seems* Like . . ."

Another important development during the preoperational stage is the emergence of **intuitive thought**, or reasoning based on personal experience or on intuitive logic rather than on any formal logical system. Children reason according to what things "seem like," that is, according to their personal experience with the objects and events involved. For example, on the way to preschool one foggy morning, our son, who was about 3½ years old, said, "Better turn your lights on—it's really *froggy* out." When asked what he meant, he explained that he had noticed a lot of this cloudy stuff in the air whenever we drove by ponds. "I know that frogs live in water, so when all the frogs breathe out, they make the air froggy." An admirable attempt, to be sure, but our son's intuitive explanation would not pass the objective tests of true logic. Evidence of intuitive thought can be seen in several characteristics of thinking that are common during the preoperational period, including *egocentrism*, *animism*, and *artificialism*.

Piaget used the term **egocentrism** to refer to a young child's inability to take another person's perspective. To young children it does seem that they are the center of the universe, and it seems that everyone must think about things just the way they do. Preoperational children are not able to understand that other people's perspectives might be different from their own. The classic demonstration of egocentrism is the three-mountain task. As pictured in Figure 8.2, experimenters show children a model of three mountains that have landmarks placed among them. A child sits at one location in relation to the mountains, and a doll sits at another location. The experimenter then asks the child to describe what the doll would see from its location. Preschool children typically describe the scene as they view it from their own location. Further, when given photographs depicting the views from each location around the table, children select the photos showing the view from their own locations, not the doll's (Piaget & Inhelder, 1948/1956). In other words, children select views based on their own personal and intuitive experience with the scene. They don't yet take into account the logical necessity that someone viewing the scene from a different place will have a different perspective. In other examples of egocentrism, children often think that the people they talk to on the telephone can see them, and they believe that their parents know what they are thinking and even know what they dream at night ("I saw my dream, why can't you?"). **Watch** on **mydevelopmentlab**

**Watch** a video on Egocentrism.
www.mydevelopmentlab.com

**Animism**—the idea that inanimate objects have conscious life and feelings—is typical of the preoperational stage (Piaget, 1929, 1930, 1951). For example, children may say that the sun is shining brightly because "it's happy," or they may put their pencil down because "it's tired." **Artificialism** is the notion that natural events or objects (e.g., the sun, moon, rain, hurricanes) are under the control of people or of superhuman agents. A child might say that the sun went down because someone switched it off, or that the moon isn't shining because someone blew it out. As children's cognitive structures encounter more and more instances in which animism and artificialism do not satisfactorily explain events, they begin to move away from these modes of intuitive thought and gradually move toward explanations based on physical facts and on a more objective logic.

THINKING CRITICALLY
Identify examples of egocentrism, animism, or artificialism from your own past or from your experiences with children you know. What prompted changes in that thinking?

## Conservation Problems

The most famous examples of preoperational thought come from children's answers to Piaget's *conservation problems.* Piaget used the term **conservation** to refer to the concept that certain basic properties of an object (e.g., volume, mass, and weight) remain the same even if its physical appearance changes (Ginsburg & Opper, 1988; Piaget, 1952, 1969, 1970; Piaget & Inhelder, 1974). **Watch** on **mydevelopmentlab**

**Watch** a video on Conservation.
www.mydevelopmentlab.com

For example, look at the liquid conservation problem shown in Figure 8.3. An experimenter fills two identical beakers with liquid to the same level, as shown on the left. The experimenter asks the child, "Do these two have the same amount of liquid, or does one have more?" The child says that they have the same amount. Then, with the child watching, the experimenter pours the contents of one beaker into a taller and skinnier beaker. When asked if the two beakers "have the same amount, or does one have more?," younger children typically claim that the taller beaker has more liquid than the shorter beaker. When asked why, they usually point to the height of the liquid surface: "See, this one is taller, so it has more." Children using preoperational thought don't seem to understand that the volume of liquid is conserved (remains the same) even though the shape of the container changes. Children give similar responses for problems involving number and mass (see Figure 8.3).

Looking at Figure 8.3, you can see why preoperational children's tendency to use intuitive thought would lead them astray. At a quick glance, it does "seem like" the taller beaker has more. Piaget, however, analyzed children's responses further and was able to pinpoint other important limitations of preoperational thought.

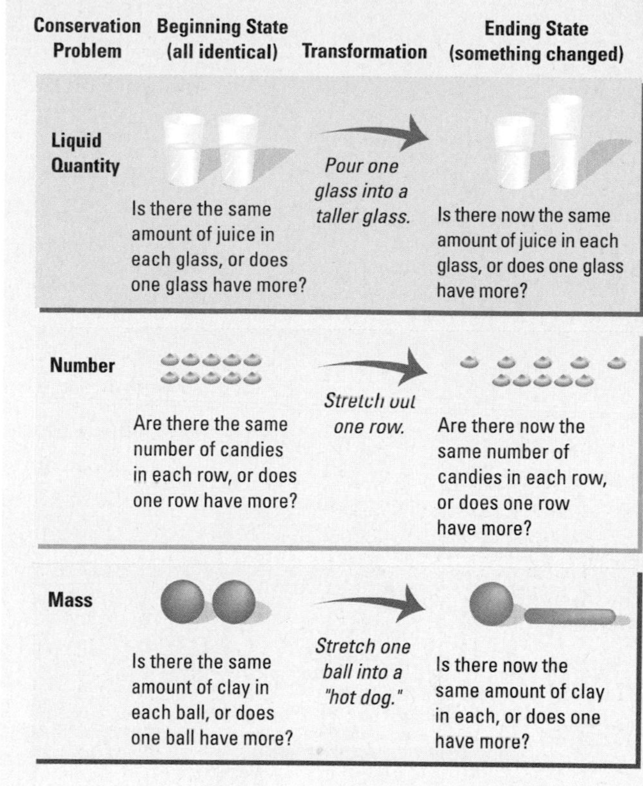


▲ FIGURE 8.3
**Conservation Problems**
Three well-known conservation problems involve liquid quantity (top), number (middle), and mass (bottom).

- First, young children show *centration* in their thinking. Centration is the tendency to focus on only one aspect of a situation at a time instead of taking several aspects into consideration. In the liquid problem, for example, children tend to focus on the height of the liquid instead of considering that the greater width of one beaker compensates for the taller height of the other.
- Second, young children focus on the *static endpoints* of the transformation (how things look before and after) rather than considering what happened in the transformation itself. Children look at the beginning state (both levels are equal on the left side of Figure 8.3), then at the ending state (one level is higher on the right side), and they conclude that the higher level must have more. They fail to consider the transformation itself—it is actually the act of pouring that shows that the amount of liquid did not change.
- Finally, children at this stage lack a grasp of *reversibility*. That is, they do not imagine what would happen if they reversed the transformation; they don't visualize pouring the liquid back into its original container to demonstrate that the amount would still be the same. Remember, their thought is *preoperational* at this stage—they don't visualize the reversible operation of pouring the liquid back.

When children focus on the height of the liquid, pay attention only to the static endpoints of the problem, and don't imagine pouring the liquid back, you can see why they usually reach such an intuitive answer as "this one is taller, so it has more."

Piaget saw the lack of mental reversibility as an important hallmark of preoperational thought. To be fully logical, our cognitive structures need to be reversible. Think about the logic of math, for example. If we have 4 and take 2 away, we need to understand that we can return to 4 by adding 2 back. Piaget believed that these dynamic mental operations were necessary for true logical thought. After continued experience with the environment, children realize that their intuitive thought does not adequately explain the events around them. As they realize the reversibility of many transformations and their thought structures become operational (reversible), we have the beginnings of the next stage of cognitive development. We will describe Stage 3 in Chapter 11.

**intuitive thought**
Thought and logic that is based on a child's personal experience rather than on a formal system of rules.

**egocentrism**
The child's inability to take another person's perspective.

**animism**
The idea that inanimate objects have conscious life and feelings.

**artificialism**
The notion that natural events or objects are under the control of people or of superhuman agents.

**conservation**
The understanding that some basic properties of objects remain the same even when a transformation changes the physical appearance.

## Piaget and Education

Before moving away from this topic, we want to make a few observations about Piaget's influence on the field of education. We note three general points about his influence.

- First, the notion of the child as an active and curious organism led to the design of interactive and hands-on curricula in schools and early childhood settings. These teaching materials encourage children to make use of their natural curiosity to explore concepts in science, mathematics, and other domains.
- Second, Piaget believed that children cannot skip stages but must move from one to another as their nervous systems biologically mature and they become cognitively ready. His stage ideas have shaped many guidelines for when to introduce different topics in schools.
- Third, educators have learned to make use of Piaget's ideas about schemes, assimilation, accommodation, disequilibrium, reflective abstraction, and similar topics (look back to Chapter 5). They do this by deliberately presenting children with puzzles,

## Perspective PROFESSIONAL — CAREER FOCUS: MEET A CONSTRUCTIVIST TEACHER

Stacie Anderson
Donnelsville, OH
First grade teacher at Donnelsville Elementary School

**How do you use Piagetian concepts in your teaching?**
It is critical to have an idea of the preexisting schemes that students already have on a topic or skill area—it sets the stage for how I introduce a lesson. Next, I observe children's thought processes as a new concept, or a new layer of the concept, is introduced. How is it fitting (assimilating) into what they already know? I check to see how the new information is fitting by asking questions and having children evaluate their own thinking and each other's responses.

**What specific activities do you use to help children construct knowledge?**
Hands-on activities are critical in first grade, and all grades in my estimation. When teaching geometric shapes, I have children sort out squares, circles, and triangles, and list what they know about each shape (the square has four sides, four corners, etc.). Then I show a rectangle and ask, "How many sides and angles does it have?" "Is it a square?" Some children will say "Yes." As we take a closer look, they recognize that the sides are different lengths. Now they understand that squares have four equal sides, but rectangles have two side lengths. Then we introduce a parallelogram, rhombus, trapezoid. . . . With counting, students build towers with Unifix cubes to represent each numeral (1 to 10). They observe that "It looks like stairs!" and "Every tower is one taller." They can visually see that each tower is one greater than the other, and this smoothly leads into the concept of adding one.

**How do you use Piaget's stages as guidelines for your curriculum or classroom activities?**
At the district level, we created benchmarks and indicators of success in critical skill areas. However, based on my experience, it is important to know that a child can exhibit various behaviors that are indicative of several of these stages. Still, first graders do think more concretely and have difficulty thinking beyond their home, family, and friends. It would be unrealistic to tackle national abstract issues with 6-year-olds!

**What education and training is required to work in your area?**
To be a licensed teacher, you need to have a degree or courses in education, and you need to be supervised as a student teacher for one year. The requirements differ in each state. Many states require teachers to get a master's degree to have a permanent teaching license, and others require an advanced degree to teach above the third grade. A praxis exam is required in most states.

QUESTION **Which concepts from Piaget's theory do you see Stacie using? Explain why her approach is considered to be a constructivist approach.**

debates, and conflicting opinions to intentionally challenge children's existing cognitive structures and to encourage children to grow in understanding. Educators encourage students to think about the implications, usefulness, and limitations of their existing cognitive structures.

To learn more about how teachers use Piaget's theory to help children learn, read the Professional Perspective box called "Career Focus: Meet a Constructivist Teacher."

## LET'S REVIEW . . .

1. According to Piaget, when children move from Stage 1 to Stage 2 in cognitive development, they begin to rely more on __________ in their thinking.
   **a.** sensorimotor impressions
   **b.** mental representations
   **c.** abstract thought
   **d.** true logic
2. As children get older, their drawings of people and other objects become more accurate and realistic. According to Piaget, this happens mostly because:
   **a.** their hand-eye coordination is improving.
   **b.** their perceptual systems are getting more accurate.
   **c.** their mental representations are maturing.
   **d.** they are relying more on sensorimotor impressions.
3. Jimmy watches as you take two identical clay balls and roll one into the shape of a hot dog. You then ask him if both pieces of clay now have the same amount, or if one piece has more clay. Jimmy points to the hot dog and responds, "This one has more because it is longer." By focusing his answer on the length of the hot dog, Jimmy is showing an example of __________.
   **a.** reversibility **b.** centration
   **c.** egocentrism **d.** transitivity
4. A 3-year-old thinks that the leaves blowing in a tree are waving "bye-bye." This is an example of __________.
   **a.** animism **b.** artificialism
   **c.** egocentrism **d.** reversibility
5. True or False: When a child gives the correct answer to conservation problems, it is a sign that the child is now in the stage of preoperational thought.
6. True or False: Piaget's theory has motivated educators to emphasize hands-on curricula and active learning in schools.

Answers: 1. b, 2. c, 3. b, 4. a, 5. F, 6. T

# Vygotsky's Sociocultural View of Cognitive Development

Of course, not everyone was satisfied with Piaget's account of cognitive development. Some theorists and practitioners have long felt that Piaget's account does not adequately consider one very important influence on cognition: the child's social environment. Lev Vygotsky is one theorist who gave the role of social interaction and culture a central place in his account of cognitive development.

AS YOU STUDY THIS SECTION, ASK YOURSELF THESE QUESTIONS:

**8.5** How does Vygotsky's own cultural background relate to the emphasis on culture and social interaction in his theory?

**8.6** What role does language play in cognitive development?

**8.7** According to Vygotsky's theory, how can adults facilitate children's development?

▲ Soviet psychologist Lev Vygotsky proposed a sociocultural theory of cognitive development that continues to gain prominence. Can you see the influence of Vygotsky's own cultural background in his theory?

**8.8** What is the zone of proximal development, and why is it important for understanding cognitive development?

**8.9** How do scaffolding and collaborative learning contribute to cognitive development?

## Vygotsky's Background: The Sociocultural Context for a New Theory

Vygotsky was born in 1896, the same year as Piaget but in Belorussia (later part of the Soviet Union). Vygotsky's family was Jewish, and they shared a rich cultural background with most of their fellow townspeople. Being Jewish, they also experienced prejudice, discrimination, and strict governmental restrictions. Vygotsky received his early education from a private tutor who taught by means of Socratic dialogue. In this method, the tutor poses questions and helps the student reason through and figure out answers rather than simply giving the student facts and information. Vygotsky graduated from the University of Moscow in 1917, the year of the Russian Revolution in which the centuries-old tsarist government fell and Vladimir Lenin came to power at the head of a new Marxist government. The new Soviet government seemed to promise an end to ethnic and religious discrimination, stating that everyone would be considered an equal Soviet citizen. Vygotsky was a committed Marxist; in particular, he was a firm believer in Marx's emphasis on the importance of social history as an influence on people's behavior and development (Kozulin, 1990; Wertsch, 1985).

In 1924 Vygotsky took a position at Moscow's prestigious Psychological Institute to help restructure the institute and develop a Marxist psychology. Over the next decade this so-called "Mozart of psychology" (Toulmin, 1978) attracted many top Soviet scholars as students and colleagues to assist in developing and testing his theoretical ideas. Unfortunately, in 1934 Vygotsky died from tuberculosis. Although he was only 38, he had already written several important books and other articles, and his brilliance was recognized by all of those who worked around him (Kozulin, 1990; Wertsch, 1985).

It might seem that such a popular figure as Vygotsky would have had an immediate impact on psychology worldwide. He did not. Much of his writing was not published, even in the Soviet Union, until decades after his death. In part this was because the research to support Vygotsky's ideas had to be completed by his students after his death. Also, even as his followers completed the work, the Soviet regime banned much of it. Vygotsky often referenced foreign scientists, philosophers, and literary works, but officials in the Soviet government saw the influence of foreigners as undesirable. For two decades, therefore, few Soviet psychologists had access to Vygotsky's work. In addition, the cold war meant that there was little hope for dissemination to Western European and American psychologists. Josef Stalin (the successor to Lenin as the Soviet leader) died in 1953 and Vygotsky's work began to be published again. After the cold war ended, Vygotsky's influence on psychology steadily increased in the United States and around the world (Kozulin, 1990; Wertsch, 1985).

**social speech**
Speech that we hear as people talk around us or to us.

**private speech**
Speech that children say aloud to themselves; later internalized to form inner speech and mental activity.

**internalization**
The process of taking external speech and making it internal and mental.

**mediation**
The process adults and more skilled peers use to introduce concepts and cognitive structures to less skilled children.

**zone of proximal development (ZPD)**
The distance between the current maximum independent performance level of the child and the tasks the child can perform if guided by adults or more capable peers.

## The Role of Speech and Language

The central theme in Vygotsky's theory is that children acquire cognitive structures from their culture and from their social interactions, primarily by listening to the language they hear around them. **Social speech** is the speech that we hear as people talk around us or to us. According to Vygotsky, children adopt important parts of social speech and make it their own **private speech**—the speech children say aloud to themselves. It is the language (speech) that carries the concepts and cognitive structures to the child, and these concepts become the "psychological tools" that the child will use (Vygotsky, 1962).

Consider the simple example of a young girl learning to draw a circle. At first the child has no concept of *circle,* so the adult uses social speech to talk her through the process. "Start your mark going around, like this [demonstrating an arc], then bring it all the way around until the marks meet each other." As the child tries to draw her own circle, she repeats the instructions aloud to herself, "I make the mark go 'round, like this, then I bring it 'round 'til it meets." The concept of *circle* was carried from the social speech (of the adult directing the child) to the private speech of the child.

Almost all children use private speech. When children are learning new concepts or difficult tasks, they often rely on the support of private speech, and the children who use private speech the most tend to be the ones who perform best in difficult tasks (Al-Namlah, Fernyhough, & Meins, 2006). **Internalization** is the process by which external activity and speech become internal and come to be executed mentally. As children master a concept, they need private speech less and less. Eventually they internalize it completely as silent, inner speech. Private speech does not simply disappear forever, however. Have you ever found yourself mumbling or talking out loud when you are working on something that is complex or difficult? Private speech seems to help all of us focus our attention, regulate our strategies, and plan our problem-solving efforts (Behrend, Rosengren, & Perlmutter, 1992; Berk, 1992; Berk & Spuhl, 1995; Emerson & Miyake, 2003; Schneider, 2002).

THINK ABOUT SUJATHA AND RK . . .
According to Vygotsky's theory, why would it be important for Sujatha and RK to spend time in the schools and classrooms listening to the verbal messages being conveyed?

THINKING CRITICALLY
Try to remember the last time that you mumbled or talked aloud to yourself when you were trying to do something difficult or challenging. How did your private speech help?

## Mediation: With a Little Help from Your Friends

In Vygotsky's theory, interpersonal interactions with adults or more-skilled peers teach, or *mediate,* the cognitive structures created in the larger culture. **Mediation** is the process of introducing concepts, knowledge, skills, and strategies to the child (Karpov & Haywood, 1998; Vygotsky, 1981). For the mediating adult, mediation involves choosing which structures to introduce to the child, deciding when and how to teach them, and helping the child understand their usefulness. For example, think about helping a young child put together a jigsaw puzzle. Many adults encourage specific puzzle-making strategies such as starting with the corners, doing the borders first, or looking for clues (e.g., matching colors, matching shapes). In addition, adults often help children think about more general skills, such as being careful when matching shapes and colors or being systematic when trying a piece in different locations. However, most adults do not try to introduce all of these things at the same time. They mediate by selecting specific strategies and highlighting them; they help the child learn a few skills, then move on to others as the child gains expertise. Gradually the child internalizes all of the strategies, along with the verbal labels for them. In the end the child can use this information as a structure and tackle jigsaw puzzles independently.

▲ How do adults provide mediation for children's learning?

Mediation can take place in structured settings (such as during formal schooling) or in informal day-to-day activities (such as when a parent talks about ecology while putting out the trash and recyclables). The key to making mediation effective is to tailor it to an appropriate level for the individual child. The structures being explained should be neither so easy that the child has already internalized them nor so difficult that the child cannot understand them. This optimal level of difficulty lies within what Vygotsky called the child's *zone of proximal development.* **Listen** on **mydevelopmentlab**

**Listen**: What exactly is a *mediator*? (Author Podcast)
www.mydevelopmentlab.com

## The Zone of Proximal Development

Vygotsky defined the **zone of proximal development (ZPD)** as the distance between a child's "actual developmental level as determined by independent problem solving" and the child's level of "potential development as determined through problem solving under adult guidance or in collaboration with more capable peers" (Vygotsky, 1978, p. 86). The ZPD refers to the range of problems a child can solve if given some assistance. As shown

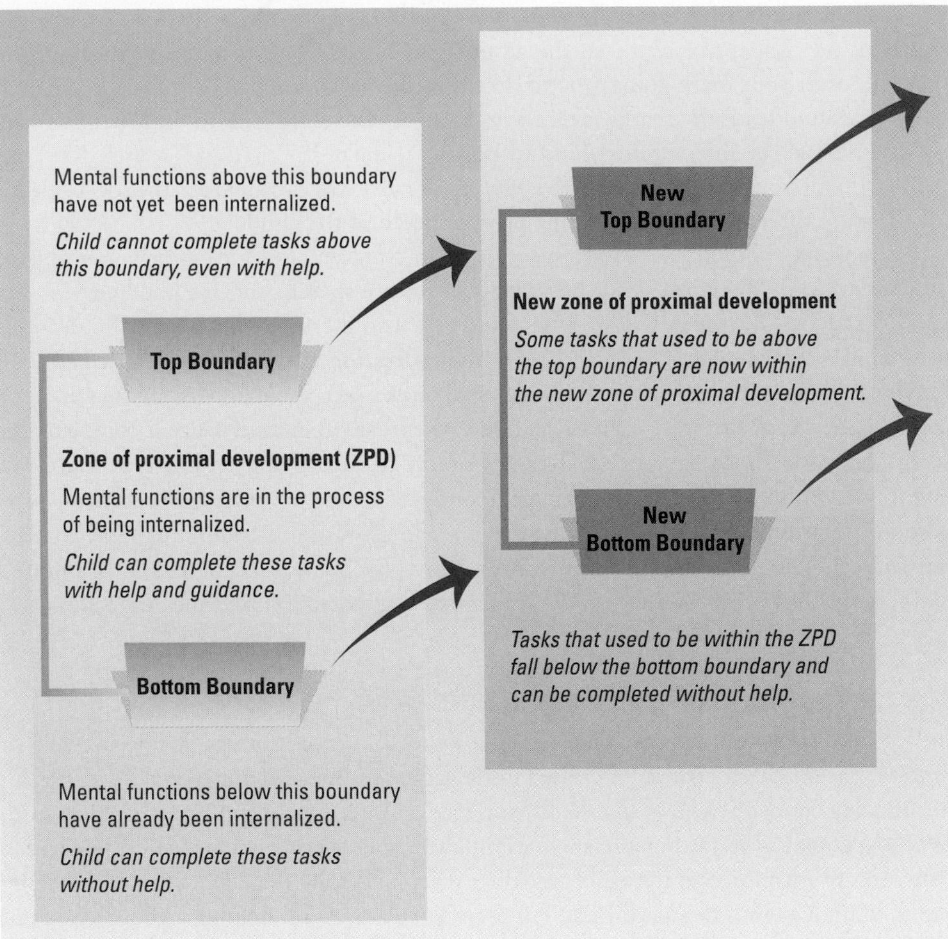


FIGURE 8.4 ▶ **The Zone of Proximal Development** The range of tasks a child is capable of completing with help and guidance defines the zone of proximal development. The bottom boundary is defined by tasks the child already can complete independently. The top is defined by tasks the child cannot complete even with help. The zone changes with development, and both boundaries move up as more mental functions are internalized. As a result, tasks that used to be above the top boundary are within the child's zone; tasks that used to be within the zone become too easy and fall below the bottom boundary.

in Figure 8.4, the bottom boundary of the ZPD consists of the most challenging problems a child can already solve independently. The top boundary of the ZPD consists of problems that the child cannot solve, no matter how much support others may offer. These tasks require higher mental functions that the child has not yet begun to internalize, so even very explicit assistance does not help. The ZPD is the zone between these two boundaries. The tasks within this zone require mental functions that the child is in the process of internalizing but has not yet completely internalized.

An important point to remember about the ZPD is that it is dynamic—the top and bottom boundaries change as the child internalizes more and more mental functions (see Figure 8.4). The boundaries move up as the natural result of effective mediation within the ZPD. An adult interacts with a child, presenting problems that challenge the child. The adult helps the child work through the problem, sometimes needing to offer a great deal of assistance at first. The child gradually learns how to solve these challenging problems. Now some of the problems that used to be within the child's ZPD are below it.

THINK ABOUT SUJATHA AND RK . . .

What could Sujatha and RK look for that would indicate that Ashwin would be appropriately challenged within his zone of proximal development? What kinds of mediation might teachers provide?

There is an important implication here for instruction—can you see what it is? According to Vygotsky, the most effective instruction involves giving children *challenging material,* along with *help in mastering it.* Although children may need extensive help at first, Vygotsky said that challenging tasks promote cognitive development, as long as a given task is not beyond the top boundary of a given child's ZPD. There is a related implication for assessment, or testing. That is, the most informative assessments are not tests of independent performance but tests of assisted performance. Such tests "take stock not only of . . . the processes of maturation that are completed" but also of "processes that are now in the state of coming into being, that are only ripening, or only developing" (Vygotsky, 1956, p. 448).

## Scaffolding and Collaborative Learning

If mediation within the ZPD is so important, how do adults and other helpers do it? Scaffolding, a concept that has grown from Vygotsky's theory, helps answer this question. **Scaffolding** is providing supportive help when a child is developing a mental function or learning to do a particular task (Wood, Bruner, & Ross, 1976; Wood & Middleton, 1975; Wood, Wood, & Middleton, 1978). Think about a building being constructed, and picture the supports that the builders set up during the construction process. These scaffolds support the workers until they complete the building. Cognitive scaffolds do exactly the same thing—they provide support for children (the "workers") as they develop the cognitive processes (the "building") needed for a particular task. Scaffolding takes place during mediation, and it can take many different forms such as doing part of a task for the child, simplifying difficult parts, talking the child through the task, or giving reminders. Any of these actions can help children complete the task and therefore assist them as they develop the necessary processes. Just as with a physical scaffold on a building, however, a cognitive scaffold is not meant to be permanent. It is a *temporary supportive structure,* meant to be gradually removed as the child's mental functions mature.

Children can also receive scaffolding and mediation from their peers. Collaborative learning is a natural outgrowth of Vygotsky's theory. With **collaborative learning**, children can work together to help one another solve problems, share their knowledge and skills, and discuss their strategies and knowledge (Gillies, 2003; Ginsburg-Block, Rohrbeck, & Fantuzzo, 2006; Slavin, 1995; Slavin, Cheung, Groff, & Lake, 2008; Slavin & Lake, 2008; Zimbardo, Butler, & Wolfe, 2003). Remember that Vygotsky emphasized that cognitive development is driven by social interaction, and that a more capable peer can be an effective mediator. Children who are struggling to learn a new concept can benefit by interacting with other children who have already grasped the concept. As with any other form of mediation, however, a collaborative learning experience must take place within each individual child's ZPD if it is to be effective.

Vygotsky would surely be delighted that his ideas have influenced the way we view cognitive development. He would be especially glad that his ideas have made a difference in educational practice. Remember that he lived in a tumultuous time, experiencing extraordinary social and intellectual upheavals. He saw firsthand how cultures and societies

**THINKING CRITICALLY**
Identify some of the scaffolds you have been offered in this textbook or in this class. Explain how they have supported your learning.

**THINK ABOUT SUJATHA AND RK . . .**
If Sujatha and RK observe children working together in groups, would this be a sign that the learning environment is conducive to cognitive development? Explain.

**scaffolding**
Support given to a child as he or she develops a new mental function or learns to perform a particular task.

**collaborative learning**
Process where children work together to help one another solve problems, share their knowledge and skills, and discuss their strategies and knowledge.

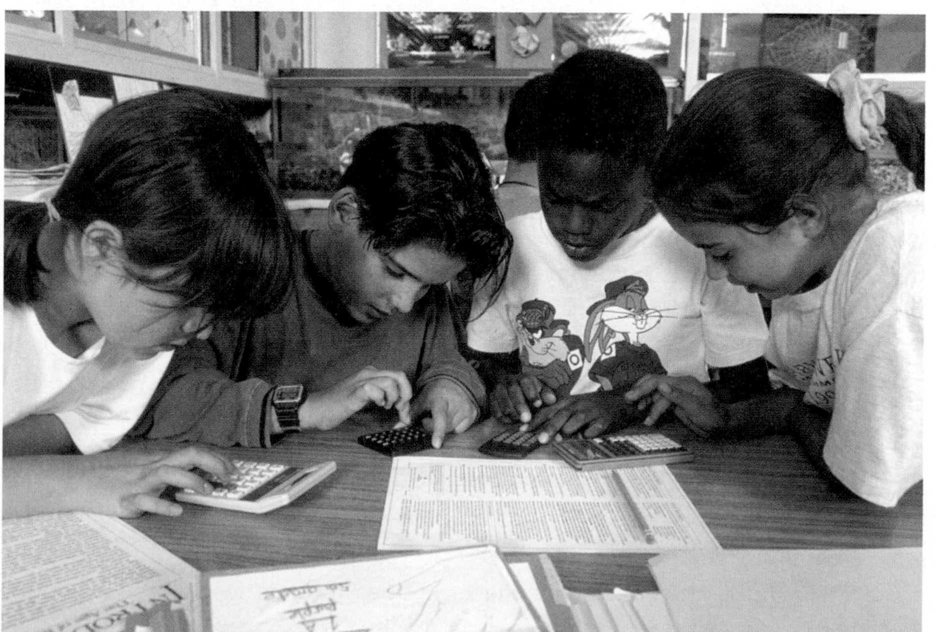

◀ Can you see Vygotsky's sociocultural theory at work in this collaborative learning group? Use the concepts of social speech, mediation, zone of proximal development (ZPD), and scaffolding to explain why peer collaboration can be an effective way for children to learn.

change over time, and he believed that such changes have a powerful influence on cognitive development. We can see that influence when we compare Vygotsky to Piaget. Piaget grew up in Switzerland, a country that prides itself on autonomy and independence; he theorized that children construct their own cognitive structures as they learn to adapt to the environment. For Piaget, the child's own experiences are primary. For Vygotsky, however, the words of the community are primary. Vygotsky believed in the collectivist philosophy of the communist Soviet Union; he proposed that children learn by adopting the cognitive structures offered by the important people—and the larger community—around the child.

**LET'S REVIEW . . .**

1. According to Vygotsky, children's thought structures develop from:
   - **a.** the language they hear around them.
   - **b.** their attempts to modify their own internal schemes.
   - **c.** their own experimentation with characteristics in the environment.
   - **d.** the biological maturation of their nervous systems.
2. When Jeremy was doing his math homework, he could be heard mumbling aloud: "I carry the 6, so that makes this 6 plus 3 equals 9." According to Vygotsky, Jeremy just gave us an example of __________.
   - **a.** social speech
   - **b.** private speech
   - **c.** inner speech
   - **d.** internalized speech
3. According to Vygotsky's theory, it is best if teachers design educational programs that work:
   - **a.** just below a child's zone of proximal development.
   - **b.** just above a child's zone of proximal development.
   - **c.** within a child's zone of proximal development.
   - **d.** against a child's zone of proximal development.
4. In contrast to Piaget, Vygotsky placed a greater emphasis on the role of __________ in children's cognitive development.
   - **a.** math and logic
   - **b.** biology and genetics
   - **c.** social interaction and language
   - **d.** the child's own subjective interpretation
5. True or False: In Vygotsky's theory, the purpose of mediation is to prevent children from internalizing new concepts.
6. True or False: In Vygotsky's theory, scaffolds are the support structures that adults and other people provide to help a child learn a difficult task.

Answers: 1. a, 2. b, 3. c, 4. c, 5. F, 6. T

# Information Processing

Jean Piaget's theory was the dominant view of cognitive development for several decades. Researchers in the 1960s and 1970s, however, began to question some of Piaget's main assumptions, especially the idea that cognitive development proceeded through broad stages. At the same time, developments in computer and information technology offered developmental psychologists an alternative model—the idea that humans process information in much the same way that a computer does. This information-processing view has shaped the majority of the research in cognitive development since the early 1970s.

AS YOU STUDY THIS SECTION, ASK YOURSELF THESE QUESTIONS:

**8.10** What is the information-processing approach?

**8.11** How do processing capacity, processing efficiency, and attention change with development?

**8.12** What is metacognition, and how does it relate to children's theory of mind?

## What Is the Information-Processing Approach?

*Information processing* is a term that comes from computer science; it refers to the way computers code information into computer symbols and how they sort, store, retrieve, and use these symbols. Information-processing psychologists have often used the computer as a metaphor for understanding how humans think and how they remember information (Munakata, 2006). In general, both computers and humans encode information into some type of symbol system; that is, they change the format of the original stimulus into something the machine or the brain can operate on. Both computers and humans process the encoded information, changing it in some way then storing it and/or producing some sort of output. In other words, both computers and humans are systems that *manipulate symbols*.

Of course, information-processing psychologists would never claim that human thought is as mechanized, systematic, logical, and accurate as a computer's—we know that it is not. Nor do computers possess the full richness of human thinking. Clearly computers do not have emotional reactions to the information they are processing. Nor do they have internal motives or desires—not yet, anyway! Regardless of how explicitly we use the computer as a metaphor, however, the information-processing approach helps us think about how humans think and has extended our understanding of cognition and its development (Klahr, 1992; Kuhn, 1992).

One of the important assumptions of the information-processing view is that *humans are limited in their capacity to process information*. In other words, you can do only so much at once. The specific limit varies tremendously from one person to another, but everybody has one. Once we reach our personal limit, we begin to make errors or forget things. Much of cognitive development consists of developing strategies for making the most of our limited capacity. We develop strategies for learning, remembering, and using information as efficiently as possible so we can free up capacity to consider new information and new problems.

▲ Though some people have more processing capacity than others, everyone has a limit; once that limit is reached, people begin to make errors or forget things.

**THINK ABOUT SUJATHA AND RK . . .**

What can Sujatha and RK look for that will tell them how well the teachers are helping students work with their limited capacities? What clues can they look for to determine whether teachers are overloading children's capacities?

## The Development of Basic Cognitive Processes

A basic fact of cognitive development is that older children are able to process more information, process it faster, and control their attention better than younger children. Let's take a closer look at how developmental changes in these basic cognitive processes lead to superior cognitive performance as children grow older.

### Changes in Processing Capacity.

**Processing capacity** is the amount of information a person can remember or think about at one time. Researchers often measure it by presenting a series of pieces of information very quickly and counting how many items a person can remember in exact order. As you can see in Figure 8.5 on page 242, measures of processing capacity show consistent and regular increases throughout childhood and into early adulthood (Case, 1985; Dempster, 1981; Gathercole, Pickering, Ambridge, & Wearing, 2004).

Changes in processing capacity help explain age differences in performance on many kinds of cognitive tasks. For example, do you remember the Piagetian conservation problem we described earlier in this chapter? When liquid is poured from a short beaker into a taller and skinnier one, young children often think that the taller one has more liquid. Piaget claimed that younger children center their thinking on only one aspect of the problem (the height of the liquid) but fail to consider the other element (the width of the beakers). Piaget believed that this was part of the child's inability to understand the logical structure of conservation. However, it is also possible that younger children's processing capacity may be too limited to allow them to work with both height and width at the

**processing capacity**
The amount of information a person can remember or think about at one time.

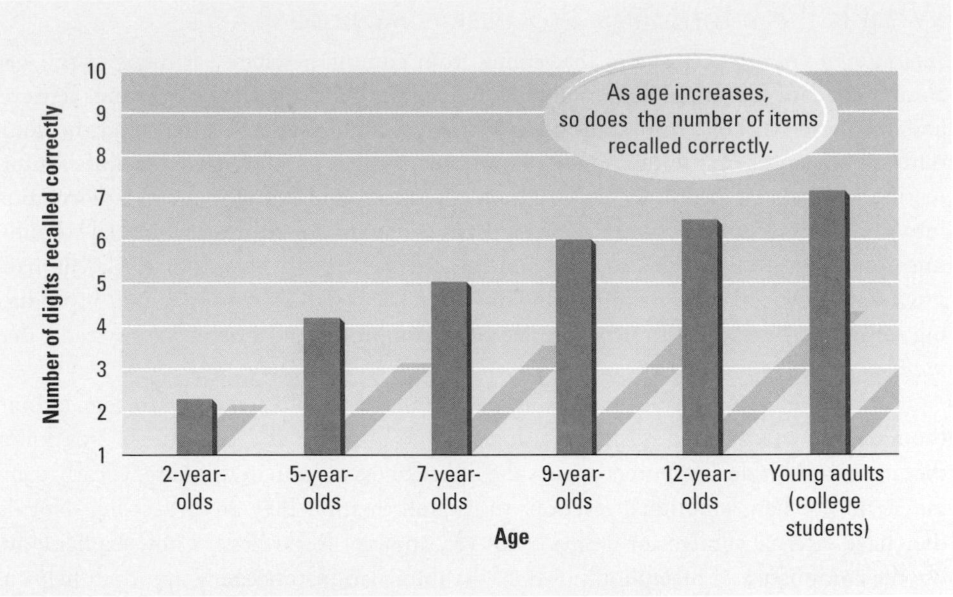


FIGURE 8.5 ▶ **Age-Related Changes in Memory Span** Adults remember about three times as much as 2-year-olds when asked to recall numbers in a specific order. Similar patterns are found in memory for words and for letters. (Adapted from Dempster, 1981, p. 66.)

same time. Perhaps younger children can switch their attention back and forth from one dimension to another, but cannot consider both of the dimensions at once. As children mature and their capacity grows, they gain the ability to consider several sources of information at the same time, and their cognitive processing therefore becomes more flexible and powerful.

▲ As skills become more automatic, they require less processing capacity. This enables people to do multiple things at the same time.

**Changes in Processing Efficiency.** Does processing capacity actually increase with development, or do older children simply learn to use the capacity they have more effectively? Some theorists focus on changes in **processing efficiency**—the speed and accuracy with which children can process information (Case, 1985; Case, Kurland, & Goldberg,, 1982; Demetriou, Christou, Spanoudis, & Platsidou, 2002). Remember the key assumption of the information-processing view: There is a limited amount of capacity available at any given time. Part of this capacity is believed to be devoted to *operating space,* where the actual manipulation of information takes place. The rest is *storage space,* a place for storing and remembering the information we are manipulating. As shown in Figure 8.6, children use less of their limited operating space as they become faster at processing information. This frees up some of the operating space for other things, like storage of more information. The result is that the older child can remember more information. A child can also use the leftover operating space to do different kinds of processing, such as considering several aspects of a problem simultaneously, relating the current information to other information, and the like.

The *automaticity* of cognitive skills is important for increasing processing efficiency (Hasher & Zachs, 1979). **Automaticity** is the ability to perform a skill with little or no conscious effort. This frees up more cognitive capacity for other tasks. For example, think about young children who are learning to read. At first, the process is very laborious: Children recognize individual letters and attempt to combine their sounds to decode words. With practice, their recognition of letters, sounds, and common letter combinations becomes very fast and requires little conscious effort—it has become automatic. Cognitive capacity is now available for other tasks, such as reading with appropriate expression, monitoring comprehension, or wondering what will happen next. Eventually some of these higher-level processes also become more automatic. This allows children to consider additional dimensions as they read, such as comparing and contrasting the current text

**processing efficiency**
The speed and accuracy with which a person can process information.

**automaticity**
The ability to carry out a process with little or no conscious effort, leaving more cognitive capacity to carry out other tasks.

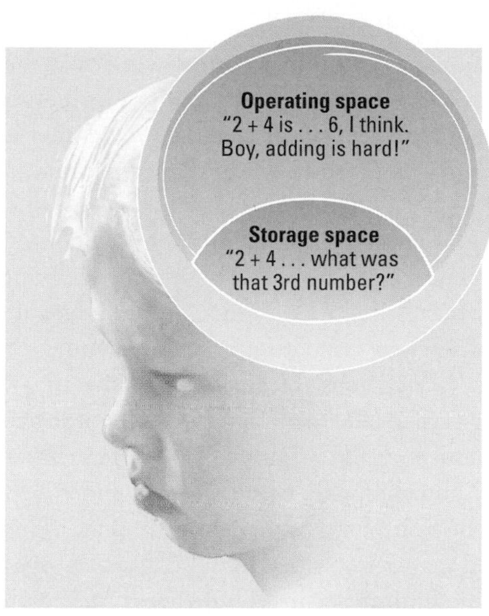


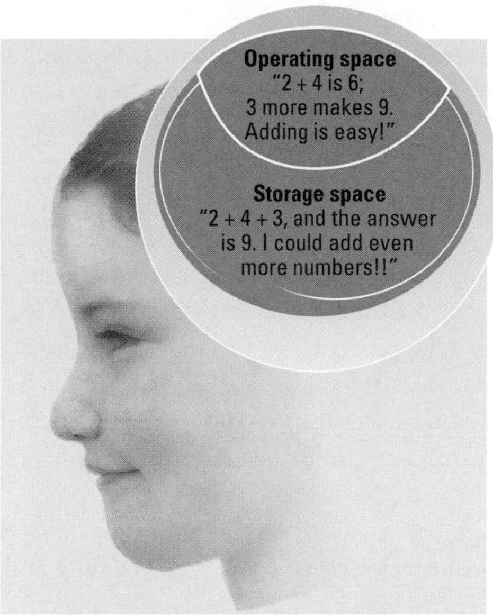


◄ FIGURE 8.6
**Storage Space and Operating Space in Working Memory**
What is 2 + 4 + 3? Younger children have difficulty with such questions because they need to use most of their processing capacity to figure out how to add the first two numbers; the capacity left available for storing and remembering other information is minimal. Adding is easy for older children, so more of their capacity is available for storage and other processes. (Based on Bjorklund, 1995.)

with others they have read. In this way, automaticity of cognitive skills enables children to move to more sophisticated and complex ways of thinking—it is one of the mechanisms that fosters cognitive development. **Listen** on **mydevelopmentlab**

**Listen**: Why does it matter if a person is cognitively *efficient*? (Author Podcast) www.mydevelopmentlab.com

Changes in Attention. **Attention** is the ability to focus on a particular stimulus (piece of information) without becoming distracted by other stimuli. As children get older they are better at maintaining their focus for longer periods of time and they also improve their ability to ignore information that can be distracting. Younger children often need help in knowing what to focus on and what to ignore. Good kindergarten teachers, for example, are skilled at directing children's attention to the topic of study (e.g., the alphabet on the blackboard) and away from other interesting sources of information (e.g., the frog in the aquarium or the noise coming in from the playground). Children gradually learn strategies that help them monitor and direct their own attentional focus, and this in turn helps them process information more deeply and accurately. Neuroscience research with adults has identified specific brain areas (specifically, the anterior cingulate gyrus and the lateral prefrontal areas) that are involved in being alert to stimuli, focusing on specific stimuli, and monitoring attention. Similar areas seem involved in attention in children, with some indication that these areas are involved in regulating attention as early as 7 months of age (Rothbart, Sheese, & Posner, 2007). Ongoing longitudinal work is tracing the relation between development of these areas of the brain and attention. Specific genes have also been identified that seem to be involved in attentional regulation, particularly those that regulate levels of the neurotransmitters dopamine and serotonin. Work with families has even found that some of these genes in children interact with quality of parenting to influence activity levels and degree of impulsivity in children (Posner, Rothbart, & Sheese, 2007; Sheese, Voelker, Rothbart, & Posner, 2007).

**attention**
The ability to focus on a particular stimulus without becoming distracted by other stimuli.

## Metacognition and the Child's Developing Theory of Mind

Do you ever think about your own thinking? Do you ever wonder how in the world you will be able to remember a complicated set of information (like this whole chapter!), or even the name or phone number of someone you just met? If so, you have engaged in what psychologists call *metacognition.* **Metacognition** is the understanding or knowledge that people have about their own thought processes and memory.

**metacognition**
The understanding or knowledge that people have about their own thought processes.

Several different types of metacognition develop during childhood. These include knowledge about cognitive *tasks* (such as knowing that a long list of words will be more difficult to remember than a short list), knowledge about cognitive *strategies* (such as knowing that simply repeating a telephone number will help you remember it for a short time), and knowledge about *people* (such as knowing that there are limits to what a person can remember).

Metacognitive skills tend to be pretty poor during early childhood, but they improve rapidly after the age of 5. Younger children are notoriously optimistic about their own memory abilities: They consistently overestimate how much they will be able to remember. However, they are more accurate when estimating how much someone else will remember on the same task (Flavell, Friedrichs, & Hoyt, 1970; Kreutzer, Leonard, & Flavell, 1975). For example, ask 4-year-old Rachel how many words she thinks she could remember from a list of 20, and she's likely to say, "I could remember them all; I'm a good rememberer!" But ask her how many her twin sister will remember, and the answer is more likely to be, "Oh, maybe 5. It's hard to remember all that." This wishful thinking on the part of young children may actually be useful because it probably motivates children to keep trying. If young children accurately predicted their own poor memory performance, they might become frustrated and give up. This would reduce their chances to discover and practice memory strategies and gain metacognitive knowledge.

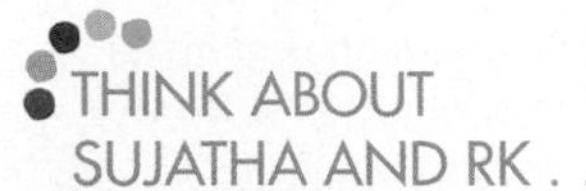
THINK ABOUT SUJATHA AND RK . . .

How can teachers help young children learn metacognitive skills? What clues can Sujatha and RK look for to indicate that the schools are doing a good job in this area?

**Theory of Mind.** In recent decades, work on metacognition has focused on how children develop their own *theory of mind.* A **theory of mind** is a coherent and integrated framework of concepts about the mind, how it works, and why it works that way (Wellman, 1990; Wellman, Cross, & Watson, 2001; Wellman & Liu, 2004). Research on children's theory of mind has looked at what children know about thinking in general and at how well they understand the thoughts of other people. **Watch** on **mydevelopmentlab**

**Watch** a video on Theory of Mind.
www.mydevelopmentlab.com

**theory of mind**
An integrated understanding of what the mind is, how it works, and why it works that way.

Even young children have some understanding of thinking as a mental activity and know it is different from physical objects and behavior. For example, children as young as 3 years old know that mental objects are different from real objects. They know that an imaginary ice cream cone is different from the real thing, and they know it is possible to carry out mental activities that could not happen in the real world, such as flying to the moon in a cardboard box (Wellman & Estes, 1986). Three-year-olds can also understand

Teachers, parents, and the overall culture have a big impact on the metacognitive skills children develop and the beliefs children hold about their efforts.

that dreams are not real life, although many young children do believe that different people have the same dreams (Woolley & Wellman, 1992).

However, children's understanding of mental activities is limited in important ways and undergoes substantial development as they get older. For example, young children often do not understand the difference between how a real object *appears* to be and how it actually is. This is called the *appearance–reality distinction,* and it is a good indicator of theory of mind. If children are not able to tell the difference between appearance and reality, it means that they are not distinguishing between their beliefs about an object (which are based on how it appears) and how it really exists. For example, in one classic study researchers introduced children to a cat named Maynard (DeVries, 1969). The researchers then put a dog mask on Maynard's face. Even though Maynard's body and tail were unchanged and remained visible while the mask was put on, 3 year-olds said that Maynard was now a dog. To them the change in appearance changed the underlying reality. In contrast, 5- and 6-year-olds had no problem understanding that Maynard was still a cat despite his change in appearance. Other work using fake rocks (pieces of sponge painted to look like rocks) and "red milk" (white milk poured into a red cup) also showed that 3-year-olds did not distinguish appearance from reality. This result was consistent even when the tasks were simplified and even after children received explicit training in distinguishing between appearance and reality (Flavell, Green, & Flavell, 1986; Flavell, Green, Wahl, & Flavell, 1987; Taylor & Hort, 1990). In other words, for young children, if it looks like a rock, it is a rock.

▲ Young children have trouble understanding the distinction between appearance and reality. If this cat wears a mask of a dog's face, 3-year-olds are likely to believe that it has turned into a dog!

Do children understand the beliefs and desires of other people? To be able to do this, children must first understand that other people's thoughts are different from their own. If they can't make this distinction, then they can't understand that other people have their own unique beliefs and desires, and there is no reason even to try to figure out what others are thinking. It's not clear whether young children understand the difference between what they know themselves and what another person knows. Several studies have found that 3-year-olds have difficulty making this distinction, and cross-cultural studies have confirmed this result (Avis & Harris, 1991; Perner, 1991; Sullivan & Wimmer, 1993; Wellman & Bartsch, 1988).

Differentiating their own beliefs from other people's beliefs is an important part of developing an accurate theory of mind, but children must go beyond that to understand that *all* people differ in their thought processes. Five-year-olds, for example, believe that two people looking at the same picture will have the same thoughts about that picture (Eisbach, 2004). Over the next few years they learn that different people can have different mental reactions even when they see the same thing.

Language plays an important role in the development of a theory of mind. Talking to children beginning at a very early age about mental states such as desires, emotions, thinking, knowing, memory, understanding, and the like seems to help them develop a theory of mind (Meins et al., 2002; Ruffman, Slade, & Crowe, 2002). Children's performance on several different theory of mind tasks seems to be related to their experience in using language to communicate with those around them (Cheung et al., 2004; Deák, Ray, & Brenneman, 2003; Lohmann & Tomasello, 2003; Nelson et al., 2003). Still, we have much yet to learn about what children understand about other people's thoughts and desires.

Recent work in neuroscience has suggested a possible neural basis for at least some aspects of theory of mind. **Mirror neurons** are neurons that fire when an individual produces an action *and* when the individual observes someone else making the action; the neurons "mirror" the behavior of someone else and produce the same pattern of neural firing as if the person him/herself produced the action. By simulating the actions of others in their own neurons, researchers hypothesize that people become able to relate to and understand others. Mirror neurons are thought to play an important role

**mirror neurons**
Neurons that fire when an individual produces an action *and* when the individual observes someone else making the action; the neurons "mirror" the behavior of someone else.

**THINKING CRITICALLY**

How good are you at reading other people's thoughts? Do you think about what other people know and want as you work or socialize with them? How is your theory of mind different from those of any children you know?

in connecting perception and action, learning through imitation, acquiring language, the development of empathy, and in understanding the actions and intentions of others. Dysfunction in the mirror neuron system has been linked to *autism spectrum disorders*, specifically the social interaction deficits that are common in these disorders. Recent evidence suggests that the basic mirror neuron system may be present at birth, but that these systems undergo a great deal of development with experience (Giudice, Manera, & Keysers, 2009; Falck-Ytter, Gredebäck, & von Hofsten, 2006; Lepage & Théoret, 2007).

**LET'S REVIEW . . .**

1. The term *processing capacity* refers to:
   a. the child's ability to understand math concepts.
   b. the amount of space a child has for storing information from the past.
   c. the amount of information a child can remember or think about at one time.
   d. the number of items that a child forgets in a given problem.
2. What does the term *metacognition* refer to?
   a. how people store and retrieve memories
   b. thought processes that are unconscious
   c. knowledge of one's own thought and memory processes
   d. the type of cognition used by younger children before they learn more mature forms of thinking
3. Renaldo pretends to play with a magic sword. He knows that the "magic" is really just pretend in his own head and that his toy sword is not really magic. Renaldo's understanding of the difference between pretend and reality is an example of his ________.
   a. cognitive strategies   b. task knowledge
   c. attentional skill   d. theory of mind
4. True or False: Processing capacity increases with age, but processing efficiency remains the same.
5. True or False: Three-year-old children are good at distinguishing appearance from reality.

Answers: 1. c, 2. c, 3. d, 4. F, 5. F

# Language Development

Several years ago, some friends came to our house for dinner, bringing their 4-year-old daughter Kelly. When Kelly asked for a second helping of pasta, she remarked, "This is the bestest, most deliciousest dinner I have *ever* eated!" Kelly's interesting grammatical construction amused us all, but we had no difficulty understanding what she meant.

Like Kelly, most children learn very quickly to express their thoughts, desires, and emotions through language. They learn new words at an incredible rate of speed. While most of us are still struggling with the intricate rules of grammar well into adulthood, young children make impressive progress in learning the complex rules of language. In this section we discuss how young children learn new words, learn rules of grammar, and learn to use language to communicate more effectively with other people. We also discuss children who are bilingual—learning more than one language at the same time.

AS YOU STUDY THIS SECTION, ASK YOURSELF THESE QUESTIONS:

**8.13** How much growth in vocabulary do we see during early childhood?

**8.14** What changes occur during early childhood in grammar and social rules of language use?

**8.15** What are the advantages and disadvantages to learning two languages at the same time? Are bilingual children at a disadvantage?

## An Expanding Vocabulary

Do you enjoy learning new vocabulary words? How many new words do you usually learn in a typical week? Consider this astounding statistic: While the average 2-year-old speaks about 200 different words, the typical 6-year-old speaks approximately 10,000 (Anglin, 1993; Ganger & Brent, 2004; Nelson, 1973). That's an average gain of about 47 words per week or nearly seven new words every day! When you consider that children typically comprehend far more words than they produce, you can appreciate the phenomenal development that takes place during these early childhood years.

How do children learn new words so quickly? As you saw in Chapter 5, children use *fast-mapping* to learn new words after only one or two exposures. They also imitate words they hear around them, and their parents shape and reinforce new word utterances. Imitation and reinforcement are not enough, however. Children also analyze language and think about the patterns they notice. They use what they know about the grammatical structure of sentences (such as word order and word endings) to figure out the meanings of new words. This process of using syntax as a cue for determining word meaning is called *syntactical bootstrapping* (Gleitman, 1990). For example, if you encountered the sentence "Will is *pidding* his cereal," the placement of the new word along with its *-ing* ending would lead you to infer that *pidding* is an action, not an object. In contrast, the placement and word structure in the sentence "Will threw his *pid*" would lead you to infer that *pid* is an object, not an action (Naigles & Hoff-Ginsburg, 1995). Evidence from MRI studies indicates that brain maturation plays an important role in this rapid increase in word learning. One study followed children from birth to 3 years and found a fast increase in vocabulary after 18 months of age—just after a period of rapid myelination in the language areas of the brain (Aslin & Schlaggar, 2006; Pujol et al., 2006).

## Learning Grammar and the Social Rules of Discourse

One of the most difficult challenges in learning any language is to learn all of the rules for properly combining words and forming sentences. Children learn these grammar rules gradually. For example, they begin to produce *wh-* questions (asking *who, what, where, when,* or *why*) by first simply placing the *wh-* word before a noun, as in "Where kitty?" Later they include a helping verb but not in the correct order, producing such questions as "Where kitty is?" Finally, they produce the correct format: "Where is the kitty?"

A similar progression takes place as children learn to produce negative sentences. Young children start by simply putting *no* at the beginning of a word or statement, as in "No peas." Next, they add improperly ordered helping words, as in "I no peas" before arriving at the proper grammatical form: "I don't want peas." By 3 years of age, children's grammatical knowledge has already developed to the point that they are able to produce complex sentences. For example, they use conjunctions (e.g., *and*) to join simple sentences, they use clauses that modify preceding nouns (e.g., "The boy who lost his dog is outside."), and they produce embedded sentences (i.e., sentences within sentences). By age 6, children are quite good at producing complex and grammatically correct sentences (de Villiers & de Villiers, 1999).

Sometime by the age of 3, most children begin adding word endings such as *-s, -ing,* or *-ed* (Brown, 1973). As children learn these rules they sometimes apply them incorrectly and produce incorrect forms of irregular words. This is called **overregularization**, and it often leads children to make mistakes with words they were able to form correctly before they learned the rules. For example, a 3-year-old may be quite capable of saying, "I saw fish in the pond," but at 4 years old, the same child might say, "I seed fishes." These errors occur when children are unable to recall the correct irregular form and so try to express their intent by applying a newly learned rule. Instances of overregularization sometimes

**overregularization**
Incorrect application of the linguistic rules for producing past tenses and plurals, resulting in incorrect forms of irregular words such as *goed* or *deers*.

**THINKING CRITICALLY**

Have you ever heard examples of overregularization? What grammatical rules did the child or children seem to be trying to apply?

cause parents to be concerned that their child is having language problems. However, these errors are nothing to worry about. Although they occur in many different languages, they are really relatively infrequent, occurring in less than 8% of the instances when children use irregular words (Marcus et al., 1992; Pinker, 1994). In fact, overregularizations actually indicate children's progress in grammatical knowledge and represent their attempts to use this knowledge to communicate. Table 8.1 gives several suggestions parents can use to help their children learn language.

**Social rules of discourse** are conventions that the speakers of a language follow when they are in a conversation with other people. The earliest social rule children acquire is *turn taking*—the idea that first one conversational partner makes a contribution to the

**TABLE 8.1**
**Facilitating Language Development: Suggestions for Parents**

**Be an active listener and participate in the conversation the child wants to have.**

- Follow your child's lead.
- Ask open-ended questions ("Tell me more").
- Encourage your child to elaborate on topics that are important to him or her.

**Provide good models.**

- If your child is "misarticulating" sounds, make the sound correctly yourself.
- Don't ask your child to repeat the words or the sound with which he or she is having "trouble."
- Correct your child by saying things like, "Oh! You want soup?" instead of, "Say *soup*, not *thoup*."

**Talk, talk, talk about events in your child's life.**

- Talk about these events in a meaningful way.
- Don't talk too fast!

**Provide a supportive atmosphere.**

- Make sure your child feels free to communicate with you.
- Provide lots of good models of speech and language.
- Be encouraging and supportive.

**Read, read, read to your child.**

- Read to your child during infancy, toddlerhood, preschool years, and beyond.
- Point to the words, talk about the pictures.
- Talk about words that rhyme, different letters, and the sounds they make.

**Have the tools of written communication available.**

- Have plenty of crayons, marking pencils, and paper available for your child.
- Encourage your child to use these tools to communicate.

**Play sound and word games.**

- "How many words are there in the sentence *I like to go to the store?*"
- "How many syllables are there in the word, *Baby?* Let's clap it out—*Ba* (clap) *by* (clap).
- "Let's play a word game. I'm thinking of *glasses*—kinds that we wear and kinds that we drink from. Can you think of another word that can mean two different things?"

**If your child shows *dysfluencies* (difficulties):**

- Let your child finish each communication; don't finish sentences for him or her.
- Model easy, slower, less complex, speech.
- Be patient!

(Bernstein, personal communication, 2003.)

**social rules of discourse**
Conventions that speakers of a language follow when having a conversation.

exchange, then the other, going back and forth until the conversation ends. Parents model this rule in child-directed speech and during countless daily activities, beginning when their children are infants. Children develop this knowledge further during early childhood and soon begin to apply it to conversations with other children as well as with adults. Other social rules of discourse, however, are not learned until later in childhood. For example, it is only around the age of 5 that children acquire the *answer-obviousness rule.* This rule says that if the answer to a question is obvious given the context and the speaker, then the listener should interpret the question as a request (or even a demand) rather than a true question. For example, suppose a mother finds her 6-year-old son jumping up and down on his bed and says, "Do you have to jump on your bed?" The child, who has acquired the answer-obviousness rule, understands that his mother is not really interested in whether or not he feels a need to jump on the bed. Instead, the mother's inquiry is an indirect way of commanding him to stop it. Other social rules of discourse involve even more sophisticated knowledge and are usually not acquired until the early school years. These include rules about saying something relevant to the topic being discussed, saying something related to what was just said in the conversation, and not repeating something that has already been said in the conversation.

▲ What would this parent really mean if she said, "Do you *have* to jump on the bed?"

It is important to remember that there can be substantial cultural differences in rules for social discourse. For example, what constitutes an "obvious" answer depends on the particular culture. African Americans, for example, do not use question-demands as frequently as white Americans, so African American children might interpret the question about jumping on the bed as a true request for information rather than a demand. Rules for turn taking differ as well. Many African American children learn at home that they must take their turn and keep their audience's attention, rather than waiting until someone else finishes and they are given a turn (Delpit, 1995; Saville-Troike, 1986).

THINKING CRITICALLY

Think of someone you know who is skilled in social rules of discourse. Now think of someone with less skill. What do they do differently?

THINK ABOUT SUJATHA AND RK . . .

What language skills can Sujatha and RK look for in their son to see if his skills are on par with other children of his age? What kinds of language mistakes or weaknesses are expected at this age?

## Bilingual Children: Learning Two Languages

Do you speak more than one language? More than six million children in the United States are **bilingual**, or fluent in two languages. In *additive bilingualism,* a person learns a second language while maintaining a first language. In *subtractive bilingualism,* a person loses fluency in the first language as a result of acquiring a second language (Bialystok & Hakuta, 1994). Different social and cultural conditions usually accompany these two types of bilingualism. When the family and larger community see acquisition of a second language as a positive asset and highly value both languages, children are more likely to show additive bilingualism. On the contrary, if people see the second language as superior and the first as inferior in some way, children will be more likely to "subtract" their first language (Hamers & Blanc, 2000). Children can get a negative message about their first language when they don't see it used in their schools or in the media, or if their peers and other social contacts do not understand it. It is not just children immigrating to the United States who experience conditions that encourage subtractive bilingualism. For example, U.S.-born Hispanic children who learn Spanish as their first language are often at a significant disadvantage when they enter a predominantly English-speaking school system. In past decades Native American children were not allowed to speak their own languages in school (Harjo, 1999). Cultural attitudes are changing, however. One recent study found that when a nonnative English speaker broke a social rule (e.g., standing too close, speaking very loudly), they were not judged negatively if they had poor fluency in English; the lack of English fluency served as a protection against negative evaluations (Molinsky & Perunovic, 2008).

**bilingual**
Fluent in two languages.

Children can become bilingual simultaneously or sequentially. *Simultaneous bilingualism* develops when a child learns two languages at the same time, starting from infancy. This situation often occurs when the child has parents who speak two languages. In *sequential bilingualism* a child learns one language first, then begins learning the second. Children who begin learning a second language by about the age of 3 usually become just as fluent in the second language as in the first. If second-language learning begins later in childhood or in adulthood, the person can use the second language effectively for communication but usually will not attain such complete fluency. The accent of the second language is particularly problematic, and most older learners never acquire a native-sounding accent. Although they usually don't achieve a natural-sounding accent or a high level of fluency, older learners actually do learn vocabulary and grammar rules faster than younger children do (Krashen, Long, & Scarcella, 1982; Snow, 1987). Some theorists argue that young children are more successful at acquiring second languages not because of a special language-learning ability but because of the younger child's greater opportunity, longer time period in which to master the second language, and less interference from a first language because it is not already automatized (Ekstrand, 1981; MacWhinney, 1992). According to this view, younger children do not have any greater ability to acquire language than older children, but they do have "a less complex task for which [they have] more time" (Hamers & Blanc, 2000, p. 75). The skills learned in the first language may also apply to learning a second language, making the second language easier to learn (Snow & Kang, 2006).

**THINK ABOUT SUJATHA AND RK . . .** What can Sujatha and RK look for in the schools that would indicate the school will properly support their bilingual son? What clues would indicate that the schools foster additive bilingualism? What would indicate subtractive bilingualism?

In the early stages of learning two languages, children may occasionally mix words and grammar from both languages. It is not clear why this mixing, or *code switching,* occurs. It may happen because a child doesn't yet understand that the two languages are separate systems, or it may happen simply because the child has acquired words to express a specific thought in one language but not yet in the other language. Parent modeling also seems to play a role. Code switching occurs more often in children whose parents also code switch. The frequency of code switching decreases as children gain more vocabulary and a stronger grasp of grammar in each language, although even adult bilingual speakers sometimes code switch intentionally.

When they are learning two languages simultaneously, research shows that children learn the vocabulary and grammar of each language separately. Bilingual and monolingual individuals use the same general brain structures when processing language, but they show different *patterns and sequences* of neural activity within these areas. In addition, neuroscientists have found different neural patterns *within the same child* in response to words from the dominant versus non-dominant language as early as 19 months of age (Abutalebi, 2008: Conboy & Mills, 2006; Conboy & Thal, 2006; Kovelman, Baker, & Petitto, 2008; Saur et al., 2009). By the early preschool years, bilingual children show clear awareness that the two languages are independent systems. At first they may restrict their use of each language to certain contexts—for example, speaking only Spanish at home but speaking only English when outside the home. By the early school years, however, the bilingual child is able to switch automatically and appropriately from one language to another in either context (Cummins, 1991; Hamers & Blanc, 2000; Lanza, 1992; Volterra & Taeschner, 1978). To learn about one family's experience with bilingualism, read the Personal Perspective box called "Meet a Bilingual Family."

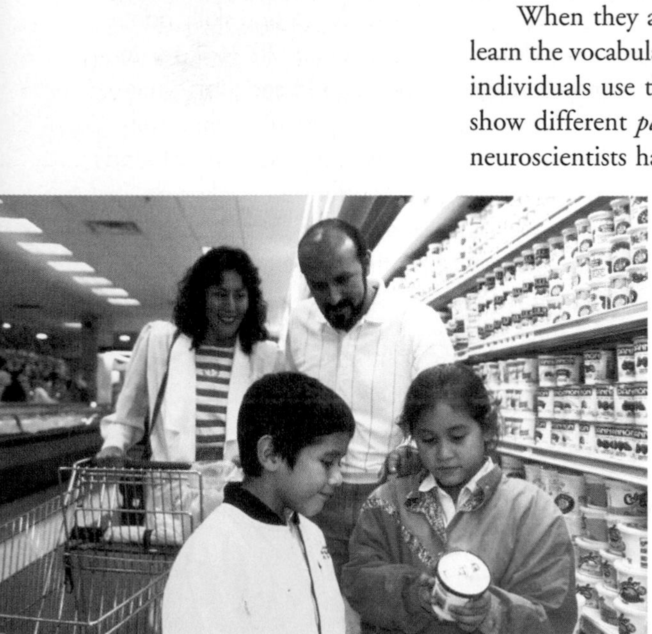

▲ Will learning two languages be a positive or a negative experience for these bilingual children?

Learning two languages is not necessarily a difficult task for children. The rate of language acquisition is slightly slower for bilingual children (Fennell, Byers-Heinlein, & Werker, 2007), but the fact that they are learning two complex and abstract systems may actually provide some cognitive advantages.

## Perspective PERSONAL — MEET A BILINGUAL FAMILY

Patrick, David, and Lori Glenn
El Paso, TX
Five-year-old bilingual child and his parents

**When did Patrick begin learning his second language (Spanish), and how is he progressing?**
Patrick was exposed to both English and Spanish from birth. Both grandmothers spoke to Patrick strictly in Spanish. His mother, Lori, read and spoke to him in Spanish most of the time; his favorite book was *Lo que le encanta a Conejito.* His grandmothers sang and recited nursery rhymes to him in Spanish, and they also watched Spanish-language television in his presence.

His paternal grandfather and I [David] always spoke to him in English. Grampa repeated "Grampa" to him whenever he was with him, and Patrick's first word, at four months, was "Grampa!" Lori stopped speaking to him in Spanish when he went to day care (at 2 years, 9 months of age) so that he would better understand English. However, his maternal grandmother, Abuela, spent every afternoon with him. So he continued to be exposed to Spanish, while his day care providers and his parents stressed English. Patrick has progressed well in English, but unfortunately, his Spanish language skills are lacking.

**What steps have you taken to help him learn either or both languages?**
We speak and read to him in both languages. We have family living in Chihuahua, Mexico, and when we are together, they speak Spanish in his presence and bring him into conversations. If he does not understand, they will speak to him in English. Funny thing is that we encourage his cousins to speak with him in Spanish, and his cousins' parents encourage them to practice their English around Patrick! It was suggested that we place him in a local magnet school with a bilingual curriculum. We have discussed the possibility of sending Patrick to school in Chihuahua for a semester.

**How does your son seem to feel about speaking two languages?**
Patrick understands Spanish fairly well, but speaks only a few words. He has his own imaginary Spanish that is mostly gibberish and sounds like the words being spoken in a conversation. He attempts to join a conversation in Spanish by using his phonetically similar made-up language; so we know he wants to converse, but just does not have the vocabulary. We attribute this to the time spent in school where English is the primary form of communication.

His 11-year-old cousin, Gerardo, is like a brother to Patrick. Gerardo is very articulate, and the Spanish language is melodious, so Patrick loves trying to imitate him. Plus, if Gerardo speaks Spanish, it's got to be cool! Or as Gerardo would say, *"Es bien padre!"*

QUESTION **What do you think is the best way to help children learn more than one language? What would you advise is the best approach for schools to take regarding bilingual children?**

Studies have found that bilingual children sometimes score higher on measures of such things as concept formation, cognitive flexibility, language awareness, ability to correct ungrammatical sentences, verbal and nonverbal creativity, and logical thinking (Bialystok, Majumder, & Martin, 2003; Diaz & Kinger, 1991; Hamers, 1996; Hamers & Blanc, 2000). Bilingual children even have the edge on certain types of appearance–reality problems, like those we discussed earlier in this chapter (Bialystok & Senman, 2004; Kovács, 2009). Because bilingual children must constantly examine and think about the particular language system they are using and the contexts for which each system is appropriate, they may develop an early awareness of the symbolic nature of language systems. This realization may encourage bilingual children to become more reflective about language and about how it can be used both for communication and as a tool for thinking (Mohanty & Perregaux, 1997).

THINKING CRITICALLY
If you are bilingual, would you say that your bilingualism is additive or subtractive? Simultaneous or sequential? Was it difficult to learn two languages? How do you understand and use both, and how do you translate between them?

**LET'S REVIEW . . .**

1. Fast-mapping and syntactical bootstrapping are two ways that children learn _______.
   **a.** new grammar rules
   **b.** new vocabulary words
   **c.** new rules of social discourse
   **d.** subtractive bilingualism
2. A child says, "Mommy goed to the store." The child's incorrect use of the *-ed* suffix in the word *goed* is an example of _______.
   **a.** overregularization
   **b.** overextension
   **c.** fast-mapping
   **d.** syntactical bootstrapping
3. Which of the following social rules of discourse do children typically learn *first?*
   **a.** turn taking
   **b.** answer obviousness
   **c.** say something relevant to the topic
   **d.** don't repeat something already said
4. True or False: Between the ages of 2 and 6, children usually learn about twenty new words per week.
5. True or False: Code switching is the process of losing fluency in the first language as a result of acquiring a second language.

Answers: 1. b, 2. a, 3. a, 4. F, 5. F

# Early Childhood Education and Kindergarten Readiness

Most children start kindergarten at the age of 5, but many children are enrolled in a preschool or nursery school program that includes an academic component in which children learn colors, shapes, the alphabet, counting, and rules for cooperating and getting along with teachers and other children in a school setting. Some programs are church-related and involve religious education, some are focused on ethnic education, and many others are run by community or public organizations. Parents enroll children to help them get an early start on academic learning, to give their children religious training, to involve their children in activities related to their ethnic backgrounds, or as a form of supervised child care while the parents work.

Other programs are designed to help children who are at special risk for falling behind after they start school. Children living in poor and disadvantaged areas, especially children in ethnic minority groups, are at a higher-than-average risk for performing poorly in school and dropping out before they graduate high school. These children can benefit from early school experiences that provide strong academic and emotional support (Hamre & Pianta, 2005). In the United States, most states now fund some type of educational program for children 4 years of age or younger, and the early indications are that these programs can help all children improve their learning and performance in school (Gormley, Gayer, Phillips, & Dawson, 2005).

In this last section of the chapter we focus on early childhood education programs that have been specifically designed to help disadvantaged children. We also explore issues related to preparation for kindergarten.

AS YOU STUDY THIS SECTION, ASK YOURSELF THESE QUESTIONS:

**8.17** What effects can early intervention programs have with children who are at risk for developmental problems?

**8.18** How do we know when children are ready to start kindergarten?

## Early Childhood Education

A key theme of this book is that children's early experiences provide a critical foundation for positive development. Unfortunately, some children's early environments do not provide strong foundations, and these children are at risk for numerous academic and social problems. Many are already behind when they enter kindergarten or first grade. Early childhood education programs have been created to improve children's readiness to benefit from formal schooling, increase their success in school, and improve the quality of their lives. We know that good early childhood programs can positive effects on children, particularly when combined with continuing high-quality education in the early elementary school years, but implementing and maintaining high-quality interventions has not been easy (Takaniushi & Bogard, 2007). What kinds of programs are common, and what do we know about their outcomes?

Two approaches that have become popular are Montessori and Reggio Emilia schools. Montessori schools emphasize several fundamental principles, including the ideas that movement and thought are closely interrelated, children thrive when given free choice to pursue things they are interested in, and order in the environment supports better learning (Lillard, 2005). Studies assessing outcomes of Montessori education show a number of positive outcomes, but they have many methodological issues such as lack of random assignment and small numbers of participants (Dohrmann, Nishida, Gartner, Lipsky, & Grimm, 2007; Lillard, 2005; Lillard & Else-Quest, 2006). Reggio Emilia schools emphasize respect for the natural curiosity, resourcefulness, and competence of children. Learning is child-controlled and involves active exploration and long-term projects in a supportive and beautiful environment. Children are encouraged to use language, art, and music to symbolically represent their ideas. This approach sees value in being confused when learning; mistakes and false starts on projects are not seen as evidence of failure but as an informative and important part of learning (Edwards, Gandini, & Forman, 1998; Fraser & Gestwicki, 2002). There is little research on this approach as of yet. However, many of the main principles in both the Montessori and Reggio Emilia approaches are consistent with many areas of developmental research and theory.

Begun in 1965 as part of President Lyndon Johnson's War on Poverty, **Project Head Start** is a federally funded, comprehensive program designed to improve academic achievement and opportunity for children from ages 3 through 5. These children receive health and social services as well as educational support, and their parents are included as an integral part of the program (Washington & Oyemade, 1987; Zigler & Styfco, 1993). Interestingly, Urie Bronfenbrenner (refer back to Chapter 1 to review his ecological systems theory) was a member of the committee that designed the program. As you can imagine, he was a strong supporter of this comprehensive approach! Project Head Start has changed over the years, going from a part-time-only program to full-time in some places. The age range for services also expanded: In 1994 Congress authorized the *Early Head Start Program,* which assists even younger children, ages newborn through 3 years. Head Start served over 908,000 children in 2007, spending almost $7,500 per child (the latest year for which data were available); 51% of these children are 4-year-olds. Project Head Start has served more than 25 million children since it began (U.S. Department of Health & Human Services, 2008).

Before Project Head Start expanded to meet the needs of more children, there was the **Abecedarian Project**. Designed to assess the impact of full-time, high-quality intervention beginning in infancy, the Abecedarian Project served primarily African American children living in poverty (Ramey, Campbell, & Blair, 1998). Infants at high risk for problems in cognitive development entered the program at 4½ months, on average, and continued until at least 5 years of age. Another well-known early intervention program was the **High/Scope Perry Preschool Program** in Ypsilanti, Michigan. This program offered high-quality, part-day (2½ hours per day) intervention during the school year (October to May) for poor African American children ages 3 to 5 (Schweinhart, Montie, Xiang, Barnett, Belfield, & Nores, 2005). The program focused on children's active involvement in directing their own learning. It also included weekly home visits to teach parents how to support their children's educational progress.

**Project Head Start**
Federally funded, comprehensive program designed to improve academic achievement and opportunity for young children.

**Abecedarian Project**
Project designed to assess the impact of full-time, high-quality intervention beginning in infancy; served primarily African American children living in poverty.

**High/Scope Perry Preschool Program**
Program offering high-quality partial-day intervention during the school year for young African American children living in poverty.

THINKING CRITICALLY

In what ways are Montessori's and the Reggio Emilia approaches to early childhood education similar to and different from Piaget's and Vygotsky's theories?

▲ The Abecedarian Project was created to help young African American children who were living in poverty and were at risk for doing poorly in school.

**Effects of Early Education Programs.** What effects have early childhood education programs had on children's development? Research has shown the following (Barnett, 1998; Ludwig & Phillips, 2007; McKey et al., 1985; Reynolds, Ou, & Topitzes, 2004; Schweinhart et al., 2005; Zigler, Styfco, & Gilman, 1993):

- Children in early intervention show an immediate gain of about 8 IQ points when compared with children who are not in such programs, but in many cases the difference "fades away" during the elementary school years. The Abecedarian Project is an exception, showing IQ differences up to 21 years of age (the oldest age tested so far), as you can see in Figure 8.7 (Campbell, Pungello, Miller-Johnson, Burchinal, & Ramey, 2001).
- The children score higher on reading and mathematics achievement tests. Studies of Head Start programs find that these differences fade, but other programs show achievement differences up to adolescence or young adulthood (see Figure 8.7).
- The children show better academic progress on other measures such as fewer students placed in special education classes and higher rates of graduation from high school, as

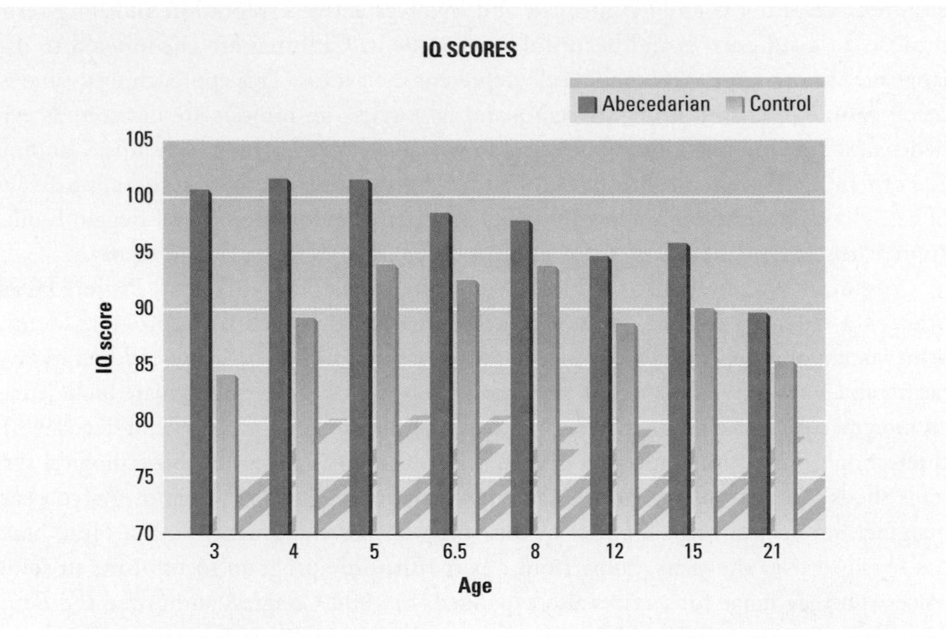


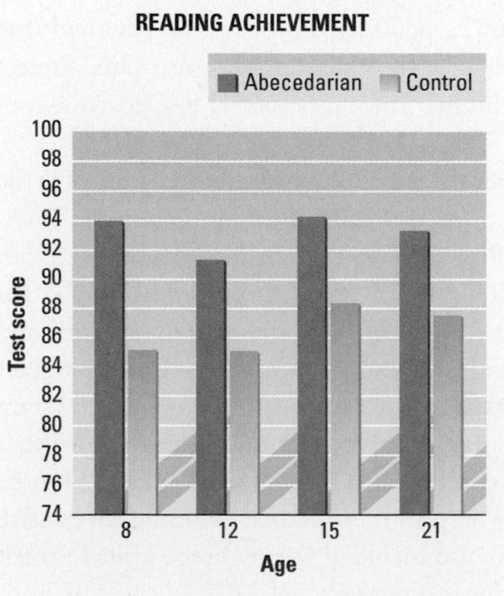


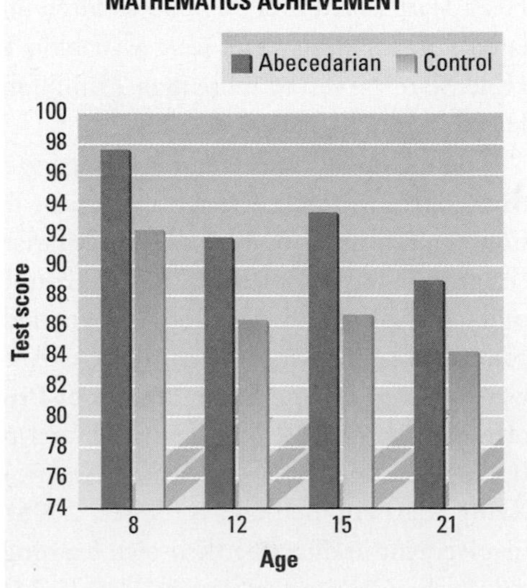


FIGURE 8.7 ▶ **IQ, Reading, and Math Scores for Children in the Abecedarian Project**
Children who participated in the Abecedarian Project continued to show higher scores for years after the program ended. (Data from Campbell et al., 2001.)

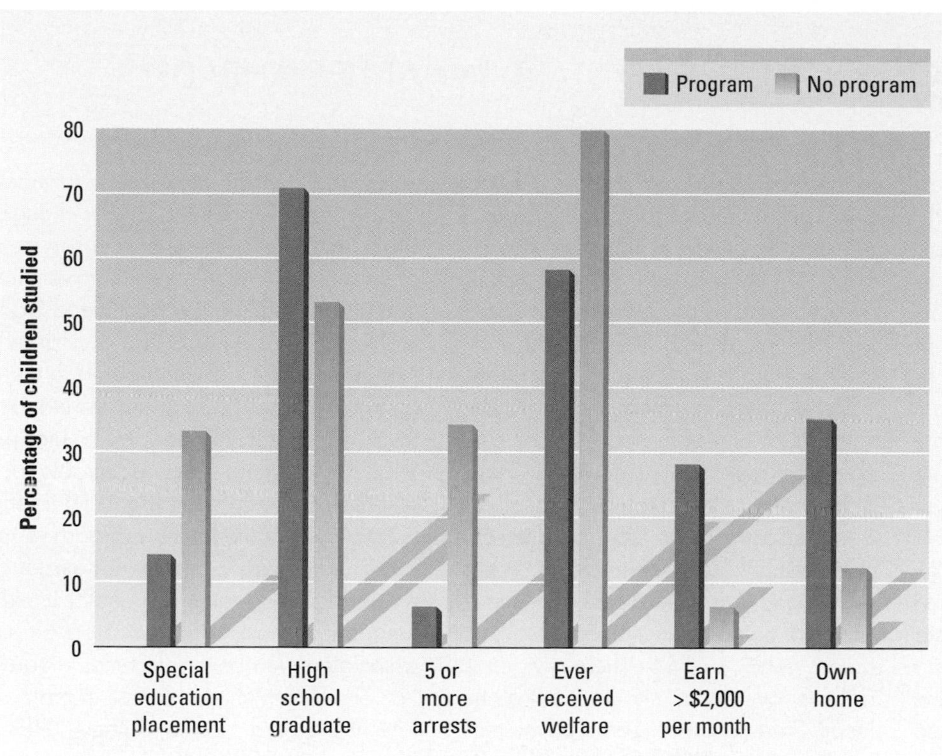


◀ FIGURE 8.8
**Results from the High/Scope Perry Preschool Project**
Children in the High/Scope Perry Preschool Project showed long-lasting benefits on measures of academic progress and of social welfare. (Adapted from Schweinhart, Barnes, & Weikart, 1993.)

shown in Figure 8.8. Children who had attended the Abecedarian Project (or its successor, called the CARE Project) were more likely to attend college than those in matched control groups (37% versus 14%, respectively) (Campbell et al., 2008).

- The children show other social and health benefits. For example, when surveyed as adults, participants in the High/Scope Perry Preschool Program were less likely to have been arrested or to have received welfare payments, and they were more likely to have a better-paying job (for the men), be employed (for the women), and own their own homes (see Figure 8.8 above) (Schweinhart et al., 2005). As a group, children in Head Start have better overall health, immunization rates, and nutrition than nonprogram children. Finally, those who participated in the Abecedarian Project during early childhood reported fewer symptoms of depression at age 21 and were more likely to report having an active lifestyle including regular exercise (Campbell et al., 2008; McLaughlin, Campbell, Pungello, & Skinner, 2007).

In general, programs such as the High/Scope Perry Preschool and Abecedarian projects show greater and longer-lasting benefits than Head Start. Why? Several factors probably play a role. Among these may be the quality of the instructional programs, the length of the programs, teacher training and pay, the numbers of at-risk children served, the seriousness of their challenges, and funding differences. However, the first large-scale evaluations of the Early Head Start Program offer encouraging results. Compared to disadvantaged children who were not enrolled in Early Head Start, the 3-year-old children in the program showed better cognitive and language skills, they were more able to maintain attention, and they were less aggressive. There were also positive effects on *parents'* skills and behaviors—parents were more emotionally supportive, read more to their children, provided more stimulation for learning, and spanked their children less (Love et al., 2002; Love et al., 2005; Love, Tartullo, Raikes, & Chazan-Cohen, 2006).

Controversy about the most effective ways to implement early intervention programs is intense. There is no better example of this than the debate that still surrounds

## Perspective SOCIAL POLICY — PROJECT HEAD START: WHAT LIES AHEAD?

Project Head Start and Early Head Start provide comprehensive health, nutrition, education, and social services to low-income children from birth to school age. Federal Head Start grants are made directly to agencies that apply for them (often public schools or community agencies). Each program site must meet specific program standards, but sites typically have some freedom in how requirements are met. Head Start programs have positive effects on children's development, but the effects have generally not been as strong or long-lasting as some other programs. The effects of Early Head Start programs look promising, but the long-term impact cannot be assessed yet (Barnett, 1998; Fenichel & Mann, 2001; Love et al., 2006; McKey et al., 1985).

There is continuing debate over Head Start. Some have questioned whether the benefits are worth the immense cost of the program (about $6.9 billion in 2007). Few argue against providing services to needy preschoolers, but many contend that including infants substantially increases the overall program cost while having limited effects. Serious questions have also been raised about whether it is ethical to limit the early educational choices of disadvantaged preschoolers. As an alternative to spending billions on a governmentally controlled program, low-income parents could be given vouchers and allowed to select from any early-education or child care arrangements, including Head Start centers. According to psychologist Sandra Scarr, "Head Start is a dinosaur, a remnant of the government-knows-best philosophy of an earlier era" and "should have to compete in the marketplace" (Scarr, 1999, p. 144). There is vigorous debate over who should control the Head Start program. Some policy makers argue that Head Start should be a state government responsibility rather than a federal one. Funding could be provided in block grants to states, with states responsible for administering the funds, developing policies about the program's implementation, overseeing quality, and integrating Head Start services with other state programs. Advocates argue that states are better able to determine the needs of the children living there and coordinate services to meet those needs. Opponents of this change argue that the comprehensive services and community and parent involvement that are hallmark strengths of Head Start would likely be lost. Critics also assert that many states are unprepared to take on the responsibilities that would be involved if this change were made. While some states do an admirable job of providing early childhood intervention to low-income families, programs in other states are poor or nonexistent; research shows that higher quality implemention of the Head Start program is associated with better outcomes regardless of whether children enroll at birth or later (Love et al., 2006; Ramey, 1999; Ripple et al., 1999).

QUESTION **Is early intervention worth its cost? How early should intervention begin, and which children should be targeted? Would a voucher system be more fair and effective? Who should control and pay for Head Start? What social policy recommendations would you make?**

Project Head Start even four decades after its beginning. To find out more about this program, read the Social Policy Perspective box above called "Project Head Start: What Lies Ahead?"

### Kindergarten Readiness

Although educators have long been interested in fostering children's readiness for schooling, defining readiness is not as easy as you might think. Schools often use chronological age to determine eligibility for entry, but several studies have shown that age is not a good predictor of academic success or learning (Carlton & Winsler, 1999; Morrison, Griffith, & Alberts, 1997). National surveys have asked parents and kindergarten teachers to identify important readiness indicators. Both parents and teachers emphasize children's overall physical health, verbal communication skills, and enthusiasm. Teachers also emphasize social skills and ability to follow classroom rules and procedures. Parents—but not most teachers—see academic knowledge, such as familiarity with the alphabet or counting skills, as an important prerequisite (Lewit & Baker, 1995). Other educators believe that self-control over behavior and emotions, the ability to keep attention focused, and impulse control are major factors that underlie readiness (Blair, 2002; Fantuzzo et al.,

2007; McClelland et al., 2007; NICHD Early Child Care Research Network, 2003). Many school districts use standardized assessments to assess readiness, but these tests show only low to moderate levels of predictive validity. In other words, the tests incorrectly identify many children as not ready for school (Carlton & Winsler, 1999; Duncan & Rafter, 2005). Studies of self-control of *cognitive* processes such as resisting temptations and distractions (rather than self-control of behavior and emotions), working memory, and cognitive flexibility (the ability to adjust to changes) indicate that these are better predictors of later school success than specific math or reading skills or overall IQ—and they can be improved through high-quality and thoughtful preschool programs (Diamond, Barnett, Thomas, & Monroe, 2007). **Watch** on **mydevelopmentlab**

**Watch** a video on Kindergarten: Ready for Success? www.mydevelopmentlab.com

How ready are our nation's children? On national surveys, kindergarten teachers rated approximately 65% of their students as ready for kindergarten on all five of the readiness characteristics the surveys assessed: rested, able to verbally communicate clearly, enthusiastic and interested, able to take turns and share, and able to sit still (Lewit & Baker, 1995). The overall health of children entering school, including immunization rates, has improved (National Education Goals Panel, 1999). One study assessed a nationally representative sample of 22,000 children. The majority of children had basic letter and number knowledge, showed good prosocial skills, persisted at tasks, were eager to learn, and could pay attention (West, Denton, & Germino-Hausken, 2000). However, almost all the measures varied according to factors such as age (older kindergartners score higher); family type (children from single-parent homes tend to score lower); mothers' education (the higher the mothers' level of education, the higher the children's scores); race/ethnicity (non-Hispanic white and Asian children score higher than African American and Hispanic children, especially on teacher ratings of behavior); and/or socioeconomic status (children from higher-income families score higher) (Stipek & Ryan, 1997). So although the majority of children seem reasonably ready for school and there have been important advancements, there is still much room for improvement.

Children old enough for school but identified as not ready present a dilemma for educators. Is it best to *redshirt,* or hold back, these children and keep them in their homes or in preschool for an additional year, place them in a transition class (either before kindergarten or between kindergarten and first grade), or retain them for an additional year of kindergarten? None of these options has been very successful in helping children catch up to peers who were not kept back (Malone, West, Flanagan, & Park, 2006). Other studies, however, have found that children who were recommended for delay, transition classes, or retention but were promoted anyway (perhaps at their parents' insistence) scored just as well on achievement tests as their classmates (Carlton & Winsler, 1999; Stipek, 2002).

THINKING CRITICALLY
Have you known a child who was held back from entering kindergarten or moving to first grade because he or she did not seem ready for school? Did it seem helpful to hold the child back?

What should we make of such contradictory findings? Some educators believe we need to rethink the idea of school readiness. They argue that it is the schools that must be ready, rather than placing the burden of readiness on the children (Carlton & Winsler, 1999; Dockett & Perry, 2003; Stipek, 2002). These educators, drawing on Vygotsky's theory of cognitive development, say that holding back children who are not ready deprives them of the "very culture and learning situations [they] need" (Carlton & Winsler, 1999, p. 346). Also, postponing school entry keeps these children in the environments that created and maintained the lack of readiness in the first place. This view challenges schools to work with children's existing abilities, scaffolding their learning experiences to help them acquire the cognitive skills our culture sees as important for learning and academic achievement. Delaying children will only produce further academic problems and may well damage both motivation and self-esteem (Rose, Medway, Cantrell, & Marus, 1983). There is abundant literature on what constitutes high-quality preschools (Bierman et al., 2008; Palermo, Hamish, Martin, Fabes, & Reiser, 2007; Gormley, Phillips, & Gayer, 2008); the difficult part is to implement these ideas consistently across the large population of diverse preschool-age children.

What factors should Sujatha and RK consider when determining their son's readiness for kindergarten?

## LET'S REVIEW . . .

1. Which of the following is true about early childhood education programs such as Head Start, High/Scope Perry Preschool, and the Abecedarian Project?
   - **a.** These programs are not cost effective.
   - **b.** These programs regularly produce permanent gains in IQ scores.
   - **c.** These programs produce improved academic progress and graduation rates.
   - **d.** These programs have little effect on social measures such as arrest records or employment.
2. According to a national survey of kindergarten teachers, what percentage of their students were fully ready for kindergarten?
   - **a.** 65%
   - **b.** 75%
   - **c.** 85%
   - **d.** 95%
3. When it comes to gauging a child's readiness for kindergarten, which characteristic is emphasized more by parents than by teachers?
   - **a.** enthusiasm
   - **b.** social skills
   - **c.** physical health
   - **d.** academic knowledge
4. True or False: Research shows that the Early Head Start Program that enrolls infants and toddlers is less effective than the regular Head Start Program.
5. True or False: Research suggests that it is best to "redshirt" children who do not seem to be socially and cognitively ready for kindergarten.

Answers: 1. c, 2. a, 3. d, 4. F, 5. F

### THINKING BACK TO SUJATHA AND RK . . .

Now that you have studied this chapter, you should be able to explain how Sujatha and RK can use cognitive development concepts to identify schools and teachers that would facilitate their son's learning and development. You should be able to list at least a dozen specific concepts and explain how each would relate to Sujatha and RK's situation.

Using Piaget's theory, Sujatha and RK would want to find classroom environments that promote active learning and look for teachers who use hands-on activities. Ashwin is in the preoperational stage, so he is learning to use his representational abilities more effectively. Art and play are important activities for exploring symbolic and representational thought. Sujatha and RK should look for signs that the teachers are sensitive to the intuitive logic commonly used by young children.

Using Vygotsky's sociocultural theory, Sujatha and RK should understand that children also learn by adopting the cognitive structures embedded in the language and culture of the classroom and the school. They should spend time observing and listening for the messages contained in the school culture. Are the messages predominantly positive—as in "All students can learn" and "Celebrate diversity"? Social speech becomes private speech. Would Sujatha and RK be proud to see their son internalize the messages heard in the schools and classrooms they visit? What kinds of mediation and scaffolding do teachers provide? Do teachers properly challenge students within their own zones of proximal development?

From the information-processing perspective, Sujatha and RK can watch for signs that the schools and teachers understand the processing limits of young children. What do they do to help children pay attention, think about, and remember information? Do they help children understand and overcome their own processing limits by teaching them metacognitive skills?

And how do the schools foster language development? Do they support bilingual children like Ashwin? Will these schools support Ashwin's specific strengths and help him meet any specific challenges that he has? By considering questions like these, Sujatha and RK can more effectively evaluate the schools to determine which one will provide the best education for their son.

8

## CHAPTER REVIEW . . .

**8.1 What evidence of Stage 2 thinking do we see in children's language, art, and play?**

In the preoperational thought stage (2 through 7 years), children can form internal mental representations. Children practice using symbols in their language (via their ability to let a word stand for an object in the environment), art (by letting marks on a paper represent people and things), and play (by using one object to stand for another).

**8.2 What is intuitive thinking and what are some examples of this?**

Intuitive thinking is thinking that is based more on personal experience than on objective logic. Egocentrism, animism, and artificialism are all indications that the young child is basing her thoughts on what things appear to be rather than on a logical understanding of what they really are.

**8.3 What do Piaget's conservation problems tell us about children's thinking?**

Children fail conservation problems because they center their thoughts on only one part of the problem, they focus on the static endpoints of the problem, and their cognitive schemes are not reversible (not yet *operational*).

**8.4 How has Piaget's theory influenced how teachers and others think about children's learning?**

Piaget's notion of the child as an active and curious organism has led to the design of interactive and hands-on curricula in schools and early childhood settings. His stage ideas have shaped guidelines for when to introduce different topics in schools. Educators have also used Piaget's ideas about schemes, assimilation, accommodation, disequilibrium, and reflective abstraction as they design and implement instruction.

**8.5 How does Vygotsky's own cultural background relate to the emphasis on culture and social interaction in his theory?**

Vygotsky experienced a rich cultural history, rapid cultural changes, and individualized tutoring. He came to believe that the broader culture determines the cognitive skills one must learn to be successful in a specific context, but that the way one learns these skills is through interpersonal interaction. Vygotsky proposed that children learn primarily by adopting the cognitive structures embedded in the language and the larger culture around them.

**8.6 What role does language play in cognitive development?**

As adults and others speak, children adopt their social speech and transform it into their own private speech. Children then internalize their private speech to form internal thought structures.

**8.7 According to Vygotsky's theory, how can adults facilitate children's development?**

Interpersonal interactions with adults (or more-skilled peers) *mediate* the cognitive structures created in the larger culture. Mediation is the process of introducing concepts, knowledge, skills, and strategies to the child; without appropriate mediation, cognitive development will not be supported.

**8.8 What is the zone of proximal development, and why is it important for understanding cognitive development?**

The zone of proximal development (ZPD) represents those tasks that the child can perform with mediation or support from more skilled mentors. If instruction is to be effective, it must take place within the individual child's ZPD.

**8.9 How do scaffolding and collaborative learning contribute to cognitive development?**

Adults and others mediate cognitive structures for children, often providing scaffolds or supports as children attempt more difficult tasks. Scaffolding and collaborative learning enable the child to work within the ZPD, above what could be accomplished initially and helping to further the development of partially mastered knowledge and skills.

**8.10 What is the information-processing approach?**

The information-processing approach views thinking as the processing of information. From this approach, it is assumed that humans manipulate symbols and that processing capacity is limited.

**8.11 How do processing capacity, processing efficiency, and attention change with development?**

Measures of processing capacity show consistent and regular increases throughout childhood and into early adulthood. Children use progressively less of their limited operating space as they become faster at processing information, which frees up some of the operating space for other things, thus increasing their processing efficiency. Older children are better able to maintain their attentional focus and ignore distracting information.

**8.12 What is metacognition, and how does it relate to children's theory of mind?**
Metacognition is the understanding or knowledge that people have about their own thought processes and memory. To be able to hold a mature theory of mind (an integrated framework of concepts about the mind, how it works, and why it works that way), one must be able to engage in metacognitive reflection and understand their own thought processes.

**8.13 How much growth in vocabulary do we see during early childhood?**
Children's dramatic vocabulary increase is accomplished through fast-mapping, imitation, syntactical bootstrapping, and by parental shaping. Increased brain myelination also plays an important role in word learning.

**8.14 What changes occur during early childhood in grammar and social rules of language use?**
Children learn grammar rules gradually. They learn rules for forming plurals and past tenses that are sometimes overregularized. Through parental modeling and social interactions, children begin to learn social rules of discourse that help them communicate effectively with other people.

**8.15 What are the advantages and disadvantages to learning two languages at the same time? Are bilingual children at a disadvantage?**
Children may develop additive or subtractive bilingualism, and may develop it successively or sequentially. Code switching often appears in the early stages of learning two languages, but its frequency decreases by the early preschool years. Bilingualism may slow the rate of language acquisition, but it may have cognitive benefits by encouraging greater reflection about language.

**8.16 What effects can early intervention programs have with children who are at risk for developmental problems?**
Programs such as Project Head Start, Early Head Start, the Abecedarian Project, and the High/Scope Perry Preschool Program were all created to help disadvantaged children succeed in school. Results vary, but the effects generally indicate improved rates of academic success, fewer school dropouts, and improved life conditions indicated by other measures.

**8.17 How do we know when children are ready to start kindergarten?**
Self-control of cognitive processes such as resisting temptations and distractions, working memory, and cognitive flexibility seem to be better predictors of later school success than specific math or reading skills or overall IQ. It does not seem to be helpful to hold younger children back before starting them in kindergarten; focus should be placed on preparing schools to educate all children.

## REVISITING THEMES

In this chapter, the *nature and nurture* theme is an underlying issue in the theories of Vygotsky and information processing (pp. 235–246), as well as in the discussion of language development and early childhood education (pp. 246–257). Vygotsky's theory acknowledges the importance of a healthy biological system, but he clearly emphasized the influence of one's social and cultural environment. Information processors describe basic processes such as processing capacity and attention, but they also emphasize the importance of developing automaticity through repeated practice and interaction with the environment. Even though some aspects of language development are strongly influenced by nature, other aspects such as learning the social rules of discourse depend on interaction within a social environment. An underlying issue in early childhood education is the importance of providing a high-quality environment to support and enhance inborn tendencies—and so influence the course of development in a positive direction.

The theme of *neuroscience* is also evident throughout this chapter. Neuroscience research is contributing to a better understanding of the genetic basis for aspects of attention (p. 243), and it is helping explain some of the reasons for the long-known "word spurt" that takes place in early childhood (p. 247). The discovery of mirror neurons is furthering our understanding of a number of aspects of development, including language and social interactions (pp. 245–246). The neural basis for bilingualism is an exciting area of research that will help us better understand the development of language (pp. 249–250).

Examples of the *diversity and multiculturalism* theme can be seen in this chapter's discussion of language development. Specifically, there are clear cultural differences in the social rules for discourse that children learn (p. 249), and the entire issue of bilingualism reflects an increased interest in and understanding of linguistic diversity—something that many parts of the world increasingly experience (pp. 249–250).

Finally, *plasticity and resilience in development* is an underlying issue in Piaget's theory (pp. 230–234); he viewed humans as active organisms always striving to understand our environment. The intuitive reasoning of the preoperational stage can be seen as attempts to actively adapt to and understand what is happening around us. Much of the interest in early childhood education programs stems from the notion of plasticity—that more positive developmental outcomes can be created by providing high-quality care early in life (pp. 252–256).

## KEY TERMS

Abecedarian Project (253)
animism (232)
artificialism (232)
attention (243)
automaticity (242)
bilingual (249)
collaborative learning (239)
conservation (233)
egocentrism (233)
High/Scope Perry Preschool Program (253)
internalization (236)
intuitive thought (233)
mediation (236)
metacognition (243)
mirror neurons (245)
operations (230)
overregularization (247)
preoperational thought (230)
private speech (236)
processing capacity (241)
processing efficiency (242)
Project Head Start (253)
scaffolding (239)
social rules of discourse (248)
social speech (236)
theory of mind (244)
zone of proximal development (ZPD) (236)

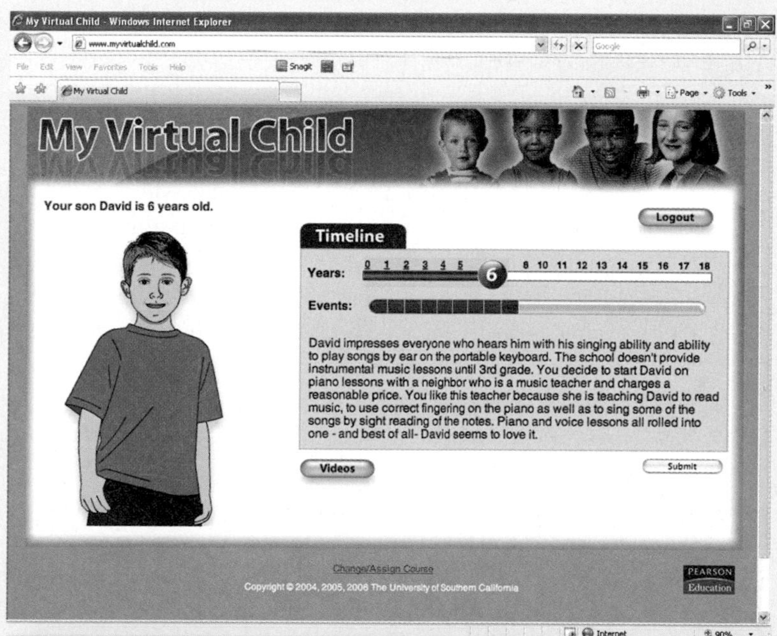


**"What decisions would you make while raising a child? What would the consequences of those decisions be?"**

Find out by accessing My Virtual Child at
**www.mydevelopmentlab.com**
and raising your own virtual child
from birth to age 18.

Watch Visit your Multimedia Library at www.mydevelopmentlab.com to watch an interview with Julie online.

# 9 EARLY CHILDHOOD

# Socioemotional Development in Early Childhood

Julie and her husband Tom have their hands full with three very active boys. Rocco (age 3) is already energetic, strong-willed, and independent. George (age 6) enjoys attention and loves making people laugh. He struggles with being so close in age to his older brother and yet not able to do all the things he does. He also gets upset with the attention his little brother Rocco receives. This causes him to act out or initiate scuffles with his brothers. Charlie is the oldest (age 8), and he seems to be more responsible, has better control over his behavior, and prefers that things run smoothly at home and school.

Sometimes, the boys will get very rough when they play. If one of the boys has a friend over to play, George sometimes acts out for attention by being destructive or arguing with the other boys. When this occurs, Julie tries to settle the dispute by talking to her boys. But this technique is often ineffective and the boys will quickly resume misbehaving. She finds that her boys respond when she raises her voice. She does not enjoy this type of approach but feels it is the only way to regain order and resolve a conflict quickly when a situation gets out of hand. The boys enjoy sports and playing outdoors. They sometimes play with girls, but mostly with other boys their age. When they are around girls, they seem to be a bit more calm and quiet.

Julie and Tom know their children understand right from wrong but sometimes feel the kids need to be reminded about appropriate behavior. They want the boys to be confident and feel good about themselves, but they are also teaching them how to respect other people. Things are going fairly smoothly in the family now, but Julie and Tom would like to learn other techniques they can use to control their boys' behavior, especially as the boys get larger and more physical. What else can they do to encourage the boys to behave well at home, at school, and with their friends? After studying this chapter you should be able to apply at least a dozen concepts and research findings that relate to Julie and Tom's story.

As you read this chapter, look for the "Think About Julie and Tom . . ." questions that ask you to think about what you're learning from their perspective.

Many parents have concerns and questions like Julie and Tom's. One of the great struggles for most parents is teaching their children good behavior and helping them learn right from wrong. During the early childhood period, children are learning who they are, how to get along with other children, and how to operate in the wider world. In this chapter we highlight these important topics, and along the way we hope that you will see useful advice for parents like Julie and Tom and for other people who raise or work with young children.

# The Social and Emotional Self

You have obviously known yourself all of your life, but have you ever wondered when you first recognized who you were? When did you first look at a photograph and say, "Hey, that's me!"? Young children have the interesting task of discovering who they are and also learning to relate properly to the other people in their lives. As children begin to play with friends and interact with other people, they need to learn self-control, how to handle their emotions, and how to behave in ways that are moral, ethical, and fair. We look at these issues of self-discovery in the first section of this chapter.

AS YOU STUDY THIS SECTION, ASK YOURSELF THESE QUESTIONS:

**9.1** What is the "self," and how do children learn to regulate their own thoughts, behaviors, and emotions?

**9.2** What do young children understand about gender—about the similarities and differences between boys and girls?

**9.3** How do young children think about moral issues, and what stages do they go through in their development of moral reasoning?

## The Self, Self-Regulation, and Emotions

**The Self.** Based on the pioneering work of William James (1890/1950), psychologists distinguish between two basic aspects of the **self**, or the characteristics, emotions, and beliefs people have about themselves. The first aspect is the **I-self**—the conscious awareness that you exist as a separate, unique person. The I-self involves understanding that you have your own individual thoughts, perceptions, emotions, experiences, and actions, and that you continue to exist across time and contexts. Also part of the I-self is a sense of *personal agency,* the understanding that your actions and emotions can affect the environment, including the behavior and emotions of other people. The second aspect of the self is the **me-self**, or what you know about yourself. The me-self includes things like the categories by which people define themselves (e.g., gender, age) as well as people's objective knowledge of their own personalities and physical and cognitive characteristics (Harter, 2006).

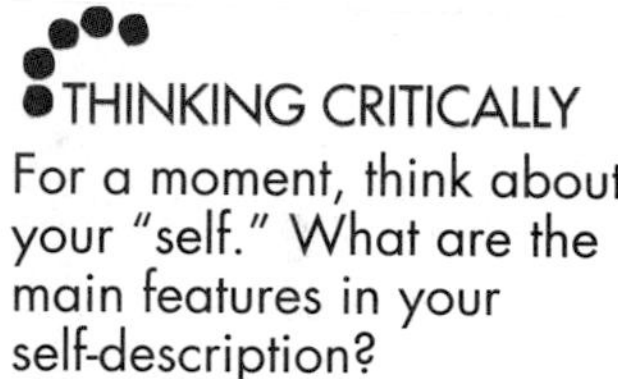
THINKING CRITICALLY
For a moment, think about your "self." What are the main features in your self-description?

Most psychologists do not believe that a sense of self is present at birth. Instead, most believe that the I-self and the me-self are cognitive constructions that children create as their cognitive skills develop. Young children construct *working models of the self,* or increasingly complex cognitive representations of who they are. These working models change as children have more experiences and interact with more people. Their developing cognitive abilities enable children to recognize and integrate their personal characteristics, compare themselves to others, and deal with contradictory information. For example, a boy may think of himself as a nice person but also may realize that sometimes he does not want to do nice things like share his toys. His developing cognitive skills help him understand that there are situations in which it is okay not to share or that there are different ways to be nice other than sharing. He can still think of himself as "nice" even though he is not behaving nicely all the time.

**self**
The characteristics, emotions, and beliefs people have about themselves, including an understanding that people are unique individuals.

**I-self**
The conscious awareness that you exist as a separate and unique person and that you can affect others.

**me-self**
What you know about yourself and how you describe yourself.

The me-self actually emerges by about 2 years of age. At first, the child's understanding of self is very concrete: "I have brown hair," and "I live in the yellow house." Younger children often give actual demonstrations of the things they mention, such as reciting

THINK ABOUT JULIE AND TOM . . .
Given Rocco's age, do you think he recognizes himself? What do you think he understands about "self" at this age?

their ABCs or running fast; their concepts are still closely tied to concrete behavior. Also, younger children's descriptions tend to be very disjointed, indicating that their self-representations are not integrated into an overall sense of self. Over the early childhood years, however, their self-descriptions become *increasingly abstract,* referring more and more to intangible qualities such as responsibility or conscientiousness. They also show *increasing differentiation* of aspects of the self and they are also more *realistic* in their assessments of their abilities. A 5-year-old, for example, may understand that he is very good at riding a bicycle but not very talented in math or spelling (Harter, 1999).

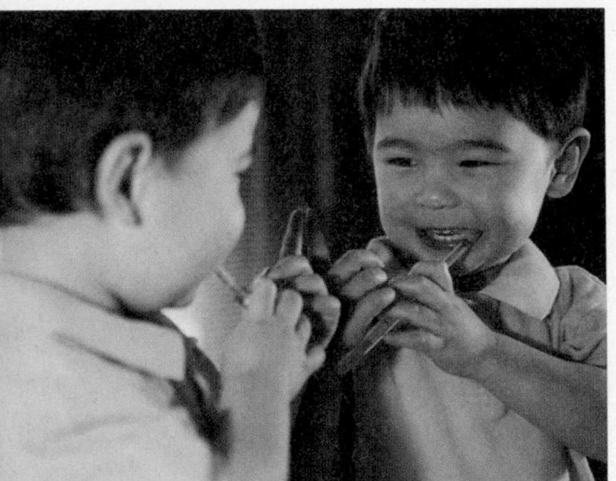

▲ What does this young child know about himself? Has he developed a me-self yet?

You can recognize that this pattern of moving from concrete to more abstract self-representations fits with Piaget's theory of cognitive development. Self-representations are concepts that children construct as they learn to understand themselves, and this process improves as cognitive development proceeds. Social interactions are also vital in helping children learn about themselves. Some theorists describe a *looking-glass self* (Cooley, 1902; Mead, 1934) which is the idea that in social situations children use other people's reactions and comments as a "social mirror into which the individual gazes to detect their opinions toward the self" (Harter, 2006, p. 511).

Researchers are also investigating links to genetics and biology, and they have found that the heritability estimates for self-concepts and self-esteem are moderate to strong, ranging from .30 to .60 depending on how and when they are measured (Hur, McGee, & Iacono, 1998; Kamakura, Ando, & Ono, 2007; Neiss, Sedikides, & Stevenson, 2006). When neuroscientists use MRI procedures to scan the brains of young children, they find that the emergence of self-representations correlates with maturity in the area of the brain where the temporal and parietal lobes meet (Lewis & Carmody, 2008). This is also the area that becomes most active when a child hears his or her own name.

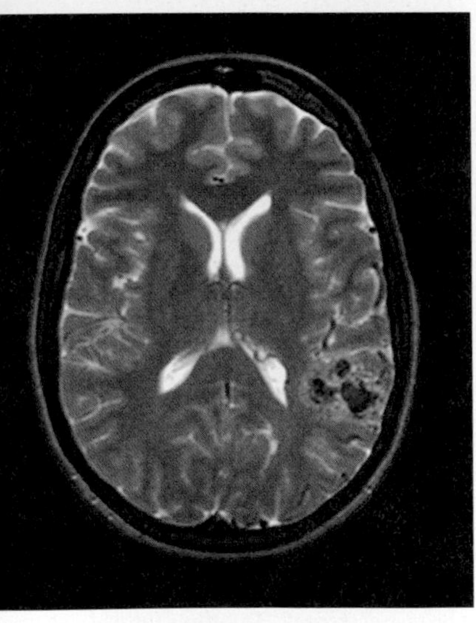

▲ Researchers study the maturity of specific areas of children's brains and link these patterns to maturity in self-representation, self-regulation, and other behaviors and mental processes.

**Self-Regulation.** One of the most important skills that children develop is the ability to control aspects of the self. **Self-regulation** is the ability to control your own thoughts, behaviors, and emotions, altering them in accordance with the demands of the situation. It includes the abilities to *inhibit* first responses, to *resist interference* from irrelevant stimulation, and to *persist* on relevant tasks even when we don't enjoy them. For example, when our son Will was young, he liked to play board games with his sisters. Will had developed reasonable self-regulation skills for his age, so he usually did not give in to the temptation to cheat when his sisters weren't looking (inhibiting first responses). Most of the time, he was able to ignore their incessant singing of "Jingle Bells" as he played (resisting interference) or distract himself by focusing on the game when he started to feel irritated by the singing (emotional regulation). Though he might not do so on his own, Will did help clean up the game and put it away when we asked, even though he didn't really want to (persisting on less enjoyable tasks). Can you envision what this scene would be like if Will and his sisters had few or no self-regulation skills? We prefer to not think about it!

**self-regulation**
The ability to control our own thoughts, behaviors, and emotions and change them to meet the demands of the situation.

Mature self-regulation requires several sophisticated cognitive skills. These include awareness of the demands of any given situation; consistent monitoring of your own behavior, thoughts, and strategies; consideration of how successfully you are meeting the demands of the situation; and the ability to change aspects of your current functioning as needed to fit the situation or to accomplish a goal. Aspects of self-regulation correlate with various positive outcomes for children and adolescents—including better academic performance, problem-solving skills, and reading comprehension; more satisfying interactions with peers; higher levels of intrinsic motivation, self-worth, perceived competence, self-efficacy, moral cognition, and moral conduct; fewer behavior problems; and lower levels of psychopathology (e.g., depression) (Eisenberg, Smith, Sadovsky, & Spinrad, 2004; Grolnick, Kurowski, & Gurland, 1999; Howse, Lange, Farran, & Boyles, 2003; Kochanska, Murray, & Cox, 1997; Ryan, Connell, & Grolnick, 1992).

How do children develop self-regulation skills? From 3 through 7 years of age children grow steadily in their abilities to inhibit first responses. For example, if you are hiding something, and you ask a child to "not peek," it is very difficult for 2- and 3-year-olds to inhibit the urge to look. Older children are much better at inhibiting responses, so they can resist peeking; they can also inhibit the urge to play more when asked to put their toys away, and they can control other behaviors as well (Rothbart, Sheese, & Posner, 2007). Several factors influence the development of self-regulation. Researchers have linked aspects of temperament (see Chapter 6) such as behavioral inhibition, effortful control, and fearfulness to several self-regulatory behaviors, including emotional regulation, cheating, compliance with adults' requests, and following rules (Kochanska, Coy, & Murray, 2001; Kochanska, Murray, & Harlan, 2000; Rothbart & Bates, 1998). Neuroscience research shows that self-regulation is related to maturation of certain areas of the brain, especially the frontal lobes and some of the pathways that lie deeper within the brain (Rothbart et al., 2007). The frontal lobes undergo two periods of rapid growth, one during infancy and another between the ages of 4 and 7—and these periods are consistent with the developmental trends in self-regulation we've described (Hudspeth & Pribram, 1990; Luria, 1973). There are also links to genetics—researchers have identified particular genes that are related to how well children can regulate their attention and behavior (Rothbart et al., 2007).

▲ One way that children learn self-regulation is by watching adults. Children internalize and imitate the behaviors and self-regulation strategies that they see in the important people around them.

But these biological links do not mean that self-regulation is completely innate. Aspects of the child's environment have a strong influence. In fact, most psychologists believe that self-regulation, though influenced by biological factors, begins with external control by others and gradually becomes internalized. For example, children learn specific strategies for regulating behavior and emotions by *modeling*—the process of imitating, practicing, and internalizing others' behavior (Schunk & Zimmerman, 1997). Children often use *private speech,* or speech they direct toward themselves (see the discussion of Vygotsky's theory in Chapter 8), to guide their problem-solving efforts and to regulate behavior, cognitive strategies, or emotions.

It also appears that the *way* adults try to direct children's behavior and emotions affects how quickly and how well self-regulatory skills develop. For example, children are more likely to change their behavior if they agree with a given request. When children comply because they agree with the request, there is a greater chance that they will view the request as being their own idea, or at least regard it as sensible, and not view it as interfering with their attempts to be independent (Kochanska et al., 2001). Compliance under these conditions may ultimately lead to more effective self-regulation. When a child disagrees but is forced to comply anyway, there is less internalization of the parents' standards, and parents tend to resort to more power-based (rather than reason-based) control tactics. When children don't comply, parents tend to get more negative and demanding, and this can cause a cycle of power and control issues in the family (Gauvain & Perez, 2008).

THINKING CRITICALLY

How well do you regulate your behavior and emotions? How could you do this more effectively?

Think for a moment about the implications of this. There will always be times when a child disagrees with parental requests, rules, or decisions. But forcing obedience through the use of power and control may delay the very thing that parents are trying to teach! Strategies that encourage internalization of social standards (e.g., explaining the rationale for a rule, involving children in establishing goals and rules, and so on) require more time and effort from caregivers but are probably more likely to produce voluntary self-regulation. Later in this chapter we explore parenting styles, including use of parental power, and their effects on children's cognitive, social, and emotional development.

THINK ABOUT JULIE AND TOM . . .

How can Julie and Tom use these concepts to help their sons learn self-regulation? What advice would you give?

**Emotions.** Infants don't fully understand that they are separate from other people and do not yet reflect on themselves as separate individuals. Consequently, their emotions

▲ This child is happy because she anticipates that she will enjoy what is inside the present. By age 5, children's emotions can be triggered by what they expect or believe will happen.

often echo the emotional states of their caregivers and other people (Saarni, Mumme, & Campos, 1998); cry contagion (crying simply because they hear another infant's cry) and imitation of facial expressions are examples. Later, as children develop the capacity for self-reflection, they begin to appreciate that their emotions are their own personal responses to the situations and events around them. For example, they understand that they can enjoy a toy or TV show even if their friends don't, or that they may be more afraid of thunderstorms than their siblings or friends.

By age 2, children are spontaneously talking about their feelings and the feelings of other people (Saarni et al., 1998). They are also becoming aware that their emotional reactions may differ from those of other people. A child's emerging *theory of mind* (see Chapter 8) helps the child understand individual differences in emotions. By 2 to 3 years of age, children understand that emotions are connected to their mental appraisals of what they want, like, don't want, and don't like (Wellman, Harris, Banerjee, & Sinclair, 1995). By the age of 5, children's understandings are more dynamic—they understand that events that confirm or disconfirm their beliefs or expectations can trigger emotions. If they think they "should" get a treat, they expect that they will be pleased, happy, or satisfied when they receive one. If they get an unexpected treat, they understand that surprise can result. Anger and sadness, however, can follow when expectations are not met. Because our beliefs, expectations, likes, dislikes, and other mental appraisals differ, we each have our own emotional reactions to events. By middle childhood, children understand these individual responses, and they are also improving their ability to control their emotions or regulate their own emotional reactions. As with other aspects of self-regulation, emotional control has a significant genetic component—identical twins are more similar in how well they regulate their emotions than are fraternal twins (Goldsmith, Pollak, & Davidson, 2008).

As children begin to understand the individualized nature of emotions, they tend to see and report their own positive emotions more than their negative emotions—they show a **positive emotion bias** (Saarni et al., 1998). For example, if you describe a hypothetical scenario, 6-year-olds predict a more positive emotional reaction for themselves than for other children (Karniol & Koren, 1987). Five-year-olds are less likely than 7-year-olds to report being sad (Glasberg & Aboud, 1982). Maybe adults value happiness in children so much that younger children bow to the social pressure, exaggerating their positive emotions and denying or minimizing sadness and other negative emotions. Boys in particular seem to get a message to hide sadness, and they become more skilled at veiling this emotion as they mature (Chaplin, Cole, & Zahn-Waxler, 2005). In one study, boys and girls expressed sadness about equally at age 6 (Fuchs & Thelen, 1988). In middle childhood, however, gender differences emerged, and by age 11 boys were only half as likely as girls to express sad feelings. Further, boys reported that they would be less likely to communicate their sadness to their fathers than to their mothers. Boys seem to learn that sadness is not socially accepted for males, and it appears that they are getting this message during early childhood. Another aspect of the positive emotion bias is that children are more accurate in recognizing other people's positive emotions and less accurate in recognizing negative emotions (Fabes, Eisenberg, Nyman, & Micheaulieu, 1991; Gross & Ballif, 1991).

## Developing Ideas about Gender

A major component of understanding the self is understanding what it means to be a boy or a girl. Some aspects of gender knowledge appear quite early in childhood. By 2½ years, children are able to apply gender labels correctly (e.g., *boy, girl, mommy, daddy*). However, young children tend to use surface features such as hairstyles and clothing to determine if someone is female or male. For example, when asked whether she was a girl or a boy and how she knew, 5-year-old Rachel pointed to her shoulder-length hair and

**positive emotion bias**
Tendency of children to report more positive than negative emotions.

replied without hesitation, "I'm a girl, because my hair is long and sometimes I wear dresses." When asked, "What if you had short hair? Would you still be a girl?" Rachel replied with exasperation, "I wouldn't *have* short hair—I'm a girl!" It is not until about the age of 8 years that most children use genital cues to determine gender and understand that surface features can vary across boys and girls (Intons-Peterson, 1988; McConaghy, 1979).

▲ Children sometimes receive explicit reinforcement for sex-typed behavior, but reinforcement can also be unspoken and subtle.

Children begin to show *gender-stereotyped preferences* even before they have a full understanding of their own gender. For example, by age 2 they begin to prefer sex-typed toys (e.g., dolls if they are female, cars if they are male). Boys show a tendency to avoid playing with "girls' toys" as early as 2 to 3 years of age (Fagot, Leinbach, & Hagan, 1986; Powlishta, Serbin, & Moller, 1993). These experiences are also reflected in their vocabulary development—by 2 years of age, more boys are using male-oriented words such as *fire truck* and more girls are using female-oriented words such as *dress* (Stennes, Burch, Sen, & Bauer, 2005). By the time children are 3 years old, they are already beginning to show **gender segregation** in their peer preferences—the tendency to play and associate with peers of their own sex. This trend increases significantly, and gender segregation remains quite marked until adolescence. We have much more to say about gender segregation later in this chapter. By the time children are 5 years old, their gender stereotypes of activities, toys, behavior, and even personality traits are quite well developed. **Watch** on **mydevelopmentlab**

**Watch** a video on Early Gender Typing.
www.mydevelopmentlab.com

*Gender stereotypes* during the late preschool and kindergarten years are also fairly rigid. For example, kindergartners react quite negatively to cross-gender behavior in peers, especially if it involves cross-gender appearance such as when a boy is wearing a dress (Signorella, Bigler, & Liben, 1993; Stoddart & Turiel, 1985). These stereotypes tend to strengthen from 3 to 8 years of age. Children who hold the strongest stereotypes at a younger age are the ones who seek out same-sex playmates the most and avoid cross-sex activities the most, so their gender stereotypes are reinforced and strengthened. In one study, girls showed this intensifying effect more so than did boys (Golombok et al., 2008). After about 8 years of age, gender stereotypes will start to become more flexible as children begin to understand that most gender norms for behavior, activities, occupations, and the like are culturally determined rather than absolute.

THINK ABOUT JULIE AND TOM . . .

Given these age trends in gender stereotyping, what should Julie and Tom expect to see with their boys?

Remember Jean Piaget's cognitive developmental theory described in Chapters 5 and 8? Lawrence Kohlberg applied Piaget's theory and proposed that knowledge of gender and gender-related behavior constitutes a cognitive category and develops in the same way as knowledge of any other cognitive category: through interaction with the world that is filtered through existing cognitive structures. According to Kohlberg, children will not have a mature understanding of gender until they achieve the Piagetian stage of concrete operations, which happens by approximately age 7 (Kohlberg, 1966). The key concept children must grasp in order to understand gender is that of **gender constancy**, or the understanding that an individual's gender remains the same despite changes in outward appearance or behavior (e.g., in hairstyle, clothing, or mannerisms). As you may notice, this idea is simply another form of the Piagetian concept of *conservation* that we described in Chapter 8.

Researchers have used Kohlberg's theory to identify three stages of gender understanding (Slaby & Frey, 1975):

- *Gender identity* (by 2½ years): Children's ability to categorize themselves and others correctly as boys or girls.
- *Gender stability* (by 4 to 5 years): The understanding that gender is a stable characteristic over time—that boys continue to be boys, and girls continue to be girls.
- *Gender constancy* (also called *gender consistency;* by 6 to 7 years): The understanding that gender is consistent across changes in outward appearance such as hairstyles or clothing.

**gender segregation**
The tendency of children to associate with others of their same sex.

**gender constancy**
The understanding that gender remains the same despite superficial changes in appearance or behavior.

Kohlberg proposed that all children progress through these stages in the same order, and studies in several different cultures have supported this sequence of development (Munroe, Shimmin, & Munroe, 1984).

## Moral Development

As children learn self-regulation and learn to understand their own emotions, they also begin to form a **conscience**—ideas children have about right and wrong. By 3 to 4 years of age, children have internalized many rules and have begun to feel guilt about their bad behavior and empathy for other children or people who have been wronged (Aksan & Kochanska, 2005). These feelings reflect the child's developing conscience and sense of *morality*, and this can be a very positive aspect of child development. **Morality** involves knowing the difference between what is right and wrong and acting on that knowledge. **Moral reasoning** refers to the many ways people think about right and wrong. We mentioned that Lawrence Kohlberg applied Piaget's theory in order to understand gender development in children; Kohlberg also applied Piaget's theory to understand morality. To study morality, Kohlberg presented children with stories that contained moral dilemmas (Kohlberg, 1969; Kohlberg, Levine, & Hewer, 1984). How did the children reason through the dilemmas? **Watch** on **mydevelopmentlab**

**Watch** a video on Moral Development. www.mydevelopmentlab.com

Pretend for a moment that someone dear to you is very sick and will soon die if they do not receive treatment. There is a new drug available that might help, but the pharmacist who developed it is asking a very high price, much more than it cost him to develop the drug. You cannot afford the price, and the druggist will not agree to sell it more cheaply or to let you pay for it later. You are becoming desperate and are considering stealing the drug. Should you? Why, or why not?

Moral dilemmas like this create a conflict between two values (e.g., saving a person's life versus obeying the law). Kohlberg believed that moral development depends on a person's level of cognitive development. You cannot think about moral issues in a sophisticated way if you do not have a fairly high level of overall cognitive development. **Perspective taking**—the ability to understand the psychological perspectives, motives, and needs of others—also is essential. To understand a person's intentions and reasons for acting, you have to be able to put yourself in the other person's place and view the situation as the other person might (Selman, 1980).

But cognitive development and perspective-taking ability alone are not enough. That is, they are *necessary but not sufficient* for moral development. Children also must directly experience and think about moral issues and dilemmas in order to understand that their current level of moral reasoning is not adequate. As you may recall, Piaget called this kind of imbalance between experiences and current understanding *cognitive disequilibrium*. Like Piaget, Kohlberg believed that moral development requires us to feel a certain degree of disequilibrium, or discomfort with our current way of thinking, to spur our cognitive construction of more complex and sophisticated reasoning about moral questions.

Kohlberg theorized that children progress through three broad levels of moral reasoning, with each level divided into two specific stages, as shown in Table 9.1. He believed that these stages were universal and constant—that all children move through the same stages in the same order. However, the pace of development and the final endpoint will differ depending on the specific moral experiences encountered, cognitive maturity, and perspective-taking ability.

Think about the meaning of the word *convention* and you'll understand why Kohlberg's levels are labeled as they are (Table 9.1). A **convention** is a rule or practice that members of a social group agree to abide by in their behavior, choices, and decisions. At Kohlberg's first level, children have not yet developed the understanding that rules are social conventions, so this is called the **preconventional level**. At this level children accept the rules of powerful others without thinking about where those rules come from, whether they are fixed or

**conscience**
Ideas children have about right and wrong.

**morality**
Knowing the difference between what is right and wrong and acting on that knowledge.

**moral reasoning**
The ways in which people think about right and wrong.

**perspective taking**
The ability to understand the psychological perspectives, motives, and needs of others.

**convention**
A rule or practice that members of a social group agree to abide by in their behaviors, choices, and decisions.

**preconventional level**
Level of moral reasoning where children do not yet understand that rules are social conventions; children accept the rules of powerful others.

**TABLE 9.1**
**Kohlberg's Levels and Stages of Moral Reasoning**

| | |
|---|---|
| **LEVEL I:** **PRECONVENTIONAL MORAL REASONING** | *Stage 1: Punishment and obedience orientation* Children decide what is right based on whether the action will be punished or rewarded, but do not consider the interests of others. They obey because adults have greater power. |
| | *Stage 2: Individualism, instrumental purpose, and exchange* Children follow rules when it serves their own needs or interests. They are aware that others have interests, and that they may conflict with their own. |
| **LEVEL II:** **CONVENTIONAL MORAL REASONING** | *Stage 3: Mutual interpersonal expectations, relationships, and interpersonal conformity* Children are concerned with living up to others' expectations. "Being good" is important, and it means having good intentions, being concerned about others, being loyal and trustworthy. |
| | *Stage 4: Social system and conscience* Children define what is right according to what fulfills duties they have agreed to carry out. They abide by laws except in extreme cases. Moral actions are those that the larger society has determined are right. |
| **LEVEL III:** **POSTCONVENTIONAL MORAL REASONING** | *Stage 5: Social contract or utility and individual rights* Values and rules are seen as relative to a particular group and can be changed. Rules should be followed for the welfare and protection of all people's rights, and what is moral is what is best for the largest number of people. Some values, such as life and liberty, are recognized as nonrelative and must be upheld regardless of socially agreed upon laws. |
| | *Stage 6: Universal ethical principles* People develop and follow their own self-chosen ethical principles, which are part of an integrated and carefully thought-out system of values. If social laws violate these principles, the person's actions will be consistent with their ethical principles. |

(Adapted from Kohlberg, 1984.)

flexible, or whether some circumstances could allow changes in the rules. In Stage 1, children determine what is "moral" on the basis of rewards or punishments, regardless of whether the intention was good or not. Is it "wrong" to take a cookie (or steal some medicine)? Well, if you get caught and punished, then it is wrong; if you are not caught and punished, then it is not wrong! In Stage 2, children are beginning to understand that others have different perspectives, but they are not able to see a situation from another's perspective. Their moral reasoning at this stage is based on meeting their own egocentric needs—what is "good" is what serves their interests. During early childhood, most children use Stage 1 reasoning to think about moral issues, and a few may use Stage 2. The remaining stages are used by older children and adolescents, so we will discuss those stages in later chapters.

As you can see, the early childhood years are a period of self-discovery. Young children are learning who they are and what they are like. Although there is much progress yet to be made, they are learning how to handle their emotional reactions and how to think about what is right and wrong. This area of development is greatly affected by the style of parenting children receive and the types of discipline procedures used by their parents. Children's self-discovery continues as they play in social groups and learn to form close friendships with other children. We explore these topics in the next sections.

**THINKING CRITICALLY**
For each of Kohlberg's stages, try to think of someone who reasons about moral issues at that stage. What has helped some of these people move to higher stages? At what stage would you place yourself?

**THINK ABOUT JULIE AND TOM . . .**
How can Julie and Tom use Kohlberg's stages to evaluate where their sons are in moral development?

## LET'S REVIEW . . .

1. The I-self is our ____________.
   a. objective knowledge of our own characteristics
   b. understanding that we exist as a separate person
   c. ability to understand events from another person's perspective
   d. accumulation of feelings about ourselves
2. Which of the following is the clearest example of self-regulation?
   a. Sarah knows what she likes and what she does not like.
   b. Mark cries when his mother leaves him all alone.
   c. Robbie would like to take his brother's toy, but he resists the temptation.
   d. Debbie is shy and does not like loud social situations.
3. Steven, a 3-year-old boy, once said that he might play with dolls someday when he grows up to be a girl. Steven's comment shows that he has not yet developed the concept of ____________.
   a. gender stability
   b. gender constancy
   c. gender segregation
   d. gender identity
4. Lawrence Kohlberg gave children stories that contained ethical dilemmas, and he asked the children to decide what they would do in the story and why. In this study, Kohlberg was studying children's ____________.
   a. gender concepts
   b. individualized emotions
   c. self-regulation
   d. moral reasoning
5. True or False: The "me-self" usually begins to emerge at about 3 years of age.
6. True or False: During early childhood, most children use what they know about rewards and punishments to determine which acts are "good" and which are "bad."

Answers: 1. b, 2. c, 3. a, 4. d, 5. F, 6. T

# Parenting

In this next section, we shed some light on parenting practices that can support the development of happy and well-adjusted children. Although parenting is never an easy task, this information should be helpful for parents or anyone else who works with children.

AS YOU STUDY THIS SECTION, ASK YOURSELF THESE QUESTIONS:

9.4 How do researchers define parental warmth and parental control?

9.5 What are the four parenting styles described by Baumrind and other researchers, and what outcomes are associated with each style?

9.6 Why is spanking an ineffective method of discipline, and what's a more positive approach that parents can use?

## Dimensions of Parenting

In studying characteristics of parenting, researchers have identified two dimensions that are especially important: *warmth* and *control.* **Parental warmth** is the degree to which parents are accepting, responsive, and compassionate with their children. Parents who are high in warmth are very supportive, nurturing, and caring. They pay close attention to their children's needs, and their parenting behaviors tend to be child-centered (focused on the needs of the child rather than on the convenience or demands of the parents). Researchers see parental warmth as existing on a broad continuum—from parents who show a high degree of warmth to those who show little or no warmth. At the lower end of the continuum are parents who are rejecting, unresponsive to their children, and more parent-centered than child-centered. This *cold* type of parenting is obviously detrimental to the child's development. Numerous studies have shown that children who experience cold parenting are more aggressive, are less popular, and perform more poorly in school. Conversely, when parenting is high in warmth, children show better social and academic

**parental warmth**
The degree to which parents are accepting, responsive, and compassionate with their children.

skills, and they show more love and respect for their parents and other people (Maccoby & Martin, 1983; Parke & Buriel, 1998).

▲ Parents high in warmth are supportive, nurturing, and caring, and pay close attention to their children's needs.

**Parental control** is the degree to which parents set limits, enforce rules, and maintain discipline with children. Parents who are high in control set firm limits on their children's behavior, and they consistently enforce rules. They are involved in their children's lives and use discipline to provide structure for their children's behaviors. Parents low in control, however, are lax, permissive, or uninvolved with their children. Like parental warmth, control is on a continuum: Some parents show a high degree of control, some only a moderate degree, and others very little control or involvement with their children.

When we look at parental warmth and parental control, it is important to consider their combined effects. When warm parents use firm control, for example, discipline tends to be child-centered, age-appropriate, and positive. When cold and rejecting parents use firm control, however, discipline can be very harsh, punitive, and even abusive. By itself, neither warmth nor control is sufficient for explaining the effects of parenting on children's developmental outcomes.

Researchers also draw a distinction between *physical control* and *psychological control.* Physical control involves the use of physical means to control children, such as hitting, spanking, pushing, and physically forcing children to do things. Psychological control uses guilt, humiliation, love withdrawal, or emotional manipulation to control children. Both forms of control can be harmful, especially when used by parents who are cold or rejecting with their children. One study of Chinese families, for example, showed that fathers who used more physical control had sons who were more physically aggressive with their peers. In this same study, psychological control by mothers was related to increases in physical and emotional aggressiveness in their daughters (Nelson, Hart, Yang, Olsen, & Jin, 2006). Therefore, the effects of physical and psychological control may depend on the parent inflicting the control and on the gender of the child who is being controlled.

## Parenting Styles

In the mid-1960s, Diana Baumrind began a longitudinal study investigating the effects of different styles of parenting. Her follow-up studies, and the many similar studies conducted by other researchers, have strongly influenced how parents and professionals think about parenting. The research has identified four distinct styles of parenting that represent the different combinations of high and low parental warmth combined with high and low parental control (Baumrind, 1973, 1991; Maccoby & Martin, 1983). Figure 9.1 (page 272) shows these four parenting styles in a 2 × 2 matrix of warmth and control. Let's look more closely at these styles. As we describe each style, consider what might happen if a 4-year-old child is caught hitting his sister. Ask yourself—what would you (or your parents) do in a situation like this? 

Watch a video on Parenting Styles. www.mydevelopmentlab.com

**Authoritative parents** are warm and exert firm control. They monitor their children closely and have clear standards and high expectations for their behavior. They tend to use disciplinary methods that are supportive rather than punitive. There is clear communication between parent and child, and the lines of communication go both ways. Authoritative parents listen carefully to their children, and they allow give-and-take on disciplinary matters in a way that is age appropriate for the child. If their 4-year-old hits another child, their first response is likely to sit with the child and have a calm discussion about the incident. "Why did you hit her?" Authoritative parents are understanding and supportive ("We know you were frustrated and angry"), but they will set boundaries for their children and institute appropriate consequences if the child does not behave ("You know the family rule is 'no hitting,' so now you will lose your TV time"). The important point is that authoritative parents are rational, consistent, and child-centered in their approaches to discipline.

**parental control**
The degree to which parents set limits, enforce rules, and maintain discipline with children.

**authoritative parents**
Parents who are warm and exert firm control.

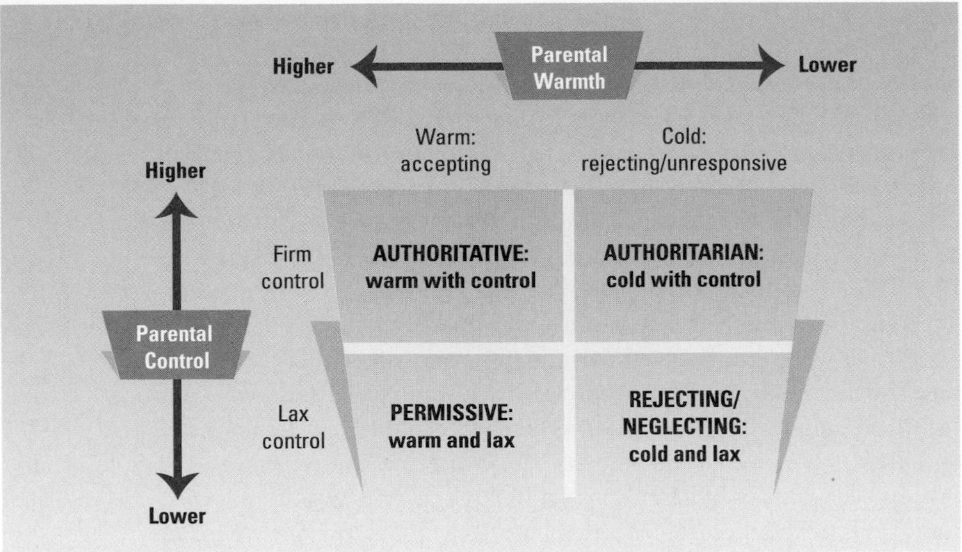


FIGURE 9.1 ▶ **Parental Warmth and Control Matrix**
Two dimensions of parenting (parental warmth and parental control) produce four styles of parenting: authoritative, authoritarian, permissive, and rejecting/neglecting. Research has associated the four styles with different outcomes for children.

Over time, authoritative parents expect their children to develop the ability to regulate their own behavior. Compared to other children, children raised by authoritative parents perform better in school, are less hostile and more popular among friends, have greater self-esteem, show more purpose and independence in their activities, and as adolescents they are more accurate in understanding their parents' values (Baumrind, 1973, 1991; Knafo & Schwartz, 2003; Parke & Buriel, 1998).

**Authoritarian parents** also exert firm control, but they do it in a way that is rejecting or unresponsive to the child. "No hitting!" they might yell. "What were you thinking!? Now you get over here right now!" Authoritarian parents set firm limits and expect that their children will behave. Their disciplinary methods tend to be harsh and punitive. Rather than having a rational discussion of an incident, they are more inclined to lower the boom immediately without regard for the child's perspective. Children raised in an authoritarian environment may feel trapped and angry but afraid to confront their parents (Parke & Buriel, 1998). They perform less well in school, are more hostile and aggressive, are less popular with their peers, and are less independent than children reared by authoritative parents (Baumrind, 1973).

**Permissive parents** are warm but have little control. They fail to set or enforce appropriate limits for their children. Permissive parents avoid confrontation with their children. Being too lenient, they do not require that their children behave in a mature and responsible manner. Sometimes permissive parents justify their style by saying they'd rather be a friend than a parent to their children. A permissive parent might dismiss misbehavior lightly ("Now you know we don't hit, so don't let me see you do that again"). At the extreme, permissive parents can become *indulgent*—beyond merely allowing their children to misbehave, they may actually encourage or foster their misbehavior: "Well, if he hit you, then you just hit him back!" As their children and teens grow older, permissive–indulgent parents may encourage or condone inappropriate behaviors such as skipping school, vandalism, alcohol or drug abuse, or sexual promiscuity. Compared to authoritatively raised children, children from permissive homes are more impulsive, perform less well in school, and are less self-assured, independent, and confident in their activities (Parke & Buriel, 1998).

**Rejecting/neglecting parents** don't set limits and are unresponsive to their children's needs. This category of parenting has two substyles: *Rejecting parents* are harsh and actively reject their children, whereas *neglecting parents* ignore their children and fail to

**authoritarian parents**
Parents who exert firm control but are rejecting or unresponsive to their children.

**permissive parents**
Parents who are warm but have little control over their children.

**rejecting/neglecting parents**
Parents who don't set limits and are unresponsive to their children's needs.

fulfill their responsibilities as parents. These parents don't monitor their children properly and may not notice misbehaviors. Rejecting/neglecting parents may be under too much stress to parent appropriately; they may not be committed to the task of raising children; or they may be depressed or otherwise psychologically or emotionally unavailable to their children. Children raised by rejecting/neglecting parents fare the worst of all. Compared to other children, rejected/neglected children grow up to show higher rates of delinquency, alcohol and drug use, and early sexual activity. They perform more poorly in school and show other disruptions in peer relations and cognitive development (Parke & Buriel, 1998). **Listen** on **mydevelopmentlab**

In her later work Baumrind expanded the number of parenting styles to seven: *authoritative, democratic, nondirective, authoritarian–directive, nonauthoritarian–directive, unengaged,* and *good enough*. She also added two dimensions in addition to parental warmth and parental control. *Maturity demands* are parents' expectations that the child will show age-appropriate behavior, self-reliance, and self-control. *Democratic communication* is the degree to which parents ask for and consider the child's feelings and opinions. As you might expect, higher levels of each are indicative of more effective parenting. Research in this area also highlights the problem of *intrusiveness,* or control that parents maintain by psychologically manipulating and inhibiting

THINKING CRITICALLY

For each of the four parenting styles, describe of a parent you know who uses (or did use) the style. How did these different styles affect the children involved?

**Listen**: Does the type of parenting style really cause differences in child outcomes? (Author Podcast)
www.mydevelopmentlab.com

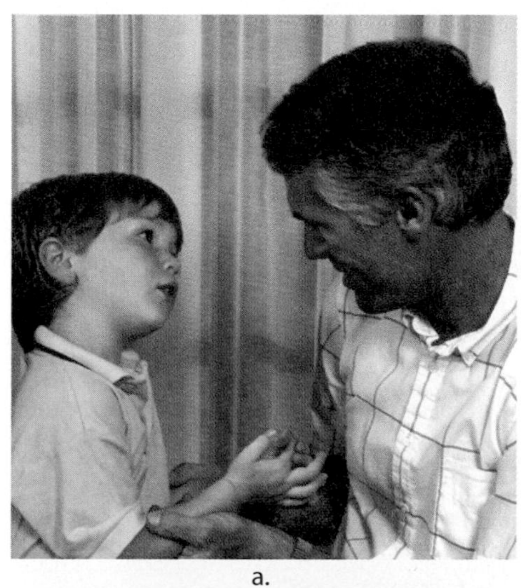

a.

b.

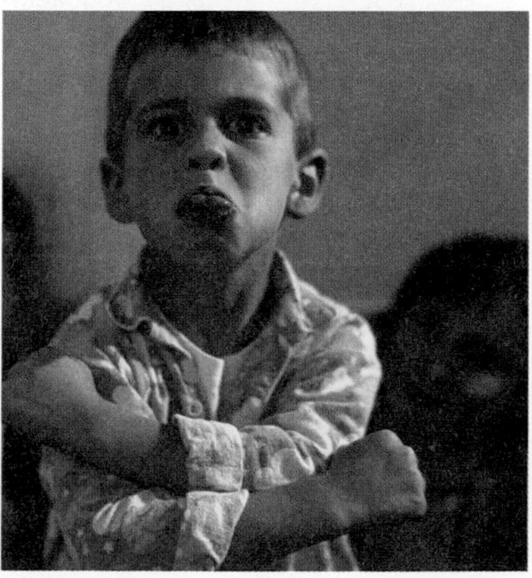

c.

d.

(a) Authoritative parents set limits and have appropriate control over children's behavior; they are warm, supportive, and respectful. (b) Authoritarian parents exert firm control, but demonstrate little warmth and respect for the child's point of view. They tend to use harsh and punitive disciplinary methods. (c) Permissive parents do not set or enforce limits, avoid confrontation with their children, and do not require their children to behave maturely or responsibly. (d) Rejecting/neglecting parents ignore or actively reject their children. They do not discipline their children, or do so harshly and inconsistently.

children. Studies have linked higher levels of intrusiveness with poorer outcomes for children and adolescents. Researchers have confirmed this finding in several different cultures, although children of "unengaged" parents still seem to fare worst of all (Barber, 2002; Baumrind, 1991).

Quality parenting is an issue of great interest and concern to all who work with children, but there is little agreement on how to improve it. One proposal involves requiring people to get a license before they can become parents. To read more about the pros and cons of this intriguing idea, read the Social Policy Perspective box called "Should Parents Have to Be Licensed?"

## Perspective SOCIAL POLICY — SHOULD PARENTS HAVE TO BE LICENSED?

We know a lot about different parenting styles and the child outcomes associated with them. As you can imagine, however, it isn't always easy to identify the "best" style. Different families' backgrounds, cultures, contexts, and temperaments may require different kinds of parenting behaviors. But have you ever seen a particularly troubling parent behavior and thought, "You ought to need a license to be a parent"?

Some are taking this idea very seriously (Lykken, 2000, 2001; Westman, 1994). They argue that parenting is a privilege and a responsibility, not a right. Requiring parents to obtain a license would communicate that parenting is just as important as all the other activities that we license, such as getting married, driving, or voting. Proponents of licensing also argue that people who wish to become foster or adoptive parents already must obtain official authorization; only parents raising their biological children need not be licensed. According to advocates of this idea, licensing would:

- Provide a way to determine parental competence "*before* rather than *after* damage to a child" (Westman, 1997, p. 201).
- Save millions of children the pain of neglect and abuse.
- Save society tremendous amounts of pain, suffering, and money. Advocates argue that incompetent parenting is a major cause of crime and violence, because it allows children to grow up unsocialized.
- Establish minimum parenting requirements, such as two parents "committed enough to be married to each other, who are mature and self-supporting, neither criminal nor incapacitated by mental illness" (Lykken, 2000, p. 599).
- Require that others who wish to raise a child (such as never-married women, divorced individuals, or gay and lesbian couples) obtain permission from a judge in family court.

As you might expect, this proposal is quite controversial. No one argues with the claim that it is better to have good parents than to have neglectful or abusive ones, but there are serious constitutionality questions about parental license requirements (Redding, 2002). In addition, licensing proponents clearly favor two-parent families, claiming that *both* biological parents should be present and committed to child rearing. Although a higher percentage of troubled youth come from single-parent rather than two-parent homes, opponents argue that the percentage is not nearly high enough to justify denying licenses to single parents (Scarr, 2000). Others point out that factors other than parenting, such as characteristics of a child's neighborhood culture, family income, and discrimination, also have important effects on children's outcomes. Opponents also maintain that it is only parents at the extremes who cause better or worse outcomes. "[P]retty good parents do not produce better children than average parents or pretty bad parents" (Harris, 2000, p. 630), and "very, very bad parents" are already addressed via (admittedly imperfect) social and child protective services. Perhaps most troubling to critics is the licensing scheme's distinct scent of social engineering. Would low-income parents be denied licenses? If so, ethnic minorities would be disproportionately affected, because they are more likely to be poor. Might not such a program limit the reproductive rights of certain groups to a greater degree than those of other segments of the population (Grigg, 1995)?

QUESTION **What do you think of parent licensing? Would it be a good way to reduce child neglect, child abuse, and violent crime? How could it be structured so as not to discriminate unfairly against lower-income and minority individuals, single adults, gay and lesbian couples, or those with less education? Who would implement it? How would policies be enforced? If parents lost their licenses, would the authorities remove their children from the home? Perhaps the idea of parent licensing is more complicated than it first appears.**

## Discipline: What's a Parent to Do?

The most important issue most parents face is how to provide appropriate discipline for their children. Psychologists use the word **discipline** to refer to the techniques parents and caregivers use to teach children appropriate behavior.

▲ Spanking is not an effective form of discipline in the long term, and it can have a variety of negative side effects.

**A Caution about Punishment.** Unfortunately, when most people think of *discipline,* they think immediately about **punishment**, or techniques used to eliminate or reduce undesirable behavior. Unless people have had special training in parenting or child development, they often overemphasize punishment when disciplining children. Too often, parents end up spanking, hitting, or yelling at children. Most parents don't want to be harsh with their children, but over time parents may lose their patience. They may feel that their problems are endless as young children fuss, fight, and get into things. With young children, 65% of parent–child interactions involve the parent telling the child *not* to do something, as in "Don't touch that!" "Get down!" or "Don't do that!" (Baumrind, 1996; Hoffman, 1975).

Surveys indicate that two-thirds of parents spank their 3-year-old children. Although spanking occurs in all types of families, the rates of spanking are somewhat higher when parents are African American, single, have lower incomes, report being frequently frustrated, or have children who have developmental delays or risks (Regalado, Sareen, Inkelas, Wissow, & Halfon, 2004; Socolar, Savage, & Evans, 2007). Reviewing the research in this area, experts report that 80% of children have been spanked, hit, or slapped by their parents by the time they reach fifth grade, and half have been hit with a belt or other object (Gershoff & Bitensky, 2007).

In the long run, spanking is not effective (Gershoff & Bitensky, 2007; Holden, 2002). When children are spanked, they eventually return to the misbehavior or replace it with other inappropriate behaviors. Hitting and spanking can cause children to fear their parents. If children try to run, or if they strike back or talk back to their parents, the hitting usually becomes more severe. Although most spanking is not legally considered physically abusive, it is true that most physical abuse begins as physical punishment—punishment that then goes too far (Straus, 2008).

Another thing to consider is the message that spanking sends to children. Do we want them to learn that "might makes right" or that it's appropriate for larger people to use physical force to get smaller people to obey? Ironically, hitting other children is the misbehavior that parents most often identify as calling for a spanking (Gershoff & Bitensky, 2007; Lehman, 1989; Straus, 1994). What message does the child get when the parent slaps or spanks them and says, "Don't hit other people!"?

Studies show that, compared to other children, children who are spanked more often are more physically violent and aggressive; are twice as likely to attack their siblings; have lower moral standards and lower self-esteem; are more likely to feel depressed; and as they grow up they are more likely to steal property, commit assaults, and commit other delinquent acts (Christie-Mizell, Pryor, & Grossman, 2008; Kerr, Lopez, Olson, & Sameroff, 2004; Mulvaney & Mebert, 2007; Straus, 1994; Straus, Sugarman, & Giles-Sims, 1997). Analyzing the results of 88 different studies, Gershoff (2002) found consistent correlations between physical punishment and increases in child aggression, delinquency, and antisocial behavior; increased rates of child abuse by parents; and poorer relationships between children and parents. Children whose parents physically punished them were less likely to internalize moral values, and later in life they were more likely to suffer from mental health problems such as low self-esteem, depression, and alcoholism. As adults they were more likely to be aggressive, commit crimes, and abuse their own children and spouses.

**discipline**
Techniques used to teach children appropriate behavior.

**punishment**
Techniques used to eliminate or reduce undesirable behavior.

A study from New Zealand showed that mothers were less supportive with their children when they were treated harshly by their own parents, so the cycle of ineffective parenting continues across generations (Belsky, Jaffee, Sligo, Woodward, & Silva, 2005). Researchers who studied families in Thailand, China, the Philippines, Italy, India, and Kenya found that physical punishment was related to higher levels of child aggression and anxiety in all of these countries (Lansford et al., 2005). When children are treated harshly by their parents, they feel vulnerable and less secure. They begin to interpret even neutral interactions as being hostile, and they react aggressively out of frustration and pent-up anger (Xu, Farver, & Zhang, 2009).

**THINKING CRITICALLY**
Were you spanked as a child? What is your opinion of the research findings regarding spanking? Why is physical punishment such a prominent feature of family life in the United States?

Of course, all of these findings on physical punishment are correlational. It could be that children and adolescents who are more violent and engage in more misbehavior simply are spanked and hit more often. One study found a mild genetic link where children who had behavioral styles that were more aggressive and defiant received more spanking from their parents, but the same researchers reported that differences in the frequencies of spanking seemed to be related more to issues related to parents than to genetics in the children (Jaffee et al., 2004). To be fair, too, we want to point out that other research suggests that the negative effects associated with spanking may be due to the style of parenting rather than to the spanking itself (Baumrind, Larzelere, & Cowan, 2002). As you can imagine, parents who rely heavily on spanking and hitting also tend to be less warm and affectionate, less involved, and less consistent in their parenting than parents who use more positive forms of discipline. **Listen** on **mydevelopmentlab**

**Listen**: Spanking laws in other nations: How do these laws work? (Author Podcast)
www.mydevelopmentlab.com

**Positive Discipline.** So, once again, what *should* parents do for discipline? There are many good books on the subject, and local community colleges and social service agencies usually offer excellent parent-education programs on effective discipline. We present here a basic positive program of discipline that is consistent with guidelines endorsed by the American Academy of Pediatrics (1998) and most parenting experts. First, remember that the term *discipline* refers to techniques used to *teach* children appropriate behavior. The emphasis is on *teaching* rather than on *punishing*. Also recognize that there is no technique that works all of the time and right away. With patience and a calm and positive approach to discipline, parents can set firm limits and help children learn to control their behavior in a way that is appropriate for their age. We recommend that parents try the following steps:

▲ With positive forms of discipline, the emphasis is on teaching rather than punishing.

1. *Manage the situation.* Parents should be aware of the situations their children are in and should try to manage each situation to reduce the temptations for misbehavior. Begin by childproofing the home. If there are items you don't want your child to touch or break, put them out of reach. Notice other infractions that occur at home, and try to rearrange things so the misbehaviors are less tempting. Make sure there are plenty of positive things for children to do and appropriate objects to explore. Too often, parents set up situations in which the most interesting thing to do is misbehave. This can be prevented.
2. *Set clear rules and limits.* Parents need to communicate clearly to children the dos and don'ts that are most important. Keep your list of rules short, or it will be difficult for you and your child to keep up with them all. Pick the issues that are most important for the child's age. With younger children you might focus on safety rules like "Stay in the yard" and "Don't touch the stove." For older children there can be clear rules about homework, expectations for household chores, and safety issues like wearing a helmet while biking or skateboarding. Try to state

rules positively so children know what they *should* do (instead of "Don't run" say "Please walk").

3. *Praise good behavior.* Have you heard the slogan "Catch them being good"? It's important to let children know when they are behaving appropriately. Work on strengthening the positive behaviors in your children. "I notice you shared with your brother today—great job!" Behaviors tend to be repeated when they are reinforced or rewarded. When children are busy behaving, they have less time to misbehave. Rewarding good behavior also helps parents keep a positive focus in their discipline.
4. *Use explanation and reasoning.* When misbehavior occurs, parents need to explain the rules and provide good reasons for compliance. A calm and reasoned discussion gives parents an opportunity to express warmth and compassion to the child and an opportunity to demonstrate positive ways to handle conflict. It also gives children a chance to express their views.
5. *If you must punish, try removing privileges or using timeouts.* If you have followed all of the preceding steps and an unwanted behavior still persists, you might consider imposing an appropriate punishment. Remember, *punishment* is a technique that reduces the frequency of an undesirable behavior, but it doesn't mean that you have to resort to hitting or yelling. It's best to tie the punishment to the infraction as much as possible. If children are fighting over video games, for example, they could lose the privilege of playing the games for the rest of the day. Any such disciplinary action should begin with the mildest form and should take the child's age into account. For a toddler, losing a favorite toy for a few minutes may make a big impact, whereas a 7-year-old may need to lose a privilege for several hours or a day to get the point. As an alternative, try a mild timeout. Remove the child from the situation and from anything that is encouraging the misbehavior to continue, and place him in a safe, quiet environment. A short timeout (about one minute per year of the child's age) gives children a few minutes to collect themselves and reflect on what they have done. It also gives you time to gather your thoughts—and reduces the likelihood that you will lash out in anger and say or do something you will regret. After the brief timeout, try explanation and reasoning again. Always be sure to praise children when their behavior improves.

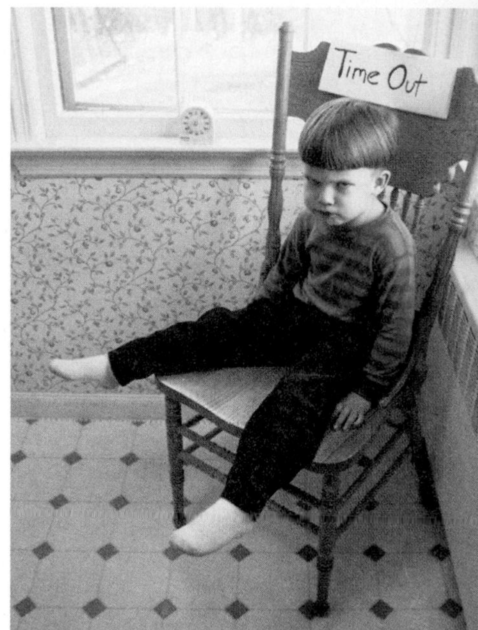


▲ Parents can use a timeout to remove a child from a situation when he is misbehaving. A safe, quiet place gives the child a chance to settle down and think about the rules.

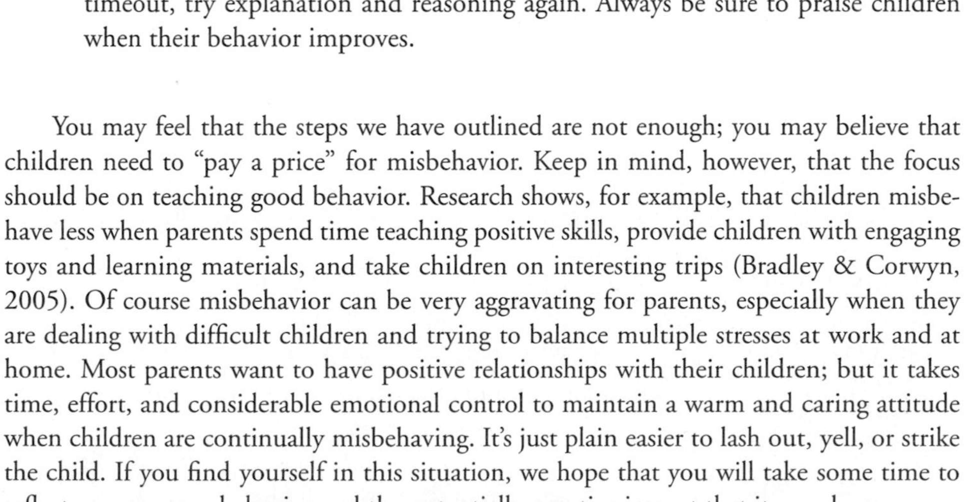

You may feel that the steps we have outlined are not enough; you may believe that children need to "pay a price" for misbehavior. Keep in mind, however, that the focus should be on teaching good behavior. Research shows, for example, that children misbehave less when parents spend time teaching positive skills, provide children with engaging toys and learning materials, and take children on interesting trips (Bradley & Corwyn, 2005). Of course misbehavior can be very aggravating for parents, especially when they are dealing with difficult children and trying to balance multiple stresses at work and at home. Most parents want to have positive relationships with their children; but it takes time, effort, and considerable emotional control to maintain a warm and caring attitude when children are continually misbehaving. It's just plain easier to lash out, yell, or strike the child. If you find yourself in this situation, we hope that you will take some time to reflect on your own behavior and the potentially negative impact that it may have.

To read more about how some parents deal with everyday situations with children of various ages, read the Personal Perspective box called "Carrots or Sticks? Family Discipline at Different Ages."

THINK ABOUT JULIE AND TOM . . .

Describe a program of positive discipline that Julie and Tom could use with their boys. What can they do when their boys are acting out or being aggressive?

## Perspective PERSONAL — CARROTS OR STICKS? FAMILY DISCIPLINE AT DIFFERENT AGES

**What methods of discipline do you use regularly? Are they effective? Are there any methods that you have tried, but found they did not work?**

**Iris and Manuel Matos: Hispanic family** We like to talk to our children about what they did wrong. It lets them know how we feel and how the situation reflects on who they are as a person. Yelling did not work at all. They could handle 5 minutes of yelling, and that was that. Spanking also did not work. When a child thinks about their mom and dad, it should be wonderful thoughts about being safe, comfort, trust, and guidance. With spanking, our children would not have the bond with us we have today because we would have instilled fear in them. To us, the most effective way is communicating with our children.

**Kristin and Marc Petraluzzi: French family (two boys, ages 2 and 4)** We use timeouts. This has not been really effective, because they have quite a few timeouts daily (the older child). When we had nowhere else to go, we tried a spanking, but that did not seem to help either. I think we just have strong characters that we are dealing with!

**Sharon Buenaventura: Asian family (three boys, ages 12, 9, and 1)** My discipline methods are based on their personalities. My eldest son, Michael, fits the mold of the "first born." On the rare occasion that I've had to discipline him, it was really more of a discussion pointing out various reasons why I did not want him to repeat his actions. Michael is quite open to our discussions and will correct his behavior willingly once the reasons are spelled out to him. My second son, Nicky, responds to timeouts and the taking away of privileges (e.g., soccer practice). Discussions do not work for Nicky. He tends to be more free-spirited and not as concerned about following the rules. Christian is still quite young, and I haven't figured out what method of discipline will work best for him. At this time, he may want to touch something that he shouldn't, and simply telling him to "look, not touch" will suffice.

One method I have discovered over the years is that "screaming" or "yelling" is definitely the least effective method for any of my boys. I find that they tend to shut me out and not really listen to anything I may be saying.

**Kim Miller: African American family (two girls, ages 14 and 11)** The 14-year-old got a poor grade on a history test because she spent more time instant-messaging her friends than studying for the test. I restricted her access to instant messaging and other unsupervised uses of the computer until she had another test and got a better grade. The key is not ever wavering from the imposed punishment—which in this case meant over 3 weeks of no instant messaging. To encourage getting in bed on time, I instituted a policy that for every minute they are late for bed, they are charged $1. The money goes in a top dresser drawer and can be earned back each night the appropriate behavior is achieved (i.e., five consecutive nights of going to bed on time will recoup $5).

QUESTION **What discipline techniques do you think are most effective? How do the strategies used in these families compare with the recommendations for positive parenting presented in this chapter**

### LET'S REVIEW . . .

1. Which of the following parent comments would best illustrate an *authoritative* parenting style?
   a. You said you'd pick up your toys! You never listen—you're in timeout for 2 hours!
   b. You didn't pick up your toys? Well, it's not that messy. You can do it some other time.
   c. Go ahead and live in a pigsty—it's your room.
   d. No TV tonight. We agreed you would clean up your toys after dinner or there would be no TV tonight.
2. Children tend to fare worst of all when their parents use the __________.
   a. authoritative style of parenting
   b. authoritarian style of parenting
   c. permissive style of parenting
   d. neglecting/rejecting style of parenting
3. Compared to other children, children who are frequently spanked tend to be __________.
   a. more aggressive, more depressed, and lower in self-esteem than other children
   b. better behaved than other children
   c. less likely to use physical means to get what they want
   d. less likely to use physical punishment with their own children

4. In the context of positive parenting, the word *discipline* means __________.
   a. punish
   b. time out
   c. reward
   d. teach
5. True or False: Authoritarian parenting is high in control and high in warmth.
6. True or False: One of the best techniques for child discipline is the use of situation management to prevent misbehavior in the first place.

Answers: 1. d, 2. d, 3. a, 4. d, 5. F, 6. T

# Friends and Play

In this section, we look at three topics that involve children's friends and play: the tendency of children to segregate into same-sex friendships, the basic types of play in early childhood, and the influence of culture on play.

AS YOU STUDY THIS SECTION, ASK YOURSELF THESE QUESTIONS:

9.7 Why do children play mostly with same-sex friends?

9.8 How do researchers define "play," and what types of play have they studied?

9.9 How do different cultures influence how children play?

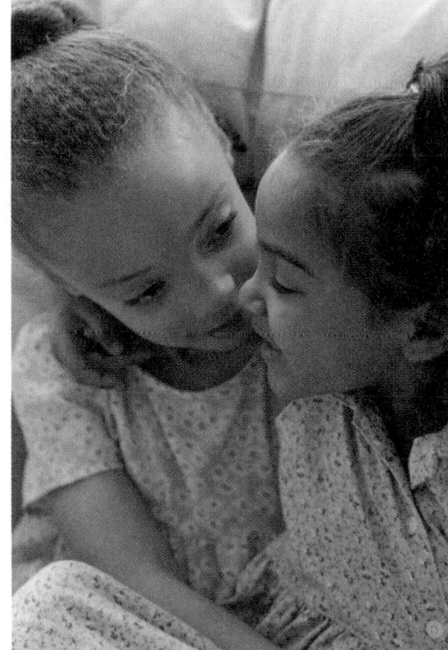

▲What do you think drew these 5-year-olds to each other as best friends? How do children of this age form close friendships?

As we mentioned in Chapter 6, toddlers form friendships based mostly on convenience—they play with whomever is available the most. During early childhood the main ingredients in forming friendships are *opportunity* and *similarity*. To become friends, children need to be available to each other for play and other activities. Children become good friends when they spend a lot of time playing together, sharing toys, and enjoying the same games and activities. Children who are neighbors, relatives, or schoolmates spend more time with each other and therefore have more opportunities to form friendships. Furthermore, children's social contacts increase dramatically when they enter school. In school, children encounter a much larger group of peers and tend to have less direct adult supervision when they are together. From the toddler period to the school-aged years, time spent with peers triples (Higgins & Parsons, 1983). Also, like adults, children are drawn to others who are like them. Friendships are more likely to form when children are similar in characteristics such as age, gender, race, attitudes, beliefs, and even play styles (Epstein, 1989; Hartup, 1989; Rubin, Lynch, Coplan, Rose-Krasnor, & Booth, 1994).

## Gender Segregation

A prominent feature of children's friendships is *gender segregation*—the tendency of children to associate with others of their same sex. Consider the situation we observed while testing 4-year-old children in a preschool. As the children returned from their outside play period, a new boy in class took a seat in a circle of chairs. Several other boys ran immediately to him, yelling, "Get up, that's where the girls sit!" Hearing this, the new boy leaped up and began to furiously dust off the back of his pants! What did he think was on the chair? Cooties?

There is no doubt that gender segregation exists. In fact, it is nearly universal, occurring in every cultural setting where children have choice in selecting social groups (Fabes, Martin, & Hanish, 2003; Whiting & Edwards, 1988). But how does it begin, and why? There are no clear answers to these questions, but we can learn more by looking at how gender segregation evolves across childhood.

By 2 to 3 years of age, children are beginning to show a clear preference for playing with other children of their own sex (Serbin, Moller, Gulko, Powlishta, & Colburne,

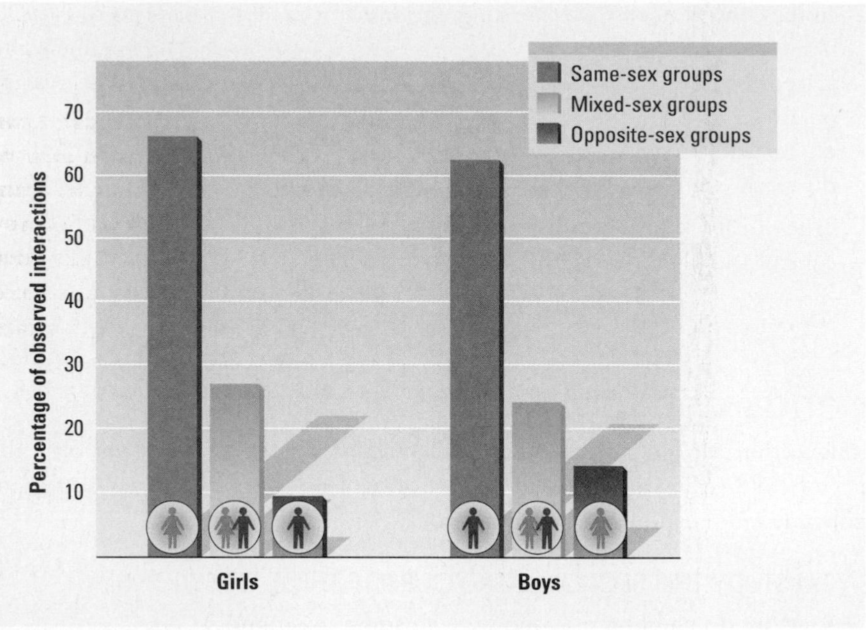


FIGURE 9.2 ▶ **Gender Interactions among Preschoolers** In free play, preschoolers (ages 3 to 6 years) choose to play with same-sex peers most often. When they do cross gender lines, they spend twice as much time playing in mixed-sex groups as with the opposite sex one-on-one. (Data from Fabes, 1994.)

1994). At this age children are more interactive and sociable when playing with same-sex friends. When they are with the opposite sex, they tend to watch or play alongside the other child rather than interact directly. Gender segregation is very prominent after the age of 3. As you can see in Figure 9.2, preschool children spend very little time playing one-on-one with the opposite sex. They spend some time in mixed-sex groups but spend most of their time, by far, playing with same-sex peers. By 6 years, segregation is so firm that if you watch 6-year-olds on the playground, you should expect to see only one girl–boy group for every 11 boy–boy or girl–girl groups (Maccoby & Jacklin, 1987).

Why does gender segregation exist? Table 9.2 summarizes several prominent theories.

Regardless of why gender segregation occurs, one of its consequences is that boys and girls grow up in different **gender cultures**—different spheres of social influence that are based on the differences between male and female groups and affiliations (Leaper, 1994; Leman, Ahmed, & Ozarow, 2005; Maccoby & Jacklin, 1987). Rough-and-tumble play, chase, keep-away games, superhero warrior games, and competitive sports are more common among boys. Physical aggression, independence, and dominance are common themes in boys' play. Girls' play, however, tends to emphasize social closeness and sensitivity. Doll play and playing house, for example, involve role playing, turn taking, nurturing, and affection. Another difference is that boys tend to play in larger groups while girls develop closer ties in smaller groups. As a consequence, girls may learn to share thoughts and feelings and practice being good listeners in intimate friendships. Boys, however, may see intimate sharing as a sign of weakness that would make them more vulnerable within their dominance hierarchies (Leaper, 1994). These different gender cultures may cause conflicts when girls and boys do begin to associate more together as they date and interact in adolescence and adulthood. Because they don't share the same gender culture, girls and boys may have difficulty understanding each other's perspectives.

What can adults do to reduce any negative effects of childhood gender segregation? Leaper (1994) provided several practical suggestions. For example, parents can model egalitarian roles at home, arrange more situations in which children can play and cooperate across genders, and reinforce and support children when they do cross stereotypical gender lines in their play. Child care providers and teachers can arrange cooperative activities among boys and girls, and they can avoid grouping children by gender when they arrange seating and form lines. They can also avoid using gender as a way to address students; for

THINKING CRITICALLY
When you were a child, how did your peers respond when they saw you playing with someone of the opposite sex? Did their reactions have an encouraging or a discouraging effect on your choice of opposite-sex playmates?

**gender cultures**
Different spheres of influence based on the differences that exist between male and female playgroups and affiliations.

**TABLE 9.2**
**Theories of Gender Segregation**

| | |
|---|---|
| Play Compatibility | • Children seek partners whose play styles match or complement their own.<br>• Among the youngest children, the first to segregate tend to be the most active and disruptive boys and the most socially sensitive girls.<br>• Both types of children prefer to play with others like them. |
| Cognitive Schemas | • Children develop *schemas* (concepts or ideas) about what boys and girls are typically like.<br>• Schemas are stereotyped and often exaggerated, such as "boys are rough and like to fight and play with trucks" and "girls are nice and like to talk and play with dolls."<br>• Children use these cognitive schemas as filters when they judge themselves and observe other children.<br>• As children learn gender schemas, their play and playmate preferences become even more segregated. |
| Operant Conditioning | • Reward and punishment contribute to gender segregation.<br>• Boys receive harsh criticism when they cross gender lines to play with girls.<br>• Although some girls revel in being "tomboys," others feel conflicted about being associated with stereotypically masculine activities.<br>• Parents, teachers, peers, the media, and others contribute to gender segregation by reinforcing sex-typed behaviors in boys and girls. |
| Psychoanalytic Theory | • Freud theorized that gender segregation occurs as children repress their sexual feelings during the latency stage of development.<br>• Children avoid interactions with the opposite sex to avoid the guilty feelings they associate with sexuality. |

Fabes, 1994; Fagot, 1977, 1994; Fagot & Patterson, 1969; Martin, 1994; Serbin et al., 1994.

example, they shouldn't shout "Boys, sit down and be quiet!" unless all of the boys were indeed being loud. Of course, it would not be prudent or practical to try to eliminate all gender differences. Nevertheless, helping children develop more flexible expectations and skills in interacting with the opposite sex could be helpful. Read the Professional Perspective box on page 282 called "Career Focus: Meet the Director of a Child Care Center" for one expert's observations and advice regarding play preferences and gender segregation.

◀ Boys and girls grow up in different gender cultures. Boys tend to engage in more rough and physical play while girls spend more time practicing interpersonal sensitivity. How do these experiences influence boys and girls differently?

# Perspective PROFESSIONAL

## CAREER FOCUS: MEET THE DIRECTOR OF A CHILD CARE CENTER

Deborah Koshansky, Ph.D.
Bright Horizons Children's Center in Washington, D.C.

**Describe the children who attend your center. How many caregivers work there?**
The Bright Horizons Children's Center in Washington, D.C., where I serve as Director, is a work-site child care program managed by Bright Horizons Family Solutions for an international financial organization. We have 91 children enrolled, ages 3 months through 5 years. We have 28 child care providers. Our family population is international in that most of the families are from countries other than the United States.

**At your center, do you often see differences in the play preferences of boys and girls?**
In our center we do see some differences in play preferences between the boys and girls. Usually this occurs initially in the 3-year-old group. It is most pronounced in the Pre-Kindergarten group and less so in the younger groups. As with any group, there is a continuum of behavior. We have some girls who enjoy rough and tumble play, construction play, and gross motor activities as much as some of the boys. Also, there are some boys who enjoy the dramatic play, art, and writing activities that usually attract the girls with greater frequency. We observe a great deal of tolerance and acceptance among the children if a child of the opposite gender joins them in play.

**Why do you think children this age prefer to play with others of their same gender and not with the other gender?**
As much as we would like to think that the genders are the same and if provided with similar encouragement and experiences we would not see gender differences, I think there are some inherent attractions for certain activities for boys and girls. My experience is that boys typically seek out more physically active activities such as superheroes, block play, or gross motor activities, while girls prefer dramatic play, art, writing, and fine-motor activities. Consequently, they self-select into those activities with other children of the same gender. We don't observe too much exclusionary behavior in our center such as "no girls allowed" or "boys don't wear dress-up clothes." I think that exclusionary behavior is more learned than innate and may reflect attitudes of adults that are transmitted to the children.

**Do you encourage children to play across gender lines? Would this be helpful?**
We don't make a practice of encouraging children to play across gender lines but we do monitor the play for exclusion. If we find that one group is excluding a child of either gender, we explore that with the children: "How can Susie participate in the dinosaur hunt?" "What role can Hank play in your family?" This is not always gender-related. It is sometimes just personalities. If we did see a pattern of gender segregation, I think it would be appropriate and useful to encourage play across genders. I would like to find subtle ways of encouraging it instead of making an overt issue of it. This could be accomplished by dividing the children into mixed-gender small groups for specific activities. This would result in some mixed groups available for free choice play at the same time. I suspect they would play together at that time with greater regularity because of the need for a certain number of children to engage in associative and cooperative play successfully. As they gain experience with each other, they would be more likely to join each other in play at other times.

**What education or training do child care providers and directors need to work in your field?**
Our center is accredited by the National Association for the Education of Young Children. Consequently, we meet the NAEYC standards for teacher qualifications. Currently, all of our teachers hold at least a Child Development Associate credential (CDA). In order to meet the new, higher accreditation standards, they are working toward earning their associate degrees in Early Childhood Education.

QUESTION **Is it appropriate and important to encourage boys and girls to play together? Why or why not? In what ways would you encourage this?**

## Types of Play

Developmental psychologists define **play** as a pleasurable activity that is actively engaged in on a voluntary basis, is intrinsically motivated, and often contains some nonliteral element (Hughes, 1999). In plain words, play is something children (and adults) choose to do, on their own, for fun. They do it for the enjoyment of the play itself, not for outside rewards or in response to outside pressures. When children are truly "playing" baseball, for example, they are doing it because they enjoy the game. If they are doing it only to win a trophy or only because their parents made them do it, then it doesn't qualify as play. Finally, most play involves a nonliteral component—some element of make-believe, pretend, or symbolism. When children are playing, they pretend that dolls can talk, toy cars can zoom around imaginary racetracks, and a stick can become a powerful sword or a magic wand.

Play allows children to explore beyond the boundaries of reality. With imagination, fantasy, and creativity, children transform the objects and people in the real world to suit their own playful purposes. Through play children have opportunities to develop muscle coordination, social interaction skills, logical reasoning and problem-solving skills, and the ability to think about the world as it really is and as it could be.

**Parten's Classic Study of Play.** In one of the classic studies of play, Mildred Parten (1932) made extensive observations of children as they engaged in free play at their preschool. The children were 1 to 5 years of age, and Parten observed them repeatedly over a period of nearly 8 months. She was particularly interested in the social nature of children's play. She identified six levels of play that ranged from completely nonsocial to highly integrated social play. **Watch** on **mydevelopmentlab**

**Watch** a video on Parten's Play Categories.
www.mydevelopmentlab.com

1. *Unoccupied behavior.* The child is not playing and not watching anyone or anything in particular. He may momentarily play with his own body, stand around, follow a teacher, or just sit alone. Example: Cody is sitting alone by the swings, apparently not playing with or watching anyone else.
2. *Onlooking.* The child spends most of his time watching other children play. He talks to the children he is watching and asks questions, but he does not engage in the play himself. He focuses on the play of a particular child or group of children, and he stays near them so he can hear and observe. Example: Cody follows Sam around the sandbox as Sam plays; Cody asks questions and talks to Sam, but he does not play directly with Sam.
3. *Solitary play.* The child plays alone, and he makes no apparent connection between his play and the play of other children around him. Although he may play close to other children, he makes no attempt to make a connection with them. Example: Cody is playing in the sandbox; Sam is playing nearby, but Cody is not talking or sharing with him, and he is not watching Sam.
4. *Parallel play.* The child plays alone but with toys that are like those used by other children around him. His play may be similar to the play of nearby children, but he plays *beside* the other children, not *with* them. Example: Cody is pouring sand into his bucket and dumping it; Cody is sitting near Sam, who is also pouring and dumping sand, but they are not playing together.
5. *Associative play.* The child plays among other children, but his play is not well coordinated with their play. He may talk with the other children and share toys and materials, but his play is still relatively independent of others. The primary interest is in associating with other children but not in coordinating their play activity. Example: Cody and Sam are playing in the sandbox together; they talk, exchange buckets, and give sand to each other, but they are still pouring and dumping their own sand.

**play**
A pleasurable activity that is actively engaged in on a voluntary basis, is intrinsically motivated, and contains some nonliteral element.

6. *Cooperative play.* The child plays with other children, and his play is integrated or coordinated with theirs. Play of this type often involves a group of children who are creating a common product, striving for a competitive goal, acting out adult situations, or playing formal games. There is a division of labor: Children play different roles, and their individual efforts contribute to a larger whole. Example: Several children are building a sand castle together. Cody is shoveling the sand into buckets while Sam dumps the sand to form spires and Sarah carefully pats and smoothes the spires. Together they build a magnificent castle!

Parten found a connection between children's ages and their types of play. She observed the lower levels of play primarily among younger children. The 1- and 2-year-olds spent most of their time in the first three levels of play: unoccupied behavior, onlooking, and solitary play. The 3- to 5-year-olds split their playtime about evenly among the upper three levels: parallel, associative, and cooperative play. Similar trends emerged in a study of young children in Taiwan (Pan, 1994). In another study, young children in the United States were given a chance to cooperate with a playmate to get a fun game to work (Brownell, Ramani, & Zerwas, 2006). Children under the age of 2 rarely ever cooperated, and when they did it seemed more accidental than planned. By age 3, however, many of the children were cooperating with each other successfully. The 3-year-olds were better at focusing their attention on the important parts of the game, and since language skills develop rapidly between ages 2 and 3, the 3-year-olds were better at using their words to coordinate their play and they were better at listening and communicating with the adults who were helping them. Play is a lot more fun when children can talk to each other and cooperate together!

Parten's observations highlighted the social nature of play. When children are young and lack social skills, they tend to play alone or beside other children—they rarely coordinate their play with peers or in a larger group. As children gain social skills, they tend to move toward more integrated play—they play with other children, and eventually they learn to coordinate their play roles to accomplish a larger group goal. When children do not make progress in learning to play socially, they are at risk for being rejected or excluded by their peers. Children who are anxious and fearful, for example, may play alone in solitary play and miss opportunities to learn to interact in more socially mature ways with other children. A cycle can erupt in which these children become even more fearful of social play, become more rejected, and become even more isolated in their solitary play (Coplan, Prakash, O'Neil, & Armer, 2004; Spinrad et al., 2004). Children do differ, however: children who are more withdrawn and solitary but have pleasant personalities tend to have more success in making friends than do those who are aggressive or act out to get attention (Gazelle, 2008). It is important that parents, preschool teachers, and other adults help children make healthy social connections with other children.

▲ Young children enjoy pretending to be superheroes and other powerful characters. What are the potential benefits of this type of sociodramatic play?

**sociodramatic play**
Play that involves acting out different social roles or characters

Sociodramatic Play. Another type of play that becomes common by 3 years of age is **sociodramatic play**—acting out different social roles and characters. Sociodramatic play may be realistic ("I'll be the daddy and you be the baby") or may involve a high degree of fantasy ("I'm queen of the empire; behold my castle!"). Sociodramatic play can serve any of the following functions for young children (Hughes, 1999):

- *Imitation of adults.* Children can act out adult roles they have observed, such as the role of a parent, teacher, cook, waiter, doctor, dentist, or veterinarian. Exploring these roles in play lets young children explore the activities of people in the larger world.
- *Reenactment of family relationships.* Children often reenact events from their family lives. Most often, sociodramatic play involves simple, everyday activities such as

"Say good-bye to Mommy 'cause she's going to work." Sometimes, however, children use sociodramatic play to process larger and more traumatic events like "Daddy and Mommy don't love each other anymore so now we have to move to another house."

- *Expression of needs.* Sociodramatic play gives children a chance to express unmet needs. For example, an only child may pretend to have a brother, or a child who misses his or her father may pretend to be playing ball with him.
- *Outlet for forbidden impulses.* Sociodramatic play gives children a safer outlet for exploring roles and activities that would not be appropriate for them in real life. Children can pretend to be highly aggressive ("Beware, I'm going to smash down your whole house!"), and they can playact love, marriage, and aspects of sexuality.
- *Reversal of roles.* Finally, in sociodramatic play children who usually feel helpless can act out more powerful roles, like those of parent, teacher, and superhero. They can turn the tables by disciplining their dolls or playmates ("Bad behavior—now you go to timeout!"), or they can be the ones giving the commands at preschool ("Now it's nap time, children"). This type of play helps children experience the more powerful perspective, and it can help them confront their anxieties about being the smaller and less powerful people in real life.

Of course, children often engage in sociodramatic play for the pure fun of acting out roles with playmates. Sometimes "You be the mommy and I'll be the baby" is simply fun, and there doesn't have to be any deeper meaning to the play.

THINKING CRITICALLY
What are your earliest memories of playing? What do you remember playing when you were very young?

The early childhood years are an especially imaginative period of pretend play. The creativity that children show in their sociodramatic play reflects the new symbolic thinking skills they are developing, as we discussed in Chapter 8. As children exercise and explore the limits of symbolic thought, their play becomes ever more imaginative. This imaginativeness, however, will yield to an increasing realism as children move into the next stage of cognitive development.

## Cultural Differences in Play

The culture in which children live has a tremendous influence on how much they play, where they play, and the main themes in their play. As an example, consider how different cultures value work and play. Children in the United States and Britain spend most of their after-school time in play, but children in Japan and Korea are more likely to spend time studying for school (Takeuchi, 1994). Japanese and Korean cultures place a high value on hard work, sacrifice, and educational achievement. In Japan, for example, students study hard in hopes of getting into the best universities and professional schools. Among the Hazda people of Tanzania, children are expected to forage for their own food by age 3; by age 10 they are expected to be productive hunters and gatherers (Lancy, 2002). Hazda children learn to work at a young age, and their parents have very little tolerance for play. In the West African nation of Senegal, children tend to live in communal "compounds" containing numerous households, all related to the eldest male in the compound (Bloch & Adler, 1994). Children play outdoors, roaming the compound in larger groups consisting mostly of siblings and cousins. As in most cultures, gender typing is clear in these children's sociodramatic play. Senegalese girls tend to playact family roles, nurturing younger children and doing domestic chores like cooking and carrying water. Senegalese boys playact farming, herding animals, fishing, and working with machines and automobiles (Bloch & Adler, 1994). Through their play these children learn the skills that are important in their culture.

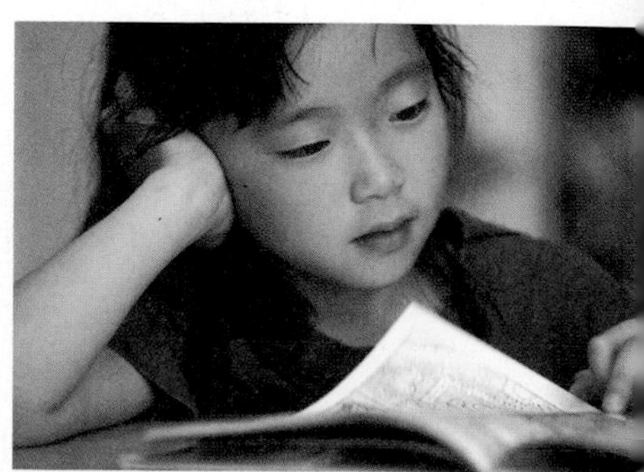

▲ Cultural values regarding work and play have an enormous influence on how children develop. Japanese children, for example, spend more time studying than do their U.S. counterparts.

Other effects of culture are apparent in the social themes and interactions in children's play. In one cross-cultural study, researchers gave 4-year-olds toy figurines to play with and

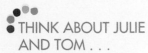

**THINK ABOUT JULIE AND TOM . . .**
How can Julie and Tom use this information on cultural differences to understand how their boys prefer to play?

asked the children to talk aloud and tell a story as they played with the figurines (Farver & Welles-Nystrom, 1997). Children in the United States incorporated significantly more aggressive words, unfriendly characters, and physical aggression in their play than did German, Swedish, or Indonesian children. American children tended to solve the problems in their stories with force and violence. In contrast, Indonesian children's story characters were the most friendly, tended to be the most helpful, and solved problems in peaceful ways. In all four cultures, the children who showed the most aggression in their play were also the most aggressive with their peers in school and were rated by teachers as performing less well in school.

Are these trends reflected in the larger society? Consider the fact that the rate of serious crime (homicide, sex offenses, assault, theft, breaking and entering, and fraud) in the United States is higher than in most other industrialized nations (Farver & Welles-Nystrom, 1997). Children's play in this country reflects our society's attitudes toward aggression. Of course, U.S. society is itself diverse, and attitudes about aggression differ among subcultures. Korean American children, for example, show more cooperation, harmony, and social sensitivity in their play; European American children are more aggressive and antagonistic (Farver, 2000; Farver & Shin, 1997). These cultural values pass from one generation to the next in children's activities as they play.

## LET'S REVIEW . . .

1. During early childhood, the main ingredients that promote friendships are similarity and __________.
   **a.** intimacy
   **b.** loyalty
   **c.** opportunity
   **d.** generosity
2. Karen and Tasha are both riding tricycles. Although they sometimes ride close together and talk to each other, they are not engaged with each other in any coordinated way. According to Parten's classification of play, Karen and Tasha are engaged in __________.
   **a.** onlooking
   **b.** solitary play
   **c.** associative play
   **d.** cooperative play
3. Imitating adults, reenacting family relationships, and expressing forbidden impulses are all functions that can be served by __________.
   **a.** solitary play
   **b.** gender segregation
   **c.** gender schemas
   **d.** sociodramatic play
4. Compared to children in Germany, Sweden, and Indonesia, children in the United States show more __________ in their play.
   **a.** aggression
   **b.** cooperation
   **c.** group harmony
   **d.** symbolic pretend
5. True or False: According to Freud's psychoanalytic theory, girls and boys avoid playing with each other because their styles of play do not match.
6. True or False: According to researchers, play is an activity that is pleasurable, voluntary, and intrinsically motivated.

Answers: 1. c, 2. c, 3. d, 4. a, 5. F, 6. T

**THINKING BACK TO JULIE AND TOM . . .**

Now that you have studied this chapter, you should be able to apply at least a dozen concepts and research findings to Julie and Tom's situation. Their sons are learning who they are and how to act in their larger social worlds. Rocco, the 3-year-old, is developing a me-self, learning what it means to be a boy, and just beginning to learn how to regulate his own behavior around other children. Children at his level of moral development are typically concerned about rewards and punishments. George and Charlie are a bit older, and they have a more developed sense of self. They also should be developing good self-regulation skills, though they may need more help in this area from their parents, teachers, and others. For parents like Julie and Tom, positive discipline techniques can help their boys learn positive behaviors that will last throughout their lives. If they put these techniques into practice, they will not need to rely so much on yelling and other negative forms of discipline.

Children at Rocco and George's age show strong gender segregation in their play. They tend to play mostly with same-sex friends. At 8 years of age, Charlie might begin to become more flexible and willing to interact more with girls (maybe!). Julie and Tom should also consider the role of culture on their boys' style of play—the culture in the U.S. tends to emphasize rough and aggressive play, especially for boys.

Using these and other concepts from this chapter, you should be able to help Julie and Tom understand their boys' developmental levels and tendencies. You should also be able to offer practical advice to help them raise their young boys, and you should be able to adjust the advice to fit families in other circumstances or other families you know.

## 9 CHAPTER REVIEW . . .

**9.1** What is the "self," and how do children learn to regulate their own thoughts, behaviors, and emotions?

The "self" refers to characteristics, emotions, and beliefs people have about themselves; it includes the I-self and the me-self. Children recognize themselves by the age of 2, and with development their sense of self becomes more abstract, domain-specific, and differentiated, but also more integrated. As a sense of self develops, children become more skilled at self-regulation—controlling and changing their thoughts, behaviors, and emotions to meet the demands of different situations.

**9.2** What do young children understand about gender—about the similarities and differences between boys and girls?

Children show gender-stereotyped preferences even before they fully understand their own gender. They prefer sex-typed toys and show high levels of gender segregation in their play by the time they are 3 years old. Gender stereotypes become increasingly rigid until early elementary school. Kohlberg proposed that gender concepts develop from gender identity, to gender stability, and then to gender constancy. Children's gender concepts greatly affect how they think about boys, girls, toys, friends, play, and other aspects of childhood.

**9.3** How do young children think about moral issues, and what stages do they go through in their development of moral reasoning?

Kohlberg proposed six stages of development of moral reasoning. Children's movement through the stages depends on their cognitive development, perspective-taking ability, and experience with moral issues. During early childhood, children's reasoning focuses on the roles of rewards and punishments (Stage 1) and on their own needs or interests (Stage 2).

**9.4** How do researchers define parental warmth and parental control?

Parental warmth is the degree to which parents are accepting, responsive, and compassionate with their children. Parents who are high in warmth are supportive, nurturing, and caring. Parental control is the degree to which parents set limits, enforce rules, and maintain discipline with children. Parental warmth and control combine to create four parenting styles.

**9.5** What are the four parenting styles described by Baumrind and other researchers, and what outcomes are associated with each style?

Authoritative parents are warm and consistent, exert firm control, listen to their children, and use supportive methods of discipline. Their children show the most positive psychological, emotional, and academic outcomes. Authoritarian parents exert firm control but show little warmth or respect and use harsh and punitive disciplinary methods. Their children tend to be more aggressive and hostile and do worse in school. Permissive parents do not set or enforce limits; they avoid confrontation with their children and do not require their children to behave maturely or responsibly. Their children tend to be more impulsive, less self-confident, and do less well in school. Rejecting/neglecting parents ignore or actively reject their children; they do not discipline their children, or do so harshly and inconsistently. Their children typically show the worst psychological, emotional, and academic outcomes.

9.6 Why is spanking an ineffective method of discipline, and what's a more positive approach that parents can use?
Spanking does not improve children's behavior over the long term, nor does it teach children appropriate behavior. Children who are spanked more often are more physically violent and aggressive, more depressed, and more likely to hit others. Positive methods of discipline include managing the situation, setting clear rules and limits, praising good behavior, using explanation and reasoning, removing privileges, and using timeouts.

9.7 Why do children play mostly with same-sex friends?
Opportunity and similarity are important bases for friendships in childhood. The prominent theories for explaining gender segregation involve play compatibility, cognitive schemas, operant conditioning, and psychoanalytic theory. There is concern that boys and girls grow up in different gender cultures, making it more difficult for them to learn to communicate effectively across genders.

9.8 How do researchers define "play," and what types of play have they studied?
Play is defined as a pleasurable activity that is actively engaged in by the child on a voluntary basis, is motivated intrinsically, and contains some nonliteral element. In her classic study Parten (1932) identified six levels of social play: unoccupied behavior; onlooking; and solitary, parallel, associative, and cooperative play. Researchers also study sociodramatic play in early childhood.

9.9 How do different cultures influence how children play?
The opportunity to play and the central themes and styles of play differ across cultures. Some examples: Compared to U.S. and British children, Japanese and Korean children spend more time studying for school and less time playing. Children in Senegal play outside in large compounds where they are watched by any member of their large extended family. Indonesians and Korean Americans tend to be cooperative and socially sensitive in their play, whereas European American children often are more aggressive.

## REVISITING THEMES

*Nature and nurture* interact to drive children's social and emotional development. Children learn from their parents, siblings, friends, and other people, and genetic links have also been established in the development of the self (p. 263), self-regulation (p. 264), aggression (pp. 275–276), and tendencies to receive physical forms of punishment (p. 276).

Research in *neuroscience* highlights the brain areas involved in forming self-representations (p. 264) and in the development of self-regulation in children (p. 265).

*Diversity and multiculturalism* was highlighted in a discussion of the cultural differences that researchers observe in children's play. Play preferences and even the spaces and time allowed for children's play differ across cultures (pp. 285–286).

Topics related to *positive development* include children's development of moral reasoning—understanding and thinking about what is right versus wrong (pp. 264–265), positive forms of parenting (pp. 270–271), and the positive techniques that parents can use to provide instructive discipline for children (pp. 276–277).

## KEY TERMS

authoritarian parents (272)
authoritative parents (271)
conscience (268)
convention (268)
discipline (275)
gender constancy (267)
gender cultures (280)
gender segregation (267)
I-self (263)
me-self (263)
moral reasoning (268)
morality (268)
parental control (271)
parental warmth (270)
permissive parents (272)
perspective taking (268)
play (283)
positive emotion bias (266)
preconventional level (268)
punishment (275)
rejecting/neglecting parents (272)
self (263)
self-regulation (264)
sociodramatic play (284)

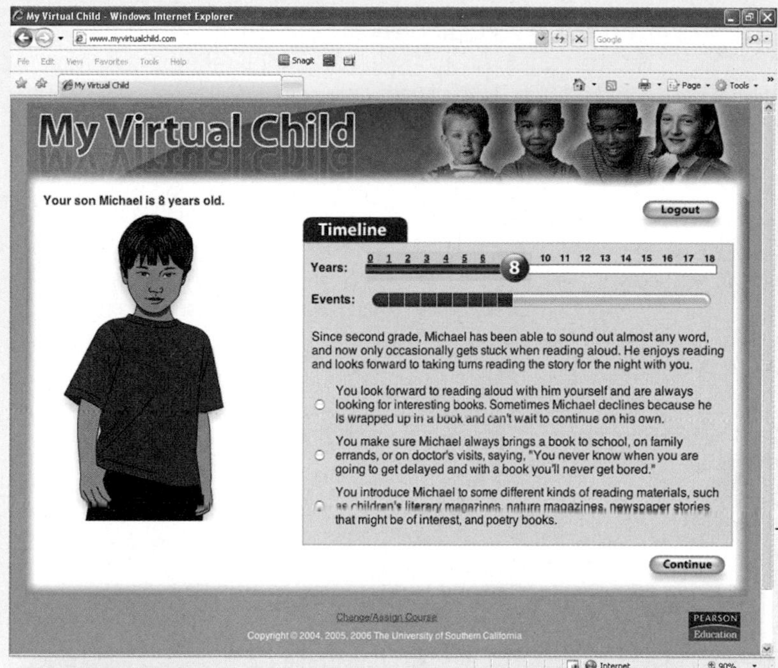


**"What decisions would you make while raising a child? What would the consequences of those decisions be?"**

Find out by accessing My Virtual Child at
**www.mydevelopmentlab.com**
and raising your own virtual child
from birth to age 18.

# PART THREE SUMMARY Early Childhood: The Playful Years

## Some Developmental Landmarks

### 3 years

- Stands on one foot
- Holds pencil between thumb and forefinger
- Speaks in sentences
- Uses correct gender labels: boy, girl, mommy, daddy
- Prefers to play with same-sex friends
- Play is full of fantasy and pretend

### 4 Years

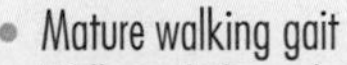

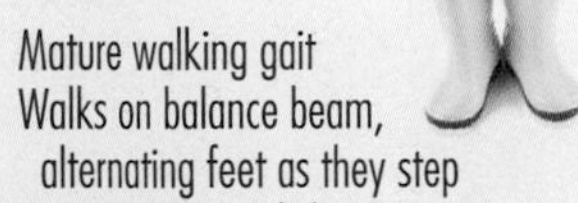

- Mature walking gait
- Walks on balance beam, alternating feet as they step
- Puts on pants and shirts
- Speaks aloud to self in private speech
- Uses rewards and punishments to make judgments about right and wrong
- Coordinates roles in play with other children

### 5 Years

- Hops several times on one foot
- Can work smaller buttons, zippers, and tools such as scissors
- Rides a two-wheel bicycle
- Can start kindergarten
- Holds four items in short-term memory
- Male versus female stereotypes are firmly formed

### 6 Years

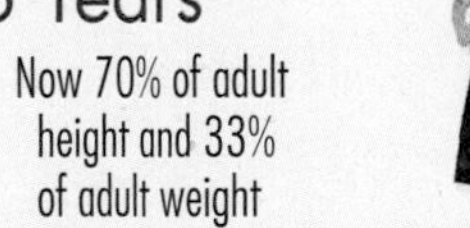

- Now 70% of adult height and 33% of adult weight
- Independent in many self-help skills such as dressing
- Vocabulary of 10,000 words
- Uses complex sentences, with accuracy
- Still has firm preference to play with same-sex friends

## Physical Development

During early childhood, children grow 2 to 3 inches and gain about 5 pounds each year. Children need a well-balanced diet to support their growth and can be picky eaters at this age, often preferring a few favorite foods, even as parents encourage healthy eating habits. Malnutrition can have serious effects. By age 3, the brain is losing more synapses than it gains, but it is still growing in other ways. As larger brain areas mature, children's abilities to control emotions, inhibit behaviors, coordinate strategies, and learn language all improve. Children show great strides in muscle strength and coordination as they learn to walk with a mature gait, run, climb, peddle bicycles, and gain fine-motor control of their hands and fingers. Parents and other caregivers can provide them places and opportunities to play and encourage children to exercise and improve their motor skills. Health and safety are major concerns as children in this age group require regular medical care and safe environments in which to live and play.

## Cognitive Development

Between the ages of 3 and 6, children's cognitive development equips them with the ability to imagine. This is a playful time when children's imaginations truly develop and their thinking becomes more internalized and fanciful. A scribble can be an ancient dinosaur, the moon can follow them home at night, and they believe the world sees everything from their perspective. Their logic is intuitive and personal, but not yet accurate. Children at this point in their development begin to pick up concepts in the social speech they hear from other people, and these concepts are internalized as they learn to mimic the speech inside their own minds. Children's capacities to process information are improving as they learn to handle more information more efficiently. Basic tasks become more automatic, freeing the mind to take in additional and more complex information. Tremendous gains are made in language development, and, by age 6, most children have a 10,000-word vocabulary and can speak using complex sentences. Some children even learn two or more languages simultaneously at this age. As the end of early childhood nears, children can begin kindergarten and formal schooling. Some children may benefit from Head Start or other early childhood education programs to help prepare them for the school years to come.

## Socioemotional Development

During this time period, children begin the task of finding out who they are. They begin to learn "right" from "wrong" and how to regulate their own behaviors. Gender plays an important role in their lives as children learn what it means to be a boy or a girl, and which gender they prefer to play with—their own! Children benefit most from parenting that is warm but firm. Spanking, hitting, and yelling have negative effects while positive forms of discipline that focus on teaching rather than punishing are more effective. Early childhood is a time when children form friendships with children who are similar to them and with whom they have opportunities to play. Play is an essential activity in early childhood as it allows children to stengthen their muscles, exercise their minds, expand their language, and learn to cooperate with other children. After age 6, fantasy and pretend give way to logic and reality. Children are now ready to enter the phase of ***Middle Childhood: The School Years.***

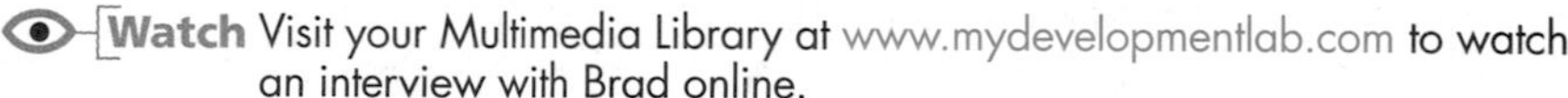
Watch Visit your Multimedia Library at www.mydevelopmentlab.com to watch an interview with Brad online.

10 MIDDLE CHILDHOOD

# Physical Development in Middle Childhood

Brad is a college student who spends his summers working with children at a YMCA camp. He especially enjoys working with children in sports and other outdoor activities. He notices that the younger children (ages 7 or so) focus more on having fun during sports, and it's important that they all get an equal chance to participate and play. The older children (11 and up) are more competitive—they focus more on winning and outperforming each other. Brad can see a huge difference in the strength, coordination, and athletic abilities of children as they mature from the younger to the older ages at his camp. What a difference a few years make!

Most of the children at the summer camp have typical abilities, but many are overweight and some have physical disabilities that limit their involvement in activities. Other children have significant difficulties with learning, concentrating, reading, or even sitting still. Brad enjoys working with a wide variety of children, and he plans to become a teacher after he graduates from college. He knows that he will have children in his classrooms who have attention-deficit/hyperactivity disorder, learning disabilities, autism, or other problems or disorders. He knows, too, that some children might even be abused or mistreated at home. He wonders what he will need to know in order to work effectively with all of these children.

What advice can you give Brad? What should he know about the more typical and less typical patterns of growth and development during middle childhood? What kinds of disabilities, disorders, and problems might he see? After studying this chapter, you should be able to use at least a dozen concepts and research findings to help Brad understand what to expect.

As you read this chapter, look for the "Think About Brad . . ." questions that ask you to consider what you're learning from Brad's perspective.

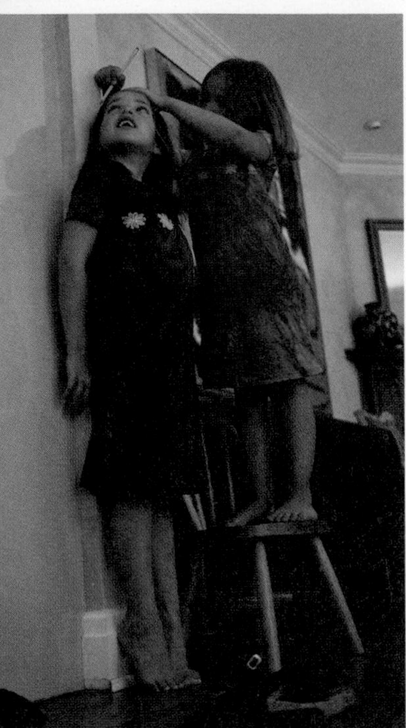

▲ Between the ages of 7 and 11 years, children on average will grow 9 inches in height and gain 35 pounds. What other trends in physical development are typical for this age range?

During the middle childhood years of ages 7 through 11, the pace of physical growth is not as obvious as during early childhood, but children are making big strides in many ways. The brain continues to change in important ways, and children's physical skills become increasingly controlled and coordinated. Children of these ages are generally quite healthy, but there are some significant threats to their health and safety, and some children begin experiencing more difficulty with disabilities due to the increasing demands of school. Like Brad, many adults want to help children of this age develop good physical activity habits and protect them from potential problems and abuse. In this chapter, we will discuss typical patterns of body and brain growth during middle childhood, along with typical development of motor skills, the advantages and potential problems with organized sports, and the impact of some of the hazards and challenges children may face.

# Growth of the Body and Brain

Children's bodies grow more slowly during the early part of middle childhood, but important changes are taking place. Unfortunately, increasing numbers of children experience problems with being overweight, which can cause immediate and long-term health problems. What are the typical patterns of body and brain growth during middle childhood, and what can be done to foster healthy growth during middle childhood? This section will address these issues.

AS YOU STUDY THIS SECTION, ASK YOURSELF THESE QUESTIONS:

**10.1** What is the average amount of growth during middle childhood, and why are so many children overweight?

**10.2** How is the brain growing and maturing during middle childhood?

## Physical Growth and Problems with Being Overweight

The average 7-year-old child stands about 4 feet tall (49 inches, to be more exact) and weighs 55 pounds. By the time children reach the age of 11, they will grow another 9 inches and gain 35 more pounds. You can look back to Figure 7.1 (on page 205) to see how the average heights and weights change across childhood.

At the age of 9, the average girl is essentially the same size as the average boy. After age 10, however, a sex difference begins to emerge in rates of physical growth. Girls begin their adolescent growth spurt a little earlier than boys. By age 11, girls are 1½ inches taller than boys and about 8 pounds heavier, on average. Boys then begin to grow at a faster rate, and they will be taller and heavier than girls by the age of 14. We will have more to say about the adolescent growth spurt and related topics in Chapter 13.

THINKING CRITICALLY

Do you recall a time during childhood when girls were taller and heavier than boys were? What effect did this have on how you felt or behaved? When did this change?

In Chapter 7 we gave the basic nutritional requirements for children and also covered the topic of child malnutrition. In this section we discuss the opposite nutritional problem—children who are overweight. In the United States, the most frequent nutritional problem is being **overweight**, defined as a body mass index at or above the 95th percentile for the child's age and sex. **Body mass index (BMI)** is an indicator of body fat based on weight and height, so a child with a BMI at or higher than 95% of all other children in the United States of the same age and sex is considered overweight. Children with a BMI between the 85th and 95th percentiles are considered at **risk of overweight** (Centers for Disease Control, 2006). As you can see in Figure 10.1, the percentage of U.S. children who were overweight has more than quadrupled from 4% to 17% since 1965. The problem is even worse among adults: A full 67% of adults over the age of 20 were overweight during the 2003–2006 test period (National Center for Health Statistics, 2009). During childhood, the problem is especially serious among certain ethnic minorities. For example, in the 6- to 11-year-old age group, 28% of Mexican American boys and 24% of African American girls are overweight (National Center for Health Statistics, 2009).

**overweight**
Having a body mass index at or above the 95th percentile for the child's age and sex.

**body mass index (BMI)**
An indicator of body fat based on weight and height.

**risk of overweight**
Having a body mass index from the 85th to the 95th percentile for the child's age and gender.

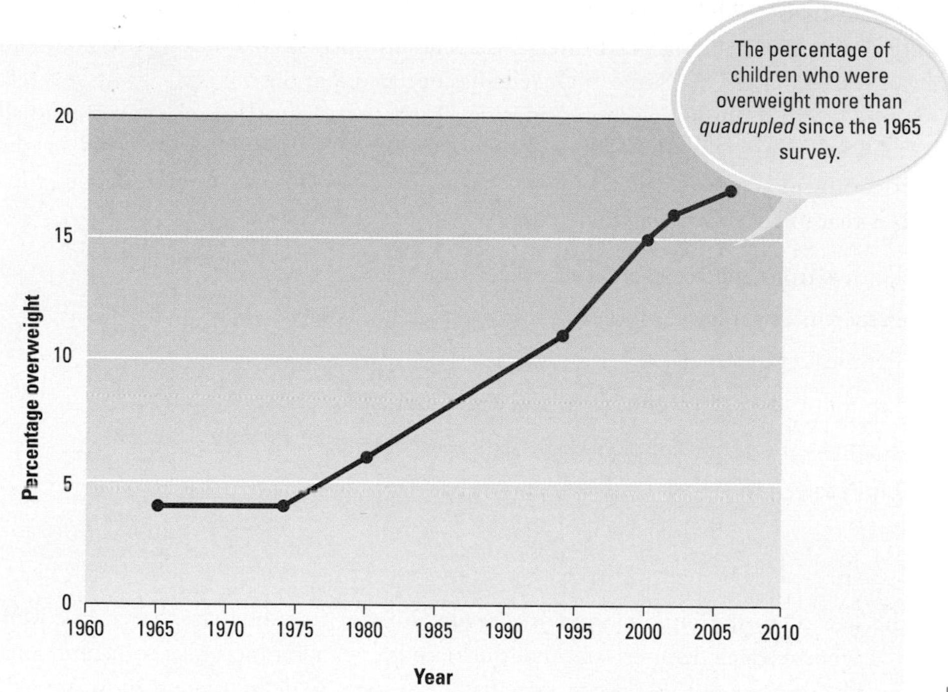


◀ FIGURE 10.1
**Percentage of Children 6 to 11 Years Old Who Were Overweight: Trend from 1965 through 2006**
(National Center for Health Statistics, 2006a, 2009.)

Families rely more and more on fast foods and processed foods, and these foods boost children's intake of calories and saturated fat. Children are also not getting enough exercise. Compared to a few decades ago, children today get less physical activity in school, they are less likely to walk to school, and their favorite hobbies and entertainment are more sedentary activities such as watching television, playing video games, and playing on computers (American Academy of Pediatrics, 2003). Because two-thirds of adults in the United States are now overweight, children today have fewer positive role models for health and fitness than in earlier decades. Obesity has been increasing world-wide, but experts estimate that the United States has the highest prevalence of obesity of any developed nation (National Center for Health Statistics, 2006b).

A mix of genetic and environmental factors (nature and nurture) contribute to being overweight. Children are more likely to be overweight when they have a high birth weight, when their mother has diabetes, or when they have other family members who are overweight. When one parent is overweight, the child's risk of being overweight increases three times. When both parents are overweight, the child's risk increases 10 times (American Academy of Pediatrics, 2003). Children living below the poverty line are 25% more likely to be overweight compared to other children (National Center for Health Statistics, 2005). Children in poor families tend to eat fewer fruits and vegetables and more foods with higher fat content, and they have fewer safe places to play outdoors and be physically active (American Academy of Pediatrics, 2003). There is also some concern that parents who are overweight themselves may not worry about their children being overweight. They may see their children as "thick," "solid," or "big-boned" rather than focus on the potential health effects of their children being overweight. They also might think that the child's size is controlled mostly by genetics and an inherited metabolism rather than by diet, exercise, and other factors that they can control (Jain et al., 2001). By examining all of these factors you can see that a child's weight is influenced by a variety of factors including genetics, neighborhood safety, and even parental attitudes.

▲ An increasing number of children in the United States are overweight. Why is this an increasing trend?

How many of the factors that contribute to being overweight did you experience during childhood? How did you deal with them, and how could the adults in your life have helped?

In childhood, as in adulthood, being overweight is a risk factor for a litany of serious health problems, including heart disease, diabetes, asthma, sleep apnea, depression, and low self-esteem. The U.S. Surgeon General has declared that obesity is the greatest threat to public health today, killing more Americans every year than AIDS, all cancers, and all accidents combined (American Medical Association, 2009). To combat the problem, the American Academy of Pediatrics (2009) has made a number of recommendations for families that include the following:

- Eat five fruits and vegetables every day.
- Prepare meals at home, and eat meals together as a family.
- Eat breakfast every day.
- Limit fast foods, take-out meals, and eating out.
- Get at least one hour of physical activity every day.
- Limit screen time to less than two hours per day.

THINK ABOUT BRAD . . .
What are some ways Brad could use these suggestions to help the children he works with now and in the future?

## Growth and Maturation of the Brain

By the age of 6, the child's brain is already 90% of its adult size (Giedd, 2003). Neuroscience research demonstrates that the brain is critical for most all of our functions, and we like to point out that it gets an early "head start" in development! In Chapters 4 and 7, we explained how the brain moves through two phases of growth and maturation: first it overproduces synapses (*synaptogenesis*), then it prunes back the circuits that are less useful in favor of the ones that are working more efficiently (*synaptic pruning*). The child's experiences activate some circuits more than others, so experience plays an important role in this survival-of-the-fittest phase of brain development when the less useful circuits are pruned—another example of the interplay of both nature and nurture in development.

The brain grows in some ways and shrinks in other ways throughout middle childhood and into the adolescent years. Until age 10, most areas of the cerebral cortex are still growing and gaining mass. Most of this gain is due to growth in the blood vessels that spread through the brain, a gain in the number of glial cells that proliferate throughout the brain and support the function of neurons, and continued myelination of the axons that make up the brain's circuits. Recall from Chapters 4 and 7 that myelination involves the growth of fatty tissues (myelin) that cover the axons that carry nerve impulses from one neuron to other neurons. After myelin grows around an axon, it insulates the nerve impulse and speeds its action across the axon by as much as 100 times (Giedd, 2003). Brain circuits become much more efficient after they become myelinated.

After age 10, the brain actually shrinks in some ways. Although it is still gaining glial cells and myelin, the rate of these gains begins to slow, and it is overtaken by a new wave of synaptic pruning. Pruning the less efficient circuits reduces the "noise" in the system, so this shrinkage is actually an important part of the maturation of the brain. As the shrinkage occurs, we see improvements in the child's functions controlled by those areas of the brain. The first areas to prune and mature in this way are the ones that control our basic sensory and motor functions (Gogtay et al., 2004). The occipital lobe on the back of the brain, for example, processes our visual signals, and it is one of the first areas to prune and mature. The motor cortex and sensory cortex also mature early, as does the area in the frontal lobe that controls smell and taste. The next areas to mature are the association areas in the parietal and temporal lobes. These areas integrate information, control language, and begin to perform our more advanced thought processes. Between the ages of 7 and 11, pruning results in a 50% loss in the circuits in the brain that control our fine-motor movements. Children at this age are beginning to master specific motor skills, for example, by playing particular sports or by practicing musical instruments. It is no coincidence that "[c]oaches and music teachers readily agree that world-class athletes or musicians almost always have been

**plasticity**
The brain's tendency to remain somewhat flexible or malleable until synaptogenesis is complete and until the brain's synapses have been pruned and locked into particular functions.

practicing their skill during this developmental stage" (Giedd, 2003, p. 138). The prefrontal cortex is one of the last areas to mature. It is located deep inside the frontal lobes, and it is responsible for abstract reasoning and complex problem solving. This last area doesn't finish its prune-and-mature process until the end of adolescence (Gogtay et al., 2004).

As you consider these developmental phases, keep in mind that brain maturity helps us perform our important mental processes and functions, but mental and physical exercise provide the stimulation needed to prune the less efficient circuits. It's a reciprocal process. Stimulation, education, exercise, and challenge all help the brain mature. In turn, the improved efficiency helps us think, remember, coordinate information, and move with greater skill. We need both sides of nature and nurture to accomplish these forms of maturation.

THINK ABOUT BRAD . . .
How could knowing about brain development help Brad be more effective as a camp counselor and teacher?

The experience-expectant phase of development that occurs early in the life cycle (see Chapter 7) provides *neural plasticity* for the developing brain. **Plasticity** is the brain's tendency to remain somewhat flexible or malleable until synaptogenesis is complete and until the brain's synapses have been pruned and locked into particular functions (Huttenlocher, 2002). For example, consider an adult who gets into an automobile accident and suffers head trauma and brain damage to the left hemisphere. Because the left hemisphere is specialized for language processing in most adults, the person will likely lose a significant amount of language function. With a strong rehabilitation regimen, the person may be able to recoup some language function, but he or she will probably experience lifelong deficits like slurred speech or trouble keeping track of complex sentence segments. Similar damage to the left hemisphere of a young child, however, will not lead to such dramatic lifelong deficits (Couperus & Nelson, 2006; Stiles, Reilly, Paul, & Moses, 2005). Thanks to neural plasticity, corresponding areas in the child's right hemisphere (or other brain areas) can take over the work of language specialization, compensating for the damage in the left hemisphere. Language processing in the right hemisphere will maintain synapses and neural circuits that, without the accident, would have been pruned away or devoted to other functions.

Plasticity is greatest before the age of 2 years, a period when new synapses are still proliferating and have not yet been pruned. From the age of 2 until adolescence, plasticity gradually declines. With declining plasticity, *sensitive periods*, or windows of opportunity, also begin to close (Knudsen, 2004). The eyes and visual centers of the brain need sensory input in the first months after birth, or their neural circuits will quickly degenerate. Plasticity lasts longer in other areas of the brain. Language centers, for example, maintain some plasticity until around the age of 12. Before age 12, children can learn a second language and speak it with the accent of a native speaker. Students who begin learning a new language after 12, however, can learn the vocabulary and syntax but have difficulty mastering the native speaker's intonations and subtle speech sounds. The ability to acquire a new accent has already been "pruned away" in the brain. The brain maintains some degree of plasticity throughout life, and this provides the capacity for recovery and resilience. After adolescence, however, the neural circuits in general are less flexible, and brain damage from accidents, stroke, or disease will have more permanent effects (Stiles et al., 2005). **Listen** on **mydevelopmentlab**

**Listen**: Is the brain fully plastic and malleable, or do particular skills become locked into the brain with development? (Author Podcast) www.mydevelopmentlab.com

## LET'S REVIEW . . .

1. Amanda and Samuel are neighbors who have always been similar in height and weight. If their rates of physical growth are typical, which of the following is likely to be true as they move through middle childhood?
   a. Samuel will get taller and heavier than Amanda and remain bigger.
   b. Amanda will get taller and heavier than Samuel and remain bigger until early adulthood.
   c. Amanda will get taller and heavier than Samuel, but Samuel will catch up; they will be equal in size after their mid-teens.
   d. Amanda will get taller and heavier than Samuel, but Samuel will catch up and be bigger by their late teens.

2. Based on the general statistics given in this section, which group of U. S. children is most likely to be overweight?
   a. Mexican American boys
   b. Caucasian boys
   c. Caucasian girls
   d. African American girls
3. Out of the areas listed below, which area of the brain is the *last* one to mature by synaptic pruning?
   a. the occipital lobe
   b. the prefrontal cortex
   c. the temporal lobe
   d. the motor cortex
4. True or False: Children in poor families are more likely to be overweight than children in non-poor families.
5. True or False: Brain maturity improves physical and mental skills, but the environment does not affect brain development.

Answers: 1. d, 2. a, 3. b, 4. T, 5. F

# Motor Development and Physcial Activity

Chapters 4 and 7 introduced you to the many physical changes of the first six years of life. The middle childhood years do not show the dramatic degrees of motor development that are found in the early years, but important changes are taking place nonetheless. Children of these ages become increasingly capable of a variety of complex and integrated physical feats. Many children during these years participate in organized sports as one way to be active and have fun while at the same time practicing a variety of physical skills. However, there is increasing concern over the level of children's physical activity. What skills do children develop during middle childhood, and how active are most children? In this section, we cover children's motor development, exercise, and participation in organized sports.

AS YOU STUDY THIS SECTION, ASK YOURSELF THESE QUESTIONS:

**10.3** In what ways do children's motor skills become more controlled and coordinated during middle childhood?

**10.4** How can adults help children get more physical activity and exercise?

**10.5** What are the benefits and concerns for children's participation in organized sports?

▲ These children have developed the motor control and coordination to do more detailed needlework. What other things will their fine- and gross-motor development enable them to do that they couldn't do when they were younger?

## Motor Development

Both gross-motor and fine-motor skills become more controlled and coordinated across the middle childhood years. For example, 6-year-old children can catch a ball—if it is relatively large, is not thrown too hard, and is thrown pretty accurately. By the time they are 11, however, most children can catch many different types of balls, easily and effectively adjusting their grasp to accommodate the different sizes. They can control their movements and run toward a ground ball during a baseball game, judge with reasonably good accuracy where the ball is going to land, coordinate their hands to catch and cover the ball—and at the same time think about which bases have runners and where and how hard they need to throw the ball in order to get the runners out! You may think of motor skills as being relevant mostly for sports and other physical activities, but they are important in many other areas as well. For example, the vast improvements in writing, artwork, playing musical instruments, and even playing video games are affected by the development of motor skills.

Overall strength improves during middle childhood—children can run faster, jump higher and farther, and throw harder than they used to. Boys tend to have greater strength than girls. Boys also continue to gain strength throughout middle childhood and adolescence, while girls' strength tends to increase until early adolescence and then stabilize. Both boys and girls show improvements in balance. Children in this age range are more flexible than older children; for example, they have a fuller range of motion when moving their arms and legs. Boys' flexibility starts to decrease at about 10 years of age, while girls' begins to decline around age 12. At all ages of middle childhood, girls show greater flexibility than boys (Gallahue & Ozmun, 1995; Keogh & Sugden, 1985).

Children also gradually gain much greater control over their movements during middle childhood. For example, they get better at adjusting their grasp when throwing and catching. They are more precise when kicking and are able to control where the ball will go and how hard they kick it. Increased control is evident in fine-motor skills as well. As students move through elementary school, handwriting improves as their fingers are able to grasp a pencil more delicately. They use their fingers and wrists more effectively, rather than just moving their whole arm when they write. Look back at Figure 8.1 (on page 231) and you will notice striking changes in the level of detail and precision in artwork. Greater control over pens, pencils, and paintbrushes allows much better precision as children fill in color and details. Improved fine-motor control is evident in many of the hobbies that children at these ages enjoy, such as accurately pressing the small buttons on hand-held electronic games and working with smaller pieces of puzzles and arts and crafts materials.

▲ Children get stronger and their balance improves during middle childhood. What other changes in motor skills has this child likely experienced?

Finally, one of the most striking developments in both gross- and fine-motor skills during middle childhood is increasing coordination of skills. Spend some time watching 7-year-olds playing baseball, then watch 11-year-olds as they play. The older children are not only better at coordinating their arms and legs as they swing a bat, they are better at anticipating when the ball will arrive and integrating this information with their swings—so that they actually hit the ball much more often! Swimmers learning new strokes are able to coordinate their arm and leg movements to produce a fluid, effective movement through the water. Some of the increased coordination is due to the brain development you read about earlier in this chapter. Increased myelination allows faster transmission of neural impulses, decreased reaction times, and increased likelihood of integrating information. With continued practice, the neurons involved in physical skills are activated together, repeatedly. Eventually, these neural pathways grow more synapses, the sensitivity of receptors increases, and they begin to fire more efficiently together—another example of the experience-dependent learning that you read about in Chapter 7 (Shonkoff & Phillips, 2000).

THINKING CRITICALLY

Think about younger children you've seen playing physical games, and compare them to 10- to 11-year-olds. What differences are there? How do maturation, brain development, and practice contribute to the differences?

## Physical Activity and Exercise

As you read in Chapter 7, health officials recommend that children get much more physical activity each day than most currently do (National Association for Sport and Physical Education, 2004). One nationally representative survey of 9- to 13-year-olds found that more than 60% of these children had not participated in any organized physical activity (i.e., one with a coach, teacher, or leader) in the week before the survey. While most of these students (77%) reported engaging in some sort of physical activity in their free time, the survey does not indicate how much time was spent in the activity (Centers for Disease Control, 2003). Girls reported significantly less free-time physical activity than boys. There were no ethnic group differences in free-time activity, but African American and Hispanic children reported less organized physical activity than white children, as shown in Figure 10.2 (page 298). The benefits of regular exercise include physical effects such as weight control, healthy lung function, and cardiovascular health. There are emotional benefits as well: children who get regular exercise tend to feel better about themselves, have higher levels of self-esteem, and report having fewer negative moods (Annesi, 2005; Parfitt & Eston, 2005; Siegel, 2006).

FIGURE 10.2 ▶
**Percentage of Children Participating in Physical Activity, by Ethnicity, 2002**
(Centers for Disease Control, 2003.)

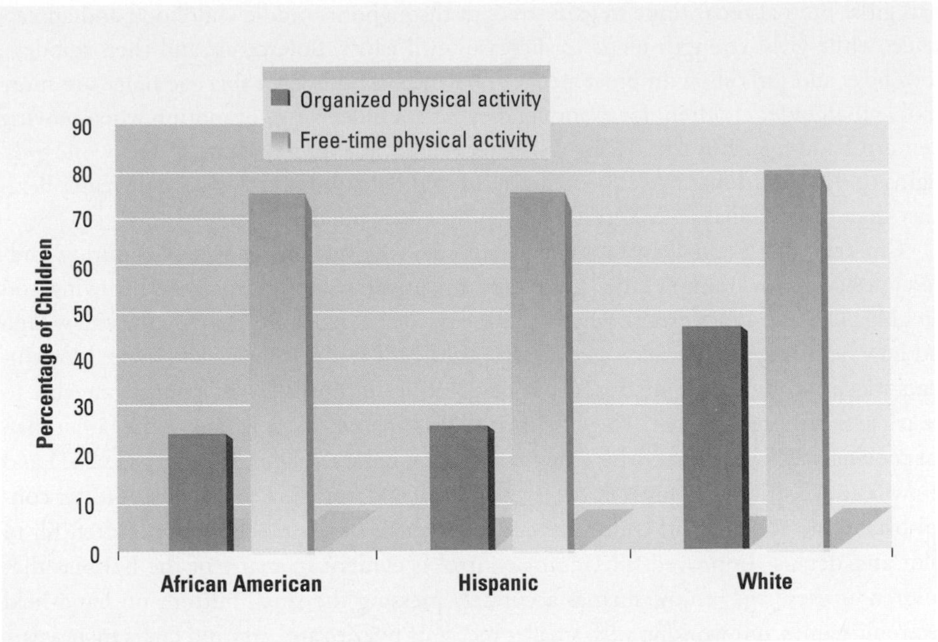

▲ Most children report getting some daily physical activity, but experts are still worried. Why?

Although most children report getting at least some physical activity, experts are still concerned. Children tend to get progressively less exercise as they move through adolescence, and some surveys indicate that only about 55% of 12th graders get regular vigorous exercise. For those children who are already less active, this may signal potentially serious health problems in adolescence and young adulthood. Unfortunately, only 28% of schools require daily physical education classes, and fewer than 10% of elementary schools provide for daily physical activity at the levels experts recommend (National Association for Sport and Physical Education & American Heart Association, 2006). Rates of physical activity during school recess vary widely, but boys are typically more physically active than girls during recess. Some have suggested that recess times be more structured to ensure that more children are active; others disagree, arguing that children already have too little free choice in their school day (Brinkman et al., 2005; Oliver, Schofield, & McEvoy, 2006).

Why don't children get more exercise? Part of the answer involves the increasing amount of time spent in sedentary activities such as watching television and playing video games, but there are other challenges as well. As shown in Figure 10.3, the cost of participating in physical activities as well as transportation difficulties are obstacles for many families, particularly for ethnic minority families and those in lower income areas. Lack of opportunities and unsafe neighborhoods also make it more difficult for some children to be physically active (Centers for Disease Control, 2003). Incorporating more physical activity into daily activities can also be challenging. For example, many children now live too far away to walk to school, and concerns about traffic keep some of those who live close enough to walk from doing so (Centers for Disease Control, 2005a). Not surprisingly, one thing that seems to help children get and stay more active is parental support of physical activity, whether in the form of

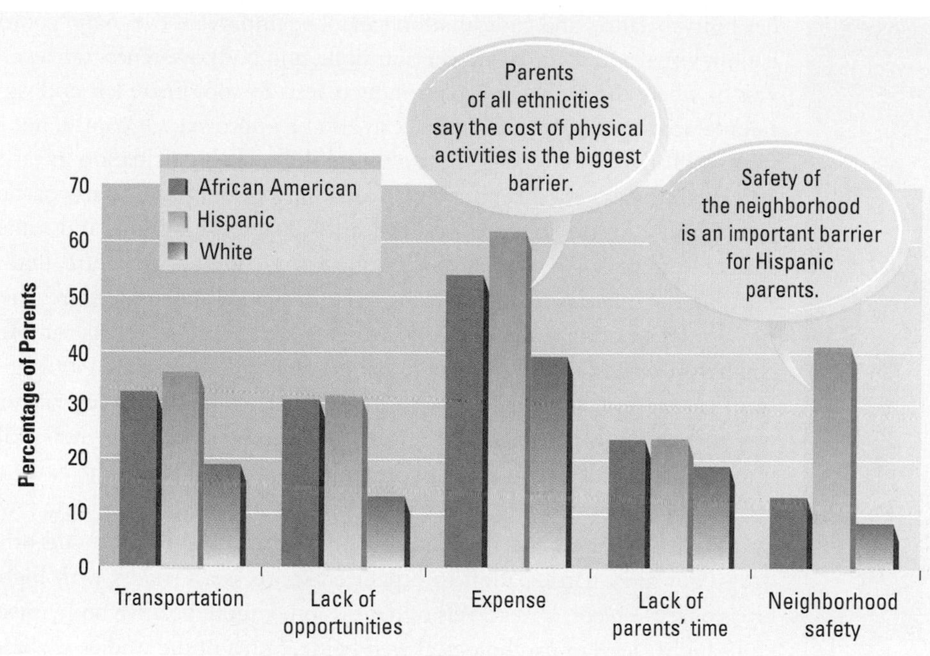


◀ FIGURE 10.3
**Barriers to Physical Activity, 2002**
(Centers for Disease Control, 2003.)

being active with the child, supporting involvement in organized sports, or ensuring that the child has time to be physically active (Gustafson & Rhodes, 2006).

One consistent finding in the research on physical activity is the existence of gender differences, particularly in the physical activities they prefer. Girls are more likely to choose games that involve fine-motor skills and small groups and that do not emphasize competition. Boys, on the other hand, are more likely to prefer larger groups, competition, and games that require risk taking (Maccoby, 2002). For boys in particular, the amount of **rough-and-tumble play** increases during middle childhood. This type of play is very physical and often involves wrestling, chasing, shoving, and other aggressive behaviors, but it is done in a friendly and nonthreatening way. It likely improves gross-motor skills and may also provide a safe context in which boys can test their strength against peers. Rough-and-tumble play becomes less and less frequent once boys reach adolescence. Physical differences in strength, hormones, and skills account for some of the gender differences in activity preferences, but social and cultural differences are also a major factor. Until recent decades, girls were not encouraged to engage in sports and strenuous physical activities; in many cases, they were actively discouraged. Adults may expect more from boys in physical activities and be more supportive of their interests and skills. We know that being physically active is an important part of a healthy lifestyle, and it is important that *both* girls and boys be encouraged to find and regularly participate in physical activities they enjoy. **Watch** on **mydevelopmentlab**

THINK ABOUT BRAD . . .
What are some specific things Brad could do to help children become more physically active and stay active?

THINKING CRITICALLY
What gender differences in physical activity preferences have you experienced? What do you think caused them?

**Watch** a video on Rough and Tumble Play.
www.mydevelopmentlab.com

**rough-and-tumble play**
Very physical, aggressive but friendly play common among boys during middle childhood.

## Organized Sports

There is no question that more children are participating in **organized sports**—sporting activities that are organized, coached, or somehow supervised by adults. Millions of children participate yearly in soccer, baseball, softball, basketball, tennis, swimming, golf, karate, dance, football, fencing, hockey—the choices include an almost mind-boggling variety. Participation in organized sports has a number of potential physical, social, and emotional benefits. Muscle strength, endurance, lung and heart functioning, speed,

**organized sports**
Sporting activities organized, coached, or supervised by adults.

▲ Increasing numbers of children participate in organized sports. What are some of the benefits of playing sports? How is this coach ensuring that her team members have a good experience?

flexibility, balance, and coordination can all be improved. Eye–hand coordination, visual and auditory perception skills, and body awareness (an awareness of where the body is in space, how it feels to coordinate left and right sides to accomplish a physical task) can also be improved. Of course, not all sports will affect every one of these physical skills, but participation in varied activities increases the likelihood of overall physical impact. Sports participation also offers the opportunity to learn valuable social skills and values, such as teamwork and cooperation, taking turns, coping with failure, understanding the importance of following rules, and good sportsmanship. There can also be emotional and cognitive benefits. For example, sports can offer children a socially acceptable way to handle feelings of frustration or aggression, an appropriate outlet for a child's naturally high energy level, and a way to help children feel good about themselves as they see their skills improve. Studies have found that participation in organized sports is associated with higher achievement test scores and greater success in school, lower rates of delinquency, and decreased likelihood of using tobacco and other drugs. For girls, participation in organized sports is associated with higher levels of self-esteem, lower levels of depression, a more positive body image, and a higher level of psychological well-being. Some of the studies are based on correlations, which makes it difficult to determine whether it is sports participation itself that accounts for the positive relationship. But others have used experimental designs and found that sports activity produces positive outcomes. Helping children establish a habit of regular physical activity encourages more sports activity in early adulthood, so it can help prevent serious future health problems such as obesity, diabetes, and heart disease (DeBate & Thompson, 2005; Fletcher, Nickerson, & Wright, 2003; Hausenblas & Fallon, 2006; Hofferth & Curtin, 2003; Hofferth & Sandberg, 2001; Humphrey, 2003; National Alliance for Youth Sports, 2003; Perkins, Jacobs, Barber, & Eccles, 2004).

Given the potential benefits, why wouldn't all parents get their children involved in organized sports? We have already mentioned money, time, transportation, and neighborhood safety considerations. Another concern about organized sports is the potential for injury. There are about 3 million sports-related injuries per year, but the rate of injury is higher for youths playing unorganized sports (e.g., a neighborhood pick-up basketball or baseball game) than organized sports. In organized youth sports, football has the highest rate and the most serious injuries. Fortunately, most injuries in organized sports are minor and the rate has decreased in recent years, thanks in part to changes in rules that restrict more aggressive play or risky moves, better safety equipment, and better training of coaches and referees. Many sports injuries are the result of contact with equipment or other players, but others are due to heat-related illness. Getting plenty of fluids is essential for athletes of any age, especially during sports practices and events in warmer weather (Committee on Sports Medicine & Fitness, 2000; Hergenroeder, 1998; Radelet, Lephart, Rubinstein, & Myers, 2002).

▲ Experts are concerned about the behavior and attitudes of some adults involved in youth sports. What impact might these adults' behavior have on the children's experience with sports?

Another increasing concern about organized sports is the behavior and attitudes of the adults involved. As sports activities become more popular, some parents and coaches put increasing pressure on children to play sports they are not developmentally ready for, play too much, practice too hard, play with an injury, or simply put too much emphasis on the competitive aspects of the sport and winning. Given that 70% of the sports programs that children participate in are organized, coached, and run by adults, the impact of these inappropriate behaviors and attitudes can be strong. Three-fourths of the 3,000 children surveyed in one study reported that they had seen out-of-control adults at their sports games; 36% of these youngsters said that parents who couldn't control themselves appropriately should be banned from the games

(National Alliance for Youth Sports, 2003)! Instead of developing their physical skills, feeling better about themselves, and having fun, children exposed to too much pressure and an overemphasis on winning can end up feeling anxious, inept, and disliking the sport altogether. Several national sports organizations now offer guidelines that emphasize positive and safe development of physical, social, and emotional skills rather than competition and winning to organizers, coaches, and parents (National Alliance for Youth Sports, 2001).

THINK ABOUT BRAD . . . How can Brad help minimize the risks and maximize the benefits of organized sports for the children with whom he's working?

**LET'S REVIEW . . .**

**1.** Which of the following children is *most* typical of motor development by the end of middle childhood?
- **a.** Josh, who can catch a beach ball thrown directly at him but not a baseball.
- **b.** Emma, who can easily hit a softball most of the time.
- **c.** Michael, whose handwriting is made up of large and ill-formed letters.
- **d.** Jasmin, who is not able to control the direction of the soccer ball when she kicks it.

**2.** Which statement best summarizes motor development during middle childhood?
- **a.** Children become more flexible.
- **b.** Children are faster but cannot effectively control their movements.
- **c.** Children more effectively control and coordinate their bodies.
- **d.** Boys and girls show similar improvements in strength, balance, and flexibility.

**3.** Which of the following is *not* a likely explanation for why children fail to get adequate exercise?
- **a.** Most children do not like to play organized sports.
- **b.** Their parents lack time or money to support more physical activity.
- **c.** Children would rather watch TV and play video games.
- **d.** Their parents are concerned about neighborhood safety.

**4.** Which of the following coaches is most likely to help the members of her fourth grade soccer team benefit from playing organized sports?
- **a.** Coach Chatam, who stresses that they need to be competitive and win as much as possible.
- **b.** Coach Marin, who just lets the team play and doesn't teach specific skills.
- **c.** Coach Danvers, who has the team practice intensely five days per week.
- **d.** Coach Budde, who has some drills during practice, makes sure everyone gets to play, and makes it fun.

**5.** True or False: Boys and girls show the same rate of rough-and-tumble play until early adolescence; then boys do more of this than girls do.

**6.** True or False: The majority of children do not get any physical activity.

Answers: 1. b, 2. c, 3. a, 4. d, 5. F, 6. F

# Health and Safety Issues

Look back to Table 7.2 on page 219 and you will see that middle childhood is a relatively safe period of time. The vast majority of fatal accidents and illnesses occur during the first year of life and after age 14. Still, a large number of accidents, serious illnesses, and deaths do occur during the intervening years, and many are preventable. Unfortunately, one of the most devastating threats to child health and safety begins to increase during the middle childhood years: sexual abuse. In this section we explore the most serious health and safety issues that children and families face during middle childhood, and we offer concrete suggestions for protecting the health and safety of children of this age.

AS YOU STUDY THIS SECTION, ASK YOURSELF THESE QUESTIONS:

**10.6** What are several things that adults can do to help protect children from the most common health and safety problems?

**10.7** What are the immediate and long-term effects of sexual abuse on children?

## Childhood Injuries and Safety Issues

In the United States, approximately 12 million children under age 12 are treated each year in hospital emergency rooms for injuries (Hunter, Helou, Saluja, Runyan, & Coyne-Beasley, 2005). The most common causes of injuries treated in emergency rooms include falls, cuts, bicycle accidents, automobile accidents, dog bites, other bites and stings, and overexertion (Centers for Disease Control, 2009). The most common causes of accidental death during middle childhood are accidents involving automobiles, drowning, fire, and burns (Centers for Disease Control, 2009). During middle childhood, children begin moving beyond the direct supervision of parents and other adults. They spend more time at home unsupervised, and they sometimes fix their own meals or work with household appliances. They ride bicycles, they walk or ride to friends' houses, and some children walk to and from school. As they gain independence, children may still lack the developmental skills they need to stay safe. When crossing a street, for example, children often misjudge the speed and distance of oncoming traffic. They may have trouble seeing over taller bushes and parked cars, just as oncoming drivers may have trouble seeing them. They may not have the cognitive maturity to understand the full extent of many dangers or how to plan ahead to avoid danger. Children can be very active, curious, and even daring at this age, but their immaturity may still lead them to underestimate the risks involved in many situations.

THINKING CRITICALLY

What health and safety risks did you experience in middle childhood? What might have helped reduce these risks for you?

Adults and other caregivers need to remind children how to stay safe, and they need to minimize the hazards that exist in and around the places where children live and play. Here are several helpful tips:

- *Home Safety.* In the U.S., 40% of children's accidental deaths and 50% of their accident-related injuries occur in or around their homes (National SAFE KIDS Campaign, 2004). There are many things parents and caregivers can do to improve safety at home. Remove or secure dangerous items such as firearms, matches, medicines, and household poisons. Prepare the house for children who will spend more time alone and will explore all through the house looking for interesting things to do. Equip the home with smoke and carbon monoxide detectors, and rehearse a family plan for fire safety. When children are alone at home, make sure that all doors and windows are locked and secure. Teach children about home safety, first aid, and how to keep strangers out of the home.
- *Automobile Safety.* Automobile accidents are the leading cause of accidental death in this age group. Remember that the majority of people who die in traffic accidents are not wearing seat belts. Every time you travel, make sure all children are secured in booster seats or seat belts that are appropriate for their size, and preferably in the back seat. Experts recommend that children use a booster seat until they are at least 8 years old or at least 4 feet and 9 inches tall (National Highway Traffic Safety Administration, 2009). When children transition out of booster seats, the seat belts should fit properly across the child's waist, and the shoulder belt should be adjusted so it does not cross the neck. Children should never ride in front seats that have air bags; the rear seat is the safest location in most vehicle crashes. Drive defensively. Never drink and drive: 32% of all traffic deaths involve alcohol, and half of the children who die in alcohol-related crashes were riding with the driver who was drinking (National Highway Traffic Safety Administration, 2007).
- *Pedestrian Safety.* Most children under the age of 10 do not understand traffic safety and do not understand traffic signs and signals. Adults need to supervise children when crossing streets until they are sure the children have the skills and the maturity in judgment they need to stay safe. Teach children to stay on sidewalks, cross only at intersections, and watch for cars backing out of driveways. Remind children to never

run into the street to chase a ball or for any other reason. When you are driving, always check carefully before backing up, and slow down in neighborhoods and other places where children play.

- *Bicycle Safety.* In the U.S., approximately 275,000 children are injured and 140 are killed on bicycles each year (Safe Kids Worldwide, 2007). Nearly all of the bicyclists killed each year were not wearing helmets (Centers for Disease Control, 2002). Wearing a helmet can reduce the risks of serious head and brain injuries by as much as 85%, but only about one-quarter of children wear helmets (Safe Kids Worldwide, 2007). The percentage of teens who wear helmets is nearly zero. Children complain that it is not "cool" to wear helmets, their friends don't wear them, they are too hot and uncomfortable, and they don't believe they will be injured on their bicycles (Centers for Disease Control, 2002). Parents and other adults can help by being good role models of helmet use and by teaching children the rules of the road for safe bicycling. When you are driving, always share the road with bicycles, and slow down around children. Children do not watch traffic carefully and they can turn or dart into traffic very suddenly. Many also do not have the coordination and skill to control their bicycles and to make sudden stops when danger approaches. Children should never ride in the dark, and they should be encouraged to take advantage of any bicycle safety programs offered in their communities.
- *Water Safety.* Drowning is another leading cause of accidental death among children. During middle childhood, children still need to be supervised closely around water. All children should learn proper swimming techniques. But even when they have good swimming skills, remember that children this age may still lack the cognitive maturity to make sound judgments about how far they are from shore, the effect of currents, and the effects of fatigue. Children should always wear proper flotation devices when in boats or participating in water sports. Diving accidents also cause serious injuries. Teach children to never dive head first into shallow water or water that was not first approved for safe diving.

▲ Bicycle riding is an excellent way to be physically active. What steps are these children taking to make sure they stay safe?

Many parenting books offer good advice on childhood safety. Table 10.1 shows some of the most common safety tips found in one review of best-selling parenting books.

Pediatricians are physicians who specialize in the treatment of children and adolescents. These physicians are often the major source of information that families have about health and safety issues. Read the Professional Perspective box on page 304 called "Career Focus: Meet a Pediatrician" to learn about one pediatrician's advice regarding health and safety for middle childhood.

**THINK ABOUT BRAD . . .**
In your opinion, what are the two most effective things Brad could do to reduce the risk of accidents and injury for his campers and future students?

**TABLE 10.1**
**The Most Common Safety Tips Offered in Best-Selling Parenting Books***

- Have a working smoke alarm in the home.
- Keep the temperature of the hot water heater to 120°F or lower.
- Never leave a child alone near water; never let children swim alone.
- Keep household products (cleaners, medicines, etc.) out of sight and reach.
- Keep matches and lighters out of sight and reach.
- Do not keep guns in the home. If you do, keep them unloaded and locked.
- Children should always wear helmets when biking and wear reflective gear when biking at night.
- Children should wear protective gear when playing sports.

*Does not include tips for infant safety.
(Hunter et al., 2005.)

## Perspective PROFESSIONAL — CAREER FOCUS: MEET A PEDIATRICIAN

Harlan R. Gephart, MD, FAAP
Woodinville, WA

**What do you see as the biggest health and safety issues for children between the ages of 7 and 11?**
One way to answer this question is to look at mortality statistics. The five leading causes of death for 5- to 9-year-olds (in descending order) are unintentional injury, malignant neoplasms (cancerous overgrowth of body cells), congenital anomalies (problems present at birth), homicide, and heart disease. In the 10- to 14-year range, suicide is third, followed by homicide and congenital anomalies. Homicide is sadly a recent newcomer to these lists! Chronic illness in childhood is also a concern. About 15% to 18% of children have ongoing health conditions that affect their functioning. The most frequent include asthma, recurrent middle ear infections, adolescent depression, ADHD, and developmental disabilities. All these conditions can persist into adulthood and impair the person's ability to be a functional and contributing citizen. Obviously, some conditions also shorten the person's life.

**Who is at greatest risk for health and safety problems, and why? What might reduce the risk?**
Poorer health status is directly related to general factors such as socioeconomic status and race/ethnicity. Increasing divorce rates and single-parent homes frequently result in lower SES, triggering a cascade of increased infections, inadequate housing, poorer nutrition, more exposure to environmental toxins, less physician contact, and reduced preventive care. There are also more specific situations that increase risk. For example, teenage pregnancies are often associated with lack of prenatal care, birth problems, prematurity, and child abuse and neglect. And there are the risks of each specific medical condition. For example, ADHD is associated with increased school and social failure, substance abuse, and driving accidents if it is not diagnosed and treated early.

These issues are very difficult to address, and experts do not always agree as to the best approaches in each situation. Yet there seems to be universal agreement, supported by data, that *early recognition and intervention* helps improve outcomes. The American Academy of Pediatrics Guidelines for treatment of ADHD, autism, hearing, vision, and many other pediatric issues emphasize this concept and provide screening and intervention tools for pediatricians.

**What education and training is needed to become a pediatrician?**
The minimal training for certification as a "qualified" pediatrician by the American Board of Pediatrics is a four-year college degree (heavily loaded with science), four years of medical school, then finally three years of specialty training in an approved pediatric residency training program. About 25% of pediatricians also obtain three additional years of training in a pediatric subspecialty such as cardiology, neonatology, allergy, etc. A thorough knowledge of child and adolescent development is crucial to a pediatrician—children are not "little adults." Because of the child's growth and development, any medical condition can have a profoundly different effect on a child than on an adult. Students who want a career in pediatrics should prepare for many arduous years of study and preparation, have a sincere love of children, and be motivated by even the small differences the practitioner can make in the daily life of children and families. Having a sense of humor is a real asset, as is an intellectual curiosity that drives one to self-examine one's practice and ask, "how do I know that what I am doing makes any difference" or "how could I do what I'm doing even better." After 42 years of practice I can look back and say it was the best vocation I could have ever chosen!

QUESTION **What can you do to reduce these health and safety risks for the children you interact with? Are there other children's health issues you think are important? If so, what can be done to address them?**

## Child Sexual Abuse

As we discussed in Chapter 7, far too many children suffer some form of maltreatment. An estimated 740,000 children were victims of neglect and abuse in 2007, with 7% of these victims suffering sexual abuse (United States Department of Health & Human Services, 2009). As we defined it in Chapter 7, *child sexual abuse* involves fondling a child's genitals or breasts, committing intercourse or other sexual acts with a child, exposing the child to indecent acts, or involving the child in pornography. The rate of confirmed cases of child sexual abuse has declined dramatically since the early 1990s, but it isn't clear how much of this drop is due to a decrease in the actual number of sexual abuse cases and how much is due to other factors such as changes in reporting and investigation procedures. Nevertheless, before they grow up, about one in every five girls and one in every nine boys in the United States will experience some form of sexual abuse. Unfortunately, the majority of victims never report their abuse (Berliner & Elliot, 2002; Finkelhor & Jones, 2004; Mash & Wolfe, 2005).

**Who's at Risk?** Child sexual abuse occurs in all ethnic, geographic, and economic groups. Sadly, children who are sexually abused are likely to experience other forms of maltreatment as well. Unlike most other forms of child maltreatment, child sexual abuse is more common in middle childhood and adolescence than in infancy and early childhood. This type of abuse is more likely to be committed by someone that the child knows, often a person with whom they have an ongoing relationship. Many people believe that only men commit child sexual abuse, but this is not true. In one study of adults who had suffered child sexual abuse, nearly 40% of the male and 6% of the female victims reported that their abuser was female (Dube et al., 2005). On average, sexual abuse continues for four years. Adolescents are the perpetrators in half the cases (Flinn, 1995; United States Department of Health and Human Services, 2001, 2006; Wekerle & Wolfe, 2003). Other risk factors include:

- *Unhealthy family environment.* The risk for child sexual abuse is higher when the relationships between family members are not appropriate or supportive, there is no healthy emotional attachment between family members, parents are absent or otherwise not available, there is a higher rate of conflict or domestic violence, and/or the child does not live with either biological parent.
- *Marital disruptions.* Child sexual abuse is more likely in separated or divorced families or when there is a stepparent in the home.
- *Individual factors.* Children who are socially isolated and have few friends are at higher risk for sexual abuse, as well as children who are physically attractive or who have gone through puberty earlier than their peers. Gay and lesbian teens are also more likely to be victims of sexual abuse (Berliner & Elliot, 2002; Mullen & Fleming, 1998; Richardson, Meredith, & Abbot, 1993; Savin-Williams, 1994).

Children who are sexually abused vary in the symptoms they exhibit, but some common signs of sexual abuse are shown in Table 10.2 (page 306).

**What Are the Effects of Child Sexual Abuse?** As with other forms of abuse, the effects of sexual abuse depend on the frequency of the abuse and the length of time over which it occurs. With child sexual abuse, the outcomes are more negative when the abuse begins at an earlier age, the episodes are frequent, physical force is involved, sexual penetration occurs, and the abuser is a close relative such as a father or

**TABLE 10.2**
**Signs That May Indicate Child Sexual Abuse**

The child:

- reports being abused
- become pregnant or has an STD, especially under age 14
- has redness, rashes, swelling in genital areas; has urinary tract infections
- shows concern that there is something wrong with his or her genitals
- becomes depressed, withdrawn, or distrustful of adults
- shows behavioral problems, anger, rebellion, or aggressiveness
- runs away
- shows suicidal behavior
- shows bizarre, seductive, sophisticated, or unusual sexual knowledge or behavior
- reports nightmares or bedwetting
- has difficulty walking or sitting
- shows symptoms of anxiety such as chronic headaches or stomach pain
- shows sudden change in appetite
- suddenly refuses to participate in physical activities
- suddenly refuses to change for gym
- shows behavior that is "too perfect"

Please note that some children show no clear signs at all!

The parent or caregiver:

- is overly protective of the child
- severely limits the child's contact with other children, especially with opposite sex
- is secretive and isolated
- is jealous or controlling with family members

(Adapted from National Clearinghouse on Child Abuse and Neglect, 2006; American Academy of Child & Adolescent Psychiatry, 2004; Darkness to Light, 2006.)

stepfather (Nash, Zivney, & Hulsey, 1993; Stien & Kendall, 2004; Wekerle & Wolfe, 1996). Outcomes are less severe when there is a relatively stable two-parent household and the abused child has a warm and supportive relationship with the mother. When mothers show anger, jealousy, or indifference, these responses compound the negative outcomes.

Some researchers have looked at the impact of trauma such as sexual abuse on brain structure and functioning. Continued abuse wreaks havoc on the body in many ways and creates a state of chronic stress that results in abnormally high levels of stress hormones such as *cortisol* (Tarullo & Gunnar, 2006). Through a complex chain of reactions, chronic high levels of cortisol-damage parts of the brain involved in memory processing and storage such as the hippocampus (Stien & Kendall, 2004). MRI scans show that women who were abused as children and now suffer from posttraumatic stress disorder (PTSD) have significantly smaller hippocampi than women who do not have PTSD or were not abused, and PET scans show that their hippocampal regions are not as active during memory tasks (Bremner et al., 2003). Patients with PTSD often report amnesia (loss of memory), problems concentrating and learning new information, and flashbacks, and these symptoms might be related to damage to the hippocampus and other areas related to memory processing. Cortisol can also damage areas of the

THINK ABOUT BRAD . . .
What signs should Brad watch for that might indicate sexual abuse of children? What should he do if he notices these things, and how can he decide if he should do something?

brain involved in regulating emotional responses. Here, PET scans with women who were abused as children and now suffer from PTSD show reduced blood flow to the prefrontal cortex, the anterior cingulate, and the amygdala. (Bremner et al., 2004). As a result of problems regulating emotional responses, patients with PTSD may overreact to negative stimuli, sometimes responding with horror or intense fear. It isn't possible to conduct experimental studies with humans to study the effects of sexual abuse or other types of trauma on the brain more directly, but research shows that the intensity of the outcomes are correlated with the severity and duration of abuse (Shonkoff & Phillips, 2000).

THINKING CRITICALLY

Does it surprise you to learn about the effects of trauma and abuse on the brain? How does this information affect how you think about the behavior of those who have been abused?

Depression is the symptom most often reported in children and adolescents following sexual abuse. In some studies, two-thirds of female victims showed depression and 42% showed evidence of suicidal thoughts in the aftermath of their abuse (Kendler, Kuhn, & Prescott, 2004; Koverola, Pound, Heger, & Lytle, 1993; Wozencraft, Wagner, & Pellegrin, 1991). Another troubling symptom often seen in abused children is an increase in sexual behavior. A study of sexually abused preschoolers found that they engaged in more sexual kissing and used sexual words more often than their peers (Friedrich, 1993). Child sexual abuse correlates with increased sexual activity during adolescence as well as with teenage pregnancy and prostitution (Wekerle & Wolfe, 1996). Drug and alcohol abuse is more likely, with female victims about three times more likely to abuse drugs than non-victims (Kendler et al., 2000). About half of abused children show signs of PTSD, and victims are at increased risk for a number of other problems such as feelings of guilt and shame, anxiety, low self-esteem, eating disorders, and running away from home. As adults, these individuals face an increased risk of continuing problems with intimate relationships and sexuality (Dube et al., 2005; Mullen & Fleming, 1998).

Despite these negative effects of sexual abuse, children and adolescents who have suffered this type of abuse can survive and learn to cope. Removal from the abusive situation is a critical first step, because all the negative outcomes are worse the longer the abuse continues. Establishing a positive and healthy relationship with caring, trusted, and appropriate adults is important, as is receiving therapy as soon as possible from a professional who is skilled in working with victims of child sexual abuse. The Personal Perspective box on page 308 called "Surviving Child Sexual Abuse: One Survivor's Story" gives a moving firsthand account of child sexual abuse and one person's ongoing efforts to cope. We warn you that this is not an easy story to read; it was even more difficult for the person to tell. The survivor in our interview wanted others to know that there is help for those who have been sexually abused, and that courses like the one you're taking now helped her learn about appropriate parenting and positive family relationships, things she never had while growing up. With knowledge and therapy, victims can become survivors—good parents and partners who can break the cycle of abuse. Those of you who have had experiences similar to those described in the interview may find that reading this account makes you feel uncomfortable and unsettled. If so, we urge you to contact your college or university counseling center, your instructor, or a local social services agency for help. You can also contact a national sexual abuse hotline such as *Darkness to Light* (1-866-FOR LIGHT; www.darkness2light.org), or the *National Child Abuse Hotline* (1-800-4ACHILD) for help and information.

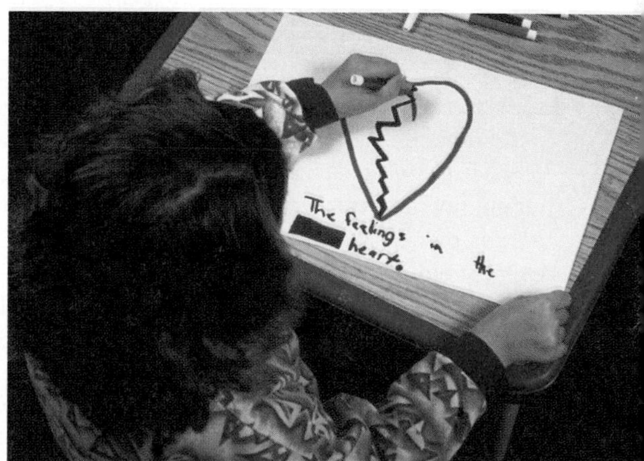

▲ This child has experienced sexual abuse, which can affect her physical, social, and emotional development. What signs might adults look for as indications of abuse?

## Perspective PERSONAL SURVIVING CHILD SEXUAL ABUSE: ONE SURVIVOR'S STORY

**Dawn**
**A small town in the Midwest**

**Dawn is a survivor. She endured years of horrific treatment at the hands of people who should have protected her. But her main message is one of hope. She wants those who have been abused to know that help is available to stop the abuse and cope with the physical and emotional scars that remain. It is ongoing and difficult work, but it is possible. Here is her story.**

My earliest memories of abuse are of my alcoholic father beating my mother and me. I even remember him beating my infant brother because he was crying—I was about 4 years old. My parents divorced, and my stepfather began immediately grooming our family for many, many years of severe sexual abuse. He would play seemingly innocent games with me, always physical, which happened mostly when my mother was at work. The games quickly led to rape a few times every week. My stepfather was violent and beat us, so I took seriously his threats to hurt us if I told. In third grade I stayed with my aunt in another state for a while. My teenage cousin, who had many behavior problems, babysat every day while my aunt worked. He soon began raping me, causing great pain and kidney infections. I wet the bed almost every night, which my aunt and uncle regularly embarrassed me about. Finally when I was 13, I told my mother about the abuse. She cursed at me and told me to leave, even after my stepfather admitted his guilt. From then on, I stayed with friends or slept outside. I married soon after I turned 18.

Why didn't anyone help? My mother could be quite violent when she was angry, so maybe she saw my stepfather's violence as acceptable. We lived in a very small town where it was just not acceptable to make waves, and the issue of abuse was only beginning to become public. I once told my best friend's mother and she became irate, accusing me of horrific lies—so I never mentioned it again. And my stepfather was respected in the community. He was from the largest family in town, taught Sunday school, and was a Boy Scout leader.

The effects of sexual abuse are pervasive. A person does not just "get over it," as has been suggested to me many times. It seeps into every part of a person's soul, mutating every cell and thought until there is nothing resembling normalcy, but this may not be evident from the outside. As an adult, I've been diagnosed with Major Depressive Disorder, Obsessive/Compulsive Disorder, Post-Traumatic Stress Disorder, and Generalized Anxiety Disorder. These are all linked to the abuse in my past, as are my lifelong eating disorders and weight-related problems. I have many issues when it comes to relationships, especially with trusting others. But the most precious thing that was ripped away from me was my true identity. I don't know the things I liked or disliked as a child, what my favorite colors were, or if I had favorite cartoon characters. I am 37 years old today and still attempting, on a daily basis, to learn who I am. Abuse strips away your identity and leaves only feelings of worthlessness, self-doubt, guilt, and shame.

In order to move on in life, it is important to seek professional help. I have been going to therapy for many, many years. I know I will need therapy on and off for life. I also use meditation, as well as reading just about everything I can about abuse. The biggest gift I have given myself, though, is continuing to learn who I am.

Adults need to know that if they were abused as children, there is no need to continue this terrible cycle. There are thousands of great books on parenting available, and classes are offered in almost every community. The cycle of abuse will not stop by itself; it takes conscious effort and much hard work, but it can be done. I feel it is important to speak out loudly about what happened to me as a child with the hope that more victims will do the same, so that people will become more aware of the extent of the effects of the abuse many children suffer. It is through awareness that we can work together to help stop the victimization of more innocent children.

QUESTION **What could teachers, relatives, neighbors, and other adults in Dawn's life have done to prevent her suffering? What signs of abuse could they have looked for?**

### LET'S REVIEW . . .

1. Aman is a 10-year-old boy who is being treated for an accident. Given his age, which of the following is most likely the cause of his accident?
   - **a.** accidental shooting
   - **b.** accidental poisoning
   - **c.** lawnmower accident
   - **d.** car accident
2. Which of the following is *most* important in keeping children safe when riding a bicycle?
   - **a.** Making sure children ride only on specially constructed bike paths.
   - **b.** Making sure children always wear a properly fitted bicycle helmet.

c. Making sure that children's bikes have nighttime lights that work properly.
d. Making sure that children never ride their bikes alone.

3. Which of the following statements about sexual abuse is *false*?
   a. Sexual abuse happens in families at all levels of income.
   b. Teens who are gay or lesbian are more likely to be sexually abused.
   c. About half of all sexual abuse perpetrators are adolescents.
   d. Almost all sexual abuse perpetrators are men.
4. Which symptom is most frequently reported among children and adolescents who have suffered sexual abuse?
   a. depression
   b. anxiety disorders
   c. conduct problems
   d. sexual promiscuity
5. True or False: The most common cause of death during middle childhood is bicycle accidents.
6. True or False: Child sexual abuse can have an effect on the physical structure and functioning of the brain.

Answers: 1. d, 2. b, 3. d, 4. a, 5. F, 6. T

# Children with Exceptional Needs

One out of every five children suffers from a mental illness or other serious developmental, emotional, or behavioral problem (Mash & Wolfe, 2005). **Children with exceptional needs** require extra help beyond what is needed by peers. Exceptional needs may be due to medical, physical, emotional, or developmental difficulties. Sometimes the needs interfere with learning because of cognitive difficulties, but other times the difficulties are caused by behavioral problems, physical disabilities, or absences from school because of medical conditions or the need for medical treatment. Because children with exceptional needs are included in regular classrooms, it is important that teachers understand a wide variety of problems and know how to effectively work with each child. Given the nature of their work, social workers, physicians, and nurses will encounter an even greater percentage of children who have serious problems. In this section, we will discuss the general approach that experts today use in thinking about problems or conditions that arise during childhood. Though there are many difficulties that children may experience, we will cover only a few in this chapter, including attention-deficit/hyperactivity disorder, communication and learning disorders, and autism spectrum disorders. Others (such as conduct disorder, oppositional defiant disorder, depression, and eating disorders) will be discussed in Chapters 12 and 13.

AS YOU STUDY THIS SECTION, ASK YOURSELF THESE QUESTIONS:

**10.8** What is the developmental psychopathology perspective, and how does it help us better understand childhood disorders?

**10.9** What is attention-deficit/hyperactivity disorder (ADHD), and what are the subtypes of this disorder?

**10.10** What are the different types of communication and learning disorders?

**10.11** What do researchers understand about autism spectrum disorders, and what treatment approaches exist for these conditions?

## What Is Developmental Psychopathology?

Before we discuss specific conditions, it is important to understand that we rarely can identify the exact cause of any disorder in a particular child. In almost every case, multiple causes or multiple conditions contribute to the problem. Today, most experts look at childhood problems from the **developmental psychopathology perspective** (Rutter & Sroufe, 2000). This view emphasizes the wide variety of factors that influence both typical and atypical paths of development. Among these factors are genetics, the interactions children have with their parents and family, the quality of their education, their peers, and many other elements in their social and cultural environments. These are many of the

**children with exceptional needs**
Children who require help beyond what is needed by peers.

**developmental psychopathology perspective**
The view that a wide variety of factors influences both typical and atypical paths of development.

same nature–nurture factors that we've discussed before. The developmental outcome of any particular child is determined by the *transactions* that occur among all of these factors. A child with a genetic predisposition for depression, for example, could develop major depression, have minor symptoms, or possibly experience no symptoms at all, depending on interactions with his or her environment. Children with no genetic predispositions can still develop major depression if they suffer severe trauma or abuse. Some children who have the odds stacked against them still manage to escape without serious problems. The point is that for any particular child we cannot determine one single cause for a disorder, disturbance, or other problem. Still, we can report the general tendencies that researchers have discovered—the factors that may contribute to each type of problem or disorder, and the effects or developmental outcomes that typically result.

It's also important to understand that it's difficult to measure how often a condition occurs. **Prevalence rates** refer to the percentages or numbers of children who show the various problems or conditions. For each condition we discuss, we give the experts' best estimates. There are no hard numbers on prevalence rates, however, because a great many children with serious problems are not diagnosed or treated. Adults often think that a child will "outgrow" a problem, or they simply fail to recognize the child's problem because many children can't communicate their feelings effectively. Often, a child's problems can go unrecognized until the child begins to fail or have problems with peers in school.

THINK ABOUT BRAD . . .
How might an understanding of developmental psychopathology and comorbidity help Brad as he works with children?

Another important point is that you can't just add up the various prevalence rates to determine how many children are affected by the total of all of these problems. A high percentage of children with disorders have more than one disorder at once—a situation referred to as **comorbidity**. For example, up to 80% of children with attention-deficit/hyperactivity disorder also have depression or some other type of anxiety, mood, or behavioral disorder (Mash & Wolfe, 2010; Pliszka, 2000). The sad fact is that childhood problems and disorders tend to cluster or co-occur in individual children.

## Attention-Deficit/Hyperactivity Disorder

As a preschooler, Tim was always on the go. Whether he was climbing and jumping on the furniture, rocking in his chair, running through the house, banging his toys, or talking constantly and loudly, it seemed that his motor was always running at high speed. When he started kindergarten, he was always interrupting other children, had a hard time waiting in line, and was too restless to sit for very long. Although his parents and teachers marveled at his energy and enthusiasm, they were exhausted trying to help him sit still, pay attention, and wait for his turn at home and school.

Most children prefer to be on the go, and they would rather learn by moving and doing than by sitting and listening quietly. But when their restlessness and high level of activity far exceed the norm for their age, then they are showing signs of **attention-deficit/hyperactivity disorder (ADHD)**. Children with ADHD are excessively active, and they have difficulty sustaining attention and controlling impulses to a degree that is unusual for their developmental levels (Mash & Wolfe, 2010). The signs of ADHD emerge early, usually before the age of 7, and they persist throughout childhood and often into adolescence and adulthood. Most children with ADHD show two phases with the disorder (Barkley, 2003):

- First, parents and caregivers notice signs of hyperactivity, usually by the time the child is 3 or 4 years of age. Tim, for example, was showing the classic signs of hyperactivity.
- Second, between the ages of 5 and 7, children with ADHD begin showing signs of inattentiveness. This side of the disorder usually becomes apparent when children begin formal schooling. They have a hard time finishing assignments, staying on task, and following rules and instructions. They can't concentrate; they seem to daydream; and they are disorganized, forgetful, and easily distracted.

**prevalence rates**
Refers to the percentages or numbers of individuals who show particular problems or conditions.

**comorbidity**
Situation in which an individual has more than one disorder or problem at the same time.

**attention-deficit/hyperactivity disorder (ADHD)**
A condition involving inablity to sustain attention, excessive activity, and deficiencies in impulse control that are unusual for the child's developmental level.

As you can imagine, this combination of hyperactivity and inattentiveness can be challenging. As children grow into middle childhood, the hyperactive symptoms tend to decrease, but the attention problems remain. Currently, clinicians recognize four types of ADHD:

1. *ADHD—predominantly inattentive*
2. *ADHD—predominantly hyperactive–impulsive*
3. *ADHD—combined*
4. *ADHD—not otherwise specified* (American Psychiatric Association, 2000).

Although parents and teachers describe as many as one-half of all children as "hyperactive," only 4% to 8% of children actually meet the clinical criteria for some type of ADHD, and ADHD rates are three times higher among boys than girls (Mash & Wolfe, 2010). The causes of ADHD are not known, but most of the research points to a genetic component and problems with areas in the frontal lobes of the brain that are responsible for attention, organization, and the inhibition and control of behavior. Researchers estimate that the heritability of ADHD is as high as .80 (Mash & Wolfe, 2010; Saudino & Plomin, 2007). Identical twins share more ADHD symptoms than do fraternal twins, and children and their biological parents share more symptoms than do adoptive families. ADHD is somewhat more common in lower socioeconomic groups, but it exists at every socioeconomic level and in every country researchers have studied (Barkley, 2003; Linnet et al., 2003). Some of the suspected causes that have *not* held up to research scrutiny include too much sugar, food allergies, bad parenting, poor school environments, urban living, and too much television—none of these have been supported conclusively as causes of ADHD in scientific research (Mash & Wolfe, 2010). **Listen** on **mydevelopmentlab**

**Listen**: Does television viewing cause ADHD? (Author Podcast) www.mydevelopmentlab.com

Family conflict is common when a child has ADHD. Children with ADHD are more talkative, defiant, and demanding than children without the disorder, and their parents (especially mothers) tend to be more negative and less rewarding (Barkley, 2003). Fathers seem to have less trouble with their ADHD children, perhaps because they spend less time with the children or because they tend to play in a rough-and-tumble style more suitable for highly active children. Parents with ADHD children tend to have more marital conflict, their separation and divorce rates are higher, they tend to consume more alcohol, and mothers are more likely to be depressed (Barkley, 2003). It is not clear whether these family problems are more a cause of ADHD or the result of the stress of dealing with difficult children with ADHD, but the evidence seems to suggest more of the latter.

In addition to family problems, children with ADHD have great difficulty in school. By the time they are adolescents, about 40% of children with ADHD have received some form of special education. One-quarter of students with ADHD get expelled from school, 35% are retained at least one grade level, and up to 30% drop out of school (Barkley, 1996). The majority do not go on to college (Barkley, 1998). Although there is little research on ADHD in adulthood, clinicians believe that nearly half of all children with ADHD carry the symptoms into their adult years—and experience significant problems in their work and social relations as a result. We should also point out that many adolescents and adults do find ways to cope with their symptoms, and many go on to college and successful careers; odds are that several of your classmates have some type of ADHD.

▲ Stimulant medications are the most effective treatment for most cases of ADHD. Only 4% to 8% of children meet the clinical criteria for ADHD, and there are concerns that many children are misdiagnosed and treated unnecessarily.

There is no cure for ADHD, but there are effective treatments. Ironically, the most frequently used and effective treatment is the use of stimulant medications. Stimulants such as Ritalin (the one prescribed most commonly) activate areas in the brain that help children control their impulses and sustain attention. Using these medications, 80% of children show significant improvements in concentration, motor control, cooperation, and the ability to stay on task (Barkley, 1998; Mash & Wolfe, 2010). Treatment is most effective when it combines medication with parent training and school interventions that reward children when they cooperate and stay on task and remove privileges or give timeouts for disruptive behaviors. These behavior management programs work best when parents and teachers apply them consistently in both home and school settings (Barkley, 1998; Owens et al., 2003).

In the United States, children's use of stimulant medications has tripled in recent decades sparking a controversy about the possible over-medication of children. Are adults prescribing medications to "control" children who really do not have diagnosable disorders? It's difficult to tell, but consider that only about 4% of children actually take stimulant medications regularly for ADHD symptoms even though as many as 8% of children have the disorder (Centers for Disease Control, 2005b). While some children may receive medication unnecessarily, medication is being given to only half of those who could benefit. Why? Parents, teachers, caregivers, and other adults often disagree when assessing the attention and activity levels of children (Mash & Wolfe, 2010). One person's "unruly" child can be merely "spunky" to someone else. The key is to use multiple sources of information and clear diagnostic criteria to make sure that all children with legitimate disorders are diagnosed and treated and that fewer children are misdiagnosed.

THINKING CRITICALLY

Have you ever known someone who has ADHD? If yes, how did it affect that person's behavior, and what treatments seemed to be most helpful?

## Communication and Learning Disorders

Pretend that you are a child in a second-grade classroom. You have an above-average IQ, and you are motivated to learn. When you try to read printed text, however, you can't make sense out of the words and sentences. The print says, "Pam saw the dog play," but you invert the *m* in "Pam" into a *w*, you reverse the letters in "saw" to read "was," and you leave out the *l* in "play." To you, the sentence reads, "Paw was the dog pay." What sense does that make? After struggling day after day, you begin to give up. While other children are reading their books, you just sit and look around. Because so much of the information and instruction given in school involves reading, you are falling behind in most of your subjects. The teacher thinks you have an attention deficit, your classmates call you names, and your parents wonder if you are just not trying. Inside, you know they are all wrong, but you can't figure out why you are having so much trouble. Actually, you are showing signs of a reading disorder—but it may be a long time before you get an official diagnosis and any real help with your difficulties in school.

**communication disorders**
Conditions in which children have significant difficulty producing speech sounds, using spoken language to communicate, or understanding what other people say.

**learning disorders**
Conditions involving difficulties with specific skills such as reading, mathematics, or writing.

Unless you have experienced a communication or learning disorder yourself, it is hard to imagine the frustrations that children with these problems feel every day in school. They are just as smart as other children are and can learn just as fast, but in some specific area they have significant difficulty with language or learning. They fall behind

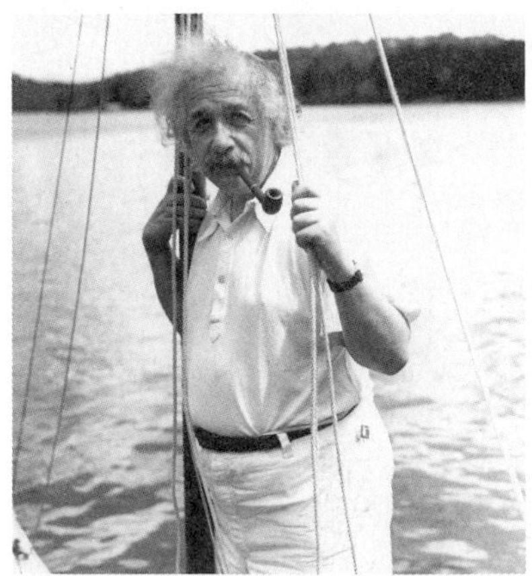

▲ Well-known people such as Albert Einstein, Thomas Edison, and Winston Churchill managed high levels of success even though they were known to have or were suspected of having learning disorders (Mash & Wolfe, 1999).

in school, they may feel rejected by their classmates, and their self-esteem plummets. Many withdraw, show signs of depression or anxiety, or act out in school.

Table 10.3 below describes the main communication and learning disorders. In **communication disorders** children have significant difficulty producing speech sounds, using spoken language to communicate, or understanding what other people say (Mash & Wolfe, 2010). **Learning disorders** (often referred to as *learning disabilities*) involve difficulties with specific skills such as reading, mathematics, or writing. With both types of disorders,

**TABLE 10.3**
Communication and Learning Disorders

| CATEGORIES OF DISORDERS | SYMPTOMS AND BEHAVIORS |
|---|---|
| **Communication Disorders** | |
| Phonological Disorder | Problems with the articulation or production of language sounds. Most frequent problems involve the *l, r, s, z,* and *th* sounds (e.g., saying "cwy" instead of "cry"). Problems persist beyond what is developmentally normal and interfere with school and social activities. About 10% of preschoolers show mild phonological problems. By age 7 years, 2% to 3% have a phonological disorder. |
| Expressive Language Disorder | Problems using words to communicate thoughts, desires, and feelings. Expression lags significantly behind the child's ability to understand language (receptive language). Speech usually begins late and progresses slowly. Limited vocabulary, short sentences, and simple grammatical structures characterize speech. Affects 2% to 3% of children. |
| Mixed Receptive-Expressive Language Disorder | Problems in expressive language combined with difficulty understanding language. Trouble making sense out of sounds, words, and sentences. Found in fewer than 3% of children. |
| Stuttering | Repeating or prolonging speech sounds (e.g., "g-g-g-g-g-go" or "Mo-ah-ah-ah-ah-mmy"). Child struggles to finish or continue sounds and words; may develop ways to avoid or compensate for problem sounds. Stuttering usually has a gradual onset between ages 2 and 7. Affects 1% of children; three times as many males as females. Usually self-correcting; 80% of children who stutter at age 5 no longer stutter by first grade. |
| **Learning Disorders** | |
| Reading Disorder | Reading ability substantially below the level expected given the child's age, intelligence, and education. Trouble recognizing basic words; common errors include letter reversals (b/d; p/q), transpositions (top/pot), letter inversions (m/w; u/n), and omissions (reading *place* instead of *palace*). Trouble decoding (separating the sounds in words). Difficulties with reading comprehension, spelling, and writing. Up to 20% of schoolchildren have significant reading problems. |
| Mathematics Disorder | Math ability is substantially below the level expected given the child's age, intelligence, and education. Trouble recognizing numbers and symbols, memorizing basic math facts (e.g., multiplication tables), aligning numbers, and understanding abstract concepts (e.g., place value and fractions). Child may also have problems with visual–spatial abilities. Disorder usually noticed when formal math instruction begins in grade 2 or 3. About 1% of children receive official diagnoses, but 6% score low enough on standardized math tests to be considered as having the disorder. |
| Writing Disorder | Writing ability is substantially below the level expected given the child's age, intelligence, and education. Problems with writing, drawing, copying figures, and other fine-motor skills involving hand–eye coordination. Large-motor skills (e.g., running, throwing, and climbing) are normal. Written work is low in interest and poorly organized; sentences are short; work contains many errors in spelling, punctuation, and grammar. Disorder affects up to 10% of children. |

(Mash & Wolfe, 2005.)

children tend to have average to above-average intelligence. They should be capable of learning quickly in school, but their disorder slows them down and disrupts their performance. Communication and learning disorders are also highly connected (comorbid).

Communication and learning disorders are sometimes thought of as "hidden" problems of childhood—they too often go undiagnosed and untreated. About 5% of U.S. students receive official diagnoses of learning disorders, but experts estimate that at least 20% of children suffer from reading disorders alone (Mash & Wolfe, 2010). Children with communication and learning disorders already receive half of all of the special education services provided in schools, and even more children could obviously benefit from these programs.

Communication and learning disorders are strongly genetic and related to abnormalities in how the brain functions. When a parent has a communication disorder, about half of that person's children also have communication disorders. Children with phonological disorder (see Table 10.3) show less than normal activation in the left temporal region of their brains, a region strongly related to language function (Wood, Felton, Flowers, & Naylor, 1991). Research has linked expressive language disorder to recurrent ear infections (Lonigan et al., 1992; Mash & Wolfe, 2010); such infections may lead to hearing loss that reduces input to the developing brain. Disruptions in prenatal brain development may also be a cause for many of these disorders (Mash & Wolfe, 2010). Even minor defects can change how the brain sorts, organizes, and brings information together from specific brain areas; and these changes in turn hamper the child's ability to interpret and make sense out of the information.

In many cases, the disorders correct themselves or the children learn ways to compensate for their difficulties. Stuttering and expressive language disorders, for example, often correct themselves by the age of 6 or 7 (Mash & Wolfe, 2010). Children who stutter can learn to slow down and breathe deeply before continuing. Speech therapists can train children with phonological disorder in articulation and help them learn to produce correct speech sounds. Children with reading, math, and writing disorders typically receive educational supports in school. They benefit from direct instruction, drill and practice, and learning strategies for breaking problems and assignments into smaller units. Counseling and therapy also can help children improve their self-esteem, cope with peer rejection, and learn how to monitor and control their own learning and thought processes. With help, families can learn to provide more effective supports for children with communication and learning disorders. On the bright side, most people with these disorders find ways to compensate and go on to live normal lives.

▲ Children with autism suffer from severe deficits in social interaction and communication. This child shows a kind of self-stimulation behavior that is typical for this disorder.

## Autism Spectrum Disorders

At the age of 9, Daniel still didn't speak, read, or write. Although he seemed to understand most of what other people said, he communicated mostly by pointing, grunting, and making nonsense sounds. For his birthday his uncle gave him a tape recorder, which Daniel began using to record short pieces of conversation he heard around him. At night he would lie in bed and replay the snippets he had recorded that day dozens of times. Using these recordings, Daniel began to teach himself to speak. As he learned two-way communication, he became fascinated with birth dates. When meeting you for the first time, he would immediately ask for your birth date and for the names and birth dates of all your pets. In a split second, Daniel would then tell you *exactly* how old your pet was, down to the very day! Eventually Daniel's skill with birth dates grew into mastery of calendars (give him any date and he could figure out which day of the week it was) and an amazing ability to multiply and divide numbers in his head. Still, Daniel avoided eye contact, didn't respond properly to human emotions, showed little attachment to his family members, and had no reciprocal friendships.

**autism spectrum disorders (ASDs)**
A group of serious developmental disorders characterized by impairments in social interaction and communication.

**Autism spectrum disorders (ASDs)** are a group of serious developmental disorders characterized by impairments in social interaction and communication. Table 10.4 lists

**TABLE 10.4**
Indicators of Autism Spectrum Disorders

| | |
|---|---|
| **Speech and Language** | • Slow language and speech development:<br>  • No meaningful gestures, no babbling by 1 year<br>  • No words by 16 months<br>  • No use of two-word combinations by 2 years<br>• Language skills seemed normal, but has regressed in use of words and other communication<br>• Does not respond to name<br>• Does not follow directions<br>• Is frequently not able to explain what is wanted<br>• At times seems to not hear well; other times hearing seems normal |
| **Social Interactions** | • Shows poor eye contact when interacting with others<br>• Does not smile in return when smiled at<br>• Does not wave goodbye<br>• Has violent or otherwise intense tantrums<br>• Prefers to play alone; not interested in interacting with other children<br>• Often seems to be absorbed in his or her own world<br>• Used to show normal social interactions, but loses social skills |
| **Behaviors** | • Shows unusual attachment to a particular toy or object<br>• Shows unusual need for a certain order of activities (e.g., becomes upset if asked to put on gloves before hat when she or he typically puts on hat first)<br>• Unusual amounts of time spent lining things up in a certain order<br>• Often repeats the same behaviors over and over; can't seem to move on to something else<br>• Seems unusually active; is uncooperative or resistant to requests or demands<br>• Frequently walks on his or her toes<br>• Is ahead of peers in some behaviors and seems very independent |

(NICHD, 2005.)

some of the more common indicators. Formerly called *autism,* ASD is a *spectrum disorder,* which means it can take forms that range from milder (such as Asperger syndrome) to more severe (such as autistic disorder) (NICHD, 2005). In addition to the problems we've seen in the case of Daniel, children with ASDs often show repetitive body motions or self-stimulation activities such as rocking their bodies or waving their fingers in front of their eyes. They are inflexible about their daily routines and become upset by changes such as a different bedtime, a new arrangement of furniture, or an attempt to take them shopping at a new store. Children with ASDs tend to score low on IQ tests (in the range of mental retardation), but a small percentage show exceptional *splinter skills* like Daniel's gift for calculating dates and numbers. Other such skills include exceptional memory for music and speed in building puzzles. Language skills tend to be severely delayed in children with ASDs. Many of these children simply repeat back words and phrases they hear (a pattern called *echolalia*) without seeming to understand what is said.

ASDs affect one out of every 150 children worldwide (Mash & Wolfe, 2010; Yeargin-Allsopp et al., 2003). They are four times more common among boys than girls. In recent years the number of children identified with ASDs has increased, perhaps due to changes in how ASDs are diagnosed. ASDs have a strong genetic component, being shared much more often

THINK ABOUT BRAD . . .
When he becomes a teacher, how can Brad tell the difference between a child with ADHD, a learning or communication disorder, or ASD? What adjustments should teachers make for these different types of disorders?

between identical twins than between fraternal twins (Bailey et al., 1995). Environmental contributors to ASDs are not well understood. For example, many parents suspected that childhood vaccinations (mostly the measles-mumps-rubella vaccine and other vaccines that contained thimerosal, a mercury-based preservative) were linked to ASDs, but scientific studies have *not* supported this link (Institute of Medicine, 2004; Mash & Wolfe, 2010). Researchers are just beginning to understand the brain mechanisms that are associated with ASDs. Early evidence indicates problems or immaturities in several important areas of the brain including the cerebellum, limbic system, hippocampus, and frontal and temporal lobes (Kabot, Masi, & Segal, 2003; Mash & Wolfe, 2010; Newsom, 1998). These areas regulate attention, language, emotion perception, and the control of planning and thought processes.

With ASDs, the effectiveness of treatment varies depending on the severity of the disorder in individual children (Mash & Wolfe, 2010; Newsom, 1998). With severe levels of autism, therapy focuses on teaching self-care skills and helping the child learn to live as independently as possible. Lifelong care and supervision will probably still be essential.

## Perspective SOCIAL POLICY: EDUCATING CHILDREN WITH EXCEPTIONAL NEEDS

Karen Singer's son was diagnosed with autism spectrum disorder (ASD) at the age of 2 when he could not speak, he did not make eye contact with other people, and he had trouble with simple demands such as sitting still in his chair (Gross, 2005). After three years of a 40-hour-a-week home program with a behavioral therapist, her son learned the communication and academic skills he needed to enter a regular kindergarten class in school. With the advances being made in behavioral therapy, an increasing number of children with ASDs, communication problems, physical or sensory disabilities, cognitive deficits, and many other types of disabilities are now attending regular school classrooms.

Today, all children are entitled by law to a free and appropriate public education. In the 1970s, the U.S. Congress passed the Individuals with Disabilities Education Act (IDEA). This law has since been amended and states that "*Each State must establish procedures to assure that, to the maximum extent appropriate, children with disabilities . . . are educated with children who are not disabled, and that special education, separate schooling, or other removal of children with disabilities from the regular educational environment occurs only when the nature or severity of the disability is such that education in regular classes with the use of supplementary aids and services cannot be achieved satisfactorily*" (as quoted by the Renaissance Group, 1999). The IDEA has done wonders to integrate children with all types of disabilities into mainstream society. Rather than attending separate schools or being pulled out for all-day special education classes, children with disabilities work alongside other children. All children can benefit. The children with disabilities have opportunities to make friends and learn from nondisabled children, and they have the challenge and stimulation offered in regular classes. Nondisabled children benefit too as they learn about diversity and see how they can adapt and have meaningful relationships with children who are different from themselves.

Unfortunately, full inclusion in regular education settings is not realistic for all children. Public schools emphasize academic skills, but they do little to help children learn the social skills they need to interact with diverse individuals. Karen Singer's son performed well in his school subjects, but by the time he entered middle school he did not feel comfortable in the regular school setting. He did not share the same teenage interests as his classmates, he was rigid about small matters such as what color ink to use on a school project, and he sometimes blurted out inappropriate remarks such as "You're stupid!" (Gross, 2005). As the years passed, he became more socially isolated, sometimes seeking the solace of the school bathroom to cry. In anguish, the Singers moved their son to a private school that specialized in disabilities, and so far their son seems more comfortable there.

Since passing the IDEA, public schools have made great strides in adapting their classrooms to accommodate students with all types of exceptional needs. We still have a long way to go, however, before all students feel equally challenged and supported in the academic realm while at the same time feeling equally accepted and comfortable in the social realm.

QUESTION **What else do you think schools should do to help all children feel comfortable? What are the other pros and cons of full inclusion in regular education settings?**

With more moderate to mild levels of ASDs, treatment can be more effective if it starts early and involves intensive one-to-one training and therapy, preferably 20 to 40 hours per week. The work focuses on improving language, teaching social skills, and helping the child learn the skills and behaviors necessary for preschool and early elementary school (Autism Society of America, 2002; Mash & Wolfe, 2010). Parent education and training are also important (Kabot et al., 2003; Whitaker, 2002). With this kind of training and therapy, children with ASDs can show impressive gains, although most will still not function like their more typical peers.

Most children with ASDs or other disabilities or disorders receive educational services in schools, and many are mainstreamed into the regular classrooms. To read more about the benefits and challenges of helping children in schools, consider the Social Policy Perspective box called "Educating Children with Exceptional Needs."

THINKING CRITICALLY

Have you ever known anyone with ASD? If so, how severe was the disorder, and what kinds of treatment or training did the person receive?

## LET'S REVIEW . . .

1. Which component of ADHD usually emerges *first* in a child's development?
   - **a.** inattention
   - **b.** hyperactivity
   - **c.** memory loss
   - **d.** aggression
2. Which of the following contributes *most* to communication and learning disorders?
   - **a.** quality of early parenting
   - **b.** quality of early education
   - **c.** genetic and biological factors
   - **d.** social and cultural factors
3. Robbie is 10 years old, but he hardly speaks. Sometimes he repeats back small bits of what you say to him, but otherwise he doesn't communicate. He spends a lot of time rocking his body back and forth or waving his fingers in front of his eyes. From this description, Robbie most likely suffers from __________.
   - **a.** autism spectrum disorder
   - **b.** a communication disorder
   - **c.** profound mental retardation
   - **d.** a severe learning disorder
4. True or False: Most children with learning disorders have below-average levels of intelligence.
5. True or False: The IDEA law requires that a child with exceptional needs be educated in classrooms with nondisabled peers regardless of the nature or extent of the disability.

Answers: 1. b, 2. c, 3. a, 4. F, 5. F

## THINKING BACK TO BRAD . . .

Now that you have studied this chapter, you should be able to explain how Brad can use information about typical physical development, safety, and the exceptional needs of some children. You should be able to list at least a dozen specific concepts and explain how each would relate to Brad and the children with whom he works.

It will be very helpful for Brad to learn about the typical levels of skills he can expect in children of these ages. This will help as he works with children in summer camps and also when he talks to parents about what's reasonable to expect from their children. It will also help him notice children who may benefit from more practice on certain skills. As they get closer to their teenage years, Brad should know that some of the girls may be bigger and taller than boys for a time. Brad is probably already aware that practicing physical skills helps improve control and coordination, but he might be interested in knowing more about the effect that these experiences have on children's brain development—and vice versa. It would also be good for him to understand that it's not very realistic to expect a high level of physical control and coordination from the kindergarten and first-graders with whom he works. Pushing them too hard may frustrate them and turn them off to exercise.

It's important for Brad to become very familiar with the rules, safety equipment, and other injury-prevention procedures in his job to guard against children getting hurt. Even this summer, he can help keep the children he is working with safe by reminding them to wear bike helmets, be careful around water, and buckle up when riding in a car. He should always be watchful for signs of abuse in the children he works with, now and in the future, to help protect children from the extreme harm these situations can cause. He can learn more about the guidelines developed by different sports and medical organizations, and share these with parents. It might even be a good idea to talk directly to parents about the goals of the summer program, emphasizing being active, giving all the children a chance to play, developing their skills, and having fun—not winning games. Brad can use the information on disorders to find ways to help all children. For example, Brad can be more patient and effective if he understands that children with ADHD may need more structure and help focusing on instructions, and children with communication disorders may need to receive instructions visually as well as verbally. Learning about the different needs that children have will help him be more effective now as a camp counselor and later in his career as a teacher. What other concepts did you find in this chapter that would be helpful for people like Brad?

# 10 CHAPTER REVIEW . . .

**10.1 What is the average amount of growth during middle childhood, and why are so many children overweight?**

On average, children gain 9 inches and 35 pounds from the ages of 7 through 11 years. For a time, girls will be taller and heavier on average than boys. Overweight conditions are caused by genetics and also by environmental factors such as children's decreased activity levels and increased consumption of fast and processed foods. Parents can be good role models and work to improve children's healthy eating and exercise habits.

**10.2 How is the brain growing and maturing during middle childhood?**

The brain gains blood vessels, glial cells, and myelination. Synaptic pruning of less efficient brain circuits decreases the size of some brain areas and improves their efficiency. Brain maturity and environmental stimulation have a reciprocal effect on each other.

**10.3 In what ways do children's motor skills become more controlled and coordinated during middle childhood?**

Both gross- and fine-motor skills become more controlled and coordinated. There are improvements in strength and balance, but flexibility decreases toward adolescence.

**10.4 How can adults help children get more physical activity and exercise?**

Most children report getting some sort of physical activity, but experts are concerned that some groups of children remain at risk for future health problems. Barriers to physical activity include children's increasing preferences for more sedentary activities, the cost of participating in sports, lack of opportunities, and unsafe neighborhoods. Parents and other adults can provide safe place to play and exercise, and they can be good role models.

**10.5 What are the benefits and concerns for children's participation in organized sports?**

Organized sports offer physical benefits such as muscle strength and endurance, cardiovascular health, improved eye–hand coordination, and increased body awareness; social skills improvements such as cooperation and good sportsmanship; and chances to develop positive emotional coping strategies and improvement of self-esteem. However, there is the potential for injury. Inappropriate behavior of adults, such as overemphasis on competition and winning, can also be detrimental.

**10.6 What are several things that adults can do to help protect children from the most common health and safety problems?**

The most common threats to safety during middle childhood are accidents; the leading cause of death is auto accidents. Parents can improve safety around their homes, insist that children are always secured in booster seats or by seat belts when riding in a car, abstain from drinking alcohol and driving, insist that children always wear a helmet when riding a bicycle, teach children how to swim, insist that they wear proper flotation devices around water, and always supervise children when they are around water.

**10.7 What are the immediate and long-term effects of sexual abuse on children?**

Child sexual abuse occurs in all ethnic, geographic, and economic groups. It is more common in middle childhood and adolescence than in earlier years and in children who have suffered other forms of maltreatment. Other risk factors include unhealthy family relationships, marital disruptions, and individual factors such as being socially isolated and being female. The effects of child sexual abuse depend on the frequency, severity, and duration of the abuse, but can include depression, abnormally sexualized behavior, drug and alcohol use, posttraumatic stress disorder, feelings of guilt and shame, and difficulties with intimate relationships. There can also be physiological effects on the brain's structure and functioning.

**10.8 What is the developmental psychopathology perspective, and how does it help us better understand childhood disorders?**

By this view, a particular developmental outcome is determined by the transactions that occur among a wide variety of developmental factors, and it is often difficult to pinpoint the exact cause(s) of a specific disorder or problem. This view helps us understand both typical and atypical paths of development and the unique circumstances that lead to the disorders suffered by individual children.

**10.9 What is attention-deficit/hyperactivity disorder (ADHD), and what are the subtypes of this disorder?**

ADHD involves the inability to sustain attention, excessive activity levels, and deficient impulse control for a child's developmental level. ADHD is associated with greater behavioral and emotional problems as children get older. There is a genetic component involved in ADHD, but environmental factors may also be involved. Children with ADHD tend to have higher levels of family conflict and difficulty in school. Treatment often involves the use of stimulant medications and behavioral management programs. Subtypes include ADHD—predominantly inattentive, ADHD—predominantly hyperactive–impulsive, ADHD—combined type, and ADHD—not otherwise specified.

**10.10 What are the different types of communication and learning disorders?**

Communication disorders involve difficulty producing speech, using spoken language to communicate, or understanding spoken language. Learning disorders refer to problems with a specific skill such as reading, mathematics, or writing. Both types of disorders disrupt performance and slow learning. They are strongly genetic and are related to specific abnormalities in brain function. Some disorders correct themselves or children learn compensation strategies; counseling, therapy, and educational supports can also be effective.

**10.11 What do researchers understand about autism spectrum disorders, and what treatment approaches exist for these conditions?**

ASDs are a group of developmental disorders characterized by impairments in social interaction and communication. Children with ASDs tend to be rigid about routines, show repetitive body movements or self-stimulation activities, and have severely delayed language skills. Most show low IQ scores, but a few show narrow areas of exceptional skill. ASDs have a strong genetic component, and they are associated with brain abnormalities in the limbic system, hippocampus, frontal, and midbrain areas. Therapy depends on the level of severity, but early intervention for children with mild to moderate ASDs can help improve language and social skills.

## REVISITING THEMES

The *nature and nurture* theme is evident with the developmental psychopathology perspective (pp. 309–310) and when considering the genetic and environmental factors that relate to children being overweight (p. 293) and having ADHD (p. 311), communication and learning disorders (pp. 312–314), and autism spectrum disorders (pp. 314–317). Nature and nurture both also influence the growth and maturation of the brain, as synapses are pruned, for example (pp. 294–295).

The *neuroscience* theme is seen in the discussion of the growth and maturation of the brain during middle childhood (pp. 294–295), discussion of brain plasticity (p. 295), ways that brain maturation support the development of motor skills (pp. 296–297), and in the damaging effects that childhood sex abuse has on the brain (pp. 305–307).

*Diversity and multiculturalism* are related to the racial and ethnic differences discussed in children being overweight (pp. 292–293) and in differences in levels and opportunities for physical activity (pp. 298–299).

*Positive development and resilience* is reflected in the discussion of how brain plasticity allows recovery and resilience in development (p. 295) and the positive benefits of participating in organized sports (pp. 299–300). Resilience is also demonstrated when children grow up to survive and possibly thrive after experiencing sexual abuse during childhood (p. 307) and when they overcome the limitations imposed by having ADHD or communication and learning disorders (p. 311, 314).

## KEY TERMS

attention-deficit/hyperactivity disorder (ADHD) (310)
autism spectrum disorders (ASDs) (314)
body mass index (BMI) (292)
children with exceptional needs (309)
communication disorders (312)
comorbidity (310)
developmental psychopathology perspective (309)
learning disorders (312)
organized sports (299)
overweight (292)
plasticity (295)
prevalence rates (310)
risk of overweight (292)
rough-and-tumble play (299)

**"What decisions would you make while raising a child? What would the consequences of those decisions be?"**

Find out by accessing My Virtual Child at
**www.mydevelopmentlab.com**
and raising your own virtual child
from birth to age 18.

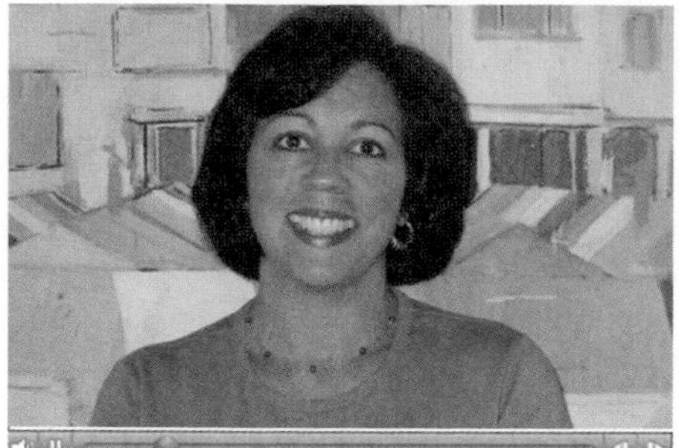

Watch Visit your Multimedia Library at www.mydevelopmentlab.com to watch an interview with Linda online.

11 MIDDLE CHILDHOOD

# Cognitive Development in Middle Childhood

Since kindergarten, Gianluca has had a lot of trouble reading. His mother, Linda, did not notice any particular problems during his preschool years, but Gianluca's kindergarten teacher brought several potential problems to Linda's attention. He had a hard time reading in class, particularly in focusing his attention and comprehending what he read. Sounds in the classroom seemed to bother him a lot—every sound seemed huge and distracted him. Gianluca also tended to read through any punctuation—he just read on and on without stopping for commas or periods. When he finished a passage, he remembered some details but it was all jumbled and he couldn't keep the facts straight. Ginaluca also had problems distinguishing between certain letters (like Ds and Bs, and Ms and Ns), and he had trouble remembering some basic words like "whose," "those," "that," and "what." Gianluca has been working with a reading specialist, and Linda works with him every day at home too. They practice the specific letters and words that he has trouble with, going over each one many times. They've also used several strategies to help him learn to focus, like separating him from the larger group during class reading times. Some of their strategies are pretty novel. For example, Linda works at an airport and uses special earplugs for ear protection. She gave Gianluca a pair to block out classroom noises and help him stay focused—and it worked! All the kids thought the earplugs were very cool, so Gianluca was happy to use them. Linda and the teacher also used a kitchen timer to challenge Gianluca to finish his work within a certain time limit. Gianluca liked this "game" and it helped him stay focused during his reading. They also try to have Gianluca read things he's especially interested in and likes, like his "Captain Underpants" superhero comic book series.

It hasn't been easy, but Linda has seen good progress in Gianluca over the last few years. He is now 10 years old and still has reading support, and a math tutor, but Linda believes that Gianluca is finally developing into a more fluent reader. After studying this chapter, you should be able to identify several potential explanations for Gianluca's difficulties with reading and suggest several things that Linda can do to help. What helpful advice can you suggest to help Gianluca continue to make progress?

As you read this chapter, look for the "Think About Linda and Gianluca . . ." questions that ask you to consider what you are learning from Linda and Gianluca's perspective.

Ginaluca has struggled with reading since kindergarten, and his family has worked to find better ways to help him learn. Nearly every day, we all find ourselves pushed to our cognitive limits. What cognitive limitations do children from the ages of 7 through 11 face? What strategies do they use to think through complicated problems? When overwhelmed with new information, how do they focus on the information that is most important? How can children at these ages improve their memory skills and avoid forgetting important information? Can their language skills help them as they try to think through problems? As a college student, you are no doubt learning new ways to process and remember the information presented in your classes and textbooks. Although you have had many years to practice learning, it can still be a struggle. Children in elementary school encounter new and complex things every day. Simple acts like reading, understanding basic facts about the world, and verbally describing their thoughts can be just as bewildering to them as physics or calculus might be to you. What kinds of thought processes, memory abilities, and language skills do children of this age have?

These are questions that we explore in this chapter. We will begin with Jean Piaget's explanation of cognitive development during middle childhood, then explore information-processing perspective research memory, knowledge, and strategy development. We will review the typical language skills of the middle childhood period and introduce you to a recent approach to understanding language development. Finally, we will talk about development within three important academic areas: mathematics, reading, and writing.

# Piaget's Stage 3: Concrete Operational Thought

In Chapter 8, you learned that children in the preoperational thought stage (roughly ages 2 to 7) can form internal mental representations and use symbols in their language, art, and play. As you learned, thinking in early childhood is intuitive (based on personal experience but not logical) and characterized by egocentrism, animism, and artificialism. Young children fail conservation problems because their cognitive schemes are not yet reversible (not "operational"), they center their thought on only one dimension of the problem, and they focus on the static endpoints of the problem. As children enter middle childhood, however, new developments take place. According to Piaget's theory, what skills and limitations are typical of children during the middle childhood years?

AS YOU STUDY THIS SECTION, ASK YOURSELF THESE QUESTIONS:

**11.1** Why does Piaget call this stage of thought *concrete operational thinking?*

**11.2** What major skills do children in the concrete operational stage show and what limitations do they still face?

## What Is Concrete Operational Thinking?

**concrete operational thought** Stage of cognitive development in which children are able to think about two or more dimensions of a problem (decentered thought), dynamic transformations, and reversible operations.

According to Piaget, children experience cognitive disequilibrium and engage in reflective abstraction (see Chapter 5). As a result, they gradually adapt their cognitive structures and reconstruct their understandings of the world. Given adequate experiences with their environment, most children progress to Piaget's third stage around 7 years of age. To these children, the conservation problems shown in Figure 8.3 (on page 233) are trivial. With the liquid conservation problem, a typical 10-year-old would say, "Of course they both still have the same amount; all you did was pour it over here. If you pour the taller one back into the short beaker, you'll see that it's just the same." Or "Sure, the taller one looks like it has more, but it is also skinnier, so it's really just the same." Children in this third stage, **concrete operational thought**, show thinking that is very different from that of the younger child. Their thought is *decentered*—they consider multiple aspects of the problem (understanding the importance of both height and width). They focus on the *dynamic transformations* in the problem (realizing that the true answer lies in the pouring). Most important, they show the *reversibility* of true mental *operations* (understanding that pouring the liquid back would show they are the same amount). In this third stage, children's cognitive structures are operational—hence the name, concrete *operational* thought. This development allows them to think about the world using objective rules of logic, freeing them from the misconceptions of intuitive thought.

THINKING CRITICALLY

Think about the last time you had to mentally reverse your thinking, such as when you were looking for an item you lost. What made this retracing of your steps more or less difficult for you? Could an 8- or 10-year-old have done this?

## Class Inclusion, Seriation, and Transitive Inference Skills

Children in the concrete operational stage also show their logical abilities when they solve *class inclusion* problems. For example, show a child a set of five dolls and three teddy bears, then ask this question: "Are there more dolls or more toys?" Children in the preoperational stage will typically answer "more dolls," because they tend to focus on only one part of the problem (dolls versus bears) and ignore the fact that all of the objects belong to the general class of toys. Most children in the concrete operational stage, however, understand that both dolls and bears are also toys. To them this is a silly question—of course there are more toys than dolls! In other words, older children understand *class inclusion*—the fact that objects can be classified in different ways and at different levels. Younger children don't understand this. When he was about 4, our younger son heard his mother referred to as "Doctor." He immediately spoke up: "She's not a doctor, she's my mommy!" Our older son just rolled his eyes. To young children, grandmothers can't also be mothers, and firemen can't also be fathers.

▲ Children in the concrete operational stage develop the ability to *seriate,* or put things into a series according to a quantitative dimension, such as height or weight. This child has no difficulty seriating these objects. How well do you think she would do if she didn't have the objects in front of her, or if she was asked to reason about the relations?

During the concrete operational stage, children develop the ability to *seriate,* or arrange a set of items into a series according to a quantitative dimension such as size, weight, or length. Seriation allows children to show another hallmark of concrete operational thought—*transitive inference,* or the process of mentally drawing inferences by comparing relations among objects. Consider the following example. Sue is taller than Jean, and Jean is taller than Lexi. Who is taller, Sue or Lexi? We can draw the inference that Sue is taller than Lexi by comparing the relationships from Sue and Jean to Jean and Lexi. Children in the preoperational stage have trouble following these transitivity problems; they may comment that they can't tell who is taller (after all, they can't see them!) or may just take a guess. With true operational logic, however, children in the concrete operational stage can represent the logical relationships and arrive at the correct answer. Research on various kinds of inferences, including transitive inferences and class inclusion problems, is consistent with Piaget's view that younger children's reasoning about inferences is consistently simpler than the reasoning of older children (Halford, 2004). Some research indicates that conservation abilities are most affected by maturation and out-of-school experiences, but class inclusion, seriation, and transitivity skills are strongly influenced by schooling (Cahan, Greenbaum, Artman, Deluya, & Gappel-Gilon, 2008).

THINK ABOUT LINDA AND GIANLUCA . . .

Would Piaget predict that Gianluca would be able to solve class inclusion, seriation, and transitivity problems? How might these skills improve his success in comprehending and using what he reads?

By age 7 most children are capable of using logical thought structures that are increasingly objective and reversible, and they can solve problems that involve class inclusion and transitivity. However, there is still one major limitation in their thinking: Their use of mental operations is still closely tied to *concrete* materials, contexts, and situations. In other words, if children have not had direct experience with the context or situation, or if the material is not tangible, then they are not successful in using their mental operations. This is why the stage is called *concrete* operational thought.

## LET'S REVIEW . . .

1. The main difference between concrete operational and preoperational thought is the ability to:
   a. reason successfully about abstract concepts.
   b. successfully use mental representation.
   c. engage in reflective abstraction.
   d. mentally reverse actions.
2. Angela knows her friend got more ice cream than she did, and that David got more than her friend. Angela cries that it isn't fair that David got more ice cream than her, even though she hasn't seen how much ice cream David has. Angela is demonstrating which of the following?
   a. objective thought
   b. reversible operations
   c. transitive inference ability
   d. class inclusion ability
3. Jimmy watches as you take two identical clay balls and roll one into the shape of a hot dog. You then ask him if both pieces of clay now have the same amount, or if one piece has more clay. Jimmy responds, "Of course they have the same amount; all you have to do is roll the hot dog back up into a ball to see that it has the same amount." Jimmy's answer shows that he understands __________.
   a. reversibility
   b. decentration
   c. static endpoints
   d. transitivity
4. True or False: When a child gives the correct answer to conservation problems, it is a sign that the child is now in the stage of preoperational thought.
5. True or False: Without the ability to seriate, a child cannot solve transitive inference problems.

Answers: 1. d, 2. c, 3. a, 4. F, 5. T

# Information Processing: Memory Development

In Chapter 8, we described changes in some of the basic elements of information processing—processing capacity, processing efficiency, and attention. Memory is influenced by all these basic processes, and memory development is one of the most studied topics in the information-processing literature. No matter what your capacity is for processing new information, and no matter how efficiently you focus your attention, it will do you very little good if you can't store the information and then remember it later. In this section we review many of the important research studies regarding the development of memory.

AS YOU STUDY THIS SECTION, ASK YOURSELF THESE QUESTIONS:

- **11.3** What are the differences between the stores model and network models of memory?
- **11.4** How does working memory change with age?
- **11.5** How does long-term memory change with age?
- **11.6** What are some of the issues in memory development, and why is each important for cognitive development?

## Two Models of Memory: Stores and Networks

**stores model (of memory)**
A model of human memory that views information as moving through a series of storage locations, from the sensory stores to short-term store to long-term store.

**chunking**
The process of recoding individual elements in memory into larger groups of information.

For decades, variations of the **stores model** of memory guided research on memory development (Atkinson & Shiffrin, 1968). This model (shown in Figure 11.1) views information as moving through a series of storage locations. Information enters the cognitive system through the *sensory store,* where large amounts of information can be maintained in their original modalities (e.g., visual, verbal, acoustic) for very brief periods of time (approximately half a second). Some of the information in the sensory store is selected and passed along to the *short-term store* (STS). The STS contains the information that you are consciously aware of at the moment, and its capacity is very limited. It can hold only between five and nine "chunks" of information (Miller, 1956). **Chunking** is the process of recoding individual elements in

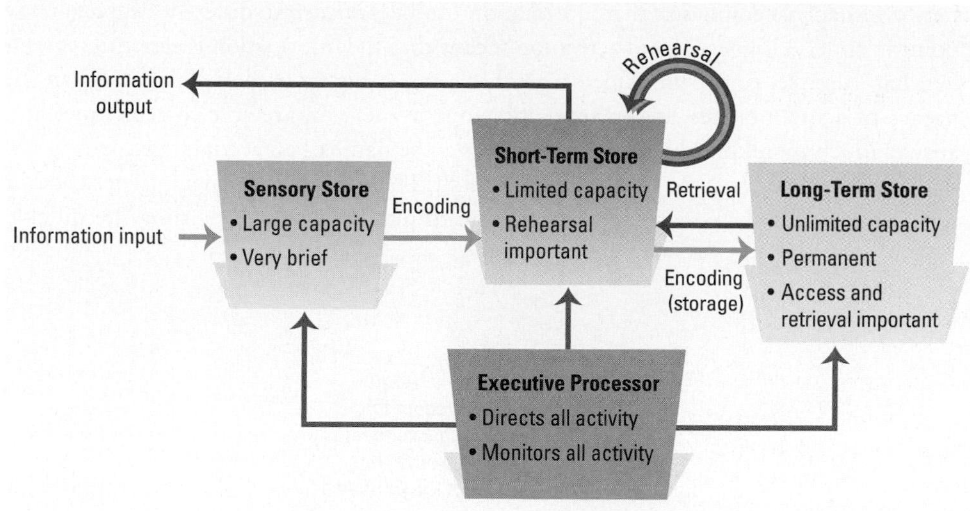


◀ FIGURE 11.1
**An Information Processing Model of Memory**
This figure shows a *stores model* of memory. Stores models view information as moving through a series of storage locations, including a sensory store, short-term store, and long-term store. An executive processor directs and monitors all activity.

memory into larger groups of information. Larger chunks mean that more information can be maintained in STS. The size of one chunk can vary tremendously, however. For a young child learning the ABCs, a chunk might consist of a single letter; for an experienced reader, a chunk could be a whole section of text. Information can be maintained in the STS for long periods of time if we actively attend to it, but it will fade and disappear within seconds if we do not. Information in the STS is also susceptible to interference from additional incoming information. Some newer research argues that interference has a bigger influence on forgetting from STS than does decay (Lewandowsky, Oberauer, & Brown, 2009). To be stored more permanently, information must be passed along to the *long-term store* (LTS). The LTS has an infinite storage capacity, and information remains there permanently even when we are not actively attending to it. Explore on mydevelopmentlab

Explore Key Processes in Stages of Memory
www.mydevelopmentlab.com

To understand the difference between the STS and LTS, notice what happens when you answer this simple question: What is your last name? If you are thinking about your last name and saying it to yourself, then it is now in your STS. But before you saw the question, you probably were not thinking about your last name. Where was your name stored then? It was in your LTS, the place where we store information that we are not consciously thinking about right now but might want to use later. According to the stores model, an *executive processor* controls all three stores and the processes that pass information among them. This processor determines which information will be attended to, and it governs the management of the system's limited capacity from moment to moment. Development of the executive function has received much attention from researchers in studies of metacognition, self-regulation, and (more recently) conscious control (Enslinger & Biddle, 2008; Marcovitch & Zelazo, 2009; Zelazo, Moscovitch & Thompson, 2007). For example, one study analyzed event-related potentials to assess frontal lobe electrical activity. Children from 7 to 16 years of age completed several tasks that required conscious cognitive control (Lamm, Zelazo, & Lewis, 2006). The specific areas of the frontal lobe that were active, and the specific patterns of activation within these areas, varied depending on the type of executive function task, age, and how well the children did on the tasks. (We discuss metacognition and self-regulation in more detail in Chapters 8 and 14.)

In recent years, **network models** of memory have largely replaced the stores model. There are several variations of network models, but in general they view memory as an interconnected network of associated information rather than as a series of separate mental storage boxes. Network models consist of *concept nodes* connected by *links*. The links vary in strength, with more heavily weighted links indicating a greater degree of association between the nodes. Rather than thinking of information as moving from STS into LTS,

**network models (of memory)** Models of human memory that view memory as an interconnected network of concept nodes connected by links of varying strength.

network theorists emphasize that information can be *activated* to different degrees at any point in time. A higher level of activation means that the information is easier to remember. For example, your own name usually has a much higher level of activation than the names of acquaintances. If someone asks your name, you are able to remember and answer much more quickly than if someone asks the name of an acquaintance.

Our son Andy loves to skateboard. Figure 11.2 below shows his memory network for topics related to skateboarding. Anytime he thinks about skateboarding, he quickly

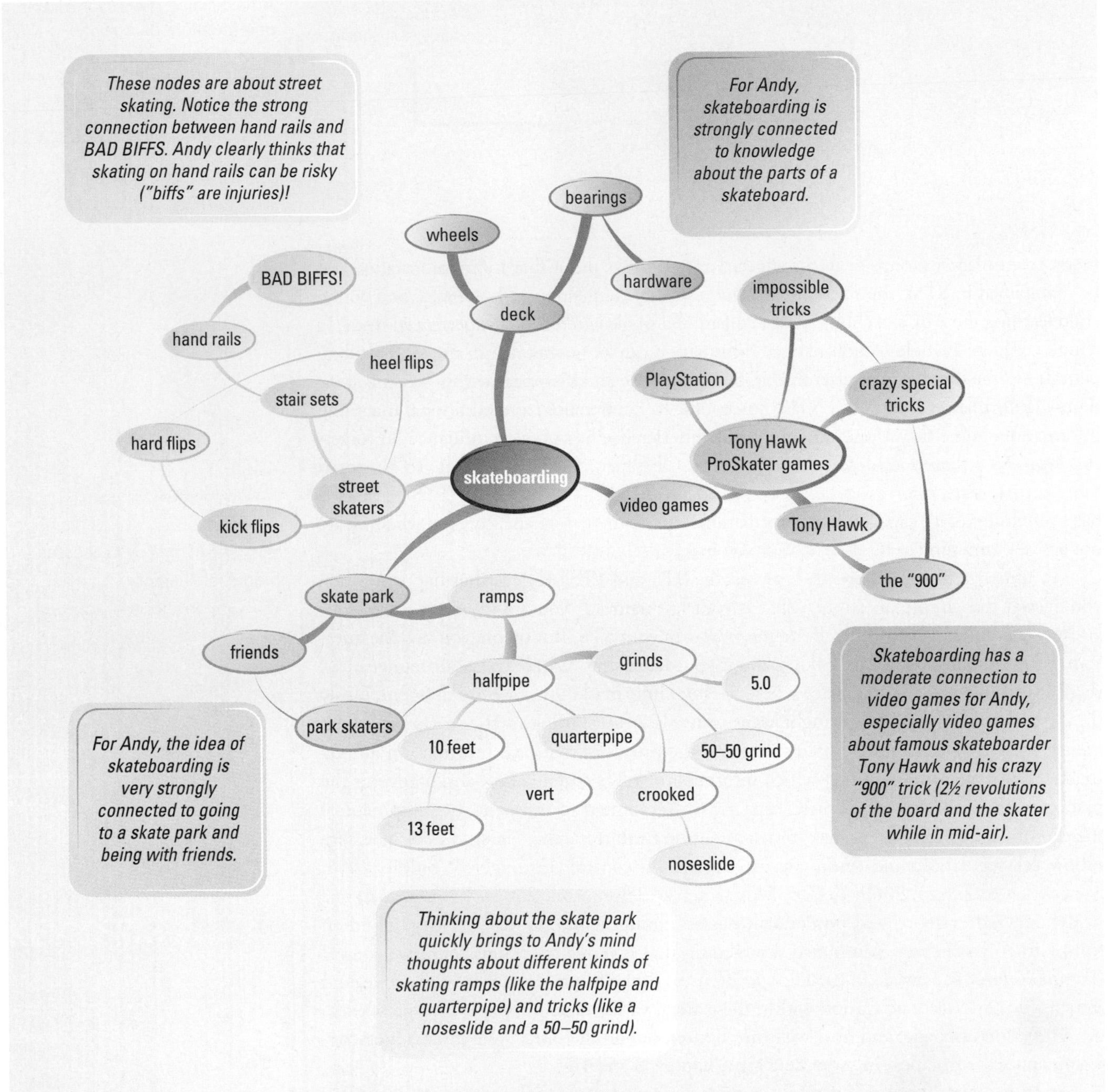

These nodes are about street skating. Notice the strong connection between hand rails and BAD BIFFS. Andy clearly thinks that skating on hand rails can be risky ("biffs" are injuries)!
For Andy, skateboarding is strongly connected to knowledge about the parts of a skateboard.
bearings
wheels
hardware
BAD BIFFS!
deck
impossible tricks
hand rails
heel flips
PlayStation
crazy special tricks
stair sets
hard flips
Tony Hawk ProSkater games
skateboarding
street skaters
video games
kick flips
Tony Hawk
the "900"
skate park
ramps
friends
grinds
5.0
halfpipe
park skaters
10 feet
quarterpipe
50–50 grind
vert
crooked
13 feet
noseslide
Skateboarding has a moderate connection to video games for Andy, especially video games about famous skateboarder Tony Hawk and his crazy "900" trick (2½ revolutions of the board and the skater while in mid-air).
For Andy, the idea of skateboarding is very strongly connected to going to a skate park and being with friends.
Thinking about the skate park quickly brings to Andy's mind thoughts about different kinds of skating ramps (like the halfpipe and quarterpipe) and tricks (like a noseslide and a 50–50 grind).

▲ FIGURE 11.2
**A Partial Network for "Skateboarding" by Andy, Age 12**
Network models of memory view memory as an interconnected network, with information stored as concept nodes connected by links. In this figure, thicker lines indicate knowledge that is strongly connected; thinner lines indicate weaker connections.

remembers his local skatepark, all of his skateboarding friends, and the ramps at the park. Trace the nodes of his network to see how the links are connected.

Nodes can be activated from either external sources (e.g., seeing an object in the environment) or internal sources (e.g., thinking about an object). Once started, the activation spreads along the connecting links like ripples on the surface of a pond, increasing the degree of activation of the nodes. The farther the activation travels from the original source, the weaker it becomes, until eventually it dies away. As a child grows, much development takes place in the memory network. The numbers of concept nodes and links increase, and the strengths of links change over time.

Try making a sketch of your cognitive nodes and links for information processing. What are the main concept nodes? How are they linked? How has your network changed as you've read this book?

## Working Memory

In the network model, the term **working memory** (WM) refers to the information that is currently active in the memory system and available for use in any mental task. From this "pool" of activated pieces of knowledge (i.e., stored information), a person focuses on some pieces for more detailed processing, but all of the activated information is considered to be in working memory (Cowan, 1995, 1997). Working memory is similar to STS in the stores model—both consist of information that a person is consciously processing at any given time. But working memory differs from STS in that information is not thought of as being moved from one storage place to another. It is simply made available, as information in a book is made available when you open the book. Another difference between STS and WM is that WM has several distinct components. One component is centrally involved in processing verbal information, another in processing auditory information, and others in allocation and monitoring of cognitive resources such as attention as well as rehearsal and temporary storage of information (Baddeley, 1986; Bayliss, Jarrold, Gunn, & Baddeley, 2003; Hamilton, Coates, & Heffernan, 2003; Handley, Capon, Copp, & Harper, 2002). The basic components of working memory are in place by the age of 6, but children learn to use each much more effectively across the school years (Gathercole, Pickering, Ambridge, & Wearing, 2004).

Like STS, working memory has two important characteristics. It is *limited* in its capacity, and the information in working memory *decays over time*. In other words, only a certain amount of information can be activated at any given time. If activation is not maintained in some way, it decays and the information is no longer readily available for use in mental tasks. This information may be permanently lost, or it may simply take more effort to activate it again. As with STS, the amount of information that can be activated in working memory ranges from five to nine chunks of information. The length of time that information can remain activated is short, estimated at approximately 30 seconds, unless we do something to keep it active. For example, we can rehearse (i.e., repeat over and over) what we are trying to remember or relate it to other pieces of information that are active in working memory. Such strategies help keep information activated and therefore available in working memory for longer periods of time.

As you learned in our discussion of the basic processes of information processing in Chapter 8, it isn't clear whether the actual capacity of working memory increases with age or whether children simply learn to use their limited capacities more effectively. But you can probably see that the way a child allocates attention has an important effect on working memory. Consciously attending to information maintains activation and keeps the information readily available, which makes it more likely to be permanently stored in the network. In addition, keeping more pieces of information active increases a child's ability to consider several items at the same time. For example, think about a child learning to read. If a child keeps the letters of a word active in working memory (e.g., *c–a–t*), she can begin to chunk them into one word (*cat*). Because she is now processing these letters as one chunk, she can keep other letters and words active at the same time (*cat–in–the–hat*). As these chunk sizes

**working memory**
The information currently active in your memory system and currently available for use in a mental task.

**long-term memory**
Memory of knowledge or events that is permanent.

**encoding**
The process of forming a mental representation of information.

**storage**
Placing information in permanent, or long-term, memory.

**accessing**
The process of finding information in memory at the desired time.

**retrieval**
In the stores model, retrieval is the process of bringing information from the long-term store to the short-term store. In network models, retrieval is the process of activating information so that it becomes a part of the working memory and thus available for use.

increase, she can activate and process other information about these chunks: She can notice similarities in word structure; she can realize that *cat* and *hat* rhyme; and she can even use some of her working memory capacity to look for other words that might rhyme (Bayliss, Jarrold, Baddeley, Gunn, & Leigh, 2005; Kuhn & Franklin, 2006).

As you might expect, working memory affects practically every cognitive task children undertake. If children could not keep information activated and accessible, they could not use the information to solve problems, answer test questions, or anything else. It is not surprising that scores on tests of short-term and working memory correlate with scores on many other cognitive abilities, including language, intelligence, reading ability, math performance, and comprehension ability. In all cases, the better a child's short-term or working memory performance, the higher the child's cognitive ability scores (Cantor, Engle, & Hamilton, 1991; Farmer & Klein, 1995; Geary, Hoard, Byrd-Craven, & DeSoto, 2004; Gillam, Cowan, & Day, 1995; Lee, Swee-Fong, Ee-Lynn, & Zee-Ying, 2004; Montgomery, 1995; Swanson & Beebe-Frankenberger, 2004).

## Long-Term Memory

**Long-term memory** is just that—memory of information or events that endures over a relatively long time period. As you saw in Figure 11.1, the stores model of memory views long-term memory as a separate store (the LTS). In contrast, network models (Figure 11.2) view long-term memory as the nonactivated part of an integrated memory network. But regardless of how different theorists view the structure of long-term memory, they agree on several fundamental characteristics. First, long-term memory is *permanent.* Once information is stored in long-term memory, it never decays—it is never truly forgotten. Second, long-term memory is *unlimited* in its capacity. This means that theoretically you can store an infinite amount of information. This does not mean, however, that you can always remember the information you want, even when you make concentrated efforts to do so. Trying to remember all of the definitions studied in yesterday's class is a prime example for most college students.

▲ This child is having a *tip-of-the-tongue* experience as he tries to remember his new teacher's name. What does this experience tell us about his access and retrieval of information in his memory?

Although long-term memory does not suffer from difficulties with decay of information or lack of storage space as working memory does, there can be problems with the initial **encoding** of information (i.e., the process of forming a mental representation of the information), **storage** of information (i.e., putting it into the LTS or into the network), **accessing** stored information (i.e., finding the right information at the desired time), and **retrieval** of stored information (i.e., activating it so that it can become part of working memory or STS and thus available for use). For example, have you ever encountered someone you know but find yourself unable to remember the person's name? The problem may be that you never encoded the person's name; this means you will never be able to remember it, because the name was never mentally represented. Maybe you encoded it but never stored it; because the name never entered your memory network, there is nothing there to remember. Or perhaps you encoded it incorrectly, so you might call the person *Helen* when her name is really *Ellen.* Maybe you encoded the name correctly but cannot access it at the moment. We often recognize a person's face (and "know" that we know the person) but fail to access or retrieve the person's name. Finally, you may be able to access the name, but the retrieval cues (things in the mind or environment that increase the likelihood you will be able to remember something) may not be adequate to actually allow you to retrieve it—or, in network model terms, fully activate it. As you might guess, it can be especially difficult to tell whether a memory problem is due to an access or a retrieval problem—access and retrieval tend to be associated, but they are not the same thing. If you've ever experienced the "tip-of-the-tongue" phenomenon, in which you know for sure that you know something but you just can't remember it at the moment, you've experienced access but an inability to retrieve.

THINKING CRITICALLY

Have you ever had a "tip-of-the-tongue" experience? How is this phenomenon explained by the network model of memory? How could it be explained by the stores model?

What develops in long-term memory? Clearly, the amount of knowledge in long-term memory grows tremendously with age—older children simply have stored more information. In addition, the organization of the stored information changes with development. Information becomes more interconnected as children understand the relations between concepts. Older children have more connections between stored concepts, and they add different types of links between concepts. For example, Figure 11.3 (page 330) shows how a child may initially connect an animal such as a dog with its network attributes, in effect representing the things a dog "has" (fur, four legs, a certain color, etc.). Eventually the child will add different kinds of links to this understanding of dogs, such as links that identify the different categories a dog belongs to and represent what a dog "is" (an animal, warm-blooded, etc.). The strengths of associations between concepts also change with development. Some connections become stronger—such as the link between "mammal" and "platypus" when a child learns that a platypus is a mammal. Others become weaker—such as the link between "mammal" and "turtle." Changes in the number, types, and strengths of interconnections of stored information are the things that create change in the organization of long-term memory.

THINK ABOUT LINDA AND GIANLUCA . . .
How can Gianluca's links between basic vocabulary and word meanings, basic letters and their sounds, and related concepts be strengthened?

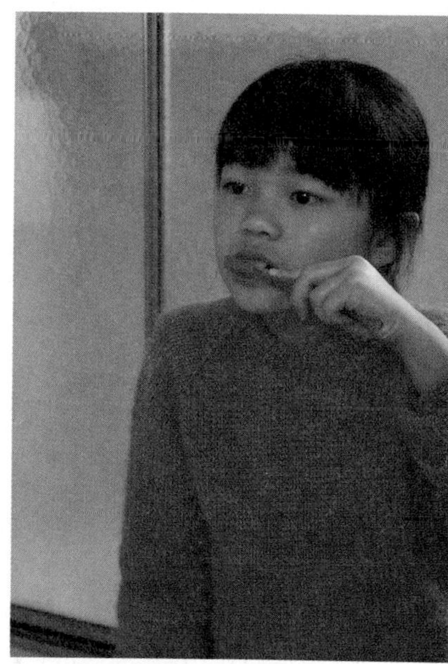

▲ Scripts are formed for events that are encountered repeatedly, like getting ready for bed.

For many years, much of the research on long-term memory concerned *semantic memory,* or knowledge of words and concepts. Children clearly develop semantic memory networks, but their earliest memories seem to be of a different type. *Episodic memory* is memory for events, or episodes, that one experiences in day-to-day life (Tulving, 1972). Some researchers have suggested that children's memories are primarily memories of events and that these episodic memories are organized into **scripts**, mental representations of the way things typically occur in certain settings or for certain events (Bauer, 2006; Nelson, 1986). For example, many children in the United States have a script for going to a fast-food restaurant. They know that you go to a counter and tell a person what you want to eat, but that you can order only the foods listed on big signs behind the counter; that you pay for the food before you get it, not after you're done eating; that you take your food to a table and throw everything away when you are finished; and that sometimes there is a playground where you can have fun.

Scripts reflect real-world events, and they indicate what usually happens for a given type of event. They form most readily for events children encounter repeatedly, such as getting ready for bed, going to visit relatives, or eating out in restaurants. Children's first scripts contain only the most central events, and even children as young as one year of age show evidence of scripts (Bauer & Dow, 1994; Bauer & Mandler, 1992; Fivush, Kuebli, & Clubb, 1992). As children grow, they need fewer encounters with an event to form a script, and the scripts become more detailed (Farrar & Goodman, 1992; Hudson, Fivush, & Kuebli, 1992). For example, a 2-year-old's script for eating in a fast-food restaurant may include only the information that first you order your food, then you play on the playground. A 9-year-old's script will likely contain many more details, such as what kinds of food are available, how loud and rowdy you can be, whether the toys that come with the kids' meals are too babyish to play with, and the fact that food must be paid for before you eat. By organizing knowledge, scripts help children predict what will happen next and help them remember events that take place (Hudson & Nelson, 1983; Hudson, Shapiro, & Sosa, 1995).

THINK ABOUT LINDA AND GIANLUCA . . .
How could Linda help Gianluca develop scripts for the stories he's reading? How would this help him be more successful in understanding and remembering what he's read?

## Other Characteristics of Memory Development

**Reconstructive Memory.** On an episode of a popular reality television show, two former friends were appearing in small-claims court. One friend (we'll call her "Kim") had purchased some expensive airline tickets for a beach vacation. She claimed that her friend "Samantha" had promised to reimburse her for one of the tickets. Kim's mother caught the girls and would not allow them to go (the girls were only 15!), but the tickets could not be returned for a refund. Samantha denied having promised to

**scripts**
Mental representations of the way things typically occur in certain settings or for certain events.

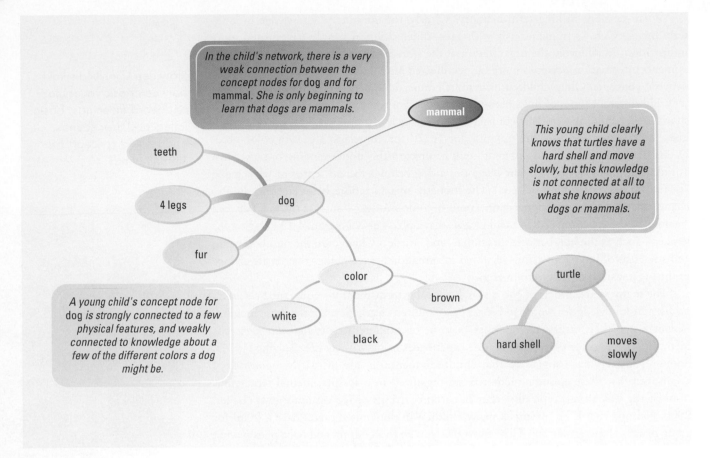

In the child's network, there is a very weak connection between the concept nodes for dog and for mammal. She is only beginning to learn that dogs are mammals.

mammal

This young child clearly knows that turtles have a hard shell and move slowly, but this knowledge is not connected at all to what she knows about dogs or mammals.

teeth

4 legs

dog

fur

color

turtle

brown

white

black

hard shell

moves slowly

A young child's concept node for dog is strongly connected to a few physical features, and weakly connected to knowledge about a few of the different colors a dog might be.

▲ FIGURE 11.3
**Developmental Changes in a Long-Term Memory Network**
A young child's initial network for the concept of "dog" is shown above; a more elaborate network for "dog" (shown on the facing page) develops as the child learns and grows. Thicker lines indicate stronger connections; thinner lines indicate weaker connections.

▲ Reconstruction in memory is vitally important for understanding eyewitness testimony, especially when the witness is a child.

**reconstructive memory**
A characteristic of human memory. We store parts of events and knowledge; during recall we retrieve the stored pieces and draw inferences about the rest.

pay for her ticket, saying that she had stated only that she would help pay for the trip. Because the trip did not take place, Samantha felt she was under no obligation to pay for anything.

Do you think of memory as a mental copy of information and events? Many people do. The story of Kim and Samantha, however, clearly illustrates that memory is anything but a "mental copy." Instead, memory is *reconstructive*. This means that only some aspects of events and some pieces of information are stored in memory—and when you try to recall the information or event, you access and retrieve these pieces then infer the rest. In other words, in **reconstructive memory** you patch together what probably happened based on the bits and pieces you actually stored, along with other relevant information from memory and from external cues. Perhaps Samantha actually said something like "I'll help pay for the trip." But Kim's reconstruction, influenced by her past eagerness to get to the beach and her present need to recover some of her lost money, was more like "She said she'd pay for her ticket." Our memory of experiences and knowledge draws on previous knowledge, memories, and the current context—it is sometimes changed in subtle ways but sometimes altered substantially.

Numerous studies have confirmed that memory can be significantly affected by what people already know, as well as by the way they are asked to recall it. For example, people

The strengths of existing links also changed with age. For example, there is now a much stronger link between dog *and* mammal.

As this child has gotten older, her network of knowledge has changed. She has added new concept nodes (shown in pink) and new links, like the one connecting dog to animal.

give very different answers to this question: "How fast was the car going when it crashed into the house?" as opposed to this one: "Can you estimate the car's speed at the time of the accident?" Can you predict which question led to higher speed estimates, and explain why? Also—and especially with children—prompted recall, which uses questions like either of the two above, produces more detailed *but more incorrect* recall than unprompted recall (e.g., responses to "Tell me all you can remember about the event") (Ceci & Bruck, 1998; Loftus & Ketcham, 1994).

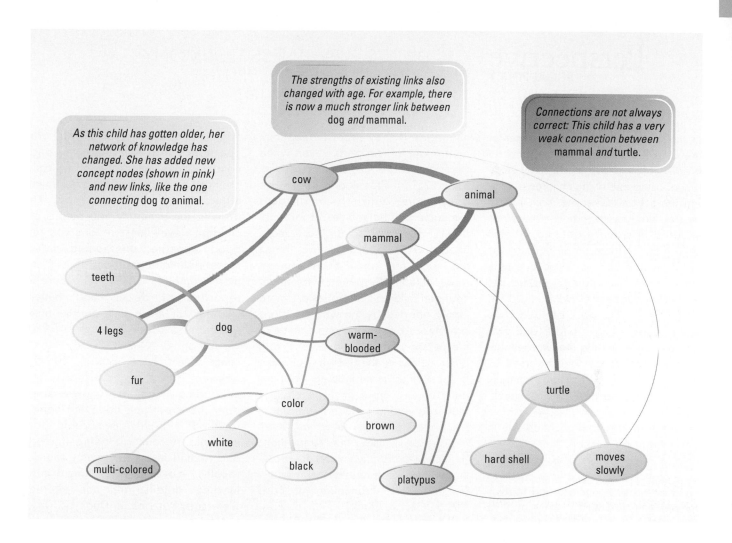

THINKING CRITICALLY

Explain several advantages and disadvantages of having reconstructive memory. Is it possible to have any memory that is not reconstructed? Why or why not?

Why does it matter whether memory is literal or reconstructed? Sometimes it doesn't. It doesn't matter whether you can remember the dialogue from a television show word for word or only the gist of the story. Other times, however, the difference is crucial. For example, read the Social Policy Perspective box on page 332 called "Children's Eyewitness Testimony: The Truth, the Whole Truth, and Nothing but the Truth?" **Listen** on **mydevelopmentlab**

**Listen**: How do we know that memory is reconstructive, and why is this important to understand? (Author Podcast) www.mydevelopmentlab.com

**Autobiographical Memory.** One of us (JLC) had a bicycle accident at about 8 years of age. Whenever I think about it, I can almost feel the pain in my knee, see the bright red of the blood, and remember the words I was thinking: "Just get home, just get home. Dad will help me." I remember remaining reasonably calm until I saw my father standing at the edge of the yard, and then bursting into tears. Do you have any such vivid memories?

## Perspective SOCIAL POLICY

## CHILDREN'S EYEWITNESS TESTIMONY: THE TRUTH, THE WHOLE TRUTH, NOTHING BUT THE TRUTH?

In the winter of 1989, a co-owner of the Little Rascals Day Care Center in North Carolina was accused of sexually abusing one of the children attending the school. Over the next several years, dozens of adults would be accused of sexually abusing 90 children. Few children made accusations early on, but after repeated questioning by parents and police and months of therapy, dozens of children did so, and seven adults were arrested. Two were found guilty at trial and two pleaded no contest to the charges, but the convictions were later reversed on appeal and the prosecution eventually dropped all charges (Ceci & Bruck, 1998).

Children are being called on in ever-increasing numbers to provide testimony in legal court cases. Often the cases involve serious crimes, such as child abuse or homicide, and the witnesses are sometimes as young as 4 years of age. Can children provide reliable and valid information under such circumstances? Are they able to tell the truth, the whole truth, and nothing but the truth? What effect does repeated questioning by therapists, police, or lawyers have on children's memories?

There is a great deal of research literature looking at these questions. Even preschoolers are *capable* of accurately reporting information, though it is often not as detailed as the reports of older children and adults and they forget more as time passes. Repeated questioning does increase the amount recalled for both children and adults, but unfortunately the additional information is not necessarily accurate. Both children and adults become more confident in their memories if they receive feedback confirming their reports—even when their reports are incorrect (Neuschatz et al., 2005)! Preschool children also have more difficulty than adults remembering the sources of information and details, so they are more likely to mistakenly think that things they were told about or even imagined actually happened to them. Younger children's memories are more easily affected by the way questions are phrased, the status and attitude of the person asking the questions, and other details of the interview context. If questioning is misleading, younger children are more likely to change their answers to include the misleading information. They may even expand on it, using the "suggestions in highly productive ways to reconstruct and at times distort reality" (Bruck, Ceci, Francouer, & Barr, 1995; Ceci & Bruck, 1998, p. 738; Schneider & Bjorklund, 1998). The false information can be integrated into memory, becoming a stable part of it to be repeated as being true when asked about the events at a later time (Brainerd, Reyna, & Brandes, 1995). In other words, the inaccurate information can essentially *become* the truth more easily for children than for adults. To make matters even more confusing, recent research shows that older children and adults can show *more* false memories than younger children, under certain types of conditions (Brainerd et al., 2008)—and experts often cannot tell for certain whether a child is reporting events that actually happened or not (Leichtman & Ceci, 1995).

The news is not all bad, however. When questions are asked in a nonmisleading way, children are questioned in a nonfrightening and nondemanding atmosphere, and children are given permission to acknowledge when they do not know the answer, the accuracy and details of children's eyewitness reports can be good. Repeated questioning under these optimal conditions results in more complete and more accurate reporting of details and better memory for the events during later questioning (Ceci & Bruck, 1998; Goodman & Quas, 2008; Pipe, Lamb, Orbach, & Esplin, 2004). Some evidence suggests that when misleading information is given long after the event and the event being recalled is highly memorable (for example, it concerns being injured and treated in an emergency room), recall is *more* accurate than if misleading details are not offered (Peterson, Parsons, & Dean, 2004). Using props during questioning (such as anatomically correct dolls) has had mixed results, but encouraging children to think more deeply by doing things such as drawing a picture about an event in addition to talking about it can increase how much is remembered (Bruck & Ceci, 1999; Butler, Gross, & Hayne, 1995; Steward & Steward, 1996).

QUESTION **If you were a social worker, prosecutor, jury member, or judge in the Little Rascals case or one like it, how would you proceed? What safeguards would you put into place to ensure that children's testimony is as accurate as possible, and what details of the questioning and therapy processes would you want to know?**

Such long-lasting memories of personally experienced events are called **autobiographical memories**, which are a special subgroup of episodic memories. They are memories of events that had a high level of personal significance. Such meaningful memories form the core experiences of a child's "life story." Not surprisingly, autobiographical memories are often quite vivid and detailed, sometimes even including emotions, sights, and sounds. Children begin to form autobiographical memories early in life and begin talking about such past events when they are as young as 2 years of age. Children's descriptions of past events become more organized and detailed between ages 3 and 6. During middle childhood, children add more background information and provide more of the contexts of the events—such as where they were, what they were thinking and feeling at the time, who was present, and the like. Children learn to describe their autobiographical memories as narratives or stories by interacting with adults; adults elaborate on the information the child provides, ask questions to clarify details or elicit more information, and teach children a cultural format to use in talking about their memories. For example, parents and children often have "remember when you . . ." conversations: "Remember when you had your big bike accident in second grade? Do you remember the bike trick you were trying to do when it happened?" Interactions like these teach children a form for describing memories, and they also help children fill in forgotten details. In other words, such conversations strengthen events that might have become inaccessible in memory so that the child is better able to remember them later (Bauer, 2006; Cleveland & Reese, 2005; Fivush, 1995; Fivush, Haden, & Adam, 1995; Howe & Courage, 2004; Howe, Courage, & Bryant-Brown, 1995). Differences in the types of interactions, such as how mothers talk with their children about past events (by elaborating on details and evaluating them versus providing fewer elaborations and evaluations) or cultural tendencies (such as storytelling as entertainment versus to teach moral lessons), affect the age of earliest memories and how detailed they are (Nelson & Fivush, 2004).

▲ *Autobiographical memories* are memories of events that are very important to the person. They are often very vivid, and can include the emotions, sights, and sounds that were present at the original event.

Autobiographical memories are interesting because they seem so different from our memory for other kinds of information, such as facts and categories. These memories are also important in helping children develop a sense of their own identity, a topic we will discuss in Chapter 15. It is not yet clear if autobiographical memories are processed differently than semantic memories at a neural level. Some evidence shows that different brain structures are involved (Svoboda & Levine, 2009), while other studies indicate that processing of autobiographical memories is distributed across multiple brain areas, including those involved in processing of facts, emotions, and visual processing (Markowitsch, 2008; Spreng, Mar, & Kim, 2009; Summerfield, Hassabis, & Maguire, 2009). Given what you've learned about the reconstructive nature of memory, however, can you see a potential problem with autobiographical memories? It can be difficult for a person to figure out how much of an autobiographical memory, particularly one of a traumatic event such as a serious accident or abuse, might be influenced by other people's interpretations of the event or even by imagining an event. Research shows that these memories are susceptible to social influence; simply hearing another person describe an early autobiographical memory influenced age judgments and confidence in early memories (Mazzoni & Memon, 2003; Niedzwienska, 2003; Peterson, Kaasa, & Loftus, 2009). To learn about how clinical psychologists deal with autobiographical memories their clients may have, read the Professional Perspective box on page 334 called "Career Focus: Meet a Child and Family Therapist."

THINKING CRITICALLY

Are your earliest memories about events? Are they autobiographical? Ask several friends about their earliest memories. Do you see a pattern?

**autobiographical memories** Memories of events of great personal importance. They are episodic memories and are often vivid and detailed.

# Perspective PROFESSIONAL — CAREER FOCUS: MEET A CHILD AND FAMILY THERAPIST

Dr. Anne Updegrove,
Licensed Clinical Psychologist and adjunct faculty at Loyola University
Chicago, IL

**In therapy situations, how do you use research information about autobiographical and reconstructive memory?**
Since therapists rely on children's reports, it is important to be familiar with research that explains what factors influence children's memory of their own experiences and events in their lives. Using research gives clinicians a sense of the "big picture" and helps us to not rely solely on our own unique experience, but to be more objective in our evaluation of children.

**In your experience, do children seem more prone than adults to making errors when they reconstruct memories in therapy?**
I don't think they make more errors. Instead, I think they remember differently and are differentially affected by how questions are asked. Children's memories tend to be less elaborate, more concrete, and often include details that may seem less relevant or more idiosyncratic. For example, a traumatized child may focus on a stuffed animal that was lost during the traumatic incident or the smell of an individual who has abused them. Also, children are more easily influenced by the way questions are asked if they sense that an adult authority figure wants them to respond in a particular way. The younger the child, the more this seems to be true.

**How do you help children accurately recall events, without leading them into inaccurate memories?**
It's difficult. We want to help clients remember as much detail as possible but without influencing the nature of their memories. We do several things to enhance accurate recall. First, clients must trust the therapist and feel that he or she is supportive and nonjudgmental. Second, questions should be open-ended. Clients should be asked to "Tell me more about that" rather than given leading questions. Good training in assessment and interviewing helps clinicians learn how to ask questions the right way. For example, clinicians learn that using the client's own words when phrasing a question reduces the possibility that you are introducing your own biases into the interview. Third, it can be helpful to ask someone to tell the story in their own words. Memories that seem unusually rehearsed or include words that children do not typically know are suspect. Likewise, if a child describes an experience in some detail that is unusual for a child to know about (for example, a sexual act), this lends credibility to the accuracy of the memory.

**What kinds of education and training are needed to work as a child or family therapist?**
Most therapists have a master's degree or a PhD in clinical psychology, counseling, or clinical social work. Course work in child development, family dynamics, assessment, and therapy is needed, with supervised practice in a therapy situation. Most states require a licensing exam.

QUESTION **What aspects of memory research seem important in clinical work as a therapist? How would you use what you have learned about memory, its processes, and its characteristics to ensure accurate memory in important situations like this?**

## LET'S REVIEW . . .

1. Which model describes human memory as a set of concept nodes with links that vary in strength?
   - **a.** the stores model
   - **b.** the network model
   - **c.** the short-term model
   - **d.** the autobiographical model

2. According to some researchers, children organize their long-term memories of events into special mental structures called ___________.
   - **a.** scripts
   - **b.** semantic networks
   - **c.** reconstructive stores
   - **d.** autobiographical networks

3. Two witnesses to a robbery offer very different reports of what happened. Which of the following *best* explains why the reports differ?
   a. autobiographical memory
   b. unintentional memory
   c. reconstructive memory
   d. episodic memory
4. True or False: As their processing speed increases, children tend to maintain less information in their working memories.
5. True or False: With development, the amount of information held in long-term memory increases, and the organization of the information changes.

Answers: 1. b, 2. a, 3. c, 4. F, 5. T

# Information Processing: Knowledge, Strategies, and New Approaches

When our two sons were about 9 and 5 years old, they asked me (JLC) to play Pokémon cards with them. Each card had a picture of a different Pokémon character. Different characters had distinctive beginning strength levels and "tricks" they could use to defeat opponents. The object was to defeat the opposing Pokémon and win the card. My sons gave me a few cards to start with and we began our game. Within minutes, I had lost all of my cards. The boys had quickly determined which Pokémon to start with, which trick to use, how much damage they had suffered, and who won the game—all before I could even figure out which of my cards had the highest beginning strength!

What could explain my sons' clear superiority with Pokémon? It wasn't overall level of intelligence. I like to think my sons are intelligent, but so am I. It was not due to their having better memory in general—just ask them about homework or if they've brushed their teeth, and it is as if they have no memory at all! The answer has to do with **knowledge base** (the amount of information a person knows about a particular topic) and **strategies** (the conscious, intentional, and controllable plans we adopt to enhance our performance).

As you may have realized by now, information processors pay a great deal of attention to how people acquire and use knowledge. In this section we explore the development of the knowledge base and strategies. We will also review recent explanations of cognitive development that have grown from the information-processing perspective and evaluate some of the pros and cons of the information-processing approach.

AS YOU STUDY THIS SECTION, ASK YOURSELF THESE QUESTIONS:

11.7 What effect does knowledge base have on cognitive development?
11.8 How do strategies develop and how does increasing strategy use foster cognitive development?
11.9 What are some newer approaches to understanding cognitive development?
11.10 What are the strengths and weaknesses of the information-processing approach to cognitive development?

## Knowledge Base

Though we haven't seen any studies of Pokémon experts (yet), researchers have looked at the effects of knowledge base in many other areas of life. Not surprisingly, the more you know about a particular topic, the more you can remember about it—but that is not the only effect of knowledge base. For example, when you get new information about a topic you already know well, you are more likely to notice details and relationships than someone who has less

**knowledge base**
The amount of information a person knows about a particular topic.

**strategies**
Conscious, intentional, and controllable plans used to improve performance.

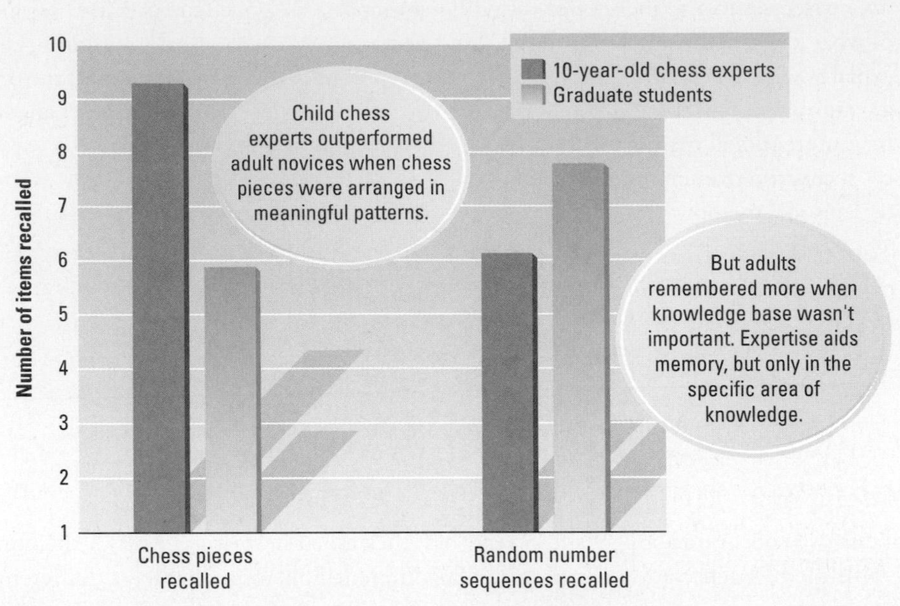
10-year-old chess experts
Graduate students
Child chess experts outperformed adult novices when chess pieces were arranged in meaningful patterns.
But adults remembered more when knowledge base wasn't important. Expertise aids memory, but only in the specific area of knowledge.
Number of items recalled
10
9
8
7
6
5
4
3
2
1
Chess pieces recalled
Random number sequences recalled

FIGURE 11.4 ▶ **Expert–Novice Differences in Memory for Chessboard Arrangements** The child chess experts showed greater memory for the chess pieces—although not for random sequences of numbers—than the graduate student novices. (Data from Chi, 1978.)

prior knowledge. You are also better able to group the information in useful ways. So my sons were good at categorizing their Pokémon cards according to the types and overall amount of "powers" they had (a useful category for the card battles), whereas I began by sorting the cards according to color and size (which is not very helpful for the battles). In other words, your knowledge base enables you to encode new information differently. You can also store the new information more effectively. In essence, you are better able to integrate the new information with previous knowledge, which increases the likelihood that you will be able to access and retrieve the new information when you need it. Finally, you are able to carry out all these processes more quickly than someone who does not know much about the topic. As you'll recall from Chapter 8, the faster you can process information, the less processing capacity you use, and the more of your limited capacity is available for other mental processes. So not only will you be able to remember more of the new information, you will be able to think about it more quickly and at a higher level than someone with less knowledge. Given all this, I suppose it isn't surprising that my sons defeated me so quickly in our Pokémon game.

▲ No matter what their age, experts have a greater knowledge base and organize their knowledge differently than novices.

The influence of prior knowledge is very clear when you study *experts* versus *novices*—that is, when you contrast people who know a lot about a given area with people who know very little about it. Some of the earliest and best-known research on expert–novice differences focused on chess players (Chi, 1978). In one well-known study the chess experts were only 10 years old, whereas the novices were graduate students. The experimenters showed both groups chess pieces in chessboard arrangements that would be likely to occur during a real game. The participants saw the pieces for about one second. Then the researchers asked them to remember the positions and place the pieces on another chessboard in the same arrangements they had viewed. The results are shown in Figure 11.4. Because of their greater knowledge of chess, the children clearly outperformed the adults. This did not happen because the children had better memories in general: When the task was to remember random sequences of numbers, the graduate students did better, as shown in Figure 11.4. In other words, greater prior knowledge of chess produced better memory, but only for chess. Expert–novice differences in memory and problem-solving performance are evident in many realms, including academic areas (e.g., mathematics, physics, information seeking, and evaluation), sports (e.g., soccer, baseball), and even hobbies and entertainment (e.g., dinosaurs, playing the word game *Scrabble*, cartoon characters like Superman or Spider-Man, or *Star Wars* characters and plots) (Brand-Gruwel, Wopereis, & Vermetten, 2005; Chi, Glaser, & Farr, 1988; Chi & Koeske, 1983; Means & Voss, 1985; Schneider, Gruber, Gold, & Opwis, 1993; Tuffiash, Roring, & Ericsson, 2007).

Perhaps the most interesting finding from all the work on expert–novice differences is that experts not only have more information but also mentally organize their knowledge about their topics differently than do novices. Instead of storing information about individual chess pieces as a novice would, chess experts mentally group entire board configurations (which are made up of many individual pieces). They store the entire thing as a single chunk in memory. They sometimes even store common *sequences* of moves as a single chunk! In other words, for a chess expert one chunk may contain dozens of individual pieces arranged in successive moves. In contrast, novices think about, store, and retrieve only a few pieces of information at a time. Experts also mentally categorize information based on general principles instead of according to surface-level characteristics (Hmelo-Silver, Marathe, & Liu, 2007; Hogan & Rabinowitz, 2009). For example, physics novices mentally store physics information according to the kinds of objects they see in the problem situation (e.g., an inclined plane). In contrast, experts mentally organize their knowledge according to general principles of physics (e.g., the principle of inertia) (Chi, Feltovich, & Glaser, 1981). As a result, physics experts can quickly recognize the underlying principles involved, categorize the general type of problem they are dealing with, and access relevant information and possible solution strategies. Meanwhile, novices are stuck trying to figure out what, if anything, the existence of an inclined plane means. A novice is like a detective who may notice clues but doesn't think about how they fit together to solve a mystery.

Given that knowledge base affects memory and knowledge organization, how does it help explain cognitive development? Young children are, in essence, "universal novices" (Brown & DeLoache, 1978). They know about fewer topics than older children, and they know less about the topics they have encountered. Because young children have less knowledge, the information in their knowledge bases is less connected than that of older children. Also, it tends to be organized according to surface features rather than according to underlying principles. All these features lead to poorer memory and less efficient cognitive processing. Information-processing psychologists agree that age differences in knowledge base play an important role in explaining cognitive development. In fact, some claim that knowledge base is the *most* important factor in explaining why adults are better than children on most cognitive tasks (Carey, 1985). Notice how different this explanation of cognitive development is from the Piagetian view.

If a rich knowledge base has such important effects, what does it take for children to acquire one? The few longitudinal studies that have been done confirm what you are probably thinking—lots of practice is absolutely necessary. In studies of both chess experts and tennis experts, it seems that practice, along with motivational factors such as interest and dedication, were more important than general aptitude measures (Renniger, Hidi, & Krapp, 1992; Schneider, 1993). How extensive a knowledge base is necessary? Not surprisingly, it appears that it takes a fairly high degree of knowledge to enhance children's performance and produce changes in the structure of their knowledge (DeMarie-Dreblow, 1991).

THINK ABOUT LINDA AND GIANLUCA . . .
What parts of Gianluca's knowledge base must improve to help him read and comprehend text more effectively? How can Linda help with this?

## Strategy Development

While reading a new book one day, 10-year-old Will encounters the word *facilitates*. He pauses and looks carefully at the picture on the page, but cannot figure out the word. He tries to sound out the individual letters but still doesn't understand the text. Finally, Will points to the word and asks his teacher for help. Will's attempts to understand the book are *strategies*—the conscious, intentional, and controllable plans that people use to improve performance at all stages of information processing (Schneider & Bjorklund, 1998). As you can see, Will tried three different strategies to encode the new word: using the context, sounding it out, and asking for help. He will probably use several other strategies to understand the story, store it in memory, and recall it later on. Information-processing psychologists have given enormous attention to children's development of cognitive strategies, because they believe that strategies have a strong impact on thinking, remembering, and solving problems.

Research has looked in depth at the development of several specific memory strategies. One strategy is *rehearsal,* or repeating information that you want to remember. Rehearsal can be a very effective memory strategy, because it increases the likelihood that information will be stored in memory. As you might expect, the amount of rehearsal is important—more rehearsal tends to produce better memory performance, but the style of rehearsal may be even more important. Older children tend to use a *cumulative* (or active) rehearsal style, in which they repeat several items together. In contrast, younger children use a more *passive* style—they repeat only the last item they are trying to remember. This passive style does not encourage further processing of other items, and it doesn't encourage the child to look for relationships among the items. Younger children can be trained to use cumulative rehearsal; doing so improves their memory performance, but they do not tend to continue using it after training (Naus, Ornstein, & Aivano, 1977).

THINK ABOUT LINDA AND GIANLUCA . . .

How could Gianluca use rehearsal, organization, and elaboration to improve his reading skills? Can you think of other strategies that might help him?

Two other useful memory strategies are *organization,* in which we use relationships among items to improve our memory for the items, and *elaboration,* in which we create visual or verbal associations to link the items. In general, all three strategies show similar changes across ages (Pressley & Hilden, 2006).

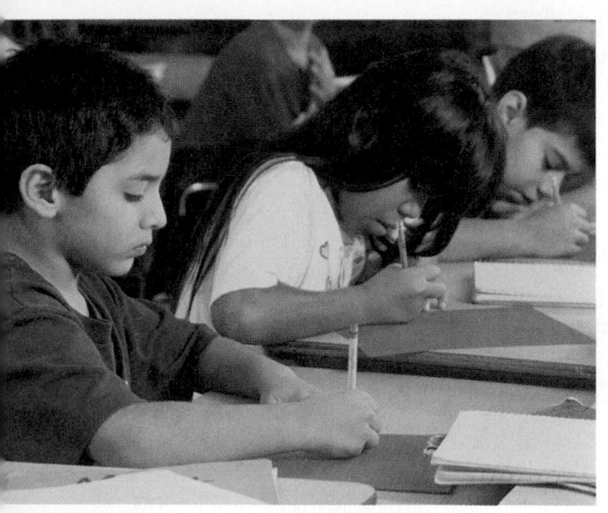

▲ These children are likely using different strategies. How might they use rehearsal, elaboration, and organization to improve their memory of their spelling words?

- Preschool children are less likely to use these strategies spontaneously than school-age children, but younger children can easily be taught to use the strategies. When used correctly, the strategies can help their memory performance.
- Even after training, younger children usually do not use the strategies as effectively or as consistently as older children. Even when younger children are trained to the point that they spontaneously use a strategy on new information, their memory of the information does not always improve (Bjorklund & Coyle, 1995; Bjorklund, Miller, Coyle, & Slawinski, 1997).
- The three strategies typically appear at different ages. Simple forms of rehearsal are found in preschool children, but organization is not common until the elementary school years, and spontaneous use of elaboration does not occur until adolescence or even later (Hasselhorn, 1992; Pressley & Afflerbach, 1995).
- Children use strategies more often and more effectively with familiar materials and meaningful, interesting activities (Rogoff & Mistry, 1990).

It is also important to keep in mind that strategies do not function in isolation. Children do not use only one strategy at a time, and they do not move neatly from less sophisticated to more sophisticated strategies. Instead, they typically use a variety of different strategies from one problem to the next. Sometimes—as with 10-year-old Will and the word *facilitates*—children use combinations of multiple strategies on a single problem (Coyle & Bjorklund, 1997; Siegler, 1995, 2007). Children's strategy development can be thought of as a series of *overlapping waves* in which children use a variety of different strategies, some simpler and some more complex. The particular strategies used most often gradually shift from the simpler to the more complex (Geary et al., 2004; Kwong & Varnhagen, 2005; Siegler, 2006; Torbeyns, Verschaffel, & Ghesquiere, 2005). The shift occurs as the child becomes more efficient in using the more complex strategy, which reduces the "cost" in terms of cognitive capacity and provides greater "benefits" in terms of better performance.

THINKING CRITICALLY

Think of a problem you had to solve recently. Did you use only one strategy or several? How (and why) have your "favorite" strategies changed over the years?

## Newer Approaches to Understanding Cognitive Development

The stores model you saw in Figure 11.1 was first proposed in the 1960s, and it is very simple compared to the models and theories of cognitive processing being developed today. In this last section we will introduce you to some of the ideas that information-processing theorists are exploring today.

**Computational Models of Thought.** Some information-processing researchers try to map the exact steps that people go through as they solve problems or perform other cognitive tasks. To test their conclusions, these researchers create computer programs that attempt to mimic the thought processes of humans. These theories of cognition that are programmed and tested on computers are known as **computational models** (Klahr & MacWhinney, 1998; Munakatu, 2006). Researchers have been developing and testing computational models of adult cognition since the early days of information processing, but we include this as a new approach because of these models' more recent use in work on children's cognitive development. There are two general types of computational models: *production systems* and *connectionist models*.

**Production systems** are sets of computerized *if–then statements,* or "productions," that state the specific actions that a person will take under certain conditions. For example, Table 11.1 (page 340) shows hypothetical productions for solving a Piagetian liquid conservation problem like those you learned about in Chapter 8. Each production specifies a *condition* that must be met before the production will be implemented (this is the *if* part) and a specific *action* that will be taken (the *then* part). When you look closely at Table 11.1, it is easy to see how production systems quickly become complex. The system must specify the many different conditions a person might encounter and the specific actions to be taken under each condition. The system also must include *decision rules* for deciding which productions to implement when the conditions of more than one production are met, when none of the conditions for any existing production are met, or when other complicating situations exist (Klahr & Siegler, 1978; Munakatu, 2006).

Researchers use production systems to clarify and test hypotheses about development. They specify the exact conditions that must be met, the exact actions that will be taken, and the exact input information needed. They then compare the computer-produced output with the solutions real children produce for similar problems. This allows the researchers to identify parts of the model that are wrong or vague. Earlier production systems emphasized matching children's performance at different ages. More recently, researchers have focused on developing self-modifying production systems, or systems that "learn," in order to simulate the actual process of developmental change (Halford et al., 1995; Siegler & Shipley, 1995; Simon & Klahr, 1995). These models provide invaluable information about the precise processes that change as a child develops (e.g., exactly what happens when a child generalizes, discriminates, or chunks information) and about the conditions under which the changes occur.

Like production systems, **connectionist models** are computational in that they are implemented in a computer simulation and focus on cognitive processes. However, they differ from most other cognitive theories in one important way: Connectionist models hypothesize that knowledge is not "stored" at all. Instead, all knowledge is believed to be reconstructed based on different patterns of activations among interconnected sets of numerous individual components (which is why these models are also sometimes called *parallel distributed processing models,* or PDP). These models reflect what is known about the workings of neurons in the brain and so are said to be "neurally inspired." They are often referred to as *neural networks.* Figure 11.5 (page 341) shows a simple connectionist model. The basic elements are its *units*—simple elements that combine to form different patterns. Each unit has a certain *level of activation*—the degree to which it is "turned on" at any given time. The individual units are connected by *links.* The links vary in how

**computational models**
Models of cognition that are programmed on computers: output of the programs is compared to human performance.

**production systems**
Sets of computerized *if–then statements* that state the specific actions that will be taken under certain conditions.

**connectionist models**
"Neurally inspired" or neural network models of cognition that view knowledge as based on patterns of activation among interconnected sets of individual units rather than stored as entire concepts.

THINK ABOUT LINDA AND GIANLUCA . . .
How would it help Gianluca to notice the conditions and actions in the texts he's trying to understand, such as for what to do with different punctuation marks? How can Linda help him notice and remember these relations?

THINKING CRITICALLY
Think of a problem that is familiar to you, then create a production system that describes how you solve the problem. By creating this system, what insights do you gain about how you think about this problem?

**TABLE 11.1**
**Examples of Possible Productions for a Piagetian Liquid Conservation Task**

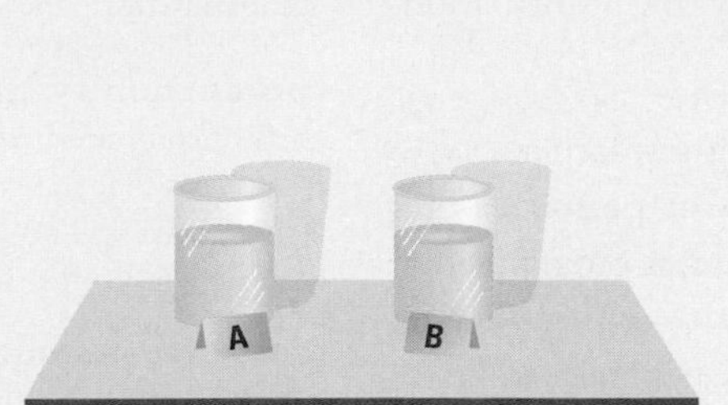


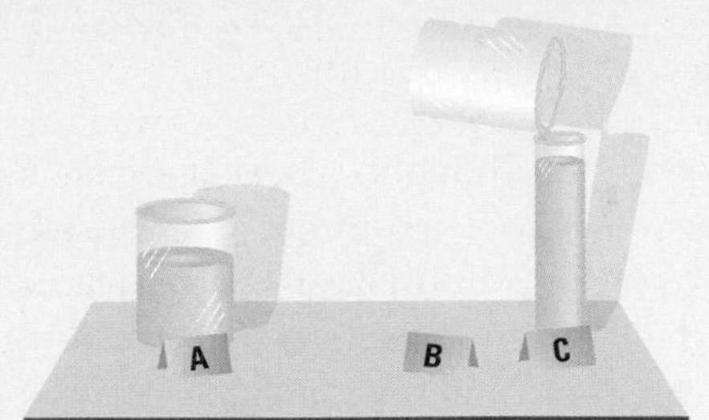


This is the same liquid conservation problem that we discussed in Chapter 8, p. 233. At the beginning of the problem, containers A and B have the same amount of liquid. The liquid in B is poured into the taller and thinner container C. The child is asked to decide if containers A and C still contain the same amount of liquid as each other, or whether one now has more.

The hypothetical production system below proposes four different ways that children can solve this problem. If these models were run on a computer, the researcher could compare the computer's output to that of real children to see how well the production system matched the children's performance.

| | |
|---|---|
| **Model I**<br>Considers only the height of liquid in each container. | P1: ((Same Height) → (Say "same"))<br>P2: ((Container C more Height) → (Say "C has more")) |
| **Model II**<br>Considers both the height and the width of the liquid in each container, but only if the height and width information are consistent. | P1: ((Same Height) → (Say "same"))<br>P2: ((Container C more Height) → (Say "C has more"))<br>P3: ((Same Height) (Container C more Width) → (Say "C has more")) |
| **Model III**<br>Considers both height and width, but not sure how to coordinate them. | P1: ((Same Height) → (Say "same"))<br>P2: ((Container C more Height) → (Say "C has more"))<br>P3: ((Same Height) (Container C more Width) → (Say "C has more"))<br>P4: ((Container C more Height) (Container C less Width) → (muddle through))<br>P5: ((Container C more Height) (Container C more Width) → (Say "C has more")) |
| **Model IV**<br>Considers both height and width of both containers, coordinating them by estimating volume. | P1: ((Same Height) → (Say "same"))<br>P2: ((Container C more Height) → (Say "C has more"))<br>P3: ((Same Height) (Container C more Width) → (Say "C has more"))<br>P4: ((Container C more Height) (Container C less Width) → (get Volume))<br>P5: ((Container C more Height) (Container C more Width) → (Say "C has more"))<br>P6: ((Same Volume) → (Say "same"))<br>P7: ((Container C more Volume) → (Say "C has more")) |

P = An individual production, or *if–then statement*; e.g., IF both containers have the same height, THEN say "same."
C = The container holding the liquid after pouring.
Height = Height of the liquid in the container.
Width = Width of the liquid in the container.
Source: Adapted from Klahr & Siegler (1978), p. 78.

strongly they are weighted, with heavily weighted links capable of transmitting activation between two units more easily than lightly weighted links. As shown in the figure, the input layer represents the signals that initially enter the network, the output layer represents the decisions made by the network, and various layers hidden in between enable the network to make a variety of different connections between the input and output layers (Munakatu, 2006; Rogers & McClelland, 2004).

Researchers "train" these connectionist models; that is, they compare a program's output to people's performance, then adjust the program to produce a better match. The main point is to match humans' *developmental changes*—to get the computer model to show the same learning patterns that humans show, including patterns of generalization to new problems. "Learning" occurs through changes in the weights of the links between units. Many different learning rules can be incorporated into the computer program, and each one has different effects on the network. The different learning rules correspond to different hypotheses about how learning takes place, and the different patterns of connections represent different levels of knowledge. By identifying the learning rules and connection patterns that provide the best fit between computer and human learning patterns,

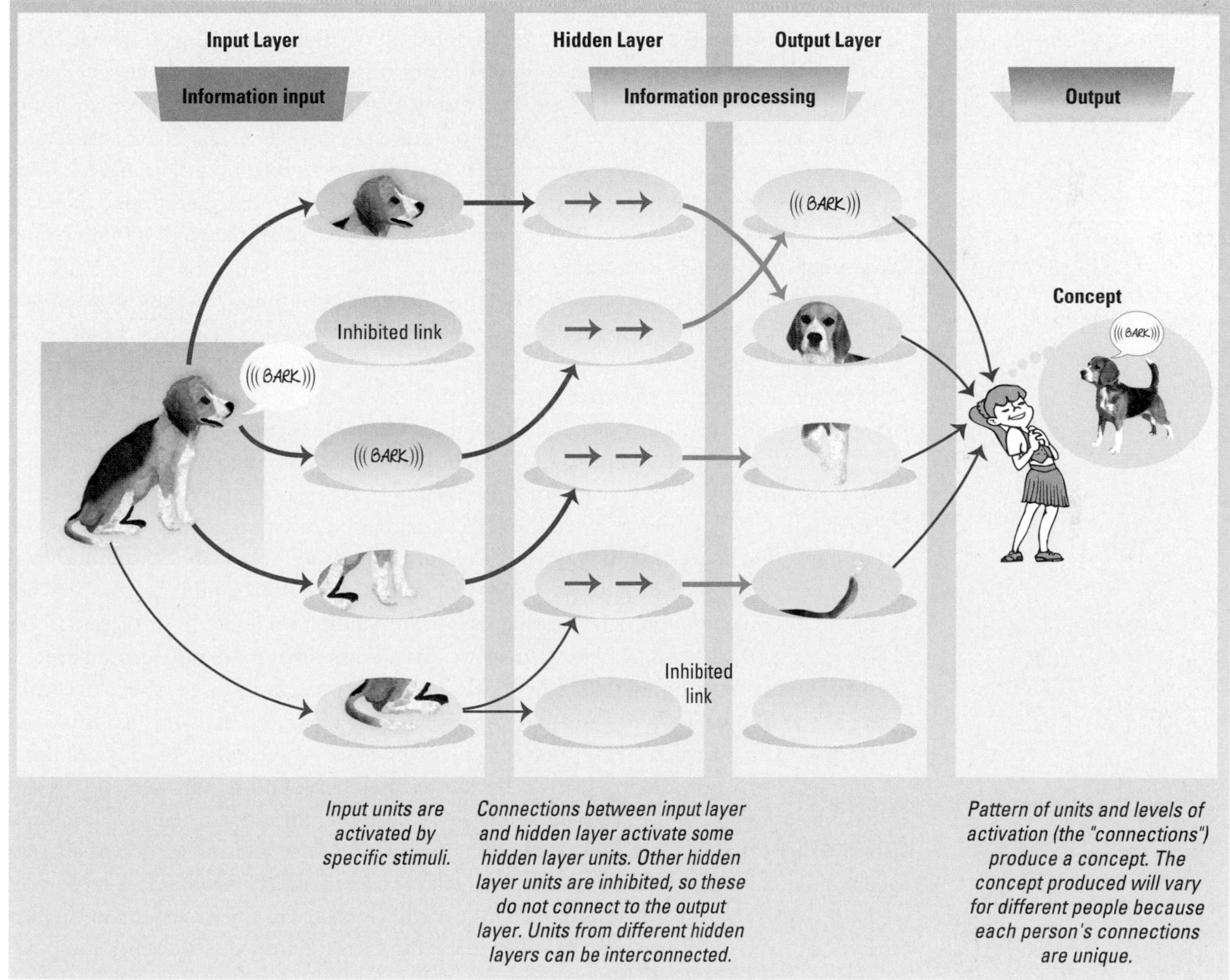


▲ FIGURE 11.5
**A Simple Connectionist Model**
The ovals are the individual units of this model. There are three different layers: an input layer, one hidden layer, and an output layer. The lines with arrows represent the links between individual units, and the different widths of lines represent degrees of strength between particular units. Notice that the input units can connect to all the output units, but not directly. Their connection is mediated by the hidden layers of units.
(Based on Klahr & MacWhinney, 1998, p. 649.)

we can begin to understand changes in human learning (Bates & Elman, 2002; Thomas & Karmiloff-Smith, 2003).

As you might expect, developing connectionist models is quite complex and time consuming, and each model must be specific to a single domain. Models have been developed and tested to investigate the learning processes in such diverse areas as learning second languages, acquiring vocabulary, learning word meanings, solving balance-scale problems, causal reasoning, and even forming emotional attachments (Klahr & MacWhinney, 1998; McClelland & Thompson, 2007; Onnis & Christiansen, 2008; Rodd, Gaskell, & Marslen-Wilson, 2004; Schapiro & McClelland, 2009; Zevin & Seidenberg, 2004).

Fuzzy Trace Theory. Think back to something you did yesterday. Now try to remember something interesting that happened several years ago. Do you remember the exact details of the events, or do you instead recall the general gist and then reconstruct the details? The main idea of **fuzzy trace theory** is that memory representations (or traces) vary on a continuum from very exact and literal traces to imprecise, general, and "fuzzy" traces based on the gist of the message (Brainerd, 2005; Brainerd & Reyna, 1993, 1995, 2004). This view says that people typically do not reason logically from precise, verbatim (or exact) recollections. Instead, we have a strong tendency toward intuitive reasoning based on the main ideas. These fuzzy memory traces are less detailed and are better integrated with our prior knowledge than verbatim traces. Better integration means that there are multiple access and retrieval cues associated with fuzzy traces. As a result, they last longer and are easier to access, less effortful to use, and less susceptible to interference and forgetting than are verbatim traces.

Young children are capable of extracting gist and storing fuzzy memory traces, but they do not do this as consistently as school-age children and adults. As a result, their memory performance is worse. It's not clear why younger children rely on verbatim traces. It is not because they can't extract gist and form fuzzy traces; studies have shown that they have this capability and that there is a gradual shift toward more gist processing during the elementary school years (Brainerd & Gordon, 1994; Brainerd, Holliday, & Reyna, 2004; Reyna & Brainerd, 1995). Perhaps this tendency has to do with younger children's relatively limited knowledge base. To extract the main ideas from an encounter, a child must have some way of identifying what the central aspects are. But until the child has at least a basic script for commonly encountered events, there is no solid basis for knowing what is relevant and important and what is not. As children encounter more variations of common events, they build a knowledge base that allows them to identify central aspects and common and important elements. This more developed knowledge base allows children to identify appropriate gists and store them as fuzzy traces. This in turn improves memory—at least when being "correct" involves recall of meaning based on making connections between common events. Recent research has found that in some situations, older children and adults actually show *more* false memories than younger children (Brainerd, Reyna, & Ceci, 2008). The same knowledge base and integration skills that allow older children and adults to extract gist may lead them to misremember important details, particularly in situations where they are likely to try to infer meaning and when they don't have verbatim memories to suppress the extraction of gist (Odegard, Holliday, Brainerd, & Reyna, 2008).

What does all this mean for the development of memory? Until recently, the answer to this question was straightforward and the implications for situations such as children's eyewitness testimony was clear. Young children are more likely to store verbatim memory traces, which might suggest that younger children would have better memory of specific events than older children. But remember that verbatim memory traces decay and become inaccessible more rapidly than fuzzy traces. Unless careful questioning takes place relatively quickly, the specifics are lost from the verbatim traces. If the questioning is misleading in

**fuzzy trace theory**
The view that memory representations vary on a continuum from exact and literal to imprecise and general memory traces based on the gist of the information or event.

some way, the likelihood of memory errors increases, because verbatim traces are more susceptible to interference. Older children's memories, on the other hand, have more fuzzy traces. Fuzzy traces are more durable and accessible; they are also less susceptible to interference, so they are less likely to be modified as a result of questioning (Ceci & Bruck, 1998; Robinson & Whitcombe, 2003; Roebers, 2002). However, the recent work showing age increases in false memories makes the situation more complicated, and there is still much research to be done. Much of the work showing increases in false memory involves memory for mundane details about everyday events. It is not yet clear whether or how the unusual and often emotionally charged situations that are often under consideration in court cases are affected (Brainerd et al., 2008).

## Information Processing: Where Does It Stand?

Since the early 1960s information processing has become the dominant model for understanding cognitive development. Through its emphasis on detailed analysis of specific cognitive processes, the computer metaphor of "thinking as the processing of information" has greatly increased our understanding of developmental change.

There are limits to this approach, however. The most obvious is that despite the detailed information it has provided, the information-processing approach does not offer a comprehensive, overarching structure for explaining cognitive development like that of Piaget's theory. We know a lot about many specific areas of development, and we have many "toy versions" of the real-life cognitive processes we wish to understand (Klahr & MacWhinney, 1998). Yet no comprehensive theory addresses the whole of cognitive development and how it might be related to other areas of development. Second, the information-processing approach has been described as "cold" cognition because of its emphasis on thoughts based on logical reasoning. Information-processing models rarely consider such factors as social interaction, emotional reactions, or motivation, even though these factors are quite important in real-life cognition. In the past, these models have also been slow to incorporate new information about the biological bases of cognitive development, though newer connectionist models are now attempting to do this. Finally, critics have long pointed out that most information-processing models depend on an "executive processor" (something that oversees all processes and determines the allocation of cognitive resources, strategy use, and the like)—but lack details on how the executive works or develops. Both fuzzy trace theory and connectionist models, which explain change without the need for an executive processor, address this criticism. In recent years, research on cognitive development has moved increasingly away from a computer metaphor for human thought and more toward computational models (Cassimatis, Bello, & Langley, 2008).

### LET'S REVIEW . . .

**1.** Children who were chess experts were compared to adults who were chess novices. What differences were found in their memory for chess pieces?

**a.** Child novices remembered as many chess pieces as adult novices.
**b.** Child experts remembered fewer chess pieces than adult experts.
**c.** Child experts remembered as many chess pieces as adult novices.
**d.** Child experts remembered more chess pieces than adult novices.

**2.** As children's knowledge bases increase, they tend to do all of the following, except ___________.

**a.** use information-processing strategies more effectively
**b.** organize information into smaller "chunks" or pieces of information
**c.** notice details about and relationships among pieces of information
**d.** encode, store, and retrieve information more quickly

3. Neural networks are an example of a __________.
   a. production system
   b. fuzzy trace model
   c. stores model
   d. connectionist model
4. Fuzzy traces tend to be:
   a. remembered longer than memories that are exact and precise.
   b. remembered for less time than memories that are exact and precise.
   c. remembered about as long as memories that are exact and precise.
   d. more effortful to use than memories that are exact and precise.
5. True or False: In connectionist models, learning is represented by changes in the weights of the links among units in the model.
6. True or False: The connectionist and fuzzy trace theories both say there is an executive processor that directs ongoing cognitive activity.

Answers: 1. d, 2. b, 3. d, 4. a, 5. T, 6. F

## Learning to Communicate: Language in Middle Childhood

Language development during early childhood is quite impressive, but it is far from complete by the time a child enters school. The middle childhood years see development in several important areas of language.

AS YOU STUDY THIS SECTION, ASK YOURSELF THESE QUESTIONS:

**11.11** What language skills do children develop between 7 and 11 years of age?

**11.12** How do 7- to 11-year-olds differ from younger children in their knowledge about and their use of language?

**11.13** What are connectionist models of language development, and what evidence supports these approaches?

### Experts in the Basics

*Semantic* knowledge, or what words mean, continues to increase dramatically over middle childhood. While a typical 2-year-old knows about 200 words and a 6-year-old about 10,000, the vocabulary of a typical 10-year-old contains about 40,000 words—and this grows to about 80,000 words by high school age (Anglin, 1993; McLaughlin, 2006). The kinds of words that older children acquire are more abstract words such as *irony* or *justice* because increases in cognitive development allow them to better understand these abstract concepts (Hulit & Howard, 2006; McGhee-Bidlack, 1991). *Phonemic* development (knowing about basic speech sounds) continues as well. As children enter elementary school, they begin to master more difficult phonemes such as *j* or *th*. During middle childhood, children continue to show increased understanding of how to use intonation (or tone of voice) to change the meaning of utterances. For example, a sentence such as "Rachel took a bracelet from Mom and she took one from Lily" can have two different meanings, depending on whether *and* or *she* is emphasized.

**metalinguistic awareness**
A person's explicit knowledge about language itself and about his or her own use of it.

**personal narratives**
Stories about personal experiences that use language to inform others about the self and that provide increased self-understanding.

The school-age years also see increases in children's mastery of grammar and *syntax* (rules for combining words into sentences). For example, English-speaking preschool children rarely use the passive voice in their speech, and show only incomplete understanding when they hear it. Sentences such as "The dog was patted by the girl" or "Donald was liked by Goofy" are quite difficult for young children and are likely to be understood as "The dog patted the girl" and "Donald liked Goofy." At ages 8 or 9, however, children begin to produce full passive sentences, though some forms of the passive voice remain difficult throughout middle childhood (Bever, 1970; Horgan, 1978; Maratsos, Kuczaj, Fox, & Chalkley, 1979). However, this sequence of grammatical development is not universal. In languages in which the passive voice is more important and frequent, such as the Southern African language Sesotho, it is understood and used correctly much earlier (by 2 to 4 years of age) (Demuth, 1990; Tomasello, 2006). By 9 to 11 years of age, children are also able to draw inferences from what they hear or read and recognize that the inferred information was not directly stated. The ability to draw inferences is essential for understanding and producing many of the more subtle uses of language, including sarcasm, humor, or metaphor (Casteel, 1993; Dews et al., 1996).

Children's *pragmatic* language skills (using language to effectively interact with others) continue to improve throughout middle childhood. Referential communication skills improve from early childhood such that older children are now able to spontaneously identify and correct ambiguities in their own and others' speech, and they are able to take effective steps to correct the ambiguities (Beal & Belgrad, 1990; Girbau, 2001; Kemper & Vernoog, 1994). Children of this age are also becoming much more skilled in the social rules of discourse. Just listen to any 10-year-old child on the phone with her friends and it's clear that they know how to have successful conversations!

## Metalinguistic Awareness and Changes in How Language Is Used

One of the most notable features of language development during the middle childhood years is the increase in **metalinguistic awareness**, or the explicit knowledge about language itself and one's own use of it (McLaughlin, 2006). Metalinguistic awareness is the result of a great deal of experience with using language along with increases in cognitive abilities, and it contributes to a number of linguistic skills. For example, one aspect of metalinguistic awareness is the understanding that a single word can have multiple meanings. This enables children to use language more flexibly and even to create and appreciate humor based on different word meanings. Metalinguistic awareness also helps children self-monitor and self-correct the speech they produce and receive, which means they can communicate more effectively. Finally, explicit knowledge of the social rules of discourse helps children have more effective and socially acceptable conversations. Not surprisingly, a higher level of metalinguistic awareness at early ages is related to higher reading ability in school (McBride-Chang, 1996; Warren-Leubecker & Carter, 1988; Zipke, 2007).

THINKING CRITICALLY

Evaluate your own metalinguistic awareness. How does this awareness affect your ability to use language effectively? How might you increase your level of metalinguistic awareness?

During middle childhood, children not only develop a more complete and explicit understanding of language, they also begin to use language in different ways. Preschool children play with language, creating nonsense words that rhyme or adding letters or syllables to create words that express strong feelings, such as "icky" or "gooey" (Ely & McCabe, 1994). School-age children continue to create words in this way, and they also begin to show a great interest in riddles and other forms of verbal humor. These kinds of language play require a more advanced understanding of language rules, especially the understanding that word meanings and syntax can be ambiguous (Ely, 1997; Ely & McCabe, 1994).

▲ These children are using their language skills to tell jokes and understand humor. How does their metalinguistic awareness help them enjoy riddles and jokes?

Finally, older children begin to use language to describe and understand important aspects of themselves. **Personal narratives** are stories about the storyteller's experiences. They involve the use of language to inform others about the self, as well as using language as a tool for increased self-understanding. While even 2-year-olds are able to give rudimentary narratives, it is during middle childhood that children become able to provide coherent narratives that fully describe and evaluate their personal experiences. For example, 4-year-olds' personal narratives tend to have a *leap-frog* structure in which they jump from one topic to another without giving a complete account of what

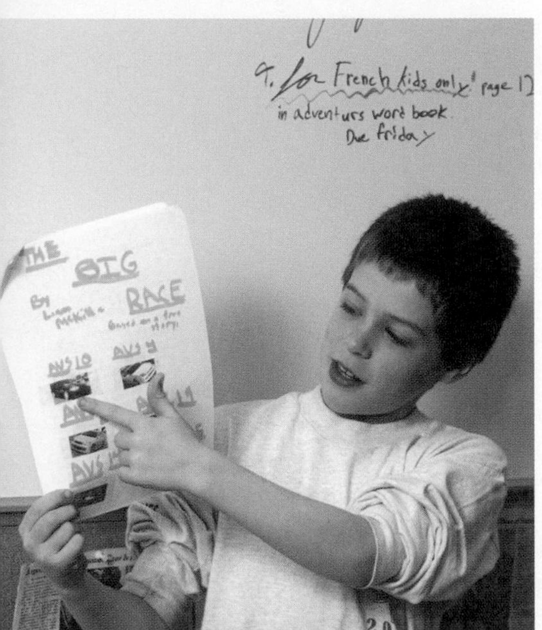


▲ Children use personal narratives to discover and communicate things about themselves. What do you think this child is communicating in his personal narrative?

**THINK ABOUT LINDA AND GIANLUCA . . .**
What are some ways in which Gianluca could use narratives to help himself understand and remember information from texts more effectively?

happened and how they felt about it. Between 4 and 8 years of age, personal narratives often have more of a *chronological* structure in which the storyteller reports a sequence of events without adding details or evaluating the events. By the age of 8 or 9, children show a *classic narrative* structure in which the story leads up to a main event (called the high point), an evaluation of how the storyteller feels about the event is offered, and then the event is resolved. Narrative skills are strong predictors of later language and literacy skills, and educational television programs can help children learn the classic narrative structure. The evaluation aspect of personal narratives will continue to increase in complexity and variety throughout adolescence (Berman & Slobin, 1994; Engel, 1995; Peterson & McCabe, 1983; Uchikoshi, 2005).

However, the preferred style of a personal narrative varies depending upon the child's culture. In addition to helping children better understand themselves, personal narratives serve to help children come to know and understand their broader cultures (Bliss & McCabe, 2008; Gee, 1992). For example, Hispanic children's narratives have been found to focus more on family relationships, while Japanese children's narratives include events that are related to a central theme rather than by time, place, or family membership. The narratives of middle- and working-class white children in North America typically focus on a single topic, while working-class African-American children tell personal narratives that are longer and include several different characters and events linked by a general theme (Ely, 1997; Michaels, 1991; Minami & McCabe, 1990). The different narrative styles reflect the values and structure of their respective cultures, and thus are one way in which language helps children come to understand the central aspects of their cultures in a very personal way.

## Connectionist Models of Language Development

In Chapter 5, we talked about several main theories of language development—the learning theory (based primarily on Skinner's operant conditioning principles and proposing that language is a learned skill), the nativist view (based on Chomsky and others' theory that language is largely a biologically programmed skill in humans), and interaction theories (with some, like Piaget, emphasizing the role of cognitive factors and others emphasizing the role of social interactions for language acquisition).

A more recent and very intriguing cognitive approach to understanding language development is based on the *connectionist models* of cognition you read about in the last section. Recall that connectionist models are neural network models in which links of varying strengths connect simple elements called *units*. Applied to language development, connectionist models say that language acquisition results from changes in the strengths of connections between units based on how closely the language produced matches external criteria. For example, imagine that a boy sees an animal that looks a lot like the animal he associates with the word *dog*. Units corresponding to characteristics of the input (the dog) stimulate the pattern of connections the boy has developed for these input features in the past, so he says, "Look at that dog." But his dad says, "Wow, look at that coyote—right in our yard!" Even though the father is not explicitly correcting his son's utterance, he is providing a model by using a specific word consistently for the new animal. As the boy continues to encounter the animal (by seeing it, seeing pictures of it, talking or thinking about it) and hear the same name, the links between the units that produce *dog* will decrease in strength, and those that lead to the production of the word *coyote* will increase. Eventually, he will come to call this animal a coyote.

The strongest support for connectionism comes from computer simulations. Researchers presented verbs to a computer with the same frequency that children typically encounter them in everyday language. Even though the computer never received and did not learn any explicit rules, it gradually learned to produce correct past tenses for both regular and irregular verbs, and it showed patterns of acquiring past tenses that were quite similar to those of children (Rumelhart & McClelland, 1986). Even more convincing are the findings that the simulation showed the same kinds of error patterns as children—and that the connectionist model successfully predicts which specific grammatical cues (such as word endings or word order) children will acquire first in specific languages. Some "lesioned" connectionist models have even been able successfully simulate children's patterns of language recovery after brain damage—an interesting computer simulation of developmental resilience (MacWhinney, 1987, 1999; Li, Zhao, & MacWhinney, 2007). However, critics argue that language development based on gradual changes in connection strengths would take far longer than it actually does for real children. A related criticism is that children often learn new words after a single exposure to them. Such *one-trial learning* can be difficult for these models to explain.

## LET'S REVIEW . . .

**1.** Which of the following children is showing metalinguistic awareness?
   **a.** Andy, who knows that *hammer* can be both a thing and an action.
   **b.** Will, who knows how to use a *hammer*.
   **c.** Rachel, who knows that *hammer* means to hit something.
   **d.** Lily, who knows that both *hammers* and *mallets* can be used to pound things.

**2.** Personal narratives are important in language development primarily because they __________.
   **a.** indicate a child's level of semantic development
   **b.** force the child to use more complex grammatical structures
   **c.** allow the child to use language to inform others about the self
   **d.** provide a way for parents to offer explicit feedback about social rules of language use

**3.** True or False: Children do not understand correct use of the passive voice in grammar until well into the middle childhood years regardless of the language they speak.

**4.** True or False: Connectionist models of language development say that children must receive direct and explicit feedback in order to learn language.

Answers: 1. a, 2. c, 3. F, 4. F

# Cognition in Context

The first sections of this chapter presented information about the development of children's cognitive skills during middle childhood. But an important part of children's lives during middle childhood involves learning in school. How do children use their cognitive abilities to deal with academic tasks? This section will discuss the development of mathematical, reading, and writing skills. Our descriptions begin with the foundations laid down during infancy and early childhood and continue past the middle childhood years, but we have included this broader range of ages in this chapter because of the importance of these academic skills in the middle childhood years.

AS YOU STUDY THIS SECTION, ASK YOURSELF THESE QUESTIONS:

**11.14** What mathematical competencies and limitations do children of different ages typically show?

**11.15** What are some important factors that predict reading skill?

**11.16** What are the major accomplishments that children achieve as they learn to write?

## Development of Mathematical Skills

**Laying the Foundation for Mathematical Skills.** Amazing but true: Researchers have found evidence that even *newborns* have rudimentary mathematical skills. Humans seem to be "born with a fundamental sense of quantity" (Geary, 1994, p. 1). For example, researchers showed newborn infants (less than one week old!) a card with two black dots (Antell & Keating, 1983). The newborns looked at the dots for a bit, then started looking away. Looking away signals boredom; in Chapter 5 we referred to this as *habituation.* When researchers then switched to a card that had three dots, the newborns regained interest in looking at the dots—they *dishabituated.* These patterns of habituation and dishabituation show that newborns can see the difference between two and three dots.

How are infants able to show such skills? They clearly cannot count objects. They have no experience with a number system, and they don't have the language skills they need to say the words that go with the numbers. Researchers propose that infants enumerate small sets by **subitizing**, a perceptual process that we all use to quickly and easily determine the basic quantity in a small set of objects. To see how subitizing works, try the following experiment. Have your friend toss three or four pennies onto a table while you have your eyes closed. Now open your eyes and, as quickly as you can, look to see how many pennies there are. Most people can "see" that there are three pennies, or four pennies, without needing to actually count each penny. There is something about the visual arrangement of the pennies that lets you know immediately how many there are.

During the preschool years, children *learn to count.* At about the age of 2, children begin to associate the counting words used in their language with the correct number of objects. By about 4 years of age, they begin to use counting as a tool to solve simple arithmetic problems rather than rely on subitizing. This represents an important advance in their mathematical skills—a child can use counting with sets of any size and in the absence of concrete objects, whereas subitizing works only with small sets and visible objects. Children quickly begin to use several different **counting strategies**, approaches to solving problems that involve counting of the quantities. For example: A child figures out that $2 + 2 = 4$ by first counting to 2 and then counting on (2 more steps) to 3 and then 4. Preschoolers learn to solve simple problems whether the change in number is visible to them, screened from their view, or even described verbally in the absence of any concrete objects. Gradually, over the later preschool and elementary school years, children increase the complexity and sophistication of their counting strategies (Aunola, Leskinen, Lerkkanen, & Nurmi, 2004 ; Geary, 2006).

**subitizing**
A perceptual process in which people quickly and easily determine how many objects are in a small set without actually counting them.

**counting strategies**
Approaches to solving math problems that involve counting of the quantities.

**strategy choice model**
The idea that children solve math problems by choosing the fastest approach that they can execute accurately.

**Watch** Hands-On Learning in Elementary Math.
www.mydevelopmentlab.com

**Mathematical Skills during the Elementary School Years.** Over the course of the elementary school years, the counting strategies children use to solve addition and subtraction problems gradually become more efficient. Table 11.2 shows some of these strategies. Younger children tend to use strategies that require more counting. This is cumbersome and increases the opportunity for errors, but it reduces the burden on their working memory. As children gain experience, they tend to move to strategies that require more memory but can be executed more quickly. Children begin to store basic math facts and simply retrieve them from memory instead of relying on counting strategies. Once a child has memorized a fact, he or she has a tool for deriving the answers to other, nonmemorized problems. For example, given the problem $5 + 8$, a child who knows that $5 + 5 = 10$ may use this known fact, reason that 8 is 3 more than 5, and add 3 to 10 to obtain the answer 13 (Ashcraft, 1992; for reviews, see Geary, 1994, and Ginsburg, Klein, & Starkey, 1998). **Watch on mydevelopmentlab**

How do elementary school children memorize and retrieve math facts? One possibility is the **strategy choice model** (Siegler & Jenkins, 1989). According to this model, "Children tend to choose the fastest approach that they can execute accurately" (Siegler, 1998, p. 286). Using a fast strategy increases the likelihood that the problem and answer

**TABLE 11.2**
**Examples of Common Counting Strategies for Addition**

| STRATEGY | EXAMPLE PROBLEM | USE OF STRATEGY |
|---|---|---|
| Counting manipulatives | 2 + 5 | Child counts two manipulatives (e.g., blocks, coins, candies), then counts five more manipulatives, then counts all seven objects. |
| Counting fingers | 2 + 5 | Child raises two fingers on one hand, then five on the other hand. Child then counts all seven fingers one at a time, moving each one as it is counted. |
| Counting all (sum) | 2 + 5 | Child counts the first number aloud "1, 2." Child then continues counting on by the second number "3, 4, 5, 6, 7"—then states the answer as "7." |
| Counting on from first | 2 + 5 | Child states the first number "2"; counts on by the second number "3, 4, 5, 6, 7"; then states the answer as "7." |
| Counting on from larger (also called minimum strategy or min) | 2 + 5 | Child states the biggest number, regardless of whether it is first or second. Here, the child says "5," then counts on by the smaller number ("6, 7"), then states the answer as "7." |
| Decomposition (deriving a fact) | 7 + 6 | Child decomposes the 6 into "3 + 3", adds 7 + 3 and gets 10, adds the other 3 to 10, and gives the answer: 13. (The child could choose to decompose the other number, 7, into 4 + 3 , add 4 + 6 to get 10, then add the remaining 3 to 10.) |
| Fact retrieval | 2 + 5 | Child retrieves the answer from long-term memory and states the answer as "7." |
| Regrouping | 16 + 23 | Child decomposes both numbers into tens and ones (16 = 10 + 6; 23 = 20 + 3), sums the tens and ones separately (10 + 20 = 30; 6 + 3 = 9), adds the subtotals (30 + 9 = 39), states answer: 39. |

(Adapted from Geary, 1994.)

will both be present in working memory, and therefore increases their degree of association. Using the most accurate strategy helps ensure that the association will develop between the problem and its *correct* answer. The more often a correct answer (e.g., 7) is associated with a problem (e.g., 4 + 3), the stronger the association between them and the more likely that the child will retrieve this answer on future occasions. If the degree of association is not strong, the child will use a *backup strategy* such as counting, guessing, or deriving an answer based on known facts or rules. According to the strategy choice model, discouraging children from using backup strategies (like counting on their fingers) may actually *delay* their memorizing basic math facts (Siegler, 1998). Can you explain why?

Though children gradually move from less to more efficient strategies, they do not rely on a single strategy for solving arithmetic problems. Instead, they consistently use a variety of strategies. The strategy choice model helps explain why. The availability of multiple strategies increases the likelihood that a child can obtain a correct answer quickly. This helps the child succeed in solving problems and helps build strong associations between problems and their correct answers. Researchers have found evidence of multiple strategies for a variety of arithmetic operations and across a wide range of student ages, abilities, and nationalities (Fuson & Kwon, 1992; Geary, 1996; LeFevre & Bisanz, 1996; Mabbott & Bisanz, 2003).

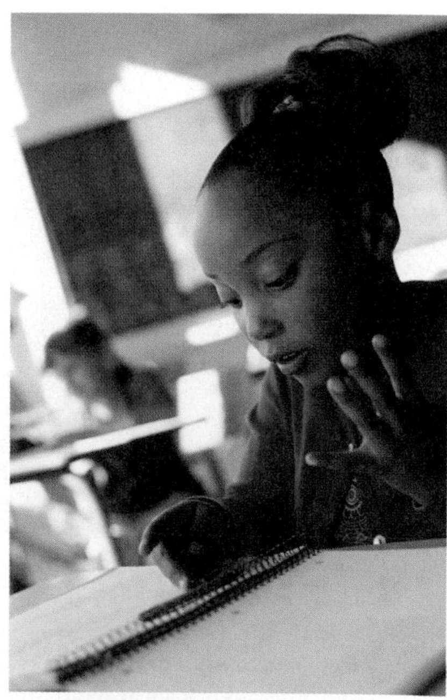

▲ When solving addition and subtraction problems, should children be allowed to use back-up strategies such as counting on their fingers?

For better or worse, elementary school children spend many hours working on mathematical *word problems*, or verbal descriptions of mathematical situations. As you may recall from personal experience, word problems can cause even the best math students to groan with dread. Several factors contribute to the difficulty of a word problem—among them the

THINKING CRITICALLY

Do you enjoy solving mathematical word problems? How are your mathematical problem-solving efforts affected by problem context and the types of relations in the problem?

THINK ABOUT LINDA AND GIANLUCA . . .

Do you think that Gianluca's reading difficulties might affect his performance in other areas, like math or science? Could Linda use Gianluca's interests or strengths in other areas to help improve his reading skills?

Listen: How is it possible to use a constructivist approach to teaching mathematics? (Author Podcast) www.mydevelopmentlab.com

number of words in the problem, the number of required arithmetic operations, and the number of mathematical terms. The context of the problem has an important effect as well. Sometimes problems are difficult because their content is simply not interesting to the child, their wording is confusing, or their context is unfamiliar. In one study, for example, Brazilian children experienced at selling products at street stands were quite good at solving word problems that had a "selling" context, even when the items named in the problems were not ones they had sold. Their performance was much worse when problems did not have the sales context, even though the required computations were identical to those in the other problems (Carraher, Carraher, & Schliemann, 1985). Unfamiliar details and situations may not provide effective cues to help children access and use relevant knowledge, or they may simply overload working memory. With familiar contexts, children have a greater chance of comprehending the situation being described, understanding what they are being asked to figure out, and being motivated to solve the problem (Mayer, Lewis, & Hegarty, 1992; Stern, 1993; Vlahovic-Štetic, Rovan, & Mendek, 2004).

Children continue to increase their knowledge of basic mathematical principles throughout their school years, although some principles take a long time to develop (Geary, 2006). Sometimes misunderstandings of fundamental math principles lead to *bugs*, or systematic errors in children's problem-solving procedures. Buggy procedures are common in all arithmetic operations, and they can persist well into the late elementary school years. During the later part of middle childhood, children begin to learn about more complex math topics such as fractions, geometry, and algebra. As they do so, they consistently attempt to build new understanding on what they already know. At times this leads to misunderstandings of new principles; but when students recognize their mistakes, they begin to debug their math knowledge and understand the accurate procedures. Instruction that builds on prior knowledge is typically more effective in helping students understand new mathematical concepts. In contrast, instruction that focuses on memorization of facts and rules gives students less opportunity to work out their buggy procedures. As a result, mistakes can take longer to correct (Clement, 1982). **Listen** on **mydevelopmentlab**

## Development of Reading Skills

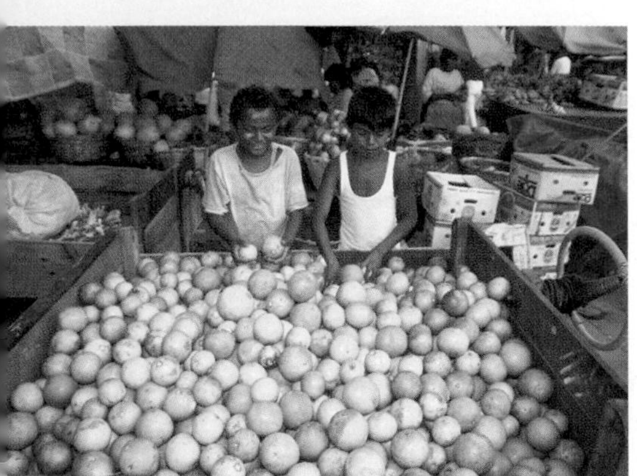

▲ These young street vendors show a great deal of math skill when they are calculating prices and making change for customers. With the traditional math problems that are used in classrooms, however, they will likely show much less skill. Context has a powerful effect on children's math problem-solving ability.

Reading is perhaps the single most important academic skill we acquire. Western cultures tend to be reading- and writing-based, so we get much of our knowledge and information through books, magazines, newspapers, instruction manuals, the Internet and television, and other print media. An expert on reading development, Jeanne Chall, surmised that "the learning and uses of literacy are among the most advanced forms of intelligence, and, compared to other forms, depend more on instruction and practice" (1983, p. 2). Chall (1983) proposed six developmental stages that describe how children typically learn to read, as summarized in Table 11.3. Chall commented that many adults may never reach the most mature stage of reading, even after four years of college.

In fact, too many people have trouble reaching even Chall's fourth stage, "Reading for New Learning." Researchers estimate that in the United States, 25% of people are poor readers and 36% of fourth graders score below the basic reading level for their grade (Adams, Treiman, & Pressley, 1998; Donahue, Voelkl, Campbell, & Mazzeo, 1999; Perie, Grigg, & Donahue, 2005). To see how volunteers can help children and adults overcome illiteracy, read the Personal Perspective box on page 352 called "Meet a Literacy Volunteer."

Two of the factors that best predict success in early reading are *familiarity with letters of the alphabet* and *phonemic awareness* (Adams et al., 1998; Leppänen, Aunola, Niemi, & Nurmi, 2008). Preschoolers who show early familiarity with letters tend to be more successful in

**TABLE 11.3**
**Chall's Six Developmental Stages in Reading**

| STAGE & AGE RANGE | DESCRIPTION OF ACTIVITIES AND SKILLS |
|---|---|
| *Prereading:* Birth to kindergarten | Parents "read" to infants and toddlers by pointing to and naming objects and colors in books and reading simple stories. Many 3-year-olds pretend to read—flipping through pages, reciting memorized stories, and creating their own stories as they point to words and pictures. By the time children enter kindergarten many of them can recite the alphabet, recognize written letters, and print their own names. These are examples of prereading skills that lay the foundation for further development. |
| *Reading/Decoding:* Grades 1–2 | Children learn to associate letters with their corresponding sounds. Using *phonics*, children sound out letters, decoding the word that is formed when they run the sounds together. With the *whole word method*, children recognize words based on context, pictures, and the shapes of the words. Readers at this stage often focus on individual words and phrases and miss the larger meaning of the story. |
| *Fluency:* Grades 2–3 | Children become more fluent in recognizing or decoding words. Rereading familiar books and reading stories with familiar or stereotyped structures, children gain speed, fluency, and confidence in their reading ability. Chall (1983) commented that children are "learning to read" by associating printed words with stories they already know and understand. |
| *Reading for New Learning:* Grades 4–8 | Fluency with words allows children to move to less familiar material. With the decoding load reduced, children can focus on meaning and messages, gaining a new way to learn new information. Fourth graders typically begin using books and printed materials to study subject areas such as science, history, and geography. In this stage children are "reading to learn," focusing on fact-based information. |
| *Multiple Viewpoints:* High school | Adolescents move beyond basic facts. They begin to appreciate layers of information representing different viewpoints or theories. *Examples:* History texts might describe events from differing perspectives; biology can be discussed at the cellular, organismic, and ecological levels. School assignments and free-reading of more mature fiction and nonfiction facilitate this development. |
| *Construction and Reconstruction:* College and adulthood | Mature readers can read multiple sources, opinions, and views and then construct their own understanding. They read to suit their purposes, whether it's to gain understanding, for entertainment, or to consider views of others. They decide how fast or to deeply to read and when to gloss, skim, or attend to detail. They know what *not* to read as well as what to read in order to suit their purposes. |

reading through the primary grades. In contrast, preschoolers who are less familiar with letters tend to have more difficulty learning to read. Children whose primary language is not English tend to be less familiar with letters and have greater difficulty learning to read in English in school. Reading difficulty really emerges, however, when children cannot blend the printed letters together to form whole words.

**Phonemic awareness** is the understanding that words are made up of smaller units of sound, or *phonemes*. This understanding involves associating printed letters with the sounds that go with them. Phonemic awareness usually begins developing during the first year of formal schooling as children learn to make the speech sounds associated with each letter and with various letter combinations. Success with phonemic awareness is a strong predictor of later reading success—even stronger than the child's overall IQ (Adams et al., 1998; Eldredge, 2005; Spira, Bracken, & Fischel, 2005; Strattman & Hodson, 2005; Vellutino & Scanlon, 1987). A major source of reading weakness is difficulty in decoding (or breaking down) printed words into their individual speech sounds. Instructional activities that emphasize phonemic awareness can facilitate reading growth. Even during the preschool years, play with letters and letter sounds is helpful. Popular TV programs like *Sesame Street* show young children how to link sounds to letters and to blend speech

**phonemic awareness**
The understanding that words are made up of smaller units of sound; also, association of printed letters with the sounds that go with them.

# Perspective PERSONAL — MEET A LITERACY VOLUNTEER

Vivian Dobrinsky
Boston, MA
*A Volunteer with Jumpstart Literacy Programs*

**Would you briefly tell us about Jumpstart and the kinds of children you serve?**
Jumpstart's goal is to build literacy, language, social, and initiative skills in young children. Motivated college students, called Corps members, work with preschool children for an entire school year, meeting twice a week for two hours at the children's preschools. During one-to-one reading, the children pick a book they want to read, and either the Corps member or the child read (or "read," in the child's case) the book. Corps members use creative strategies to help the children think critically about what they were reading, engage their interest, and introduce them to various components of reading such as noticing letters or words on a page. We have circle time where all the Corps members and children sing songs, read a book together, or to do a quick activity. There is also a choice time where four pre-planned and prepared choices are made available for the children. Throughout the sessions, Corps members work to help children build self-confidence and initiative, literacy, and problem solving skills.

**Why did you decide to become involved in this program?**
At first I joined Jumpstart because I thought it would look good on my resume and that it would give me more teaching experience. However, as I learned more about Jumpstart, I realized what an amazing opportunity it was to be able to work with a child one-to-one and to make a difference in her life. I realized how important early intervention is and how valuable it was to show a child the importance of what she was learning *and* to show her what an important person she was. I also found myself agreeing with Jumpstart's philosophy. Nothing was done for the child or forced on the child. Activities were child-initiated and the process of learning and growing was deemed more important than the product. The strategies we used honored each child's individuality and let each progress at his/her own pace. The partnership between Corps member and child was to enable the child to be independent, to develop confidence, and to help her grow in various areas Being able to help a child learn important skills such as reading or problem solving is an amazing experience. Teaching these skills to young children is providing them with lifelong foundations and tools for success. Without these basic essential skills, it is incredibly hard for a child to grow and feel confident in him/herself.

**What are some of the specific things you do to help children learn to read?**
The first step is actually to read with them and instill an enjoyment of reading. Children need to have an interest, a desire to read, and also to understand the purpose of reading. We try to provide books having to do with the child's interests. We use fun voices and props (such as a puppet or story felt board) to help tell the story. I also often ask for a child to "read" to me. By practicing the act of "reading" the images on a page, a child begins to understand books, which will eventually lead to reading words. I also make books with the children. When they feel the accomplishment of writing their own story, they often become more interested in books around them. While copying words or writing their names, I often sound out each letter as they write. By making the children aware of the sounds that each letter makes, they begin to understand how letters and sounds can be put together to make words—this helps them in reading, as well as writing and general speaking abilities. Jumpstart uses the Dialogic Reading method, and I learned several specific techniques that are part of this method. For example, the acronym PEER stands for Prompt, Evaluate, Expand, and Recall; and CROWD stands for Completion, Repeating, Open-ended questions, Wh-questions, and Distancing. These techniques help adults engage children in a shared reading experience that builds vocabulary and other language and literacy skills, and they help the adult understand the child's thought process.

**What advice do you have for others who are interested in a literacy program?**
Be ready for anything. The child you are working with may not be interested in books at the beginning but with hard work and creativity you can change a child's perceptions of books. Also, find ways to engage the child's interests such as using open-ended and thoughtful questions, or using puppets to act out the plotline. Work at the child's pace and remember that the process is much more important than the product. The purpose isn't for a child to be able to read, but for a child to be motivated to *want* to read and to develop the underlying skills that support later literacy. Once a child is motivated, it will be much easier for him/her to learn. If a child is interested in just one page of a book and wants to spend 15 minutes on just that one page, it is important to follow the child's lead.

QUESTION **What effects might programs like this one have on young children's literacy skills? Do you think such programs can help children become "smarter"? Explain your reasoning.**

sounds (e.g., "Today's program is brought to you by the letter *T* as in *Toy, Tiger,* and *Teddy*").

Once children develop phonemic awareness, it is important that they pick up speed in recognizing whole words: They need to *automatize* their recognition of words (Eldredge, 2005). Strong readers quickly learn to recognize words, increasing their reading fluency. Reitsma (1983, 1989) studied second graders who were reading at and below grade level. After accomplished readers reread and decoded unfamiliar words a few times, they became significantly faster at recognizing those words. Less accomplished readers, however, showed little or no gain in recognition speed. When children fail to automatize word recognition, they must continue to decode words by sounding out the individual letters and speech sounds. The decoding process occupies a great deal of processing capacity, so struggling readers have less capacity available to attend to meaning and get less out of their reading. These kinds of decoding and automaticity difficulties are common in children with learning disabilities in reading.

▲ As children become more accomplished readers, they become better at understanding the meaning of text and considering different interpretations. How has automaticity in reading enabled this child to enjoy reading to her class?

In sum, when it comes to reading, "the rich get richer." Children with strong decoding skills and phonemic awareness are better able to sound out words. With repeated exposures, they automatize their word recognition. This makes it easier for them to read—and as a result they tend to read more. Increased reading further enhances their reading skills; it also exposes them to a broader array of knowledge and information, which, in turn, facilitates their cognitive development. When you consider all that we can learn through reading, you can see why it is critically important that children get off to a good start in the early reading stages (see Adams et al., 1998, for a review).

In recent years, there has been a great deal of neuroscience research on reading (Schlaggar & McCandliss, 2007). Initially, the focus was on describing the neural basis of skilled reading and identifying differences between skilled readers and those with reading disabilities. Researchers are now starting to focus on changes in neural processing as reading skill develops. Thus far, this body of work indicates that visual and phonological (sound) properties of words are processed in different areas of the brain, but that specific neural circuits between the occipital and temporal lobes develop as the visual and sound properties of words are experienced together. With increased skill in reading, activation patterns shift to a greater localization in specific areas within the left hemisphere. Adult readers with dyslexia (one type of reading disability) show less activation in these connecting areas, and one study found that successful reading intervention resulted in patterns of activation similar to nondisabled readers (Eden et al., 2004). Different locations in the brain are involved in processing different languages, depending on the visual properties of the written symbols. For example, there are higher levels of activation in areas involved in visual attention and visuospatial processing when reading Chinese (in which characters are related to syllables) than when reading English (in which letters are related to sounds). Even more interesting is the finding that Chinese individuals with dyslexia show reduced brain activation in areas involved in processing Chinese but *not* in areas typically involved in processing English (Siok, Niu, Jin, Perfetti, & Tan, 2008). This leads to "the intriguing question of whether dyslexic readers in one language would be typical readers in another" (Varma, McCandliss, & Schwartz, 2008, pg. 147). While neuroscientists have learned much about the neural basics of connecting letters with sounds and processing single words, they are only beginning to investigate the complicated interactions involved in processing and comprehending longer texts (Varma et al., 2008).

**THINK ABOUT LINDA AND GIANLUCA . . .**
What effect do you think that reading practice has had on Ginaluca's neural connections? In turn, how have these neural changes affected his reading skills?

## Development of Writing Skills

You probably know from experience that reading and writing skills are highly correlated (Spivey & King, 1989). Children who learn the alphabet early, become skilled decoders, and automatize word recognition will later have a strong foundation for spelling and some of the other mechanics of writing. Also, children who can read and synthesize text from multiple perspectives will likely write more effectively because they can keep the perspective of the audience in mind. Furthermore, both reading and writing show similar developmental progressions. That is, children move from early mastery of the alphabet, to greater fluency and confidence with words and language, to greater sophistication in comprehension and the ability to use reading and writing to suit their purposes or fulfill their goals. In this section we outline some of the major accomplishments that children achieve in the writing process as they move from the early phases of inventive spelling to the more mature phase of successful revision.

**Inventive Spelling.** In the early phases of writing, children struggle to learn spelling. Before they memorize conventional word spellings, they frequently invent their own made-up versions, a process called **inventive** (sometimes called *invented*) **spellings**. For example, a beginner might write *two* as *tu* or *sometimes* as *sumtyms.* We are all painfully aware of the myriad complexities, letter blends, and spelling exceptions that exist in English. Schools today generally accept and encourage inventive spelling, teaching beginners to focus more on their meaning and message than on writing mechanics. Research indicates that inventive spelling does not interfere with children's ability to learn to correctly spell words later on. Instead, as children construct their own spellings, they gain practice with letter sounds and blends, enhancing their phonemic awareness. The use of inventive spelling therefore correlates with later success in conventional spelling, word recognition, and reading fluency (Adams et al., 1998; Ouellette & Sénéchal, 2008; Uhry & Shepard, 1993).

**Mechanics and Intermediate Writing.** During the elementary school years, children gradually learn conventional spellings and begin to form increasingly complex sentence structures. In the earlier grades children must devote most of their processing capacity to the technical requirements of writing: spelling, capitalization, punctuation, and the formation of complete sentences. Children tend to write from an egocentric perspective—they have a difficult time keeping the needs of the reader in mind. Organization also tends to be lacking. Beginning writers tend to engage in **knowledge telling**, a strategy in which children simply add ideas to their essays as they come to mind (Bereiter & Scardamalia, 1987). Even high school and college writers show this strategy, in fact. It seems that many assignments in formal education encourage students to "dump in" all they know about a topic. Few assignments require or encourage students to write creatively, so children often rely on rudimentary and stereotyped structures during this intermediate phase of their writing development. As children gain more experience and knowledge about the writing process (including better understanding of their writing goal, audience needs, different genres, and the structure of stories and informational texts) they gradually begin to restrict the content of their written work to information that is more directly relevant to the writing task at hand (Bereiter & Scardamalia, 1987; Graham, 2006; Olinghouse & Graham, 2009).

**inventive spellings**
Incorrect spellings that children create by sounding out words and writing the associated letters.

**knowledge telling**
Adding or "dumping" in ideas as they come to mind; a failure to selectively organize ideas in writing.

THINK ABOUT LINDA AND GIANLUCA . . .
How could Ginaluca use his writing skills to improve his reading skills? How might this help him?

THINKING CRITICALLY
When writing, how much time do you spend on planning and revising your text? Look back at one of your past writing assignments; can you see revisions that might have improved it?

**Planning and Revising.** Young writers have particular difficulty knowing when and what to revise. Once weaknesses are pointed out, however, they do seem capable of correcting most mistakes. As students move into more mature phases of writing, they spend increasing amounts of time on planning and revising. Before writing their first sentence, mature writers spend time gathering facts and sources and organizing their ideas; the first draft is not the last draft. They realize that good writing evolves through the dynamic process of *recursive revision.* That is, after planning and writing, they reevaluate their plan and rewrite several times. In early revisions accomplished writers attend above all to the meaning and message of their writing. They tend to defer the mechanics of spelling, grammar, and punctuation to later revisions (Adams et al., 1998). Strong writers become skilled at reviewing their own material from the reader's perspective—even reading it aloud—and continually revise their work to meet their writing goals. Unfortunately, a recent national survey of high school teachers indicated that many students are not often asked to write multiparagraph pieces or to analyze and interpret information in their writing (Kiuhara, Graham, & Hawkin, 2009).

In this chapter we have described the cognitive skills of children during the middle childhood years, from ages 7 to 11. We described the skills and limitations of these ages according to Piagetian theory. We discussed in detail the important developments in memory, knowledge base, strategies, and language skills, and we introduced recent views of cognition and language development. To offer a glimpse of how children put their cognitive skills to use in one important practical setting—school—we also described the development of three important academic skills. Hopefully, it is clear to you that children of this age have an amazing array of cognitive skills, and that these skills are built upon the cognitive foundation developed during the infancy, toddler, and early childhood periods. While they still face important limitations, anyone who works with children of these ages cannot help but be impressed with the level and range of skills most children show during the middle childhood years.

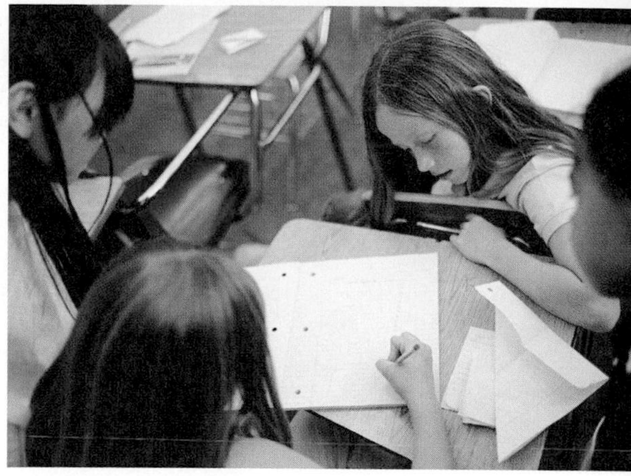

▲ These children are working together to plan and revise their stories in a writer's workshop. What writing skills are these children displaying?

## LET'S REVIEW . . .

1. Which of the following is *true* regarding the effect of context familiarity on solving story problems?
   **a.** Children become bored with familiar contexts and so pay less attention to problem details.
   **b.** Familiar contexts provide more effective cues for children to use relevant knowledge.
   **c.** Unfamiliar contexts encourage more effective strategies and reduce working memory load.
   **d.** There is no difference in problem difficulty for unfamiliar versus familiar contexts.
2. This year Jeremy is able to learn new material by reading textbooks. Before, he could barely understand individual words and sentences. Now Jeremy can process the meaning of text passages and absorb new information. Jeremy's ability to learn by reading shows that he is in Jeanne Chall's stage of ____________.
   **a.** reading/decoding
   **b.** fluency
   **c.** reading for new learning
   **d.** multiple viewpoints
3. One important part of learning to read is the understanding that words are made up of smaller units of sound. What is this concept called?
   **a.** word fluency
   **b.** phonemic awareness
   **c.** automatizing word recognition
   **d.** the prereading component
4. True or False: According to the strategy choice model, children who are discouraged from using counting strategies to solve mathematics problems may take longer to memorize and retrieve basic math facts.
5. True or False: The use of inventive spelling in the early elementary school years interferes with children's ability to learn to spell words correctly in the later school years.

Answers: 1. b, 2. c, 3. b, 4. T, 5. F

## THINKING BACK TO LINDA AND GIANLUCA . . .

Now that you have studied this chapter, you should be able to list at least a dozen specific concepts and explain how Linda could use each to help Gianluca. According to Piaget, Gianluca is probably in the stage of concrete operational thinking. Linda may be able to help him use his ability to mentally reverse actions and his developing abilities to integrate information and draw inferences to better comprehend what he reads. Gianluca probably has at least basic class inclusion and transitive inference skills, but he may need more experience with these kinds of problems before he can successfully apply them to what he reads. You probably noticed the effects of Gianluca's limited processing capacity and overloaded working memory. By the time he finishes the effortful task of reading a passage, he doesn't have enough capacity left over to think about how it all fits together and connect the new information to what he already knows! If Linda can help Gianluca develop automaticity in recalling the sounds of basic letters, meanings of vocabulary words, and the structure of different types of text passages, he can focus on other aspects of the text and how it relates to other topics. One of Gianluca's biggest challenges has been focusing his attention. Gianluca is doing much better at focusing on reading rather than being distracted by classroom noises, but perhaps Linda can help him further develop the attentional skills of identifying and selectively attending to the most important parts of what he is reading.

Linda can help Gianluca's memory for new vocabulary and concepts become better organized and easier to access by helping him practice and use this new information. Using "story webs" or organizing the main topics and supporting details will strengthen the associations in his memory network, making retrieval of the most important information faster and more accurate; then he'll be able to use the information from what he's reading to answer questions and to solve problems. After more experiences with similar kinds of text passages, Gianluca will probably develop some scripts for common types of stories, which will help him figure out what's likely to happen and what to expect in similar types of stories. It might be helpful to encourage Gianluca to connect his reading and writing skills. He could write a personal narrative; Linda has already encouraged him to write his own stories, which seemed to motivate him. These activities could help Gianluca better understand the connection between reading and how language skills are useful in describing, understanding, and communicating about the real-life situations he encounters every day. Linda has helped Gianluca develop several different strategies, both for focusing his attention and comprehending text. Perhaps he is getting old enough to learn to identify useful strategies on his own, and maybe even develop his own new strategies.

Linda and Gianluca's situation provides a good example of how research on cognitive development helps people solve real-life problems. Teachers and parents alike can benefit from understanding how factors such as mental reversibility, processing efficiency, knowledge base, and learning specific strategies contribute to memory and problem solving. The information-processing view in particular can offer specific ideas about what is causing problems for a child; it also offers specific ideas about how to help the child improve.

# 11

## CHAPTER REVIEW . . .

**11.1** Why does Piaget call this stage of thought *concrete operational thinking*?

Cognitive operations are *reversible* mental structures. Schemes in this stage are reversible ("operational"), but logic at this stage still requires tangible, or concrete, material or experience.

**11.2** What major skills do children in the concrete operational stage show and what limitations do they still face?

In the concrete operational stage (7 to 11 years of age), children can solve conservation problems, and they can represent multiple dimensions of the problems and the dynamic transformations involved. Logic is more objective and allows the child to understand class inclusion and transitive inference, but children are not yet able to apply their logic systematically or to abstract concepts.

**11.3** What are the differences between the stores model and network models of memory?

The stores model proposes a series of storage locations (sensory store, short-term memory, long-term memory) into which information is placed. It focuses on characteristics of each store and how an executive processor directs the use of processing capacity within the stores. Network models view memory as an interconnected system of concept nodes connected by links. These models focus on how information is organized and on how activation spreads along the links.

**11.4** How does working memory change with age?

Functional capacity of working memory changes with age, even if actual capacity may not. The size of chunks that can be kept active in working memory and the speed with which activation spreads within the memory network both increase with age.

**11.5** How does long-term memory change with age?

In long-term memory, the amount of knowledge and its organization change with age. Children get better at encoding information, storing it in long-term memory, accessing, and retrieving it.

**11.6** What are some of the issues in memory development, and why is each important for cognitive development?

Memory is reconstructive rather than based on mental copies, which means that memory can and often does contain many errors. Younger children's reconstructions are affected more than older children's by several factors. Autobiographical memories, or memories of personally important events, help form the basis for a child's sense of self.

**11.7** What effect does knowledge base have on cognitive development?

Greater knowledge in a domain leads to more effective and efficient processing of new information in that domain. Experts organize their knowledge differently than novices, which allows them to quickly identify important aspects of a situation and focus on problem solutions.

**11.8** How do strategies develop and how does increasing strategy use foster cognitive development?

Young children's strategy use is inconsistent and inflexible and does not always improve their performance. Younger children can be trained to use a strategy, but they often do not generalize it. Parental and cultural expectations and encouragement strongly influence strategy use. Children seem to have a variety of strategies available, and development consists of changes in which strategy is used most often. Increasingly sophisticated and accurate strategy use allows children to solve problems more efficiently, which in turn allows them to use limited attention and other cognitive resources more effectively.

**11.9** What are some newer approaches to understanding cognitive development?

New in the developmental sphere are computational models—theories of cognition that are programmed into and run on a computer. Researchers compare the programs' output with that of real children in order to better explain development. Production systems are sets of computerized *if–then* statements that specify the actions involved in a cognitive task. Connectionist models contain many simple units arranged into layers and connected by links of different weights. Fuzzy trace theory says that memory traces vary from verbatim to imprecise and general. Verbatim traces require more effort to store and use and are more likely to be forgotten or modified. Older children and adults tend to store and reason with fuzzy traces, while younger children tend to use verbatim traces.

**11.10** What are the strengths and weaknesses of the information-processing approach to cognitive development?

The information-processing view emphasizes detailed analysis of specific processes and highlights the importance of cognitive efficiency and the knowledge base. However, it does not offer an overarching theory to explain all of cognitive development. Nor does it address social or emotional issues in cognitive development.

**11.11** What language skills do children develop between 7 and 11 years of age?

Vocabulary development continues, and more abstract words are learned. Children become skilled in the use of passive voice, making inferences, referential communication, and social rules of discourse.

**11.12** How do 7- to 11-year-olds differ from younger children in their knowledge about and their use of language?

Metalinguistic awareness improves with age, which enables older children to use language more flexibly and better understand subtle humor compared to younger children. Children begin to use language in different ways, becoming more skilled at language play such as riddles. They use language as a tool for informing others about themselves and to better understand themselves through personal narratives.

**11.13** What are connectionist models of language development, and what evidence supports these approaches?

Cognitive connectionist models explain language development as progressive changes in the strength of connections among cognitive units. Evidence from computer simulations support these models in that they shown the same patterns of learning and errors as children learning language.

**11.14 What mathematical competencies and limitations do children of different ages typically show?**
Even young infants can distinguish between small sets and recognize the effects of addition and subtraction through subitizing. Preschoolers develop several counting strategies, and strategy efficiency increases throughout elementary school. Children develop strong associations between problems and correct answers and become able to retrieve answers, though they continue to use multiple strategies to solve arithmetic problems. Word problems are difficult for many students; problems with unfamiliar contexts and involving static relations between sets are especially difficult. Buggy procedures in mathematics result from lack of understanding of math principles.

**11.15 What are some important factors that predict reading skill?**
Chall identified six stages of reading development. For young children, familiarity with the alphabet and phonemic awareness predict later reading success. After learning to decode or recognize whole words, children must automatize word recognition. Consistent practice is important for developing these skills.

**11.16 What are the major accomplishments that children achieve as they learn to write?**
Reading and writing skills are correlated and follow similar developmental pathways. Early writers use inventive spellings. After automatizing proper spellings, children can focus on other technical requirements of writing. Early writers tend to be egocentric, have poor organization, and use unsophisticated "knowledge-telling" strategies. As writers mature, they engage in more planning and revising.

## REVISITING THEMES

In this chapter, the *nature and nurture* theme can be seen in the mathematical skills that of infants. Through the process of subitizing, even newborns can determine the basic quantity in a small set of objects (p. 348).

The theme of *neuroscience* is evident throughout this chapter. The newer connectionist models of cognitive development are "neurally-inspired" and attempt to incorporate what is currently known about how neural processing works (pp. 339–343). Neuroscience research is proceeding at a fast pace, with research investigating the underlying neural processes involved in cognitive monitoring and other executive cognitive processes (p. 325), autobiographical memory (p. 333), and the development of reading (p. 353).

Examples of *diversity and multiculturalism* can be seen in this chapter's discussions of autobiographical memory (p. 333), language development (p. 346), mathematics (p. 350), and reading (p. 353). Cultural differences were noted in the sequence of grammatical development and in the style of personal narratives (p. 345).

Finally, examples of *positive development and resilience* can be seen in the discussion of language and strategy development. Increasing metalinguistic awareness allows children to make more effective use of their language skills to communicate with others (p. 345); some connectionist models of language development are looking in detail at the underlying processes that allow recovery of language functions following brain injuries (p. 347). Work on children's use of strategies, in mathematics specifically (pp. 348–350), emphasizes the use of multiple strategies even within a single problem. This flexible use of cognitive processes enables children to successfully adapt to a variety of problems and situations.

## KEY TERMS

accessing (328)
autobiographical memories (333)
chunking (324)
computational models (339)
concrete operational thought (322)
connectionist models (339)
counting strategies (348)
encoding (328)
fuzzy trace theory (342)
inventive spelling (354)
knowledge base (335)
knowledge telling (354)
long-term memory (328)
metalinguistic awareness (344)
network models (of memory) (325)
personal narratives (344)
phonemic awareness (351)
production systems (339)
reconstructive memory (330)
retrieval (328)
scripts (329)
storage (328)
stores model (of memory) (324)
strategies (335)
strategy choice model (348)
subitizing (348)
working memory (327)

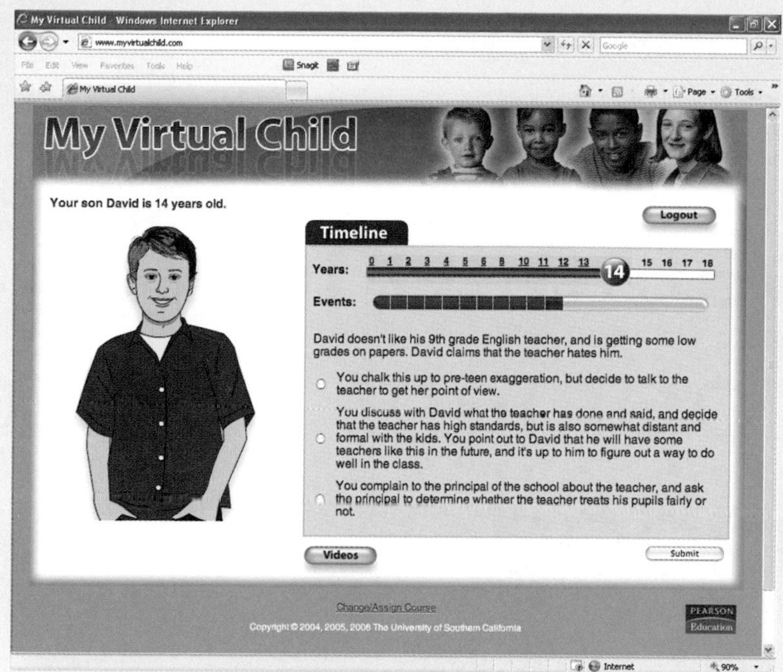


**"What decisions would you make while raising a child? What would the consequences of those decisions be?"**

Find out by accessing My Virtual Child at
**www.mydevelopmentlab.com**
and raising your own virtual child
from birth to age 18.

**Watch** Visit your Multimedia Library at www.mydevelopmentlab.com to watch an interview with Laurel's mother, Pam, online.

12 MIDDLE CHILDHOOD

# Socioemotional Development in Middle Childhood

Laurel is an outgoing and bubbly 9-year-old who is popular and well-liked by her peers. She's friendly with a wide range of children at school, and she has one friend who is especially tight. Laurel had a close relationship with one of the boys in her class, but he moved away. They still correspond by e-mail (her mother says it's very cute!). Laurel loves school, but she's a bit of a perfectionist. She spends a lot of time comparing herself to her peers, and she's rather tough on herself. She looks in the mirror a lot and comments that she's overweight. Pam, her mother, reminds her to focus on being "the best you can be." Laurel enjoys reality TV shows and police dramas and otherwise uses the same media as most of her peers: e-mail, instant messaging, and the typical social networking sites.

Laurel's parents separated when she was four, and they are now divorced. Her father moved to a different state and they don't have much contact. Laurel feels that he abandoned her. Laurel is emotionally very close to her mother, but she's having trouble accepting the fact that her mother is dating and needs her own personal time. Even at age 9, Laurel is still sleeping with her mother. Pam tried a few behavior modification techniques, and even resorted to outright bribery with a new cell phone and TV in her bedroom, but Laurel refuses to sleep in her own room. Although Laurel really enjoys school and spending time with her friends, she becomes very upset if she's separated from her mother for any prolonged period of time.

How do Laurel's experiences and concerns compare to those of other children in middle childhood? What advice could you give her mother for helping Laurel overcome her separation concerns? Is her parents' divorce an issue here, and will Laurel's perfectionism become a problem at this age? How will Laurel's friendships, school experiences, and use of technology and the media change as she develops through middle childhood? After studying this chapter, you should be able to apply at least a dozen concepts and research findings to understand Laurel's situation. What advice would you give?

As you read this chapter, look for the "Think About Laurel . . ." questions that ask you to consider what you're learning from Laurel's perspective.

Many children have concerns like Laurel's. Middle childhood is an important phase for children's social and emotional development. During this time, children notice how their talents and abilities compare to their peers, some children become more popular and some less popular, and some children seek challenge and excitement while others withdraw and feel more helpless. Divorce, remarriage, and stepfamilies are a reality for many children of this age, and as they get older children are exposed to many more messages from TV, movies, music, and the Internet. From family to friends to the media, children's lives are shaped by a wide array of social forces. The concepts and research findings presented in this chapter should help you understand how children become themselves in part through their interactions with the important people around them. We begin the chapter by looking at how children understand themselves and their own emotional reactions.

Schools and the Media

- Children's Beliefs and Teachers' Expectations about Schooling
- Classroom Climate and Grouping Practices in Schools
- Children and the Media
- Children and Television
- Video Games, Computers, and the Internet

▲ During middle childhood children compare themselves to their peers. This social comparison helps them define who they are and makes them aware that they may not be as competent in some areas as their peers are.

# The Social and Emotional Self

In Chapter 9 we discussed how children develop a sense of who they are during early childhood. A sense of "I-self" and "me-self" emerge during the early childhood years as young children create working models of who they are. As children continue to develop, their sense of self becomes more abstract and complex. The elementary school years are an important time of **social comparison.** In defining themselves, children at this age place special importance on how they measure up compared to their peers. They look around at their classmates and other children their age and ask: "Am I as tall, as fast, as smart as they are?" "Do kids like me as much as they like other kids?" By comparing themselves to their peers, children learn more about who they are and what their relative strengths and weaknesses are. Middle childhood is also an important time for children to learn to control their emotional reactions, learn to help other people, and learn to control their aggressive behavior. These are just a few of the topics that are important to consider as children learn more about who they are and how they fit in the larger social world.

AS YOU STUDY THIS SECTION, ASK YOURSELF THESE QUESTIONS:

**12.1** How do children evaluate themselves and their own talents, abilities, and weaknesses and how does this evaluation process relate to a sense of self-esteem?

**12.2** What changes take place in the development of emotions during middle childhood?

**12.3** What gender differences do we see in how boys and girls behave at this age?

**12.4** How do children think about moral issues, and how does this relate to their tendencies to help other people?

**12.5** Why are some children more aggressive than others?

THINK ABOUT LAUREL . . .

How is the social comparison process going for Laurel? Is it typical for children of this age to compare themselves to their peers? What do they learn?

**social comparison** The process in which children compare their own qualities and performances to those of their peers.

## Self-Evaluations

**Self-representations** are the ways people describe themselves. Self-representations are also called *self-concepts,* and they are the characteristics and facts about ourselves that make up the *me-self* we described in Chapter 9. **Self-evaluations** are the judgments people make about themselves, and these judgments lead to **self-esteem** or the emotions people feel about themselves. An example of a self-representation (description) that a child might have is "I am tall and fast." The self-evaluation (judgment) might then be "It is great to be tall and fast," leading to a feeling of self-esteem (emotion), of being proud to be tall and fast. In this example,

**self-representations** The ways people describe themselves; also called *self-concepts.*

**self-evaluations** The judgments people make about themselves.

**self-esteem** The emotions people feel about themselves.

you can see how a description leads to a judgment and then to an emotion. Psychologically, it is important that children have an accurate understanding of themselves and feel good about themselves. Children should have reasonably high self-esteem, but their self-esteem needs to be based on judgments and self-representations that are accurate and realistic.

Self-evaluations tend to be unrealistically optimistic during early childhood as most young children believe they are more capable than they really are ("I can run *super* fast," and "I'm the best reader ever!"). Self-evaluations become more realistic during middle childhood as children compare themselves to other children and get a more accurate view of how their capabilities compare. By age 7, children form an overall judgment of themselves, or *global self-evaluation* (Harter, 1998; Stipek, Recchia, & McClintic, 1992).

Children begin to distinguish between their *real selves* and their *ideal selves*—between the performance and attributes children actually have and the qualities they would like to have. Two aspects of this comparison process are important: the actual discrepancy between the ideal and the real in areas that are important to the child, and the degree of social support the child receives from parents and/or peers (Harter, 1999). For example, if a girl would like to be a soccer star (the ideal self) but is not very athletic (the real self), the discrepancy is large. If athletics are not important to the girl, then even a large discrepancy in this domain will have little effect on her self-evaluation. In contrast, if physical skills and athletics are important to the child, her self-evaluation in this domain is likely to suffer. However, if the girl's parents and peers are very supportive of her attempts to play soccer, focusing on her improvements and praising her efforts, then her self-evaluation will be less negative. Some aspects of her self-evaluation may even become very positive (e.g., "I'm a hard worker," "I'm not afraid to try to learn new things"). The worst cases seem to be situations in which children perceive support as being *contingent on* performance. In other words, if a child who is not athletic feels that others will support and accept her only if she plays soccer well, then she must contend with both a large discrepancy and potential loss of support—and is likely to develop a negative self-evaluation and low self-esteem.

▲ If parents are supportive of a child's efforts, even a big discrepancy between the child's real and ideal selves is not necessarily harmful.

During middle childhood, children make judgments about themselves in many areas including athletics, academics, social skills, and physical appearance. It is interesting to note that of all the areas of self-evaluation that researchers have studied, perceived physical appearance consistently shows the highest correlation with overall self-esteem. Correlations range from .65 to a remarkable .82 (Harter, 1998). This strong relationship is apparent from early childhood through adulthood; for males and females; across different population groups (e.g., people with learning disabilities, gifted students, or behaviorally disruptive adolescents); across different ethnic groups; and in different countries, including Ireland, Australia, Greece, Japan, and the United States (Gardner, Friedman, & Jackson, 1999; James, Phelps, & Bross, 2001). Concern about physical appearance seems to be especially detrimental for girls, who report significantly greater dissatisfaction with their physical selves than do boys, starting at about fourth grade and continuing through adulthood. Although the cultural emphasis on physical appearance is strong for both genders, it appears to take its toll most strongly on girls by presenting unrealistic standards for comparison. Not surprisingly, girls who report that their self-esteem is based on physical appearance also tend to show especially low levels of self-esteem (Harter, 1993).

How can we help children develop more positive self-evaluations? Table 12.1 offers some helpful suggestions.

## Emotional Development

In early childhood, children learn that emotions represent their own reactions to situations and events and that children can differ from each other in their emotional responses. Middle childhood is a period when children learn to control and regulate their own

**TABLE 12.1**
**Fostering Positive Self-Evaluations**

| | |
|---|---|
| Early care-giving promotes a secure emotional attachment | • Learn to read your child's cues. Respond to them, and then watch to see if the need has been met.<br>• Watch and listen; let the child initiate when feasible. Don't always rush in to start an interaction.<br>• Provide an environment that is sensitive to your child's temperament. Don't try to push a reluctant child too hard or too fast, or constrain an active child for too long.<br>• Provide many opportunities to play and interact with others, including you.<br>• Express delight in your child's early accomplishments; even if every other child also does the same thing, it is a new accomplishment for *this* child!<br>• Provide comfort to your child when he seeks it from you. Communicate in words; use facial and physical gestures, and organize activities that tell your children that they are worthy, lovable, and capable. |
| Provide positive support and encouragement. Outcomes may matter, but also stress effort and improvement | • Praise a good outcome (e.g., "What a beautiful painting! I'm so proud it was chosen for the art show!"). But also point out the process and the effort (e.g., "Was it fun to come up with those colors? I noticed that you put in a lot of work on that project").<br>• Support the *effort* and recognize *progress*, even if the outcome isn't good<br>• Help your child set realistic goals and subgoals so the difference between his real and ideal selves is not so great.<br>• Remind your child that she doesn't have to excel in everything. Some things are truly just for fun! |
| Provide instruction and guidance to help your child improve | • Make time to help your child with the things you know how to do.<br>• Work with others (e.g., teachers, coaches, and friends) to provide good models for knowledge and skills you do not have.<br>• Think creatively. Find ways to use your child's strengths to improve her weaknesses (e.g., a child who is not a good reader but is very social might enjoy doing a dramatic reading of a story to her family, friends, or stuffed animals).<br>• Make teaching interactions as pleasant as possible (e.g., make up card games or money games to practice math skills; play word rhyming games to practice phonics for reading). |
| Give honest feedback | • Don't lie or exaggerate, especially as children move into elementary school. They usually know when they have not done well and will simply learn to not believe you. Be honest, but in a gentle and kind way.<br>• Talk about specific things the child can do to improve, and provide help. Spend time with the child working on the skills, offer guidance, do an activity with the child, etc. Different approaches will work with different children.<br>• Offer balanced feedback. Point out what went well as well as what went poorly.<br>• Point out examples of both strengths and weaknesses in yourself, other family members, and your child's friends to help them understand that *no one* is great at everything. |
| Teach goal-setting skills | • Help your child set specific and reasonable goals.<br>• As children get older, model how to set goals that are explicit, long-term goals as well as smaller, more immediate goals, and how to make a plan for accomplishing them.<br>• Help children develop and use a system for tracking progress toward their goals (e.g., a chart, calendar, or written log of progress). Notice and comment on progress toward goals. |
| Emphasize strengths | • All children do some things well.<br>• Remind them of their strengths and offer specific examples of them. |

emotional reactions, and they improve their abilities to accurately read the emotions of other people. Children need to learn that their emotional reactions affect other people. To get along effectively, we all need to learn to manage our own emotions, and we need skill in predicting and interpreting other people's emotions.

Children who learn positive emotional skills from their parents seem to have more success making friends. Children of emotionally expressive mothers tend to receive high regard from their peers (Cassidy, Parke, Butkovsky, & Braungart, 1992). An interesting longitudinal study linked adults' levels of empathy (ability to feel other people's emotions) with childhood experiences. The study found that when empathic adults were children, their fathers were more involved in their care and their mothers were more tolerant of dependent behavior, were more likely to restrict the children's aggression, and were more satisfied in their roles as mothers (Koestner, Franz, & Weinberger, 1990). You can imagine that parents who fit this description would tend to model positive control of emotions for their children.

THINK ABOUT LAUREL . . .

How do you think Laurel's relationship with her mother will affect how Laurel learns to control and express her emotions? What else would you like to know about their relationship in order to assess this?

Of course, the reverse is also true. Children of mothers who are chronically depressed, for example, are often prone to feelings of guilt and helplessness. Although they try hard to make their mothers feel happy, they cannot succeed, and they often believe it is their fault (Zahn-Waxler & Robinson, 1995). Even subtle differences in emotional treatment can affect children—research with twins shows that the twin who is treated more negatively and less warmly by the mother tends to have more behavioral problems than the twin who is treated more warmly (Caspi et al., 2004).

An interesting research finding is that children sometimes have difficulty reading the emotions expressed by people from ethnic backgrounds other than their own. For example, one group of researchers showed children photographs of adult and child actors who were making happy, sad, angry, and fearful faces (Collins & Nowicki, 2001). Most of the people in the photographs were European American actors. When asked to name the emotions shown in the photographs, African American children (around 10 years of age) made more mistakes than did European American children. African American children also had more difficulty judging emotions from tones of voice when European American adults were speaking. In another study Canadian children (all white and varying in age from about 5 to 10 years old) identified the emotion of disgust more accurately when it was shown by White actors than when it was expressed by Asian actors (Gosselin & Larocque, 2000). A surprising finding, however, was that these same children identified the emotions of fear and surprise more accurately when demonstrated by the Asian actors. The researchers speculated that ethnic groups differ somewhat in the extent to which they lower their eyebrows, stretch their lips, wrinkle their noses, and make other facial movements when expressing emotions. Some of these patterns of movement are easier to see in Asian faces, for example; other patterns may be more apparent when expressed by Whites of European descent. When interacting with other people, we need to read their emotions accurately so we can appropriately respond. These studies, however, remind us that there may be ethnic group differences in how people express, read, and interpret emotions. **Simulate** on **mydevelopmentlab**

**Simulate** Recognizing Facial Expressions of Emotions www.mydevelopmentlab.com

Accuracy in reading emotions is an important social skill. Children who are adept at reading emotions tend to be liked more by their peers (Denham, McKinley, Couchoud, & Holt, 1990). They know when they are making their friends happy, when to back off if their friends become frustrated, and when to console friends who are sad or dejected. As we mentioned in Chapter 9, children have a bias toward positive emotions. Children tend to like other children who are happy and know how to control their emotions. As one group of researchers put it, "feeling good . . . makes it easier for a child to enter the peer world" and "greases the cogs of ongoing social interaction" (Denham et al., 2003, p. 251). Conversely, children who have difficulty controlling their emotions are more likely to suffer problems such as anger and depression (Eisenberg et al., 2005) and would presumably have more difficulty making and keeping friends.

## Gender Differences

As we mentioned before, children show strong gender segregation in their social activities and play. By the time children reach middle childhood, they already have firm ideas about their own gender and about how boys and girls typically differ. Prevailing stereotypes in Western cultures portray boys as more active and aggressive and girls as more emotional and helpful. The research evidence supports some of these images, but not all. On average, boys do show higher activity levels than girls. They are more likely to engage in outdoor play, in rough play, and in activities that cover large areas of physical space (Eaton & Enns, 1986; Lindsey, Mize, & Pettit, 1997; Maccoby, 1998). Girls, on the other hand, perform better on tasks involving flexibility and fine-motor coordination. These differences increase with age.

Beginning at an early age, boys show more physical aggression, such as hitting or kicking, than girls, and this difference continues throughout childhood and into adulthood (Baillargeon et al., 2007; Card, Stucky, Sawalani, & Little, 2008; Coie & Dodge, 1998; Hyde, 2005). Boys also show higher levels of assertiveness than girls, though the difference is not as large as for physical aggressiveness (Feingold, 1994). Studies have found gender differences in physical aggressiveness and assertiveness across numerous countries (Bettencourt & Miller, 1996; Coie & Dodge, 1998; Maccoby & Jacklin, 1974). It's also important to realize that aggression can take different forms. **Relational aggression** seeks to hurt others by destroying social relationships. Examples include threats to withdraw friendship ("I won't be your best friend anymore!"), social exclusion ("You can't be in our group!"), or harmful gossip ("She said she didn't like you anymore!"). Girls are significantly more likely than boys to show relational aggression (Crick & Grotpeter, 1995). By the time children are 5, they already understand these differences, and they expect boys to be more physically aggressive and girls to engage in more relational aggression (Giles & Heyman, 2005). **Watch** on **mydevelopmentlab**

**Watch** a video on Relational Aggression. www.mydevelopmentlab.com

Researchers have not found consistent gender differences in helping behavior or emotions. Girls often receive ratings from others and evaluate themselves as more helpful, cooperative, and sympathetic, but their actual behavior is not consistently different from that of boys. However, girls are more likely to seek and to receive help than are boys, and some studies indicate that girls are more easily influenced than boys (Eisenberg & Fabes, 1998; Ruble & Martin, 1998). When attempting to influence others, boys are more likely to use threats and physical force. Girls tend to use verbal persuasion or, if that does not work, simply to stop their efforts to influence the other person (Serbin, Moller, Gulko, Powlishta, & Colburne, 1994).

## Moral and Prosocial Reasoning

**Moral Reasoning.** Look back to Chapter 9 (on page 269) to review Lawrence Kohlberg's stages of moral reasoning. By age 10, the majority of children are still reasoning at Stage 1 or 2 (Colby, Kohlberg, Gibbs, & Lieberman, 1983). A few children begin to show evidence of conventional moral reasoning, however, as they begin to grasp the idea that rules are social conventions and they are able to understand things from other

**relational aggression** Withdrawing friendship or otherwise disrupting or threatening social relationships as a way to hurt other people.

◀ Boys show higher levels of physical aggression throughout childhood and adolescence, but girls show higher levels of relational aggression.

people's perspectives. At the conventional level, children follow rules because they believe it's important to maintain their personal social standing or the social order as a whole. They begin to see how others might view their actions and to understand how their actions can affect other people. In Stage 3 children primarily follow rules in order to gain the approval of their parents, family, teachers, and friends.

**prosocial reasoning**
How children think about helping others, including their reasons for deciding whether to help another person.

Simulate Helping a Stranger
www.mydevelopmentlab.com

Prosocial Reasoning. Another aspect of moral reasoning involves **prosocial reasoning**, or children's thought processes as they decide whether or not to help someone. Nancy Eisenberg presented children and young people from preschool through 12th grade with prosocial dilemmas—situations in which helping someone else would require some kind of personal sacrifice (Eisenberg, 1986; Eisenberg, Carlo, Murphy, & Van Court, 1995). For example, in one scenario a girl on her way to a birthday party was asked to help another child who was hurt. Stopping to help would mean missing the ice cream, cake, and games. Should the girl help, and if so, why? Simulate on mydevelopmentlab

On the basis of the responses she received, Eisenberg proposed that prosocial reasoning develops through the levels shown in Table 12.2. It is easy to see the parallels between the levels of prosocial reasoning and Kohlberg's levels of general moral reasoning: With

**TABLE 12.2**
**Developmental Levels of Prosocial Reasoning**

| LEVEL | AGES | DESCRIPTION |
|---|---|---|
| Hedonistic orientation | Preschool to the beginning of elementary school | • The child is concerned with his or her own needs and consequences for himself or herself.<br>• Child will help if it benefits himself or herself now or in the future, or if he or she likes or needs the other person.<br>• *Example:* "I'd help because then he'd let me ride his new bike." |
| Needs-of-others orientation | Some preschool children; many elementary school children | • The child is concerned with the needs of others, even if they conflict with his or her own needs.<br>• There is little evidence of sympathy for the other person or of guilt over not helping.<br>• *Example:* "I'd help because he's hurt and needs help." |
| Approval and/or stereotyped orientation | Elementary school to high school | • The child is concerned with being accepted by others and gaining approval.<br>• Decisions about helping or not are often based on stereotyped views of what "good" or "bad" people do.<br>• *Example:* "I'd help because my dad would be really proud of me." |
| Empathic orientation | Older elementary school to high school | • The child shows sympathy for the other person's situation.<br>• The child expresses guilt for not helping and positive feelings for helping.<br>• There are sometimes vague references to internalized values or responsibilities.<br>• *Example:* "I'd help because he must feel really sad. It would help him feel better, and I'd feel good about helping." |
| Strongly internalized values orientation | Small number of high school students | • The child is concerned with following his or her own internalized values, norms, beliefs, or duties.<br>• Violating the internal standards can cause loss of self-respect.<br>• *Example:* "It's important to help people who are hurt. If we all did that all the time, our world would be a much better place." |

(Adapted from Eisenberg, Lennon, & Roth, 1983.)

age, children move from a sole concern with their own needs to a concern with social approval, and finally to reasoning based on broader principles. As in Kohlberg's theory, Eisenberg's theory views overall cognitive development and perspective-taking ability as important in the development of prosocial reasoning. However, her theory does not assume that prosocial reasoning levels are universal. According to Eisenberg, both environmental and emotional factors, such as parenting and feelings of empathy, affect the development and use of prosocial reasoning (Eisenberg & Fabes, 1998).

Studies in several different countries have supported the sequence of levels Eisenberg proposed (Eisenberg, 1986; Eisenberg et al., 1995). However, the type of request affects whether children engage in any reasoning at all about whether to help. When a request for help is simple and involves little or no cost, it seems that children give very little thought to what they should do: They simply help (Eisenberg & Shell, 1986; Miller, Eisenberg, Fabes, & Shell, 1996). The social environment also affects prosocial reasoning. For example, children in an Israeli kibbutz, which emphasizes communal values and equality, showed lower levels of needs-oriented reasoning and higher levels of an internalized values orientation (Eisenberg, 1986). In addition, prosocial reasoning is influenced by parental relationships. Parenting that is warm in emotional tone, communicates expectations of mature behavior, and provides explanations seems to encourage higher levels of prosocial reasoning (Janssens & Dekovic, 1997). Families that value, model, expect, and explicitly encourage and discuss prosocial reasoning and good behavior are more likely to see it in their children. Exposure to violence in movies and video games reduces the likelihood of helping another person, both in terms of noticing when help is needed and in how long it takes to help (Bushman & Anderson, 2009).

## Aggression, Conduct Problems, and Resilient Children

**Aggression.** All children show aggressiveness at times, particularly during the early childhood years and most often during conflicts over possessions. Aggressiveness is a relatively stable characteristic. Figure 12.1 shows the results of one longitudinal study that

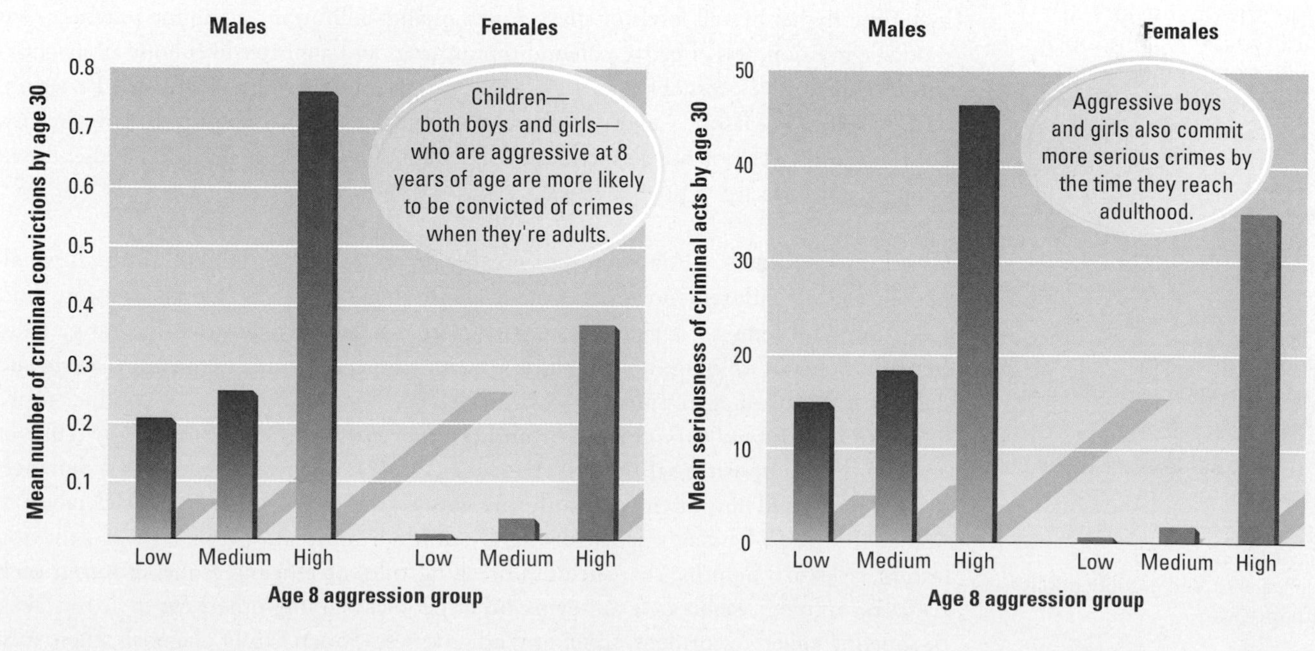


▲ FIGURE 12.1
**The Stability of Aggressiveness**
One longitudinal study found that children rated as aggressive at 8 years of age continued showing aggressive behaviors more than 20 years later (Huesmann et al., 1984).

assessed aggressive behavior over 22 years. As you can see, children who were rated as aggressive at 8 years of age were significantly more likely to be convicted of criminal offenses and to commit more serious crimes. They were also more likely to commit domestic violence against spouses or children. Other studies have shown similar patterns across early and middle childhood (Hart, Olsen, Robinson, & Mandleco, 1997; Huesmann, Eron, Lefkowitz, & Walder, 1984; Newman, Caspi, Moffitt, & Silva, 1997). Twin studies have indicated a genetic predisposition toward aggressive behavior (Plomin, 1990). Clearly some children are at higher risk for aggressive behavior.

▲ Some children tend to interpret ambiguous or innocent events as hostile and to react defensively and with aggression.

As we have seen for the development of prosocial emotions and behavior, the family environment also plays a key role in a child's aggressiveness. An aggressive, out-of-control child may live in what has been called a *coercive home environment* (Patterson, 1995, 1997). In such families, coercive discipline and conflict resolution strategies such as yelling, threats, orders, and physical punishment are the norm. Both parents and children frequently behave aggressively, and levels of anger and hostility are high. Parents rarely acknowledge or reinforce prosocial behavior, focusing instead on misbehavior. In addition, coercive parents tend to interpret ambiguous events in negative ways, seeing threats where there really aren't any (Dodge, Pettit, & Bates, 1994; Patterson, 1995, 1997). Even when the home environment is not openly coercive, parents may indirectly encourage aggression by failing to adequately supervise their children's activities and social relationships or to place appropriate limits on behavior.

Finally, cultural conditions can encourage aggressive behavior. Within the United States some subcultures are clearly more aggressive than others. Poverty is an important factor, however. Males living in large urban areas show higher levels of aggressive behavior, and the rates are especially high for African American males (Atwater, 1992; Graham, Hudley, & Williams, 1992). Poor white children show as much aggressive behavior as African Americans, but a smaller percentage of white children live in poverty. Many factors associated with lower socioeconomic status help explain higher rates of aggressiveness, including higher overall levels of stress, lower-quality education, discipline practices that model aggression, less effective parental monitoring, and a greater likelihood of associating with aggressive peers (Dodge et al., 1994; Kupersmidt, Briesler, DeRosier, Patterson, & Davis, 1995; Mason, Cauce, Gonzales, & Hiraga, 1996). Exposure to community, domestic, and peer violence all increase the likelihood of aggressive behavior, and children of all ages are affected (Osofsky, 1999).

THINKING CRITICALLY

Has your home environment affected your level of aggressive behavior? In what ways? Looking back, would you change your home situation in any way?

Conduct Problems. Almost everyone breaks rules from time to time. A small percentage of children, however, engage in frequent or severe forms of acting out. **Conduct problems** are a general category of rule-breaking behaviors that range from frequent bouts of whining, yelling, and throwing temper tantrums to the more severe and dangerous forms of aggression and destructiveness. Two specific types of conduct problems are *oppositional defiant disorder* and *conduct disorder*. Approximately 6–10% of children have **oppositional defiant disorder (ODD)**, a repetitive pattern of defiance, disobedience, and hostility toward authority figures (Kann & Hanna, 2000; McMahon & Wells, 1998). To be diagnosed with ODD, children must show a pattern of behavior, lasting at least 6 months, that includes breaking rules or refusing requests; losing their tempers; arguing; deliberately annoying other people; blaming others for their mistakes; or showing anger, resentment, spite, or vindictiveness. For an ODD diagnosis, these misbehaviors also must be more frequent than with children of similar age and must cause disruptions in children's school performance and social relationships.

Another 2–9% of children have **conduct disorder (CD)**; they consistently violate the basic rights of other people or break major societal rules (McMahon & Wells, 1998).

**conduct problems**
A general category of rule-breaking behaviors.

**oppositional defiant disorder (ODD)**
A conduct problem involving a repetitive pattern of defiance, disobedience, and hostility toward authority figures.

**conduct disorder (CD)**
A conduct problem involving consistent violations of other people's basic rights or the breaking of major societal rules.

Examples include harming people or animals, fighting, bullying, using weapons, being cruel, destroying property, setting fires, stealing, lying, running away from home, and other serious violations. To be diagnosed with CD, a child must show a persistent pattern of serious violations during the past 12 months, with at least one violation within the last 6 months. ODD and CD are typically treated with counseling, behavior therapy, family therapy, and sometimes prescription medications.

**Resilient Children.** Some children have all of the odds stacked against them—they live in poor neighborhoods where they frequently witness violence, they attend low-quality schools, and they experience harsh or even abusive parenting. Yet, they manage to survive in life, and some even thrive. These are **resilient children**—children who succeed, achieve, or otherwise have positive developmental outcomes despite growing up under negative conditions (Garmezy, 1985; Luthar, 2006; Rutter, 1987). Resilient children present some of the most interesting cases in child development. One classic study of resilient children was conducted by Emmy Werner, a child psychologist who tracked the lives of all children born in 1955 on the island of Kauai, Hawaii (Werner, 1989, 2000; Werner & Smith, 2001). Werner categorized approximately 10% of the children as resilient. These children developed into competent, caring, happy adults even though they were born into poverty, had mothers with little education, and grew up in families with considerable distress, alcoholism, or mental illness. Like other researchers, Werner was able to identify several factors that seemed to protect these resilient children from negative developmental outcomes. They had pleasant personalities, they had average or above-average intelligence, and they managed to maintain a positive tie with a member of their family or with an important adult in their school or church—all these factors helped resilient children avoid the pitfalls and temptations that ensnared their less fortunate peers. By studying resilient children you can see that some children manage to escape the negative influences in life, and these lessons may help us reach other children who are living in unfortunate circumstances.

**resilient children**
Children who succeed, achieve, or otherwise have positive developmental outcomes despite growing up under negative conditions.

## LET'S REVIEW . . .

1. If the discrepancy between Diana's *real self* and her *ideal self* is large and Diana cares about this area of herself, which of the following is most likely to be true about her self-evaluation?
   - **a.** It will be high.
   - **b.** It will not be affected.
   - **c.** It will be low even if her parents are supportive.
   - **d.** It will be low if her parents are not supportive.
2. Which of the following is shown more often by girls than by boys?
   - **a.** threats
   - **b.** assertiveness
   - **c.** physical aggression
   - **d.** relational aggression
3. Samuel says it would be wrong to steal candy because his parents would be very upset and disappointed in such a behavior. Samuel is probably reasoning at which of Kohlberg's stages?
   - **a.** Stage 1
   - **b.** Stage 2
   - **c.** Stage 3
   - **d.** Stage 4
4. Children who beat the odds and manage to live successful lives even though they grew up under negative circumstances are referred to as ___________.
   - **a.** resilient
   - **b.** vulnerable
   - **c.** risk-free
   - **d.** relationally secure
5. True or False: During middle childhood, children's self-esteem is not related to how physically attractive children perceive themselves to be.
6. True or False: Overall, girls engage in more helping behaviors than do boys.

Answers: 1. d, 2. d, 3. c, 4. a, 5. F, 6. F

# Families

In Chapter 9 we focused on parenting styles and types of discipline used in families—two topics important for children of all ages. In this chapter we will focus on the structure of the modern American family. Over the last 50 years, there has been a steady decrease in the numbers of children who live with both of their parents, and the percentage who live with one parent has more than doubled (U.S. Census Bureau, 2009). In Figure 12.2 you can compare these trends for Caucasian, African American, and Hispanic children. You can see that the majority of African American children are now living in single-parent homes. What are the effects of these varying family structures on children? Is family structure itself the overriding factor in a child's experience, or are other factors more important? In this section we explore divorce, single-parent families, and stepfamilies, and we consider how these family structures relate to children's social and emotional development.

AS YOU STUDY THIS SECTION, ASK YOURSELF THESE QUESTIONS:

**12.6** What are the main outcomes associated with divorce, and what factors explain these outcomes?

**12.7** What effects might living in never-married households or in stepfamilies have on children?

## Children and Divorce

Have you experienced a divorce in your family? Even if you have not, you probably know several people who have. Each year in the United States, there are about 47% as many divorces as marriages (U.S. Census Bureau, 2006). This rate has held steady for at least the last 15 years. Before they turn age 18, nearly half of all children in the U.S. will experience a family divorce (Lansford, 2009). Given these statistics, it is imperative that parents, teachers, child care workers, developmental psychologists, clinicians, and legal

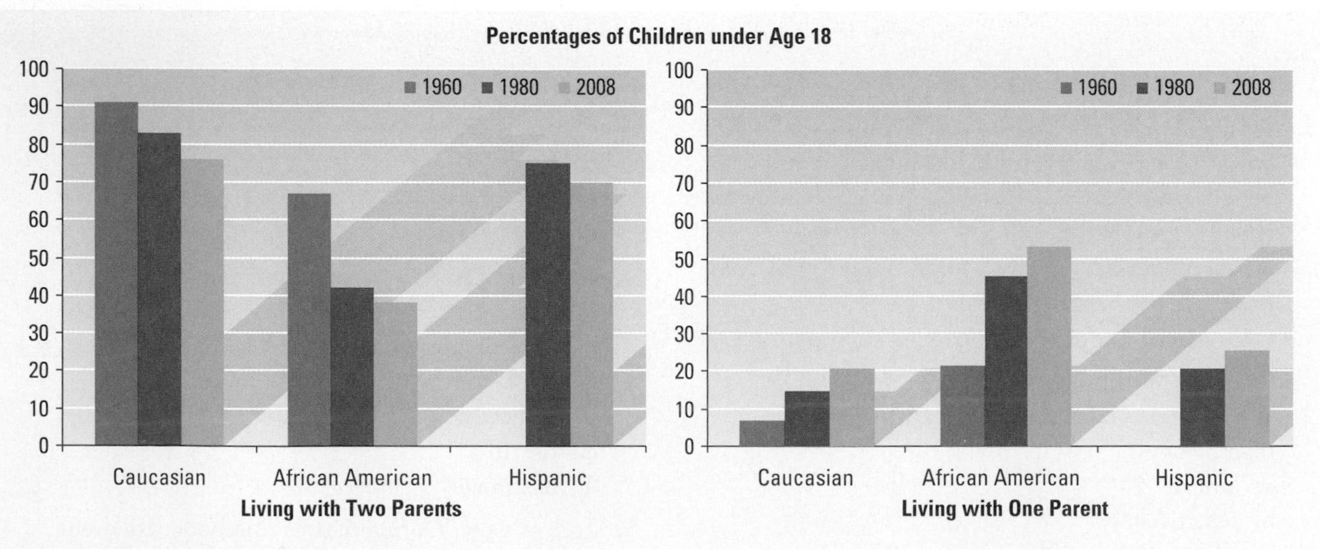


▲ FIGURE 12.2

**Percentages of Children Living with Two Parents or with One Parent.**
Since 1960, the percentages of children under age 18 living with both parents have steadily declined. The percentages living with one parent have increased. A small percentage of children do not live with either parent. In 2008, 54% of African American children lived with one parent, and only 38% lived with both parents. Data for 1960 for Hispanics are not available. Data are from the U.S. Census Bureau (2009).

professionals understand the effects divorce has on children. All of us who work with children need to know how best to help children cope with the changes and emotions that occur when parents divorce.

When compared to children whose parents are still married, children with divorced parents show more problems, including:

- more feelings of depression, distress, grief, anger, anxiety, shame, fear of abandonment, and feelings of responsibility for the divorce;
- more disobedience, aggression, antisocial behavior, criminal behavior, and lack of self-control;
- lower grades in school, lower school attendance, and higher drop-out rates in high school;
- lower rates of college attendance, and lower annual incomes in adulthood;
- higher rates of teenage pregnancy, and
- lower marriage rates, higher cohabitation rates, and higher divorce rates when they do marry.

Differences are usually small to moderate in size, but they have been consistent across several decades of research (Amato, 1999, 2000; Amato & Keith, 1991; Conger & Chao, 1996; Emery, 1999a; Hetherington & Stanley-Hagan, 1995; Lansford, 2009; McLanahan, 1999; Wallerstein, Lewis, & Blakeslee, 2000).

Children of divorced parents often feel pressure to grow up faster as a result of their parents' divorce. In part, this feeling may develop because of **parentification,** a reversal of roles in which the child takes on responsibilities usually handled by parents (Hetherington, 1999; Johnston, 1990). Parentification can be instrumental, involving increased responsibility for household tasks and care of siblings. Or it can take an emotional form, in which a child provides emotional support or acts as an advisor or confidant for a parent. Moderate levels of parentification can have positive effects for both boys and girls. However, high levels are related to problems such as depression, anxiety, compulsive caretaking, anger, and irritation, especially for girls. Girls receive such treatment from both mothers and fathers more often than do boys. But emotional parentification precipitated by fathers seems especially difficult for boys to deal with; it is related to anxiety, depression, rebellion, resistance, and withdrawal from the family. Parentification occurs not only in divorced families but in situations of maternal depression and in families experiencing high levels of marital conflict (Emery, 1999a; Hetherington, 1999).

Not surprisingly, the hardest time for most children seems to be the first 2 to 4 years following a divorce (Buchanan, Maccoby, & Dornbusch, 1996; Emery, 1999a). Some studies, however, suggest that more subtle effects of divorce may not become apparent until children reach adolescence or young adulthood and begin attempting to form their own intimate and stable relationships. Sometimes called the **sleeper effect** of divorce, this finding may indicate that children deal with issues stemming from their parents' divorce at each developmental stage they pass through (Bray, 1999; Hetherington, Cox, & Cox, 1982; Sun & Li, 2002). Table 12.3 (page 372) shows the "agree" responses to various statements of well-functioning college students with divorced parents and of students with continuously married parents. As you can see, students still seem to harbor painful feelings about their parents' divorces, even though more than 80% felt that divorce was the right thing for their families. Compared to students with continuously married parents, children with divorced parents had significantly higher ratings of distress on ten of the items (Laumann-Billings & Emery, 2000).

**What Factors Explain the Effects of Divorce?** A decline in both the quantity and quality of parenting accounts for a significant portion of the effects of divorce (Clarke-Stewart, Vandell, McCartney, Owen, & Booth, 2000; Fisher, Leve, O'Leary, & Leve,

Is comparing children in divorced families to children in married families the best way to study the effects of divorce? What other comparisons would be useful here?

▲ With parentification, children feel pressure to grow up faster and assume responsibilities that are normally reserved for parents. Moderate levels of parentification can have positive effects on children, but higher levels can create problems.

**parentification**
Role reversal in which a child assumes responsibilities usually taken care of by parents.

**sleeper effect (of divorce)**
Subtle effects of divorce that may not become apparent until children reach adolescence or young adulthood and have difficulty forming intimate and stable relationships.

**TABLE 12.3**
**Psychological Distress among Well-Adjusted College Students of Divorced Parents**

| ITEM TO BE RATED | PERCENTAGES OF YOUNG ADULTS WHO AGREED OR STRONGLY AGREED WITH THE STATEMENT | |
|---|---|---|
| | DIVORCED PARENTS | CONTINUOUSLY MARRIED PARENTS |
| My father caused most of the trouble in my family. | 60 | 19* |
| I feel like I might have been a different person if my father/mother had been a bigger part of my life. | 51 | 20* |
| I worry about big events like graduations or weddings, when both my parents will have to come. | 50 | 10* |
| I had a harder childhood than most people. | 48 | 14* |
| I wish I had more time with Dad/Mom. | 47 | 19* |
| My childhood was cut short. | 34 | 17* |
| I have not forgiven Dad. | 30 | 6* |
| I have not forgiven Mom. | 7 | 4 |
| I sometimes wonder if my father even loves me. | 29 | 10* |
| I feel doomed to repeat my parents' problems in my own relationships. | 18 | 15 |
| My father is still in love with my mother. | 14 | 78* |
| My mother is still in love with my father. | 11 | 82* |
| My parents' divorce still causes struggles for me. | 49 | Not Applicable |
| I really missed not having my father around as much after my parents' separation. | 48 | Not Applicable |
| Even though it was hard, divorce was the right thing for my family. | 81 | Not Applicable |
| I probably would be a different person if my parents had not gotten divorced. | 73 | Not Applicable |

*Difference between children of divorced and married parents is statistically significant.
(Adapted from Laumann-Billings & Emery, 2000.)

2003; Hilton, 2002; McLanahan, 1999). Even people with good parenting skills can become overwhelmed by the emotional stress of divorce. Many children also become more difficult to manage during this time of change in routines, residences, and rules. Parenting frequently becomes more authoritarian, neglecting, or permissive (Hetherington et al., 1982). If custodial parents are able to maintain good parenting practices, remaining involved with and responsive to their children, their children fare much better (Buchanan et al., 1996; DeGarmo, Forgatch, & Martinez, 1999).

Experts agree that open conflict between parents is very detrimental. It results in worse outcomes for children whether the parents divorce or stay married, especially if the conflict is angry or violent or places the child in the middle (El-Sheikh & Harger, 2001; Emery, 1982; Katz & Woodin, 2002). One study documented an unfortunate cycle: As parents argued more about their children's disruptive behaviors, the children engaged in even more disruptive behavior, which in turn was related to even more parental arguments (Jenkins, Dunn, O'Connor, Rasbash, & Simpson, 2005). Sadly, the amount of conflict experienced by a child may actually increase after a divorce as parents fight over access to children, money, resources, and other issues. Boys tend to be exposed to more conflict than girls, and conflict is greater in stepfamilies than in biological families that are still intact (Jenkins et al., 2005). Even when children manage to avoid most of the conflict, they might still worry and show emotional problems (Rhoades, 2008).

Divorce puts a financial strain on many families as the parents separate and need to find ways to make ends meet on less household income. Families often move, and children feel the strain when they lose their familiar home, friends, schools, and neighborhoods. Community services and social networks can be very helpful in the divorce transition, but maintaining social connections is challenging when families move.

▲ Open conflict between parents is very detrimental for children, whether parents divorce or remain married. Unfortunately, conflict does not necessarily decrease following a divorce.

Experts agree that it's important to see divorce as a process rather than as a single event. This process can begin years before parents actually separate, and it may not end until long after the legal end of the marriage. From the **divorce-stress-adjustment perspective,** the divorce process initiates many events that parents and children find stressful. It is these stressors that increase the risk of negative outcomes for both parents and children (Amato, 2000; Emery, 1999b; Hetherington, Bridges, & Insabella, 1998). As Figure 12.3 (page 374) shows, according to this model the overall effect of divorce depends on several factors. Stressors such as the decrease in financial resources, loss of custody, and parental conflict all have an impact on the child's emotions and behavior. The individual child's specific vulnerabilities, such as a difficult temperament or a genetic predisposition to psychological problems such as depression, may make it more difficult for the child to cope with the stressors. However, the existence of protective factors, such as social support or good coping skills, helps ease the transition. In the end, the outcome for the child is a result of this mixture of stressors, specific vulnerabilities, and protective factors.

Some researchers do not believe that it's the divorce itself that causes many of the negative outcomes for children. Instead, according to the **selection model,** certain characteristics of the parents, such as antisocial personality traits or poor parenting skills, cause both the divorce and children's problems (Amato, 2000; Harris, 1998). This perspective is called the selection model because negative traits cause certain parents to be "selected" out of marriage, and the same traits have negative effects on their children. For example, an abusive father can have a negative effect on his children, and he is more likely to be divorced by his wife. If the children show negative effects after the divorce (aggression or poor school performance, for example), the effects may result more from having lived with the abusive father than from the divorce itself. The effects may have occurred whether the parents divorced or not. Of course both models could operate at the same time (D' Onofrio et al., 2006). Some problems may be due to factors related to the parents (the selection model) and some due to the divorce itself (the divorce-stress-adjustment perspective). It is difficult to disentangle these effects when researchers are studying a complex system such as family life.

**divorce-stress-adjustment perspective**
A model used to understand divorce outcomes; emphasizes that a complex interaction of stressors, specific vulnerabilities, and protective factors determine an individual child's adjustment to divorce.

**selection model**
A model used to understand divorce outcomes; emphasizes that certain characteristics of parents (e.g., abusiveness) rather than the divorce itself cause children's negative outcomes.

**Positive Outcomes of Divorce.** Divorce does have some positive outcomes. For both boys and girls, the ending of a high-conflict marriage can produce beneficial effects, provided that the divorce reduces the degree of conflict. Children in high-conflict intact families score significantly lower on measures of psychological adjustment and self-esteem than children in divorced families (Amato & Keith, 1991; Booth & Amato, 2001; Hanson, 1999; Hetherington, 1999; Hetherington & Kelly, 2002; Jekielek, 1998). Some children, especially daughters, benefit from the development of very close relationships with their mothers after divorce (Amato & Booth, 1997; Arditti, 1999). Following a divorce, moderate demands on children to take more responsibility for household tasks, care for siblings, and provide emotional support to parents and other family members can lead to greater social responsibility, competence, and empathy during adulthood. As we mentioned before, however, excessive demands of this type lead to parentification and are

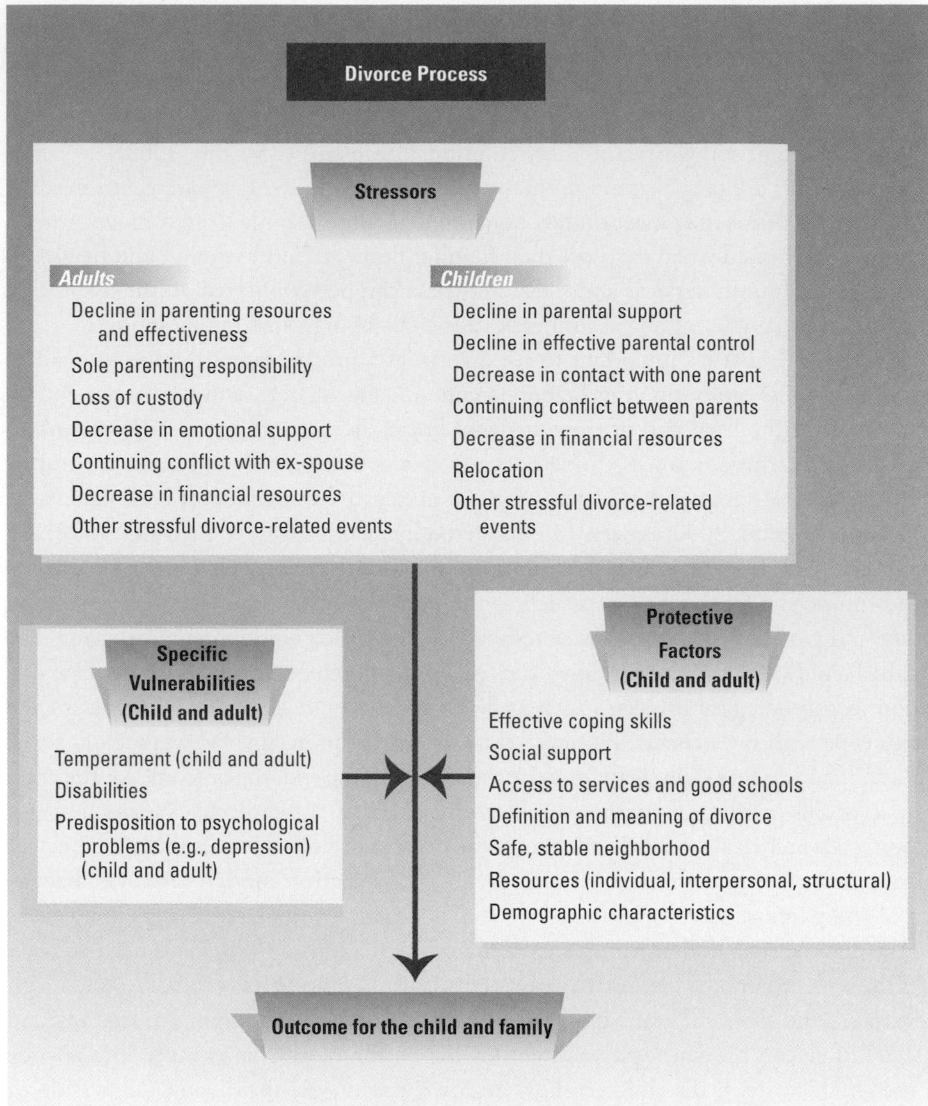


FIGURE 12.3 ▶ **The Divorce-Stress-Adjustment Perspective** The divorce-stress-adjustment perspective views divorce as a process affected by many different stressors specific vulnerabilities, and protective factors. All of these factors interact and affect a child's developmental outcomes. (Adapted from Amato, 2000.)

detrimental to both boys and girls (Hetherington, 1999). When a parent shows high levels of antisocial behavior such as aggression, emotional and financial impulsivity, drug and alcohol problems, and coercive discipline, children fare better the less time they spend with the parent (Jaffee, Moffitt, Caspi, & Taylor, 2003).

Regardless of the outcomes, divorce is a complicated process that individual children experience in individual ways. Psychologists and others who work with divorcing families have identified things parents and other adults can do to help children cope with divorce (Pedro-Carroll, 2001; Wallerstein, 2001). Table 12.4 summarizes some of their suggestions. As you will notice, some of these suggestions may be very difficult for divorcing parents to implement, but when parents are able to follow them, they will help children make more positive adjustments.

## Never-Married Households and Stepfamilies

**Never-Married Households.** In 2007, 40% of all children born in the United States were born to mothers who were not married (Hamilton, Martin, & Ventura, 2009). The rates of childbearing outside of marriage vary widely by ethnic group. For example, in 2006 there was a higher percentage of births outside of marriage for African American

**TABLE 12.4**
Helping Children Cope with Divorce

**Minimize conflict during and after divorce**. Place children's needs above your own when negotiating custody, finances, schooling, and so on. Do not belittle your ex-spouse to children. Do not place children in the middle of parental disputes and ask them to (or imply that they should) take sides.

**Minimize the number of changes children must experience at one time**. Avoid moving if possible; in any case, make as few residence changes as you can. Help the child maintain contact with familiar friends, teachers, schools, and other community resources. Introduce necessary changes gradually whenever possible.

**Prevent children from becoming family caretakers**. Join a support group for divorced parents or call upon friends and family for emotional and practical support rather than burdening children with adult responsibilities.

**Develop and maintain an effective parenting style**. Remain involved and affectionate, but make certain to provide appropriate supervision.

**Seek help and support**. Ask for help from friends and family, as well as counseling from a professional with training in child development. Try family and/or parent-based therapies to improve parenting skills and the quality of parent–child relationships.

**Develop consistent rules for behavior and expectations**. Ideally, both parents should implement the same rules and support each other. Try to agree on what is expected of the child, on consequences, and on routines for monitoring the child's behavior and activities.

**Help children maintain consistent contact with both parents**. Maintain a regular schedule of visits with the noncustodial parent, adjusting the schedule as the child's needs and interests change. Maintain regular telephone, e-mail, or letter contact, especially if a parent lives too far away for frequent visitation. Make sure to remember special events like the child's birthday or holidays. Demonstrate interest in and support for the child's activities by attending recitals, athletic events, and the like at least occasionally.

**Seek professional help for children in pain and distress**. Try school-based group interventions to help reduce distress or change children's beliefs about divorce. Seek individual therapy for children suspected of having more serious problems, such as conduct disorders or depression. Teach children active coping skills, like problem solving and seeking support from others, and help them establish the belief that they can deal effectively with the stresses they are experiencing. Try to provide a model of effective, positive, and proactive problem solving before, during, and after a divorce.

**Help youngsters develop positive interpersonal skills**. Work to develop the skills necessary to establish and maintain intimate relationships, then model these skills for your children through your own healthy interpersonal relationships. Counselors and therapists can include interpersonal skills training in their therapy with children. Parents can request that these issues be addressed.

**Minimize financial decline as much as possible**. Find out about legal or social programs that help support families in transition (e.g., programs that help parents obtain child support payments or find housing, job placement, or educational training assistance).

**Prevent divorce when possible and appropriate**. When possible and appropriate, try to prevent divorce by strengthening a weak marriage and by learning how to deal with conflicts in constructive ways. Try to resolve or minimize conflicts between family and other obligations (e.g., workplace demands).

Amato (2000); Buchanan et al. (1996); Emery, Kitzman, & Waldron (1999); Hetherington (1999); Meyer (1999); Sandler, Tein, Mehta, Wolchik, & Ayers (2000); Wallerstein et al. (2000).

(70%) and Hispanic mothers (50%) than for non-Hispanic white mothers (27%) (Martin et al., 2009). Most of the outcomes associated with divorce also hold true for children whose parents never married. In some cases, in fact, the risks to children of never-married parents are somewhat greater. Financial security is a particularly important factor. Single women head the vast majority of never-married households. Unmarried mothers tend to have relatively low incomes, and they are less likely to receive child support from the fathers of their children than are divorced mothers (Meyer, 1999). Like divorced single parents, never-married single parents tend to have fewer parenting resources and thus show less effective parenting. They also tend to move more frequently, which reduces their access to supportive community connections.

Today increasing numbers of well-educated and financially secure women are becoming single mothers by choice. These women are better off in terms of education and financial resources, but little is known about whether their children fare better than those of other never-married parents. There is also little research on never-married households headed by fathers. Early work on these households shows inconsistent findings. Some research indicates that children have similar levels of well-being regardless of whether they live in single-father or in single-mother homes (Downey, Ainsworth-Darnell, & Dufur, 1998). Other studies have found that children in single-father homes are more troubled, and during adolescence they are at higher risk for substance abuse and violent or risky behavior (Breivik & Olweus, 2006; Jablonska & Lindberg, 2007). It's possible, however, that their problems are the reason for and not the result of these children's being placed with their fathers (Buchanan et al., 1996).

**Stepfamilies.** What happens to children when parents remarry after a divorce? Just as with children of divorced and never-married parents, the picture is complicated. When mothers remarry, the family's financial status may improve, which in turn increases the quality of services and educational opportunities available to the children. However, some groups of children experience greater benefits of remarriage than others. For example, living with a stepfather can increase a boy's chances of finishing high school, attending and graduating from college, and finding subsequent job opportunities. If the stepfamily remains stable over many years and provides appropriate care for the children, it can have a positive effect on children's intimate relationships when they reach adulthood. If children are able to maintain good relationships with both biological parents and stepparents, they can end up with even *more* access to parenting resources than children with continuously married biological parents (Amato, 1999a; Hetherington et al., 1998; McLanahan, 1999; Wallerstein et al., 2000). Most stepchildren seem to have reasonably positive views of their stepfathers. Close relationships between stepchildren and stepparents have positive effects on children's academic achievement and psychological well-being, and introducing a stepparent even in adolescence can be beneficial to children's adjustment (Amato, 1999a; Buchanan et al., 1996; Hetherington & Jodl, 1994).

But stepfamilies also present special challenges. Although remarriage has the potential to increase financial security, there is also the risk that it may worsen children's financial circumstances. Some experts point out that remarried parents, particularly remarried fathers, may feel pressure to provide first for their new spouse's children from a prior marriage or for biological children they have with their new spouse. As a consequence, these parents may decrease financial and/or emotional support to their biological children from a previous marriage, especially if these biological children do not live with them (Wallerstein et al., 2000). Additionally, although this is not inevitable, the quality of parenting is often even lower in remarried families than in single-mother households. The rules change, family members take on different roles, and it takes time to sort things out and establish new routines and responsibilities. There may be competition between the children and their

THINKING CRITICALLY
What are some of the common themes that run through the research findings on divorced, never-married, and stepfamilies?

stepfather for the mother's time and attention, leaving the mother with less time than before to parent effectively. Such competition may be more stressful for girls than for boys, especially if daughters have been providing friendship and close emotional support to their divorced mothers. Stepfathers tend to be less involved and less emotionally supportive than continuously married biological fathers, and they provide less discipline and supervision of children (Hetherington & Clingempeel, 1992). All in all, even though stepparents have the potential to positively affect their stepchildren's development, children in remarried families are typically no better off in their behavioral and psychological outcomes, and sometimes show worse outcomes, than children of single-parent families (Amato, 1994).

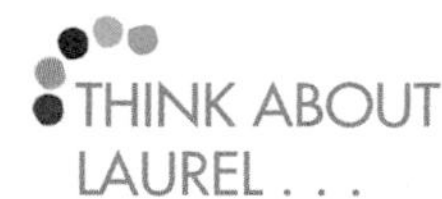


Given Laurel's reaction to her mother's dating, what issues do you think would arise if Laurel's mother remarried?

## LET'S REVIEW . . .

1. According to the divorce-stress-adjustment model, the overall effect of a divorce on children's outcomes depends on ____________.
   a. genetically based personality traits
   b. the emotional health and parenting skills of the parents
   c. how the family adjusts to the stress of financial loss after the divorce
   d. children's vulnerabilities in combination with stressors and protective factors
2. Which of the following is *not* one of the causes of the negative effects of divorce?
   a. Families often move after a divorce.
   b. Conflict between parents often continues after a divorce.
   c. Parenting usually becomes more authoritative after a divorce.
   d. Families usually have fewer financial resources after a divorce.
3. With never-married households, the most important factor leading to negative outcomes for children seems to be ____________.
   a. fewer financial resources in the family
   b. depression in the single parent
   c. the social stigma of living in a single-parent home
   d. the frequent moves and transitions that occur with these families
4. Most children living in stepfamilies:
   a. have relatively negative views of their stepparents.
   b. are no better off in outcomes than are children in single-parent households.
   c. experience a higher quality of parenting than children in single-parent households.
   d. have significantly worse outcomes than children living in single-parent households.
5. True or False: Boys handle parentification more effectively when it comes from their fathers than when it comes from their mothers.
6. True or False: Compared to boys in single-mother homes, boys who live with stepfathers tend to do more poorly in school and are less likely to attend college.

Answers: 1. d, 2. c, 3. a, 4. b, 5. F, 6. F

# Play, Friends, and Peer Popularity

Early childhood was a time of fantasy and make-believe play when young children were exercising their newfound symbolic thinking abilities. During middle childhood, children's thinking becomes more logical, and their play during this period follows suit. Middle childhood is also an important time for children to form friendships and become "best friends" with special peers and playmates. As they interact more frequently with children their own age at school and in play, some children become popular while other children become less popular or even rejected by peers. In this section, we turn to what researchers have discovered about the important world of children's play, friends, and peer popularity.

### AS YOU STUDY THIS SECTION, ASK YOURSELF THESE QUESTIONS:

**12.8** What are the main characteristics in play during middle childhood, and what are the connections that cause children to become best friends?

**12.9** What are the characteristics associated with children who are more popular among their peers, and what about those who are less popular?

**12.10** How do researchers understand peer popularity, and how do children respond when they are rejected by their peers?

## Play and Best Friends

As we described in Chapter 11, by 7 years of age, most children have entered Piaget's stage of concrete operational thought. Their thought processes become more logical and realistic, and fantasy and pretend tend to give way to seeing the world more as it really is. Children now enjoy play activities and games that involve structured rules. Children can follow the rules in board games; counting games like "one potato, two potato" take on a real logical force; and the rules and strategies of video games can occupy some children for hours. Although elements of fantasy can still be fun, it is now the logic in the games that becomes the focus of interest. Children's collections give more evidence of their new sense of logic, order, and organization. At this age, children collect sports cards, action figures, dolls, and other toys more for the interest of acquiring and organizing them than for the fun of playing with them. Negotiating trades and developing strategies for improving such collections are important exercises in logical thought (Hughes, 1999).

During middle childhood, play often involves acquiring and improving physical skills. Hitting a baseball, jumping rope, climbing trees, riding bicycles, and skateboarding are common examples of skill-based play. Mastery of skills is important to children—they often push the limits of their skills and demonstrate their mastery by performing stunts that become increasingly complex and dangerous. Jumping a ramp on a skateboard or hanging by a knee from a tree limb can alarm parents but it gives children a sense of accomplishment and even impresses peers. During the grade school years, children demonstrate their skills in order to establish their positions in peer groups (Hughes, 1999). Many children, too, become involved in organized sports, as we discussed in Chapter 10. When the fun of participating in the game is children's main motivation, then involvement in sports can rightly qualify as play. If, however, children participate in sports because parents or coaches pressure them, or for the sake of winning alone, then their activity has moved out of the proper realm of play. **Watch** on **mydevelopmentlab**

**Watch** a video on Friends. www.mydevelopmentlab.com

*Best friends* is a special category of friends. A child's relationship with a best friend is closer and more exclusive than relationships with the casual acquaintances most children refer to as "friends." The number of best friends that children have tends to increase until about age 11, and then children become much more selective in whom they designate as their best friends (Epstein, 1986; Rubin, Bukowski, & Parker, 1998). In one study that is often cited, Bigelow (1977) asked Canadian and Scottish schoolchildren what they expected in their best (same-sex) friends. First graders most frequently reported that having common activities was important. By the eighth grade the most important trait was an admirable character, followed by common activities, acceptance, and loyalty and commitment. Only girls mentioned the potential for intimacy (sharing personal thoughts and feelings) as an important feature, and only after the fifth grade. Children rarely mentioned physical attractiveness as an important characteristic in best friends. Also rarely mentioned were shared personal characteristics (such as both friends being shy). Other researchers find that loyalty, faithfulness, and generosity define close friendships during middle childhood. "He shares his best things with me," "She sticks by me when other kids tease me," and "She doesn't ignore me when her other friends are around" are common descriptions of best friends during this period of childhood (Berndt, 1986; Bigelow, 1977; Rubin et al., 1998; Smollar & Youniss, 1982). To read more about how two best friends describe their relationship, read the Personal Perspective box: "We Are Best Friends."

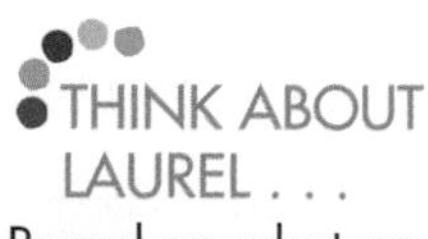


Based on what we know about "best friends," what can Laurel expect to give and to receive in her close friendships with other children?

## Perspective PERSONAL WE ARE BEST FRIENDS

Sophia Martin (age 7) and Mariana Hertel (age 8)
Ellicott City, MD

**Why are you best friends?**
Sophia: Mariana is my best friend because she makes me laugh.
Mariana: Because we have a lot in common.

**What makes you best friends?**
Sophia: We have a lot in common.
Mariana: We are best friends because we like playing with each other.

**Why do you like each other best?**
Sophia: Because I think Mariana is very nice.

**How long have you been friends?**
Sophia and Mariana: For 4 years.

**How did you meet?**
Sophia: When Mariana said, "Can you be my friend?"
Mariana: We met at La Petite (daycare center).

**What do you like to do together?**
Sophia: Play horses at school.
Mariana: We like to play horses with each other.

QUESTION **As these girls enter middle childhood, how do their reasons for being best friends compare with those identified by researchers? Are their reasons typical for middle childhood?**

### Peer Popularity

Picture yourself as a child in a third-grade classroom. A researcher comes in and explains to the whole class that she would like to know how children pick their friends. She then gives each child a list of all of the children in the class. She asks you to look down the list of names and select the children you "like best" and the ones you "like least." Whom do you pick?

As you can imagine, when the researcher collects the lists, some names will have received a lot of positive nominations (many selections for "like best"). There will be other children, unfortunately, with a lot of negative nominations (many selections for "like least"). Others will get a mixture of positive and negative nominations or practically no nominations at all. This **peer nomination technique** is the method researchers employ most often to measure social status in childhood. Using this rather simple polling technique, researchers have identified numerous characteristics that distinguish popular and unpopular children. In this next section, we will describe the differences between popular and unpopular children, and we will also consider some of the important consequences that occur when some children are rejected by their peers.

Figure 12.4 (page 380) shows how researchers typically categorize children using the peer nomination technique. As you can see in the figure, five categories of children emerge from the nomination patterns: *popular, rejected, controversial, average,* and *neglected.*

**Popular children** are the ones who receive a large number of "like best" nominations. These children are well liked. In general, popular children are friendly, cooperative, sociable, and sensitive to the needs of others (Rubin, Bukowski, & Parker,, 2006). They like to interact with other children, they are helpful, and they show good leadership skills. Popular children also have good communication skills: They speak clearly and are good listeners. Although they can be assertive, popular children are usually not aggressive in a way that interferes with the other children's happiness.

One of the special characteristics researchers have noted in popular children is their easy and nondisruptive manner when joining activities or new groups of children (Dodge,

**peer nomination technique**
A polling technique used to identify categories of popular and unpopular children.

**popular children**
Children whom a large number of peers have chosen as classmates they "like best."

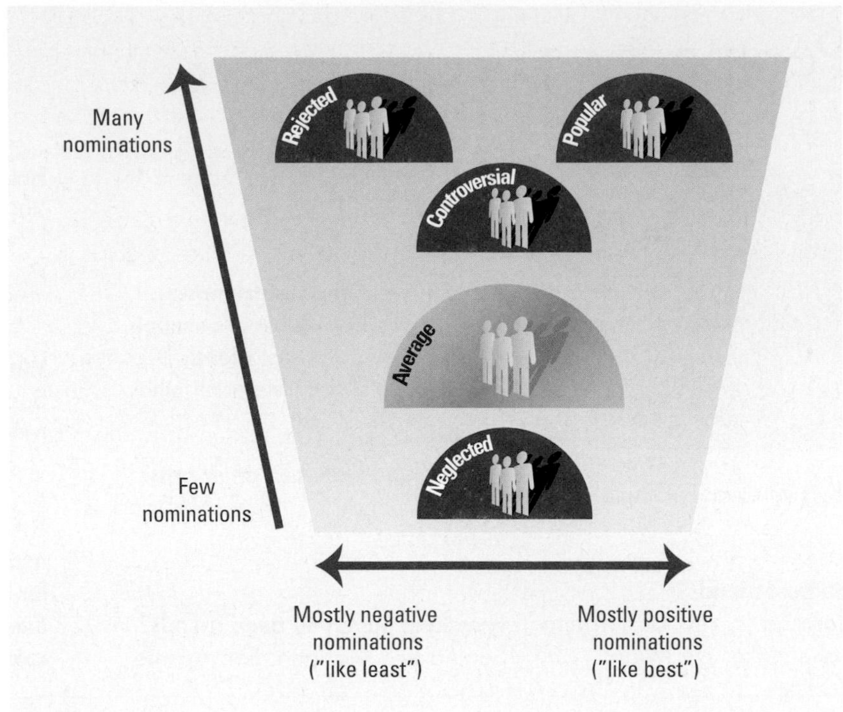


FIGURE 12.4 ▶ **Peer Nomination Categories**
With the peer nomination technique, researchers ask children to name peers they "like best" and "like least." The number and types of nominations (positive and negative) determine categories. For example, "rejected" children are those who receive a large number of negative nominations; "neglected" children are those who receive few nominations of either type.

Pettit, McClaskey, & Brown, 1986; Putallaz, 1983). If, for example, they come to the playground at recess and find that other children are already playing kickball, popular children are likely to find an easy and friendly way to join the game. They may begin by hanging around other children who are waiting for a turn to kick, then gradually move onto the team as other children accept them. They are sensitive to social cues from other children, and they back away if others seem offended by their presence. Rather than being overbearing, popular children find a way to join activities without drawing a lot of attention to themselves. They ease in gradually without disrupting the game for others. Later, after they have gained acceptance from the other children, they may take on a leadership role or may become more of the center of attention. **Simulate** on **mydevelopmentlab**

**Simulate** Measuring Popularity in Young Children www.mydevelopmentlab.com

**Rejected children** also receive a large number of nominations—but the nominations are of the "like least" variety. These children are actively disliked. This category typically includes two subtypes that are very different from each other. On the one hand, researchers classify about half of all rejected children as *rejected–aggressive* (French, 1988; Rubin et al., 2006). Rejected–aggressive children are physically aggressive (they often hit, push, and bully other children), and they are also verbally abusive (they threaten and tease others). To join the kickball game, for example, they may grab the ball, declare that "it's my turn to kick!" and threaten violence against anyone who challenges them. Alternatively, rejected–aggressive children may disrupt the game and try to start a new game of their own: "C'mon, this game's for sissies; let's go play some real football instead!" Girls in the rejected category are less likely than boys to use physical aggression or direct verbal assaults. Instead, they use more *relational aggression*—withdrawing friendship or otherwise disrupting or threatening social relationships. For example, rejected girls are more likely to force their way into a game by saying, "If you don't let me play, I won't be your best friend anymore!"

Another 20% or so of rejected children are withdrawn and timid, and they fall under the *rejected–withdrawn* heading. Not all withdrawn children are rejected; out of the children who are most withdrawn in a class, only about one-quarter actually receive "like least" nominations (Rubin et al., 2006). When children are younger, they are less likely to dislike classmates who are withdrawn. By later childhood, however, some withdrawn children

**rejected children**
Children who are actively disliked; a large number of peers have chosen them as classmates they "like least."

become outcasts and experience considerable disdain from their peers. In many cases there is something about rejected–withdrawn children that puts off or annoys other children. For example, they may dress or behave oddly, or they may blatantly refuse to participate or cooperate with other children. The climate of the classroom or school can also play a role—children who are withdrawn and timid tend to fare worse in classrooms that are disorganized, chaotic, or hostile (Gazelle, 2006).

The remaining children in the rejected category fall between the aggressive and withdrawn subtypes. Though they are "liked least," it is not clear how these children differ from other peers who may simply be considered "shy."

**Controversial children** are an especially intriguing group. These children receive large numbers of both positive and negative nominations: A lot of children pick them as "like best," but just as many pick them as "like least." This category tends to be very small in most groups of children, and researchers have not studied it in great detail. In one study, however, it appeared that although controversial boys were more aggressive, active, disruptive, and angry than average children, they were also more helpful and cooperative and showed more leadership than average (Coie & Dodge, 1988).

**Average children** receive moderate numbers of both "like best" and "like least" nominations. That is, unlike children in the controversial category, average children don't receive a large number of either type of nomination. These children tend to show good social skills, but some are more aggressive than popular children and others are a bit more withdrawn.

**Neglected children** receive very few "like best" or "like least" peer nominations. Instead, these children seem to be mostly ignored by other children. As you might imagine, neglected children don't interact with other children very often. They tend to be less sociable than the average child, but they are also less negative, disruptive, and aggressive than average. They seem to actively avoid aggressive confrontations (Coie & Dodge, 1988; Rubin et al., 2006). Most neglected children do not show high levels of social anxiety or wariness of other children. Remember that when social withdrawal becomes more extreme, children sometimes receive enough "like least" nominations to place them in the rejected category. Also, membership in the neglected category is not very stable (Rubin et al., 2006). When researchers wait just a few months and repeat the peer nomination process, they often find that many names in the previous neglected group have moved into other categories. Finally, note carefully how children in the neglected category differ from rejected children. *Neglected children* don't receive many nominations at all—they are mostly ignored. In contrast, *rejected children* are actively disliked and receive a large number of negative nominations.

The peer nomination technique reveals clear associations between levels of popularity and certain personality characteristics. Popular children tend to be sociable and friendly and to enter groups easily. Children who are less popular tend to be either more aggressive or withdrawn. Looking at this research, you might infer that a sociable and friendly manner causes some children to become popular, and that aggression and withdrawal lead to unpopularity. However, we must again caution that these associations are merely correlational. We don't know for certain what is the cause and what is the effect. Children who are already popular have an easier time being friendly with other children. On the other hand, children who are rejected at a young age tend to become more hostile and aggressive as the years pass (Dodge et al., 2003). Although we assume that it is the social characteristics of children that lead, at least in part, to their peer nomination category, in the end we cannot be sure. It is logically possible that the popularity or unpopularity comes first and the social characteristics (like friendliness or aggressiveness) follow afterward.

Also note that we are using the term "popular" in this section to refer to children who are well-liked by other children. In another connotation, people often use the term "popular" to refer to children or teens who have high social status (they are looked up to or

THINKING CRITICALLY

What other techniques or methods can you think of to measure peer popularity? What are the advantages and disadvantages of these techniques?

THINK ABOUT LAUREL . . .

How do you think Laurel's peers would rate her peer popularity? In which peer nomination category do you think she would be placed?

**controversial children**
Children who receive large numbers of both "like best" and "like least" nominations.

**average children**
Children who receive moderate numbers of both "like best" and "like least" nominations.

**neglected children**
Children who have very few peers who like them best or least.

held in high regard). Research findings can differ depending on which form of the word is used (Schwartz, Gorman, Nakamoto, & McKay, 2006). For example, adolescents who are well-liked tend to be less aggressive than others, and they tend do well in school. Some adolescents who are aggressive, however, still have high social status (they are "popular" in their schools) but they tend to perform poorly in school. In some cases, their popularity even increases as their grades and performance fall in school. These aggressive teens may not be well-liked, but other teens agree that they are still popular as leaders of certain social crowds. Aggressive children are not very popular during the early grade school years, but during the high school years some of these teens become more popular as they also become more aggressive (Xie, Li, Boucher, Hutchins, & Cairns, 2006). **Listen** on **mydevelopmentlab**

**Listen**: What is the difference between the terms "peer popularity" and "popular"? (Author Podcast) www.mydevelopmentlab.com

The peer nomination technique has also been used to study racial discrimination in classrooms. African American children, for example, receive more negative nominations (e.g., "like least") when they are in classes with low percentages of African American students (Jackson, Barth, Powell, & Lochman, 2006). When they feel isolated in smaller numbers, minority children may feel intimidated by the majority racial group in the class. As their percentages increase in classrooms, African American children tend to have more social interactions with classmates and more positive opportunities—and African Americans in these classrooms receive more "like best" and other positive peer nominations. It's not just with race: Even when children are divided artificially into "red groups" and "blue groups," they tend to perceive their own group as better and more friendly, and they develop negative stereotypes about the "other" group (Patterson & Bigler, 2006). Teachers, parents, and others can help children reduce their stereotyping by encouraging them to play and make friends across racial, ethnic, religious, and other group lines. Research shows that children have fewer racial biases when they have more opportunity to socialize with children from different groups (McGlothlin & Killen, 2006).

## A Social Cognition Model of Peer Relations, and Helping Rejected Children

It is clear that children differ in how they behave in social situations. Some children are more friendly, generous, and cooperative; others tend to be more aggressive or withdrawn. Looking at how children process information in social settings can shed light on some of these differences. Drawing on information-processing theory and cognitive psychology, Ken Dodge and his associates have developed a **social cognition model** to explain some of the important differences in how different children perceive, interpret, and respond to information in social settings (Crick & Dodge, 1994; Dodge, 1986). According to Dodge's model of social cognition, a child's response depends on how he or she processes social events during these steps:

- *Perceiving the information.* How did the event look and sound? Did the child notice all of the details in the event?
- *Interpreting the information.* What does the child think about what he sees and hears? Is the interpretation positive, or is it negative and suspicious?
- *Considering potential responses and enacting one.* Children use their perceptions and interpretations to determine their range of responses. Which potential response they choose to enact depends on the interpretation they make.

**social cognition model**
A model that explains how different children perceive, interpret, and respond to information in social settings.

Now consider how this model relates to peer popularity. Research suggests that popular children have a positive bias when they process social information—they tend to perceive and interpret social situations as being comfortable and friendly (Rubin et al., 2006). When negative events do happen, these children are likely to interpret them as being innocent. Rejected children, however, tend to have negative biases that lead to negative interpretations. Rejected–aggressive children tend to see even innocent events as threats. For example, they might interpret an accidental bump in the school hallway as a provocation to fight. Their negative interpretations lead to aggressive responses—to revenge, attack, or self-defense. Because these children are overly negative and aggressive, their peers tend to reject them. Many rejected–withdrawn children have difficulty acting out social responses (Stewart & Rubin, 1995). Although they may know how to respond appropriately, they are reluctant to take the risk. In turn, other children may misinterpret their withdrawal as a sign of disinterest or contempt. By interpreting events negatively or by failing to act out positive responses, some children create circumstances that lead to social failure. Their maladaptive social cognitions cause these children to become unpopular among their peers.

THINKING CRITICALLY

Rather than basing the model of information processing, how would a model of peer popularity or social relationships look if were based instead on the theory of operant conditioning? What if it was based on social learning theory? Refer back to Chapter 1 for these theories.

Unfortunately, the negative social experiences some children face in their early years can continue as they get older. Compared to popular children, rejected children are seven times more likely to fail a grade in school and nearly four times more likely to drop out of school before tenth grade (Kupersmidt & Coie, 1990; Ollendick, Weist, Borden, & Greene, 1992). Children who are less accepted by their classmates in school tend to get lower grades and tend to be rated by teachers as more anxious, fearful, and depressed (Flook, Repetti, & Ullman, 2005). Correlations also exist between peer rejection and higher rates of delinquency, arrest, violent behavior, and substance abuse (Kupersmidt & Coie, 1990; Ollendick et al., 1992). Children who show behavior problems during the early school years tend to be more rejected and have fewer friends in the later school years, and they report more feelings of being lonely and depressed (Pedersen, Vitaro, Barker, & Borge, 2007). Reviewing the research in this area, one pair of authors concluded that "childhood peer relations have been identified as one of the most powerful predictors of concurrent and future mental health problems, including the development of psychiatric disorders" (Mueller & Silverman, 1989, p. 529).

Accounts of peer rejection often emerge when communities try to understand incidents of school violence. Consider the case of Charles "Andy" Williams, a 15-year-old high school freshman. Williams opened fire on students and teachers from the high school bathroom. In an 8-minute shooting spree, Williams killed two students and wounded 11 other students, a security guard, and a student teacher. Some students described Williams as an "outsider," a "nerd," and a "dork." Others reported being close friends with Williams. One friend commented that Williams was the most trustworthy friend he ever had, and a prior girlfriend described him as "real nice" and "very popular" (ABC News, 2001; *New York Times,* 2001). Nevertheless, peer rejection was the focus of the early investigation into the shootings. Some witnesses reported that Williams was smiling as he shot, as if he was getting back at people who had rejected him.

▲ Many social interactions are somewhat ambiguous. When her friends are whispering, how will the girl in this photo interpret the situation? According to the social cognition model, her interpretation will determine the type of response she gives.

Peer rejection is a powerful force in children's lives, especially when the child being rejected is also ridiculed, harassed, or bullied. Although rejection leads to murder and suicide only in rare instances, it is associated with countless other acts of lesser violence, delinquency, isolation, and loneliness. Fortunately, intervention programs have shown some promise in helping children gain acceptance among peers (Asher, Parker, & Walker, 1996; Frey et al., 2005). School psychologists, counselors, and other professionals can now use videotapes, adult and peer coaching, role-playing, and direct instruction to help rejected and neglected children develop the social skills they need. By successfully making and keeping friends, these children and adolescents may be able to avoid despair and its destructive effects.

## LET'S REVIEW . . .

1. Which statement below best summarizes the type of friendships children have during middle childhood?
   - **a.** "He is my friend because he sticks by me when other kids make fun of me."
   - **b.** "She is my friend because she is my neighbor and we play together a lot."
   - **c.** "She is my friend because we are in the same class in school."
   - **d.** "He is my friend because he is smart like me."
2. A lot of children in Jenny's class really like her, but many other children strongly dislike her. With the peer nomination technique, Jenny would be categorized as __________.
   - **a.** rejected
   - **b.** neglected
   - **c.** average
   - **d.** controversial
3. Rejected children tend to be __________ while neglected children are more __________.
   - **a.** disliked; ignored
   - **b.** withdrawn; aggressive
   - **c.** liked; disliked
   - **d.** passive; aggressive
4. Research using the social cognition model of peer popularity suggests that rejected–withdrawn children have difficulty:
   - **a.** perceiving social cues in a positive way.
   - **b.** interpreting social cues in a positive way.
   - **c.** enacting appropriate social responses.
   - **d.** understanding the difference between their perception and interpretation of social cues.
5. True or False: Structured rules and logic become the focus of play during middle childhood.
6. True or False: An important skill that many popular children have is an ability to join groups without disturbing the group or drawing too much attention to themselves.

Answers: 1. a, 2. d, 3. a, 4. c, 5. T, 6. T

# Schools and the Media

Children spend an enormous amount of time in school, and when they are home they are often watching TV, playing video games, or using computers or other forms of media. Children are certainly influenced by their parents and peers, but schools and the media are two contexts that expose children to an even wider social world. In this final section of the chapter we look at attitudes children have about school, how children are affected by teachers and the climate and structure of classrooms, and how children interact with TV, video games, computers, and other forms of media.

AS YOU STUDY THIS SECTION, ASK YOURSELF THESE QUESTIONS:

- **12.11** How are children affected by their own beliefs about school and learning and by the expectations that teachers have of them?
- **12.12** How does the climate in the classroom affect children, and what are the effects of grouping children by their abilities?
- **12.13** What kinds of media do children use?
- **12.14** Does watching violence on TV cause children to be more aggressive?
- **12.15** What are researchers finding out about the effects of video games, computers, and children's use of the Internet?

## Children's Beliefs and Teachers' Expectations about Schooling

**achievement motivation** The degree to which a person chooses to engage in and keep trying to accomplish challenging tasks.

Children's Beliefs. **Achievement motivation** is the degree to which a person chooses to engage in and keep trying to accomplish challenging tasks. Children's achievement motivation involves a complex interplay between their beliefs about why they do or do not achieve, their values concerning the importance of and expected benefit from achieving, and their psychological goals (Wigfield, Eccles, Schiefele, Roeser, & Davis-Kean, 2006). Psychologists call children's beliefs about why they succeed or fail **attributions.** Attributions tend to focus on five factors: ability, effort, luck, task difficulty, and strategy use (Alderman, 1999; Weiner, 1992). Notice how some of these factors are *internal* (ability, effort, strategy use), whereas others are *external* (luck, task difficulty). Some are *stable* over time, whereas others are *unstable* or changeable (such as luck or task difficulty; ability can be viewed as either). Some are more *controllable* (like effort and strategy use), whereas others are *uncontrollable* (like luck).

THINK ABOUT LAUREL . . .

How can achievement motivation be helpful for Laurel in school? What are the benefits of this type of motivation?

The attributions a child makes about performance have important effects on the child's behavior and achievement motivation. For example, some children develop a **mastery orientation.** They attribute their successes to their own hard work and abilities—internal and controllable factors—and their failures to factors that they can either control (such as effort or strategy) or change (such as task difficulty). These children tend to believe that they can improve their abilities. They focus on *learning goals,* attempting tasks that are more difficult because they believe this helps them learn new skills and therefore increase their overall abilities. These children tend to be high in achievement motivation, because successes on challenging tasks validate their beliefs that they are able and work hard. Failures simply mean that they need to work harder or try a different strategy.

Other children, however, develop a more **helpless orientation.** These children attribute their failures to their own basic lack of ability, and they attribute successes to external and uncontrollable factors such as luck. They tend to avoid challenging tasks, because failure would tell them they are low in ability. They do not persist on difficult tasks, because to keep trying would be to experience continuous reminders of their lack of ability. In these children's minds, if they were capable, they wouldn't have to try so hard, and continued effort won't help them improve their abilities. So why keep trying? Instead, these children focus on *performance goals,* seeking out tasks they are sure they can do well. Unfortunately, this orientation sets up a negative cycle in which children consistently avoid the very situations that could help them develop important new skills (Dweck & Leggett, 1988; Elliott & Dweck, 1988; Weiner, 2000).

THINKING CRITICALLY

Is your attribution orientation more mastery oriented or more helpless oriented? Why do you think you developed the orientation you have? How could you change your orientation if you wanted to?

Parents' and teachers' feedback can strongly influence the specific views that children develop, particularly how much emphasis adults place on factors such as intelligence (which children cannot change) and effort (which children can change) (Dweck, 2001; Wigfield et al., 2006). Culture also plays an important role. An interesting cross-cultural study showed that Chinese children tend to associate learning with the personal virtues of diligence, persistence, and concentration (Li, 2004). In Chinese society, children who lack these virtues are often viewed as irresponsible, or even immoral, because they don't strive to be good. American children, however, tend to view learning as a task to be tackled, and they emphasize the learner's ability and use of strategies in tackling the task. For the Chinese, learning is a moral value, but with Americans it is more of a practical task to be accomplished.

**attributions**
Individuals' beliefs about why they or others succeed or fail.

**mastery orientation**
The tendency to attribute success to internal and controllable factors such as hard work and ability, and to attribute failure to controllable or changeable factors such as effort, strategy, or task difficulty.

**helpless orientation**
The tendency to attribute success to external and uncontrollable factors such as luck, and to attribute failure to internal and stable factors such as lack of ability.

**Teachers' Expectations.** Not surprisingly, teachers have an important influence on child development. As we just noted, teachers communicate their beliefs about ability in the kind of feedback they offer. Teachers' beliefs also affect the goals they set for learning, classroom activities, grouping practices, and rewards (Ames, 1992). Additionally, teachers' beliefs about learning and teaching shape classroom practice and interaction. For example, teachers who hold a constructivist view of learning (a view based on the theories of Piaget and Vygotsky, as presented in Chapters 5 and 8) are more likely than teachers with behavioral views to think of themselves as guides for learning. Constructivist teachers tend to encourage student exploration and questioning, value students' perspectives, adjust the curriculum to fit students' needs, and emphasize thinking processes rather than

▲ A warm and supportive classroom climate improves students' motivation and achievement. Such an atmosphere requires a supportive teacher who has good classroom management and effective teaching skills.

final answers (Elliott, Kratochwill, Cook, & Travers, 2000). Interestingly, teachers' beliefs about their own teaching effectiveness are correlated with student achievement. Teachers who believe they can teach even the most challenging students work harder to do so, and their students benefit (Tschannen-Moran, Woolfolk Hoy, & Hoy, 1998).

One classic study demonstrated the potential power of teacher expectations (Rosenthal & Jacobson, 1968). In this study, researchers told teachers that certain students would probably show large intellectual gains during the upcoming year. In fact, the researchers randomly selected the list of "intellectual bloomers." By the end of the year, however, these children showed significantly greater increases in IQ scores than other children in the teachers' classes. This type of change is a **self-fulfilling prophecy:** a prediction that comes true because a person believes it will and behaves in ways that produce the expected outcome. As you might expect, the possibility that self-fulfilling prophecies were at work in school achievement stirred a great deal of interest when the study first came out. However, critics pointed out that the effects were not as substantial as they initially seemed. Significant differences were found only in first and second grades, and they may have occurred because of large gains on the part of only five children. Critics also noted several problems with the design and analysis of the study (Elashoff & Snow, 1971; Snow, 1995).

THINKING CRITICALLY

Identify examples of "warmer" and "cooler" classroom climates you have experienced. Why did they feel like this to you? What could have made a cooler climate feel warmer?

## Classroom Climate and Grouping Practices in Schools

**Classroom Climate.** As you probably know from personal experience, classrooms can differ dramatically in the kind of emotional environment or **classroom climate** they offer. Classroom climate reflects the general attitudes, social and emotional responses, and perceptions of the individuals in the class; in other words, it is the way the classroom feels to those in it (Zahn, Kagan, & Widaman, 1986). Many different factors affect classroom climate, including student characteristics and behaviors (e.g., self-regulation skills, attentional abilities, attitudes, and engagement); teacher characteristics (e.g., levels of warmth and supportiveness, friendliness, expectations, and effectiveness of direction and feedback); and even the physical arrangement of the classroom and the number of students in the class (Chang, 2003; Eccles & Roeser, 1999; MacAulay, 1990; NICHD Early Child Care Research Network, 2004; Wentzel & Watkins, 2002). A positive classroom climate is associated with higher student motivation and achievement, but simply being a warm and friendly teacher is not enough to produce a positive climate. Good classroom management and effective teaching skills are essential. Teachers must establish and maintain clear procedures and rules for activities and behavior; at the same time, they must allow children to make choices, follow individual interests, and actively participate in class decisions and discussions. These practices help build a classroom climate in which students develop feelings of competence and autonomy—feelings conducive to higher student engagement, motivation, and learning (Ben-Ari & Eliassy, 2003; Deci & Ryan, 1985).

**Grouping Practices.** A teacher's or a school's approach to grouping can have an important effect on children's achievement and motivation. There is considerable debate about **ability grouping,** the practice of placing children in instructional groups based on their ability levels. Particularly controversial is *between-class ability grouping,* or tracking, in which students within a grade attend separate classes according to ability level. Common in secondary schools, this practice can have positive effects for high-ability students, but the long-term effects for students in lower-ability or non-college tracks are generally negative (Eccles & Roeser, 1999; Slavin, 1990). Often the quality of instruction in lower-ability classes is not as good as in higher-ability classes. Students' contact with peers of

**self-fulfilling prophecy**
A prediction that comes true because people believe the prediction and behave in ways that produce the expected outcome.

**classroom climate**
The social and emotional environment within a classroom; the way the classroom feels to those in it.

**ability grouping**
Placing children in instructional groups based on their ability levels.

different ability levels is also very limited, which makes it harder for lower-ability students to develop friendships with classmates who might model stronger academic skills and motivation (Garmon, Nystrand, Berends, & LePore, 1995; Slavin, 1990).

It is vital that each child begin school ready to learn, experience early success to gain a solid foundation for learning, and learn that effort and persistence make a difference. Each child must feel that school is relevant and important in his or her life, and each must feel individually known and valued by teachers and staff. These are challenging goals that require the active involvement of all who care about children's academic success and overall quality of life. Helping children feel welcomed and valued is especially difficult when the children come from immigrant families or families that do not speak English as their first language. To read more about programs designed to help children learn to be bilingual, see the Social Policy Perspective box called "Bilingual Education in the Schools."

## Perspective SOCIAL POLICY: BILINGUAL EDUCATION IN THE SCHOOLS

In 2002, Massachusetts voters elected to end bilingual education as it was then practiced. Both California and Arizona have passed similar voter referenda, but Colorado's voters rejected such a measure (Zehr, 2002). What is bilingual education, and why is it so controversial?

In the current debate, the term *bilingual education* refers to several different types of programs, all of which have the ultimate goal of helping non–English-speaking children learn English. Ironically, very few of the programs try to help students become truly bilingual—that is, fluent and literate in two languages. Two main types of programs are in contention. In *transitional bilingual education* (TBE), instruction is mostly in the child's native language. TBE provides some English instruction and gradually increases the use of English as students' English skills increase. In contrast, with *structured English immersion* (SEI) instruction is mostly in English from the earliest stages, using students' native language only as needed.

Those trying to end TBE forms of bilingual education argue that TBE programs simply do not work. Children spend many years in TBE yet still score lower on measures of achievement than students in SEI programs (Baker, 1998). Critics also claim that TBE programs enroll almost exclusively Spanish-speaking children and Creole-speaking Haitian children, essentially segregating these children from mainstream education (Baker, 1998; Rossell & Baker, 1996). These advocates of reform point to several examples of SEI programs across the country (e.g., in California, Texas, Virginia, and Maryland), and they cite improvements on California test scores under SEI as evidence that these programs work, work better, and work more quickly than TBE—exactly what children need if they are to compete in classrooms and the job market (Baker, 1998; Zehr, 2001).

Opponents of the reform measures argue that research reviews showing SEI's superiority are flawed, using only a handful of studies, and that critics have misinterpreted the reported changes in test scores in California. In fact, reform opponents claim that the rate of test score improvement has been *slower* under SEI and that changes in other areas (e.g., smaller class sizes) could just as well explain improvements. Also, they point out, in some areas scores for students in SEI programs have remained the same or even dropped (Krashen, 1999; Orr & Hakuta, 2000). Some argue that laws ending TBE are discriminatory, equating school underachievement with bilingual education and language difference with cognitive disability (Attinasi, 1998). They also claim that the newly mandated SEI programs follow an inappropriate model. The early studies took place in Canada; their explicit goal was true bilingualism, they used bilingual teachers, and they served students from middle-class backgrounds who were already fluent and literate in one language. Finally, one summary of the research concludes that immersion or early-exit programs (SEI) may keep students where they are in terms of achievement but do not help them catch up (Crawford, 1997). Several years after the Massachusetts law was passed, one study concluded that some schools have developed successful programs for English-language learners, but many have not (Smith, Coggins, & Cardoso, 2008).

QUESTION **What do you think of bilingual education? How does this debate relate to issues of classroom climate and effective schools? Which approach to bilingual education makes the most sense to you?**

## Children and the Media

▲ Children in the United States spend many hours watching television, with much of the time unsupervised by adults.

More kinds of media are available to children today than ever before. Television, movies, radio, books, and magazines now compete with video games, computer games, MP3s, cell phones, and the Internet for children's attention. Many children have virtually unlimited access to various media, beginning at a very young age—one survey reported that 60% of infants and toddlers watch TV or videos for one to two hours on an average day (Rideout & Hamel, 2006). By the time they are 8 years old, 68% of children have a TV, 49% have a video game player, and 31% have a computer in their bedrooms (Comstock & Scharrer, 2006; Mistry, Minkovitz, Strobino, & Borzekowski, 2007; Rideout, Roberts, & Foehr, 2005). Television is by far the most commonly used medium at all ages; during middle childhood, children spend an average of two to three hours each day watching television (Comstock & Scharrer, 2006; Rideout et al., 2005). While adolescents use the Internet more frequently than do children, the age of first Internet use is quickly falling (Greenfield & Yan, 2006). Despite the wider array of media available today compared to a few years ago, the total amount of time spent using media has remained quite stable at just over 6 hours per day. But the way children and teens use media has changed—26% report using more than one type of media at the same time (Rideout et al., 2005).

Statistics on overall use of media can mask differences between specific subgroups, however. For example, boys spend substantially more time playing video games than girls, with 11- to 14-year-old boys being the heaviest users of video games. Boys also prefer action/adventure, sports, and violent themes more than girls. Girls (particularly from age 15 to 17) are more likely than boys to be "power communicators and information seekers," spending more time using e-mail, text messaging, and searching for various kinds of information on the Internet (Lenhart, Madden, & Hitlin, 2005, p. iv). Girls, beginning in middle childhood, spend more time than boys reading books and magazines, and listening to music (Griffiths & Hunt, 1995; Huston & Wright, 1998; Lenhart et al., 2005; Roberts, Foehr, Rideout, & Brodie, 1999; *U.S. Teens & Technology,* 1997).

Children from lower-income households have less access to and spend less time using computers and the Internet, though again, access to computers at school may be helping reduce this difference. Low-income children who take advantage of programs that provide home Internet services show higher reading scores and grades (Jackson et al., 2006). Children in lower-SES (socioeconomic status) households spend more time watching television and are more likely than their higher-SES peers to have a television in their bedrooms. Younger children from lower-SES households spend less time with books and magazines, and older children spend more time listening to music (Newburger, 2001; Roberts et al., 1999; U.S. Department of Education, 2001).

## Children and Television

**TV and Aggression.** The amount of violence portrayed on television is staggering. Researchers estimate that by the time the average child in the United States leaves elementary school, that child will have viewed more than 8,000 murders and 100,000 other violent acts on network TV alone. This doesn't include cable channels or DVD movies! Saturday-morning cartoons and late-afternoon and early-evening programs, all aired at times when children are most likely to be watching, have the highest rates of violent acts (Comstock & Scharrer, 2006; Huston et al., 1992). In addition, TV often portrays violence as good, without consequence, causing no pain or suffering, and even funny. In short, very different from real-life violence. **Watch** on **mydevelopmentlab**

**Watch** a video on Television Violence.
www.mydevelopmentlab.com

But even if children view violence regularly on television, does it affect their behavior? Meta-analyses of the many studies investigating this issue conclude that TV violence has a moderate negative impact on children's behavior. The effect is similar for boys and girls, and it is larger for children than adults (Bushman & Huesmann, 2001; Hogben, 1998; Huston & Wright, 1998; Paik & Comstock, 1994). Neuroscience research indicates that watching violent TV scenes activates different areas of children's brains than watching nonviolent scenes; violent scenes produce higher levels of activation in areas involved in processing episodic memories, emotion, attention, and motor programming (Murray, et al., 2006). Though the relationship to behavior is not clear yet, more activation in these areas may enhance the storage and fast retrieval of aggressive information—possibly setting the stage for a tendency toward more aggressive behavior.

One well-known study followed a sample of boys and girls for 22 years. The researchers looked at the relationship between the amount and level of violence of the television they watched as children and their aggressive behavior in adulthood (Eron, Huesmann, Lefkowitz, & Walder, 1972; Huesmann & Miller, 1994). Figure 12.5 shows results for the boys in their study. For boys, watching TV violence at age 8 was the best predictor of aggressiveness at age 18, and those who watched the most TV at age 8 were most likely to engage in violent criminal behavior by age 30. But couldn't it be that children who had aggressive tendencies chose to watch more violent TV *and* engaged in more violent behavior, so the violence of TV was not a causative factor? Boys who were already aggressive at age 8 did watch more TV. But even among these already aggressive children, the boys who watched more TV had committed more serious criminal offenses by age 30 than those who watched less. It seems there is a bidirectional effect: More aggressive children prefer more violent TV, but TV violence increases their aggression even more. Later studies showed similar relationships between TV violence and later aggression in women in several countries (though not in all countries studied), even after researchers statistically controlled for the influences of earlier aggression, intelligence level, and social class (Bushman & Huesmann, 2001; Huesmann, Moise-Titus, Podolski, & Eron, 2003). **Listen** on **mydevelopmentlab**

Establishing a relationship is one thing, but even a strong correlation does not prove a causal link. Experimental studies are needed for this, and there have been many experimental tests of the short-term effects of television violence on children's aggressive behavior. Probably the best-known examples were experiments conducted by Albert Bandura (developer of the social learning theory we described in Chapter 1). Bandura randomly

**Listen**: Why is there such a concern over violence in the media? (Author Podcast) www.mydevelopmentlab.com

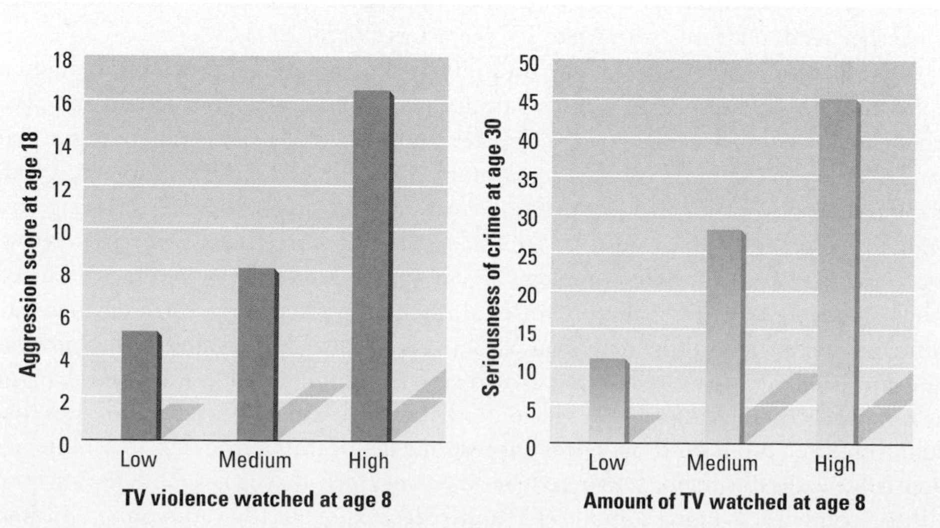


FIGURE 12.5
**TV Watching and Aggression**
Watching violent television during childhood predicts aggressiveness during adolescence and amount of violent crime in adulthood. These data are for males, but similar results have been found for females (Eron, 1987; Eron et al., 1972).

▲ Albert Bandura's experimental studies show that children who observe violent behavior act more aggressive immediately afterward. This child has just finished watching an aggressive model. Can you see the effect on her behavior?

assigned children to view either violent or nonviolent video clips, then observed their behavior afterwards while they played with one another or with toys. Children who viewed the violent videos behaved more aggressively with both people and objects. Bandura found this effect across genders, across ethnicities, and regardless of whether children showed preexisting aggressive tendencies (Bandura, 1977). It seems that watching violence on television causes children to behave more aggressively in the short term; and there is increasing evidence of a long-term effect as well (Anderson et al., 2003; Comstock & Scharrer, 2006; Hopf, Huber, & Weib, 2008).

**Positive Effects of TV.** Research has found moderate to large positive associations between watching educational programming such as *Mister Rogers' Neighborhood, Sesame Street,* and *Blue's Clues* and positive behaviors such as helping, sharing, talking about feelings, persisting on tasks, using imagination, donating, offering comfort, and cooperating (Hearold, 1986; Mares & Woodard, 2001). These positive effects are larger among younger children (peaking at about age 7), children from middle- and upper-income homes, and children whose parents watch with them and/or follow up the program with reinforcing activities.

THINKING CRITICALLY

What are some of the positive and some of the negative messages that you observe on television? What effects do you think these might have on children?

Studies of educational programs show that more positive and realistic portrayals of ethnic minorities and women can have positive effects on children's beliefs. In addition, the presence of African American characters on television can have positive effects on African American children's self-esteem (Bogatz & Ball, 1977; Gorn, Goldberg, & Kanningo, 1976; Huston & Wright, 1998; Signorielli, 2001). However, self-esteem among African Americans is lower when they watch more sports and music videos and when they tend to identify with white TV characters (Ward, 2004).

The American Academy of Pediatrics (2001) discourages TV viewing for children under the age of 2 because it takes away from time spent in social interactions and play, which are known to foster language, cognitive, and social skills. Some experts argue that early TV viewing can lead to attentional problems such as ADHD later in childhood. Others, however, claim that the increased stimulation supports better learning and brain development. Some studies have found significant correlations between TV viewing before age 3 and attention problems several years later, but these findings occurred when children watched primarily entertainment programming and not when the content was educational (Zimmerman & Christakis, 2007). Other studies find no relationship (Obel et al., 2004). Notice that these studies are correlational—they cannot determine a causal relationship or rule out other factors. Finally, research indicates that young children can learn from video, but it seems that learning from live social interaction is far easier for them. One recent review concluded that it is simply too early to either "condemn . . . or promote" TV and video exposure for very young children (Courage & Setliff, 2009, p. 76).

## Video Games, Computers, and the Internet

**Video Games.** Video games (e.g., Xbox and PlayStation) are most popular with boys about 8 to 12 years old. Even boys in this age bracket spend less time playing such games than you might expect, with most (79%) playing less than one hour per day. As you probably know, the majority of video games are fast-paced, visually based games that demand close attention and fast reactions. In the short term these games improve a variety of skills, including spatial skills (e.g., anticipating and predicting where targets will appear on the screen), the ability to interpret visual images like pictures and diagrams, response times to visual targets, and strategies for keeping track of things happening at several different screen locations (Ferguson, 2007; Huston & Wright, 1998; Subrahmanyam, Kraut, Greenfield, & Gross, 2001). Long-term effects and the transfer of these skills to other contexts aren't clear yet. Some correlational research indicates that more time spent using video games is associated with lower grades and lower SAT scores, but experimental studies that would address a cause-and-effect relationship are lacking (Anand, 2007).

Unfortunately, the majority of video games involve at least some aggression and violence. Though this was not true of the earliest games, the amount and severity of aggression (particularly of direct "human" aggression) has increased with each game generation. Experimental studies indicate that playing a violent video game for even a brief time increases aggressive thoughts and behavior. Meta-analyses report a moderate and significant effect of video game violence on players' aggressive behavior, thoughts, feelings, and physiological arousal (Anderson, 2004; Anderson & Bushman, 2001). The effects were similar in males and females, in children and adults, and in experimental and correlational studies. Children who play video games are just as socially involved with peers as those who don't play, but little is known about the social impact of heavy game playing (more than 30 hours per week) on either short-term or long-term outcomes (Subrahmanyam et al., 2001).

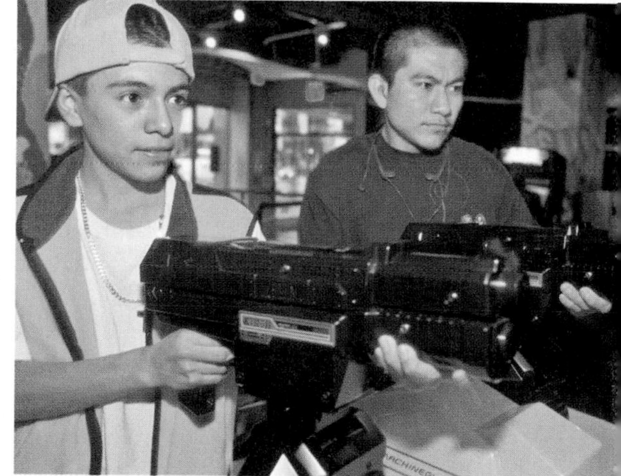

▲ Boys between the ages of 8 and 12 play video games more often than other children. Video games can improve a variety of spatial skills, but the majority of games contain violent content that may increase aggressive thoughts and behavior.

Neuroscience studies examining chronic exposure to violent video games have found decreased activation in brain areas involved in evaluating emotional information and in self-control, as well as less physiological arousal (measured as heart rate and skin conductance) when presented with violent stimuli. These results indicate that a history of playing violent video games is associated with being less sensitive to violent stimuli and with less self-control (Bartholow, Bushman, & Sestir, 2006; Carnagey, Anderson, & Bartholow, 2007; Carnagey, Anderson, & Bushman, 2007). However, it's important to remember that these studies are correlational—they cannot show whether exposure to violent games caused the brain patterns identified. Furthermore, not everyone agrees that there is a significant link between playing violent video games and aggression. Some researchers point to a variety of methodological flaws, such as the way aggression is measured, and a bias toward publishing studies that find significant differences in aggression as a result of playing violent video games (Ferguson, 2010; Ferguson & Kilburn, 2009).

**Computer Games and the Internet.** Computer software games are typically more education oriented than video games. They often require more conceptual, logical, and cognitive strategy skills and less fast physical response. These programs can successfully introduce even very young children to computers. They can help teach basic concepts in reading and math; and they can help build children's divergent thinking skills, confidence, and enjoyment in using computers. They also can prompt students to think about the cognitive strategies they are using as well as learn how to organize their thinking and to make use of feedback (Huston & Wright, 1998; Wartella, Caplovitz, & Lee, 2004).

Children's access to the Internet is increasing at breakneck speed, but we are only beginning to understand the effects on children of spending time online. More than 80% of 12- to 18-year-olds go online, and half do so every day (Lenhart et al., 2005). Many use the Internet for schoolwork, but the most frequent reason for logging on is to communicate with friends (both friends they already knew and new friends they "met" online) via instant messaging, e-mail, social networking sites such as Facebook and Twitter, and chat rooms. Almost half of kindergartners and first graders in one study reported interacting with another person online, and online gaming (which often involves playing with others online) is becoming increasingly popular among all ages, even kindergartners (Gross, 2004; Kraut, Scherlis, Mukhopadhyay, Manning, & Kiesler, 1996; McQuade & Sampat, 2008). Depending on how young people use the Internet, working online certainly could affect cognitive skills such as problem-solving ability and information search skills, but studies are just beginning to explore such effects.

Ironically, some earlier studies found that greater use of the Internet by teens was associated with decreased face-to-face social involvement, greater loneliness, and increases in depression (Kraut et al., 1996). The *social compensation hypothesis* suggests that teens who are lonely and have few friends to begin with are more likely to choose Internet over face-to-face involvement, substituting online activity for social interactions (Subrahmanyam et al., 2001). But more recent studies have found that adolescents use the Internet most often to communicate with people they already know and are friends with, serving to strengthen the closeness of their friendships—called the *rich-get-richer hypothesis.* Almost half those surveyed report also making new friends online (Lenhart & Madden, 2007; Valkenburg & Peter, 2007, 2009). One recent study found that more Internet use was associated with *higher* quality of friendships (though with less positive relationships with parents); moderate Internet use was associated with a more positive attitude toward academics than either high levels of use or not using the Internet at all (Willoughby, 2008). Whom a teen interacts with and the particular Web sites visited are clearly important. For example, teens at risk for problem behaviors such as self-injury, eating disorders, or gambling can easily find websites and chat rooms where they can socialize with others who have the same tendencies. While these online relationships can provide social support, they can also introduce vulnerable teens to new strategies for engaging in these behaviors; some even explicitly encourage the problems (Whitlock, Powers, & Eckenrode, 2006).

When we were young, our parents despaired over the terrible influence of hard rock music and sci-fi films like the original *Star Wars* movie. In our parents' generation, Elvis was considered evil. For today's parents, the worry is violent video games and the Internet. Yet in each generation, most children emerge intact and healthy. There is no question that media have an influence—why else would companies continue to pour money into advertising their products in the media? But as systems theories of child development remind us, media constitute *one of several* important influences. Parenting practices, the overall culture, and individual child factors interact with the types of media and media content children regularly experience to influence complex characteristics and behaviors like reading, aggression, prejudice, and helping others. It simply makes sense for parents and other adults to monitor the amount and content of the media children are using. Adults must think carefully about the kinds of influences children are exposed to on a regular basis and make conscious decisions based on the individual children involved. It isn't television *per se* that has positive or negative effects, but what is portrayed and how families handle it: "The medium is not the message. The message is the message!" (Anderson, Huston, Schmitt, Linebarger, & Wright, 2001, p. 134). To learn more about how people who work in media use their knowledge of child development in positive ways, read the Professional Perspective box called "Career Focus: Meet a Marketing Executive."

# Perspective PROFESSIONAL CAREER FOCUS: MEET A MARKETING EXECUTIVE

Jan Craige Singer
Watertown, MA
President/partner at BIG BLUE DOT

**What kind of work do you do?**
At BIG BLUE DOT, we work with clients who want to reach children from toddlers to teens and everyone in between. Our services include broadcast design, Web site design, logos, print and packaging, and branding. We are a mix of graphic designers, producers, brand strategists, and child development specialists dedicated solely to the universe of kids. This blend enables us to deliver fresh, smart, fun, age-appropriate solutions to companies that care about kids. Having an understanding of how kids learn, think, and make sense of the world is at the very core of the work we do. Each time we solve a new design problem, we find a deeper understanding of what kids want at specific stages of development and how our clients can reach children from tots to teens.

**What training do you have in child development, and how has this knowledge been useful?**
My professional background includes TV marketing, promotion, and programming. It wasn't until I had my own children and had the opportunity to develop programming ideas for the Discovery Channel and the Learning Channel that I realized creating great educational and entertaining stuff for kids was what I enjoyed doing the most. I took a few years off to stay home with my son and daughter and decided to go to graduate school to find out how kids really learn. I now have an EdM from Harvard in child development. I sought out a company where I could combine my love and respect for children with a creative atmosphere. I'm happy to say I found it at BIG BLUE DOT.

**Are there many people in your profession who have knowledge and training about child development? What's a specific example of how this knowledge affected your work?**
Children are the primary target for our clients. They come to us for our knowledge and expertise in reaching kids. It's remarkable how many of the larger entertainment companies have full-time child development experts on staff to help them understand the children they are trying to appeal to. Recently we worked with Suave on a new line of personal care products for *tweens* (8- to 12-year-olds). Though they hired us for our kid knowledge, the first thing we did was explain the world of tweens by creating a visual tween audit document. This way, our client had something tangible to refer to during the creative process. The audit explored characteristics of both boys and girls in the 8 to 12 age group such as the social awareness of the opposite sex, the development of tight groups of friends, caring about how they look, looking for social acceptance, knowing the rules but starting to push the limits a little. We also knew it was important to appeal to both boys and girls, so we searched for a common theme that was rather unisex in nature. We presented several different packaging concepts to Suave. They all reflected the interests and attitudes of tweens in music and dance, adventure and sports, urban cool, ecology and the environment, and mythology and magic.

**What advice would you offer to students interested in child development who are considering going into this profession?**
I would advise students to think about the incredible opportunity and not forget the responsibility that is unique in marketing to kids. If you love kids, you'll love thinking about them, studying them, designing and creating for them every day. And if you really love kids, you can use your understanding of them to help companies be respectful, honest, playful, educational, and entertaining in the messages and products that they bring to kids.

QUESTION **Can you see how marketing professionals such as Jan Craige Singer can use knowledge of child development in ways that help children? What other concepts from this chapter (and other chapters) could someone use in the marketing profession?**

## LET'S REVIEW . . .

1. Jacqueline, a fourth grader, said, "I like to try things that are a little hard for me, because when I finally can do them, it makes me smarter!" Jacqueline has __________.
   **a.** a mastery orientation
   **b.** a helpless orientation
   **c.** an immature view of ability
   **d.** performance goals
2. Overall, research suggests that violence on television __________.
   **a.** has no lasting effect on children's behavior
   **b.** affects boys' but not girls' aggressive behavior
   **c.** has a small immediate effect, but no long-term effects on children
   **d.** has a moderate effect on aggressive behavior in children
3. According to the research, which statement below is *true* regarding children playing video games?
   **a.** Video games have a greater negative effect on children's behavior than watching violent television.
   **b.** There is no evidence that video games have a negative effect on children's behavior.
   **c.** Video games can help children improve several different spatial skills.
   **d.** Video games increase the amount of children's social interactions.
4. According to research, students between the ages of 12 and 18 use the Internet most often for __________.
   **a.** schoolwork
   **b.** finding news information
   **c.** communicating with friends
   **d.** participating in chat rooms
5. True or False: Self-fulfilling prophecies are based on reliable information about past behavior and achievement patterns.
6. True or False: Compared to other children, children in families with higher financial incomes are the ones most likely to have televisions in their bedrooms.

Answers: 1. a, 2. d, 3. c, 4. c, 5. F, 6. F

## THINKING BACK TO LAUREL . . .

Now that you have studied this chapter, you should be able to apply at least a dozen concepts and research findings to Laurel's situation. First, it is typical for children her age to compare themselves to their peers. Social comparison is an important way children learn about themselves and their relative talents and abilities, although children do sometimes learn that they are not as competent as their peers or don't measure up as well in some areas. Laurel is showing some concern about her weight and physical appearance—her mother, Pam, should continue to help Laurel accept and appreciate herself through this self-evaluation process. Laurel is well-liked and popular among her peers, so all indications are that she already has positive social skills and good emotional control. She can build on these strengths as she begins to develop more close friendships, though she needs to learn how her emotional attachment to her mother is affecting her mother's life.

Laurel is struggling with issues surrounding her parents' divorce. She feels abandoned by her father, and she might be relying too much on her mother for security and emotional support. Feelings of abandonment are common among children of divorce, but Laurel's reactions seem to be a bit extreme—perhaps because her father moved out of state. According to the divorce-stress-adjustment perspective, it can take time for children to adjust to the strains of a divorce, but it's already been five years since Laurel's parents separated. Laurel should at least be sleeping in her own room and more willing to give Pam the freedom to date and have some personal life of her own. These are issues that Laurel and Pam need to focus on for improvement, and Pam should also watch for other effects of divorce that might crop up later for Laurel. Otherwise, Laurel enjoys school and likely has strong achievement motivation. As Laurel excels in school, her teachers will have high expectations for her and this will likely continue a positive self-fulfilling cycle in school.

These are just a few of the concepts you can use from this chapter to better understand Laurel's situation. These, along with many other concepts and research findings presented in this chapter, can help you gain more insight into the many social and emotional issues faced by children Laurel's age.

12

## CHAPTER REVIEW . . .

**12.1** How do children evaluate themselves and their own talents, abilities, and weaknesses and how does this evaluation process relate to a sense of self-esteem?

By 7 years of age, children develop a global self-evaluation and begin comparing themselves with their peers. Self-esteem is unrealistically high in early childhood but becomes more realistic during the elementary school years. The degree of discrepancy between a child's real and ideal selves, in combination with the supportiveness of parents and peers, affects self-evaluation. Perceived physical attractiveness is an important component of children's self-esteem.

**12.2** What changes take place in the development of emotions during middle childhood?

During middle childhood, children learn to control and regulate their own emotional reactions, and they improve their abilities to accurately read the emotions of other people. Children who can read and control their emotions have more success making friends; they tend to have parents with positive emotional control. Children can have difficulty reading emotions in people from different racial or ethnic backgrounds.

**12.3** What gender differences do we see in how boys and girls behave at this age?

Boys show higher activity levels and greater physical aggression than girls, but girls show more relational aggression.

**12.4** How do children think about moral issues, and how does this relate to their tendencies to help other people?

Girls are often rated higher in prosocial behavior and empathy, but their actual prosocial behavior is not consistently different than boys'. By age 10, most children still show preconventional moral reasoning, but a few begin showing conventional (Stage 3) reasoning. With prosocial reasoning, children progress from a focus on their own needs to social approval to reasoning based on broader principles.

**12.5** Why are some children more aggressive than others?

Aggressiveness seems to be a stable characteristic—children who are aggressive at a young age are more likely than others to commit aggressive acts into adulthood.

**12.6** What are the main outcomes associated with divorce, and what factors explain these outcomes?

Children of divorced parents are at increased risk for a variety of negative behavioral, emotional, academic, and occupational outcomes. Lack of money, ineffective parenting, and loss of community connections are factors. According to the divorce-stress-adjustment perspective, the effects of divorce depend on interactions among the stresses produced, specific vulnerabilities in the child, and a variety of protective factors. The selection model suggests that long-lasting effects are due to parent characteristics rather than to the divorce itself.

**12.7** What effects might living in never-married households or in stepfamilies have on children?

Children whose parents do not marry are similar in outcomes to children of divorce. With stepfamilies, outcomes are better when the family remains stable, financial resources improve, and parenting becomes more effective; otherwise problems can occur or continue.

**12.8** What are the main characteristics in play during middle childhood, and what are the connections that cause children to become best friends?

During middle childhood, children's thought processes become more logical and realistic, and their play follows a similar trend. Games with rules, toy collections, and practicing physical skills and sports become the focus. Children increase their numbers of "best friends" until about age 11, then they become more selective in forming close friendships. Having activities in common, loyalty, faithfulness, and generosity are important elements in forming friendships during middle childhood.

12.9 What are the characteristics associated with children who are more popular among their peers, and what about those who are less popular?

The peer nomination technique is used frequently to categorize children into popular, rejected, controversial, average, and neglected categories. Popular children tend to be more helpful, have good leadership skills, and are adept at joining groups and activities without being disruptive. Less popular children tend to be more aggressive or withdrawn.

12.10 How do researchers understand peer popularity, and how do children respond when they are rejected by their peers?

The social cognition model focuses on how children perceive and interpret social cues and on how they consider and enact social responses. Popular children tend to have a positive bias in perceiving and interpreting cues, while rejected–aggressive children often perceive innocent cues as threats and rejected–withdrawn children have difficulty enacting positive social responses. Media accounts of school shootings and violence sometimes note that the perpetrators feel rejected by peers, and this highlights the need to identify and provide help for rejected students.

12.11 How are children affected by their own beliefs about school and learning and by the expectations that teachers have of them?

Achievement motivation and attributions are important. Children with a mastery orientation attribute their successes to their own hard work and abilities and focus on learning goals. Children with a helpless orientation attribute success to external and uncontrollable factors such as luck and focus more on performance goals. Teachers' expectations are important and sometimes result in self-fulfilling prophecies about students' performance.

12.12 How does the climate in the classroom affect children, and what are the effects of grouping children by their abilities?

A positive classroom climate is associated with higher student motivation and achievement, but teachers must also have classroom management and effective teaching skills. The effects of between-class ability grouping depend on the students' ability levels; the effects on students in lower-ability tracks are generally negative.

12.13 What kinds of media do children use?

Media use begins at a very young age. TV is the most commonly used medium at all ages; use of the Internet is beginning at younger and younger ages. There are gender differences in the types of media used. Children from lower-income households have less access to and spend less time using computers and the Internet.

12.14 Does watching violence on TV cause children to be more aggressive?

Media have mixed effects on children. Educational television can improve academic skills and prosocial behavior. Watching violence on TV causes more aggressive thoughts and behavior in the short term and is correlated with long-term levels of aggressive behavior.

12.15 What are researchers finding out about the effects of video games, computers, and children's use of the Internet?

Video games can improve spatial skills, but their violent content may increase aggression, physiological arousal, and is related to patterns of brain activation involving desensitization to violence and less self-control. Computer software can effectively teach academic skills. Even young children use the Internet to play games and interact with friends. A moderate amount of time online does not harm social relationships and is associated with more positive attitudes towards academics.

## REVISITING THEMES

The impact of parenting and family environment on prosocial (p. 367) and aggressive behavior (pp. 367–368) demonstrates the theme of *nature and nurture*.

The *neuroscience* theme was included in the discussion of exposure to violence in the media; chronic exposure to violence is associated with different patterns of physiological responses and brain activation (p. 391).

*Diversity and multiculturalism* were demonstrated by comparing statistics on family structures among different racial and ethnic groups within the U.S. (pp. 370, 374–376) and in a discussion of how peer popularity relates to racial discrimination in some schools (p. 382). Difficulties in reading emotions across ethnicities (p. 364), and cross-cultural research on prosocial reasoning was also discussed (p. 367).

*Positive development and resilience* were highlighted regarding the positive effects of divorce in some families (pp. 373–374), suggestions for helping children cope with divorce (p. 375), the positive influences in stepfamilies (p. 376), and with discussion about how children connect with best friends and become popular with their peers (pp. 378–380). The section on resilient children identifies characteristics that help these children overcome difficult situations (p. 369).

## KEY TERMS

ability grouping (386)
achievement motivation (384)
attributions (385)
average children (381)
classroom climate (386)
conduct disorder (CD) (368)
conduct problems (368)
controversial children (381)
divorce-stress-adjustment perspective (373)
helpless orientation (385)
mastery orientation (385)
neglected children (381)
oppositional defiant disorder (ODD) (368)
parentification (371)
peer nomination technique (379)
popular children (379)
prosocial reasoning (366)
rejected children (380)
relational aggression (365)
resilient children (369)
selection model (373)
self-esteem (361)
self-evaluations (361)
self-fulfilling prophecy (386)
self-representations (361)
sleeper effect (of divorce) (371)
social cognition model (382)
social comparison (361)

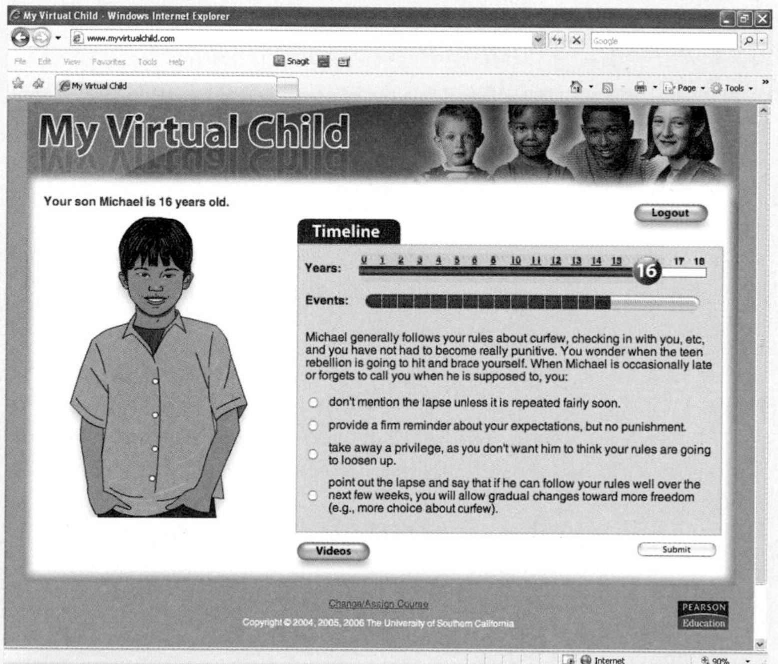


**"What decisions would you make while raising a child? What would the consequences of those decisions be?"**

Find out by accessing My Virtual Child at
**www.mydevelopmentlab.com**
and raising your own virtual child
from birth to age 18.

# PART FOUR SUMMARY Middle Childhood: The School Years

## Physical Development

Children typically gain 9 inches and 35 pounds during middle childhood. Girls will be taller and heavier than boys for a time. Changes in the brain over these ages lead to increased efficiency of brain functioning. Motor skills become more controlled and coordinated, and strength and balance improve. These changes allow impressive improvements in children's physical skills across many areas such as sports, handwriting, and playing musical instruments. Many children begin to participate in organized sports, which offer many physical, social, and emotional benefits. Most 7- to 11-year-old children are healthy, but health threats include accidents, the risk of sexual abuse, and weight problems. ADHD, learning and communication disorders, and autism can become more problematic as children strive to meet the increasing demands of school. Adults can help protect children's safety and establish a healthy foundation for later years by encouraging good eating habits, making sure that children take proper precautions when biking and playing sports, watching for signs of abuse, and advocating for fair and appropriate education of children with disabilities

## Cognitive Development

Children from 7 to 11 years become able to use objective logic and think about several different dimensions of problems. Their memory and thinking become more organized and efficient. These changes allow children to think at higher levels and solve increasingly complex problems. They learn a great deal about a wide variety of topics—their knowledge base becomes quite impressive. Children make more, and more accurate, connections between the concepts they have learned, and they acquire many different strategies for remembering, reasoning, and solving problems. During this time period children become more sophisticated in their language skills, using language flexibly and playfully as a tool to better understand themselves, interact socially, and have fun. Children of these ages spend a great deal of time in school, and they show impressive gains in core areas of reading, mathematics, and writing.

## Socioemotional Development

During middle childhood, children notice how their talents and abilities compare to their peers, and they begin to think about differences between their real and ideal selves. Their self-evaluations become more realistic, and their self-esteem may decline. When confronted with moral issues, most children still primarily consider themselves first when deciding what they should do, but a few are beginning to think about society's laws and conventions. Divorce, remarriage, and stepfamilies are a reality for many children of this age. The impact of these family structures depends a great deal on finances, quality of parenting, and connections with the community. Children of these ages enjoy playing games with rules, developing toy collections, and practicing physical skills and sports. Friendships are based on having activities in common, loyalty, faithfulness, and generosity. Motivation to achieve and beliefs about effort and ability become increasingly important factors in children's school success. By the end of middle childhood, children have broadened their knowledge, experiences, and skills and become much more mature and capable of coping with physical, cognitive, and social challenges. They are ready to enter the phase of ***Adolescence: The Transition toward Adulthood.***

## Some Developmental Landmarks

### 7 years

- Average 4 feet tall and 55 pounds
- Logical thinking skills improve
- When reading, recognizes words faster
- Forms an overall opinion of self
- Will help others if it benefits the self
- Friendships are based on common activities

### 8 years

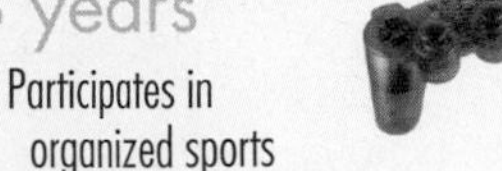

- Participates in organized sports
- Memory improves
- Better at controlling emotions
- Shows concern for others
- Video games popular

### 9 years

- Control and coordination of motor skills increases
- Effectively uses organizational strategies to improve memory
- Can identify and correct ambiguities in speech
- Shows increasing interest in riddles and verbal humor
- Increasing concern with gaining approval from others
- Influence of media increases

### 10 years

- Synaptic pruning results in shrinkage of some brain areas
- Flexibility in boys decreases
- Knowledge increases and becomes more organized
- 40,000-word vocabulary
- Self-evaluations more realistic
- Internet increasingly used

### 11 years

BFF!

- Average 5 feet tall and 90 pounds
- Girls are 1½ inches taller and 8 pounds heavier than boys
- Rough play in boys decreases
- Understands social rules
- Reading to learn
- Deep friendships form

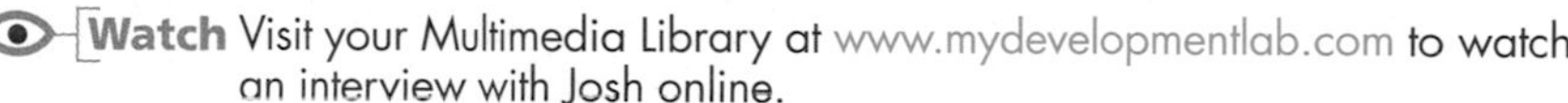
**Watch** Visit your Multimedia Library at www.mydevelopmentlab.com to watch an interview with Josh online.

13 ADOLESCENCE

# Physical Development in Adolescence

Sixteen-year-old Josh looks a lot older than he is. Last year when he was a freshman, people often mistook him for a junior! He has to admit that it's nice to get the respect from students and teachers that goes along with looking older, and he knows it isn't easy to look younger than your friends. Like many guys his age, Josh spends a lot of time thinking about girls. He knows some people in his class have already had sex, but many others have not—and many say they have but he's not sure they're telling the truth. His friends find health class to be an awkward and embarrassing time, and most of them use it as a "blow-off class." Josh knows a girl who got pregnant last year so he's well aware of the importance of using protection, but having condoms on hand seems a little too planned. He and his friends think age 16 is too young to be sexually active, but others see turning 16 as a reason to do it because they are "so old." While they all know that it's possible to get STDs, none of them really believe that will happen to them. Fortunately, Josh has been a part of the conversations that his parents have had with his older brothers, so he is aware of the importance of these choices—and he knows he can talk with his parents about them and other important choices. Josh is also well aware of how easy it would be to get alcohol and marijuana. If he wanted to, it would probably take him less than a day to get any substance he wanted. He estimates that about half his class started using drugs and/or alcohol freshman year—way too many, in his opinion. Many try these things so they can associate with upperclassmen, or to rebel against parents. Josh has seen many friends go into a downward spiral because of their alcohol/drug use. He knows that he doesn't want to risk his grades, his music, or his future.

Is Josh typical in the things he's thinking about? What kinds of physical issues do most adolescents face, and how can parents and teachers help? How many adolescents are sexually active, and how many experiment with drugs and alcohol? After studying this chapter, you should be able to identify at least a dozen research findings or concepts that will help Josh as he thinks about these issues.

As you read this chapter, look for the "Think About Josh . . ." questions that ask you to consider what you're learning from Josh's perspective.

# Growth of the Body and Brain During Adolescence

*Adolescence* is the period of life that serves as a transition between childhood and adulthood. It is a time of tremendous physical, cognitive, and socioemotional development. Individuals enter this period looking like children, but in a few short years they blossom into young adults. Like Josh, many teens worry about whether their physical development is keeping up with, or is too far ahead of, their peers. While many of the physical changes of adolescence are easily seen, some of the most important are hidden—important changes are taking place in the brain that will enable adolescents to improve on directing their behaviors, thoughts, and emotions. In this chapter, we'll discuss the normal physical changes of adolescence. We'll also talk about several important health and safety issues, including sexual activity, nutrition and exercise, sleep, substance use, depression and suicide, and teen driving.

AS YOU STUDY THIS SECTION, ASK YOURSELF THESE QUESTIONS:

13.1 What is the typical sequence of events in puberty?

13.2 What are the psychological effects of early and late maturation for boys and for girls?

13.3 What major changes take place in the brain during adolescence, and how are these changes related to adolescent behavior?

## Puberty

One of the most recognized landmarks of adolescent development is **puberty**, the process of physical maturation that leads to the physical capability to reproduce. During puberty, there are rapid increases in height, weight, and strength as well as changes in the amount and distribution of body muscle and fat. The *primary sex characteristics* (the organs needed for reproduction) mature and begin producing eggs and sperm. *Secondary sex characteristics* (physical indicators of sexual maturation that do not involve the sex organs) also develop. Table 13.1 summarizes these changes.

The primary factors governing the onset of puberty are genetics and two types of sex hormones: **androgens** (male hormones) and **estrogens** (female hormones). Puberty involves several different glands in the body's endocrine system, the system of organs that produce, secrete, and regulate levels of a variety of body hormones (chemicals secreted by the endocrine system that affect the functioning of other cells). The biological processes are diagrammed in Figure 13.1. (page 402) Leptin, a protein produced by fat cells, plays an important role in initiating puberty in females (Susman & Rogol, 2004). Rising levels of leptin signal that there is enough body fat to support menstruation and pregnancy. Leptin causes the hypothalamus to increase production of several hormones called *releasing factors,* which then stimulate the pituitary gland to increase production of other hormones. In both males and females, increasing levels of hormones from the pituitary gland signal the release of sex hormones from the gonads (ovaries in females and testes in males). The sex hormones stimulate the growth and maturation of the reproductive systems as well as secondary sexual characteristics, and they provide feedback to the hypothalamus about current levels of sex hormones. This feedback loop from hypothalamus to pituitary gland to gonads and back to the hypothalamus, known as the *HPG axis,* regulates the levels of sex hormones. It is functional early in life, but the levels of hormones it maintains gradually change during late

**puberty**
The process of physical maturation that leads to the physical capability to reproduce.

**androgens**
One type of sex hormone, released in greater concentration by males.

**estrogens**
One type of sex hormone, released in greater concentration by females.

**TABLE 13.1**
Physical Changes That Occur at Puberty

| FEMALES | MALES |
|---|---|
| **Stage 1:** Begins from 8 to 12 years<br>• No visible signs of physical development<br>• Growth in ovaries<br>• Hormone production begins | **Stage 1:** Begins from 9 to 14 years<br>• No visible signs of physical development<br>• Hormone production begins |
| **Stage 2:** Begins from 8 to 14 years<br>• Rapid increases in height and weight<br>• Hair growth begins in pubic area and underarms<br>• Breasts begin to develop<br>• Sweat and oil glands become more active | **Stage 2:** Begins from 11 to 13 years<br>• Rapid increases in height and weight<br>• Growth in testicles<br>• Scrotum becomes darker in color.<br>• Hair growth begins in pubic area, legs, underarms |
| **Stage 3:** Begins from ages 9 to 15 years<br>• Breast development continues<br>• Hips start to widen<br>• Vaginal secretions begin<br>• Continued growth of body and pubic hair<br>• Height and weight continue to increase | **Stage 3:** Begins from 12 to 14 years<br>• Growth of penis, scrotum, and testicles<br>• Continued growth of body and pubic hair<br>• Muscles become larger and shoulders become broader.<br>• Sweat and oil glands become more active<br>• Height and weight continue to increase |
| **Stage 4:** Begins from 10 to 16 years<br>• Continued growth of body and pubic hair<br>• Breast development continues<br>• Ovulation occurs<br>• *Menarche* occurs, but menstrual periods may be irregular | **Stage 4:** Begins from 13 to 16 years<br>• Sperm production begins<br>• Voice begins to break or crack, then deepens<br>• Height and weight continue to increase<br>• Continued growth of penis and testicles<br>• Continued growth of body and pubic hair |
| **Stage 5:** Begins from 12 to 19 years<br>• Adult height is reached<br>• Breast development is complete<br>• Body hair is adult color and texture<br>• Ovulation and menstrual periods usually occur regularly | **Stage 5:** Begins from 14 to 18 years<br>• Adult height is reached<br>• Growth of facial and chest hair begins<br>• Penis and testicles are full adult size<br>• Body hair is adult color, texture, and distribution |

Adapted from: U.S. Department of Health & Human Services (2009, March 27). *Sexual development and reproduction.* Accessed April 21, 2009 from www.4parents.gov/index.html.

childhood and early adolescence based on genetic factors and input from other sources, such as leptin levels.

The HPG axis is what most people think of as puberty, but it is only one part of it—*gonadarche.* The pituitary gland also stimulates the adrenal gland to release hormones that contribute to the development of secondary sex characteristics and increased sexual attraction. This process is called *adrenarche.* It occurs about two years earlier than gonadarche, which means that increased sexual attraction and subtle changes in secondary sex characteristics begin happening much earlier than most people think—around 7 years of age in both males and females (Sussman & Rogol, 2004).

Sexual maturation tends to occur earlier in girls than in boys. Many girls show noticeable changes by age 10 or 11, but most boys enter puberty a year or two later. For most girls, **menarche** (the first menstrual period) occurs at 12 or 13, though African American girls start to menstruate earlier than girls of other ethnicities (Chumlea et al., 2003; Rosenfeld, Lipton, & Drum, 2008). The average age at menarche, however, has

**menarche**
The first menstrual period for females, usually occurring around 12 to 13 years of age.

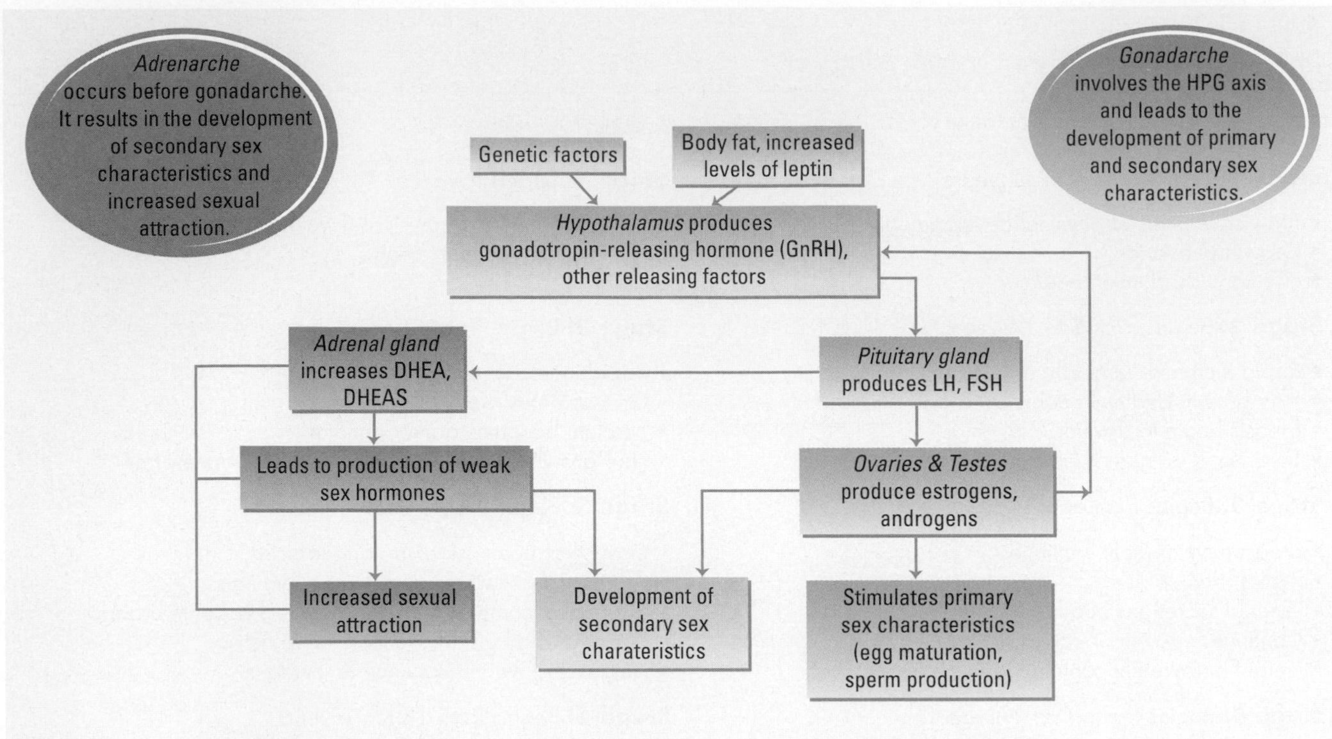


▲ FIGURE 13.1
**The Biological Processes of Puberty**
*Gonadarche*, shown in the right side of the figure, involves the HPG axis and results in the development of the primary sex characteristics. *Adrenarche*, shown on the left side, results in the development of sexual attraction and contributes to secondary sex characteristics. Adrenarche begins around ages 7 to 10, about two years before the onset of gonadarche.

**adolescent growth spurt**
The increase in growth associated with the onset of puberty.

**body image**
The way a person thinks about his or her body and how it looks to others.

**early maturation**
When the physical changes of puberty occur earlier than they do in the majority of one's peers.

**late maturation**
When the physical changes of puberty do not occur until after they do in the majority of one's peers.

**Watch** a video on Secular Trends.
www.mydevelopmentlab.com

been decreasing. In the United States, for example, the average age at menarche fell from 13.8 in 1920 to 12.8 around 1960 and is currently estimated at 12.4 (Chumlea et al., 2003; Marshall & Tanner, 1986; Tanner, 1991). Over the last 100 years, children have grown larger and matured faster than in previous generations. Improved nutrition and overall health have contributed greatly to this long-term pattern, called the *secular trend.* Weight gain is related to menarche; perhaps improved nutrition and health cause earlier weight gain, signaling the female body to begin the reproductive phase of life. Although the same secular trend has occurred in other industrialized nations, girls in the United States have always reached menarche a bit earlier than girls in other nations. The reasons for this are not known. The secular trend toward earlier puberty appears to be slowing, but not for all groups (Sun et al., 2005). While the overall average age of menarche has not changed over the past few decades in the United States, there is evidence of earlier onset of puberty over the last few decades for non-Hispanic White boys and for Mexican American boys and girls (Chumlea et al., 2003; Herman-Giddens, 2006; Sun et al., 2005). **Watch** on **mydevelopmentlab**

The **adolescent growth spurt** is an increase in growth that begins with the onset of puberty. As we've seen, sex hormones at puberty trigger the process of sexual maturation. This release of sex hormones also stimulates the release of additional growth hormones from the pituitary gland. As Figure 13.2 indicates, boys and girls grow at about the same rate until adolescence. Then comes the growth spurt, usually peaking around 12 years of age for girls. For boys the growth spurt peaks a few years later, usually around 14 years.

This lag in growth spurt means that there is a short time period between the ages of 11 and 14, when females are taller than males, on average. The growth spurt lasts longer for boys, however. By the time he reaches 18 years of age, the average male is now about 5 inches taller than the average female. Both sexes have nearly reached their adult heights. In both sexes the long bones (e.g., in the arms and legs) may continue to grow slightly until age 25, and minor growth in the vertebral column can continue until age 30 (Tanner, 1978).

▲ Do you recall the age period when the girls in your class were taller than the boys? After being about equal in height throughout childhood, girls enter their adolescent growth spurt at an earlier age than boys. By the end of adolescence, boys will stand 5 inches taller (on average) than girls.

## Early and Late Maturation

Of course, these are just the physical changes associated with puberty and sexual maturation—but what about the psychological effects? For many adolescents puberty is a confusing and awkward time. Their bodies are changing rapidly and in dramatic ways, and these changes affect their thoughts and emotions. As you'll learn in Chapters 14 and 15, adolescents' developing cognitive skills and changing social roles affect how they cope with their rapidly changing bodies. No longer children, teenagers may look toward late adolescence and adulthood with mixed feelings of excitement and apprehension. Researchers have devoted considerable attention to adolescents' changing **body image**, or the way a person thinks about his or her body and how it looks to others. During adolescent growth, boys tend to add muscle mass and height, and with these changes they tend to become more satisfied with their bodies (Duncan, Ritter, Dornbusch, Gross, & Carlsmith, 1985; Simmons & Blyth, 1987). In contrast, girls tend to add more fat tissue, and many become less satisfied with their bodies. This is particularly true among girls who reach menarche before age 12, because their build tends to be shorter and stockier by late adolescence.

In **early maturation**, the physical changes of puberty occur in a child before these changes occur in the majority of other children of the same age. In **late maturation**, the physical changes do not occur until after the majority of one's peers. Early and late

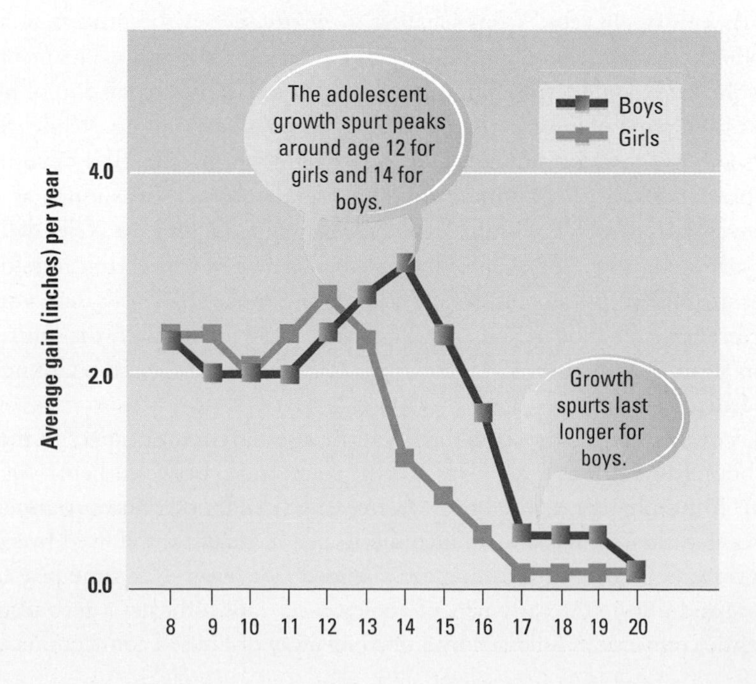


◀ FIGURE 13.2
**Height Curves for Girls and Boys**
These curves show the average height gained per year from late childhood through adolescence. (National Center for Health Statistics, 2000b.)

▲ Adolescents go through puberty at very different times. What advantages and disadvantages do you think early maturing girls experience? What about later maturing girls?

THINKING CRITICALLY

Did you begin puberty earlier or later than other adolescents your age? How did your rate of maturation affect your feelings about yourself and how you compared with your classmates?

maturation can have an important psychological impact. A study of nearly 5,000 girls in Scotland, for example, showed that girls who matured earlier perceived their bodies as "too fat." More late-maturing girls saw themselves as "too thin" (Williams & Currie, 2000). Girls with both types of negative body image tended to have lower self-esteem. Early-maturing girls also tend to have older friends, engage in more delinquency, have more problems in school, begin dating at a younger age, and tend to have more problems with depression and substance abuse (Magnusson, 1988; Simmons & Blyth, 1987; Stice, Presnell, & Bearman, 2001; Wiesner & Ittel, 2002). You can imagine how the social context can put added pressure on early-maturing girls—they receive more attention from boys and may feel somewhat alienated from slower-developing girls their own age. For more on this issue, read the Personal Perspective box on page 405 called "Meet a Young Adolescent."

Early maturation can enhance the self-image of boys, however (Nottelmann et al., 1987; Simmons & Blyth, 1987). Thanks to their size and strength, early-maturing boys have an advantage in sports. Also, peers may see their more developed musculature, facial hair, and deeper voices as being attractive. Late-maturing boys often feel uncomfortable about comparing themselves with their more developed peers. On the negative side, however, early-maturing boys tend to engage in more delinquent behavior and feel more hostile and distressed than do boys who mature later, (Duncan et al., 1985; Ge, Brody, Conger, Simons, & Murry, 2002; Ge, Conger, & Elder, 2001). Being larger and stronger than most of their peers, these boys often affiliate with older adolescents. They may get into situations they are not prepared to handle—and get into trouble as a result.

## Brain Development

Until recently, most researchers believed that brain development was for the most part complete before adolescence. However, the adolescent brain appears to still be under construction in many ways.

As you might recall from Chapter 4, *myelination* is the process in which the fatty myelin sheath is deposited on the axons of neurons in the brain. The myelin sheath insulates the axon, and increased myelination leads to faster transmission of neural impulses, faster processing of information, and faster speed of responding. While most brain pathways are myelinated in infancy and early childhood, myelination of some areas such as the prefrontal cortex continues throughout adolescence with as much as a 92% increase in myelination of some brain areas between ages 10 and 20 (Giedd, Shaw, Wallace, Gogtay, & Lenroot, 2006). This increased efficiency of neural transmission is one reason teens are able to process information faster and more efficiently than younger children. Increased myelination is sometimes referred to as increases in the white matter in the brain (Kail & Salthouse, 1994; Keating, 2004; National Research Council and Institute of Medicine, 2000).

A more recent discovery is that there are also important changes in the gray matter of the brain (the neurons themselves and the connections between them). Again, as you may recall from Chapter 4, the brain during early childhood shows *synaptogenesis,* a rapid increase in the number of neural connections (or synapses) followed by *synaptic pruning,* or a decrease as connections that are not used fade away. The same process happens just before and during the early part of adolescence. This indicates a second growth spurt in synaptic connections followed by a pruning away of unused connections. The motor and

## Perspective PERSONAL — MEET A YOUNG ADOLESCENT

Hannah Lee Vestal
Bristol, TN
Age 15, discussing the impact of physical changes during adolescence

**Which physical changes do you and your friends notice most? What differences do you notice between early and late "bloomers"?**

I notice a lot of physical changes in myself and in others. I notice hair, clothing, body, nails, and much more. But, for some reason, I think I am always looking for faults; I always notice them so much. I think developed girls look at not-so-developed girls and wish they could be that way, and vice versa! I see some late "bloomers" who are very self-conscious and limit their clothing due to the fact that they are not fully developed. But I also see late bloomers who are very comfortable with themselves and their bodies, so they are more willing to wear the clothing of choice. Some early bloomers (like me) are a lot more inclined to cover themselves and hide the fact that they have bloomed. But again, I see some early bloomers who embrace the fact that they are developed. They sometimes wear low-cut shirts or strapless tops, which I guess is good in a way. They are so comfortable with themselves that they *can* wear those clothes.

**What do you think are the most exciting, awkward, and stressful aspects of puberty?**

Starting to date, friends, and drugs. Starting to date is very difficult because if you don't date, you start to feel like you are ugly and no one wants to date you. Dating makes you feel very critical of yourself. It makes you want to change things about yourself, mainly your looks. If you do date, you might feel pressured to do things you aren't ready for. Friends can also be very stressful. High school is like one big soap opera, one that you can't miss a single episode of. The drama of who's dating who and the "he said, she said" stuff is very aggravating and childish. But pressure from friends is not as bad as TV and politicians make it out to be, at least not at my school. Drugs are readily available, but I have never been asked if I would like to take drugs, smoke anything, or drink. I think to get involved in that stuff you have to go looking for it. Teens can't blame all their mess-ups on pressure, because it's not really there as much as adults think. Most of it is in the individual.

**What advice would you give adults about an adolescent's perspective during puberty?**

I think parents should be very honest with their children, especially at this age. If you tell your kids about the experiences you had, they'll learn more from that than they would from watching a movie on it or reading a book about it. If you tell your kids if or how your experiences changed your life, for good or bad, they will respect that. They'll tell you more and trust you. I know I can talk to my mom about almost anything. She won't yell at me, but will listen and tell me how she feels, and about her experiences and the effects they had on her.

QUESTION **What have you learned so far in this book that could help adolescents cope successfully with the "soap opera" of adolescence?**

sensory areas of the brain show decreases in gray matter first, while brain areas involved in integrating information and making associations show decreases later. Like the general patterns of maturation and puberty discussed earlier, girls tend to show decreases of gray matter earlier than boys. Synaptic pruning highlights the importance of experience in adolescence because the connections that are pruned are those that are not used. Given that teens have far more control than infants over how they spend their time, teens may actually be able to control to some extent how their brains "grow" through their choices of activities during these critical years (Giedd et al., 1999; Giedd et al., 2006; Marsh, Gerber, & Peterson, 2008; Paus, 2005).

Myelination, synaptogenesis, and synaptic pruning are especially evident in the **prefrontal cortex** of the adolescent's brain. This area (a large part of the frontal lobe, located behind the forehead) is especially important in planning, judgment and decision making, and inhibiting impulsive responding. There is also evidence that, contrary to what we used to think, some new neurons are formed throughout adolescence and into adulthood in certain areas such as the hippocampus, which is heavily involved in storing memory of facts and relations between places and events (Blakemore & Choudhury, 2006; Dahl & Spear, 2004; Eriksson et al., 1998; Keating, 2004).

The relative lateness in maturation of the prefrontal cortex has implications for many aspects of self-regulation. For example, adolescents are known for reacting quickly and emotionally to things. The traditional explanation is that hormones are to blame. However, differences in the relative functioning of brain structures may also be involved (Giedd et al., 2006). One study compared adolescents and adults in their understanding of emotional cues in facial expressions (Baird et al., 1999). Compared to adults, teens were less accurate in identifying the emotions being portrayed and they showed significantly more activity in the *amygdala,* a part of the brain's temporal lobe that is important in processing emotional stimuli and distinguishing among different emotions. In contrast, adults showed more activity in the *frontal lobes,* the area of the brain associated with rational thinking, goal-directed behavior, and inhibiting impulsive responses. Other research suggests that continued development of connections between the prefrontal cortex and brain areas involved in processing emotions (e.g., the amygdala, basal ganglia) may also be involved (Casey, Getz, & Galvan, 2008; Paus, 2005). So adolescents' classic emotion-based responding may also have a basis in the relative immaturity of parts of their frontal lobes.

▲ During puberty, adolescents sometimes react impulsively and emotionally, partly because of immaturity in their prefrontal cortex. Could this teen be misunderstanding her parents' emotional cues?

Finally, adolescents experience changes in the levels of several different neurotransmitters (e.g., glutamate, GABA, dopamine, and serotonin) in both the prefrontal cortex and the limbic system of the brain. The limbic system (which includes the amygdala mentioned previously) is important for processing and responding to emotional and stressful stimuli. Dopamine levels in the brain are very sensitive to stress, and dopamine plays a role in assessing the motivational value of stimuli. During adolescence, changes in the prefrontal cortex and the limbic system combine with changes in the levels of dopamine to these brain areas to increase the degree of emotionality and reaction to stress. But these changes also make adolescents *less* responsive to rewards. As a result, adolescents may increase their risk-taking behaviors as a way to seek more novel and engaging stimuli (Spear, 2000).

THINK ABOUT JOSH . . .
What effect might brain development be having on Josh's emotions and his decisions about sex and drug use?

As you'll learn later in this chapter, many of the major threats to adolescent health and well-being involve impulsive behavior, taking risks, and generally making poor decisions in areas such as sexual behavior, substance use, and driving. Adolescents can control their impulses and behavior, but immaturity of the prefrontal cortex, weaker connections between this area and the limbic system, and changing neurotransmitter levels may make this more difficult than adults realize (Steinberg, 2008). In addition, we are just beginning to understand the potential long-term impact of some of these impulsive behaviors on a brain that is still developing. For example, heavy alcohol consumption may have more negative effects on adolescents than on adults because of differences in brain structure and function (Brown, Tapert, Granholm, & Delis, 2000; Dahl & Spear, 2004; Keating, 2004; Tapert, Caldwell, & Burke, 2004/2005).

**prefrontal cortex**
A large part of the frontal lobe of the brain that is important for planning, judgment, decision making, and inhibiting impulsive responding.

## LET'S REVIEW . . .

1. The secular trend in puberty onset is due to ____________.
   a. genetic changes over the last 100 years
   b. better nutrition and health over the last 100 years
   c. increases in the release of sex hormones from the ovaries and testes with age
   d. the decreasing age of the adolescent growth spurt over the last 100 years
2. When comparing early- versus late-maturing girls, which of the following is *true?*
   a. Early-maturing girls are more likely than late maturers to think they are too thin.
   b. Early-maturing girls begin dating at about the same time as late-maturing girls.
   c. Late-maturing girls tend to have friends who are younger than themselves.
   d. Early-maturing girls tend to have more problems with depression and substance use.
3. Which of the following would be a more likely consequence of late maturation in adolescents' prefrontal cortex?
   a. Adolescents will show higher levels of sexual attraction than younger children.
   b. Adolescents will be more responsive to rewards.
   c. Adolescents will show higher levels of impulsive behavior than older individuals.
   d. Adolescents will handle stressful situations better than older individuals.
4. True or False: The process of sexual maturation begins in the sex organs.
5. True or False: Compared to adults, teens show less activity in their frontal lobes when processing emotional stimuli.

Answers: 1. b, 2. d, 3. c, 4. F, 5. T

# Sexual Activity during Adolescence

One of the hallmarks of physical development in adolescence is increased interest in sex. Many adolescents become sexually active, but there is great variation in when and why they become sexually active. The majority of the research literature on sexual activity in adolescence has focused on the negative consequences that can occur; there is little information to guide teens and parents as to what is a *good* age to become sexually active (Savin-Williams & Diamond, 2004). When do most teens become sexually active, and what reasons do they give for having or not having sex? The sexual landscape has changed tremendously over the last few decades due to social changes as well as diseases that have serious long-term effects. What do teens know about these issues, and how consistently do they use their knowledge for safer sexual practices?

AS YOU STUDY THIS SECTION, ASK YOURSELF THESE QUESTIONS:

**13.4** How common is sexual activity during adolescence, and why do some teens become sexually active relatively early while others wait?

**13.5** Do adolescents use contraception appropriately?

**13.6** What approaches to sex education are commonly used, and how effective are these programs in delaying sexual activity or increasing safer sex practices among teens?

## Patterns of Sexual Activity

The majority of adolescents in the United States have had sexual intercourse by the time they finish high school. Figure 13.3 (page 408) shows the percentages of adolescents who reported ever having sexual intercourse. These data from a nationwide survey of high school students show that one-third of adolescents have had intercourse by the ninth

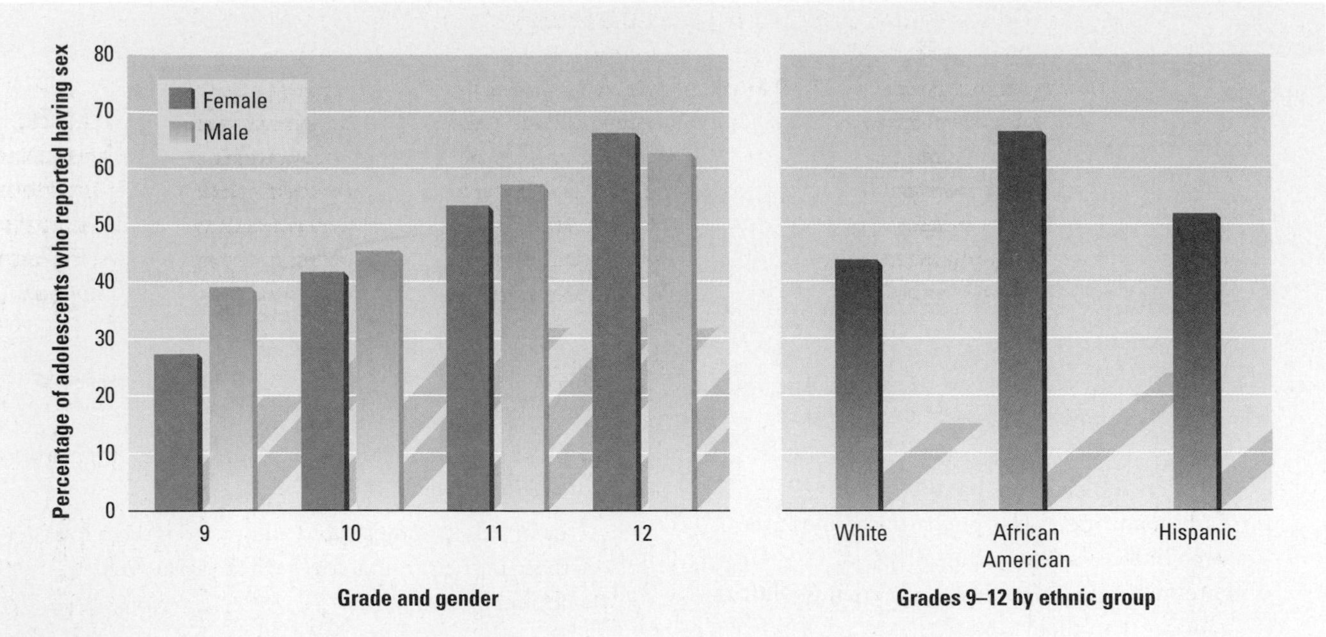


▲ FIGURE 13.3
**Percentages of High School Students Who Have Ever Had Sexual Intercourse**
This graph shows the percentages of male and female high school students who reported in a nationwide survey that they have ever had sexual intercourse. The bars at the right show percentages by ethnic group. (Data from Eaton et al., 2008.)

Do these patterns of sexual activity match what you remember from high school? What were the main pressures at that age for engaging in sexual activity? Why do you think some students abstained from sexual activity?

grade, and nearly two-thirds by 12th grade. African Americans are much more likely than Hispanics or non-Hispanic Whites to have engaged in sexual intercourse. In other data from the survey, 26% of African American males reported that they had sexual intercourse before the age of 13. In contrast, among all high school students (including male African Americans), 10% of males and 4% of females reported sexual intercourse before age 13 (Eaton et al., 2008). Rates of engaging in oral sex are much higher than for sexual intercourse, with 55% of 15 to 19 year olds and 18% of teens between the ages of 12 and 15 reporting that they had engaged in oral sex at least once (CDC, 2009; Halpern-Felsher, Cornell, Kropp, & Tschann, 2005; McKay, 2004).

Why do some adolescents become sexually active at an early age while others wait? The reasons vary, but several tendencies do exist and are summarized in Table 13.2. In general, adolescents who engage in earlier sexual activity are more likely to perform poorly in school, to achieve lower intelligence-test scores, to lack clear educational goals, to live in single-parent homes, to report poor parental communication and lack of parental support, to be more impulsive, and to use alcohol and other drugs and engage in binge drinking. The top reasons teens give for being sexually active are peer pressure, curiosity, and the idea that "everyone does it." Girls also cite pressure from boys as a top reason, and girls who mature earlier and look older are more likely to be sexually active than those who mature later (Dunn, Bartee, & Perko, 2003; Katchadourian, 1990; Raffaelli & Crockett, 2003; Savin-Williams & Diamond, 2004). Among teens who had abstained from sex, 65% told researchers they abstained because they feared **sexually transmitted diseases** (or STDs, diseases that are transmitted mostly through sexual contact), 62% feared pregnancy, 50% feared parents, and 29% feared they would lose their reputations among friends (Katchadourian, 1990). Watch on **mydevelopmentlab**

**sexually transmitted diseases (STDs)**
A disease transmitted primarily through sexual contact.

**Watch** Virginity: Cool?
www.mydevelopmentlab.com

Lack of parental supervision is also an important factor in teens' sexual activity. One study reported that higher levels of parental supervision were significantly linked to lower

**TABLE 13.2**
**Factors Associated with Earlier and Later Sexual Activity among Teens**

| EARLIER SEXUAL ACTIVITY | LATER SEXUAL ACTIVITY |
|---|---|
| • Poverty<br>• History of sexual abuse<br>• Violence in home<br>• Peer pressure (perceived, actual) | • Higher income<br>• Higher adult expectations of them |
| **INDIVIDUAL FACTORS**<br>• Early puberty<br>• Less religious affiliation<br>• Poor impulse control<br>• Alcohol, drug use (especially binge drinking)<br>• Thrill seeking, risk-taking personality | **INDIVIDUAL FACTORS**<br>• More religious affiliation<br>• Better impulse control |
| **PARENTAL FACTORS**<br>• Poor relationship with parents<br>• Lack of parental support<br>• Poor parental monitoring<br>• Single-parent household | **PARENTAL FACTORS**<br>• Good relationship with parents<br>• Good parental monitoring<br>• Good parenting skills<br>• Dual-parent household<br>• Parental disapproval of early sexual activity |
| **COGNITIVE AND EDUCATIONAL FACTORS**<br>• Lack of school, career goals<br>• Poor school performance<br>• Lower IQ scores | **COGNITIVE AND EDUCATIONAL FACTORS**<br>• Clear school, career goals<br>• Better school performance |

levels of sexual activity, fewer sexual partners, and lower incidence of STDs, especially for boys (Cohen, Farley, Taylor, Martin, & Schuster, 2002). The majority of high school students said the most frequent place they had sex was in their own homes (74% of boys and 87% of girls) and more than half said they had sex at home after school—when their parents were not home. Supervision of adolescents is a difficult issue for parents, especially for those parents who work outside of the home. Unfortunately, there are fewer supervised after-school activities available to middle and high school youths than there are for younger kids. At some point, parents do need to "loosen the reins" and allow teens more unsupervised time. The questions are how much, how soon, and under what conditions—difficult questions to answer.

The impact of peer pressure and the belief that "everyone is doing it" are more complicated than they may first appear. For example, Latino and African American girls report experiencing pressure to become sexually active, but also to conform to traditional norms to not be sexually permissive—and these pressures come from both girls and boys (O'Sullivan & Meyer-Bahlberg, 2003). It also seems that adolescents' beliefs about what their peers are doing matters more than the actual behavior. Sometimes teens misperceive the behavior of their peers and *think* that more of their peers are engaging in sexual activities than really are—they end up conforming to a "peer pressure" that isn't even real and engaging in sexual activities that they believe are not appropriate (Buhi & Goodson, 2007; Lewis, Lee, Patrick, & Fossos, 2007; Martens et al., 2006; Roche & Ramsbey, 1993; Wallace, Miller, & Forehand, 2008). Notice, however, that perceived peer pressure can influence adolescents to abstain from sexual activity as well. In one study of more than 1,000 African American 9- to 12-year-olds, those who believed their peers were not sexually active were less likely to be sexually active themselves; this was true for both the males

THINK ABOUT JOSH . . .
What important information should Josh have as he thinks about sexual activity? How could his parents improve the odds that he'll make thoughtful decisions regarding sex?

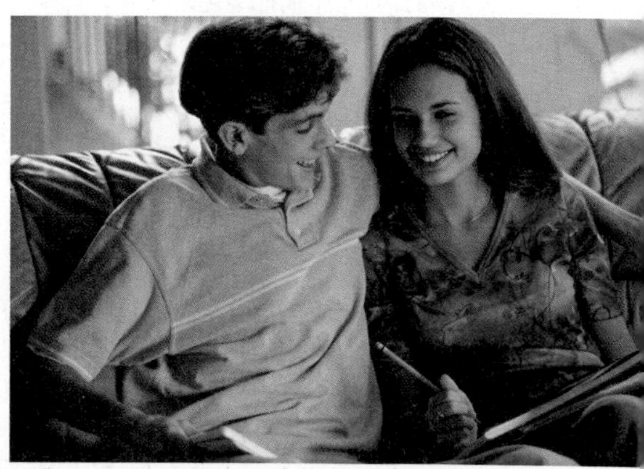
▲ Lack of parental supervision is an important risk factor for many teen behaviors, including early sexual activity and drug use. What can the families of these teens do to help reduce their risks?

and females surveyed (Wallace et al., 2008). In talking to teens about becoming sexually active, it is important to help them realize when they may be overestimating the sexual activity of their peers and not let their behavior be influenced by these misperceptions. **Listen** on **mydevelopmentlab**

**Listen**: What kinds of misperceptions do teens have about their peers' sexual behavior? (Author Podcast) www.mydevelopmentlab.com

## Contraceptive Use in Adolescence

Not surprisingly, many adults are concerned about adolescents' consistent and correct use of **contraception**, methods used to prevent pregnancy and sexually transmitted diseases. More adolescents report using contraception (particularly condoms and birth control pills) now than in past years. But teens are still notoriously inconsistent in this regard. For example, as you can see in Figure 13.4, 45% of adolescent girls under age 16 in a recent survey did not use any contraception at first intercourse. More teens who consider themselves to be sexually active report using contraception at last intercourse—83% of females and 91% of males used some method. However, it is difficult to tell from these surveys whether sexually active teens *always* use some form of contraception and whether they correctly use contraceptives; several studies indicate that they do not (Kourtis et al., 2006). The best predictor of consistent contraceptive use is age—though not perfect, older teens are more reliable than younger ones. Family factors are also important. Teens who have good relationships with their families are less likely to be sexually active, and they're more likely to consistently use contraceptives if they are sexually active (Abma, Martinez, Mosher, & Dawson, 2004; Breheny & Stephens, 2004; Mosher, Martinez, Chandra, Abma, & Willson, 2004; Santelli, Lowry, Brener, & Robin, 2000).

▲ Many teens aren't mature enough to admit that they are sexually active and need to consistently use contraception. What factors do you think encouraged this teenage boy to be more responsible?

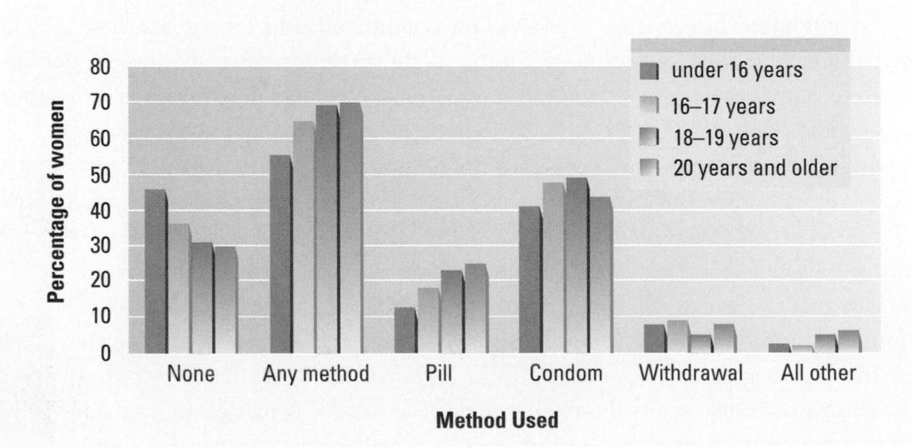


▲ FIGURE 13.4
**Women's Use of Contraceptives at First Intercourse**
This figure shows the percentage of women who did and did not report using contraception at first intercourse. Of those who reported using contraceptives, the percentages of women using different types of contraceptives are also shown. Younger teens are less likely to use any type of contraception. Condoms are the most often used type of protection of all ages surveyed. *Note: Any method* includes all methods reported by women in the survey such as surgical sterilization, hormonal methods, barrier and chemical methods, IUD, rhythm methods, withdrawal, and other. (Data from Mosher et al., 2004.)

**contraception**
Methods such as condoms and birth control pills used to prevent pregnancy and sexually transmitted diseases.

# Perspective SOCIAL POLICY THE SEX EDUCATION DEBATE

In 2001 the Surgeon General of the United States, David Satcher, released a report about sex education in U.S. schools. After reviewing hundreds of scientific studies of teenage pregnancy, teen rates of sexually transmitted disease, and adolescent sexual activity, Satcher recommended that sex education programs teach the importance of abstaining from sex but also teach teens who are already sexually active how to prevent STDs and unintended pregnancies (Alan Guttmacher Institute, 2002).

The issue of teaching teens how to use condoms and other methods of pregnancy and disease prevention has been hotly debated since the federal government began playing a role in sex education in the 1980s. In 1981 Congress passed the Adolescent Family Life Act (AFLA), creating a federally funded program to prevent teen pregnancy by teaching abstinence and self-discipline in the schools. Later, a welfare reform law passed in 1996 and a maternal and child health block grant passed in 2000 began providing additional federal funds to promote *abstinence-only* programs in schools. Abstinence-only programs condemn all sex outside of marriage (for people of any age), and they completely prohibit any positive discussion of contraception. Abstinence-only programs may discuss condoms and other contraceptive methods only in order to explain how often they fail in preventing pregnancy and disease in adolescents.

Since the 1980s U.S. schools overall have shifted toward the abstinence-only approach. They have moved away from giving teens detailed information about how to obtain and use condoms and other contraceptive methods. According to a nationwide survey published in 1999, out of the school districts with sex education programs, 35% mandated the abstinence-only approach; 51% required that abstinence be taught as the preferred method but allowed some discussion of contraception in preventing pregnancy and STDs; and only 14% offered the kind of comprehensive approach recommended by Satcher (Alan Guttmacher Institute, 2002).

Conservative lawmakers and some religious groups worry that teaching children and adolescents about condoms and contraception sends the wrong moral message—the message that premarital sex is acceptable. Satcher and others argue that the reality is that most teens *are* sexually active and need accurate and unbiased information about how to protect themselves. In a 1995 survey fewer than 60% of teenage males (ages 15 to 19) said they received information in school about birth control and STDs before their first sexual intercourse (Lindberg et al., 2000). Less than half had instruction on how to say no to sex, and fewer than 40% were taught how to put on a condom. Only half said they spoke to their parents about these issues. Girls are more likely to get these messages, with about 70% reporting formal education about birth control, HIV/AIDS, STDs, and abstinence before their first intercourse. Other surveys indicate that 81% of parents want their children's schools to provide comprehensive sex education that includes abstinence as well as condom use, birth control, abortion, and disease prevention. About half of all teens say they want more information about these and other sex-related topics (Kaiser Family Foundation, 2002).

Satcher's report pointed out that there was no available research evidence that abstinence-only programs work in preventing or delaying teen sex. Comprehensive programs that teach abstinence and contraception, however, have been associated with slight delays in the onset of sexual activity, reductions in the numbers of sexual partners, and increased contraceptive use among sexually active teens. The teenage pregnancy rate did decline slightly during the 1990s, with most of the decline due to increased use of contraception; however, the rate has increased in recent years (Alan Guttmacher Institute, 2002; Hamilton et al., 2009; Kirby, 2007).

The debate still rages. Abstinence promotion was a prominent feature of George W. Bush's 2000 presidential campaign. During the early part of the Bush administration, information about condom use, ways to reduce sex among teenagers, and abortion were removed from government Web sites. On the other side, a federal judge in New Orleans ordered Louisiana to change its federally funded abstinence programs because some programs used the federal funds to advance religious beliefs (Clymer, 2002; Liptak, 2002; Santelli, Ott, Lyon, Rogers, & Summers, 2006).

The battle over sex education in schools involves conflicting views on government control, religious morals, family and personal values, and the realities of teen sex. The stakes are high, given our nation's high rate of teen pregnancy and the devastating consequences of HIV infection and other STDs.

QUESTION **What should schools do? What role should the federal government play? What kinds of information and values do you think should be taught in sex education classes?**

Why don't teens consistently use contraception? Many teens do not seem able or willing to admit to themselves that they are sexually active or that they plan to be. Consistent contraceptive use, especially hormonal methods like birth control pills, requires that adolescents recognize they are sexually active and plan for sex far in advance of the act itself—something that is incompatible with many teens' views of sexual activity as being spontaneous. Not surprisingly, teens who are able to talk with their partners about contraception and their intent to use it are more likely to do so; but as we just learned, many teens have trouble showing this level of maturity, planning, and reasoned decision making about sex. Some teens do not use contraceptives because they're afraid their parents will discover that they are sexually active. Others say they do not know where to get contraceptives or that they aren't easily available. Surprisingly, despite the years of sex education that most teens have, some still have misunderstandings about sex and pregnancy or hold misconceptions about the need for contraceptives and how to use them. For example, some teens believe that if they do not have sex frequently, they do not need contraceptives, or that taking a single birth control pill shortly before or after having sex will protect them. Some teens simply don't believe that things like pregnancy or STDs will happen to them. The belief that one is special and invincible is called the *personal fable,* and is related to cognitive development during adolescence (see Chapter 14). Finally, for some adolescents, lack of contraceptive use is part of a broader pattern of risk-taking behaviors and impulsivity (Averett, Rees, & Argus, 2002; Iuliano, Speizer, Santelli, & Kendall, 2006; Kaplan, 2004; Miller & Moore, 1990).

## Sexual Knowledge and Sex Education

THINKING CRITICALLY

**Was the sex education program in your school system adequate and effective? How do you think it could be improved?**

Almost all public school systems provide sex education programs. Churches and community organizations such as Planned Parenthood, the YMCA, Boy Scouts, and Girl Scouts also offer these programs. Most teens are often not willing to openly talk with their parents about sex, and they don't have independent access to health care or their own health insurance. Without school and community programs, where would they get reliable information? Almost everyone agrees that it is essential to provide sex education in schools, but there is heated debate about what to teach in sex-ed classes. Read about the debate between *abstinence-only* and *comprehensive* sex-ed programs in the Social Policy Perspective box (page 411) called "The Sex Education Debate."

Given all these educational efforts, what do teens know about sex, sexuality, pregnancy, STDs, and contraception? Early reports were discouraging. For example, high school students in one early study had an average score of 42% on an assessment of sexual knowledge, despite the fact that many were already sexually active (Carver, Kittleson, & Lacey, 1990; Padilla & Baird, 1991; Trussell, 1988). Fortunately, later studies found that teens have better knowledge of how to prevent pregnancy. In general, students' knowledge of sex and contraception is increased by participating in sex education programs, though they don't always participate in these programs before they become sexually active (Kirby, 2002, 2007; Lindberg, Ku, & Sonenstein, 2000). However, a surprising number of teens have little knowledge of what STDs are, how they are spread, and how to prevent them. For example, only one-third of teens in one study knew that chlamydia is an STD. Another found that many teens in their sample believed that condoms *cause* STDs. Knowledge is only one of the many factors that influence sexual behavior, but recent drops in the rate of teen pregnancy may indicate that students are putting their knowledge of contraception into practice. More efforts are needed regarding STDs (Downs, deBruin, Murray, & Fischhoff, 2006; Duncan, Ritter, Dornbusch, Gross, & Carlsmith, 1985; Garside, Ayres, & Owen, 2001; Halpern-Felsher et al., 2005; Lagerberg, 2004).

## LET'S REVIEW . . .

1. Based on research of adolescents' knowledge of sex after participating in sex education programs, which of the following is *true?*
   - **a.** Adolescents' knowledge about sex is improved, but many still do not have a good understanding of STDs and how to prevent them.
   - **b.** Adolescents are very knowledgeable about sex, STDs, and contraception.
   - **c.** Despite participation in sex education programs, adolescents know little about sex, STDs, and contraception.
   - **d.** Adolescents' knowledge about sex is improved, but there is little evidence that they use this knowledge to prevent pregnancy and STDs.
2. Teens who are sexually active do not use contraception consistently because they ________.
   - **a.** are less likely to become pregnant than older sexually active individuals
   - **b.** do not have sex frequently enough to warrant the use of contraception
   - **c.** believe that contraceptive methods are not effective in preventing pregnancy and infections
   - **d.** believe that pregnancy and STDs won't happen to them
3. Regarding the reasons for becoming sexually active, which of the following is *false?*
   - **a.** Girls report pressure from boys as the biggest factor for becoming sexually active.
   - **b.** Teens' perceptions of their peers' sexual activity are accurate.
   - **c.** Girls report pressure to be active as well as the conflicting pressure to not be sexually active.
   - **d.** Both boys and girls who have less parental supervision are more likely to be sexually active.
4. Which of the following is a risk factor for early sexual activity?
   - **a.** Later physical maturation compared to peers
   - **b.** Fear of STD infection
   - **c.** Lack of adequate parental supervision
   - **d.** Lack of knowledge about sex
5. True or False: The majority of teens have had sexual intercourse by the age of 18.
6. True or False: Oral sex eliminates the risk of STD infection.

Answers: 1. a, 2. d, 3. b, 4. c, 5. T, 6. F

# Special Concerns about Teenage Sexual Activity

Most adults recognize that an important part of adolescence involves understanding sexual needs and learning to meet these needs in a mature way. Three important issues that arise are preventing STDs, preventing teenage pregnancy, and keeping adolescents safe from sexual assault. Who is at risk? What are the outcomes and how can they be prevented?

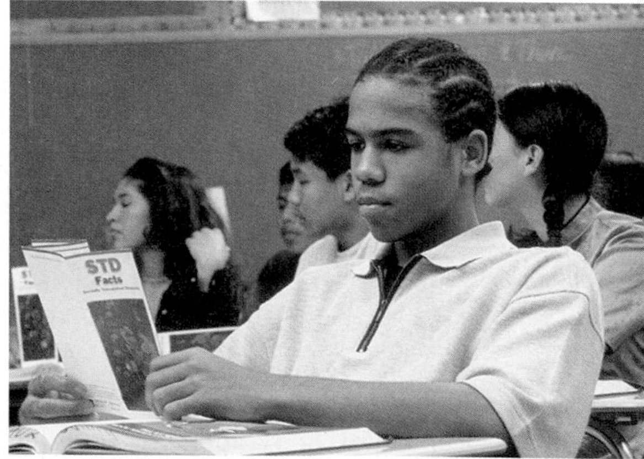


▲ Many teens do not have accurate knowledge about STDs, how they are transmitted, and how they are treated. How can parents and schools help teens become more aware of these infections and how to protect themselves?

AS YOU STUDY THIS SECTION, ASK YOURSELF THESE QUESTIONS:

**13.7** Why are adolescents at higher risk for STDs, and how can they reduce their risk?

**13.8** What are the risk factors for and outcomes of teen pregnancy?

**13.9** Which teens are at a highest risk for suffering a sexual assault?

## Sexually Transmitted Diseases and Adolescents

Sexually transmitted diseases, or STDs, constitute a major concern for teenage sexual activity, and rightly so. Adolescents and young adults from the ages of 15 to 24 account for almost half of all new cases of STDs each year, even though they only make up 25% of the sexually active population. One recent national study found that one in four teen girls have an STD—and nearly one-half of African American teen girls have an STD. Figure 13.5 (page 414) shows the rates of infection for chlamydia and gonorrhea, two STDs for which the highest rates of infection are among teens (CDC, 2008).

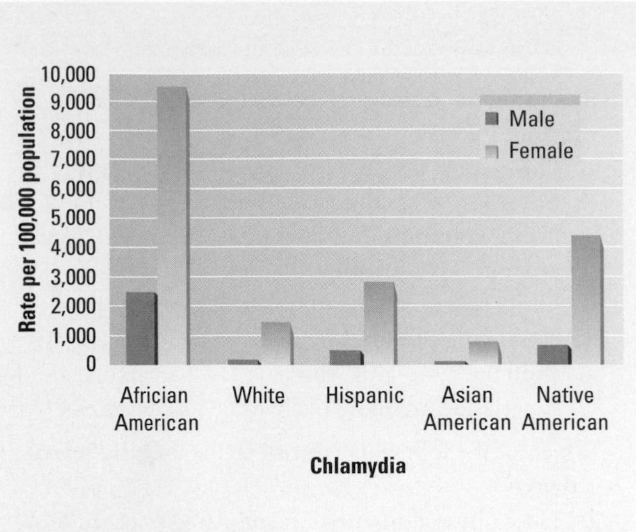


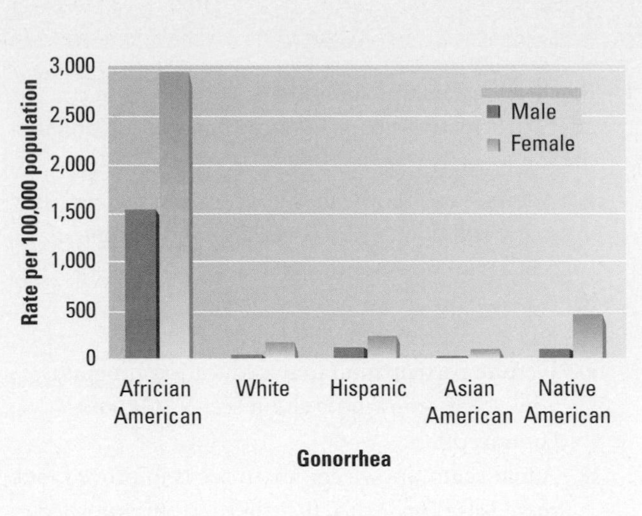


▲ FIGURE 13.5
**Rate of Chlamydia and Gonorrhea Infection among Teens Age 15 to 19, by Ethnicity**
This figure shows the rate of reported infection among teens for chlamydia and gonorrhea, two of the most common STDs. These graphs show that females in general, and African American females in particular, are at high risk. (Data from CDC, 2008.)

**Chlamydia**, caused by bacteria, is one of the most commonly reported diseases in the United States. It is known as a "silent" disease because it often produces no symptoms. It is spread through vaginal, oral, or anal sexual contact, and is much more commonly diagnosed in women. Though not serious in the short term, chlamydia can lead to infertility if untreated. Babies born to women with chlamydia are at risk for preterm birth, eye and respiratory tract infections, and pneumonia (CDC Fact Sheets on Sexually Transmitted Diseases, 2009).

**Gonorrhea** is also caused by a bacteria spread by vaginal, oral, or anal sex. Symptoms are often mild and mistaken for kidney or bladder infections, and include pain or burning during urination, a discharge, bleeding, or a sore throat (CDC Fact Sheets on Sexually Transmitted Diseases, 2009). Gonorrhea can lead to infertility in both men and women, and to serious blood or joint problems. An infected mother can pass the infection to her baby during birth, which can cause blindness, joint infection, or serious blood infection in the infant. Both chlamydia and gonorrhea can be easily cured with antibiotics, but treatment does not reverse any damage that is done before treatment begins.

**chlamydia**
A common STD caused by a bacteria that often produces no symptoms, but that can lead to infertility if untreated.

**gonorrhea**
A common STD caused by a bacteria with often mild symptoms, but that can lead to infertility, blood, or joint problems if untreated.

**human papillomavirus (HPV)**
A common STD caused by any of a group of viruses with more than 100 different strains. Persistent infection is the main risk factor for cervical cancer.

**Human papillomavirus (HPV)** is a group of viruses with more than 100 different strains. Infection sometimes produces visible warts in the genital area, but there are often no symptoms. Infection with HPV is very common; at least 50% of sexually active men and women will be infected at some point. Persistent infection with some HPV strains, although rare, is the main risk factor for cervical cancer (CDC Fact Sheets on Sexually Transmitted Diseases, 2009). There is no cure for HPV, but a vaccine that appears to reduce the likelihood of becoming infected with some strains of the virus was recently approved by the U.S. Food and Drug Administration. Many doctors are now recommending that girls receive the vaccination before becoming sexually active—at 11 to 12 years of age (Koutsky et al., 2002; Lo, 2006; Poland et al., 2005).

As you probably noticed, all three of these infections can be difficult to recognize because they often have mild symptoms or none at all. This makes it even more important for sexually active individuals of any age to have regular screenings for these and other STDs. (Several other STDs that have serious consequences for fetuses were discussed in Chapter 3.)

As you can see in Figure 13.5, the rate of STD infection varies by ethnicity. Rates for most of these infections are higher among ethnic minorities. For example, in 2007, 70% of the reported cases of gonorrhea occurred in African Americans. It is important to remember that ethnic minority status is frequently confounded with other factors that are associated with higher rates of STDs such as poverty, lack of access to health care, and living in communities that have higher rates of STDs (CDC, 2008; Upchurch, Mason, Kusunoki, & Kriechbaum, 2004).

Adolescents are more likely to engage in casual sex and, as we learned in the last section, are less likely to use protection than adults. For both these reasons, sexually active teens are at high risk for STDs. In addition, adolescent females are at an increased risk for some STDs because the cervix is not fully mature (CDC, 2005). Many of these infections have vague symptoms or none at all so teens are often not aware that they carry them. Unfortunately, infection puts them at risk for a number of serious health risks. Having an STD makes people of any age more susceptible to other infections, including HIV. Someone who has an STD is also more likely to pass HIV on to someone else—the concentration of HIV in semen is up to 10 times higher in men who have both gonorrhea and HIV than in those who have only HIV (Wasserheit, 1992). Women with STDs are also at increased risk of pelvic inflammatory disease (PID), an infection of reproductive organs that can lead to infertility or ectopic (tubal) pregnancies. PID is frequently associated with the two STDs mentioned above that are commonly found in teens—chlamydia and gonorrhea. More teens are beginning to use condoms, but more effective efforts are needed to reduce STDs in adolescents.

THINKING CRITICALLY

What did you and your peers know about STDs when you were 13, 14, and 15 years old? How did this knowledge (or lack of it) affect your choices about sexual activities?

▲ Teens who live in poverty, both external and internal, are at higher risk for teen pregnancy. What problems does this young woman face, and how can her family and community help her?

## Teenage Pregnancy

Each year almost 750,000 U.S. teenage girls become pregnant. About 30% of U.S. teens will become pregnant *at least once* before they turn 20 years old. Adolescent girls account for about 12% of all pregnancies and 10% of all births each year (Hamilton, Martin, & Ventura, 2009; National Campaign to Prevent Teen Pregnancy, 2008; Ventura, Abma, Mosher, & Henshaw, 2008). Increased use of contraception and delaying having sex until later ages have contributed to a steep decline in teenage pregnancy rates over the last 20 years, but this may be changing; teen birth rates have increased by 5% in recent years, with the largest increase seen in Native American teens (Hamilton et al., 2009; Santelli et al., 2004). Also concerning is that teen pregnancy rates in the U.S. rates are twice as high as in Canada, three times higher than in France, and four times higher than in Germany. As you can see in Figure 13.6, pregnancy rates are higher for African Americans, and most adolescent pregnancies result in live births (Advocates for Youth, 2008; McKay, 2006; Ventura et al., 2008). **Watch** on **mydevelopmentlab**

**Watch** a video on Teenage Pregnancy.
www.mydevelopmentlab.com

**Who Is at Risk for Teenage Pregnancy?** Most experts agree that living in poverty is the biggest risk factor for teenage pregnancy (Santelli et al., 2000). As you probably realize, however, it's not a lack of money that increases the risk. Poverty is associated with many factors related to teen pregnancy including poorer educational systems, lack of educational and job opportunities, family instability, less parental monitoring, and early age of first intercourse. Earlier age of first intercourse increases the risk of pregnancy in large part because younger teens are much less likely than older teens to use contraception reliably. Younger age of intercourse is also related to other family and personal problems, such as poorer parental monitoring and increased risk-taking. Regardless of socioeconomic status, lack of parental supervision increases the risk of a teen pregnancy. Growing up in a single-parent home, poor academic performance, cognitive deficits, aggressiveness and social withdrawal during childhood, and alcohol and other drug use in early adolescence all increase the risk of teen pregnancy (Serbin et al., 1998; Stack, Serbin, Schwartzman, & Ledingham, 2005).

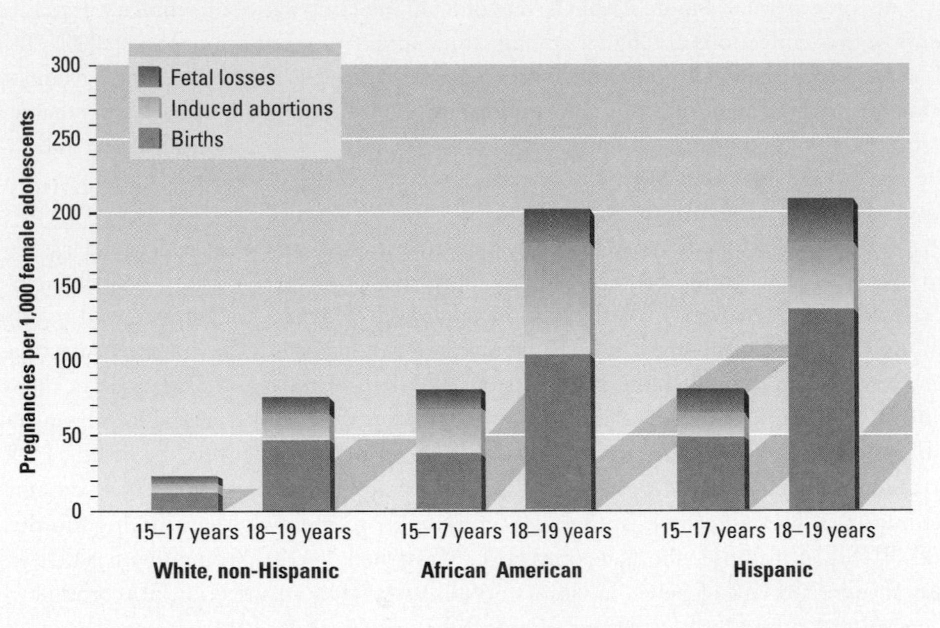


FIGURE 13.6 ▶ **Teenage Pregnancy Rates** Pregnancy rates and pregnancy outcomes among 15- to 19-year-olds in the United States vary at different ages and among different ethnic groups. The data here come from a 2004 survey. (Ventura et al., 2008.)

Individual cognitive factors also play a role. One study assessed the locus of control and self-efficacy (both are related to feelings of control over outcomes and competence) along with educational and career expectations of almost 2,000 eighth grade girls from a large national data set. Four years later, teens who reported becoming pregnant by 12th grade were compared to nonpregnant teens of the same race and age. By eighth grade, those who would later become pregnant showed significantly lower self-efficacy, higher external locus of control, and lower expectations regarding their overall educational achievement. In essence, these teens seem to suffer from an "internal poverty," or the belief that they were less able to achieve their goals and that their lives were under others' control rather than their own (Young, Martin, Young, & Ting, 2001, p. 290; Young, Turner, & Denny, 2004). Expectations about life options also play a role in teen pregnancy, with those who perceive fewer or more negative life options at a higher risk. For these teens, becoming pregnant may not represent a great loss of potential because, in their eyes, they did not have many positive options in the first place. Therefore, they see a pregnancy as causing less disruption to their lives, which may lead them to be less concerned about consistent use of contraception (Bickel, Weaver, Williams, & Lange, 1997; Bissel, 2000). Some teens even see pregnancy as a positive option that provides purpose and meaning to their lives, particularly if poor academic achievement limits their opportunities. At least, they may not believe they would have been better off if they had remained childless (SmithBathe, 2005; Young et al., 2001).

Less is known about risk factors for becoming a teenage father. Only about 7% of teen boys become fathers. Most are poor, do not do well in school (many have dropped out of high school), and are more likely to engage in drug use and delinquent activities than teens who are not fathers. Many come from single-parent and lower-income homes, and from homes in which parents showed the poor discipline practices of *coercive homes* that we described in Chapter 12. Teen fathers show some of the same cognitive deficits as teen mothers, such as poor planning skills and childhood aggression. Substance use and involvement in deviant peer groups were also related to teen parenthood, all of which suggests a pattern of poor impulse control (Fagot, Pears, Capaldi, Crosby, & Leve, 1998; Miller-Johnson, Winn, Coie, Malone, & Lochman, 2004; Trad, 1995).

THINK ABOUT JOSH . . .
Does Josh have any of the risk factors for teen pregnancy? What can his family and community do to reduce the chances of his becoming a teen father?

Finally, one important risk factor for teen pregnancy is having already had a baby. In 2007, 19.5% of all teen births were repeat births; these young women had already given birth to at least one child. The rates of repeat births ranged from 16% for White teens to 23% for Native American teens (Hamilton et al., 2009).

THINKING CRITICALLY

What supports exist in your community for teens who become pregnant? What steps could your school or community take to improve the outcomes for teen parents and their children.

**The Impact of Teen Parenthood.** Unintended pregnancies can place severe strains on adolescents. These teens are often not physically or emotionally ready to bear and raise children. Teenage parenthood is associated with a number of negative outcomes, including poorer educational achievement, less financial stability (both short term and long term), and disruptions in emotional development such as identity development (Coley & Chase-Lansdale, 1998; Furstenberg, Brooks-Gunn, & Chase-Lansdale, 1989; Hofferth, Reid, & Mott, 2001; Planned Parenthood, 2006; Stoiber & McIntyre, 2006).

The children of teenage parents fare less well than those of older parents. As infants they are more likely to suffer from preterm birth, low birth weight, birthing complications, and infant mortality; second children of teen mothers have an even higher mortality rate (Cowden & Funkhouser, 2001). This may be due in part to the fact that younger mothers are less likely to receive consistent prenatal care, and they are less knowledgeable about and less inclined to engage in healthy behaviors during pregnancy and avoid unhealthy ones. The parenting skills of teen parents are often not well-developed, and their children are at increased risk for accidents, illnesses, child abuse, and neglect. Adolescent mothers are more likely to show an unresponsive parenting style and they tend to have unrealistic expectations of their children. Both teen mothers and fathers use discipline styles that are more negative, directive, and physical—much like the coercive parenting described in Chapter 12. These young parents are less empathetic toward their children, less patient, less verbal, and provide less stimulating environments for their babies. Problems for children of adolescent parents tend to worsen as they get older, especially for sons. They are at greater risk for educational, behavioral, emotional, and financial problems—including early parenthood themselves (Bunting & McAuley, 2004; Fagot et al., 1998; Pogarsky, Thornberry, & Lizotte, 2006).

▲ Not all teen pregnancies have dire outcomes. If the young parents are able to continue their education, delay having a second child, and form supportive and positive relationships with family and friends, these young families can be more successful.

Clearly, teen parenthood is associated with a host of problems for mothers, fathers, and babies. What is less clear, however, is the extent to which these problems are the *result* of, rather than the *cause* of, teen parenthood. For example, the educational achievement differences between teen mothers and those who delay having a child are frequently in place long before early parenthood, though they do tend to worsen afterward. A number of the behavioral problems shown by the children of young parents, such as early aggressiveness and poor impulse control, are very similar to the behaviors that put these parents at risk for early parenthood in the first place. Are these educational and behavioral problems due to early parenthood *per se*, to the poorer parenting skills of young parents, or to genetically related tendencies shared by these parents and children? The research has only begun to sort out these issues. Finally, the pervasive effects of poverty, both as a contributing factor to teen pregnancy and a result of young parenthood, may have a bigger impact on outcomes for teenage moms, dads, and their children than early parenthood itself (Bissell, 2000; Coley & Chase-Lansdale, 1998; Furstenberg et al., 1989; Levine, Pollack, & Comfort, 2001).

There is a great deal of diversity in the outcomes for teen parents and their children (Furstenberg et al., 1989; Klein & The Committee on Adolescence, 2005; Schiefelbein, Sussman, & Dorn, 2005). Many teen parents eventually achieve stability, especially if they are able to continue their education and delay having subsequent children. A stable marriage can contribute to better outcomes, but unstable relationships are associated with worse outcomes. While becoming a teenage parent is clearly not optimal, it does not necessarily doom the parents and children to negative outcomes. Prevention programs that foster self-esteem, feelings of self-competence, hopefulness, and plans for the future, and that help adolescents remain engaged in school help reduce the occurrence of teenage pregnancy (Bennett & Assefi, 2005; Klein & The Committee on Adolescence, 2005).

## Forced Sexual Behavior

Unfortunately, many teens report that they were forced to have sex. **Rape** refers to sexual intercourse as a result of physical force or psychological coercion, while **sexual assault** refers to sexual contact due to physical force or psychological coercion that may or may not involve penetration. **Sexual harrassment** refers to any sort of unwanted behavior of a sexual nature and includes unwelcome sexual requests, demands, rumors, jokes, taunts, or other actions that create a hostile or offensive environment.

▲ Date rape and other types of sexual assault are far too common. What can these teens do to reduce the likelihood of becoming victims of sexual assault?

Adolescents are at higher risk for rape and other sexual assault than any other age group. Most victims are female, and most know the person who assaults them. Estimates of the prevalence of forced sex vary widely. Some studies report that about 11% of girls and 5% of boys will experience forced sex at some point; for many, this will happen to them before the age of 12. Other studies estimate that as many as 68% of adolescents will suffer *acquaintance* or *date rape* (in which the victim knows, or is on a date with, the perpetrator). Research studies have shown that twenty-six percent of college-aged men report having attempted acquaintance or date rape. The rate of sexual harrassment is even higher—in one study, 83% of adolescent girls and 79% of adolescent boys reported that they had experienced it, and 25% said they experienced it frequently (Abma et al., 2004; American Association of University Women, 2001; National Center for Victims of Crime, 2006; Rickert & Weimann, 1998; Tjaden & Thoennes, 2006).

Why are adolescents at higher risk of sexual assault? They usually have more freedom than younger children in terms of where they go and who they are with, they often want to experiment with new behaviors and therefore take more risks than older or younger individuals, they may not yet be skilled in "reading the signs" that indicate a potentially dangerous situation is developing, and they are in close contact with many other adolescents for a large part of the day during the school year (Howard & Wang, 2005; Rickert & Weimann, 1998).

Which adolescents are at highest risk for sexual assault? Unfortunately, one of the best predictors of being a victim of rape in adolescence is having been a victim of rape during childhood (Clements, Speck, Crane, & Faulkner, 2004; Rickert, Wiemann, Vaughan, & White, 2004). As you learned in Chapter 10, the consequences of childhood sexual abuse are severe and far-reaching and, for many youth, the abuse does not stop. Other predictors of sexual assault during adolescence are early age for first date and early sexual activity, both of which place teens in situations where sexual coercion and rape are more likely. Drug use, particularly use of alcohol, is also associated with sexual assault for adolescents. For perpetrators of sexual violence, drug and alcohol use increases the chance of misinterpreting cues from the victim as sexual invitations. In addition, others may not hold perpetrators as responsible for their behavior if they were intoxicated; ironically, victims who are intoxicated may be viewed as more to blame (Johnson, Kuck, & Schander, 1997; Rickert & Weimann, 1998). For victims, alcohol and other drugs make it harder to cope with or escape the situation. One particular drug, flunitrazepam (Rohypnol), has received a lot of attention. This so-called *date rape drug* produces sleepiness, decreased anxiety and muscle control, and may cause amnesia. These effects put the victim at greater risk of not only being sexually assaulted but also unable to remember details that might be helpful in reporting and prosecuting an attack. Rape-tolerant attitudes also play an important role in the risk for rape. In some studies, date and acquaintance rape were not considered to be rape at all, or there was a stronger tendency in these situations to blame the victim. Both male and female high school students are more likely to assign blame to the victim if she dresses provocatively, though some studies find that more males assign this blame than females (White & Kurpius, 2002).

**rape**
Sexual intercourse as a result of physical force or psychological coercion.

**sexual assault**
Sexual contact due to physical force or psychological coercion that may or may not involve penetration.

**sexual harassment**
Any unwanted behavior of a sexual nature that creates a hostile or offensive environment.

As you might expect, forced sexual activity has a number of negative consequences. Victims report feeling afraid, anxious, sad, and hopeless. Feelings of depression are common for both males and females, and they are worse when the victim knows the attacker. Victims may also experience problems with academic achievement, risky sexual behavior, increased drug and alcohol use, and increased risk of post-traumatic stress disorder. Not surprisingly, the more severe an assault and the longer the attacks continue before they are stopped, the more emotionally, psychologically, and physically difficult it is for the victims (Clements et al., 2004; Demaris & Kaukinen, 2005; National Center for Victims of Crime, 2006). Some prevention programs have been effective in changing both males' and females' attitudes and behaviors associated with sexual assault and in increasing knowledge of strategies for preventing rape. Awareness of sexual harassment and assault has been heightened, and guidelines have been published to help schools develop policies for preventing and reporting unwanted sexual activities. Given the statistics on adolescent sexual assault and harassment, however, there remains a need to improve and expand these programs (American Council on Education, 1992).

THINKING CRITICALLY

Think about the pressures on adolescents to engage in sexual activity and the high prevalence of forced sexual activity. What steps could a school or community take to create safer environments for both boys and girls?

**LET'S REVIEW . . .**

1. Compared to White teens, teens who are ethnic minorities are at higher risk for STDs because a higher percentage of ethnic minority teens tend to ____________.
   - **a.** use drugs at a higher rate
   - **b.** live in poverty
   - **c.** avoid using health care even though it is easily available
   - **d.** live in places where STDs are uncommon so they don't want to be screened for them
2. Why is poverty a risk factor for teen pregnancy?
   - **a.** Poor teens are more likely to see a pregnancy as disrupting their future plans.
   - **b.** Poor teens tend to become sexually active later and have less knowledge about contraception.
   - **c.** Poor teens have fewer job and education opportunities.
   - **d.** Poor teens are more aggressive and socially withdrawn during childhood.
3. Which of the following teen girls is at highest risk of a teenage pregnancy?
   - **a.** Olivia, who loves school and enjoys working on school-related activities with her friends
   - **b.** Julia, who believes that success in life is mostly about being lucky
   - **c.** Bernadette, who plans to be a clinical psychologist
   - **d.** Maya, whose parents check up on her regularly
4. Which of the following teens is at highest risk for becoming a victim of sexual assault?
   - **a.** Brady, who binge drinks regularly
   - **b.** Tevin, who is not yet sexually active at age 16
   - **c.** Daniel, who helped organize his school's sexual assault prevention program
   - **d.** Sam, who suffers from depression
5. True or False: The biggest risk factor for teenage pregnancy is aggressiveness during childhood.
6. True or False: Children of teen parents tend to have significant problems early in life, but their problems get better as they get older.

Answers: 1. b, 2. c, 3. b, 4. a, 5. F, 6. F

# Adolescent Health Issues

In terms of physical illness and chronic health problems, adolescents are much healthier than the rest of the population. Leading causes of death among adults such as heart disease, cancer, and stroke are far less prevalent during adolescence (Miniño, Arias, Kochanek, Murphy, & Smith, 2002). However, experts have become increasingly concerned with

▲ Teens eat out much more frequently than in years past and overeat fat and sugars. How can teens, parents, and communities improve the health habits of adolescents?

adolescents' health. One reason is that adolescence is a time when long-lasting behavior patterns begin. If adolescents can be encouraged to develop positive health habits, they may avoid problems in adulthood. Experts also recognize that the major things that threaten adolescent health are *completely preventable.* For example, the leading cause of death by far among adolescents is unintentional injury, particularly motor vehicle accidents. Many adolescents each year compromise their health by misusing alcohol and other drugs; others suffer from depression and may even attempt suicide. Clearly, encouraging adolescents to develop positive health behaviors and avoid negative ones will reduce their risk for health problems and injury.

AS YOU STUDY THIS SECTION, ASK YOURSELF THESE QUESTIONS:

**13.10** What is the state of adolescent nutrition and exercise today?

**13.11** Which teens are at a higher risk for substance abuse problems?

**13.12** What other health-related issues do teens face?

## Nutrition and Exercise

**anorexia nervosa**
A serious eating disorder involving distorted body image, intense fear of gaining weight, and refusal to maintain a healthy weight.

**bulimia nervosa**
A serious eating disorder with binge eating, followed by purging, fasting, or excessive exercise.

**Watch** a video on Adolescent Behavior: Health and Lifestyle Choices.
www.mydevelopmentlab.com

You're probably well aware that the average teen today does not have very good eating habits. But just how good (or bad) is the state of adolescent nutrition? Recent surveys found that only 22% of high school students eat the recommended five servings of fruits and vegetables daily—unless you count french fries and potato chips. In fact, for any given category in the USDA's Food Pyramid (grains, vegetables, fruits, meat and beans, milk), fewer than half the teens surveyed ate the recommended number of servings. But their intake of fat and sugars was much higher than recommended. Two-thirds exceeded the guidelines for overall fat intake and almost 75% ate too much saturated fat—the kind that is associated with a host of health problems (Enns, Mickle, & Goldman, 2003; Grunbaum et al., 2004). Adolescents are also more likely than other age groups to have inconsistent eating patterns. Skipping meals is quite common, with about 20% of teens not eating breakfast and 50% not eating lunch. Skipping meals often leads to adolescents eating more snacks, and snack choices are often as bad or worse than meal choices (Siega-Riz, Cavadini, & Popkin, 2001). All foods are much more available to teens than in past generations, but the availability of fast food in particular plays an important role in the teens' food choices. Increased portion sizes encourage many to overeat less healthy foods. Family eating habits are also important—more families eat away from home than in the past and parents often provide poorer models of food choices for children (Briefel & Johnson, 2004). **Watch** on **mydevelopmentlab**

What about exercise? About two-thirds of adolescents engage in regular vigorous physical activity, though less than one-third do so in a physical education class at school. Teens are less physically active than younger children, however, and teen girls are significantly less likely to get regular physical exercise than teen boys. Teens who are more physically active see themselves as healthier, have a more positive body image, and have healthier overall lifestyles. Both teen boys and girls report that they are more likely to exercise regularly when they have a friend to exercise with, when they like the activity they engage in, and when they think of exercise as something that is typical among their friends (Godin, Anderson, & Lambert, 2005; Tergerson & King, 2002). The level of physical activity among minority females is lower than among Whites, but they have similar perceptions of the benefits (e.g., staying in shape) and negative aspects of exercise (e.g., getting hurt, sweating, having to deal with aggressive players, and embarrassment) (Grieser, Vu, & Bedimo-Rung, 2006). Higher levels of support from parents and peers is related to higher levels of regular physical activity (DeBourdeaudhuij, Lefevre, & Deforche, 2005; Gustafson & Rhodes, 2006). One important factor that is

THINK ABOUT JOSH . . .
What steps can Josh take as a teen to improve his lifelong health? What are some things his parents and his school could do to encourage Josh to develop positive health habits?

sometimes overlooked in attempts to increase physical activity in children and teens is neighborhood safety. Teens who live in neighborhoods that are perceived as being less safe are less likely to engage in physical activity (Molnar, Gortmaker, & Bull, 2004).

THINKING CRITICALLY

What were your diet and exercise patterns like when you were an adolescent? How could they have been healthier?

**Eating Disorders.** As you may have experienced yourself, there is considerable pressure toward unhealthy thinness for children and teens, especially for girls and women. For example, consider the story of Sarah. At the age of 13, Sarah was already thinner than most girls her age, but she still believed that she was fat and unattractive. On a typical day Sarah ate a plain piece of toast in the morning and a cup of yogurt and fruit for dinner. She rarely snacked. She exercised vigorously every day, determined to lose another 5 to 10 pounds. By the time she was 15, Sarah weighed only 85 pounds (more than 25% less than the average weight for her age). Because of her severe weight loss, she stopped having menstrual periods, but she was still determined to lose more weight. Sarah was never satisfied with how she looked, and she felt that she was losing control of her weight. In despair, Sarah tried to end her life by taking an overdose of sleeping pills. Fortunately, her parents found her before it was too late, and they admitted her to the hospital. Before she was released from the hospital, she gained 14 pounds. Sarah and her parents now attend counseling sessions, and only time will tell if she will recover from her condition.

You have probably recognized that Sarah suffers from **anorexia nervosa**. This serious condition involves a distorted body image, an intense fear of gaining weight, and the refusal to maintain a minimally healthy body weight. People with anorexia, like Sarah, have an irrational view of their own bodies. By objective standards they are already thin, but they are still convinced that they are fat and unattractive. They show a relentless determination to be even more thin. People with anorexia have a very restricted diet, and they attempt to lose additional weight through vigorous exercise or by purging food through self-induced vomiting or the misuse of laxatives or enemas.

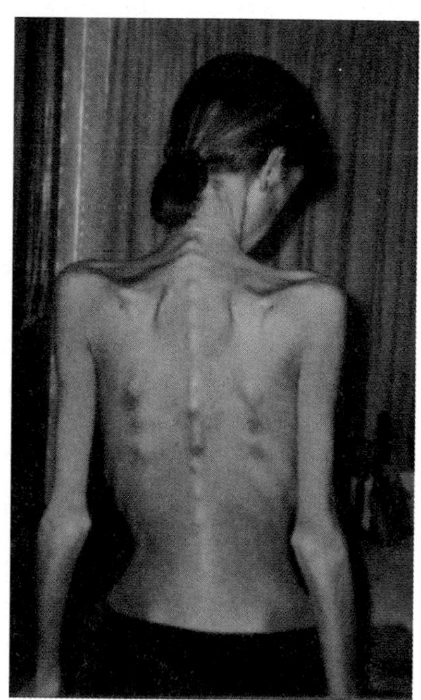

▲ Some teens suffer from serious eating disorders. What does this young woman see when she looks in the mirror? What are some of the factors that might have led to her illness?

**Bulimia nervosa**, or bulimia, is a related condition that involves cycles of binge eating (consumption of huge amounts of food) followed by purging, fasting, or excessive exercise as a means to compensate for overeating. People with bulimia experience a loss of control during binge episodes: They know they are overeating, but they feel powerless to stop. Afterwards, they feel intense guilt. In contrast to some anorexics, who purge after eating only small amounts of food, bulimics purge after uncontrolled eating binges.

Both types of eating disorders are most common among female adolescents. Approximately one out of every 100 female adolescents is anorexic; two to three times as many are bulimic (Hudson, Hiripi, Pope & Kessler, 2007; Mash & Wolfe, 1999). In the past these disorders were rare in males, but body dissatisfaction and eating disorders may be increasing among male adolescents, along with use of anabolic steroids and other untested supplements to increase muscle mass (Labre, 2002; McCabe & Ricciardelli, 2004). Anorexia typically appears between the ages of 14 and 18, whereas bulimia usually emerges in later adolescence. There is a mild to moderate genetic link to eating disorders. These disorders tend to run in families, and compared to nonidentical twins, identical twins are three to five times more likely to share an eating disorder (Hsu, Chesler, & Santhouse, 1990; Mazzeo et al., 2009). Researchers believe that adolescents can inherit emotional tendencies that make them vulnerable to eating disorders. Too often, these vulnerabilities can combine with low self-esteem, family pressures, and the strong societal message that "thin is beautiful" to lead to eating disorders (Davison & Birch, 2002; Stice & Whitenton, 2002). Unfortunately, eating disorders have a higher death rate than any other psychiatric disorder (Sullivan, 1995).

THINKING CRITICALLY

Have you known anyone with an eating disorder? What impact did it have on his or her life? Did this person receive treatment? Was it effective?

We all know that society places too much emphasis on being thin. The mass media are full of images of attractive women who are significantly thinner than the general population. In fact many models are so thin that they are unhealthy. Very few adolescent girls can "measure up" to these unreasonable standards. Most adolescent girls are not satisfied with their body image, and 80% diet to control their weight (Mash & Wolfe, 1999). For ethnic minority teens, the stress of trying to fit into the majority culture adds additional pressures (Perez, Voelz, Pettit, & Joiner, 2002). Striving to be thin, some adolescent girls spiral into a

## Perspective PROFESSIONAL — CAREER FOCUS: MEET AN EATING DISORDERS COUNSELOR

Douglas Bunnell, PhD, FAED
Wilton, CT
Counselor specializing in treatment of eating disorders; past president of the National Eating Disorders Association

**What eating disorders are common in teens? What factors lead to an eating disorder?**
Most teens with eating disorders have tried to diet by restricting their food intake. Some go on to develop full-blown anorexia nervosa, but many are not able to sustain the food restriction. They develop symptoms such as binge eating. This often leads to guilt and anxiety about weight gain and can provoke overexercising, using laxatives, or inducing vomiting. Eating disorders are never caused by a single factor. There is no question that cultural messages about the importance of being thin help create tremendous body image distress in teens, boys and girls alike. This is a pervasive risk factor for developing eating disorders. Teens who have other risk factors, such as predisposing genetics, anxiety, or depression are most likely to develop a serious eating disorder.

**What symptoms and effects do teens with eating disorders and their families experience?**
Eating disorders are serious illnesses that have an enormous impact on both the individual and the people who know and love her or him. Teens with eating disorders often feel anxious and depressed. Many feel that nothing they accomplish can make them feel satisfied, so they push themselves to incredible lengths just to feel "good enough." They can develop dangerous cardiac problems, weakened bones, and serious dental problems. Their families also struggle.

**What kinds of treatments are available? How can parents and teens prevent eating disorders?**
Eating disorders are complicated illnesses. Treatment has to be equally complex, but it can be hard to find, expensive, and it can take a long time. Most patients have an individual or family therapist who helps them develop new ways to cope with their feelings. Family therapy is often the most effective treatment. Patients may work with a nutritionist for help with meal planning and eating disorder behaviors. Psychiatric medications can be very helpful—a medical doctor is an important part of every patient's treatment team. Many patients can be treated as outpatients, but a significant number will need a residential or hospital-based program. The structure and supervision of these programs often make it easier for patients to give up their symptoms. Teaching children to decode cultural messages about body image may help them resist the pressure to be thin at any cost. Identifying early warning signs of an eating disorder like body image distress, attempts to diet when there is no need to lose weight, ritualized eating habits, or evidence of purging can help by starting treatment before more serious symptoms occur.

**What advice do you have for students who are considering a career in this area?**
Clinicians need to be fully aware of the mental, psychological, relational, and biological aspects of adolescence, because eating disorders are mostly teen disorders. Whether their specialty is medicine, psychology, nutrition, or social work, students need to be able to integrate information from a wide variety of perspectives. Patients with eating disorders may be reluctant to let themselves get help. Clinicians need to be empathic, informed, and creative to establish a connection with them. The best background is one that exposes you to a wide variety of literature, arts, science, and humanities. There are no simple answers with these disorders and clinicians need to be comfortable with complexity and ambiguity. They also need to be a bit stubborn while still being respectful and caring.

QUESTION **What can families and communities do to help their children and adolescents cope with the pervasive cultural messages about being thin?**

dangerous cycle of anorexia or bulimia. For many anorexics, food is the only thing they feel they can control. For bulimics, binging and purging is another symptom of their lack of control over life events. Psychological therapy and medications have shown promise in treating adolescent eating disorders (DeAngelis, 2002). Some recent approaches combine a school-based prevention program that addresses issues of body image, cultural ideals, and self-esteem with a more intensive family-based program for students identified as being at high risk of developing eating disorders (Varnado-Sullivan & Zucker, 2004). Severe cases, like Sarah's, may require hospitalization to force weight gain or to treat other symptoms such as suicidal behavior or chronic depression. To read more about eating disorders, their impact on teens and their families, and how they are treated, read the Professional Perspective box (page 422) called "Career Focus: Meet an Eating Disorders Counselor."

## Substance Use and Abuse

A major threat to adolescent health is substance use and abuse. **Substance use** can be somewhat difficult to define, but in general it refers to ingesting any legal or illegal substance that alters psychological functioning on more than a few occasions. **Substance abuse** refers to the use of a substance (legal or illegal) to the extent that it creates difficulties in day-to-day life. How prevalent is substance use and abuse? A large nationwide survey of U.S. high school students indicated that two-thirds of ninth graders had tried alcohol, over 40% had tried tobacco, and almost one-third had tried marijuana (Eaton et al., 2008). Many of these students reported trying these substances before 13 years of age (8% tried marijuana, 14% tried cigarettes, and 24% tried more than just a few sips of alcohol). As Figure 13.7 shows, much smaller percentages of ninth graders had tried cocaine and other drugs. Use of inhalants (sniffing glue, paint, or aerosols) is a more recent phenomenon: More ninth

**substance use**
Ingesting on more than a few occasions any substance that alters psychological functioning.

**substance abuse**
The use of a substance that alters psychological functioning to the extent that it creates difficulties in day-to-day life.

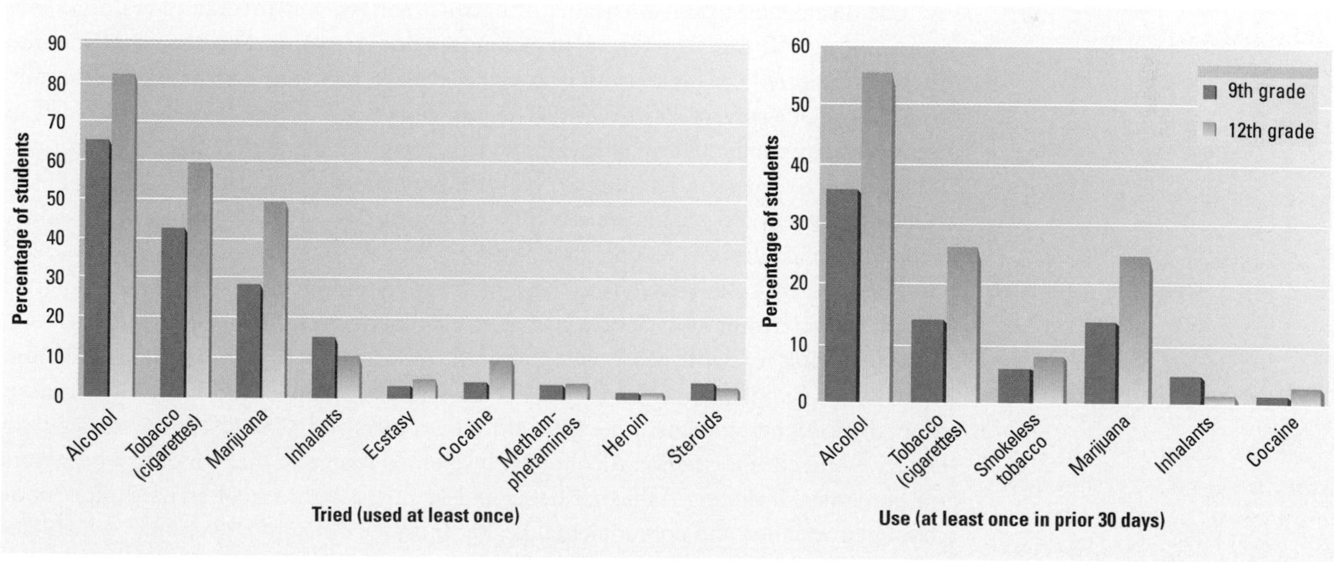


▲ FIGURE 13.7
**Alcohol and Drug Use in 9th and 12th Grades**
The data graphed here come from a nationwide survey of high school students. Compare the percentages of students in the ninth and 12th grades who reported trying and using alcohol and other drugs. *Note: Tried* means used the substance at least once; *use* means used the substance at least once during the 30 days prior to the survey. *Cocaine* includes powder, "crack," and "freebase"; *inhalants* include sniffing glue or breathing aerosols, paints, or sprays; *heroin* includes "smack," "junk," and "China white." (Data from Eaton et al., 2008.)

**TABLE 13.3**
High School Students' Alcohol and Drug Use by Ethnic Group

| | NON-HISPANIC WHITE | AFRICAN AMERICAN | HISPANIC |
|---|---|---|---|
| Use alcohol | 47 | 35 | 48 |
| Use tobacco (cigarettes) | 23 | 12 | 17 |
| Use tobacco (smokeless) | 10 | 1.2 | 5 |
| Use marijuana | 20 | 22 | 19 |
| Use cocaine | 3 | 1 | 5 |
| Tried inhalants | 14 | 9 | 14 |
| Tried ecstasy | 6 | 4 | 7 |
| Tried methamphetamines | 5 | 2 | 6 |
| Tried heroin | 2 | 2 | 4 |
| Binge drink | 30 | 13 | 27 |

*Note: Use* means the students used the substance at least once during the 30 days prior to the survey. *Tried* means the students ever used that drug in any form. *Binge drink* means drinking 5 or more drinks within a couple hours. (Eaton et al., 2008.)

graders than 12th graders reported ever having tried inhalants. Use of both ecstasy (also known as MDMA) and methamphetamines by high schoolers has declined by almost half since 2003 (11% report trying ecstasy in 2003 versus 6% in 2007; 8% reported trying methamphetamines in 2003 versus 4% in 2007) (Eaton et al., 2008; Grumbaum et al., 2004)

Table 13.3 shows ethnic differences in substance use from the same nationwide survey. Use of alcohol, tobacco, cocaine, inhalants, ecstasy, and methamphetamines was lower among African Americans than among non-Hispanic Whites or Hispanics. Hispanics reported the highest use of cocaine, ecstasy, methamphetamines, and heroin. Other large-scale surveys show that the rate of using many illegal drugs has declined in recent years, by about 10% among 12th graders. However, the use of inhalants, sedatives, and the addictive prescription drug OxyContin has increased (Cleveland & Wiebe, 2003; Dishion & Owen, 2002; Eaton et al., 2008; Grumbaum et al., 2004; Johnston, O'Malley, Bachman, & Schulenberg, 2006).

The rates of alcohol and tobacco (and increasingly, marijuana) use are concerning. As you read, a majority of teens have at least tried alcohol by the time they reach high school, and many drink regularly. Most obtain alcohol from their own homes. **Binge drinking**, defined as consuming five or more drinks on a single occasion, is also relatively common among high school students, with 17% of ninth graders and 37% of 12th graders saying they have binged at least once. Alcohol use by teens is related to many problem behaviors and outcomes, including traffic accidents and fatalities, early sexual activity, rape, poor school performance, and poorer mental health. It can be difficult to tease apart which factors lead to and which result from alcohol use, but alcohol use by teens is clearly linked to many problems. Cigarette smoking has declined significantly since the mid-1990s. Although this trend is weakening, teens tend to hold more negative attitudes toward smoking and its health risks than in past years, there is less cigarette advertising that targets them, and they see more antismoking advertising. The skyrocketing cost of cigarettes is probably also a factor in lower rates of cigarette use (Johnston et al., 2006). The rate of teens who use smokeless tobacco has remained steady at 7% to 8% since 1999. Finally, marijuana is by far the most frequently used drug that is illegal for both adolescents and

**binge drinking**
Consuming five or more alcoholic drinks on a single occasion.

adults. It rivals tobacco in the percentage of teens who are regular users (20% of teens report that they used marijuana in the past 30 days; 25% reported they used some form of tobacco) (Eaton et al., 2008).

Substance use usually starts during adolescence, and it usually begins with legal-for-adults drugs such as alcohol and tobacco. If it progresses, marijuana is typically used next, then other illegal drugs. Alcohol, tobacco, and marijuana are often called **gateway drugs** because the vast majority of those who use harder drugs first used one of these three. Across several studies, 90% of those who used illegal drugs first used marijuana, and the risk of using marijuana is 65 times greater for those who have smoked cigarettes or used alcohol compared to those who have not. Earlier and more frequent use of the gateway drugs is also associated with a greater chance of using harder illegal drugs. The gateway theory does not say that progression to harder drugs is inevitable or even likely—in fact, most who use alcohol, tobacco, and marijuana do not go on to harder drug use. But monitoring the use of these substances is still important for parents because it is a signal for potential problems, particularly if their adolescent shows other risk factors for drug abuse (Fergusson, Boden, & Horwood, 2006; Kandel, 2002; Kandel, Yamaguchi, & Chen, 1992).

THINKING CRITICALLY

What effects of substance use and abuse have been seen in your community? Which risk factors contribute to the problem, and which protective factors could be made stronger?

**Risk Factors for Drug Use.** One risk factor for drug use is simply being an adolescent. Adolescents are far more likely to experiment with alcohol and drugs than younger or older individuals. But not all teens who experiment are at equal risk of developing problems or having negative long-term outcomes. Many who experiment or only use occasionally do not experience long-term effects—as long as they escape short-term negative outcomes such as accidents and sexual risk-taking. As you might expect, early onset of use (e.g., using alcohol before age 14 or illegal drugs before age 15) is associated with increasing use over time and greater risk for alcohol and drug disorders (Chassin et al., 2004). But what risk factors can adults watch for before substance use begins?

▲ Like many adolescents, these teens are experimenting with alcohol and tobacco. Why do some teens choose not to drink and smoke? What are the effects of occasional substance use and of heavier substance use during adolescence?

Characteristics of the individual are related to substance use. Those who develop substance problems are more likely to be sensation seeking, aggressive, impulsive, and have poor behavioral control—and many of these qualities are evident between 3 and 5 years of age. Problems with cognitive skills related to self-regulation such as planning, organizing, and selective attention are also related to increased risk of substance abuse. A history of antisocial behavior, including aggressiveness and conduct problems, is also a risk factor (Chassin et al., 2004; Dubow, Boxer, & Huesmann, 2008; Zucker, Donovan, Masten, Mattson, & Moss, 2008).

Teens' beliefs, values, and experiences also play a role in whether they use alcohol and drugs. Those who believe that alcohol and drugs are a threat to their health or their future goals are less likely to use them, while those that think of drug use as less risky and more fun are at increased risk. Teens who describe themselves as more religious are less likely to try alcohol or drugs. Those who experience high levels of stress are at an increased risk. Having experienced physical or sexual abuse in childhood or witnessed family or neighborhood violence increases the risk. For these teens, substance use may be an attempt to cope with circumstances that are overwhelming to them (McIntosh, MacDonald, & McKeganey, 2005; Merrill, Salazar, & Gardner, 2001; Wallace, Brown, & Bachman, 2003).

Family factors are important in predicting substance problems. Those with a family history of substance abuse are at higher risk, probably for several reasons. Families may share a genetic susceptibility for drug use and dependence, and parents who abuse alcohol or drugs provide a model of substance use for their children. Prenatal exposure to alcohol or drugs may increase the sensitivity of receptors for the substances in the child's brain or may contribute to conduct and self-control problems in the child. Alcohol and drugs are also likely to be more available in homes with a family history of substance use.

**gateway drugs**
Drugs such as alcohol, tobacco, and marijuana that are typically used prior to the onset of using harder drugs such as cocaine and heroin.

Parenting practices are also important. Harsh, inconsistent, or permissive discipline is associated with higher levels of substance use. Not surprisingly, poor parental monitoring increases the risk as well because these parents have less knowledge of what their teens are doing and who they're with. More authoritative parenting (high in warmth and responsiveness, but with appropriate expectations and discipline) is associated with lower levels of substance use. A close relationship with parents reduces the likelihood of drug use, probably because these parents monitor their adolescents more closely and perhaps have more influence on their teens' friendships. Parents also communicate their beliefs and values about substance use by their behavior and through discussions with their children, and they can reinforce positive connections with peers, school, clubs, churches, and other organizations that affect the risk of substance use.

Having friends who use alcohol and other drugs is consistently found to be one of the strongest predictors of teen substance use (Chassin et al., 2004; Collins, Johnson, & Becker, 2007; Duan, Chou, Andreeva, & Pentz, 2009; Garnier & Stein, 2002; Park, Weaver, & Romer, 2009). Friends who use provide a model of substance use, opportunity to engage in substance use, access to the substances, and reinforcement for using. Of course, it is difficult to know exactly how to interpret this relationship. Do teens who are more likely to use substances *select* friends who are also likely to do so? Or are teens who would otherwise be unlikely to use drugs being *influenced to use* by their friends? As you might expect, it can be difficult for research to sort out these possibilities but it seems that both selection and socialization influences are important. Regardless, it's a good idea for parents to monitor who their teens are spending time with and get to know their teen's friends.

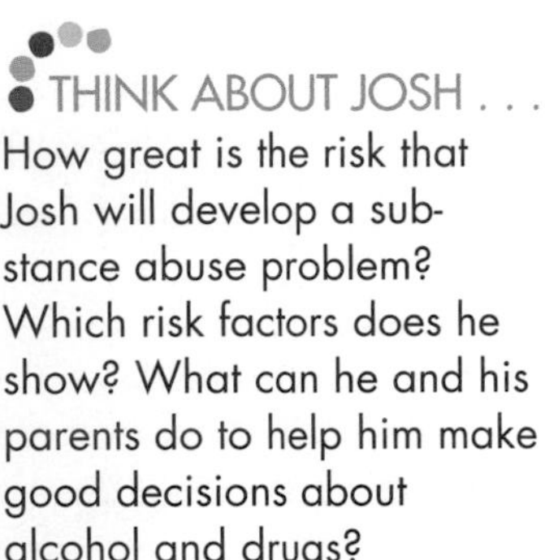

THINK ABOUT JOSH . . . How great is the risk that Josh will develop a substance abuse problem? Which risk factors does he show? What can he and his parents do to help him make good decisions about alcohol and drugs?

As you can see, adolescents with more difficult temperaments, cognitive difficulties, and poor self-control of behavior and emotions are at higher risk for substance problems. These individual vulnerabilities may interact with more coercive or lax parenting practices, leading to problems with schooling and lack of acceptance into a positive peer group. These children and teens may then become increasingly involved with deviant peer groups that model, reinforce, and provide opportunities to engage in substance use—much the same way that these elements work together to produce conduct problems, aggression, and delinquent behavior (see Chapters 12 and 15).

## Other Health Issues during the Adolescent Years

**Adolescents Need More Sleep.** It will probably come as no surprise to you that many adolescents don't get enough sleep. One large study found that only 20% of high school students averaged at least 9 hours of sleep on school nights and almost half slept 8 hours or less. Most students know that they do not get enough sleep, though their parents believe their teens get enough sleep at least a few nights each week (National Sleep Foundation, 2006; Wolfson & Carskadon, 1998). But adolescents and young adults *need* as much sleep as younger children to be alert and function well during the day—about 9.2 hours. Lack of sleep is associated with greater levels of depression and anxiety, poorer grades in school, lapses of attention, slower cognitive and motor reactions, mental errors, poorer task performance, decreased motivation, and increased risk of accidents. Difficulties with regulating emotions and attention may be due to the effect of sleep deprivation on the prefrontal cortex. As you learned earlier in this chapter, this area of the brain is still undergoing important developmental changes during adolescence and lack of sleep may affect this development in ways we do not yet understand (Dahl & Spear, 2004; Mitru, Millrood, & Mateika 2002). Remember, though, that the problems associated with lack of sleep are based on correlations so we can't be certain if less sleep is causing these difficulties, the difficulties are causing sleep problems, or if some other factor such as having a more anxiety-prone personality is causing both.

▲ Most teens do not get enough sleep, which leads to problems with concentrating, staying alert, and performing tasks. What role might biological changes in circadian rhythms play in this student's difficulties staying awake?

As you may have experienced, sleep deprivation can lead teenagers to nap during the day. Some have *microsleeps* in which they fall asleep from a few seconds up to a minute but aren't aware that they've been asleep—clearly a dangerous situation if they happen to be driving at the time! Many attempt to catch up on lost sleep on weekends, but it's not clear whether this is a good strategy. Some studies have found that inconsistency in weekday versus weekend bedtimes is associated with more sleep-related difficulties such as having a hard time falling asleep and needing more than one reminder to get up. The strategies that teens (indeed, that many of us) use to cope with daytime sleepiness often involve consuming some form of caffeine, which can create even more sleep problems (Millman, 2005; O'Brien & Mindell, 2005; Orbeta, Overpeck, Ramcharran, Kogan, & Ledsky, 2006).

Why do adolescents get less sleep than they need? Parents don't monitor bedtimes as closely as with younger children, and teens often have more demands on their time and tasks to complete before they go to bed such as homework, jobs, volunteer activities, sports practices, music lessons, clubs, and the like. Television, instant messaging, online social networking, and other technological distractions also keep them up late. But there may also be a biological reason for their later bedtimes. As adolescents go through puberty, circadian rhythms that help regulate many of the body's systems (including the sleep/wake cycle) change to a **delayed phase preference**—so teens simply aren't sleepy until later at night (Carskadon, Viera, & Acebo, 1993; Carskadon, Wolfson, Acebo, Tzischinsky, & Seifer, 1998; Millman, 2005; National Sleep Foundation, 2006).

Research on the biology of adolescent sleep patterns has led to attempts to change school start times. Between 35% and 50% of high schools in the United States begin by 7:30 a.m. (Millman, 2005). However, high school students perform better in afternoon classes than in morning classes, and they report being less alert in earlier classes. Early start times are also associated with higher levels of sleep deprivation and overall daytime sleepiness (Carskadon et al., 1998; Hansen, Janssen, Schiff, Zee, & Dubocovich, 2005). In 1997 the Minneapolis school district changed the start times for its schools so that older students started later, affecting 50,000 students at all grades. High schoolers reported feeling more alert, tardiness due to oversleeping decreased, and teachers reported fewer students sleeping in class. The effects on student behavior and grades were less clear. Only about one-third of teachers in one survey reported that behavior improved. Grades were higher than in comparison schools, but it's not clear whether this was because of later start times or differences in grading practices (Kubow, Wahlstrom, & Bemis, 1999). Not all students seemed to benefit from the changes. Middle schoolers, whose school start time changed from 7:40 a.m. to 9:40 a.m., seemed tired and impatient by the end of the day and many had to miss late afternoon classes because of conflicts with sports and other after-school activities. Changing school start times also presents challenges with scheduling buses, sports practices, and other after-school activities, as well as conflicts with teens' after-school job schedules.

What can Josh do to make sure he gets enough sleep? Why is it important that he do this?

Depression. Most of us use the word *depression* to refer to the kind of sadness and loss of energy that periodically occurs in our lives. **Clinical depression**, however, refers to a constellation of symptoms that can include sadness, loss of interest in activities, feelings of worthlessness, sleep problems, and changes in appetite (Kazdin & Marciano, 1998). The symptoms are prolonged, lasting longer than normal for periods of grief or loss. It is normal, for example, for someone to feel intense sadness for several months after losing a loved one. But when the symptoms continue for an unusually long time, then clinical depression is indicated. With depression, the symptoms also cause significant distress and impair the person's ability to perform at school, at work, and in social situations.

**delayed phase preference**
Changes in natural circadian rhythms during puberty that cause teens to become sleepy later in the evening and awaken later in the morning.

**clinical depression**
A condition that involves sadness, loss of interest in activities, feelings of worthlessness, sleep problems, and changes in appetite that persist for an unusually long time.

Adolescents who are depressed tend to have low self-esteem and they have negative thoughts about themselves and the events around them. They are less popular among

▲ It is normal for children to feel intense sadness after experiencing a significant loss. It is considered to be a clinical depression when the symptoms continue after an unusually long time and when they impair the child's ability to perform at school and in social situations.

their peers and are more likely to feel rejected and isolated. They tend to perform poorly in school, and are more likely to miss assignments, miss school, and fail a grade. When they become adults, they are at an increased risk for having marriage problems, being unemployed, abusing drugs, and engaging in criminal activity (Kazdin & Marciano, 1998).

Depression is relatively rare (less than 1%) among preschoolers, increases during the elementary school years (up to 2%), and increases again during adolescence (to around 2% to 8%). There is some evidence that, during childhood, depression is more common among boys than girls. By puberty, however, depression is five times more common among girls than boys (Kazdin & Marciano, 1998; Substance Abuse, 2008). When boys are angry, they tend to act out their feelings in physical and sometimes aggressive ways, but girls are socialized from an early age to hold these feelings inside. Researchers believe that many more children and adolescents suffer from serious symptoms of depression, even if they don't meet the full criteria for a clinical disorder. The rates of depression seem to be significantly increasing. The most serious forms of clinical depression run in families. The heritability index for depression is as high as .60, with identical twins much more likely to share symptoms of depression than fraternal twins (Nurnberger & Gershon, 1992). The milder forms of depression, however, do not have a consistent genetic link. Depression is also thought to be related to faulty cognitive processes (pessimistic and negative thought patterns), learned behaviors, and stressful life events.

Children and adolescents who suffer from depression tend to show significant improvements after receiving psychotherapy. Therapy is especially effective when it focuses on decreasing negative and destructive thought processes, improving self-esteem, enhancing social skills, and techniques for relaxation and the management of anxiety (Kazdin & Marciano, 1998). Surprisingly, the antidepressant medications (such as *Prozac*) that seem to work for adults don't work as well with younger individuals. Some studies with children have failed to show that antidepressants work any better than placebo (sugar) pills. Studies with teens indicate that a combination of cognitive behavior therapy and antidepressant medication is more effective than either approach alone. There is continuing concern about the possibility of serious side effects such as increased risk of suicidal thoughts and actions in children, teens, and young adults, particularly during the first few months of treatment (Bridge et al., 2007; Kazdin & Marciano, 1998; Mash & Wolfe, 1999; TADS team, 2007; Tsapakis, Soldani, Tondo, & Baldessarini, 2008). Unfortunately, 70% to 80% of depressed adolescents do not receive treatment of any kind (Kazdin & Marciano, 1998). Because they are more withdrawn, and their symptoms are turned inward, depressed adolescents are often overlooked. Parents, teachers, and others often expect adolescents to be moody and dramatic, and the symptoms of depression are sometimes mistaken for a "phase that will pass."

**Causes of Death.** The leading cause of death among adolescents is unintentional injury, led by motor vehicle accidents. In fact, a national study found that the *only* group of adolescents for whom unintentional injuries were not the leading cause of death were 15- to 19-year-old African American males—homicide was the leading cause of death in this group. Homicide and suicide are within the top six causes of adolescent death for all ethnic groups except 10- to 14-year-old Asian American females—for this group, accidents were the leading cause of death and homicide was third, but suicide was not in the top 10 causes (Heron, 2007).

**Adolescent Drivers.** The statistics are striking. For every mile they drive, 16-year-old drivers are seven times more likely to have an accident than 25- to 29-year-olds. Despite accounting for only about 5% of licensed drivers, teens are involved in 12% of fatal crashes. Accidents involving teens are especially likely during the first six months after obtaining a license, when driving at night (between 9 p.m and 6 a.m.), when carrying passengers, and when drinking alcohol. Teenagers are less likely than adults to wear seatbelts, which increases the likelihood of serious injury when they are in an accident. Teens' greater tendencies to take risks accounts for some of their increased accident rate, but simple inexperience with driving is also a major contributor (CDC Injury Fact Book, 2002; Sherman, Lapidus, Gelven, & Banco, 2004; Williams, 2003).

*Graduated driver licensing* laws (GDL laws) have been enacted by many states to reduce the frequency of teen vehicle accidents. GDL laws typically have a six-month period of supervised driving, then an intermediate period during which teens are allowed to drive unsupervised in lower risk conditions (e.g., daytime, with limited numbers of passengers), and finally full licensure. Since enacting GDL, states report reductions in teen accidents ranging from 5% to 60%, so it seems these laws can be effective (Sherman et al., 2004; Simons-Morton, Hartos, Leaf, & Preusser, 2005). States vary in how strictly they enforce GDL laws, and the accident rate for teens is still higher than for older drivers even in states where these laws are enforced. Experts point out that "parents remain the true enforcers of driving privileges among teenagers, because parents can control access to the car" (Simons-Morton et al., 2005, p. 447). Parents are encouraged to closely monitor their teens' driving skills, control how often and under what conditions their teen is allowed to drive, and establish and enforce restrictions in accordance with appropriate driving behaviors.

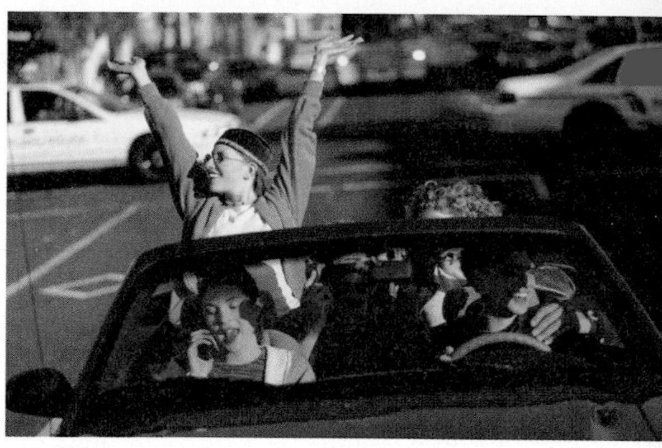

▲ Teen drivers have more accidents than any other age group, especially in the first six months after getting their licenses. What should parents do to help their teens gain experience and avoid accidents?

**THINK ABOUT JOSH . . .**
How can Josh and his parents reduce the likelihood that Josh will have an accident when he gets his license? Will GDL laws be enough, or should his parents do more?

**Suicide.** Suicide is a leading cause of death among teens (Heron, 2007). It is estimated that between 3% and 11% of all adolescents have attempted suicide at some point (Lewinsohn, Rohde, & Seeley, 1994). In one set of studies, researchers interviewed a large representative sample of adolescents in the state of Oregon (Andrews & Lewinsohn, 1992; Lewinsohn, Rohde, & Seeley, 1993; Lewinsohn et al., 1994). When interviewed again one year later, 26 (out of 1,508) of the adolescents reported that they had attempted suicide since the first interview. That means that, in one year alone, 1.7% of the adolescents attempted suicide!

What distinguished these 26 adolescents from the ones who did not attempt suicide? Adolescents were more likely to attempt suicide when they were born to teenage mothers, suffered from depression or other psychological disorders, had suicidal thoughts or ideas during the first interview, had a friend who attempted suicide recently, or had low self-esteem. Similar evidence indicates that adolescents are more likely to attempt suicide when they live in single-parent homes, their parents have less education, they lack support from family and friends, and they show problems with appetite (Lewinsohn et al., 1994). Also, females are about three times more likely than males to attempt suicide, but males are more than four times more likely to die from their suicide attempts (Lewinsohn et al., 1994; Stillion & McDowell, 1996). Suicide rates are nearly twice as high among Latino American adolescents as among African American or White teens. Researchers speculate that in Latino families that recently immigrated to the United States, teens are especially stressed by the conflict between their Latino culture and mainstream America (Canino & Roberts, 2001). Researchers are still trying to assemble a list of risk factors that might indicate which adolescents are at especially high risk for trying to take their own lives, but as you can tell from this discussion, a great many adolescents show one or more of the risks. It is therefore very difficult to identify (in advance) which ones will actually make suicide attempts.

Since 1960, the rate of suicide deaths has remained steady for the whole U.S. population, but it has steadily increased for younger individuals. For 15- to 24-year-olds, there were about five suicides per 100,000 individuals in 1960 and about 10 per 100,000 by 2005. It is rare for younger children to actually commit suicide, but as many as one in five say that they

**THINKING CRITICALLY**

Researchers can identify risk factors that are associated with depression and suicide, yet people still cannot accurately predict which individual teens will make suicide attempts. Explain why. Will we ever be able to make accurate predictions? Why or why not?

**Listen**: Do adolescents in other countries face similar health concerns as those in the U.S.? (Author Podcast) www.mydevelopmentlab.com

have seriously thought about killing themselves (Kung, Hoyert, Xu, & Murphy, 2008; Stillion & McDowell, 1996). These numbers should give us all reason to pause and consider how children's lives have changed in recent decades. Researchers have not yet identified the specific causes of the increase in suicide rates, but you can imagine that speculation centers on changes in family structure, the increased pace of life, and the loss of family support systems. One way to reduce the rate is to make sure that the symptoms of depression (and other psychological disturbances) are noticed and treated at an earlier age.

Although G. Stanley Hall (1904) and other theorists characterized adolescence as a time of "storm and stress," most teens do manage to work their way through puberty and adolescent transitions in a relatively peaceful manner. In this chapter, we described the many physical changes that characterize the move toward adulthood, as well as some of the major challenges to adolescent health and safety. Good relationships with parents make these transitions easier, and affiliating with a positive peer group can influence teens to use positive and adaptive coping strategies. As we saw at earlier ages, physical changes have an important influence on cognitive and socioemotional development, but adolescents' health and safety are also clearly influenced by cognitive and social development. We will talk more about these areas of development in the next two chapters. **Listen** on **mydevelopmentlab**

## LET'S REVIEW . . .

1. Which of the following is *true* about adolescents and sleep?
   - **a.** On average, teens get about 9.2 hours of sleep per night.
   - **b.** Teens' circadian rhythms lead them to become sleepy later at night than when they were younger.
   - **c.** Changing to later school start times does not affect teens' school performance.
   - **d.** Teens need less sleep than younger children.
2. For most drugs, the rate of use is lowest for which of the following ethnicities?
   - **a.** African American
   - **b.** Hispanic
   - **c.** White
   - **d.** Native American
3. Which of the following best defines the gateway drug effect theory?
   - **a.** Teens who use harder drugs begin doing so before or at the same time as using alcohol.
   - **b.** Teens who use harder drugs almost always started out with alcohol, tobacco, or marijuana.
   - **c.** Teens who use alcohol, tobacco, or marijuana will likely progress to using harder drugs.
   - **d.** Teens who use alcohol, tobacco, or marijuana are not at any higher risk for progressing to harder drugs.
4. GDL laws are intended to __________.
   - **a.** keep teens from driving until they are older
   - **b.** get parents more involved in teaching their teens to drive
   - **c.** explicitly teach teens how to drive in high-risk situations
   - **d.** reduce the number of motor vehicle accidents for teens
5. True or False: A majority of teens report that they get regular vigorous exercise.
6. True or False: Anorexia and bulimia are most likely caused by a combination of genetic, social, and psychological factors.

Answers: 1. b, 2. a, 3. b, 4. d, 5. T, 6. T

**THINKING BACK TO JOSH . . .**

Now that you have studied this chapter, you should be able to help Josh better understand the things he's thinking about and help him make good choices. The things he's thinking about and the choices he's faced with are not at all unusual. Many teens think about whether their physical development is normal. You might help him understand that even though early maturing guys like him seem to have lots of advantages, they also face potential problems with getting into situations they aren't socially or emotionally mature enough to handle. Helping Josh think about how he might handle peer pressure and difficult situations might be helpful. Because of his early maturation, Josh may be focused on his physical size and appearance, but you might tell him about the important ways in which his brain is developing too—this might help him understand why parents and teachers worry about impulsive teenage behavior and rash decisions!

The fact that Josh is thinking about sex is also very normal for someone his age. Remind him to think about what the sex education classes are teaching him, but expand on the information a little to help him see how the sexual decisions he makes can have important consequences for his education and future goals. To help him make more informed decisions, talk with him about the emotional aspects of sexual activity as well as his goals for the future, and encourage him to talk with his parents about these things. Josh seems to have learned from his friend's pregnancy, but he may still need help understanding the importance of being sexually responsible—both to prevent pregnancy and to protect himself from STDs. If possible, have a frank discussion about the different sexual practices his friends might be boasting about, like oral sex. It might be interesting for him to learn that many teens overestimate the sexual activity of their peers, so that he can make more informed decisions about sexual activity.

Making decisions about alcohol and marijuana are difficult issues for many teens. Josh seems to have a very good relationship with his parents and can talk with them about this. While teens do like to experiment, it would help for Josh to know where his parents stand regarding drinking and drugs, and why. It seems that Josh understands that while occasional users might not suffer long-term ill effects, the short-term risks like car accidents can be very high. It seems that Josh is reasonably involved in school, and very interested in music. It might be helpful to encourage him to think how he might begin making more health-enhancing choices (like getting proper nutrition, exercise, and sleep) and fewer health-compromising choices (like poor nutrition, using alcohol and drugs, and engaging in unsafe sex).

# 13 CHAPTER REVIEW . . .

**13.1 What is the typical sequence of events in puberty?**

With the onset of puberty, sex hormones (androgens and estrogens) initiate increased growth and sexual maturation. These changes typically begin earlier for girls than for boys.

**13.2 What are the psychological effects of early and late maturation for boys and for girls?**

Early maturation in girls is associated with a stockier and shorter build during later adolescence, less satisfaction with body image, lower self-esteem, a tendency to affiliate with older peers, increased delinquency and problems in school, and earlier dating behavior. Early maturation in boys may give them an advantage in sports and social situations, but also an increased risk of delinquency.

**13.3 What major changes take place in the brain during adolescence, and how are these changes related to adolescent behavior?**

The neurons in the brain become increasingly myelinated during adolescence. Their brains show synaptogenesis just before and synaptic pruning during the early part of adolescence, particularly in the prefrontal cortex. Changing levels of several neurotransmitters in the prefrontal cortex and the limbic system may make adolescents less responsive to rewards, which explains in part why adolescents are more prone to taking risks.

**13.4** How common is sexual activity during adolescence, and why do some teens become sexually active relatively early while others wait?

A majority of adolescents have had sexual intercourse by 12th grade, though age of first intercourse varies by ethnicity and gender. In recent years, adolescents are waiting until they are older to have intercourse, though rates of oral sex have increased. Factors that predict earlier sexual activity include lack of parental support and supervision, impulsivity, alcohol use, and peer pressure. Teens' sexual activity may be affected by misperceptions of peers' sexual activity.

**13.5** Do adolescents use contraception appropriately?

More adolescents use contraception than in past years, but many still do not use them consistently or correctly. Older teens are more consistent than younger ones, and teens who have good relationships with parents are more likely to consistently use contraceptives when they become sexually active. Some teens do not acknowledge that they are sexually active, are not mature enough to admit they are having sex, have misunderstandings about how to effectively obtain and use contraception, or believe they are immune from negative consequences.

**13.6** What approaches to sex education are commonly used, and how effective are these programs in delaying sexual activity or increasing safer sex practices among teens?

Both abstinence-only and comprehensive sex-ed programs are commonly used. Students' knowledge of sex and contraception is increased by participating in sex education programs. Despite these programs, some teens have less knowledge about STDs than educators would like.

**13.7** Why are adolesescents at higher risk for STDs, and how can they reduce their risk?

Teens have better knowledge than in past years regarding contraception, but many still do not understand STDs very well. Teens are at higher risk for STDs, and many STDs can have few symptoms initially but serious consequences later.

**13.8** What are the risk factors for and outcomes of teen pregnancy?

Fewer teens become pregnant now than in the last few decades. Poverty is the biggest risk factor for teen pregnancy, and lack of parental supervision also increases the risk. Teen moms are also more likely to suffer from low self-efficacy and external locus of control. Both teen moms and dads tend to have histories of aggression, and alcohol and other drug use. Educational and financial outcomes for teen moms and dads are negative; their children have higher rates of physical, behavioral, and cognitive problems. Teens who continue their education, delay having a second child, and are supported by family and/or community programs fare better.

**13.9** Which teens are at a highest risk for suffering a sexual assault?

Adolescents who were victimized during childhood are at greatest risk. Other risk factors include early dating and early sexual activity, and drug use by either the teen or his or her parents. Teens who suffer a sexual assault may suffer from fear, anxiety, sadness, depression, academic difficulties, increased drug/alcohol use, and risky sexual behavior.

**13.10** What is the state of adolescent nutrition and exercise today?

Few teens get the recommended daily servings for any category of the USDA food pyramid, but most overconsume fat and sugars. Most adolescents report getting regular vigorous exercise. A small percentage of teens develop eating disorders such as anorexia and bulimia—serious disorders of body image and control that can be fatal if not treated.

**13.11** Which teens are at a higher risk for substance abuse problems?

Many teens experiment with alcohol, tobacco, and marijuana. A strong predictor of teen substance use is having friends who use alcohol and/or drugs, but impulsivity, parental substance use, and lack of parental monitoring are also important.

**13.12** What other health-related issues do teens face?

Most adolescents need more sleep than they get, which can lead to academic, behavioral, and emotional problems as well as increased accidents. Social factors, increased responsibilities, decreased parental monitoring, early school start times, and biologically based changes in circadian rhythms all play a role. The rate of depression increases during adolescence. Use of antidepressant medications can help, especially if combined with psychotherapy, but there are ongoing concerns about serious side effects of these medications. The leading causes of adolescent death are accidents (particularly motor vehicle accidents), homicide, and suicide.

## REVISITING THEMES

The theme of *nature and nurture* is illustrated by the secular trend and the effects of early and late maturation (pp. 402–403). The discussion of teens' risk-taking (p. 406) also highlights the interaction of brain development (nature) and social setting (nurture), and both genes and the environment contribute to the development of eating disorders (p. 421) and depression (p. 427).

*Positive development and resilience* can be seen in the positive peer pressure that teens can exert on one another to abstain from early sexual activity (p. 409). The research on diversity in teen pregnancy outcomes also illustrates that some teens are able to successfully cope with this challenging situation (p. 417).

*Diversity and multiculturalism* were demonstrated by comparing statistics on sexual activity (p. 408), rates of STDs (p. 415), and drug use among different racial and ethnic groups within the U.S. (p. 424).

The *neuroscience* theme was evident throughout the discussion of brain development during adolescence (pp. 404–406). Teens' delayed sleep preferences, and the effect of sleep deprivation on brain functioning (pp. 426–427), also involve neuroscience.

## KEY TERMS

adolescent growth spurt (402)
androgens (400)
anorexia nervosa (420)
binge drinking (424)
body image (402)
bulimia nervosa (420)
chlamydia (414)
clinical depression (427)
contraception (410)
delayed phase preference (427)
early maturation (402)
estrogens (400)
gateway drugs (425)
gonorrhea (414)
human papillomavirus (HPV) (414)
late maturation (402)
menarche (401)
prefrontal cortex (406)
puberty (400)
rape (418)
sexual assault (418)
sexual harrassment (418)
sexually transmitted diseases (STDs) (408)
substance abuse (423)
substance use (423)

**"What decisions would you make while raising a child? What would the consequences of those decisions be?"**

Find out by accessing My Virtual Child at **www.mydevelopmentlab.com** and raising your own virtual child from birth to age 18.

Watch Visit your Multimedia Library at www.mydevelopmentlab.com to watch an interview with Leo online.

# 14 ADOLESCENCE

# Cognitive Development in Adolescence

## Piaget's Stage 4: Formal Operational Thought

- What Is Formal Operational Thought?
- Adolescent Egocentrism
- Evaluating Piaget's Theory

## Recent Sociocultural Views of Cognitive Development

- Situated Cognition
- Guided Participation and Communities of Practice
- Thinking as Socially Shared Cognition: Two Heads Are Better Than One

## Intelligence

- Theories of Intelligence
- Assessing Intelligence
- Extremes of Intelligence: Intellectual Disability and Giftedness
- Ethnic Differences and Questions about Cultural Bias

## Learning to Communicate: Language in Adolescence

- The Adolescent Register
- Social and Cultural Dialects

*(Continued)*

Leo is a 16-year-old Latina who is nearing the end of her junior year in high school. She is working hard to keep up in school. Though English and history continue to be fun and relatively easy for her, math and chemistry are a lot more challenging. She finds them complicated, dull, and boring, and doesn't see their connection to her life. She enjoys working in study groups with friends, but finds that this is sometimes more distracting than helpful. Diagnosed with ADD at age 7, Leo only recently began taking medication for this disorder. The medication has helped, but it is still difficult for Leo to finish her schoolwork.

Leo really wants to get a part-time job so she'll have spending money over the summer. She's thinking about working during the school year, but her parents worry that this will interfere with her schoolwork and drama club, something she loves to do. Leo has also spent a lot of time thinking about what she'll do after she finishes high school. She has always wanted to go to college, and her parents encourage this, but Leo's recent academic struggles make her a little worried. She always thought she was fairly smart, and believes that the key is to use what she knows effectively. She likes writing, especially short stories, and loves acting, but she knows that this is a risky career path to pursue—there are lots of unemployed actors out there!

Are Leo's cognitive skills and intelligence causes for concern? Should she have a more definite post-high school plan? Is working during the school year a good idea? After studying this chapter, you should be able to identify several potential reasons for Leo's difficulties and be able to suggest several things that might help. What helpful advice can you suggest?

As you read this chapter, look for the "Think About Leo . . ." questions that ask you to consider what you're learning from Leo's perspective.

Leo is dealing with several important issues and will soon be making some important decisions about her future. Like many teens her age, schoolwork seems to demand higher levels of thinking about abstract concepts. She wonders what kind of careers might inspire her to succeed. What cognitive skills are typical for teens of this age, and how do they use these skills? In this chapter we will describe theories of adolescent cognitive development, how adolescents use language, and different theories of intelligence. Finally, we will talk about one important way that adolescents must learn to apply their cognitive skills—to make decisions.

# Piaget's Stage 4: Formal Operational Thought

In earlier chapters, you learned about Piaget's view of the cognitive skills and limitations of children from infancy through age 11, up to the end of the concrete operational stage. By the end of the middle childhood years, children have developed impressive reasoning abilities. They can use logical thought structures that are increasingly objective and reversible, and they can solve problems that involve class inclusion and transitivity. As they enter adolescence, their thinking finally becomes abstract—they no longer need to have direct experience with tangible materials to be able to reason logically. According to Piaget's theory, what are the characteristics of this highest level of cognitive development?

AS YOU STUDY THIS SECTION, ASK YOURSELF THESE QUESTIONS:

**14.1** What new forms of logical thought and cognitive advances emerge during the formal operational stage?

**14.2** What is *adolescent egocentrism*, and why is it important for understanding adolescents' thinking and behavior?

**14.3** What are the main criticisms and contributions of Piaget's theory?

## Cognition in Context: Adolescents Making Decisions



## What Is Formal Operational Thought?

According to Piaget, it is during adolescence that cognitive development reaches its fullest potential—**formal operational thought**. Formal operational thought is characterized by five important higher-level cognitive abilities: hypothetico-deductive reasoning; reasoning logically about abstract concepts; separating reality from possibilities; considering all logical possible combinations; and thinking about one's own thinking (Inhelder & Piaget, 1958; Kaplan, 2004). However, they are still limited by adolescent egocentrism, especially during the early part of adolescence.

**Hypothetico-Deductive Reasoning.** For Piaget, one of the most important achievements in cognitive development is the ability to use hypothetico-deductive reasoning. **Hypothetico-deductive reasoning** is the use of *deductive reasoning* (reasoning from general principles to particular conclusions) to systematically manipulate several variables, test hypotheses about their effects in a systematic way, and reach correct conclusions. Piaget tested adolescents' developing use of hypothetico-deductive reasoning by using several tasks, many of which involved physics or chemistry (Ginsburg & Opper, 1988; Inhelder & Piaget, 1958). In his famous pendulum problem, children and adolescents of different ages were given a set of weights and strings of different lengths. As you can see in Figure 14.1, the weights could be hung from the strings and swung like pendulums. The investigators asked the children and adolescents to determine what caused the pendulums to swing at different rates. Was it the length of the string, the amount of weight, or how high the weight was held before it was released? The answer can be found on page 440. Children in the concrete operational stage are not good at systematically testing all of the factors; they tend to report whatever answer seems to be correct after conducting only a few tests. Adolescents using formal operations, however, start by considering all of the variables and all of their possible combinations, reasoning that any single factor could be responsible for the pendulum's rate of swing. They then systematically test each factor one at a time, holding the other factors constant, until they arrive at the correct solution. The adolescent shows hypothetico-deductive reasoning, or formal scientific reasoning—the ability to plan systematic tests to explore multiple variables.

**formal operational thought**
Piaget's final stage of cognitive development, when an adolescent gradually learns to use hypothetico-deductive reasoning and to extend logical thinking to abstract concepts.

**hypothetico-deductive reasoning**
The ability to use deductive reasoning (reasoning from general to specific facts) to systematically manipulate several variables, test the effects in a systematic way, and reach correct conclusions in complex problems; scientific reasoning.

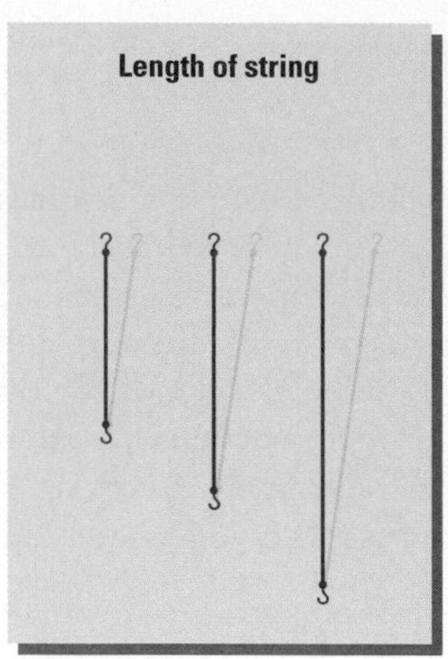

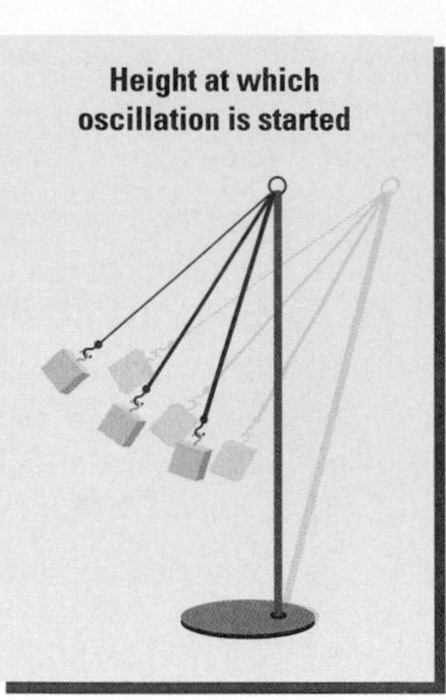


FIGURE 14.1 ▶
**Piaget's Pendulum Problem**
The pendulum problem asks you to figure out what causes the rate of the swing to vary. Is it the length of the string, the amount of weight at the end, or the height from which the weight is dropped? What tests would you conduct to isolate the relevant factor?

Abstract Thought. A second major development that takes place during the formal operational stage is the adolescent's growing ability to engage in abstract thought. **Abstract thought** is the ability to think about things that are not concrete or tangible, such as general concepts or ideas. During the stage of formal operations, the adolescent learns to think logically about such abstract concepts as truth, justice, fairness, and morality. "Whereas earlier the adolescent could love his mother or hate a peer, now he can love freedom or hate exploitation" (Ginsburg & Opper, 1979, p. 201). Such concepts are at the heart of many important social, political, and ethical issues faced the world over. Not only are adolescents beginning to comprehend these concepts, they also develop the ability to reason flexibly about them and understand their relativity. For example, adolescents gradually become able to understand that *justice* may mean very different things to different people, depending on the context and intent of an action. They learn that it can be difficult to assess the justness of any particular action without considering these complex factors. The black-and-white meanings of childhood have given way to the grays of adulthood.

THINK ABOUT LEO . . .
Could Leo's problems with her math and chemistry classes be related to her skills in hypothetico-deductive reasoning and abstract thought? How would Piaget suggest she improve these skills?

Separating Reality from Possibilities. Related to the developing skill of abstract thinking is the adolescent's increasing ability to separate what is real from what is possible. You saw an example of this in the pendulum problem. When solving the problem, adolescents took as their starting point *all possible solutions;* this allowed them to efficiently reach an accurate solution. Piaget argued that during the formal operational stage, the direction of thinking about reality and possibility actually reverses: Possibility is not thought of as an extension of an existing situation, but instead reality is thought of as only one of many possible outcomes (Inhelder & Piaget, 1958). As you can probably imagine, the ability to envision how things *could* be offers an exhilarating freedom—adolescents are no longer bound by reality but can imagine all kinds of different situations, from the swinging of a pendulum to the nature of justice to the career path they might choose. As a result, adolescents may become very idealistic about the possibilities for their own lives, the environment, or for those in difficult and unfair situations around the world. They sometimes become discouraged when they compare the reality they or others experience with these idealistic visions. The ability to envision multitudes of possibilities can also lead adolescents to spend extraordinary amounts of time speculating on all the possible outcomes of seemingly simple actions—as when they spend four hours discussing whether to wear *this* dress or *that* dress to a school social event. Although these behaviors may drive parents crazy, they really are signs of increasing cognitive maturity!

**abstract thought**
Thought about things that are not real or things that are only possibilities.

**combinational logic**
The ability to generate and systematically consider all possible combinations of a set of elements.

**adolescent egocentrism**
A cognitive immaturity seen in adolescents—their inability to distinguish between one's own abstract reasoning and thoughts and the reasoning and thoughts of others.

**imaginary audience**
Adolescents' belief that other people are just as concerned with their behavior, feelings, thoughts, and appearance as they are themselves.

**personal fable**
False beliefs that adolescents have about their own thoughts, influence, and risks.

Combinational Logic. The pendulum problem in Figure 14.1 also illustrates the use of **combinational logic**, or the adolescent's ability to generate and systematically consider all possible combinations of a set of elements. When asked to solve the pendulum problem, younger children may test the factors individually (the weight, the length of the string, or the height), and some may haphazardly combine them. But adolescents are much more likely to generate all the possible combinations of the three factors and conduct systematic tests. As you might imagine, the ability to use combinational logic along with hypothetico-deductive logic is essential for solving problems in chemistry, physics, and other academic areas. But it is also helpful in thinking about social and personal problems. For example, suppose an adolescent is thinking about what career path she might follow. She may realize that she has multiple interests, skills, and goals such as writing, traveling, helping others, creating new products, and spending time with friends and family. Using combinational thinking will help her think through different ways to combine these elements and, hopefully, achieve her goals.

THINKING CRITICALLY

Does one need to think at the level of formal operations in order to graduate from college? Try to think of examples of coursework you've had in college that required each of the five changes discussed. Do any of your examples require a combination of these types of thinking?

**Reflective Thinking.** As a result of many of the developing abilities we have just described, adolescents are able to think about their own thinking, a skill that Piaget called *reflective thinking*. They are able to critically analyze their thoughts, opinions, and beliefs and construct their own theories about how their thoughts develop, change, and compare with others' thoughts. As you may recall from Chapter 8 information-processing psychologists call the ability to analyze one's own thoughts *metacognition* and, like Piaget, believe it plays an important role in mature thinking.

▲ Adolescents' increasing ability to imagine how things *could* be may lead them to be idealistic—but they may also become discouraged when comparing their idealistic visions with reality.

## Adolescent Egocentrism

Although adolescents are developing impressive thinking skills, Piaget observed that they still show a level of immaturity. He defined **adolescent egocentrism** as a young person's inability to distinguish between his or her own abstract reasoning and thoughts and those of others (Inhelder & Piaget, 1958). Two particular forms of adolescent egocentrism have been described (Elkind, 1967). The first is the **imaginary audience**, or adolescents' belief that other people are just as concerned with their behavior, feelings, thoughts, and appearance as they are themselves. This leads to a sometimes excruciating degree of self-consciousness. Many adolescents feel "on stage," as if everyone else were noticing every embarrassing thing they do. The second facet of adolescent egocentrism involves the **personal fable**, or false beliefs that adolescents have about their own thoughts, influence, and risk (Aalsma, Lapsley, & Flannery, 2006; Elkind, 1967). Adolescents tend to believe that they and their newly abstract thoughts are unique—that no one has ever thought about issues in the same way they do, and that no one else (especially parents!) could ever understand the way they feel. Another aspect of the personal fable is the feeling of invulnerability: "Don't worry, nothing's going to happen to me." It is often suggested that such feelings lead adolescents to believe they can engage in very risky behavior—like unprotected sexual activity or drinking and driving—without adverse consequences. However, new research questions whether this is true. While some adolescents develop personal fables, not all do—and egocentrism in general remains a part of thinking into adulthood (Holland & Klaczynski, 2009). As we discussed in Chapter 13, adolescents' risk-taking behavior may have more to do with immaturity in the brain's prefrontal cortex (which is associated with impulse control and executive functioning) than perception of risk (Blakemore & Choudhury, 2006). We will discuss other aspects of adolescent decision making later in this chapter.

THINKING CRITICALLY

Do you ever recall having an imaginary audience? What examples of personal fable can you think of from your own adolescent experiences or from those of other adolescents you have known?

With the achievement of the cognitive skills described here, young adults gradually attain what Piaget considered mature cognition. They become able to reason about anything, real or imagined, and have the capability to use scientific reasoning to solve complex problems. But this does not mean that no further changes in cognition occur. On the contrary, Piaget claimed that we never reach a permanent state of equilibrium.

THINKING CRITICALLY

In what ways do adults think differently than adolescents? Do you believe many adults are capable of postformal reasoning? If so, cite some examples that you have observed. If not, explain why you think not.

THINK ABOUT LEO . . .

In what way is Leo's thinking likely to change over the next few years? How will these changes help her deal with schoolwork and her decisions?

He believed that we are forever adapting and reorganizing our cognitive structures and working "toward *better* equilibrium" (Piaget, 1985, p. 26). Piaget did not, however, envision further major reorganizations of cognitive structure or the development of qualitatively more advanced or different kinds of thought. Others disagree, arguing that older adolescents and adults show *postformal reasoning,* characterized by (Kaplan, 2004; Labouvie-Vief, 2006):

- Increasing emphasis on what is *practical within a given context* (Labouvie-Vief, 1980);
- Increasing ability to accept contradiction in the world;
- *Relativistic reasoning,* the understanding that knowledge is subjective and depends on the experiences and perspective of the individual; and
- Judgments and decisions based on increasing *wisdom,* or knowledge and beliefs about what it means to live a "good life," including an understanding of how to balance one's own well-being with others' (Baltes & Kunzmann, 2004; Baltes & Staudinger, 2000).

## Evaluating Piaget's Theory

Many important aspects of Piaget's views on cognitive development have been supported by research. In general, children do seem to move from being more egocentric to less egocentric. They also move from being less systematic and less able to reason logically to being more able to think in these ways. Many studies over many years have also replicated Piaget's results on tasks such as object permanence and conservation, if the experimenters conduct the tasks in the same ways as Piaget conducted them. Finally, studies from different cultures indicate that children seem to pass through Piaget's four stages in the same order—although the age brackets of the stages show great variability. Also, whether children ever achieve the formal operational stage depends on several different factors such as educational level and the kinds of cognitive skills valued in a culture (Gelman & Baillargeon, 1983; Ginsburg & Opper, 1988; Harris, 1983; Opper, 1977).

Research studies have also, however, highlighted two important weaknesses in Piaget's theory. First, as discussed in Chapter 5, Piaget underestimated the abilities of children, especially during infancy (Gelman & Baillargeon, 1983; Haith & Benson, 1998; Wellman & Gelman, 1998). At the same time, it turns out that Piaget may have *overestimated* the abilities of most adolescents and adults. Researchers believe that only 50% to 60% of 18- to 20-year-olds in industrialized countries use formal operations and that the rates are even lower in nonindustrialized countries (Commons, Miller, & Kuhn, 1982; Keating, 1980). Research also questions how consistently adolescent egocentrism is found. Studies have suggested that it may indicate more about young adolescents' attempts to develop an identity and psychologically separate from their families than a general cognitive immaturity (Vartanian, 2000, 2001). As we noted earlier, many researchers are finding evidence of changes in the types of thought well beyond adolescence.

A second general criticism addresses the notion of developmental stages. Piaget's theory implies that as children reorganize their cognitive structures, they rise to a higher and qualitatively different level of logical thought. Once achieved, these new structures and organizations presumably apply across all contexts. In real life, however, it is not clear that this is the case (Gelman, 2000; Gelman & Baillargeon, 1983; Harris, 1983; Larivée, Normandeau, & Parent, 2000). Let's take conservation problems as an example. Research shows that most children pass tests on number conservation problems by age 6 or 7; they pass weight conservation problems by age 9 or 10; but they don't pass volume conservation problems until about age 11 or 12 (Ginsburg & Opper, 1988). If children understand the concept of conservation (showing decentered and reversible thought) in the number problem, why don't they transfer this understanding to the weight and volume problems until years later? How do we mark the transition from preoperational to concrete operational thought? Does it occur when a child passes the number conservation problem, or do we wait until the child comprehends conservation in all its forms? Not only is it difficult to define these transitions, but children also frequently show evidence of being in two or more stages at once. For these and other reasons, many modern-day researchers reject the concept of broad cognitive developmental stages (Flavell, Miller, & Miller, 1993). Debate about this issue continues, with supporters of Piagetian-type stages arguing that researchers fail to define concepts precisely, misunderstand Piaget's claims, draw questionable conclusions about infant capabilities based on only one type of data (i.e., looking time) and do not consider the relationship between stage transitions and what is known about brain maturation (Desrochers, 2008; Kagan, 2008).

What is least criticized is Piaget's constructivist view of development. Children do seem to be active participants in their own learning and development, assimilating new information into their existing cognitive structures, and modifying or reorganizing their structures when necessary to fit new information. The process of adaptation that Piaget observed in sea mollusks seems a fitting analogy for the adaptive processes children engage in as they achieve cognitive maturity.

**Piaget's Legacy.** Piaget's theory of cognitive development has left a legacy that no other theory in developmental psychology has even approached. His contributions can be summarized as follows.

- Piaget changed *psychology's view of young children.* Before, theorists saw children as passive organisms capable only of reacting to events. After Piaget, they realized that children actively seek to understand their environments and actively initiate events simply to see how things work.
- Piaget gave to future generations a *vast store of facts about children* and child development. This knowledge came both directly—from Piaget's own research, observations, and writings—and indirectly, from the research that others conducted attempting to either support or refute his theory.
- Piaget's theory has had *important applications in the field of education*, as we discussed in Chapter 8. The notion of children as active and curious organisms and the ideas of cognitive readiness, cognitive disequilibrium, and reflective abstraction are all due at least in part to Piaget's theory.
- Piaget's work and writing stimulated *vast amounts of research* in a variety of areas of child development. In doing this work, researchers developed new methodologies, tested new ideas of how children think, and opened and pursued new areas of inquiry. There is an old saying in scientific circles that the clear sign of a good theory is not whether the theory is ultimately shown to be right or wrong, but how much research and knowledge it stimulates. Whether or not any aspects of Piaget's theory are ultimately shown to be true, the theory can be considered great by this standard alone.

## LET'S REVIEW . . .

**1.** All of the following are abilities that develop during the formal operational period *except* __________.

**a.** the ability to mentally reverse actions
**b.** the ability to mentally separate what is real from what is possible
**c.** the ability to critically analyze one's own thoughts
**d.** the ability to think about general principles and arrive at specific conclusions

**2.** When asked to help figure out why the DVD player won't work, which of the following suggestions shows evidence of formal operational thought?

**a.** Remembering that the problem last time was that the cord wasn't plugged in.
**b.** Checking that both the power cord and the connections to the screen are tight.

c. Thinking through the possible sources of the problem and systematically testing them one-by-one.
d. Thinking through the possible sources of the problem and systematically testing them both alone and in all possible combinations.

3. According to Piaget, the imaginary audience and the personal fable are both parts of __________
   a. intuitive thought
   b. object thought
   c. conservation problems
   d. adolescent egocentrism
4. True or False: Compared to young adults, adolescents show less evidence of wisdom in their reasoning.
5. True or False: One criticism of Piaget's theory is that he underestimated the cognitive abilities of adolescents.

Answers: 1. a, 2. d, 3. d, 4. T, 5. F

*Answer to the pendulum problem in Figure 14.1:* Length of the string is the factor that determines how fast the pendulum swings.

# Recent Sociocultural Views of Cognitive Development

In Chapter 8, you learned about another approach to cognitive development, the sociocultural view of Lev Vygotsky. Vygotsky's theory served as the foundation for several more recent views of cognitive development. These views emphasize the important influence of social interaction and the larger cultural context on cognitive development, and they reveal how Vygotsky's theory has stimulated researchers to think about cognitive development in new ways.

AS YOU STUDY THIS SECTION, ASK YOURSELF THESE QUESTIONS:

**14.4** What is the situated cognition view of cognitive development and how is it consistent with Vygotsky's theory?

**14.5** How does guided participation in communities of practice explain cognitive development?

**14.6** What is socially shared cognition?

## Situated Cognition

"If you were selling candy, would you make more profit by selling one piece for 200 cruzeiros or by selling three pieces for 500 cruzeiros?" When Geoffrey Saxe (1988) asked Brazilian schoolchildren questions like this, he found that most were not able to answer correctly. But when he went into city streets in Brazil and asked children who were not attending school at all, he got accurate answers. Why the difference? Those he interviewed in the streets were vendors who sold things to support themselves and their families. Although they lacked formal education in mathematics, they had developed their own strategies for solving complicated problems. The street vendors probably would not have succeeded in school math tests, because these tests tend to use problems that are rather abstract and taken out of context. Within their familiar context, however, the vendors were quite adept. Similar results have been found in the cultures of other countries, such as Beirut (Jurdak & Shahin, 1999). These mathematical skills were situation-specific—an example of *situated cognition.*

**situated cognition**
The idea that we cannot fully understand children's thinking and cognition without considering the context in which it occurs.

The **situated cognition** view of cognitive development holds that thinking always takes place within a specific context, and always in relation to a particular problem, situation, or interaction. According to this view you cannot really understand thought or its quality or level without also examining the context in which the thought takes place. For example, suppose you ask a sixth grader, "Find the value of X in the expression 6X = 750." She may have trouble finding the answer, perhaps saying she hasn't "had algebra yet." But tell her that she and her friends are getting $750 for band camp and it has to be divided equally among all six girls, and watch how quickly she figures out how much money each girl will get. Embedding questions in concrete and meaningful contexts enables people to solve problems that they cannot otherwise understand. The situated cognition view emphasizes that the particular kinds of thinking that occur in different cultures result from adaptations to the particular contexts in which the members of the cultures find themselves. The key factors are the kinds of problems people encounter frequently and the cognitive structures that they find to be effective. In sum, this view reminds us that to properly understand cognitive development, we need also to consider its social and cultural context (Sternberg & Grigorenko, 2006). In keeping with this view, many educators strive to teach cognitive skills within contexts—drawing on the types of situations most important within their students' cultures.

## Guided Participation and Communities of Practice

Another recent sociocultural view emphasizes **guided participation** within a *community of practice.* A community of practice is a broad term that refers to the people, activities, and social interactions that take place as people work together to learn and accomplish goals. The central idea here is that development consists of a person's gradually increasing participation in sociocultural activity—with gradually decreasing guidance and support from those around them (Cox, 2005; Handley, Sturdy, Finsham, & Clark, 2006; Lave & Wenger, 1991; Rogoff, 2003; Rogoff, Mistry, Göncü, & Mosier, 1993; Wenger, 1998). For example, think about a high school student (a participant) learning about auto mechanics (a community of practice). Initially, he does not understand concepts of engine timing, compression, and torque, so his participation is marginal. But he is a *legitimate peripheral participant* (Lave & Wenger, 1991, 1996), which means that he is involved in the activity to the degree that his current skill allows. He can clean tools, check air pressure in tires, and help change the oil. As he learns more, his degree of participation increases and its nature changes. He can now perform a basic engine tune-up, change spark plugs, drain a radiator, and even replace an exhaust system—but he is still not able to diagnose more than simple problems without help, and he needs guidance on more complicated repairs. His participation continues to change as he gradually becomes more of a *central participant,* able to do a great deal of the work himself and even teach the basics to other, less central participants.

▲ This adolescent boy is a *legitimate peripheral participant* in auto mechanics, contributing to the extent he can right now. With guidance and support from those who know more about this area, his participation will increase.

The guided participation view is similar to Vygotsky's in that more central participants initially guide the activity, and the learner gradually takes on increasing responsibility. But whereas Vygotsky emphasized how learners internalize the psychological tools represented in their cultures, the guided participation view instead emphasizes how a person's social roles or shared interactions with other people change as the person develops. Also, whereas Vygotsky tended to focus on the internalization of such things as a culture's language or number system, the guided participation view emphasizes participation in more routine, day-to-day activities.

THINKING CRITICALLY

Identify an activity in which you have moved from being a legitimate peripheral participant to being a more central participant. What skills and knowledge did you learn as a legitimate peripheral participant, and how did they help you become more of a central participant?

## Thinking as Socially Shared Cognition: Two Heads Are Better Than One

Vygotsky claimed that even after children internalize cognitive structures, thought is still a social phenomenon because its roots are in social interaction. Other researchers also emphasize this point, describing cognition as a socially shared activity rather than an individual

**guided participation**
The idea that children are involved in sociocultural activities to the degree that their level of cognitive development allows.

activity (Resnick, Levine, & Teasley, 1991; Wertsch, Tulviste, & Hagstrom, 1993). In this view, cognition does not involve an individual's activities alone, or even an individual's contributions to a social interaction. This view holds that thinking extends "beyond the skin" of the individual and includes the "thinking" of pairs and groups of people (Wertsch et al., 1993, p. 337). It does not make sense to ask, "Whose idea is that?" because thought takes place across the members of a group—it is **socially shared cognition**. This theory does not deny that an individual can think independently. But it argues that even "independent" thought is the culmination of many others' input. Thinking resides in the dynamic interactions between individuals within the group, not solely inside the head of any individual.

THINK ABOUT LEO . . . What aspects of these sociocultural views could be used to help make Leo's study groups more effective in helping her learn?

**Listen**: How can thinking be "socially shared"? (Author Podcast) www.mydevelopmentlab.com

The three views we have summarized here all draw on different aspects of Vygotsky's theory. These modern sociocultural views of cognition are still in the formative stages. But the key point is that today's sociocultural cognition theorists no longer see thought as something that takes place inside one individual's head and consists of abstract skills applied across many different problems and contexts. Instead, they view cognition as much more complex. They suggest that cognition makes use of specific features and contexts and involves individuals collaborating to create ideas and think in ways that no individual could accomplish alone. In short, they see cognition as a very dynamic, social, and interactive process. **Listen** on **mydevelopmentlab**

## LET'S REVIEW . . .

**1.** Children show more advanced cognitive processing when they are tested within contexts that are familiar and well practiced. This is one of the main points of the:

**a.** socially shared cognition view.
**b.** guided participation view.
**c.** social speech view.
**d.** situated cognition view.

**2.** Which of the following would be an example of development in the guided participation view?

**a.** John moves from watching children play basketball to playing in the game himself.
**b.** Sue and Lisa work together to solve a problem that neither could solve alone.
**c.** Henri can read his favorite books at home but has trouble reading the practice sheets in school.
**d.** Tonya needs social scaffolds to help her understand algebra problems.

**3.** True or False: The sociocultural theories are a reaction against Vygotsky's view of cognitive development.

**4.** True or False: According to the sociocultural view, cognition is the product of social interaction more than the private construction of individual thinkers.

Answers: 1. d, 2. a, 3. F, 4. T

# Intelligence

Piaget's theory of cognitive development, Vygotsky's sociocultural theory, information processing, sociocultural views—each of these theories attempts to explain the development of cognitive skills. In many important ways, each theory can be thought of as explaining the development of intelligence. But intelligence can be defined in many different ways. Most of the psychological research on intelligence comes from the Western, industrialized perspective of Europe and the United States. Theorists within this perspective generally define **intelligence** as the ability to learn, think logically about abstract concepts, and adapt to the environment—very similar to Piaget's views of formal operational thought. Even within this Western perspective, however, there has been great disagreement about how to define and understand human intelligence, and even greater disagreement about how to fairly measure intelligence. In this section we will introduce you to three different approaches to

**socially shared cognition**
The idea that thought is a shared group activity and that the thoughts held by an individual are derived at least in part from dynamic interactions occurring between people and in groups.

**intelligence**
As generally defined in Western cultures, the ability to learn, think logically about abstract concepts, and adapt to the environment.

intelligence: the psychometric approach, Sternberg's triarchic theory, and Gardner's multiple-intelligences approach. We will also discuss some frequently used intelligence tests, as well as the issue of cultural bias in using these assessments.

**psychometric approach**
The attempt to quantify people's psychological skills and abilities, usually by means of paper-and-pencil tests and/or physical measurements.

**general intelligence (*g*)**
A broad thinking ability or mental power that underlies all intellectual tasks and functions; the ability to see how things relate and fit together.

**specific intelligence (*s*)**
Abilities people have in particular areas, such as reading, verbal, and spatial skills.

**fluid ability**
A biological-based ability to think and perceive relations among elements.

**crystallized ability**
The body of specific knowledge and skills acquired in a particular culture.

AS YOU STUDY THIS SECTION, ASK YOURSELF THESE QUESTIONS:

**14.7** What are the major similarities and differences among the different theories of intelligence?

**14.8** How is intelligence assessed?

**14.9** What characterizes the upper and lower extremes of intelligence, and how can we explain why these extremes develop?

**14.10** What might explain ethnic group differences in intelligence test scores, and what can be done to ensure the fairness of these tests?

## Theories of Intelligence

Psychometric Approaches. With the **psychometric approach** to studying intelligence, researchers use paper-and-pencil tests and/or physical measurements in an attempt to quantify people's psychological skills and abilities. One of the most influential psychometric theorists was Charles Spearman (1863–1945), who gathered information on school children in a village in England. Spearman studied children's physical and perceptual attributes as well as children's cleverness, common sense, and exam scores in various subject areas. Spearman found strong positive correlations among all his measures and proposed a *two-factor theory of intelligence* to explain his results (Spearman, 1904, 1927). The first factor he called **general intelligence (*g*)**. General intelligence is a broad ability that applies to some extent to all intellectual tasks—essentially, the ability to see how things relate and fit together. Spearman thought that it was neurologically based, and he saw *g* as providing the driving force behind most intellectual accomplishments (Spearman, 1923, p. 5). Spearman called his second factor **specific intelligence (*s*)**, referring to the abilities people have in particular areas, such as reading, verbal, and spatial skills.

The biggest area of disagreement among different psychometric theories is the question of how many abilities fall under the heading of "intelligence." For example, Louis Thurstone identified seven mental abilities that he saw as separate and distinct from general intelligence (Thurstone, 1938; Thurstone & Thurstone, 1941). J. P. Guilford identified at least 150 abilities as important in defining intelligence (Guilford, 1967, 1982). John Horn and Raymond B. Cattell proposed two broad factors, **fluid ability** and **crystallized ability**, along with several other more specific factors (Horn & Cattell, 1966). Fluid ability, much like Spearman's *g* is a biologically based ability to think. It essentially involves the ability to perceive relations among elements, and it peaks by around age 18. In contrast, crystallized ability consists of the knowledge and skills people acquire in a particular culture. Crystallized ability includes such things as number ability, mechanical skills, and vocabulary, and it can increase throughout adulthood.

How is Leo's view of intelligence related to Spearman's concepts of *g* and *s*?

The important point to remember about these later psychometric theories of intelligence is this: They began to challenge the idea that a *g*-factor theory like Spearman's could adequately explain differences among individuals' intellectual performance. The controversy reminds us that there has always been disagreement about whether each person has a level of "general" intelligence underlying performance across all tasks. Modern cognitive psychologists have argued that psychometric theories place too much emphasis on static indicators of intelligence (such as facts and vocabulary) and disregard the cognitive *processes* involved in intelligent thought. These criticisms have led to new theories of intelligence that take more contemporary cognitive and neuropsychological views into account (Garlick, 2002).

Do you agree with the idea of a *g* factor in intelligence that underlies all intellectual accomplishments? Explain why or why not.

Explore Sternberg's Triarchic Theory of Intelligence www.mydevelopmentlab.com

▲ Robert Sternberg's triarchic theory describes how mental processes, experience, and the environmental context all interact to produce intelligent thought and behavior.

THINKING CRITICALLY

Think of a task you've completed, such as taking an exam. Identify which aspects of the task were carried out by each type of component.

**triarchic theory of intelligence**
Theory of intelligence emphasizing how mental processes, experience, and situational contexts relate to intellectual thought.

**componential subtheory**
Describes how mental processes work together to give us intellectual thought ("analytical intelligence").

**experiential subtheory**
Describes how we become more intelligent as we master new tasks and perform them more automatically ("creative intelligence").

**Sternberg's Triarchic Theory.** Starting in the early 1980s, Yale University psychologist Robert Sternberg developed a **triarchic theory of intelligence**. Sternberg's theory embraces the information-processing concept you read about in earlier chapters. It describes the mental processes involved in thinking as well as the aspects of experience and the environmental context for intelligence. The theory is called "triarchic" because it consists of three interrelated subtheories, as shown in Figure 14.2. Explore on mydevelopmentlab

The **componential subtheory** describes how mental processes work together to give us intellectual thought (Sternberg, 1985, 1999). In this subtheory a "component" is a mental process (such as planning, reading, or remembering) that gathers or works with information. Sternberg described three types of components (he is famous for doing things in threes!). *Knowledge-acquisition components* selectively encode, combine, and compare information, allowing us to acquire new knowledge. *Performance components* perform tasks such as sorting, classifying, remembering, and otherwise processing information. *Metacomponents* "supervise" and evaluate the functioning of the other two types of components.

As an example, Sternberg described how these three components work together when we write a paper (Sternberg, 1988). We use metacomponents to define a topic, decide on an organization, monitor the writing progress, and evaluate the finished product. Thanks to *performance components,* we can do such things as retrieve appropriate words from memory, remember how to use the word-processing system on our computer, or remember the rules of grammar. Knowledge-acquisition components help us during the research phase, allowing us to sift through vast amounts of information and decide what to include in the paper. Because these mental components enable us to analyze information, they are sometimes called *analytical intelligence.* Analytical intelligence is the type of intelligence that is usually measured in typical paper-and-pencils tests.

The **experiential subtheory** addresses the role of novelty and experience in intelligence. According to this subtheory, we become more intelligent as we master new tasks and learn how to perform them more automatically. For example, think of adolescents learning to drive. At first processes such as steering, braking, and accelerating are new, so new drivers have to think hard about each one. With more experience they begin to carry out more and more of the processes automatically. Eventually the processes flow smoothly and together, so the drivers are able to control a car's speed and direction easily. Now

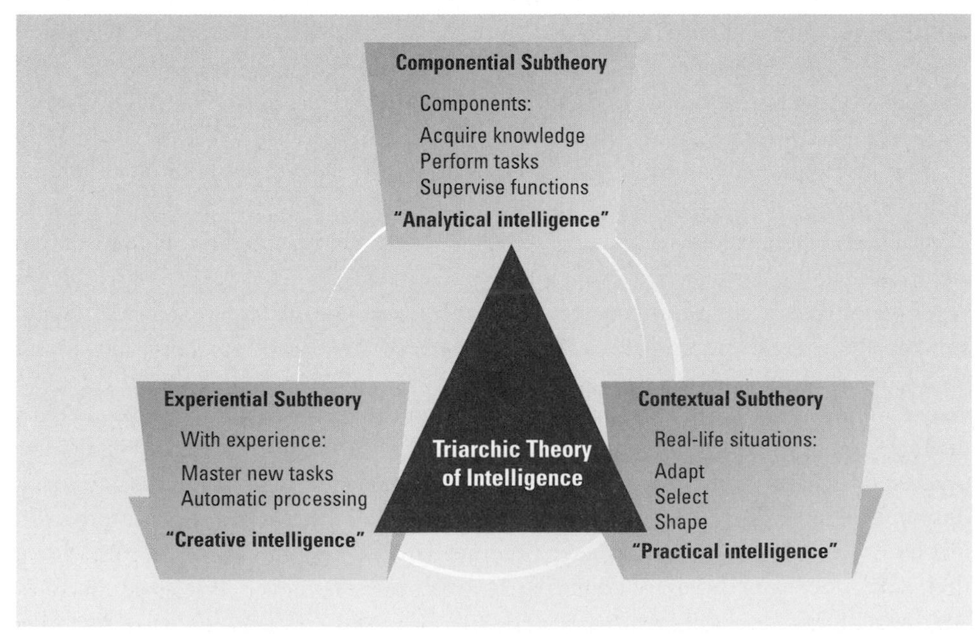


FIGURE 14.2 ▶ **Sternberg's Triarchic Theory of Intelligence** In Sternberg's theory, analytic intelligence, experience, and real-life contexts combine to yield intelligent thought and behavior.

adolescents can begin to deal with other aspects of driving—looking ahead at intersections, noticing other drivers' behavior, and noticing the effects of different weather conditions. Like driving, most complex tasks are difficult to perform at first, but with experience become more automatic. This frees up more mental capacity for other aspects of the task. As you can see, this part of Sternberg's theory uses the concept of *automaticity,* which we discussed in Chapter 8. The experiential subtheory ties in with what we typically call *creative intelligence.* That is, some people are quick at figuring out new tasks—they see new patterns easily and find creative new ways to solve problems.

The **contextual subtheory** describes individuals' abilities to show intelligent behavior in real-life contexts. That is an aspect of intelligent behavior that Sternberg thought was missing in most other theories of intelligence (Sternberg, 1985). It involves adapting to, selecting, and shaping real-life situations. (Yes, *another* set of three.) When placed in a new situation, people usually try first to *adapt to* their environment: They try to achieve a good fit between themselves and the environment without changing either in any significant way. Sometimes, however, they must do something to improve the fit. One possibility is to *select* a different environment; another is to attempt to *shape* the existing environment. Sternberg (1985) used the example of marriage to illustrate these three processes. If a marriage is not satisfying in some way, a person will try first to adapt by ignoring the negatives and focusing on the marriage's positive aspects. If that does not work, then the person may select a different environment by leaving the marriage—or may try to shape the existing environment by changing its unsatisfactory aspects. Some people are especially good at dealing with their environments. Contextual intelligence is related to what most people call *common sense, street smarts,* or *practical intelligence.*

**contextual subtheory**
Describes how intelligent behavior is related to real-life situations as people adapt to, select, and/or shape their environments ("practical intelligence").

**theory of multiple intelligences**
Theory of intelligence emphasizing multiple intelligences that operate relatively independently of one another; the theory includes eight intelligences.

Sternberg's theory is an ambitious attempt to account for the varied facets of intelligent behavior. His comprehensive explanation is a strength of this theory. Another strength is that empirical research studies have investigated each of the subtheories and have provided at least modest support for many of the ideas (Sternberg, 1985). However, critics charge that although the theory is comprehensive, it is not clear how the three subtheories relate to one another. Nor is it clear why some elements are included but other possible elements are not. Finally, Sternberg does not link his components and processes to the biology of intelligence or to what is known about how the brain functions (Gardner, Kornhaber, & Wake, 1996).

THINK ABOUT LEO . . .
How might Sternberg's theory help Leo deal with her concerns about her intelligence and her fears about succeeding in college?

**Gardner's Theory of Multiple Intelligences.** In 1983 Harvard psychologist Howard Gardner proposed a **theory of multiple intelligences**. This theory defines *an intelligence* as a "biopsychological potential to process information that can be activated in a cultural setting to solve problems or create products that are of value in a culture" (Gardner, 1999, p. 34). Notice several important aspects of this definition. First, Gardner is not defining *intelligence;* rather, he is defining *an intelligence.* This is the heart of his theory. Gardner proposes that intelligence is neither a unitary *g* factor, nor a broad factor made up of subcomponents or specific abilities. Instead, he argues that there are several different types of intelligence, each relatively independent of the others. A person's overall level of functioning is determined by his profile of strengths and weaknesses among these different intelligences in interaction with a particular cultural setting. A second important point is that an intelligence is a *biopsychological potential;* this means that there is an underlying biological, and most likely genetic, component. Being genetic, however, does not mean that this potential is unaffected by the environment. A particular biopsychological potential *may or may not be fully realized,* depending on environmental factors. Cultural values, opportunities, and individual choices all affect the developing intelligence. For example, think of a girl born with strong logical–mathematical potential. If she grows up in a culture that does not allow females to be educated, such as under the former Taliban government in Afghanistan, it is very unlikely that the girl will fulfill this particular potential. In other

▲ What will happen with this girl's biopsychological potential if she has a genetic strength for math and science but grows up in a culture that forbids her from pursuing these topics in school? How has your culture affected your intellectual potential?

▲ Howard Gardner believes there is more than one type of intelligence. His theory of multiple intelligences includes eight different types.

THINK ABOUT LEO . . .
How would you describe Leo's profile of intelligences? How could she use her strengths to improve her weaknesses? How could her parents and teachers help with this?

THINKING CRITICALLY
For each intelligence proposed by Gardner, identify a person you know who is strong in this intelligence. What would your own profile look like across these types of intelligences?

Explore Gardner's Multiple Intelligences. www.mydevelopmentlab.com

countries, girls may go to school, but the culture may steer them toward more "domestic" topics and away from advanced mathematics. Finally, even if the culture is encouraging, the girl herself may decide not to pursue math; again, her mathematics potential is not going to be fully realized.

Gardner identifies eight intelligences, shown in Table 14.1 (Gardner, 1983, 1999). Clearly, he is not the first to identify several of these areas—all the theorists we have discussed recognize at least two, and sometimes many more, factors. Gardner differs from other approaches, though, in that he does not base his analysis solely on statistical analysis of a battery of paper-and-pencil tests. Instead, he identified a set of specific criteria to determine whether a given skill qualifies as an intelligence. These criteria include not only psychometric findings but also such things as the potential for isolation by brain damage (which indicates a biological basis for the skill), an evolutionary history (to explain why the intelligence would have evolved), identifiable core operation(s) (to specify the skills involved in the intelligence), and the existence of exceptional people (both those with strength and those with weakness in the particular intelligence). Thus, Gardner's analysis depends on support from more than just psychometric test scores.

Gardner emphasizes that all eight intelligences exist to some degree in every individual, because the intelligences are part of being human. However, each person has a different *profile of intelligences*—a different combination of strengths and weaknesses (Chen & Gardner, 2005). According to Gardner, it is important that parents and educators recognize each child's individual strengths and weaknesses and provide adequate opportunities for each child to activate his or her own areas of strength. When looking at a school curriculum, for example, we need to recognize that one size doesn't fit all. In addition to covering areas such as reading, math, and science, we need to offer opportunities in art, music, sports, and technical training. Exploring these options lets students activate their unique potentials or strengthen their individual intellectual profiles.

Gardner's theory has broadened our view of what constitutes intelligence. He is not without critics, however (Kincheloe, 2004). One complaint is that Gardner's roster of intelligences really does not further our understanding of the concept of intelligence. They argue that the theory blurs the distinction between intelligence and other, nonintellectual, human characteristics (Herrnstein & Murray, 1994). Critics also have pointed out that Gardner's measures of the intelligences often correlate with one another, perhaps weakening the argument that they are independent. Gardner responds that this intercorrelation occurs because of the types of tests that have traditionally been available. If more appropriate measures existed for each of the intelligences, he suggests, we could test their independence more fairly (Gardner et al., 1996; Scarr, 1985). Finally, it is not clear what coordinates the intelligences when they work together on a given task. Gardner says that the intrapersonal intelligence may play this role; but critics claim that such coordination necessarily implies a *g* factor—the very concept that Gardner was reacting against. Explore on mydevelopmentlab

## Assessing Intelligence

As you have just learned, experts have never agreed on how to define intelligence. Even so, there have been many attempts to try to assess intelligence for practical purposes such as selecting those who might do well in various types of training programs or identifying those who may need extra help in learning. The first practical intelligence scale was developed by Alfred Binet and Theodore Simon in 1905 to help French schools predict which children would perform well in regular education settings and which would benefit from special education. The scale posed a series of increasingly difficult questions, such as pointing to an object in a picture, defining a common word, and explaining the difference between "boredom" and "weariness" (Gregory, 1996). Then each child's progress through the tests was compared to the average pattern shown by other children of the same age (called *age norms*).

**TABLE 14.1**
Eight Types of Intelligences Proposed by Gardner, with Examples of Occupations Involving Each Type

| TYPE OF INTELLIGENCE | DESCRIPTION AND EXAMPLES |
|---|---|
| *Linguistic intelligence* | • Acute sensitivity to spoken and written language; includes abilities to learn languages, use language effectively to achieve specific goals<br>• *Examples:* Lawyers, speakers, writers, and poets |
| *Logical–mathematical intelligence* | • Recognizing and using abstract relations to logically analyze problems, carry out mathematical operations, and investigate issues scientifically<br>• Gardner believes that Piaget's theory of cognitive development is mostly a description of the development of this intelligence<br>• *Examples:* Mathematicians, computer programmers, accountants, engineers, and scientists |
| *Musical intelligence* | • Sensitivity to aspects of sound (such as tone, pitch, and rhythm) and skill in creating and communicating with sounds and musical patterns<br>• *Examples:* Composers, conductors, audio engineers, and acousticians |
| *Bodily–kinesthetic intelligence* | • The ability to use the whole body, or parts of it, to solve problems or make products; involves a high degree of control over fine- and gross-motor skills<br>• *Examples:* Dancers, athletes, surgeons, craftspeople, actors, and mechanics |
| *Spatial intelligence* | • The abilities to perceive, transform, and re-create spatial information for large-scale or small-scale projects<br>• *Examples:* Sailors, pilots, engineers, surgeons, sculptors, and painters |
| *Interpersonal intelligence* | • The capacity to understand and work effectively with other people, including understanding other people's motivations, intentions, and desires<br>• *Examples:* Successful salespeople, politicians, teachers, clinicians, and religious leaders |
| *Intrapersonal intelligence* | • The ability to understand and regulate your own emotions; involves sensitivity to and understanding of own desires, fears, intentions, and capacities<br>• Gardner believes intrapersonal intelligence allows people to build accurate "mental models" of themselves and to use these models to make good personal decisions.<br>• *Examples:* Writers, therapists, and communities' "wise elders" |
| *Naturalist intelligence* | • Skill in recognizing and classifying plants and animals, including an ability to distinguish among species and chart relations among species<br>• *Examples:* Biologists, environmentalists, hunters, fishermen, farmers, gardeners, and cooks |

Through these comparisons, Binet and Simon stated, they could determine "how much above or below average" a child was (Simon & Binet, 1905, as quoted in Thorndike & Lohman, 1990, p. 13).

In 1916, Lewis Terman, an American psychologist at Stanford University, published his own modified version of the Binet–Simon scale (Gregory, 1996). Terman's test popularized the term intelligence quotient (IQ), defined as mental age (MA) divided by chronological age (CA). Later it became popular to multiply the result by 100 to eliminate decimals, giving the formula (MA ÷ CA) × 100. With this formula, a child who shows a mental age of 12 on the test, but who is actually 15 years old, would score an IQ of 80 [(12 ÷ 15) × 100 = 80]. A child who shows a mental age of 15 on the test, but has a chronological age of only 12, would score an IQ of 125 [(15 ÷ 12) × 100 = 125]. A 12-year-old who shows a mental age of 12 on the test would have an IQ of 100

▲ Howard Gardner proposes that there are several different types of intelligence. What types of intelligences are shown by the people in these photos?

[(12 ÷ 12) × 100 = 100]. With this scoring system, 100 is the average IQ for children of a given age. Scores below 100 show performance that is below what is typical for that age, and scores above 100 show above-average performance.

**Intelligence Testing Today.** Today, psychologists and other mental health professionals often use intelligence tests to help diagnose and treat numerous problems in children and adolescents, including cognitive deficits; learning disabilities; attention deficits; problems with specific processes such as reading, spatial reasoning, or memory; emotional disturbance, brain disorder, or serious mental illness. Taken alone, intelligence scores do not provide enough information to enable a practitioner to make any of these diagnoses. In combination with clinical interviews (e.g., of the child, parents, and teachers), physical examinations, and results from other psychological tests and observations, however, the scores can add an important piece to the larger puzzle.

There are two essential ingredients that any assessment device needs: *reliability* and *validity.* The term **reliability** refers to the consistency of scores when a test is repeated under the same or similar conditions. If the same person takes an intelligence test twice, the results should be about the same both times (assuming there has been no intervention between test sessions aimed at improving intelligence). Otherwise, how could we trust that either score was accurate? Correlations between two administrations of a test above .80 indicate a high degree of reliability (Sattler, 2001). A test's **validity** is its ability to measure what it intends to measure—in this case, intelligence. Intelligence tests are considered valid when the scores accurately predict which children will perform better or worse in school, when they predict success in other areas of life (such as job performance), or when the scores on one intelligence test correlate highly with scores on other tests that are also presumed to measure intelligence.

Today there are two widely used intelligence tests. A few sample items like those from each are shown in Figure 14.3. The *Stanford-Binet Intelligence Scale: Fifth Edition* (or *SB5*) is based on Terman's original 1916 test (Roid, 2003). The SB5 provides an overall intelligence score along with scores in five subareas (fluid reasoning, knowledge, quantitative reasoning, visual-spatial processing, and working verbal memory), and it yields both a verbal and a nonverbal IQ score. Test items have been reviewed for several sources of possible bias (gender, ethnic, cultural, religious, regional, and socioeconomic status) to make the test as culturally fair as possible. David Wechsler constructed the *Wechsler Scales* in the 1930s to use with the diverse patients he treated in the psychiatric unit of Bellevue Hospital in New York. He began his work with adults, but gradually developed a family of intelligence scales designed for people as young as 2.5 years. Each scale provides an overall, or composite, intelligence score and two general subscale scores: verbal and performance. The verbal subscale includes subtests in basic information, vocabulary, arithmetic, comprehension, and similarities. The performance subscale includes picture completion, block design, and object assembly. Additional verbal and performance subtests are available but vary across the tests.

**reliability**
The consistency of scores when a test is repeated under the same or similar conditions.

**validity**
The ability of a test to measure what it intends to measure (e.g., intelligence).

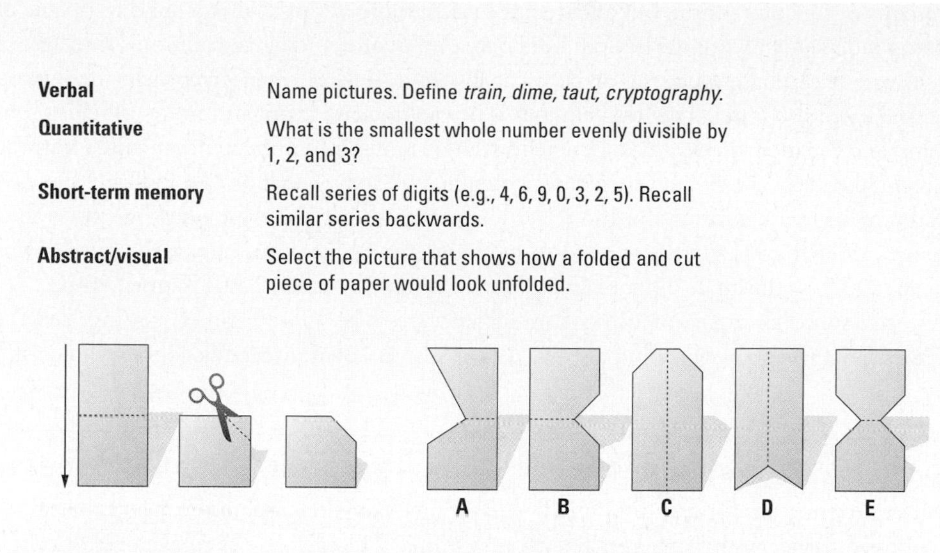
Verbal
Name pictures. Define *train, dime, taut, cryptography.*
Quantitative
What is the smallest whole number evenly divisible by 1, 2, and 3?
Short-term memory
Recall series of digits (e.g., 4, 6, 9, 0, 3, 2, 5). Recall similar series backwards.
Abstract/visual
Select the picture that shows how a folded and cut piece of paper would look unfolded.
A
B
C
D
E

**Verbal**

| | |
|---|---|
| **Basic information** | Who discovered the North Pole? What is the capital of France? |
| **Vocabulary** | Define *summer, poet, obstreperous.* |
| **Arithmetic** | If a suit sells for one-half of the regular price, what is the cost of a $120 suit? |
| **Comprehension** | Why are we tried by a jury of our peers? |
| **Similarities** | In what way are *inch* and *mile* alike? |

**Performance**

| Picture completion | Block design | Object assembly |
|---|---|---|
| What is missing from this picture? | Reproduce the design below using four or nine blocks. | Arrange the pieces into a meaningful object. |

◀ FIGURE 14.3
**Sample Intelligence Test Items**
The *Stanford–Binet Intelligence Scale,* 5th ed. (top) and the *Wechsler Intelligence Scale for Children,* 4th ed. (bottom) include items such as the questions shown here. (Sattler, 2001)

Both the SB5 and the Wechsler scales were standardized using large samples representing all income and ethnic segments of the U.S. population, and both have reliability correlations of .90 or higher. Both tests also show adequate validity in terms of predicting later school success (correlations ranged from .50 to .65) and correlating with other measures of intelligence (Kamphaus, 2001; Roid, 2003; Sattler, 2001; Zhu & Weiss, 2005).

New Assessment Approaches. Traditional intelligence tests have been a useful tool, but critics have argued that these "static" tests focus on past learning and independent performance rather than assessing a child's *potential* for future learning. **Dynamic assessment (DA)** procedures attempt to assess learning potential by using a test-teach-test format, measuring how much a child's performance improves after receiving instruction. DA is based on Vygotsky's concept of the zone of proximal development (see Chapter 5). There are several

**dynamic assessment (DA)**
A Vygotskian-based approach which assesses learning potential by measuring the degree of improvement in performance after receiving instruction.

variants of DA procedures, but all attempt to determine not just what a child is capable of doing independently (or the bottom boundary of the zone, and what traditional intelligence tests assess), but also what she or he is capable of achieving when given help (or the top boundary of the zone). The less help that is needed to solve more and more difficult problems, and the more quickly a child benefits from instruction, the greater that child's learning potential (Elliott, 2003; Sternberg & Grigorenko, 2002). Research on DA indicates that DA can provide useful information about learning potential that is not provided by static assessments, though more work is needed to fully understand what this approach offers (Fuchs et al., 2007; Sternberg & Grigorenko, 2002; Swanson & Lussier, 2001; Tzuriel, 2001).

For some examples of uses of intelligence tests in a professional setting, see the Professional Perspective box on page 451 called "Career Focus: Meet a School Psychologist."

## Extremes of Intelligence: Intellectual Disability and Giftedness

Most current tools for assessing intelligence come from the psychometric approaches we described earlier in this chapter. These tests compare people's scores to averages of others of the same chronological age, so most people by definition show average intelligence scores. But what about those whose IQ scores are significantly below or above average? What outcomes are common for these individuals?

### Intellectual Disability.

Children with intellectual disability (also known as *mental retardation* or *cognitive disability*) learn more slowly than other children, have more difficulty solving problems, and show language and communication deficits. As a result, they perform less well in school and have more difficulty making friends and engaging in social activities. With special services and support, children with mild to moderate levels of intellectual disability can adjust to many of the normal challenges in life. They can attend regular classrooms, learn to care for themselves, and develop friendships with peers. With more severe levels, a child may need extensive support merely to negotiate everyday activities such as brushing his teeth and getting dressed. Approximately 2% to 3% of the U.S. population has an intellectual disability. There are three components to the formal definition of **intellectual disability**.

1. *Below-normal intellectual functioning* (usually indicated by an IQ of less than 70 or 75)
2. *Deficits in adaptive behavior,* the daily activities required for personal and social independence (e.g., communicating needs to others, eating, dressing, grooming, toileting, following rules, and working and playing with others) (American Association on Intellectual and Developmental Disabilities, 2009)
3. *An onset early in life* (before age 18) (American Psychiatric Association, 2000; Hodapp & Dykens, 2003)

Literally thousands of biological and environmental factors can cause intellectual disabilities. The most severe forms tend to result from genetic disorders. Down syndrome and fragile-X syndrome (see Chapter 2) are the two most common types of genetic disorders that cause intellectual disability. Together these two disorders alone affect one in every 500 children born, and more than 700 other genetic diseases also can contribute to MR (Hodapp & Dykens, 2003). Intellectual disability can also result from prenatal damage to the brain and nervous system by toxins such as alcohol and drugs. As you read in Chapter 3, prenatal alcohol exposure is the leading *known* cause of intellectual disability in the United States (Abel & Sokol, 1987; Institute of Medicine, 1996). Intellectual disability can occur when infants suffer oxygen deprivation or other traumas during birth, and when they are born prematurely.

**intellectual disability**
A condition characterized by below-normal intellectual functioning, deficits in adaptive behavior, and an onset early in life (before age 18).

## Perspective PROFESSIONAL — CAREER FOCUS: MEET A SCHOOL PSYCHOLOGIST

Sandy Roland, PhD, Licensed Specialist in School Psychology
Richardson Independent School District in Dallas and Richardson, TX

**In what circumstances are intelligence tests useful in your practice?**
Intelligence tests are used to acquire a general level of functioning of the child when considering what strategies may help the child progress in learning. Mainly, we use intelligence tests when determining if a child has intellectual disability or a learning disability. Intelligence scores are also sometimes helpful when a child is being screened or evaluated for ADHD.

**How do you decide what tests to use?**
The child's age, developmental level, special needs, and background are important to consider when choosing an intelligence test. First, the test must have norms for the age of the child. Second, it is important to consider the child's developmental level and if he/she has any special needs such as a physical disability or speech/language impairment. Finally, the background of the child, including cultural differences and socioeconomic challenges, needs to be considered. We have a wide range of tests to choose from including developmental screenings, neuropsychological batteries, nonverbal tests, and the typical Wechsler-like tests.

**What do scores on intelligence tests tell you about a child?**
Scores usually tell us a lot about a child, but there are times when the scores are not as useful as the information gained from observation during the testing session. Most tests yield at least one composite score, usually, a score to describe the overall cognitive ability of a child. Many tests have subtest scores that give additional information that can be used when looking at a profile of strengths and weaknesses for the child. Cognitive processing and problem solving can also be gauged. During the test, observing the frustration level of the child is also a very important result of the testing situation.

**What precautions do you take when interpreting and using scores?**
It is important to make sure that the most appropriate test is given to the child and if the most appropriate is unavailable, then the next appropriate test can be used with some precautions. If the child's frustration level is too high and he/she "shuts down" during the testing session, it should be noted. If the child's attention has to be constantly redirected to the task at hand, if speech/language issues make the testing session difficult, or if there are language or cultural differences to consider, then caution should be used in interpreting those scores.

**Describe the education and training required to become a school psychologist.**
In Texas we need the LSSP (Licensed Specialist in School Psychology) certification. This is a master's level certification. Practicum and internship are required, as well as a year of post-internship supervision before working independently. Many school psychologists also have a doctorate degree.

QUESTION **Do you think educators should use intelligence tests to determine which students qualify for services or to gauge students' progress? Why or why not? How should eligibility and progress be determined?**

After children are born, numerous factors in the environment can affect mental development. The best-known environmental factors related to intellectual disability include exposure to lead and other toxins, poor nutrition, lack of stimulation, and parents who are illiterate or mentally retarded themselves. Rates of intellectual disability are higher among children living in poverty, minority children, and males (Hodapp & Dykens, 2003). Mental health researchers often refer to intellectual disability caused by lack of educational opportunity and stimulation as *cultural–familial retardation*. Intellectual disability also can have multiple causes. For example, children may inherit low intelligence from their parents; on top of this, they may suffer poor nutrition, and their parents may fail to provide a stimulating learning environment. When both parents have intellectual disability, the odds are more than 40% that their children also will

**TABLE 14.2**
**Four Levels of Intellectual Disability**

| LEVEL OF INTELLECTUAL DISABILITY | APPROXIMATE IQ* |
|---|---|
| Mild | 50 to 70 or 75 |
| Moderate | 35 to 50 |
| Severe | 20 to 40 |
| Profound | Below 20 or 25 |

*Note:* An IQ score of 100 indicates an "average" level of intelligence. (Mash & Wolfe, 2005.)

have this condition. The odds drop to 20% when only one parent has intellectual disability and to less than 10% when neither parent has intellectual disability (Mash & Wolfe, 1999).

Clinicians typically divide intellectual disability into the four levels shown in Table 14.2. Approximately 85% of people with intellectual disability are in the mild category (Mash & Wolfe, 2005). Toddlers and preschoolers with mild intellectual disability usually show only small delays. When they reach early elementary school, however, they fall behind in academic subjects. With some special education and support, these children can learn up to the sixth- or seventh-grade level. They may have only minor problems with peers and other social relationships, and after finishing school they can live and work independently or with a modest amount of supervision. At the other end of the scale, 1% to 2% of all people with intellectual disability are in the profound category. As infants, they show serious delays in sensory and motor functions, and by the age of 4 they are still responding like typical 1-year-olds (Mash & Wolfe, 2005). These children need considerable training to learn to perform self-care activities such as eating, dressing, and toileting. They will need lifelong care. At present, most people with profound intellectual disability in the United States eventually go to live in group homes or residential facilities. Almost all cases of profound intellectual disability have a genetic or biological cause.

▲This teenager needs help with many of the self-care activities that most of us take for granted. Deficits in adaptive behavior, low IQ, and early onset (before age 18) are all elements of intellectual disability.

There are several things family members and other people can do to help children with intellectual disability improve the quality of their lives (Mash & Wolfe, 2005; Ramey & Ramey, 1992). They can encourage children with intellectual disability to explore the environment so they can learn and gather information, and work with them on basic learning skills such as labeling, sorting, and comparing objects. Children with intellectual disability need consistent care from a responsible adult—someone they can trust and depend on. Caregivers can also help by celebrating the achievements and developmental milestones of children with intellectual disability, and protecting them from harmful teasing, punishment, and criticism. None of these steps can erase the disability, but they can go a long way in helping the child live a more happy and satisfying life.

**gifted (or talented) children** Children who show extraordinary achievement in one or more areas.

Gifted and Talented Children. **Gifted (or talented) children** show achievement that is well above average in one or more areas—usually in language, math, music, art, or athletics. Some children are *globally gifted:* They show exceptional talent in all areas. Other children are *unevenly gifted:* They are exceptional in one or two areas but are at (or below) average levels in others. While a high IQ score may be an indicator of giftedness, it is not the only one: some talent areas are not included on intelligence tests, and such tests do not consider a child's cultural context when used as indicators of talent (Sternberg, 2007). Winner (1996) describes three characteristics that are typical of gifted (or talented) children.

1. Gifted children are *precocious*. They begin learning early and progress faster than others.
2. Gifted children *march to their own drummer.* They don't need much assistance to master information in their favorite subjects. They often teach themselves, have their own way of learning and unique ways of organizing and sorting information, and they don't always conform to the conventional learning methods of schools.
3. Gifted children have a *rage to master*—an intense craving for information and an obsessive need to make sense out of their favorite topics. They devour information, spend endless hours on their chosen subjects, and rarely engage in any other pursuits. Parents don't push them to achieve; instead, gifted children push their parents for more materials and stimulation.

Neuroscience research is just beginning to investigate the neural processing of gifted versus average individuals. One study found that mathematically gifted male adolescents activate different brain regions when completing mental rotation tasks (bilateral activation of the parietal and frontal cortex, as well as the anterior cingulate rather than right hemisphere activation of the parietal cortex typically found) (O'Boyle et al., 2005). Another found that professional pianists show activation of several different brain regions when creating music through improvisation than when reproducing music they had previously created (Bengtsson, Csíkszentmihályi, & Ullén, 2007). More research is needed to understand how and when different patterns of brain activation develop, and how they are related to specific skills in talented individuals.

One of the most ambitious longitudinal studies in history was begun by Lewis Terman in 1921 to study the development of highly gifted individuals. Contrary to common stereotypes, Terman found that gifted and talented individuals were not neurotic, frail, eccentric, or emotionally sensitive individuals. Instead, they were larger, healthier, and generally more well adjusted than most other children. Overall, they tended to live longer, enjoyed better health, had a lower divorce rate, and were happier than most people (Holahan, Holahan, Velasquez, & North, 2008; Shurkin, 1992; Terman, 1925). More recent research has found that gifted and talented adolescents are more focused in school, spend much of their free time working in their talent areas, and spend more time alone than their "average" peers. Their parents tend to have more education, and their families have higher incomes, as well as more supportive and positive family environments. For example, most talented teenagers rate their family interactions as more affectionate, cohesive, flexible, and happy than other students (Csikszentmihalyi, Rathunde, & Whalen, 1997; Shurkin, 1992; Terman, 1925). If others had these benefits, how many more would show exceptional talent?

Have you ever had a "rage to master" a particular topic? What was the experience like, and what do you think motivated you? If you haven't experienced this intense level of motivation, what subject comes closest to motivating you to learn at a higher level?

## Ethnic Differences and Questions about Cultural Bias

Imagine the challenges that faced many immigrants arriving in the United States in the early 1900s. Often malnourished, exhausted, and in poor health after a long journey in a crowded ship, they stepped out on Ellis Island. Anxious to find relatives and explore their new country, they learned that first they must take several tests. One was an intelligence test—perhaps the Stanford–Binet, which was a French test translated into English. If the immigrants didn't speak English, then they would take a version retranslated into their native languages. The test administrators would then compare their scores to the norms established by U.S.-born citizens who were tested under far more comfortable conditions. Is it surprising that the immigrants' scores were lower? Furthermore, could the questions in the French and American tests adequately measure the general intelligence of people raised in Hungary, Russia, Italy, African nations, or other parts of the world? Did the questions even make sense to people from other cultures? In other words, were the tests culturally fair?

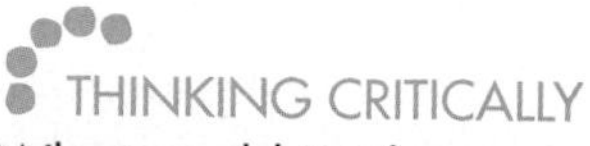


What would it take to develop an intelligence test that is truly culturally fair?

Numerous studies conducted since the 1960s have documented differences in intelligence scores among various U.S. ethnic groups (see Gregory, 1996, and Sattler, 2001, for reviews). Typically, composite scores for non-Hispanic whites are about 100. Asians score slightly higher, African Americans score about 15 points lower, and Hispanics score between whites and African Americans. You must keep in mind that these are group differences; scores vary much more *within* these groups than *among* them. It is impossible to predict any one person's score based on the person's ethnic group identity. Still, these group differences have generated a fierce debate about the cultural fairness of intelligence tests. To read more about the social implications of ethnic differences in IQ scores, see the Social Policy Perspective box this page called "Ethnicity and IQ."

Because of intelligence tests' potential for cultural bias, some critics have argued that these tests should not be used with students from ethnic minority groups. Some of the most common arguments *against* testing are listed on the beginning of page 455 (Onwuegbuzie & Daley, 2001; Sattler, 2001).

## Perspective SOCIAL POLICY — ETHNICITY AND IQ

How important is intelligence for doing well in school, getting a good job, and for explaining social problems like poverty, unemployment, crime, and poor parenting? Why are there persistent differences in the average IQ scores of different ethnic groups? These questions have been addressed for decades, with heated debate about the answers and their implications for social policies.

Heated controversy centered on *The Bell Curve,* a book that presents intelligence as a general trait, significantly influenced by genetics and successfully estimated by IQ tests (Herrnstein & Murray, 1994). The authors argue that differences in intelligence play a central role in many of the vexing problems faced by society such as poverty, unemployment, crime, education, and poor home environment, and that "large proportions of the people who exhibit the behaviors and problems that dominate the nation's social policy agenda have limited cognitive ability" (Herrnstein & Murray, 1994, p. 386).

The biggest controversy centers on the discussion of ethnic differences in IQ scores. While most experts agree that there are consistent differences in the average IQ scores of different ethnic groups, there is heated disagreement as to why. Herrnstein and Murray argue that the differences are not due to poverty, education, or test bias, but to real differences in cognitive abilities. They acknowledge that the environment undoubtedly plays a role in the development of intelligence, and that differences within groups is greater than between them, but argue that increasing intelligence has proven to be difficult. Finally, they urge consideration of social policies that recognize the central role of intelligence. For example, they urge a return to emphasizing quality education for gifted students because these students will benefit more from good education than less intelligent students. They also advocate a re-examination of affirmative action policies in education and employment to give preference to disadvantaged individuals only when their qualifications are very similar to those of nondisadvantaged peers. "The assumption of no innate differences among groups suffuses American social policy. That assumption is wrong" and it is important to open a dialogue to discuss these differences (Murray, 2005).

Reaction to *The Bell Curve* was swift, furious, and often negative. Critics claim the book does not describe problems in the data they use to support their arguments, the theories and data on which it is based have been replaced by newer views of intelligence and cognitive processing, and that the social policy recommendations are "exotic, neither following from the analyses nor justified on their own terms" (Gardner, 1995, p. 23; Fraser, 1995). Others believe that the authors dismiss the impact of such things as poverty, discrimination, and testing bias far too quickly, and overemphasize a narrowly defined view of intelligence to explain complex social problems (Edwards & Fuller, 2005; Fish, 2002; Miele, 1995; Neisser, 1998; Neisser et al., 1996).

QUESTION **What role do you think intelligence plays in the important social issues we currently face? What are the social policy implications of thinking of intelligence as a strongly genetically influenced general factor that is difficult to change? If you were developing social policies to address such things as poverty, crime, and fairness in educational and job opportunities, what role would group differences in intelligence play in your thinking?**

- *Intelligence tests are culturally biased.* The developers of most tests are middle-class whites who bring their own experiences to test construction. If they lack knowledge of other cultures, they may inadvertently create biased instruments. Some test items require knowledge that is specific to middle-class white culture. Cultural bias disadvantages test takers from minority cultures.
- *Minorities have less test-taking skill and experience.* Ethnic minority groups tend to focus more on oral skills, so paper-and-pencil tests may not be a good fit with their learning styles. Children from these groups also may have had less practice with standardized tests. Because the tests reflect the values and norms of the dominant majority, these children may be less motivated to perform at their highest levels or may not appreciate the importance and implications of doing well on the test.
- *Most test examiners are white.* Communication and rapport between white examiners and minority children may be less than optimal, and this may depress scores.
- *Test results lead to inadequate and inferior educational placements.* Because of their lower test scores, schools often disproportionately place minority children in special education classes, where curriculum and support may fall short of what other children receive. Special education placements also create negative expectancies in teachers and other school officials—and even in the minds of minority children themselves. In this negative cycle, called *stereotype threat,* the child begins to accept the negative views and expectations; this can lead to poorer intellectual performance (Steele & Aronson, 1995; Wout, Shih, Jackson, & Sellers, 2009).

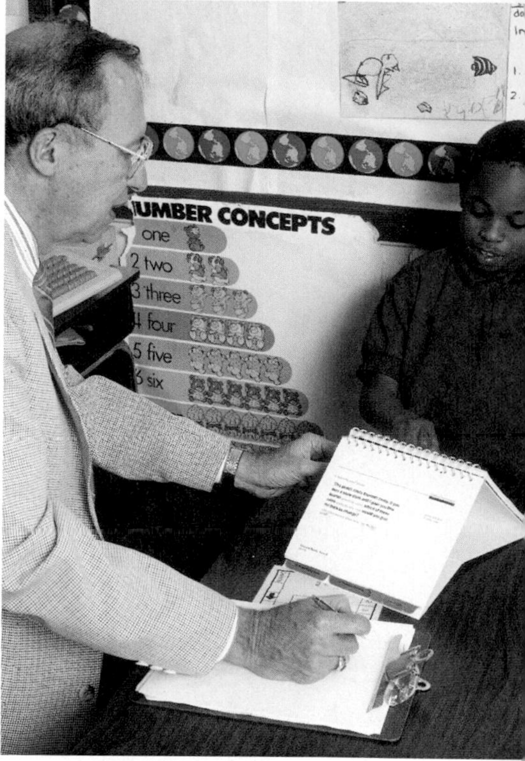


▲ Does racial uneasiness between examiner and child affect children's performance on IQ tests? What other potential problems must we consider when comparing IQ scores across different ethnic groups?

In view of these arguments, examiners administering psychological tests need to be sensitive to cultural differences. They should always interpret test results with caution, and they should never base special education placements or other diagnoses solely on the results of a single test. However, it's also important to evaluate criticisms of cultural bias in the light of objective research data. For example, it might seem that the verbal subscales of intelligence tests, which involve vocabulary, factual knowledge, and text comprehension (e.g., define the word *obfuscate*), would reflect more cultural bias than nonverbal subscales involving picture completion, object assembly, and block design (e.g., use blocks to copy a design). However, Taylor and Richards (1991) researched this question and found that African American children actually scored *higher* on the verbal subscales of the WISC–R (an earlier version of the WISC–IV) than they did on the nonverbal subscales. Further, when people have identified test items as culturally biased, test statistics often showed the same ethnic group differences on those items as on the whole test. Sometimes, in fact, results on these "biased" items favor ethnic minorities (Sattler, 2001).

One factor with a clear link to IQ scores is socioeconomic status, or SES. When SES and other living conditions are the same, IQ differences between non-Hispanic whites and African Americans are far smaller—less than five points in some studies (Sattler, 1992). After all, ethnic minority groups make up a disproportionately high percentage of families living in poverty in the United States. Children living in poverty have worse schools and fewer educational opportunities, both leading to lower IQ scores.

Jerome Sattler (1992, 2001), a researcher and expert in childhood assessment, summarized arguments that *favor* using intelligence tests with minority students.

- *Tests are useful in evaluating present functioning.* The subscales of intelligence tests can help educators identify students' cognitive strengths and weaknesses. Some subscale profiles may suggest brain damage or psychological difficulties; more specific tests can then follow up on these potential problems. A significant drop in IQ score can signal the need for follow-up.

THINK ABOUT LEO . . .
How might Leo's ethnicity impact her performance on intelligence tests? What steps can she, her parents, and test administrators take to make assessments more fair for her?

- *Tests help students get access to special programs.* When used properly, test scores can be an important part of the justification for providing special education programming and other services that some children need—services to which they are legally entitled.
- *Tests help families, educators, and communities evaluate programs.* By helping to document gains and losses, IQ scores can help hold schools and programs accountable for benefiting all children. When test scores reveal significant differences among ethnic groups, these findings can stimulate special interventions to address inequalities. Rather than seeing the tests as marred by bias, we can see them as tools for identifying bias in existing systems.
- *Finally, tests are useful in indicating future functioning.* Binet originally designed his scales to predict future school performance, and this is still one of the most important uses of intelligence tests today. IQ scores do correlate with academic success and performance.

Biases that exist in intelligence tests reflect the values and assumptions that operate in the dominant culture. The reality is that educational opportunities, and the likelihood of success in school and work, also reflect the dominant culture. Childhood IQ scores provide early evidence of this effect. They demonstrate the importance of achieving a truly multiethnic and pluralistic society where students of all cultures have an equal chance of success, achievement, and happiness.

## LET'S REVIEW . . .

**1.** Most experts agree that intelligence involves ___________

**a.** the ability to learn
**b.** the ability to think logically about abstract concepts
**c.** the ability to adapt to the environment
**d.** all of the above

**2.** Now in fifth grade, Lisa has practiced her division math facts so thoroughly that she can fly through her flash cards at an impressive speed. Which subtheory in Sternberg's triarchic theory of intelligence would relate most closely to Lisa's speed with division facts?

**a.** the componential subtheory
**b.** the experiential subtheory
**c.** the contextual subtheory
**d.** the metacomponent subtheory

**3.** Intellectual disability that results from lack of educational opportunity and stimulation is referred to as ___________

**a.** moderate intellectual disability
**b.** profound intellectual disability
**c.** early-starter retardation.
**d.** cultural–familial retardation.

**4.** Which of the following is *not* one of the reasons critics believe that intelligence tests are unfair assessments for ethnic minority children?

**a.** Tests can indicate future functioning.
**b.** Minorities have less skill and experience in taking standardized tests.
**c.** Most test examiners are white.
**d.** Tests lead to inadequate and inferior educational placements.

**5.** True or False: In Gardner's theory of multiple intelligences, linguistic intelligence is the root of all of the other types of intelligence, and people tend to be intelligent in the other areas only when they are high in linguistic intelligence.

**6.** True or False: When income levels are the same, average IQ scores for African Americans are much more similar to those of non-Hispanic whites.

Answers: 1. d, 2. b, 3. d, 4. a, 5. F, 6. T

# Learning to Communicate: Language in Adolescence

As you learned in Chapter 5, language development during childhood is quite impressive, but it is far from complete by the time a child enters adolescence. The teenage years see development in several important aspects of language. Some of these developments seem almost intentionally designed to keep parents and other adults from knowing what adolescents are talking about! Others aspects arise from the social and cultural contexts in which a teen develops.

AS YOU STUDY THIS SECTION, ASK YOURSELF THESE QUESTIONS:

**14.11** What is the adolescent register and what role does it play in adolescent development?

**14.12** What are dialects, and what advantages and disadvantages do they present?

## The Adolescent Register

During adolescence children begin to use language as a tool for identifying peer groups and for excluding those outside their peer group. The **adolescent register** is a special form of speech that adolescents use to identify themselves as belonging to a particular social, cultural, or generational group (Romaine, 1984). If you have ever overheard a group of adolescents talking with one another, you will recognize that their patterns of language include several distinctive features, including phonemes and syntax that are markedly different from those used by younger and older speakers of the same language. In particular, the adolescent register has an interesting vocabulary that includes many novel slang terms. Think back to movies from or about prior decades—can you recall any of the odd-sounding words and phrases that adolescents used? What was *groovy* in the 1960s, *cool* in the 1970s, and *awesome* in the 1990s became *phat* in the early 2000s; yesterday's *drama queens* are today's *emos.* Although adolescent registers exist across social, regional, and ethnic groups, the specific terms, syntax, and phonemes vary widely. Also, because the purpose of an adolescent register is to identify an adolescent as belonging to a particular generation, place, and group, registers change quickly. As adolescents grow to adulthood, the patterns and terms that marked their groups either fade away or, in some cases, become part of the overall culture. (Pretty cool, huh?)

THINKING CRITICALLY

What was your adolescent register? How was it different from those of your parents or of members of other social and ethnic groups?

**adolescent register**
Special form of speech adolescents use to identify themselves as belonging to a particular social, cultural, or generational group.

◀ What features of their adolescent registers do you think these teenagers are using?

▲ African American English (AAE), spoken by many African Americans, includes elements of several western African languages, Portuguese, Dutch, and French. Like other cultural dialects, AAE is a consistent system with its own linguistic rules and vocabulary, not an incorrect form of Standard American English.

## Social and Cultural Dialects

Even though people in different geographic regions and cultural groups within a country may all speak the same language, there are often differences in vocabulary, grammar/syntax, pragmatics, and style of language interactions. A **dialect** is a consistent and systematic variety of a single language that is shared by a certain subgroup of speakers (McLaughlin, 2006; Oetting, 2003a). In contrast, an *accent* consists of audible speech characteristics or differences in how words are pronounced and is one component of a dialect. A given language usually has several dialects, some of which are associated with specific geographic regions (e.g., Boston English, Southern English) and others with ethnic and cultural groups (e.g., African American English). A dialect may get its name from a particular ethnic group, but not all members of that ethnic group will necessarily speak the dialect—nor will members of the ethnic group be the only people who can speak it. Dialects develop in response to social and cultural conditions, not according to race, although these factors often go together (Hulit & Howard, 2006).

The most studied social dialect of Standard American English is *African American English* (AAE), also known as *Black English* or *Ebonics* (Green, 2002; Wolfram & Thomas, 2002). AAE is a distinct dialect of English, complete with its own linguistic rules and vocabulary, not a simplistic or incorrect form of Standard American English. *Hispanic English* and *Asian English* are other common dialects. As with AAE, not all Hispanic American or Asian American children use these dialects. Also, Hispanic and Asian populations in the United States come from a variety of different Spanish and Asian language backgrounds, so these dialects can vary a great deal. All these dialects show consistent differences from Standard American English in vocabulary, phonology, and grammar rules (Cheng, 1987; Hulit & Howard, 2006; McLaughlin, 2006; Taylor, 1986).

Different dialects are simply different from one another; no one dialect is inherently better or worse than any other. Even though dialects differ in systematic ways, they also share many similarities (Oetting, 2003a; Oetting & McDonald, 2001). However, the reality is that people often make negative judgments about those who speak a dialect other than their own. People may rate dialect speakers as lower in competence, professionalism, intelligence, ambition, education, success, and wealth—even when the raters are themselves speakers of the dialects (Atkins, 1993; Luhman, 1990). Often such judgments affect the treatment of people who speak different dialects in schools or workplaces. There is a tendency to treat such individuals as less competent and less intelligent, and speaking a dialect in educational and work settings often brings reprimands or even punishments (Romaine, 1995). Perhaps wider understanding that social dialects have their own complex rule systems and develop as a result of cultural and social circumstances might decrease these negative and unfair judgments (Oetting, 2003b).

THINK ABOUT LEO . . .

Is it likely that Leo speaks a dialect of English? If so, how might this affect how she is treated by others who do not speak the same dialect?

THINKING CRITICALLY

Do you, or does anyone you know, speak a dialect of English? What are some examples of the dialect's vocabulary and grammar? Do you think speaking a dialect is likely to affect people's judgments about the person? If so, in what ways?

**dialect**
A consistent and systematic variety of a single language that is shared by a certain subgroup of speakers.

### LET'S REVIEW . . .

1. The adolescent register helps adolescents identify themselves as ____________.
   a. being members of adult society
   b. being popular among peers
   c. belonging to a particular generation
   d. being aware of the abstract nature of language

2. The adolescent register
   a. is similar across ethnic groups in the specific vocabulary and syntax used.
   b. did not exist until the most recent generation of adolescents.

c. indicates poor understanding of a language's vocabulary and syntax.
d. is replaced by new forms as new generations reach adolescence.

3. True or False: A dialect has consistent linguistic rules and contains its own distinctive vocabulary.

4. True or False: People who speak dialects themselves do not rate other dialect speakers as lower in competence or intelligence, ambition, education, success, and wealth.

Answers: 1. c, 2. d, 3. T, 4. F

# Cognition in Context: Adolescents Making Decisions

As adolescents develop, they are increasingly called upon to use their intelligence in a variety of different ways. They have more freedom to make decisions about day-to-day matters as well as serious and far-reaching issues. Deciding what courses to take, how much effort to put into studying, whether to continue with further schooling past high school, which extracurricular activities to participate in, when they are ready for sexual activity, and whether to try drugs and alcohol are only a few of the choices most adolescents face. How well do adolescents make decisions? In this section we will briefly review research on adolescent decision making in general, then talk in more detail about adolescents' choices of jobs and careers.

AS YOU STUDY THIS SECTION, ASK YOURSELF THESE QUESTIONS:

**14.13** What cognitive skills and processes are involved in making decisions?

**14.14** How do adolescents think about possible jobs and occupational goals?

**14.15** What is the *forgotten third,* and what can be done to help improve their economic prospects?

## How Well Do Adolescents Make Decisions?

*Decision making* is a complex process. It involves the coordination of a number of cognitive skills, including recognizing that there is a decision to be made; generating alternatives and identifying possible problems or biases with each; objectively evaluating the likelihood that an alternative will produce the results you want, and the likely consequences whether it does or does not; and taking into consideration the social, personal, and emotional contexts at each step in the process. It also often involves *inhibiting* the first impulses one has about how to behave in a given situation, and knowing whether you know enough about the situation to trust your first instinct. It all happens with at least some degree of uncertainty, because we can never be sure if a decision is the "right" one or not until it has already been made. Adolescent decision making also frequently takes place very quickly—they are more likely than adults to be called upon to make fast decisions with uncertain information in emotionally-charged situations (Halpern, 2003, Halpern-Felsher, 2009; Holland & Klaczynski, 2009).

Think back to our discussions of formal operations, and to the information-processing and brain development research in earlier chapters, and it is easy to understand why we might expect adolescents to be better than children at making sound decisions. For example, generating alternatives requires the ability to think about abstract possibilities and use combinational logic, and evaluating possibilities is aided by systematic logical thinking. Determining likely consequences is based in part on reasoning about logical conclusions and abstract concepts as well as reflective thinking. As information-processing psychologists point out, adolescents also have a great deal more knowledge and a greater repertoire of strategies to bring to bear when making decisions. Their cognitive processing is faster and more efficient, in part due to increased brain myelination—this enables them to keep several perspectives in mind at once and allows them to compare and contrast possible courses of action.

The research in this area supports the conclusion that adolescents are better than children at making "good" decisions, or ones that reflect reasonably careful consideration of different options. By 14 years of age, adolescents are able to evaluate options and defend their decisions. As you might expect, older adolescents (over age 14) show better performance than younger ones in a variety of decision-making skills. Younger teens tend to use less of the information that is available to them, are not as good at identifying possible negative consequences, and are not as good at determining whether the source of information is credible or not (Kaplan, 2004; Keating, 1990). Younger adolescents may also be more susceptible to peer pressure in their decision making, and may give more weight to what adults think of as less important factors (such as appearance or being viewed positively by their friends).

However, it is also clear that decision-making skills continue to improve throughout adolescence and into adulthood. For example, one study asked adolescents ranging in age from 11 to 17 and 23-year-old young adults to help a teen think through a decision (such as whether to have cosmetic surgery or whether to live with her mother or her father following a divorce). Compared to the adolescents, young adults were more likely to consider the risks and benefits of the decisions and to suggest that the teen seek help from an impartial expert (Halpern-Felsher & Cauffman, 2001; Lewis, 1981). It's also important to keep in mind that most of the studies comparing adolescent and adult decision-making processes involve hypothetical dilemmas in laboratory settings, with plenty of time for considering options and evaluating available information. It's been suggested that the differences in decision making may be greater than we realize when the choices involve personally relevant issues in emotional, real-world contexts. Recent work indicates that two processes may be involved in making decisions—an analytic and rational process, and a faster intuitive process. The analytical and rational process involves thoughtful consideration of the risks and benefits of different possible decisions as well as relevant prior knowledge. Although teens may weigh costs and benefits differently than adults and may not have as much prior knowledge, they are good at using this type of decision-making process by mid- to late-adolescence. The second process is a much faster intuitive process—decisions are based on experience, emotion, and whether the behavior "feels right" in the moment. Intuitive processing is faster, requires less cognitive effort, and is more automatic. It might surprise you to learn that as we get older, we tend to rely *more* on intuitive decision making. Adults are better than adolescents in intuitive processing because their intuitions are based on greater experience. They are also better able to override this intuitive system when necessary, in part because of brain maturation. As we mentioned in Chapter 13, both the gray matter and white matter of the prefrontal cortex and its connections with the emotion centers of the brain develop throughout adolescence, which means that adults' impulse control increases and their emotional reactivity declines—both of which contribute to better control over decision making (Halpern-Felsher, 2009; Holland & Klaczhnski, 2009; Steinberg, 2008; Steinberg & Scott, 2003).

THINKING CRITICALLY

Think about a difficult decision you had to make during your adolescence. How did you think through the issue—what factors did you consider? What roles did analytic versus intuitive decision making play? How would you think about it differently now?

The issue of adolescent decision making can have critical real-world implications, particularly when considering issues such as legal rights and responsibilities and risky behavior. At what age should one be legally allowed to seek health care without parental permission? At what age should teens be prosecuted as adults for criminal activities? And, if adolescents use analytic and intuitive decision-making processes that are similar to adults, why do they have the reputation of engaging in risky behaviors with potentially devastating consequences? What are the relative influences of brain development, perceived costs and benefits, analytic versus intuitive processing, and prior knowledge—and how can program developers use this information to encourage teens to make more positive decisions for long-term well-being (Beckman, 2004; Goldberg, Halpern-Felsher, & Millstein, 2002; Gruber, 2001; Holland & Klaczynski, 2009; Steinberg & Scott, 2003)? The research on decision making, and adolescent cognitive development in general, will be important to consider as society makes these decisions and tries to understand these adolescent behaviors. **Listen** on **mydevelopmentlab**

**Listen**: Why do adolescents take risks? (Author Podcast)
www.mydevelopmentlab.com

## Making Vocational Choices

One of the biggest decisions that adolescents must grapple with is what occupation to work toward. It may surprise you to learn that the foundations for making choices about vocations begin well before adolescence, as even young children begin recognizing and developing their talents, attitudes, and needs (Hartung, Porfeli, & Vondracek, 2005). Occupational development is a developmental process, with individuals first observing and thinking about the occupations they see around them and becoming progressively more specific and realistic about their choices (Super, 1957). During early and middle adolescence, increasing cognitive skills enable adolescents to think more realistically about their own skills and interests as well as to consider what is required in different occupations.

What factors influence the specific vocational decisions that an individual makes? Several factors are involved, including one's interests, values regarding the rewards one wants from working, and several aspects of the social context such as socioeconomic status, parents, peers, the job market, gender, and ethnicity. One well-known theory of career choice was developed by John Holland (1997) and focuses on the role of personality, particularly a person's interests. According to Holland, successful career choice involves making a good match between one's interests and the demands of their occupational environment. Holland argued that interests can be organized into six general occupational categories, as shown in Figure 14.4, and that different occupational environments are more suited to some categories than others. For example, someone whose personality characteristics are more investigative would likely be better suited to and more satisfied with a career in a scientific or technical field rather than in a clerical or sales position. According to Holland, a good fit will increase the likelihood of career satisfaction, achievement, and stability as well as greater overall well-being. In general, these relationships are supported by research, though some studies find stronger relations than others (Luzzo & MacGregor, 2001; Mullis & Mullis, 1997). In addition, predicting occupational success may be more complicated than finding a good match between personality and occupational demands, particularly for members of minority groups. These individuals may have the interests, desire, and talents to succeed in a specific career but have to contend with discrimination or other barriers in educational or job opportunities (Brown, 1995; Greenlee, Damarin, & Walsh, 1988).

Other researchers emphasize the role of *work values,* or the types of rewards a person wishes to get from work, rather than interests *per se* when explaining career choice (Johnson, 2002). For example, some people are very motivated by money when making job choices while others seek job stability, opportunities to be creative, power over others, helping others, or having time for recreation. Adolescents may be unrealistic in this regard. For example, teens rate many different types of rewards as being very important, and say they are very confident they will find a job that meets them all (Schneider & Stevenson, 1999). As they gain more experience in the work world, work values change. Emphasis on making a lot of money, helping others, and enjoying relationships with

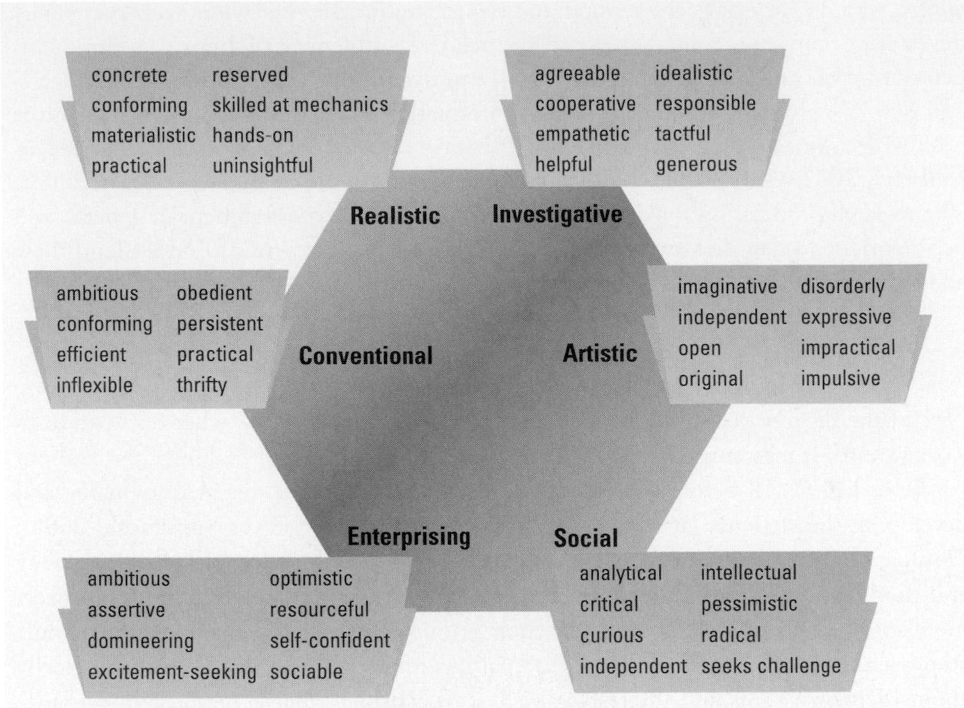


FIGURE 14.4 ▶ **Holland's Six Occupational Categories** In Holland's theory, an individual's pattern of interests can be categorized into the six occupational categories shown here. The better the match between these interest categories and the demands of the occupation, the more satisfied and successful the person will be.

coworkers decreases while job stability and opportunities to be creative continue to be important (Johnson, 2002).

This research is an important reminder of one of the main difficulties of relying on interest-based or work value-based models when talking with adolescents about career decisions: These things can change. While some 18-year-olds are quite sure of their identities, interests, and values, others are not. By this age they may have a general sense of their interests and talents but are still in the process of exploring alternatives and trying different possibilities (Duffy & Sedlacek, 2007; Tracey, Robbins, & Hofsess, 2005). Adolescents and young adults are making vocational choices at later ages now than in past decades, and work environments themselves can have an important influence on the development of interests and values. Many adolescents will transition in and out of full-time work several times before they settle on one career path, and most will hold part-time employment almost continuously from high school postsecondary education (Staff & Mortimer, 2008). As with many aspects of development, the factors involved have bidirectional effects.

It is also important to remember that vocational decisions are not based solely on the individual's characteristics. Instead, they are made within and significantly affected by the social context. For example, overall socioeconomic status affects many job-relevant factors, including the occupational models the adolescent sees, job opportunities, types of schooling and training available, work values, degree and types of career exploration available and encouraged, and family connections to list only a few (Mullis, Mullis, & Gerwels 1998; Steinberg, 2005). Adolescents are also affected by expectations of their families and their culture. For example, stereotypes of appropriate careers for women and cultural expectations to balance family and work affect young women's thinking about careers. Cultural values regarding group connectedness and community responsibility require that adolescents and young adults from some ethnic minority backgrounds balance these values with occupational environments that may be quite different (Kaplan, 2004). Given the complexities of vocational decision making, it is not surprising that it takes many years to make career decisions.

THINK ABOUT LEO . . .
In general, what occupational category(ies) might best describe Leo? What work values does she seem to be developing?

## The Forgotten Third: Improving the Transition from School to Work

When considering vocational decision making, the majority of attention is focused on adolescents who will attend college (defined as two- or four-year programs that grant a degree). In the late 1980s, a report drew nationwide attention to the fact that almost half of adolescents do not go to college after high school—and for those that don't, these individuals received little support, training, or help beyond high school (William T. Grant Foundation Commission on Work, Family and Citizenship, 1988). In fact, the report concluded that high schools were doing little to prepare adolescents for going directly to the work world either in terms of encouraging higher-level thinking or teaching job-specific trade skills. More recent data show that more students are going on to attend some college (so there is only a "forgotten third") but the economic prospects of the third who do not attend college are even worse than before, with lower wages and higher unemployment. Even though more students are attending college, graduation rates have increased only slightly, with 29% of young adults completing a bachelor's degree in 2008 compared with 22% in 1971. There are clear ethnic differences in postsecondary education graduation—33% of white, 20% of African American, and 13% of Hispanic students graduate from college (Halperin, 1998; Jennings & Rentner, 2005; Snyder, Dillow, & Hoffman, 2009).

▲The school-to-work transition for adolescents who do not further their schooling after high school graduation can be difficult. How can schools and potential employers help ease this transition?

It is in everyone's interest to improve the economic prospects for those who do not attend or complete college. A host of economic, social, and health outcomes are positively related to having a more stable and higher-paying job. Fortunately, increasing attention is being given to improving the *school-to-work transition* (American Youth Policy Forum & Center for Workforce Development, 2000; Bowles & Brand, 2009; Hamilton & Hamilton, 2004). For example, school and work settings are offering increasing alternatives. **Watch** on **mydevelopmentlab**

**Watch** On the Job Learning www.mydevelopmentlab.com

- *Cooperative educational programs.* Schools and work places cooperate to provide paid work experience with specific skill goals as part of the student's schooling. These programs are often offered as part of a school's vocational educational curriculum.
- *Internships.* Interns are placed in a work setting either during the school year or summer. Work hours, responsibilities, and compensation are negotiated among the student, work supervisor, and academic supervisor.
- *Youth apprenticeships.* These are formal, structured, systematic programs with the explicit goal of teaching the skills of a specific trade to a certain standard.
- *Service-learning experiences.* These experiences combine the opportunity to learn skills while performing a service for others. They are unpaid and short-term activities, but may be required as part of a school's community service expectations.

For school-to-work experiences to be beneficial and successful, the quality of *mentoring* the students receive must be considered. **Mentoring** refers to adults in the work and/or school setting taking responsibility for teaching and advising the student to make sure that the work being done contributes to students' learning. Good mentoring in school-to-work programs helps adolescents achieve competence in the academic skills and knowledge required by the job, responsibility in their personal job-related actions, the skills and willingness to behave and communicate according to the norms of the professions, and the skills and willingness to learn effectively and perform well in school in general (Hamilton & Hamilton, 2004). Good mentoring can also help students build important social networks, which will help them find full-time employment after they graduate. When done well, school-to-work mentoring programs have positive effects on a variety of social, academic, and occupational outcomes though the size of the effects are relatively modest (DuBois, Holloway, Valentine, & Cooper, 2002). To learn more about the experiences of one of the Forgotten Third, read the Personal Perspective box on page 464 called "I Graduated—Now What?"

**mentoring**
The process of taking responsibility for teaching and advising students in a work or school setting to ensure student learning.

## Perspective PERSONAL I GRADUATED—NOW WHAT?

Donna Rowland
Pittsburgh, PA

**Why did you decide to not continue your schooling after high school?**
It was more of an assumption than a decision. I grew up in a very blue-collar environment. Going off to college was not something that was discussed or even thought about in my immediate family. I did have friends that went on to college, and I would look at them with such amazement and curiosity. Why were they going off to college and leaving me behind to jump-start a future with really no knowledge? I am not bitter about my decision, but I do daydream about what I might have been and what my life would be like now had I gone to college.

**What was the school-to-work transition like for you?**
I was looking for that glamorous secretarial position, not realizing that you have to start out as the lowly file clerk. You could always find employment as a sales clerk or cashier but that was not something I wanted to do. My first job was processing payment checks in the credit office of a major department store. It doesn't sound like much fun or excitement, but this was my entrance into the business world. What I do remember are the great friends I made and what fun we had planning what we were going to do on the weekend.

**What could the school system have done to make the transition easier?**
I was in the academic program in high school, so in some ways I was not as efficient as those who concentrated on their typing and shorthand skills—Yes, I did say shorthand! It would have been beneficial if my school had an intern program. This would have prepared the people not going on to college for what the real world had to offer. That in itself may have convinced more of us to try to further their education.

**Looking back, would you change anything about your decision-making process, your choices, or your preparation for life after high school?**
This is a very hard question to answer. I am very pleased with my life but there are times when I think about what I would have done differently. I love art and spend a lot of my free time painting. This talent might have been channeled into a profession such as an art teacher. I love children and if someone had shown me how these two could have come together, I might have pursued a career as an elementary art teacher.

QUESTION **What school-to-work programs would you design to ease the school-to-work transition and help students become more aware of their options as well as the real world of work? What elements seem most important, and why?**

Finally, what about the effects of simply working for pay during adolescence—not as part of a structured school-to-work program? Most teenagers have part-time jobs, usually in retail or service jobs as cashiers, cooks, stock handlers/baggers, or fast-food servers. Working more than 20 hours per week during the school year is associated with poorer grades and increased negative behaviors. Some of this negative effect may be due to selection factors (i.e., students who work longer hours may also be less interested and less successful in school to begin with). In general, however, adolescents who balance work, school, and extracurricular activities (spending less than 20 hours per week working for pay) are most successful in high school and beyond (Mortimer, 2003; Staff, Mortimer, & Uggen, 2004). As you might expect, number of hours worked is not the only important factor in thinking about the effects of teen employment. Working conditions that encourage school–work connections and provide opportunities to learn new career-related skills reduce the chances of school problems, drug and alcohol use, and criminal activity. These working conditions, which school-to-work transition programs try to encourage, also have the positive effects of helping teens become more independent, confident, and responsible as well as helping them develop work values and beliefs that will help them succeed in the adult workplace (Staff et al., 2004). The little evidence available for younger teens (less than age 16) is not consistent. Some studies find no negative relationship between school-year employment on academic engagement or achievement, perhaps because parents are more likely to limit the working hours for these teens and the types of jobs they have (lawn care, babysitting) are less likely to conflict with school (Sabia, 2009). However, another study of more than 5,000 fifth graders found more substance use, aggression, and home problems in youth working more than a few hours per week (Ramchand et al., 2009). These are correlational studies—what issues must you be careful about when interpreting their results?

In this chapter, we have described important cognitive changes that occur during adolescence as well as several ways to think about and assess intelligence. We also described how adolescents use these skills to make decisions about daily aspects of their lives and their future occupations. As we look back over the course of cognitive development, it is clear that adolescents have made tremendous strides in their abilities to reason, and have become very capable at making important decisions. Their cognitive skills will continue to grow in important ways over the rest of their lives, but adolescents' reasoning is quite impressive indeed!

THINK ABOUT LEO . . .
How could a part-time job help Leo as she thinks about her future? What type of job might help her most, and what should she be cautious about?

## LET'S REVIEW . . .

1. Adolescents are better decision makers than younger children because of adolescents'
   a. less detailed knowledge base
   b. more mature cognitive skills
   c. slower cognitive processing
   d. greater emphasis on peer opinion
2. According to Holland's theory of career decision making, which of the following factors would be *most* important for a high school guidance counselor to know in order to help a teen make occupational plans?
   a. what the teen's parents do for an occupation
   b. the teen's ethnic background
   c. the teen's work values
   d. the teen's interests
3. Compared to adults, adolescents' work values __________
   a. are more idealistic
   b. focus more on having free time for recreation
   c. are less realistic
   d. are very similar and do not change much with age
4. True or False: By age 14, most adolescents are just as good as adults at making decisions.
5. True or False: The economic conditions for teens who do not continue their schooling after high school graduation are better now than they were two decades ago.

Answers: 1. b, 2. d, 3. c, 4. F, 5. F

## THINKING BACK TO LEO . . .

Now that you have studied this chapter, you should be able to help Leo understand more about her cognitive strengths and weaknesses, as well as how she might use her skills to make important decisions in her life. You can explain some of the higher level thinking skills that Piaget's theory predicts will develop during adolescence. This theory may help Leo see how skills like hypothetico-deductive reasoning, abstract thought, and combinational thinking are needed more in her coursework than before. Understanding adolescent egocentrism might help her better understand her own and her friends' behaviors, and prompt her to think more carefully about important choices and taking risks. Knowledge of situated and socially shared cognition may give her some ideas of how to better use her study groups and aspects of both her in-school and out-of-school contexts to understand the concepts she is learning. Understanding more about her developing ability to separate reality from possibilities may also help Leo as she thinks through the pros and cons of working and possible options for her future. She may be comforted to know that things will not always seem so confusing—her skills will become more mature and she will probably develop aspects of postformal reasoning.

It would be helpful to tell Leo about some of the ways of conceptualizing intelligence. Perhaps if she thinks about the different factors, components, or types of intelligence, she might see her own profile of skills more clearly. You could work with her to identify her areas of strength (like verbal skills) and help her find ways to use those to improve her skills and performance in weaker areas. She and her parents should also be made aware of the potential bias of the standardized tests she may have taken (and will surely take, if she decides to apply for college admissions) and take whatever steps they can to ensure that these assessments are fair and used appropriately.

Working while still in high school offers some benefits, but Leo should be careful to balance her work, school, and other activities. Leo's parents might try to find people within her general areas of interest to provide mentoring for her; perhaps her school or local businesses offer structured school-to-work programs. Participating in these might help Leo understand the usefulness of what she is learning in school, connect her schoolwork to the real world, develop mature work values, and think of herself as a legitimate peripheral participant in a field that interests her. Leo and her parents should definitely work with one another and the school system to help prepare her for her transition after high school, whether she attends college or not.

# 14 CHAPTER REVIEW . . .

**14.1** What new forms of logical thought and cognitive advances emerge during the formal operational stage?

Adolescents develop the abilities to use hypothetico-deductive reasoning, abstract thought, combinational logic, reflective thought, and separate reality from possibilities. They can systematically work through all possible solutions to complex problems and are able to envision how things *could* be in contrast to how they really exist.

**14.2** What is *adolescent egocentrism,* and why is it important for understanding adolescents' thinking and behavior?

Adolescent egocentrism is the inability to distinguish between one's own thoughts and those of others. Adolescents show egocentrism in the form of the imaginary audience and the personal fable; these factors may play a role in the decisions adolescents make about taking risks.

**14.3** What are the main criticisms and contributions of Piaget's theory?

Piaget underestimated children's abilities, and there does not seem to be evidence for the unified stages he proposed. Still, Piaget left a tremendous legacy for child development. He emphasized the active, constructive nature of children's learning, and many of the cognitive developmental trends he observed have been verified by research.

**14.4** What is the situated cognition view of cognitive development and how is it consistent with Vygotsky's theory?

Like Vygotksy, the situated cognition view emphasizes adaptation to the cultural context. Situated cognition holds that all thinking takes place within a context, and that development cannot be understood or measured without considering the situation.

**14.5** How does guided participation in communities of practice explain cognitive development?

The guided participation defines development as gradually increasing participation in day-to-day sociocultural activity accompanied by gradually decreasing guidance and support from others. This view also emphasizes the changes that take place in social roles and shared interactions with development.

**14.6** What is socially shared cognition?

Socially shared cognition is a view of cognitive development that emphasizes the shared nature of thinking; Working together, children can construct more advanced cognitive products than when working alone. Thinking resides in the dynamic interactions between individuals within the group, not solely inside the head of any individual.

**14.7** What are the major similarities and differences among the different theories of intelligence?

The psychometric approach relies on numerous paper-and-pencil tests and physical measures; the data are analyzed to identify a smaller set of factors that underlie intelligence. Sternberg proposed three subtheories: componential, experiential, and contextual that explain how one acquires skills, processes information, and copes with the environment. Gardner proposed eight independent types of intelligence. People inherit biopsychological potentials to be stronger or weaker in each intelligence but environmental factors and individual choices are important for developing these potentials.

**14.8** How is intelligence assessed?

Binet and Simon developed the first practical intelligence test to determine which French schoolchildren would benefit from special education. Frequently used intelligence tests today are the most recent edition of the Stanford–Binet scale (SB5) and the series of assessments developed by David Wechsler. All provide an overall IQ score as well as subtest scores. Newer approaches called dynamic assessment are based on Vygotsky's developmental theory.

**14.9** What characterizes the upper and lower extremes of intelligence, and how can we explain why these extremes develop?

Intellectual disability refers to below-normal intellectual functioning, deficits in adaptive behavior, and an onset before age 18. Thousands of biological and environmental factors can cause intellectual disability. Gifted children are precocious, march to their own drummers, and have a "rage to master." Most gifted children are healthy, well adjusted, and well liked by peers; most come from families with the financial and emotional resources to support giftedness.

**14.10** What might explain ethnic group differences in intelligence test scores, and what can be done to ensure the fairness of these tests?

Consistent differences between ethnic groups have been found on intelligence tests, although there is much more variability within groups than between, and ethnic group differences are smaller when SES levels are equal. Critics have concerns about possible bias in test items, testing situations, and use of test results. Provided they are used and interpreted properly, tests can be useful in evaluating individuals and programs, qualifying children for needed services, and predicting future school functioning.

**14.11** What is the adolescent register and what role does it play in adolescent development?

The adolescent register is a special form of speech used by adolescents to identify themselves as belonging to a particular social, cultural, or generational group. It exists in unique forms in all these groups, and changes quickly over time.

**14.12** What are dialects, and what advantages and disadvantages do they present?

Social dialects are consistent and systematic varieties of a single language shared by a certain subgroup of speakers. They develop in response to social and cultural conditions, and facilitate communication among people who share these conditions. People who speak social dialects are often subject to negative judgments.

**14.13** What cognitive skills and processes are involved in making decisions?

Adolescents are better than younger children in many decision-making skills, but they weigh risks and benefits differently than do adults. Teens can use both analytic and intuitive decision making processes, but their intuitive decision are based on less knowledge than adults; they are also less able than adults to override the intuitive process.

**14.14** How do adolescents think about possible jobs and occupational goals?

Development of occupational interests starts well before adolescence. Holland's theory of career choice emphasizes a good match between an individual's interests and occupation, while others emphasize the role of work values. Other factors are also involved, such as SES and cultural values.

**14.15** What is the *forgotten third,* and what can be done to help improve their economic prospects?

The forgotten third is the percentage of students in the United States who do not continue their schooling after high school graduation. The transition from school to work is especially difficult for these students, and their economic prospects are difficult. Several transition programs can ease the transition, and the role of quality mentoring by an adult is key. Working for pay during high school offers several benefits as long as adolescents are careful to balance work with school demands and extracurricular activities.

## REVISITING THEMES

Gardner's theory of intelligence (pp. 445–446), with its emphasis on biopsychosocial potential, demonstrates the theme of *nature and nurture*. This theme is also evident in the discussion of the genetic and environmental contributors to intellectual disability (p. 450).

The *neuroscience* theme was addressed in the discussion of the relationship of brain maturation and adolescent decision making (p. 459), intellectual disability (p. 450), and new work on different brain activation in gifted and talented individuals (p. 453).

*Positive development and resilience* can be seen in the discussion of multiple facets of intelligence, as in Sternberg's consideration of street smarts and successfully adapting the environment to better fit one's particular strengths (p. 445). Positive development can also be seen in the supportive homes of gifted and talented individuals (p. 452). The effective elements of school-to-work transition programs can also serve to foster positive development (p. 463).

*Diversity and multiculturalism* were included in the discussion of cross-cultural research on Piaget's theory (p. 438), the situated cognition view's emphasis on understanding the cultural context in which cognition develops (p. 440), and the impact of speaking a social dialect (p. 458). Ethnic differences on intelligence tests and college completion, and the discussion of issues involved in fair testing, also address this theme (p. 453).

## KEY TERMS

abstract thought (436)
adolescent egocentrism (436)
adolescent register (457)
combinational logic (436)
componential subtheory (444)
contextual subtheory (445)
crystallized ability (443)
dialect (458)
dynamic assessment (449)
experiential subtheory (444)
fluid ability (443)
formal operational thought (435)
general intelligence (*g*) (443)
gifted (or talented) children (452)
guided participation (441)
hypothetico-deductive reasoning (435)
imaginary audience (436)
intelligence (442)
intellectual disability (450)
mentoring (463)
personal fable (436)
psychometric approach (443)
reliability (448)
situated cognition (440)
socially shared cognition (442)
specific intelligence (*s*) (443)
theory of multiple intelligences (445)
triarchic theory of intelligence (444)
validity (448)

**Watch** Visit your Multimedia Library at www.mydevelopmentlab.com to watch an interview with Camila online.

15 ADOLESCENCE

# Socioemotional Development in Adolescence

Camila just turned 16. She and her parents love each other, but lately it seems like they argue about everything; getting chores and homework done, getting off the phone, her friends, her clothes, school—you name it! The arguments that bother Camila most are about things she believes are her own personal choices. Why should her parents object if she wants another piercing? It's her body and she's the one who is responsible for it. Her parents always tell her that she needs to be responsible, but how can she when they won't let her do or have anything to be responsible for? Camila is really hoping to take her driver's license test soon, if her parents will let her. She can't wait for the freedom a driver's license can offer, but she's pretty sure her parents won't let her drive as much as she'd like. Her family just moved to a very quiet (*too* quiet) suburb, and she would love to be able to drive back to her old place in the city. But she probably won't be able to get a car for a long time. Her parents are both out of work right now so they don't have much money.

Camila knows that the time is coming when she'll need to think more seriously about her future. She's thought about being a veterinarian, or maybe a therapist, but still isn't sure. She's feels pretty confused about it all so she mostly tries to avoid thinking about it. Right now she just enjoys hanging out with her friends, going downtown or to the mall, reading a good book—and she loves playing her video games. Camila has had several good friends since middle school and they keep in very close touch. Camila knows that most kids experiment with drugs and alcohol. Unfortunately, she's seen some of her good friends go too far and develop serious problems. In a lot of ways, she feels closer to her friends than to her family, which sometimes makes her feel a little confused. After all, isn't family supposed to always come first?

Are the concerns and feelings Camila is having about her future, her family, and her friends normal for this age? After studying this chapter, you should be able to identify several potential reasons for her concerns and suggest several things that might help.

(*Continued*)

As you read this chapter, look for the "Think About Camila . . ." questions that ask you to consider what you're learning from Camila's perspective.

Contexts of Development
- Adolescents in School
- Differences in Academic Performance
- Cultural Contexts for Development

Like Camila, many adolescents feel excitement, anxiety, eagerness to experience adult activities, and fear of not being able to handle adult responsibilities—sometimes all within a matter of minutes! Adolescents face three central developmental tasks in their socioemotional development: *identity*, *autonomy*, and *intimacy*. This is a time when individuals begin to develop a clearer sense of their skills, interests, personal and occupational goals. They usually develop close friendships during these years as well as experience the first feelings of romance and sexual attraction. The family still exerts a strong influence on attitudes and behavior, but the impact of peers increases substantially as adolescents gradually become more independent. With their increased freedom and more mature thinking skills, some adolescents encounter conflicts between their developing moral guidelines and what they experience; many begin to think about ethical dilemmas in more mature ways. As with younger children, adolescents' development is affected by the different social contexts in which they live, such as the schools they attend as well as their overall cultural context. The concepts and research findings presented in this chapter should help you understand the many aspects of adolescent social and emotional development. It is also important to remember that, although these developmental tasks are typically discussed as socioemotional tasks, all three are directly affected by the physical and cognitive developments you learned about in Chapters 13 and 14.

# Who Am I? Adolescents' Understanding of Themselves

As you might recall from Chapter 1, Erik Erikson believed that one of the central developmental tasks for adolescent socioemotional development is to develop a clear sense of their own identities. **Identity** refers to a person's self-definition, including a knowledge and understanding of the combination of skills, interests, and characteristics that make her a unique person. In this section, we will describe the development of several different aspects of identity: identity status and ethnic identity, sexual orientation, and morality.
**Watch** on **mydevelopmentlab**

**Watch** Adolescence: Identity and Role Development. www.mydevelopmentlab.com

AS YOU STUDY THIS SECTION, ASK YOURSELF THESE QUESTIONS:

**15.1** What are the four identity statuses described by Marcia?

**15.2** What factors contribute to the development of sexual orientation?

**15.3** What evidence supports Kohlberg's theory of moral development, and what are some of the criticisms of this theory?

## Identity

Adolescents' developing self-representation becomes an important issue as young people strive to develop their own identities. You may recall Erik Erikson's famous theory of psychosocial development (see Table 1.2 on page 12 in Chapter 1) (Erikson, 1968). Erikson believed that adolescents grapple with the stage of *identity versus role confusion*. Their increasing cognitive abilities enable them to think about abstract qualities of the self, to compare their "real selves" to their "ideal selves," and to think about other "possible selves." During adolescence, too, social demands increase rapidly: Teenagers take on different roles and responsibilities in areas such as work, religion, politics, and sexual relationships. Erikson proposed that adolescents must come to a resolution of who they are and what they believe. In other words, they must integrate in some way the many aspects of their self-representation and develop a sense of identity. If adolescents do not resolve the crisis of identity, their unclear sense of self will make it more difficult to deal with the crises that will arise during the adulthood years (i.e., intimacy, generativity, and integrity).

**identity**
A person's self-definition, including a knowledge and understanding of the combination of skills, interests, and characteristics that make him or her a unique person.

**identity achievement**
A state of identity development in which a person has experienced and worked through the crisis and has made a commitment.

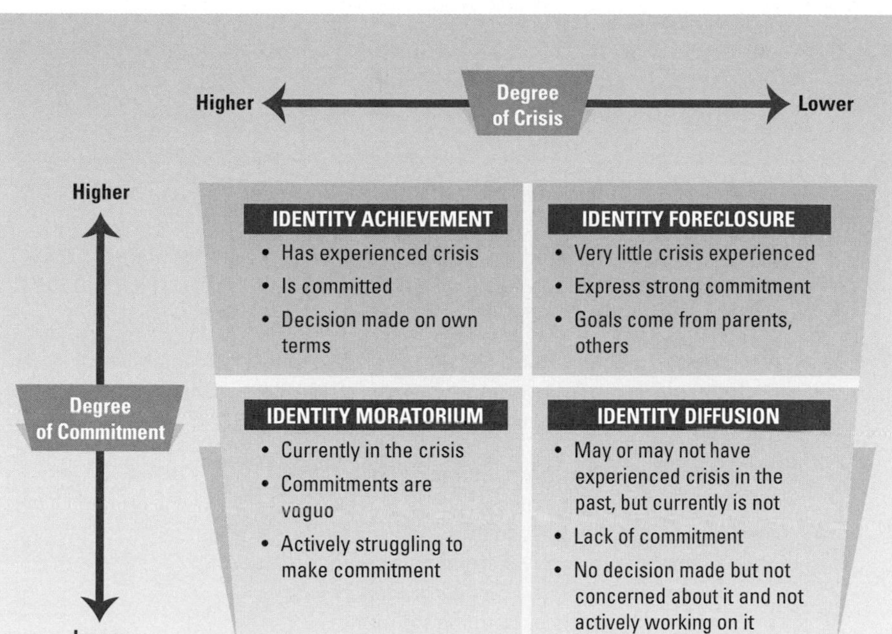


◀ FIGURE 15.1
**The Four Identity Statuses of James Marcia**
Each of Marcia's identity statuses reflects the degree of *crisis* experienced and the degree of *commitment* reached. (Based on Marcia, 1966.)

Identity Status. James Marcia put forth a well-known elaboration of Erikson's theory, as shown in Figure 15.1 (Marcia, 1966). Marcia proposed two components of adolescent identity development. The first component is a *crisis* (sometimes referred to as *exploration*). In this crisis we question and think about what we know about ourselves, how it all fits together, and how it compares to the ideal vision we have of ourselves. Second, after some period of questioning and thought, we may make a *commitment* to an identity, reaching some conclusion or decision about ourselves. As shown in Figure 15.1, Marcia described four possible identity statuses during adolescence.

1. **Identity achievement** is the status in which an adolescent has experienced and worked through the crisis and has made a commitment.
2. **Identity foreclosure** is the status in which an adolescent has experienced very little crisis but has made a commitment based on what others have said he is and should be. The adolescent has taken on an identity without much self-examination or questioning.
3. **Identity diffusion** is the status in which an adolescent may or may not have experienced a crisis, but is not currently in a state of crisis. The adolescent in identity diffusion either has stopped trying to reach a commitment or for some reason is still unable to do so—there is a clear *lack* of commitment.
4. **Identity moratorium** is the status of an adolescent who is still in the process of working through the crisis. The experience of the crisis is relatively high, but commitment is low.

As you might expect, adolescents who experience the period of crisis before making a commitment show greater complexity in their self-concepts than those in the foreclosed identity status, who have not experienced a period of exploration (Low, 1999).

The Development of Ethnic Identity. Adolescents who are members of an ethnic minority must also develop an **ethnic** or racial **identity**—an understanding of their ethnic backgrounds and a feeling of belonging within their minority groups. The groundwork for this development occurs during middle childhood, when minority children first begin to identify themselves as members of specific minority groups. Children as young as 5 understand the differences between themselves and majority-group children and typically prefer children of their own

THINK ABOUT CAMILA . . .

In which identity status do you think Camila is? Does it seem that her changing interests and confusion are typical for her age, or do they indicate a problem? Why or why not?

**identity foreclosure**
A state of identity development in which a person has experienced very little crisis but has made a commitment based on what others have said he or she is and should be.

**identity diffusion**
A state of identity development in which a person is not currently in a state of crisis, but there is a lack of commitment. The person either has stopped trying or is unable to reach a commitment.

**identity moratorium**
A state of identity development in which a person is still in the process of working through the crisis.

**ethnic identity**
A person's understanding of his or her ethnic background and a feeling of belonging to a minority group.

**TABLE 15.1**
**Phinney's Three-Stage Model of Ethnic Identity Development**

| STAGE | DESCRIPTION |
|---|---|
| Unexamined Ethnic Identity | • Child holds an identity based on outside sources, or has no clear sense of identity<br>• A foreclosed or diffused identity status<br>• May be based on positive image (e.g., from parents)<br>• May be based on negative image (e.g., stereotypes) |
| Ethnic Identity Search | • Increasing cognitive abilities and social experiences combine to prompt reexamination and questioning of ethnic identity<br>• A period of moratorium |
| Achieved Ethnic Identity | • Adolescent settles on an ethnic identity<br>• Achieved identity status<br>• Can resolve the crisis by:<br>· *Distancing* themselves from their ethnic culture;<br>· Adopting a *blended bicultural identity,* in which aspects of both the majority and ethnic culture are adopted;<br>· Adopting an *alternating bicultural identity,* in which two different identities are created and the individual switches between them depending on the social context;<br>· Making a *complete commitment* to their ethnicity, even if it means loss of acceptance and access to the majority culture. |

(Phinney, 1990.)

ethnicity (Aboud & Doyle, 1995; Wright, 1998). According to Phinney (1990), the development of ethnic identity takes place in three stages during adolescence, as shown in Table 15.1.

If you examine Phinney's stages, you will notice parallels to Marcia's identity statuses. Minority teens may begin with an *unexamined ethnic identity.* In this stage, as in the foreclosed identity status, adolescents have not gone through a period of exploration or questioning but they have clear feelings about their ethnicity based on outside sources. These sources may convey a positive image, such as an image held by parents; or they may convey a more negative identity, such as stereotypes from the majority culture (Spencer & Dornbusch, 1990). Alternatively, the unexamined stage may be more of an identity diffusion status in which adolescents have not really explored identity issues and have no clear sense of ethnicity. The second stage, *ethnic identity search,* is a period of identity moratorium during which teenagers reexamine their ethnic identities and search for what makes sense to them personally. This questioning process occurs when teens apply their growing cognitive abilities to social experiences—typically, experiences that in some way highlight their ethnicities, such as encounters with people of other ethnicities or personal experiences of prejudice. The *resolution of conflict* stage is comparable to Marcia's achieved identity status. In this stage adolescents come to a resolution regarding their ethnicities that is comfortable and makes sense to them. Developing an ethnic identity is often a long and difficult process, however. It is made more difficult because ethnic minority adolescents often must deal with stress and conflict created by racial discrimination at the same time (Fisher, Wallace, & Fenton, 2000; Verkuyten, 2003).

▲ Adolescents from ethnic minority groups progress through several stages as they develop an ethnic identity.

# Perspective PERSONAL DEVELOPING AN ETHNIC IDENTITY

Angela Watkins
Atlanta, GA
African American professor, author, and parent

**How did your ethnic identity develop?**
I was born during a most promising time for African Americans—the Civil Rights Movement was in full motion, and it was a time of massive social change. My agents of socialization were African Americans in positions of authority, power, and influence. My family members were key players in the Civil Rights Movement. I grew up in Ebenezer Baptist Church in Atlanta, Georgia, the church of world-renowned Civil Rights leader, Reverend Dr. Martin Luther King, Jr. The administrators, teachers, and babysitters that I interacted with in preschool and elementary school were African Americans. Each had a clear sense of ethnicity and an unspoken responsibility to continue the struggle for justice and equality. I remember learning words like "slavery," "Jim Crow," "Ku Klux Klan," "segregation," and "discrimination" early in life. I also remember messages of empowerment that counteracted such evil. Throughout my childhood I observed African American pride and dignity firsthand. Although I was keenly aware of racial differences and the evils of racism, I was also aware of the possibilities of active protest.

My teenage years were more challenging, consumed by a personal struggle for ethnic identity congruence. Others' perceptions of me were critically important. I looked for confirmation of my intelligence, my worth, and my potential for success. I remember many positive and affirming experiences, which buffered me for the more difficult ones of prejudice that I often faced. It was clear that society viewed whites as cleaner, better, and smarter and African Americans as less clean, less intelligent, and of lesser value. Fortunately, the buffers I had, coupled with the excellent models in my immediate and extended family, church, and school, saved me from a life of delusion, depression, and defeat.

Now I am married, with a 6-year-old daughter and a flourishing career. Although I am still reminded of the prestige of whites and the subordination of blacks every morning when I turn on the television, now I am more confident, secure, and proud. I have learned to appreciate the history of our resilience, despite slavery and oppression, and I recognize our brilliance and significant inventions. I reject demeaning messages and seek out inspiration and truth. I share these truths in my courses, my writings, and in daily interactions with family and friends. I actively advocate positive social change and participate in acts of protest. Now my own story of survival empowers me. An added benefit is that as I have learned to embrace my own ethnicity, I have a greater appreciation for other cultures of the world.

**How have you approached teaching your children about their ethnic heritage?**
The task of instilling a healthy sense of ethnic pride in my daughter is a challenging one. At times I wish that I could free her from the evil and the pain. I see her confusion as she notices particular inequalities and tries to understand them. She wants to know why she sees so many white people in magazines, on television, in books, in stores, and in hotels. She ponders the meaning behind her observation of a little white girl who bought a black "Bratz" doll. She has noticed that her skin is light, compared to mine, and wonders if it's okay. I want to give her both the truth of the harsh realities and the richness of our culture. I surround her with symbols of African American culture, black art in our home, a host of books with African American characters and names, black dolls, educational software infused with our cultural flair, black music (spirituals, blues, gospel, and jazz), and greeting cards with African American faces and expressions. I also expose her to lessons of African American history. We watch documentaries that give accurate portrayals of our people. We participate in the Kwanza celebration (a traditional 7-day emphasis on Africentric value systems that occurs around the Christmas holiday season). We attend plays and concerts that highlight the beauty and uniqueness of our culture. We talk a lot. She asks lots of questions and I try to answer them all. I want her to be as equipped as I am to navigate the dominant society and to appreciate the many cultures of the world. I realize that until she develops a love of her own ethnicity, she will not be able to accept and appreciate those who are different. She must learn to be multicultural and to respect diversity. In fact, that is a lesson for us all!

QUESTION **What can parents and community do to help a child develop a positive ethnic identity? What challenges do you think children from ethnic backgrounds face in their development of identity?**

Teens may go about resolving ethnic identity conflicts in a variety of ways, as Table 15.1 indicates. *Acculturation strategies*—the particular strategies a family uses to deal with differences between the customs and beliefs of their ethnic background and the majority culture—affect the development of ethnic identity (Berry, 1993; Phinney, 2003; Saito, 2003). For example, some families emphasize and celebrate their ethnicities as a proud cultural heritage. Such families are likely to encourage their children to learn more about and be proud of their backgrounds. In some cultures, identity development is less a process of individual discovery and more of coming to understand one's role within the family. The further minority adolescents progress through the three stages, the better their levels of psychological adjustment and self-esteem (Phinney, Cantu, & Kurtz 1997). To learn more about how one family has accomplished the task of developing an ethnic identity, read the Personal Perspective box on page 473 called "Developing an Ethnic Identity."

How can Camila's parents help her as she tries to develop her own identity? Are there things they should not do?

THINKING CRITICALLY

In which identity status do you believe you are? Why? If you are from an ethnic background, in what stage of ethnic identity development are you?

Watch Adolescence: Identity and Role Development and Ethnicity. www.mydevelopmentlab.com

Remember that identity is multifaceted; an adolescent may reach commitment in some facets well before others. Culture plays an important role in identity development by suggesting such things as how long it is acceptable to remain in moratorium and what kinds of identities are acceptable to consider (we will discuss culture's influence on identity in more detail later in this chapter). Relationships with parents also affect how adolescents deal with issues of identity. Both younger children and adolescents benefit from parenting that is supportive and accepting, that lets youngsters express themselves, but that also provides reasonable expectations and limits for behavior (Harter, 2006). Contrary to what many people believe, parents continue to be just as important in their children's lives during adolescence as they were during childhood, even as the influence of friends increases (Lamborn & Steinberg, 1993). Watch on **mydevelopmentlab**

## Sexual Orientation

One aspect of self-understanding that becomes prominent during adolescence is sexual orientation. Most children begin experiencing feelings of sexual attraction during late childhood or early adolescence. **Sexual orientation** is the tendency to be attracted to people of the same sex (homosexual orientation), of the opposite sex (heterosexual orientation), or of both sexes (bisexual orientation). Why an individual develops a specific sexual orientation is a matter of great debate, as you are probably well aware. The basic issue is the one we have discussed throughout this text: What are the relative influences of nature (genetics and biology) and nurture (the environment in which a child develops), and how do these two factors interact?

When studying sexual orientation, we need to distinguish between sexual attraction, sexual behavior, and sexual identity (Savin-Williams, 2006). Homosexual *identity* is a sexual identity in which the person is sexually attracted primarily to people of the same sex—the individual identifies him/herself as being homosexual. Homosexuals include *gay males* and *lesbian females*. *Bisexuals* have an attraction to both sexes. Homosexual *behavior*, however, is simply a sexual encounter with someone of the same sex; homosexual *attraction* is a sexual desire directed toward people of the same sex. When experimenting with sexuality, adolescents may have some type of homosexual experience or attraction. These same-sex experiences may be exploratory and not lead to a homosexual orientation in adulthood. In fact, one consistent finding in the research on sexual orientation is that most people who experience same-sex attraction or who engage in same-sex behavior do not have a homosexual identity (Pederson & Kristiansen, 2008; Savin-Williams, 2006; Savin-Williams & Ream, 2007).

**sexual orientation**
Tendency to be attracted to people of the same sex (homosexual orientation), of the opposite sex (heterosexual orientation), or to both sexes (bisexual orientation).

**Development of a Homosexual Identity.** Researchers estimate that 1% to 3% of adults in the United States identify themselves as gay, lesbian, or bisexual (Mosher, Chandra, & Jones, 2005; Savin-Williams, 2006). Some differences between homosexual and heterosexual individuals are apparent during childhood. For example, homosexual men and women report having had cross-gender interests during childhood more often than heterosexuals, and ratings of home videos show higher rates of gender nonconforming behavior and appearance in children who later develop a homosexual orientation (Rieger, Linsenmeier, Gygax, & Bailey, 2008).

Homosexual identity has often been described as developing through several stages, from a realization during childhood of being somehow different from peers, to confusion about sexual identity during adolescence, to eventually adopting a homosexual identity and "coming out" to others (Ruble, Martin, & Berenbaum, 2006; Troiden, 1988). But rather than a single sequence of stages, there may be several developmental pathways of sexual identity development. All involve *identity formation* (exploration and growing awareness of a homosexual orientation, and engaging same-sex activity) and *identity integration* (accepting and becoming committed to a sexual identity). But the sequence of these milestones, the age at which they are achieved, and how long it takes to form and integrate sexual identity probably depend on several factors, including the particular sexual orientation that is developing, gender, past experiences (such as sexual abuse), and social context (such as having supportive social relationships) (Diamond, 2008; Peplau & Huppin, 2008; Rosario, Schrimshaw, & Hunter, 2008; Rosario, Schrimshaw, Hunter, & Levy-Warren, 2009). Stage models may also overemphasize the stability of sexual identity. Particularly for women, there are more *fluid sexual identities* which include categories such as "mostly heterosexual," "mostly homosexual," and "unlabeled" in addition to homosexual, heterosexual, and bisexual. Over a 10-year period, two-thirds of the lesbian and bisexual women in one study changed how they categorize their sexual identity. These findings have led some researchers to argue that sexual identity might be better thought of as a difference in the degree of attraction toward same or opposite sex people, rather than qualitatively distinct and stable orientations (Diamond, 2008; Pederson & Kristiansen, 2008; Thompson & Morgan, 2008).

One of the myths about homosexuality is what researchers call the *heterosexual assumption*—the idea that all adolescents are heterosexual at first and "discover" their homosexuality only after having several failed relationships with members of the opposite sex (Hunter & Mallon, 2000). For most gay people this assumption couldn't be further from the truth. After extensive interviews with gay and bisexual men aged 17 to 23, for example, Savin-Williams (1995) reported that most of the men experienced homosexual sex first. If they tried heterosexual relations at all, they did so later and with much less frequency. On average these gay and bisexual men had their first homosexual experiences at age 14 and their first heterosexual experiences later. Most did not try heterosexual sex until after they graduated from high school. Across their sexual histories the men reported having sex with an average of eight male partners and only one female partner. Most of the men noticed at an early age that they were attracted to the same sex. Some reported having same-sex attractions from their earliest memories; the average was at 8 years old, although a few had their first male attraction as late as age 16. Individuals obviously differ, but it is clear that in most of these men their attraction to other males emerged at an early age and before any attraction they may have had to the opposite sex.

**Causes of Sexual Orientation.** Descriptions of different childhood characteristics of heterosexual and homosexual individuals are interesting and indicate that orientations may begin to develop early in life—but they do not explain *why* children have these characteristics. There may be a genetic influence: Twin studies have found higher concordance in homosexuality in identical than in nonidentical twins (Bailey & Pillard, 1991). Neuroscience studies have identified differences between homosexual and heterosexual men in the corpus callosum, a brain structure believed to be strongly influenced by genetics (Witelson et al., 2008). Prenatal hormone levels may play a role as well. For example, there is a relationship between abnormal prenatal hormone levels and later behavior, personality characteristics, and sexual orientation. Girls exposed to higher than normal prenatal levels of *androgens* (male hormones) tend to show traits and preferences more typical of males, and males exposed to lower than normal levels of androgens show more female-typical patterns and choices (Berenbaum & Snyder, 1995; Meyer-Bahlburg et al., 1995; Meyer-Bahlburg, Dolezal, Baker, & New, 2008; Ruble et al., 2006). Autopsy studies have found that some areas of the brains of homosexual men are more similar to those of heterosexual women than of heterosexual men; remember, however, that differences in brain structure could result from biological factors or from differences in experience (Byrnes, 2001; LeVay, 1993; Swaab, Gooren, & Hofman, 1995). Reinforcement, punishment, and observational learning—all aspects of the environment—also play a role.

One interesting theory tries to integrate the findings on biological and environmental influences (Bem, 1996, 2000, 2008). Called the "exotic becomes erotic" theory, it proposes that children are born with biologically based traits that predispose them to prefer male-typical (more active, rough, and energetic) or female-typical (less active and less aggressive) activities; they are drawn to peers with similar interests and feel similar to them. During childhood, each group will tend to view the other as different ("exotic") and undesirable, and these perceptions will cause arousal. Children interpret this arousal as dislike, discomfort, or sometimes even anger or fear. Puberty then changes things—a lot! At this point youngsters cognitively reinterpret the arousal and gradually come to experience it as attraction ("erotic"). As a result, most adolescents develop sexual attraction toward members of the group they have not identified themselves as belonging to. The key factor is not a child's overall activity level and degree of aggressiveness but how different the child feels from his or her own or opposite-sex peers during childhood.

Some evidence supports the "exotic becomes erotic" idea. Gender segregation during early and middle childhood is very strong, and young children often describe the opposite sex as undesirable and different ("yucky," to use one 6-year-old's word). Homosexual men and women report higher levels of childhood cross-gender play and preferences, as well as feelings of being different from others of their gender (Bailey & Zucker, 1995; Ruble et al., 2006). However, others have suggested that the process may work in the opposite way. That is, rather than behavioral differences leading to feelings of being different from others of the same sex, it may be that feelings of being different lead to progressively more atypical gender behavior and a homosexual self-concept (Carver, Egan, & Perry, 2004; Hammack, 2005; Nicolosi & Byrd, 2002; Ruble et al., 2006). Clearly, the development of sexual identity is complex and more research is needed.

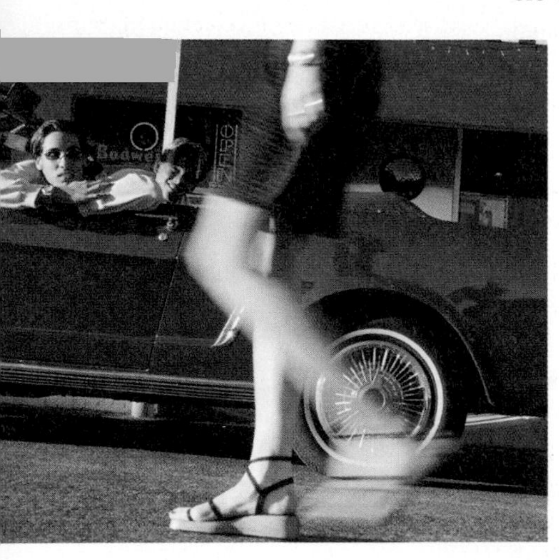

▲ The development of sexual attraction is complex. One theory describes the process as moving from a dislike of those we see as different from ourselves (*exotic*) to thinking of them as sexually attractive (*erotic*).

### The Experience of Being Gay.

Although homosexuality is becoming more widely accepted in today's culture, gay men and lesbians still experience tremendous discrimination and harsh treatment from peers and family. Most homosexuals are keenly aware that heterosexuals view their same-sex attraction as "different" or "deviant." The vast majority of lesbian and gay adolescents report that they feel separated and emotionally isolated from their peers. In one national survey, over 80% were called names or threatened at school, almost half had been pushed or shoved, and one-quarter had been physically assaulted at school (Kosciw, Diaz & Greytak, 2008; Savin-Williams, 1994). Many are victims of violent physical attacks, and you may be surprised to learn that most of these attacks actually come from members of the teenagers' own families (Hunter, 1990; Savin-Williams, 1994). The verbal and physical abuse that many homosexual students receive from peers, parents, and others is harmful to their sense of self-worth and mental health. Compared to their heterosexual peers, homosexual youths are at a much higher risk of failing a grade in school, skipping school, dropping out of school, running away from home, being kicked out of their own homes, and/or engaging in substance abuse and prostitution. Suicide continues to be a major concern—the suicide rate is two to three times higher among homosexual than among heterosexual youths. When gay and lesbian adolescents try to take their own lives, family conflict is the reason cited most often (Bos, Sandfort, de Bruyn, & Hakvoort, 2008; D'Augelli et al., 2005; Eisenberg & Resnick, 2006; Savin-Williams, 1994).

Among gay and lesbian youths who do show positive development, self-acceptance is the best predictor of positive growth (Hershberger & D'Augelli, 1995). A general sense of personal worth and a positive view of their sexual orientation are critical for these adolescents' healthy development. Strong family support is also important: It can provide a buffer against the harsh treatment the adolescent receives at school and elsewhere (Bos et al., 2008; Eisenberg & Resnick, 2006). Many homosexuals report that they find great comfort in having good friends who understand and appreciate their sexual orientations (Bos et al., 2008; Hunter & Mallon, 2000).

THINKING CRITICALLY

Do you know anyone who has a homosexual orientation? What family and friendship supports or challenges has this person experienced, and what effect have these experiences had?

## Morality

Another aspect of self-understanding that adolescents often struggle with is figuring out a set of personal values and morals to guide their behavior. As you might recall from Chapter 9, Lawrence Kohlberg described three levels of moral reasoning (look back at Table 9.1 on page 269 to review Kohlberg's levels). While most adolescents continue to think about moral issues at Kohlberg's earlier levels (preconventional and conventional), some will progress to the third level.

▲ At Stage 6, the highest level of Lawrence Kohlberg's theory of moral reasoning, a person's thinking about moral issues is based on self-chosen abstract ethical principles that apply to all humans. While Mother Teresa clearly achieved Stage 6, few people appear to function consistently at this level.

### Kohlberg's Level III.

The highest level of Kohlberg's theory is the **postconventional level**, at which people move beyond social conventions as the basis for moral reasoning. They no longer obey societal rules without at least questioning them. They understand that others can have opinions that are different from their own, and that different opinions can be equally "right." In Stage 5, they obey rules and laws because this helps protect the rights of individuals. Laws (conventions) can be interpreted and changed for greater fairness, however. In Stage 6, individuals reason about moral issues on the basis of self-chosen, abstract ethical principles that they apply to all humans and social systems. People at this stage may choose to disobey laws they believe are immoral rather than violating their ethical principles. They accept the legal or social consequences of breaking the rules. Adolescents certainly grapple with moral issues and some may achieve the postconventional level, but people usually do not attain this level until adulthood, if ever. Kohlberg emphasized that it is the way a person *reasons* about the issue that determines the level of moral reasoning, not the specific choice the person makes.

### Later Work and Research on Kohlberg's Theory.

Kohlberg revised his theory several times. In later work, he said that some aspects of moral development (the levels of reasoning) are universal, whereas others (the particular moral values developed and choices made) depend on the specific social conditions in which a child develops. Kohlberg also acknowledged that Stage 6 is rare in real life; it may be more of a theoretical endpoint than a stage many people actually achieve. However, he also speculated that there may be a seventh stage that goes past the postconventional level. The seventh stage would represent an "ethical orientation arising from . . . existential or religious experience and thinking rather than from moral experience alone" (Kohlberg & Power, 1981, p. 354).

THINKING CRITICALLY

Think of someone who reasons about moral issues at Kohlberg's Stage 6 or the possible Stage 7. What has helped them develop to these levels? At what level would you place yourself?

Research has supported several aspects of Kohlberg's theory. For example, Figure 15.2 (page 478) shows some of the results of a well-known 20-year longitudinal study of Kohlberg's original sample. Participants showed the expected sequence of stages from Stage 1 up to Stage 5, with no evidence of skipping stages or of falling back to lower stages once they had reached a higher level. The correlation between age and stage of moral development was

**postconventional level**
The level of moral reasoning at which people base moral reasoning on an understanding of social contract and utility and universal ethical principles.

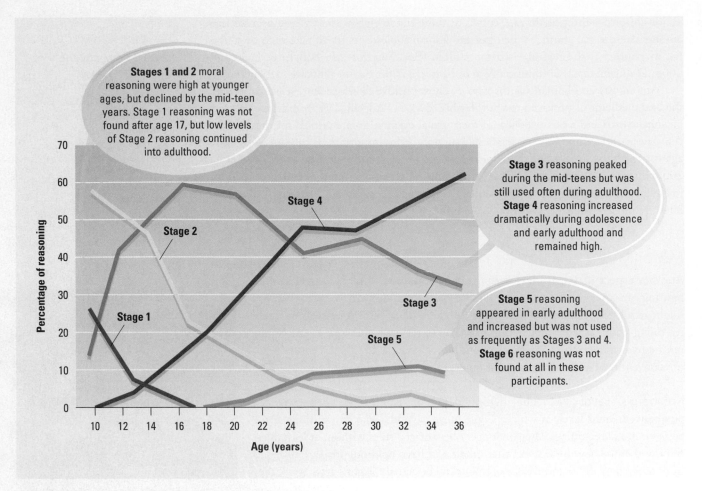

**Stages 1 and 2** moral reasoning were high at younger ages, but declined by the mid-teen years. Stage 1 reasoning was not found after age 17, but low levels of Stage 2 reasoning continued into adulthood.

**Stage 3** reasoning peaked during the mid-teens but was still used often during adulthood. **Stage 4** reasoning increased dramatically during adolescence and early adulthood and remained high.

**Stage 5** reasoning appeared in early adulthood and increased but was not used as frequently as Stages 3 and 4. **Stage 6** reasoning was not found at all in these participants.

Percentage of reasoning

Age (years)

Stage 1

Stage 2

Stage 3

Stage 4

Stage 5

▲ FIGURE 15.2
**Follow-Up Research on Kohlberg's Theory of Moral Development**
A 20-year follow-up of Lawrence Kohlberg's original sample supported the sequence of stages proposed in his developmental theory of moral reasoning. Ages and stages of moral reasoning showed strong correlations. (Adapted from Colby et al., 1983.)

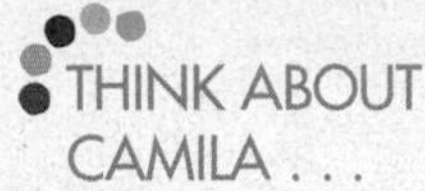

THINK ABOUT CAMILA . . .
Does Camila's ambivalence about a career reflect a higher level of moral reasoning and concern with abstract ethical issues?

THINKING CRITICALLY
Why does one need to be able to think at a formal operational level in order to morally reason at the post-conventional level? Does being able to think at a high level guarantee a high level of reasoning about moral issues?

.78, indicating a strong positive relationship. Other studies have verified the predicted sequences across several different cultures (Boom, Wouters, & Keller, 2007; Colby, Kohlberb, Gibbs, & Lieberman., 1983; Dawson, 2002; Snarey, Reimer, & Kohlber, 1985; Tietjen & Walker, 1985; Walker, 1989). There is also good support for Kohlberg's ideas about the relationship among cognitive development, perspective-taking skill, and moral development (Krebs & Gillmore, 1982; Selman, 1976; Walker & Hennig, 1997).

**Other Moral Orientations and Moral Domains.** Nevertheless, critics have raised important questions about Kohlberg's model. Cross-cultural studies support his sequence of stages, but they have also found that people in less technologically advanced and more rural cultures move through the stages more slowly and achieve a lower end stage than those in more advanced and urban cultures (Snarey, 1995). These findings are not necessarily a problem for Kohlberg's theory; to the degree that different cultures provide different kinds of experience with moral issues, the theory would expect differences (Kohlberg, 1969; Snarey et al., 1985). However, these results could be due to a bigger issue: a fundamental difference between the moral orientation of these cultures and the orientation Kohlberg's theory reflects. Critics argue that Kohlberg's stages are based on a *justice orientation* of morality. That is, in Kolhberg's theory morality involves justice, individual responsibility, and preservation of individual rights. In some cultures, however, justice is not the factor people emphasize when making moral judgments. For example, some cultures emphasize a morality based on *community,* in which social order, status, and duty to others are key. Others emphasize *divinity,* which involves restraint from sinful acts, duty to a God, and the sanctity of people, objects, or places. Others, like Kohlberg's, emphasize *autonomy* and focus on justice, preservation of individual rights, and fairness (Shweder, Much, Mahapatra, & Park, 1997; Turiel, 2006). Kohlberg's theory (and the dilemmas used to test it) reflects an orientation that may not be relevant in other cultures. Therefore, the theory may apply to only a small or unimportant part of moral development in these cultures. If so, then conclusions about the people's levels of moral reasoning or the universality of moral development will be incomplete or even invalid.

A similar criticism has arisen regarding the validity of Kohlberg's model for women. In 1982, Carol Gilligan proposed that women's moral reasoning derives from a *care ethic,* which emphasizes concern for the welfare of others, preservation of interpersonal relationships, and an obligation to take care of others (Gilligan, 1982). Gilligan said that Kohlberg's emphasis on autonomy, justice, and impartial fairness is more consistent with a traditionally male perspective. She argued that Kohlberg's theory does not fully consider

▲ Cultures differ in their moral orientations. Some emphasize community, others divinity, and others autonomy. Kohlberg's stages of moral reasoning may pertain more to some cultures than others.

the elements that are central to women's moral reasoning. Are her criticisms supported by research? No and yes. There is little evidence of systematic gender differences in studies using Kohlberg's materials and stages. That is, when participants offer reasons involving care for others, the materials do not systematically score these reasons as being at a lower level (Jadack, Hyde, Moore, & Keller, 1995; Jaffee & Hyde, 2000; Walker, 1995). However, a care orientation does exist and females are somewhat more likely to use it, especially when reasoning about personal and real-life issues (Garmon, Basinger, Gregg, & Gibbs, 1996; Wark & Krebs, 1996). But it is not the case that males do not use a care orientation. Instead, it appears that both men and women can and do use both care and justice orientations. It's just that the typical moral issues encountered by each gender may lead men to use a justice orientation more often and women to use a care orientation more often (Clopton & Sorell, 1993; Gilligan & Attanucci, 1988).

Other studies have questioned the degree to which moral reasoning is consistent across contexts. For example, when reasoning about real-life moral dilemmas instead of hypothetical ones, people use a lower level of moral reasoning, report having strong emotions as they think about the dilemma, and often suggest several different strategies for addressing the dilemma (Walker & Hennig, 1997; Walker, Pitts, Hennig, & Matsuba, 1995). Moral reasoning also seems to be different for different types of moral issues such as protection of human rights versus matters of individual choice; in other words, moral reasoning is more domain-specific than Kohlberg believed. Finally, Kohlberg's theory does not consider how emotions such as guilt, fear, shame, sympathy, or empathy affect moral reasoning (Krebs & Denton, 2005; Nucci, 1996; Turiel, 2006).

In sum, as with Piaget's theory of cognitive development, it appears that levels of moral reasoning can be influenced significantly by features of the context and are more domain-specific than Kohlberg believed. In addition, as you might have gathered from the discussion so far in this chapter and from Chapters 9 and 12, moral development is multifaceted and includes many aspects of reasoning, emotion, context, and behavior—*reasoning* about what is morally right in a given situation by no means guarantees moral *behavior*.

## LET'S REVIEW . . .

**1.** Andrew has tried three different majors in college. After carefully considering his interests and skills, he believes he has finally found the best major for him. Andrew is probably in which of Marcia's identity statuses?

- **a.** foreclosure
- **b.** moratorium
- **c.** achieved
- **d.** diffusion

**2.** Which of the following best exemplifies the *resolution of conflict* stage of ethnic identity development?

- **a.** Sage is proud to be a Chippewa tribal member, but she's never really thought much about what it means.
- **b.** At times, Choong-youl is unhappy about his culture's emphasis on family, especially when his friends want him to do something that his family disapproves of.
- **c.** Marta is trying to learn more about her ethnic background.
- **d.** LaToya struggled for a while, but she found ways to blend her cultural values and her professional training as a doctor.

**3.** Which of the following quotes from a 10-year-old boy is the best example of Daniel Bem's "exotic becomes erotic" theory of the development of sexual orientation?

- **a.** "Girls really stink."
- **b.** "Boys really stink."
- **c.** "Everybody stinks and they always did."
- **d.** "Girls used to really stink, but they don't seem to stink so much anymore."

**4.** Research on Kohlberg's stages of moral reasoning has found that ____________.

- **a.** the sequence of stages is consistent across many cultures

**b.** the sequence of stages is not valid for cultures that emphasize autonomy and justice.
**c.** the sequence of stages applies only to Western cultures
**d.** the sequence of stages is evident in men but not in women

**5.** True or False: The care ethic proposed by Gilligan is used by women but not by men.

Answers: 1. c, 2. d, 3. d, 4. a, 5. F

# Social Relationships: Family

A second major developmental task that adolescents face is to develop emotional and behavioral **autonomy**, or the ability to be independent in thought and action. Autonomy also involves being able to control impulses and accept responsibility for your own behavior. Developing autonomy can become a source of conflict between teens and parents, especially during early and middle adolescence. As you learned in earlier chapters, parenting style and family structure can have an impact on children's outcomes. In this section, we will discuss the nature and function of conflict during adolescence, as well as research on the characteristics of three family structures we have not yet considered: adoptive, gay or lesbian, and ethnic families.

AS YOU STUDY THIS SECTION, ASK YOURSELF THESE QUESTIONS:

**15.4** Why do adolescents and their parents argue, and how can families cope positively with this conflict?

**15.5** What are the effects of growing up in adoptive, gay/lesbian, and ethnic families, and what developmental challenges does each face?

## Teens Developing Autonomy: Conflict with Parents

**Conflict between Teens and Parents.** G. Stanley Hall, often considered the "father" of the study of adolescent development, strongly believed that adolescence was a time of *storm and stress,* during which frequent and intense levels of teen–parent conflict were to be expected. In fact, the prevailing view for many years was that if there was *not* conflict, then something was wrong. Conflict was seen as an indication that the adolescent was developing a unique identity and becoming emotionally and behaviorally independent. Little conflict meant the adolescent was not trying to separate or parents were not allowing separation to happen. In early research, indeed, it seemed that adolescent–parent relationships were characterized by frequent and rather intense conflict (Laursen & Collins, 1994; Steinberg, 2001).

On closer examination, however, the story seems more complicated—and fortunately more positive. Recent research indicates that stormy and stressful encounters between parents and teens are not the norm. Much of the early research was based on families seeking mental health services. When *nonclinical* samples were studied, 75% of teens reported positive relationships with parents; most who reported poorer relationships had experienced family difficulties well before adolescence (Rutter, Graham, Chadwick, & Yule, 1976). One study interviewed teens about conflicts with their parents on three different randomly selected days. On average, these teens reported conflicts with their parents only about once every three days (Montemayor, 1982). Girls report more conflicts than boys, and both report more conflicts with moms than with dads; they also report spending more time with moms than with dads. As teens get older, the rate of conflict with moms decreases more than the rate with dads (Collins & Laursen, 2004).

THINKING CRITICALLY
How frequent and how intense was the conflict you and your parents experienced? How did your family cope with it, and how might you have dealt with it more positively?

**autonomy**
The ability to be independent in thought and action, control impulses, and accept responsibility for one's behavior.

However, it would be inaccurate to say that there is *no* conflict during this period of development. Adolescents and their parents do disagree, but they typically argue about everyday issues rather than major issues such as educational importance, religious values, sexual activity, or drug use (Gecas & Seff, 1990; Montemayor, 1982). Teens and parents most often argue about things like clothes and music, keeping the teen's bedroom clean enough and doing household chores, curfew and bedtimes, appropriate age for dating, and choice of leisure activities. Whether teens will argue about parents' rules depends on how the teen views the issue involved. For example, teens are more likely to resist their parents' rules when they see the issue as one of a personal choice (such as what clothes to wear or how clean to keep their rooms) than when they believe the issue involves something parents have a right to regulate, as when a moral or safety issue is involved (such as knowing when the teen is expected to be home or whether to drink alcohol). When the expectations of either the teen or the parents are violated, conflict is more likely to occur (Steinberg, 2001).

▲ Many teens recover quickly from arguments with parents but parents see the conflicts as much more meaningful and involving more important issues.

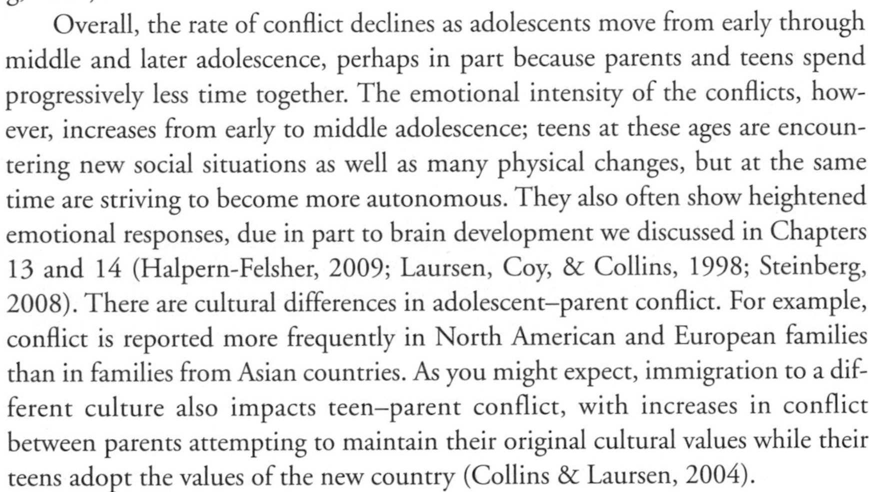

Overall, the rate of conflict declines as adolescents move from early through middle and later adolescence, perhaps in part because parents and teens spend progressively less time together. The emotional intensity of the conflicts, however, increases from early to middle adolescence; teens at these ages are encountering new social situations as well as many physical changes, but at the same time are striving to become more autonomous. They also often show heightened emotional responses, due in part to brain development we discussed in Chapters 13 and 14 (Halpern-Felsher, 2009; Laursen, Coy, & Collins, 1998; Steinberg, 2008). There are cultural differences in adolescent–parent conflict. For example, conflict is reported more frequently in North American and European families than in families from Asian countries. As you might expect, immigration to a different culture also impacts teen–parent conflict, with increases in conflict between parents attempting to maintain their original cultural values while their teens adopt the values of the new country (Collins & Laursen, 2004).

Much of the focus in this area of research has been on what the adolescent experiences. But one author notes that "the popular image of the individual sulking in the wake of a family argument may be a more accurate portrayal of the emotional state of the *parent,* rather than the teenager" (Steinberg, 2001, p. 5). Many teens seem to recover rather quickly from quarrels while parents, especially mothers, see the conflicts as much more meaningful and involving more important issues—so moms tend to be more concerned about disagreements. In addition, many parents of teens are entering middle age and are coping with physical and emotional issues that often arise during this period of life. Finally, parents may have difficulty coping with the fact that their teens no longer view them as positively as they did when the teens were younger. In teens' eyes, parents become astoundingly less capable and less intelligent—and teens are not very skilled at hiding their change of opinion from their parents (Steinberg, 2001).

**Dealing Effectively with Adolescent–Parent Conflict.** So if some conflict is inevitable, how should parents deal with it? The first thing to remember is that even though conflict is not a pleasant thing, it can have some positive effects such as improved reasoning and conflict resolution skills, increased understanding of others' perspectives, and enhanced identity development. In fact, adolescents who experience moderate levels of conflict with their parents perform better in school and have fewer overall adjustment difficulties than *either* those who report higher levels of conflict or no conflict at all (Adams & Laursen, 2001; Collins & Laursen, 2004; Kaplan, 2004). Second, just because teenagers argue with their parents from time to time does not mean they do not have a close relationship overall. Indeed, in families with healthy and secure attachment between parents and teens, conflict serves the positive function of helping the family talk about issues that need attention, revise expectations, and renegotiate rules to allow increasing autonomy to the teen within appropriately changing boundaries. This type of interaction can have the effect of actually improving the overall relationship (Collins & Laursen, 2004).

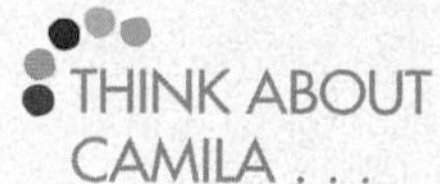

THINK ABOUT CAMILA . . .

Does the conflict between Camila and her parents seem atypical in any way? How can they deal with it constructively?

A key in effectively handling conflict and achieving positive and productive outcomes is something you read about in Chapter 9—*authoritative parenting*. As you might recall, this parenting style involves developmentally appropriate expectations and firm, consistent limits within the context of warmth, involvement, and supportiveness. During adolescence, a third dimension also seems to become important: **psychological autonomy granting**, or encouraging adolescents to develop their own individual opinions and beliefs (Steinberg, 2001). This style of parenting is associated with a number of positive social, cognitive, and behavioral outcomes as well as positive identity development. The effects have been found for both males and females and across a number of ethnic groups (Collins & Laursen, 2004; Steinberg, 2001). It does not operate in isolation, however. One longitudinal study found that better "quality" conflict (less negative, more positive interactions) resulted from better quality parenting in interaction with aspects of the child's disposition—less negative emotion, more self-control, and greater resilience (ability to bounce back after stressful or negative events) (Eisenberg et al., 2008). Unfortunately, most parent–teen conflicts are resolved by submission (one party giving in) or disengagement (the topic is dropped and one party leaves the conflict) instead of through compromise (Laursen & Collins, 1994). Developing a more authoritative parenting style might help families deal more constructively with conflict as their teens strive for autonomy.

## Family Structures

**Adopted Adolescents.** Millions of adolescents grow up in adoptive families, whether adopted by relatives, stepparents, nonrelated adults, or adults of a different country or ethnicity. Adopted individuals do much better on many psychological, educational, social, and emotional measures than those in residential institutions, long-term foster care, or returned from foster care to parents who are unable or unwilling to parent effectively (Morgan, 1998; Triseliotis & Hill, 1990). Greater financial resources and stability, higher-quality parenting, highly motivated parents, significant parental emotional involvement and support, and a clear long-term parental commitment help adopted adolescents develop a stronger sense of identity and enable them to take advantage of available financial and community resources. Children in transracial adoptions, in which parents of one racial group adopt a child of a different race, are the same as children adopted by same-race parents in terms of racial self-identity, general adjustment, or self-esteem (Baden, 2002; Feigelman, 2000; Silverman & Feigelman, 1990; Vroegh, 1997).

▲ Most adopted individuals adjust well and function normally, even though they do face some challenges. What potential issues might this child and her adoptive parents need to cope with?

Most adopted individuals adjust well and function normally. However, they do face special challenges and are at greater risk for negative outcomes than biological offspring, particularly when the problems become more severe (Miller, Fan, Christensen, Grotevant, & van Dulmen, 2000). Adopted children and adolescents are more likely than others to be referred for psychological treatment and more likely to show aggressive and delinquent behavior, learning disabilities, drug use, and school adjustment problems. In general, adopted children have greater difficulty when they are older (e.g., over 5 years of age) at the time of adoption, perhaps more because of negative early experiences than because of adoption. Adopted boys seem to have more difficulty than adopted girls. Sometimes problems do not emerge during infancy or early childhood but seem to emerge as children move through middle childhood and adolescence. However, adopted children show better scores on measures such as participation in academic clubs, prosocial behavior, self-reports of social problems, and self-reported withdrawal. The majority of adopted individuals report being satisfied with their adoptive status and report feeling

**psychological autonomy granting**
A dimension of parenting that involves encouraging adolescents to develop their own individual opinions and beliefs.

emotionally attached to their adoptive parents (Brodzinsky, 1990, 1993; Howe, 1998; Kirschner, 1995; Miller et al., 2000; Morgan, 1998; Sharma, McGue, & Benson, 1996, 1998; Stams, Juffer, Rispens, & Hoksbergen, 2000; Triseliotis, 2000).

**Families with Lesbian or Gay Parents.** Researchers estimate that anywhere from 1 to 14 million children and adolescents in the United States have lesbian or gay parents (Cooper & Cates, 2006; Patterson, 1992). The majority were born while their biological parents were in heterosexual marriages. An increasing number of lesbians, however, are using donor insemination to conceive biological children or are adopting or providing foster care for children. More gay men are also adopting children, providing foster care, or fathering their own biological children. Does exposure to a gay or lesbian lifestyle disrupt the adolescent's developing sense of identity or cause any other negative developmental outcomes? Charlotte Patterson (1992, 2006) conducted thorough reviews of the research and concluded that "more than two decades of research has failed to reveal important differences in the adjustment or development of children or adolescents reared by same-sex couples compared to those reared by other-sex couples" (2006, p. 241). Those with lesbian parents are well adjusted and show positive relationships with their parents. They are no different from children raised by heterosexual parents in activity preferences, interests, popularity, social skills, occupational goals, sociability, hyperactivity, emotional difficulty, behavior problems, moral maturity, or measures of intelligence (Bos, van Balen, & van den Boom, 2005; Golombok et al., 2003; MacCallum & Golombok, 2004).

In her review, Patterson found that children and adolescents raised by lesbian or gay parents showed no disturbances in gender identity. Compared to those raised by heterosexual parents, they were just as happy with the gender to which they belonged and had no wish to be the opposite sex. Sexual orientation also did not differ. Children raised by gay or lesbian parents were not more likely to become homosexuals themselves. This finding is particularly interesting in view of the fact that these adolescents received significant portions of their genes from gay or lesbian parents and grew up in environments created in part by those same parents.

Finally, courts vary a great deal in custody and adoption rulings involving gay parents. Some award child custody on the condition that the homosexual parent *not* live with his or her romantic partner—even though the research evidence actually shows advantages for children whose gay or lesbian parents live with committed partners (Patterson, 1992, 2006). One study documented higher self-esteem in daughters of lesbian mothers living with partners than in girls whose lesbian mothers lived alone (Huggins, 1989). Mothers in lesbian partnerships are more likely to arrange male role models for their children. Lesbian couples who conceived children by donor insemination showed as much awareness of parenting skills as heterosexual mothers and more awareness than heterosexual fathers, and both lesbian partners were equally involved in the child's activities (Flaks, Ficher, Masterpasqua, & Joseph, 1995; MacCallum & Golombok, 2004; Vanfraussen, Ponjaert-Kristoffersen, & Brewaeys, 2003). In short, it is evident that lesbian and gay parents can and do provide healthy living environments for children.

**Ethnically Diverse Families.** Ethnic minority families are the fastest growing segment of the U.S. population, as shown in Table 15.2. In earlier decades most of the research on family ethnicity focused on negative factors and outcomes. As you are no doubt aware, the rates of poverty, crime, homicide, incarceration, and other such problems are higher among minority groups than among White European Americans. Researchers compared ethnically diverse families to White families and emphasized things that were "going wrong" in minority-group families. This **cultural deficit perspective** assumed negative outcomes were due to ways in which minority families were not "measuring up" to the majority population.

**cultural deficit perspective**
Research perspective that assumed the problems associated with minority group families were due to the ways these families were not "measuring up" to the standards of majority White families.

**TABLE 15.2**
Growth in U.S. Ethnic Diversity 1990–2007 (Figures in Millions)

| RACE OR LATINO ORIGIN | 1990 | 2000 | 2007 | PERCENT INCREASE FROM 1990 | GROWTH RATE VS. WHITE GROWTH RATE |
|---|---|---|---|---|---|
| Whites (non-Latino)* | 188.9 | 194.6 | 198.6 | 5 | — |
| Latinos (of any race)* | 22.4 | 35.3 | 45.4 | 103 | 20.6 times faster |
| African Americans | 30.4 | 34.7 | 37.3 | 24 | 4.8 times faster |
| Asian Americans and Pacific Islanders | 7.3 | 10.6 | 13.7 | 88 | 17.6 times faster |
| Native Americans and Alaskans | 2.0 | 2.5 | 2.4 | 20 | 4.0 times faster |
| Other races | 9.8 | 15.4 | 18.7 | 91 | 18.2 times faster |
| More than one race | NA | 6.8 | 6.5 | −.04 | — |

*The total U.S. population in the year 2007 was 301.6 million. The U.S. Census considers race separately from Latino origin. In the 2000 Census, 48% of Latinos identified themselves as White. In this table we present the number of Whites who did not identify themselves as Latino (estimated for 1990 and 2000 by subtracting 48% of the Latinos totals from the 1990 and 2000 census total for Whites). The 2000 Census was the first to allow respondents to identify themselves as belonging to more than one race (e.g., White *and* Asian).

(U.S. Census Bureau, 2009).

Recently, however, researchers have learned that many of the negative outcomes associated with minority families are due more to poverty and difficulties in the neighborhoods that many minority families live in than to ethnic culture itself (Caspi, Taylor, Moffitt, & Plomin, 2000; Leventhal & Brooks-Gunn, 2000; McLoyd, 1998; Pinderhughes, Dodge, Bates, Pettit, & Zelli, 2000). A more positive approach to looking at minority families, the **strength and resilience perspective**, has emerged (Parke & Buriel, 2006). Researchers are now exploring ways in which minority families have survived in spite of historical patterns of racism, bigotry, and inequality.

What characteristics of ethnic families have contributed to their strength and resilience? Table 15.3 on page 486 summarizes some of the characteristics of several ethnic groups identified by researchers. One important factor seems to be the central role that the family often plays, particularly the extended family. For example, Latino parents teach children that their personal identity is inseparable from the larger identity of the family (*la familia*). In many ethnic groups, people value family and group cooperation over competition and personal achievement. Researchers have noted that African American families tend to show a strong sense of family and family obligation, fluid household boundaries (and great willingness to have relatives move into and out of the household), frequent interaction with relatives, frequent extended-family gatherings for holidays and special occasions, and a strong system of mutual aid and support among family members (Hatchett & Jackson, 1999; Parke & Buriel, 2006). Asian American families teach their children to be obedient and loyal to their parents and to place the family above individual needs. Extended-family systems have also been crucial in helping Native Americans cope with the discrimination and many forms of adversity they have faced. Even when living in urban areas, Native Americans often organize around several households of relatives that operate like a communal village (Parke & Buriel, 2006).

Think about a family you know that fosters strength and resilience in their teens. What parenting practices do they use? How do these practices help their children become more resilient?

**strength and resilience perspective**
Research perspective that explores ways that minority families have survived in spite of historical patterns of racism, bigotry, and inequality.

**TABLE 15.3**
**Sources of Ethnic Groups' Strength and Resilience**

| ETHNIC GROUP | REFERS TO | FAMILY FACTORS | CULTURAL TRADITIONS |
|---|---|---|---|
| Latino | Primarily immigrants from Mexico, Central and South America, Puerto Rico, Cuba, and descendants of Spanish explorers | Personal identity connected to family identity<br>Emphasis on extended-family systems<br>First few years following immigration often spent living with extended-family members | Cooperation<br>Group harmony<br>Respect<br>Obedience and respect for elders<br>Traditional gender roles |
| African American | Primarily descendants of slaves originally from West African tribes | Emphasis on extended-family systems<br>Strong sense of family and family obligation<br>Frequent interactions with relatives<br>Grandmothers play important role in moral and religious focus, provide sense of family solidarity<br>Emphasis on strict discipline, especially among working-class and poor families | West African traditions of spirituality, harmony, and communalism<br>Emphasis on ethnic pride |
| Asian American | Immigrants from 28 countries or ethnic groups from Far East and Southeast Asia, including India, China, Philippines, Vietnam, Cambodia, Laos, Japan, Korea, Pakistan, Thailand, Hmong | Father dominant but emotionally distant<br>Emphasis on *chiao shun* and *guan* styles of strict discipline among some groups | Religious traditions of respect for elders and family harmony<br>Obedience and loyalty to parents<br>Family needs placed above individual needs<br>Traditional gender roles |
| Native American and Alaskan | Numerous peoples including 450 different tribal units with more than 100 different languages, among them Cherokee, Navajo, Chippewa, Sioux, Pueblos, Aleuts, Eskimos | Emphasis on extended-family systems, communal village structure<br>Grandparents play important official and symbolic role<br>Prior government policies disrupted family structure, producing lack of cultural and family role models | Cooperation<br>Partnership<br>Respect for elders<br>Increasing emphasis on ethnic pride |

(Boykin & Toms, 1985; Chao, 1994; Parke & Buriel, 2006; Reed, 1982; Trimble & Medicine, 1993.)

▲ Asian American parents tend to be strict, but they are generally caring and loving rather than harsh and punitive. Their *chiao shun* and *guan* styles are linked to superior school performance in their children.

An emphasis on strict discipline is also characteristic of many ethnic groups. Both working-class African American parents and Latino families tend to rely on physical punishment, power assertion, and obedience in their efforts to control their children (Parke & Buriel, 2006). However, this approach to discipline correlates more with poverty and dangerous neighborhoods than with ethnicity—lower-income Whites also tend to use strict authoritarian discipline, while middle-class African American parents tend to use a more authoritative approach. Lower-income parents may use physical discipline to try to protect their children in dangerous communities and as a way to emphasize the importance of performing well in school (Kelley, Sanchez-Hucles, & Walker, 1993; Parke & Buriel, 2006).

Mothers in China are more restrictive and controlling than Euro-American mothers (Chiu, 1987). As Chinese Americans adapt to life in the United States, they tend to take on parenting styles that lie between these two extremes. In her cross-cultural studies, Chao (1994, 2001) has pointed out that the strict control used by Chinese parents is not the same as the harsh and punitive style used by authoritarian parents in the United States. Chinese parents practice the concepts of *chiao shun* (meaning "training" or "teaching") and *guan* ("to govern" or "to care for or love"). They model appropriate behaviors for their children, and they govern their children firmly but with great care and love. Whereas harsh and punitive parenting (the authoritarian style) correlates with poor school performance in Euro-American students, children raised in the strict *chiao shun* and *guan* style used by many Asian American parents show superior school performance (Chao, 1994; Dornbusch, Ritter, Leiderman, Roberts, & Fraleigh, 1987). This type of cross-cultural research reminds us that we cannot always view other cultures through the same lenses that we develop using Euro-American research samples.

A sense of ethnic pride can help buffer some of the hardships that ethnic children often face. Many African American families foster ethnic pride in their children as a way to help them confront the discrimination they will face in U.S. society (Parke & Buriel, 2006). In a national study of African American families, the children who were eventually more successful and upwardly mobile were the ones whose parents had emphasized ethnic pride, the importance of self-development, and an awareness of the racial barriers that they would face (Bowman & Howard, 1985). Similarly, Native Americans are increasingly working to build ethnic pride in their children, both to reconnect with the traditions of their cultures and to support their children's development. We all benefit by recognizing the unique strengths demonstrated by cultures and ethnic groups other than our own.

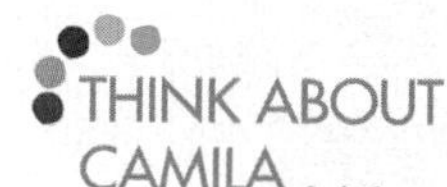

THINK ABOUT CAMILA . . .

What parenting practices might Camila's parents try to help their daughter develop resilience? How might these practices differ if this family were of a different ethnic background?

**LET'S REVIEW . . .**

1. It is normal for adolescent–parent conflict to ______________.
   - **a.** be frequent and intense
   - **b.** decline in frequency and emotional intensity from early to middle to later adolescence
   - **c.** be more upsetting for moms than for adolescents
   - **d.** occur more often over moral and safety issues than over issues of personal choice
2. Which of the following is *not* true of adopted children?
   - **a.** Most adopted children adjust well and are emotionally attached to their adoptive parents.
   - **b.** Adopted children are at greater risk than nonadopted children for many negative outcomes.
   - **c.** Children who were older when adopted are at greater risk for poorer outcomes than those adopted at a younger age.
   - **d.** Transracial adoptees have more difficulty with identity development than adoptees with same-race parents.
3. The cultural deficit perspective on ethnic families tends to focus on which of the following?
   - **a.** negative outcomes experienced by ethnic families
   - **b.** ways in which ethnic families have survived and succeeded
   - **c.** the role of the extended family in ethnic families
   - **d.** differences in parenting styles between ethnic and nonethnic families
4. True or False: Regardless of cultural background, strict parenting styles are associated with poor school performance in children.
5. True or False: Children raised by gay or lesbian parents are no more likely to be homosexuals themselves than are children raised by heterosexual parents.

Answers: 1. c, 2. d, 3. a, 4. F, 5. T

# Social Relationships: Peers

A third important developmental task for adolescents is to develop **intimacy**, both within the context of friendships and in romantic relationships. Intimacy is an emotional attachment to another person and involves sharing important personal information and trusting one another to hold confidences and be supportive. Earlier, we described the development of sexual orientation, but how do adolescents learn the skills needed to make and maintain intimate relationships? What impact do peers have on teens' behavior? And when are

**intimacy**
An emotional attachment to another person that involves sharing important personal information and trusting others to hold confidences and be supportive.

adolescents ready to move from nonromantic friendship groups to dating in couples? In this section, we will discuss the nature of friendships and dating during the teenage years.

AS YOU STUDY THIS SECTION, ASK YOURSELF THESE QUESTIONS:

**15.6** Why are friendships important during adolescence?

**15.7** What are cliques and crowds, and how do they affect adolescents' development?

**15.8** What influence does peer pressure have on adolescent behavior?

**15.9** How do adolescents spend their leisure time?

## Friends and Peers in Adolescence

Intimate friends share their most personal thoughts and feelings. They trust each other to keep personal secrets, and they use each other as a safe base for exploring issues and problems that they may not discuss with anyone else, including parents, teachers, and close siblings. During adolescence, intimacy and self-disclosure distinguish best friends from other friends. Intimacy emerges in early adolescence for girls but only in later adolescence for most boys (Berndt, 1986). Adolescents spend twice as much time with their friends (outside of the classroom) as with their parents, siblings, and other adults (Csikszentmihalyi & Larson, 1984). As Savin-Williams and Berndt (1990) put it:

> Adolescents typically report that they enjoy their activities with friends more than any other. With friends, they feel that they are understood and can fully be themselves. Friends spend much time together simply talking about themselves, other adolescents, or events in the wider world. They relax, joke, watch television or videos, and participate in sports. These moments of enjoyment and companionship contribute to a generational sense of belonging with others who are respected and liked. (p. 279)

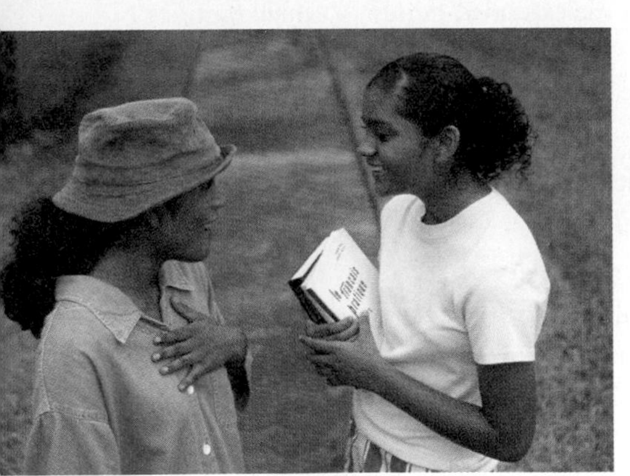

▲ Beginning in adolescence, our closest friends are the people we can trust and with whom we share our personal thoughts and feelings. A shared sense of intimacy bonds best friends together.

In their review of the research literature on adolescent friendships and peer relations, Savin-Williams and Berndt (1990) found that adolescents who have close and supportive friendships tend to have higher self-esteem, to understand other people's feelings better, and to be more generally popular among their peers. In school they are better behaved, receive higher grades, and score higher on tests of intelligence. Adolescents who do not have close friendships don't fare as well (Rubin, Bukowski, & Parker, 2006). Keep in mind, however, that these findings are correlational. In other words, we don't know the direction of the causal link between friendships and adolescent development. Do close and supportive friendships facilitate social and academic growth, or do adolescents who are more socially and academically skilled attract more close friends?

How do teens develop the skills needed to start and maintain intimate friendships and, later, romantic relationships? One view is based on the attachment research that you read about in Chapter 6. According to Alan Sroufe and his colleagues, children internalize the significant relationships they have early in life and use those early experiences as a basis for understanding what it means to have an intimate relationship (Hazan & Shaver, 1987; Roisman, Collins, & Sroufe, 2005; Sroufe, Egeland, & Carlson, 2005). A different view emphasizes the role of peers more strongly. Harry Stack Sullivan (1953) says that youngsters develop *chumships,* or close nonromantic relationships, over the course of late childhood and early adolescence. It is within these chumships that teens learn the skills needed to have successful intimacy such as loyalty, trustworthiness, honesty, and supportiveness. After these skills are developed to some degree, teens begin to shift the focus of their intimacy to romantic relationships. The chumships allow young teens to "practice" intimacy without the added element of romantic attraction. Perhaps attachment relations in early childhood set the stage for the development of intimacy and serve as a foundation for early nonromantic relationships, and chumships both modify teens' understanding of intimacy and help them develop specific relationship skills.

When it comes to forming friendships, similarity is still the rule in adolescence. Adolescents who become close friends tend to share similar attitudes; educational aspirations; religious and political orientations; and patterns of drinking, drug use, and delinquency (Rubin et al., 2006; Savin-Williams & Berndt, 1990). As we mentioned earlier, shared intimacy is an important feature of adolescent friendships. Strong bonds form when intimate friends share personal stories and help one another cope with problems. Although it can be difficult to maintain friendships as adolescents move through the transitions from middle school to high school and later into college or work, many lifelong friends trace their relationships back to their adolescent years.

THINK ABOUT CAMILA . . .

In what ways have Camila's family and friends helped her develop the skills she needs to develop intimate friendships?

## Cliques and Crowds

Another aspect of adolescent peer relations is the emergence of *cliques* and *crowds*. **Cliques** are small groups, usually including three to nine friends, who hang out together on a voluntary basis (Rubin et al., 2006). Friends in cliques are almost always of the same sex and race. By the age of 11, most children report being a member of a clique, and this social group forms the context for most of their peer interactions (Crockett, Losoff, & Petersen, 1984). Most cliques are closed circles—members often put down or exclude people outside their clique, even though they understand that excluding peers is sometimes wrong and harmful (Horn, 2003). Between ages 11 and 18, however, bonds within individual cliques loosen and adolescents begin associating simultaneously with several loosely defined cliques (Rubin et al., 2006).

**Crowds** are larger groups made up of individuals who have similar reputations or share primary attitudes or activities (Brown, 2004). When asked to describe the different groups of students that make up their schools, teenagers typically identify crowds such as *jocks, brains, nerds, druggies, goths, populars, normals, nobodies,* and *loners.* Specific names for crowds vary across geographic locations and schools, but they tend to fall into these general categories.

Individual students usually can't pick their favorite crowd to join. Instead, they acquire crowd "membership" based on stereotyped perceptions held across the school population. Your crowd designation has to do mostly with what other people think about you and who they think you are like. In one study researchers asked students to guess which crowd their peers had assigned them to. Although 75% of the "jocks" and "druggies" correctly guessed their crowd assignment, only 15% of the "nobodies" and "loners" were accurate (Brown, Clasen, & Niess, 1987). In many schools, students see members of ethnic minority groups as separate crowds—the Hispanic crowd, the African American crowd, and so on (Brown & Klute, 2003). Perhaps because of the prejudice and discrimination they experience, ethnic minority students may feel more comfortable associating with other members of their racial or ethnic group. In other cases, perhaps ethnic groups are segregated because of cultural differences in behavior, dress, religion, or other characteristics.

THINKING CRITICALLY

Describe the different "crowds" that you recall from your high school. Which crowd did you fit best with? What effect did your crowd have on your identity?

Research has shown a link between self-esteem and membership in particular crowds. In one midwestern community, students in junior and senior high schools rank-ordered five crowds that they identified in their schools (Brown & Lohr, 1987). Most admired were the *jocks,* followed (in order) by *populars, normals, druggies/toughs,* and *nobodies.* Not surprisingly, self-esteem scores were highest among students who were jocks and populars, moderate among normals and druggies/toughs, and lowest for nobodies. For outsiders (students who were not associated with any of the crowds), self-esteem depended on how much they cared about being in a crowd. Self-esteem was relatively high among outsiders

**cliques**
Small groups, of usually three to nine friends, who spend time together on a voluntary basis.

**crowds**
Groups of adolescent peers who have similar reputations or share primary attitudes or activities.

who gave little importance to crowd membership, but it was low among students who wanted to—but didn't—belong to a crowd.

Just as clique memberships loosen by mid-adolescence, crowd affiliations begin to soften by the end of high school. Researchers have commented on the cohesiveness that often develops among high school seniors (Rubin et al., 2006). Differences and animosities seem to fade a bit as members of the different crowds reflect back on their years together and look ahead to what awaits them after they leave school. **Watch** on **mydevelopmentlab**

**Watch** a video on Adolescence: Social Changes. www.mydevelopmentlab.com

▲ In early adolescence, members of the same larger crowd begin pairing off and dating. Cross-sex intimacy (the ability to share personal thoughts and feelings with a member of the opposite sex) typically develops faster in girls than in boys.

**From Gender Segregation to Dating.** Although most cliques form among same-sex peers in early adolescence, many relationships do form across the sexes by middle adolescence. The classic study of the transition from gender segregation to dating is a naturalistic field study that Dexter Dunphy (1963) performed in Sydney, Australia. Dunphy observed that young adolescents (around age 13) congregated in same-sex cliques containing between three and nine close friends. Then group-to-group interactions began to occur between male and female cliques. As you probably recall from your own adolescence, these interactions often begin as teasing and chasing. Eventually, however, they evolve into relationships that are more cooperative. In Dunphy's study the cross-sex interactions occurred almost exclusively between cliques in the same larger crowd (between male jocks and female jocks, for example), so the cross-sex relationships were among adolescents who had similar attitudes, values, and economic status. When asked to choose partners in social situations, adolescents picked members of their own clique most often. They chose other members of their crowd (not in their clique) less frequently. Only rarely (6% of the time) did they select partners outside their crowds. In the next phase, the higher-status members of each clique began heterosexual dating. Gradually, the boundaries between cliques dissolved as more members began dating. Now the most recognizable social unit was the crowd, in which some members were dating and some were not. By late adolescence (ages 18 to 21), Dunphy reported, crowd boundaries also began to dissolve as more couples paired off for dating. This pattern echoes the trends we described earlier, with clique boundaries softening earlier in adolescence and crowds blending by high school graduation. **Watch** on **mydevelopmentlab**

**Watch** a video on Peer Groups in Adolescence. www.mydevelopmentlab.com

## Peer Pressure, Delinquent Behavior, and Aggression

Conformity to peer pressure is highest during early adolescence, peaking around age 14. Parents often worry that peers will influence their teens to do things they shouldn't, like drink alcohol or use drugs. After all, as you learned in Chapter 13, the best predictor of drug and alcohol use is having friends who do these things. Another concern is that some adolescent crowds can put pressure on peers to engage in violence or aggression (Espelage, Holt, & Henkel, 2003). One report from the U.S. surgeon general indicated that having antisocial or delinquent peers was one of the strongest risk factors for adolescent violence (U.S. Department of Health and Human Services, 2001). But is peer pressure to blame for delinquent behavior? Involvement in delinquent activity is relatively common during adolescence (especially for boys), and most delinquent acts such as stealing or trespassing are committed by middle adolescent boys in groups. Further, boys who are more autonomous compared to their peers are less likely to engage in delinquent acts—so it seems that peer pressure does play a role.

THINKING CRITICALLY

What are examples of both positive and negative peer pressure you experienced during adolescence?

Fortunately, most adolescents who begin delinquent behavior during adolescence do not continue it. Some, however, show a **life-course persistent pattern** in which they engage in antisocial and delinquent behavior from childhood and continuing into adulthood (Moffitt, 1993). Peer pressure is not the main factor for these adolescents' behavior. They have several things working against them from an early age, including a difficult temperament, subtle cognitive deficits, poor impulse control, poor parenting, high-conflict

**life-course persistent pattern** A pattern of antisocial and delinquent behavior that begins in childhood and continues into adulthood.

home environments (such as the coercive homes you read about in Chapter 12), and dangerous neighborhoods. This combination leads to academic and behavior problems. At greatest risk are adolescents who are aggressive and also unpopular. These teens tend to be rejected by nonaggressive peers, so they often seek the company of other aggressive and rejected adolescents, and sometimes form groups that further encourage violence and aggression. Most studies of delinquent and aggressive behavior focus on boys; the few that examine girls' delinquent behavior find similar factors to be involved (Carroll et al., 2006; Dodge, Coie, & Lynam, 2006; Farrington, 2004; Moffitt, Caspi, Dickson, Silva, & Stanton, 1996). Juvenile delinquency is a difficult problem with no easy answers. The number of juveniles, particularly girls, entering the justice system has increased significantly over the past decade. To learn more about how the justice system helps youths, see the Professional Perspective box called "Career Focus: Meet a Juvenile Probation Officer."
**Listen** on **mydevelopmentlab**

The good news about peer pressure is that, for most adolescents, the strongest pressures actually tend to be positive. Adolescents claim that the greatest peer pressures they experience are to get along with others, get good grades, graduate from high school, and

**Listen**: How can parents, schools, and communities help prevent a child from developing a life-course persistent pattern of antisocial behavior? (Author Podcast) www.mydevelopmentlab.com

## Perspective PROFESSIONAL — CAREER FOCUS: MEET A JUVENILE PROBATION OFFICER

Nancy Magowan
Philadelphia, PA
Juvenile probation officer in the Family Division of the Common Pleas Court, Special Offender Unit

**What are the most common offenses that youths supervised by the Special Offender Unit commit?**
The Special Offender Unit supervises juveniles who are placed in a residential treatment facility for mental therapy and treatment. The offenses include assault, theft, robbery, auto theft, burglary, controlled substance offenses, criminal conspiracy, and sexual offenses such as rape, indecent assault, indecent exposure, and involuntary deviate sexual intercourse.

**What do juvenile probation officers do to help youths avoid future offenses?**
Once the juvenile completes treatment and is recommended for discharge from the facility, we develop a Probation Supervision Plan. The plan holds the youth accountable for his/her actions, offers some restoration to the victim, protects the community, and develops the youth's competencies. I monitor the youth's progress and success. I often connect the youth with community-based support programs that provide educational or vocational schooling, substance abuse treatment, individual or family therapy, and employment services. We customize the plans to meet the needs of each youth.

**What do you think is the most important thing that can be done to prevent behavior problems, violence, and crime among youths?**
Preventing youth from entering the juvenile justice system is an ongoing and difficult task. The breakdown of the family seems to affect so many. Family support, guidance, and encouragement are key in a youth's ability to develop positive and appropriate social skills and self-esteem to adjust to the challenges of adolescence and life. Communication among parents, schools, and support programs is essential to maintain continuity and encouragement for the young people in our society in their efforts to succeed. Empowering youth with education and emphasizing their strengths will help reduce the juvenile crime rate.

**What education and training is needed to work in your occupation?**
After I got my bachelor's degree in Administration of Justice from Penn State University and did an internship at the court where I work now, most of my training was on the job. Additional training and education (40-plus hours) is provided and required by the courts on a yearly basis. My only regret regarding education is not being bilingual.

QUESTION **What delinquent behavior should families watch for that might indicate the beginnings of delinquent behaviors? What can parents and communities do to prevent delinquent behaviors and encourage adolescents to focus on positive activities?**

attend college (Brown, 1990). While some students do commit delinquent acts and behave aggressively, many do not. And adolescents are just as concerned by aggressiveness in their peers as adults are—after all, they are the most frequent victims of delinquent and aggressive behavior (Dodge et al., 2006). Since the tragic school shootings at Columbine High School in Colorado and other places across the country, communities and schools have struggled to confront the issue of aggression and school safety. All agree that something must be done, but there is no consensus on what steps to take. For more information about this issue, read the Social Policy Perspective box called "How Should We Deal with Aggressive Students?" **Watch** on **mydevelopmentlab**

**Watch** Students Discuss Columbine.
www.mydevelopmentlab.com

## Perspective SOCIAL POLICY — HOW SHOULD WE DEAL WITH AGGRESSIVE STUDENTS?

**BURLINGTON, WISCONSIN** (November 1998). Five teens were arrested and expelled after their plans to kill school staff and 12 children were reported to police. The boys confessed; three received probation and two were ordered to undergo psychiatric treatment (Kertscher, 1999; Kertscher, Spice, Johnson, Krantz, & Ortiz, 1998). A similar incident, thwarted by a friend who contacted police, occurred in Green Bay, Wisconsin (Phelps, 2006).

**LITTLETON, COLORADO** (April 1999). Eric Harris and Dylan Klebold entered Columbine High School carrying two shotguns, a rifle, a pistol, and numerous bombs. They killed 12 students and one teacher, and seriously wounded about 23 others before killing themselves (Luzadder & Vaughan, 1999).

**CASENOVIA, WISCONSIN** (September 2006). Weston Schools principal John Klang was shot and killed by Eric Hainstock, a 15-year-old ninth grader at the school. Hainstock was reportedly upset over being teased by classmates, as well as for being reprimanded for behavior problems and having tobacco in school ("Principal Killed . . .", 2006).

**BEDFORD, TEXAS** (March 2002). A high school junior was expelled from school after a guard found a 10-inch bread knife in the bed of his truck. The student says the knife fell from a box of his grandmother's belongings that he was taking to a thrift shop ("High School Expels Junior," 2002).

Reports like these have become all too common over the last decade; violence in schools seems to have reached epidemic levels. But how frequent are violent behavior and crime among children and youth? In reality, the rate of many of the most violent school crimes actually decreased across the 1990s. By 2000 fewer students reported carrying a weapon to school, and students reported feeling more secure at school. Children are far more likely to be victims of crime when they are *not* at school (Kaufman et al., 2001, 2000). However, the rate of threats and injuries with weapons on school property remained constant across the 1990s, as did the number of physical fights not involving weapons. Although horrifying incidents like the Columbine massacre are rare, even one such tragedy is too many.

How should communities and schools deal with aggressive students? The majority of public schools in the United States have adopted some form of *zero tolerance policy* toward firearms, violence, alcohol, and drugs. These policies mandate a specific punishment (often expulsion) for specific offenses. Unfortunately, critics argue, in practice these well-intentioned policies often use suspension and expulsion to punish both serious and trivial incidents. The policies are used inconsistently across schools and disproportionately affect minority students; compared to White students, Black students are two to three times more likely to be suspended, and Black students receive harsher punishments for less serious offenses (Skiba & Knesting, 2001). Above all, critics say, there is little evidence that zero tolerance policies are effective in reducing student aggression—and they may actually increase students' risk of dropping out of school and engaging in juvenile delinquency (Browne, Losen, & Wald, 2001; Skiba & Knesting, 2001). Other approaches advocate prevention; they focus on early identification and treatment of such things as truancy, bullying (treating both the bullies and the victims), anger, and aggression through school-based group therapy run by trained psychologists or counselors (Larson & Lochman, 2002). School and districtwide policies and staff training emphasizing conflict resolution skills, effective discipline strategies, and social skills training have helped produce more prosocial environments in some schools (Gagnon & Leone, 2001). Many experts point out that aggression and school violence have multiple causes; schools, parents, and the overall community must coordinate their efforts and resources to deal with these problems effectively.

QUESTION **What policies seem to work best with aggressive students and school violence? How can schools balance the needs and rights of students against the urgency of identifying and dealing with potential problems so as to prevent violence? What social policy suggestions would you make?**

## Leisure Time in Adolescence

Adolescence brings a shift from the concrete and realistic thought of the grade school child to the more hypothetical and idealistic thought characteristic of the formal operational stage. In some sense this represents a return to the fantasy of earlier years, but this time adolescents use their imaginations to speculate about how the world could be or should be (Hughes, 1999). Movies, TV, music, video games, and surfing the Internet (particularly instant messaging and social networking Web sites) are popular; they give adolescents opportunities to escape the realities of life, explore more exciting possibilities, and connect with one another (Lenhart & Madden, 2007). Activities that enable adolescents to be around one another, sharing their ideas and interests, often lead to dating and other intimate contacts. Even when alone, adolescents use music, TV, online Web sites, and similar activities as ways to explore their own interests, examine how they fit with peers, and reflect on where they are going in their lives. Self-understanding, sexual attraction, and intimate communication are important aspects of leisure-time activities in adolescence (Hughes, 1999).

As Figure 15.3 shows, adolescents devote more time to screen media (including TV, DVDs, videos, and movies) than to homework, and their hours spent watching screen media outnumber hours spent reading books and magazines by almost 5 to 1. Adolescents from 15 to 18 years of age report an average of 1 hour 22 minutes a day in non-school-related computer activities—but 3 hours and 40 minutes watching television (Roberts, Foehr, & Rideout, 2005). Adolescents don't spend all of their time watching TV or online, of course. They put a considerable amount of time into doing homework, paid employment, and household chores (a combined total of about 2 hours per day). Adults often complain that adolescents waste too much time watching TV, but research data suggest that their criticism may be misdirected. According to one British study, for example, 12- to 15-year-olds and 16- to 24-year-olds spent approximately 2.7 hours per day watching TV, but adults (25 to 54 years old) spent 3.5 hours glued to the tube (Gunter & McAleer, 1997). Older adults (ages 55 and up) watched nearly 5 hours per day! Estimates of media usage by teens are complicated by the fact

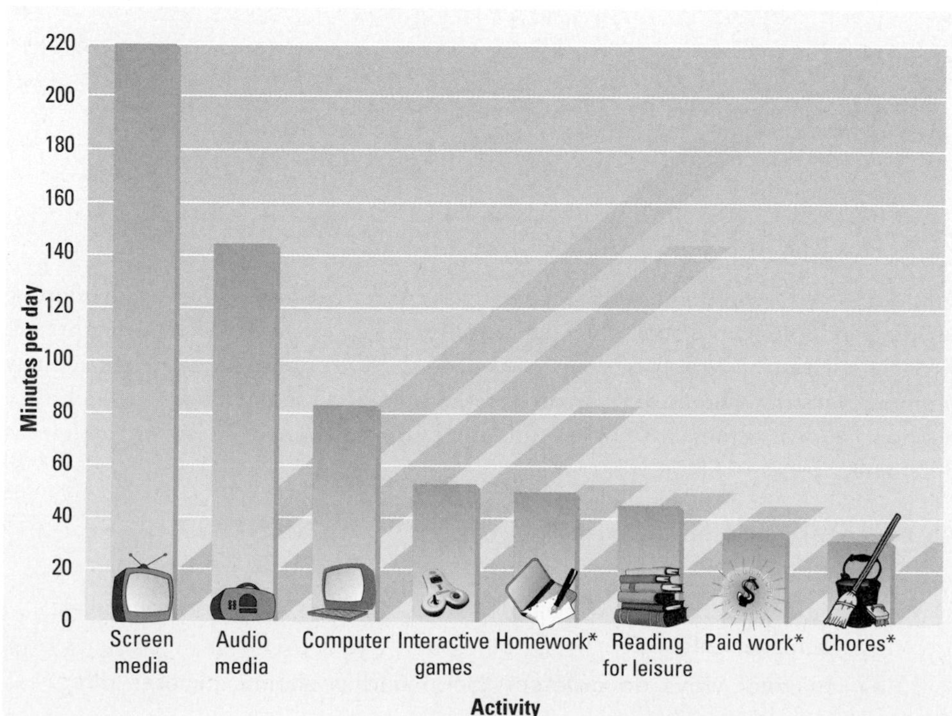


◀ FIGURE 15.3
**Common Activities in Adolescence**
Shown here are average minutes per day that U.S. adolescents spend in various activities, based on reports from students mostly 15 to 18 years old (data in categories with * are from 7th to 12th graders). *Screen media* includes TV, DVDs, video, and movies. *Audio media* includes CDs, radio, tapes, and MP3 players. *Interactive games* includes video and computer games. *Reading for leisure* includes reading books and magazines. (Data from Roberts, Foehr, & Rideout, 2005.)

that many teenagers do several things at once, *multitasking* at every possible opportunity. For example, 15- to 18-year-olds average 6.5 hours of media use per day but 25% of this involves using two or more media sources at once—so their actual media exposure is 8 hours and 44 minutes per day (Foehr, 2006; Roberts et al., 2005). Of course, many adolescents also engage in more active such as organized sports, skateboarding, or dancing. At this age, however, they tend to focus selectively on the one or two activities in which they excel (Hughes, 1999). Even in adolescence, these activities still qualify as play: They are pleasurable, and the adolescent engages in them actively, voluntarily, and for intrinsic motivations.

## LET'S REVIEW . . .

**1.** Which statement best summarizes the type of friendships children have during adolescence?
   **a.** "He's my friend because we have known each other forever."
   **b.** "She's my friend because she is my neighbor and we play soccer together a lot."
   **c.** "She's my friend because we are in the same class in school."
   **d.** "He's my friend because we can talk about things that upset me and he'll keep it secret."

**2.** According to Harry Stack Sullivan, which of the following is *most* important for the development of successful intimate relationships in adolescence?
   **a.** having close nonromantic relationships during late childhood
   **b.** having a secure attachment to caregivers during infancy
   **c.** having a lot of loyal and honest friends
   **d.** having friends who are similar to yourself in important ways

**3.** Research on adolescent crowds indicates that self-esteem is highest among ________.
   **a.** druggies/toughs
   **b.** nobodies
   **c.** normals
   **d.** jocks

**4.** True or False: Most adolescents experience stronger peer pressure to engage in positive behaviors than in negative behaviors.

**5.** True or False: In general, adolescents who do *not* have close friendships have just as good outcomes as those who do have close friendships.

Answers: 1. d, 2. a, 3. d, 4. T, 5. F

# Contexts of Development

Adolescents do not face the developmental tasks of forming their identity, developing intimate relationships, and achieving autonomy in a vacuum. Their attempts are strongly affected by aspects of their social context. Two contexts that are particularly important are the schools they attend and the overall cultural context in which they develop. In this section, we will examine the impact of these contexts on adolescent development.

AS YOU STUDY THIS SECTION, ASK YOURSELF THESE QUESTIONS:

**15.10** What impact does the school context have on adolescent development?

**15.11** How do U.S. students compare to those in other countries in academic achievement?

**15.12** In what ways do different social and economic cultures affect development?

## Adolescents in School

**School Climate and Structure.** Just as classroom climate can encourage certain goals, activities, beliefs, emotions, and behavior, overall school climate influences students and teachers alike (Roeser, Midgley, & Urdan, 1996). Schoolwide practices such as honor roll assemblies, public posting of honor rolls, and class ranking on student report cards and permanent records encourage a schoolwide emphasis on ability, competition, and social comparison. In contrast, recognition of effort and improvement, coupled with instruction that encourages mastery, produces a schoolwide learning orientation (Eccles & Roeser, 1999; Roeser & Eccles, 1998).

THINK ABOUT CAMILA . . .

How good do you think Camila's stage–environment fit has been in the past few years? What is her school doing well, and what could they do to improve the fit?

School structure has important effects as students transition to middle school or junior high. At this point schools typically increase the emphasis on competition, grades, teacher control, and social comparison. At the same time, schools decrease individual attention and support from teachers and provide fewer opportunities for students to maintain close networks of friendships. Long-lasting declines in students' self-esteem, motivation, and achievement can occur—particularly for students who are at academic risk or are more psychologically vulnerable (Eccles, Lord, Roeser, Barber, & Jozefowicz, 1997). This mismatch between school structure and adolescents' developmental needs is an example of a poor **stage–environment fit**: a poor match between the environment and the cognitive, social, and emotional needs of a particular stage of development (Eccles, 2004; Eccles & Roeser, 1999). School structures can be modified to be more appropriate for middle school students by encouraging learning-oriented goals (rather than performance-oriented goals); using cooperative learning techniques; focusing honors and awards on initiative, effort, and improvement; allowing students more control in classroom and school decision making; and scheduling regular advisory sessions so teachers get to know individual students and identify potential problems early (Anderman & Maehr, 1994; Eccles, 2004; Seidman & French, 1997). ((•• **Listen** on **mydevelopmentlab**

((•• **Listen**: How is schooling different in different countries across the world? (Author Podcast) www.mydevelopmentlab.com

## Differences in Academic Performance

How do students in the United States compare to those in other countries in academic achievement? In the latest international assessment of mathematics and science achievement, U.S. 15 year olds ranked 35th in math and 29th in science out of 57 countries assessed—well below the scores of the top-ranked countries (Baldi, Jin, Skemer, Green, & Herget, 2007). Twelfth graders have fared even worse in international comparisons, ranking 19th in math and 16th in science out of 21 countries assessed in past years (Mullis et al., 1998). Findings like these are disappointing, particularly because of the heavy emphasis on educational improvement over the past few decades.

Researchers have examined educational practices in the United States, Japan, China, and Taiwan and found interesting differences between practices in Asian cultures (which often lead the world in math and science scores) and in the United States. Differences have been especially apparent in such areas as beliefs about effort and ability, active engagement in learning activities, parent expectations and involvement, and how time on academics is spent by students and teachers (Lee, 1998; Shen, 2001; Stevenson & Lee, 1990). It would be unrealistic to propose that the same educational practices that work in Asian cultures be implemented wholesale in the United States as there are quite different cultural systems operating (Shen, 2001). But some school systems have attempted changes inspired by Asian educational practices. For example, one study found that extending the school year by 30 days produced higher achievement scores in several areas (Frazier & Morrison, 1998). It's interesting to note that many of the practices long advocated by educational researchers and developmental psychologists are common in Asian cultures. Examples include active learning by students, emphasis on effort rather than

**stage–environment fit**
The degree to which the environment is successful in meeting the cognitive, social, and emotional needs of a child in a particular stage of development.

▲ Middle school practices such as publicly posting honor rolls emphasize competition and ability rather than cooperation and effort at a time when students need greater support and chances to maintain friendships. This is an example of a poor *stage–environment fit*, and it can produce long-lasting negative effects—especially for young adolescents who are at academic risk or psychologically vulnerable.

ability, and focus on problem solving and conceptual knowledge. As you're probably well aware, many U.S. schools have made changes to try to improve education, but it will likely take several years before we can see the effects of these changes.

What about ethnic group differences among U.S. students? As Figure 15.4 shows, the 2007 National Assessment of Educational Progress found large ethnic group differences in math achievement. Similar differences were found in all the subjects tested. While the gaps have narrowed substantially since 1971, most have narrowed little or none since 1990 (Grigg, Lauko, & Brockway, 2006; Lee, Grigg, & Dion, 2007; Rampey, Dion, & Donahue, 2009; Salahu-Din, Persky, & Miller, 2008). Although the rate of dropping out of school declined for all ethnicities during the 1970s and 1980s, ethnic differences persist. For example, the dropout rate among Hispanic students (39.4%) is almost four times the rate for non-Hispanic White students (10.6%); African American students' dropout rate (19.9%) is almost twice that of White students (Crissey, 2009).

Why do substantial ethnic differences remain in spite of years of attention and concern? Poverty and its effects are a crucial factor. Ethnic minority students are far more likely to live in poverty than are White students. Poverty affects the quality of schools available, money available for materials and enrichment activities, parents' abilities and opportunities to help, and students' overall health, to name but a few factors (Byrnes, 2008; Skiba, Knesting, & Bush, 2002). Cultural differences also are important, particularly the extent to which schools are compatible with students' home cultures and the degree to which children's cultures value the kinds of skills taught in schools (Byrnes, 2008). One important result of cultural incompatibility is that students are less likely to care about their performance, put in extra effort, or seek help. Schools that are sensitive to the cultures of their students and try to involve parents can have a positive impact on children's academic achievement (Fan & Chen, 2001; Parker, Boak, Griffin, Ripple, & Peay, 1999).

▲ Asian cultures place a strong emphasis on hard work. In these societies, there are high expectations for students' achievement and active involvement in learning. Teachers have more preparation time than in the United States; children have ample recess time; and parents are very involved in their children's schoolwork.

Is it true that boys are better than girls in mathematics, as so many people seem to believe? It depends on students' ages as well as on the particular area of mathematics being assessed. The only consistent differences found in elementary school favor girls, both for computation and for grades in math (Halpern, 2000). Girls continue to earn higher math grades, but their superior performance in computation disappears after about age 15. Gender differences favoring boys appear at adolescence and increase during high school, but only in areas involving mathematics problem solving. Since the late 1970s boys have consistently scored about 10% higher than girls on the math portion of the Scholastic Aptitude Test (SAT). However, on national assessments of fourth, eighth, and twelfth graders, math gender differences have decreased since the early 1980s, and the most recent national assessment shows no significant differences at any of these grade levels (Byrnes, 2008; Rampey et al., 2009;). Some studies find that girls hold less positive attitudes toward math, show less interest in math, and receive less encouragement for engaging in math-related activities (Eccles, Wigfield, & Schiefele, 1998; Maccoby, 1998). Schools have struggled with these issues for many years, but stereotypes still exist.

In more general cognitive skills the largest and most consistent gender differences are in verbal, language, and certain spatial skills (Halpern, 2000; Hyde, 2007; Hyde & Linn, 1988). The biggest differences in verbal skills during school-age years—all favoring girls—are in spelling, overall language measures, and writing. Some of these differences get smaller during adolescence, whereas others (e.g., writing) remain. Boys score higher in some spatial skills such as mental rotation (the ability to visualize how an object would look if you viewed it from a different angle). Differences in these areas emerge at around 9 to 13 years and widen throughout adolescence (Masters & Sanders, 1993; Voyer, Voyer, & Bryden, 1995).

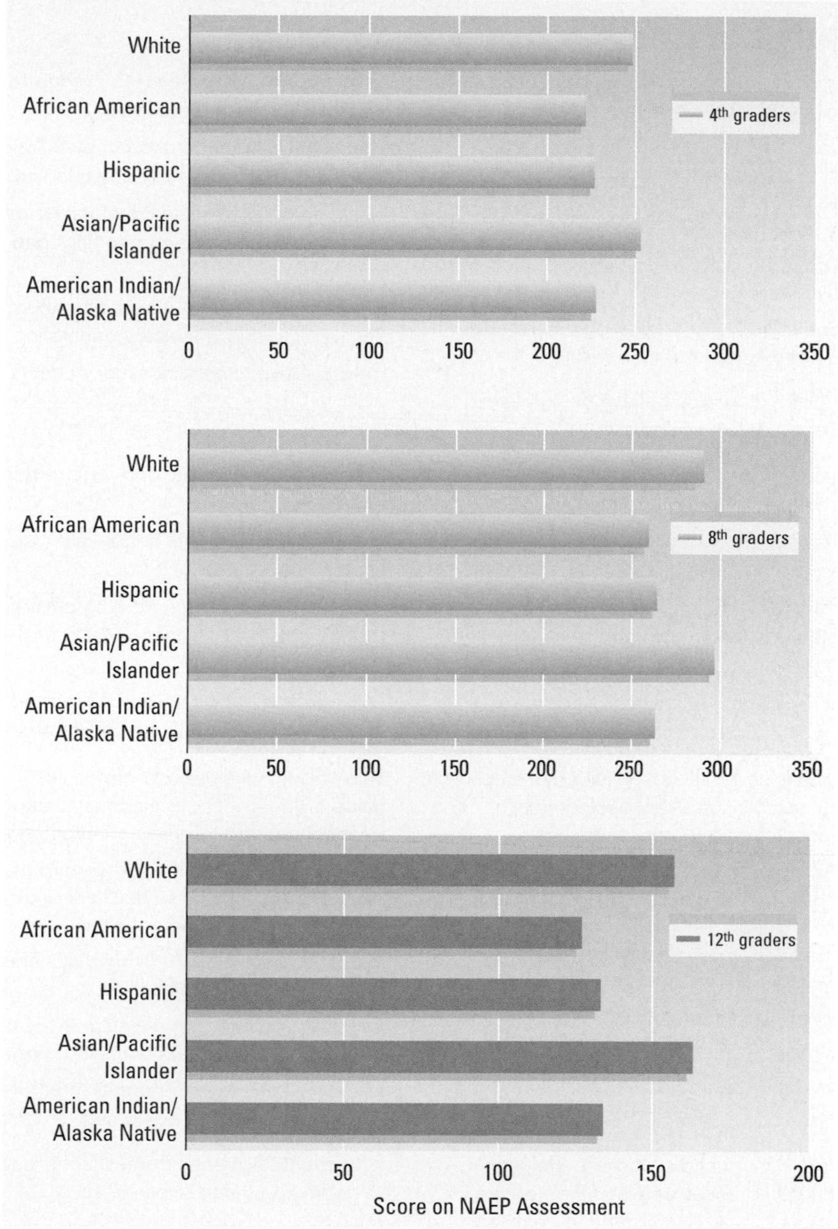


◀ FIGURE 15.4
**Ethnic Group Differences in Achievement**
This figure shows the ethnic group differences in math. Ethnic group differences in achievement are large in all subject areas tested. Maximum possible score was 500 for 4th and 8th graders; 300 for 12th graders. *Note*: Data for 4th and 8th grades are from the year 2007; 12th grade are from the year 2005 (year 2007 data not available). (Grigg, Donahue, & Dion, 2007; Lee et al., 2007).

**How Can We Prevent Problems in Schooling?** What can we do to prevent difficulties in schooling? You may soon be in a position to help, perhaps by working in health and social services, early childhood education, schools, or government or private agencies. You may also have children of your own. Table 15.4 (page 498) presents suggestions for all of us who work with children, from preschool through high school. It is vital that each student begin school ready to learn, experience early success to gain a solid foundation for learning, and learn that effort and persistence make a difference. Each child must feel that school is relevant and important in his or her life, and each must feel individually known and valued by teachers and schools. These are challenging goals that require active involvement of all who care about students' academic success and overall quality of life.

## Cultural Contexts for Development

Throughout this book we have often mentioned the influence of culture when explaining why children behave, think, or feel in certain ways. In every chapter we have pointed out

**TABLE 15.4**
Preventing Problems with Schooling

| STRATEGIES | PARENTS CAN . . . | SCHOOLS CAN . . . |
|---|---|---|
| **Promote school readiness** to help children get off to a good start academically | Immunize children, encourage good eating and exercise habits, and make sure children get enough sleep.<br>Use quality preschool programs that teach basic skills and encourage positive attitudes toward learning and schooling.<br>Read to children *daily* and encourage them to use descriptive words.<br>Encourage curiosity and questions. Encourage children's efforts, not just their results.<br>Let your child know you believe he can learn through effort and persistence. | Offer specific suggestions to parents for increasing school readiness.<br>Thoroughly screen all preschoolers to identify those at highest need of early intervention.<br>Establish an environment that values and encourages curiosity, questioning, and enthusiasm for learning.<br>Develop policies that emphasize effort, persistence, and a mastery orientation.<br>Hold positive expectations for students. |
| **Help create a positive school environment** to help children feel comfortable, confident, and happy to be in school | Be involved in your child's school. Volunteer, and attend school events.<br>Meet with your child's teacher(s) periodically, even if your child is not having any problems.<br>Request teachers who emphasize effort, persistence, and mastery, and who have positive expectations for children.<br>Consider the climate of your child's class—is it warm and supportive or chilly and uninviting? | Encourage meaningful and regular parent involvement.<br>Take steps to eliminate negative classroom environments.<br>Hold regular in-service training on strategies that foster positive classroom climates and mastery learning orientations.<br>Make strong efforts to keep class sizes below 20 students, especially at early grade levels. |
| **Think about the consequences of school structure and policies** to provide a good stage–environment fit | Ask questions about school policies that emphasize grades or competition. Ask how learning orientations, effort, and persistence are encouraged.<br>Support programs in middle/junior high schools that make it a friendlier place for students, like block schedules or homeroom "advisory" programs.<br>Watch for signs that your child is having difficulty transitioning to a new school. | Think about whether school policies focus too much on ability. Try to emphasize effort, persistence, and learning orientations more often.<br>Consider having "advisory" programs and/or block-type schedules so teachers and students can get to know one another better.<br>Watch for signs that individual students are having adjustment difficulties.<br>Establish routines that are student-friendly and teach self-management and self-control strategies.<br>Maintain contact with parents to ensure that children's needs are being met. |
| **Understand different cultures** to make school more relevant and interesting for students | Get to know your child's teachers. Help them understand differences between their culture and yours.<br>Help organize a multicultural event in your child's class or school. Try to understand *why* the school curriculum contains the things it does.<br>Try to find reasons that make sense to your child.<br>Point out to your child examples of the content and skills he or she is learning, especially for topics your child thinks are irrelevant. | Plan events that encourage parents and teachers to get to know one another.<br>Offer in-service training to help teachers understand the cultures, expectations, and customs of their students.<br>Encourage teachers to incorporate information about their students' cultural backgrounds into instruction.<br>Ask community members about school topics that seem irrelevant to them or their children. Get suggestions to improve the relevance of the curriculum. |
| **Do more than just teach content** so students' non-academic needs are not an obstacle to learning | Help children develop positive, supportive friendships.<br>Encourage children to talk about school—about what they're learning, what they like or don't like, and why.<br>Encourage your child to develop positive relationships with other trusted adults such as teachers. | Talk with students about attitudes toward learning, strategies for self-control, and how to deal with strong or negative emotions.<br>Provide counseling services or referrals for students having academic, social, or emotional difficulties.<br>Serve as an information resource for academic as well as nonacademic services and issues. |

(Anderman & Maehr, 1994; Deci & Ryan, 1985; Dweck, 2001; Eccles, 2004; Fan & Chen, 2001; Ford & Harris, 2000; Good & Brophy, 2003; Keith et al., 1998; Parker et al., 1999; Seidman & French, 1997.)

differences among cultures. But what is *culture,* and how does it affect development? In this section we will discuss types of cultures and consider their impact on children's development.

**Cultural Orientations: Individualism and Collectivism.** A **culture** is a system of shared customs and meanings that allows individuals to participate as members of a group and that is transmitted from one generation to the next (Cole, 1999; Goodenough, 1994). A culture includes clearly specified rules (such as laws) as well as attitudes, beliefs, goals, values, and traditions. Cultures can be vastly different in their specific customs and meanings, but one important dimension on which people often compare cultures has to do with their emphasis on the group or on the individual. For example, think about how you describe yourself. Do you tend to use terms that emphasize your individuality or your relationships with others? Now think honestly about how responsible you feel for the well-being of your friends and family: Would you readily sacrifice your own desires, independence, and happiness for their sake? Psychologists have posed questions like these to people from a variety of different places. Their responses can be categorized as having an individualistic or collectivistic general cultural orientation.

**Individualism** involves the general belief that people are independent of each other. Individualistic cultures focus on an individual's "rights above duties, a concern for oneself and immediate family, an emphasis on personal autonomy and self-fulfillment," and an identity based on personal accomplishments (Oyserman, Coon, & Kemmelmeier, 2002, p. 4). In contrast, **collectivism** is the view that individuals are interdependent members of a social group and that the greatest concern is with the group's goals, values, and well-being. In collectivism the emphasis is on fulfilling duties to others, even if it means sacrificing your own desires and happiness; identity has to do with group beliefs, accomplishments, and characteristics rather than individual ones. Group membership in such a culture may be based on kinship, religion, ethnicity, or something else. Researchers often talk about whole countries as having an individualistic or collectivistic cultural orientation, but any specific individual within the country may not have the same orientation. Within a given country there can be large differences in how strictly individuals adhere to the overall cultural orientation or to any of the culture's specific customs or meanings (Chirkov, Ryan, Kim, & Kaplan, 2003; Triandis, 1995).

Studies have found differences related to individualism and collectivism in many cultural beliefs and behaviors relevant for development, including parenting practices, emotional attachment type, attitudes toward academic effort and ability, school discipline strategies, cooperation and competition, conflict resolution, helping behaviors, and preferences for working alone versus in groups (Greenfield, Suzuki, & Rothstein-Fisch, 2006; Oyserman et al., 2002; Rothbaum, Weisz, Pott, Miyake, & Morelli, 2000). For example, many European Americans (not to mention developmental researchers) view authoritative parenting as effective because it encourages outcomes such as self-reliance, self-regulation, and exploration—outcomes that an individualistic cultural orientation finds desirable. But as you learned earlier in this chapter, this parenting style is not the norm and these outcomes are not the goal in other, less individualistic cultures such as those of East Asian and African countries (Greenfield et al., 2006).

As you have probably guessed, researchers often describe Western cultures like that of the United States as individualistic. Within U.S. culture, they typically see European Americans as the most individualistic. East Asian cultures such as those of China and Japan are often thought of as more collectivistic. However, recent research is challenging some of the established beliefs about individualistic and collectivistic cultures. It appears that some theories and measures may be biased toward one orientation or the other; also, some studies question the traditional beliefs about which cultures show strong tendencies toward one orientation or the other (Oyserman et al., 2002; Rothbaum et al., 2000).

**culture**
A system of shared customs and meanings that allow individuals to participate as a member of a group and that are transmitted from one generation to the next.

**individualism**
A cultural orientation based on the belief that people are independent of each other; emphasizes individual rights, self-fulfillment, and personal accomplishments.

**collectivism**
A cultural orientation based on the belief people are interdependent members of a social group; emphasizes duty to others and group goals, values, and well-being.

THINKING CRITICALLY

Do you consider your cultural orientation to be individualistic or collectivistic? If you've known anyone with a different cultural orientation, describe any differences you have noticed.

Do you see indications of a collectivist or individualistic cultural orientation in Camila and her family? How might their cultural orientations affect their beliefs, behavior, and expectations?

**What's the Neighborhood Like? Urban and Rural Poverty.** In recent years, developmental researchers have focused a great deal of attention on characteristics of the neighborhoods in which children live. Neighborhoods often consist of people who are similar in important ways; for example, in attitudes, beliefs, ethnicity, language, and/or behavior. The resources a community supports, the private and public behavior it encourages, the parenting practices it encourages, and the social activities it organizes and allows can all affect children for better or for worse, directly and indirectly (Furstenberg & Hughes, 1997). One factor that stands out is the impact of living in a poor neighborhood. Living in poverty has pervasive negative effects on children's development.

**Poverty: A Culture of Economics.** As of 2007, the overall poverty rate for U.S. families was 12.5%. This is among the lowest in two decades, but the rate has risen every year since 2000. Look carefully at Figure 15.5. What does this figure show about the poverty status of *children and adolescents* as a group relative to the overall population? Although the situation is improving, the poverty rate of children up to age 18 is still almost 1.5 times higher than the rate for all ages. In other words, children, particularly young children, are more likely to live in poverty than any other age group. This is especially true for African American and Hispanic children; three out of 10 children in these ethnic groups live in poverty. Even more striking is the fact that over half (55%) of families living in poverty include at least one person who works *full-time* and *year-round;* 39% live with parents who have at least some college education (DeNavas-Walt, Proctor, & Smith, 2008; Douglas-Hall & Chau, 2008). In 2008, the U.S. Census Bureau defined the poverty level as a total annual income of not more than $14,000 for a household of two people ($21,200 for four). What difficulties do you think a family of four would have on this income? Given recent economic conditions, what trends in poverty rates would you predict for the next few years?

In general, children and adolescents living in poverty face seriously limited options and many difficulties in their day-to-day lives. Lack of resources, continuous hassles, and relatively frequent negative life events create high levels of stress for all family members, and the

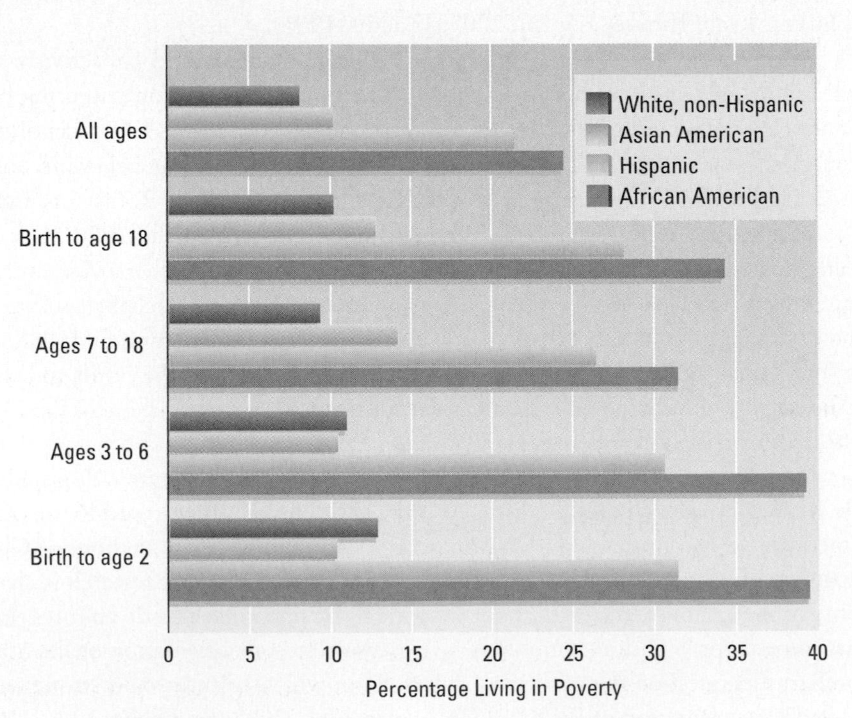


FIGURE 15.5 ▶ **Percentages of U.S. Age Groups Living in Poverty, 2007** People living in poverty in the United States include more children than any other age group—especially children under the age of 2. African American and Hispanic children are especially at risk. (U.S. Census Bureau, 2008.)

stress never seems to abate. The younger a child is and the longer the child lives in poverty, the larger the impact tends to be. The more poverty risk factors an individual experiences (such as poor health, inadequate parenting, and low social support), the worse the effect. Living in poverty affects well-being in numerous ways, including the following (Bradley & Corwyn, 2002; Brooks-Gunn, Klebanov, Liaw, & Duncan, 1995; Duncan & Brooks-Gunn, 1997; Linver, Brooks-Gunn, & Kohen, 2002; McLoyd, Aikens, & Burton, 2006):

THINKING CRITICALLY

Think about the things you've done in the last week or so. How might these activities have been different or more difficult (or easy) if you were poor or if you were wealthy?

- Children living in poverty are more likely than children who are not poor to suffer physical health problems, including higher rates of preterm birth, low birth weight, illnesses, injuries, poisoning, parental neglect, exposure to toxic substances, and abuse (Pelton, 1989). They have less access to adequate health care and lower rates of immunizations, so illnesses and injuries often progress to more serious levels before they receive treatment.
- Poverty correlates significantly with lower IQ scores, lower academic achievement, and lower scores on a variety of cognitive measures (Bradley, Corwyn, & Whiteside-Mansell, 1996). Poor children are less ready for school in terms of knowledge, cognitive skills, social skills, and self-regulation.
- Children and teenagers living in poverty tend poorer-quality schools and have far fewer opportunities for positive extracurricular and enrichment activities than other children. They are also more likely to repeat grade levels and eventually to drop out of school (Battin-Pearson et al., 2000; Zill, Moore, Smith, Stief, & Coiro, 1995).
- Parents living in poverty rely more often on power-assertive discipline tactics (e.g., issuing commands and using physical punishment) and are less likely to use reasoning, involve their children in decisions, or give praise for proper behavior (Bradley, Corwyn, McAdoo, & Coll, 2001). Parenting can be less consistent and less child-centered, although this often depends on whether other problems arise (Halpern, 1993).
- Homelessness is a very real possibility. Families with children make up one-third of the homeless population; children under age 18 account for almost one-fourth of this population. Homeless children have even more health and developmental problems than other poor children (Molnar, Roth, & Klein, 1990; Smith & Smith, 2001; U.S. National Coalition for the Homeless, 2001).
- Children living in poverty have higher rates of social and emotional difficulties from an early age, including substance abuse, behavior problems, mental illness, suicide, personality disorders, and lower self-esteem and self-confidence. Poverty in itself may not directly cause these difficulties, but it creates stressful environmental conditions that make them more likely to develop.

▲ In addition to the obstacles poor children face, inner-city adolescents living in poverty must deal with higher levels of violent crime, bad housing, lack of positive options, less support from parents, temptation from gangs and drugs, and a sense of isolation from the larger community.

Children from ethnic minority backgrounds are far more likely to live in poverty and spend longer living in poverty than non-Hispanic White children. Many of the ethnic-group differences we have noted in other chapters (e.g., differences in parenting practices, academic achievement and school completion, early pregnancy, and low birth weight, to name a few) at least partly reflect the impacts of poverty. For many outcomes, in fact, differences between ethnic groups fade or disappear when analysts take the effects of poverty into account. Moving from a poor neighborhood to one with little poverty has many positive effects, including decreased emotional distress, less reliance on harsh parenting practices, and less violent behavior (DeAngelis, 2001).

THINK ABOUT CAMILA . . .

What effect might the lack of money in Camila's family have on her? How can she and her family deal with these effects?

**The Inner City.** Inner-city poverty is an especially difficult context for children and adolescents. Almost one-quarter of all children in U.S. inner cities are living in poverty. All of the effects of poverty we've already discussed weigh especially heavily on those living in

▲ Community-bridging families help children find and take advantage of opportunities by closely monitoring their activities and friendships, maintaining social support networks, encouraging their involvement in positive activities, and expecting them to help with family responsibilities.

inner-city poverty, and the vast majority of these children are members of ethnic minorities (Brooks-Gunn, Duncan, & Aber, 1997). There are additional problems as well. Crime, particularly violent crime, is much more frequent in the inner city. Housing is often substandard, crowded, and inconsistent. Positive options are less available, and negative options like gangs and drug use are more common. Children and parents alike focus more on the present than on the future; "simply surviving in the inner city is viewed by these families as evidence" of success (Brookins, Petersen, & Brooks, 1997, p. 54; Burton, Obeidallah, & Allison, 1996). Parents lack financial and emotional resources, often facing chronic unemployment or inconsistent employment as well as insufficient support and help from the community. Often there is a sense of social isolation from other parts of the city, and families may keep to themselves because of fear for children's safety. Inner-city children have far less academic success, with a 50% high school dropout rate in some areas. These outcomes limit options for these children even further and serve to perpetuate the cycle of poverty for the next generation.

How can families living in poor neighborhoods find a way out? Numerous social programs try to help create economic opportunities and improve the educational success of inner-city youth, with varying degrees of success (Brown & Richman, 1997; Lehman & Smeeding, 1997). Although there is no doubt that neighborhood factors are important, a child's family can overcome the influence of a poor neighborhood. For example, researchers have identified several family behaviors that help inner-city African American adolescents be more successful (Jarrett, 1995). These behaviors characterize *community-bridging families,* which can help children find and take advantage of opportunities within and outside the immediate neighborhood. For example, community-bridging families:

- Establish and maintain networks among family members (immediate and extended) that provide support and resources
- Restrict children's interaction with people whose lifestyles are inconsistent with the family's goals and values; this reduces children's exposure to negative influences
- Carefully and consistently monitor their children's activities and friendships
- Encourage involvement in positive activities—activities that increase contact with like-minded families and friends and help children develop their skills and talents
- Expect children to contribute to the family's well-being through chores, responsibilities, part-time jobs, and the like, all of which help increase children's self-esteem and family cohesion

THINK ABOUT CAMILA . . .

What aspects of community-bridging families might be helpful to Camila and her family? How could they use these ideas to help Camila as she moves through adolescence?

THINKING CRITICALLY

Do you know any "community-bridging" families? Think about what kinds of things they do differently than other families and how this affects their children's development.

**Rural Poverty.** The fact that the poverty rate in rural areas is almost as high as in inner cities is often overlooked. In the year 2007, for example, 25% of children in inner cities and 22% of children in rural areas were poor, compared to 12.5% of children in suburbs (Children's Defense Fund, 2008). Like all poor children, children living in rural poverty face more difficulties and stress than nonpoor children. They experience many of the effects we have reviewed, with one possible, but important, exception. One extensive study of rural Iowa farm children found that family ties are often strong and serve to connect several generations, and that strong social networks connect these farm communities (Elder & Conger, 2000). Strong family loyalty also is frequent in Appalachian poor families. At least for these rural families, poverty does not seem to disrupt social supports as much as it does in the inner city (Crockett, Shanahan, & Jackson-Newsom, 2000; Wilson & Peterson, 2000).

**acculturation**
The process of learning the language, values, customs, and social skills of a new culture.

**Coming to America: Immigration and Acculturation.** Throughout the history of the United States, immigrants have coped with the stresses of settling in a new country, usually arriving with few resources and little knowledge of the language and customs. **Acculturation** is the process of learning the language, values, customs, and social skills of a new culture (Chun, Organista, & Marin, 2003; Parke & Buriel, 2006). It is a lengthy process, often spanning several generations, and it can create conflict and stress for families, particularly during adolescence. For example, when adolescents speak different languages than their parents (i.e., the parents talk to their children in the native language, but the children usually respond in English), the teenagers report less communication and closeness with their parents than do teenagers who use the same language as their parents (Tseng & Fuligni, 2000). In addition, U.S.-born adolescents in immigrant families tend to change their values and beliefs more rapidly than their parents, creating a bigger difference in values between parents and adolescents in these families than in other immigrant or nonimmigrant families. Because many immigrants come from cultures that emphasize respect for and obedience to adults, this difference can create much family stress and disruption. The more differences there are in the acculturation of parents and children, the more family conflict there tends to be (Farver, Narang, & Bhadha, 2002; Phinney, Ong, & Madden., 2000).

▲ The poverty rate in rural areas is almost as high as in inner cities, and children in rural poverty suffer many of the same effects as the inner-city poor. The rural poor are from a wide range of ethnic backgrounds, cultures, and geographic regions.

Regardless of their countries of origin, immigrants must develop strategies in order to adapt successfully. For example, studies find that Mexican immigrants emphasize and strengthen family ties; this strategy provides additional sources of economic, emotional, and social support. They also cultivate **biculturalism**, or adoption of two cultural orientations at the same time. Biculturalism allows families to maintain the cultural values they brought from their homeland but also understand and function successfully in the new culture. The adolescents (and sometimes even younger children) of immigrants often find themselves serving as **child cultural brokers**—as interpreters not only of the language but also of the culture of the new country for their parents and other family members (Parke & Buriel, 2006). This can be a difficult position for children. They must try to represent the family to members of the majority culture and to cope with important adult responsibilities like legal matters, tax forms, and insurance claims. Child cultural brokers are supposed to teach their parents about these matters and other subtleties of the new culture, but they must do it in a way that allows their parents to maintain their status and respect within the family and community. Being a child cultural broker can have some positive effects, too; these children can develop a greater knowledge of U.S. culture, greater sensitivity to the challenges facing their parents, and stronger bonds with their parents.

▲ Adolescence can be a stressful time for immigrant families. This adolescent is likely to have adopted American customs faster than her parents, which can lead to conflict. Her grandparent is likely to maintain an identity of her country of origin, while the girl and her parents are likely to have an Asian American ethnic identity.

Immigrants to the United States gradually acculturate to the mainstream culture, but it's important to remember that mainstream U.S. culture also changes. Latinos and Asian Americans are the fastest-growing ethnic minority groups in the United States, and each of these groups represents a varied collection of home cultures and languages. As the population of the United States becomes more diverse, the mainstream culture will evolve to incorporate new customs and reflect this rich diversity.

**biculturalism**
Adopting two cultural orientations at the same time.

**child cultural brokers**
Children of immigrants who serve as interpreters of the language and culture of the new country for their family members.

**Explaining Culture's Influence.** In essence, culture provides a "set of lenses for seeing the world" (Triandis, 1994, p. 13). For example, consider an experience one of the authors had in East Germany in 1989, just months after the fall of the Communist government. The citizens there often said, "It's not possible," as in "It's not possible to go there" (because the store was closed) or "It's not possible to do that" (because a sign was posted prohibiting parking, smoking, or loitering). The phrase sounded odd to an American. A lifetime in the United States led us to believe that problems can be overcome

▲ Children of immigrants may find themselves serving as cultural brokers. This son is expected to teach his parents about the majority culture and represent his family to others, but he must also make sure his parents retain status and respect both inside and outside the family.

given enough effort, time, and resources. Under communism, however, citizens had learned that government regulations were not mere requests—they were absolute requirements. Being steeped in communist culture led East Germans to the very different belief that trying to remove obstructions was futile and perhaps even dangerous.

Think back to the layers of Bronfenbrenner's ecological systems theory, shown in Figure 1.3 on page 16, and look at the many different systems that affect development directly or indirectly. All of these systems exist within and are affected by a specific cultural setting. At the broadest levels (the macrosystem and the exosystem), culture affects the options that are available to children and families, the resources they have to draw on, the governmental policies and laws that help or hurt them, the types of neighborhoods they live in, and the types of lifestyles they have and wish for. On more individual levels (the microsystem and the mesosystem), culture affects how and with whom social interactions take place; what kinds of parenting are considered appropriate; what people see as important or problematic, possible or impossible; what constitutes acceptable versus inappropriate behavior; and what children expect of themselves and others. In short, culture permeates all these levels to affect children's thoughts, emotions, beliefs, and behaviors. Yet so often we aren't even aware of the pervasive effects of our own culture—that is, until we encounter someone else's culture! Because cultural beliefs and customs are so thoroughly ingrained, it's not surprising that we sometimes misconstrue cultural differences as deficits. We are so accustomed to doing and thinking about things in the ways our own culture considers correct that we forget there are often other, equally correct, ways to go about things. "Like the air one breathes, under ordinary conditions, these values frameworks do not rise to conscious awareness" (Greenfield & Suzuki, 1998, p. 1060).

In this chapter we described three central developmental tasks adolescents face in their socioemotional development—identity, autonomy, and intimacy—along with several factors that influence their efforts to accomplish these tasks. Families, peers, and social context have a substantial impact. We discussed each influence as a separate topic, but it is important to remember that these and other factors all interact to influence the adolescent's development.

THINKING CRITICALLY

Have you experienced any cultural differences that led to misunderstanding or confusion? Describe what happened and how it could have gone more smoothly.

## LET'S REVIEW . . .

1. Which of the following does *not* explain the negative effect of the transition to junior high after sixth grade?
   - **a.** Junior high schools usually decrease individual attention but increase competition.
   - **b.** Students are given too much control too quickly over school-related decisions.
   - **c.** Teachers rely too heavily on competitive learning techniques and performance-oriented goals.
   - **d.** Class structure in junior high schools makes it harder to maintain friendship networks.
2. Andre has been offered a well-paying job that requires moving far away from his parents and extended family. His family does not want him to leave their town, so Andre does not take the job because he doesn't want to go against his family's wishes. Andre is most likely ________.
   - **a.** individualistic in his cultural orientation
   - **b.** collectivistic in his cultural orientation
   - **c.** neutral in his cultural orientation
   - **d.** European American
3. Which of the following is *true* about the effects of poverty on child development?
   - **a.** Poor children have more physical health problems than other children.
   - **b.** Poor children perform just as well in school as other children.
   - **c.** Poor children's parents are just as consistent and child centered as other parents.
   - **d.** Poor children are more likely to attend preschool than other children.

4. Twelve-year-old Miguel helps his parents with paperwork for their medical forms, translates for them when they must deal with their landlord, and helps them understand which kinds of stores are likely to negotiate prices and which are not. Miguel is a(n) _________.
   a. individualist
   b. collectivist
   c. child cultural broker
   d. community bridger

5. True or False: Ethnic differences in academic achievement scores are large and stable.

6. True or False: Community bridging families protect their children by severely restricting the children's interactions with all community members.

Answers: 1. b, 2. b, 3. a, 4. c, 5. T, 6. F

## THINKING BACK TO CAMILA . . .

Now that you have studied this chapter, you should be able to apply at least a dozen concepts and research findings to Camila's situation. The description of Camila clearly shows that she is dealing with all three of the socioemotional developmental tasks of adolescence: identity, autonomy, and intimacy. Her thoughts (or avoidance of them!) about what she wants to do in the future and her changes of mind about her interests are a normal part of the identity exploration process. While it's frustrating for Camila, it's important for her to think about a variety of different possibilities. This will increase the likelihood that she'll find an area that is a good fit for her interests and talents. The fact that she connects well with school is great. This is likely to help her continue to explore different subject areas and paths to continue her education. Even so, it would be a good idea for Camila's parents to monitor her interests in school, her overall grades, and her overall involvement. Perhaps they can work with her teachers and a guidance counselor as Camila moves toward her junior and senior years of high school to help her as she starts identifying areas of strength and interest.

Camila is also working to develop autonomy, evidenced by the conflicts she's having with her parents. Although it may seem that they are arguing more than other families, the amount and degree of conflict do not seem excessive. It may serve the positive purpose of helping Camila learn to deal with conflict and increased responsibility, and it may help her parents learn to allow Camila more autonomy as she is ready for it. It will be important for her parents to maintain appropriate expectations and offer positive support, but also recognize Camila's need to become more independent. The conflicts Camila and her parents are having may actually help them learn to communicate more clearly and build a stronger relationship, factors that may help buffer Camila from any of the ill effects of stress they may be having right now due to their recent move and job losses.

Finally, Camila is also continuing to develop the skills she'll need for forming successful and positive intimate relationships. Overall, her friends have helped her make positive decisions, and she is learning to resist negative peer pressure to make her own decisions. She is also learning the difficult lesson that friendships sometimes change as people mature and their interests change. The friendship skills she has developed, along with the model of relationships she has experienced in her family, will be important as she moves to intimate romantic relationships.

# 15

## CHAPTER REVIEW . . .

**15.1 What are the four identity statuses described by Marcia?**
Two components of identity development have been proposed (crisis, commitment) resulting in four identity statuses (moratorium, foreclosed, achieved, and diffused). Adolescents from ethnic minority groups work to develop an ethnic identity, possibly moving through several stages.

**15.2 What factors contribute to the development of sexual orientation?**
The development of a sexual orientation begins in childhood and involves identity formation and identity integration. The reasons for developing a particular sexual orientation are not completely understood but genetic factors, prenatal hormones, and the environment may all play a role. Teens with a homosexual orientation face increased risk of emotional, behavioral, and physical difficulties.

**15.3 What evidence supports Kohlberg's theory of moral development, and what are some of the criticisms of this theory?**
Kohlberg's postconventional level of moral reasoning begins in adolescence, but few people reason consistently at this level. The justice orientation of Kohlberg's theory is less central in some cultures. Men and women use both care and justice orientations when thinking about moral issues. Moral reasoning is not as consistent across tasks as Kohlberg's theory suggests.

**15.4 Why do adolescents and their parents argue, and how can families cope positively with this conflict?**
Some conflict over day-to-day issues is common and helps families address issues and learn to resolve conflict, and it indicates the adolescent is working toward autonomy. Parents, rather than teens, seem to be most bothered by conflict. Authoritative parenting, with the additional factor of psychological autonomy granting, helps adolescents constructively deal with conflict.

**15.5 What are the effects of growing up in adoptive, gay/lesbian, and ethnic families, and what developmental challenges does each face?**
Most adopted children and teenagers are well adjusted, but they do face challenges that nonadopted individuals do not. There is increased risk of psychological, behavioral, and academic problems, and some problems emerge in late childhood and adolescence. Being raised by gay or lesbian parents is not associated with negative developmental outcomes. Ethnic minority families and immigrant families often face challenges that majority group children do not, such as an increased risk of poverty and discrimination. Research has identified a number of characteristics of families that foster these teens' strength and resilience. A strict discipline style is common in many ethnic groups, but may be a protective response to dangerous neighborhoods.

**15.6 Why are friendships important during adolescence?**
The skills to form intimate relationships may be based in part on the attachment relations the child has with parents early in life, but childhood friendships also teach relationship skills.

**15.7 What are cliques and crowds, and how do they affect adolescents' development?**
Adolescents form closely knit cliques and socialize in larger crowds. Crowd membership can affect behavior, identity, relationships, and emotions in both positive and negative ways. Eventually, clique and crowd members begin interacting, which will lead to dating and eventual disintegration of the crowd structure.

**15.8 What influence does peer pressure have on adolescent behavior?**
Most, but not all, peer pressure is toward positive behaviors. Some adolescents face challenges from early childhood that increase their likelihood of ongoing delinquent behavior.

**15.9 How do adolescents spend their leisure time?**
Adolescents spend more time watching screen media than any other type of media. They also spend almost one hour each day listening to music, on the computer, playing interactive games, and doing homework; they often do several of these things at one time.

**15.10 What impact does the school context have on adolescent development?**
School structure is not always supportive of the emotional, social, physical, and cognitive changes that young adolescents face. When there is a poor match between the environment and the cognitive, social, and emotional needs of a particular stage of development, students' cognitive and emotional development can suffer.

**15.11 How do U.S. students compare to those in other countries in academic achievement?**
Cross-national assessments of achievement indicate that U.S. students fare worse than expected. Comparisons of American and Asian educational systems and beliefs have

found interesting differences. There are substantial and consistent ethnic group differences in academic performance despite years of attempts to address the differences. Gender differences in cognitive skills are most consistent in verbal, language, and some spatial skills, but similarities in academic achievement between boys and girls far outweigh the differences.

**15.12** In what ways do different social and economic cultures affect development?

A culture's overall orientation affects every system of development, including parenting practices, attitudes toward academic effort and achievement, and responsibility to family. Poverty affects all aspects of development directly and/or indirectly through lack of opportunity, lack of having basic needs met, increased difficulty of accomplishing day-to-day tasks, increased likelihood of poor parenting practices, and increased risk of social and emotional problems. Community bridging families create strong family networks and connections to protect and support children and adolescents. Children and adolescents in immigrant families must cope with the process of *acculturation,* which can span several generations and create conflict during the adolescent years. Children and teens in immigrant families frequently become the cultural brokers for their parents, interpreting language as well as important adult responsibilities.

## REVISITING THEMES

Several topics in this chapter address the theme of *positive development and resilience.* The strengths of ethnic families that were identified (p. 474) and the characteristics of community-bridging families (p. 502) offer clear examples of ways in which families can help their children overcome difficult circumstances. This theme can also be found in the discussion of ethnic identity development (pp. 471–474) and of acculturation strategies used by immigrant families (p. 474); both highlight ways in which people of various ethnicities and countries of origin go about developing an ethnic and cultural identity. Other examples of this theme are seen in the discussion of positive approaches for dealing with teen-parent conflict (pp. 482–483) and the role of family support as a buffer for gay youth (p. 477).

The theme of *diversity and multiculturalism* is also clear in several parts of this chapter, including in the discussion of ethnic identity development (pp. 471–474), the acculturation process (p. 503), differences in moral orientation across cultures (pp. 478–480), cultural differences in patterns of parent-adolescent conflict (p. 482), and academic achievement differences (pp. 495–496).

The *nature and nurture* theme was found in the section on causes of sexual orientation, including the "exotic becomes erotic" theory (p. 476), which integrates biological and environmental factors. This theme is also found in the discussion of the life-course persistent pattern of aggressive and delinquent behavior (pp. 490–491).

The *neuroscience* theme was addressed in the discussion of causes of sexual orientation (pp. 475–476), and in the role of brain maturation in teens' greater emotional responding during conflicts with their parents (p. 482).

## KEY TERMS

acculturation (502)
autonomy (481)
biculturalism (503)
child cultural brokers (503)
cliques (489)
collectivism (499)
crowds (489)
cultural deficit perspective (484)
culture (499)
ethnic identity (471)
identity (470)
identity achievement (470)
identity diffusion (471)
identity foreclosure (471)
identity moratorium (471)
individualism (499)
intimacy (487)
life-course persistent pattern (490)
postconventional level (477)
psychological autonomy granting (483)
sexual orientation (474)
stage–environment fit (495)
strength and resilience perspective (485)

# PART FIVE SUMMARY Adolescence: Transition toward Adulthood

## Some Developmental Landmarks

### 12–14 years

- Girls' growth spurt peaks
- Girls experience first menstruation, boys experience first ejaculation
- Body image becomes more important
- Increasing ability to think logically about abstract concepts
- Become more self-conscious
- Believe they are invulnerable
- Begin to explore different identities
- Risk of depression increases
- Conflict with parents
- Time spent with peers increases

### 14–16 years

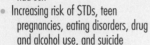

- Boys' growth spurt peaks
- Over 30% of teens have had sex

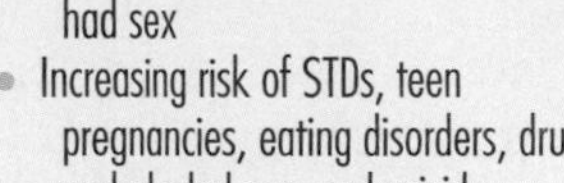

- Increasing risk of STDs, teen pregnancies, eating disorders, drug and alcohol use, and suicide
- Rate of physical exercise declines, especially for girls
- Friendships are based on shared intimacy and similar values, behaviors, and attitudes
- Increasing time spent in mixed gender crowds
- Conformity to peer pressure peaks
- Decision-making skills improve
- Use of teen "slang" words increases
- Teens become increasingly independent from parents

### 16–19 years

- Two-thirds have had sex
- Consistency in use of contraceptives increases
- Lack of sleep increases risk of accidents, errors, and other problems
- Risk of injury and death due to auto accidents increases
- Increasing emphasis on practicality instead of idealism
- Begin to make decisions about education and careers
- Most have part-time jobs
- May begin to question society's rules and develop personal ethical principles
- Rate of conflict with parents declines
- Crowds decrease in importance, dating becomes common

## Physical Development

Puberty produces drastic changes in appearance—adolescents enter this period looking like children and leave it looking like physically mature adults. The timing of puberty varies across adolescents, and those who mature significantly earlier or later than peers may experience different social and emotional effects. Continued brain development enables better reasoning and planning skills but also makes adolescents less responsive to rewards, which contributes to risk-taking behaviors. Two-thirds of adolescents are sexually active by 12th grade. Many are inconsistent in their use of contraceptives, which puts them at high risk for STDs and unintended pregnancies. Teen parenthood is associated with many problems for both parents and children, but outcomes are better if the teens stay in school, delay having another child, and receive support. Overall, adolescence is one of the healthiest periods of life, despite the fact that many teens do not eat well-balanced diets, get less vigorous exercise than recommended, and get too little sleep. Major threats to health and safety are most often the result of auto accidents and risk-taking behaviors such as drug and alcohol use and unprotected sexual activity. The risks of depression, suicide, and eating disorders also increase.

## Cognitive Development

Adolescents gradually develop the abilities to think logically and systematically about abstract, hypothetical problems and possibilities. In later adolescence, thinking may progress even further to the understanding that knowledge is relative rather than absolute and that practical aspects of a situation often must take precedence over ideals when solving a problem. Intellectual skills are defined differently depending on the theory of intelligence, and they continue to develop throughout adolescence. Adolescents often intentionally use slang words and phrases to set them apart from other generations. Decision-making skills improve, gradually including a more thorough consideration of risks and benefits. Teens begin making important decisions about schooling and careers as well as behaviors such as sexual activity and experimentation with drugs and alcohol.

## Socioemotional Development

Adolescents face three main developmental tasks in their socioemotional development: identity, autonomy, and intimacy. They explore different possible selves and are influenced by their cliques and crowds. Crowd membership is less important to older adolescents, who are more secure in their identities and relationships. Most families experience some conflict between teens and parents, especially during early adolescence. Conflict can help teens become independent as long as the conflict is dealt with constructively and is not too intense or frequent. Adolescents build on skills learned in relationships with parents and childhood friends to create intimate friendships and romantic relationships. Important contexts that affect socioemotional development include adolescents' school settings, background culture, and poverty status.

By the end of adolescence, most teenagers have developed a deeper understanding of their individual preferences, skills, and limitations. Most have become relatively autonomous, no longer dependent on parents for making decisions and regulating behavior and emotions. Most have learned how to have good social relationships. Clearly, development does not end with adolescence—there are many important physical, cognitive, and socioemotional changes that happen during adulthood as well. Looking back over the chapters in this book, however, it's clear that adolescents have made tremendous accomplishments on their path to maturity.

# A Few Last Thoughts

Throughout this book, we have emphasized many of the different factors that influence children's development. We'd like to leave you with a few general points to keep in mind.

## Children's Development Is Complex

Children develop physically, emotionally, socially, and cognitively—and all these aspects interact with one another as well as with children's overall family and cultural context. As you have seen over and over, it is usually difficult to give one specific answer to the question of *why:* Why do children do, think, or feel what they do? Why do some children thrive even in the worst of living conditions? Why do others seem to have such difficulty even when they have many advantages? While this complexity may be frustrating at times, it is important to understand that usually there are no quick and easy solutions to the issues that children and their families face.

## Think about Children's Development from Several Different Perspectives

Throughout this book we have emphasized different perspectives—from the different explanations that theorists offer for a developmental phenomenon, to the different professions that deal with children, to the different ways to understand and interpret the data from a single experiment. People (and even entire professions) see things differently, focus on different aspects of a situation, and consider different types of solutions. By trying to look at an issue through another person's eyes we can better understand it. For example, while taking a walk one day with our then 8-year-old skateboarder son, we commented on the remodeling that our neighbors had done to their house. We noticed the inviting front porch and beautifully restored brickwork along the front of the home. Our son had a very different perspective. He exclaimed, "Wow, those steps would be awesome to ollie [meaning, jump over on a skateboard]!" We hadn't even noticed the steps, but our son analyzed them in detail and saw that they offered exciting possibilities. Different people think in different ways; this has a profound impact on what they notice, what they see as a problem, and what they see as possible solutions.

## Be Active in Your Thinking about and Analysis of Child Development Information

As we've pointed out numerous times, sometimes research data can be interpreted in different ways, and often things are more complex than they seem on the surface. Cultivate the habit of asking why a result makes sense and thinking about how the information might be useful to you in your professional and personal life. The more deeply you think about the information you've encountered, the more likely you are to remember it, to use it in the future, and to understand the vast amount of new information you'll encounter in the years to come.

## Most Importantly, Be an Active Advocate for Children

This textbook has given you a foundation for your knowledge of development. You're not expected to be an expert on children and adolescents—no one could be after only one course! But you have gained valuable information that many people you work with, live with, or meet in your life may not have. Build on what you've learned, and use your knowledge to help make children's lives more healthy, positive, and supported. Children depend on caring and supportive adults to help them learn and develop in positive ways. Take the responsibility seriously and help provide the best environment you can for all the children you interact with!

# Glossary

**Abecedarian Project** Project designed to assess the impact of full-time, high-quality intervention beginning in infancy; served primarily African American children living in poverty. (p. 253)

**ability grouping** Placing children in instructional groups based on their ability levels. (p. 386)

**abstract thought** Thought about things that are not real or things that are only possibilities. (p. 436)

**accessing** The process of finding information in memory at the desired time. (p. 328)

**accommodation** The process of modifying old schemes or creating new ones to better fit assimilated information. (p. 149)

**acculturation** The process of learning the language, values, customs, and social skills of a new culture. (p. 502)

**achievement motivation** The degree to which a person chooses to engage in and keep trying to accomplish challenging tasks. (p. 384)

**adaptation** In cognitive development, the process of changing a cognitive structure or the environment (or both) in order to understand the environment. (p. 147)

**adolescent egocentrism** A cognitive immaturity seen in adolescents—their inability to distinguish between one's own abstract reasoning and thoughts and the reasoning and thoughts of others. (p. 436)

**adolescent growth spurt** The increase in growth associated with the onset of puberty. (p. 402)

**adolescent register** Special form of speech adolescents use to identify themselves as belonging to a particular social, cultural, or generational group. (p. 457)

**adoption studies** Comparisons between measurements of children and their adoptive and biological parents used to estimate the genetic contribution to traits and characteristics. (p. 65)

**afterbirth** The third and last stage of birth, in which the placenta and other membranes are delivered through the birth canal. (p. 95)

**allele** An alternative version of a gene; alleles operate in pairs across matched chromosomes. (p. 41)

**amniocentesis** Procedure used to detect chromosomal and genetic abnormalities in the fetus. A needle is inserted through the mother's abdomen and uterus and into the amniotic sac, and fetal cells are withdrawn from the amniotic fluid. (p. 54)

**androgens** One type of sex hormone, released in greater concentration by males. (p. 400)

**animism** The idea that inanimate objects have conscious life and feelings. (p. 232)

**anorexia nervosa** A serious eating disorder involving distorted body image, intense fear of gaining weight, and refusal to maintain a healthy weight. (p. 420)

**Apgar test** A brief assessment of the newborn conducted at 1 and 5 minutes after birth; used to identify newborns who are at risk and need medical attention. (p. 100)

**artificialism** The notion that natural events or objects are under the control of people or of superhuman agents. (p. 232)

**assimilation** The process of bringing new objects or information into a scheme that already exists. (p. 149)

**attachment** An emotional tie to a specific other person or people that endures across time and space. (p. 174)

**attention** The ability to focus on a particular stimulus without becoming distracted by other stimuli. (p. 243)

**attention-deficit/hyperactivity disorder (ADHD)** A condition involving inablity to sustain attention, excessive activity, and deficiencies in impulse control that are unusual for the child's developmental level. (p. 310)

**attributions** Individuals' beliefs about why they or others succeed or fail. (p. 385)

**authoritarian parents** Parents who exert firm control but are rejecting or unresponsive to their children. (p. 272)

**authoritative parents** Parents who are warm and exert firm control. (p. 271)

**autism spectrum disorders (ASDs)** A group of serious developmental disorders characterized by impairments in social interaction and communication. (p. 314)

**autobiographical memories** Memories of events of great personal importance. They are episodic memories and are often vivid and detailed. (p. 333)

**automaticity** The ability to carry out a process with little or no conscious effort, leaving more cognitive capacity to carry out other tasks. (p. 242)

**autonomy** The ability to be independent in thought and action, control impulses, and accept responsibility for one's behavior. (p. 481)

**average children** Children who receive moderate numbers of both "like best" and "like least" nominations. (p. 381)

**behaviorism** An American movement to develop a psychology that was objective and scientific, focusing on the principles of classical conditioning and operant conditioning. (p. 11)

**biculturalism** Adopting two cultural orientations at the same time. (p. 503)

**bilingual** Fluent in two languages. (p. 249)

**binge drinking** Consuming five or more alcoholic drinks on a single occasion. (p. 424)

**body image** The way a person thinks about his or her body and how it looks to others. (p. 402)

**body mass index (BMI)** An indicator of body fat based on weight and height. (p. 292)

**bulimia nervosa** A serious eating disorder with binge eating, followed by purging, fasting, or excessive exercise. (p. 420)

**Caesarean section (C-section) births** Surgical procedure in which the baby is removed through an incision made through the mother's abdomen and into the uterus. (p. 87)

**canalization** Genetic limits on the effects of the environment. In experiential canalization, in contrast, it is the environment that limits the expression of genes. (p. 59)

**cephalocaudal pattern** Pattern of growth where areas in the head and upper body tend to form and grow before the areas in the lower body grow. (p. 78)

**cerebral palsy (CP)** A serious disorder caused by damage to one or more areas of the brain that control muscle movement and coordination. (p. 216)

**child cultural brokers** Children of immigrants who serve as interpreters of the language and culture of the new country for their family members. (p. 503)

**child development** Field of study in which researchers from many disciplines work to describe and understand the important changes that take place as children grow through childhood. (p. 2)

**child maltreatment** A general category including all situations in which parents or other persons in charge of a child's well-being harm the child or otherwise neglect the child's needs. (p. 220)

**child sexual abuse** Abuse that includes fondling a child's genitals or breasts, committing intercourse or other sexual acts with a child, exposing the child to indecent acts, or involving the child in pornography. (p. 220)

**children with exceptional needs** Children who require help beyond what is needed by peers. (p. 309)

**chlamydia** A common STD caused by a bacteria that often produces no symptoms, but that can lead to infertility if untreated. (p. 414)

**chorionic villus sampling (CVS)** Procedure used to detect chromosomal and genetic abnormalities in the fetus. A catheter (tube) is inserted into the uterus, and cells are taken from the chorionic layer of the placenta around the fetus. Chromosomes are removed to conduct genetic tests. (p. 56)

**chromosomes** Strands of deoxyribonucleic acid (DNA) molecules that contain the genetic codes. (p. 38)

**chunking** The process of recoding individual elements in memory into larger groups of information. (p. 324)

**classical conditioning** A kind of learning through association where neutral stimuli are paired with unconditioned stimuli until they come to evoke conditioned responses. (p. 11)

**classroom climate** The social and emotional environment within a classroom; the way the classroom feels to those in it. (p. 386)

**clinical depression** A condition that involves sadness, loss of interest in activities, feelings of worthlessness, sleep problems, and changes in appetite that persist for an unusually long time. (p. 427)

**cliques** Small groups, of usually three to nine friends, who spend time together on a voluntary basis. (p. 489)

**co-sleeping** Practice where infants and young children sleep with one or both parents. (p. 115)

**cognitive development** Component of development related to changes in how children perceive the world, think, remember information, and communicate. (p. 3)

**cognitive developmental theory** A theory that focuses on how children adjust their own understanding as they explore and learn about the world. (p. 13)

**collaborative learning** Process where children work together to help one another solve problems, share their knowledge and skills, and discuss their strategies and knowledge. (p. 239)

**collectivism** A cultural orientation based on the belief people are interdependent members of a social group; emphasizes duty to others and group goals, values, and well-being. (p. 499)

**colostrum** A thick, yellowish substance in breast milk containing important antibodies. (p. 116)

**combinational logic** The ability to generate and systematically consider all possible combinations of a set of elements. (p. 436)

**communication disorders** Conditions in which children have significant difficulty producing speech sounds, using spoken language to communicate, or understanding what other people say. (p. 312)

**comorbidity** Situation in which an individual has more than one disorder or problem at the same time. (p. 310)

**componential subtheory** Describes how mental processes work together to give us intellectual thought ("analytical intelligence"). (p. 444)

**compulsive compliance** A behavior pattern seen among some physically abused children, marked by ready and quick responses aimed at pleasing adults by complying with their demands and wishes. (p. 223)

**computational models** Models of cognition that are programmed on computers: output of the programs is compared to human performance. (p. 339)

**conception** The process of fertilization where a sperm cell combines with an egg cell to create a new organism. (p. 75)

**concrete operational thought** Stage of cognitive development in which children are able to think about two or more dimensions of a problem (decentered thought), dynamic transformations, and reversible operations. (p. 322)

**conduct disorder (CD)** A conduct problem involving consistent violations of other people's basic rights or the breaking of major societal rules. (p. 368)

**conduct problems** A general category of rule-breaking behaviors. (p. 368)

**connectionist models** "Neurally inspired" or neural network models of cognition that view knowledge as based on patterns of activation among interconnected sets of individual units rather than stored as entire concepts. (p. 339)

**conscience** Ideas children have about right and wrong. (p. 268)

**conservation** The understanding that some basic properties of objects remain the same even when a transformation changes the physical appearance. (p. 233)

**constructivist view** The view that people construct their own knowledge and understanding of the world by using what they already know and understand to interpret new experiences. (p. 146)

**contact comfort** The comfortable feeling that infants gain by clinging to a soft attachment figure. (p. 174)

**contextual subtheory** Describes how intelligent behavior is related to real-life situations as people adapt to, select, and/or shape their environments ("practical intelligence"). (p. 445)

**contraception** Methods such as condoms and birth control pills used to prevent pregnancy. (p. 410)

**controversial children** Children who receive large numbers of both "like best" and "like least" nominations. (p. 381)

**convention** A rule or practice that members of a social group agree to abide by in their behaviors, choices, and decisions. (p. 268)

**coordinated imitation** Interaction in which toddler playmates take turns imitating each other and are aware that they are being imitated. (p. 196)

**correlational method** Research method that measures the degree to which two or more variables are related or associated. (p. 21)

**counting strategies** Approaches to solving math problems that involve counting of the quantities. (p. 348)

**critical periods** Segments of time when structures are first forming and are most vulnerable to damage. (p. 79)

**cross-sectional method** A type of research design that studies development by comparing groups of children of different ages against one another at the same point in time. (p. 25)

**crowds** Groups of adolescent peers who have similar reputations or share primary attitudes or activities. (p. 489)

**crystallized ability** The body of specific knowledge and skills acquired in a particular culture. (p. 443)

**cultural deficit perspective** Research perspective that assumed the problems associated with minority group families were due to the ways these families were not "measuring up" to the standards of majority white families. (p. 484)

**culture** A system of shared customs and meanings that allow individuals to participate as a member of a group and that are transmitted from one generation to the next. (p. 499)

**delayed phase preference** Changes in natural circadian rhythms during puberty that cause teens to become sleepy later in the evening and awaken later in the morning. (p. 427)

**descriptive methods** Research methods that describe a behavior of interest, such as how often it occurs and under what conditions. (p. 20)

**developmental psychopathology perspective** The view that a wide variety of factors influences both normal and abnormal paths of development. (p. 309)

**dialect** A consistent and systematic variety of a single language that is shared by a certain subgroup of speakers. (p. 458)

**differentiation** Process that occurs during cell division in which each new cell, as it divides, is committed to becoming a particular structure and serving a particular function. (p. 75)

**difficult temperament** Temperament in which a child is frequently negative, is easily frustrated, withdraws from new situations, is slow to adapt to change, and shows irregular patterns of eating and sleeping. (p. 187)

**dilation** The gradual opening of the cervix caused by labor contractions during the first stage of birth. (p. 93)

**discipline** Techniques used to teach children appropriate behavior. (p. 275)

**dishabituation** The recovery or increase in infant's response when a familiar stimulus is replaced by one that is novel. (p. 142)

**divorce-stress-adjustment perspective** A model used to understand divorce outcomes; emphasizes that a complex interaction of stressors, specific vulnerabilities, and protective factors determine an individual child's adjustment to divorce. (p. 373)

**dizygotic (DZ) twins** Fraternal (fraternal) twins. These twins form when two eggs are fertilized by two different sperm cells. (p. 46)

**DNA** Two strands of molecules that twist around each other like a spiral staircase, connected by a series of nucleotide bases (adenine, thymine, guanine, and cytosine). (p. 38)

**dominant–recessive relationship** Relationship between genes where the dominant allele will govern a particular trait, and the recessive allele will be repressed. To express a recessive trait, the individual needs to inherit two recessive alleles—one on each chromosome. (p. 49)

**Down syndrome** Trisomy 21, a genetic disorder that occurs when there is an extra 21st chromosome. Low IQ, facial defects, heart problems, and shortened life span are characteristic problems. (p. 53)

**dynamic assessment (DA)** A Vygotskian-based approach which assesses learning potential by measuring the degree of improvement in performance after receiving instruction. (p. 449)

**dynamic systems theories** Theories that use models from mathematics and physics to understand complex systems of development. (p. 17)

**early maturation** When the physical changes of puberty occur earlier than they do in the majority of one's peers. (p. 402)

**easy temperament** Temperament in which a child is primarily positive, smiles easily, is adaptive and flexible, and has regular patterns of eating and sleeping. (p. 187)

**ecological systems theory** Theory focusing on the complex set of systems and interacting social layers that can affect children's development. (p. 15)

**egocentrism** The child's inability to take another person's perspective. (p. 233)

**embryonic stage** The second stage of prenatal development, weeks 3 through 8. The embryo forms tissue representing every system and major part of the body. (p. 78)

**emotion contagion** The tendency of the emotional cues displayed by one person to generate similar cues or emotional states in other people. (p. 192)

**encoding** The process of forming a mental representation of information. (p. 328)

**equilibration** The dynamic process of moving between states of cognitive disequilibrium and equilibrium. (p. 149)

**estrogens** One type of sex hormone, released in greater concentration by females. (p. 400)

**ethnic identity** A person's understanding of his or her ethnic background and a feeling of belonging to a minority group. (p. 471)

**ethology** An area of study focusing on the adaptive significance and survival value of behaviors. (p. 15)

**experience-dependent development** Development of specific skills (such as riding a skateboard) in which new synapses form to code the experience. (p. 209)

**experience-expectant development** Development of universal skills (such as hand–eye coordination) in which excess synapses form and are pruned according to experience. (p. 208)

**experiential subtheory** Describes how we become more intelligent as we master new tasks and learn how to perform them more automatically ("creative intelligence"). (p. 444)

**experiment** Method where researchers systematically manipulate an independent variable to deter mine if it causes a difference in a dependent variable. (p. 24)

**fertilization** The union of the father's sperm cell with the mother's egg, yielding one fertilized cell with a unique combination of genes along 46 chromosomes—23 from the father and 23 from the mother. (p. 41)

**fetal alcohol effects (FAE)** Individual or multiple birth defects caused by prenatal exposure to alcohol. Lowered IQ, hyperactivity, growth deficiencies, and physical malformations can exist alone or in combinations but not in a way that indicates FAS. (p. 84)

**fetal alcohol syndrome (FAS)** A syndrome of birth defects caused by prenatal exposure to alcohol. Includes growth deficiencies, head and facial malformations, and central nervous system dysfunction. (p. 83)

**fetal distress** A condition that indicates that the fetus is at risk; usually includes a sudden lack of oxygen (anoxia), a change in fetal heart rate, and/or a change in fetal respiration. (p. 99)

**fetal stage** The third and final stage of prenatal development, lasting from 8 weeks after conception until birth. (p. 79)

**fine motor development** Process of coordinating intricate movements with smaller muscles. (p. 127)

**fluid ability** A biological-based ability to think and perceive relations among elements. (p. 443)

**formal operational thought** Piaget's final stage of cognitive development, when an adolescent gradually learns to use hypothetico-deductive reasoning and to extend logical thinking to abstract concepts. (p. 435)

**fuzzy trace theory** The view that memory representations vary on a continuum from exact and literal to imprecise and general memory traces based on the gist of the information or event. (p. 342)

**G x E interaction** The interacting effects of genetics and the environment on the development of traits and characteristics. (p. 58)

**gateway drugs** Drugs such as alcohol, tobacco, and marijuana that are typically used prior to the onset of using harder drugs such as cocaine and heroin. (p. 425)

**gender constancy** The understanding that gender remains the same despite superficial changes in appearance or behavior. (p. 267)

**gender cultures** Different spheres of influence based on the differences that exist between male and female playgroups and affiliations. (p. 280)

**gender segregation** The tendency of children to associate with others of their same sex. (p. 267)

**gene** A segment of DNA that provides an instruction for a particular structure, function, or trait. (p. 39)

**general intelligence** A broad thinking ability or mental power that underlies all intellectual tasks and functions. (p. 443)

**genotype** The genetic code a person inherits. (p. 59)

**germinal stage** The first stage of prenatal development, from conception through 2 weeks. (p. 76)

**gifted (or talented) children** Children who show extraordinary achievement in one or more areas. (p. 452)

**glial cells** Specialized cells in the nervous system that support neurons in several ways. (p. 208)

**gonorrhea** A common STD caused by a bacteria with often mild symptoms, but that can lead to infertility, blood, or joint problems if untreated. (p. 414)

**goodness of fit** The degree to which the child's temperament and environment are compatible or complementary, leading to better developmental outcomes. (p. 189)

**gross motor development** Process of coordinating movements with the large muscles in the body. (p. 127)

**guided participation** The idea that children are involved in sociocultural activities to the degree that their level of cognitive development allows. (p. 441)

**habituation** The tendency of infants to reduce their response to stimuli that are presented repeatedly. (p. 141)

**habituation–dishabituation technique** Technique used to test infant perception. Infants are shown a stimulus repeatedly until they respond less (habituate) to it. Then a new stimulus is presented. (p. 141)

**helpless orientation** The tendency to attribute success to external and uncontrollable factors such as luck, and to attribute failure to internal and stable factors such as lack of ability. (p. 385)

**heritability** A mathematical estimate of the degree of genetic influence for a given trait or behavior. (p. 64)

**High/Scope Perry Preschool Program** Program offering high-quality partial-day intervention during the school year for young African American children living in poverty. (p. 253)

**holophrases** Single words used to express an entire idea or sentence. (p. 167)

**Human Genome Project** A multinational effort by governments and scientists to map the 3 billion pairs of nucleotide bases and the genes contained in human chromosomes. (p. 39)

**human papillomavirus (HPV)** A common STD caused by any of a group of viruses with more than 100 different strains. Persistent infection is the main risk factor for cervical cancer. (p. 414)

**hypotheses** Specific inferences drawn from theories; researchers test hypotheses by collecting scientific observations. (p. 7)

**hypothetico-deductive reasoning** The ability to use deductive reasoning (reasoning from general to specific facts) to systematically manipulate several variables, test the effects in a systematic way, and reach correct conclusions in complex problems; scientific reasoning. (p. 435)

**I-self** The conscious awareness that you exist as a separate and unique person and that you can affect others. (p. 263)

**identity** A person's self-definition, including a knowledge and understanding of the combination of skills, interests, and characteristics that make him or her a unique person. (p. 470)

**identity achievement** A state of identity development in which a person has experienced and worked through the crisis and has made a commitment. (p. 470)

**identity diffusion** A state of identity development in which a person is not currently in a state of crisis, but there is a lack of commitment. The person either has stopped trying or is unable to reach a commitment. (p. 471)

**identity foreclosure** A state of identity development in which a person has experienced very little crisis but has made a commitment based on what others have said he or she is and should be. (p. 471)

**identity moratorium** A state of identity development in which a person is still in the process of working through the crisis. (p. 471)

**imaginary audience** Adolescents' belief that other people are just as concerned with their behavior, feelings, thoughts, and appearance as they are themselves. (p. 436)

**implantation** Process in which the zygote embeds itself into the inner lining of the mother's uterus. (p. 78)

**individualism** A cultural orientation based on the belief that people are independent of each other; emphasizes individual rights, self-fulfillment, and personal accomplishments. (p. 499)

**Individuals with Disabilities Education Act (IDEA)** Federal law requiring that services be provided to assist all children with disabilities. (p. 216)

**infant mortality** Deaths that occur between birth and 1 year of age. (p. 111)

**infantile amnesia** Inability to remember things and events occurring before the age of 3 or 4. (p. 211)

**information-processing approach** A theoretical approach focusing on how children perceive, store, and retrieve information, and on how they solve problems and communicate with others. (p. 14)

**insecure–avoidant attachment** In Ainsworth's classification, an unhealthy type of attachment that is indicated when infants do not use their caregivers as a safe base for exploring unfamiliar environments, do not prefer the caregiver over unfamiliar adults, and are not visibly distressed by separation. Such infants ignore or avoid their caregivers when reunited after separation. (p. 178)

**insecure–disorganized (or disoriented) attachment** An unhealthy type of attachment that is indicated when infants seem confused or dazed or show contradictory behaviors in the Strange Situation. Infants may be calm and then become angry, or they may be motionless or apprehensive. (p. 179)

**insecure–resistant attachment** In Ainsworth's classification, an unhealthy type of attachment that is indicated when infants seek the proximity of their caregiver but do not seem to gain comfort from the contact. (p. 179)

**intellectual disability** A condition characterized by below-normal intellectual functioning, deficits in adaptive behavior, and an onset early in life (before age 18). (p. 450)

**intelligence** As generally defined in Western cultures, the ability to learn, think logically about abstract concepts, and adapt to the environment. (p. 442)

**intermodal perception** The process of combining or integrating information across sensory modalities. (p. 142)

**internalization** The process of taking external speech and making it internal and mental. (p. 236)

**intimacy** An emotional attachment to another person that involves sharing important personal information and trusting others to hold confidences and be supportive. (p. 487)

**intuitive thought** Thought and logic that is based on a child's personal experience rather than on a formal system of rules. (p. 233)

**inventive spellings** Incorrect spellings that children create by sounding out words and writing the associated letters. (p. 354)

**knowledge base** The amount of information a person knows about a particular topic. (p. 335)

**knowledge telling** Adding or "dumping" in ideas as they come to mind; a failure to selectively organize ideas in writing. (p. 354)

**kwashiorkor** Disease caused by a lack of protein in the diet. Children are severely malnourished, with a swollen belly. (p. 206)

**language acquisition device (LAD)** A brain mechanism in humans that is specialized for acquiring and processing language. (p. 158)

**language** An arbitrary system of symbols (words) that is rule-governed and allows communication about things that are distant in time or space. (p. 156)

**late maturation** When the physical changes of puberty do not occur until after they do in the majority of one's peers. (p.402)

**learning disorders** Conditions involving difficulties with specific skills such as reading, mathematics, or writing. (p. 312)

**learning theory** Theory that sees language as a skilled behavior that children learn through operant conditioning, imitation, and modeling. (p. 157)

**life-course persistent pattern** A pattern of antisocial and delinquent behavior that begins in childhood and continues into adulthood. (p. 490)

**locomotor skills** Skills used to move around, such as walking, running, and climbing. (p. 212)

**long-term memory** Memory of knowledge or events that is permanent. (p. 328)

**longitudinal method** A type of research design that studies development by measuring or observing the same children across time as they grow and mature. (p. 25)

**low birth weight** Weight less than 5½ pounds at birth (2 pounds lighter than average). (p. 83)

**malnutrition** Nutritional deficiency caused by an inadequate intake of calories, protein, vitamins, and minerals. (p. 206)

**malpresentation** Improper positioning of the fetus in the mother's uterus. (p. 99)

**mastery orientation** The tendency to attribute success to internal and controllable factors such as hard work and ability, and to attribute failure to controllable or changeable factors such as effort, strategy, or task difficulty. (p. 385)

**mature tripod grasp** Placing the base of the hand on the writing surface for support, holding the pencil with the index finger and thumb, and moving the wrist along with finer movements in the fingers to guide the pencil more precisely. (p. 213)

**me-self** What you know about yourself and how you describe yourself. (p. 263)

**mediation** The process adults and more skilled peers use to introduce concepts and cognitive structures to less skilled children. (p. 236)

**meiosis** "Reduction division," the type of cell division that occurs during the formation of gametes (sperm and eggs). (p. 44)

**menarche** The first menstrual period for females, usually occurring around 12 to 13 years of age. (p. 401)

**mentoring** The process of taking responsibility for teaching and advising students in a work or school setting to ensure student learning. (p. 463)

**metacognition** The understanding or knowledge that people have about their own thought processes. (p. 243)

**metalinguistic awareness** A person's explicit knowledge about language itself and about his or her own use of it. (p. 344)

**mirror neurons** Neurons that fire when an individual produces an action *and* when the individual observes someone else making the action; the neurons "mirror" the behavior of someone else. (p. 245)

**miscarriage** Naturally occurring loss of pregnancy during the first 20 weeks of gestation. (p. 78)

**mitosis** "Copy division," the type of cell division that occurs when chromosomes are copied into each new cell. (p. 44)

**monozygotic (MZ) twins** Identical twins. These twins form when one zygote divides to make two zygotes. (p. 44)

**moral reasoning** The ways in which people think about right and wrong. (p. 268)

**morality** Knowing the difference between what is right and wrong and acting on that knowledge. (p. 268)

**mutual gaze** Intent eye contact between two people, as when young infants stare at each other. (p. 195)

**myelination** A form of neuron maturation in which the fatty insulation (myelin sheath) grows around the axons. (p. 120)

**nativist theory** Theory that sees language as an innate human capability that develops when language input triggers a *language acquisition device* in the brain. (p. 158)

**nature** The biological forces (e.g., genetics) that govern development. (p. 4)

**neglect** Failure to provide for a child's basic physical, educational, or psychological needs. (p. 220)

**neglected children** Children who have very few peers who like them best or least. (p. 381)

**network models (of memory)** Models of human memory that view memory as an interconnected network of concept nodes connected by links of varying strength. (p. 325)

**neurons** Specialized cells that process information and allow communication in the nervous system. (p. 119)

**neuroscience** Study of the brain and the nervous system. (p. 4)

**niche-picking** The tendency to pick activities and environments that fit with our genetic predispositions. (p. 60)

**nonshared environment** Experiences and aspects of the environment that differ across people. (p. 64)

**nurture** The environmental supports and conditions that impact development. Also refers to learning and experience. (p. 4)

**object permanence** The fact that objects, events, and people continue to exist even when they are out of a child's direct line of sensory input or motor action. (p. 152)

**operant conditioning** A type of learning where a person's actions are reinforced or punished. (p. 12)

**operations** Logical processes that can be reversed. (p. 230)

**oppositional defiant disorder (ODD)** A conduct problem involving a repetitive pattern of defiance, disobedience, and hostility toward authority figures. (p. 368)

**organization** The tendency to integrate separate elements into increasingly complex higher-order structures. (p. 147)

**organized sports** Sporting activities organized, coached, or somehow supervised by adults. (p. 299)

**organogenesis** Organ formation: Process where each major organ and system in the body differentiates within the embryo. (p. 79)

**overregularization** Incorrect application of the linguistic rules for producing past tenses and plurals, resulting in incorrect forms of irregular words such as *goed* or *deers*. (p. 247)

**overweight** Having a body mass index at or above the 95th percentile for the child's age and gender. (p. 292)

**ovulation** Release of an egg (ovum) from the female ovary. (p. 75)

**palmar grasp** An immature grasp, holding the pencil in the palm and moving the whole arm to draw. (p. 213)

**parental control** The degree to which parents set limits, enforce rules, and maintain discipline with children. (p. 271)

**parental warmth** The degree to which parents are accepting, responsive, and compassionate with their children. (p. 270)

**parentification** Role reversal in which a child assumes responsibilities usually taken care of by parents. (p. 371)

**peer nomination technique** A polling technique used to identify categories of popular and unpopular children. (p. 379)

**perception** The cognitive process of organizing, coordinating, and interpreting sensory information. (p. 138)

**permissive parents** Parents who are warm but have little control over their children. (p. 272)

**personal fable** False beliefs that adolescents have about their own thoughts, influence, and risks. (p. 436)

**personal narratives** Stories about personal experiences that use language to inform others about the self and that provide increased self-understanding. (p. 344)

**perspective taking** The ability to understand the psychological perspectives, motives, and needs of others. (p. 268)

**phenotype** The observable trait a person shows, resulting in part from the genotype they inherit. (p. 59)

**phonemic awareness** The understanding that words are made up of smaller units of sound; also, association of printed letters with the sounds that go with them. (p. 351)

**physical abuse** Abuse that causes physical harm to a child. (p. 220)

**physical development** Component of development related to growth in size, strength, and muscle coordination. (p. 2)

**Piaget's cognitive developmental theory** Theory that sees language as one of several abilities that depend on overall cognitive development. Proper cognitive development is a necessary prerequisite for normal language development. (p. 162)

**plasticity** The brain's tendency to remain somewhat flexible or malleable until synaptogenesis is complete and until the brain's synapses have been pruned and locked into particular functions. (p. 295)

**play** A pleasurable activity that is actively engaged in on a voluntary basis, is intrinsically motivated, and contains some nonliteral element. (p. 283)

**popular children** Children whom a large number of peers have chosen as classmates they "like best." (p. 379)

**positive emotion bias** Tendency of children to report more positive than negative emotions. (p. 266)

**positive psychology** Refers to a new emphasis in psychology on the study of happiness and positive development. (p. 6)

**postconventional level** The level of moral reasoning at which people base moral reasoning on an understanding of social contract and utility and universal ethical principles. (p. 477)

**preconventional level** Level of moral reasoning where children do not yet understand that rules are social conventions; children accept the rules of powerful others. (p. 268)

**preferential-looking technique** Technique used to test infant visual perception. If infants consistently look longer at some patterns than at others, researchers infer that the infants can see a difference between the patterns. (p. 138)

**prefrontal cortex** A large part of the frontal lobe of the brain that is important for planning, judgment, decision making, and inhibiting impulsive responding. (p. 406)

**premature (or prematurity)** Refers to babies who are born earlier or smaller than average. (p. 83)

**prenatal development** Development of the organism that occurs before (pre) its birth (natal). (p. 75)

**preoperational thought** Thought characterized by the use of mental representations (symbols) and intuitive thought. (p. 230)

**prepared childbirth** Classes or training that typically provides education about labor and delivery, selective relaxation and controlled breathing, and the help of a labor coach to help mothers with childbirth. (p. 96)

**preterm birth** Births that occur before 37 weeks of gestation. (p. 83)

**prevalence rates** Refers to the percentages or numbers of individuals who show particular problems or conditions. (p. 310)

**private speech** Speech that children say aloud to themselves; later internalized to form inner speech and mental activity. (p. 236)

**probabilistic epigenesis** The likelihood that specific environmental conditions will activate specific genes that lead to particular traits or behavioral outcomes. (p. 62)

**processing capacity** The amount of information a person can remember or think about at one time. (p. 241)

**processing efficiency** The speed and accuracy with which a person can process information. (p. 242)

**production systems** Sets of computerized *if–then statements* that state the specific actions that will be taken under certain conditions. (p. 339)

**programmed cell death** Process by which many neurons die during periods of migration and heavy synaptogenesis. (p. 120)

**Project Head Start** Federally funded, comprehensive program designed to improve academic achievement and opportunity for young children. (p. 253)

**prosocial reasoning** How children think about helping others, including their reasons for deciding whether to help another person. (p. 366)

**proximodistal pattern** Pattern of growth where areas closer to the center of the body tend to form and grow before the areas toward the extremities grow. (p. 79)

**psychoanalytic theories** Theories that focus on the structure of personality and how the conscious and unconscious portions of the self influence behavior and development. (p. 9)

**psychological abuse** Abuse that includes verbal put-downs and other behavior that terrorizes, threatens, rejects, or isolates children. (p. 220)

**psychological autonomy granting** A dimension of parenting that involves encouraging adolescents to develop their own individual opinions and beliefs. (p. 483)

**psychometric approach** The attempt to quantify people's psychological skills and abilities, usually by means of paper-and-pencil tests and/or physical measurements. (p. 443)

**puberty** The process of physical maturation that leads to the physical capability to reproduce. (p. 400)

**punishment** Techniques used to eliminate or reduce undesirable behavior. (p. 275)

**range of reaction** The range of possible phenotypes that exist for a particular genotype. (p. 59)

**rape** Sexual intercourse as a result of physical force or psychological coercion. (p. 418)

**reconstructive memory** A characteristic of human memory. We store parts of events and knowledge; during recall we retrieve the stored pieces and draw inferences about the rest. (p. 330)

**reflective abstraction** The process of noticing and thinking about the implications of information and experiences. (p. 149)

**reflexes** Involuntary movements that are elicited by environmental stimuli. (p. 126)

**rejected children** Children who are actively disliked; a large number of peers have chosen them as classmates they "like least." (p. 380)

**rejecting/neglecting parents** Parents who don't set limits and are unresponsive to their children's needs. (p. 272)

**relational aggression** Withdrawing friendship or otherwise disrupting or threatening social relationships as a way to hurt other people. (p. 365)

**reliability** The consistency of scores when a test is repeated under the same or similar conditions. (p. 448)

**resilient children** Children who rise above adversity to become successful or otherwise develop in positive ways. (p. 6)

**resilient children** Children who succeed, achieve, or otherwise have positive developmental outcomes despite growing up under negative conditions. (p. 369)

**retrieval** In the stores model, retrieval is the process of bringing information from the long-term store to the short-term store. In network models, retrieval is the process of activating information so that it becomes a part of the working memory and thus available for use. (p. 328)

**risk of overweight** Having a body mass index from the 85th to the 95th percentile for the child's age and gender. (p. 292)

**rough-and-tumble play** Very physical, aggressive, but friendly play common among boys during middle childhood. (p. 299)

**scaffolding** Support given to a child as he or she develops a new mental function or learns to perform a particular task. (p. 239)

**scheme** An organized pattern of physical or mental action. (p. 147)

**scientific method** Process where researchers test hypotheses by making systematic observations. (p. 19)

**scripts** Mental representations of the way things typically occur in certain settings or for certain events. (p. 329)

**secure attachment** In Ainsworth's classification system, the healthy type of attachment between an infant and a caregiver. It is indicated when the infant seeks contact with the caregiver, clings, and is soothed by the caregiver and when the infant uses the caregiver as a safe base for exploring unfamiliar environments. Other indicators include *separation anxiety* and *stranger anxiety*. (p. 178)

**selection model** A model used to understand divorce outcomes; emphasizes that certain characteristics of parents (e.g., abusiveness) rather than the divorce itself cause children's negative outcomes. (p. 373)

**self** The characteristics, emotions, and beliefs people have about themselves, including an understanding that people are unique individuals. (p. 263)

**self-conscious emotions** Emotions that relate to people's self-images or what people think about themselves; include shame, embarrassment, guilt, and pride. (p. 194)

**self-esteem** The emotions people feel about themselves. (p. 361)

**self-evaluations** The judgments people make about themselves. (p. 361)

**self-fulfilling prophecy** A prediction that comes true because people believe the prediction and behave in ways that produce the expected outcome. (p. 386)

**self-regulation** The ability to control our own thoughts, behaviors, and emotions and change them to meet the demands of the situation. (p. 264)

**self-representations** The ways people describe themselves; also called *self-concepts.* (p. 361)

**sensitive responsiveness** A quality of infant care in which caregivers respond quickly and warmly to the baby's signals and adjust their responses to allow the infant to direct some of the interactions. (p. 180)

**sensorimotor play** Play that evolves mostly around the practice of sensory activity and the development of new motor actions. (p. 195)

**sensorimotor thought** Thought that is based only on sensory input and physical (motor) actions. (p. 149)

**separation anxiety** Distress infants experience when separated from their primary caregivers. (p. 178)

**sex chromosomes** The 23rd pair of chromosomes (in humans), specialized to determine the sex of the child and other characteristics. Males are XY and females are XX. (p. 48)

**sexual assault** Sexual contact due to physical force or psychological coercion that may or may not involve penetration. (p. 418)

**sexual harassment** Any unwanted behavior of a sexual nature that creates a hostile or offensive environment. (p. 418)

**sexual orientation** Tendency to be attracted to people of the same sex (homosexual orientation), of the opposite sex (heterosexual orientation), or to both sexes (bisexual orientation). (p. 474)

**sexually transmitted diseases (STDs)** A disease transmitted primarily through sexual contact. (p. 408)

**shared environment** Experiences and aspects of the environment that are common across all individuals who are living together. (p. 64)

**situated cognition** The idea that we cannot fully understand children's thinking and cognition without considering the context in which it occurs. (p. 440)

**sleeper effect** Subtle effects of divorce that may not become apparent until children reach adolescence or young adulthood and have difficulty forming intimate and stable relationships. (p. 371)

**slow-to-warm-up temperament** Temperament in which a child shows mildly negative responses to new stimuli and situations but with repeated exposure gradually develops a quiet and positive interest. (p. 187)

**small for gestational age (SGA)** Born below the 10th percentile of birth weight for gestational age; indicates serious health risks. (p. 111)

**social cognition model** A model that explains how different children perceive, interpret, and respond to information in social settings. (p. 382)

**social comparison** The process in which children compare their own qualities and performances to those of their peers. (p. 361)

**social interactionist theory** Theory proposing that language development results from the interaction of biological and social factors and that social interaction is required. (p. 163)

**social learning** A type of learning where children observe and imitate the behaviors of others. (p. 12)

**social policy** Attempts to improve the lives of children and families by using child development research to affect laws, regulations, and programs. (p. 30)

**social referencing** The tendency of infants and children to look for emotional cues from parents and other caregivers to get information in uncertain situations. (p. 193)

**social rules of discourse** Conventions that speakers of a language follow when having a conversation. (p. 248)

**social speech** Speech that we hear as people talk around us or to us. (p. 236)

**socially shared cognition** The idea that thought is a shared group activity and that the thoughts held by an individual are derived at least in part from dynamic interactions occurring between people and in groups. (p. 442)

**sociocultural theory** A theory that focuses on how language and culture influence the growth of thought in children. (p. 14)

**sociodramatic play** Play that involves acting out different social roles or characters. (p. 284)

**socioemotional development** Component of development related to changes in how children interact with other people (e.g., family members, peers, and playmates) and manage their emotions. (p. 3)

**specific intelligence** Abilities people have in particular areas, such as reading, verbal, and spatial skills. (p. 443)

**stage–environment fit** The degree to which the environment is successful in meeting the cognitive, social, and emotional needs of a child in a particular stage of development. (p. 495)

**stillbirth** Naturally occurring loss of pregnancy after 20 weeks of gestation. (p. 78)

**storage** Placing information in permanent, or long-term, memory. (p. 328)

**stores model (of memory)** A model of human memory that views information as moving through a series of storage locations, from the sensory stores to short-term store to long-term store. (p. 324)

**Strange Situation** A structured laboratory procedure that is used to observe attachment behavior in human infants. (p. 176)

**stranger anxiety** Wariness or fear of unfamiliar adults. (p. 177)

**strategies** Conscious, intentional, and controllable plans used to improve performance. (p. 335)

**strategy choice model** The idea that children solve math problems by choosing the fastest approach that they can execute accurately. (p. 348)

**strength and resilience perspective** Research perspective that explores ways that minority families have survived in spite of historical patterns of racism, bigotry, and inequality. (p. 485)

**subitizing** A perceptual process in which people quickly and easily determine how many objects are in a small set without actually counting them. (p. 348)

**substance abuse** The use of a substance that alters psychological functioning to the extent that it creates difficulties in day-to-day life. (p. 423)

**substance use** Ingesting on more than a few occasions any substance that alters psychological functioning. (p. 423)

**Sudden Infant Death Syndrome (SIDS)** Sudden death of an infant before 1 year of age that is not explained by autopsy, medical history, or investigation of the scene of death. (p. 116)

**symbolic play** Play in which children use make-believe and pretend to embellish objects and actions. (p. 198)

**symbolic (representational) thought** The ability to form symbols (or mental representations) that stand for objects or events in the world. (p. 150)

**synaptic pruning** Process in which unused synapses are lost (pruned). (p. 208)

**synaptogenesis** One form of neuron maturation in which dendrites and axons branch out to form an enormously large number of connections with neighboring neurons. (p. 120)

**telegraphic speech** Speech that includes only words that are essential to get the meaning across, leaving out unessential words. (p. 167)

**temperament** The infant or child's behavioral style or primary pattern of reacting to the environment. (p. 187)

**teratogen** Any substance or condition that might disrupt prenatal development and cause birth defects. (p. 81)

**theory** An explanation of how facts fit together, allowing us to understand and predict behavior. (p. 7)

**theory of mind** An integrated understanding of what the mind is, how it works, and why it works that way. (p. 244)

**theory of multiple intelligences** Theory of intelligence emphasizing that we all have multiple intelligences that operate relatively independently of one another; the theory includes eight intelligences. (p. 445)

**triarchic theory of intelligence** Theory of intelligence emphasizing how mental processes, experience, and situational contexts relate to intellectual thought. Includes componential, experiential, and contextual subtheories. (p. 444)

**twin studies** Comparisons between measurements of identical and fraternal twins, used to estimate the genetic contribution to traits and characteristics. (p. 64)

**ultrasonography (ultrasound)** Images of the fetus inside the mother's womb produced by sound waves. Ultrasound can be used to help physicians monitor fetal growth and detect physical defects. (p. 54)

**validity** The ability of a test to measure what it intends to measure (e.g., intelligence). (p. 448)

**very low birth weight** Weight less than 3½ pounds at birth (4 pounds lighter than average); indicates greater potential for health risks. (p. 109)

**visual acuity** The ability to see fine detail. (p. 123)

**working memory** The information currently active in your memory system and currently available for use in a mental task. (p. 327)

**X-linked (sex-linked) traits** Traits that differ in rate of occurrence between males and females, caused by dominant and recessive alleles on the X and Y chromosomes. (p. 52)

**zone of proximal development (ZPD)** The distance between the current maximum independent performance level of the child and the tasks the child can perform if guided by adults or more capable peers. (p. 236)

**zygote** Term used to refer to the human organism after the fertilized egg cell begins to divide. (p. 43)

# References


Aalsma, M. C., Lapsley, D. K., & Flannery, D. J. (2006). Personal fables, narcissism, and adolescent adjustment. *Psychology in the Schools, 43,* 481–491.

ABC News. (2001). An evil smile: Witnesses say suspect looked like he was "getting even." Retrieved March 6, 2001, from abcnews.go.com/sections/us/dailynews/shooting_calif010306.html.

Abel, E. L. (1992). Paternal exposure to alcohol. In T. B. Sonderegger (Ed.), *Perinatal substance abuse: research findings and clinical Implications* (pp. 132–160). Baltimore: The Johns Hopkins University Press.

Abel, E. L. (1993). Paternal alcohol exposure and hyperactivity in rat offspring: Effects of amphetamine. *Neurotoxicology and Teratology, 15,* 445–449.

Abel, E. L. (2004). Paternal contribution to fetal alcohol syndrome. *Addiction Biology, 9,* 127–133.

Abel, E. L., & Sokol, R. J. (1987). Incidence of fetal alcohol syndrome and economic impact of FAS-related anomalies. *Drug and Alcohol Dependence, 19,* 51–70.

Abma, J. C., Martinez, G. M., Mosher, W. D. & Dawson, B. S. (2004). *Teenagers in the United States: Sexual activity, contraceptive use, and childbearing, 2002.* National Center for Health Statistics. Vital Health Statistics Series 23 (24). Retrieved May 27, 2005, from www.cdc.gov/nchs/data/series/sr_23/sr23_024.pdf.

Aboud, F. E., & Doyle, A. B. (1995). The development of in-group pride in black Canadians. *Journal of Cross-Cultural Psychology, 26,* 243–254.

Abutalebi, J. (2008). Neural aspects of second language representation and language control. *Acta Psychologica, 128,* 466–478.

Adams, M. J., Treiman, R., & Pressley, M. (1998). Reading, writing, and literacy. In W, Damon (Ed.), *Handbook of Child Psychology, Vol. 4.* New York: John Wiley & Sons, Inc.

Adams, R., & Laursen, B. (2001). The organization and dynamics of adolescent conflict with parents and friends. *Journal of Marriage and the Family, 63,* 97–110.

Adams, R. J., Courage, M. L., & Mercer, M. E. (1994). Systematic measurement of human neonatal color vision. *Vision Research, 34,* 1691–1701.

Adams, R. J., Maurer, D., & Davis, M. (1986). Newborns' discrimination of chromatic from achromatic stimuli. *Journal of Experimental Child Psychology, 41,* 267–281.

Advocates for Youth (August, 2008). *Adolescent sexual health in Europe and the U.S.—Why the difference?* Washington, DC: Advocates for Youth. Retrieved April 25, 2009 from www.advocatesforyouth.org.

Ahnert, L., Pinquart, M., & Lamb, M. E. (2006). Security of children's relationships with nonpartental care providers: A meta-analysis. *Child Development, 74,* 664–679.

Ainsworth, M. D. S. (1973). The development of infant–mother attachment. In B. M. Caldwell & H. N. Ricciuti (Eds.), *Review of child development research* (Vol. 3, pp. 1–94). Chicago: University of Chicago Press.

Ainsworth, M. D. S., & Wittig, B. A. (1969). Attachment and exploratory behavior of one-year-olds in a Strange Situation. In B. M. Foss (Ed.), *Determinants of infant behavior* (Vol. 4, pp. 111–136). London: Methuen.

Ainsworth, M. D. S., Blehar, M. C, Waters, E., & Wall, S. (1978). *Patterns of attachment: A psychological study of the Strange Situation.* Hillsdale, NJ: Erlbaum.

Ainsworth, M. S. (1967). *Infancy in Uganda.* Baltimore: The Johns Hopkins University Press.

Akhtar, N., & Tomasello, M. (2000). The social nature of words and word learning. In R. M. Golinkoff, K. Hirsh-Pasek, L. Bloom., L. B. Smith, A. L. Woodward, N. Akhtar, M. Tomasello, & G. Hollich, *Becoming a word learner: A debate on lexical acquisition* (pp. 115–135). Oxford, England: Oxford University Press.

Aksan, N., & Kochanska, G. (2005). Conscience in childhood: Old questions, new answers. *Developmental Psychology, 41,* 506–516.

Al-Namlah, A. S., Fernyhough, C., & Meins, E. (2006). Sociocultural influences on the development of verbal mediation: Private speech and phonological recoding in Saudi Arabian and British samples. *Developmental Psychology, 42,* 117–131.

Alan Guttmacher Institute (2002). State-level policies on sexuality, STD education. Retrieved January 6, 2003, from www.guttmacher.org/pubs/ib_5-01.html.

Alderman, M. K. (1999). *Motivation for achievement: Possibilities for teaching and learning.* Mahwah, NJ: Erlbaum.

Aliyu, M. H., Wilson, R. E., Zoorob, R., Chakrabarty, S., Alio, A. P., Kirby, R. S., & Salihu, H. M. (2008). Alcohol consumption during pregnancy and the risk of early stillbirth among singletons. *Alcohol, 42,* 369–374.

Altman, L. K. (2000, June 27). Reading the book of life: The doctor's world; genomic chief has high hopes, and great fears, for genetic testing. *The New York Times.* Retrieved February 15, 2002, from www.nytimes.com.

Amato, P. R. (1994). The implications of research findings on children in stepfamilies. In A. Booth & J. Dunn (Eds.), *Stepfamilies: Who benefits? Who does not?* (pp. 81–87). Hillsdale, NJ: Erlbaum.

Amato, P. R. (1999). Children of divorced parents as young adults. In E. M. Hetherington (Ed.), *Coping with divorce, single parenting, and remarriage: A risk and resiliency perspective* (pp. 147–163). Mahwah, NJ: Erlbaum.

Amato, P. R. (2000). The consequences of divorce for adults and children. *Journal of Marriage and the Family, 62,* 1269–1287.

Amato, P. R., & Booth, A. (1997). *A generation at risk: Growing up in an era of family upheaval.* Cambridge, MA: Harvard University Press.

Amato, P. R., & Keith, B. (1991). Parental divorce and the well-being of children: A meta-analysis. *Psychological Bulletin, 110,* 26–46.

American Academy of Child & Adolescent Psychiatry (2004). *Child sexual abuse.* Retrieved June 22, 2006, from www.aacap.org/publications/factsfam/sexabuse.htm.

American Academy of Pediatrics (2001). Children, adolescents, and television. *Pediatrics, 107,* 423–426.

American Academy of Pediatrics (2003). Prevention of Pediatric Overweight and Obesity. *Pediatrics, 112*(2), 424–430.

American Academy of Pediatrics (2005a). Policy Statement. The changing concept of Sudden Infant Death Syndrome: Diagnostic coding shifts, controversies regarding the sleeping environment, and new variables to consider in reducing risk. *Pediatrics, 116 (2),* 1245–1255.

American Academy of Pediatrics (2005b). Breastfeeding and the use of human milk. *Pediatrics, 115 (2),* 496–506.

American Academy of Pediatrics (2009). Prevention and treatment of childhood overweight and obesity: What families can do. Retrieved May 9, 2009, from www.aap.org/healthtopics/overweight.cfm.

American Academy of Pediatrics. (1998). Guidance for effective discipline. *Pediatrics, 101,* 723–728.

American Association of University Women (2001). *Hostile hallways: Bullying, teasing, and sexual harassment in school.* Washington, DC: AAUW.

American Association on Intellectual and Developmental Disabilities (2009). Definition of Intellectual Disability. Retrieved May 2, 2009, from www.aamr.org/content_100.cfm?navID=21.

American Council on Education (1992). *Sexual harassment on campus: A policy and program of deterrance.* Washington, DC: American Council on Education.

American Medical Association (2009). Obesity. Promoting Healthier Lifestyles. Chicago: American Medical Association. Last accessed May 9, 2009, from www.ama-assn.org/ama/pub/physician-resources/public-health/promoting-healthy-lifestyles/obesity.shtml.

American Psychiatric Association (2000). *Diagnostic and statistical manual of mental disorders-IV-TR.* Arlington, VA: American Psychiatric Association.

American Psychiatric Association (2000). *Diagnostic and statistical manual of mental disorders—TR* (4th ed.). Washington, DC.

American Psychological Association. www.apa.org/ethics/.

American Youth Policy Forum & Center for Workforce Development (June 2000). *Looking forward: School-to-work principles and strategies for sustainability.* Washington, DC. Retrieved July 14, 2005, from www.aypf.org.

Ames, C. (1992). Classrooms: Goals, structures, and student motivation. *Journal of Educational Psychology, 84,* 261–271.

Anand, V. (2007). A study of time management: The correlation between video game usage and academic performance markers. *CyberPsychology & Behavior, 10,* 552–559.

Anderman, E. M., & Maehr, M. L. (1994). Motivation and schooling in the middle grades. *Review of Educational Research, 64,* 287–309.

Anderson, C. (2004). An update on the effects of playing violent video games. *Journal of Adolescence, 27*(1), 113.

Anderson, C. A., & Bushman, B. J. (2001). Effects of violent video games on aggressive behavior, aggressive cognition, aggressive affect, physiological arousal, and prosocial behavior: A meta-analytic review of the scientific literature. *Psychological Science, 12,* 353–359.

Anderson, C. A., Berkowitz, L., Donnerstein, E., Huesmann, L. R., Johnson, J. D., Linz, D., Malamuth, N. M., & Wartella, E. (2003). The influence of media violence on youth. *Psychological Science in the Public Interest, 4*(3), 81–110.

Anderson, D. K., Rhees, R. W., & Fleming, D. E. (1985). Effects of prenatal stress on differentiation of the sexually dimorphic nucleus of the preoptic area (SDN–POA) of the rat brain. *Brain Research, 332,* 113–118.

Anderson, D. R., Huston, A. C., Schmitt, K. L., Linebarger, D. L., & Wright, J. C. (2001). Early childhood television viewing and adolescent behavior. *Monographs of the Society for Research in Child Development, 66* (Serial No. 264), 1–156.

Andersson, H. W. (1996). The Fagan Test of Infant Intelligence: Predictive validity in a random sample. *Psychological Reports,* 78, 1015–1026.

Andraca, I., Pino, P., LaParra, A., & Castillo, F. R. (1998). Risk factors for psychomotor development among infants born under optimal biological conditions. *Revista de Saude Publica, 32,* 138–147. As cited in Santos et al., 2001.

Andrews, J. A., & Lewinsohn, P. M. (1992). Suicidal attempts among older adolescents: Prevalence and co-occurrence with psychiatric disorders. *Journal of the American Academy of Child and Adolescent Psychiatry, 31,* 655–662.

Anglin, J. M. (1993). Vocabulary development: A morphological analysis. *Monographs of the Society for Research in Child Development, 58* (10, Serial No. 238).

Annesi, J. J. (2005). Improvements in self-concept associated with reductions in negative mood in preadolescents enrolled in an after-school physical activity program. *Psychological Reports, 97,* 400–404.

Antell, S., & Keating, D. (1983). Perception of numerical invariance in neonates. *Child Development, 54,* 695–701.

Anuntaseree, W., Mo-suwan, L., Vasiknanonte, P., Kuasirikul, S., Ma-a-lee, A., & Choprapawon, C. (2008). Factors associated with bed sharing and sleep position in Thai neonates. *Child: Care, Health, and Development, 34*(4), 482–490.

Apgar, V. (1953). A proposal for a new method of evaluation in the newborn infant. *Current Research in Anesthesia and Analgesia, 32,* 260.

Arditti, J. A. (1999). Rethinking relationships between divorced mothers and their children: Capitalizing on family strengths. *Family Relations, 48,* 109–119.

Arendt, R. E., Short, E .J., & Singer, L. T. (2004). Children prenatally exposed to cocaine: Developmental outcomes and environmental risks at seven years of age. *Journal of Developmental and Behavioral Pediatrics, 25,* 83–90.

Ashcraft, M. H. (1992). Cognitive arithmetic: A review of data and theory. *Cognition, 44,* 75–106.

Asher, S. R., Parker, J. G., & Walker, D. L. (1996). Distinguishing friendship from acceptance: Implications for intervention and assessment. In W. M. Bukowski, A. F. Newcomb, & W. W. Hartup (Eds.), *The company they keep: Friendship in childhood and adolescence* (pp. 366–405). New York: Cambridge University Press.

Ashford, J., van Lier, P. A. C., Timmermans, M., Cuijpers, P., & Koot, H. M. (2008). Prenatal smoking and internalizing and externalizing problems in children studied from childhood to late adolescence. *Journal of the American Academy of Child and Adolescent Psychiatry, 47*(7), 779–787.

Aslin, R. & Schlaggar, B. (2006). Is myelination the precipitating neural event for language development in infants and toddlers. *Neurology, 66,* 304–305.

Aslin, R. N., Jusczyk, P. W., & Pisoni, D. B. (1998). Speech and auditory processing during infancy. In D. Kuhn & R. S. Siegler (Eds.), Cognitive, language, and perceptual develoment, Vol. 2 (pp. 147–198), in W. Damon (Gen. Ed.), *Handbook of child psychology.* New York: John Wiley & Sons.

Associated Press, (1999, January 15). Mom wins parole after drug rehab. *The State* (Columbia, SC, newspaper), p. B1.

Atkins, C. P. (1993). Do employment recruiters discriminate on the basis of nonstandard dialect? *Journal of Employment Counseling, 30,* 108–118.

Atkinson, R. C., & Shiffrin, R. M. (1968). Human memory: A proposed system and its control processes. In K. W. Spence & J. T. Spence (Eds.), *The psychology of learning and motivation: Advances in research and theory* (Vol. 2, pp. 89–195). New York: Academic Press.

Attinasi, J. J. (1998). English only for California children and the aftermath of proposition 227. *Education, 119,* 263–284.

Atwater, E. (1992). *Adolescence* (2nd ed.). Englewood Cliffs, NJ: Prentice Hall.

Aunola, K., Leskinen, E., Lerkkanen, M., & Nurmi, J. (2004). Developmental dynamics of math performance from preschool to grade 2. *Journal of Educational Psychology, 96,* 699–713.

Autism Society of America (2002). What is autism? Retrieved June 28, 2002, from www.autism-society.org.

Averett, S. L., Rees, D. I. & Argus, L. M. (2002). The impact of government policies and neighborhood characteristics on teenage sexual activity and contraceptive use. *American Journal of Public Health, 92,* 1773–1778.

Avis, J., & Harris, P. L. (1991). Belief-desire reasoning among Baka children: Evidence for a universal conception of mind. *Child Development, 62,* 460–467.

Baddeley, A. D. (1986). *Working memory.* New York: Oxford University Press.

Baden, A. L. (2002). The psychological adjustment of transracial adoptees: An application of the cultural-racial identity model. *Journal of Social Distress and the Homeless, 11,* 167–191,

Bahrick, L. E. (2000). Increasing specificity in the development of intermodal perception. In D. Muir & A. Slater (Eds.), *Infant development: The essential readings* (pp. 119-136). Malden, MA: Blackwell Publishers.

Bailey, A., LeCouteur, A., Gottesman, I., Bolton, P., Simonoff, E., Yuzda, E., & Rutter, M. (1995). Autism as a strongly genetic disorder: Evidence from a British twin study. *Psychological Medicine, 25,* 63–77.

Bailey, J. M., & Pillard, R. C. (1991). A genetic study of male sexual orientation. *Archives of General Psychiatry, 48,* 1089–1096.

Bailey, J. M., & Zucker, K. J. (1995). Childhood sex-typed behavior and sexual orientation: A conceptual analysis and quantitative review. *Developmental Psychology, 31,* 43–55.

Baillargeon, R. (1993). The object concept revisited: New directions in the investigation of infants' physical knowledge. In C. E. Granrud (Ed.), *Visual perception and cognition in infancy* (pp. 265–315). Hillsdale, NJ: Erlbaum.

Baillargeon, R. (2004). Infants' reasoning about hidden objects: Evidence for event-general and event-specific expectations. *Developmental Science, 7,* 391–424.

Baillargeon, R. (2008). Innate ideas revisited: For a principle of persistence in infants' physical reasoning. *Perspectives on Psychological Science, 3,* 2–13.

Baillargeon, R., Zoccolillo, M., Keenan, K., Wu, H., Côté, S., Pérusse, D., et al. (2007). Gender differences in physical aggression: A prospective population-based survey of children before and after 2 years of age. *Developmental Psychology, 43*(1), 13–26.

Baird, A. A., Burber, S. A., Rein, D. A., Maas, L. C., Steingard, R. J., Renshaw, P. F., Cohen, B. M., & Yurgelun-Todd, D. A (1999). Functional magnetic resonance imaging of facial affect recognition in children and adolescents. *Journal of the American Academy of Child and Adolescent Psychiatry, 38,* 195–199.

Baker, K. (1998). Structured English immersion: Breakthrough in teaching limited-English-proficient students. *Phi Delta Kappan, 80,* 199–204.

Bakermans-Kranenburg, M. J., van Ijzendoorn, M. H., Bokhorst, C. L., & Schuengel, C. (2004). The importance of shared environment in infant–father attachment; A behavioral genetic study of the Attachment Q-sort. *Journal of Family Psychology, 18,* 545–549.

Baldi, S., Jin, Y., Skemer, M., Green, P. J., and Herget, D. (2007). *Highlights from PISA 2006: Performance of U.S. 15-year-old students in science and mathematics literacy in an international context* (NCES 2008–016). National Center for Education Statistics, Institute of Education Sciences, U.S. Department of Education. Washington, DC. Retrieved May 10, 2009, from nces.ed.gov/pubsearch/pubsinfo.asp?pubid=2008016.

Baldwin, D. A., Markman, E. M., Bill, B., Desjardins, R. N., Irwin, R. N., & Tidball, G. (1996). Infants' reliance on social criterion for establishing word-object relations. *Child Development, 67,* 3135–3153.

Baltes, P. B., & Kunzmann, U. (2004). The two faces of wisdom: Wisdom as a general theory of knowledge and judgment about excellence in mind and virtue vs. wisdom as everyday realization in people and products. *Human Development, 47,* 290–299.

Baltes, P. B., & Staudinger, U. M. (2000). Wisdom: A metaheuristic (pragmatic) to orchestrate mind and virtue toward excellence. *American Psychologist, 55,* 122–136.

Bandura, A. (1977). *Self-efficacy: The exercise of control.* New York: W. H. Freeman.

Bandura, A., & Walters, R. (1963). *Social learning and personality development.* New York: Holt, Rinehart, & Winston.

Barber, B. K. (2002). *Intrusive parenting: How psychological control affects children and adolescents.* Washington, DC: American Psychological Association.

Barkley, R. A. (1996). Attention-Deficit/Hyperactivity Disorder. In E. J. Mash & R. A. Barkley (Eds.), *Child psychopathology* (pp. 63–112). New York: Guilford Press.

Barkley, R. A. (1998). Attention-Deficit/Hyperactivity Disorder. In E. J. Mash & R. A. Barkley (Eds.), *Treatment of childhood disorders* (pp. 55–110). New York: Guilford Press.

Barkley, R. A. (2003). Attention-Deficit/Hyperactivity Disorder. In E. J. Mash & R. A. Barkley (Eds.), *Child psychopathology* (2nd ed., pp. 63–112). New York: Guilford Press.

Barlow, S. M., Knight, A. F., & Sullivan, F. M. (1979). Prevention by diazepam of adverse effects of maternal restraint stress on postnatal development and learning in the rat. *Teratology, 19,* 105–110.

Barnett, D., Ganiban, J., & Cicchetti, D. (1999). Maltreatment, negative expressivity, and the development of Type D attachments from 12 to 24 months of age. *Monographs of the Society for Research in Child Development, 64*(3), 97–118.

Barnett, W. S. (1998). Long-term effects on cognitive development and school success. In W. S. Barnett & S. S. Boocock (Eds.), *Early care and education for children in poverty: Promises, programs, and long-term results,* (pp. 11–44). Albany: State University of New York Press.

Barrera, M. E., & Maurer, D. (1981). Recognition of mother's photographed face by the three-month-old infant. *Child Development,* 52, 714–716.

Bartholow, B., Bushman, B., & Sestir, M. (2006). Chronic violent video game exposure and desensitization to violence: Behavioral and event-related brain potential data. *Journal of Experimental Social Psychology, 42*(4), 532–539.

Bates, E. A., & Elman, J. L. (2002). Connectionism and the study of change. In M. H. Johnson, Munakata, Y., & R. O. Gilmore (Eds.), *Brain development and cognition: A reader* (2nd ed.) (pp. 420–440). Malden, MA: Blackwell Publishers.

Battin-Pearson, S., Newcomb, M. D., Abbott, R. D., Hill, K. G., Catalano, R. F., & Hawkins, J.D. (2000). Predictors of early high school drop-out: A test of five theories. *Journal of Educational Psychology, 92,* 568–582.

Bauer, P. J. (2006). Event memory. In D. Kuhn & R. S. Siegler (Eds.), *Cognitive, language, and perceptual develoment,* Vol. 2 (pp. 373–425), in W. Damon (Gen. Ed.), *Handbook of child psychology.* New York: Wiley.

Bauer, P. J., & Dow, G. A. (1994). Episodic memory in 16- and 20-month-old children: Specifics are generalized but not forgotten. *Developmental Psychology, 30,* 403–417.

Bauer, P. J., & Mandler, J. M. (1992). Putting the horse before the cart: The use of temporal order in recall of events by one-year-old children. *Developmental Psychology, 28,* 441–452.

Baumrind, D. (1973). The development of instrumental competence through socialization. In A. D. Pick (Ed.), *Minnesota symposia on child psychology* (Vol. 7, pp. 3–46). Minneapolis: University of Minnesota Press.

Baumrind, D. (1991). Effective parenting during the early adolescent transition. In P. A. Cowan & M. Heatherington (Eds.), *Family transitions* (pp. 111–164). Hillsdale, NJ: Erlbaum.

Baumrind, D. (1996). The discipline controversy revisited. *Family Relations, 45,* 405–414.

Baumrind, D., Larzelere, R. E., & Cowan, P. A. (2002). Ordinary physical punishment: Is it harmful? Comment on Gershoff (2002). *Psychological Bulletin, 128,* 580–589.

Baydar, N., & Greek, A. (1997). A longitudinal study of the effects of the birth of a sibling during the first six years of life. *Journal of Marriage & the Family, 59*(4), 939–957.

Baydar, N., & Hyle, P. (1997). A longitudinal study of the effects of the birth of a sibling during preschool and early grade school years. *Journal of Marriage and the Family, 59*(4), 957–966.

Bayliss, D. M., Jarrold, C., Baddeley, A. D., Gunn, D. M., & Leigh E. (2005). Mapping the developmental constraints on working memory span performance. *Developmental Psychology, 41,* 579–597.

Bayliss, D. M., Jarrold, C., Gunn, D. M., & Baddeley, A. D. (2003). The complexities of complex span: Explaining individual differences in working memory in children and adults. *Journal of Experimental Psychology: General, 132,* 71–92.

Beal, C., & Belgrad, S. (1990). The development of message evaluation skills in young children. *Child Development, 61,* 705–712.

Beauchamp, G. K., Cowart, B. J., Mennella, J. A., & Marsh, R. R. (1994). Infant salt taste: Developmental, methodological, and contextual factors. *Developmental Psychobiology, 27,* 353–365.

Beckman, M. (2004). Crime, culpability, and the adolescent brain. *Science, 305*(5684), 596–599.

Behme, C., & Deacon, S. (2008). Language learning in infancy: Does the empirical evidence support a domain specific language acquisition device? *Philosophical Psychology, 21,* 641–671

Behrend, D. A., Rosengren, K. S., & Perlmutter, M. (1992). The relation between private speech and parental interactive style. In R. M. Diaz & L. E. Berk (Eds.), *Private speech: From social interaction to self-regulation* (pp. 85–100). Hillsdale, NJ: Erlbaum.

Beilin, H. (1994). Jean Piaget's enduring contribution to developmental psychology. In R. D. Parke, P. A. Ornstein, J. J. Rieser, & C. Zahn-Waxler (Eds.), *A century of developmental psychology* (pp. 257–290). Washington, DC: American Psychological Association.

Beller, E. K., & Pohl, A. (1986, April). *The Strange Situation revisited.* Paper presented at the biennial meeting of the International Conference on Infant Studies, Beverly Hills, CA.

Bellugi, U., & St. George, M. (Eds.). (2001). *Journal from cognition to brain to gene: Perspectives from Williams syndrome.* Cambridge, MA: The MIT Press.

Belsky, J., & Isabella, R. (1985). Marital and parent–child relationships in family of origin and marital change following the birth of a baby: A retrospective analysis. *Child Development, 56,* 342–349.

Belsky, J., & Rovine, M. J. (1988). Nonmaternal care in the first year of life and the security of infant–parent attachment. *Child Development, 59,* 157–167.

Belsky, J., Jaffee, S. R., Sligo, J., Woodward, L., & Silva, P. A. (2005). Intergenerational transmission of warm-sensitive-stimulating parenting: A prospective study of mothers and fathers of 3-year-olds. *Child Development, 76,* 384–396.

Bem, D. J. (1996). Exotic becomes erotic: A developmental theory of sexual orientation. *Psychological Review, 103,* 320–335.

Bem, D. J. (2000). Exotic becomes erotic: Interpreting the biological correlates of sexual orientation. *Archives of Sexual Behavior, 29,* 531–548.

Bem, D. J. (2008). Is there a causal link between childhood gender nonconformity and adult homosexuality? *Journal of Gay & Lesbian Mental Health, 12,* 61–79.

Ben-Ari, R., & Eliassy, L. (2003). The differential effects of the learning environment on student achievement motivation: A comparison between frontal and complex instruction strategies. *Social Behavior and Personality, 31,* 143–166.

Bengtsson, S. L., Csíkszentmihályi, M., & Ullén, R. (2007). Cortical regions involved in the generation of musical structures during improvisation in pianists. *Journal of Cognitive Neuroscience, 19,* 830–842.

Benham-Deal, T. (2005). Preschool children's accumulated and sustained physical activity. *Perceptual and Motor Skills,* 100, 443–450.

Bennett, D. S., Bendersky, M., & Lewis, M. (2008). Children's cognitive ability from 4 to 9 years old as a function of prenatal cocaine exposure, environmental risk, and maternal verbal intelligence. *Developmental Psychology, 44,* 919–928.

Bennett, S. E., & Assefi, N. P. (2005). School-based teenage pregnancy prevention programs: A systematic review of randomized controlled trials. *Journal of Adolescent Health, 36,* 72–81.

Bentur, Y. (1994). Ionizing and nonionizing radiation in pregnancy. In G. Koren (Ed.), *Maternal–fetal toxicology: A clinician's guide* (pp. 515–572). New York: Marcel Dekker, Inc.

Bentur, Y., & Koren, G. (1994). The common occupational exposures encountered by pregnant women. In G. Koren (Ed.), *Maternal–Fetal toxicology: A clinician's guide* (pp. 425–445). New York: Marcel Dekker, Inc.

Bereiter, C., & Scardamalia, M. (1987). *The psychology of written composition.* Hillsdale, NJ: Erlbaum.

Berenbaum, S. A., & Snyder, E. (1995). Early hormonal influences on childhood sex-typed activity and playmate preferences: Implications for the development of sexual orientation. *Developmental Psychology, 31,* 31–42.

Berk, L. E. (1992). Children's private speech: An overview of theory and the status of research. In R. M. Diaz & L. E. Berk (Eds.), *Private speech: From social interaction to self-regulation,* (pp. 17–53). Hillsdale, NJ: Erlbaum.

Berk, L. E., & Spuhl, S. T. (1995). Maternal interaction, private speech, and task performance in preschool children. *Early Childhood Research Quarterly, 10,* 145–169.

Berkowitz, G. S., & Kasl, S. V. (1983). The role of psychosocial factors in spontaneous preterm delivery. *Journal of Psychosomatic Research, 27,* 283–290.

Berkowitz, G. S., Skovron, M. L., Lapinski, R. H., & Berkowitz, R. L. (1990). Delayed childbearing and the outcome of pregnancy. *The New England Journal of Medicine, 322,* 659–664.

Berliner, L., & Elliot, D. M. (2002). Sexual abuse of children. In J. E. B. Myers, L. Berliner, J. Briere, C. T. Hendrix, T. A. Reid, & C. A. Jenny, (Eds.), *The APSAC handbook on child maltreatment* (2nd ed.) (pp. 55–78). Thousand Oaks, CA: Sage Publications.

Berman, R. A., & Slobin, D. I. (1994). *Relating events in narrative: A crosslinguistic developmental study.* Hillsdale, NJ: Erlbaum.

Berndt, T. J. (1986). Children's comments about their friendships. In M. Perlmutter (Ed.), *Cognitive perspectives on children's social and behavioral development* (pp. 189–212). Hillsdale, NJ: Lawrence Erlbaum Associates.

Bernstein, N., & Chivers, C. J. (2000, May 19). Disabled girl is found dead, amid signs of malnutrition. *New York Times.* Retrieved August 2, 2002, from www.nytimes.com.

Berry, J. W. (1993). Ethnic identity in plural societies. In M. E. Bernal & G. P. Knight (Eds.), *Ethnic identity: Formation and transmission among Hispanic and other minorities* (pp. 271–296). Albany, NY: SUNY Press.

Bettencourt, B. A., & Miller, N. (1996). Gender differences in aggression as a function of provocation: A meta-analysis. *Psychological Bulletin, 119,* 422–447.

Bever, T. G. (1970). The cognitive basis for linguistic structure. In J. R. Hayes (Ed.), *Cognition and the development of language* (pp. 279–362). New York: Wiley.

Bhatt, R. S., Bertin, E., Hayden, A., & Reed, A. (2005). Face processing in infancy: Developmental changes in the use of different kinds of relational information. *Child Development,* 76, 169–181.

Bialystok, E., & Hakuta, K. (1994). *In other words: The science and psychology of second-language acquisition.* New York: Basic Books.

Bialystok, E., & Senman, L. (2004). Executive processes in appearance-reality tasks: The role of inhibition of attention and symbolic representation. *Child Development, 75,* 562–579.

Bialystok, E., Majumder, S., & Martin, M. M. (2003). Developing phonological awareness: Is there a bilingual advantage? *Applied Psycholinguistics, 24,* 27–44.

Bickel, R., Weaver, S., Williams, T., & Lange, L. (1997). Opportunity, community, and teen pregnancy in an Appalachian state. *Journal of Educational Research, 90,* 175–181.

Bierman, K., Domitrovich, C., Nix, R., Gest, S., Welsh, J., Greenberg, M., et al. (2008). Promoting academic and social-emotional school readiness: The Head Start REDI Program. *Child Development, 79*(6), 1802–1817.

Bigelow, B. J. (1977). Children's friendship expectations: A cognitive–developmental study. *Child Development, 48,* 246–253.

Bishop, E. G., Cherny, S. S., Corley, R., Plomin, R., DeFries, J. C., & Hewitt, J. K. (2003). Development genetic analysis of general cognitive ability from 1 to 12 years in a sample of adoptees, biological siblings, and twins. *Intelligence, 31,* 31–50.

Bissel, M. (2000). Socio-economic outcomes of teen pregnancy and parenthood: A review of the literature. *The Canadian Journal of Human Sexuality, 9,* 191–204.

Bjorklund, D. F. (1989). *Children's thinking: Developmental function and individual differences.* Pacific Grove, CA: Brooks/Cole.

Bjorklund, D. F. (1995). *Children's thinking: Developmental functions and individual differences.* Pacific Grove, CA: Brooks/Cole Publishing Company.

Bjorklund, D. F., & Coyle, T. R. (1995). Utilization deficiencies in the development of memory strategies. In F. E. Weinert & W. Schneider (Eds.), *Memory performance and competencies: Issues in growth and development* (pp. 161–180). Hillsdale, NJ: Erlbaum.

Bjorklund, D. F., Miller, P. H., Coyle, T. R., & Slawinski, J. L. (1997). Instructing children to use memory strategies: Evidence of utilization deficiencies in memory training studies. *Developmental Review, 17,* 411–422.

Black, J. E., & Greenough, W. T. (1986). Induction of pattern in neural structure by experience: Implications for cognitive development. In M. E. Lamb, A. L. Brown, & B. Rogoff (Eds.), *Advances in developmental psychology* (Vol. 4, pp. 1–50). Hillsdale, NJ: Erlbaum.

Blair, C. (2002). School readiness: Integrating cognition and emotion in a neurobiological conceptualization of children's functioning at school entry. *American Psychologist, 57,* 111–127.

Blakemore, S. & Choudhury, S. (2006). Development of the adolescent brain: Implications for executive function and social cognition. *Journal of Child Psychology & Psychiatry, 47,* 296–312.

Bliss, L., & McCabe, A. (2008). Personal narratives: Cultural differences and clinical implications. *Topics in Language Disorders, 28,* 162–177.

Bloch, M. N., & Adler, S. M. (1994). African children's play and the emergence of the sexual division of labor. In J. L. Roopnarine, J. E. Johnson, & F. H. Hooper (Eds.), *Children's play in diverse cultures* (pp. 148–178). Albany: State University of New York Press.

Bloom, L., Lightbrown, P., & Hood, L. (1975). Structure and variation in child language. *Monographs of the Society for Research in Child Development,* 40, Serial No. 160.

Boccia, M., & Campos, J. J. (1989). Maternal emotional signals, social referencing, and infants' reactions to strangers. In N. Eisenberg (Ed.), *New directions for child development* (Vol. 44, pp. 25–49). San Francisco: Jossey-Bass.

Bogatz, G. A., & Ball, S. (1977). *The second year of "Sesame Street": A continuing evaluation.* Princeton, NJ: Educational Testing Service.

Bohannon, J. N., & Bonvillian, J. D. (1997). Theoretical approaches to language acquisition. In J. B. Gleason (Ed.), *The development of language* (pp. 259–316). Needham Heights, MA: Allyn and Bacon.

Bohannon, J. N., & Padgett, R. (1996). Useful evidence on negative evidence. *Developmental Psychology,* 32, 551–555.

Bojanowski, J. (2005). Sickle cell disease. *The Gale Encyclopedia of Genetic Disorders* (2nd ed.), Vol. 1, 1181–1188. Detroit, MI: Thomson Gale.

Bondas-Salonen, T. (1998). How women experience the presence of their partners at the births of their babies. *Qualitative Health Research, 8,* 784–800.

Boom, J., Wouters, H., & Keller, M. (2007). A cross-cultural validation of stage development: A Rasch re-analysis of longitudinal socio-moral reasoning data. *Cognitive Development, 22,* 213–229.

Booth, A., & Amato, P. R. (2001). Parental predivorce relations and offspring postdivorce well-being. *Journal of Marriage and the Family, 63,* 197–212.

Bornstein, M. H., & Arterberry, M. E. (1999). Perceptual development. In M. H. Bornstein & M. E. Lamb (Eds.), *Developmental psychology: An advanced textbook,* 4th ed. (pp. 231–274). Mahwah, NJ: Erlbaum.

Bortfeld, H., Wruck, E., & Boas, D. A. (2007). Assessing infants' cortical response to speech using near-infrared spectroscopy. *NeuroImage, 34,* 407–415.

Bos, H. M. W., Sandfort, T. G. M., de Bruyn, E. H, & Hakvoort, E. M. (2008). Same-sex attraction, social relationships, psychosocial functioning, and school performance in early adolescence. *Developmental Psychology, 44,* 59–68.

Bos, H. M. W., van Balen, F., & van den Boom, D. C. (2005). Lesbian families and family functioning: An overview. *Patient Education and Counseling, 59,* 263–275.

Bouchard, T. J. (2004). Genetic influence on human psychological traits. *Current Directions in Psychological Science, 13,* 148–151.

Bouchard, T. J., & McGue, M. (1981). Familial studies of intelligence: A review. *Science, 212,* 1055–1059.

Bouchard, T. J., Jr. (1994). Genes, environment, and personality. *Science, 264,* 1700–1701.

Bouchard, T. J., Jr. (1997). Experience producing drive theory: How genes drive experience and shape personality. *Acta Paediatr Supplement, 422,* 60–64.

Bower, T. G. R. (1974). The evolution of sensory systems. In R. B. MacLeod & H. L. Pick, Jr. (Eds.), *Perception: Essays in honor of James J. Gibson* (pp. 141–165). Ithaca, NY: Cornell University Press.

Bowlby, J. (1958). The nature of the child's tie to his mother. *International Journal of Psycho-Analysis, 39,* 350–373.

Bowlby, J. (1969). *Attachment and loss: Attachment* (Vol. 1). New York: Basic Books.

Bowlby, J. (1988). *A secure base: Parent-child attachment and healthy human development.* New York: Basic Books.

Bowles, A., & Brand, B. (2009) *Learning around the clock: Benefits of expanded learning opportunities for older youth.* Washington, DC: American Youth Policy Forum. Retrieved May 2, 2009, from www.aypf.org/publications/index.htm.

Bowman, P. J., & Howard, C. S. (1985). Race-related socialization, motivation and academic achievement: A study of Black youth in three-generation families. *Journal of the American Academy of Child Psychiatry, 24*, 134–141.

Boyd, D. & Bee, H. (2006). *Lifespan development* (4th ed). Boston, MA: Allyn & Bacon.

Boykin, A. W., & Toms, F. D. (1985). Black child socialization: A conceptual framework. In H. P. McAdoo & J. L. McAdoo (Eds.), *Black children: Social, educational, and parental environments* (pp. 33–51). Newbury Park, CA: Sage.

Bradley, R. H., & Corwyn, R. F. (2002). Socioeconomic status and child development. *Annual Review of Psychology, 53*, 371–399.

Bradley, R. H., & Corwyn, R. F. (2005). Productive activity and the prevention of behavior problems. *Developmental Psychology, 41*, 89–98.

Bradley, R. H., Corwyn, R. F., & Whiteside Mansell, L. (1996). Life at home: Same time, different places. *Early Developmental Parenting, 5*, 251–269.

Bradley, R. H., Corwyn, R. F., McAdoo, H. P., & Coll, C. G. (2001). The home environments of children in the United States. Part I: Variations by age, ethnicity, and poverty status. *Child Development, 72*, 1844–1867.

Brainerd, C. J. (2005). Fuzzy-trace theory: Memory. In C. Izawa & N. Ohta (Eds.), *Human learning and memory: Advances in theory and application: The 4th Tsukuba international conference on memory* (pp. 219–238). Mahwah, NJ: Erlbaum.

Brainerd, C. J., & Gordon, L. L. (1994). Development of verbatim and gist memory for numbers. *Developmental Psychology, 30*, 163–177.

Brainerd, C. J., & Reyna, V. F. (1993). Memory independence and memory interference in cognitive development. *Psychological Review, 100*, 42–67.

Brainerd, C. J., & Reyna, V. F. (1995). Learning rate, learning opportunities, and the development of forgetting. *Developmental Psychology, 31*, 251–262.

Brainerd, C. J., & Reyna, V. F. (2004). Fuzzy-trace theory and memory development. *Developmental Review, 24*, 396–439.

Brainerd, C. J., Holliday, R. E., & Reyna, V. F. (2004). Behavioral measurement of remembering phenomenologies: So simple a child can do it. *Child Development, 75*, 505–522.

Brainerd, C. J., Reyna, V., & Brandes, E. (1995). Are children's false memories more persistent than their true memories? *Psychological Science, 4*, 141–148.

Brainerd, C., Reyna, V., & Ceci, S. (2008). Developmental reversals in false memory: A review of data and theory. *Psychological Bulletin, 134*, 343–382.

Brand-Gruwel, S., Wopereis, I., & Vermetten, Y. (2005). Information problem solving by experts and novices: Analysis of a complex cognitive skill. *Computers in Human Behavior, 21*, 487–508.

Braungart, J. M., Plomin, R., DeFries, J. C., & Fulker, D. W. (1992). Genetic influence on tester-rated infant temperament as assessed by Bayley's Infant Behavior Record: Nonadoptive and adoptive siblings and twins. *Developmental Psychology, 28*, 40–47.

Bray, J. H. (1999). From marriage to remarriage and beyond: Findings from the developmental issues in stepfamilies research project. In E. M. Hetherington (Ed.), *Coping with divorce, single parenting, and remarriage: A risk and resiliency perspective* (pp. 253–271). Mahwah, NJ: Erlbaum.

Brazelton, T. B. (1962). A child-oriented approach to toilet training. *Pediatrics, 29*(1), 121–128.

Breheny, M. & Stephens, C. (2004). Barriers to effective contraception and strategies for overcoming them among adolescent mothers. *Public Health Nursing, 21*, 220–227.

Breivik, K., & Olweus, D. (2006). Adolescents' adjustment in four post-divorce family structures: Single mother, stepfather, joint physical custody and single father families. *Journal of Divorce & Remarriage, 44*, 99–124.

Bremner, J. D., Vermetten, E., Vythilingam, M., Afzal, N., Schmahl, C., Elzinga, B., & Charney, D. S. (2004). Neural correlates of the classic color and emotional Stroop in women with abuse-related posttraumatic stress disorder. *Biological Psychiatry, 55*, 612–620.

Bremner, J. D., Vythilingam, M., Vermetten, E., Southwick, S. M., McGlashan, T., Nazeer, A., et al. (2003). MRI and PET study of deficits in hippocampal structure and function in women with childhood sexual abuse and posttraumatic stress disorder. *American Journal of Psychiatry, 160*(5), 924–932.

Bridge, J. A., Iyengar, S., Salary, C. B., Barbe, R. P., Birmaher, B., Pincus, H. A., et al. (2007). Clinical response and risk for reported suicidal ideation and suicide attempts in pediatric antidepressant treatment: A meta-analysis of randomized controlled trials. *Journal of the American Medical Association, 297*, 1683–1696.

Briefel, R. R., & Johnson, C. L. (2004). Secular trends in dietary intake in the United States. *Annual Review of Nutrition, 24*, 401–431.

Bril, B., & Sabatier, C. (1986). The cultural context of motor development: Postural manipulations in the daily life of Bambara babies (Mali). *International Journal of Behavioral Development, 9*, 439–453.

Bringuier, J. (1980). *Conversations with Jean Piaget.* Chicago: The University of Chicago Press.

Brinkman, B., Cook, K. L., Kahan, D., Elliott, G., Myrick, S., Greene, B., Snow, J., Stein, J. U, & Springs, O. (2005). Should recess be more structured and supervised in order to increase students' physical activity? *JOPERD: The Journal of Physical Education, Recreation & Dance, 76*, 9–49.

Brodzinsky, D. M. (1990). A stress and coping model of adoption adjustment. In D. M. Brodzinsky & M. D. Schechter (Eds.), *The psychology of adoption* (pp. 3–24). New York: Oxford University Press.

Brodzinsky, D. M. (1993). Long-term outcomes in adoption. In R. E. Behrman (Ed.), *The future of children: Adoption* (pp. 153–166). Los Altos, CA: Center for the Future of Children, the Davis and Lucile Packard Foundation.

Bronfenbrenner, U. (1989). Ecological systems theory. In R. Vasta (Ed.), *Annals of child development* (Vol. 6, pp. 187–251). Greenwich, CT: JAI Press.

Bronfenbrenner, U. (1995). The bioecological model from a life course perspective: Reflections of a participant observer. In P. Moen, G. H. Elder, Jr., & K. Lüscher (Eds.), *Examining lives in context* (pp. 599–618). Washington, DC: American Psychological Association.

Bronfenbrenner, U. (Ed.) (2005). *Making human beings human: Bioecological perspectives on human development.* Thousand Oaks, CA: SAGE Publications.

Brookins, G. K., Petersen, A. C., & Brooks, L. M. (1997). Youth and families in the inner city: Influencing positive outcomes. In H. J. Walberg, O. Reyes, & R. P. Weissberg (Eds.), *Children and youth: Interdisciplinary perspectives* (pp. 45–66). Thousand Oaks, CA: Sage Publications.

Brooks-Gunn, J., Duncan, G. J., & Aber, J. L. (1997) (Eds.). *Neighborhood poverty: Vol. I. Context and consequences for children.* New York: Russell Sage Foundation.

Brooks-Gunn, J., Klebanov, P., Liaw, F., & Duncan, G. (1995). Toward an understanding of the effects of poverty upon children. In H. E. Fitzgerald, B. M. Lester, & B. Zuckerman (Eds.), *Children of poverty: Research, health, and policy issues* (pp. 3–37). New York: Garland Publishing, Inc.

Broome, M. E., & Koehler, C. (1986). Childbirth education: A review of effects on the woman and her family. *Family & Community Health, 9*, 33–44.

Brown, A. L., & DeLoache, J. S. (1978). Skills, plans, and self-regulation. In R. S. Siegler (Ed.), *Children's thinking: What develops?* (pp. 3–35). Hillsdale, NJ: Erlbaum.

Brown, B. B. (1990). Peer groups and peer cultures. In S. S. Feldman & G. R. Elliott (Eds.), *At the threshold: The developing adolescent* (pp. 171–196). Cambridge, MA: Harvard University Press.

Brown, B. B. (2004). Adolescents' relationships with peers. In R. M. Lerner & L. Steinberg (Eds.), *Handbook of adolescent psychology* (2nd ed.) (pp. 363–394). Hoboken, NJ: John Wiley & Sons, Inc.

Brown, B. B., & Klute, C. (2003). Friendships, cliques, and crowds. In G. R. Adams & M. D. Berzonsky (Eds.), *Blackwell handbook of adolescence* (pp. 330-348). Malden, MA: Blackwell Publishing, Ltd.

Brown, B. B., & Lohr, M. J. (1987). Peer-group affiliation and adolescent self-esteem: An integration of ego-identity and symbolic-interaction theories. *Journal of Personality and Social Psychology, 52*, 47–55.

Brown, B. B., Clasen, D. R., & Niess, J. D. (1987, April). *Smoke in the looking glass: Adolescents' perceptions of their peer group status.* Paper presented at the biennial meeting of the Society for Research in Child Development, Baltimore (as cited in Brown, 1989).

Brown, E., & Brownell, C. (1990). Individual differences in toddlers' interaction styles. Paper presented at the International Conference on Infant Studies, Montreal, Canada. (As cited in Rubin et al., 1998.)

Brown, M. T. (1995). The career development of African Americans: Theoretical and empirical issues. In F. T. L. Leong (Ed.)., *Career development and vocational behavior of racial and ethnic minorities* (pp. 7–36). Mahwah, NJ: Erlbaum.

Brown, P., & Richman, H. A. (1997). Neighborhood effects and state and local policy. In J. Brooks-Gunn, G. J. Duncan, & J. L. Aber (Eds.), *Neighborhood poverty: Vol. II. Policy implications in studying neighborhoods* (pp. 164–181). New York: Russell Sage Foundation.

Brown, R. (1973). *A first language: The early stages*. Cambridge, MA: Harvard University Press.

Brown, R., & Hanlon, C. (1970). Derivational complexity and the order of acquisition in child speech. In J. R. Hayes (Ed.), *Cognition and the development of language* (pp. 11–53). New York: John Wiley & Sons.

Brown, S. A., Tapert, S. F., Granholm, E. & Delis, D. C. (2000). Neurocognitive functioning of adolescents: Effects of protracted alcohol use. *Alcoholism: Clinical and Experimental Research, 24*, 164–171.

Brown, W. H., Pfeiffer, K. A., McIver, K. L., Dowda, M., Addy, C. L., & Pate, R. R. (2009). Social and environmental factors associated with preschoolers' nonsedentary physical activity. *Child Development, 80*, 45–58.

Browne, J. A., Losen, D. J., & Wald, J. (2001). Zero tolerance: Unfair, with little recourse. In R. J. Skiba & G. G. Noam (Eds.), *Zero tolerance: Can suspension and expulsion keep schools safe?* (pp. 73–100). San Francisco: Jossey-Bass.

Brownell, C. A., Ramani, G. B., & Zerwas, S. (2006). Becoming a social partner with peers: Cooperation and social understanding in one- and two-year-olds. *Child Development, 77*, 803–821.

Bruck, M., & Ceci, S. J. (1999). The suggestibility of children's memory. *Annual Review of Psychology, 50*, 419–439.

Bruck, M., Ceci, S. J., Francouer, E., & Barr, R. J. (1995). "I hardly cried when I got my shot!": Influencing children's reports about a visit to their pediatrician. *Child Development, 66*, 193–208.

Bruner, J. S. (1983). *Child's talk: Learning to use language*. New York: Norton.

Buchanan, C. M., Maccoby, E. E., & Dornbusch, S. M. (1996). *Adolescents after divorce*. Cambridge, MA: Harvard University Press.

Buhi, E., & Goodson, P. (2007). Predictors of adolescent sexual behavior and intention: A theory-guided systematic review. *Journal of Adolescent Health, 40*(1), 4–21.

Bunting, L. & McAuley, C. (2004). Research review: Teenage pregnancy and parenthood: The role of fathers. *Child and Family Social Work, 9*, 295–303.

Burnham, M. M., Goodlin-Jones, B. L., Gaylor, E. E., & Anders, T. F. (2002). Nighttime sleep-wake patterns and self-soothing from birth to one year of age: a longitudinal intervention study. *Journal of Child Psychology and Psychiatry, 43*(6), 713–725.

Burstein, I., Kinch, R. A., & Stern, L. (1974). Anxiety, pregnancy, labor, and the neonate. *American Journal of Obstetrics and Gynecology, 118*, 195–199.

Burton, L. M., Obeidallah, D. A., & Allison, K. (1996). Ethnographic insights on social context and adolescent development among inner-city African American teens. In R. Jessor, A. Colby, & R. Schweder (Eds.), *Ethnography and human development: Context and meaning in social inquiry* (pp. 395–418). Chicago: University of Chicago Press.

Bushman, B., & Anderson, C. (2009). Comfortably numb: Desensitizing effects of violent media on helping others. *Psychological Science, 20*(3), 273–277.

Bushman, B. J., & Huesmann, L. R. (2001). Effects of televised violence on aggression. In D. G. Singer & J. L. Singer (Eds.), *Handbook of children and the media* (pp. 223–254). Thousand Oaks, CA: Sage.

Butler, S., Gross, J., & Hayne, H. (1995). The effect of drawing on memory performance in young children. *Developmental Psychology, 31*, 597–608.

Buyske, S., Bates, M., Gharani, N., Matise, T., Tischfield, J., & Manowitz, P. (2006). Cognitive traits link to human chromosomal regions. *Behavior genetics, 36*(1), 65–76.

Byrnes, J. P. (2001). *Minds, brains, and education: Understanding the psychological and educational relevance of neuroscientific research*. New York: Guilford.

Byrnes, J. P. (2008). *Cognitive Development and Learning in Instructional Contexts* (3rd ed.). Boston, MA: Allyn & Bacon.

Cahan, S., Greenbaum, C., Artman, L., Deluya, N., & Gappel-Gilon, Y. (2008). The differential effects of age and first grade schooling on the development of infralogical and logico-mathematical concrete operations. *Cognitive Development, 23*(2), 258–277.

Camey, X. C., Barrios, C. G., Guerrero, X. R., Nuñez-Urquiza, R. M., Hernández, D. G., & Glass, A. L. (1996). Traditional birth attendants in Mexico: Advantages and inadequacies of care for normal deliveries. *Social Science & Medicine, 43*(2), 199–207.

Campbell, F. A., Pungello, E. P., Miller-Johnson, S., Burchinal, M., & Ramey, C. T. (2001). The development of cognitive and academic abilities: Growth curves from an early childhood educational experiment. *Developmental Psychology, 37*, 231–242.

Campbell, F. A., Wasik, B. H., Pungello, E., Burchinal, M., Barbarin, O., Kainz, K., Sparling, J. J., & Ramey, C. T. (2008). Young adult outcomes of the Abecedarian and CARE early childhood educational interventions. *Early Childhood Research Quarterly, 23*, 452–466

Campos, J. J., Langer, A., & Krowitz, A. (1970). Cardiac responses on the visual cliff in prelocomotor human infants. *Science, 170*, 196–197.

Canino, G., & Roberts, R. E. (2001). Suicidal behavior among Latino youth. *Suicide and Life-Threatening Behavior, 31*, 122–131.

Cantor, J. R., Engle, W., & Hamilton, G. (1991). Short-term memory, working memory, and verbal abilities: How do they relate? *Intelligence, 15*, 229–246.

Card, N., Stucky, B., Sawalani, G., & Little, T. (2008). Direct and indirect aggression during childhood and adolescence: A meta-analytic review of gender differences, intercorrelations, and relations to maladjustment. *Child Development, 79*(5), 1185–1229.

Carey, G., & DiLalla, D. L. (1994). Personality and psychopathology: Genetic perspectives. *Journal of Abnormal Psychology, 103*(1), 32–43.

Carey, S. (1977). The child as a word learner. In M. Halle, J. Bresnan, & G. A. Miller (Eds.), *Linguistic theory and psychological reality* (pp. 264–293). Cambridge, MA: MIT Press.

Carey, S. (1985). Are children fundamentally different kinds of thinkers and learners than adults? In S. F. Chipman, J. W. Segal, & R. Glaser (Eds.), *Thinking and learning skills*, Vol. 2 (pp. 485–517). Hillsdale, NJ: Erlbaum.

Carlton, M. P., & Winsler, A. (1999). School readiness: The need for a paradigm shift. *School Psychology Review, 28*, 338–352.

Carnagey, N., Anderson, C., & Bartholow, B. (2007). Media violence and social neuroscience: New questions and new opportunities. *Current Directions in Psychological Science, 16*(4), 178–182.

Carnagey, N., Anderson, C., & Bushman, B. (2007). The effect of video game violence on physiological desensitization to real-life violence. *Journal of Experimental Social Psychology, 43*(3), 489–496.

Carpenter, M., Nagell, K., & Tomasello, M. (1998). Social cognition, joint attention, and communicative competence from 9 to 15 months of age. *Monographs of the Society for Research in Child Development* (Serial No. 255), *63*(4).

Carraher, T. N., Carraher, D. W., & Schliemann, A. D. (1985). Mathematics in the streets and in the schools. *British Journal of Developmental Psychology, 3*, 21–29.

Carroll, A., Hemingway, F., Bower, J., Ashman, A., Houghton, S., & Durkin, K. (2006). Impulsivity in juvenile delinquency: Differences among early-onset, late-onset, and non-offenders. *Journal of Youth and Adolescence, 35*, 519–529.

Carskadon, M. A., Vieira, C. & Acebo, C. (1993). Association between puberty and delayed phase preference. *Sleep, 16*, 258–262.

Carskadon, M. A., Wolfson, A. R., Acebo, C., Tzischinsky, O. & Seifer, R. (1998). Adolescent sleep patterns, circadian timing, and sleepiness at a transition to early school days. *Sleep, 21*, 871–881.

Carver, P. R., Egan, S. K., & Perry, D. G. (2004). Children who question their heterosexuality. *Developmental Psychology, 40*, 43–53.

Carver, V. C., Kittleson, M. J. & Lacey, E. P. (1990). Adolescent pregnancy: A reason to examine gender differences in sexual knowledge, attitudes and behavior. *Heath Values: Health, Behavior, Education and Promotion, 14*, 24–29.

Case, R. (1985). *Intellectual development: Birth to adulthood*. New York: Academic Press.

Case, R., Kurland, M., & Goldberg, J. (1982). Operational efficiency and the growth of short-term memory span. *Journal of Experimental Child Psychology, 33*, 386–404.

Caselli, M. C., Bates, E., Casadio, P., Fenson, J., Fenson, L., Sanderl, L., & Weir, J. (1995). A cross-linguistic study of early lexical development. *Cognitive Development, 10*, 159–199.

Casey, B., Getz, S., & Galvan, A. (2008). The adolescent brain. *Developmental Review, 28*, 62–77.

Caspi, A., Moffitt, T. E., Morgan, J., Rutter, M., Taylor, A., Arseneault, L., Tully, L., Jacobs, C., Kim-Cohen, J., & Polo-Tomas, M. (2004). Maternal expressed emotion predicts children's antisocial behavior problems: Using monozygotic-twin differences to identify environmental effects on behavioral development. *Developmental Psychology, 40*, 149–161.

Caspi, A., Taylor, A., Moffitt, T. E., & Plomin, R. (2000). Neighborhood deprivation affects children's mental health: Environmental risks identified in a genetic design. *Psychological Science, 11*, 338–342.

Cassidy, J., Parke, R. D., Butkovsky, L., & Braungart, J. M. (1992). Family–peer connections: The roles of emotional expressiveness within the family and children's understanding of emotions. *Child Development, 63*, 603–618.

Cassimatis, N., Bello, P., & Langley, P. (2008). Ability, breadth, and parsimony in computational models of higher-order cognition. *Cognitive Science, 32*, 1304–1322.

Casteel, M. A. (1993). Effects of inference necessity and reading goal on children's inferential generation. *Developmental Psychology, 29*, 346–357.

Caughey, A., Hopkins, L., & Norton, M. (2006). Chorionic villus sampling compared with amniocentesis and the difference in the rate of pregnancy loss. *Obstetrics and Gynecology, 108*(3 Pt. 1), 612–616.

CDC (2009). *Sexual risk behaviors.* Retrieved April 22, 2009, from www.cdc.gov/HealthyYouth/sexualbehaviors/index.htm

CDC (December, 2008). *Sexually transmitted disease surveillance, 2007.* Atlanta, GA: U.S. Department of Health and Human Services. Retrieved April 23, 2009, from www.cdc.gov/std/stats07/main.htm.

CDC (September, 2005). *Sexually transmitted disease surveillance, 2004.* Atlanta, GA: U.S. Department of Health and Human Services. Retrieved May 29, 2005, from www.cdc.gov/std/stats/04pdf/2004SurveillanceAll.pdf.

CDC Fact Sheets on Sexually Transmitted Diseases (2009). Retrieved April 23, 2009, from www.cdc.gov/std/healthcomm/fact_sheets.htm

CDC Injury Fact Book (2002). *Teens Behind the Wheel.* Retrieved May 30, 2006, from www.cdc.gov/ncipc/fact_book/27_Teens_Behind_Wheel.htm.

Ceci, S. J., & Bruck, M. (1998). Children's testimony: Applied and basic issues. In W. Damon, I. E. Sigel, & K. A. Renninger (Eds.), *Handbook of child psychology* (5th ed.), Vol 4: *Child psychology in practice* (pp. 713–774).

Cederholm, M., Haglund, B., & Axelsson, O. (2005). Infant morbidity following amniocentesis and chorionic villus sampling for prenatal karyotyping. *BJOG: An International Journal of Obstetrics & Gynaecology, 112*(4), 394–402.

Centers for Disease Control (2002). Bicycle-related injuries. Retrieved December 6, 2005, from www.cdc.gov/ncipc/fact_book/11_bicycle_related_injuries.htm.

Centers for Disease Control (2003). Physical activity levels among children aged 9–13 years—United States, 2002. *Morbidity and Mortality Weekly Report, 52*, 785–788. Retrieved June 20, 2006, from www.cdc.gov/mmwr/PDF/wk/mm5233.pdf.

Centers for Disease Control (2005a). Barriers to children walking to or from school—United States, 2004. *Morbidity and Mortality Weekly Report, 54*, 949-952. Retrieved June 20, 2006, from www.cdc.gov/mmwr/PDF/wk/mm5438.pdf.

Centers for Disease Control (2005b). Mental health in the United States: Prevalence of diagnosis and medication treatment for attention-deficit/hyperactivity disorder—United States, 2003. *Morbidity and Mortality Weekly Report, 54*(34), 842–847. Retrieved May 10, 2009, from www.cdc.gov/mmwr/PDF/wk/mm5434.pdf.

Centers for Disease Control (2006). BMI—Body mass index: About BMI for children and teens. Retrieved June 24, 2006, from www.cdc.gov/nccdphp/dnpa/bmi/childrens_BMI/about_childrens_BMI.htm.

Centers for Disease Control (2009). Unintentional injuries, ages 7–11, United States, 2006; and 10 leading causes of nonfatal injury, ages 7–11, United States, 2007. Both are results from custom searchers conducted using the WISQARS system at the CDC site. Last accessed May 10, 2009, from www.cdc.gov/injury/wisqars/index. html.

Centers for Disease Control and Prevention (2001). Racial disparities in median age at death of persons with Down Syndrome—United States, 1968–1997. *Morbidity and Mortality Weekly Report, 50* (22), 463–465. Retrieved October 25, 2008, from www.cdc.gov/mmwr/preview/mmwrhtml/mm5022a3.htm.

Centers for Disease Control and Prevention (CDC). (2005). Fetal alcohol syndrome. From the National Center on Birth Defects and Developmental Disabilities. Retrieved June 9, 2006, from www.cdc.gov/ncbddd/fas/faqs.htm.

Centers for Disease Control and Prevention (CDC). (June, 2008). Stillbirths. Retrieved December 23, 2008, from www.cdc.gov/ncbddd/bd/stillbirths.htm.

Centers for Disease Control and Prevention (CDC). (November, 2007a). Sexually transmitted disease surveillance, 2006. Atlanta: U.S. Department of Health and Human Services. Retrieved December 30, 2008, from www.cdc.gov/std/stats/toc2006.htm.

Centers for Disease Control and Prevention (CDC). (October, 2007b). HIV/AIDS and pregnancy and childbirth. Atlanta: Department of Health and Human Services. Retrieved December 30, 2008, from www.cdc.gov/hiv/topics/perinatal/index.htm.

Cernoch, J. M., & Porter, R. H. (1985). Recognition of maternal axillary odors by infants. *Child Development, 56*, 1593–1598.

Chall, J. S. (1983). *Stages of reading development.* New York: McGraw-Hill Book Company.

Chang, L. (2003). Variable effects of children's aggression, social withdrawal, and prosocial leadership as functions of teacher beliefs and behaviors. *Child Development, 74*, 535–548.

Chao, R. K. (1994). Beyond parental control and authoritarian parenting style: Understanding Chinese parenting through the cultural notion of training. *Child Development, 65*, 1111–1119.

Chao, R. K. (2001). Extending research on the consequences of parenting styles for Chinese Americans and European Americans. *Child Development, 72*, 1832–1843.

Chaplin, T. M., Cole, P. M., & Zahn-Waxler, C. (2005). Parental socialization of emotion expression: Gender differences and relations to child adjustment. *Emotion, 5*, 80–88.

Chassin, L., Hussong, A., Barrera, M., Molina, B. S. G., Trim, R. & Ritter, J. (2004). Adolescent substance use. In R. M. Lerner & L. Steinberg (Eds.), *Handbook of adolescent psychology* (pp. 665–696). Hoboken, NJ: John Wiley & Sons, Inc.

Chen, J., & Gardner, H. (2005). Assessment based on multiple-intelligences theory. In D.P. Flanagan, & P. L. Harrison (Eds.), *Contemporary intellectual assessment: Theories, tests, and issues* (pp. 77–102). New York: Guilford Press.

Chen, X., Wen, S. W., Krewski, D., Fleming, N., Yang, Q., & Walker, M. C. (2008). Paternal age and adverse birth outcomes: Teenager or 40+, who is at risk? *Human Reproduction, 23*(6), 1290–1296.

Cheng, L. L. (1987). Cross-cultural and linguistic considerations in working with Asian populations. *ASHA, 29*, 33–38.

Cherny, S. S., Fulker, D. W., Emde, R. N., Robinson, J., Corley, R. P., Reznick, J. S., et al. (1994). A developmental-genetic analysis of continuity and change in the Bayley mental development index from 14 to 24 months: The MacArthur Longitudinal Twin Study. *Psychological Science, 5*, 354–360.

Chess, S., & Thomas, A. (1995). *Temperament in clinical practice.* New York: Guilford Press.

Cheung, H., Hsuan-Chih, C., Creed, N., Ng, L., Wang, S. P., & Mo, L. (2004). Relative roles of general and complementation language in theory-of-mind development: Evidence from Cantonese and English. *Child Development, 75*, 1155–1170.

Chi, M. T. H. (1978). Knowledge structure and memory development. In R. Siegler (Ed.), *Children's thinking: What develops?* (pp. 73–96) Hillsdale, NJ: Erlbaum.

Chi, M. T. H., & Koeske, R. D. (1983). Network representation of a child's dinosaur knowledge. *Developmental Psychology, 19*, 29–39.

Chi, M. T. H., Feltovich, P. J., & Glaser, R. (1981). Categorization and representation of physics problems by experts and novices. *Cognitive Science, 5*, 121–152.

Chi, M. T. H., Glaser, R., & Farr, M. (Eds.) (1988). *The nature of expertise.* Hillsdale, NJ: Erlbaum.

Childers, J. B., & Tomasello, M. (2002). Two-year-olds learn novel nouns, verbs, and conventional actions from massed or distributed exposures. *Developmental Psychology*, 38, 967–978.

Children's Defense Fund (2001). *The state of America's children yearbook 2001.* Washington, DC: CDF Publications.

Children's Defense Fund (2008). *Each day in America; child health; and Census 2000 supplementary survey: Poverty status during previous 12 months, by age.* Three reports retrieved October 20, 2008, from www.childrensdefense.org.

Children's Defense Fund (2008). *State of America's children, 2008.* Retrieved May 10, 2009, from www.childrensdefense.org/child-research-data-publications/data/state-of-americas-children-2008-report.html.

Ching, J., & Newton, N. (1982). A prospective study of psychological and social factors in pregnancy related to preterm and low-birth-weight deliveries. In H. J. Prill & M. Stauber (Eds.), *Advances in psychosomatic obstetrics and gynecology* (pp. 384–385). New York: Springer-Verlag.

Chirkov, V., Ryan, R. M., Kim, Y., & Kaplan, U. (2003). Differentiating autonomy from individualism and independence: A self-determination theory perspective on internalization of cultural orientations and well-being. *Journal of Personality and Social Psychology, 84,* 97–101.

Chiu, L. H., (1987). Child-rearing attitudes of Chinese, Chinese-American, and Anglo-American mothers. *International Journal of Psychology, 22,* 409–419.

Chomsky, N. S. (1957). *Syntactic structures.* The Hague: Mouton.

Chomsky, N. S. (1981). *Lectures on government and binding.* New York: Foris.

Christie-Mizell, C. A., Pryor, E. M., & Grossman, E. R. B. (2008). Child depressive symptoms, spanking, and emotional support: Differences between African American and European American youth. *Family Relations, 57,* 335–350.

Chugani, H. T. (1998). A critical period of brain development: Studies of cerebral glucose utilization with PET. *Preventive Medicine, 27*(2), 184–188.

Chumlea, W. C., Schubert, C. M., Roche, A. F., Kulin, H. E., Lee, P. A., Himes, J. H., & Sun, S. S. (2003). Age at menarche and racial comparisons in U.S. girls. *Pediatrics, 111,* 110–113.

Chun, K. M., Organista, P. B., & Marin, G. (Eds.) (2003). *Acculturation: Advances in theory, measurement, and applied research.* Washington, DC: American Psychological Association.

Cicchetti, D., Toth, S., & Bush, M. (1988). Developmental psychopathology and incompetence in childhood: Suggestions for intervention. In B. B. Lahey & A. E. Kazdin (Eds.), *Advances in clinical child psychology* (Vol. 11, pp. 1–77). New York: Plenum.

Clarke-Stewart, K. A., Vandell, D. L., McCartney, K., Owen, M. T., & Booth, C. (2000). Effects of parental separation and divorce on very young children. *Journal of Family Psychology, 14,* 304–326.

Clement, J. (1982). Algebra word problem solutions: Thought processes underlying a common misconception. *Journal for Research in Mathematics Education, 13,* 16–30.

Clements, P. T., Speck, P. M., Crane, P. A., & Faulkner, M. J. (2004). Issues and dynamics of sexually assaulted adolesents and their families. *International Journal of Mental Health Nursing, 13,* 267–274.

Cleveland, E. S., & Reese, E. (2005). Maternal structure and autonomy support in conversations about the past: Contributions to children's autobiographical memory. *Developmental Psychology, 41,* 376–388.

Cleveland, H. H., & Wiebe, R. P. (2003). The moderation of adolescent-to-peer similarity in tobacco and alcohol use by school levels of substance use. *Child Development, 74,* 279–291.

Cloninger, C. R., Adolfsson, R., & Svrakic, N. M. (1996). Mapping genes for human personality. *Nature Genetics, 12,* 3–4.

Clopton, N. A., & Sorell, G. T. (1993). Gender differences in moral reasoning: Stable or situational? *Psychology of Women Quarterly, 17,* 85–101.

Clymer, A. (2002, November 26). Critics say government deleted sexual material from web sites to push abstinence. *New York Times.* Retrieved January 6, 2003, from www.nytimes.com.

Cnattingius, S., Forman, M. R., Berendes, H. W., & Isotalo, L. (1992). Delayed childbearing and risk of adverse perinatal outcome. *Journal of the American Medical Association, 19,* 886–890.

Cohen, D. A., Farley, T. A., Taylor, S. N., Martin, D. H., & Schuster, M. A. (2002). When and where do youths have sex? The potential role of adult supervision. *Pediatrics, 110,* e66. Retrieved May 28, 2006, from www.pediatrics.org/cgi/content/full/110/6/e66.

Cohen, L. B., & Cashon, C. H. (2006). Infant cognition. In D. Kuhn & R. S. Siegler (Eds.), *Cognition, perception, and language,* Vol. 2 (pp. 214–251), in W. Damon & R. M. Lerner (Gen. Eds.), *Handbook of child psychology,* 6th ed. New York: John Wiley & Sons.

Cohen, L. B., DeLoache, J. S., & Strauss, M. S. (1979). Infant visual perception. In J. D. Osofsky (Ed.), *Handbook of infant development* (pp. 393–438). New York: John Wiley & Sons.

Cohen, L. B., Gelber, E. R., & Lazar, M. A. (1971). Infant habituation and generalization to differing degrees of stimulus novelty. *Journal of Experimental Child Psychology,* 11, 379–389.

Coie, J. D., & Dodge, K. A. (1988). Multiple sources of data on social behavior and social status. *Child Development, 59,* 815–829.

Coie, J. D., & Dodge, K. A. (1998). Aggression and antisocial behavior. In W. Damon & N. Eisenberg (Eds.), *Handbook of child psychology: Vol 3. Social, emotional, and personality development* (pp. 779–862). New York: Wiley.

Colby, A., Kohlberg, L., Gibbs, J. C., & Lieberman, M. (1983). A longitudinal study of moral judgment. *Monographs of the Society for Research in Child Development, 48*(1–2, Serial No. 200).

Cole, M. (1999). Culture in development. In M. H. Bornstein & M. E. Lamb (Eds.), *Developmental psychology: An advanced textbook* (pp. 73–123). Mahwah, NJ: Erlbaum.

Coley, R. L., & Chase-Lansdale, P. L. (1998). Adolescent pregnancy and parenthood: Recent evidence and future direction. *American Psychologist, 53,* 152–166.

Collins, D., Johnson, K., & Becker, B. (2007). A meta-analysis of direct and mediating effects of community coalitions that implemented science-based substance abuse prevention interventions. *Substance Use & Misuse, 4,* 985–1007.

Collins, M., & Nowicki, S. (2001). African American children's ability to identify emotion in facial expressions and tones of voice of European Americans. *Journal of Genetic Psychology, 162,* 334–346.

Collins, W. A., & Laursen, B. (2004). Parent-adolescent relationships and influences. In R. M. Lerner & L. Steinberg (Eds.), *Handbook of Adolescent Psychology* (2nd ed.) (pp. 331–361). Hoboken, NJ: John Wiley & Sons, Inc.

Colombo, J., & Bundy, R. S. (1981). A method for the measurement of infant auditory selectivity. *Infant Behavior & Development, 4,* 219–233.

Committee on Sports Medicine & Fitness (2000). Injuries in youth soccer: A subject review. *Pediatrics, 105,* 659–661.

Commons, M. L., Miller, P. M., & Kuhn, D. (1982). The relation between formal operational reasoning and academic course selection and performance among college freshmen and sophomores. *Journal of Applied Developmental Psychology, 3,* 1–10.

Comstock, G., & Scharrer, E. (2006). Media and popular culture. In W. Damon & R. M. Lerner (Series Ed.) and K. A. Renninger & I. E. Sigel (Vol. Eds.), *Handbook of Child Psychology: Vol. 4. Child Psychology in Practice* (pp. 817–863). New York: John Wiley & Sons.

Conboy, B., & Mills, D. (2006). Two languages, one developing brain: event-related potentials to words in bilingual toddlers. *Developmental Science, 9*(1), F1–F12.

Conboy, B. T., & Thal, D. J. (2006). Ties between the lexicon and grammar: Cross-sectional and longitudinal studies of bilingual toddlers. *Child Development, 77,* 712–735.

Conger, R. D., & Chao, W. (1996). Adolescent depressed mood. In R. L. Simons (Ed.), *Understanding differences between divorced and intact families* (pp. 157–175). Thousand Oaks, CA: Sage.

Cooley, C. H. (1902). *Human nature and the social order.* New York: Charles Scribner's Sons.

Cooper, L. & Cates, P. (2006). *Too high a price: The case against restricting gay parenting* (2nd ed.). New York: American Civil Liberties Union Foundation. Retrieved May 10, 2009, from www.aclu.org/lgbt/ parenting/27496pub20061113.html.

Cooper, R. P., & Aslin, R. N. (1994). Developmental differences in infant attention to the spectral properties of infant-directed speech. *Child Development, 65,* 1663–1677.

Coplan, R. J., Prakash, K., O'Neil, K., & Armer, M. (2004). Do you "want" to play? Distinguishing between conflicted shyness and social disinterest in early childhood. *Developmental Psychology, 40,* 244–258.

Copper, R. L., Goldenberg, R. L., Creasy, R. K., DuBard, M. B., Davis, R. O., Entman, S. S., Iams, J. D., & Cliver, S. P. (1993). A multicenter study of preterm birth weight and gestational age-specific neonatal mortality. *American Journal of Obstetrics and Gynecology, 168,* 78–84.

Cornelius, M. D., Goldschmidt, L., Day, N. L., & Larkby, C. (2002). Alcohol, tobacco and marijuana use among pregnant teenagers: Six-year follow-up of offspring growth effects. *Neurotoxicology and Teratology, 24*(6), 703–710.

Cornell, T. L., Fromkin, V. A., & Mauner, G. (1993). A linguistic approach to language processing in Broca's aphasia: A paradox resolved. *Current Directions in Psychological Science,* 247–52.

Corrigan, R. (1987). A developmental sequence of actor-object pretend play in young children. *Merrill-Palmer Quarterly, 33,* 87–106.

Couperus, J. W., & Nelson, C. A. (2006). Early brain development and plasticity. In K. McCartney & D. Phillips (Eds.), *Blackwell handbook of early childhood development* (pp. 85–105). Malden, MA: Blackwell Publishing.

Courage, M. L., & Setliff, A. E. (2009). Debating the impact of television and video material on very young children: Attention, learning, and the developing brain. *Child Development Perspectives, 3*, 72–78.

Cowan, N. (1995). *Attention and memory: An integrated framework.* New York: Oxford University Press.

Cowan, N. (1997). The development of working memory. In N. Cowan & C. Hulme (Eds.), *The development of memory in childhood* (pp. 163–200). Hove East Sussex, UK: Psychology Press.

Cowan, N., Nugent, L. D., Elliot, E. M., Ponomarev, I., & Saults, J. S. (1999). The role of attention in the development of short-term memory: Age differences in the verbal span of apprehension. *Child Development, 70*, 1082–1097.

Cowden, A. J. & Funkhouser, E. (2001). Adolescent pregnancy, infant mortality, and source of payment for birth: Alabama residential live births, 1991–1994. *Journal of Adolescent Health, 29*, 37–45.

Cox, A. (2005). What are communities of practice? A comparative review of four seminal works. *Journal of Information Science, 31*, 527–540.

Coyle, T. R., & Bjorklund, D. F. (1997). Age differences in, and consequences of, multiple- and variable-strategy use on a multitrial sort-recall task. *Developmental Psychology, 33*, 372–380.

Crawford, J. (1997). *Best evidence: Research foundations of the Bilingual Education Act.* Washington, DC: National Clearinghouse for Bilingual Education. Retrieved on December 24, 2002, from www.ncela.gwu.edu/ncbepugs/reports/bestevidence/.

Crick, N. R., & Dodge, K. A. (1994). A review and reformulation of social information-processing mechanisms in children's social adjustment. *Psychological Bulletin, 115*, 74–101.

Crick, N. R., & Grotpeter, J. K. (1995). Relational aggression, gender, and social–psychological adjustment. *Child Development, 66*, 710–722.

Crissey, S. R. (2009). Educational attainment in the United States: 2007. Current Population Reports. Washington, DC: U.S. Census Bureau. Retrieved May 10, 2009, from www.census.gov/population/www/socdemo/educ-attn.html.

Crittenden, P. M., & DiLalla, D. L. (1988). Compulsive compliance: The development of an inhibitory coping strategy in infancy. *Journal of Abnormal Child Psychology, 16*, 585–599.

Crockett, L. J., Shanahan, M. J., & Jackson-Newsom, J. (2000). Rural youth: Ecological and life course perspectives. In R. Montemayor, G. R. Adams, & T. P. Gullotta (Eds.), *Adolescent diversity in ethnic, economic, and cultural contexts* (pp. 43–74). Thousand Oaks, CA: Sage Publications.

Crockett, L., Losoff, M., & Petersen, A. C. (1984). Perceptions of the peer group and friendship in early adolescence. *Journal of Early Adolescence, 4*, 155–181.

Cronenwett, L. R. & Newmark, L. L. (1974). Fathers' responses to childbirth. *Nursing Research, 23*, 210–217.

Crook, C. K. (1987). Taste and olfaction. In P. Salapatek & L. B. Cohen (Eds.), *Handbook of infant perception* (Vol. 1, pp. 237–264). New York: Academic Press.

Crosnoe, R., & Elder, G. H., Jr. (2002). Adolescent twins and emotional distress: The interrelated influence of nonshared environment and social structure. *Child Development, 73*, 1761–1774.

Csikszentmihalyi, M., & Larson, R. (1984). *Being adolescent: Conflict and growth in the teenage years.* New York: Basic Books.

Csikszentmihalyi, M., Rathunde, K., & Whalen, S. (1997). *Talented teenagers: The roots of success and failure.* Cambridge, England: Cambridge University Press.

Cuevas, K., Rovee-Collier, C., & Learmonth, A. (2006). Infants form associations between memory representations of stimuli that are absent. *Psychological Science, 17*(6), 543–549.

Cummins, J. (1991). Interdependence of first- and second-language proficiency in bilingual children. In E. Bialystok (Ed.), *Language processing in bilingual children* (pp. 70–89). Cambridge: Cambridge University Press.

Curtiss, S. (1977). *Genie: A psycholinguistic study of a modern-day "wild child."* New York: Academic Press.

Curtiss, S. (1981). Dissociations between language and cognition: Cases and implications. *Journal of Autism and Developmental Disorders, 11*, 15–30.

D'Alessandro, M. P. (2002). Rickets, vitamin–D resistant. Retrieved March 1, 2002, from www.vh.org.

D'Augelli, A. R., Grossman, A. H., Salter, N. P., Vasey, J. J., Starks, M. S., & Sinclair, K. O. (2005). Predicting the suicide attempts of lesbian, gay, and bisexual youth. *Suicide and Life-Threatening Behavior, 35*, 646–660.

Dahl, R. E., & Spear, L. P. (2004). *Adolescent brain development: Vulnerabilities and opportunities.* New York: New York Academy of Sciences.

Dalterio, S. L., & Fried, P. A. (1992). The effects of marijuana use on offspring. In T. B. Sonderegger (Ed.), *Perinatal substance abuse: Research findings and clinical applications* (pp. 161–183). Baltimore: The Johns Hopkins University Press.

Darkness 2 Light (2006). Darkness2light.org.

Davenport-Slack, B., & Boylan, C. H. (1974). Psychological correlates of childbirth pain. *Psychosomatic Medicine, 36*, 215–223.

Davison, K. K., & Birch, L. L. (2002). Processes linking weight status and self-concept among girls ages 5 to 7 years. *Developmental Psychology, 38*, 735–748.

Dawson, G., Carver, L., Meltzoff, A. N., Panagiotides, H., McPartland, J., & Webb, S. J. (2002). Neural correlates of face and object recognition in young children with autism spectrum disorder, developmental delay, and typical development. *Child Development, 73*, 700–717.

Dawson, T. (2002). New tools, new insights: Kohlberg's moral judgment stages revisited. *International Journal of Behavioral Development, 26*, 154–166.

de Haan, M., & Nelson, C. (1999). Brain activity differentiates face and object processing in 6-month-old infants. *Developmental Psychology, 35*, 1113–1121.

de Onis, M., Monteiro, C., Akré, J., & Clugston, G. (2002). The worldwide magnitude of protein–energy malnutrition: An overview from the WHO Global Database on Child Growth. Retrieved March 22, 2002, from www.WHO.int/whosis/cgrowth/bulletin.htm.

de Villiers, J. G., & de Villiers, P. A. (1999). Language development. In M. H. Bornstein & M. E. Lamb (Eds.), *Developmental psychology: An advanced textbook* (4th ed.) (pp. 313–373). Hillsdale, NJ: Erlbaum.

de Waal, F. B. M. (1999). The end of nature versus nurture. *Scientific American, 281*(6), 94–99.

Deák, G. O., Ray, S. D., & Brenneman, K. (2003). Children's perseverative appearance-reality errors are related to emerging language skills. *Child Development, 74*, 944–964.

DeAngelis, T. (2001). Movin' on up? *Monitor on Psychology,* July/August, 2001, 70–73.

DeAngelis, T. (2002). Promising treatments for anorexia and bulimia. *Monitor on Psychology, 33*, 38–41.

DeBate, R. D., & Thompson, S. H. (2005). Girls on the run: Improvements in self-esteem, body size satisfaction and eating attitudes/behavior. *Eating and Weight Disorders, 10*, 25–32.

DeBourdeaudhuij, I., Lefevre, J. & Deforche, B. (2005). Physical activity and psychosocial correlates in normal weight and overweight 11 to 19 year olds. *Obesity Research, 13*, 1097–1105.

DeCasper, A. J., & Fifer, W. P. (1980). Of human bonding: Newborns prefer their mothers' voices. *Science, 208*, 1174–1176.

DeCasper, A. J., & Spence, M. J. (1986). Prenatal maternal speech influences newborns' perception of speech sounds. *Infant Behavior and Development, 9*, 133–150.

Deci, E. L., & Ryan, R. M. (1985). *Intrinsic motivation and self-determination in human behavior.* New York: Plenum.

DeGarmo, D. S., Forgatch, M. S., & Martinez, C. R. (1999). Parenting of divorced mothers as a link between social status and boys' academic outcomes: Unpacking the effects of socioeconomic status. *Child Development, 70*, 1231–1245.

Delaney-Black, V., Covington, C., Nordstrom, B., Ager, J., Janisse, J., Hannigan, J. H., et al. (2004). Prenatal cocaine: Quantity of exposure and gender moderation. *Journal of Developmental and Behavioral Pediatrics, 25*, 254–263.

Delpit, L. (1995). *Other people's children: Cultural conflict in the classroom.* New York: New Press/W. W. Norton.

DeMarie-Dreblow, D. (1991). Relation between knowledge and memory: A reminder that correlation does not imply causality. *Child Development, 62*, 484–498.

Demaris, A. & Kaukinen, C. (2005). Violent victimization and women's mental and physical health: Evidence from a national sample. *Journal of Research in Crime and Delinquency, 42*, 384–411.

Demetriou, A., Christou, C., Spanoudis, G., & Platsidou, M. (2002). The development of mental processing: Efficiency, working memory, and thinking. *Monographs of the Society for Research in Child Development, 67*(1); Serial No. 268.

Dempster, F. N. (1981). Memory span: Sourcs of individual and developmental differences. *Psychological Bulletin, 89*, 63–100.

Demuth, K. (1990). Subject, topic and Sesotho passive. *Journal of Child Language, 17*, 67–84.

DeNavas-Walt, C., Proctor, D. B., & Smith, J. C. (2008). U.S. Census Bureau, Current Population Reports, P60-235, *Income, Poverty, and Health Insurance Coverage in the United States: 2007*. U.S. Government Printing Office, Washington, DC, 2008.

Denham, S. A., Blair, K. A., DeMulder, E., Levitas, J., Sawyer, K., Auerbach-Major, S., & Queenan, P. (2003). Preschool emotional competence: Pathway to social competence? *Child Development, 74*, 238–256.

Denham, S. A., McKinley, M., Couchoud, E. A., & Holt, R. (1990). Emotional and behavioral predictors of preschool peer ratings. *Child Development, 61*, 1145–1152.

Dennis, W., & Dennis, M. G. (1939/1991). The effect of cradling practices upon the onset of walking in Hopi children. *Journal of Genetic Psychology, 152*, 563–573. *Note*: This article was published in 1991 but was first received by the journal editor in 1939.

Desnick, R. J., & Kaback, M. M. (2001). *Tay–Sachs disease*. Academic: San Diego, CA.

Desrochers, S. (2008). From Piage to specific Genevan developmental models. *Child Development Perspectives, 2*, 7–12.

Devlin, B., Daniels, M., & Roeder, K. (1997). Heritability of IQ, *Nature, 388*, 468–471.

DeVries, R. (1969). Constancy of generic identity in the years three to six. *Monographs of the Society for Research in Child Development, 34* (Serial No. 127).

Dews, S., Winner, E., Kaplan, J., Rosenblatt, E., Hunt, M., Lim, K., McGovern, A., Qualter, A., & Smarsh, B. (1996). Children's understanding of the meaning and functions of verbal irony. *Child Development, 67*, 3071–3085.

Diamond, A., Barnett, W., Thomas, J., & Munro, S. (2007, November 30). Preschool program improves cognitive control. *Science, 318*(5855), 1387–1388.

Diamond, D., Heinicke, C., & Mintz, J. (1996). Separation-individuation as a family transactional process in the transition to parenthood. *Infant Mental Health Journal, 17*(1), 24–42.

Diamond, L. M. (2008). Female bisexuality from adolescence to adulthood: Results from a 10-year longitudinal study. *Developmental Psychology, 44*, 5–14.

Diaz, R. M., & Kinger, C. (1991).Towards an explanatory model of the interaction between bilingualism and cognitive development. In E. Bialystok (Ed.), *Language processing in bilingual children* (pp. 167–192). Cambridge: Cambridge University Press.

Dick, D., Aliev, F., Kramer, J., Wang, J., Hinrichs, A., Bertelsen, S., et al. (2007). Association of CHRM2 with IQ: Converging evidence for a gene influencing intelligence. *Behavior Genetics, 37*(2), 265–272.

DiPietro, J. A., Novak, M. F. S. X., Costigan, K. A., Atella, L. D., & Reusing, S. P. (2006). Maternal psychological distress during pregnancy in relation to child development at age two. *Child Development, 77*, 573–587.

Dishion, T. J., & Owen, L. D. (2002). A longitudinal analysis of friendships and substance use: Bidirectional influence from adolescence to adulthood. *Developmental Psychology, 38*(4), 480–491.

Dockett, S., & Perry, B. (2003). The transition to school: What's important? *Educational Leadership, 60*(7), 30–33.

Dodge, K. A. (1986). A social information processing model of social competence in children. In M. Perlmutter (Ed.), *Minnesota symposium on child psychology* (Vol. 18, pp. 77–125). Hillsdale, NJ: Erlbaum.

Dodge, K. A., Coie, J. D., & Lynam, D. (2006). Aggression and antisocial behavior in youth. In W. Damon & R. Lerner (Series Ed.) & N. Eisenberg (Vol. Ed.), *Handbook of Child Psychology: Vol. 3. Social, emotional, and personality development* (6th ed., pp. 719–788). New York: Wiley.

Dodge, K. A., Lansford, J. E., Burks, V. S., Bates, J. E., Pettit, G. S., Fontaine, R., & Price, J. M. (2003). Peer rejection and social information-processing factors in the development of aggressive behavior problems in children. *Child Development, 74*(2), 374–393.

Dodge, K. A., Pettit, G. S., & Bates, J. E. (1994). Socialization mediators of the relation between socioeconomic status and child conduct problems. *Child Development, 65*, 649–665.

Dodge, K. A., Pettit, G. S., McClaskey, C. L., & Brown, M. W. (1986). Social competence in children. *Monographs of the Society for Research in Child Development, 51*(2), 1–80.

Dohrmann, K. R., Nishida, T., Gartner, A., Lipsky, D. & Grimm, K. (2007). High school outcomes for students in a public Montessori program. *Journal of Research in Childhood Education, 22*, 205–217.

Domsch, H., Lohaus, A., & Thomas, H. (2009). Prediction of childhood cognitive abilities from a set of early indicators of information processing capabilities. *Infant Behavior and Development, 32*, 91–102.

Donahue, P. L., Voelkl, K. E., Campbell, J. R., & Mazzeo, J. (1999). *NAEP 1998 reading report card for the nation and the states*. Washington, DC: U.S. Department of Education, Office of Educational Research and Improvement.

D' Onofrio, B. M., Turkheimer, E., Emery, R. E., Slutske, W. S., Heath, A. C., Madden, P. A., & Martin, N. G. (2006). A genetically informed study of the processes underlying the association between parental marital instability and offspring adjustment. *Developmental Psychology, 42*, 486–499.

Doris, J. L., Meguid, V., Thomas, M., Blatt, S., & Eckenrode, J. (2006). Prenatal cocaine exposure and child welfare outcomes. *Child Maltreatment, 11*(4), 326–337.

Dornbusch, S. M., Ritter, P. L., Leiderman, P. H., Roberts, D. F., & Fraleigh, M. J. (1987). The relation of parenting style to adolescent school performance. *Child Development, 58*, 1244–1257.

Douglas-Hall, A., & Chau, M. (2008). *Basic facts about low income children: Birth to age 18*. New York: National Center for Children in Poverty. Retrieved June 1, 2009, from www.nccp.org/publications/pub_845.html.

Downey, D. B., Ainsworth-Darnell, J. W., & Dufur, M. J. (1998). Sex of parent and children's well-being in single-parent households. *Journal of Marriage and the Family, 60*, 878–893.

Downs, J. S., deBruin, W. B., Murray, P. J. & Fischhoff, B. (2006). Specific STI knowledge may be acquired too late. *Journal of Adolescent Health, 38*, 65–67.

Dragonas, T. G. (1992). Greek fathers' participation in labour and care of the infant. *Scandinavian Journal of Caring Sciences, 6*, 151–159.

Duan, L., Chou, C., Andreeva, V., & Pentz, M. (2009). Trajectories of peer social influences as long-term predictors of drug use from early through late adolescence. *Journal of Youth & Adolescence, 38*, 454–465.

Dube, S. R., Whitfield, C. L., Brown, D. W., Felitti, V. J., Dong, M., & Giles, W. H. (2005). Long-term consequences of childhood sexual abuse by gender of victim. *American Journal of Preventative Medicine, 28*, 430–438.

DuBois, D. L., Holloway, B. E., Valentine, J. C., & Cooper, H. (2002). Effectiveness of mentoring programs for youth: A meta-analytic review. *American Journal of Community Psychology, 30*, 157–197.

Dubow, E. F., Boxer, P., & Huesmann, L. R. (2008). Childhood and adolescent predictors of early and middle adulthood alcohol use and problem drinking: the Columbia County Longitudinal Study. *Addiction, 103*, 36–47.

Duffy, R. D. & Sedlacek, W. E. (2007). What is most important to students' long-term career choices. *Journal of Career Development, 34*, 149–163.

Duncan, G. J., & Brooks-Gunn, J. (1997) (Eds.). *Consequences of growing up poor*. New York: Russell Sage Foundation.

Duncan, J., & Rafter, E. (2005). Concurrent and predictive validity of the Phelps Kindergarten Readiness Scale-II. *Psychology in the Schools, 42*(4), 355–359.

Duncan, P. D., Ritter, P. L., Dornbusch, S. M., Gross, R. T., & Carlsmith, J. M. (1985). The effects of pubertal timing on body image, school behavior, and deviance. *Journal of Youth and Adolescence*, 14, 227–235.

Dunn, M. S., Bartee, R. T. & Perko, M. A. (2003). Self-reported alcohol use and sexual behaviors of adolescents. *Psychological Reports, 92*, 339–348.

Dunphy, D. (1963). The social structure of urban adolescent peer groups. *Sociometry, 26*, 230–246.

Durrett, M. E., Otaki, M., & Richards, P. (1984). Attachment and the mother's perception of support from the father. *International Journal of Behavioral Development, 7*, 167–176.

Dweck, C. S. (2001). The development of ability conceptions. In A. Wigfield & J. S. Eccles (Eds.), *Development of achievement motivation* (pp. 57–88). San Diego, CA: Academic Press.

Dweck, C. S., & Leggett, E. L. (1988). A social–cognitive approach to motivation and personality. *Psychological Review, 95*, 256–273.

Eaton, D. K., Kann, L., Kinchen, S., Shanklin, S., Ross, J., & Hawkins, J. (June, 2008). Youth Risk Behavior Surveillance—United States, 2007. *MMWR Surveillance Summaries, 57,* No. SS-4. Retrieved April 23, 2009, from www.cdc.gov/healthyyouth/yrbs/pubs_mmwr.htm.

Eaton, W. O., & Enns, L. R. (1986). Sex differences in human motor activity level. *Psychological Bulletin, 100,* 19–28.

Eccles, J. S. (2004). Schools, academic motivation, and stage-environment fit. In R. M. Lerner & L. Steinberg (Eds.), *Handbook of adolescent psychology* (2nd ed.) (pp. 125–153). Hoboken, NJ: John Wiley & Sons, Inc.

Eccles, J. S., & Roeser, R. W. (1999). School and community influences on human development. In M. H. Bornstein & M. E. Lamb (Eds.), *Developmental psychology: An advanced textbook* (pp. 503–554). Mahwah, NJ: Erlbaum.

Eccles, J. S., & Roeser, R. W. (1999). School and community influences on human development. In M. H. Bornstein & M. E. Lamb (Eds.), *Developmental psychology: An advanced textbook* (pp. 503–554). Mahwah, NJ: Erlbaum.

Eccles, J. S., Lord, S. E., Roeser, R. W., Barber, B. L., & Jozefowicz, D.M.H. (1997). The association of school transitions in early adolescence with developmental trajectories through high school. In J. Schulenberg, J. Maggs, & K. Hurrelmann (Eds.), *Health risks and developmental transitions during adolescence* (pp. 283–320). New York: Cambridge University Press.

Eccles, J. S., Wigfield, A., & Schiefele, U. (1998). Motivation to succeed. In W. Damon & N. Eisenberg (Eds.), *Handbook of child psychology: Vol. 3. Social, emotional, and personality development* (pp. 1018–1095). New York: John Wiley & Sons, Inc.

Eckerman, C. O. (1979). The human infant in social interaction. In R. Cairns (Ed.), *The analysis of social interactions: Methods, issues, and illustrations* (pp. 163–178). Hillsdale, NJ: Lawrence Erlbaum Associates.

Eckerman, C. O. (1993). Imitation and toddlers' achievement of co-ordinated action with others. In J. Nadel & L. Camaioni (Eds.), *New perspectives in early communicative development* (pp. 116–138). London: Routledge.

Eden, G., Jones, K., Cappell, K., Gareau, L., Wood, F., Zeffiro, T., et al. (2004). Neural changes following remediation in adult developmental dyslexia. *Neuron, 44,* 411–422.

Edwards, C., Gandini, L., & Forman, G. (1998). *The hundred languages of children: The Reggio Emilia approach—advanced reflections.* Westport, CT: Ablex Pubublishing Corporation.

Edwards, O., & Fuller, D. (2005). Implications of the Cattell-Horn-Carroll theory on ethnic differences in IQ. *Psychological Reports, 97,* 891–897.

Egeland, B., & Farber, E. A. (1984). Infant-mother attachment: Factors related to its development and changes over time. *Child Development, 55,* 753–771.

Eimas, P. D., Siqueland, E. R., Jusczyk, P., & Vigorito, J. (1971). Speech perception in infants. *Science, 71,* 303–306.

Eisbach, A. O. (2004). Children's developing awareness of diversity in people's trains of thought. *Child Development, 75,* 1694–1707.

Eisenberg, M. E., & Resnick, M. D. (2006). Suicidality among gay, lesbian and bisexual youth: The role of protective factors. *Journal of Adolescent Health, 39,* 662–668.

Eisenberg, N. (1986). *Altruistic emotion, cognition, and behavior.* Hillsdale, NJ: Erlbaum.

Eisenberg, N., & Fabes, R. A. (1998). Prosocial development. In W. Damon & N. Eisenberg (Eds.), *Handbook of child psychology: Vol. 3. Social, emotional, and personality development* (pp. 701–778). New York: Wiley.

Eisenberg, N., & Shell, R. (1986). The relation of prosocial moral judgment and behavior in children: The mediating role of cost. *Personality and Social Psychology Bulletin, 12,* 426–433.

Eisenberg, N., Carlo, G., Murphy, B., & Van Court, P. (1995). Prosocial development in late adolescence: A longitudinal study. *Child Development, 66,* 1179–1197.

Eisenberg, N., Guthrie, I. K., Murphy, B. C., Shepard, S. A., Cumberland, A., & Carlo, G. (1999). Consistency and development of prosocial dispositions: A longitudinal study. *Child Development, 70,* 1360–1372.

Eisenberg, N., Hofer, C., Spinrad, T. L., Gershoff, E. T., Valiente, C., Losoya, S., Zhou, Q., Cumberland, A., Liew, J., Reiser, M., & Maxon, E. (2008). Understanding mother-adolescents conflict disccuions: Concurrent and across-time prediction from youths' dispositions and parenting. *Monographs of the Society for Research in Child Development, 73,* 1–180.

Eisenberg, N., Lennon, R., & Roth, K. (1983). Prosocial development: A longitudinal study. *Developmental Psychology, 19,* 846–855.

Eisenberg, N., Sadovsky, A., Spinrad, T. L., Fabes, R. A., Losoya, S. H., Valiente, C., Reiser, M., Cumberland, A., & Shepard, S. A. (2005). The relations of problem behavior status to children's negative emotionality, effortful control, and impulsivity: Concurrent relations and prediction of change. *Developmental Psychology, 41,* 193–211.

Eisenberg, N., Smith, C. L., Sadovsky, A., & Spinrad, T. L. (2004). Effortful control: Relations with emotion regulation, adjustment, and socialization in childhood. In R. F. Baumeister & K. D. Vohs (Eds.), *Handbook of self regulation: Research, theory, and applications* (pp. 259–282). New York: Guilford.

Eisenberg, R. (1976). *Auditory competence in early life: The roots of communicative-behavior.* Baltimore: University Park Press.

Ekstrand, L. H. (1981). Theories and facts about early bilingualism in native and migrant children. As cited in J. F. Hamers & M. H. A. Blanc (2000). *Bilinguality and bilingualism* (2nd ed.). Cambridge: Cambridge University Press.

El-Sheikh, M., & Harger, J. (2001). Appraisals of marital conflict and children's adjustment, health, and physiological reactivity. *Developmental Psychology, 37,* 875–885

Elashoff, J. D., & Snow, R. E. (1971). *Pygmalion reconsidered.* Worthington, OH: Charles A. Jones.

Elder, G. H., Jr., & Conger, R. D. (2000). *Children of the land: Adversity and success in rural America.* Chicago: University of Chicago Press.

Eldredge, J. L. (2005). Foundations of fluency: An exploration. *Reading Psychology, 26,* 161–182.

Elias, L. J., & Saucier, D. M. (2006). *Neuropsychology: Clinical and experimental foundations.* Boston: Pearson Education.

Elkind, D. (1967). Egocentrism in adolescence. *Child Development, 38,* 1025–1034.

Elliott, E. S., & Dweck, C. S. (1988). Goals: An approach to motivation and achievement. *Journal of Personality and Social Psychology, 54,* 5–12.

Elliott, J. (2003). Dynamic assessment in educational settings: Realising potential. *Educational Review, 55,* 15–32.

Elliott, S. N., Kratochwill, T. R., Cook, J. L., & Travers, J. F. (2000). *Educational psychology: Effective teaching, effective learning* (3rd ed.). Boston: McGraw-Hill.

Ely, R. (1997). Language and literacy in the school years. In J. B. Gleason (Ed.), *The development of language* (pp. 398–439). Boston, MA: Allyn and Bacon.

Ely, R., & McCabe, A. (1994). The language play of kindergarten children. *First Language, 14,* 19–35.

Embury, S., Hebbel, R., Mohandas, N., & Steinberg, M. (Eds.) (1994). *Sickle cell disease: Basic principles and clinical practice.* New York: Raven Press.

Emde, R. M., Plomin, R., Robinson, J., Corley, R., DeFries, J., Fulker, D. W., et al. (1992). Temperament, emotion, and cognition at fourteen months: the MacArthur Longitudinal Twin Study. *Child Development, 63,* 1437–1455.

Emerson, M. J., & Miyake, A. (2003). The role of inner speech in task switching: A dual-task investigation. *Journal of Memory & Language, 48,* 148–168.

Emery, R. E. (1982). Interparental conflict and the children of discord and divorce. *Psychological Bulletin, 92,* 310–330.

Emery, R. E. (1999a). *Marriage, divorce, and children's adjustment* (2nd ed.). Thousand Oaks, CA: Sage.

Emery, R. E. (1999b). Postdivorce family life for children: An overview of research and some implications for policy. In R. A. Thompson & P. R. Amato (Eds.), *The postdivorce family: Children, parenting, and society* (pp. 3–27). Thousand Oaks, CA: Sage.

Emery, R. E., Kitzman, K. M., & Waldron, M. (1999). Psychological interventions for separated and divorced families. In E. M. Hetherington (Ed.), *Coping with divorce, single parenting, and remarriage: A risk and resiliency perspective* (pp. 323–344). Mahwah, NJ: Erlbaum.

Engel, S. (1995). *The stories children tell: Making sense of the narratives of children.* New York: W.H. Freeman.

Enns, C. W., Mickle, S. J., & Goldman, J. D. (2003). Trends in food and nutrient intakes by adolescents in the United States. *Family Economics and Nutrition Review, 15,* 15–27.

Epstein, H. T. (1978). Growth spurts during brain development: Implications for educational policy and practice. In J. S. Chall & A. F. Mirsky (Eds.), *Education and the brain: The seventy-seventh yearbook of the national society for the study of education* (pp. 343–370). Chicago: University of Chicago Press.

Epstein, J. L. (1986). Friendship selection: Developmental and environmental influences. In E. Mueller & C. Cooper (Eds.), *Process and outcome in peer relationships.* New York: Academic Press.

Epstein, J. L. (1989). The selection of friends: Changes across the grades and in different school environments. In T. J. Berndt & G. W. Ladd (Eds.), *Peer relationships in child development* (pp. 158–187). New York: Wiley.

Erikson, E. H. (1968). *Identity: Youth and crisis.* New York: Norton. As cited in Thomas, R. M. (1992), *Comparing theories of child development.* Belmont, CA: Wadsworth, pp. 163–164.

Erikson, E. H. (1968). *Identity: Youth and crisis.* New York: Norton.

Eriksson, P. S., Perfilieva, E., Bjork-Eriksson, T., Alborn, A. M., Nordborg, C., Peterson, D. A. & Gage, F. H. (1998). Neurogenesis in the adult human hippocampus. *Nature Medicine, 4,* 1313–1317.

Eron, L. D. (1987). The development of aggressive behavior from the perspective of a developing behaviorism. *American Psychologist, 42,* 435–442.

Eron, L. D., Huesmann, L. R., Lefkowitz, M. M., & Walder, L. O. (1972). Does television violence cause aggression? *American Psychologist, 27,* 253–263.

Eslinger, P., & Biddle, K. (2008). Prefrontal cortex and the maturation of executive functions, cognitive expertise, and social adaptation. *Executive functions and the frontal lobes: A lifespan perspective* (pp. 299–316). Philadelphia, PA: Taylor & Francis.

Espelage, D. L., Holt, M. K., & Henkel, R. R. (2003). Examination of peer-group contextual effects on aggression during early adolescence. *Child Development, 74*(1), 205–220.

Fabes, R. A. (1994). Physiological, emotional, and behavioral correlates of gender segregation. In W. Damon (Ed.), *New directions for child development* (No. 65, pp. 19–34). San Francisco: Jossey-Bass.

Fabes, R. A., Eisenberg, N., Nyman, M., & Michealieu, Q. (1991). Young children's appraisals of others' spontaneous emotional reactions. *Developmental Psychology, 27,* 858–866.

Fabes, R. A., Martin, C. L., & Hanish, L. D. (2003). Young children's play qualities in same-, other-, and mixed-sex peer groups. *Child Development, 74*(3), 921–932.

Fabes, R., & Martin, C. L. (2003). *Exploring child development*, 2nd ed. Boston: Allyn & Bacon.

Fagan, J. F. (2000). A theory of intelligence as processing: Implications for society. *Psychology, Public Policy, and Law, 6,* 168–179.

Fagan, J., Holland, C., & Wheeler, K. (2007). The prediction, from infancy, of adult IQ and achievement. *Intelligence, 35*(3), 225–231.

Fagot, B. I. (1977). Consequences of moderate cross-gender behavior in preschool children. *Child Development, 48,* 902–907.

Fagot, B. I. (1994). Peer relations and the development of competence in boys and girls. In W. Damon (Ed.), *New directions for child development* (No. 65, pp. 53–65). San Francisco: Jossey-Bass.

Fagot, B. I., & Patterson, G. R. (1969). An in vivo analysis of reinforcing contingencies for sex-role behaviors in the preschool child. *Developmental Psychology, 1,* 563–568.

Fagot, B. I., Leinbach, M. D., & Hagan, R. (1986). Gender labeling and the adoption of sex-typed behaviors. *Developmental Psychology, 22,* 440–443.

Fagot, B. I., Pears, K. C., Capaldi, D. M., Crosby, L. & Leve, C. S. (1998). Becoming an adolescent father: Precursors and parenting. *Developmental Psychology, 34,* 1209–1219.

Falck-Ytter, T., Gredeback, G., & von Hofsten, C. (2006). Infants predict other people's action goals. *Nature Neuroscience, 9,* 878–879.

Falorni, M. L., Fornasarig, A., & Stefanile, C. (1979). Research about anxiety effects on the pregnant woman and her newborn child. In L. Carenza & L. Zichella (Eds.), *Emotion and reproduction. Proceedings of the Serono Symposium* (Vol. 20B, pp. 1147–1153). London: Academic Press.

Fan, X., & Chen, M. (2001). Parental involvement and students' academic achievement: A meta-analysis. *Educational Psychology Review, 13,* 1–22.

Fantuzzo, J., Bulotsky-Shearer, R., McDermott, P., McWayne, C., Frye, D., & Perlman, S. (2007). Investigation of dimensions of social-emotional classroom behavior and school readiness for low-income urban preschool children. *School Psychology Review, 36*(1), 44–62.

Fantz, R. L. (1956). A method for studying early visual development. *Perceptual Motor Skills, 6,* 13–15.

Fantz, R. L. (1961). The origin of form perception. *Scientific American, 204,* 66–72.

Fantz, R. L. (1963). Pattern vision in newborn infants. *Science, 140,* 296–297.

Farmer, M. E., & Klein, R. M. (1995). The evidence for a temporal processing deficit linked to dyslexia: A review. *Psychonomic Bulletin and Review, 2,* 460–493.

Farrar, J. (1992). Negative evidence and grammatical morpheme acquisition. *Developmental Psychology, 28,* 90–98.

Farrar, M. J., & Goodman, G. S. (1992). Developmental changes in event memory. *Child Development, 63,* 173–187.

Farrington, D. P. (2004). Conduct disorder, aggression, and delinquency. In R. M. Lerner & L. Steinberg (Eds.), *Handbook of adolescent psychology* (2nd ed.) (pp. 627–664). Hoboken, NJ: John Wiley & Sons, Inc.

Farver, J. A. M., Narang, S. K., & Bhadha, B. R. (2002). East meets West: Ethnic identity, acculturation, and conflict in Asian Indian families. *Journal of Family Psychology, 16,* 338–350.

Farver, J. M. (2000). Within cultural differences. *Journal of Cross-Cultural Psychology, 31,* 583–602.

Farver, J. M., & Shin, Y. L. (1997). Social pretend play in Korean- and Anglo-American preschoolers. *Child Development, 68,* 544–556.

Farver, J. M., & Welles-Nystrom, B. (1997). Toy stories. *Journal of Cross-Cultural Psychology, 28,* 393–420.

Fee, E. J., & Shaw, K. (1998). Pitch modifications in Mi'kmaq child-directed speech. In E. V. Clark (Ed.), *The proceedings of the twenty-ninth annual child language research forum* (pp. 47–54). Chicago, IL: Center for the Study of Language and Information.

Feigelman, W. (2000). Adjustments of transracially and inracially adopted young adults. *Child and Adolescent Social Work Journal, 17,* 165–183.

Feingold, A. (1994). Gender differences in personality: A meta-analysis. *Psychological Bulletin, 116,* 429–456.

Feinman, S., & Lewis, M. (1983). Social referencing at ten months: A second-order effect on infants' responses to strangers. *Child Development, 54,* 878–887.

Fenichel, E., & Mann, T. L. (2001). Early head start for low-income families with infants and toddlers. *Reports from the Field, 11*(1), 135–141.

Fennell, C. T., Byers-Heinlein, K., & Werker, J. F. (2007). Using speech sounds to guide word learning: The case of bilingual infants. *Child Development 78,* 1510–1525.

Ferguson, C. J. (2007). Evidence for publication bias in video game violence effects literature: A meta-analytic review. *Aggression & Violent Behavior, 12*(4), 470–482.

Ferguson, C. J. & Kilburn, J. (2009). The public health risks of media violence: A meta-analytic review. *The Journal of Pediatrics, 154,* 759–763.

Ferguson, C. J., (2010). *Violent crime: clinical and social implications.* Los Angeles, CA: Sage.

Fergusson, D. M., Boden, J. M. & Horwood, L. J. (2006). Cannabis use and other illicit drug use: Testing the cannabis gateway hypothesis. *Addiction, 101,* 556–569.

Fernald, A. (1992). Human maternal vocalizations to infants as biologically relevant signals: An evolutionary perspective. In J. H. Barkow, L. Cosmides, & J. Tooby (Eds.), *The adaptive mind: Evolutionary psychology and the generation of culture.* New York: Oxford University Press.

Fernald, A., & O'Neill, D. K. (1993). Peek-aboo across cultures: How mothers and infants play with voices, faces and expectations. In K. Macdonald (Ed.), *Parent-child play* (pp. 391–428). Albany: State University of New York Press.

Field, T. M., Woodson, R., Greenberg, R., & Cohen, D. (1982). Discrimination and imitation of facial expressions by neonates. *Science, 218,* 179–181.

Finkelhor, D. (1994). The international epidemiology of child sexual abuse. *Child Abuse and Neglect, 18,* 409–417.

Finkelhor, D., & Jones, L. M. (2004). Explanations for the decline in child sexual abuse cases. *Juvenile Justice Bulletin, January 2004.* U.S. Department of Justice, Office of Justice Programs, Office of Juvenile Justice and Delinquency Prevention. Retrieved June 22, 2006, from www.ncjrs.gov/pdffiles1/ojjdp/199298.pdf.

Fischer, K. W., & Bidell, T. R. (1998). Dynamic development of psychological structures in action and thought. In W. Damon (Series Ed.) & R. M. Lerner (Vol. Ed.), *Handbook of child psychology: Vol. 1. Theoretical models of human development* (5th ed., pp. 467–561). New York: Wiley.

Fish, J. M. (2002). *Race and intelligence: Separating science from myth.* Mahwah, NJ: Erlbaum.

Fisher, C. B., Wallace, S. A., & Fenton, R. E. (2000). Discrimination distress during adolescence. *Journal of Youth and Adolescence, 29,* 679–695.

Fisher, P. A., Leve, L. D., O'Leary, C. C., & Leve, C. (2003). Parental monitoring of children's behavior: Variation across stepmother, stepfather, and two-parent biological families. *Family Relations, 52,* 45–52.

Fivush, R. (1995). Language, narrative, and autobiography. *Consciousness and Cognition, 4,* 100–103.

Fivush, R., Haden, C., & Adam, S. (1995). Structure and coherence of preschoolers' personal narratives over time: Implications for childhood amnesia. *Journal of Experimental Child Psychology, 60,* 32–56.

Fivush, R., Kuebli, J., & Clubb, P. A. (1992). The structure of events and event representations: A developmental analysis. *Child Development, 63,* 188–201.

Flaks, D. K., Ficher, I., Masterpasqua, F., & Joseph, G. (1995). Lesbians choosing motherhood: A comparative study of lesbian and heterosexual parents and their children. *Developmental Psychology, 31,* 105–114.

Flavell, J. H., Friedrichs, A. G., & Hoyt, J. D. (1970). Developmental changes in memorization processes. *Cognitive Psychology, 1,* 324–340.

Flavell, J. H., Green, F. L., & Flavell, E. R. (1986). Development of knowledge about the appearance-reality distinction. *Monographs of the Society for Research in Child Development, 51* (Serial No. 212).

Flavell, J. H., Green, F. R., Wahl, K. E., & Flavell, E. R. (1987). The effects of question clarification and memory aids on young children's performance on appearance-reality tasks. *Cognitive Development, 2,* 127–144.

Flavell, J. H., Miller, P. H., & Miller, S. A. (1993). *Cognitive development* (3rd ed.). Englewood Cliffs, NJ: Prentice Hall.

Flavell, J. R. (1985). *Cognitive development* (2nd ed.). Englewood Cliffs, NJ: Prentice Hall.

Fletcher, A. C., Nickerson, P., & Wright, K. L. (2003). Structured leisure activities in middle childhood: Links to well-being. *Journal of Community Psychology, 31,* 641–659.

Flinn, S. K. (1995). *Child sexual abuse I: An overview.* Advocates for Youth. Retrieved June 22, 2006, from www.advocatesforyouth.org/publications/factsheet/fsabuse1.htm.

Flom, R., & Bahrick, L. E. (2007). The development of infant discrimination of affect in multimodal and unimodal stimulation: The role of intersensory redundancy. *Developmental Psychology, 43,* 238–252.

Flook, L., Repetti, R. L., & Ullman, J. B. (2005). Classroom social experiences as predictors of academic performance. *Developmental Psychology, 41,* 319–327.

Foehr, U. G. (2006). *Media multitasking among American youth: Prevalence, predictors, and pairings.* Menlo Park, CA: Kaiser Family Foundation. Retrieved May 10, 2009, from www.kff.org/entmedia/7592.cfm.

Fogel, A. (1979). Peer- vs. mother-directed behavior in 1- to 3-month-old infants. *Infant Behavior and Development, 2,* 215–226. In T. J. Berndt & G. W. Ladd (Eds.), *Peer relationships in child development* (pp. 46–70). New York: Wiley.

Fogelman, K. (1980). Smoking in pregnancy and subsequent development of the child. *Child Care Health and Development, 6,* 233–249.

Ford, D. Y., & Harris, J. J. (2000). A framework for infusing multicultural curriculum into gifted education. *Roeper Review, 23,* 4–10.

Foreman, M. A. (1995). Foreword. In S. Chess & A. Thomas, *Temperament in clinical practice* (pp. v–viii). New York: Guilford Press.

Fowler, A. E. (1998). Language in mental retardation: Associations with and dissociations from general cognition. In J. A. Burack, R. M. Hodapp, & E. Zigler (Eds.), *Handbook of mental retardation and development* (pp. 290–333). New York: Cambridge University Press.

Fox, N. A., Kimmerly, N. L., & Schafer, W. D. (1991). Attachment to mother/attachment to father: A meta-analysis. *Child Development, 62,* 210–225.

Fox, R., Aslin, R. N., Shea, S. L., & Dumais, S. T. (1980). Stereopsis in human infants. *Science, 207,* 323–324.

Fracasso, M. P., Busch-Rossnagel, N. A., & Fisher, C. B. (1993). The relationship of maternal behavior and acculturation to the quality of attachment in Hispanic infants living in New York City. *Hispanic Journal of Behavioral Sciences, 16,* 143–154.

Frankenburg, W. K., Dodds, J., Archer, P., Bresnick, B., Maschka, P., Edelman, N., & Shapiro, H. (1992). *Denver II: Training manual.* Denver: Denver Developmental Materials, Inc.

Franks, L. (2008). An insight into Chinese maternity services. *British Journal of Midwifery, 16*(8), 536–538.

Fraser, S. (1995). *The bell curve wars: Race, intelligence, and the future of America.* New York: Basic Books.

Fraser, S., & Gestwicki, C. (2002). *Authentic childhood: Exploring Reggio Emilia in the classroom.* Albany, NY: Delmar/Thomson Learning.

Frazier, J. A., & Morrison, F. J. (1998). The influence of extended-year schooling on growth of achievement and perceived competence in early elementary school. *Child Development, 69,* 495–517.

French, D. C. (1988). Heterogeneity of peer rejected boys: Aggressive and nonaggressive subtypes. *Child Development, 59,* 976–985.

Fretts, R. C., Schmittdiel, J., McLean, F. H., Usher, R. H., Goldman, M. B. (1995). Increased maternal age and the risk of fetal death. *The New England Journal of Medicine, 333,* 953–957.

Frey, K. S., Hirschstein, M. K., Snell, J. L., Edstrom, L. V., MacKenzie, E. P., Broderick, C. J. (2005). Reducing playground bullying and supporting beliefs: An experimental trial of the *Steps to Respect* program. *Developmental Psychology, 41,* 479–491.

Friedrich, W. N. (1993). Sexual behavior in sexually abused children. *Violence Update, 3,* 1–7.

Frosch, C. A., Mangelsdorf, S. C., & McHale, J. L. (1998). Correlates of marital behavior at six months postpartum. *Developmental Psychology, 34,* 1438–1449.

Fuchs, D., & Thelen, M. H. (1988). Children's expected interpersonal consequences of communicating their affective state and reported likelihood of expression. *Child Development, 59,* 1314–1322.

Fuchs, D., Fuchs, L. S., Compton, D. L., Bouton, B., Caffrey, E., & Hill, L. (2007). Dynamic assessment as responsiveness to intervention. *Teaching Exceptional Children, 39,* 58–63.

Furman, B., & Appelman, Z. (2005). Genetic diagnosis in multiple pregnancies: Amniocentesis versus chorionic villus sampling. *Ultrasound Review of Obstetrics & Gynecology, 5*(1), 69–74.

Furstenberg, F. F., & Hughes, M. E. (1997). The influence of neighborhoods on children's development: A theoretical perspective and a research agenda. In J. Brooks-Gunn, G. J. Duncan, & J. L. Aber (Eds.), *Neighborhood poverty: Vol. II. Policy implications in studying neighborhoods* (pp. 23–47). New York: Russell Sage Foundation.

Furstenberg, F. F., Brooks-Gunn, J. & Chase-Lansdale, L. (1989) Teenaged pregnancy and childbearing. *American Psychologist, 44,* 313–320.

Fuson, K. C., & Kwon, Y. (1992). Korean children's single-digit addition and subtraction: Numbers structured by ten. *Journal for Research in Mathematics Education, 23,* 148–165.

Gabbard, C. P. (1992). *Lifelong motor development* (2nd ed.). Madison, WI: Brown & Benchmark.

Gagnon, J. C., & Leone, P. E. (2001). Alternative strategies for school violence prevention. In R. J. Skiba & G. G. Noam (Eds.), *Zero tolerance: Can suspension and expulsion keep schools safe?* (pp. 101–126). San Francisco: Jossey-Bass.

*Gale Encyclopedia of Genetic Disorders,* Vol. 2. (2005). Detroit: Thomson Gale.

Gallahue, D. L., & Ozmun, J. C. (1995). *Understanding motor development: Infants, children, adolescents, adults* (3rd ed.). Madison, WI: Brown & Benchmark.

Gallahue, D. L., & Ozmun, J. C. (1995). *Understanding motor development: Infants, children, adolescents, adults.* Madison, WI: Wm. C. Brown Communications, Inc.

Galloway, J. C., & Thelen, E. (2004). Feet first: Object exploration in young infants. *Infant Behavior & Development, 27,* 107–112.

Ganger, J., & Brent, M. R. (2004). Reexamining the vocabulary spurt. *Developmental Psychology, 40,* 621–632.

Gardner, H. (1983). *Frames of mind: The theory of multiple intelligences.* New York: Basic Books.

Gardner, H. (1995). Cracking open the IQ box. In S. Fraser (Ed.), *The bell curve wars: Race, intelligence, and the future of America* (pp. 23–35). New York: Basic Books.

Gardner, H. (1999). *Intelligence reframed: Multiple intelligences for the 21st century.* New York: Basic Books.

Gardner, H., Kornhaber, M. L., & Wake, W. K. (1996). *Intelligence: Multiple perspectives.* Fort Worth, TX: Harcourt Brace College.

Gardner, R. M., Friedman, B. N., & Jackson, N. A. (1999). Body size estimations, body dissatisfaction, and ideal size preferences in children six through thirteen. *Journal of Youth and Adolescence, 28,* 603–618.

Garlick, D. (2002). Understanding the nature of the general factor of intelligence: The role of individual differences in neural plasticity as an explanatory mechanism. *Psychological Review, 109,* 116–136.

Garmezy, N. (1985). Stress-resistant children: The search for protective factors. In J. E. Stevenson (Ed.), *Recent research in developmental psychopathology* (pp. 213–233). Oxford: Pergamon Press.

Garmon, A., Nystrand, M., Berends, M., & LePore, P. C. (1995). An organizational analysis of the effects of ability grouping. *American Education Research Journal, 32,* 687–715.

Garmon, L.C., Basinger, K.S., Gregg, V.R., & Gibbs, J.C. (1996). Gender differences in stage and expression of moral judgment. *Merrill-Palmer Quarterly, 42,* 418–437.

Garnier, H., & Stein, J. (2002). An 18-year model of family and peer effects on adolescent drug use and delinquency. *Journal of Youth & Adolescence, 31,* 45–56.

Garside, R., Ayres, R., & Owen, M. (2001). "They never tell you about the consequences": Young people's awareness of sexually transmitted infections. *International Journal of STD & AIDS, 12,* 582–588.

Gathercole, S. E., Pickering, S. J., Ambridge, B., & Wearing, H. (2004). The structure of working memory from 4 to 15 years of age. *Developmental Psychology, 40,* 177–190.

Gaultney, J. F, & Gingras, J. L. (2005). Fetal rate of behavioral inhibition and preference for novelty during infancy. *Early Human Development, 81,* 379–386.

Gauvain, M., & Perez, S. M. (2008). Mother-child planning and child compliance. *Child Development, 79*(3), 761–775.

Gazelle, H. (2006). Class climate moderates peer relations and emotional adjustment in children with an early history of anxious solitude: A child X environment model. *Developmental Psychology, 42,* 1179–1192.

Gazelle, H. (2008). Behavioral profiles of anxious solitary children and heterogeneity in peer relations. *Developmental Psychology, 44*(6), 1604–1624.

Ge, X., Brody, G. H., Conger, R. D., Simons, R. L., &Murry, V. M. (2002). Contextual amplification of pubertal transition effects on deviant peer affliation and externalizing behavior among African American children. *Developmental Psychology, 38,* 42–54.

Ge, X., Conger, R. D., & Elder, G. H. (2001). The relation between puberty and psychological distress in adolescent boys. *Journal of Research on Adolescence, 11,* 49–70.

Geary, D. (1994). *Children's mathematical development: Research and practical applications.* Washington, DC: American Psychological Association.

Geary, D. C. (1996). International differences in mathematical achievement: Their nature, courses, and consequences. *Current Directions in Psychological Science, 5,* 133–137.

Geary, D. C. (2006). Development of mathematical understanding. In D. Kuhn & R. S. Siegler (Eds.), *Cognitive, language, and perceptual develoment,* Vol. 2 (pp. 777–810), in W. Damon (Gen. Ed.), *Handbook of child psychology*. New York: Wiley.

Geary, D. C., Hoard, M. K., Byrd-Craven, J., & DeSoto, M. C. (2004). Strategy choices in simple and complex addition: Contributions of working memory and counting knowledge for children with mathematical disability. *Journal of Experimental Child Psychology, 88,* 121–151.

Gecas, V., & Seff, M. (1990). Families and adolescents: A review of the 1980s. *Journal of Marriage and the Family, 52,* 941–958.

Gee, J. P. (1992). *The social mind: Language, ideology and social practice.* New York: Bergin & Garvey.

Gelman, R. (2000). Domain specificity and variability in cognitive development. *Child Development, 71,* 854–856.

Gelman, R., & Baillargeon, R. (1983). A review of some Piagetian concepts. In P. H. Mussen (Series Ed.) & J. H. Flavell & E. M. Markman (Vol. Eds.), *Handbook of child psychology: Vol. 3. Cognitive development* (pp. 163–230). New York: Wiley.

Gershkoff-Stowe, L., & Thelen, E. (2004). U-shaped changes in behavior: A dynamic systems perspective. *Journal of Cognition & Development, 5,* 11–36.

Gershoff, E. T. (2002). Corporal punishment by parents and associated child behaviors and experiences: A meta-analytic and theoretical review. *Psychological Bulletin, 128,* 539–579.

Gershoff, E. T., & Bitensky, S. H. (2007). The case against corporal punishment of children: Converging evidence from social science research and international human rights law and implications for U.S. public policy. *Psychology, Public Policy, and Law, 13*(4), 231–272.

Gibbs, C. P., Krischer, J., Peckham, B. M., Sharp, H., & Kirschbaum, T. H. (1986). Obstetric anesthesia: A national survey. *Anesthesiology, 65,* 298–306.

Gibson, E. J., & Walk, R. D. (1960). The "visual cliff." *Scientific American, 202,* 64–71.

Gibson, E. J., & Walker, A. S. (1984). Development of knowledge of visual-tactual affordances of substance. *Child Development, 55,* 453–460.

Giedd, J. N. (2003). The anatomy of mentalization: A view from developmental neuroimaging. *Bulletin of the Menninger Clinic, 67*(2), 132–142.

Giedd, J. N., Blumenthal, J., Jeffries, N. O., Castellanos, F. X., Liu, H., Zijdenbos, A., Paus, T., Evans, A. C. & Rapoport, J. L. (1999). Brain development during childhood and adolescence: A longitudinal MRI study. *Nature Neuroscience, 2,* 861–863.

Giedd, J. N., Shaw, P., Wallace, G., Gogtay, N., & Lenroot, R. K. (2006). Anatomic brain imaging studies of normal and abnormal brain development in children and adolescents. In D. Cicchetti & D. J. Cohen (Eds.), *Developmental Psychopathology* (2nd ed.)*; Vol. 2: Developmental Neuroscience* (pp. 127–196).

Giles, J. W., & Heyman, G. D. (2005). Young children's beliefs about the relationship between gender and aggressive behavior. *Child Development, 76,* 107–121.

Gillam, R. B., Cowan, N., & Day, L. S. (1995). Sequential memory in children with and without language impairment. *Journal of Speech and Hearing Research, 38,* 393–402.

Gillies, R. M. (2003). The behaviors, interactions, and perceptions of junior high school students during small-group learning. *Journal of Educational Psychology, 95,* 137–147.

Gilligan, C. (1982). *In a different voice: Psychological theory and women's development.* Cambridge, MA: Harvard University Press.

Gilligan, C., & Attanucci, J. (1988). Two moral orientations: Gender differences and similarities. *Merrill-Palmer Quarterly, 34,* 223–237.

Ginsburg, H. P., & Opper, S. (1988). *Piaget's theory of intellectual development* (3rd ed.). Englewood Cliffs, NJ: Prentice Hall.

Ginsburg, H. P., Klein, A., & Starkey, P. (1998). Development of children's mathematical thinking: Connecting research with practice. In W. Damon, I. E. Sigel, & K. A. Renninger (Eds.), *Handbook of child psychology (Vol. 4): Child psychology in practice.* New York: John Wiley & Sons, Inc.

Ginsburg, H., & Opper, S. (1979). *Piaget's theory of intellectual development* (2nd ed.). Englewood Cliffs, NJ: Prentice-Hall.

Ginsburg-Block, M., Rohrbeck, C., & Fantuzzo, J. (2006). A meta-analytic review of social, self-concept, and behavioral outcomes of peer-assisted learning. *Journal of Educational Psychology, 98,* 732–749.

Girbau, D. (2001). Children's referential communication failure: The ambiguity and abbreviation message. *Journal of Language & Social Psychology, 20,* 81–89.

Giudice M., Manera V., Keysers, C. (2009) Programmed to learn? The ontogeny of mirror neurons. *Developmental Science, 12,* 350–36.

Glaberson, W. (2002, March 5). Judge rebukes city officials for removing children from homes of battered women. *New York Times.* Retrieved August 2, 2002, from www.nytimes.com.

Glasberg, R., & Aboud, F. (1982). Keeping one's distance from sadness: Children's self-reports of emotional experience. *Developmental Psychology, 18,* 287–293.

Gleason, J. B. (1997). *The development of language.* Boston, MA: Allyn and Bacon.

Gleitman, L. (1990). The structural sources of verb meanings. *Language Acquisition, 1,* 3–55.

Godin, G., Anderson, D. & Lambert, L. D. (2005). Identifying factors associated with regular physical activity in leisure time among Canadian adolescents. *American Journal of Health Promotion, 20,* 20–27.

Gogtay, N., Giedd, J. N., Lusk, L., Hayashi, K. M., Greenstein, D., Vaituzis, A. C., Nugent, T. F., III, Herman, D. H., Clasen, L. S., Toga, A. W., Rapoport, J. L., & Thompson, P. M. (2004). Dynamic mapping of human cortical development during childhood through early adolescence. *Proceedings of the National Academy of Science, 101*(21), 8174–8179.

Goldberg, J. H., Halpern-Felsher, B. L., & Millstein, S. G. (2002). Beyond in vulnerability: The importance of benefits in adolescents' decision to drink alcohol. *Health Psychology, 21,* 477–484.

Goldin-Meadow, S. (2006). Nonverbal communication: The hand's role in talking and thinking. In D. Kuhn & R. S. Siegler (Eds.), *Cognition, perception, and language,* Vol. 2 (pp. 336–369), in W. Damon & R. M. Lerner (Gen. Eds.), *Handbook of child psychology*, 6th ed. New York: John Wiley & Sons.

Goldschmidt, L., Richardson, G. A., Willford, J., & Day, N. L. (2008). Prenatal marijuana exposure and intelligence test performance at age 6.

*Journal of the American Academy of Child and Adolescent Psychiatry, 47*(3), 254–263.

Goldsmith, H. H., Pollak, S. D., & Davidson, R. J. (2008). Developmental neuroscience perspectives on emotion regulation. *Child Development Perspectives, 2*(3), 132–140.

Golinkoff, R. M., Mervis, C., & Hirsh-Pasek, K. (1994). Early object labels: The case for a developmental lexical principles framework. *Journal of Child Language, 21*, 125–155.

Golombok, G., Perry, B., Burson, A., Murray, C., Mooney-Somers, J., Stevens, M., & Golding, J. (2003). Children with lesbian parents: A community study. *Developmental Psychology, 39*, 20–33.

Golombok, S., Lycett, E., MacCallum, F., Jadva, V., Murray, C., Rust, J., et al. (2004a). Parenting infants conceived by gamete donation. *Journal of Family Psychology, 18*, 443–452.

Golombok, S., MacCallum, F., & Goodman, E. (2001). The "test-tube" generation: Parent–child relationships and the psychological well-being of in vitro fertilization children at adolescence. *Child Development, 72*, 599–608.

Golombok, S., MacCallum, F., Goodman, E., & Rutter, M. (2002). Families with children conceived by donor insemination: A follow-up at age twelve. *Child Development, 73*, 952–968.

Golombok, S., Murray, C., Jadva, V., MacCallum, F., & Lycett, E. (2004b). Families created through surrogacy arrangements: Parent-child relationships in the 1st year of life. *Developmental Psychology, 40*, 400–411.

Golombok, S., Rust, J., Zervoulis, K., Croudace, T., Golding, J., & Hines, M. (2008). Developmental trajectories of sex-typed behavior in boys and girls: A longitudinal general population study of children aged 2.5–8 years. *Child Development, 79*(5), 1583–1593.

González-Frankenberger, B., Harmony, T., Ricardo-Garcell, J., Porras-Kattz, E., Fernández-Bouzas, A., Santiago, E., & Avecilla-Ramírez, G. (2008). Habituation of visual evoked potentials in healthy infants and in infants with periventricular leukomaliacia. *Clinical Neurophysiology, 119*, 2879–2886.

Good, T. L., & Brophy, J.E. (2003). *Looking in classrooms* (9th ed.). Boston: Allyn & Bacon.

Goodall, J. (1986). *The chimpanzees of Bombe: Patterns of behavior*. Cambridge, MA: Harvard University Press.

Goode, E. (1999, August 3). Mozart for baby? Some say, maybe not. *New York Times*. Retrieved September 14, 2000, from www.nytimes.com.

Goodenough, W. H. (1994). Toward a working theory of culture. In R. Borotsky (Ed.), *Assessing cultural anthropology* (pp. 262–273). New York: McGraw-Hill.

Goodman, G., & Quas, J. (2008). Repeated interviews and children's memory: It's more than just how many. *Current Directions in Psychological Science, 17*(6), 386–390.

Goodsitt, J., Morse, P., VerHoeve, J., & Cowan, N. (1984). Infant speech recognition I multisyllabic contexts. *Child Development, 55*, 903–910.

Goossens, F. A., & van IJzendoorn, M. H. (1990). Quality of infants' attachments to professional caregivers: Relation to infant–parent attachment and day-care characteristics. *Child Development, 61*, 832–837.

Gopnik, A. (1984). The acquisition of "gone" and the development of the object concept. *Journal of Child Language, 11*, 273–292.

Gopnik, A., & Meltzoff, A. (1984). Semantic and cognitive development in 15- to 21-month old children. *Journal of Child Language, 11*, 495–513.

Goren, C. C., Sarty, M., & Wu, P. Y. K. (1975). Visual following and pattern discrimination of face-like stimuli by newborn infants. *Pediatrics, 56*, 544–549.

Gormley, W. T. Jr., Gayer, T., Phillips, D., & Dawson, B. (2005). The effects of universal pre-K on cognitive development, *Developmental Psychology, 41*, 872–884.

Gormley, W., Phillips, D., & Gayer, T. (2008, June 27). Preschool programs can boost school readiness. *Science, 320*(5884), 1723–1724.

Gorn, G. I., Goldberg, M. E., & Kanningo, R. N. (1976). The role of educational television in changing intergroup attitudes to children. *Child Development, 47*, 277–280.

Gosselin, P., & Larocque, C. (2000). Facial morphology and children's categorization of facial expressions of emotions: A comparison between Asian and Caucasian faces. *Journal of Genetic Psychology, 161*, 346–358.

Gostin, L.O. (2001). The rights of pregnant women: The Supreme Court and drug testing. *Hastings Center Report, 31*(5), 8–9.

Gottesman, I. I. (1963). Genetic aspects of intelligent behavior. In N. Ellis (Ed.), *Handbook of mental deficiency* (pp. 253–296). New York: McGraw-Hill.

Gottesman, I. I. (1991). *Schizophrenia genetics: The origins of madness*. New York: Freeman.

Gottlieb, G. (1991). *Individual development and evolution: The genesis of novel behavior*. New York: Oxford University Press.

Gottlieb, G. (1997). *Synthesizing nature-nurture: Prenatal roots of instinctive behavior*. Mahwah, NJ: Erlbaum.

Gottlieb, G. (2003). On making behavioral genetics truly developmental. *Human Development, 46*, 337–355.

Graham, S. (2006). Writing. In P. A. Alexander & P. H. Winne (Eds.), *Handbook of educational psychology* (2nd ed.) (pp. 457–478). Mahwah, NJ: Erlbaum.

Graham, S., Hudley, C., & Williams, E. (1992). Attributional and emotional determinants of aggression among African-American and Latino young adolescents. *Developmental Psychology, 28*, 731–740.

Green, L. J. (2002). *African American English: A linguistic introduction*. New York: Cambridge University Press.

Greenfield, P., & Yan, Z. (2006). Children, adolescents, and the Internet: A new field of inquiry in developmental psychology. *Developmental Psychology, 42*, 391–394.

Greenfield, P. M., & Suzuki, L. K. (1998). Culture and human development: Implications for parenting, education, pediatrics, and mental health. In W. Damon, I. E. Sigel, & K. A. Renninger (Eds.), *Handbook of child psychology, Vol. 4: Child psychology in practice* (pp. 1059–1109). New York: John Wiley & Sons.

Greenfield, P. M., Suzuki, L. K., & Rothstein-Fisch, C. (2006). Cultural pathways through human development. In W. Damon & R. M. Lerner (Series Eds.), K. A. Renninger, & I. E. Sigel (Vol. Eds.), *Handbook of child psychology, Vol. 4: Child psychology in practice* (pp. 665–699). New York: John Wiley & Sons.

Greenlee, S. P., Damarin, F. L., & Walsh, W. G. (1988). Congruence and differentiation among Black and White males in two non-college-degreed occupations. *Journal of Vocational Behavior, 32*, 298–306.

Greenough, W. T., & Black, J. E. (1999). Experience, neural plasticity, and psychological development. In N. A. Fox, L. A. Leavitt, & J. G. Warhol (Eds.), *The role of early experience in infant development* (pp. 29–40). Johnson & Johnson Pediatric Institute.

Gregory, R. (1996). *Psychological testing: History, principles, and applications* (2nd ed.). Boston: Allyn & Bacon.

Gregory, S. G., Barlow, K. F., McLay, K. E., Kaul, R., Swarbreck, D., Dunham, A., et al., (2006). The DNA sequence and biological annotation of human chromosome 1. *Nature, 441*, 315–321.

Grieser, M., Vu, M. B. & Bedimo-Rung, A. L. (2006). Physical activity attitudes, preferences, and practices in African American, Hispanic, and Caucasian girls. *Health Education & Behavior, 33*, 40–51.

Griffiths, M. D., & Hunt, N. (1995). Computer game playing in adolescence: Prevalence and demographic indicators. *Journal of Community and Applied Social Psychology, 5*, 189–193.

Grigg, W. N. (1995). Are you fit to be a parent? *The New American, 11*(2), www.thenewamerican.com/ [retrieved on January 9, 2003].

Grigg, W., Donahue, P., and Dion, G. (2007). *The nation's report card: 12th-grade reading and mathematics 2005* (NCES 2007.468). U.S. Department of Education, National Center for Education Statistics. Washington, DC: U.S. Government Printing Office. Retrieved May 9, 2009, from nces.ed.gov/pubsearch/pubsinfo.asp? pubid=2007468.

Grigg, W., Lauko, M., & Brockway, D. (2006). *The nation's report card: science 2005* (NCES 2006–466). U.S. Department of Education, National Center for Education Statistics. Washington, DC: U.S. Government Printing Office. Retrieved May 10, 2009, from nces.ed.gov/pubsearch/pubsinfo.asp?pubid=2006466.

Grolnick, W. S., Kurowski, C. O., & Gurland, S. T. (1999). Family processes and the development of children's self-regulation. *Educational Psychologist, 34*, 3–14.

Gross, A. L., & Ballif, B. (1991). Children's understanding of emotion from facial expressions and situations: A review. *Developmental Review, 11*, 368–398.

Gross, E. F. (2004). Adolescent Internet use: What we expect, what teens report. *Journal of Applied Developmental Psychology, 25*, 633–649.

Gross, J. (1998, January 18). On the case: A special report. Child welfare foot soldier treads fine line. *New York Times*. Retrieved August 2, 2002, from www.nytimes.com.

Gross, J. (2005, February 26). As autistic children grow, so does social gap. *The New York Times*, retrieved February 13, 2006, from www.nytimes.com.

Grossmann, K. E., Grossmann, K., Huber, F., & Wartner, U. (1981). German children's behavior towards their mothers at 12 months and their fathers at 18 months in Ainsworth's Strange Situation. *International Journal of Behavioral Development, 4*, 157–181.

Gruber, J. (2001). *Risky behavior among youths: An economic analysis.* Chicago: University of Chicago Press.

Grunbaum, J., Kann, L., Kinchen, S., Ross, J., Hawkins, J., Lowry, R., et al. (May, 2004). Youth risk behavior surveillance—United States, 2003. *MMWR Surveillance Summaries, 53*, No. SS-2. Retrieved April 25, 2009, from www.cdc.gov/healthyyouth/yrbs/pubs_mmwr.htm.

Guilford, J. P. (1967). *The nature of human intelligence.* New York: McGraw-Hill.

Guilford, J. P. (1982). Cognitive psychology's ambiguities: Some suggested remedies. *Psychological Review, 89*, 48–59.

Gulli, L. (2005). Huntington's disease. *The Gale Encyclopedia of Genetic Disorders* (2nd ed., Vol. 1, pp. 646–649). Detroit, MI: Thomson Gale.

Gunter, B., & McAleer, J. (1997). *Children and television.* London: Routledge.

Gustafson, S. L., & Rhodes, R. E. (2006). Parental correlates of physical activity in chlidren and early adolescents. *Sports Medicine, 36*, 79–97.

Guttmacher Institute. (2006). U.S. teenage pregnancy statistics: National and state trends and trends by race and ethnicity. New York: Guttmacher Institute. Retrieved December 30, 2008 from www.guttmacher.org/pubs/2006/09/12/USTPstats.pdf.

Hahn, C. (2001). Review: Psychosocial well-being of parents and their children after assisted reproduction. *Journal of Pediatric Psychology*, 26, 525–538.

Hainline, L. (1998). The development of basic visual abilities. In A. Slater (Ed.), *Perceptual development: Visual, auditory, and speech perception in infancy* (pp. 5–50). East Sussex, UK: Psychology Press, Ltd.

Haith, M. M., & Benson, J. B. (1998). Infant cognition, In W. Damon (Series Ed.) & D. Kuhn & R. S. Siegler (Vol. Eds.), *Handbook of child psychology: Vol. 2. Cognition, perception, and language* (5th ed., pp. 199–254). New York: Wiley.

Halford, G. S. (2004). The development of deductive reasoning: How important is complexity? *Thinking & Reasoning, 10*, 123–145.

Halford, G. S., Smith, S. B., Dickson, J. C., Mayberry, M. T., Kelly, M. E., Bain, J. D., & Stewart, J. E. M. (1995). Modeling the development of reasoning strategies: The roles of analogy, Knowledge, and capacity. In T. Simon & G. Halford (Eds.), *Developing cognitive competence: New approaches to process modeling* (pp. 77–156). Hillsdale, NJ: Erlbaum.

Hall, G. S. (1904). *Adolescence: Its psychology and its relations to physiology, anthropology, sociology, sex, crime, religion, and education* (Vols. 1 and 2). New York: Appleton.

Halperin, S. (Ed.) (1998). *The forgotten half revisited: American youth and young families, 1988–2008.* Washington, DC: American Youth Policy Forum.

Halpern, D. F. (2000). *Sex differences in cognitive abilities* (3rd ed.). Hillsdale, NJ: Erlbaum.

Halpern, D. F. (2003). *Thought & knowledge: An introduction to critical thinking* (4th ed.). Mahwah, NJ: Erlbaum.

Halpern, R. (1993). Poverty and infant development. In C. H. Zeanah, Jr. (Ed.), *Handbook of infant mental health* (pp. 73–86). New York: The Guilford Press.

Halpern-Felsher, B. (2009). Adolescent decision making: An overview. *The Prevention Researcher, 16*, 3–7.

Halpern-Felsher, B. L., & Cauffman, E. (2001). Costs and benefits of a decision: Decision-making competence in adolescents and adults. *Journal of Applied Developmental Psychology, 22*, 257–273.

Halpern-Felsher, B. L., Cornell, J. L., Kropp, R. Y. & Tschann, J. M. (2005). Oral versus vaginal sex among adolescents: Perceptions, attitudes, and behavior. *Pediatrics, 115*, 845–851.

Hamers, J. F. (1996). Cognitive and language development of bilingual children. In I. Parasnis (Ed.), *Cultural and language diversity and the deaf experience* (pp. 51–75). Cambridge: Cambridge University Press.

Hamers, J. F., & Blanc, M. H. A. (2000). *Bilinguality and bilingualism* (2nd ed.). Cambridge: Cambridge University Press.

Hamilton, B. E., Martin, J. A., & Ventura, S. J. (2009). Births: Preliminary data for 2007. *National Vital Statistics Reports, 57*(12). Retrieved April 24, 2009, from www.cdc.gov/nchs/products/nvsr.htm.

Hamilton, B. E., Martin, J. A., & Ventura, S. J., (2009). Births: Preliminary data for 2007. *National Vital Statistics Reports, 57*(12), p. 13. Hyattsville, MD: National Center for Health Statistics. Last accessed March 25, 2009, from www.cdc.gov/nchs/data/nvsr/nvsr57/nvsr57_12.pdf.

Hamilton, C. J., Coates, R. O., & Heffernan, T. (2003). What develops in visuo-spatial working memory development? *European Journal of Cognitive Psychology, 15*, 43–70.

Hamilton, S. F., & Hamilton, M. A. (2004). Contexts for mentoring: Adolescent-adult relationships in workplaces and communities (pp. 395–428). In R. M. Lerner & L. Steinberg (Eds.), *Handbook of Adolescent Psychology* (2nd ed.), Hoboken, NJ: John Wiley & Sons.

Hammack, P. L. (2005). The life course development of human sexual orientation: An integrative paradigm. *Human Development, 48*, 267–290.

Hamre, B. K., & Pianta, R. C. (2005). Can instructional and emotional support in the first-grade classroom make a difference for children at risk of school failure? *Child Development, 76*, 949–967.

Handley, K., Sturdy, A., Finsham, R., & Clark, T. (2006). Within and beyond communities of practice: Making sense of learning through participation, identity and practice. *Journal of Management Studies, 43*, 641–653.

Handley, S. J., Capon, A., Copp, C., & Harper, C. (2002). Conditional reasoning and the Tower of Hanoi: The role of spatial and verbal working memory. *British Journal of Psychology, 93*, 501–518.

Hansen, M., Janssen, I., Schiff, A., Zee, P. C. & Dubocovich, M. L. (2005). The impact of school daily schedule on adolescent sleep. *Pediatrics, 115*, 1555–1561.

Hanson, T. L. (1999). Does parental conflict explain why divorce is negatively associated with child welfare? *Social Forces, 77*, 1283–1316.

Harjo, S. S. (1999). The American Indian experience. In H. P. McAdoo (Ed.), *Family ethnicity: Strength in diversity* (pp. 63-71). Thousand Oaks, CA: Sage Publications, Inc.

Harlow, H. F., & Zimmermann, R. R. (1959). Affectional responses in the infant monkey. *Science, 130*, 421–432.

Harris, J. R. (1998). *The nurture assumption: Why children turn out the way they do.* New York: Free Press.

Harris, J. R. (2000). The outcome of parenting: What do we really know? *Journal of Personality, 68*, 625–637.

Harris, P. L. (1983). Infant cognition. In P. H. Mussen (Series Ed.) & M. M. Haith & J. J. Campos (Vol. Eds.), *Handbook of child psychology: Vol. 2. Infancy and developmental psychobiology* (pp. 689–782). New York: Wiley.

Hart, B., & Risley, T. R. (1995). *Meaningful differences in the everyday experience of young American children.* Baltimore: Paul H. Brookes.

Hart, C. H., Olsen, S. F., Robinson, C. C., & Mandleco, B. L. (1997). The relation of childhood personality types to adolescent behavior and development: A longitudinal study of Icelandic children. *Developmental Psychology, 33*, 195–205.

Harter, S. (1993). Causes and consequences of low self-esteem in children and adolescents. In R. F. Baumeister (Ed.), *Self-esteem: The puzzle of low self-regard* (pp. 87–116). New York: Plenum.

Harter, S. (1998). The development of self-representations. In W. Damon & N. Eisenberg (Eds.), *Handbook of child psychology: Vol 3. Social, emotional, and personality development* (pp. 553–617). New York: Wiley.

Harter, S. (1999). *The construction of the self: A developmental perspective.* New York: Guilford Press.

Harter, S. (2006). The self. In W. Damon & R. M. Lerner (Series Eds.) & N. Eisenberg (Vol. Ed.), *Handbook of child psychology, Vol 3: Social, emotional, and personality development* (6th ed., pp. 505–570). New York: John Wiley & Sons.

Hartung, P. J., Porfeli, E. J., & Vondracek, F. W. (2005). Child vocational development: A review and reconsideration. *Journal of Vocational Behavior, 66*, 385–419.

Hartup, W. W. (1989). Behavioral manifestations of children's friendships. In T. J. Berndt & G. W. Ladd (Eds.), *Peer relationships in child development* (pp. 46–70). New York: Wiley.

Harwood, K., McLean, N., & Durkin, K. (2007). First-time mothers' expectations of parenthood: What happens when optimistic expectations are not matched by later experiences? *Developmental Psychology, 43*(1), 1–12.

Harwood, R. L. (1992). The influence of culturally derived values on Anglo and Puerto Rican mothers' perceptions of attachment behavior. *Child Development, 63*, 822–839.

Hasher, L., & Zachs, R. T. (1979). Automatic and effortful processes in memory. *Journal of Experimental Psychology: General, 108*, 356–388.

Hasselhorn, M. (1992). Task dependency and the role of category typicality and metamemory in the development of an organizational strategy. *Child Development, 63*, 202–214.

Hatchett, S. J., & Jackson, J. S. (1999). African American extended kin systems: An empirical assessment in the National Survey of Black Americans. In H. P. McAdoo (Ed.), *Family ethnicity: Strength in diversity* (2nd ed., pp. 171–190). Thousand Oaks, CA: Sage.

Hauck, F. R., Signore, C., Fein, S. B., & Raju, T. N. K. (2008). Infant sleeping arrangements and practices during the first year of life. *Pediatrics, 122*, S113–120.

Hausenblas, H. A. & Fallon, E. A. (2006). Exercise and body image: A meta-analysis. *Psychology & Health, 21*, 33–47.

Haviland, J. M., & Lelwica, M. (1987). The induced affect response: 10-week-old infants' responses to three emotion expressions. *Developmental Psychology, 23*, 97–104.

Hay, D. F., & Ross, H. S. (1982). The social nature of early conflict. *Child Development, 53*, 105–113.

Hazan, C. & Shaver, P. (1987). Romantic love conceptualized as an attachment process. *Journal of Personality and Social Psychology, 52*(3), 511–524.

He, F., Lidow, I. A., & Lidow, M. S. (2006). Consequences of paternal cocaine exposure in mice. *Neurotoxicology and Teratology, 28*(2), 198–209.

Hearold, S. (1986). A synthesis of 1043 effects of television on social behavior. In G. Comstock (Ed.), *Public communication and behavior* (Vol. 1, pp. 65–133). New York: Academic Press.

Heinicke, C. M., & Guthrie, D. (1996). Prebirth marital interactions and postbirth marital development. *Infant Mental Health Journal, 17*(2), 140–151.

Hergenroeder, A. C. (1998). Prevention of sports injuries. *Pediatrics, 101*, 1057–1063.

Herman, J. L. (1992). *Trauma and recovery: The aftermath of violence—from domestic abuse to political terror.* New York: Basic Books. As cited in Werkerle & Wolfe (1996), p. 508.

Herman-Giddens, M. E. (2006). Recent data on pubertal milestones in United States children: The secular trend toward earlier development. *International Journal of Androogy, 29*, 241–246.

Heron, M. (2007). Deaths: Leading causes for 2004. *National Vital Statistics Reports, 56*(5). Retrieved April 25, 2009, from www.cdc.gov/nchs/products/nvsr.htm.

Herpes.com (2002). "Good" virus/"Bad" virus: The truth about HSV-1 and HSV-2; Herpes and pregnancy; and Transmission. All articles retrieved March 1, 2002, from www.herpes.com.

Herrnstein, R. J., & Murray, C. (1994). *The bell curve: Intelligence and class structure in American life.* New York: Free Press.

Hershberger, S. L., & D'Augelli, A. R. (1995). The impact of victimization on the mental health and suicidality of lesbian, gay, and bisexual youths. *Developmental Psychology, 31*, 65–74.

Hetherington, E. M. (1999). Should we stay together for the sake of the children? In E. M. Hetherington (Ed.), *Coping with divorce, single parenting, and remarriage: A risk and resiliency perspective* (pp. 93–116). Mahwah, NJ: Erlbaum.

Hetherington, E. M., & Clingempeel, W. G. (1992). Coping with marital transitions. *Monographs of the Society for Research in Child Development, 57* (No. 2–3). Chicago: University of Chicago Press.

Hetherington, E. M., & Jodl, K. M. (1994). Stepfamilies as settings for child development. In A. Booth & J. Dunn (Eds.), *Stepfamilies: Who benefits? Who does not?* (pp. 55–79). Hillsdale, NJ: Erlbaum.

Hetherington, E. M., & Kelly, J. (2002). *For better or for worse: Divorce reconsidered.* New York: W. W. Norton.

Hetherington, E. M., & Stanley-Hagan, M. M. (1995). Parenting in divorced and remarried families. In M. H. Bornstein (Ed.), *Handbook of parenting: Vol. 3. Status and social conditions of parenting* (pp. 233–254). Mahwah, NJ: Erlbaum.

Hetherington, E. M., Bridges, M., & Insabella, G. M. (1998). What matters? What does not? *American Psychologist, 53*, 167–184.

Hetherington, E. M., Cox, M., & Cox. R. (1982). Effects of divorce on parents and children. In M. E. Lamb (Ed.), *Nontraditional families: Parenting and child development* (pp. 233–288). Hillsdale, NJ: Erlbaum.

Hetherington, E. M., Reiss, D., & Plomin, R. (Eds.) (1994). *Separate social worlds of siblings: The impact of nonshared environment on development.* Hillsdale, NJ: Erlbaum.

Higgins, E. T., & Parsons, J. E. (1983). Social cognition and the social life of the child: Stages as subcultures. In E. T. Higgins, D. N. Ruble, & W. W. Hartup (Eds.), *Social cognition and social development* (pp. 15–62). Cambridge, England: Cambridge University Press.

High school expels junior after guard finds knife in truck. (2002, March 21). *New York Times.* Retrieved August 7, 2002, from www.nytimes.com.

Hilton, J. M. (2002). Children's behavior problems in single-parent and married-parent families: Development of a predictive model. *Journal of Divorce and Remarriage, 37*, 13–36.

Hmelo-Silver, C., Marathe, S., & Liu, L. (2007). Fish swim, rocks sit, and lungs breathe: Expert-novice understanding of complex systems. *Journal of the Learning Sciences, 16*, 307–331.

Ho, M.-W. (1984). Environment and heredity in development and evolution. In M.-W. Ho & P. T. Saunders (Eds.), *Beyond neo-Darwinism: An introduction to the new evolutionary paradigm* (pp. 267–289). London: Academic Press.

Hodapp, R. M., & Dykens, E. M. (2003). Intellectual disability (intellectual disabilities). In E. J. Mash & R. A. Barkley (Eds.), *Child psychopathology* (2nd ed.). (pp. 486–519). New York: Guilford Press.

Hodnett, E. D., & Osborn, R. W. (1989). Effects of continuous intrapartum professional support on childbirth outcomes. *Research in Nursing and Health, 12*, 289–297.

Hoehl, S., & Striano, T. (2008). Neural processing of eye gaze and threat-related emotional facial expressions in infancy. *Child Development, 79*, 1752–1760.

Hofferth, S. L., & Curtin, S. C. (2003). *Leisure time activities in middle childhood.* Paper presented at the Positive Outcomes Conference, Washington, DC, March 12–13, 2003. Retrieved June 21, 2006, from www.childtrends.org/Files/HofferthCurtinPaper.pdf.

Hofferth, S. L., & Sandberg, J. F. (2001). How American children use their time. *Journal of Marriage and the Family, 63*, 295–308.

Hofferth, S. L., Reid, L. & Mott, F. L. (2001). The effects of early childbearing on schooling over time. *Family Planning Perspectives, 33*, 259–267.

Hoffman, M. L. (1975). Moral internalization, parental power, and the nature of parent–child interaction. *Developmental Psychology, 11*, 228–239.

Hoffman-Plotkin, D., & Twentyman, C. T. (1984). A multimodal assessment of behavioral and cognitive deficits in abused and neglected preschoolers. *Child Development*, 55, 794–802.

Hogan, T., & Rabinowitz, M. (2009). Teacher expertise and the development of a problem representation. *Educational Psychology, 29*, 153–169.

Hogben, M. (1998). Factors moderating the effect of televised aggression on viewer behavior. *Communication Research, 25*, 220–247.

Holahan, C., Holahan, C., Velasquez, K., & North, R. (2008). Longitudinal change in happiness during aging: The predictive role of positive expectancies. *International Journal of Aging & Human Development, 66*, 229–241.

Holden, C. (1995). More on genes and homosexuality. *Science*, 268, 1571.

Holden, G. W. (2002). Perspectives on the effects of corporal punishment: Comment on Gershoff (2002). *Psychological Bulletin, 128*, 590–595.

Holland, J. L. (1997). *Making Vocational Choices* (3rd ed.). Lutz, FL: Psychological Assessment Resources.

Holland, J. D. & Klaczynski, P. A. (2009). Intuitive risk taking during adolescence. *The Prevention Researcher, 16*, 8–11.

Hopf, W. H., Huber, G. L., & Weiβ, R. H. (2008). Media violence and youth violence: A 2-year longitudinal study. *Journal of Media Psychology, 20*, 79–96.

Horgan, D. (1978). The development of the full passive. *Journal of Child Language, 5*, 65–80.

Horn, J., & Cattell, R. B. (1966). Refinement and test of the theory of fluid and crystallized general intelligences. *Journal of Educational Psychology, 57*(5), 253–270.

Horn, S. S. (2003). Adolescents' reasoning about exclusion from social groups. *Developmental Psychology, 39*(1), 71–84.

Howard, D. E., & Wang, M. Q. (2005). Psychosocial correlates of U.S. adolescents who report a history of forced sexual intercourse. *Journal of Adolescent Health, 36*, 372–379.

Howe, D. (1998). *Patterns of adoption: Nature, nurture, and psychosocial development.* Oxford: Blackwell Science, Ltd.

Howe, M. L., & Courage, M. L. (2004). Demystifying the beginnings of memory. *Developmental Review, 24,* 1–5.

Howe, M. L., Courage, M. L., Bryant-Brown, L. (1995). Reinstating preschoolers' memories. *Developmental Psychology, 29,* 854–869.

Howes, C. (1988). Peer interaction of young children. *Monographs of the Society for Research in Child Development*, 53 (Serial no. 217), pp. 1–78.

Howse, R. B., Lange, G., Farran, D. C., & Boyles, C. D. (2003). Motivation and self-regulation as predictors of achievement in economically disadvantaged young children. *Journal of Experimental Education, 71,* 151–174.

Hsu, L. K. G., Chesler, B. E., & Santhouse, R. (1990). Bulimia nervosa in eleven sets of twins: A clinical report. *International Journal of Eating Disorders, 9,* 275–282.

Hudson J. I., Hiripi, E., Pope, H. G., & Kessler, R. C. (2007). The prevalence and correlates of eating disorders in the National Comorbidity Survey Replication. *Biological Psychiatry, 61*, 348–58.

Hudson, J. A., & Nelson, K. (1983). Effects of script structure on children's story recall. *Developmental Psychology, 19*, 625–635.

Hudson, J. A., Fivush, R., & Kuebli, J. (1992). Scripts and episodes: The development of event memory. *Applied Cognitive Psychology, 6*, 483–505.

Hudson, J. A., Shapiro, L. R., & Sosa, B. B. (1995). Planning in the real world: Preschool children's scripts for familiar events. *Child Development, 66*, 984–998.

Hudspeth, W. J. & Pribram, K. H. (1990). Stages of brain and cognitive maturation. *Journal of Educational Psychology, 82*, 881–884.

Huesman, L. R., Eron, L. D., Lefkowitz, M. M., & Walder, L. O. (1984). Stability of aggression over time and generations. *Developmental Psychology, 20,* 1120–1134.

Huesmann, L. R., & Miller, L. S. (1994). Long-term effects of repeated exposure to media violence in childhood. In L. R. Huesmann (Ed.), *Aggressive behavior: Current perspectives* (pp. 153–186). New York: Plenum.

Huesmann, L. R., Moise-Titus, J., Podolski, C., & Eron, L. D. (2003). Longitudinal relations between children's exposure to TV violence and their aggressive and violent behavior in young adulthood: 1977–1992. *Developmental Psychology, 38,* 201–221.

Huggins, S. L. (1989). A comparative study of self-esteem of adolescent children of divorced lesbian mothers and divorced heterosexual mothers. *Journal of Homosexuality, 18*, 123–135.

Hughes, F. P. (1999). *Children, play, and development.* Boston: Allyn & Bacon.

Huizink, A. C., & Mulder, E. J. H. (2006). Maternal smoking, drinking or cannabis use during pregnancy and neurobehavioral and cognitive functioning in human offspring. *Neuroscience and Biobehavioral Reviews, 30*, 24–41.

Hulit, L. M., & Howard, M. R. (1997). *Born to talk: An introduction to speech and language development.* Boston, MA: Allyn and Bacon.

Hulit, L. M., & Howard, M. R. (2006). *Born to talk: An introduction to speech and language development* (4th ed.). Boston, MA: Allyn and Bacon.

Human Genome Project, U.S. Department of Energy (2008a). Genomics and its impact on science and society: The human genome project and beyond, Washington, D.C. Retrieved November 22, 2008, from www.ornl.gov/sci/techresources/Human_Genome/publicat/primer2001/primer11.pdf.

Human Genome Project, U.S. Department of Energy (2008b). Genetics privacy and legislation. Washington, D.C. Retrieved November 28, 2008, from www.ornl.gov/sci/techresources/Human_Genome/elsi/legislat.shtml.

Humphrey, J. H. (2003). *Child development through sports.* New York: The Haworth Press.

Hunter, J. (1990). Violence against lesbian and gay male youths. *Journal of Interpersonal Violence, 5*, 295–300.

Hunter, J., & Mallon, G. P. (2000). Lesbian, gay, and bisexual adolescent development: Dancing with your feet tied together. In B. Greene & G. L. Croom (Eds.), *Education, research, and practice in lesbian, gay, bisexual, and transgendered psychology: A resource manual* (pp. 226–243). Thousand Oaks, CA: Sage.

Hunter, W. M., Helou, S., Saluja, G., Runyan, C. W., & Coyne-Beasley, T. (2005). Injury prevention advice in top-selling parenting books. *Pediatrics, 116*(5), 1080–1088.

Hur, Y., McGue, M., & Iacono, W. G. (1998). The structure of self-concept in female preadolescent twins: A behavioral genetic approach. *Journal of Personality and Social Psychology, 74*, 1069–1077.

Huston, A. C., & Wright, J. C. (1998). Mass media and children's development. In W. Damon, I. E. Sigel, & K. A. Renninger (Eds.), *Handbook of child psychology: Vol. 4. Child psychology in practice* (pp. 999–1058). New York: Wiley.

Huston, A. C., Donnerstein, E., Fairchild, H., Feshbach, N. D., Katz, P. A., Murray, J. P., Rubinstein, E. A., Wilcox, B. L., & Zuckerman, D. (1992). *Big world, small screen: The role of television in American society.* Lincoln: University of Nebraska Press.

Huttenlocher, P. R. (1990). Morphometric study of human cerebral cortex development. *Neuropsychologia, 28*, 517–527.

Huttenlocher, P. R. (1999). Synaptogenesis in human cerebral cortex and the concept of critical periods. In N. A. Fox, L. A. Leavitt, & J. G. Warhol (Eds.), *The role of early experience in infant development* (pp. 15–28). Johnson & Johnson Pediatric Institute.

Huttenlocher, P. R. (2002). *Neural plasticity: The effects of environment on the development of the cerebral cortex.* Cambridge, MA: Harvard University Press.

Huttenlocher, P. R., & Dabholkar, A. S. (1997). Regional differences in synaptogenesis in human cerebral cortex. *Journal of Comparative Neurology, 387*, 167–178.

Hyde, J. (2005). The gender similarities hypothesis. *American Psychologist, 60*(6), 581–592.

Hyde, J. S. (2007). New directions in the study of gender similarities and differences. *Current Directions in Psychological Science, 16*, 259–263.

Hyde, J. S., & Linn, M. C. (1988). Gender differences in verbal ability: A meta-analysis. *Psychological Bulletin, 104*, 53–69.

Inhelder, B., & Piaget, J. (1958). *The growth of logical thinking from childhood to adolescence: An essay on the construction of formal operational structures.* New York: Basic Books.

Institute of Medicine (2004). *Immunization safety review: Vaccines and autism.* Washington, DC. Retrieved May 10, 2009, from www.iom.edu/CMS/3793/4705/20155.aspx.

Institute of Medicine, Committee to Study Fetal Alcohol Syndrome (1996). In K. Stratton, C. Howe, & F. Battaglia (Eds.), *Fetal alcohol syndrome: diagnosis, epidemiology, prevention, and treatment.* Washington D. C.: National Academy Press.

Intons-Peterson, M. J. (1988). *Children's concepts of gender.* Norwood, NJ: ABLEX.

Isabella, R. A. (1995). The origins of infant-mother attachment: Maternal behavior and infant development. *Annals of Child Development, 10*, 57–81.

Isabella, R. A., & Belsky, J. (1991). Interactional synchrony and the origins of infant-mother attachment: A replication study. *Child Development, 62*, 373-384.

Isabella, R. A., Belsky, J., & von Eye, A. (1989). Origins of infant–mother attachment: An examination of interactional synchrony during the infant's first year. *Developmental Psychology, 25*, 12–21.

Istvan, J. (1986). Stress, anxiety, and birth outcomes: A critical review of the evidence. *Psychological Bulletin, 100*, 331–348.

Iuliano, A. D., Speizer, I. S., Santelli, J. & Kendall, C. (2006). Reasons for contraceptive nonuse at first sex and unintended pregnancy. *American Journal of Health Behavior, 30*, 92–102.

Ivkovic, V., Vitart, V., Rudan, I., Janicijevic, B., Smolej-Narancic, N., Skaric-Juric, T., et al. (2007). The Eysenck personality factors: Psychometric structure, reliability, heritability and phenotypic and genetic correlations with psychological distress in an isolated Croatian population. *Personality and Individual Differences, 42*, 123–133.

Jablonska, B., & Lindberg, L. (2007). Risk behaviours, victimisation and mental distress among adolescents in different family structures. *Social Psychiatry and Psychiatric Epidemiology, 42*, 656–663.

Jackson, L. A., vonEye, A., Biocca, F. A., Barbatsis, G., Zhao, Y., & Fitzgerald, H. E. (2006). Does home Internet use influence the academic performance of low-income children? *Developmental Psychology, 42*, 429–435.

Jackson, M. F., Barth, J. M., Powell, N., & Lochman, J. E. (2006). Classroom contextual effects of race on children's peer nominations. *Child Development, 77*, 1325–1337.

Jacobson, J. L., & Jacobson, S. W. (1996). Intellectual impairment in children exposed to polychlorinated biphenyls in utero. *New England Journal of Medicine, 335,* 783–789.

Jacobson, J. L., & Jacobson, S. W. (2002). Effects of prenatal alcohol exposure on child development. *Alcohol Research & Health, 26,* 282–286.

Jacobson, J. L., Jacobson, S. W., & Humphrey, H. E. B. (1990). Effects of in utero exposure to polychlorinated biphenyls (PCBs) and related contaminants on cognitive functioning in young children. *Journal of Pediatrics, 116,* 38–45.

Jadack, R. A., Hyde, J. S., Moore, C. F. & Keller, M. L. (1995). Moral reasoning about sexually transmitted diseases. *Child Development, 66,* 167–177.

Jaffee, S., & Hyde, J. S. (2000). Gender differences in moral orientation: A meta-analysis. *Psychological Bulletin, 126,* 703–726.

Jaffee, S. R., Caspi, A., Moffitt, T. E., Polo-Tomas, M., Price, T. S., & Taylor, A. (2004). The limits of child effects: Evidence for genetically mediated child effects on corporal punishment but not on physical maltreatment. *Developmental Psychology, 40,* 1047–1058.

Jaffee, S., R., Moffitt, T. E., Caspi, A., & Taylor, A. (2003). Life with (or without) father: The benefits of living with two biological parents depend on the father's antisocial behavior. *Child Development, 74,* 109–126.

Jain, A., Sherman, S. N., Chamberlin, L. A., Carter, Y., Powers, S. W., & Whitaker, R. C. (2001). Why don't low-income mothers worry about their preschoolers being overweight? *Pediatrics, 107*(5), 1138–1146.

James, K. A., Phelps, L., & Bross, A. L. (2001). Body dissatisfaction, drive for thinness, and self-esteem in African American college females. *Psychology in the Schools, 38,* 491–495.

James, W. (1890/1950). *The principles of psychology.* New York: Dover. (Originally published in 1890.)

Janson, H., & Mathiesen, K. S. (2008). Temperament profiles from infancy to middle childhood: Development and associations with behavior problems. *Developmental Psychology, 44,* 1314–1328.

Janssens, J. M. A. M., & Dekovic, M. (1997). Child rearing, prosocial moral reasoning, and prosocial behavior. *International Journal of Behavioral Development, 20,* 509–527.

Jarrett, R. L. (1995). Growing up poor: The family experiences of socially mobile youth in low-income African American neighborhoods. *Journal of Adolescent Research, 10,* 111–135.

Jekielek, S. M. (1998). Parental conflict, marital diruption and children's emotional well-being. *Social Forces, 76,* 905–935.

Jenkins, J., Dunn, J., O'Connor, T. G., Rasbash, J., & Simpson, A. (2005). Mutual influence of marital conflict and children's behavior problems: Shared and nonshared family risks. *Child Development, 76,* 24–39.

Jennings, J., & Rentner, D. S. (2005). Youth and school reform: From the forgotten half to the forgotten third. Washington, DC: Center on Education Policy. Retrieved July 13, 2005, from www.ctredpol.org/policy_papers/

Johnson, B. E., Kuck, D. L., & Schander, P. R. (1997). Rape myth acceptance and sociodemographic characteristics: A multidimensional analysis. *Sex Roles, 36,* 693–708.

Johnson, J. S., & Newport, E. L. (1989). Critical period effects in second language learning: The influence of maturational state on the acquisition of English as a second language. *Cognitive Psychology, 21,* 60–99.

Johnson, M. K. (2002). Social origins, adolescent experiences, and work value trajectories during the transition to adulthood. *Social Forces, 80,* 1307–1341.

Johnson, S. P., Amso, D., & Slemmer, J. A. (2003). Development of object concepts in infancy: Evidence for early learning in an eye-tracking paradigm. *Proceedings of the New York Academy of Sciences, 100,* 10568–15073.

Johnston, J. (1990). Role diffusion and role reversal: Structural variations in divorced families and children's functioning. *Family Relations, 39,* 405–413.

Johnston, L. D., O'Malley, P. M., Bachman, J. G. & Schulenberg, J. E. (2006). *Monitoring the future: National results on adolescent drug use, Overview of key findings, 2005.* (NIH Publication No. 06-5882). Bethesda, MD: National Institute on Drug Abuse. Retrieved May 30, 2006 from monitoringthefuture.org/.

*Journal of Gene Medicine* (2008). Gene therapy clinical trials worldwide. Retrieved October 25, 2008, from www.wiley.co.uk/genetherapy/clinical.

Jurdak, M., & Shahin, I. (1999). An ethnographic study of the computational strategies of a group of young street vendors in Beirut. *Educational Studies in Mathematics, 40,* 155–172.

Kabot, S., Masi, W., & Segal, M. (2003). Advances in the diagnosis and treatment of autism spectrum disorders. *Professional Psychology: Research and Practice, 34,* 26–33.

Kagan, J. (1997). Temperament and the reactions to unfamiliarity. *Child Development, 68,* 139–143.

Kagan, J. (2008). In defense of qualitative changes in development. *Child Development, 79,* 1606–1624.

Kagan, J. Arcus, D., & Snidman, N. (1993). The idea of temperament: Where do we go from here? In R. Plomin & G. E. McClearn (Eds.), *Nature, nurture, and psychology* (pp. 197–210). Washington, DC: American Psychological Association.

Kagan, J., Arcus, D., Snidman, N., Feng, W. Y., Hendler, J., & Greene, S. (1994). Reactivity in infants: A cross-national comparison. *Developmental Psychology, 30,* 342–345.

Kagan, J., Reznick, J. S., & Snidman, N. (1988). Biological bases of childhood shyness. *Science, 240,* 167–171.

Kail, R., & Salthouse, T. A. (1994). Processing speed as a mental capacity. *Acta Psychologica, 86,* 199–225.

Kaiser Family Foundation (2002, March). Sex education in the U.S.: Policy and politics. Retrieved January 7, 2003, from www.kff.org/content/2002/3224.

Kaltenbach, K., & Finnegan, L. (1992). Methadone maintenance during pregnancy: Implications for perinatal and developmental outcome. In T. B. Sonderegger (Ed.), *Perinatal substance abuse: Research findings and clinical applications* (pp. 239–253). Baltimore: The Johns Hopkins University Press.

Kamakura, T., Ando, J., & Ono, Y. (2007). Genetic and environmental effects of stability and change in self-esteem during adolescence. *Personality & Individual Differences, 42,* 181–190.

Kamerman, S. B. (2000). Parental leave policies: An essential ingredient in early childhood education and care policies. *Social Policy Report, 14*(2). Ann Arbor, MI: The Society for Research in Child Development.

Kamphaus, R. W. (2001). *Clinical assessment of child and adolescent intelligence* (2nd ed.). Boston: Allyn & Bacon.

Kandel, D. B. (2002). *Stages and pathways of drug involvement: Examining the gateway hypothesis.* New York: Cambridge University Press.

Kandel, D. B., Yamaguchi, K. & Chen, K. (1992). Stages of progression in drug involvement from adolescence to adulthood: Further evidence for the gateway theory. *Journal of Studies on Alcohol, 53,* 447–457.

Kandel, E. R., Schwartz, J. H., & Jessell, T. M. (2000). *Principles of neural science* (4th ed.). New York: McGraw-Hill.

Kann, R. T., & Hanna, F. J. (2000). Disruptive behavior disorders in children and adolescents: How do girls differ from boys? *Journal of Counseling & Development, 78,* 267–274.

Kaplan, P. S. (2004). *Adolescence.* Boston: Houghton Mifflin.

Karniol, R., & Koren, L. (1987). How would you feel? Children's inferences regarding their own and others' affective reactions. *Cognitive Development, 2,* 271–278.

Karpov, Y. V., & Haywood, H. C. (1998). Two ways to elaborate Vygotsky's concept of mediation. *American Psychologist, 53,* 27–36.

Katchadourian, H. (1990). Sexuality. In S. S. Feldman & G. R. Elliott (Eds.), *At the threshold: The developing adolescent* (pp. 330–351). Cambridge, MA: Harvard University Press.

Katz, L. F., & Woodin, E. M. (2002). Hostility, hostile detachment, and conflict engagement in marriages: Effects on child and family functioning. *Child Development, 73,* 636–652.

Kaufman, J., & Zigler, E. (1989). The intergenerational transmission of child abuse and the prospect of predicting future abusers. In D. Cicchetti & V. Carlson (Eds.), *Child maltreatment: Research and theory on the causes and consequences of child abuse and neglect* (pp. 129–150). New York: Cambridge University Press.

Kaufman, P., Chen, X., Choy, S. P., Peter, K., Ruddy, S. A., Miller, A. K., Fleury, J. K., Chandler, K. A., Planty, M. G., & Rand, M. R. (2001). *Indicators of school crime and safety, 2001.* Washington, DC: U.S. Departments of Education and Justice. NCES 2002-113/NCJ-190075. Retrieved August 8, 2002, from nces.ed.gov.

Kaufman, P., Chen, X., Choy, S. P., Ruddy, S. A., Miller, A. K., Fleury, J. K., Chandler, K. A., Rand, M. R., Klaus, P., & Planty, M. G. (2000). *Indicators of school crime and safety, 2000.* Washington, DC: U.S.

Departments of Education and Justice. NCES 2001-017/NCJ-184176. Retrieved August 8, 2002, from nces.ed.gov.

Kavšek, M. (2004). Predicting later IQ from infant visual habituation and dishabituation: A meta-analysis. *Journal of Applied Developmental Psychology*, 25, 369–393.

Kazdin, A. E., & Marciano, P. L. (1998). Childhood and adolescent depression. In E. J. Mash & R. A. Barkley (Eds.), *Treatment of childhood disorders* (pp. 211–248). New York: Guilford Press.

Keating, D. P. (1980). Thinking processes in adolescence. In J. Adelson (Ed.), *Handbook of adolescent psychology* (pp. 211–246). New York: Wiley.

Keating, D. P. (1990). Adolescent thinking. In S. S. Feldman & G. R. Elliott (Eds.), *At the threshold: The developing adolescent* (pp. 54–89). Cambridge, MA: Harvard University Press.

Keating, D. P. (2004). Cognitive and brain development. In R. M. Lerner & L. Steinberg (Eds.), *Handbook of adolescent psychology* (2nd ed.) (pp. 45–84). Hoboken, NJ: John Wiley & Sons, Inc.

Keith, T. Z., Keith, P. B., Quirk, K. J., Sperduto, J., Santillo, S., & Killings, S. (1998). Longitudinal effects of parent involvement on high school grades: Similarities and differences across gender and ethnic groups. *Journal of School Psychology, 36,* 335-363.

Keller, M. C., Coventry, W. L., Heath, A. C., & Martin, N. G., (2005). Widespread evidence for non-additive genetic variation in Cloninger's and Eysenck's personality dimensions using a twin plus sibling design. *Behavior Genetics*, *35*, 707–721.

Kelley, M. L., Sanchez-Hucles, J., & Walker, R. (1993). Correlates of disciplinary practices in working- to middle-class African-American mothers. *Merrill-Palmer Quarterly, 39*, 252-264.

Kellman, P. J., & Arterberry, M. E. (2006). Infant visual perception. In D. Kuhn & R. S. Siegler (Eds.), *Cognition, perception, and language*, Vol. 2 (pp. 109–160), in W. Damon & R. M. Lerner (Gen. Eds.), *Handbook of child psychology*, 6th ed. New York: John Wiley & Sons.

Kemper, R. L., & Vernoog, A. R. (1994). Metalinguistic awareness in first graders: A qualitative perspective. *Journal of Psycholinguistic Research, 22*, 41–57.

Kendler, K. S., Bulik, C. M., Silberg, J., Hettema, J. M., Myers, J., & Prescott, C. A. (2000). Childhood sexual abuse and adult psychiatric and substance use disorders in women: An epidemiological and co-twin control analysis. *Archives of General Psychiatry, 57*, 953–959.

Kendler, K. S., Kuhn, J. W., & Prescott, C. A. (2004). Childhood sexual abuse, stressful life events and risk for major depression in women. *Psychological Medicine, 34*, 1475–1482.

Kendler, K. S., Neale, M. C., Kessler, R. C., Heath, A. C., & Eaves, L. J. (1993). A test of the equal-environment assumption in twin studies of psychiatric illness. *Behavior Genetics*, *23*(1), 21–27.

Keogh, J., & Sugden, D. (1985). *Movement skill development*. New York: Macmillian.

Kerr, D. C. R., Lopez, N. L., Olson, S. L., & Sameroff, A. J. (2004). Parental discipline and externalizing behavior problems in early childhood: The roles of moral regulation and child gender. *Journal of Abnormal Child Psychology, 32*, 369–383.

Kertscher, T. (1999, April 6). Burlington teenager gets probation. *Milwaukee Journal Sentinel.* Retrieved July 19, 2002, fromproquest. umi.com.

Kertscher, T., Spice, L., Johnson, M., Krantz, C., & Ortiz, V. (1998, November 19). Pewaukee High student arrested after threat. In separate case, three Burlington teens charged with planning killings. *Milwaukee Journal Sentinel.* Retrieved July 19, 2003, from proquest.umi.com.

Kilani-Schoch, M., Balčiuniené, I., Korecky-Kröll, K., Laaha, S., & Dressler, W. (2009). On the role of pragmatics in child-directed speech for the acquisition of verb morphology. *Journal of Pragmatics*, *41*, 219–239.

Kim, J., & Cicchetti, D. (2006). Longitudinal trajectories of self-esteem processes and depressive symptoms among maltreated and nonmaltreated children. *Child Development*, *77*, 624–639.

Kincheloe, J. L. (2004). *Multiple intelligences reconsidered*. New York: Peter Lang.

Kirby, D. (2002). Effective approaches to reducing adolescent unprotected sex, pregnancy, and childbearing. *The Journal of Sex Research, 39*, 51–57.

Kirby, D. (2007). Abstinence, *sex*, and STD/HIV education programs for teens: Their impact on sexual behavior, pregnancy, and sexually transmitted disease: Preview. *Annual Review of Sex Research*, *18*, 143–177.

Kirschner, D. (1995). Adoption psychopathology and the "adopted child syndrome." In *The Hatherleigh guide to child and adolescent therapy* (pp. 103–123). New York: Hatherleigh Press.

Kiuhara, S., Graham, S., & Hawken, L. (2009). Teaching writing to high school students: A national survey. *Journal of Educational Psychology, 101*, 136–160.

Klahr, D. (1992). Information processing approaches to cognitive development. In M. H. Bornstein & M. E. Lamb (Eds.), *Developmental psychology: An advanced textbook* (3rd ed., pp. 273–335). Hillsdale, NJ: Erlbaum.

Klahr, D., & MacWhinney, B. (1998). Information processing. In W. Damon, D. Kuhn, & R. S. Siegler (Eds.), *Handbook of child psychology* (5th ed.), *Vol 2: Cognition, perception, and language* (pp. 631–678). New York: John Wiley & Sons.

Klahr, D., & Siegler, R. S. (1978). The representation of children's knowledge. In H. W. Reese & L. P. Lipsitt (Eds.), *Advances in child development and behavior* (Vol. 12, pp. 61–116). New York: Academic Press.

Klaus, M. H., & Kennell, J. H. (1976). *Maternal-infant binding*. St. Louis: Mosby.

Klein, J. D. & The Committee on Adolescence (2005). Adolescent pregnancy: Current trends and issues. *Pediatrics, 116*, 281–286. Retrieved May 28, 2006, from pediatrics.aappublications.org/cgi/content/full/116/1/281.

Knafo, A., & Plomin, R. (2006). Prosocial behavior from early to middle childhood: Genetic and environmental influences on stability and change. *Developmental Psychology*, *42*, 771–786.

Knafo, A., & Schwartz, S. H. (2003). Parenting and adolescents' accuracy in perceiving parental values. *Child Development, 74,* 595–611.

Knudsen, E. I. (2004). Sensitive periods in the development of the brain and behavior. *Journal of Cognitive Neuroscience, 16*(8), 1412–1425.

Kochanska, G., Coy, K. C., & Murray, K. T. ( 2001). The development of self-regulation in the first four years of life. *Child Development, 72*, 1091–1111.

Kochanska, G., Murray, K. T., & Harlan, E. T. (2000). Effortful control in early childhood: Continuity and change, antecedents, and implications for social development. *Developmental Psychology, 36*, 220–232.

Kochanska, G., Murray, K., & Coy, K. C. (1997). Inhibitory control as a contributor to conscience in childhood: From toddler to early school age. *Child Development, 68*, 263–277.

Koenig, L. B., McGue, M., Krueger, R. F., & Bouchard, T. J. (2007). Religiousness, antisocial behavior, and altruism: Genetic and environmental mediation. *Journal of Personality*, *75*, 265-290.

Koestner, R., Franz, C., & Weinberger, J. (1990). The family origins of empathetic concern: A 26-year longitudinal study. *Journal of Personality and Social Psychology, 58,* 709–717.

Kohlberg, L. (1969). Stage and sequence: The cognitive-developmental approach to socialization. In D. Goslin (Ed.), *Handbook of socialization theory and research* (pp. 347–480). Chicago: Rand McNally.

Kohlberg, L., & Power, C. (1981). Moral development, religious thinking, and the question of a seventh stage. In L. Kohlberg, *Essays on moral development: Vol. I. The philosophy of moral development: Moral stages and the idea of justice* (pp. 311–372). Cambridge: Harper & Row.

Kohlberg, L., Levine, C., & Hewer, A. (1984). The current formulation of the theory. In L. Kohlberg, *Essays on moral development: Vol. II. The psychology of moral development: The nature and validity of moral stages* (pp. 212–319). San Francisco: Harper & Row.

Kohlberg, L. A. (1966). A cognitive-developmental analysis of children's sex role concepts and attitudes. In E. E. Maccoby (Ed.), *The development of sex differences* (pp. 82–173). Stanford, CA: Stanford University Press.

Kohlberg, L. A. (1969). Stage and sequence: The cognitive-developmental approach to socialization. In D. Goslin (Ed.), *Handbook of socialization theory and research* (pp. 347–480). Chicago: Rand McNally.

Kohlberg, L. A. (1984). Moral stages and moralization: The cognitive-developmental approach. In L. Kohlberg, *Essays on moral development: Vol. II. The psychology of moral development: The nature and validity of moral stages* (pp. 170–211). San Francisco, CA: Harper & Row Publishers.

Kolb, B. (1999). Neuroanatomy and development overview. In N. A. Fox, L. A. Leavitt, & J. G. Warhol (Eds.), *The role of early experience in infant development* (pp. 5–14). Johnson & Johnson Pediatric Institute.

Kolb, B., & Fantie, B. (1989). Development of the child's brain and behavior. In C. R. Reynolds & E. F. Janzen (Eds.), *Handbook of clinical child neuropsychology* (pp. 17–40). New York: Plenum.

Kolb, B., Gibb, R., & Dallison, A. (1999). Early experience, behavior, and the changing brain. In N. A. Fox, L. A. Leavitt, & J. G. Warhol (Eds.), *The role of early experience in infant development* (pp. 41–63). Johnson & Johnson Pediatric Institute.

Kolb, B., Wilson, B., & Taylor, L. (1992). Developmental changes in the recognition and comprehension of facial expression: Implications for frontal lobe function. *Brain and Cognition, 20*(1), 74–84.

Kollar, E. J., & Fisher, C. (1980). Tooth induction in chick epithelium: Expression of quiescent genes for enamel synthesis. *Science, 207,* 993–995.

Korkman, M., Kettunen, S., & Autti-Rämö, I. (2003). Neurocognitive impairment in early adolescence following prenatal alcohol exposure of varying duration. *Child Neuropsychology, 9,* 117–128.

Korkman, M., Liikanen, A., & Fellman, V. (1996). Neuropsychological consequences of very low birth weight and asphyxia at term: Follow-up until school age. *Journal of Clinical and Experimental Neuropsychology, 18,* 220–233.

Kosciw, J. G., Diaz, E. M., & Greytak, E. A. (2008). *2007 National School Climate Survey: The experiences of lesbian, gay, bisexual and transgender youth in our nation's schools.* New York: GLSEN

Kourtis, A. P., Kraft, J. M., Gavin, L., Kissin, D., McMichen-Wright, P., & Jamieson, D. J. (2006). Prevention of sexually transmitted human immunodeficiency virus (HIV) infection in adolescents. *Current HIV Research, 4,* 209–219.

Koutsky, L. A., Ault, K. A., Wheeler, C. M., Brown, D. R., Barr, E., Alvarez, F. B., Chiacchierini, L. M., & Jansen, K. U. (2002). A controlled trial of a human papillomavirus type 16 vaccine. *New England Journal of Medicine, 347*(21), 1645–1651.

Kovács, Á. (2009). Early bilingualism enhances mechanisms of false-belief reasoning. *Developmental Science, 12,* 48–54.

Kovelman, I., Baker, S., & Petitto, L. (2008). Bilingual and monolingual brains compared: A functional magnetic resonance imaging investigation of syntactic processing and a possible neural signature of bilingualism. *Journal of Cognitive Neuroscience, 20,* 153–169.

Koverola, C., Pound, J., Heger, A., & Lytle, C. (1993). Relationship of child sexual abuse to depression. *Child Abuse and Neglect, 17,* 393–400.

Kozulin, A. (1990). *Vygotsky's psychology: A biography of ideas.* Cambridge, MA: Harvard University Press.

Krashen, S. (1999). What the research really says about structured English immersion. *Phi Delta Kappan, 80,* 705–706.

Krashen, S., Long, M., & Scarcella, R. (1982). Age, rate, and eventual attainment in second language acquisition. In S. Krashen, R. Scarcella, & M. Long (Eds.), *Child-adult differences in second language acquisition* (pp. 161–174). Rowley, MA: Newbury House.

Kraut, R., Scherlis, W., Mukhopadhyay, T., Manning, J., & Kiesler, S. (1996). The HomeNet field trial of residential Internet services. *Communications of the ACM, 39,* 55–63.

Krebs, D., & Gillmore, J. (1982). The relationship among the first stages of cognitive development, role-taking abilities, and moral development. *Child Development, 53,* 877–886.

Krebs, D., & Denton, K. (2005). Toward a more pragmatic approach to morality: A critical evaluation of kohlberg's model. *Psychological Review, 112,* 629–649.

Kreutzer, M. A., Leonard, C., & Flavell, J. H. (1975). An interview study of children's knowledge about memory. *Monographs of the Society for Research in Child Development, 40* (Serial No. 159).

Krishner, H. S. (1995). *Classical aphasia syndromes.* New York: Marcel Dekker.

Kubow, P. K., Wahlstrom, K. L., & Bemis, A. E. (1999). Starting time and school life: Reflections from educators and students. *Phi Delta Kappan, 80,* 366–371.

Kuhl, P. K., Andruski, J. E., Christovich, I. A., Christovich, L. A., Kozhevnikova, E. V., Ryskina, V. L., Stolyarova, E. I., Sundberg, U., & Lacerda, F. (1997). Cross-language analsyis of phonetic units in language addressed to infants. *Science, 277*(1 August), 684–686.

Kuhl, P. K., Conboy, B., Padden, D., Nelson, T., & Pruitt, J. (2005). Early speech perception and later language development: Implications for the "critical period." *Language Learning and Development, 1,* 237–264.

Kuhl, P., & Rivera-Gaxiola, M. (2008). Neural substrates of language acquisition. *Annual Review of Neuroscience, 31*(1), 511–534.

Kuhn, D. (1992). Cognitive development. In M. H. Bornstein & M. E. Lamb (Eds.), *Developmental psychology: An advanced textbook* (3rd ed., pp. 211–272). Hillsdale, NJ: Erlbaum.

Kuhn, D., & Franklin, S. (2006). The second decade: What develops (and how). In D. Kuhn & R. S. Siegler (Eds.), *Cognitive, language, and perceptual develoment,* Vol. 2 (pp. 953–993), in W. Damon (Gen. Ed.), *Handbook of child psychology.* New York: Wiley.

Kung, H. C., Hoyert, D. L., Xu, J. Q., & Murphy, S. L. (2008). Deaths: Final data for 2005. *National Vital Statistics Reports, 56*(10). Hyattsville, MD: National Center for Health Statistics. Retrieved April 25, 2009, from http://www.cdc.gov/nchs/data/nvsr/nvsr56/nvsr56_10.pdf.

Kupersmidt, J. B., & Coie, J. D. (1990). Preadolescent peer status, aggression, and school adjustment as predictors of externalizing problems in adolescence. *Child Development, 61,* 1350–1362.

Kupersmidt, J. B., Briesler, P. C., DeRosier, M. E., Patterson, C. J., & Davis, P. W. (1995). Childhood aggression and peer relations in the context of family and neighborhood factors. *Child Development, 66,* 360–375.

Kwong, T. E., & Varnhagen, C. K. (2005). Strategy development and learning to spell new words: Generalization of a process. *Developmental Psychology, 41,* 148–159.

Labouvie-Vief, G. (1980). Beyond formal operations: Uses and limits of pure logic in life-span development. *Human Development, 23,* 141–161.

Labouvie-Vief, G. (2006). Emerging structures of adult thought. In J. J. Arnett & J. L. Tanner (Eds.), *Emerging adults in America: Coming of age in the 21st century* (pp. 59–84). Washington, DC: American Psychological Association.

Labre, M. P. (2002). Adolescent boys and the muscular male body ideal. *Journal of Adolescent Health, 30*(4, supplement), 233–242.

Lagerberg, D. (2004). Sexual knowledge and behavior in South African students: A case for prevention with focus on behavior. *Acta Paediatrica, 93,* 159–161.

Laible, D., Panfile, T., & Makariev, D. (2008). The quality and frequency of mother-toddler conflict: Links with attachment and temperament. *Child Development, 79,* 426–443.

Lamaze, F. (1958). *Painless childbirth.* London: Burke.

Lamb, M. E. (1987). Predictive implications of individual differences in attachment. *Journal of Consulting and Clinical Psychology, 55,* 817–824.

Lamb, M. E., Hwang, C. P., Frodi, A., & Frodi, M. (1982). Security of mother– and father–infant attachment and its relation to sociability with strangers in traditional and non-traditional Swedish families. *Infant Behavior and Development, 5,* 355–367.

Lamb, M. E., Thompson, R. A., Gardner, W., & Charnov, E. L. (1985). *Infant–mother attachment: The origins and developmental significance of individual differences in Strange Situation behavior.* Hillsdale, NJ: Lawrence Erlbaum Associates.

Lamborn, S. D., & Steinberg, L. (1993). Emotional autonomy redux: Revisiting Ryan and Lynch. *Child Development, 64,* 483–499.

Lamm, C., Zelazo, P., & Lewis, M. (2006). Neural correlates of cognitive control in childhood and adolescence: Disentangling the contributions of age and executive function. *Neuropsychologia, 44*(11), 2139–2148.

Lancy, D. F. (2002). Cultural constraints on children's play. In J. L. Roopnarine (Ed.), *Conceptual, social-cognitive, and contextual issues in the fields of play. Play & Culture Studies,* Vol. 4 (pp. 53–60). Westport, CT: Ablex.

Langlois, J. H., Roggman, L. A., Casey, R. J., Ritter, J. M., Rieser-Danner, A., & Jenkins, V. Y. (1987). Infant preferences for attractive faces: Rudiments of a stereotype? *Developmental Psychology, 23,* 363–369.

Lansford, J. E. (2009). Parental divorce and children's adjustment. *Perspectives on Psychological Science, 4*(2), 140–152.

Lansford, J. E., Chang, L., Dodge, K. A., Malone, P. S., Oburu, P., Palmérus, K., Bacchini, D., Pastorelli, C., Bombi, A. S., Zelli, A., Tapanya, S., Chaudhary, N., Deater-Deckard, K., Manke, B., & Quinn, N. (2005). Physical discipline and children's adjustment: Cultural normativeness as a moderator. *Child Development, 76,* 1234–1246.

Lanza, E. (1992). Can bilingual two-year-olds code-switch? *Journal of Child Language, 19,* 633–658.

Larivée, S., Normandeau, S., & Parent, S. (2000). The French connection: Some contributions of French-language research in the post-Piagetian era. *Child Development, 71,* 823–839.

Larson, J., & Lochman, J. E. (2002). *Helping schoolchildren cope with anger.* New York: Guilford Press.

Laumann-Billings, L., & Emery, R. E. (2000). Distress among young adults from divorced families. *Journal of Family Psychology, 14,* 671–688.

Laursen, B., & Collins, W. A. (1994). Interpersonal conflict during adolescence. *Psychological Bulletin, 115,* 197–209.

Laursen, B., Coy, K. C., & Collins, W. A. (1998). Reconsidering changes in parent-child conflict across adolescence: A meta-analysis. *Child Development, 69*, 817–832.

Lave, J., & Wenger, E. (1991). *Situated learning: Legitimate peripheral participation.* Cambridge, England: Cambridge University Press.

Lave, J., & Wenger, E. (1996). Practice, person, social world. In H. Daniels (Ed.), *An introduction to Vygotsky* (pp. 143–150). London: Routledge.

Leaper, C. (1994). Exploring the consequences of gender segregation on social relationships. In W. Damon (Ed.), *New directions for child development* (No. 65, pp. 67–86). San Francisco: Jossey-Bass.

Lee, J., Grigg, W., & Dion, G. (2007). *The nation's report card: Mathematics 2007* (NCES 2007–449). National Center for Education Statistics, Institute of Education Studies, U.S. Department of Education, Washington, D.C. Retrieved May 9, 2009, from nces.ed.gov/pubsearch/pubsinfo.asp?pubid=2007494.

Lee, K., Swee-Fong, N., Ee-Lynn, N., & Zee-Ying, L. (2004). Working memory and literacy as predictors of performance on algebraic word problems. *Journal of Experimental Child Psychology, 89*, 140–158.

Lee, S. (1998). Mathematics learning and teaching in the school context: Reflections from cross-cultural comparisons. In S. G. Paris & H. M. Wellman (Eds.), *Global prospects for education: Development, culture, and schooling* (pp. 45–77). Washington, DC: American Psychological Association.

LeFevre, J., & Bisanz, J. (1996). Multiple routes to solution of single-digit multiplication problems. *Journal of Experimental Psychology: General, 125*, 284–307.

Lehman, B. A. (1989, March 13). Spanking teaches the wrong lesson. *Boston Globe*, p. 27.

Lehman, J. S., & Smeeding, T. M. (1997). Neighborhood effects and federal policy. In J. Brooks-Gunn, G. J. Duncan, & J. L. Aber (Eds.), *Neighborhood poverty: Vol. I. Context and consequences for children* (pp. 251–278). New York: Russell Sage Foundation.

Leichtman, M. D., & Ceci, S. J. (1995). The effect of stereotypes and suggestions on preschoolers' reports. *Developmental Psychology, 31*, 568–578.

Leman, P. J., Ahmed, S., & Ozarow, L. (2005). Gender, gender relations, and the social dynamics of children's conversations. *Developmental Psychology, 41*, 64–74.

Lemoine, P., Harousseau, H., Borteyru, J. P., & Menuet, J. C. (1968). Les enfants de parents aicooliques: Anomalies observies. A proposos de 127 cas. [Children of alcoholic parents: Abnormalities observed in 127 cases.] *Ouest Medicine, 21*, 476–482. As cited in Mattson & Riley, 1998.

Lenhart, A. & Madden, M. (2007). *Teens, privacy & online social networks.* Washington, DC: Pew Internet & American Life Project. Accessed April 11, 2009, from www.pewinternet.org/Reports/2007/ Teens-Privacy-and-Online-Social-Networks.aspx.

Lenhart, A., & Madden, M. ( 2007). *Teens, privacy, and online social networks.* Washington, DC: Pew Internet & American Life Project. Retrieved June 1, 2009, from www.pewinternet.org/~/media//Files/Reports/2007/PIP_Teens_Privacy_SNS_Report_Final.pdf.pdf.

Lenhart, A., Madden, M., & Hitlin, P. (2005). *Teens and Technology.* Washington, DC: Pew Internet & American Life Project. Accessed April 11, 2009, from www.pewinternet.org/Reports/2005/Teens-and-Technology.aspx.

Lenneberg, E. H. (1967). *Biological foundations of language.* New York: John Wiley & Sons.

Lepage, J.-F., & Théoret, H. (2007). The mirror neuron system: grasping others' actions from birth? *Developmental Science, 10*, 513–529.

Leppänen, J. M., Moulson, M. C., Vogel-Farley, V. K., & Nelson, C. A. (2007). An ERP study of emotional face processing in the adult and infant brain. *Child Development, 78*, 232–245.

Leppänen, U., Aunola, K., Niemi, P., & Nurmi, J. (2008). Letter knowledge predicts Grade 4 reading fluency and reading comprehension. *Learning & Instruction, 18*, 548–564.

Lerner, R. M. (2006). Developmental science, developmental systems, and contemporary theories of human development. In W. Damon & R. M. Lerner (Series Eds.) & R. M. Lerner (Vol. Ed.), *Handbook of child psychology: Vol. 1. Theoretical models of human development* (6th ed., pp. 1–17). Hoboken, NJ: Wiley.

LeVay, S. (1993). *The sexual brain.* Cambridge: MIT Press.

Leventhal, T., & Brooks-Gunn, J. (2000). The neighborhoods they live in: The effects of neighborhood residence on child and adolescent outcomes. *Psychological Bulletin, 126*, 309–337.

Levine, J. A., Pollack, H. & Comfort, M. E. (2001). Academic and behavioral outcomes among the children of young mothers. *Journal of Marriage & Family, 63*, 355–369.

Levy, Y., Tennenbaum, A., & Ornoy, A. (2000). Spontaneous language of children with specific neurological syndromes. *Journal of Speech, Language, and Hearing Research, 43*, 351–365.

Lewandowsky, S., Oberauer, K., & Brown, G. (2009). No temporal decay in verbal short-term memory. *Trends in Cognitive Sciences, 13*(3), 120–126.

Lewinsohn, P. M., Rohde, P., & Seeley, J. R. (1993). Psychosocial characteristics of adolescents with a history of suicide attempt. *Journal of the American Academy of Child and Adolescent Psychiatry, 32*, 60–68.

Lewinsohn, P. M., Rohde, P., & Seeley, J. R. (1994). Psychosocial risk factors for future adolescent suicide attempts. *Journal of Consulting and Clinical Psychology, 62*, 297–305.

Lewis, B. A., Singer, L. T., & Short, E. J. (2004). Four-year language outcomes of children exposed to cocaine in utero. *Neurotoxicology & Teratology, 26*, 617–627.

Lewis, C. C. (1981). How adolescents approach decisions: Changes over grades seven to twelve and policy implications. *Child Development, 52*, 538–544.

Lewis, M. (1993). Self-conscious emotions: Embarrassment, pride, shame, and guilt. In M. Lewis & J. Haviland (Eds.), *The handbook of emotions* (pp. 563–573). New York: Guilford Press.

Lewis, M. W., Misra, S., Johnson, H. L., & Rosen, T. S. (2004). Neurological and developmental outcomes of prenatally cocaine-exposed offspring from 12 to 36 months. *American Journal of Drug & Alcohol Abuse, 30*, 299–321.

Lewis, M., & Carmody, D. P. (2008). Self-representation and brain development. *Developmental Psychology, 44*(5), 1329–1334.

Lewis, M., Lee, C., Patrick, M., & Fossos, N. (2007). Gender-specific normative misperceptions of risky sexual behavior and alcohol-related risky sexual behavior. *Sex Roles, 57*, 81–90.

Lewit, E. M., & Baker, L. S. (1995). School readiness. *The Future of Children, 5*, 128–139.

Li, J. (2004). Learning as a task or a virtue: U.S. and Chinese preschoolers explain learning. *Developmental Psychology, 40*, 595–605.

Li, P., Zhao, X., & MacWhinney, B. (2007). Dynamic self-organization and early lexical development in children. *Cognitive Science, 31*, 581-612.

Li-Repac, D. C. (1982). *The impact of acculturation on the child-rearing attitudes and practices of Chinese-American families: Consequences for the attachment process.* Unpublished doctoral dissertation, University of California–Berkeley.

Lillard, A. S., & Else-Quest, N. (2006). Evaluating Montessori education. *Science, 313*, 29.

Lillard, A. S. (2005). *Montessori: The science behind the genius.* New York: Oxford University Press.

Lindberg, L. D., Ku, L. & Sonenstein, F. (2000). Adolescents' reports of reproductive health education, 1988 and 1995. *Family Planning Perspectives, 32*, 220–226.

Lindsey, E. W., Mize, J., & Pettit, G. S. (1997). Differential play patterns of mothers and fathers of sons and daughters: Implications for children's gender role development. *Sex Roles, 17*, 643–661.

Linnett, K. M., Dalsgaard, S., Obel, C., Wisborg, K., Henriksen, T. B., Rodriguez, A., et al. (2003). Maternal lifestyle factors in pregnancy risk of attention deficit hyperactivity disorder and associated behaviors: Review of the current evidence. *American Journal of Psychiatry, 160*, 1028–1040.

Linver, M. R., Brooks-Gunn, J., & Kohen, D. E. (2002). Family processes as pathways from income to young childrens' development. *Developmental Psychology, 38*, 719–734.

Liptak, A. (2002, July 26). Judge orders abstinence program changed. *New York Times.* Retrieved January 6, 2003, from www.nytimes.com.

Lo, B. (2006). HPV vaccine and adolescents' sexual activity. *British Medical Journal, 332*, 1106–1107.

Locke, J. L. (1993). *The child's path to spoken language.* Cambridge, MA: Harvard University Press.

Loehlin, J. C., & Nichols, R. C. (1976). *Heredity, environment, and personality.* Austin: University of Texas Press.

Loehlin, J. C., Horn, J. M., & Willerman, L. (1994). Differential inheritance of mental abilities in the Texas Adoption Project. *Intelligence, 19*, 325–336.

Loehlin, J. C., Jönsson, E. G., Gustavsson, J. P., Stallings, M. C, Gillespie, N. A., Wright, M. J., & Martin, N. G. (2005). Psychological masculinity-femininity via the gender diagnosticity approach: Heritability and consistency across ages and populations. *Journal of Personality, 73,* 1295–1320.

Loftus, E. F., & Ketcham, K. (1994). *The myth of repressed memory.* New York: St. Martin's Press.

Lohmann, H., & Tomasello, M. (2003). Language and social understanding: Commentary on Nelson et al. *Human Development, 46,* 47–50.

Lonigan, C. J., Fischel, J. E., Whitehurst, G. J., Arnold, D. S., & Valdez-Menchaca, M. C. (1992). The role of otitis media in the development of expressive language disorder. *Developmental Psychology, 28,* 430–440.

Lorenz, K. Z. (1973/1977). *Behind the mirror: A search for a natural history of human knowledge.* New York: Harcourt Brace Jovanovich.

Love, J. M., Kisker, E. E., Ross, C. M., Schochet, P. Z., Brooks-Gunn, J., Paulsell, D., Boller, K., Constantine, J., Vogel, C., Fuligni, A. A., & Brady-Smith, C. (2002). *Making a difference in the lives of infants and toddlers and their families: The impact of Early Head Start.* Department of Health and Human Services Document, Retrieved July 11, 2003, from www.headstartinfo.org/cgi-bin/pubcatstore.cfm.

Love, J. M., Kisker, E. E., Ross, C., Raikes, H., Constantine, J., Boller, K., Brooks-Gunn, J., Chazan-Cohen, R., Tarullo, L. B., Brady-Smith, C., Fuligni, A. S., Schochet, P. Z., Paulsell, D., & Vogel, C. (2005). The effectiveness of Early Head Start for 3-year-old children and their parents: Lessons for policy and programs. *Developmental Psychology, 41,* 885–901.

Love, J. M., Tarullo, L. B., Raikes, H., & Chazan-Cohen, R. (2006). Head Start: What do we know about its effectiveness? What do we need to know? In K. McCartney & D. Phillips (Eds.), *Blackwell handbook of early childhood development* (pp. 550–575). Malden, MA: Blackwell Publishing.

Low, J. M. (1999). Differences in cognitive complexity of adolescents with foreclosed and achieved identity status. *Psychological Reports, 85,* 1093–1099.

Luciano, M., Wright, M., Duffy, D., Wainwright, M., Zhu, G., Evans, D., et al. (2006). Genome-wide scan of IQ finds significant linkage to a quantitative trait locus on 2q. *Behavior Genetics, 36*(1), 45–55.

Lugwig, J., & Phillips, D. (2007). The benefits and costs of Head Start. *SRCD Social Policy Report, 21*(3). Accessed October 1, 2007, from srcd.org/documents/publications/spr/21-3_early_childhood_education.pdf.

Luhman, R. (1990). Appalachian English stereotypes: Language attitudes in Kentucky. *Language in Society, 19,* 331–348.

Luo, X., Kranzler, H. R., Zuo, L., Wang, S., & Gelernter, J. (2007). Personality traits of agreeableness and extraversion are associated with ADH4 variation. *Biological Psychiatry, 61,* 599–608.

Luria, A. R. (1973). *The working brain: An introduction to neuropsychology.* New York: Basic.

Luthar, S. S. (2006). Resilience in development: A synthesis of research across five decades. In D. Cicchetti & D. J. Cohen (Eds.), *Developmental Psychopathology* (2nd ed), *Vol. 3: Rish, disorder, and adaptation* (pp. 739–795). Hoboken, NJ: J. B. Wiley & Sons.

Luzadder, D., & Vaughan, K. (1999, December 12). Inside the Columbine investigation. *Rocky Mountain News* (Denver). Retrieved January 3, 2003, from denver.rockymountainnews.com.

Luzzo, D. A., & MacGregor, M. W. (2001). Practice and research in career counseling and development 2000. *Career Development Quarterly, 50,* 98–140.

Lykken, D. T. (2000). The causes and costs of crime and a controversial cure. *Journal of Personality, 68,* 559–605.

Lykken, D. T. (2001). Parental licensure. *American Psychologist, 56,* 885–894.

Lyons-Ruth, K., Connell, D. B., Zoll, D., & Stahl, J. (1987). Infants at social risk: Relations among infant maltreatment, maternal behavior, and infant attachment behavior. *Developmental Psychology, 23,* 223–232.

Mabbott, D. J., & Bisanz, J. (2003). Developmental change and individual differences in children's multiplication. *Child Development, 74,* 1091–1107.

MacAulay, D. J. (1990). Classroom environment: A literature review. *Educational Psychology, 10,* 239–253.

MacCallum, F., & Golombok, S. (2004). Children raised in fatherless families from infancy: A follow-up of children from lesbian and single heterosexual mothers at early adolescence. *Journal of Child Psychology & Psychiatry, 45,* 1407–1419.

MacCallum, F., Golombok, S., & Brinsden, P. (2007). Parenting and child development in families with a child conceived through embryo donation. *Journal of Family Psychology, 21*(2), 278–287.

Maccoby, E. E. (1998). *The two sexes: Growing up apart, coming together.* Boston: Harvard University Press.

Maccoby, E. E. (2002). Gender and group process: A developmental perspective. *Current Directions in Psychological Science, 11,* 54–58.

Maccoby, E. E., & Jacklin, C. N. (1974). *The psychology of sex differences.* Stanford, CA: Stanford University Press.

Maccoby, E. E., & Jacklin, C. N. (1987). Gender segregation in childhood. In E. H. Reese (Ed.), *Advances in child development and behavior* (Vol. 20, pp. 239–287). New York: Academic Press.

Maccoby, E. E., & Martin, J. A. (1983). Socialization in the context of the family: Parent–child interaction. In P. H. Mussen (Ed.), *Handbook of child psychology* (Vol. 4, pp. 1–101). New York: Wiley.

MacWhinney, B. (Ed.) (1987). *Mechanisms of language acquisition.* Hillsdale, NJ: Erlbaum.

MacWhinney, B. (1992). Transfer and competition in second language learning. In R. J. Harris (Ed.) *Cognitive processing in bilinguals.* Amsterdam, North Holland: Elsevier.

MacWhinney, B. (Ed.) (1999). *The emergence of language.* Hillsdale, NJ: Erlbaum

Madigan, S, Moran, G., & Pederson, D. R. (2006). Unresolved states of mind, disorganized attachment relationships, and disrupted interactions of adolescent mothers and their infants. *Developmental Psychology, 42,* 293–304.

Maes, H. H. M., Neale, M. C., & Eaves, L. J. (1997). Genetic and environmental factors in relative body weight and human adiposity. *Behavior Genetics, 27*(4), 325–351.

Magnusson, D. (1988). *Individual development from an interactional perspective: A longitudinal study.* Hillsdale, NJ: Erlbaum.

Main, M., & George, C. (1985). Responses of abused and disadvantaged toddlers to distress in agemates: A study in the day care setting. *Developmental Psychology, 21,* 407–412.

Main, M., & Hesse, E. (1990). Parents' unresolved traumatic experiences are related to infant disorganized attachment status: Is frightened and/or frightening parental behavior the linking mechanism? In M. T. Greenberg, D. Cicchetti, & E. M. Cummings (Eds.), *Attachment in the preschool years: Theory, research, and intervention* (pp. 161–182). Chicago: University of Chicago Press.

Main, M., & Solomon, J. (1986). Discovery of an insecure–disorganized/disoriented attachment pattern. In T. B. Brazelton & M. W. Yogman (Eds.), *Affective development in infancy* (pp. 95–124). Norwood, NJ: Ablex Publishing.

Main, M., & Solomon, J. (1990). Procedures for identifying infants as disorganized/disoriented during the Ainsworth Strange Situation. In M. T. Greenberg, D. Cicchetti, & E. M. Cummings (Eds.), *Attachment in the preschool years: Theory, research, and intervention* (pp. 121–182). Chicago: University of Chicago Press.

Malone, L. M., West, J., Flanagan, K. D., & Park, J. (2006). *The early reading and mathematics achievement of children who repeated kindergarten or who began school a year late* (NCES 2006-064). U.S. Department of Education, National Center for Education Statistics. Washington, DC: U.S. Government Printing Office.

Mandel, D., Kemler Nelson, D. G., & Jusczyk, P. W. (1996). Infants remember the order of words in a spoken sentence. *Cognitive Development, 11,* 181–196.

Maratsos, M. (1983). Some current issues in the study of the acquisition of grammar. In J. H. Flavell & E. M. Markman (Eds.), *Handbook of child psychology,* Vol. 3. *Cognitive development* (pp. 707–786). New York: John Wiley & Sons.

Maratsos, M., & Matheney, L. (1994). Language specificity and elasticity: Brain and clinical syndrome studies. *Annual Review of Psychology, 45,* 487–516.

Maratsos, M., Kuczaj, S. A., Fox, D. E. C., & Chalkley, M. A. (1979). Some empirical studies in the acquisition of transformational relations: Passives, negatives and the past tense. In W. A. Collins (Ed.), *Children's language and communication* (pp. 1–45). Hillsdale, NJ: Erlbaum.

Marcia, J. E. (1966). Development and validation of ego identity status. *Journal of Personality and Social Psychology, 38,* 551–558.

Marcovitch, S., & Zelazo, P. (2009). A hierarchical competing systems model of the emergence and early development of executive function. *Developmental Science, 12*(1), 1–18.

Marcus, G. F., Pinker, S., Ullman, M., Hollander, M., Rosen, T. J., & Xu, F. (1992). Overregularization in language acquisition. *Monographs of the Society for Research in Child Development, 57* (4, Serial No. 228).

Mares, M., & Woodard, E. H. (2001). Prosocial effects on children's social interactions. In D. G. Singer & J. L. Singer (Eds.), *Handbook of children and the media* (pp. 183–203). Thousand Oaks, CA: Sage.

Markowitsch, H. (2008). Autobiographical memory: A biocultural relais between subject and environment. *European Archives of Psychiatry & Clinical Neuroscience, 258*, 98–103.

Marlier, L., & Schall, B. (2005). Human newborns prefer human milk: Conspecific milk odor is attractive without postnatal exposure. *Child Development, 76*, 155–168.

Marsh, R., Gerber, A., & Peterson, B. (2008). Neuroimaging studies of normal brain development and their relevance for understanding childhood neuropsyciatric disorders. *Journal of the American Academy of Child & Adolescent Psychiatry, 47*, 1233–1251.

Marshall, W. A., & Tanner, J. M. (1986). Puberty. In F. Falkner & J. M. Tanner (Eds.), *Human growth* (2nd ed., Vol. 2, pp. 171–209). New York: Plenum Press.

Martens, M., Page, J., Mowry, E., Damann, K., Taylor, K., & Cimini, M. (2006). Differences between actual and perceived student norms: An examination of alcohol use, drug use, and sexual behavior. *Journal of American College Health, 54*, 295–300.

Martin, C. L. (1994). Cognitive influences on the development and maintenance of gender segregation. In W. Damon (Ed.), *New directions for child development* (No. 65, pp. 35–51). San Francisco: Jossey-Bass.

Martin, G. B., & Clark, R. D. (1982). Distress crying in neonates: Species and peer specificity. *Developmental Psychology, 18*, 3–9.

Martin, J. A., Hamilton, B. E., Sutton, P. D., Ventura, S. J., Menacker, F., & Kirmeyer, S. (September 29, 2006). Births: Final data for 2004. *National Vital Statistics Reports, 55*(1), Hyattsville, MD: National Center for Health Statistics.

Martin, J. A., Hamilton, B. E., Sutton, P. D., Ventura, S. J., Menacker, F., Kirmeyer, S., & Mathews, T. J. (January, 2009). Births: Final data for 2006. *National Vital Statistics Reports, 57*(7), 1–104. Hyattsville, MD: National Center for Health Statistics. Retrieved January 17, 2009, from www.cdc.gov/nchs/data/nvsr/nvsr57/nvsr57_07.pdf

Martin, J. A., Hamilton, B. E., Sutton, P. D., Ventura, S. J., Menacker, F., Kirmeyer, S., & Munson, M. L. (December, 2007). Births: Final data for 2005. *National Vital Statistics Reports, 56*(6), 1–104. Hyattsville, MD: National Center for Health Statistics. Retrieved January 19, 2009, from www.cdc.gov/nchs/data/nvsr/nvsr56/nvsr56_06.pdf.

Martin, J. A., Hamilton, B. E., Sutton, P. D., Ventura, S. J., Menacker, P. H., Kirmeyer, S., & Mathews, T. J. (2009). Births: Final data for 2006. *National Vital Statistics Reports, 57*(7), p. 54. Hyattsville, MD: National Center for Health Statistics. Last accessed March 25, 2009, from www.cdc.gov/nchs/data/nvsr/nvsr57/nvsr57_07.pdf.

Martin, J. A., Hamilton, B. E., Sutton, P. D., Ventura, S. J., Menacker, F., & Kirmeyer, S. (2006). Births: Final data for 2004. *National Vital Statistics Reports, 55*(1), 1–104. Hyattsville, MD: National Center for Health Statistics. Retrieved June 10, 2007, from www.cdc.gov/nchs/data/nvsr/nvsr55/nvsr55_01.pdf.

Martin, J. C. (1992). The effects of maternal use of tobacco products or amphetamines on offspring. In T. B. Sonderegger (Ed.), *Perinatal substance abuse: Research findings and clinical applications* (pp. 279–305). Baltimore: The Johns Hopkins University Press.

Martin, N. G., & Heath, A. C. (1993). The genetics of voting: An Australian twin-family study. *Behavior Genetics, 23*, 558.

Martin, N. G., Eaves, L. J., Heath, A. C., Jardine, R., Feingold, L. M., & Eysenck, H.J. (1986). Transmission of social attitudes. *Proceedings of the National Academy of Sciences, USA, 83*, 4364–4368.

Masataka, N. (1996). Perception of motherese in a signed language by 6-month-old deaf infants. *Developmental Psychology, 32*, 874–879.

Masataka, N. (1998). Perception of motherese in Japanese sign language by 6-month-old hearing infants. *Developmental Psychology, 34*, 241–246.

Mash, E. J., & Wolfe, D. A. (1999). *Abnormal child psychology.* Belmont, CA: Brooks/Cole.

Mash, E. J., & Wolfe, D. A. (2005). *Abnormal Child Psychology* (3rd ed.). Belmont, CA: Wadsworth.

Mash, E. J., & Wolfe, D. A. (2010). *Abnormal child psychology* (4th ed.). Belmont, CA: Wadsworth.

Mason, C. A., Cauce, A. M., Gonzales, N., & Hiraga, Y. (1996). Neither too sweet nor too sour: Problem peers, maternal control, and problem behavior in African American adolescents. *Child Development, 67*, 2115–2130.

Masters, M. S., & Sanders, B. (1993). Is the gender difference in mental rotation disappearing? *Behavior Genetics, 23*, 337–341.

Mathews, T. J., & MacDorman, M. F. (2006). Infant mortality statistics from the 2003 period linked birth/infant death data set. *National Vital Statistics Reports, 54*(16), pp. 1–32. Hyattsville, MD: National Center for Health Statistics. Retrieved June 10, 2007, from www.cdc.gov/nchs/data/nvsr/nvsr54/nvsr54_16.pdf.

Mattson, S. N., & Riley, E. P. (1998). A review of the neurobehavioral deficits in children with fetal alcohol syndrome or prenatal exposure to alcohol. *Alcoholism: Clinical and Experimental Research, 22*, 279–294.

Maurer, D., & Salapatek, P. (1976). Developmental changes in the scanning of faces by young infants. *Child Development*, 47, 523–527.

Mayer, R. E., Lewis, A., & Hegarty, M. (1992). Mathematical misunderstandings: Qualitative reasoning about quantitative problems. In J. I. D. Campbell (Ed.), *Advances in psychology, Vol. 91: The nature and origins of mathematical skills* (pp. 137–153). Oxford, England: North-Holland.

Mayes, L. C., Granger, R. H., Frank, M. A., Schottenfeld, R., & Bornstein, M. (1993). Neurobehavioral profiles of infants exposed to cocaine prenatally. *Pediatrics, 91*, 778–783.

Mayes, L., & Bornstein, M. H. (1995). Information processing and developmental assessments in 3-month-old infants exposed prenatally to cocaine. *Pediatrics, 95*, 539–545.

Mayo Clinic (2003, March 17). HIV/AIDS. Retrieved March 21, 2003, from www.MayoClinic.com.

Mazzeo, S. E., Mitchell, K. S., Bulik, C. M., Reichborn-Kjennerud, T., Kendler, K. S., & Neale, M. C. (2009). Assessing the heritability of anorexia nervosa symptoms using a marginal maximal likelihood approach. *Psychological Medicine, 39*, 463–473.

Mazzoni, G., & Memon, A. (2003). Imagination can create false autobiographical memories. *Psychological Science, 14*, 186–188.

McBride-Chang, C. (1996). Models of speech perception and phonological processing in reading. *Child Development, 67*, 1836–1856.

McCabe, M. P. & Ricciardelli, L. A. (2004). Body image dissatisfaction among males across the lifespan: A review of past literature. *Journal of Psychosomatic Research, 56*, 675–685.

McCall, R. B., & Carriger, M. S. (1993). A meta-analysis of infant habituation and recognition memory performance as predictors of later IQ. *Child Development, 64*, 57–79.

McCartney, K., Harris, M. J., & Bernieri, F. (1990). Growing up and growing apart: A developmental meta-analysis of twin studies. *Psychological Bulletin, 107*, 226–237.

McClelland, J., & Thompson, R. (2007). Using domain-general principles to explain children's causal reasoning abilities. *Developmental Science, 10*, 333–356.

McClelland, M., Cameron, C., Connor, C., Farris, C., Jewkes, A., & Morrison, F. (2007). Links between behavioral regulation and preschoolers' literacy, vocabulary, and math skills. *Developmental Psychology, 43*(4), 947–959.

McConaghy, M. J. (1979). Gender permanence and the genital basis of gender: Stages in the development of constancy of gender identity. *Child Development, 50*, 1223–1226.

McCord, J. (1983). A forty year perspective on effects of child abuse and neglect. *Child Abuse and Neglect, 7*, 265–270.

McElwain, N. L., Booth-LaForce, C., Lansford, J. E., Wu, X., & Dyer, W. J. (2008). A process model of attachment-friend linkages: Hostile attribution biases, language ability, and mother–child affective mutuality as intervening mechanisms. *Child Development, 79*, 1891–1906.

McGhee-Bidlack, B. (1991). The development of noun definitions: A metalinguistic analysis. *Journal of Child Languages, 18*, 417–434.

McGlothlin, H., & Killen, M. (2006). Intergroup attitudes of European American children attending ethnically homogeneous schools. *Child Development, 77*, 1375–1386.

McHale, J. P., Kazali, C., & Rotman, T. (2004). The transition to coparenthood: Parents' prebirth expectations and early coparental adjustment at 3 months postpartum. *Development & Psychopathology, 16*, 711–733.

McIntosh, J., MacDonald, F., & McKeganey, N. (2005). The reasons why children in their pre and early teenage years do or do not use illegal drugs. *International Journal of Drug Policy, 16*, 254–261.

McKay, A. (2004). Oral sex among teenagers: Research, discourse, and education. *The Candian Journal of Human Sexuality, 13*, 201–203.

McKay, A. (2006). Trends in teen pregnancy in Canada with comparisons to U.S.A. and England/Wales. *The Canadian Journal of Human Sexuality, 15*, 157–161.

McKenna, J. J., Ball, H. L., & Gettler, L. T. (2007). Mother-infant cosleeping, breastfeeding and Sudden Infant Death Syndrome: What biological anthropology has discovered about normal infant sleep and pediatric sleep medicine. *Yearbook of Physical Anthropology, 50,* 133–161.

McKey, R., Condelli, L., Ganson, H., et al. (1985). *The impact of Head Start on children, families, and communities* (Final report of the Head Start Evaluation, Synthesis, and Utilization Project). Washington, DC: U.S. Department of Health and Human Services.

McKusick, V. A. (1998). *Mendelian inheritance in man: A catalog of human genes and genetic disorders* (12th ed., Vols. 1–3). Baltimore: The Johns Hopkins University Press.

McLanahan, S. S. (1999). Father absence and the welfare of children. In E. M. Hetherington (Ed.), *Coping with divorce, single parenting, and remarriage: A risk and resiliency perspective* (pp. 117–145). Mahwah, NJ: Erlbaum.

McLaughlin, A., Campbell, F., Pungello, E., & Skinner, M. (2007). Depressive symptoms in young adults: The influences of the early home environment and early educational child care. *Child Development, 78*(3), 746–756.

McLaughlin, S. (2006). *Introduction to language development* (2nd ed.). San Diego, CA: Singular Publishing Group, Inc. and Clifton Park, NY: Thomson Delmar Learning.

McLoyd, V. C. (1998). Socioeconomic disadvantage and child development. *American Psychologist, 53,* 185–204.

McLoyd, V. C., Aikens, N. L., & Burton, L. M. (2006). Childhood poverty, policy, and practice. In W. Damon & R. M. Lerner (Series Eds.) and K. A. Renninger & I. E. Sigel (Vol. Eds.), *Handbook of child psychology: Vol. 4. Child psychology in practice* (pp. 700–775). New York: John Wiley & Sons.

McMahon, R. J., & Wells, K. C. (1998). Conduct problems. In E. J. Mash & R. A. Barkley (Eds.), *Treatment of Childhood Disorders* (pp. 111–207). New York: Guilford Press.

McQuade, S. C. & Sampat, N. (2008). *Survey of Internet and at-risk behaviors.* Rochester, NY: Rochester Institute of Technology. Accessed April 11, 2009, from hdl.handle.net/1850/7652.

Mead, G. H. (1934). *Mind, self, and society from the standpoint of a social behaviorist.* Chicago: University of Chicago Press.

Means, M., & Voss, J. (1985). Star wars: A developmental study of expert and novice knowledge structures. *Memory and Language, 24,* 746–757.

Meijer, A. M., & van den Wittenboer, G. L. H. (2007). Contribution of infants' sleep and crying to marital relationship of first-time parent couples in the 1st year after childbirth. *Journal of Family Psychology, 21*(1), 49–57.

Meins, E., Fernyhough, C., Wainwright, R., Gupta, M. D., Fradley, E., & Tuckey, M. (2002). Maternal mind-mindedness and attachment security as predictors of theory of mind understanding. *Child Development, 73,* 1715–1726.

Meisels, S. J., & Atkins-Burnett, S. (2000). The elements of early childhood assessment. In J. P. Shonkoff & S. J. Meisels (Eds.), *Handbook of early childhood intervention* (2nd ed.) (pp. 231–257). New York: Cambridge University Press.

Meltzoff, A. N., & Borton, R. W. (1979). Intermodal matching by human neonates. *Nature, 282,* 403–404.

Meltzoff, A. N., & Moore, M. K. (1983). Newborn infants imitate adult facial gestures. *Child Development, 54,* 702–709.

Meltzoff, A. N., & Moore, M. K. (1989). Imitation in newborn infants: Exploring the range of gestures imitated and the underlying mechanisms. *Developmental Psychology, 25,* 954–962.

Merrill, R. M., Salazar, R. D. & Gardner, N. W. (2001). Relationship between family religiosity and drug use behavior among youth. *Social Behavior and Personality, 29,* 347–358.

Messinger, D. S., Bauer, C. R., Das, A., Seifer, R., Lester, B. M., Lagasse, L. L., et al. (2004). The maternal lifestyle study: Cognitive, motor, and behavioral outcomes of cocaine-exposed and opiate-exposed infants through three years of age. *Pediatrics, 113*(6), 1677–1686.

Meyer, D. R. (1999). Compliance with child support orders in paternity and divorce cases. In R. A. Thompson & P. R. Amato (Eds.), *The post-divorce family: Children, parenting, and society* (pp. 127–157). Thousand Oaks, CA: Sage.

Meyer-Bahlburg, H., Dolezal, C., Baker, S., & New, M. (2008). Sexual orientation in women with classical or non-classical congenital adrenal hyperplasia as a function of degree of prenatal androgen excess. *Archives of Sexual Behavior, 37,* 85–99.

Meyer-Bahlburg, H. F. L., Ehrhardt, A. A., Rosen, L. R., Gruen, R. S., Veridiano, N. P., Vann, F. H., & Neuwalder, H. F. (1995). Prenatal estrogens and the development of homosexual orientation. *Developmental Psychology, 31,* 12–21.

Michaels, S. (1991). The dismantling of narrative. In A. McCabe & C. Peterson (Eds.), *Developing narrative structure* (pp. 303–351). Hillsdale, NJ: Erlbaum.

Michels, T. C., & Tiu, A. Y. (2007). Second trimester pregnancy loss. *American Family Physician, 76,* 1341–1346.

Mick, E., Biederman, J., Faraone, S. V., Sayer, J., & Kleinman, S. (2002). Case-control study of attention-deficit hyperactivity disorder and maternal smoking, alcohol use and drug use during pregnancy. *Journal of the American Academy of Child and Adolescent Psychiatry, 41*(4), 378–385.

Miele, F. (1995). *Skeptic Magazine* interview with Robert Sternberg on *The bell curve. Skeptic, 3,* 72–80.

Miller, B. & Moore, K. (1990). Adolescent sexual behavior, pregnancy, and parenting: Resarch through the 1980s. *Journal of Marriage and the Family, 52,* 1025–1044.

Miller, B. C., Fan, X., Christensen, M., Grotevant, H. D., & van Dulmen, M. (2000). Comparisons of adopted and nonadopted adolescents in a large, nationally representative sample. *Child Development, 71,* 1458–1473.

Miller, G. A. (1956). The magical number seven, plus or minus two: Some limits on our capacity for processing information. *Psychological Review, 63,* 81–97.

Miller, P. A., Eisenberg, N., Fabes, R. A., & Shell, R. (1996). Relations of moral reasoning and vicarious emotion to young children's prosocial behavior toward peers and adults. *Developmental Psychology, 32,* 210–219.

Miller-Johnson, S., Winn, D. C., Coie, J. D., Malone, P. S., & Lochman, J. (2004). Risk factors for adolescent pregnancy reports among African American males. *Journal of Research on Adolescence, 14,* 471–495.

Millman, R. P. (2005). Excessive sleepiness in adolescents and young adults: Causes, consequences, and treatment strategies. *Pediatrics, 115,* 1774–1786.

Minami, M., & McCabe, A. (1990). Haiku as a discourse regulation device: A stanza analysis of Japanese children's personal narratives. *Language in Society, 20,* 577–599.

Miniño, A. M., Arias, E., Kochanek, K. D., Murphy, S. L. & Smith, B. L. (2002). Deaths: Final data for 2000. *National Vital Statistics Reports, 50*(15). Hyattsville, MD: National Center for Health Statistics.

Mistry, K. B., Minkovitz, C. S., Strobino, D. M., & Borzekowski, D. L. G. (2007). Children's television exposure and behavioral and social outcomes at 5.5 years: Does timing of exposure matter? *Pediatrics, 120,* 762–769.

Mitru, G., Millrood, D. L. & Mateika, J. H. (2002). The impact of sleep on learning and behavior in adolescents. *Teachers College Record, 104,* 704–726.

Moerk, E. L. (1992). *A first language taught and learned.* Baltimore: Paul H. Brooks Publishing.

Moerk, E. L. (2000). *The guided acquisition of first language skills.* Stamford, CT: Ablex.

Moffitt, T. E. (1993). Adolescence-limited and life-course-persistent antisocial behavior: A developmental taxonomy. *Psychological Review, 100,* 674–701.

Moffitt, T. E., Caspi, A., Dickson, N., Silva, P., & Stanton, W. (1996). Childhood-onset versus adolescent-onset antisocial conduct problems in males: Natural history from ages 3 to 18 years. *Development and Psychopathology, 8,* 399–424.

Mohanty, A. K., & Perregaux, C. (1997). Language acquisition and bilingualism. In J. W. Berry, P. R. Dasen, & T. S. Saraswathi (Eds.), *Handbook of cross-cultural psychology. Vol 2: Basic processes and human development.* 2nd ed. Boston, MA: Allyn & Bacon.

Moir, D. D. (1986). *Pain relief in labour: A handbook for midwives* (5th ed.). Edinburgh: Churchill Livingstone.

Molinsky, A., & Perunovic, W. (2008). Training wheels for cultural learning: Poor language fluency and its shielding effect on the evaluation of culturally inappropriate behavior. *Journal of Language & Social Psychology, 27,* 284–289.

Molnar, B. E., Gortmaker, S. L. & Bull, F. C. (2004). Unsafe to play? Neighborhood disorder and lack of safety predict reduced physical activity among urban children an adolescents. *American Journal of Health Promotion, 18,* 378–386.

Molnar, J., Roth, W., & Klein, T. (1990). Constantly compromised: The impact of homelessness on children. *Journal of Social Issues, 46,* 109–124.

Montague, D. P. F., & Walker-Andrews, A. S. (2001). Peekaboo: A new look at infants' perception of emotion expressions. *Developmental Psychology, 37*, 826–838.

Montemayor, R. (1982). The relationship between parent-adolescent conflict and the amount of time adolescent spend alone and with parents and peers. *Child Development, 53*, 1512–1519.

Montgomery, J. W. (1995). Sentence comprehension in children with specific language impairment: The role of phonological working memory. *Journal of Speech and Hearing Research, 38*, 187–199.

Moore, D. S., Spence, M. J., & Katz, G. S. (1997). Six-month-olds' categorization of natural infant-directed utterances. *Developmental Psychology, 33*, 980–989.

Moore, K. L., & Persaud, T. V. N. (1998). *The developing human: Clinically oriented embryology* (6th ed.). Philadelphia: W. B. Saunders Company.

Moore, M. K., & Meltzoff, A. N. (2007). Factors affecting infants' manual search for occluded objects and the genesis of object permanence. *Infant Behavior & Development, 31*,168–180.

Morelli, G. A., Rogoff, B., Oppenheim, D., & Goldsmith, D. (1992). Cultural variation in infants' sleeping arrangements: Questions of independence. *Developmental Psychology, 28*, 604–613.

Morgan, J., Bonamo, K. M., & Travis, L. L. (1995). Negative evidence on negative evidence. *Developmental Psychology*, 31, 180–197.

Morgan, P. (1998). *Adoption and the care of children.* London: IEA Health and Welfare Unit.

Morrison, F. J., Griffith, E. M., & Alberts, D. M. (1997). Nature–nurture in the classroom: Entrance age, school readiness, and learning in children. *Developmental Psychology, 33*, 254–262.

Morrow, C. E., Vogel, A. L., & Anthony, J. C. (2004). Expressive and receptive language functioning in preschool children with prenatal cocaine exposure. *Journal of Pediatric Psychology, 29*, 543–554.

Mortimer, J. T. (2003). *Working and growing up in America.* Cambridge, MA: Harvard University Press.

Mosher, W. D., Chandra, A. & Jones, J. (2005). Sexual behavior and selected health measures: Men and women 15–44 years of age, United States, 2002. *Advance data from vital and health statistics, no. 362.* Hyattsville, MD: National Center for Health Statistics.

Mosher, W. D., Martinez, G. M., Chandra, A., Abma, J. C. & Willson, S. J. (2004). Use of contraception and use of family planning services in the United States: 1982–2002. *Advance data from vital and health statistics, no. 350.* Hyattsville, MD: National Center for Health Statistics. 2004. Retrieved May 28, 2006, from www.cdc.gov/nchs/data/ad/ad350.pdf.

Mueller, E., & Silverman, N. (1989). Peer relations in maltreated children. In D. Cicchetti & V. Carlson (Eds.), *Child maltreatment: Theory and research on the causes and consequences of child abuse and neglect* (pp. 529–578). New York: Cambridge University Press.

Mullen, P. E., & Fleming, J. (1998). Long-term effects of child sexual abuse. *Issues in Child Abuse Prevention, 9.* National Child Protection Clearinghouse. Retrieved June 22, 2006, from www.aifs.gov.au/nch/issues9.html.

Mullis, A. K., & Mullis, R. L. (1997). Vocational interests of adolescents: Relationships between self-esteem and locus of control. *Psychological Reports, 81*, 1363–1371.

Mullis, I. V. S., Martin, M. O., Beaton, A. E., Gonzalez, E. J., Kelly, D. L., & Smith, T. A. (1998). *Mathematics and science achievement in the final year of secondary school: IEA's third international mathematics and science study (TIMSS).* Chestnut Hill, MA: Center for the Study of Testing, Evaluation, and Educational Policy, Boston College.

Mullis, R. L., Mullis, A. K., & Gerwels, D. (1998). Stability of vocational interests among high school students. *Adolescence, 33*, 699–707.

Mulvaney, M. K., & Mebert, C. J. (2007). Parental corporal punishment predicts behavior problems in early childhood. *Journal of Family Psychology, 21*(3), 389–397.

Munakata, Y. (2006). Information processing approaches to development. In D. Kuhn & R. Siegler (Vol. Eds.) and W. Damon & R. M. Lerner (Eds.-in-Chief), *Handbook of child psychology* (6th ed., Vol. 1, pp. 426–463). Hoboken, NJ: John Wiley & Sons.

Munroe, R. H., Shimmin, H. S., & Munroe, R. L. (1984). Gender understanding and sex role preferences in four cultures. *Developmental Psychology, 20*, 673–682.

Murray, C., & Golombok, S. (2005). Going it alone: Solo mothers and their infants conceived by donor insemination. *American Journal of Orthopsychiatry, 75*, 242–253.

Murray, C. (2005). The inequality taboo. *Commentary, 120*, 13–22.

Murray, J., Liotti, M., Ingmundson, P., Mayberg, H., Pu, Y., Zamarripa, F., et al. (2006). Children's brain activations while viewing televised violence revealed by fMRI. *Media Psychology, 8*(1), 25–37.

Murray, L., de Rosnay, M., Pearson, J., Bergeron, C., Schofield, E., Royal-Lawson, M., & Cooper, P. J. (2008). Intergenerational transmission of social anxiety: The role of social referencing processes in infancy. *Child Development, 79*, 1049–1064.

Naeye, R., & Peters, E. (1984). Mental development of children whose mothers smoked during pregnancy. *Obstetrics and Gynecology, 64*, 601–607.

Naigles, L. G., & Hoff-Ginsburg, E. (1995). Input to verb learning: Evidence for the plausibility of syntactic bootstrapping. *Developmental Psychology, 31*, 827–837.

Naigles, L., & Gelman, S. A. (1995). Overextensions in comprehension and production revisited: Preferential-looking in a study of dog, cat, and cow. *Journal of Child Language, 22*, 19–46.

Nantais, K. M., & Schellenberg, E. G. (1999). The Mozart effect: An artifact of preference. *Psychological Science, 10*, 370–373.

Nash, M. R., Zivney, O. A., & Hulsey, T. (1993). Characteristics of sexual abuse associated with greater psychological impairment among children. *Child Abuse and Neglect, 17*, 401–408.

Nathanielsz, P. W. (1992). *Life before birth: The challenges of fetal development.* New York: W. H. Freeman and Company.

National Alliance for Youth Sports (2001). *Standards.* Retrieved June 22, 2006 from June 22, 2006, from www.nays.org/TimeOut/National%20Standards.pdf.

National Alliance for Youth Sports (2003). *Recommendations for Communities.* Retrieved June 22, 2006, from www.nays.org/nays_community_recommendations.pdf.

National Association for Sport and Physical Education & American Heart Association (2006). *2006 Shape of the nation report: Status of physical education in the USA.* Reston, VA: National Association for Sport and Physical Education. Retrieved June 20, 2006, from www.aahperd.org/naspe/ShapeOfTheNation/PDF/ShapeOfTheNation.pdf

National Association for Sport and Physical Education (2002). *Active Start: A statement of physical activity guidelines for children birth to five years.* Reston, VA: National Association for Sport and Physical Education.

National Association for Sport and Physical Education (2004). *Physical activity for children: A statement of guidelines for children ages 5–12* (2nd ed.). Reston, VA: National Association for Sport and Physical Education. Online statement last accessed May 10, 2009, from www.aahperd.org/Naspe/template.cfm?template=ns_children.html.

National Campaign to Prevent Teen Pregnancy (2008). *Fact Sheet: How is the 3 in 10 statistic calculated?* Retrieved April 25, 2009, from www.thenationalcampaign.org/resources/pdf/FactSheet_3in10_April2008.pdf.

National Center for Biotechnology Information (2009). *NCBI map viewer.* Accessed April 13, 2009, from www.ncbi.nlm.nih.gov/mapview/maps.cgi?taxid=9606&CHR=X&maps=genes-r,pheno,morbid,genec&R1=on&query=FMR1&VERBOSE=ON&ZOOM=3.

National Center for Chronic Disease Prevention and Health Promotion (2004). *Breastfeeding practices: Results from the 2003 National Immunization Survey.* Retrieved September 10, 2004, from www.cdc.gov/breastfeeding/data/NIS_data/.

National Center for Health Statistics (2000b). *National health and nutrition examinations survey: Clinical growth charts.* Retrieved October 21, 2002, from www.cdd.gov/nchs/about/major/nhanes/growthcharts/clinical_charts.htm#clin1.

National Center for Health Statistics (2004). *2000 CDC growth charts: United States, for the U.S. Department of Health and Human Services and the Centers for Disease Control and Prevention.* Last accessed November 7, 2005, from www.cdc.gov/growthcharts/.

National Center for Health Statistics (2005). *Health, United States, 2005, with chartbook on trends in the health of Americans* (pp. 320–324). Hyattsville, MD: National Center for Health Statistics. Retrieved December 13, 2005, from www.cdc.gov/nchs/hus.htm.

National Center for Health Statistics (2006a). *Prevalence of overweight among children and adolescents: United States, 2003–2004. NCHS Health E-Stats.* Hyattsville, MD: National Center for Health Statistics. Retrieved May 9, 2009, from www.cdc.gov/nchs/products/pubs/pubd/hestats/overweight/overwght_child_03.htm.

National Center for Health Statistics (2006b). *Obesity still a major problem.* Hyattsville, MD: National Center for Health Statistics. Retrieved

May 9, 2009, from www.cdc.gov/nchs/pressroom/06facts/obesity 03_04.htm.

National Center for Health Statistics (2009). *Health, United States, 2008, with chartbook* (pp. 42–43, 275–279). Hyattsville, MD: National Center for Health Statistics. Retrieved May 9, 2009, from www.cdc.gov/nchs/data/hus/hus08.pdf#076.

National Center for Health Statistics (2009). *Health, United States, 2008, with chartbook*. Hyattsville, MD: U.S. Government Printing Office. Last accessed March 7, 2009, from www.cdc.gov/nchs/data/hus/hus08.pdf.

National Center for Health Statistics. (2000). *Growth charts.* Retrieved September 10, 2004, from www.cdc.gov/nchs/data/nhanes/growthcharts/wtageinf.txt.

National Center for Health Statistics. (2007). *Health, United States, 2007, with chartbook on trends in the health of Americans* (pp. 145, 276–278). Hyattsville, MD: National Center for Health Statistics. Retrieved December 30, 2008, from www.cdc.gov/nchs/data/hus/hus07.pdf#068.

National Center for Victims of Crime (2006). *Sexual assault fact sheet.* Accessed May 27, 2006 from www.ncvc.org/ncvc/AGP.Net/Components/documentViewer/Download.aspxnz?DocumentID=39727.

National Clearinghouse on Child Abuse and Neglect (2006). *Recognizing child abuse and neglect: Signs and symptoms.* Retrieved June 22, 2006, from nccahch.acf.hhs.gov.

National Education Goals Panel. (1999). *The National Education Goals report: Building a nation of learners.* Washington, DC: U.S. Government Printing Office.

National Highway Traffic Safety Administration (2007). *Traffic safety facts: 2007* (reports on "Children" and "Alcohol-impaired driving"). Last accessed May 9, 2009, at www.nhtsa.dot.gov/.

National Highway Traffic Safety Administration (2009). *Chart on correct usage of child seats (Child passenger safety: A parent's primer).* Last accessed May 9, 2009, at www.nhtsa.dot.gov/portal/site/nhtsa/menuitem.9f8c7d6359e0e9bbbf30811060008a0c/.

National Human Genome Research Institute (April, 2009). *Genetic Information Nondiscrimination Act (GINA) of 2008.* Retrieved April 13, 2009, from www.genome.gov/24519851.

National Institute on Drug Abuse (2001). *Pregnancy and drug use trends. NIDA InfoFax.* Retrieved March 3, 2002, from www.nida.nih.gov/infofax/pregnancytrends.html.

National Research Council and Institute of Medicine. (2000). *From neurons to neighborhoods: The science of early childhood development.* J. P. Shonkoff & D. A. Phillips, Eds. Board on Children, Youth, and Families, Commission on Behavioral and Social Sciences and Education. Washington, DC: National Academy Press.

National SAFE KIDS Campaign (2004). *Childhood injury fact sheet.* Washington, DC: NSKC. Retrieved December 6, 2005, from www.usa.safekids.org/tier3_printable.cfm?content_item_id=1030&folder_id=540.

National Sleep Foundation (2006). *2006 Sleep in American poll.* Washington, DC: National Sleep Foundation. Retrieved April 25, 2009, from www.sleepfoundation.org/site/c.huIXKjM0IxF/b.2419037/k.1466/2006_Sleep_in_America_Poll.htm.

National Sleep Foundation (2009). *Children's sleep habits.* Retrieved February 14, 2009, from www.sleepfoundation.org/site/ c.huIXKjM0IxF/b.4809577/k.BB1D/Sleep_and_Children.htm.

Naus, M. J., Ornstein, P. A., & Aivano, S. (1977). Developmental changes in memory: The effects of processing time and rehearsal instructions. *Journal of Experimental Child Psychology, 23,* 237–251.

Neiss, M. B., Sedikides, C., & Stevenson, J. (2006). Genetic influences on level and stability of self-esteem. *Self and Identity, 5,* 247–266.

Neisser, U. (1998). *The rising curve: Long-term gains in IQ and related measures.* Washington, DC: American Psychological Association.

Neisser, U., Boodoo, G., Bouchard, T. J., Boykin, A. W., Brody, N., Ceci, S. J., Halpern, D. F., Loehlin, J. C., Perloff, R., Sternberg, R. J., & Urbina, S. (1996). Intelligence: Knowns and unknowns. *American Psychologist, 51,* 77–101.

Nelson, C. A. (2001). The development and neural bases of face recognition. *Infant and Child Development, 10*(1–2), 3–18.

Nelson, D. A., & Crick, N. R. (2002). Parental psychological control: Implications for childhood physical and relational aggression. In B. K. Barber (Ed.), *Intrusive parenting: How psychological control affects children and adolescents* (pp. 168–189). Washington, DC: American Psychological Association.

Nelson, C. A., & Horowitz, F. D. (1983). The perception of facial expressions and stimulus motion by two- and five-month-old infants using holographic stimuli. *Child Development, 54,* 868–877.

Nelson, D. A., Hart, C. H., Yang, C., Olsen, J. A., & Jin, S. (2006). Aversive parenting in China: Associations with child physical and relational aggression. *Child Development, 77,* 554–572.

Nelson, K. (1973). Structure and strategy in learning to talk. *Monographs of the Society for Research in Child Development, 38* (Serial No. 149).

Nelson, K. (1986). *Event knowledge: Structure and function in development.* Hillsdale, NJ: Erlbaum.

Nelson, K., & Fivush, R. (2004). The emergence of autobiographical memory: A social cultural developmental theory. *Psychological Review, 111,* 486–511.

Nelson, K., Skwerer, D. P., Goldman, S., Henseler, S., Presler, N., & Walkenfeld, F. F. (2003). Entering a community of minds: An experiential approach to "theory of mind." *Human Development, 46,* 24–46.

Nettlebladt, P., Fagerstrom, C., & Udderberg, N. (1976). The significance of reported childbirth pain. *Journal of Psychosomatic Research, 20,* 215–221.

Neuschatz, J. S., Preston, E. L., Burkett, A. D., Toglia, M. P., Lampinen, J. M., Neuschatz, J. S., Fairless, A. H., Lawson, D. S., Powers, R. A., & Goodsell, C. A., (2005). The effects of post-identification feedback and age on retrospective eyewitness memory. *Applied Cognitive Psychology, 19,* 435–453.

Newburger, E. C. (2001). Home computers and Internet use in the United States: August 2000. *Current Population Reports.* Washington, DC: U.S. Census Bureau. Retrieved July 8, 2002, from www.census.gov.

Newman, D. L., Caspi, A., Moffitt, T. E., & Silva, P. A. (1997). Antecedents of adult interpersonal functioning: Effects of individual differences in age 3 temperament. *Developmental Psychology, 33,* 206–217.

Newman, R. S. (2005). The cocktail party effect in infants revisited: Listening to one's name in noise. *Developmental Psychology, 41,* 352–362.

Newport, E. L. (1990). Maturational constraints on language learning. *Cognitive Science, 14,* 11–28.

Newsom, C. (1998). Autistic disorder. In E. J. Mash & R. A. Barkley (Eds.), *Treatment of childhood disorders* (2nd ed., pp. 416-467). New York: Guilford Press.

Newton, R. W., & Hunt, L. P. (1984). Psychosocial stress in pregnancy and its relation to low birth weight. *British Medical Journal, 288,* 1191–1194.

NICHD (2005). *Autism overview: What we know.* Retrieved June 17, 2005, from www.nichd.nih.gov/publications/pubs/autism_overview_2005.pdf.

NICHD Early Child Care Research Network (1997). The effects of infant child care on infant-mother attachment security: Results of the NICHD study of early child care. *Child Development, 68,* 860–879.

NICHD Early Child Care Research Network (2001). Child-care and family predictors of preschool attachment and stability from infancy. *Developmental Psychology, 37,* 847–862.

NICHD Early Child Care Research Network. (2003). Do children's attention processes mediate the link between family predictors and school readiness? *Developmental Psychology, 39,* 581–593.

NICHD Early Child Care Research Network. (2004). Does class size in first grade relate to children's academic and social performance or observed classroom processes? *Developmental Psychology, 40,* 651–664.

Nichols, R. C. (1978). Twin studies of ability, personality, and interests. *Homo, 29,* 158–173.

Nicolosi, J., & Byrd, A. D. (2002). A critique of Bem's "exotic becomes erotic" theory of sexual orientation development. *Psychological Reports, 90,* 931–946.

Niedzwienska, A. (2003). Distortion of autobiographical memories. *Applied Cognitive Psychology, 17,* 81–91.

Nottelmann, E. D., Susman, E. J., Blue, J. H., Inoff-Germain, G., Dorn, L. D., Loriaux, D. L., Cutler, G. B., & Chrousos, G. P. (1987). Gonadal and adrenal hormone correlates of adjustment in early adolescence. In R. M. Lerner & T. T. Foch, *Biological-psychosocial interactions in early adolescence.* Hillsdale, NJ: Erlbaum.

Nucci, L. P. (1996). Morality and the personal sphere of action. In E. Reed, E. Turiel, & T. Brown (Eds.), *Values and knowledge* (pp. 41–60). Hillsdale, NJ: Erlbaum.

Nurnberger, J. I., & Gershon, E. S. (1992). Genetics. In E. S. Paykel (Ed.), *Handbook of affective disorders* (2nd ed., pp. 131–148). New York: Guilford Press.

*New York Times* (2001). Shooting at California school leaves 2 dead and 13 hurt. Retrieved March 6, 2001, from www.nytimes.com/2001/03/06/national/06SHOO.html.

O'Boyle, M., Cunnington, R., Silk, T., Vaughan, D., Jackson, G., Syngeniotis, A., et al. (2005). Mathematically gifted male adolescents activate a unique brain network during mental rotation. *Cognitive Brain Research, 25*, 583–587.

O'Brien, E. M. & Mindell, J. A. (2005). Sleep and risk-taking behavior in adolescents. *Behavioral Sleep Medicine, 3*, 113–133.

O'Connor, M. J., & Whaley, S. E. (2007). Brief intervention for alcohol use by pregnant women. *American Journal of Public Health, 97*(2), 252–258.

O'Reilly, A. W. (1995). Using representations: Comprehension and production of actions with imagined objects. *Child Development, 66*, 999–1010.

O'Sullivan, L. R., & Meyer-Bahlberg, H.F.L. (2003). African American and Latina inner-city girls' reports of romantic and sexual development. *Journal of Social and Personal Relationships, 20*, 221–238.

Østensjø, S., Carlberg, E. B., & Vøllestad, N. K. (2003). Everyday functioning in young children with cerebral palsy: Functional skills, caregiver assistance, and modifications of the environment. *Developmental Medicine and Child Neurology, 45*(9), 603–612.

Østensjø, S., Carlberg, E. B., & Vøllestad, N. K. (2004). Motor impairments in young children with cerebral palsy: Relationship to gross motor function and everyday activities. *Developmental Medicine and Child Neurology, 46*(9), 580–589.

Obel, C., Henriksen, T., Dalsgaard, S., Linnet, K., Skajaa, E., Thomsen, P., et al. (2004). Does children's watching of television cause attention problems? Retesting the hypothesis in a Danish cohort. *Pediatrics, 114*(5), 1372–1374.

Odegard, T., Holliday, R., Brainerd, C., & Reyna, V. (2008). Attention to global gist processing eliminates age effects in false memories. *Journal of Experimental Child Psychology, 99*, 96–113.

Oetting, J. B. (2003a). Dialect speakers. In R. Kent (Ed.), *MIT encyclopedia of communication sciences and disorders.* Cambridge, MA: MIT Press.

Oetting, J. B. (2003b). Dialect vs. disorder. In R. Kent (Ed.), *MIT encyclopedia of communication sciences and disorders* Cambridge, MA: MIT Press.

Oetting, J. B., & McDonald, J. L. (2001). Nonmainstream dialect use and specific language impairment. *Journal of Speech, Language, and Hearing Research, 44*, 207–223.

Olinghouse, N., & Graham, S. (2009). The relationship between the discourse knowledge and the writing performance of elementary-grade students. *Journal of Educational Psychology, 101*, 37–50.

Oliver, M., Schofield, G., & McEvoy, E. (2006). An integrated curriculum approach to increasing habitual physical activity in children: A feasibility study. *Journal of School Health, 76*, 74–79.

Ollendick, T. H., Weist, M. D., Borden, M. G., & Greene, R. W. (1992). Sociometric status and academic, behavioral, and psychological adjustment: A five-year longitudinal study. *Journal of Consulting and Clinical Psychology, 60*, 80–87.

Oller, D. K., & Eilers, R. E. (1988). The role of audition in infant babbling. *Child Development*, 59, 441–449.

Onnis, L., & Christiansen, M. (2008). Lexical categories at the edge of the word. *Cognitive Science, 32*, 184–221.

Onwuegbuzie, A. J., & Daley, C. E. (2001). Racial differences in IQ revisited: A synthesis of nearly a century of research. *Journal of Black Psychology, 27*, 209–220.

Opper, S. (1977). Concept development in Thai urban and rural children. In P. R. Dasen (Ed.), *Piagetian psychology: Cross-cultural contributions* (pp. 89–122). New York: Gardner Press.

Orbeta, R. L., Overpeck, M. D., Ramcharran, D., Kogan, M. D., & Ledsky, R. (2006). High caffeine intake in adolescents: Associations with difficulty sleeping and feeling tired in the morning. *Journal of Adolescent Health, 38*, 451–453.

Organisation for Economic Co-operation and Development. (2006). OECD health data 2006—frequently requested data. Retrieved June 10, 2007, from www.oecd.org/document/16/0,3343,en_2825_495642_2085200_1_1_1_1,00.html

Orr, J. E., & Hakuta, K. (2000). Inadequate conclusions from an inadequate assessment: What can SAT-9 scores tell us about the impact of Proposition 227 in California? *Bilingual Research Journal, 24*, 141–155.

Osofsky, J. D. (1999). The impact of violence on children. *The Future of Children, 9*, 33–49.

Ouellette, G., & Sénéchal, M. (2008). Pathways to literacy: A study of invented spelling and its role in learning to read. *Child Development, 79*, 899–913.

Owens, E. B., Hinshaw, S. P., Arnold, L. E., Cantwell, D. P., Elliott, G., Hechtman, L., Jensen, P. S., Newcorn, J. H., Severe, J. B., Vitiello, B., Kraemer, H. C., Abikoff, H. B., Conners, C. K., Greenhill, L. L., Hoza, B., March, J. S., Pelham, W. E., Swanson, J. M., & Wells, K. C. (2003). Which treatment for whom for ADHD? Moderators of treatment response in the MTA. *Journal of Consulting and Clinical Psychology, 71*, 540–552.

Oyserman, D., Coon, H. M., & Kemmelmeier, M. (2002). Rethinking individualism and collectivism: Evaluation of theoretical assumptions and meta-analyses. *Psychological Bulletin, 128*, 3–72.

Padilla, A. M. & Baird, T. L. (1991). Mexican-American adolescent sexuality and sexual knowledge: An exploratory study. *Hispanic Journal of Behavioral Sciences, 13*, 95–104.

Paik, H., & Comstock, G. (1994). The effects of television violence on antisocial behavior: A meta-analysis. *Communication Research, 21*, 516–546.

Palermo, F., Hanish, L., Martin, C., Fabes, R., & Reiser, M. (2007). Preschoolers' academic readiness: What role does the teacher–child relationship play? *Early Childhood Research Quarterly, 22*(4), 407–422.

Pam, A., Kemker, S. S., Ross, C. A., & Golden, R. (1996). The "equal environments assumption" in MZ–DZ twin comparisons: an untenable premise of psychiatric genetics? *Acta Geneticae Medicae et Gemellologiae: Twin Research, 45*(3), 349–360.

Pan, H. W. (1994). Children's play in Taiwan. In J. L. Roopnarine, J. E. Johnson, & F. H. Hooper (Eds.), *Children's play in diverse cultures* (pp. 31–50). Albany, NY: State University of New York Press.

Parfitt, G., & Eston, R.G. (2005). The relationship between children's habitual activity level and psychological well-being. *Acta Paediatrica, 94*, 1791–1797.

Park, S., Weaver, T., & Romer, D. (2009). Predictors of the transition from experimental to daily smoking among adolescents in the United States. *Journal for Specialists in Pediatric Nursing, 14*, 102–111.

Parke, R. D., & Buriel, R. (1998). Socialization in the family: Ethnic and ecological perspectives. In W. Damon & N. Eisenberg (Eds.), *Handbook of child psychology: Vol. 3. Social, emotional, and personality development* (pp. 463–552). New York: Wiley.

Parke, R. D., & Buriel, R. (2006). Socialization in the family: Ethnic and ecological perspectives. In W. Damon & R. Lerner (Series Ed.) & N. Eisenberg (Vol. Ed.), *Handbook of Child Psychology: Vol. 3. Social, emotional, and personality developmenty* (6th ed., pp. 429–504). New York: Wiley.

Parker, F. L., Boak, A. Y., Griffin, K. W., Ripple, C., & Peay, L. (1999). Parent-child relationship, home learning environment, and school readiness. *School Psychology Review, 28*, 413–425.

Parten, M. B. (1932). Social participation among pre-school children. *Journal of Abnormal and Social Psychology, 27*, 243–269.

Partridge, T. (2005). Are genetically informed designs genetically informative? Comment on McGue, Elkins, Walden, and Iacono (2005) and quantitative behavioral genetics. *Developmental Psychology, 41*, 985–988.

Pasco Fearon, R. M., van IJzendoorn, M. H., Fonagy, P., Bakersmans-Kranenburg, M. J., Schuengel, C., & Bokhorst, C. L. (2006). In search of shared and nonshared environmental factors in security of attachment: A behavior-genetic study of the association between sensitivity and attachment security. *Developmental Psychology, 42*, 1026–1040.

Patterson, C. J. (1992). Children of lesbian and gay parents. *Child Development, 63*, 1025–1042.

Patterson, C. J. (2006). Children of lesbian and gay parents. *Current Directions in Psychological Science, 15*, 241–244.

Patterson, G. R. (1995). Coercion—a basis for early age of onset for arrest. In J. McCord (Ed.), *Coercion and punishment in long-term perspective* (pp. 81–105). New York: Cambridge University Press.

Patterson, G. R. (1997). Performance models for parenting: A social interactional perspective. In J. E. Grusec & L. Kuczynski (Eds.), *Parenting and children's internalization of values* (pp. 193–226). New York: Wiley.

Patterson, M. M., & Bigler, R. S. (2006). Preschool children's attention to environmental messages about groups: Social categorization and the origins of intergroup bias. *Child Development, 77*, 847–860.

Paus, T. (2005). Mapping brain maturation and cognitive development during adolescence. *Trends in Cognitive Sciences, 9*, 60–68.

Pear, R. (1996, March 17). Many states fail to fulfill child welfare. *New York Times*. Retrieved August 2, 2002, from www.nytimes.com.

Pedersen, N. L. (1993). Genetic and environmental continuity and change in personality. In T. J. Bouchard, Jr. & P. Propping (Eds.), *Twins as a tool of behavioral genetics* (pp. 147–162). West Sussex, England: Wiley.

Pedersen, S., Vitaro, F., Barker, E. D., & Borge, A. I. H. (2007). The timing of middle-childhood peer rejection and friendship: Linking early behavior to early-adolescent adjustment. *Child Development, 78*, 1037–1051.

Pederson, W. & Kristiansen, H. W. (2008). Homosexual experience, desire and identity among young adults. *Journal of Homosexuality, 54*, 68–102.

Pedro-Carroll, J. (2001). The promotion of wellness in children and families: Challenges and opportunities. *American Psychologist, 56*, 993–1004.

Pelton, L. (1989). *For reasons of poverty: A critical analysis of the public child welfare system in the United States*. New York: Praeger.

Peña, M., Maki, A., Kovacic D., Dehaene-Lambertz, G., Koizumi, H., Bouquet, F., & Mehler, J. (2003). Sounds and silence: An optical topography study of language recognition at birth. *Proceedings of the National Academy of Sciences of the United States of America, 100*, 11702–11705.

Pennington, B. F., Moon, J., Edgin, J., Stedron, J., & Nadel, L. (2003). The neuropsychology of Down syndrome: Evidence for hippocampal dysfunction. *Child Development, 74*, 75–93.

Peplau, L. A. & Huppin, M. (2008). Masculinity, femininity and the development of sexual orientation in women. *Journal of Gay & Lesbian Mental Health, 12*, 145–165.

Perez, M., Voelz, Z. R., Pettit, J. W., & Joiner, T. E., Jr. (2002). The role of acculturative stress and body dissatisfaction in predicting bulimic symptomology across ethnic groups. *International Journal of Eating Disorders, 31*, 442–454.

Perie, M., Grigg, W., & Donahue, P. (2005). *The nation's report card: Reading 2005* (NCES 2006-451). U.S. Department of Education, National Center for Education Statistics. Washington, DC: U.S. Government Printing Office. Retrieved June 11, 2006, from nces.ed.gov/nationsreportcard/pdf/main2005/2006451.pdf

Perkins, D. F., Jacobs, J. E., Barber, B. L., & Eccles, J. S. (2004). Childhood and adolescent sports participation as predictors of participation in sports and physical fitness activities during young adulthood. *Youth & Society, 35*, 495–520.

Perner, J. (1991). *Understanding the representational mind*. Cambridge, MA: MIT Press.

Peterson, C., & McCabe, A. (1983). *Developmental psycholinguistics: Three ways of looking at a child's narrative*. New York: Plenum.

Peterson, C., Parsons, T., & Dean, M. (2004). Providing misleading and reinstatement information a year after it happened: Effects on long-term memory. *Memory, 12*, 1–13.

Peterson, T., Kaasa, S., & Loftus, E. (2009). Me too!: Social modeling influences on early autobiographical memories. *Applied Cognitive Psychology, 23*(2), 267–277.

Phelps, N. (2006). Teen says he had to stop school plot. Retrieved October 14, 2006, from www.thenorthwestern.com/apps/pbcs.dll/article? AID=20060921/OSH/309210013/1128/OSHnews.

Phinney, J. S. (1990). Ethnic identity in adolescents and adults: Review of research. *Psychological Bulletin, 108*, 499–514.

Phinney, J. S. (2003). Ethnic identity and acculturation. In K. M. Chun, P. B. Organista, & G. Marín (Eds.), *Acculturation: Advances in theory, measurement, and applied research* (pp. 63–81). Washington, DC: American Psychological Association.

Phinney, J. S., Cantu, C. L., & Kurtz, D. A. (1997). Ethnic and American identity as predictors of self-esteem among African American, Latino, and White adolescents. *Journal of Youth and Adolescence, 26*, 165–185.

Phinney, J. S., Ong, A., & Madden, T. (2000). Cultural values and intergenerational value discrepancies in immigrant and non-immigrant families. *Child Development, 71*, 528–539.

Piaget, J. (1929). *The child's conception of the world*. New York: Harcourt, Brace & World.

Piaget, J. (1930). *The child's conception of physical causality*. New York: Harcourt, Brace & World. (Original work published in 1926.)

Piaget, J. (1951). *Play, dreams, and imitation in childhood*. New York: Norton.

Piaget, J. (1952). *The child's conception of number* (trans. C. Gattegno & F. M. Hodgson). London: Routledge & Paul.

Piaget, J. (1952a). *The origins of intelligence in children* (trans. M. Cook). New York: International Universities Press.

Piaget, J. (1952b). *The origins of intelligence in children*. New York: Norton.

Piaget, J. (1954a). *The origins of intelligence*. New York: Basic Books.

Piaget, J. (1954b). *The construction of reality in the child* (trans. M. Cook). New York: Basic Books.

Piaget, J. (1969). *The child's conception of time*. London: Routledge & Kegan Paul.

Piaget, J. (1970). *The child's conception of movement and speed*. London: Routledge & Kegan Paul.

Piaget, J. (1971). *Biology and knowledge* (trans. B. Walsh). Chicago: University of Chicago Press.

Piaget, J. (1985). *The equilibration of cognitive structures*. Chicago: University of Chicago Press.

Piaget, J., & Inhelder, B. (1948/1956). *The child's conception of space*. London: Routledge & Kegan Paul. (Original work published in 1948.)

Piaget, J., & Inhelder, B. (1974). *The child's construction of quantities: Conservation and atomism* (trans. A. J. Pomerans). London: Routledge & Kegan Paul.

Pinderhughes, E. E., Dodge, K. A., Bates, J. E., Pettit, G. S., & Zelli, A. (2000). Discipline responses: Influences of parents' socioeconomic status, ethnicity, beliefs about parenting, stress, and cognitive-emotional processes. *Journal of Family Psychology, 14*, 380–400.

Pinker, S. (1994). *The language instinct*. New York: William Morrow.

Pipe, M-E., Lamb, M. E., Orbach, Y., & Esplin, P. W. (2004). Recent research on children's testimony about experienced and witnessed events. *Developmental Review, 24*, 440–468.

Planned Parenthood (2006). *Pregnancy and childbearing among U.S. teens*. Retrieved May 26, 2006, from www.plannedparenthood.org/.

Pliszka, S. R. (2000). Patterns of psychiatric comorbidity with attention-deficit/hyperactivity disorder. *Child and Adolescent Psychiatric Clinics of North America, 9*, 525–540.

Plomin, R. (1986). *Development, genetics, and psychology*. Hillsdale, NJ: Erlbaum.

Plomin, R. (1990). *Nature and nurture: An introduction to behavioral genetics*. Pacific Grove, CA: Brooks/Cole.

Plomin, R., & DeFries, J. C. (1998). The genetics of cognitive abilities and disabilities. *Scientific American, 278*, 62–69.

Plomin, R., & McGuffin, P. (2003). Psychopathology in the postgenomic era. *Annual Review of Psychology, 54*, 205–228.

Plomin, R., DeFries, J. C., Craig, I. W., & McGuffin, P. (2003). *Behavioral genetics in the postgenomic era*. Washington, DC: APA.

Plomin, R., Emde, R. N., Braungart, J. M., Campos, J., Corley, R., et al. (1993). Genetic change and continuity from 14 to 20 months: The MacArthur Longitudinal Twin Study. *Child Development, 64, 1354–1376.*

Plomin, R., Owen, M. J., & McGuffin, P. (1994). The genetic basis of complex human behaviors. *Science, 264*, 1733–1739.

Pogarsky, G., Thornberry, T. P., & Lizotte, A. J. (2006). Developmental outcomes for children of young mothers. *Journal of Marriage & Family, 68*, 332–344.

Poland, G. A., Jacobson, R. M., Koutsky, L. A., Tamms, G. M., Railkar, R., Smith, J. F., Bryan, J. T., Cavanaugh, P. F., Jansen, K. U. & Barr, E. (2005). Immunogenicity and reactogenicity of a novel vaccine for human papillomavirus 16: A 2-year randomized controlled clinical trial. *Mayo Clinic Proceedings, 80*(5), 601–610.

Pollak, S. D., Vardi, S., Putzer Bechner, A. M., & Curtin, J. J. (2005). Physically abused children's regulation of attention in response to hostility. *Child Development, 76*, 968–977.

Pollatou, E., Karadimou, K., & Gerodimos, V. (2005). Gender differences in musical aptitude, rhythmic ability and motor performance in preschool children. *Early Child Development and Care, 175*(4), 361–369.

Posada, G., Carbonell, O. A., Alzate, G., & Plata, S. J. (2004). Through Columbian lenses: Ethnographic and conventional analyses of maternal care and their associations with secure base behavior. *Developmental Psychology, 40*, 508–518.

Posada, G., Jacobs, A., Richmond, M. K., Carbonell, O. A., Alzate, G., Bustamante, M. R., & Quiceno, J. (2002). Maternal caregiving and infant security in two cultures. *Developmental Psychology, 38*, 67–78.

Posner, M., Rothbart, M., & Sheese, B. (2007). Attention genes. *Developmental Science, 10*, 24–29.

Powlishta, K. K., Serbin, L. A., & Moller, L. C. (1993). The stability of individual differences in gender typing: Implications for understanding gender segregation. *Sex Roles, 29*, 723–737.

Pressley, M., & Afflerbach, P. (1995). *Verbal protocols of reading: The nature of constructively responsive reading*. Hillsdale, NJ: Erlbaum.

Pressley, M., & Hilden, K. (2006). Cognitive strategies. In D. Kuhn & R. S. Siegler (Eds.), *Cognitive, language, and perceptual develoment,* Vol. 2 (pp. 511–556), in W. Damon (Gen. Ed.), *Handbook of child psychology*. New York: Wiley.

Principal Killed at Wisconsin school; 9th-grader charged (2006, September 30). CNN.com. Retrieved October 14, 2006, from www.CNN.com.

Propper, C., Moore, G. A., Mills-Koonce, W. R., Halpern, C. T., Hill-Soderlund, A. L., Calkins, S. D., Carbone, M. A., & Cox, M. (2008). Gene-environment contributions to the development of infant vagal reactivity: The interaction of dopamine and maternal sensitivity. *Child Development, 79*, 1377–1394.

Pujol, J., Soriano-Mas, C., Ortiz, H., Sebastián-Gallés, N., Losilla, J.M., & Deus, J. (2006). Myelination of language-related areas in the developing brain. *Neurology, 66*, 339–343.

Putallez, M. (1983). Predicting children's sociometric status from their behavior. *Child Development, 54*, 1417–1426.

Quercia, N. (2005). Fragile X syndrome. *The Gale Encyclopedia of Genetic Disorders* (2nd ed., Vol. 1, pp. 472–475). Detroit, MI: Thomson Gale.

Quinn, P. C., Uttley, L., Lee, K., et al. (2008). Infant preference for female faces occurs for same–but not other–race faces. *Journal of Neuropsychology, 2*, 15–26.

Rabain-Jamin, J., & Wornham, W. L. (1993). Practices and representations of child care and motor development among West Africans in Paris. *Early Development and Parenting, 2*, 107–119.

Radelet, M. A., Lephart, S. M., Rubinstein, E. N., & Myers, J. B. (2002). Survey of the injury rate for children in community sports. *Pediatrics, 110*(3), e28. Retrieved June 22, 2006, from www.pediatrics.org/cgi/content/full/110/3/e28.

Raffaelli, M., & Crockett, L. J. (2003). Sexual risk taking in adolescence: The role of self-regulation and attraction to risk. *Developmental Psychology, 39*, 1036–1046.

Ramchand, R., Elliott, M., Mrug, S., Grunbaum, J., Windle, M., Chandra, A., et al. (2009). Substance use and delinquency among fifth graders who have jobs. *American Journal of Preventive Medicine, 36*, 297–303.

Ramey, C. T., & Ramey, S. L. (1992). Effective early intervention. *Intellectual Disability, 6*, 337–345.

Ramey, C. T., Campbell, F. A., & Blair, C. (1998). Enhancing the life course for high-risk children: Results from the Abecedarian Project. In J. Crane (Ed.), *Social programs that work* (pp. 163–183). New York: Russell Sage Foundation.

Ramey, S.L. (1999). Head Start and preschool education: Toward continued improvement. *American Psychologist, 54*, 344–346.

Rampey, B. D., Dion, G. S., and Donahue, P. L. (2009). *NAEP 2008 trends in academic progress* (NCES 2009-479). National Center for Education Statistics, Institute of Education Sciences, U.S. Department of Education, Washington, DC. Retrieved May 10, 2009, from nces.ed.gov/pubsearch/pubsinfo.asp?pubid=2009479.

Rauscher, F. H., Shaw, G. L., & Ky, K. N. (1993). Music and spatial task performance. *Nature, 365*, 611.

Rauscher, F. H., Shaw, G. L., & Ky, K. N. (1995). Listening to Mozart enhances spatial-temporal reasoning: Towards a neurophysiological basis. *Neuroscience Letters, 185*, 44–47.

Rauscher, F. H., Shaw, G. L., Levine, L. J., Wright, E. L., Dennis, W. R., & Newcomb, R. L. (1997). Music training causes long-term enhancement of preschool children's spatial-temporal reasoning. *Neurological Research, 19*, 2–8.

Redding, R. E. (2002). The impossibility of parental licensure. *American Psychologist, 57*, 987–988.

Reed, J. (1982). Black Americans in the 1980s. *Population Bulletin, 37*, 1–37.

Regalado, M., Sareen, H., Inkelas, M., Wissow, L. S., & Halfon, N. (2004). Parents' discipline of young children: Results from the National Survey of Early Childhood Health. *Pediatrics, 113*, 1952–1958.

Reitsma, P. (1983). Printed word learning in beginning readers. *Journal of Experimental Child Psychology, 36*, 321–339.

Reitsma, P. (1989). Orthographic memory and learning to read. In P. G. Aaron & R. M. Joshi (Eds.), *Reading and writing disorders in different orthographic systems* (pp. 51–73). The Hague, The Netherlands: Kluwer Academic.

Rempel, L. A., & Rempel, J. K. (2004). Partner influence on health behavior decision-making: Increasing breastfeeding duration. *Journal of Social and Personal Relationships, 21*, 92–111.

Renaissance Group (1999). Legal requirements: Children that learn together, learn to live together. Retrieved February 13, 2006, from www.uni.edu/coe/inclusion/legal/index.html.

Renniger, A., Hidi, S., & Krapp, A. (Eds.) (1992). *The role of interest in learning and development*. Hillsdale, NJ: Erlbaum.

Resnick, L. B., Levine, J. M., & Teasley, S. D. (Eds.). (1991). *Perspectives on socially shared cognition*. Washington, DC: American Psychological Association.

Reyna, V. F., & Brainerd, C. J. (1995). Fuzzy-trace theory: An interim synthesis. *Learning and Individual Differences, 7*, 1–75.

Reynolds, A. J. (2000). *Success in early intervention: The Chicago child–parent centers*. Lincoln: University of Nebraska Press.

Reynolds, A. J., & Robertson, D. L. (2003). School-based early intervention and later child maltreatment in the Chicago longitudinal study. *Child Development, 74*, 3–26.

Reynolds, A. J., Ou, S., & Topitzes, J. W. (2004). Paths of effects of early childhood intervention on educational attainment and delinquency: A confirmatory analysis of the Chicago child-parent centers. *Child Development, 75*, 1299–1328.

Reynolds, A. J., Temple, J. A., Robertson, D. L., & Mann, E. A. (2001). Long-term effects of an early childhood intervention on educational achievement and juvenile arrest: A 15-year follow-up of low-income children in public schools. *JAMA: Journal of the American Medical Association*, 285, 2339–2346.

Rhoades, K. A. (2008). Children's responses to interparental conflict: A meta-analysis of their associations with child adjustment. *Child Development, 79*, 1942–1956.

Richardson, K. & Norgate, S. H. (2006). A critical anlaysis of IQ studies of adopted children. *Human Development, 49*, 319–335.

Richardson, M. F., Meredith, W., & Abbot, D. A. (1993). Sex-typed role in male adolescent sexual abuse survivors. *Journal of Family Violence, 8*, 89–100.

Rickert, V. J., & Wiemann, C. M. (1998). Date rape among adolescents and young adults. *Journal of Peiatric Adolescent Gynecology, 11*, 167–175.

Rickert, V. I., Wiemann, C. M., Vaughan, R. D., & White, J. W. (2004). Rates and risk factors for sexual violence among an ethnically diverse sample of adolescents. *Archives of Pediatrics and Adolescent Medicine, 158*, 1132–1139.

Rideout, V. J., & Hamel, E. (2006). *The media family: Electronic media in the lives of infants, toddlers, preschoolers and their parents*. Menlo Park, CA: Kaiser Family Foundation.

Rideout, V., Roberts, D. F., & Foehr, U. G. (2005). *Generation M: Media in the lives of 8–18 year olds*. Menlo Park, CA: Kaiser Family Foundation. Accessed October 1, 2007, from www.kff.org/entmedia/ 7251.cfm.

Rieger, G., Linsenmeier, J. A. W., Gygax, L., & Bailey, J. M. (2008). Sexual orientation and childhood gender nonconformity: Evidence from home videos. *Developmental Psychology, 44*, 46–58.

Ripple, C. H., Gilliam, W. S., Chanana, N., & Zigler, E. (1999). Will fifty cooks spoil the broth? The debate over entrusting Head Start to the states. *American Psychologist, 54*, 327–343.

Rivera-Gaxiola, M., Silva-Pereyra, J., & Kuhl, P. (2005). Brain potentials to native and non-native speech contrasts in 7- and 11-month-old American infants. *Developmental Science*, *8*, 162–172.

Rivkin, M. J., Davis, P. E., Lemaster, J. L., Cabral, H. J., Warfield, S. K., Mulkern, R. V., Robson, C. D., Rose-Jacobs, R., & Frank, D. A. (2008). Volumetric MRI study of brain in children with intrauterine exposure to cocaine, alcohol, tobacco, and marijuana. *Pediatrics, 121*(4), 741–750.

Roberts, D. F., Foehr, U. G., & Rideout, V. (2005). *Generation M: Media in the lives of 8–18 year olds*. Menlo Park, CA: Kaiser Family Foundation. Retrieved May 10, 2009, from www.kff.org/entmedia/tv.cfm.

Roberts, D. F., Foehr, U. G., Rideout, V. J., & Brodie, M. (1999). *Kids and media @ the new millennium*. Menlo Park, CA: Kaiser Family Foundation.

Robinson, E. J., & Whitcombe, E. L. (2003). Children's suggestibility in relation to their understanding about sources of knowledge. *Child Development, 74*, 48–62.

Robinson, L. L., Buckley, J. D., Daigle, A. E., Wells, R., Benjamin, D., & Hammond, G. D. (1989). Maternal drug use and risk of childhood nonlymphoblastic leukemia among offspring: an epidemiologic investigation implicating marijuana (a report from the Children's Cancer Study Group). *Cancer, 63*, 1904–1911.

Roche, J. P., & Ramsbey, T. W. (1993). Premarital sexuality: A five-year follow-up study of attitudes and behavior by dating stage. *Adolescence, 28*, 67–80.

Rodd, J. M., Gaskell, M. G., & Marslen-Wilson, W. D. (2004). Modelling the effects of semantic ambiguity in word recognition. *Cognitive Science, 28*, 89–104.

Roebers, C. M. (2002). Confidence judgments in children's and adults' event recall and suggestibility. *Developmental Psychology, 38*, 1052–1067.

Roeser, R. W., & Eccles, J. S. (1998). Adolescents' perceptions of middle school: Relation to longitudinal changes in academic and psychological adjustment. *Journal of Research on Adolescence, 88*, 123–158.

Roeser, R. W., Midgley, C. M., & Urdan, T. C. (1996). Perceptions of the school psychological environment and early adolescents' psychological and behavioral functioning in school: The mediating role of goals and belonging. *Journal of Educational Psychology, 88*, 408–422.

Roffward, H., Muzio, J., Dement, W. (1966). Ontogenetic development of the human sleep-dream cycle. *Science, 152*, 604–619.

Rogers, T. T., & McClelland, J. L. (2004). *Semantic cognition: A parallel distributed processing approach*. Cambridge, MA: MIT Press.

Rogoff, B. (2003). *The cultural nature of human development*. London: Oxford University Press.

Rogoff, B., & Mistry, J. (1990). The social and functional context of children's remembering. In R. Fivush & J. A. Hudson (Eds.), *Knowing and remembering in young children* (pp. 197–222). Cambridge, England: Cambridge University Press.

Rogoff, B., Mistry, J., Göncü, A., & Mosier, C. (1993). Guided participation in cultural activity by toddlers and caregivers. *Monographs of the Society for Research in Child Development, 58* (8, Serial No. 236).

Roid, G. (2003). *Stanford-Binet Intelligence Scales, Fifth Edition*. Itasca, IL: Riverside.

Roisman, G. I., & Fraley, R. C. (2008). A behavior-genetic study of parenting quality, infant attachment security, and their covariation in a nationally representative sample. *Developmental Psychology, 44*, 831–839.

Roisman, G. I., Collins, W. A., & Sroufe, L. A. (2005). Predictors of young adults' representations of and behavior in their current romantic relationship: Prospective tests of the prototype hypothesis. *Attachment & Human Development, 7*(2), 105–121.

Romaine, S. (1984). *The language of children and adolescents—the acquisition of communicative competence*. New York: Blackwell.

Romaine, S. (1995). *Bilingualism* (2nd ed.). Oxford, England: Blackwell.

Rosario, M., Schrimshaw, E. W., & Hunter, J. (2008). Predicting different patterns of sexual identity development over time among lesbian, gay, and bisexual youth: A cluster analytic approach. *American Journal of Community Psychology, 42*, 266–282.

Rosario, M., Schrimshaw, E. W., Hunter, J, & Levy-Warren, A. (2009). The coming-out process of young lesbian and bisexual women: Are there butch/femme differences in sexual identity development? *Archives of Sexual Behavior, 38*, 34–49.

Rose, J. S., Medway, F. J., Cantrell, V. L., & Marus, S. H. (1983). A fresh look at the retention–promotion controversy. *Journal of School Psychology, 21*, 201–211.

Rose, R. J. (1995). Genes and human behavior. In J. T. Spence, J. M. Darley, & D. J. Foss (Eds.), *Annual review of psychology* (Vol. 46, pp. 625–654). Palo Alto, CA: Annual Reviews Inc.

Rose, S. A., & Ruff, H. A. (1987). Cross-modal abilities in human infants. In J. D. Osofsky (Ed.), *Handbook of infant development* (2nd ed., pp. 318–362). New York: John Wiley & Sons.

Rose, S. A., & Wallace, I. F. (1985). Cross-modal and intramodal transfer as predictors of mental development in fullterm and preterm infants. *Developmental Psychology, 21*, 949–962.

Rose, S. A., Feldman, J. F., & Jankowski, J. J. (2009). A cognitive approach to the development of early language. *Child Development, 80*, 134–150.

Rosenblith, J. R., & Sims-Knight, J. E. (1985). *In the beginning: Development in the first two years*. Belmont, CA: Brooks-Cole.

Rosenfeld, R. L., Lipton, R. B. & Drum, M. L. (2008). Thelarche, pubarche, and menarche attainment in children with normal and elevated body mass index. *Pediatrics, 123*, 84–88.

Rosenthal, R., & Jacobson, L. (1968). *Pygmalion in the classroom: Teacher expectation and pupils' intellectual development*. New York: Holt, Rinehart & Winston.

Rosick, E. (2005). Cystic fibrosis. *The Gale Encyclopedia of Genetic Disorders* (2nd ed., Vol. 1, pp. 315–322). Detroit, MI: Thomson Gale.

Ross, H. S. (1982). Establishment of social games among toddlers. *Developmental Psychology, 18*, 509–518.

Rossell, C. H., & Baker, K. (1996). The educational effectiveness of bilingual education. *Research in the Teaching of English, 30*, 7–74.

Roth, R. (2000). *Making women pay: The hidden costs of fetal rights*. Ithaca, NY: Cornell University Press.

Rothbart, M. K. (1981). Measurement of temperament in infancy. *Child Development, 52*, 569–578.

Rothbart, M. K. (2001). *Mary Rothbart's temperament laboratory at the University of Oregon*. Last accessed November 17, 2004, at www.uoregon.edu/~maryroth/.

Rothbart, M. K., & Bates, J. E. (1998). Temperament. In W. Damon & N. Eisenberg (Eds.), *Handbook of child psychology (Vol. 3): Social, emotional, and personality development* (pp. 105–176). New York: John Wiley & Sons, Inc.

Rothbart, M. K., Ahadi, S. A., & Hershey, K. L. (1994). Temperament and social behavior in childhood. *Merrill-Palmer Quarterly, 40*, 21–39.

Rothbart, M. K., Sheese, B. E., & Posner, M. I. (2007). Executive attention and effortful control: Linking temperament, brain networks, and genes. *Child Development Perspectives, 1*, 2–7.

Rothbaum, F., Weisz, J., Pott, M., Miyake, K., & Morelli, G. (2000). Attachment and culture: Security in the United States and Japan. *American Psychologist, 55*, 1093–1104.

Rovee-Collier, C., & Cuevas, K. (2009). Multiple memory systems are unnecessary to account for infant memory development: An ecological model. *Developmental Psychology, 45*(1), 160–174.

Rovee-Collier, C. K., & Gerhardstein, P. (1997). The development of infant memory. In N. Cowan & C. Hulme (Eds.), *The development of memory in childhood* (pp. 5-40). Hove East Sussex, UK: Psychology Press.

Rowe, D. C. (2003). Assessing genotype-environment interactions and correlations in the postgenomic era. In R. Plomin, J. C. Defries, I. W. Craig, & P. McGuffin (Eds.), *Behavioral genetics in the postgenomic era* (pp. 71–86). Washington, DC: APA.

Rubin, K. H., Bukowski, W. M., & Parker, J. G. (2006). Peer interactions, relationships, and groups. In N. Eisenberg (Vol. Ed.) and W. Damon and R. M. Lerner (Eds.), *Handbook of child psychology* (Vol. 3, 6th ed., pp. 571–645). New York: Wiley.

Rubin, K. H., Bukowski, W., & Parker, J. G. (1998). Peer interactions, relationships, and groups. In W. Damon (Ed.), *Handbook of child psychology* (Vol. 3, 5th ed., pp. 619–700). New York: Wiley.

Rubin, K. H., Burgess, K. B., Dwyer, K. M., & Hastings, P. D. (2003). Predicting preschoolers' externalizing behaviors from toddler temperament, conflict, and maternal negativity. *Developmental Psychology, 39*, 164–176.

Rubin, K. H., Lynch, D., Coplan, R., Rose-Krasnor, L., & Booth, C. L. (1994). "Birds of a feather . . .": Behavioral concordances and preferential personal attraction in children. *Child Development, 65*, 1778–1785.

Ruble, D. N., & Martin, C. L. (1998). Gender development. In W. Damon & N. Eisenberg (Eds.), *Handbook of child psychology: Vol. 3. Social, emotional, and personality development* (pp. 933–1016). New York: Wiley.

Ruble, D. N., & Martin, C. L., & Berenbaum, S. A. (2006). Gender development. In W. Damon & R. Lerner (Series Ed.) & N. Eisenberg (Vol. Ed.), *Handbook of child psychology: Vol. 3. Social, emotional, and personality development* (6th ed., pp. 858–932). New York: Wiley.

Ruff, H. A. (1984). Infants' manipulative exploration of objects: Basic cognitive processes and individual differences. In M. H. Bornstein & A. W. O'Reilly (Eds.), *The role of play in the development of thought* (pp. 5–15). San Francisco: Jossey-Bass.

Ruffman, T., Slade, L., & Crowe, E. (2002). The relation between children's and mothers' mental state language and theory-of-mind understanding. *Child Development, 73*, 734–751.

Rumelhart, D. E., & McClelland, J. L. (1986). On learning the past tenses of English verbs. In J. L. McClelland, D. E. Rumelhart, & and PDP Research Group, *Parallel distributed processing: Explorations in the microstructure of cognition, Vol. 2: Psychological and biological models* (pp. 216–271). Cambridge, MA: The MIT Press.

Rutter, M. (1987). Psychosocial resilience and protective mechanisms. *American Journal of Orthopsychiatry, 57*, 316–331.

Rutter, M. (2002). Nature, nurture, and development: From evangelism through science toward policy and practice. *Child Development, 73*, 1–21.

Rutter, M. (2006). *Genes and behavior: Nature-nurture interplay explained.* Malden, MA: Blackwell.

Rutter, M., & Sroufe, L. A. (2000). Developmental psychopathology: Concepts and challenges. *Development and Psychopathology, 12,* 265–296.

Rutter, M., Graham, P., Chadwick, R., Yule, W. (1976). Adolescent turmoil: Fact or fiction? *Journal of Child Psychology and Psychiatry, 17,* 35–56.

Ryan, R. M., Connell, J. P., & Grolnick, W. S. (1992). When achievement is not intrinsically motivated: A theory of self-regulation in school. In A. K. Boggiano & T. S. Pittman (Eds.), *Achievement and motivation: A social-developmental perspective* (pp. 167–188). New York: Cambridge University Press.

Saarni, C., Campos, J. J., Camras, L. A., & Witherington, D. (2006). Emotional development: Action, communication, and understanding. In N. Eisenberg (volume editor) and W. Damon and R. M. Lerner (Eds.), *Handbook of child psychology* (6th ed., Vol. 3, pp. 226–299). New York: John Wiley & Sons.

Saarni, C., Mumme, D. L., & Campos, J. J. (1998). Emotional development: Action, communication, and understanding. In W. Damon (Ed.), *Handbook of child psychology* (Vol. 3, pp. 237–309). New York: Wiley.

Sabia, J. (2009). School-year employment and academic performance of young adolescents. *Economics of Education Review, 28,* 268–276.

Sachs, J., & Devine, J. (1976). Young children's use of age-appropriate speech styles in social interaction and role-playing. *Journal of Child Language, 3,* 81–98.

Sachs, J., Bard, B., & Johnson, M. L. (1981). Language learning with restricted input: Case studies of two hearing children of deaf parents. *Applied Psycholinguistics, 2*(1), 33–54.

Sack, K. (1998, January 15). Georgia's governor seeks musical start for babies. *New York Times.* Retrieved September 17, 2000, from www.nytimes.com.

Safe Kids Worldwide (2007). Bicycle, rollerblade, and skateboard injuries. Washington, DC: Safe Kids Worldwide. Last accessed May 10, 2009, from www.usa.safekids.org/tier3_cd_2c.cfm?content_item_id=25251&folder_id=540.

Saffran, J. R., Werker, J. F., & Werner, L. A. (2006). The infant's auditory world: Hearing, speech, and the beginnings of language. In D. Kuhn & R.S. Siegler (Eds.), *Cognition, perception, and language,* Vol. 2 (pp. 58–108), in W. Damon & R. M. Lerner (Gen. Eds.), *Handbook of child psychology,* 6th ed. New York: John Wiley & Sons.

Sagi, A., & Hoffman, M. L. (1976). Empathetic distress in the newborn. *Developmental Psychology, 12,* 175–176.

Sagi, A., & Lewkowicz, K. S. (1987). A cross-cultural evaluation of attachment research. In L. W. C. Tavecchio & M. H. van IJzendoorn (Eds), *Attachment in social networks* (pp. 427–459). Amsterdam, The Netherlands: Elsevier.

Sagi, A., Lamb, M. E., Lewkowicz, K. S., Shoham, R., Dvir, R., & Estes, D. (1985). Security of infant-mother, -father, and metapelet attachments among kibbutz-reared Israeli children. In I. Bretherton & E. Waters (Eds.), *Growing points of attachment theory and research. Monographs of the Society for Research in Child Development, 50* (Serial No. 209), 257–275.

Sagi, A., van IJzendoorn, M. H., Aviezer, O., Donnell, F., & Mayseless, O. (1994). Sleeping out of home in a kibbutz communal arrangement: It makes a difference for infant–mother attachment. *Child Development, 65,* 992–1004.

Saito, L. T. (2003). *Ethnic identity and motivation: Socio-cultural factors in the educational achievement of Vietnamese American students.* Levittown, PA: LFB Scholarly.

Salahu-Din, D., Persky, H., & Miller, J. (2008). *The nation's report card: Writing 2007* (NCES 2008–468). National Center for Education Statistics, Institute of Education Sciences, U.S. Department of Education, Washington, DC. Retrieved May 10, 2009, from nces.ed.gov/pubsearch/pubsinfo.asp?pubid=2008468.

Salzinger, S., Kaplan, S., Pelcovitz, D., Samit, C., & Krieger, R. (1984). Parent and teacher assessment of children's behavior in child maltreating families. *Journal of the American Academy of Child Psychiatry, 23,* 458–464.

Samakoglu, S., Lisowski, L., Budak-Alpdogan, T., Usachenko, Y., Acuto, S., Di Marzo, R., et al. (2006). A genetic strategy to treat sickle cell anemia by coregulating globin transgene expression and RNA interference. *Nature Biotechnology, 24*(1), 89–94.

Sandler, I. N., Tein, J., Mehta, P., Wolchik, S., & Ayers, T. (2000). Coping efficacy and psychological problems of children of divorce. *Child Development, 71,* 1099–1118.

Santelli, J. S., Lowry, R., Brener, N. D., & Robin, L. (2000). The association of sexual behaviors with socioeconomic status, family structure, and race/ethnicity among US adolescents. *American Journal of Public Health, 90,* 1582–1588.

Santelli, J., Abma, J., Ventura, S., Lindberg, L., Morrow, B., Anderson, J. E., Lyss, S. & Hamilton, B. E. (2004). Can changes in sexual behaviors among high school students explain the decline in teen pregnancy rates in the 1990s? *Journal of Adolescent Health, 35,* 80–90.

Santelli, J., Ott, M. A., Lyon, M., Rogers, J. & Summers, D. (2006). Abstinence-only education policies and programs: A position paper of the Society for Adolescent Medicine. *Journal of Adolescent Health, 38,* 83–87.

Santos, D. C. C., Gabbard, C., & Goncalves, V. M. G. (2001). Motor development during the first year: A comparative study. *Journal of Genetic Psychology, 162,* 143–154.

Sattler, J. (1992). *Assessment of children* (3rd ed.). San Diego, CA: Jerome M. Sattler.

Sattler, J. (2001). *Assessment of children* (4th ed.). San Diego, CA: Jerome M. Sattler.

Saudino, K. J., & Plomin, R. (2007). Why are hyperactivity and academic achievement related? *Child Development, 78,* 972–986.

Saur, D., Baumgaertner, A., Moehring, A., Büchel, C., Bonnesen, M., Rose, M., et al. (2009). Word order processing in the bilingual brain. *Neuropsychologia, 47,* 158–168.

Savage-Rumbaugh, S., Shanker, S. G., & Taylor, T. J. (1998). *Apes, language, and the human mind.* Oxford, England: Oxford University Press.

Saville-Troike, M. (1986). Anthropological considerations in the study of communication. In O. L. Taylor (Ed.), *Nature of communication disorders in culturally and linguistically diverse populations* (pp. 47–72). San Diego, CA: College-Hill Press.

Savin-Williams, R. (1994). Verbal and physical abuse as stressors in the lives of lesbian, gay male, and bisexual youths: Associations school problems, running away, substance abuse, prostitution, and suicide. *Journal of Consulting and Clinical Psychology, 62,* 261–269.

Savin-Williams, R. C. & Diamond, L. M. (2004). Sex. In R. M. Lerner & L. Steinberg (Eds.), *Handbook of Adolescent Psychology,* 2nd ed. (pp. 189–231). Hoboken, NJ: Wiley.

Savin-Williams, R. C. (1995). An exploratory study of pubertal maturation timing and self-esteem among gay and bisexual male youths. *Developmental Psychology, 31,* 56–64.

Savin-Williams, R. C. (2006). Who's gay? Does it matter? *Current Directions in Psychological Science, 15I,* 40–44.

Savin-Williams, R. C., & Berndt, T. J. (1990). Friendship and peer relations. In S. S. Feldman & G. R. Elliott (Eds.), *At the threshold: The developing adolescent* (pp. 277–307). Cambridge, MA: Harvard University Press.

Savin-Williams, R. C., & Ream, G. L. (2007). Prevalence and stability of sexual orientation components during adolescence and young adulthood. *Archives of Sexual Behavior, 36,* 385–395.

Saxe, G. B. (1988). The mathematics of child street vendors. *Child Development, 59,* 1415–1425.

Saxton, M. (1997). The contrast theory of negative input. *Journal of Child Language, 24,* 139–161.

Saxton, M. (2000). Negative evidence and negative feedback: Immediate effects on the grammaticality of child speech. *First Language, 20* (60, Pt. 3), 221–252.

Scarr, S. (1985). Constructing psychology: Making facts and fables for our times. *American Psychologist, 40,* 499–512.

Scarr, S. (1992). Developmental theories for the 1990s: Development and individual differences. *Child Development, 63,* 1–19.

Scarr, S. (1999). Freedom of choice for poor families. *American Psychologist, 54,* 144.

Scarr, S. (2000). Toward voluntary parenthood. *Journal of Personality, 68,* 615–623.

Scarr, S., & McCartney, K. (1983). How people make their own environments: A theory of genotype-environment effects. *Child Development, 54,* 424–435.

Scarr, S., Weinberg, R. A., & Waldman, I. D. (1993). IQ correlations in transracial adoptive families. *Intelligence, 17,* 541–555.

Schall, B., Marlier, L., & Soussignan, R. (1998). Olfactory function in the human fetus: Evidence from selective neonatal responsiveness to the odor of amniotic fluid. *Behavioral Neuroscience, 112,* 1438–1449.

Schapiro, A., & McClelland, J. (2009). A connectionist model of a continuous developmental transition in the balance scale task. *Cognition, 110,* 395–411.

Schiefelbein, V. L., Sussman, E. J. & Dorn, L. D. (2005). Self-competence mediates earlier and later anxiety in adolescent mothers: A 3-year longitudinal perspective. *Journal of Research on Adolescence, 15*, 625–655.

Schlaggar, B., & McCandliss, B. (2007). Development of neural systems for reading. *Annual Review of Neuroscience, 30*, 475–503.

Schmidt-Hieber, C., Jonas, P., & Bischofberger, J. (2004). Enhanced synaptic plasticity in newly generated granule cells of the adult hippocampus. *Nature, 429* (May), 184–187.

Schneider, B. L., & Stevenson, D. (1999). *The ambitious generation: America's teenagers, motivated but directionless.* New Haven: Yale University Press.

Schneider, J. F. (2002). Relations among self-talk, self-consciousness, and self-knowledge. *Psychological Reports, 91*, 807–812.

Schneider, W. (1993). Acquiring expertise: Determinants of exceptional performance. In K. A. Keller, F. J. Monks, & A. H. Passow (Eds.), *International handbook of research on and development of giftedness and talent* (pp. 311–324). Oxford, UK: Pergamon Press.

Schneider, W., & Bjorklund, D. F. (1998). Memory. In W. Damon, D. Kuhn, & R. S. Siegler (Eds.), *Handbook of child psychology* (5th ed), *Vol. 2: Cognition, perception, and language* (pp. 467–521). New York: John Wiley & Sons.

Schneider, W., Gruber, H., Gold, A., & Opwis, K. (1993). Chess expertise and memory for chess positions in children and adults. *Journal of Experimental Child Psychology, 56*, 328–349.

Schum, T. R., Kolb, T. M., McAuliffe, T. L., Simms, M. D., Underhill, R. L., & Lewis, M. (2002). Sequential acquisition of toilet-training skills: A descriptive study of gender and age differences in normal children. *Pediatrics, 109*(3). Retrieved September 20, 2004, from www.pediatrics.org/cgi/content/full/109/3/e48.

Schunk, D. H., & Zimmerman, B. J. (1997). Social origins of self-regulatory competence. *Educational Psychologist, 32*, 195–208.

Schutzman, D. L., Frankenfield-Chernicoff, M., Clatterbaugh, H. E., & Singer, J. (1991). Incidence of intrauterine cocaine exposure in a suburban setting. *Pediatrics, 88*, 825–827.

Schwartz, D., Gorman, A. H., Nakamoto, J., & McKay, T. (2006). Popularity, social acceptance, and aggression in adolescent peer groups: Links with academic performance and school attendance. *Developmental Psychology, 42*, 1116–1127.

Schwartz, G. M., Izard, C. E., & Ansul, S. E. (1985). The 5-month-old's ability to discriminate facial expressions of emotion. *Infant Behavior and Development, 8*, 65–77.

Schweinhart, L. J., Barnes, H. V., & Weikart, D. P. (1993). *Significant benefits: The High/Scope Perry Preschool study through age 27* (Monographs of the High/Scope Educational Research Foundation, Number Ten). Ypsilanti, MI: The High/Scope Press.

Schweinhart, L. J., Montie, J., Xiang, Z., Barnett, W. S., Belfield, C. R., & Nores, M. (2005). *Lifetime effects: The High/Scope Perry Preschool study through age 40.* (Monographs of the High/Scope Educational Research Foundation, 14). Ypsilanti, MI: High/Scope Press.

Schweinle, A., & Wilcox, T. (2004). Intermodal perception and physical reasoning in young infants. *Infant Behavior and Development, 27*(2), 246–265.

Seidman, E., & French, S. E. (1997). Normative school transitions among urban adolescents: When, where, and how to intervene. In H. J. Walberg, O. Reyes, & R. P. Weissberg (Eds.), *Children and youth: Interdisciplinary perspectives* (pp. 166–189). Thousand Oaks, CA: Sage.

Sekizawa, A., Purwosunu, Y., Matsuoka, R., Koide, K., Okazaki, S., Farina, A., et al. (2007). Recent advances in non-invasive prenatal DNA diagnosis through analysis of maternal blood. *The Journal of Obstetrics and Gynaecology Research, 33*(6), 747–764.

Selman, R. L. (1976). Social-cognitive understanding: A guide to educational and clinical practices. In T. Likona (Ed.), *Moral development and behavior: Theory, research, and social issues* (pp. 299–316). New York: Holt, Rinehart, and Winston.

Selman, R. L. (1980). *The growth of interpersonal understanding.* New York: Academic Press.

Serbin, L. A., Cooperman, J. M., Peters, P. L., Lehoux, P. M., Stack, D. M., & Schwartzman, A. E. (1998). Intergenerational transfer of psychosocial risk in women with childhood histories of aggression, withdrawal, or aggression and withdrawal. *Developmental Psychology, 34*, 1246–1262.

Serbin, L. A., Moller, L. C., Gulko, J., Powlishta, K. K., & Colburne, K. A. (1994). The emergence of gender segregation in toddler playgroups. In C. Leaper (Ed.), *Childhood gender segregation: Causes and consequences. New directions for child development* (Vol. 65, pp. 7–17). San Francisco: Jossey-Bass.

Serbin, L. A., Moller, L. C., Gulko, J., Powlishta, K. K., & Colburne, K. A. (1994). The emergence of gender segregation in toddler playgroups. In W. Damon (Ed.), *New directions for child development* (No. 65, pp. 7–17). San Francisco: Jossey-Bass.

Sexton, J., & Swarns, R. L. (1997, November 15). Pictures of Sabrina: A special report. A slide into peril, with no one to catch her. *New York Times.* Retrieved August 2, 2002, from www.nytimes.com.

Sharma, A. R., McGue, M. K., & Benson, P. L. (1996). The emotional and behavioral adjustment of United States adopted adolescents: I. A comparison study. *Children and Youth Services Review, 18*, 77–94.

Sharma, A. R., McGue, M. K., & Benson, P. L. (1998). The psychological adjustment of United States adopted adolescents and their nonadopted siblings. *Child Development, 69*, 791–802.

Sheese, B., Voelker, P., Rothbart, M., & Posner, M. (2007). Parenting quality interacts with genetic variation in dopamine receptor D4 to influence temperament in early childhood. *Development and Psychopathology, 19*, 1039–1046.

Shen, C. (2001). Social values associated with cross-national differences in mathematics and science achievement: A cross-national analysis. *Assessment in Education, 8*, 193–223.

Sherman, K., Lapidus, G., Gelven, E. & Banco, L. (2004). New teen drivers and their parents: What they know and what they expect. *American Journal of Health Behavior, 28*, 387–396.

Shonkoff, J. P., & Phillips, D. A. (2000). *From neurons to neighborhoods: The science of early childhood development.* Washington, DC: National Academy Press.

Shurkin, J. N. (1992). *Terman's kids: The groundbreaking study of how the gifted grow up.* Boston: Little, Brown and Company.

Shweder, R. A., Much, N. C., Mahapatra, M., & Park, L. (1997). The "Big Three" of morality (autonomy, community, and divinity) and the "Big Three" explanations of suffering. In A. Brandt & P. Rozin (Eds.), *Morality and health* (pp. 119–169). Stanford: Stanford University Press.

Sickle cell anemia. (2008). Retrieved November 25, 2008, from http://www. mayoclinic.com.

Siega-Riz, A. M., Cavadini, C. & Popkin, B. M. (2001). U.S. teens and the nutrient contribution and differences of their selected meal patterns. *Family Economics & Nutrition Review, 13*, 15–26.

Siegel, D. (2006). The effects of physical activity on the health and well-being of youths. *JOPERD: The Journal of Physical Education, Recreation & Dance, 77*, 11.

Siegler, R. (2007). Cognitive variability. *Developmental Science, 10*, 104–109.

Siegler, R. S. (1995). Children's thinking: How does change occur. In W. Schneider & F. E. Weinert (Eds.), *Memory performance and competencies: Issues in growth and development* (pp. 405–430). Hillsdale, NJ: Erlbaum.

Siegler, R. S. (1998). *Children's thinking* (3rd ed). Upper Saddle River, NJ: Prentice Hall.

Siegler, R. S. (2006). Microgenetic analyses of learning. In D. Kuhn & R. S. Siegler (Eds.), *Cognitive, language, and perceptual develoment,* Vol. 2 (pp. 464–510), in W. Damon (Gen. Ed.), *Handbook of child psychology.* New York: Wiley.

Siegler, R. S., & Jenkins, E. (1989). *How children discover strategies.* Hillsdale, NJ: Erlbaum.

Siegler, R. S., & Shipley, C. (1995). Variation, selection, and cognitive change. In T. Simon & G. Halford (Eds.), *Developing cognitive competence: New approaches to process modeling* (pp. 31–76). Hillsdale, NJ: Erlbaum.

Signorella, M. L., Bigler, R. S., & Liben, L. S. (1993). Developmental differences in children's gender schemata about others: A meta-analytic review. *Developmental Review, 13*, 147–183.

Signorielli, N. (2001). Television's gender role images and contribution to stereotyping: Past, present, and future. In D. G. Singer & J. L. Singer (Eds.), *Handbook of children and the media* (pp. 341–358). Thousand Oaks, CA: Sage.

Silverman, A. R., & Feigelman, W. (1990). Adjustment in interracial adoptees: An overview. In D. M. Brodzinsky & M. D. Schechter (Eds.), *The psychology of adoption* (pp. 187–200). New York: Oxford University Press.

Simmons, R. G., & Blyth, D. A. (1987). *Moving into adolescence: The impact of pubertal change and school context.* New York: Aldine De Gruyter.

Simner, M. L. (1971). Newborn's response to the cry of another infant. *Developmental Psychology, 5*, 136–150.

Simon, T., & Klahr, D. (1995). A theory of children's learning about number conservation. In T. Simon & G. Halford (Eds.), *Developing cognitive competence: New approaches to process modeling* (pp. 315–354). Hillsdale, NJ: Erlbaum.

Simons-Morton, B. G., Hartos, J. L., Leaf, W. A. & Preusser, D. F. (2005). Persistence of effects of the checkpoints program on parental restrictions of teen driving privileges. *American Journal of Public Health, 95,* 447–452.

Singer, L. T., Arendt, R., Minnes, S., Farkas, K., Salvator, A., Kirchner, H. L., et al. (2002). Cognitive and motor outcomes of cocaine-exposed infants. *Journal of the American Medical Association, 287,* 1952–1959.

Siok, W., Niu, Z., Jin, Z., Perfetti, C., & Tan, L. (2008). A structural–functional basis for dyslexia in the cortex of Chinese readers. *Proceedings of the National Academy of Sciences of the United States of America, 105,* 5561–5566.

Skiba, R. J., & Knesting, K. (2001). Zero tolerance, zero evidence: An analysis of school disciplinary practice. In R. J. Skiba & G. G. Noam (Eds.), *Zero tolerance: Can suspension and expulsion keep schools safe?* (pp. 17–43). San Francisco: Jossey-Bass.

Skiba, R. J., Knesting, K., & Bush, L. D. (2002). Culturally competent assessment: More than unbiased tests. *Journal of Child and Family Studies, 11,* 61–78.

Skinner, B. F. (1957). *Verbal behavior.* Englewood Cliffs, NJ: Prentice Hall.

Slaby, R. G., & Frey, K. S. (1975). Development of gender constancy and selective attention to same-sex models. *Child Development, 46,* 849–856.

Slater, A. (1997). Can measures of infant habituation predict later intellectual ability? *Archives of Disease in Childhood,* 77, 474–476. Retrieved June 12, 2006, from adc.bmjjournals.com/cgi/content/full/77/6/474.

Slavin, R. E. (1990). Achievement effects of ability grouping in secondary schools: A best-evidence synthesis. *Review of Education Research, 60,* 471–499.

Slavin, R. E. (1995). *Cooperative learning* (2nd ed.). Boston: Allyn & Bacon.

Slavin, R., & Lake, C. (2008). Effective programs in elementary mathematics: A best-evidence synthesis. *Review of Educational Research, 78,* 427–515.

Slavin, R., Cheung, A., Groff, C., & Lake, C. (2008). Effective reading programs for middle and high schools: A best-evidence synthesis. *Reading Research Quarterly, 43,* 290–322.

Slobin, D. I. (1979). *Psycholinguistics.* Glenview, IL: Scott, Foresman.

Slobin, D. I. (1982). Universal and particular in the acquisiton of language. In E. Wanner & L. Gleitman (Eds.) *Language acquistion: The state of the art* (pp. 128–170). Cambridge, UK: Cambridge University Press.

Slobin, D. I. (1985a). *The crosslinguistic study of language acquisition: Vol. 1. The data.* Hillsdale, NJ: Erlbaum.

Slobin, D. I. (1985b). Crosslinguistic evidence for the language-making capacity. In D. I. Slobin (Ed.), *The crosslinguistic study of language acquisition: Vol. 2. Theoretical issues.* (pp. 1157–1249). Hillsdale, NJ: Erlbaum.

Smith, A. C., & Smith, D. I. (2001). *Emergency and transitional shelter population: 2000.* U.S. Census Bureau, Census Special Reports, Series CENSR/01–2. Washington, DC: U.S. Government Printing Office.

Smith, J., Coggins, C., & Cardoso, J. (2008). Best practices for English language learners in Massachusetts: Five years after the Question 2 mandate. *Equity & Excellence in Education, 41*(3), 293–310.

Smith, J. C. (2001). *Rett syndrome in boys.* Accessed March 1, 2002, from www.rettsyndrome.org.

Smith, P. K., & Noble, R. (1987). Factors affecting the development of caregiver–infant relationships. In L. W. C. Tavecchio & M. H. van IJzendoorn (Eds.), *Attachment in social networks* (pp. 93–134). Amsterdam, The Netherlands: Elsevier.

SmithBathe, L. (2005). Examining assumptions about teen mothers. *American Journal of Nursing, 105,* 13.

Smollar, J., & Youniss, J. (1982). Social development through friendship. In K. H. Rubin & H. S. Ross (Eds.), *Peer relationships and social skills in childhood* (pp. 279–298). New York: Springer.

Snarey, J. R. (1995). In a communitarian voice: The sociobiological expansion of Kohlbergian theory, research, and practice. In W. M. Kurtines & J. L. Gerwirtz (Eds.), *Moral development: An introduction* (pp. 109–134). Boston: Allyn & Bacon.

Snarey, J. R., Reimer, J., & Kohlberg, L. (1985). The development of social-moral reasoning among kibbutz adolescents: A longitudinal cross-cultural study. *Developmental Psychology, 20,* 3–17.

Snow, C. (1972). Mother's speech to children learning language. *Child Development, 43,* 549—565.

Snow, C. E. (1987). Relevance of the notion of a critical period to language acquisition. In M. Bornstein (Ed.), *Sensitive periods in development: An interdisciplinary perspective* (pp. 183–209). Hillsdale, NJ: Erlbaum.

Snow, C. E., & Kang, J. Y. (2006). Becoming bilingual, biliterate, and bicultural. In K. A. Renninger & I. E. Sigel (Vol. Eds.) and W. Damon & R. M. Lerner (Eds.-in-chief), *Handbook of child psychology* (6th ed., Vol. 1, pp. 75–102). Hoboken, NJ: Wiley.

Snow, R. E. (1995). Pygmalion and intelligence. *Current Directions in Psychological Science, 4,* 169–171.

Snyder, T. D., Dillow, S. A., and Hoffman, C. M. (2009). *Digest of education statistics 2008* (NCES 2009-020). National Center for Education Statistics, Institute of Education Sciences, U.S. Department of Education. Washington, DC. Retrieved May 2, 2009, from nces.ed.gov/pubsearch/pubsinfo.asp?pubid=2009020.

Society for Research in Child Development. www.srcd.org/index.php?option=com_content&task=view&id=68&Itemid=499.

Socolar, R. R. S., Savage, E., & Evans, H. (2007). A longitudinal study of parental discipline of young children. *Southern Medical Journal, 100,* 472–477.

Sokol, R. J., Delaney-Black, V., Nordstrom, B. (2003). Fetal alcohol spectrum disorder. *Journal of the American Medical Association, 290,* 2996–2999.

Sorce, J. F., Emde, R. N., Campos, J., & Klinnert, M. D. (1985). Maternal emotional signaling: Its effect on the visual cliff behavior of 1-year-olds. *Developmental Psychology, 21,* 195–200.

Spear, L. P. (2000). The adolescent brain and age-related behavioral manifestations. *Neuroscience & Biobehavioral Reviews, 24,* 417–463.

Spearman, C. (1904). General intelligence, objectively determined and measured. *American Journal of Psychology, 15,* 201–293.

Spearman, C. (1923). *The nature of "intelligence" and the principles of cognition.* London: Macmillan.

Spearman, C. (1927). *The abilities of man.* New York: Macmillan.

Spelke, E. S. (1979). Perceiving bimodally specified events in infancy. *Developmental Psychology, 15,* 626–636.

Spelke, E. S. (1991). Physical knowledge in infancy: Reflections on Piaget's theory. In S. Carey & R. Gelman (Eds.), *The epigenesis of mind* (pp. 133–169). Hillsdale, NJ: Erlbaum.

Spencer, M. B., & Dornbusch, S. M. (1990). Challenges in studying minority youth. In S. S. Feldman & G. R. Elliott (Eds.), *At the threshold: The developing adolescent* (pp. 123–146). Cambridge, MA: Harvard University Press.

Spinrad, T. L., Eisenberg, N., Harris, E., Hanish, L., Fabes, R. A., Kupanoff, K., Ringwald, S., & Holmes, J. (2004). The relation of children's everyday nonsocial peer play behavior to their emotionality, regulation, and social functioning. *Developmental Psychology, 40,* 67–80.

Spira, E. G., Bracken, S. S., & Fischel, J. E. (2005). Predicting improvement after first-grade reading difficulties: The effects of oral language, emergent literacy, and behavior skills. *Developmental Psychology, 41,* 225–234.

Spivey, N. N., & King, J. R. (1989). Readers as writers composing from sources. *Reading Research Quarterly, 24,* 7–26.

Spreng, R., Mar, R., & Kim, A. (2009). The common neural basis of autobiographical memory, prospection, navigation, theory of mind, and the default mode: A quantitative meta-analysis. *Journal of Cognitive Neuroscience, 21*(3), 489–510.

Sroufe, L. A., Egeland, B, Carlson, E. A., & Collins, W. A. (2005). *The development of the person: The Minnesota study of risk and adaptation from birth to adulthood.* New York: Guilford Press.

Sroufe, L. A., Egeland, B., & Carlson, E. (2005). Placing early attachment experiences in developmental context: The Minnesota longitudinal study. In K. E. Grossmann, K. Grossmann, & E. Waters (Eds.), *Attachment from infancy to adulthood: The major longitudinal studies* (pp. 48–70). New York: Guildford Publications, Inc.

Stack, D. M., Serbin, L. A. Schwartzman, A. E., & Ledingham, J. (2005). Girls' aggression across the life course: Long-term outcomes and intergenerational risk. In D. J. Pepler, K. C. Madsen, C. Webster, & K. S. Levene (Eds.), *The development and treatment of girlhood aggression* (pp. 253–283). Mahwah, NJ: Erlbaum.

Stadtler, A. C., Gorski, P. A., & Brazelton, T. B. (1999). Toilet training methods, clinical interventions, and recommendations. *Pediatrics, 103*(6), 1359–1361.

Staff, J., & Mortimer, J. (2008). Social class background and the school-to-work transition. *New Directions for Child & Adolescent Development, 119,* 55–69.

Staff, J., Mortimer, J. T., & Uggen, C. (2004). Work and leisure in adolescence (pp. 429–450). In R. M. Lerner & L. Steinberg (Eds.), *Handbook of adolescent psychology* (2nd ed.), Hoboken, NJ: John Wiley & Sons, Inc.

Stams, G. J. M., Juffer, F., Rispens, J., & Hoksbergen, R. A. C. (2000). The development and adjustment of 7-year-old children adopted in infancy. *Journal of Child Psychology & Psychiatry, 41*, 1025–1037.

Standley, K., Soule, B., & Copans, S. (1979). Dimensions of prenatal anxiety and their influence on pregnancy outcome. *American Journal of Obstetrics and Gynecology, 135*, 22–26.

Stark, R., Bernstein, L., & Demorest, M. (1993). Vocal communication in the first 18 months of life. *Journal of Speech and Hearing Research, 36*, 548–558.

Starkey, P., Spelke, E. S., & Gelman, R. (1983). Detection of intermodal numerical correspondences by human infants. *Science, 222*, 179–181.

Starr, C., & Taggart, R. (1998). *Biology: The unity and diversity of life.* Belmont, CA: Wadsworth.

Stechler, G., & Halton, A. (1982). Prenatal influences on human development. In B. B. Wolman (Ed.), *Handbook of developmental psychology* (pp. 175–189). Englewood Cliffs, NJ: Prentice-Hall.

Steele, C. M., & Aronson, J. (1995). Stereotype threat and the intellectual test performance of African Americans. *Journal of Personality & Social Psychology, 69*, 797–811.

Steele, K. M., Bass, K. E., & Crook, M. D. (1999). The mystery of the Mozart effect: Failure to replicate. *Psychological Science, 10*, 366–369.

Steinberg, L. (2001). We know some things: Parent-adolescent relationships in retrospect and prospect. *Journal of Research on Adolescence, 11*, 1–19.

Steinberg, L. (2005). *Adolescence* (7th ed.). Boston, MA: McGraw Hill.

Steinberg, L. (2008). A social neuroscience perspective on adolescent risk-taking. *Developmental Review, 28*, 78–106.

Steinberg, L., & Scott, E. S. (2003). Less guilty by reason of adolescence: Developmental immaturity, diminished responsibility, and the juvenile death penalty. *American Psychologist, 58*, 1009–1018.

Steiner, J. E. (1979). Human facial expressions in response to taste and smell stimulation. In H. Reese & L. Lipsitt (Eds.), *Advances in child development and behavior* (Vol. 13, pp. 257–295). New York: Academic Press.

Stennes, L. M., Burch, M. M., Sen, M. G., & Bauer, P. J. (2005). A longitudinal study of gendered vocabulary and communicative action in young children. *Developmental Psychology, 41*, 75–88.

Stern, E. (1993). What makes certain arithmetic word problems involving comparison of sets so difficult for children? *Journal of Educational Psychology, 85*, 7–23.

Sternberg, R. J. & Grigorenko, E. L. (2002). *Dynamic testing: The nature and measurement of learning potential.* Cambridge, UK: Cambridge University Press.

Sternberg, R. J. (1985). *Beyond IQ: A triarchic theory of human intelligence.* Cambridge, England: Cambridge University Press.

Sternberg, R. J. (1988). *The triarchic mind: A new theory of human intelligence.* New York: Viking.

Sternberg, R. J. (1999). The theory of successful intelligence. *Review of General Psychology, 3*, 292–316.

Sternberg, R. J. (2007). Cultural dimensions of giftedness and talent. *Roeper Review, 29*, 160–165.

Sternberg, R. J., & Grigorenko, E. L. (2006). Cultural intelligence and successful intelligence. *Group & Organizational Management, 31*, 27–39.

Stevenson, H. W., & Lee, S. (1990). Contexts of achievement: A study of American, Chinese, and Japanese children. *Monographs of the Society for Research in Child Development, 55*(1–2, Serial No. 221).

Stevenson, J. (1992). Evidence for genetic etiology in hyperactivity in children. *Behavior Genetics, 22*(3), 337–344.

Steward, M. S., & Steward, D. S. (1996). Interviewing young children about body touch and handling. *Monographs of the Society for Research in Child Development, 61* (Serial No. 248).

Stewart, S. L., & Rubin, K. H. (1995). The social problem-solving skills of anxious–withdrawn children. *Development and Psychopathology, 7*, 323–336.

Stice, E., & Whitenton, K. (2002). Risk factors for body dissatisfaction in adolescent girls: A longitudinal investigation. *Developmental Psychology, 38*(5), 669–678.

Stice, E., Presnell, K., & Bearman, S. K. (2001). Relation of early menarche to depression, eating disorders, substance abuse, and comorbid psychopathology among adolescent girls. *Developmental Psychology, 37*(5), 608–619.

Stien, P. T., & Kendall, J. (2004). *Psychological trauma and the developing brain.* New York: The Haworth Press, Inc.

Stiles, J., & Thal, D. (1993). Linguistic and spatial cognitive development following early focal brain injury: Patterns of deficit and recovery. In M. Johnson (Ed.), *Brain development and cognition: A reader* (pp. 272–291). Oxford: Blackwell Publishers.

Stiles, J., Reilly, J., Paul, B., & Moses, P. (2005). Cognitive development following early brain injury: Evidence for neural adaptation. *Trends in Cognitive Sciences, 9*(3), 136–143.

Stillion, J. M., & McDowell, E. E. (1996). *Suicide across the life span* (2nd ed.). Washington, DC: Taylor & Francis.

Stipek, D. (2002). At what age should children enter kindergarten? A question for policy makers and parents. *SRCD Social Policy Report, 16*(2). Accessed October 1, 2007, from srcd.org/documents/publications/SPR/spr16-2.pdf.

Stipek, D., Recchia, S., & McClintic, S. (1992). Self-evaluation in young children. *Monographs of the Society for Research in Child Development, 57* (1, Serial No. 226).

Stipek, D. J., & Ryan, R. H. (1997). Economically disadvantaged preschoolers: Ready to learn but further to go. *Developmental Psychology, 33*, 711–723.

Stoddart, T., & Turiel, E. (1985). Children's concepts of cross-gender activities. *Child Development, 56*, 1241–1252.

Stoel-Gammon, C., & Otomo, K. (1986). Babbling development of hearing-impaired and normally hearing subjects. *Journal of Speech and Hearing Disorders, 51*, 33–41.

Stoiber, K. C., & McIntyre, H. (2006). Adolescent pregnancy and parenting. In G. G. Bear & K. M. Minke (Eds.), *Children's needs III: Development, prevention, and intervention* (pp. 705–719). Washington, DC: National Association of School Psychologists.

Strattman, K., & Hodson, B. W. (2005). Variables that influence decoding and spelling in beginning readers. *Child Language Teaching & Therapy, 21*, 165–191.

Straus, M. A. (1994). *Beating the devil out of them: Corporal punishment in American families.* New York: Lexington Books.

Straus, M. A. (2008). The special issue on prevention of violence ignores the primordial violence. *Journal of Interpersonal Violence, 23*(9), 1314–1320.

Straus, M. A., & Stewart, J. H. (1999). Corporal punishment by American parents: National data on prevalence, chronicity, severity, and duration, in relation to child and family characteristics. *Clinical Child and Family Psychology Review, 2*, 55–70.

Straus, M. A., Sugarman, D. B., & Giles-Sims, J. (1997). Spanking by parents and subsequent antisocial behavior of children. *Archives of Pediatric and Adolescent Medicine, 151*, 761–767.

Stright, A. D., Gallagher, K. C., & Kelley, K. (2008). Infant temperament moderates relations between maternal parenting in early childhood and children's adjustment in first grade. *Child Development, 79*, 186–200.

Subrahmanyam, K., Kraut, R., Greenfield, P., & Gross, E. (2001). New forms of electronic media. In D. G. Singer & J. L. Singer (Eds.), *Handbook of children and the media* (pp. 73–99). Thousand Oaks, CA: Sage.

Substance Abuse and Mental Health Services Administration, Office of Applied Studies (May 13, 2008). *The NSDUH report—major depressive episode among youths aged 12 to 17 in the United States: 2004 to 2006.* Rockville, MD. Retrieved April 25, 2009, from oas.samhsa.gov/2k8/youthDepress/youthDepress.htm.

Sullivan, A. (2000, July 23). The way we live now: 7-23-00: Counter culture; promotion of the fittest. *The New York Times.* Retrieved February 15, 2002, from www.nytimes.com.

Sullivan, H. S. (1953). *The interpersonal theory of psychiatry.* New York: Norton.

Sullivan, K., & Wimmer, E. (1993). Three-year-olds' understanding of mental states: The influence of trickery. *Journal of Experimental Child Psychology, 56*, 135–148.

Sullivan, P. F. (1995). Mortality in anorexia nervosa. *American Journal of Psychiatry, 152*, 1073–1074.

Summerfield, J., Hassabis, D., & Maguire, E. (2009). Cortical midline involvement in autobiographical memory. *NeuroImage, 44*(3), 1188–1200.

Sun, S. S., Schubert, C. M., Liang, R., Roche, A. F., Kulin, H. E., Lee, P. A., Himes, J. H., & Chumlea, W. C. (2005). Is sexual maturity occurring earlier among U.S. children? *Journal of Adolescent Health, 37*, 345–355.

Sun, Y., & Li, Y. (2002). Children's well-being during parents' marital disruption process: A pooled time-series analysis. *Journal of Marriage and Family, 64*, 472–488.

Super, C. (1976). Environmental effects on motor development: The case of "African infant precocity." *Developmental Medicine and Child Neurology, 18*, 561–567.

Super, D. E. (1957). *The psychology of careers: An introduction to vocational development*. New York: Harper.

Sussman, E. J., & Rogol, A. (2004). Puberty and psychological development. In R. M. Lerner & L. S. Steinberg (Eds.), *Handbook of adolescent psychology* (2nd ed.), pp. 15–44. Hoboken, NJ: John Wiley & Sons, Inc.

Suttle, C. M., Banks, M. S., & Graf, E. W. (2002). FPL and sweep VEP to tritan stimuli in young human infants. *Vision Research, 42*(26), 2879–2891.

Svoboda, E., & Levine, B. (2009). The effects of rehearsal on the functional neuroanatomy of episodic autobiographical and semantic remembering: A functional magnetic resonance imaging study. *Journal of Neuroscience, 29*(10), 3073–3082.

Swaab, D. F., Gooren, L. J. G., & Hofman, M. A. (1995). Brain research, gender, and sexual orientation. *Journal of Homosexuality, 28*, 283–301.

Swanson, H. L., & Lussier, C. M. (2001). A selective synthesis of the experimental literature on dynamic assessment. *Review of Educational Research, 71*, 321–349.

Swanson, H. L., & Beebe-Frankenberger, M. (2004). The relationship between working memory and mathematical problem solving in children at risk and not at risk for serious math difficulties. *Journal of Educational Psychology, 96*, 471–491.

Swarns, R. L. (1999, January 30). Children go to foster care needlessly, suit charges. *The New York Times*. Retrieved August 2, 2002, from www.ntimes.com.

Szeverenyi, P., Hetey, A., Kovacsne, Z. T., & Muennich, A. (1995). Does the father's presence at delivery have an influence on the parental judgment of the father–child relationship? *Magyar Pszichologiai Szemle, 51*, 83–95.

TADS Team (2007). The treatment for adolescents with depression study (TADS): Long-term effectiveness and safety outcomes. *Archives of General Psychiatry, 64*, 1132–1144.

Tager-Flusberg, H., Boshart, J., & Baron-Cohen, S. (1999). Reading the windows to the soul: Evidence of domain-specific sparing in Williams syndrome. *Journal of Cognitive Neuroscience, 10*, 631–639.

Takahashi, K. (1986). Examining the Strange-Situation procedure with Japanese mothers and 12-month-old infants. *Developmental Psychology, 22*, 265–270.

Takahashi, K. (1990). Are the key assumptions of the "Strange Situation" procedure universal? A view from Japanese research. *Human Development, 33*, 23–30.

Takanishi, R., & Bogard, K.L. (2007). Effective educational programs for young children: What we need to know. *Child Development Perspectives, 1*, 40–45.

Takeuchi, M. (1994). Children's play in Japan. In J. L. Roopnarine, J. E. Johnson, & F. H. Hooper (Eds.), *Children's play in diverse cultures* (pp. 51–72). Albany: State University of New York Press.

Tanner, J. M. (1978). *Fetus into man: Physical growth from conception to maturity*. Cambridge, MA: Harvard University Press.

Tanner, J. M. (1991). Menarche, secular trend in age of. In R. M. Lerner, A. C. Petersen, & J. Brooks-Gunn (Eds.), *Encyclopedia of adolescence* (Vol. 2, pp. 637–641). New York: Garland Publishing, Inc.

Tapert, S. F., Caldwell, L. & Burke, C. (2004/2005).Alcohol and the adolescent brain. *Alcohol Research & Health, 28*, 205–212.

Tarullo, A. R., & Gunnar, M. R. (2006). Child maltreatment and the developing HPA axis. *Hormones and Behavior, 50*, 632–639.

Tasbihsazan, R., Nettelbeck, T., & Kirby, N. (2003). Predictive validity of the Fagan Test of Infant Intelligence. *British Journal of Developmental Psychology, 21*, 585–597.

Taylor, M., & Hort, B. (1990). Can children be trained in making the distinction between appearance and reality? *Child Development, 5*, 89–99.

Taylor, N., Donovan, W., & Leavitt, L. (2008). Consistency in infant sleeping arrangements and mother-infant interaction. *Infant Mental Health Journal, 29*(2), 77–94.

Taylor, O. L. (1986). *Nature of communication disorders in culturally and linguistically diverse populations*. San Diego, CA: College-Hill Press.

Taylor, R., & Richards, S. (1991). Patterns of intellectual differences of black, Hispanic, and white children. *Psychology in the Schools, 28*, 5–9.

Teeter, P. A., & Semrud-Clikeman, M. (1997). *Child neuropsychology: assessment and interventions for neurodevelopmental disorders*. Boston: Allyn & Bacon.

Teicher, M. H. (2002). Scars that won't heal: The neurobiology of child abuse. *Scientific American, 286*(3), 68–75.

Tergerson, J. L., & King, K. A. (2002). Do perceived cues, benefits, and barriers to physical activity differ between male and female adolescents? *Journal of School Health, 72*, 374–380.

Terman, L. M. (1925). *Genetic studies of genius, Vol. 1: Mental and physical traits of a thousand gifted children*. Stanford, CA: Stanford University Press.

Terrace, H. S., Petitto, L. A., Sanders, R. J., & Bever, T. G. (1980). On the grammatical capacity of apes. In K. E. Nelson (Ed.), *Children's language*. New York: Gardner Press.

Thapar, A., Fowler, T., & Rice, F. (2003). Maternal smoking during pregnancy and Attention Deficit Hyperactivity Disorder symptoms in offspring. *American Journal of Psychiatry, 160*, 1985–1989.

Thelen, E. (1989). The (re)discovery of motor development: Learning new things from an old field. *Developmental Psychology, 25*, 946–949.

Thelen, E., & Smith, L. B. (2006). Dynamic systems theories. In W. Damon & R. M. Lerner (Series Eds.) & R. M. Lerner (Vol. Ed.), *Handbook of child psychology: Vol. 1. Theoretical models of human development* (6th ed., pp. 258–312). Hoboken, NJ: Wiley.

Thelen, E., Fisher, D. M., & Ridley-Johnson, R. (1984). The relationship between physical growth and a newborn reflex. *Infant Behavior and Development, 7*, 479–493.

Thiessen, E. D., Hill, E. A., & Saffran, J. R. (2005). Infant-directed speech facilitates word segmentation. *Infancy, 7*(1), 53–71.

Thomas, A., & Chess, S. (1977). *Temperament and development*. New York: Brunner/Mazel.

Thomas, M., & Karmiloff-Smith, A. (2003). Connectionist models of development, developmental disorders, and individual differences. In R. J. Sternberg, J. Lautrey, & Lubart, T. (Eds.), *Models of intelligence: International perspectives* (pp. 133–150). Washington, DC: American Psychological Association.

Thomas, R. M. (2000). *Comparing theories of child development*. Belmont, CA: Wadsworth Publishing Company.

Thompson, E. M., & Morgan, E. M. (2008). "Mostly straight" young women: Variations in sexual behavior and identity development. *Developmental Psychology, 44*, 15–21.

Thompson, M. W., McInnes, R. R., & Willard, H. F. (1991). *Thompson & Thompson genetics in medicine* (5th ed.). Philadelphia: W. B. Saunders Company.

Thompson, P. M., Giedd, J. N., Woods, R. P., MacDonald, D., Evans, A. C., & Toga, A. W. (2000). Growth patterns in the developing brain detected by using continuum mechanical tensor maps. *Nature, 404*, 190–193.

Thompson, R. A. (1998). Early sociopersonality development. In W. Damon (Ed.), *Handbook of child psychology* (Vol. 3, pp. 25–104). New York: John Wiley & Sons.

Thompson, R. A. (2006). The development of the person: Social understanding, relationships, conscience, self. In N. Eisenberg (volume editor) and W. Damon and R. M. Lerner (Eds.), *Handbook of child psychology* (6th ed., Vol. 3, pp. 24–98). New York: John Wiley & Sons.

Thorndike, R., & Lohman, D. (1990). *A century of ability testing*. Chicago: Riverside.

Thurstone, L. L. (1938). *Primary mental abilities*. Chicago: University of Chicago Press.

Thurstone, L. L., & Thurstone, T. G. (1941). *Factorial studies of intelligence*. Chicago: University of Chicago Press.

Tietjen, A., & Walker, L. (1985). Moral reasoning and leadership among men in a Papua, New Guinea village. *Developmental Psychology, 21*, 982–992.

Tjaden, P., & Thoennes, N. ( 2006). *Extent, nature, and consequences of rape victimization: Findings from the National Violence against Women Survey*. Washington, DC: National Institute of Justice. Retrieved April 24, 2009, from www.cdc.gov/ViolencePrevention/sexualviolence/datasources.html

Tomasello, M. (1995). Language is not an instinct. *Cognitive Development, 10*, 131–156.

Tomasello, M. (2006). Acquiring linguistic construction. In D. Kuhn & R. S. Siegler (Eds.), *Cognition, perception, and language*, Vol. 2 (pp. 255–298), in W. Damon & R. M. Lerner (Gen. Eds.), *Handbook of child psychology*, 6th ed.. New York: John Wiley & Sons.

Tomasello, M. (2006). Acquiring linguistic constructions. In D. Kuhn & R. S. Siegler (Eds.), *Cognitive, language, and perceptual development,* Vol. 2 (pp. 255–298), in W. Damon (Gen. Ed.), *Handbook of child psychology*. New York: Wiley.

Tomkins, A. J., & Kepfield, S. S. (1992). Policy responses: When women use drugs during pregnancy: Using child abuse laws to combat substance abuse. In T. B. Sonderegger (Ed.), *Perinatal substance abuse: Research findings and clinical applications* (pp. 306–345). Baltimore: The Johns Hopkins University Press.

Torbeyns, J., Verschaffel, L., & Ghesquiere, P. (2005). Simple addition strategies in a first-grade class with multiple strategy instruction. *Cognition & Instruction, 23,* 1–21.

Toulmin, S. (1978, September). The Mozart of psychology. *New York Review of Books.* As cited in Wertsch, (1985).

Tracey, J. G., Robbins, S. B., & Hofsess, C. D. (2005). Stability and change in interests: A longitudinal study of adolescents from grades 8 through 12. *Journal of Vocational Behavior, 66,* 1–25.

Trad, P. V. (1995). Mental health of adolescent mothers. *Journal of the American Academy of Child and Adolescent Psychiatry, 34,* 130–142.

Trasler, J. M., & Doerksen, T. (1999) Teratogen update: Paternal exposures—reproductive risks. *Teratology, 60,* 161–172.

Trehub, S. E. (1976). The discrimination of foreign speech contrasts by infants and adults. *Child Development, 47,* 466–472.

Triandis, H. C. (1994). *Culture and social behavior.* New York: McGraw-Hill.

Triandis, H. C. (1995). *Individualism and collectivism.* Boulder, CO: Westview Press.

Trimble, J. E., & Medicine, B. (1993). Diversification of American Indians: Forming an indigenous perspective. In U. Kim & J. W. Berry (Eds.), *Indigenous psychologies* (pp. 133–151). Newbury Park, CA: Sage.

Triseliotis, J. (2000). Identity formation and the adopted person revisited. In A. Treacher & I. Katz (Eds.), *The dynamics of adoption* (pp. 81–97). London: Jessica Kingsley Publishers.

Triseliotis, J., & Hill, M. (1990). Contrasting adoption, foster care, and residential rearing. In D. M. Brodzinsky & M. D. Schechter (Eds.), *The psychology of adoption* (pp. 107–120). New York: Oxford University Press.

Troiden, R. R. (1988). Homosexual identity development. *Journal of Adolescent Health Care, 9,* 105–113.

Trussell, J. (1988). Teenage pregnancy in the United States, *Family Planning Perspectives,* 20, 262–272.

Tsao, R., Liu, H., & Kuhl, P. K. (2004). Speech perception in infancy predicts language development in the second year of life: A longitudinal study. *Child Development, 75,* 1067–1084.

Tsapakis, E. M., Soldani, F., Tondo, L., & Baldessarini, R. J. (2008). Efficacy of antidepressants in juvenile depression: Meta-analysis. *The British Journal of Psychiatry, 193,* 10–17.

Tschannen-Moran, M., Woolfolk Hoy, A., & Hoy, W. K. (1998). Teacher efficacy: Its meaning and measure. *Review of Educational Research, 68,* 202–248.

Tseng, V. & Fuligni, A. J. (2000). Parent-adolescent language use and relationships among immigrant families with East Asian, Filipino, and Latin American backgrounds. *Journal of Marriage and the Family, 62,* 465–476.

Tuffiash, M., Roring, R., & Ericsson, K. (2007). Expert performance in SCRABBLE: Implications for the study of the structure and acquisition of complex skills. *Journal of Experimental Psychology: Applied, 13,* 124–134.

Tulving, E. (1972). Episodic and semantic memory. In E. Tulving & W. Donaldson (Eds.), *Organization of memory* (pp. 382–403). New York: Academic Press.

Turati, C., Cassia, V. M., Simion, F., & Leo, I. (2006). Newborns' face recognition: Role of inner and outer facial features. *Child Development, 77,* 297–311.

Turati, C., Simion, F., Milani, I., & Umiltá, C. (2002). Newborns' preferences for faces: What is crucial? *Developmental Psychology, 38*(6), 875–882.

Turati, C., Valenza, E., Leo, I., & Simion, F. (2005). Three-month-olds' preference for faces and its underlying visual processing mechanisms. *Journal of Experimental Child Psychology, 90,* 255–273.

Turiel, E. (2006). The development of morality. In W. Damon & N. Eisenberg (Eds.), *Handbook of child psychology: Vol. 3. Social, emotional, and personality development* (pp. 863–932). New York: John Wiley & Sons, Inc.

Tzuriel, D. (2001). Dynamic assessment of learning potential. In J. J. W. Andrews, D. H. Saklofski, & H. L. Janzen (Eds.), *Handbook of psychoeducational assessment: Ability, achievement, and behavior in children* (pp. 451–496). San Diego: Academic Press.

U.S. Census Bureau (2008). Annual social and economic (ASEC) supplement. Accessed May 3, 2009, from pubdb3.census.gov/macro/032008/pov/new34_000.htm.

U.S. Census Bureau (2009). *2007 American community survey 1-year estimates.* Retrieved May 10, 2009, from factfinder.census.gov/servlet/DatasetMainPageServlet?_lang=en&_ts=260024123223&_ds_name=ACS_2007_1YR_G00_&_program=ACS.

U.S. Census Bureau. (2006). America's children in brief: Key national indicators of well-being, 2006. Last accessed July 28, 2006, from www.childstats.gov/amchildren06/tables.asp.

U.S. Census Bureau. (2009). Families and living arrangements. Historical time series: Living arrangements of children, Tables CH-1 to CH-4. Last accessed March 25, 2009, from www.census.gov/population/www/socdemo/hh-fam.html#history.

U.S. Department of Education. (2001). National Center for Education Statistics. *Internet access in U.S. public schools and classrooms: 1994–2000* (NCES 2001-071), by A. Cattagni & E. F. Westat. Washington, DC: U.S. Government Printing Office.

U.S. Department of Energy (2008). Gene gateway—Exploring genes and genetic disorders. Washington, D.C. Retrieved November 28, 2008, from genomics.energy.gov/.

U.S. Department of Health & Human Services (2008). Head Start Program fact sheet fiscal year 2008. Retrieved March 15, 2009, from http://eclkc.ohs.acf.hhs.gov/hslc/About%20Head%20Start/dHeadStart progr. htm.

U.S. Department of Health & Human Services (2009, March 27). *Sexual development and reproduction.* Retrieved April 21, 2009, from www.4parents.gov/index.html.

U.S. Department of Health and Human Services. (2001). *Youth violence: A report of the Surgeon General.* Rockville, MD: U.S. Department of Health and Human Services, Centers for Disease Control and Prevention, National Center for Injury Prevention and Control; Substance Abuse and Mental Health Services Administration, Center for Mental Health Services; and National Institutes of Mental Health, National Institute of Mental Health.

U.S. National Coalition for the Homeless (2001). Homeless families with children (NCH fact sheet #7). Retrieved July 19, 2002, from www.nationalhomeless.org/families.html.

*U.S. Teens & Technology* [on-line]. (1997). Retrieved July 11, 2002, from www.nsf.gov/lpa/nstw/teenov.htm.

Uchikoshi, Y. (2005). Narrative development in bilingual kindergartners: Can *Arthur* help? *Developmental Psychology, 41,* 464–478.

Uhlmann, W. R. (2000, February 29). When genes are decoded, who should see the results?: "Every one of us is at risk." *The New York Times.* Retrieved February 15, 2002, from www.nytimes.com.

Uhry, J. K., & Shepard, M. J. (1993). Segmentation/spelling instruction as part of a first-grade reading program: Effects on several measures of reading. *Reading Research Quarterly,* 28, 218–233.

United Cerebral Palsy. (2005) United Cerebral Palsy. Last accessed October 27, 2005 from www.ucp.org.

United States Department of Agriculture (USDA) (2008). Food security in the United States: Key statistics and graphics; and Food security in the United States: Definitions of hunger and food security. Both articles from the USDA Economic Research Service, Briefing Rooms, retrieved April 4, 2009, from www.ers.usda.gov/Briefing/FoodSecurity/.

United States Department of Health and Human Services (DHHS) (2001). *Youth violence: A report of the surgeon general.* Rockville, MD: U.S. Department of Health and Human Services.

United States Department of Health and Human Services (DHHS) (2006). *Child maltreatment, 2004.* Washington, DC: U.S. Government Printing Office. Retrieved June 22, 2006, from www.acf.hhs.gov/programs/cb/pubs/cm04/cm04.pdf.

United States Department of Health and Human Services (DHHS) (2009). *Child maltreatment 2007.* Administration on Children, Youth and Families. U.S. Government Printing Office: Washington, DC. Retrieved April 4, 2009, from www.acf.hhs.gov/programs/cb/pubs/cm07/cm07.pdf.

United States Department of Health and Human Services (DHHS) Administration on Children, Youth, and Families. (2001). *Child maltreatment 1999.* Washington, DC: U.S. Government Printing Office.

Upchurch, D. M., Mason, W. M., Kusunoki, Y. & Kriechbaum, M. J. (2004). Social and behavioral determinants of self-reported STD among adolescents. *Perspectives on Sexual and Reproductive Health, 36,* 276–287.

Vaish, A., Carpenter, M., & Tomasello, M. (2009). Sympathy through affective perspective taking and its relation to prosocial behavior in toddlers. *Developmental Psychology, 45,* 534–543.

Valenzuela, M. (1990). Attachment in chronically underweight young children. *Child Development, 61,* 1984–1996.

Valkenburg, P. M., & Peter, J. (2007). Preadolescents' and adolescents' online communication and their closeness to friends. *Developmental Psychology, 43,* 267–277.

Valkenburg, P., & Peter, J. (2009). The effects of instant messaging on the quality of adolescents' existing friendships: A longitudinal study. *Journal of Communication, 59*(1), 79–97.

van IJzendoorn, M. H., Goldberg, S., Kroonenberg, P. M., & Frenkel, O. J. (1992). The relative effects of maternal and child problems on the quality of attachment: A meta-analysis of attachment in clinical samples. *Child Development, 63,* 840–858.

van IJzendoorn, M. H., Goossens, F. A., Kroonenberg, P. M., & Tavecchio, L. W. C. (1985). Dependent attachment: B4-children in the Strange Situation. *Psychological Reports, 57,* 439–451.

Vandell, D. L., & Mueller, E. C. (1980). Peer play and friendships during the first two years. In H. C. Foot, A. J. Chapman, & J. R. Smith (Eds.), *Friendship and social relations in children* (pp. 181–208). New York: John Wiley & Sons.

Vandell, D. L., & Wilson, K. S. (1982). Social interaction in the first year: Infants' social skills with peers versus mother. In K. H. Rubin & H. S. Ross (Eds.), *Peer relationships and social skills in childhood* (pp. 187–208). New York: Springer-Verlag.

Vandell, D. L., Wilson, K. S., & Buchanan, N. R. (1980). Peer interaction in the first year of life: An examination of its structure, content, and sensitivity to toys. *Child Development, 51,* 481–488.

Vanfraussen, K., Ponjaert-Kristoffersen, I., & Brewaeys, A. (2003). Family functioning in lesbian families created by donor insemination. *American Journal of Orthopsychiatry, 73,* 78–90.

Varma, S., McCandliss, B. D., & Schwartz, D. L. (2008). Scientific and pragmatic challenges for bridging education and neuroscience. *Educational Researcher, 37,* 140–152.

Varnado-Sullivan, P. J. & Zucker, N. (2004). The body logic program for adolescents. *Behavior Modification, 28,* 854–875.

Vartanian, L. R. (2000). Revisiting the imaginary audience and personal fable constructs of adolescent egocentrism: A conceptual review. *Adolescence, 35,* 639–661.

Vartanian, L. R. (2001). Adolescents' reactions to hypothetical peer group conversations: Evidence for an imaginary audience? *Adolescence, 36,* 347–380.

Vellutino, F. R., & Scanlon, D. M. (1987). Phonological coding, phonological awareness, and reading ability: Evidence from a longitudinal and experimental study. *Merrill-Palmer Quarterly, 33,* 321–363.

Venter, J. C., Adams, M. D., Myers, E.W., Li, P. W., Mural, R. J., Sutton, G. G., et al., (2001). The sequence of the human genome. *Science, 291,* 1304–1351.

Ventura, S. J., Abma, J. C., Mosher, W. D., & Henshaw, S. K. (2008). Estimated pregnancy rates by outcome for the United States, 1990–2004. *National Vital Statistics Reports, 56*(15). Retrieved April 24, 2009, from www.cdc.gov/nchs/products/nvsr.htm.

Verkuyten, M. (2003). Postive and negative self-esteem among ethnic minority early adolescents: Social and cultural sources and threats. *Journal of Youth & Adolescence, 32,* 267–277.

Vichinsky, E. (2002). New therapies in sickle cell disease. *Lancet, 360,* 629–631.

Vihman, M., & Miller, R. (1988). Words and babble at the threshold of language acquisition. In M. Smith & J. Locke (Eds.), *The emergent lexicon: The child's development of a linguistic vocabulary* (pp. 151–184). New York: Academic Press.

Viken, R. J., Rose, R. J., Kaprio, J., & Koskenvuo, M. (1994). A developmental-genetic analysis of adult personality: Extraversion and neuroticism from 18 to 59. *Journal of Personality and Social Psychology, 66,* 722–730.

Vlahovic-Stetic, V., Rovan, D., & Mendek, Z. (2004). The role of students' age, problem type and situational context in solving mathematical word problems. *Review of Psychology, 11,* 25–33.

Volterra, V. & Taeschner, T. (1978). The acquisition and development of language by bilingual children. *Journal of Child Language, 5,* 311–326.

Voyer, D., Voyer, S, & Bryden, M. P. (1995). Magnitude of sex differences in spatial abilities: A meta-analysis and consideration of critical variables. *Psychological Bulletin, 117,* 250–270.

Vroegh, K. S. (1997). Transracial adoptees: Developmental status after 17 years. *American Journal of Orthopsychiatry, 67,* 568–575.

Vygotsky, L. S. (1956). *Izbrannye psikhologicheskie issledovaniya [Selected psychological investigations].* Moscow: Izdatel'stvo Akademii Pedagogicheskikh Nauk. As cited in Wertsch & Tulviste, 1992.

Vygotsky, L. S. (1962). *Thought and language.* New York: John Wiley & Sons.

Vygotsky, L. S. (1978). *Mind in society: The development of higher psychological processes.* Cambridge, MA: Harvard University Press.

Vygotsky, L. S. (1981). The genesis of higher mental functions. In J. V. Wertsch (Ed.), *The concept of activity in Soviet psychology* (pp. 144–188). Armonk, NJ: M. E. Sharpe.

Waddington, C. H. (1942). Canalization of development and the inheritance of acquired characters. Nature, 150, 563–564.

Waddington, C. H. (1957). *The strategy of the genes.* London: Allen and Unwin.

Waddington, C. H. (1974). A catastrophe theory of evolution. *Annals of New York Academy of Sciences, 231,* 37.

Walker, L. J. & Hennig, K. H. (1997). Moral development in the broader context of personality. In S. Hala (Ed.), *The development of social cognition* (pp. 297–327). Hove, UK: Psychology Press.

Walker, L. J. (1989). A longitudinal study of moral reasoning. *Child Development, 60,* 157–166.

Walker, L. J. (1995). Sexism in Kohlberg's moral psychology? In W. M. Kurtines & J. L. Gerwirtz (Eds.), *Moral development: An introduction* (pp. 83–107). Boston: Allyn & Bacon.

Walker, L. J., Pitts, R., Hennig, K., & Matsuba, M. K. (1995). Reasoning about morality and real-life moral problems. In M. Killen & D. Hart (Eds.), *Morality in everyday life: Developmental perspectives* (pp. 371–407). New York: Cambridge University Press.

Walker, S. O., Petrill, S. A., Spinath, F.M., & Plomin, R. (2004). Nature, nurture and academic achievement: A twin study of teacher assessments of 7-year-olds. *British Journal of Educational Psychology, 74,* 323–342.

Walker-Andrews, A. S., & Lennon, E. M. (1985). Auditory-visual perception of changing distance by human infants. *Child Development, 56,* 544–548.

Wallace, J. M., Brown, T. N., & Bachman, J. G. (2003). The influence of race and religion on abstinence from alcohol, cigarettes, and marijuana among adolescents. *Journal of Studies on Alcohol, 64,* 843–848.

Wallace, S., Miller, K., & Forehand, R. (2008). Perceived peer norms and sexual intentions among African American preadolescents. *AIDS Education & Prevention, 20,* 360–369.

Wallerstein, J. S. (2001). The challenges of divorce for parents and children. In J. C. Westman (Ed.), *Parenthood in America: Undervalued, underpaid, under siege* (pp. 127–139). Madison: University of Wisconsin Press.

Wallerstein, J. S., Lewis, J. M., & Blakeslee, S. (2000). *The unexpected legacy of divorce: A 25-year landmark study.* New York: Hyperion.

Wang, Q. (2003). Infantile amnesia reconsidered: A cross-cultural analysis. *Memory, 11,* 65–80.

Ward, L. M. (2004). Wading through the stereotypes: Positive and negative associations between media use and black adolescents' conceptions of self. *Developmental Psychology, 40,* 284–294.

Wark, G. R., & Krebs, D. L. (1996). Gender and dilemma differences in real-life moral judgments. *Developmental Psychology, 32,* 220–230.

Warren-Leubecker, A., & Carter, B. W. (1988). Reading and growth in metalinguistic awareness: Relations to socioeconomic status and reading readiness skills. *Child Development, 59,* 728–742.

Wartella, E., Caplovitz, A. G., & Lee, J. H. (2004). From Baby Einstein to Leapfrog, from Doom to the Sims, from instant messaging to Internet chat rooms: Public interest in the role of interactive media in children's lives. *SRCD Social Policy Report, 18*(4). Accessed October 1, 2007, from srcd.org/Documents/Publications/SPR/spr18-4.pdf.

Washington, V., & Oyemade, U. J. (1987). *Project Head Start: Past, present, and future trends in the context of family needs.* New York: Garland.

Wasserheit, J. N. (1992). Epidemiologic synergy: Interrelationships between human immunodeficiency virus infection and other sexually transmitted diseases. *Sexually Transmitted Diseases, 9,* 61–77.

Watson, J. B. (1924). *Behaviorism.* Chicago: University of Chicago Press.

Watson, J. B. (1930). *Behaviorism.* Chicago: The University of Chicago Press. (Original edition published in 1924.)

Watson, J. B., & Rayner, R. (1920). Conditioned emotional reactions. *Journal of Experimental Psychology, 3,* 1–14.

Waxman, S. R., & Lidz, J. L. (2006). Early word learning. In D. Kuhn & R. S. Siegler (Eds.), *Cognition, perception, and language,* Vol. 2 (pp. 299–335), in W. Damon & R. M. Lerner (Gen. Eds.), *Handbook of child psychology,* 6th ed. New York: John Wiley & Sons.

Weiner, B. (1992). *Human motivation: Metaphors, theories, and research.* Newbury Park, CA: Sage.

Weiner, B. (2000). Intrapersonal and interpersonal theories of motivation from an attributional perspective. *Educational Psychology Review, 12,* 1–14.

Wekerle, C., & Wolfe, D. A. (1996). Child maltreatment. In E. J. Mash & R. A. Barkley (Eds.), *Child psychopathology* (pp. 492–537). New York: Guilford Press.

Wekerle, C., & Wolfe, D. A. (2003). Child maltreatment. In E. J. Mash & R. A. Barkley (Eds.), *Child psychopathology* (pp. 632–684). New York: Guilford Press.

Welles-Nystrom, B. (2005). Co-sleeping as a window into Swedish culture: Considerations of gender and health care. *Scandanavian Journal of Caring Sciences, 19,* 354–360.

Wellman, H., Harris, P. L., Banerjee, M., & Sinclair, A. (1995). Early understanding of emotion: Evidence from natural language. *Cognition and Emotion, 9,* 117–149.

Wellman, H. M. (1990). *The child's theory of mind.* Cambridge, MA: MIT Press.

Wellman, H. M., & Bartsch, K. (1988). Young children's reasoning about beliefs. *Cognition, 30,* 239–277.

Wellman, H. M., & Estes, D. (1986). Early understanding of mental entities: A reexamination of childhood realism. *Child Development, 57,* 910–923.

Wellman, H. M., & Gelman, S. A. (1998). Knowledge acquisition in foundational domains. In W. Damon (Series Ed.) & D. Kuhn & R. S. Siegler (Vol. Eds.), *Handbook of child psychology: Vol. 2. Cognition, perception, and language* (5th ed., pp. 523–573). New York: Wiley.

Wellman, H. M., & Liu, D. (2004). Scaling of theory-of-mind tasks. *Child Development, 75,* 523–541.

Wellman, H. M., Cross, D., & Watson, J. (2001). Meta-analysis of theory-of-mind development: The truth about false belief. *Child Development, 72,* 655–684.

Wenger, E. (1998). *Communities of practice: Learning, meaning, and identity.* Cambridge, England: Cambridge University Press.

Wentzel, K. R., & Watkins, D. E. (2002). Peer relationships and collaborative learning as contexts for academic enablers. *School Psychology Review, 31,* 366–377.

Werker, J. F., & Tees, R. C. (1984). Cross-language speech perception: Evidence for perceptual reorganization during the first year of life. *Infant Behavior and Development, 7,* 49–63.

Werker, J., & Tees, R. (1984). Cross-language speech perception: Evidence for perceptual reorganization during the first year of life. *Infant Behavior and Development, 7,* 49–64.

Werner, E. E. (1989). High-risk children in young adulthood: A longitudinal study from birth to 32 years. *American Journal of Orthopsychiatry, 59,* 72–81.

Werner, E. E. (2000). Protective factors and individual resilience. In J. P. Shonkoff & S. J. Meisels (Eds.), *Handbook of early childhood intervention* (2nd ed., pp. 115–132). Cambridge: Cambridge University Press.

Werner, E. E., & Smith, R. S. (2001). *Journeys from childhood to midlife: Risk, resilience, and recovery.* Ithaca, NY: Cornell University Press.

Wertsch, J. V. (1985). *Vygotsky and the social formation of mind.* Cambridge, MA: Harvard University Press.

Wertsch, J. V., Tulviste, P., & Hagstrom, F. (1993). A sociocultural approach to agency. In E. A. Forman, N. Minick, & C. A. Stone (Eds.), *Contexts for learning* (pp. 336–356). New York: Oxford University Press.

Wertsch, J., & Tulviste, P. (1992, July). L.S. Vygotsky and contemporary developmental psychology. *Developmental Psychology, 28*(4), 548. Retrieved May 26, 2009, from Academic Search Premier database.

West, J., Denton, K., & Germino-Hausken, E. (2000). *America's kindergarteners.* Washington, DC: U.S. Department of Education, National Center for Education Statistics.

Westman, J. C. (1994). *Licensing parents: Can we prevent child abuse and neglect?* New York: Insight Books.

Westman, J. C. (1997). Reducing governmental interventions in families by licensing parents. *Child Psychiatry and Human Development, 27,* 193–205.

What is Tay–Sachs disease? (2007). Retrieved October 25, 2008, from www.ntsad.org.

Whitaker, P. (2002). Supporting families of preschool children with autism: What parents want and what helps. *Autism, 6,* 411–426.

White, B. H., & Kurpius, S. E. R. (2002). Effects of victim sex and sexual orientation on perceptions of rape. *Sex Roles, 46,* 191–200.

Whiting, B. B., & Edwards, C. P. (1988). *Children of different worlds.* Cambridge, MA: Harvard University Press.

Whitlock, J. L., Powers, J. L., & Eckenrode, J. (2006). The virtual cutting edge: The Internet and adolescent self-injury. *Developmental Psychology, 42,* 407–417.

Wiesner, M., & Ittel, A. (2002). Relations of pubertal timing and depressive symptoms to substance use in early adolescience. *Journal of Early Adolescence, 22*(1), 5–23.

Wigfield, A., Eccles, J. S., Schiefele, U., Roeser, R. W., & Davis-Kean, P. (2006). Development of achievement motivation. In W. Damon & R. M. Lerner (Ser. Ed.) and N. Eisenberg (Vol. Ed.), *Handbook of child psychology. Vol. 3. Social, emotional, and personality development* (pp. 933–1002). New York: John Wiley & Sons.

Wilcox, A. J., Baird, D. D., & Weinberg, C. R. (1999). Time of implantation of the conceptus and loss of pregnancy. *The New England Journal of Medicine, 340,* 1796–1799.

Wilcox, T., Nadel, L. & Rosser, R. (1996). Location memory in healthy preterm and full-term infants. *Infant Behavior and Development, 19,* 309–323.

William T. Grant Foundation Commission on Work, Family and Citizenship (1988). *The forgotten half: Pathways to success for America's youth and young families: Final report.* Washington, DC: William T. Grant Foundation Commission on Work, Family, and Citizenship.

Williams, A. F. (2003). Teenage drivers: Patterns of risk. *Journal of Safety Research, 34,* 5–15.

Williams, J. M., & Currie, C. (2000). Self-esteem and physical development in early adolescence: Pubertal timing and body image. *Journal of Early Adolescence,* 20, 129–149.

Willoughby, T. (2008). A short-term longitudinal study of Internet and computer game use by adolescent boys and girls: Prevalence, frequency of use, and psychosocial predictors. *Developmental Psychology, 44*(1), 195–204.

Wilson, G. S. (1992). Heroin use during pregnancy: Clinical studies of long-term effects. In T. B. Sonderegger (Ed.), *Perinatal substance abuse: research findings and clinical applications* (pp. 224–238). Baltimore: The Johns Hopkins University Press.

Wilson, S. M., & Peterson, G. W. (2000). Growing up in Appalachia: Ecological influences on adolescent development. In R. Montemayor, G. R. Adams, & T. P. Gullotta (Eds.), *Adolescent diversity in ethnic, economic, and cultural contexts* (pp. 75–109). Thousand Oaks, CA: Sage Publications.

Winner, E. (1996). *Gifted children: Myths and realities.* New York: Basic Books.

Witelson, S. F. (1987). Neurobiological aspects of language in children. *Child Development, 58,* 653–688.

Witelson, S., Kigar, D., Scamvougeras, A., Kideckel, D., Buck, B., Stanchev, P., et al. (2008). Corpus callosum anatomy in right-handed homosexual and heterosexual men. *Archives of Sexual Behavior, 37,* 857–863.

Wolfram, W., & Thomas, E. R. (2002). *The development of African American English.* Oxford, England: Blackwell Publishers.

Wolfson, A. R., & Carskadon, M. A. (1998). Sleep schedules and daytime functioning in adolescents. *Child Development, 69,* 875–887.

Wood, D., & Middleton, D. (1975). A study of assisted problem-solving. *British Journal of Psychology, 66,* 181–191.

Wood, D., Bruner, J. S., & Ross, G. (1976). The role of tutoring in problem-solving. *Journal of Child Psychology and Psychiatry, 17,* 89–100.

Wood, D., Wood, H., & Middleton, D. (1978). An experimental evaluation of four face-to-face teaching strategies. *International Journal of Behavioral Development, 2,* 131–147.

Wood, F., Felton, R., Flowers, L., & Naylor, C. (1991). Neurobehavioral definition of dyslexia. In D. D. Duane & D. B. Gray (Eds.), *The reading brain: The biological basis of dyslexia* (pp. 1–25). Parkton, MD: York Press.

Woodward, A. L., Markman, E. M., & Fitzsimmons, C. M. (1994). Rapid word learning in 13- and 18-month-olds. *Developmental Psychology, 30,* 553–566.

Woolley, J. D., & Wellman, H. M. (1992). Children's conceptions of dreams. *Cognitive Development, 7,* 365–380.

World Health Organization (2003). Nutrition data banks: Global data bank on breastfeeding. Retrieved September 13, 2004, from www.who.int/nut/db_bfd.htm.

World Health Organization (2005). Global database on child growth and malnutrition. Last accessed September 30, 2005, at www.who.int/nutgrowthdb/database/en/.

Wout, D. A., Shih, M. J., Jackson, J. S., & Sellers, R. M. (2009). Targets as perceivers: How people determine when they will be negatively stereotyped. *Journal of Personality and Social Psychology, 96,* 349–362.

Wozencraft, T., Wagner, W., & Pellegrin, A. (1991). Depression and suicidal ideation in sexually abused children. *Child Abuse and Neglect, 15,* 505–511.

Wright, M. A. (1998). *I'm chocolate, you're vanilla.* San Francisco: Jossey-Bass Publishers.

Xie, H., Li, Y., Boucher, S. M., Hutchins, B. C., & Cairns, B. D. (2006). What makes a girl (or a boy) popular (or unpopular)? African American children's perceptions and developmental differences. *Developmental Psychology, 42,* 599–612.

Xu, Y., Farver, J. A. M., & Zhang, Z. (2009). Temperament, harsh and indulgent parenting, and Chinese children's proactive and reactive aggression. *Child Development, 80,* 244–258.

Yazigi, R. A., Odem, R. R., & Polakoski, K. L. (1991). Demonstration of specific binding of cocaine to human spermatozoa. *Journal of the American Medical Association, 266,* 1956–1959.

Yeargin-Allsopp, M., Rice, C., Karapurkar, T., Doernberg, N., Boyle, C., & Murphy, C. (2003). Prevalence of autism in a U.S. metropolitan area. *Journal of the American Medical Association, 289,* 49–55.

Young, T. M., Martin, S. S., Young, M. E., & Ting, L. (2001). Internal poverty and teen pregnancy. *Adolescence, 36,* 289–304.

Young, T., Turner, J., & Denny, G. (2004). Examining external and internal poverty as antecedents of teen pregnancy. *American Journal of Health Behavior, 28,* 361–373.

Zachopoulou, E., Tsapakidou, A., & Derri, V. (2004). The effects of a developmentally appropriate music and movement program on motor performance. *Early Childhood Research Quarterly, 19,* 631–642.

Zahn, G. L., Kagan, S., & Widaman, K. F. (1986). Cooperative learning and classroom climate. *Journal of School Psychology, 24,* 351–362.

Zahn-Waxler, C., & Robinson, J. (1995). Empathy and guilt: Early origins of feelings of responsibility. In J. Tangney & K. Fischer (Eds.), *Self-conscious emotions* (pp. 143–173). New York: Guilford Press.

Zehr, M. A. (2001). English-language learners post improved California test scores. *Education Week, 21*(1), September 5, 2001.

Zehr, M. A. (2002). Colorado extends bilingual education, but Massachusetts voters reject it. *Education Week, 22*(11), November 13, 2002.

Zelazo, P. R. (1983). The development of walking: New findings and old assumptions. *Journal of Motor Behavior, 15,* 99–137.

Zelazo, P. R., Zelazo, N. A., & Kolb, S. (1972). "Walking" in the newborn. *Science, 176,* 314–315.

Zelazo, P., Moscovitch, M., & Thompson, E. (2007). *The Cambridge handbook of consciousness.* New York: Cambridge University Press.

Zevin, J. D., & Seidenberg, M. S., (2004). Age-of-acquisition effects in reading aloud: Tests of cumulative frequency and frequency trajectory. *Memory & Cognition, 32,* 31–38.

Zhu, J., & Weiss, L. (2005). The Wechsler scales. In D. P. Flanagan & P. L. Harrison (Eds.), *Contemporary intellectual assessment: Theories, tests, and issues* (pp. 297–324). New York: Guilford Press.

Zigler, E., & Styfco, S. J. (1993). *Head Start and beyond: A national plan for extended childhood intervention.* New Haven, CT: Yale University Press.

Zigler, E., Styfco, S. J., & Gilman, E. (1993). The national Head Start program for disadvantaged preschoolers. In E. Zigler & S. J. Styfco (Eds.), *Head Start and beyond: A national plan for extended childhood intervention* (pp. 1–41). New Haven, CT: Yale University Press.

Zill, N., Moore, K. A., Smith, E. W., Stief, T., & Coiro, M. J. (1995). The life circumstances and development of children in welfare families: A profile based on national survey data. In P. L. Chase-Lansdale & J. Brooks-Gunn (Eds.), *Escape from poverty: What makes a difference for children?* (pp. 39–59). Cambridge, UK: Cambridge University Press.

Zimbardo, P. G., Butler, L. D., & Wolfe, V. A. (2003). Cooperative college examinations: More gain, less pain when students share information and grades. *The Journal of Experimental Education, 71,* 101–125.

Zimmerman, F., & Christakis, D. (2007). Associations between content types of early media exposure and subsequent attentional problems. *Pediatrics, 120*(5), 986–992.

Zipke, M. (2007). The role of metalinguistic awareness in the reading comprehension of sixth and seventh graders. *Reading Psychology, 28,* 375–396.

Zucker, R. A., Donovan, J. E., Masten, A. S., Mattson, M. E., & Moss, H. B. (2008). Early developmental processes and the continuity of risk for underage drinking and problem drinking. *Pediatrics, 121,* S252–272. Retrieved April 23, 2009, from www.pediatrics.org.

Zwelling, E. (2008). The emergence of high-tech birthing. *Journal of Obstetric, Gynecologic, and Neonatal Nursing, 37*(1), 85–93.

# Credits

## Figure and Table Credits

**Figure 1.1(A-E),** Getty Images, Inc.; Nancy Sheehan/PhotoEdit Inc.; Bob Daemmrich/PhotoEdit Inc.; © Corbis, All rights reserved; Michael Newman/PhotoEdit Inc.
**Figure 1.2,** Elizabeth Crews/The Image Works
**Figure 1.3,** Daniel Pangbourne © Dorling Kindersley
**Figure 1.6,** Pedersen, Vitaro, Barker, & Borge (2007). *Child Development*, v78 n4 p1037–1051 Jul–Aug 2007. Blackwell Publishing. Reprinted with permission.
**Figure 2.1,** CNRI/SPL/Photo Researchers, Inc.
**Figure 2.3,** National Center for Biotechnology Information, 2009.
**Figure 2.4,** U.S. Department of Energy, 2008.
**Figure 2.9,** Will Hart/PhotoEdit Inc.
**Figure 2.11,** UHB Trust/Getty Images Inc. - Stone Allstock
**Figure 2.12,** From H. Bee & D. Boyd (2004). *Lifespan Development*, 3/e. Published by Allyn and Bacon, Boston, MA. Copyright © 2004 by Pearson Education. By permission of the publisher.
**Figure 2.14,** Adapted from CH. Waddington. (1974). *A catastrophe theory of evolution. Annals of the New York Academy of Sciences*. 231. 32–42. Adapted with permission.
**Figure 2.15,** Based on Gottlieb, 1991.
**Figure 2.16,** Plomin & DeVries, 1998.
**Table 2.1,** Moore & Persaud, 1998.
**Table 2.2,** From Starr/Taggart. *Ecology and Behavior* 8e. Copyright © 1998 Brooks/Cole, a part of Cengage Learning, Inc. Reproduced by permission. www.cengage.com/permissions.
**Table 2.3,** *The Gale Encyclopedia of Genetic Disorders*, 2005; Thompson et al., 1991.
**Table 2.4,** 1. Plomin, Owen, & McGuffin, 1994; 2. Nichols, 1978; 3. Loehlin & Nichols, 1976; 4. Walker, Petrill, Spinath, & Plomin., 2004; 5. McCartney, Harris, & Bernieri, 1990; 6. Martin, Eaves, Heath, Jardine, Feingold, & Eysenck, 1986; 7. Koenig, McGue, Krueger, & Bouchard., 2007; 8. Loehlin, Jönsson, Gustavsson, Stallings, Gillespie, Wright, & Martin, 2005; 9. Rose, 1995; 10. Stevenson, 1992; 11. Plomin, 1990; 12. Maes, Neale, & Eaves, 1997. 13. Rutter, 2006.
**Figure 3.3,** Data from Martin et al., 2007.
**Figure 3.4,** Adapted from Moore, K.L. & Persaud, T.V.N. (1998). *The developing human: clinically oriented embryology*. Philadephia: W. B. Saunders.
**Figure 3.5,** Moore & Persaud, 1998.
**Table 3.2,** Marijuana: Dalterio & Fried, 1992; Goldschmidt, Richardson, Willford, & Day, 2008; and Robinson et al, 1989. Heroin: Kaltenback & Finnegan, 1992; and Wilson, 1992. Environmental pollutants: Bentur, 1994; Bentur & Koren, 1994; J. Jacobson & S. Jacobson, 1996; J. Jacobson, S. Jacobson, & Humphrey, 1990; and Moore & Persaud, 1998. Maternal diseases: Moore & Persaud, 1998. Stress: Anderson, Rhees, & Fleming, 1985; Barlow et al., 1979; Berkowitz & Kasl, 1983; Burstein et al., 1974; Ching & Newton, 1982; DiPietro et al., 2006; Falorni et al., 1979; Istvan, 1986; Newton & Hunt, 1984; and Standley et al., 1979.)
**Figure 4.1,** Jonathan Nourok/PhotoEdit Inc.
**Figure 4.2,** Data for the U.S. from Mathews & MacDorman (2006); all other nations from Organisation for Economic Co-operation and Development (2006).
**Figure 4.3,** National Center for Health Statistics, 2000.
**Figure 4.4,** Feldman, Robert. *Child Development*, 4e, p. 125, fig 5-6. © 2007 Pearson Education.
**Figure 4.5,** National Center for Chronic Disease Prevention and Health Promotion, 2004.
**Figure 4.7,** From Richard Fabes, Carol Lynn Martin, *Exploring Child Development*, 2/e. Published by Allyn and Bacon, Boston, MA. © 2004 by Pearson Education. Reprinted by permission of the publisher.
**Figure 4.8,** From Richard Fabes, Carol Lynn Martin, *Exploring Child Development*, 2/e. Published by Allyn and Bacon, Boston, MA. © 2004 by Pearson Education. Reprinted by permission of the publisher.
**Figure 4.9,** Fantz, 1961.
**Figure 4.10,** Mark Richards/PhotoEdit/Courtesy of Joe Campos & Rosanne Kermoian
**Figure 4.11(A-F),** (from top left), Elizabeth Crews/Elizabeth Crews Photography; Elizabeth Crews/Elizabeth Crews Photography; Laura Dwight/Laura Dwight Photography; Elizabeth Crews/Elizabeth Crews Photography; © Corbis, All rights reserved; Laura Dwight/Laura Dwight Photography
**Figure 4.12(B-D),** (from top right), Laura Dwight/Laura Dwight Photography; © Corbis All Rights Reserved; Elizabeth Crews/Elizabeth Crews Photography
**Figure 5.1,** Based on Fantz, 1961.
**Figure 5.2,** Based on Fantz, 1963.
**Figure 5.3,** Goren, Sarty, & Wu, 1975. Reproduced with permission from *Pediatrics* October 1975, 56, 544-549. Copyright © 1975 by the AAP.
**Figure 5.4,** Based on Maurer & Salapatek, 1976.
**Figure 5.5,** Based on Cohen, Gelber, & Lazar, 1971.
**Figure 5.7,** Wilcox, Nadel & Rosser, *Infant Behavior and Development 19* (1996), pg. 314. Reprinted by permission of Elsevier Science.
**Figure 5.8,** Based on Fabes & Martin, 2003.
**Figure 5.9,** Based on Johnson & Newport, 1989. Reprinted from *Cognitive Psychology, 21*. J.S. Johnson & E.L. Newport, Critical period effects in second language leaming: The influence of maturational state on the acquisition of English as a second language, p. 79. Copyright © 1989, with permission from Elsevier.
**Table 5.3,** Adapted from Hulit & Howard, 1997.
**Table 5.4,** Adapted from Nelson, 1973.
**Figure 6.1,** Nina Leen/Getty Images/Time Life Pictures
**Figure 6.3,** Based on Sorce et al., 1985.

**Table 6.3,** Data for U.S. general population taken from a review by van IJzendoorn, Goldberg, Kroonenberg, & Frankel (1992). All other data taken from Thompson (1998), who reviewed studies by Beller & Pohl (1986); Durrett, Otaki, & Richards (1984); Fracasso, Busch-Rossnagel, & Fischer (1993); Goossens & van IJzendoorn (1990); Grossmann, Grossmann, Huber, & Wartner (1981); Lamb, Hwang, Frodi, & Frodi (1982); Li-Repac (1982); Sagi, Lamb, Lewkowicz, Shoham, Dvir, & Estes Sagi et al. STET (1985); Sagi & Lewkowicz (1987); Sagi, van IJzendoorn, Aviezer, Donnell, & Mayseless (1994); Smith & Noble (1987); Takahashi (1986, 1990); Valenzuela (1990); and van IJzendoorn, Goossens, Kroonenberg, & Tavecchio (1985). We excluded data from high-risk groups.
**Table 6.5,** Thomas & Chess, 1977.
**Figure 7.1,** National Center for Health Statistics, 2004.
**Figure 7.2,** Brennan Linsley/AP Wide World Photos
**Figure 7.3,** P.R. Huttenlocher & A.S. Dabholkar, 1997. *Regional differences in synaptogenesis in human cerebral cortex. Journal of Comparative Neurology,* 387. 167–178. Copyright © 1997, John Wiley & Sons, Inc. Reprinted with permission of Wiley-Liss, Inc., a subsidiary of John Wiley & Sons, Inc.
**Figure 7.4,** From J. Keogh & D. Sugden, *Movement Skill Development.* Macmillan. Copyright © by J. Keogh and D. Sugden.
**Figure 7.5,** Data are from the U.S. Department of Human Services (2009).
**Figure 7.6,** U.S. Department of Health and Human Services, 2009.
**Table 7.1,** World Health Organization, 2005 and their report written by de Onis, Monteiro, Akré, & Clugston, 2002.
**Table 7.2,** Data are from Kung, Hoyert, Xu, & Murphy, 2008.
**Table 7.3,** Data are from the U.S. Department of Health and Human Services (2009).
**Table 7.4,** Kim & Cicchetti, 2006; Hoffman-Plotkin & Twentyman, 1984; Main & George, 1985; McCord, 1983; Nelson & Crick, 2002; Pollak, Vardi, Putzer Bechner, & Curtin et al., 2005; Salzinger, Kaplan, Pelcovitz, Samit, & Krieger et al., 1984; Wekerle & Wolfe, 2003.
**Figure 8.1,** Artwork showing the development of mental representation; drawings by children Brooks Wendler, Lily Cook, and Rachel Cook.
**Figure 8.2,** From H. Bee & D. Boyd (2006). *Lifespan Development,* 4/e. Published by Allyn and Bacon, Boston, MA. Copyright © 2006 by Pearson Education. By permission of the publisher.
**Figure 8.5,** Adapted from Dempster, 1981, p. 66.
**Figure 8.6,** Based on Bjorklund, 1995.
**Figure 8.7,** Data from Campbell et al., 2001.
**Figure 8.8,** Adapted from L.J. Schweinert, H.V. Bames, & D.P. Weikart. (1993). *Significant benefits: The High/Scope Peny Preschool study through age 27* (Monographs of the High/Scope Educational Research Foundation, Number 10), pp. xvi–xvii. Ypsilanti, MI: The High/Scope Press.
**Table 8.1,** Bernstein, personal communication, 2003.
**Figure 9.9,** Data from Fabes, 1994.
**Table 9.1,** Adapted from Kohlberg, 1984.
**Table 9.2,** Fabes, 1994; Fagot, 1977, 1994; Fagot & Patterson, 1969; Martin, 1994; Serbin et al., 1994.
**Figure 10.1,** National Center for Health Statistics, 2006a, 2009.
**Figure 10.2,** Centers for Disease Control, 2003.
**Figure 10.3,** Centers for Disease Control, 2003.
**Table 10.1,** From Wanda M. Hunter, Samah Helou, Gitanjali Saluja, Carol W. Runyan & Tamara Coyne-Beasley, "Injury Prevention Advice in Top-Selling Parenting Books." *Pediatrics 116*(5), pp. 1080–1088. Reproduced with permission from *Pediatrics 116*(5), 1080–1088, Table 5, Copyright © 2005 by the AAP.
**Table 10.2,** Adapted from National Clearinghouse on Child Abuse and Neglect, 2006; American Academy of Child & Adolescent Psychiatry, 2004; Darkness to Light, 2006.
**Table 10.3,** Mash & Wolfe, 2005.
**Table 10.4,** NICHD, 2005.
**Figure 11.4,** Data from Chi, 1978.
**Figure 11.5,** Based on Klahr & MacWhinney, 1998, p. 649
**Table 11.2,** Adapted from Geary, D.C. (1994). *Children's mathematical development: Research and practical applications.* Washington, DC: American Psychological Association.
**Figure 12.1,** From Huesmann, L. R., Eron, L. D., Leflcowitz, M. M.,& Walder, L. O. (1984). Stability of aggression over time and generations. *Developmental Psychology.* 20(6), p. 1125. Reprinted with permission.
**Figure 12.2,** Data are from the U.S. Census Bureau (2009).
**Figure 12.3,** Adapted from Amato, 2000, pp. 1269–1287.
**Figure 12.5,** Adapted from Eron, L.D. (1987). The development of aggressive behavior from the perspective of a developing behaviorism. *American Psychologist 42*(5). Adapted with permission. Aggression score from Eron, Huesmann, Leflcowitz, & Walder (1972).
**Table 12.2,** Adapted from Eisenberg et al., 1983.
**Table 12.3,** Adapted from Laumann-Billings & Emery, 2000.
**Table 12.4,** Amato, 2000; Buchanan et al. (1996); Emery, Kitzman, & Waldron (1999); Hetherington, 1999; Meyer, 1999; Sandler Tein, Mehta, Wolchik, & Ayers (2000); Wallerstein et al. (2000).
**Figure 13.2,** National Center for Health Statistics, 2000b.
**Figure 13.3** Data from Eaton et al., 2008.
**Figure 13.4,** Data from Mosher et al., 2004.
**Figure 13.5,** Data from CDC, 2008.
**Figure 13.6,** Data from Ventura et al., 2008.
**Figure 13.7,** Data from Eaton et al., 2008.
**Table 13.1,** Adapted from: U.S. Department of Health & Human Services (2009, March 27). Sexual development and reproduction. Accessed April 21, 2009 from http://www.4parents.gov/index.html.
**Table 13.3,** Eaton et al., 2008. Results from the 2007 National Survey on Drug Use and Health: National Findings. DEPARTMENT OF HEALTH AND HUMAN SERVICES Substance Abuse and Mental Health Services Administration (SAMHSA).

**Figure 14.3,** Sattler. (2001). *Assessment of children*, 4th ed. San Diego, CA: Jerome M. Sattler. - CREDIT LINE FOR TOP - Wechsler Intelligence Scale for Children, Fourth Edition (WISC®-IV). Copyright © 2003 NCS Pearson, Inc. Reproduced with permission. All rights reserved. "Wechsler Intelligence Scale for Children" and "WISC" are trademarks, in the US and/or other countries, of Pearson Education, Inc. or its affiliates(s).
**Table 14.2,** Mash & Wolfe, 2005. *Abnormal Child Psychology*. Wadsworth Publishing.
**Figure 15.1,** Based on Marcia, 1966.
**Figure 15.2,** Adapted from A. Colby, L. Kohlberg, J. Gibbs, & M. Liebennan. (1983). A longitudinal study of moral judgment. Monograph of the *Society for Research in Child Development*, 40(1-2, Serial No. 200)
**Figure 15.3,** Data from Roberts, Foehr, & Rideout, 2005
**Figure 15.4,** Lee, Grigg, & Dion, 2007; Grigg, Donahue, & Dion, 2007. Washington: National Center for Education Statistics.
**Figure 15.5,** U.S. Census Bureau, 2008.
**Table 15.1,** Phinney, 1990.
**Table 15.2,** U.S. Census Bureau, 2009
**Table 15.3,** Boykin & Toms, 1985; Chao, 1994; Parke & Buriel, 2006; Reed, 1982; Trimble & Medicine, 1993
**Table 15.4,** Anderman & Maehr, 1994; Deci & Ryan, 1985; Dweck, 2001; Eccles, 2004; Fan & Chen, 2001; Ford & Harris, 2000; Good & Brophy, 2003; Keith et al., 1998; Parker et al., 1999; Seidman & French, 1997.

## Photo Credits

### CHAPTER 1

p.2, EyeWire Collection/Getty Images - Photodisc-Royalty Free; p.3, Kathy McLaughlin/The Image Works; p.4, Ellen Sinisi/The Image Works; p.5, Scott K. Holland, PhD; p.5, © Matthew Cavanaugh/Corbis, All Rights Reserved; p.9, Image Works/Mary Evans Picture Library Ltd; p.11, Library of Congress; p.11, Professor Ben Harris, University of New Hampshire; p.13, Nina Leen/Getty Images/Time Life Pictures; p.13, Jon Brenneis/Getty Images/Time Life Pictures; p.14, Wayne Behling, with permission of Judith Behling Ford; p.15, © Novosti/Sovfoto; p.15, Nena Leen/Getty Images/Time Life Pictures; p.17, AP Wide World Photos

### CHAPTER 2

p.40, SSPL/The Image Works; p.41, OnRequest Images/Photolibrary.com; p.43, Alix/Photo Researchers, Inc.; p.44, Jamie Commissaris; p.45, Collection CNRI/Phototake NYC; p.48, Custom Medical Stock Photo, Inc.; p.61, Getty Images, Inc.; p.64, Photolibrary.Com Royalty-Free; p.67, Bob Daemmrich/The Image Works; p.69, © Viviane Moos/Corbis All Rights Reserved

### CHAPTER 3

p.75, Photo Lennart Nilsson/Albert Bonniers Forlag; p.77, Dr. Yorgos Nikas/Phototake NYC; p.78, ICAMona Lisa/Eurelios/Phototake NYC; p.79, Photo Lennart Nilsson/Albert Bonniers Forlag; p.80, (left) Photo Lennart Nilsson/Bonnier Alba AB, A Child Is Born, Dell Publishing Company; p.80, (right) Photo Lennart Nilsson/Albert Bonniers Forlag; p.80, Photo Lennart Nilsson/Albert Bonniers Forlag; p.86, Stevie Grand/Photo Researchers, Inc.; p.90, Nick Emm/Alamy Images; p.92, Tim Kiusalaas/Masterfile Corporation; p.95, © Dumbarton Oaks, Pre-Columbian Collection, Washington, DC; p.96, Hattie Young/Photo Researchers, Inc.; p.98, Chip East/Reuters Limited; p.98, Ruth Jenkinson/MIDIRS/Photo Researchers, Inc.; p.100, © Corbis, All rights reserved; p.102, Laura Dwight/Laura Dwight Photography

### PART ONE SUMMARY

p.107, R. Gino Santa Maria/Shutterstock; Shutterstock; Vadim Ponomarenko/Shutterstock; Shane W. Thompson/Shutterstock; Gelpi/Shutterstock; Yuri Arcurs/Shutterstock

### CHAPTER 4

p.109, David Young-Wolff/PhotoEdit Inc.; p.110, Dynamic Graphics Value/Superstock Royalty Free; p.112, Chad Ehlers/Alamy Images; p.114, (left) Spencer Grant/PhotoEdit Inc.; p.114, (right) © Corbis, All Rights Reserved; p.115, Peter Arnold/Peter Arnold, Inc.; p.116, © Corbis, All Rights Reserved; p.117, Getty Images, Inc.; p.119, CNRI/Photo Researchers, Inc.; p.121, Anatomical Travelogue/Photo Researchers, Inc.; p.125, William P. Fifer, New York State Psychiatric Institute, Columbia University; p.125, Dion Ogust/The Image Works; p.126, © Corbis, All Rights Reserved; p.131, © Corbis, All Rights Reserved; p.131, Mike Greenlar/The Image Works; p.132, BananaStock/Alamy Images

### CHAPTER 5

p.144, Michael Newman/PhotoEdit Inc.; p.146, Corbis, All rights reserved; p.146, Geri Engberg/The Image Works; p.150, © Corbis, All Rights Reserved; p.152, Laura Dwight Photography; p.156, © Corbis All Rights Reserved; p.157, Cleo Photography/PhotoEdit Inc.; p.159, Susan Kuklin/Photo Researchers, Inc.; p.163, Peter Southwick/Stock Boston; p.168, Laura Dwight/Laura Dwight Photography

### CHAPTER 6

p.174, Laura Dwight/Laura Dwight Photography; p.176, Harlow Primate Laboratory/University of Wisconsin; p.177, Mary Ainsworth, University of Virginia. Photo by Daniel Grogan; p.180, Michael Newman/PhotoEdit Inc.; p.181, © Corbis, All rights reserved; p.182, Getty Images, Inc.; p.183, Dynamic Graphics Group/IT Stock Free/Alamy Images; p.185, Ellen Senisi/The Image Works; p.188, (left) ANA/The Image Works; p.188, (right) Royalty-Free/Corbis RF; p.193, Bob Daemmrich/PhotoEdit Inc.; p.194, Jim Whitmer/Jim Whitmer Photography; p.195, © Corbis, All rights reserved; p.198, Laura Dwight/Laura Dwight Photography

### PART TWO SUMMARY

p.202, Adrov Andriy/Shutterstock; Cara Purdy/Shutterstock; Svitlana Kataieva/Shutterstock; Ruslan Stadnik/iStockPhoto; joingate/Shutterstock

## CHAPTER 7

p.204, Bob Daemmrich/The Image Works; p.207, Robin Nelson/PhotoEdit Inc.; p.210, Getty Images, Inc.; p.211, John Russell/AP Wide World Photos; p.212, (left) Nancy Sheehan/Photolibrary.com; p.212, (right) Peter Griffith/Masterfile Corporation; p.213, Laura Dwight/Laura Dwight Photography; p.214, Michelle D. Bridwell/ PhotoEdit Inc.; p.216, Richard Hutchings/PhotoEdit Inc.; p.218, G. Tompkinson/Photo Researchers, Inc.; p.219, Rommel/Masterfile Corporation; p.223, © Corbis, All rights reserved

## CHAPTER 8

p.231, Jonathan Skow/Getty Images, Inc. - Stone Allstock; p.236, Sovfoto/Eastfoto; p.237, © Corbis, All Rights Reserved; p.241, Laura Dwight Photography; p.242, Getty Images, Inc.; p.245, Barbara Peacock/Corbis-NY; p.249, Royalty-Free/Corbis RF; p.250, Greenberg, Jeff/Photolibrary.com -; p.253, Robin Nelson/PhotoEdit Inc.

## CHAPTER 9

p.264, Photo Researchers, Inc.; p.266, © Ken Seet/Corbis, All rights reserved; p.271, Bananastock/Jupiter Images; p.273, Bob Daemmrich/The Image Works; p.264, Getty Images, Inc.; p.265, David Young-Wolff/PhotoEdit Inc.; p.267, Blend Images/Alamy Images; p.273, Tony Freeman/PhotoEdit Inc.; p.273, Murez, Steve/Getty Images Inc. - Image Bank; p.273, Myrleen Ferguson Cate/PhotoEdit Inc.; p.273, Michael Newman/PhotoEdit Inc.; p.277, Cindy Roesinger/Photo Researchers, Inc.; p.279, © Corbis, All rights reserved; p.281, James Shaffer/PhotoEdit Inc.; p.281, Laura Dwight/Laura Dwight Photography; p.284, Image Bank/Getty Images; p.285, Ingram/Jupiter Images - FoodPix - Creatas

## PART THREE SUMMARY

p.290, Morgan Lane Photography/Shutterstock; MaFord/Shutterstock; Roman Sigaev/Shutterstock; PhotoNAN/ Shutterstock

## CHAPTER 10

p.293, Bob Daemmrich/Stock Boston; p.296, © Corbis, All rights reserved; p.297, ImageState/Alamy Images; p.298, Myrleen Ferguson Cate/PhotoEdit Inc.; p.300, Brand X Pictures/Alamy Images; p.300, Getty Images, Inc.; p.303, Myrleen Ferguson Cate/PhotoEdit Inc.; p.307, Rob Crandall/Stock Connection; p.311, Lezlie Sterling/Zuma Press; p.312, AP Wide World Photos; p.312, Corbis- NY; p.312, Getty Images, Inc. - Hulton Archive Photos; p.315, Robin Sachs/PhotoEdit Inc.; p.292, © Corbis, All rights reserved

## CHAPTER 11

p.323, © Corbis, All rights reserved; p.328, © Corbis, All Rights Reserved; p.329, Lawrence Migdale/Stock Boston; p.330, Jim Pickerell/The Image Works; p.333, David J. Sams/Stock Boston; p.336, David Young-Wolff/PhotoEdit Inc.; p.338, Robert E. Daemmrich/Stone/Getty Images; p.345, Getty Images, Inc.; p.346, Laura Dwight/Laura Dwight Photography; p.349, © Corbis, All rights reserved; p.353, image100/Alamy Images; p.355, Image Source/Alamy Images

## CHAPTER 12

p.361, Eric R. Berndt/Unicorn Stock Photos; p.362, © Corbis, All rights reserved; p.365, (left) Bob Daemmrich/The Image Works; p.365, (right) Tony Freeman/PhotoEdit Inc.; p.368, Richard Hutchings/PhotoEdit Inc.; p.371, Lon C. Diehl/PhotoEdit Inc.; p.373, Royalty-Free/Corbis RF; p.383, Catherine Ledner/Getty Images, Inc. - Stone Allstock; p.386, © Corbis, All rights reserved; p.388, David Young-Wolff/PhotoEdit Inc.; p.390, (from left) Albert Bandura, D. Ross & S.A. Ross, Imitation of film-mediated aggressive models. "Journal of Abnormal and Social Psychology," 1963, 66. p.8; p.391, Andrew Lichtenstein/The Image Works

## PART FOUR SUMMARY

p.398, Elnur/Shutterstock; Dmitry Terentjev/Shutterstock; Yuganov Konstantin/Shutterstock; Morgan Lane Photography/Shutterstock; Shutterstock

## CHAPTER 13

p.403, Richard Hutchings/Digital Light Source/Peter Arnold, Inc.; p.404, Jon Feingersh/Masterfile Corporation; p.406, Royalty-Free/Corbis RF; p.409, PunchStock - Royalty Free; p.410, Peter D. Byron/PhotoEdit Inc.; p.413, Will Hart; p.415, Getty Images, Inc.; p.418, Brand X Pictures/Alamy Images; p.420, Pixtal/Superstock Royalty Free; p.421, Staffordshire Sentinel/Solo/Zuma/Newscom; p.425, Photodisc/Getty Images; p.426, Royalty-Free/Corbis RF; p.428, © Corbis, All rights reserved; p.429, Photodisc/Getty Images

## CHAPTER 14

p.437, Bob Daemmrich/PhotoEdit Inc.; p.441, Photodisc/Getty Images; p.444, AP Wide World Photos; p.445, Wang Lei/AP Wide World Photos; p.448, © Corbis, All rights reserved; p.448, Bob Daemmrich/Stock Boston; p.448, © Corbis, All rights reserved; p.452, James Shaffer/PhotoEdit Inc.; p.455, Laura Dwight/Laura Dwight Photography; p.457, David Young-Wolff/PhotoEdit Inc.; p.458, Yva Momatuik/Stock Boston; p.467, © Corbis, All rights reserved

## CHAPTER 15

p.472, Jim Witmer/AUTHOR PROVIDED; p.476, Purestock/Alamy Images; p.479, Vicki Silbert/PhotoEdit Inc.; p.479, Kamal Kishore/Corbis- NY; p.479, Spencer Grant/PhotoEdit Inc.; p.482, John Powell/Topham/The Image Works; p.483, AGE Fotostock America, Inc.; p.488, Alan Veldenzer/Photolibrary.com; p.490, Image Bank/Getty Images; p.496, HIRB/Photolibrary.com; p.496, Digital Vision/Getty Images/Digital Vision; p.501, Peter Byron/PhotoEdit Inc.; p.502, © Corbis, All rights reserved; p.503, Peter Blakely/Corbis- NY; p.503, Kindra Clineff/Photolibrary.com; p.504, Richard Lord/The Image Works

## PART FIVE SUMMARY

p.508, Michal Rozanski/iStockPhoto; RoJo Images/Shutterstock; Volodymyr Kyrylyuk/Shutterstock

# Name Index

# Subject Index